Expert
WSS 3.0 and MOSS 2007 Programming

Dr. Shahram Khosravi

Wiley Publishing, Inc.

Expert WSS 3.0 and MOSS 2007 Programming

Published by
Wiley Publishing, Inc.
10475 Crosspoint Boulevard
Indianapolis, IN 46256
www.wiley.com

Published simultaneously in Canada

ISBN-13: 978-0-470- 38137-3

ISBN-10: 0-7645-381371

Manufactured in the United States of America

10 9 8 7 6 5 4 3 2 1

Library of Congress Cataloging-in-Publication Data is available from the publisher.

For general information on our other products and services please contact our Customer Care Department within the United States at (800) 762-2974, outside the United States at (317) 572-3993 or fax (317) 572-4002.

Wiley also publishes its books in a variety of electronic formats. Some content that appears in print may not be available in electronic books.

To my parents

About the Author

Shahram Khosravi, Ph.D., is a lead technical consultant, architect, author, and instructor specializing in Microsoft Windows SharePoint Services (WSS) 3.0, Microsoft Office SharePoint Server (MOSS) 2007, SharePoint 2007 workflow programming, Windows Workflow Foundation (WF), ASP.NET, Windows Communication Foundation (WCF), ASP.NET AJAX, IIS7 and ASP.NET Integrated Programming, ASP.NET, web services, .NET, and XML technologies such as XSD, XSLT, XPath, SOAP, and WSDL. He also has years of experience in object-oriented analysis, design, and programming; architectural and design patterns; service-oriented analysis, design, and programming; 3D computer graphics programming; user interface design; and usability.

He is the sole author of the following six books: *Professional SharePoint 2007 Workflow Programming, Expert WSS 3.0 and MOSS 2007 Programming, Professional ASP.NET 2.0 and .NET 3.0 Programming (ASP.NET Internals plus ASP.NET AJAX, IIS 7, Windows Workflow Foundation, and Workflow Communication Foundation), ASP.NET AJAX Programmer's Reference with ASP.NET 2.0 or ASP.NET 3.5, Professional IIS7 and ASP.NET Integrated Programming*, and *Professional ASP.NET 2.0 Server Control and Component Development*. He has written articles on the ASP.NET, ASP.NET, .NET, and XML technologies for the industry's leading journals, including *Dr. Dobb's Journal, asp.netPRO* magazine, and Microsoft MSDN Online.

Credits

Executive Editor
Chris Webb

Development Editor
Julie M. Smith

Technical Editors
Sherry Neal
Cori Schlegel

Production Editor
Daniel Scribner

Copy Editor
Kim Cofer

Editorial Manager
Mary Beth Wakefield

Production Manager
Tim Tate

Vice President and Executive Group Publisher
Richard Swadley

Vice President and Executive Publisher
Joseph B. Wikert

Project Coordinator, Cover
Lynsey Stanford

Proofreading
Publication Services

Indexing
Ron Strauss

Acknowledgments

My deepest gratitude and appreciation go to my beautiful wife, Xiaodong Gong, for her unwavering support throughout this exciting project. This book could not have been written without her complete support and encouragement. Xiaodong, thanks very much for your continuous love, companionship, patience, sacrifice, support, and understanding.

Huge thanks go to Chris Webb, the executive editor for the book, for giving me the opportunity to work on this great project and for all his support throughout the process. Special thanks go to Jim Minatel, the senior acquisitions editor for the book, for all his help and guidance. Huge thanks go to Julie Smith, the development editor for the book. I greatly appreciate all your input, comments, and advice throughout the process. Julie, it's been such a great pleasure working with you on this exciting project. Special thanks go to Cori Schlegel and Sherry Neal, the book's technical editors. Thank you for all your input and comments. Additional thanks go to Daniel Scribner, the book's production editor. Thanks also go to Kim Cofer, the copy editor.

Contents

Introduction **xxiii**

Chapter 1: The SharePoint 2007 Architecture **1**

ASP.NET Hosting Environment **1**
Hosting ASP.NET 1
HttpWorkerRequest 2
Internet Information Services (IIS) **3**
Application Pools 4
SharePoint Extensions **6**
SPApplicationPool 6
SPIisWebSite 8
SPWebApplication 11
SPWebApplicationBuilder 14
SPWebService 16
ISAPIRuntime **18**
ASP.NET HTTP Runtime Pipeline **19**
HttpApplication 23
SPHttpApplication 26
SPRequestModule 28
SPVirtualPathProvider 30
IHttpHandlerFactory and IHttpHandler 32
Summary **52**

Chapter 2: CAML, Features, Custom Actions, and Application Pages **53**

Collaborative Application Markup Language (CAML) **53**
CAML Queries 57
Features **63**
An Example of a Feature 66
SharePoint Solution Package **70**
Application Pages **70**
Inline Approach 73
Code-Behind Approach 83
Summary **96**

Chapter 3: List Types **97**

What Is SharePoint Forms Infrastructure, Anyway? **97**
Creating a New List 98
Adding a New List Item 101
Viewing a List Item 102
Editing a List Item 103
Display, New, and Edit List Item Forms 104
List Types **119**
GroupByHeader 133
<GroupByFooter> 140
<ViewFields> 142
<Query> 142
<ViewBody> 143
List Provisioning **150**
Graphical List Provisioning 150
Declarative List Provisioning 152
Imperative List Provisioning 154
Custom List Item Forms **159**
Summary **161**

Chapter 4: Form-Rendering Controls **163**

SharePoint Rendering Server Controls **163**
SPControl **165**
ListFormPageTitle **166**
ListProperty **169**
TemplateBasedControl **172**
Template Property 177
AlternateTemplate Property 184
TemplateOverride 185
ControlTemplate 186
CreateChildControls 187
CustomTemplate and CustomAlternateTemplate 189
RenderContext 191
FormComponent **192**
ControlMode 196
ItemContext 198
Fields 199
Item 199
ItemId 199
List 200

ListId 200
ListItem 200
FormToolBar 201
RequiredFieldMessage 208
ListFieldIterator 210
Summary 213

Chapter 5: Field Types 215

SPField 215
SPFieldBoolean 220
SPFieldMultiChoice 223
SPFieldChoice 229
Field Type Definition 231
HeaderPattern 242
DisplayPattern 249
EditPattern 249
NewPattern 256
Field-Rendering Controls 256
FieldMetadata 256
CompositeField 260
FieldDescription 262
FieldProperty 263
FieldLabel 264
BaseFieldControl 268
FormField 280
Variable Field Type Property Rendering 286
Property Schema 287
Variable Field Type Property Editor 287
Implementing a Custom Field Type 289
Implementing a Custom Field Type Class 290
Implementing a Custom Field-Rendering Control 293
Implementing a Field Type Definition 297
Using the Custom Field Type 298
Summary 301

Chapter 6: Site Columns and Site Content Types 303

Site Columns 303
Graphical Approach 304
Declarative Approach 305
Site Content Types 313
Summary 336

Chapter 7: Site Definitions and Site Provisioning Providers **337**

Site Definitions **337**
onet.xml 339
WebTemp*.xml 372
Site Definition Best Practices 375
Site Provisioning Provider **383**
Summary **395**

Chapter 8: Advanced SharePoint Programming **397**

Web Configuration Modification **397**
RSS 402
RssHandler 403
Extending STSADM **416**
Feature Receiver **423**
Developing Custom Timer Jobs **428**
SPOneTimeSchedule 431
SPMinuteSchedule 431
SPHourlySchedule 432
SPDailySchedule 432
SPMonthlySchedule 432
SPWeeklySchedule 433
SPYearlySchedule 433
Feature Activation **440**
Feature Dependency 440
Feature Stapling 442
Summary **444**

Chapter 9: Event Receivers **445**

Overview **445**
List Event Receiver **446**
SPEventPropertiesBase 449
Implementing a Custom List Event Receiver 450
Item Event Receiver **464**
Binding Item Event Handlers to a Site Content Type 470
Binding Item Event Handlers to a List Instance 472
Web Event Receiver **474**
Binding a Web Event Handler to an Existing Site 476
Binding a Web Event Handler to an Existing Site Definition Configuration 478

Binding a Web Event Handler to a New Site Definition Configuration (First Approach) 480
Binding a Web Event Handler to a New Site Definition Configuration (Second Approach) 482
Summary **486**

Chapter 10: SharePoint Web Parts **487**

What Is the ASP.NET Web Parts Framework? **487**
SharePoint Extensions to ASP.NET Web Parts Framework **491**
SPWebPartManager 491
WebPartZone 492
Editor and Catalog Zones 494
Switching Display Modes 495
Developing WebPart Server Controls 495
Main Components of the Web Parts Framework **496**
Part **498**
Web Part **499**
RssUrl 502
CreateChildControls 502
AddContainer 504
AddItemToContainer 504
Deploying a Custom WebPart Server Control **504**
Bin versus GAC 505
Web Part Description File 507
Implementing IWebPart **515**
IWebActionable **515**
EditorPart **518**
Developing Custom EditorPart Controls **518**
CreateChildControls 520
SyncChanges 521
ApplyChanges 521
RssReaderWebPart3 Control 521
Templated Web Parts **525**
TemplateBasedWebPart 525
TemplateBasedWebPart1 532
Deploying Web Parts 534
Connecting WebPart Controls **535**
Implementing Web Parts that Support Connections 541
Summary **571**

Chapter 11: Code Access Security (CAS) 573

What CAS Provides 574
Security Syntax 575
Declarative Security Syntax 576
Imperative Security Syntax 578
GAC versus Bin 579
Security Demands 580
Demand 581
Link Demand 582
Inheritance Demand 583
Security Requests 583
Minimum 584
Optional 584
Refuse 584
Granting Permissions 585
AllowPartiallyTrustedCallersAttribute 595
Summary 595

Chapter 12: Deployment 597

Why Use a SharePoint Solution Package? 597
Cabinet and DDF Files 599
Solution Manifest 601
Deployment Scenarios 604
Deploying a SharePoint Web Part Solution 604
Deploying a SharePoint Site Definition Solution 620
Summary 625

Chapter 13: Business Data Catalog 627

BDC Metadata XML Schema 628
MetadataObject 629
IndividuallySecurableMetadataObject 630
LocalizedDisplayNames 631
Properties 632
AccessControlList 634
LobSystem Document Element 636
Type Attribute 637
Version Attribute 637
SystemUtility 638
ConnectionManager 639
EntityInstance 640

LobSystemInstances **651**
Entities **657**
InstanceCount **664**
Identifiers **665**
Methods **671**
Parameters **684**
FilterDescriptors **708**
MethodInstances **723**
Finder 729
Enterprise Search and Indexing 730
Scalar 731
Actions **731**
Associations **734**
Example **740**

Index **763**

Introduction

Welcome to *Expert WSS 3.0 and MOSS 2007 Programming*. This book provides you with in-depth coverage of the WSS 3.0 and MOSS 2007 development framework. The discussions of the book are presented in the context of numerous detailed step-by-step recipes and real-world examples where these recipes are used. This book uses an approach based on detailed code-walkthroughs and in-depth technical discussions to help you develop the skills you need to become a proficient WSS 3.0 and MOSS 2007 developer.

What This Book Covers

The book is divided into 13 chapters:

Chapter 1, "The SharePoint 2007 Architecture," discusses the main architectural components of IIS and ASP.NET and shows you how these components are extended to add support for SharePoint functionalities. The chapter begins with coverage of the ASP.NET hosting environment, where HTTP worker requests and runtime classes are discussed. The chapter then covers IIS concepts such as web sites and application pools followed by the discussions of the related SharePoint object model classes such as SPApplicationPool, SPIis, SPWebApplication, SPWebApplicationBuilder, and SPWebService. You learn these object model classes in the context of numerous code examples.

Next, the ASP.NET HTTP Runtime Pipeline and the SharePoint extensions to this pipeline, such as SPHttpApplication, SPRequestModule, SPVirtualPathProvider, and SPHttpHandler, are discussed in depth. You also learn about the ASP.NET dynamic compilation model and the role it plays in SharePoint.

Chapter 2, "CAML, Features, Custom Actions, and Application Pages," begins with coverage of the Collaborative Application Markup Language (CAML), which is used to perform SharePoint queries and define SharePoint components in declarative fashion. The rest of the chapter uses CAML to implement features and custom actions. This chapter uses code examples to show you how to perform CAML queries on SharePoint data. It then dives into SharePoint features and uses examples to show you how to implement your own SharePoint features as well as how to install and activate them. Finally, this chapter provides in-depth coverage of SharePoint application pages, where you can learn two different approaches to implementing your own custom application pages. The chapter also uses numerous examples to show how to implement and deploy custom SharePoint actions.

Chapter 3, "List Types," first provides an introduction to the SharePoint forms infrastructure to demonstrate how this infrastructure enables the user interactions with SharePoint abstractions such as site collections, sites, list types, lists, list items, content types, site columns, field types, and so on. You get in-depth coverage of the internal workings of the page template for standard SharePoint display, edit, and new list item forms; the ListFormWebPart Web part; the SPForm class; and some of the standard rendering template controls that are used to render these list item forms.

You then look at the first SharePoint abstraction, that is, list types, where you learn how to implement and deploy your own custom list types and how to use CAML and SharePoint web services to provision instances of your custom list types. The chapter provides in-depth coverage of the schema.xml file that defines the schema of a SharePoint list type. The chapter finally shows you how to implement custom display, edit, and new list item forms for your own custom list types.

Chapter 4, "Form-Rendering Controls," provides complete coverage of the form-rendering server controls, which constitute a major portion of the SharePoint forms infrastructure. The chapter dives into the internal implementation of the standard SharePoint form-rendering server controls such as SPControl, ListFormPageTitle, ListProperty, TemplateBasedControl, FormComponent, FormToolBar, RequiredFieldMessage, and ListFieldIterator to help you gain the skills you need to implement your own custom form-rendering server controls.

Chapter 5, "Field Types," teaches you the skills you need to implement your own custom field types and deploy them to SharePoint. The chapter first provides the internal implementation of the standard SharePoint field types such as SPField, SPFieldBoolean, SPFieldMultiChoice, and SPFieldChoice to help you gain the required skills to implement custom field types. It then walks through an example to demonstrate how to implement a field type definition.

The chapter then covers field-rendering server controls where the internal implementation of the standard SharePoint field-rendering server controls such as FieldMetadata, CompositeField, FieldDescription, FieldProperty, FieldLabel, BaseFieldControl, and FormField are discussed to help you learn the required skills for implementing custom field-rendering server controls.

Next, the chapter covers variable field type property rendering. It demonstrates how to use CAML instructions inside a field type definition to render variable field type properties. The chapter then shows how to implement a variable field type editor to enable more complex rendering of variable field type properties. The chapter finally implements a custom field type, a custom field rendering control, and a custom field type definition.

Chapter 6, "Site Columns and Site Content Types," begins with showing how to implement site columns in CAML and how to use features to deploy them to SharePoint. Then it covers site content types, where you learn how to derive from an existing site content type to implement a custom site content type. The discussions in the chapter are presented in the context of the implementation of sample custom site columns and site content types. The chapter then demonstrates how to implement a custom edit list item form and attach it to a site content type to have SharePoint render the form every time the user attempts to edit an item of the specified content type.

Chapter 7, "Site Definitions and Site Provisioning Providers," dives into site definitions and site provisioning providers and uses examples to show you how to implement your own custom site definitions and site provisioning providers. The chapter provides you with a recipe for implementing a custom site definition and implements a site definition where this recipe is used.

You get full coverage of the XML structure of the onet.xml and webtemp*.xml files, where you learn how to implement and deploy these two XML files for your custom site definition. You also learn about site definition best practices through examples. The chapter then provides a recipe for implementing site provisioning providers and implements a custom site provisioning provider where this recipe is used.

Chapter 8, "Advanced SharePoint Programming," covers the advanced SharePoint programming topics including web configuration modification via the SharePoint object model, extending the STSADM command-line utility to add support for custom operations, feature receivers, developing custom timer jobs, feature dependency, and feature stapling.

The chapter begins with detailed coverage of SPWebConfigModification. It then provides a recipe for implementing a custom HTTP handler and implements a custom HTTP handler where this recipe is used. Next, it shows you how to implement a site provisioning provider that uses the SharePoint object model to add entries for the custom HTTP handler to the web.config file.

The chapter then demonstrates how to implement ISPStsAdmCommand to extend the functionality of the STSADM command-line utility to add support for custom operations. The chapter then demonstrates how to implement and deploy a feature receiver to execute custom code in response to feature-related events including installing, activating, uninstalling, and deactivating features.

The chapter then provides a recipe for implementing a custom timer job and implements a custom timer job where this recipe is used. You get full coverage of SPJobDefinition, SPOneTimeSchedule, SPMinuteSchedule, SPHourlySchedule, SPDailySchedule, SPMonthlySchedule, SPWeeklySchedule, and SPYearlySchedule.

Next, the chapter covers feature dependency, where you learn how to use feature dependency to ensure that all the features on which a feature depends are activated before the feature itself is activated. The chapter finally teaches you how to implement a stapling feature to staple your features to existing site definition configurations so your features are automatically activated every time a user provisions a site from these site definition configurations, even though your features are not directly referenced from the respective <SiteFeatures> or <WebFeatures> elements of the respective onet.xml files.

Chapter 9, "Event Receivers," provides in-depth coverage of the three main types of event receivers and uses numerous examples to help you gain the skills you need to implement your own event receivers. The chapter starts with list event receivers, which enable you to respond to events that SharePoint lists first. You learn how to bind your custom list event handlers to list types, list instances, site content types, and list content types.

Next it discusses item event receivers. You can use these event receivers to execute custom code in response to events that a list item raises. You also learn how to bind your custom item event handlers to site content types and list instances. Finally, the chapter covers web event receivers, which enable you to run custom code when a site fires a specified event. The chapter also teaches you how to bind your web event handlers to existing sites, existing site definition configurations, and new site definition configurations.

The chapter also discusses SPEventReceiver, SPListEventReceiver, SPListEventProperties, SPEventPropertiesBase, SPEventReceiverDefinition, SPItemEventReceiver, SPItemEventProperties, SPWebEventReceiver, and SPWebEventProperties.

Chapter 10, "SharePoint Web Parts," first discusses the ASP.NET Web Parts Framework, where you learn how SharePoint manages to extend this framework. Next, the chapter provides in-depth coverage of the main components of the Web Parts Framework such as Part, WebPart, IWebPart, IWebActionable, IPersonalizable, and IWebEditable. The chapter then shows you how to implement a custom Web part and how to deploy it to SharePoint.

The chapter discusses Web part description files (.webpart) in detail and shows how to add them to the Web Part Gallery through SharePoint features. The chapter then dives into editor parts where it uses a couple of examples to show how to implement your own custom editor parts. Next, the chapter implements a couple of template-based Web parts, which delegate the responsibility of rendering their HTML markup text to user controls, which are deployed to the ControlTemplates folder in the file system of each front-end web server. The chapter then provides in-depth coverage of Web part connections and implements Web parts that support Web part connections, enabling them to connect to other Web part to share data with them.

Chapter 11, "Code Access Security (CAS)," provides in-depth coverage of CAS and the fundamental role that it plays in SharePoint Web part solutions. The chapter begins with an overview of what CAS provides. It then dives into declarative and imperative security syntaxes. Next, the chapter discusses the three types of security demands: Demand, LinkDemand, and InheritanceDemand. The chapter then covers the three types of security requests: minimum, optional, and refuse. The chapter finally dives into the topic of granting permissions to assemblies where the XML structure of a security policy file is covered in-depth.

Chapter 12, "Deployment," provides in-depth coverage of SharePoint deployment, where you learn how to package your SharePoint solution in a single deployment package and deploy it as a single unit. The chapter first discusses why you need to use SharePoint solution packages. It then covers cabinet files and the structure of a Data Description File (DDF). Next, the chapter covers the XML structure of a SharePoint manifest file and the role this file plays in SharePoint deployment. The chapter finally presents two deployment scenarios in the context of real-world deployment examples.

Chapter 13, "Business Data Catalog," provides comprehensive coverage of the Business Data Catalog (BDC) XML markup language in the context of real-world examples where you learn how to use this markup language to enable a SharePoint portal site to bring in business data from various database and web service LOB applications and expose them as if they were SharePoint data.

This chapter among many others covers metadata objects, individually securable metadata objects, localization, Access Control Lists (ACLs), LOB systems, LOB system instances, entities, entity identifiers, methods, method parameters, type descriptors, filter descriptors, method instances including finders and specific finders, ID enumerators, and scalars, actions, and associations. The chapter also walks you through a step-by-step process to load and examine a BDC application definition file in the SharePoint Central Administration web application.

1

The SharePoint 2007 Architecture

SharePoint 2007 is an extension of ASP.NET and IIS. This chapter walks through the main architectural components of IIS and ASP.NET and shows you how these components are extended to add support for SharePoint functionalities.

Because IIS is one of the many options for hosting ASP.NET, the discussion begins with the coverage of the ASP.NET hosting environment where HTTP worker requests and runtime classes are discussed. Next, the chapter covers IIS concepts such as web sites and application pools followed by discussions of the related SharePoint object model classes. The ASP.NET HTTP Runtime Pipeline and the SharePoint extensions to this pipeline are discussed in depth. You'll also learn about the ASP.NET dynamic compilation model and the role it plays in SharePoint.

ASP.NET Hosting Environment

One of the great architectural characteristics of the ASP.NET Framework is its isolation from its hosting environment, which allows you to run your ASP.NET applications in different hosting scenarios such as IIS 5.0, IIS 5.1, IIS 6.0, IIS 7.0, or even a custom managed application. This section discusses these architectural aspects of the ASP.NET Framework as well as the most common hosting scenario, IIS.

Hosting ASP.NET

As mentioned, ASP.NET can be hosted in different environments, such as IIS 5.0, IIS 6.0, IIS 7.0, or even a custom managed application such as a console application. Hosting ASP.NET in a given environment involves two major components:

- **Worker request class.** This is a class that directly or indirectly inherits from the HttpWorkerRequest abstract base class. As you'll see later, an ASP.NET component named HttpRuntime uses the worker request class to communicate with the underlying environment. All worker request classes implement the HttpWorkerRequest API, which isolates HttpRuntime from the environment-specific aspects of the communications between HttpRuntime and the underlying environment. This allows ASP.NET to be hosted in any environment as long as the environment comes with a worker request class that implements the HttpWorkerRequest API.

- **Runtime class.** By convention, the name of this class ends with the word *Runtime*. The runtime class must perform two tasks for every client request. These tasks are to:
    - Instantiate and initialize an instance of the appropriate worker request class.
    - Call the appropriate method of HttpRuntime, passing in the worker request instance to process the request.

The worker request and runtime classes are discussed in the following sections.

HttpWorkerRequest

As mentioned previously, this API isolates HttpRuntime from its environment, allowing ASP.NET to be hosted in different types of environments. For example, as you can see from Listing 1-1, the HttpWorkerRequest class exposes a method named CloseConnection that HttpRuntime calls to close the connection with the client without knowing the environment-specific details that close the connection under the hood. Or HttpRuntime calls the FlushResponse method (see Listing 1-1) to flush the response without knowing the environment-specific details that flush the response under the hood.

Listing 1-1: The HttpWorkerRequest API

```
public abstract class HttpWorkerRequest
{
  public virtual void CloseConnection();
  public abstract void EndOfRequest();
  public abstract void FlushResponse(bool finalFlush);
  public virtual byte[] GetPreloadedEntityBody();
  public virtual int GetPreloadedEntityBody(byte[] buffer, int offset);
  public abstract string GetQueryString();
  public virtual int ReadEntityBody(byte[] buffer, int size);
  public abstract void SendResponseFromFile(string filename, long offset,
                                            long length);
  public abstract void SendResponseFromMemory(byte[] data, int length);
}
```

ASP.NET comes with several standard implementations of the HttpWorkerRequest API, each one specifically designed to handle the communications with a specific hosting environment such as IIS 5.1, IIS 6.0, IIS 7.0, and so on. ASP.NET also comes with a standard implementation of the HttpWorkerRequest API called SimpleWorkerRequest, which you can use to host ASP.NET in custom managed environments, such as a console application.

Runtime Class

The ASP.NET 2.0 Framework comes with two important runtime classes named ISAPIRuntime and PipelineRuntime. Each class is described next:

- **ISAPIRuntime.** This is the runtime class for ISAPI-based IIS environments, including IIS 5, IIS 6, and IIS 7 running in ISAPI mode.
- **PipelineRuntime.** This is the runtime class for IIS 7 running in integrated mode.

These runtime classes are very different from one another because they represent different runtime environments. However, they both feature a method (though each method is different) that processes the request:

- ISAPIRuntime uses the ProcessRequest method.
- PipelineRuntime uses the GetExecuteDelegate method.

The request processing method for each runtime class takes two important steps. First, it instantiates and initializes an instance of the appropriate worker request class. Second, it passes the instance to the appropriate method of HttpRuntime to process the request.

Internet Information Services (IIS)

Microsoft Internet Information Services (IIS), the Windows web server, is an integral part of the Windows 2000 Server, Windows XP Professional, Windows Server 2003, Windows Vista, and Windows Server 2008 operating systems. IIS is an instance of a Win32 executable named inetinfo.exe, which is located in the following folder on your machine:

```
%SystemRoot%\System32\inetsrv
```

The version of IIS running on your machine depends on your OS version. Each IIS version presents a somewhat different ASP.NET request processing model. An ASP.NET request processing model is a set of steps taken to process incoming requests. These steps vary from one IIS version to another. We'll only cover IIS 6.0 here.

One of the great architectural advantages of IIS 6.0 is its extensibility model, which allows you to write your own ISAPI extension and filter modules to extend the functionality of the web server. An ISAPI extension module is a Win32 DLL that can be loaded into the IIS process (inetinfo.exe) itself or another process.

IIS communicates with ISAPI extension modules through a standard API that contains an important function named HttpExtensionProc as shown in the following code snippet:

```
DWORD WINAPI HttpExtensionProc (LPEXTENSION_CONTROL_BLOCK lpECB);
```

This function takes a parameter named lpECB that references the Extension_Control_Block data structure associated with the current request. Every ISAPI extension is specifically designed to process requests for resources with specific file extensions. For example, the asp.dll ISAPI extension handles requests for resources with an .asp file extension. Every version of ASP.NET comes with a specific version of the

ISAPI extension module named aspnet_isapi.dll. This module, like any other ISAPI module, is a Win32 dynamic link library (DLL). As such it's an unmanaged component. The ASP.NET ISAPI extension module (aspnet_isapi.dll) is located in the following folder on your machine:

```
%SystemRoot%\Microsoft.NET\Framework\versionNumber\aspnet_isapi.dll
```

Upon installation, ASP.NET automatically registers the ASP.NET ISAPI extension module with the IIS metabase for handling requests for resources with the ASP.NET-specific file extensions such as .aspx, .asmx, .asax, .ashx, and so on. The IIS metabase is where the IIS configuration settings are stored. You can use the Application Configuration dialog to access the IIS metabase.

IIS passes the Extension_Control_Block data structure to the HttpExtensionProc method of the ASP.NET ISAPI extension module, and is then finally passed into the ProcessRequest method of the ISAPIRuntime class. This is discussed in greater detail later in the chapter.

Application Pools

IIS 6.0 allows you to group your web applications into what are known as *application pools* (see Figure 1-1). Web applications residing in the same application pool share the same worker process. The worker process is an instance of the w3wp.exe executable.

Because different application pools run in different worker processes, application pools are separated by process boundaries. This has the following important benefits:

- Because web applications do not run inside the IIS process, application misbehaviors will not affect the IIS process itself. This dramatically improves the reliability and stability of the web server.
- Because application pools are isolated by process boundaries, application failure in one pool has no effect on applications running in other pools.

  Because upgrades and troubleshooting are done on a per application pool basis, upgrading and troubleshooting one pool has no effect on other pools. This provides tremendous benefits to system administrators because they don't have to restart the whole web server or all applications running on the web server to perform a simple upgrade or troubleshooting that affects only a few applications.

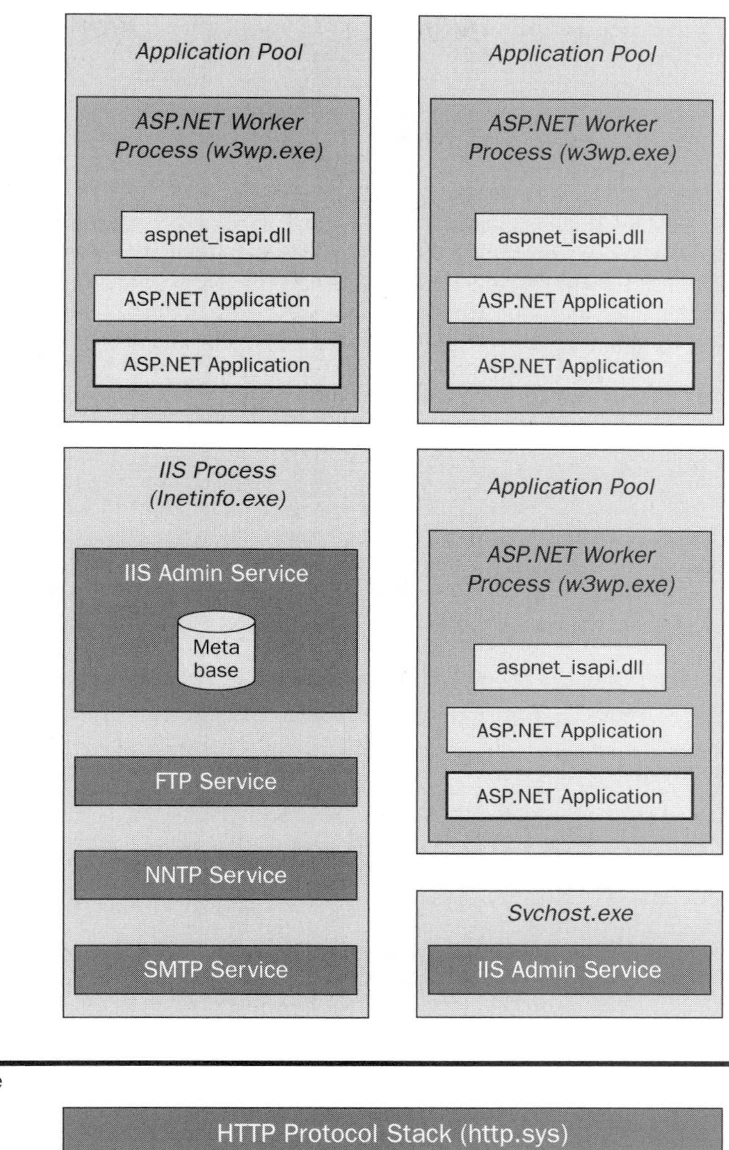

Figure 1-1: The default_aspx class

The w3wp.exe executable is an IIS 6.0-specific executable located in the following IIS-specific directory on your machine:

```
%SystemRoot%\System32\inetsvc\w3wp.exe
```

As such, you have to configure the w3wp worker process from the Internet Information Services (IIS) 6.0 Manager.

IIS 6.0 introduces a new kernel-mode component named the HTTP Protocol Stack (http.sys) that eliminates the need for interprocess communications between the worker process and the IIS process. Earlier IIS versions use the user-mode Windows Socket API (WinSock) to receive HTTP requests from the clients and to send HTTP responses back to the clients. IIS 6.0 replaces this user-mode component with the kernel-mode http.sys driver. Here is how this driver manages to avoid the interprocess communications.

When you add a new virtual directory for a new web application belonging to a particular application pool, IIS 6.0 registers this virtual directory with the kernel-mode http.sys driver. The main responsibility of http.sys is to listen for an incoming HTTP request and pass it onto the worker process responsible for processing requests for the associated application pool. http.sys maintains a kernel-mode queue for each application pool, allowing it to queue the request in the kernel-mode request queue of the associated application pool. The worker process then picks up the request directly from the kernel-mode request queue. As you can see, this avoids the interprocess communications between the web server and worker process. When the worker process is done with processing the request, it returns the response directly to http.sys, avoiding the interprocess communication overhead.

http.sys not only eliminates the interprocess communication overhead but also improves the availability of your applications. Here's why: Imagine that the worker process responsible for processing requests for a particular application pool starts to misbehave. http.sys will keep receiving HTTP requests and queueing them in the associated kernel-level queue while the WWW Service is starting a new worker process to process the requests. The users may feel a little delay, but their requests will not be denied.

Another added performance benefit of http.sys is that it caches the response in a kernel-mode cache. Therefore the next requests are directly serviced from this kernel-mode cache without switching to the user mode.

SharePoint Extensions

SharePoint extends IIS and ASP.NET to add support for SharePoint functionality. This section provides more detailed information about these extensions and the roles they play in the overall SharePoint architecture. The SharePoint object model also contains types whose instances represent typical IIS entities such as application pools, web sites, and so on. These types allow you to program against these entities within your managed code.

SPApplicationPool

SharePoint represents each IIS application pool with an instance of a type named SPApplicationPool, which allows you to program against IIS application pools from your managed code. Here are some of the public properties of the SPApplicationPool class that you can use in your managed code:

- **CurrentIdentityType.** This property gets or sets an IdentityType enumeration value that specifies the type of identity (such as the type of Windows account) under which this application pool is running. The possible values are LocalService, LocalSystem, NetworkService, and SpecificUser.
- **DisplayName.** This read-only property gets the display name of this application pool.

- **Farm.** This read-only property gets a reference to the SPFarm object that represents the SharePoint farm where this application pool resides.
- **Id.** This property gets or sets a GUID that uniquely identifies this application pool.
- **Name.** This property gets or sets a string that contains the name of this application pool.
- **Password.** This property gets or sets a string that specifies the password of the Windows account under which this application pool is running.
- **Username.** This property gets or sets a string that specifies the username of the Windows account under which this application pool is running.
- **Status.** This property gets or sets an SPObjectStatus enumeration value that specifies the current status of this application pool. The possible values are Disabled, Offline, Online, Provisioning, Unprovisioning, and Upgrading.

Here are some of the public methods of the SPApplicationPool class:

- **Delete.** This method deletes the application pool.
- **Provision.** This method creates the application pool.
- **Unprovision.** This method removes the application pool.
- **Update.** This method updates and commits the changes made to the application pool.
- **UpdateCredentials.** This method updates and commits the credentials under which the application pool is running.

Listing 1-2 presents an example that shows you how to use the SPApplicationPool class to program against the IIS application pools.

Listing 1-2: A page that displays the application pools running in the local farm

```
<%@ Page Language="C#" %>
<%@ Assembly Name="Microsoft.SharePoint, Version=12.0.0.0, Culture=neutral,
PublicKeyToken=71E9BCE111E9429C" %>
<%@ Import Namespace="Microsoft.SharePoint" %>
<%@ Import Namespace="Microsoft.SharePoint.Administration" %>
<%@ Import Namespace="System.ComponentModel" %>
<%@ Import Namespace="System.Collections.Generic" %>

<!DOCTYPE html PUBLIC "-//W3C//DTD XHTML 1.0 Transitional//EN"
"http://www.w3.org/TR/xhtml1/DTD/xhtml1-transitional.dtd">

<script runat="server">
  void Page_Load(object sender, EventArgs e)
  {
    SPWebServiceCollection wsc = new SPWebServiceCollection(SPFarm.Local);

    foreach (SPWebService ws in wsc)
    {
      SPApplicationPoolCollection apc = ws.ApplicationPools;
```

(continued)

Listing 1-2 *(continued)*

```
          foreach (SPApplicationPool ap in apc)
          {
            Response.Write(ap.Name);
            Response.Write("</br>");
          }
        }
      }
    </script>

    <html xmlns="http://www.w3.org/1999/xhtml">
    <head runat="server">
      <title>Untitled Page</title>
    </head>
    <body>
      <form id="form1" runat="server">
      <div>
      </div>
      </form>
    </body>
    </html>
```

SPIisWebSite

SharePoint runs on top of IIS. As such, it uses IIS web sites. An IIS web site is an entry point into IIS and is configured to listen for incoming requests on a specific port over a specific IP address and/or with a specific host header. Upon installation, IIS creates an IIS web site named Default Web Site and configures it to listen for incoming requests on port 80. You have the option of creating one or more IIS web sites and configuring them to listen for incoming requests on other ports and/or IP addresses supported on the IIS web server.

One of the great things about IIS web sites is that their security settings can be configured independently. For example, you can have an IIS web site such as Default Web Site that acts as an Internet-facing web site for your company, allowing anonymous users to access its contents. You can then create another IIS web site to act as an intranet-facing web site and configure it to use integrated Windows authentication, allowing only users with Windows accounts on the web server or a trusted domain to access its content.

SharePoint's object model comes with a class named SPIisWebSite whose instances represent IIS web sites. The following list presents the public properties of this class:

- **Exists.** This gets a Boolean value that specifies whether the IIS web site that the SPIisWebSite object represents exists in the metabase.
- **InstanceId.** This gets an integer value that uniquely identifies the IIS web site that the SPIisWebSite represents.
- **ServerBindings.** This gets or sets a string array where each string in the array specifies a server binding that the IIS web site that the SPIisWebSite object represents serves.

- **ServerComment.** This gets or sets a string that contains the display name of the IIS web site that the SPIisWebSite object represents.
- **ServerState.** This gets an SPIisServerState enumeration value that specifies the server state. The possible values are Continuing, Paused, Pausing, Started, Starting, Stopped, and Stopping.

The following list presents the public methods of the SPIisWebSite class:

- **Provision.** This provisions (creates) the IIS web site that the SPIisWebSite object represents.
- **Unprovision.** This unprovisions (removes) the IIS web site that the SPIisWebSite object represents.
- **Update.** This commits all changes to the registry.

You can create an instance of this class to access a specified IIS web site from within your managed code as shown in Listing 1-3.

Listing 1-3: An application page that shows how to access an IIS web site

```
<%@ Page Language="C#" %>
<%@ Assembly Name="Microsoft.SharePoint, Version=12.0.0.0, Culture=neutral,
PublicKeyToken=71E9BCE111E9429C" %>
<%@ Import Namespace="Microsoft.SharePoint" %>
<%@ Import Namespace="Microsoft.SharePoint.Administration" %>
<%@ Import Namespace="System.Globalization" %>

<!DOCTYPE html PUBLIC "-//W3C//DTD XHTML 1.0 Transitional//EN"
"http://www.w3.org/TR/xhtml1/DTD/xhtml1-transitional.dtd">

<script runat="server">
  void Page_Load(object sender, EventArgs e)
  {
    HttpContext context = HttpContext.Current;
    int instanceId = int.Parse(context.Request.ServerVariables["INSTANCE_ID"],
                               NumberFormatInfo.InvariantInfo);
    SPIisWebSite site = new SPIisWebSite(instanceId);
    lbl.Text = "Exists: " + site.Exists + "<br/>";
    lbl.Text += "InstanceId: " + site.InstanceId + "<br/>";
    lbl.Text += "Server bindings served by this IIS Web site:<br/>";
    foreach (string serverBinding in site.ServerBindings)
    {
      lbl.Text += "    Server Binding  " +
                  serverBinding + "<br/>";
    }
    lbl.Text += "<br/>";
    lbl.Text += "ServerComment: " + site.ServerComment + "<br/>";
    lbl.Text += "Server State: " + site.ServerState + "<br/>";
  }
</script>

<html xmlns="http://www.w3.org/1999/xhtml">
```

(continued)

Listing 1-3 *(continued)*

```
<head runat="server">
  <title>Untitled Page</title>
</head>
<body>
  <form id="form1" runat="server">
  <div>
    <asp:Label ID="lbl" runat="server" />
  </div>
  </form>
</body>
</html>
```

As Listing 1-3 shows, the Page_Load method of this application page first accesses the current ASP.NET HTTP context as shown next:

```
HttpContext context = HttpContext.Current;
```

Next, it uses the current ASP.NET HTTP context to access the instance ID of the current IIS web site, which hosts the current SharePoint web application:

```
    int instanceId = int.Parse(context.Request.ServerVariables["INSTANCE_ID"],
                               NumberFormatInfo.InvariantInfo);
```

Then, it instantiates an SPIisWebSite object to represent the current IIS web site:

```
    SPIisWebSite site = new SPIisWebSite(instanceId);
```

Next, it iterates through the properties of this SPIisWebSite and prints their values:

```
    lbl.Text = "Exists: " + site.Exists + "<br/>";
    lbl.Text += "InstanceId: " + site.InstanceId + "<br/>";
    lbl.Text += "Server bindings served by this IIS Web site:<br/>";
    foreach (string serverBinding in site.ServerBindings)
    {
      lbl.Text += "    Server Binding  " +
                  serverBinding + "<br/>";
    }
    lbl.Text += "<br/>";
    lbl.Text += "ServerComment: " + site.ServerComment + "<br/>";
    lbl.Text += "Server State: " + site.ServerState + "<br/>";
```

As the following application page shows, you can also update the properties of an IIS web site:

```
<%@ Page Language="C#" %>
<%@ Assembly Name="Microsoft.SharePoint, Version=12.0.0.0, Culture=neutral,
PublicKeyToken=71E9BCE111E9429C" %>
<%@ Import Namespace="Microsoft.SharePoint" %>
<%@ Import Namespace="Microsoft.SharePoint.Administration" %>
```

```
<%@ Import Namespace="System.Globalization" %>

<!DOCTYPE html PUBLIC "-//W3C//DTD XHTML 1.0 Transitional//EN"
"http://www.w3.org/TR/xhtml1/DTD/xhtml1-transitional.dtd">

<script runat="server">
  void Page_Load(object sender, EventArgs e)
  {
    HttpContext context = HttpContext.Current;
    int instanceId = int.Parse(context.Request.ServerVariables["INSTANCE_ID"],
                               NumberFormatInfo.InvariantInfo);
    SPIisWebSite site = new SPIisWebSite(instanceId);
    site.ServerComment = "My " + site.ServerComment;
    site.Update();
  }
</script>

<html xmlns="http://www.w3.org/1999/xhtml">
<head runat="server">
  <title>Untitled Page</title>
</head>
<body>
  <form id="form1" runat="server">
  <div>
    <asp:Label ID="lbl" runat="server" />
  </div>
  </form>
</body>
</html>
```

As this code listing shows, this application page first creates an SPIisWebSite object to represent the current IIS web site as discussed earlier. Then, it sets the value of the ServerComment property on this SPIisWebSite object. Finally, it invokes the Update method on this SPIisWebSite object to commit the change.

SPWebApplication

SharePoint takes an IIS web site through a one-time configuration process to enable it to host SharePoint sites. Such an IIS web site is known as a web application in SharePoint terminology. This configuration process adds a wildcard application map to the IIS metabase to have IIS route all incoming requests targeted to the specified IIS web site to the aspnet_isapi.dll ISAPI extension module. Because this ISAPI extension module routes the requests to ASP.NET in turn, it ensures that all requests go through the ASP.NET HTTP Runtime Pipeline and are properly initialized with ASP.NET execution context before they are routed to SharePoint. This avoids a lot of the awkward problems associated with request processing in previous versions of SharePoint.

The SharePoint object model comes with a class named SPWebApplication that you can use to program against web applications from your managed code.

The following list describes some of the public properties of the SPWebApplication class:

- **AllowAccessToWebPartCatalog.** This gets or sets a Boolean value that specifies whether sites in the web application can use Web parts from the global Web part catalog.
- **AllowPartToPartCommunication.** This gets or sets a Boolean value that specifies whether the web application allows Web parts to communicate with each other to share data.
- **ApplicationPool.** This gets or sets the SPApplicationPool object that represents the application pool in which the web application is running.
- **BlockedFileExtensions.** This gets a Collection<string> object that contains the list of blocked file extensions. Files with such file extensions cannot be uploaded to the sites in the web application or downloaded from the sites in the web application.
- **ContentDatabases.** This gets the SPContentDatabaseCollection collection that contains the SPContentDatabase objects that represent the content databases that are available to the web application.
- **DaysToShowNewIndicator.** This gets or sets an integer value that specifies how many days the New icon is displayed next to new list items or documents.
- **DefaultTimeZone.** This gets or sets an integer value that specifies the default time zone for the web application.
- **DisplayName.** This gets the string that contains the display name of the web application.
- **Farm.** This gets the SPFarm object that represents the SharePoint farm in which the web application resides.
- **Features.** This gets the SPFeatureCollection collection that contains the SPFeature objects that represent the features activated for the web application.
- **Id.** This gets or sets the GUID that uniquely identifies the web application.
- **IsAdministrationWebApplication.** This gets or sets a Boolean value that indicates whether the web application is the Central Administration application.
- **Name.** This gets or sets a string that contains the name of the web application.
- **Properties.** This gets a property bag that is used to store properties for the web application. SharePoint automatically stores and retrieves the custom objects that you place in this property bag.
- **Sites.** This gets a reference to the SPSiteCollection collection that contains the SPSite objects that represent all site collections in the web application.
- **Status.** This gets or sets the SPObjectStatus enumeration value that specifies the status of the web application. The possible values are Disabled, Offline, Online, Provisioning, Unprovisioning, and Upgrading.
- **WebService.** This gets a reference to the SPWebService object that contains the web application.

The following list presents the public methods of the SPWebApplication class:

- **Delete.** This deletes the web application that the SPWebApplication object represents.
- **GrantAccessToProcessIdentity.** This takes a string that contains a username as its argument and grants the user access to the process identity of the SharePoint web application. This basically gives the user full control.
- **Lookup.** This takes a string that contains the URL of a web application and returns a reference to the SPWebApplication object that represents the web application.
- **Provision.** This provisions (creates) the web application that the SPWebApplication object represents on the local server.
- **Unprovision.** This unprovisions (removes) the web application that the SPWebApplication object represents from all local IIS web sites.
- **Update.** This serializes the state of the web application and propagates changes to all web servers in the server farm.
- **UpdateCredentials.** This commits new credentials (username or password) to the database.
- **UpdateMailSettings.** This commits the new email settings. These email settings are used to send emails.

Use one of the following methods to access the SPWebApplication object that represents a given SharePoint web application:

- The SPSite object that represents a SharePoint site collection exposes a property named WebApplication. WebApplication returns a reference to the SPWebApplication object that represents the SharePoint web application that hosts the site collection.
- The SPWeb object that represents a SharePoint site exposes a property named WebApplication returning a reference to the SPWebApplication object that represents the SharePoint web application that hosts the site.
- The SharePoint object model comes with a class named SPWebService that mainly acts as a container for SPWebApplication objects representing a SharePoint farm's collection of web applications. The SPWebService object for a given SharePoint farm exposes a collection property of type SPWebApplicationCollection named WebApplications that contains the farm's web applications. Use the name or GUID of a web application as an index into this collection to return a reference to the SPWebApplication object that represents the web application.
- The SPWebApplication class exposes a static method named Lookup. This method takes a URI object that specifies the URI of a web application and then returns the SPWebApplication object that represents it.

The following code listing presents a web page that uses the SharePoint object model to display the names of all web applications in the local farm:

```
<%@ Page Language="C#" %>
<%@ Assembly Name="Microsoft.SharePoint, Version=12.0.0.0, Culture=neutral,
PublicKeyToken=71E9BCE111E9429C" %>
<%@ Import Namespace="Microsoft.SharePoint" %>
<%@ Import Namespace="Microsoft.SharePoint.Administration" %>

<!DOCTYPE html PUBLIC "-//W3C//DTD XHTML 1.0 Transitional//EN"
"http://www.w3.org/TR/xhtml1/DTD/xhtml1-transitional.dtd">

<script runat="server">
  void Page_Load(object sender, EventArgs e)
  {
    SPWebServiceCollection wsc = new SPWebServiceCollection(SPFarm.Local);
    foreach (SPWebService ws in wsc)
    {
      SPWebApplicationCollection wac = ws.WebApplications;
      foreach (SPWebApplication wa in wac)
      {
        Response.Write(wa.Name);
        Response.Write("<br/>");
      }
    }
  }
</script>

<html xmlns="http://www.w3.org/1999/xhtml">
<head runat="server">
  <title>Untitled Page</title>
</head>
<body>
  <form id="form1" runat="server">
  <div>
  </div>
  </form>
</body>
</html>
```

SPWebApplicationBuilder

Use an instance of the SPWebApplicationBuilder class to create an instance of the SPWebApplication class. The SPWebApplicationBuilder instance automatically provides default values for all the required settings, allowing you to override only the desired settings.

The following list presents the public properties of the SPWebApplicationBuilder class:

- **AllowAnonymousAccess.** This gets or sets a Boolean value that indicates whether anonymous users are allowed to access the new web application.

- **ApplicationPoolId.** This gets or sets a string that contains the GUID that uniquely identifies the application pool in which the new web application is created.
- **ApplicationPoolPassword.** This gets or sets the password of the Windows account under which the new application pool for the web application is to run.
- **ApplicationPoolUsername.** This gets or sets a string that contains the username of the Windows account under which the new application pool for the new web application is to run.
- **CreateNewDatabase.** This gets or sets a Boolean value that indicates whether to create a new content database for the web application.
- **DatabaseName.** This gets or sets a string that specifies the name for the new content database.
- **DatabasePassword.** This gets or sets a string that specifies the password for the new content database.
- **DatabaseServer.** This gets or sets a string that contains the database server name and instance in which to create the new content database.
- **DatabaseUsername.** This gets or sets a string that contains the username for the new content database.
- **Id.** This gets or sets the GUID that uniquely identifies the web application.
- **IdentityType.** This gets or sets an IdentityType enumeration value that specifies the process identity type of the application pool for the web application. The possible values are LocalService, LocalSystem, NetworkService, and SpecificUser.
- **Port.** This gets or sets an integer that specifies the port number of the new web application.
- **RootDirectory.** This gets or sets the DirectoryInfo object that represents the file system directory in which to install static files such as web.config for the new web application.
- **ServerComment.** This gets or sets a string that contains the server comment for the web application.
- **WebService.** This gets or sets the SPWebService object that represents the web service that contains the web application.

The following list presents the methods of the SPWebApplicationBuilder class:

- **Create.** This takes no arguments, uses the specified settings, creates a new web application, and returns a WebApplication object that represents the newly created web application.
- **ResetDefaults.** This takes no arguments and initializes all values with the best defaults that SharePoint can determine.

The following code listing creates and provisions a new web application:

```
<%@ Page Language="C#" %>
<%@ Assembly Name="Microsoft.SharePoint, Version=12.0.0.0, Culture=neutral,
PublicKeyToken=71E9BCE111E9429C" %>
<%@ Import Namespace="Microsoft.SharePoint" %>
<%@ Import Namespace="Microsoft.SharePoint.Administration" %>
<%@ Import Namespace="System.ComponentModel" %>
<%@ Import Namespace="System.Collections.Generic" %>

<!DOCTYPE html PUBLIC "-//W3C//DTD XHTML 1.0 Transitional//EN"
"http://www.w3.org/TR/xhtml1/DTD/xhtml1-transitional.dtd">

<script runat="server">
  void Page_Load(object sender, EventArgs e)
  {
    SPWebApplicationBuilder wab = new SPWebApplicationBuilder(SPFarm.Local);
    wab.Port = 12000;
    SPWebApplication wa = wab.Create();
    wa.Provision();
  }
</script>

<html xmlns="http://www.w3.org/1999/xhtml">
<head runat="server">
  <title>Untitled Page</title>
</head>
<body>
  <form id="form1" runat="server">
  <div>
  </div>
  </form>
</body>
</html>
```

SPWebService

The SPWebService acts as a container for SPWebApplication objects that represents one or more web applications in a SharePoint farm. The following list presents the public properties of this class:

- **AdministrationService.** This is a static property that gets a reference to the SPWebService object that contains the SPWebApplication object that represents the SharePoint Central Administration web application.
- **ApplicationPools.** This gets a reference to the SPApplicationPoolCollection collection that contains the SPApplicationPool objects that represent the IIS application pools available to the web service that this SPWebService object represents.
- **ContentService.** This gets a reference to the SPWebService object that contains the SPWebApplication objects that represent the content web applications.

- **DefaultDatabaseInstance.** This gets or sets a reference to the SPDatabaseServiceInstance object that represents the default named SQL Server installation for new content databases.
- **DefaultDatabasePassword.** This gets or sets a string that contains the default password for new content databases.
- **DefaultDatabaseUsername.** This gets or sets a string that contains the default username for new content databases.
- **DisplayName.** This gets a string that contains the display name of the web service that this SPWebService object represents.
- **Farm.** This gets a reference to the SPFarm object that represents the SharePoint farm where this web service resides.
- **Features.** This gets a reference to the SPFeatureCollection collection that contains SPFeature objects that represent farm-level scoped features.
- **Id.** This gets or sets the GUID that uniquely identifies this web service.
- **Name.** This gets or sets a string that contains the name of this web service. The name of the web service uniquely identifies the service.
- **Properties.** This gets a reference to a hash table where you can store arbitrary name/value pairs. SharePoint automatically takes care of persistence and retrieval of this pair just like it does for any other persistable SharePoint data.
- **Status.** This gets or sets the SPObjectStatus enumeration value that specifies the status of this web service. The possible values are Disabled, Offline, Online, Provisioning, Unprovisioning, and Upgrading.
- **WebApplications.** This gets a reference to an SPWebApplicationCollection collection that contains the SPWebApplication objects that represent the web applications that this web service contains.

The following list contains the public methods of the SPWebService class:

- **Delete.** This removes the web service from the SharePoint farm.
- **Provision.** This provisions the web service into the local server by making the necessary changes to the local server.
- **Unprovision.** This unprovisions the web service by making the necessary changes to the local server to clean up after deleting the object.
- **Update.** This commits and propagates the change made to this web service to all the machines in the farm.

The following code listing iterates through the application pools for each web service and prints their names:

```
<%@ Page Language="C#" %>
<%@ Assembly Name="Microsoft.SharePoint, Version=12.0.0.0, Culture=neutral,
PublicKeyToken=71E9BCE111E9429C" %>
<%@ Import Namespace="Microsoft.SharePoint" %>
<%@ Import Namespace="Microsoft.SharePoint.Administration" %>

<!DOCTYPE html PUBLIC "-//W3C//DTD XHTML 1.0 Transitional//EN"
"http://www.w3.org/TR/xhtml1/DTD/xhtml1-transitional.dtd">

<script runat="server">
  void Page_Load(object sender, EventArgs e)
  {
    SPWebServiceCollection wsc = new SPWebServiceCollection(SPFarm.Local);
    foreach (SPWebService ws in wsc)
    {
      SPApplicationPoolCollection apc = ws.ApplicationPools;
      foreach (SPApplicationPool ap in apc)
      {
        Response.Write(ap.Name);
        Response.Write("<br/>");
      }
    }
  }
</script>

<html xmlns="http://www.w3.org/1999/xhtml">
<head id="Head1" runat="server">
  <title>Untitled Page</title>
</head>
<body>
  <form id="form1" runat="server">
  <div>
  </div>
  </form>
</body>
</html>
```

ISAPIRuntime

As discussed earlier, when a request arrives, the HttpExtensionProc function of the ASP.NET ISAPI extension module is invoked and the Extension_Control_Block data structure is passed into it. The HttpExtensionProc function uses this data structure to communicate with IIS. The same Extension_Control_Block data structure is finally passed into the ProcessRequest method of the ISAPIRuntime object (see Listing 1-4).

Listing 1-4: The ProcessRequest method of ISAPIRuntime

```
public int ProcessRequest(IntPtr ecb, int iWRType)
{
  HttpWorkerRequest request =  CreateWorkerRequest(ecb, iWRType);
  HttpRuntime.ProcessRequest(request);
  return 0;
}
```

The ProcessRequest method of ISAPIRuntime, like the request processing method of any runtime class, first instantiates and initializes the appropriate HttpWorkerRequest object and then calls the ProcessRequest static method of an ASP.NET class named HttpRuntime and passes the newly instantiated HttpWorkerRequest object into it. HttpRuntime is the entry point into what is known as the ASP.NET HTTP Runtime Pipeline. This pipeline is discussed in detail in the next section.

ASP.NET HTTP Runtime Pipeline

The main responsibility of this pipeline is to process incoming requests and to generate the response text for the client. Listing 1-5 presents the internal implementation of the ProcessRequest method.

Listing 1-5: The ProcessRequest method of HttpRuntime

```
public static void ProcessRequest(HttpWorkerRequest wr)
{
  HttpContext context1 = new HttpContext(wr, true);
  IHttpHandler handler1 = HttpApplicationFactory.GetApplicationInstance(context1);

  if (handler1 is IHttpAsyncHandler)
  {
    IHttpAsyncHandler handler2 = (IHttpAsyncHandler)handler1;
    context1.AsyncAppHandler = handler2;
    handler2.BeginProcessRequest(context1, _handlerCompletionCallback,
                                 context1);
  }
  else
  {
    handler1.ProcessRequest(context1);
    FinishRequest(context1.WorkerRequest, context1, null);
  }
}
```

ProcessRequest performs these three main tasks:

- It instantiates an instance of an ASP.NET class named HttpContext, passing in the HttpWorkerRequest object. This HttpContext instance represents the ASP.NET execution context for the current request:

```
HttpContext context1 = new HttpContext(wr, true);
```

- It calls the GetApplicationInstance method of an ASP.NET class named HttpApplicationFactory to return an instance of an ASP.NET class that implements the IHttpHandler. This class inherits from another ASP.NET class named HttpApplication. ASP.NET represents each ASP.NET application with one or more HttpApplication objects. Also notice that HttpRuntime passes the HttpContext object into the GetApplicationInstance method:

```
IHttpHandler handler1 = HttpApplicationFactory.GetApplicationInstance(context1);
```

- It checks whether the object that GetApplicationInstance returns implements the IHttpAsyncHandler interface. If so, it calls the BeginProcessRequest method of the object to process the current request asynchronously:

```
httpApplication.BeginProcessRequest(context1, _handlerCompletionCallback,
                                    context1);
```

  If not, it calls the ProcessRequest method of the object to process the request synchronously:

```
handler1.ProcessRequest(context1);
```

  HTTP requests are always processed asynchronously to improve the performance and throughput of ASP.NET applications. As such, GetApplicationInstance always invokes the BeginProcessRequest method.

Notice that HttpRuntime passes the HttpContext object to HttpApplicationFactory, which is then passed to HttpApplication. HttpRuntime, HttpApplicationFactory, and HttpApplication, together with some other components discussed later in this chapter, form a pipeline of managed components known as the ASP.NET HTTP Runtime Pipeline. Each component in the pipeline receives the HttpContext object from the previous component, extracts the needed information from the object, processes the information, stores the processed information back into the object, and passes the object to the next component in the pipeline.

Each incoming HTTP request is processed with a distinct ASP.NET HTTP Runtime Pipeline. No two requests share the same pipeline. The HttpContext object provides the context within which an incoming HTTP request is processed.

Every application domain contains a single instance of the HttpApplicationFactory object. The HttpApplicationFactory class features a field named _theApplicationFactory that returns this single instance. The main responsibility of the GetApplicationInstance method of HttpApplicationFactory is to return an instance of a class to represent the current application. The type of this class depends on whether the application uses the global.asax file. This file is optional but every application can contain only a single instance of the file, which must be placed in the root directory of the application. The instances of the file placed in the subdirectories of the root directory are ignored.

If the root directory of an application doesn't contain the global.asax file, the GetApplicationInstance method returns an instance of an ASP.NET class named HttpApplication to represent the current application. If the root directory does contain the file, the GetApplicationInstance method returns an instance of a class that derives from the HttpApplication class to represent the application.

This HttpApplication-derived class is not one of the standard classes such as HttpApplication that ships with the ASP.NET Framework. Instead it's a class that the GetApplicationInstance method dynamically generates on the fly from the content of the global.asax file. In other words, the GetApplicationInstance method automatically turns what's inside the global.asax file into a class that derives from HttpApplication, dynamically compiles this class into an assembly, and creates an instance of this dynamically generated compiled class to represent the application.

Listing 1-6 presents the internal implementation of the GetApplicationInstance method.

Listing 1-6: The internal implementation of the GetApplicationInstance method

```
public class HttpApplicationFactory
{
  private Stack _freeList;
  private int _numFreeAppInstances;

  internal static IHttpHandler GetApplicationInstance(HttpContext context)
  {
    GenerateAndCompileAppClassIfNecessary(context);
    HttpApplication appInstance = null;
    lock (_freeList)
    {
      if (_numFreeAppInstances > 0)
      {
        appInstance = (HttpApplication)_freeList.Pop();
        _numFreeAppInstances--;
      }
    }
    if (appInstance == null)
    {
      appInstance = InstantiateAppInstance();
      appInstance.InitializeAppInstance();
    }
    return appInstance;
  }
}
```

The GetApplicationInstance method performs these tasks. First, it calls the GenerateAndCompileAppClassIfNecessary method of the HttpApplicationFactory:

```
GenerateAndCompileAppClassIfNecessary(context);
```

The GenerateAndCompileAppClassIfNecessary method takes these steps. First, it determines whether the root directory of the application contains the global.asax file. If so, it instantiates an instance of an ASP.NET class named ApplicationBuildProvider. As the name suggests, ApplicationBuildProvider is the build provider responsible for generating the source code for the class that represents the global.asax file. As mentioned earlier, this class inherits from the HttpApplication base class.

After generating the source code for this class, the GenerateAndCompileAppClassIfNecessary method uses the AssemblyBuilder to dynamically compile this source code into an assembly and loads the assembly into the application domain. This dynamic code generation and compilation process is performed only when the first request hits the application. The process is repeated only if the timestamp of the global.asax and root web.config file of the application change. The timestamp of a file could change for a number of reasons. One obvious case is when you change the content of a file. Another less obvious case is when you run a program such as an antivirus program that changes this timestamp even though the content of the file hasn't changed. If the timestamp of the global.asax file changes, the global.asax file is recompiled when the next request arrives.

Now back to Listing 1-6. The HttpApplicationFactory maintains a pool of HttpApplication-derived instances that represent the current application. In other words, more than one instance may be processing requests for the same application to improve the performance. When a request hits the application, GetApplicationInstance checks whether there's a free HttpApplication-derived instance available. If so, it returns that instance:

```
lock (_freeList)
{
  if (_numFreeAppInstances > 0)
  {
    appInstance = _freeList.Pop();
    _numFreeAppInstances--;
  }
}
```

Notice that the HttpApplicationFactory maintains the pool members in an internal instance of the Stack class named _freeList. As the previous listing shows, GetApplicationInstance simply calls the Pop method of this internal Stack object to access the free HttpApplication object and decrements the number of available HttpApplication objects by one. Also notice that GetApplicationInstance locks the Stack object before it accesses it because the same Stack object is accessed by multiple threads handling multiple requests.

If the pool has no free HttpApplication object available, GetApplicationInstance calls the InstantiateAppInstance method to create a new HttpApplication object:

```
if (appInstance == null)
{
  appInstance = InstantiateAppInstance();
  appInstance.InitializeAppInstance();
}
```

Notice that GetApplicationInstance finally calls the InitializeAppInstance method of the newly instantiated HttpApplication-derived object to initialize it. What this initialization process entails is discussed later in this chapter.

As mentioned, the GetApplicationInstance method parses the content of the global.asax file into a class that derives from HttpApplication. This means that you can have this method generate a different type of class by implementing and adding the global.asax file to your application. The global.asax file like many other ASP.NET files can have an associated code-behind class. You must use the Inherits attribute of the @Application directive inside the global.asax file to specify the complete information about this code-behind class, which contains the fully qualified name of the type of the class, including its complete namespace containment hierarchy and the complete information about the assembly that contains the class such as assembly name, version, culture, and public key token.

SharePoint uses the same approach to introduce a code-behind class named SPHttpApplication. This means that the objects that represent a given application are instances of a dynamically generated class that inherits from SPHttpApplication. As such, SharePoint applications are represented by instances of the SPHttpApplication class. This class like any code-behind class used in the global.asax file inherits from the HttpApplication class, which means that it exposes the same familiar API as HttpApplication class, which you can use to program against SharePoint applications. As such, we first need to study the HttpApplication class.

HttpApplication

The HttpApplication class is the base class for the class that represents the current application. As such, it provides its subclass with the base functionality that it needs to process the request. Recall that the GetApplicationInstance method of HttpApplicationFactory invokes the InitializeAppInstance method of HttpApplication on the newly instantiated HttpApplication-derived instance to initialize the instance. This method performs these tasks. First, it reads the contents of the <httpModules> sections of the configuration files. The <httpModules> section of a configuration file contains zero or more <add> child elements where each <add> element is used to register an ASP.NET component known as an HTTP module.

Listing 1-7 presents the portion of the <httpModules> section of the root web.config file, which registers the standard ASP.NET HTTP modules.

Listing 1-7: The <httpModules> section of the root web.config file

```
<configuration>
  <system.web>
    <httpModules>
      <add name="OutputCache" type="System.Web.Caching.OutputCacheModule" />
      <add name="Session" type="System.Web.SessionState.SessionStateModule" />
      <add name="WindowsAuthentication"
       type="System.Web.Security.WindowsAuthenticationModule" />
      <add name="FormsAuthentication"
       type="System.Web.Security.FormsAuthenticationModule" />
      ...
    </httpModules>
  </system.web>
</configuration>
```

An HTTP module is a class that implements the IHttpModule interface. Recall from the previous section that HttpRuntime creates an instance of a class named HttpContext, which provides the execution context for the current request. Each module must extract the required information from the HttpContext object, process the information, then store the processed information back in the object.

For example, the FormsAuthenticationModule authenticates the request, creates an IPrincipal object to represent the security context of the current request, and assigns this object to the User property of the HttpContext object. Listing 1-8 presents the definition of the IHttpModule interface.

Listing 1-8: The IHttpModule interface

```
public interface IHttpModule
{
  void Dispose();
  void Init(HttpApplication context);
}
```

InitializeAppInstance reads the contents of the <httpModules> section of the root web.config and other configuration files. Notice that the <add> element features two important attributes, that is, name and type, which respectively contain the friendly name and type information of the HTTP module. The friendly name provides an easy way to reference an HTTP module. The type attribute contains the complete type information needed to instantiate the module.

InitializeAppInstance first uses the value of the type attribute of each <add> element and .NET reflection to dynamically instantiate an instance of the associated HTTP module. It then calls the Init method of each HTTP module to initialize the module. As Listing 1-8 shows, every HTTP module implements the Init method.

The main function of the Init method of an HTTP module is to register event handlers for one or more of the events of the HttpApplication object. HttpApplication exposes a bunch of application-level events as described in the following table. Notice that this table lists the events in the order in which they are fired.

Event	Description
BeginRequest	Fires when ASP.NET begins processing the request
AuthenticateRequest	Fires when ASP.NET authenticates the request
PostAuthenticateRequest	Fires after ASP.NET authenticates the request
AuthorizeRequest	Fires when ASP.NET authorizes the request
PostAuthorizeRequest	Fires after ASP.NET authorizes the request
ResolveRequestCache	Fires when ASP.NET is determining whether the request can be serviced from the cache
PostResolveRequestCache	Fires after ASP.NET determines that the request can indeed be serviced from the cache bypassing the execution of the request handler
MapRequestHandler	Fires when ASP.NET determines the request handler
PostMapRequestHandler	Fires after ASP.NET determines the HTTP request handler
AcquireRequestState	Fires when ASP.NET acquires the request state
PostAcquireRequestState	Fires after ASP.NET acquires the request state
PreRequestHandlerExecute	Fires before ASP.NET executes the request handler
RequestHandlerExecute	Fires when ASP.NET executes the request handler

Event	Description
PostRequestHandlerExecute	Fires after ASP.NET executes the request handler
ReleaseRequestState	Fires when ASP.NET stores the request state
PostReleaseRequestState	Fires after ASP.NET stores the request state
UpdateRequestCache	Fires when ASP.NET is caching the response
PostUpdateRequestCache	Fires after ASP.NET caches the response so the next request is serviced from the cache bypassing the execution of the request handler
LogRequest	Fires when ASP.NET is logging the request
PostLogRequest	Fires after ASP.NET logs the request
EndRequest	Fires when ASP.NET ends processing the request
Disposed	Fires when ASP.NET releases all resources used by the application

The following three events could be raised at any time during the lifecycle of a request:

Event	Description
Error	Fires when an unhandled exception is thrown
PreSendRequestContent	Fires before ASP.NET sends the request content or body
PreSendRequestHeaders	Fires before ASP.NET sends the request HTTP headers

So far, I've covered the synchronous versions of the events of the HttpApplication object. The asynchronous version of each event follows this same format: AddOnXXXAsync where XXX is the placeholder for the event name. AddOnXXXAsync is a method that registers an event handler for the specified events. For example, in the case of the BeginRequest event, this method is AddOnBeginRequestAsync.

Now back to the InitializeAppInstance method of HttpApplication. So far, you've learned that this method instantiates and initializes the registered HTTP modules. Next it instantiates an instance of a class named ApplicationStepManager.

To understand the role of ApplicationStepManager, you need to understand how HttpApplication processes the request. The request processing of HttpApplication consists of a set of execution steps, which are executed in order. Each execution step is represented by an object of type IExecutionStep. The IExecutionStep interface features a method named Execute. As the name suggests, this method executes the step. Each IExecutionStep object is associated with a particular event of HttpApplication. For example, there's an IExecutionStep object associated with the BeginRequest event of HttpApplication.

As the name implies, ApplicationStepManager manages the building and executing the IExecutionStep objects associated with the HttpApplication events. ApplicationStepManager exposes two methods named BuildSteps and ExecuteStage where the former creates these IExecutionStep objects and the latter calls the Execute method of these IExecutionStep objects to execute them. Now let's see who calls these two methods of ApplicationStepManager.

After instantiating the ApplicationStepManager, the InitializeAppInstance method of HttpApplication calls the BuildSteps method to create the IExecutionStep objects associated with the HttpApplication events. These objects are instantiated and added to an internal collection in the same order as their associated events. The order of these events was discussed in the previous table.

Next, you see who calls the ExecuteStage method. Recall that the ProcessRequest method of HttpRuntime calls the BeginProcessRequest method of the HttpApplication object as shown in the boldfaced section of the following code listing:

```
public static void ProcessRequest(HttpWorkerRequest wr)
{
  HttpContext context1 = new HttpContext(wr, true);
  IHttpHandler handler1 = HttpApplicationFactory.GetApplicationInstance(context1);

  IHttpAsyncHandler handler2 = (IHttpAsyncHandler)handler1;
  context1.AsyncAppHandler = handler2;
  handler2.BeginProcessRequest(context1, _handlerCompletionCallback, context1);
}
```

BeginProcessRequest internally calls the ExecuteStage method of the ApplicationStepManager, which, in turn, iterates through the internal collection that contains the IExecutionStep objects and calls their Execute methods in the order in which they were added to the collection.

SPHttpApplication

Launch the Windows Explorer and navigate to the physical root directory of your SharePoint web application, which is located in the following folder on the file system of the front-end web server:

```
Local_Drive:\inetpub\wwwroot\wss\VirtualDirectories
```

There you should see the global.asax file. SharePoint automatically adds this file every time you create a new SharePoint web application. If you open this file in your favorite editor, you should see the following:

```
<%@ Assembly Name="Microsoft.SharePoint"%>
<%@ Application Language="C#"
Inherits="Microsoft.SharePoint.ApplicationRuntime.SPHttpApplication" %>
```

As you can see, the global.asax file contains two directives. The @Assembly directive references the Microsoft.SharePoint.dll assembly, which contains the ApplicationRuntime namespace. Note that the Inherits attribute of the @Application directive instructs ASP.NET to use SPHttpApplication as the base class for the class that it dynamically creates and instantiates. Recall that instances of this dynamically generated class represent the SharePoint web application.

Listing 1-9 presents the internal implementation of the SPHttpApplication class.

Listing 1-9: The internal implementation of the SPHttpApplication class

```
public class SPHttpApplication : HttpApplication
{
  private ReaderWriterLock readerWriterLock = new ReaderWriterLock();
  private List<IVaryByCustomHandler> varyByCustomHandlers =
                                              new List<IVaryByCustomHandler>();

  [SharePointPermission(SecurityAction.Demand, ObjectModel = true)]
  public sealed override string GetVaryByCustomString(HttpContext context,
                                                     string custom)
  {
    StringBuilder stringBuilder = new StringBuilder();
    readerWriterLock.AcquireReaderLock(-1);
    try
    {
      foreach (IVaryByCustomHandler varyByCustomHandler in varyByCustomHandlers)
      {
        stringBuilder.Append(
              varyByCustomHandler.GetVaryByCustomString(this, context, custom));
      }
    }
    finally
    {
      readerWriterLock.ReleaseReaderLock();
    }
    return stringBuilder.ToString();
  }

  [SharePointPermission(SecurityAction.Demand, ObjectModel = true)]
  public override void Init()
  {
    AppDomain currentAppDomain = AppDomain.CurrentDomain;
    if (currentAppDomain != null)
      currentAppDomain.UnhandledException +=
               new UnhandledExceptionEventHandler(UnhandledExceptionHandler);
  }

  public void RegisterGetVaryByCustomStringHandler(IVaryByCustomHandler
                                                   varyByCustomHandler)
  {
    if (varyByCustomHandler!= null)
    {
      readerWriterLock.AcquireWriterLock(-1);
      try
      {
        varyByCustomHandlers.Add(varyByCustomHandler);
      }
      finally
```

(continued)

Listing 1-9 *(continued)*

```
        {
          readerWriterLock.ReleaseWriterLock();
        }
      }
    }

    public void DeregisterGetVaryByCustomStringHandler(IVaryByCustomHandler
                                                       varyByCustomHandler)
    {
      if (varyByCustomHandler != null)
      {
        readerWriterLock.AcquireWriterLock(-1);
        try
        {
          varyByCustomHandlers.Remove(varyByCustomHandler);
        }
        finally
        {
          readerWriterLock.ReleaseWriterLock();
        }
      }
    }
  }
```

As you can see, the SPHttpApplication class overrides the GetVaryByCustomString and Init methods of the HttpApplication base class. Note that SPHttpApplication exposes a public method named RegisterGetVaryByCustomStringHandler that takes an IVaryByCustomHandler handler and adds it to an internal list. When ASP.NET finally invokes the GetVaryByCustomString method, this method iterates through these IVaryByCustomHandler handlers and invokes their GetVaryByCustomString methods, passing in these three parameters: a reference to the SPHttpApplication object, a reference to the current HttpContext object, and the string that contains the custom parameter. The GetVaryByCustomString method then collects the string values returned from the GetVaryByCustomString methods of these handlers in a string and returns this string to its caller.

SPRequestModule

When you create a new SharePoint web application, SharePoint automatically adds a web.config file to the root directory of the application. This file, among many other settings, includes the <httpModules> configuration section shown in Listing 1-10.

As discussed earlier, the InitializeAppInstance method of SPHttpApplication reads the content of the <httpModules> configuration section, instantiates the registered HTTP modules, and invokes their Init methods to allow them to register event handlers for one or more of the SPHttpApplication events. Note that the InitializeAppInstance method invokes the Init methods of the registered HTTP modules in the order in which these modules are added inside the <httpModules> configuration section. Therefore, the HTTP modules that are added first get to register their event handlers first. This means that when the respective events are raised, their registered event handlers are the first to be invoked.

SharePoint comes with an HTTP module of its own named SPRequestModule that registers event handlers for most of these events. SharePoint uses these event handlers to initialize the SharePoint runtime environment. Because these initializations must be performed before any other ASP.NET HTTP modules get to perform their own tasks, SharePoint first adds the <clear/> element as the first element of the <httpModules> configuration section to clear up all the registered ASP.NET HTTP modules and then registers the SPRequestModule HTTP module (see Listing 1-10). SharePoint adds all the ASP.NET HTTP modules back inside the <httpModules> element after the SPRequestModule module. This ensures that the SPRequestModule HTTP module initializes the SharePoint runtime environment before any ASP.NET HTTP module gets involved.

Listing 1-10: The content of the web.config file

```
<configuration>
 <system.web>
    <httpModules>
      <clear />
      <add name="SPRequest"
      type="Microsoft.SharePoint.ApplicationRuntime.SPRequestModule,
            Microsoft.SharePoint, Version=12.0.0.0, Culture=neutral,
            PublicKeyToken=71e9bce111e9429c" />
      <add name="OutputCache" type="System.Web.Caching.OutputCacheModule" />
      <add name="FormsAuthentication"
      type="System.Web.Security.FormsAuthenticationModule" />
      <add name="UrlAuthorization"
      type="System.Web.Security.UrlAuthorizationModule" />
      <add name="WindowsAuthentication"
      type="System.Web.Security.WindowsAuthenticationModule" />
      <add name="RoleManager" type="System.Web.Security.RoleManagerModule" />
      <add name="PublishingHttpModule"
      type="Microsoft.SharePoint.Publishing.PublishingHttpModule,
            Microsoft.SharePoint.Publishing, Version=12.0.0.0, Culture=neutral,
            PublicKeyToken=71e9bce111e9429c" />
      <add name="Session" type="System.Web.SessionState.SessionStateModule" />
    </httpModules>
  </system.web>
</configuration>
```

Listing 1-11 presents the portion of the internal implementation of the Init method of the SPRequestModule.

Listing 1-11: The portion of the implementation of the Init method of the SPRequestModule

```
public sealed class SPRequestModule : IHttpModule
{
  void IHttpModule.Init(HttpApplication app)
  {
    if (app is SPHttpApplication)
    {
      if (!_virtualPathProviderInitialized)
      {
        lock (_virtualServerDataInitializedSyncObject)
        {
          if (!_virtualPathProviderInitialized)
          {
            SPVirtualPathProvider virtualPathProvider =
                                            new SPVirtualPathProvider();
            HostingEnvironment.RegisterVirtualPathProvider(virtualPathProvider);
            _virtualPathProviderInitialized = true;
          }
        }
      }
    }

    else
      return;

    app.BeginRequest += new EventHandler(this.BeginRequestHandler);
    app.PostResolveRequestCache +=
                        new EventHandler(this.PostResolveRequestCacheHandler);
    app.PostMapRequestHandler += new EventHandler(this.PostMapRequestHandler);
    app.ReleaseRequestState += new EventHandler(this.ReleaseRequestStateHandler);
    app.PreRequestHandlerExecute +=
                        new EventHandler(this.PreRequestExecuteAppHandler);
    app.PostRequestHandlerExecute +=
                        new EventHandler(this.PostRequestExecuteHandler);
    app.AuthenticateRequest += new EventHandler(this.AuthenticateRequestHandler);
    app.PostAuthenticateRequest +=
                        new EventHandler(this.PostAuthenticateRequestHandler);
    app.Error += new EventHandler(this.ErrorAppHandler);
    app.EndRequest += new EventHandler(this.EndRequestHandler);
  }
}
```

As you can see, the Init method first instantiates and registers an instance of a class named SPVirtualPathProvider and then registers event handlers for different events of the SPHttpApplication object representing the current SharePoint web application. As discussed earlier, these event handlers are responsible for initializing the SharePoint runtime environment.

SPVirtualPathProvider

SharePoint site pages are normally provisioned from a page template, which resides on the file system of each front-end web server on a SharePoint farm. A site page remains in a state known as *ghosted* until it is customized. When a request for a ghosted site page arrives, SharePoint checks whether this is the first request for any site page instance of the associated page template. If so, SharePoint loads the page template from the file system into memory and passes it to the ASP.NET page parser, which in turn parses the page template into a dynamically generated class, compiles the class into an assembly, loads the assembly into the current application domain, instantiates an instance of the compiled class, and then passes the request into it for processing.

When another request for a site page that is an instance of the same page template arrives, the same compiled class is used to process the request. Because this compiled class represents the page template, which resides in the file system of the front-end web server, as opposed to the requested site page, it is as if the requester requested the page template as opposed to the site page, hence the name *ghosted*.

As a result, all requests for a SharePoint web application's site pages that are instances of the same page template are processed through the same compiled class, which is already loaded into memory. This improves the performance of the ghosted site pages dramatically. As you can see, SharePoint ghosted site pages are processed just like a normal ASP.NET page.

When you customize a SharePoint site page in the SharePoint Designer and save the changes, the SharePoint Designer stores the content of the site page file into the content database. This alters the state of the site page from ghosted to unghosted. When a request for an unghosted site page arrives, SharePoint must load the page from the content database and pass that to the ASP.NET page parser. In other words, the page template on the file system is no longer used to process a request for an unghosted page, hence the name *unghosted*.

Because the ASP.NET page parser in ASP.NET 1.1 can only parse pages loaded from the file system, the previous version of SharePoint comes with its own page parser, which allows it to parse files loaded from the content database. Unfortunately the SharePoint page parser is not as rich as the ASP.NET page parser. For example, it does not handle user controls.

ASP.NET 2.0 has changed all that. ASP.NET 2.0 has moved the logic that loads the page from the page parser to a dedicated component known as virtual path provider. This component is a class that inherits a base class named VirtualPathProvider. The ASP.NET 2.0 page parser communicates with these components through the VirtualPathProvider API. It is the responsibility of the configured virtual path provider, not the page parser, to load the ASP.NET page from whatever data source it is designed to work with.

SharePoint 2007 comes with an implementation of the VirtualPathProvider API named SPVirtualPathProvider that incorporates the logic that loads an ASP.NET page from

- The file system of the front-end web server if the page being loaded is an application page or a ghosted site page (and this is the first request for any instance of the associated page template)
- The content database if the page being loaded is an unghosted site page

This means that SharePoint 2007 no longer uses its own page parser. When a request for an ASP.NET page arrives, the SPVirtualPathProvider loads the page from the appropriate source and passes it along to the ASP.NET 2.0 page parser for parsing.

As the following excerpt from Listing 1-11 shows, the Init method of the SPRequestModule HTTP module instantiates an instance of the SPVirtualPathProvider and uses the RegisterVirtualPathProvider static method of the HostingEnvironment class to register it with ASP.NET:

```
SPVirtualPathProvider virtualPathProvider = new SPVirtualPathProvider();
HostingEnvironment.RegisterVirtualPathProvider(virtualPathProvider);
```

Take these steps if you need to customize the behavior of the SPVirtualPathProvider:

1. Implement a custom virtual path provider that inherits the VirtualPathProvider base class where your implementation of the methods of this base class should delegate to the associated methods of the previous virtual path providers. Keep in mind that ASP.NET chains the registered virtual path providers together.
2. Implement a custom HTTP module where your implementation of the Init method must use the RegisterVirtualPathProvider static method of the HostingEnvironment class to register your custom virtual path provider with ASP.NET.
3. Add your HTTP module after the SPRequestModule inside the <httpModules> configuration section of the web.config file of the SharePoint web application. This ensures that the SPRequestModule HTTP module gets to register the SPVirtualPathProvider first so this virtual provider path comes before your custom virtual path provider in the chain of virtual path providers. This allows your virtual path provider's implementation of the methods of the VirtualPathProvider base class to use the Previous property to delegate to the associated methods of the SPVirtualPathProvider.

IHttpHandlerFactory and IHttpHandler

HttpApplication features an event named MapRequestHandler, which like any other HttpApplication event is associated with an IExecutionStep object. The main responsibility of the Execute method of this IExecutionStep object is to find a class that either knows how to handle the current request or knows the class that knows how to handle the current request. The class that knows how to handle HTTP requests for a resource with a specified file extension is known as an HTTP handler. The class that knows the HTTP handler that handles HTTP requests for a resource with a specified file extension is known as an HTTP handler factory. All HTTP handlers implement an interface named IHttpHandler. Listing 1-12 presents the definition of this interface.

Listing 1-12: The IHttpHandler interface

```
public interface IHttpHandler
{
  void ProcessRequest(HttpContext context);
  bool IsReusable { get; }
}
```

The following table describes the members of the IHttpHandler interface:

Member	Description
ProcessRequest	The main function of this method is to process the request, that is, to generate the response text sent to the client.
IsReusable	This gets a Boolean value that specifies whether the same IHttpHandler instance can be reused to handle other requests.

All HTTP handler factories implement an interface named IHttpHandlerFactory. Listing 1-13 contains the definition of this interface.

Listing 1-13: The IHttpHandlerFactory interface

```
public interface IHttpHandlerFactory
{
  IHttpHandler GetHandler(HttpContext context, string requestType, string url,
                          string pathTranslated);
  void ReleaseHandler(IHttpHandler handler);
}
```

The GetHandler method takes four parameters: the current HttpContext object, the HTTP verb used to make the request, the virtual path of the requested file, and the physical path of the requested file.

As discussed earlier, the main responsibility of the Execute method of the IExecutionStep object associated with the MapRequestHandler event of HttpApplication is to determine the HTTP handler that knows how to process requests for the resource with the specified file extension or the HTTP handler factory that knows the HTTP handler. The Execute method uses the <httpHandlers> section of the configuration files to make this determination. Listing 1-14 shows the portion of the <httpHandlers> section of the web.config file of an ASP.NET application.

Listing 1-14: The portion of the <httpHandler> section

```
<configuration>
  <system.web>
    <httpHandlers>
      <add path="*.aspx" verb="*" type="System.Web.UI.PageHandlerFactory" />
      <add path="*.ashx" verb="*" type="System.Web.UI.SimpleHandlerFactory" />
      <add path="*.asmx" verb="*"
       type="System.Web.Services.Protocols.WebServiceHandlerFactory,
             System.Web.Services, Version=2.0.0.0, Culture=neutral,
             PublicKeyToken=b03f5f7f11d50a3a" />
      ...
    </httpHandlers>
  </system.web>
</configuration>
```

Note that the <add> element features three important attributes: path, verb, and type. The type attribute contains a comma-separated list of up to five substrings that provide the Execute method of the associated IExecutionStep object with the complete type information needed to instantiate the specified implementation of the IHttpHandlerFactory or IHttpHandler. The only required substring is the first substring, which contains the fully qualified name of the type of the specified implementation of the IHttpHandlerFactory or IHttpHandler.

The path attribute specifies the virtual path of the resource(s) that the specified implementation of the IHttpHandlerFactory or IHttpHandler handles. For example, as Listing 1-14 shows, PageHandlerFactory handles requests for ASP.NET pages, that is, files with the file extension .aspx. Or, WebServiceHandlerFactory handles requests for ASP.NET web services, that is, files with the file extension .asmx.

The verb attribute contains a comma-separated list of HTTP verbs. The * value specifies that all HTTP verbs are supported. For example, PageHandlerFactory handles requests for ASP.NET pages no matter what HTTP verb the client uses to make the request.

The Execute method of the IExecutionStep object associated with the MapRequestHandler event searches the content of the <httpHandlers> section for the IHttpHandlerFactory or IHttpHandler implementation that handles the request for the file with the specified file extension. For example, if the client has made the request for an ASP.NET page, that is, a file with the file extension .aspx, the Execute method will look for an <add> element whose path attribute has been set to *.aspx or something such as * that includes the file extension .aspx. The method then reads the value of the type attribute of this <add> element and uses that information and .NET reflection to dynamically instantiate an instance of the specified IHttpHandlerFactory or IHttpHandler implementation. For example, if the request is made for an ASP.NET page, the Execute method instantiates an instance of the PageHandlerFactory class.

What the Execute method does next depends on whether the type or class that the type attribute specifies is an HTTP handler or HTTP handler factory. If it's an HTTP handler, Execute simply calls the ProcessRequest method of the handler to process the request. Recall that every HTTP handler implements the ProcessRequest method of the IHttpHandler interface. If it's an HTTP handler factory, Execute first calls the GetHandler method of the handler factory to return the HTTP handler responsible for processing the request and then calls the ProcessRequest method of the HTTP handler to process the request.

For example, in the case of a request for a resource with the file extension .aspx, the Execute method calls the GetHandler method of PageHandlerFactory to return an instance of the HTTP handler responsible for processing the request. This HTTP handler is a class that inherits from the Page base class.

SPHttpHandler

ASP.NET comes with a special HTTP handler named DefaultHttpHandler, which allows you to custom handle the incoming requests. Doing so involves four steps:

1. Add a wildcard application map to the IIS metabase to have IIS route all requests to the aspnet_isapi.dll ISAPI extension module.
2. Implement a custom HTTP handler that inherits from DefaultHttpHandler.
3. Add the following <remove> element as the first child element of the <httpHandlers> configuration section of the web.config file at the root directory of your ASP.NET application:

```
<remove verb="GET,HEAD,POST" path="*" />
```

   As you can see, this <remove> element removes all the HTTP handler factories and HTTP handlers registered for handling requests made through any HTTP verb for resources with any file extension (path="*"). This effectively removes all the ASP.NET registered HTTP handler factories and HTTP handlers.

4. Add your custom HTTP handler immediately after the preceding <remove> child element.

SharePoint follows this same four-step process to custom handle all SharePoint requests. Following these steps, SharePoint comes with a custom HTTP handler named SPHttpHandler that inherits from the DefaultHttpHandler HTTP handler.

When you create a SharePoint web application, SharePoint automatically adds the <httpHandlers> configuration section shown in Listing 1-15 to the web.config file at the root directory of the web application.

Listing 1-15: The web.config file

```
<configuration>
 <system.web>
   <httpHandlers>
     <remove verb="GET,HEAD,POST" path="*" />

     <add verb="GET,HEAD,POST" path="*"
     type="Microsoft.SharePoint.ApplicationRuntime.SPHttpHandler,
           Microsoft.SharePoint, Version=12.0.0.0, Culture=neutral,
           PublicKeyToken=71e9bce111e9429c" />
     ...

    </httpHandlers>
  </system.web>
</configuration>
```

So far you've learned how to configure IIS and ASP.NET to route all requests to a custom DefaultHttpHandler-derived HTTP handler for processing. This HTTP handler, like any other HTTP handler, exposes a method named ProcessRequest. As the name implies, this method processes the request. Listing 1-16 presents the internal implementation of the DefaultHttpHandler HTTP handler.

Listing 1-16: The DefaultHttpHandler HTTP handler

```
public class DefaultHttpHandler : IHttpAsyncHandler
{
  private HttpContext context;
  private NameValueCollection executeUrlHeaders;

  public virtual IAsyncResult BeginProcessRequest(HttpContext context,
                               AsyncCallback asyncCallback, object asyncState)
  {
    this.context = context;
    string virtualPath = OverrideExecuteUrlPath();
    ...
    return context.Response.BeginExecuteUrlForEntireResponse(virtualPath,
                                 executeUrlHeaders, asyncCallback, asyncState);
    }
    ...
  }

  public virtual void EndProcessRequest(IAsyncResult asyncResult);

  public virtual void OnExecuteUrlPreconditionFailure() { }

  public virtual string OverrideExecuteUrlPath()
  {
    return null;
  }

  protected NameValueCollection ExecuteUrlHeaders { get; }
  protected HttpContext Context {get;}
  public virtual bool IsReusable {get;}
}
```

Note that this HTTP handler implements the IHttpAsyncHandler interface, which in turn extends the standard IHttpHandler to add support for asynchronous request processing. Listing 1-17 presents the definition of this interface.

Listing 1-17: The IHttpAsynchronousHandler interface

```
public interface IHttpAsyncHandler : IHttpHandler
{
  IAsyncResult BeginProcessRequest(HttpContext context, AsyncCallback cb,
                                   object extraData);
  void EndProcessRequest(IAsyncResult result);
}
```

As you can see, the IHttpAsyncHandler interface exposes the following two methods:

- **BeginProcessRequest.** This method takes a reference to the current HttpContext object, a reference to an AsyncCallback delegate, and a reference to an optional object and returns an IAsyncResult instance. The caller of this method must wrap a callback method in the AsyncCallback delegate. When the HTTP handler is done with processing the current request, it automatically invokes this callback method, passing in the same IAsyncResult object that the BeginProcessRequest method returns. This object exposes a property named AsyncState that references the optional object that the caller passed into the BeginProcessRequest as the third argument.
- **EndProcessRequest.** This method takes an IAsyncResult object. It is the responsibility of the callback method wrapped in the AsyncCallback delegate to call the EndProcessRequest method.

In effect, the IHttpAsyncHandler interface allows you to process the request asynchronously where your callback method is automatically invoked after the handler is done with processing request. Now back to the DefaultHttpHandler HTTP handler's implementation of the BeginProcessRequest method as shown in Listing 1-16. As you can see, this method first calls the OverrideExecuteUrlPath method:

```
string virtualPath = OverrideExecuteUrlPath();
```

The DefaultHttpHandler HTTP handler's implementation of the OverrideExecuteUrlPath method does not do anything. It simply returns null. It is the responsibility of the HTTP handler that derives from the DefaultHttpHandler to override this method where it must take two important steps. First, it must populate the ExecuteUrlHeaders NameValueCollection property with the appropriate request headers. Second, it must return the appropriate virtual path for the request.

After calling the OverrideExecuteUrlPath method and accessing the virtual path for the request, the BeginProcessRequest method of DefaultHttpHandler invokes the BeginExecuteUrlForEntireResponse method on the HttpResponse object that represents the current HTTP request, passing in the virtual path of the requested resource, the NameValueCollection collection that contains the names and values of the request headers, the AsyncCallback delegate discussed earlier, and the object that was passed in as the third argument of the BeginProcessRequest method:

```
return context.Response.BeginExecuteUrlForEntireResponse(virtualPath,
                                  executeUrlHeaders, asyncCallback, asyncState);
```

Listing 1-18 presents the internal implementation of the BeginExecuteUrlForEntireResponse method.

Listing 1-18: The BeginExecuteUrlForEntireResponse method

```
public sealed class HttpResponse
{
  internal IAsyncResult BeginExecuteUrlForEntireResponse(string pathOverride,
                        NameValueCollection requestHeaders,
                        AsyncCallback asyncCallback, object asyncState)
  {
    string userName = context.User.Identity.Name;
    string authenticationType = context.User.Identity.AuthenticationType;

    string rewrittenUrl = Request.RewrittenUrl;
    if (pathOverride != null)
      rewrittenUrl = pathOverride;

    string requestHeadersStr;
    if (requestHeaders != null)
    {
      if (requestHeaders.Count > 0)
      {
        StringBuilder stringBuilder = new StringBuilder();
        for (int i = 0; i < requestHeaders.Count; i++)
        {
          stringBuilder.Append(requestHeaders.GetKey(i));
          stringBuilder.Append(": ");
          stringBuilder.Append(requestHeaders.Get(i));
          stringBuilder.Append("\r\n");
        }
        requestHeadersStr = stringBuilder.ToString();
      }
    }

    byte[] entityBody = context.Request.EntityBody;

    IAsyncResult asyncResult =
       this.workerRequest.BeginExecuteUrl(
                        rewrittenUrl, null, requestHeadersStr, true, true,
                        this.workerRequest.GetUserToken(), userName,
                    authenticationType, entityBody, asyncCallback, asyncState);
    headersWritten = true;
    ended = true;
    return asyncResult;
  }
}
```

This method first accesses the username of the Windows account under which the current request is executing:

```
string userName = context.User.Identity.Name;
```

Next, it determines the authentication type:

```
string authenticationType = context.User.Identity.AuthenticationType;
```

Then, it specifies the virtual path for the request:

```
string rewrittenUrl = Request.RewrittenUrl;
if (pathOverride != null)
  rewrittenUrl = pathOverride;
```

Next, it iterates through the NameValueCollection collection and creates a string consisting of an "\r\n" separated list of substrings, each substring consisting of two parts separated by a colon character where the first part is a request header name and the second part is the value of the header:

```
string requestHeadersStr = null;
if (requestHeaders != null)
{
  if (requestHeaders.Count > 0)
  {
    StringBuilder stringBuilder = new StringBuilder();
    for (int i = 0; i < requestHeaders.Count; i++)
    {
      stringBuilder.Append(requestHeaders.GetKey(i));
      stringBuilder.Append(": ");
      stringBuilder.Append(requestHeaders.Get(i));
      stringBuilder.Append("\r\n");
    }
    requestHeadersStr = stringBuilder.ToString();
  }
}
```

Then, it determines the body of the request:

```
byte[] entityBody = context.Request.EntityBody;
```

Finally, it invokes the BeginExecuteUrl method on the HttpWorkerRequest to execute the specified URL, passing in the virtual path of the requested resource, request headers, username of the Windows account, authentication type, body of the request, the AsyncCallback delegate discussed earlier, and the optional object discussed earlier:

```
IAsyncResult asyncResult =
       this.workerRequest.BeginExecuteUrl(
                          rewrittenUrl, null, requestHeadersStr, true, true,
                          this.workerRequest.GetUserToken(), userName,
                      authenticationType, entityBody, asyncCallback, asyncState);
```

Recall that the HttpWorkerRequest facilitates the communications between ASP.NET and its host, which is IIS in this case. In other words, the BeginExecuteUrl method of the HttpWorkerRequest method in effect starts a new request with a new URL and new request headers.

As you can see, the DefaultHttpHandler HTTP handler provides a powerful approach to custom request processing where you can restart a whole new request with a new URL and new set of custom request headers. Your custom DefaultHttpHandler-derived HTTP handler must override the OverrideExecuteUrlPath method of the DefaultHttpHandler where it must determine the new URL and the new set of custom request headers needed for the new request.

One of the great things about using a DefaultHttpHandler-derived HTTP handler is that all requests, regardless of the HTTP verbs used to make them and regardless of the file extensions of the requested resources, go through all the registered HTTP modules. Each HTTP module performs a specific preprocessing task on each request and stores the outcome of this task in the HttpContext object. For example, the FormAuthenticationModule HTTP module instantiates and initializes an IPrinciple object and assigns it to the User property of the HttpContext object to represent the security context of the request. This means that the new request for the new URL with new set of custom request headers now carries with it the outcome of all the HTTP modules that the previous request went through. As a matter of fact, as you can see from Listing 1-18, the BeginExecuteUrlForEntireResponse method of the current HttpResponse object passes the username and authentication types as arguments into the BeginExecuteUrl method of the HttpWorkerRequest object. In other words, all requests, regardless of the HTTP verbs used to make them and regardless of the file extensions of the requested resources, get authenticated and authorized through the same ASP.NET authentication and authorization modules.

SPHttpHandler inherits from DefaultHttpHandler and overrides its OverrideExecuteUrlPath method as shown in Listing 1-19 to determine the new URL and new set of custom request headers for the new request.

Listing 1-19: The internal implementation of SPHttpHandler

```
public sealed class SPHttpHandler : DefaultHttpHandler
{
  public override string OverrideExecuteUrlPath()
  {
    base.ExecuteUrlHeaders.Add("VTI_TRANSLATE",
                            base.Context.Request.ServerVariables["HTTP_TRANSLATE"]);
    base.ExecuteUrlHeaders.Remove("TRANSLATE");
    base.ExecuteUrlHeaders.Add("VTI_REQUEST_METHOD",
                                 base.Context.Request.HttpMethod);
    bool invalidUnicode = false;
    string url = SPHttpUtility.UrlPathEncode(base.Context.Request.RawUrl,
                                                  true, true, ref invalidUnicode);
    base.ExecuteUrlHeaders.Add("VTI_SCRIPT_NAME", url);
    base.ExecuteUrlHeaders.Add(this.AppDomainIdHeader,
                AppDomain.CurrentDomain.Id.ToString(CultureInfo.InvariantCulture));
    base.ExecuteUrlHeaders.Add(this.ContentLengthHeader,
       base.Context.Request.ContentLength.ToString(CultureInfo.InvariantCulture));
    if (SPSecurity.AuthenticationMode == AuthenticationMode.Windows)
      base.ExecuteUrlHeaders.Add(this.AuthModeHeader, "Windows");

    else
```

(continued)

Listing 1-19 *(continued)*

```
      {
        uint num;
        base.ExecuteUrlHeaders.Add(this.AuthModeHeader, "Forms");
        if (SPSecurity.UseMembershipUserKey &&
            base.Context.User.Identity.IsAuthenticated)
        {
          string userKey = UTF7Encode(SPUtility.GetFullUserKeyFromLoginName(
                                                base.Context.User.Identity.Name));
          base.ExecuteUrlHeaders.Add(this.MembershipUserKeyHeader, userKey);
        }
        string membershipProviderName = UTF7Encode(Membership.Provider.Name);
        base.ExecuteUrlHeaders.Add(this.AuthProviderHeader, membershipProviderName);
        string roles;
        SPSecurity.GetRolesForUser(out num, out roles);
        if (num > 0)
        {
          base.ExecuteUrlHeaders.Add(this.RoleCountHeader,
                                     num.ToString(CultureInfo.InvariantCulture));
          base.ExecuteUrlHeaders.Add(this.RolesHeader, UTF7Encode(roles));
        }
      }
      HttpCookieCollection cookies = base.Context.Response.Cookies;
      if ((cookies != null) && (cookies.Count > 0))
      {
        bool supportsHttpOnly = SupportsHttpOnly();
        for (int i = 0; i < cookies.Count; i++)
        {
          string cookieName = this.ManagedCookiesHeader + "_" +
                         i.ToString(CultureInfo.InvariantCulture);
          string cookieValue = UTF7Encode(this.GetCookieString(cookies[i],
                                    supportsHttpOnly));
          base.ExecuteUrlHeaders.Add(cookieName, cookieValue);
        }
      }
      ...
    }
  }
```

The OverrideExecuteUrlPath method of SPHttpHandler, like the OverrideExecuteUrlPath method of any other DefaultHttpHandler-derived HTTP handler, first populates the ExecuteUrlHeader NameValueCollection collection with the appropriate header names and values. Recall that the BeginProcessRequest method of DefaultHttpHandler passes the content of this collection as a parameter into the BeginExecuteUrlForEntireResponse method of the current HttpResponse object.

Note that OverrideExecuteUrlPath also stores the authentication and authorization information into the ExecuteUrlHeader NameValueCollection collection:

```
if (SPSecurity.AuthenticationMode == AuthenticationMode.Windows)
  base.ExecuteUrlHeaders.Add(this.AuthModeHeader, "Windows");

else
{
  uint num;
  base.ExecuteUrlHeaders.Add(this.AuthModeHeader, "Forms");
  if (SPSecurity.UseMembershipUserKey &&
      base.Context.User.Identity.IsAuthenticated)
  {
    string userKey = UTF7Encode(SPUtility.GetFullUserKeyFromLoginName(
                                          base.Context.User.Identity.Name));
    base.ExecuteUrlHeaders.Add(this.MembershipUserKeyHeader, userKey);
  }
  string membershipProviderName = UTF7Encode(Membership.Provider.Name);
  base.ExecuteUrlHeaders.Add(this.AuthProviderHeader, membershipProviderName);
  string roles;
  SPSecurity.GetRolesForUser(out num, out roles);
  if (num > 0)
  {
    base.ExecuteUrlHeaders.Add(this.RoleCountHeader,
                                  num.ToString(CultureInfo.InvariantCulture));
    base.ExecuteUrlHeaders.Add(this.RolesHeader, UTF7Encode(roles));
  }
}
```

OverrideExecuteUrlPath also stores response cookies into this collection:

```
HttpCookieCollection cookies = base.Context.Response.Cookies;
if ((cookies != null) && (cookies.Count > 0))
{
  bool supportsHttpOnly = SupportsHttpOnly();
  for (int i = 0; i < cookies.Count; i++)
  {
    string cookieName = this.ManagedCookiesHeader + "_" +
                  i.ToString(CultureInfo.InvariantCulture);
    string cookieValue = UTF7Encode(this.GetCookieString(cookies[i],
                                supportsHttpOnly));
    base.ExecuteUrlHeaders.Add(cookieName, cookieValue);
  }
}
```

In summary, thanks to the SPHttpHandler HTTP handler, regardless of whether it targets ASP.NET or non-ASP.NET resources, all requests go through all the HTTP modules in the ASP.NET HTTP Runtime Pipeline, including the SPRequestModule HTTP module. This has two important effects. First, because all requests go through the SPRequestModule HTTP module, they're all initialized with the SharePoint execution context. Second, because all requests go through all ASP.NET HTTP modules, they're all initialized with the ASP.NET execution context.

Developing Custom HTTP Handler Factories, HTTP Handlers, and HTTP Modules

Deep integration of SharePoint and ASP.NET 2.0 allows you to implement your own custom HTTP handler factories, HTTP handlers, and HTTP modules, and plug them into the ASP.NET HTTP Runtime Pipeline to customize this pipeline.

ASP.NET Dynamic Compilation

Let's begin our discussion with a simple example. Create a new ASP.NET web site in Visual Studio and add the simple ASP.NET web page named default.aspx to it, as shown in Listing 1-20.

Listing 1-20: The default.aspx page

```
<%@ Page Language="C#" AutoEventWireup="true" CodeFile="Default.aspx.cs"
Inherits="Default" %>
<html xmlns="http://www.w3.org/1999/xhtml">
<body>
  <form id="form1" runat="server">
    <div>
      <table>
        <tr>
          <td align="right">
            Display Name:</td>
          <td>
            <asp:TextBox runat="server" ID="DisplayNameTbx" /></td>
        </tr>
        <tr>
          <td align="right">
            Email:</td>
          <td>
            <asp:TextBox runat="server" ID="EmailTbx" /></td>
        </tr>
        <tr>
          <td colspan="2" align="center">
            <asp:Button runat="server" ID="SubmitBtn"
            OnClick="SubmitCallback" Text="Submit" />
          </td>
        </tr>
        <tr>
          <td colspan="2" align="left">
            <asp:Label runat="server" ID="Info" />
          </td>
        </tr>
      </table>
    </div>
  </form>
</body>
</html>
```

Now introduce a compilation error and hit F5 to compile the page. You should get the page shown in Figure 1-2, which has a link titled Show Complete Compilation Source. Click the link to access the code partly shown in Listing 1-21.

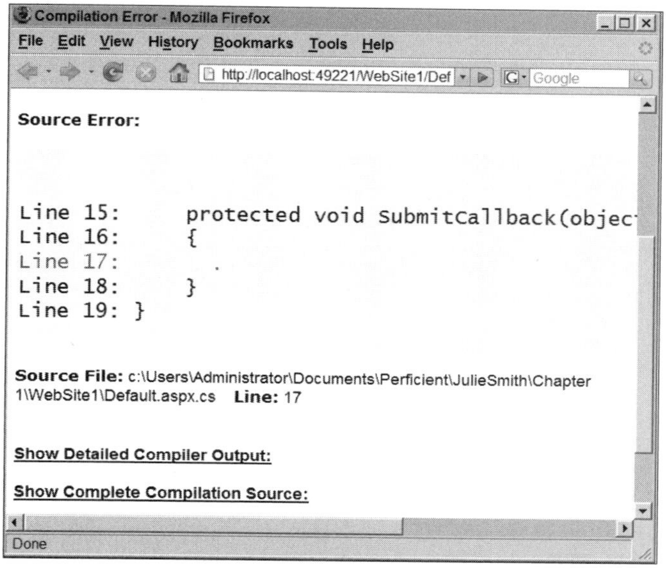

Compilation Error - Mozilla Firefox

File Edit View History Bookmarks Tools Help

http://localhost:49221/WebSite1/Def

Source Error:

```
Line 15:     protected void SubmitCallback(objec
Line 16:     {
Line 17:         .
Line 18:     }
Line 19: }
```

Source File: c:\Users\Administrator\Documents\Perficient\JulieSmith\Chapter 1\WebSite1\Default.aspx.cs **Line:** 17

Show Detailed Compiler Output:

Show Complete Compilation Source:

Done

Figure 1-2: The error page

Listing 1-21: The Compilation Source

```
namespace ASP
{
  ...
  public class default_aspx : Default, System.Web.IHttpHandler
  {
    ...
    private TextBox @__BuildControlDisplayNameTbx()
    {
      TextBox @__ctrl;
      @__ctrl = new TextBox();
      this.DisplayNameTbx = @__ctrl;
      @__ctrl.ApplyStyleSheetSkin(this);
      @__ctrl.ID = "DisplayNameTbx";
      return @__ctrl;
    }
    ...
  }
}
```

When you hit F5, the ASP.NET build environment performs these tasks:

1. Parses the MySimplePage.aspx markup file shown in Listing 1-20.
2. Generates the source code partly shown in Listing 1-21. Notice that this source code contains a class named default_aspx belonging to a namespace named ASP. You can think of this class as the programmatic representation of the MySimplePage.aspx markup file shown in Listing 1-20.
3. Stores this source code in a file in the following directory on your machine:

```
%SystemRoot%\Microsoft.NET\Framework\versionNumber\ASP.NET Temporary Files
```

   By default, the ASP.NET build environment deletes this file after it compiles it into an assembly. However, you can change this default behavior by setting the Debug attribute on the @Page directive to true. This will allow you to view this file in a text editor.

4. Compiles the preceding source code file into an assembly and stores the assembly in the ASP.NET Temporary Files directory.
5. Loads the compiled assembly into the application domain that contains the ASP.NET application to make the dynamically generated default_aspx class available to the managed code running in the application domain.

In other words, the ASP.NET build environment converts the markup code shown in Listing 1-20 into the procedural code partly shown in Listing 1-21. You may be wondering why this conversion from markup to procedural code is necessary. As a matter of fact, the older web development technologies such as ASP don't do this conversion. Instead, they interpret the markup. This is very similar to what browsers do when they're displaying an HTML page. The browsers scan through the HTML page and interpret the HTML markup they run into. For example, when they see a <table> HTML element, they take it that they're asked to render a table. The great thing about markup programming is its convenience. Writing code in an HTML-like markup language is more convenient than writing code in a procedural language such as C# or VB.NET and significantly improves the developer productivity. Markup programming is also the basis on which visual designers such as Visual Studio operate. The disadvantage of markup programming is the performance-degradation due to the underlying interpretation mechanism.

This is where the ASP.NET build environment comes into play. The ASP.NET build environment allows you or visual designers to use markup programming to implement your ASP.NET web page and transparently compiles your markup code into procedural code. This allows you to enjoy both the convenience and productivity boost of markup programming and the performance boost of procedural programming. Who says you can't have your cake and eat it too?

The GetHandler method of the PageHandlerFactory internally uses the ASP.NET page parser to parse a requested ASP.NET page such as the one shown in Listing 1-20 into a class that inherits from the Page base class. The name of this class follows the ASP.NET internal naming convention. According to this convention, the name of the class consists of two parts. The first part is the name of the ASP.NET page being processed. The second part, on the other hand, is the file extension of the ASP.NET page, that is, .aspx. For example, the name of the HTTP handler that handles requests for the default.aspx file is default_aspx. All dynamically generated classes such as default_aspx belong to an assembly named ASP. To see this in action, create an ASP.NET Web Site project in Visual Studio and add a Web Form to this page. Then switch to the code-behind file for this page and start typing ASP as shown in Figure 1-3.

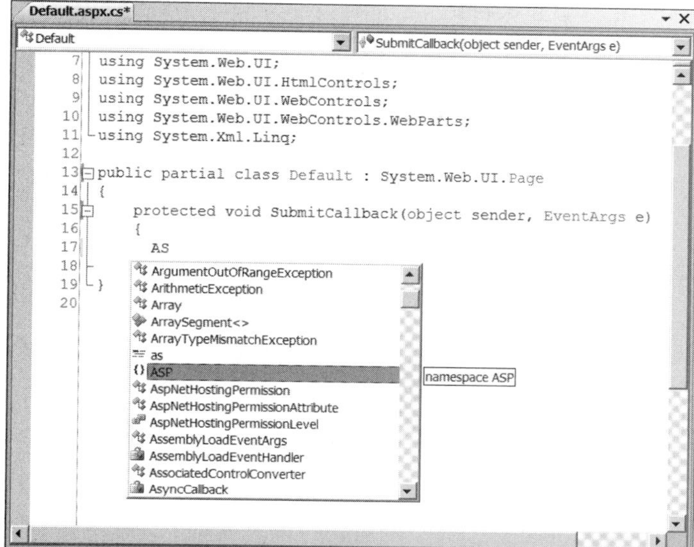

Figure 1-3: The default_aspx class

As you can see, this popup menu contains an entry for the ASP namespace. If you add a dot after ASP, you should see the menu shown in Figure 1-4.

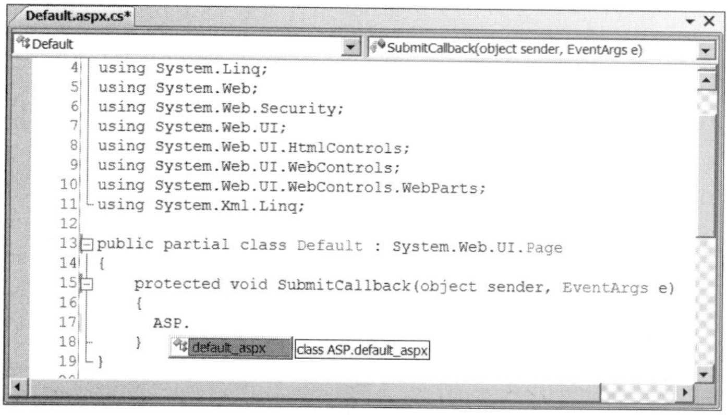

```
Default.aspx.cs*
Default                                   SubmitCallback(object sender, EventArgs e)
using System.Linq;
using System.Web;
using System.Web.Security;
using System.Web.UI;
using System.Web.UI.HtmlControls;
using System.Web.UI.WebControls;
using System.Web.UI.WebControls.WebParts;
using System.Xml.Linq;

public partial class Default : System.Web.UI.Page
{
    protected void SubmitCallback(object sender, EventArgs e)
    {
      ASP.
    }   default_aspx   class ASP.default_aspx
}
```

Figure 1-4: Temporary files for the application

As the tooltip shows, the ASP namespace contains a class named default_aspx. Note that the name of the class is the concatenation of the file name (default) and the file extension (aspx) separated by an underscore (_) character as discussed earlier.

As mentioned, the ASP.NET build environment temporarily stores the source code for this dynamically generated class in the Temporary ASP.NET Files directory. This directory contains one directory for each ASP.NET application that has ever run on the machine. The directory is named after the virtual root directory of its associated ASP.NET application. A couple of directories down this root directory, you can find the temporary files that contain the dynamically generated classes such as default_aspx. As mentioned, the ASP.NET build environment deletes these files immediately after the compilation process ends, unless you set the Debug attribute on the @Page directive of the ASP.NET page to true.

Next, take a look at the contents of the directory that contains the temporary files for the application. You'll start with hash.web file, which is located in the hash folder. This file contains the hash value for this directory. ASP.NET uses this hash value to generate hash values that are used as part of the names of the files contained in this directory. As you'll see later, these hash values ensure the uniqueness of the names of these files. Next, we'll discuss these four files: App_Web_jgyyqxek.0.cs, App_Web_jgyyqxek.1.cs, App_Web_jgyyqxek.2.cs, and App_Web_jgyyqxek.dll. Listing 1-22 will help you understand the role and significance of these four files.

Recall that Listing 1-20 contains the content of the Default.aspx file. Notice that this file registers an event handler named SubmitCallback for the Click event of the Submit button. The Default.aspx.cs code-behind file contains the implementation of this event handler as shown in Listing 1-22.

Listing 1-22: The code-behind file

```
using System;

public partial class Default : System.Web.UI.Page
{
  protected void SubmitCallback(object sender, EventArgs e)
  {
    Info.Text = "<b>Display Name: </b>" + DisplayNameTbx.Text + "<br/>";
    Info.Text += "<b>Email: </b>" + EmailTbx.Text;
  }
}
```

The App_Web_jgyyqxek.1.cs file contains the class defined in the code-behind file, that is, the Default class. Notice that this class references the server controls defined in the markup file, that is, Default.aspx. Also note that the class does not expose these server controls as protected fields as it used to do in Visual Studio 2003. Thanks to partial classes the addition of these tool-generated protected fields is no longer necessary when you're developing your pages. When you hit F5 to build and run the application, ASP.NET automatically generates another partial class exposing the required protected fields. The App_Web_jgyyqxek.0.cs file contains this partial class as shown in Listing 1-23.

Listing 1-23: The App_Web_jgyyqxek.0.cs file

```
public partial class Default : System.Web.SessionState.IRequiresSessionState
{
  protected global::System.Web.UI.WebControls.TextBox DisplayNameTbx;
  protected global::System.Web.UI.WebControls.TextBox EmailTbx;
  protected global::System.Web.UI.WebControls.Button SubmitBtn;
  protected global::System.Web.UI.WebControls.Label Info;
  protected global::System.Web.UI.HtmlControls.HtmlForm form1;
  ...
}
```

You may be wondering why the Default class shown in Listing 1-23 implements the IRequiresSessionState interface. What is this interface anyway? This interface is a marker interface; that is, it doesn't have any methods, properties, or events. Implementing this interface marks the implementor (the class that implements the interface) as a class that needs write access to the session data. The Default class shown in Listing 1-23 implements this interface when the value of the EnableSessionState attribute on the @Page directive is set to true (default).

When a compiler sees a partial class like the Default class shown in Listing 1-22 (App_Web_jgyyqxek.1.cs), it knows that the definition of this class is not complete and the class is missing some members. Therefore the compiler doesn't attempt to compile the class. Instead it first merges the partial Default classes shown in Listings 1-22 and 1-23 into a complete Default class as shown in Listing 1-24.

Listing 1-24: The complete Default class

```
public class Default : System.Web.UI.Page,
                       System.Web.SessionState.IRequiresSessionState
{
  protected global::System.Web.UI.WebControls.TextBox DisplayNameTbx;
  protected global::System.Web.UI.WebControls.TextBox EmailTbx;
  protected global::System.Web.UI.WebControls.Button SubmitBtn;
  protected global::System.Web.UI.WebControls.Label Info;
  protected global::System.Web.UI.HtmlControls.HtmlForm form1;
  ...

  protected void SubmitCallback(object sender, EventArgs e)
  {
    Info.Text = "<b>Display Name: </b>" + DisplayNameTbx.Text + "<br/>";
    Info.Text += "<b>Email: </b>" + EmailTbx.Text;
  }
}
```

Next, the ASP.NET build environment uses the PageBuildProvider to generate the source code for the class that represents the markup file, that is, the Default.aspx file shown in Listing 1-20. The App_Web_jgyyqxek.0.cs file contains the source code for this class as shown in Listing 1-21. Notice that this class inherits from the Default class shown in Listing 1-24.

Finally, Listing 1-25 presents the content of the App_Web_jgyyqxek.2.cs file. Notice that this file simply defines a fast object factory for the default_aspx type. The PageBuilderProvider calls the GenerateTypeFactory method of the AssemblyBuilder to generate this fast object factory class.

Listing 1-25: The type factory

```
namespace @__ASP
{
  internal class FastObjectFactory_app_web_jgyyqxek
  {
    static object Create_ASP_default_aspx()
    {
      return new ASP.default_aspx();
    }
  }
}
```

Notice that the directory whose content is shown on the right panel of the Windows Explorer shown in Figure 1-5 contains the following files that capture the information that the compiler generates:

- **jgyyqxek.cmdline.** This file contains the command line used to compile the code:

```
/t:library /utf8output
/R:"C:\Windows\assembly\GAC_32\System.EnterpriseServices\2.0.0.0__b03f5f7f11d50a3a\
System.EnterpriseServices.dll"
/R:"C:\Windows\assembly\GAC_MSIL\System.Core\3.5.0.0__b77a5c561934e089\
System.Core.dll"
...
/out:"C:\Windows\Microsoft.NET\Framework\v2.0.50727\Temporary ASP.NET Files\
website1\a49191ca\d589c0e2\App_Web_jgyyqxek.dll"
/D:DEBUG /debug+ /optimize- /w:4 /nowarn:1659;1699;1701 /warnaserror-
"C:\Windows\Microsoft.NET\Framework\v2.0.50727\Temporary ASP.NET Files\website1\
a49191ca\d589c0e2\App_Web_jgyyqxek.0.cs"
"C:\Windows\Microsoft.NET\Framework\v2.0.50727\Temporary ASP.NET Files\website1\
a49191ca\d589c0e2\App_Web_jgyyqxek.1.cs"
"C:\Windows\Microsoft.NET\Framework\v2.0.50727\Temporary ASP.NET Files\website1\
a49191ca\d589c0e2\App_Web_jgyyqxek.2.cs"
```

  As the boldfaced portions of this listing shows, this command line compiles the App_Web_jgyyqxek.0.cs, App_Web_jgyyqxek.1.cs, and App_Web_jgyyqxek.2.cs files into an assembly named App_Web_jgyyqxek.dll.

- **gyyqxek.out.** This file contains any text that the compiler generates while it's compiling.
- **jgyyqxek.err.** This file contains any error text that the compiler generates.

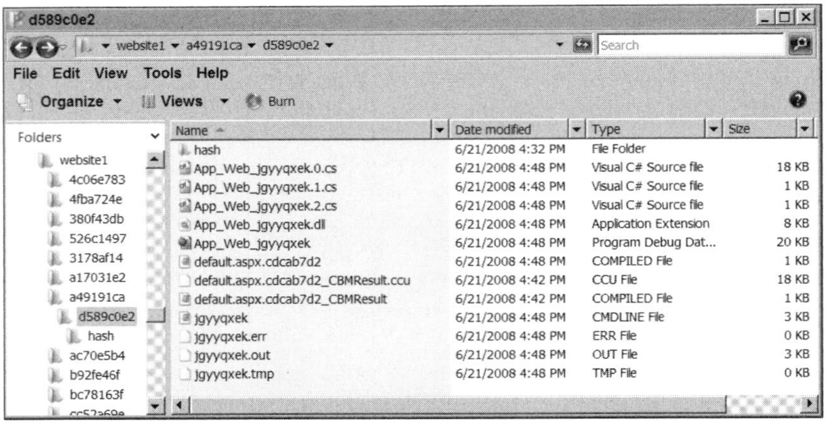

Figure 1-5: The dynamically generated files for an ASP.NET application

There is one more important file in the right panel of the Windows Explorer; Listing 1-26 shows the content of this file.

Listing 1-26: The default.aspx.cdcab7d2 compiled file

```
<?xml version="1.0" encoding="utf-8"?>
<preserve resultType="3" virtualPath="/WebSite1/Default.aspx"hash="ffffff8cb1ce302"
filehash="28511aded9d26a0a" flags="110000" assembly="App_Web_jgyyqxek"
type="ASP.default_aspx">
  <filedeps>
    <filedep name="/WebSite1/Default.aspx" />
    <filedep name="/WebSite1/Default.aspx.cs" />
  </filedeps>
</preserve>
```

As discussed earlier, the ASP.NET build environment compiles the App_Web_jgyyqxek.0.cs, App_Web_jgyyqxek.1.cs, and App_Web_jgyyqxek.2.cs files (the default_aspx class) into App_Web_jgyyqxek.dll (which is stored in the ASP.NET Temporary Files directory), loads this compiled assembly into the application domain where the current application is running, instantiates the default_aspx class, and calls its ProcessRequest method to process the current request.

Now let's see what happens when the next request for the same page (Default.aspx) arrives. ASP.NET first reads the content of the default.aspx.cdcab7d2 file shown in Listing 1-26. Notice that this file is an XML file with a document element named <preserve> that features the following important attributes:

- **virtualPath.** The virtual path of the Default.aspx file
- **type.** The fully qualified name of the type or class that represents the Default.aspx file, that is, the ASP.default_aspx class
- **assembly.** The name of the assembly that contains the ASP.default_aspx class

ASP.NET retrieves two important pieces of information from the default.aspx.cdcab7d2 file: the name of the class that represents the Default.aspx file and the name of the assembly that contains this file. ASP.NET then simply locates this assembly in the application domain and calls the type factory shown in Listing 1-25 to create an instance of the ASP.default_aspx class and finally calls the ProcessRequest method of this instance to process the request. In other words, processing the second request does not go through the code generation and compilation steps that the first request went through. Therefore, the second request will not experience the code generation and compilation delay that the first request experienced. As you'll see later, SharePoint application pages and page templates for ghosted site pages are processed through this same exact ASP.NET compilation model. In other words, these pages are treated just like any other normal ASP.NET pages. That is why SharePoint application pages and ghosted site pages perform much better than unghosted site pages.

Notice that the <preserve> document element features a single child element named <filedeps>, which contains one or more <filedep> elements where each <filedep> element features an attribute that specifies the virtual path of the file that the ASP.default_aspx class depends on. When one of these files changes, ASP.NET checks whether the assembly that contains the ASP.default_aspx class contains other classes. If so, it doesn't delete the assembly. Instead it uses the same code generation and compilation steps discussed in this chapter to compile a new assembly and loads this assembly into the application domain where the current application is running. This means that now both the old assembly and the new assembly are running side-by-side inside the application domain. This is possible because the assembly name contains a randomly generated hash value that ensures the uniqueness of the assembly names. In other words, each time ASP.NET compiles a new assembly, it gives it a new name.

If the old assembly doesn't contain any other classes, ASP.NET attempts to remove it from the ASP.NET Temporary Files directory. If another request is using this assembly, the assembly cannot be deleted because it's locked. If that is the case, ASP.NET simply renames the assembly to App_Web_jgyyqxek.dll .delete. The assemblies that are marked as deleted are deleted when the application restarts. Even though ASP.NET may not be able to remove the old assembly, it can still go ahead with building the new assembly and loading it into the application domain, which means that now we have two different versions of the same assembly running side-by-side inside the application domain.

This raises the following question: What happens to the old assembly when the request using it ends? Unfortunately, you cannot unload an assembly from an application domain, which means that the old assembly will remain in the application domain until the application domain shuts down even though no one is using this assembly. This is because the application domain is the CLR unloading unit. You have to unload the entire application domain in order to unload an assembly. Unloading an application domain unloads all the assemblies loaded into the application domain.

Therefore, every time you make a little change in the Default.aspx or Default.aspx.cs file, ASP.NET loads a new assembly into the application domain without unloading the old ones. In other words, after several recompiles, you end up littering the application domain with a bunch of useless assemblies. That is why ASP.NET puts an upper limit on the number of allowable recompiles. When an application domain reaches this limit, ASP.NET automatically unloads the application domain, which automatically unloads all the assemblies loaded into the application domain.

Keeping unused old assemblies in web server memory causes major problems for SharePoint web servers that host thousands of sites, each with numerous site pages. As an example let's consider the home pages of these sites. The home page of a site is a site page provisioned from a page template named default.aspx. When a site page is provisioned from a page template it remains in ghosted state until it is customized. When the first request for the home page of a site arrives, if this is the first request made to any instance of the default.aspx page template, that is, if the home page of no other sites has been requested yet, the SPVirtualPathProvider simply loads the default.aspx page template from the file system of the front-end web server and passes it along to the ASP.NET page parser for the standard ASP.NET compilation processing as just thoroughly discussed where:

- The default.aspx page template is parsed into a dynamically generated class named ASP.default_aspx
- The ASP.default_aspx class is dynamically compiled into an assembly, which is stored in the ASP.NET Temporary Files folder on the file system of the front-end web server
- An instance of the ASP.default_aspx class is dynamically instantiated and assigned to the task of processing the request

The next request for the home page of the same site or any other sites in the same SharePoint application will be directly served from the same assembly where a new instance of the ASP.default_aspx class is instantiated and assigned to the task of processing the request. In other words, the first two steps of the previous three steps are not repeated for the next request to the home pages of the same or other sites of the same web applications. As you can see, this is a great boost in performance for these requests.

Now imagine the case where the site administrators of these sites, which could be thousands of them, customize the home pages of these sites in the SharePoint Designer. When a site administrator saves his or her changes, the SharePoint Designer saves the content of the home page in the content database. This means that each site now has its own version of the default.aspx page template stored in the content database. When a request for the home page of one of these sites arrives, the SPVirtualPathProvider loads the associated version of the default.aspx page template from the content database and passes it along to ASP.NET parser for the standard ASP.NET compilation processing discussed earlier.

This means that now each version of the default.aspx page template, that is, each site page, which could run into thousands, is compiled into a separate assembly. As you can see, we end up having literally thousands of assemblies in the web server memory and consequently the application domain reaches it upper limit of assemblies and unloads. As you can imagine, this is simply not scalable in large SharePoint web applications. You may be wondering why not simply unload the assembly right after the request for its associated site page is processed. As mentioned earlier .NET does not allow unloading individual assemblies from an application domain. When an assembly is loaded into memory it must remain in memory until the application domain is unloaded.

That is why unghosted site pages do not go through the standard ASP.NET compilation process, which means that they are not compiled into assemblies. Instead they are simply parsed and interpreted on the fly. This is known as no-compile mode and these pages are known as no-compile pages. When a request for an unghosted site page arrives and the SPVirtualPathProvider determines that the requested resource is an unghosted site page, SPVirtualPathProvider downloads the unghosted site page from the content database into the web server memory and passes it along to the ASP.NET page parser as usual. However, SPVirtualPathProvider also instructs the ASP.NET page parser to process the unghosted site page in no-compile mode. This allows SharePoint to unload the page from memory after the request is processed to release precious web server resources for next requests. This is obviously a much more scalable solution than compiled pages.

This, however, introduces a restriction on site pages. Because site pages are not compiled into assemblies, they cannot contain inline code. There is also a security aspect involved here. Because site pages are stored in the content database, by default, they are processed in safe mode where no inline code is allowed, and where the site pages can only contain server controls that are registered as safe controls. These security measures are in place to ensure that no one can mount an attack on the content database and consequently an attack on the web server by injecting malicious inline code or server controls into a site page.

When you implement a custom server control that you want to be used in site pages, you must add an entry into the web.config file of the SharePoint web application to register your server control as a safe control before anyone can use it in a site page. This entry is an element named <SafeControl>, which exposes the following attributes:

- **Assembly.** This is the complete information about the assembly that contains the server controls being registered as safe, including assembly name, version, culture, and public key token.
- **Namespace.** This is the complete namespace containment hierarchy of the server controls being registered as safe.
- **Type.** This is the type of the server control being registered as safe. Set this attribute to * to register all server controls in the specified namespace in the specified assembly as safe.
- **Safe.** Set this attribute to true to register the specified server controls as safe.
- **AllowRemoteDesigner.** Set this attribute to true to allow the remote designer.

When you provision a SharePoint web application, SharePoint automatically registers all standard ASP.NET and SharePoint server controls as safe. The following excerpt for the web.config file of a typical SharePoint web application shows a few of these SafeControl entries:

```
<configuration>
  <SharePoint>
    <SafeControls>
      <SafeControl Assembly="System.Web, Version=1.0.5000.0, Culture=neutral,
                             PublicKeyToken=b03f5f7f11d50a3a"
      Namespace="System.Web.UI.WebControls" TypeName="*" Safe="True"
      AllowRemoteDesigner="True" />

      <SafeControl Assembly="System.web, Version=1.0.5000.0, Culture=neutral,
                           PublicKeyToken=b03f5f7f11d50a3a"
      Namespace="System.Web.UI.HtmlControls" TypeName="*" Safe="True"
      AllowRemoteDesigner="True" />

      <SafeControl Assembly="System.Web, Version=2.0.0.0, Culture=neutral,
                             PublicKeyToken=b03f5f7f11d50a3a"
      Namespace="System.Web.UI" TypeName="*" Safe="True"
      AllowRemoteDesigner="True" />

     <SafeControl Assembly="Microsoft.SharePoint, Version=12.0.0.0,
                            Culture=neutral, PublicKeyToken=71e9bce111e9429c"
     Namespace="Microsoft.SharePoint.WebControls" TypeName="*" Safe="True"
     AllowRemoteDesigner="True" />
    </SafeControls>
  </SharePoint>
</configuration>
```

Keep in mind that when you provision a site page from a page template, the site page remains in ghosted state until it is customized. As discussed earlier, requests for ghosted site pages are processed through a normal ASP.NET compiled page scenario where the SharePoint safe mode is not involved. This means that the page template could in principle contain inline code and unsafe server controls. However, as soon as someone customizes the site page, SharePoint will process the next requests through the safe mode. Therefore the next requests will get an exception if the page template contains inline code and/or unsafe server controls. To avoid this problem, you should never contain inline code and/or unsafe server controls in your page templates.

Summary

This chapter provided an in-depth coverage of the SharePoint 2007 architecture and its main components. You learned how SharePoint extends ASP.NET and IIS to add support for SharePoint-specific functionality and features. The chapter discussed the main ASP.NET and IIS components and the SharePoint extensions to these components. You also learned a great deal about the ASP.NET HTTP Runtime Pipeline and the ASP.NET dynamic compilation and the role they play in SharePoint.

The next chapter moves on to the Collaborative Application Markup Language (CAML) and shows you how to use these power markup languages to query SharePoint data and to implement various SharePoint components. You'll also learn a great deal about custom actions, features, and application pages.

2

CAML, Features, Custom Actions, and Application Pages

SharePoint comes with an XML-based markup language known as Collaborative Application Markup Language (CAML) that you can use to perform SharePoint queries and define SharePoint components in a declarative fashion. The first part of this chapter covers this markup language. The rest of the chapter uses CAML to implement features and custom actions. This chapter also shows you how to implement application pages, which can be accessed from custom actions on the SharePoint menus.

Collaborative Application Markup Language (CAML)

As a SharePoint developer, you need to have a solid understanding of Collaborative Application Markup Language (CAML) and how to use it in your own SharePoint applications to query SharePoint data, define features, create site templates, and so on.

The structure of CAML, like the structure of many other eXtensible Markup Languages (XML), is defined and described in terms of the XML constructs of the XML Schema markup language. Such a description is an XML document stored in one or more XML files. The XML files that define the XML schema of CAML are located in the following folder on your machine:

```
Local_Drive:\Program Files\Common Files\microsoft shared\Web Server
Extensions\12\TEMPLATE\XML
```

One of the great ways to learn about CAML is to study the XML schema document that describes its structure. As an example, let's study the portion of the XML schema document that describes the structure of a CAML query. A CAML query is used to query SharePoint data. A CAML query is an instance of a schema type named CamlQueryRoot as defined in Listing 2-1, which is an excerpt from the CAML XML schema document.

Listing 2-1: The definition of the CamlQueryRoot type

```
<xs:complexType name="CamlQueryRoot" mixed="true">
  <xs:all>
    <xs:element name="Where" type="LogicalJoinDefinition"
    minOccurs="0" maxOccurs="1" />

    <xs:element name="OrderBy" type="FieldRefDefinitions"
    minOccurs="0" maxOccurs="1" />

    ...
  </xs:all>
</xs:complexType>
```

As you can see from Listing 2-1, a CAML query contains two XML elements named <Where> and <OrderBy>. The <Where> element is of the LogicalJoinDefinition schema type, which is defined in the portion of the CAML XML schema document shown in Listing 2-2.

Listing 2-2: The definition of the LogicalJoinDefinition type

```
<xs:complexType name="LogicalJoinDefinition">
  <xs:sequence>
    <xs:choice minOccurs="0" maxOccurs="unbounded">
      <xs:element name="Eq" type="LogicalTestDefinition" />
      <xs:element name="Geq" type="LogicalTestDefinition" />
      <xs:element name="Gt" type="LogicalTestDefinition" />
      <xs:element name="Leq" type="LogicalTestDefinition" />
      <xs:element name="Lt" type="LogicalTestDefinition" />
      <xs:element name="Neq" type="LogicalTestDefinition" />
      <xs:element name="And" type="ExtendedLogicalJoinDefinition" />
      <xs:element name="Or" type="ExtendedLogicalJoinDefinition" />
      <xs:element name="IsNull" type="LogicalTestDefinition" />
      <xs:element name="IsNotNull" type="LogicalTestDefinition" />
      <xs:element name="BeginsWith" type="LogicalTestDefinition" />
      <xs:element name="Contains" type="LogicalTestDefinition" />
      ...
    </xs:choice>
  </xs:sequence>
</xs:complexType>
```

As you can see, the <Where> element can contain one or more of the following child elements:

- **Eq.** Equal to
- **Geq.** Greater than or equal to
- **Gt.** Greater than
- **Leq.** Less than or equal to
- **Lt.** Less than
- **Neq.** Not equal to
- **And.** And
- **Or.** Or
- **IsNull.** Is null
- **IsNotNull.** Is not null
- **BeginsWith.** Begins with
- **Contains.** Contains

As Listing 2-2 shows, all these child elements are of the LogicalTestDefinition schema type, with the exception of the <And> and <Or> elements, which are of the ExtendedLogicalJoinDefinition schema type. The definition of the ExtendedLogicalJoinDefinition schema type is very similar to the definition of the LogicalJoinDefinition schema type. This means that the <And> and <Or> elements, just like the <Where> element, can contain one or more of the <Eq>, <Geq>, <Gt>, <Leq>, or <Lt> elements, and so on.

Listing 2-3 presents the portion of the CAML XML schema document that defines the LogicalTestDefinition schema type.

Listing 2-3: The definition of the LogicalTestDefinition type

```
<xs:complexType name="LogicalTestDefinition">
  <xs:sequence>
    <xs:choice minOccurs="0" maxOccurs="unbounded">
      <xs:element name="FieldRef" type="FieldRefDefinition" />
      <xs:element name="Value" type="ValueDefinition" />
      ...
    </xs:choice>
  </xs:sequence>
</xs:complexType>
```

As you can see from Listing 2-3, the child elements of the <Where>, <And>, and <Or> elements (that is, <Eq>, <Geq>, <Gt>, and so on) can contain zero or more <FieldRef> and <Value> elements, which are of the FieldRefDefinition and ValueDefinition schema types, respectively. Listing 2-4 presents the portion of the CAML XML schema document that defines these two schema types.

Listing 2-4: The definitions of the FieldRefDefinition and ValueDefinition types

```
<xs:complexType name="FieldRefDefinition" mixed="true">
  <xs:simpleContent>
    <xs:extension base="xs:string">
      <xs:attribute name="Alias" type="xs:string" />
      <xs:attribute name="Ascending" type="TRUEFALSE" />
      <xs:attribute name="CreateURL" type="xs:string" />
      <xs:attribute name="DisplayName" type="xs:string" />
      <xs:attribute name="Explicit" type="TRUEFALSE" />
      <xs:attribute name="ID" type="xs:string" />
      <xs:attribute name="Key" type="xs:string" />
      <xs:attribute name="Name" type="xs:string" />
      <xs:attribute name="RefType" type="xs:string" />
      <xs:attribute name="ShowField" type="xs:string" />
      <xs:attribute name="TextOnly" type="TRUEFALSE" />
      <xs:attribute name="Type" type="ReferenceType" />
    </xs:extension>
  </xs:simpleContent>
</xs:complexType>

 <xs:complexType name="ValueDefinition" mixed="true">
  <xs:complexContent>
    <xs:restriction base="xs:anyType">
      <xs:sequence>
        <xs:choice minOccurs="0" maxOccurs="unbounded">
          <xs:element name="Today" type="xs:string"
          minOccurs="0" maxOccurs="1" />
          <xs:element name="UserID" type="xs:string" nillable="true" />
          <xs:element name="ListProperty" type="QueryListProperty" />
          <xs:element name="Now" type="xs:string" />
          <xs:element name="Month" type="xs:string" />
          <xs:element name="XML" type="xs:string" />
        </xs:choice>
      </xs:sequence>
      <xs:attribute name="Type" type="xs:string" />
    </xs:restriction>
  </xs:complexContent>
```

As you can see, the <FieldRef> element does not have any child elements and only supports attributes that describe the field that the element references. The <Value> element exposes a single attribute named Type, which specifies the data type of the value that the element represents, and can contain child elements such as <Today>, which represents the today's date.

As Listing 2-1 shows, the <OrderBy> element is of the FieldRefDefinitions schema type. Listing 2-5 presents the portion of the CAML XML schema document that defines this schema type.

Listing 2-5: The definition of the FieldRefDefinitions type

```
<xs:complexType name="FieldRefDefinitions" mixed="true">
  <xs:sequence>
    <xs:element name="FieldRef" type="FieldRefDefinition"
    minOccurs="0" maxOccurs="unbounded" />
  </xs:sequence>
</xs:complexType>
```

As you can see, the <OrderBy> element can contain zero or more <FieldRef> child elements.

In summary, a CAML query normally contains a <Where> and an <OrderBy> element. The <Where> element acts more like the SQL Where clause; that is, it filters the data. The <OrderBy> element acts more like the SQL Order By clause; that is, it sorts the data. The <Where> element contains zero or more logical elements such as <Eq>, <Neq>, <Geq>, <Leq>, <Lt>, and <Gt> elements where each element contains zero or more <FieldRef> and <Value> elements. A <FieldRef> element is basically a reference to a field. A <Value> element is basically a reference to a value such as today's date. This is very similar to the SQL Where clause where logical expressions are used to filter data based on database fields. The <OrderBy> element contains zero or more <FieldRef> elements, where each element references a field. This is very similar to the SQL Order By clause, which sorts the data based on the specified database fields.

CAML Queries

This section looks at a few CAML query examples. All these examples query a SharePoint Contacts list named Clients, so the first thing you'll need to do is add this list. Figure 2-1 shows the Clients list.

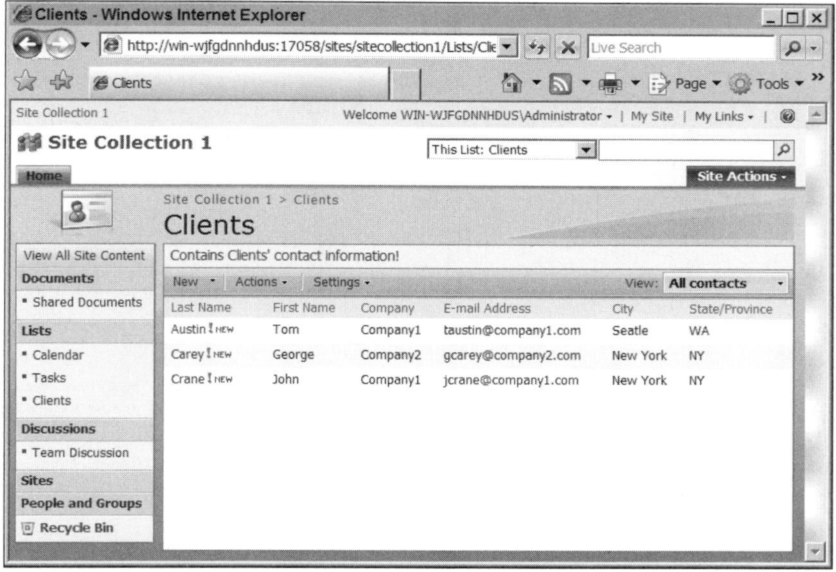

Figure 2-1: The Client list

Listing 2-6 presents an example of a CAML query that provides the Clients list for those clients that work for a company named Company1 and then sorts the data based on the clients' last name. Note that the <FieldRef> child element of the <OrderBy> element references a field named LinkTitle as opposed to the last name. This is because the last name of clients is stored internally in a field named LinkTitle. As this example shows, one of the challenges with CAML queries is to figure out the actual names of the underlying fields. You'll see an easy way to do this shortly.

Listing 2-6: An example of a CAML query

```
<Query>
  <Where>
    <Eq>
      <FieldRef Name='Company' />
      <Value Type='Text'>Company1</Value>
    </Eq>
  </Where>
  <OrderBy>
   <FieldRef Name='LinkTitle' />
  </OrderBy>
</Query>
```

Listing 2-7 presents another CAML query where the <And> element is used to create a filter with two operators.

Listing 2-7: Another example of a CAML query

```
<Query>
  <Where>
    <And>
      <Eq>
        <FieldRef Name='Company' />
        <Value Type='Text'>Company1</Value>
      </Eq>
      <Eq>
        <FieldRef Name='WorkCity' />
        <Value Type='Text'>Seattle</Value>
      </Eq>
    </And>
  </Where>
  <OrderBy>
    <FieldRef Name='LinkTitle' />
  </OrderBy>
</Query>
```

This CAML query queries the Clients list for clients who work for Company1 in Seattle and sorts the data based on the clients' last names. Again notice that the <FieldRef> child element of the second <Eq> element references a field named WorkCity as opposed to City. This is because the actual name of the underlying field is WorkCity as opposed to City.

Next, you're going to write managed code that uses the SharePoint object model to run the previous CAML queries against the Clients list.

In general, there are three ways to programmatically interact with the SharePoint object model:

- Implementing and deploying a SharePoint component, such as an application page or Web part, which contains managed code using the SharePoint object model.
- Implementing a .NET application such as a console, Windows, or web application that contains managed code that uses the SharePoint object model. Such .NET applications must run locally on a SharePoint server. In other words, such .NET applications must run on a server where WSS 3.0 or MOSS 2007 is installed. These .NET applications are normally administrative tools that are run by system administrators to perform administrative tasks. These .NET applications basically extend the functionality of the SharePoint framework to add support for features that the framework does not support out of the box.
- Implementing a .NET application such as a console, Windows, or web application that uses a SharePoint web service to interact with the SharePoint object model. Such .NET applications do not have to run on a SharePoint server. As a matter of fact, such .NET applications are normally client applications that run on machines where WSS 3.0 or MOSS 2007 is not installed. For example, you could have a client application that stores data in SharePoint lists and uses a SharePoint web service to manipulate the data. Keep in mind that the SharePoint objects are not remotable. In other words, you cannot use .NET remoting to access the SharePoint object model. You have to access the SharePoint object model through a SharePoint web service or WCF service.

Now launch Visual Studio 2008 and add a new console application. Then add a reference to the Microsoft.SharePoint.dll assembly. This assembly is located in the following directory on your machine:

```
Local_Drive:\Program Files\Common Files\microsoft shared\Web Server Extensions\12\ISAPI
```

Next, add the code shown in Listing 2-8 to your new Program.cs file.

Listing 2-8: The content of the Program.cs file

```
using System;
using Microsoft.SharePoint;

namespace ConsoleApplication2
{
  class Program
  {
    static void Main(string[] args)
    {
      using (SPSite site = new SPSite("Enter the site collection URL here"))
      {
        using (SPWeb web = site.OpenWeb())
        {
          SPList list = web.Lists["Clients"];
          SPView view = list.Views["All contacts"];
          SPQuery query = new SPQuery(view);
```

(continued)

Listing 2-8 *(continued)*

```
            query.ViewFields = "<FieldRef Name='LinkTitle'/>" +
                               "<FieldRef Name='FirstName'/>" +
                               "<FieldRef Name='Company'/>" +
                               "<FieldRef Name='WorkCity'/>";
            query.Query = "<Where>" +
                            "<Eq>" +
                              "<FieldRef Name='Company' />" +
                              "<Value Type='Text'>Company1</Value>" +
                            "</Eq>" +
                          "</Where>" +
                          "<OrderBy>" +
                            "<FieldRef Name='LinkTitle' />" +
                          "</OrderBy>";

            SPListItemCollection items = list.GetItems(query);

            foreach (SPListItem item in items)
            {
              Console.WriteLine("Last Name: " + item["LinkTitle"].ToString());
            }

            Console.ReadLine();
          }
        }
      }
    }
  }
```

If you run this code, you should get the result shown in Figure 2-2.

Figure 2-2: The query result

This code listing takes the following steps:

1. First, it uses the SPSite constructor, passing in the site collection URL, to instantiate an SPSite object that represents the site collection. In other words, this SPSite object is the programmatic representation of the site collection with the specified name. Because the SPSite class implements the IDisposable interface, this code listing uses the SPSite object within the context of the "using" C# statement so its Dispose method is automatically invoked when the object goes out of scope.
2. Next, it invokes the OpenWeb method on this SPSite object to instantiate and to return an SPWeb object representing the site associated with the URL used in the SPSite constructor. In other words, this SPWeb object is the programmatic representation of this site. Because the SPWeb class implements the IDisposable interface, this code listing uses the SPWeb object within the context of the "using" C# statement so its Dispose method is automatically invoked when the object goes out of scope.

3. Then it passes the name of the list, which is "Clients," as an index into the Lists collection property of this SPWeb object in order to return the SPList object that represents this list. Note that the Lists collection is of the SPListCollection type. As the name suggests, SPListCollection is a collection of SPList objects where each SPList object represents a particular list in the specified site.
4. The code listing then passes the name of the default view of the Clients list, or "All contacts," as an index into the Views collection property of the SPList object for returning the SPView object that represents this default view. SharePoint views play the same roles as SQL Server views.
5. Next, the code listing instantiates an SPQuery object, passing in the SPView object. As the name suggests, this SPQuery object represents your CAML query over the specified view. Note that the Query string property of this SPQuery object is set to the CAML query.
6. The code listing then invokes the GetItems method on the SPList object representing the Clients list, passing in the SPQuery object in order to return the SPListItemCollection that contains the SPListItem objects that represent those items in the Clients list that meet the criteria specified in the CAML query.
7. Finally, the code listing iterates through the SPListItem objects in the SPListItemCollection and uses the "LinkTitle" as an index into each enumerated SPListItem object to return the value of the LinkTitle field of the list item that the SPListItem object represents.

Note that the CAML query assigned to the Query property of the SPQuery object in Listing 2-8 does not contain the <Query> document element shown in Listing 2-6. This is because the SPQuery object under the hood adds this document element.

A console application is just one option when it comes to developing an administrative application that runs locally on the server on which SharePoint is running. Another option is a web application. The following code listing presents the web version of the console application shown in Listing 2-8:

```
<%@ Page Language="C#" %>
<%@ Assembly Name="Microsoft.SharePoint, Version=12.0.0.0, Culture=neutral,
PublicKeyToken=71E9BCE111E9429C" %>
<%@ Import Namespace="Microsoft.SharePoint" %>
<!DOCTYPE html PUBLIC "-//W3C//DTD XHTML 1.0 Transitional//EN"
"http://www.w3.org/TR/xhtml1/DTD/xhtml1-transitional.dtd">

<script runat="server">
  void Page_Load(object sender, EventArgs e)
  {
    using (SPSite site = new SPSite("EnterSiteCollectionURLHere"))
    {
      using (SPWeb web = site.OpenWeb())
      {
        SPList list = web.Lists["Clients"];
        SPView view = list.Views["All contacts"];
        SPQuery query = new SPQuery(view);
        query.ViewFields = "<FieldRef Name='LinkTitle'/>" +
                           "<FieldRef Name='FirstName'/>" +
                           "<FieldRef Name='Company'/>" +
                           "<FieldRef Name='WorkCity'/>";
```

(continued)

(continued)

```
        query.Query = "<Where>" +
                        "<Eq>" +
                          "<FieldRef Name='Company' />" +
                          "<Value Type='Text'>Company1</Value>" +
                        "</Eq>" +
                      "</Where>" +
                      "<OrderBy>" +
                        "<FieldRef Name='LinkTitle' />" +
                      "</OrderBy>";

        SPListItemCollection items = list.GetItems(query);

        foreach (SPListItem item in items)
        {
          Response.Write("Last Name: " + item["LinkTitle"].ToString() + "<br/>");
        }
      }
    }

  }
</script>

<html xmlns="http://www.w3.org/1999/xhtml">
<head runat="server">
  <title>Untitled Page</title>
</head>
<body>
  <form id="form1" runat="server">
  <div>
  </div>
  </form>
</body>
</html>
```

Yet another option is a Windows application. I'll leave that to you as an exercise.

As mentioned earlier, one of the challenges in writing a CAML query is determining the actual names of the underlying fields. Listing 2-9 presents the managed code that displays the actual names of the underlying fields.

Listing 2-9: Displaying the actual field names

```
using System;
using Microsoft.SharePoint;

namespace ConsoleApplication3
{
  class Program
  {
    static void Main(string[] args)
```

```
        {
          SPSite site = new SPSite("Enter site collection URL!");
          SPWeb web = site.OpenWeb();
          SPList list = web.Lists["Clients"];
          SPView view = list.Views["All contacts"];
          SPQuery query = new SPQuery(view);
          Console.WriteLine(query.ViewXml);
          Console.ReadLine();
        }
      }
    }
```

If you run this code, you should get the result shown in Figure 2-3. The SPQuery exposes a string property named ViewXml. This is a string property that returns the XML document defining the specified view, which is the default view in this case. This XML document contains the actual names of the underlying fields.

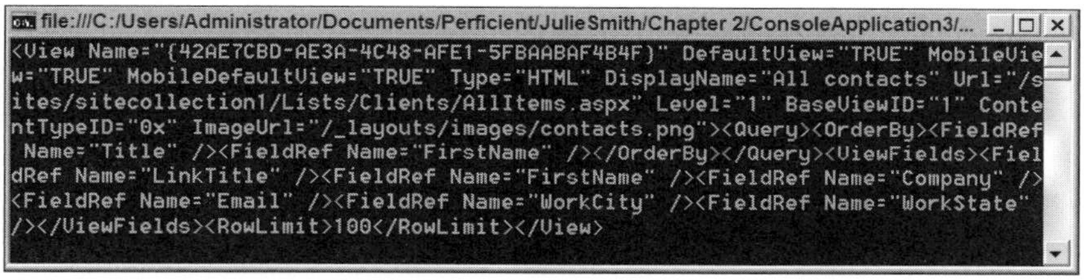

```
file:///C:/Users/Administrator/Documents/Perficient/JulieSmith/Chapter 2/ConsoleApplication3/...
<View Name="{42AE7CBD-AE3A-4C48-AFE1-5FBAABAF4B4F}" DefaultView="TRUE" MobileVie
w="TRUE" MobileDefaultView="TRUE" Type="HTML" DisplayName="All contacts" Url="/s
ites/sitecollection1/Lists/Clients/AllItems.aspx" Level="1" BaseViewID="1" Conte
ntTypeID="0x" ImageUrl="/_layouts/images/contacts.png"><Query><OrderBy><FieldRef
 Name="Title" /><FieldRef Name="FirstName" /></OrderBy></Query><ViewFields><Fiel
dRef Name="LinkTitle" /><FieldRef Name="FirstName" /><FieldRef Name="Company" />
<FieldRef Name="Email" /><FieldRef Name="WorkCity" /><FieldRef Name="WorkState"
/></ViewFields><RowLimit>100</RowLimit></View>
```

Figure 2-3: The XML document defining the view

Features

A feature is a way to package functionality and reuse it across different SharePoint sites and site templates. Every feature contains an XML file named feature.xml, which defines the feature-level attributes and references other XML files that define the elements that make up the feature. The feature.xml file and the XML files that it references are all written in CAML. This is an example of cases where CAML is not used for querying SharePoint data. As you can see, CAML is much more than just another query language.

The feature.xml file contains an XML document that defines the feature. The structure of this XML document, like the structure of many other XML documents, is described by the XML constructs of the XML schema markup language. One great way to understand the structure of the XML document that describes a feature is to study its associated XML schema. As mentioned earlier, all the XML schema documents are stored in files on the file system of the front-end web server in the following directory:

```
Local_Drive:\Program Files\Common Files\microsoft shared\Web Server Extensions\12\
TEMPLATE\XML
```

The feature.xml file, like any other XML file, has a single element known as document element. The document element in this case is an element named <Feature>. The following excerpt defines this element. As you can see, this element is of the FeatureDefinition schema type:

```
<xs:element name="Feature" type="FeatureDefinition"/>
```

The document element of an XML document is different from its root element. The root element contains the document element and other elements that reside outside of the document element.

Listing 2-10 presents the portion of the CAML XML schema that defines this type.

Listing 2-10: The definition of the FeatureDefinition type

```
<xs:complexType name="FeatureDefinition">
  <xs:all>
    <xs:element name="ElementManifests" type="ElementManifestReferences"
    minOccurs="0" maxOccurs="1" />
    <xs:element name="Properties" type="FeaturePropertyDefinitions"
    minOccurs="0" maxOccurs="1" />
    <xs:element name="ActivationDependencies" minOccurs="0" maxOccurs="1"
    type="FeatureActivationDependencyDefinitions" />
  </xs:all>
  <xs:attribute name="Id" type="UniqueIdentifier" use="required" />
  <xs:attribute name="Title" type="LocalizableString" />
  <xs:attribute name="Description" type="LocalizableString" />
  <xs:attribute name="Version" type="FeatureVersion" />
  <xs:attribute name="Scope" type="FeatureScope" use="required" />
  <xs:attribute name="ReceiverAssembly" type="AssemblyStrongName" />
  <xs:attribute name="ReceiverClass" type="AssemblyClass" />
  <xs:attribute name="Creator" type="LocalizableString" />
  <xs:attribute name="DefaultResourceFile" type="xs:string" />
  <xs:attribute name="Hidden" type="TRUEFALSE" />
  <xs:attribute name="SolutionId" type="UniqueIdentifier" />
  <xs:attribute name="ActivateOnDefault" type="TRUEFALSE" />
  <xs:attribute name="AutoActivateInCentralAdmin" type="TRUEFALSE" />
  <xs:attribute name="AlwaysForceInstall" type="TRUEFALSE" />
  <xs:attribute name="RequireResources" type="TRUEFALSE" />
  <xs:attribute name="ImageUrl" type="RelativeFilePath" use="optional" />
  <xs:attribute name="ImageUrlAltText" type="LocalizableString" use="optional" />
</xs:complexType>
```

As you can see, the <Feature> element contains zero or one <ElementManifests>, <Properties>, and <ActivationDependencies> elements. The <Feature> element also exposes the following attributes:

- **Id.** You must set the value of this attribute to a GUID that uniquely identifies this feature. Visual Studio comes with a handy tool named guidgen.exe, which is located in the following directory on your machine:

```
Local_Drive:\Program Files\Microsoft Visual Studio 9.0\Common7\Tools
```

  This tool allows you to generate a GUID and copy it to the clipboard. Figure 2-4 shows this tool in action.

- **Title.** Use this attribute to specify a title or name for your feature. SharePoint will display this title to users on the SharePoint page that allows users to activate or deactivate features.
- **Description.** Use this attribute to specify a short description for your feature. SharePoint will display this description to users on the SharePoint page that allows users to activate or deactivate features.

- **Hidden.** Use this Boolean attribute to specify whether you want SharePoint to make your feature available to users on the SharePoint page that allows users to activate or deactivate features. A hidden feature can only be activated or deactivated via command line or SharePoint object model.
- **ImageUrl.** Use this attribute to specify an icon for your feature. SharePoint will display this icon next to the title of your feature on the SharePoint page that allows users to activate or deactivate features.
- **ImageUrlAltText.** Use this attribute to specify text that will be displayed in place of the feature icon when the icon file is not available.
- **Scope.** Use this attribute to specify the scope at which users can activate or deactivate your feature. The possible values are:
    - **Farm.** Use this value to allow users to activate or deactivate your feature at a farm level. Features activated at this level are available only to the web applications of that farm.
    - **WebApplication.** Use this value to allow users to activate or deactivate your feature at a web application level. Features activated at this level are available only to the site collections of that web application.
    - **Site.** Use this value to allow users to activate or deactivate your feature at a site collection level. Features activated at this level are available only to the descendant sites of that site collection.
    - **Web.** Use this value to allow users to activate or deactivate your feature at a site level. Features activated at this level are available only to the descendant sites of that site.
- **Version.** Use this attribute to specify the version of your feature. Use this format for the version: major.minor[.build[.revision]]. An example would be 1.0.0.0.
- **ReceiverClass.** Use this attribute to specify the fully qualified name of the type of the class, including its complete namespace containment hierarchy, which handles the feature events.
- **ReceiverAssembly.** Use this attribute to specify the assembly, which contains the class specified in the ReceiverClass attribute.

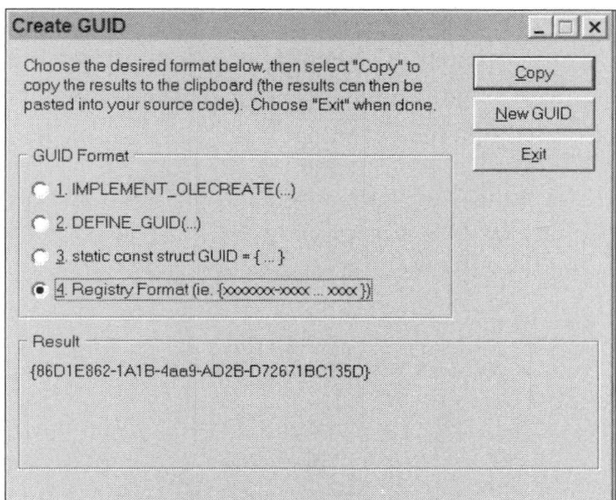

Figure 2-4: The guidgen.exe tool

As mentioned, the <Feature> element contains zero or one <ElementManifests> child element of the ElementManifestReferences schema type. Listing 2-11 presents the portion of the CAML XML schema that defines this schema type.

Listing 2-11: The definition of the ElementManifestReferences type

```
<xs:complexType name="ElementManifestReferences">
  <xs:sequence>
    <xs:choice minOccurs="0" maxOccurs="unbounded">
      <xs:element name="ElementManifest" type="ElementManifestReference"
      minOccurs="0" maxOccurs="unbounded" />
      <xs:element name="ElementFile" type="ElementManifestReference"
      minOccurs="0" maxOccurs="unbounded" />
    </xs:choice>
  </xs:sequence>
</xs:complexType>
```

As you can see, the <ElementManifests> element contains zero or more <ElementManifest> and <ElementFile> child elements of the ElementManifestReference schema type. Listing 2-12 presents the portion of the CAML schema that defines this schema type.

Listing 2-12: The definition of the ElementManifestReference type

```
<xs:complexType name="ElementManifestReference">
  <xs:sequence></xs:sequence>
  <xs:attribute name="Location" type="RelativeFilePath" use="required" />
</xs:complexType>
```

As this code listing demonstrates, the <ElementManifest> and <ElementFile> elements do not contain any child element and expose a single attribute named Location, which specifies the location of a file. This file in the case of the <ElementManifest> element contains an XML document written in CAML that describes the elements that make up the feature. This file in the case of the <ElementFile> element is a file such as an .aspx file that supports the feature.

An Example of a Feature

This section walks you through the process of defining and deploying a simple feature. This feature packages functionality that adds a custom menu item to the Site Actions menu. This custom menu item will allow users to navigate to the Google web site.

1. Visual Studio provides IntelliSense support for XML manipulation among many other benefits. One way to enable the IntelliSense support for CAML is to copy the CAML schema files into the following Visual Studio directory on your machine:

```
Local_Drive:\Program Files\Microsoft Visual Studio 9.0\Xml\Schemas
```

The CAML schema files are four files named CoreDefinitions.xsd, CamlView.xsd, CamlQuery.xsd, and wss.xsd, all of which are located in the following directory on your machine:

```
Local_Drive:\Program Files\Common Files\microsoft shared\Web Server Extensions\12\
TEMPLATE\XML
```

2. Now launch Visual Studio 2008 and create a new Class Library project named GoogleMenuItem. You must deploy your custom feature into a folder named FEATURES, which is a subfolder of another standard folder named TEMPLATE on the file system of the front-end SharePoint web server:

```
Local_Drive:\Program Files\Common Files\microsoft shared\Web Server Extensions\12\
TEMPLATE\FEATURES
```

3. You may want to create a folder with the same name as your custom feature inside the FEATURES folder to avoid name conflicts with other features. In this case, you'll name your feature GoogleMenuItem and consequently you'll need to create a new folder named GoogleMenuItem under the FEATURES folder.

4. You may also want to display the Google icon next to the menu item. This means that you need to deploy the icon file to the file system of the front-end web server. The TEMPLATE folder contains a subfolder named Images where you need to deploy the icon file. You may want to create a folder with the same name as your custom feature inside the Images folder to avoid name conflicts with the image files of other features. In this case, you should create a folder named GoogleMenuItem within the Images folder.

   One way to make the deployment easier is to create the same folder hierarchy inside your Visual Studio Class Library as shown in Figure 2-5.

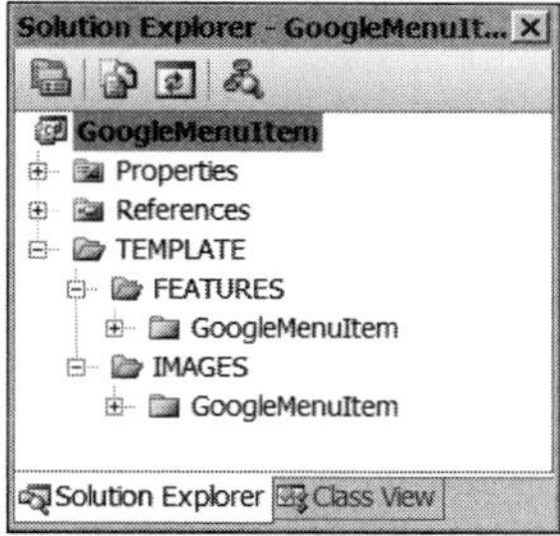

Figure 2-5: The folder hierarchy of the project

   As this figure shows, the GoogleMenuItem Class Library project contains a folder named TEMPLATE, which in turn contains two subfolders named FEATURES and IMAGES. This basically mirrors the same folder hierarchy as the one on the file system of the front-end web server.

5. Next go ahead and add a new XML file named GoogleMenuItem.xml to the GoogleMenuItem folder in this project and add the XML document shown in Listing 2-13 to this file.

Listing 2-13: The content of the GoogleMenuItem.xml file

```
<?xml version="1.0" encoding="utf-8" ?>
<Elements xmlns="http://schemas.microsoft.com/sharepoint/">
  <CustomAction
  Id="12D1CB00-6DDA-4ce6-B834-23C1C8493417"
  GroupId="SiteActions"
  Location="Microsoft.SharePoint.StandardMenu"
  Title="Google Web site"
  Description="Select to navigate to the Google Web site."
  ImageUrl="/_layouts/images/GoogleMenuItem/google.png">
    <UrlAction Url="http://www.google.com"/>
  </CustomAction>
</Elements>
```

This XML document defines a custom menu item, which takes the user to the Google site. Note that the Id attribute of the <CustomAction> element is set to a GUID that uniquely identifies this menu item. As discussed earlier, you can click the New GUID button on the guidgen.exe tool shown in Figure 2-4 to generate a new GUID, click the Copy button to copy the new GUID to the clipboard, and finally paste the GUID into the XML document as the value of the Id attribute.

So far you've used CAML to implement the XML document that defines your custom menu item as shown in Listing 2-13. Next, you need to use CAML to implement the XML document that defines the feature that will package your custom menu item and allow you to deploy it in a reusable fashion where it can be used across different sites and site templates.

Add a new XML file named feature.xml to the GoogleMenuItem subfolder of the FEATURES folder of the GoogleMenuItem Class Library project and add the XML document shown in Listing 2-14 to this XML file.

Listing 2-14: The content of the feature.xml file

```
<?xml version="1.0" encoding="utf-8" ?>
<Feature
xmlsn="http://schemas.microsoft.com/sharepoint/"
Id="24E9C1DC-2860-4724-8437-E1B68F4B8613"
Title="GoogleMenuItem"
Description="This feature contains the GoogleMenuItem menu item!"
Hidden="False"
ImageUrl="/_layouts/images/GoogleMenuItem/google.png"
Scope="Site"
Version="1.0.0.0">
 <ElementManifests>
   <ElementManifest Location="GoogleMenuItem.xml"/>
 </ElementManifests>
</Feature>
```

As you can see, the feature.xml file contains an <ElementManifest> element that references the GoogleMenuItem.xml file. Also note that you've set the ImageUrl attribute of the <CustomAction> (see Listing 2-13) and <Feature> (see Listing 2-14) elements to the URL of the google.png image file.

Next, you need to take the following steps:

1. Create a new folder named GoogleMenuItem inside the FEATURES directory in the following location on the file system of the front-end web server:

```
Local_Drive:\Program Files\Common Files\microsoft shared\Web Server Extensions\12\
TEMPLATE\FEATURES
```

2. Create a new folder named GoogleMenuItem inside the IMAGES directory in the following location on the file system of the front-end web server:

```
Local_Drive:\Program Files\Common Files\microsoft shared\Web Server Extensions\12\
TEMPLATE\ IMAGES
```

3. Copy the feature.xml and GoogleMenuItem.xml files into the GoogleMenuItem folder in Step 1.
4. Copy the google.png image file into the GoogleMenuItem folder in Step 2. You can use any desired image file to represent this feature.
5. Restart the IIS.

You can automate all five of the previous tasks by doing the following:

1. Adding a batch file named mybatchfile.bat to the root directory of the GoogleMenuItem Class Library project and then adding the following listing to this batch file:

```
@SET TEMPLATE="c:\program files\common files\microsoft shared\web server
extensions\12\Template"

@SET STSADM="c:\program files\common files\microsoft shared\web server
extensions\12\bin\stsadm"

Echo Copying the GoogleMenuItem feature's files
xcopy /e /y TEMPLATE\* %TEMPLATE%

Echo Installing the GoogleMenuItem feature
%STSADM% -o InstallFeature -filename GoogleMenuItem\feature.xml -force

Echo Restarting the IIS
IISRESET
```

2. Adding the following to the "Post-build event command line" section of the Properties dialog box of the GoogleMenuItem Class Library project:

```
cd $(ProjectDir)
mybatchfile.bat
```

   This instructs Visual Studio to run the preceding two command lines after each build.

After deploying the GoogleMenuItem feature, if you navigate to the Site Features Collection page, you should see this feature listed among other features. Next, you need to click the Activate button to activate the feature. This will automatically add the Google menu item to the Site Actions menu. If you select this menu item, it will automatically redirect you to the Google web site.

SharePoint Solution Package

The examples and recipes presented in this and the next chapters do not use SharePoint solution packages for deployment. Instead they use a manual approach to make the steps involved in the deployment of SharePoint solutions explicit so you can gain a better understanding of these steps. For example, as you saw, this manual approach requires you to directly create the required folders in the file system of the front-end web server and copy the required files into these folders.

This manual approach is taken for educational purposes. You should not use this manual approach to deploy your SharePoint solutions to a production machine. Instead you should use SharePoint solution packages. A SharePoint solution package automatically creates the specified folders and copies the specified files to these folders.

Implementing a SharePoint solution package requires you to know what files you need to deploy and to which folders on the file system of each front-end web server in the server farm to deploy these files. The manual approach explicitly specifies what these files are and where they should be deployed. I'll postpone the discussion of SharePoint solution packages to Chapter 12, where you learn how to use SharePoint solution packages to deploy your solutions.

Application Pages

As discussed in the previous chapter, SharePoint supports two types of pages known as application pages and site pages. Here are the major differences between application and site pages:

- Users cannot customize an application page in Office SharePoint Designer 2007. Site pages, on the other hand, are user-customizable, meaning that users can open them in Office SharePoint Designer 2007 and customize them.
- Application pages are deployed in the physical folder in the following standard folder in the file system of each front-end web server:

```
Local_Drive:\Program Files\Common Files\microsoft shared\Web Server Extensions\12\
TEMPLATE\LAYOUTS
```

- When an IIS web site goes through the one-time transformation process turning it into a SharePoint web application, SharePoint adds a new virtual directory named _layouts to this IIS web site. It then maps it to the previous physical folder on the file system of the front-end web server, as you can see from Figure 2-6, which shows the IIS Manager. If you click the Basic Setting link on the Actions pane, it will launch the dialog box shown in Figure 2-7. As the "Physical path" text box in this dialog box shows, the _layouts virtual directory is mapped to the previously mentioned physical path. Thanks to this mapping, the clients of your application page can simply append the /_layouts/ApplicationSpecificDirectory/YourApplicationPage.aspx to the URL of every site on web server to access your page.

As you'll see later, as a best practice, you should always create an application-specific directory under the LAYOUTS physical folder and deploy your application page to this directory as opposed to deploying your application page directory to the LAYOUTS directory itself to avoid possible name conflicts with other deployed application pages.

- Site pages are provisioned from page templates. These page templates are deployed in the same directory as the features that contain these page templates. Recall that features are deployed in the following folder in the file system of the front-end web server:

```
Local_Drive:\Program Files\Common Files\microsoft shared\Web Server Extensions\12\
TEMPLATE\FEATURES
```

- As discussed in the previous chapter, as a best practice you should create an application-specific folder under the FEATURES folder and deploy your feature to this folder. You also need to create another folder such as PageTemplates in your feature folder and then deploy your page template in this folder. Note that there is no virtual directory on the IIS web site that maps to the physical folder containing your page template. This means that there is no way for the clients to directly access your page template. This is because it is not the page template that clients access, but an instance of the page template instead. As you'll see later, the provisioning logic that provisions a site page from a page template determines the URL for the site page, which is the URL that the clients must use to access it. As you can imagine, you can provision different site pages with different URLs from the same page template. As the name suggests, a page template is a template from which site pages are provisioned. Site pages are provisioned from page templates, whereas application pages stand on their own.
- Application pages are dynamically compiled into assemblies the first time they're accessed. This means that the first request for an application page suffers performance degradation due to the compilation overhead. However, the next requests for the same application page are serviced through the same assembly. As such, the next requests are processed much faster. Because application pages are compiled, they can contain inline code. Ghosted site pages benefit from the same performance boost as an application page does because their associated page templates are compiled just like application pages. This remains as long as site pages are not customized. When a site page is customized, it is no longer processed like an application page. Instead it is processed through what is known as no-compile mode. As such, site pages (and consequently page templates) mustn't contain inline code.
- Application pages do not require you to register your custom controls as safe controls because application pages are not processed through safe mode processing. Site pages, on the other hand, use safe mode processing where inline code and/or unsafe server controls are not allowed.

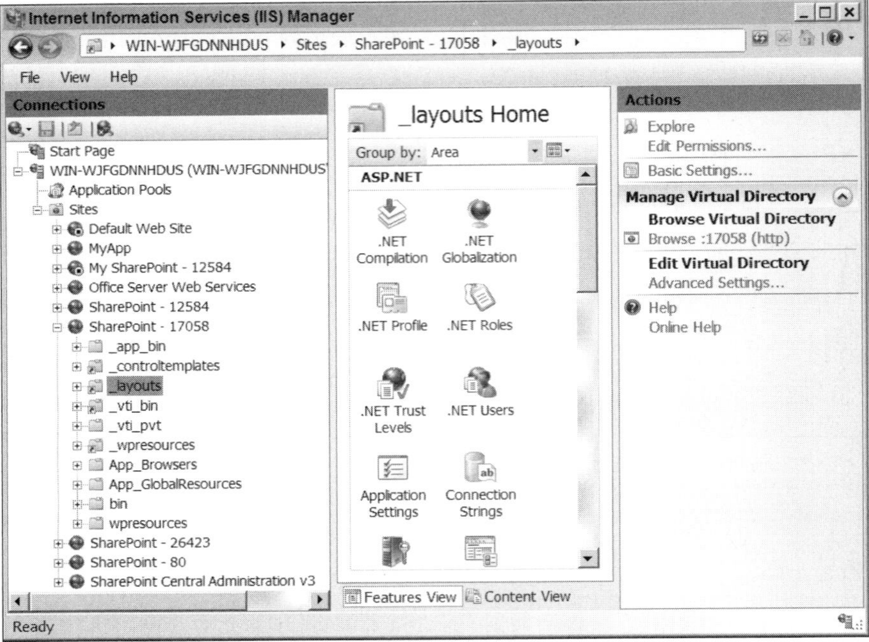

Figure 2-6: The IIS Manager

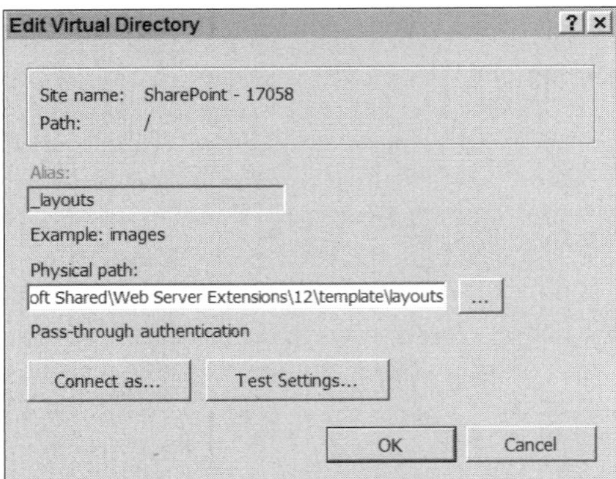

Figure 2-7: Edit Virtual Directory

There are two types of application pages as far as adding code goes. You can add the code inline within the .aspx page or in a separate code-behind file. The recommended practice is to add the code in a separate code-behind file because it separates business logic from the user interface. Next, you'll use both approaches to implement an example, beginning with the inline approach.

Inline Approach

As the name implies, in an inline approach you add the code inline within the .aspx page. The code is added within a <script> HTML element whose runat attribute is set to server. Use the inline approach as follows:

1. Launch Visual Studio 2008 and add a new Class Library named ClassLibrary1.
2. This Class Library project by default contains a file named Class1.cs. Delete this file from this project.
3. Add a reference to the Microsoft.SharePoint.dll assembly, which is located in the following directory:

```
Local_Drive:\Program Files\Common Files\Microsoft Shared\Web Server Extensions\12\ISAPI
```

   You're going to need this assembly because you're going to program against the SharePoint object model.

4. Add a reference to the System.Web.dll assembly.
5. Add a new text file named Default.aspx to the project.

   Implementing a custom application page normally involves using ASP.NET and SharePoint server controls. The SharePoint server controls are in a namespace named Microsoft.SharePoint.WebControls inside the Microsoft.SharePoint.dll assembly. Next, you learn how to add these server controls to the Visual Studio Toolbox so you can drag and drop them on the designer surface.

6. Right-click the Toolbox and select Add Tab from the popup menu as shown in Figure 2-8.

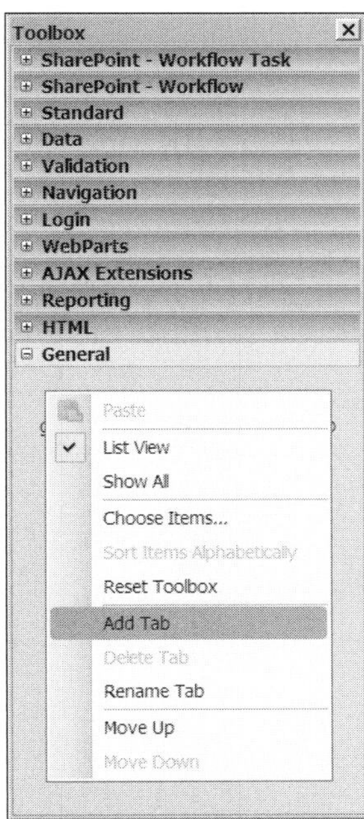

Figure 2-8: The popup menu containing the Add Tab menu option

This will add a new tab to the Toolbox. Name this tab SharePoint Controls, as shown in Figure 2-9.

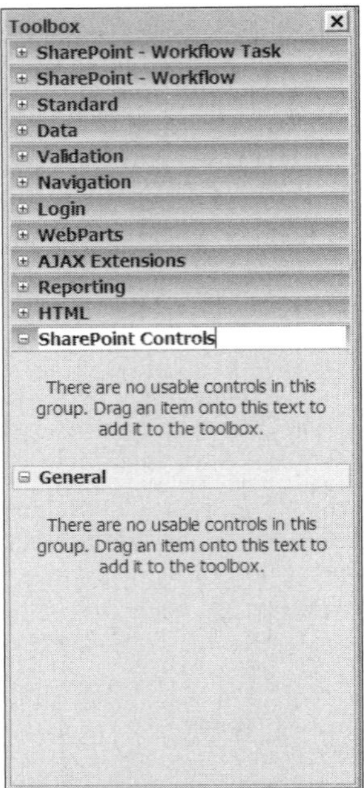

Figure 2-9: Toolbox with a new tab for SharePoint server controls

7. Next, right-click inside the new tab in the Toolbox and select Choose Items, as shown in Figure 2-10.

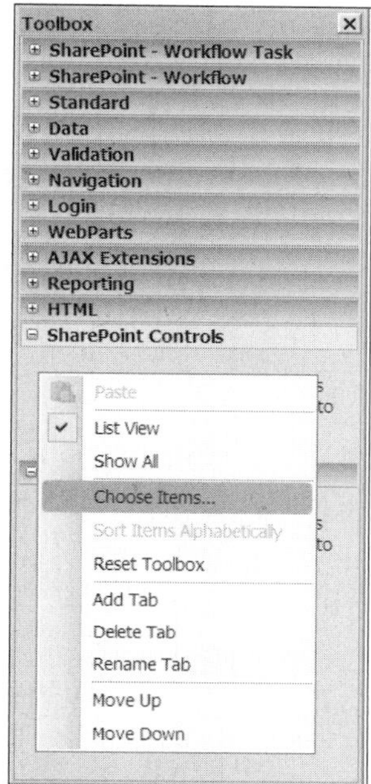

Figure 2-10: The popup menu containing the Choose Items menu option

This pops up the Choose Toolbox Items dialog box shown in Figure 2-11.

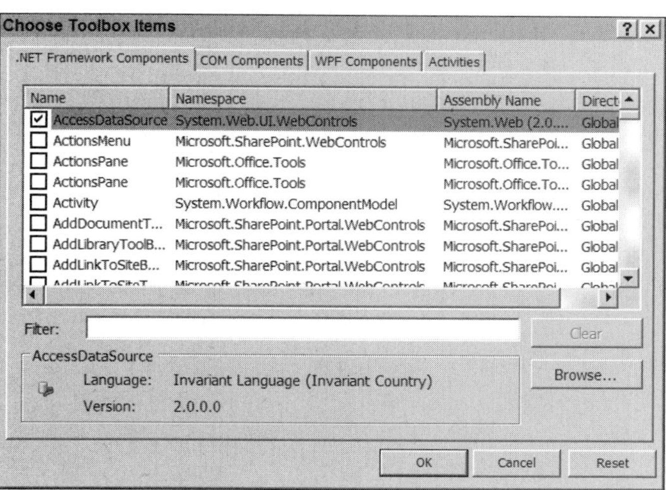

Figure 2-11: The Choose Toolbox Items dialog

8. Click the Browse button, navigate to the following folder, and then select the Microsoft.SharePoint.dll assembly as shown in Figure 2-12.

```
Local_Drive:\Program Files\Common Files\Microsoft Shared\Web Server Extensions\12\
ISAPI
```

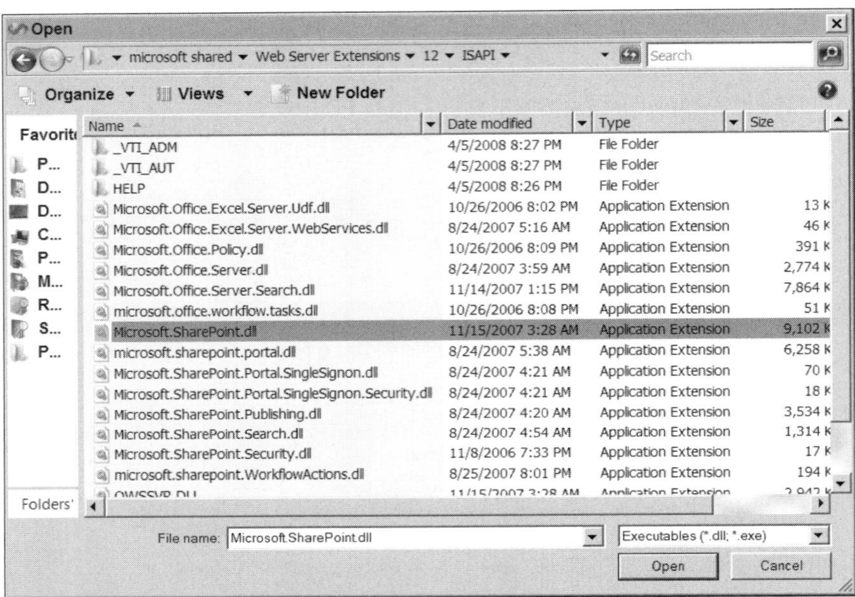

Figure 2-12: The Microsoft.SharePoint.dll assembly

This will take you back to the Choose Toolbox Items dialog box. Notice that this dialog box automatically highlights all available components in the Microsoft.SharePoint.dll directory as shown in Figure 2-13. You can sort the list by namespace and scroll to the Microsoft.SharePoint namespace to view these components.

9. Toggle the checkbox on one of these highlighted components. This will select all highlighted components. This saves you from having to toggle all selected checkboxes. Click the OK button on the Choose Toolbox dialog to add these controls to the Toolbox.

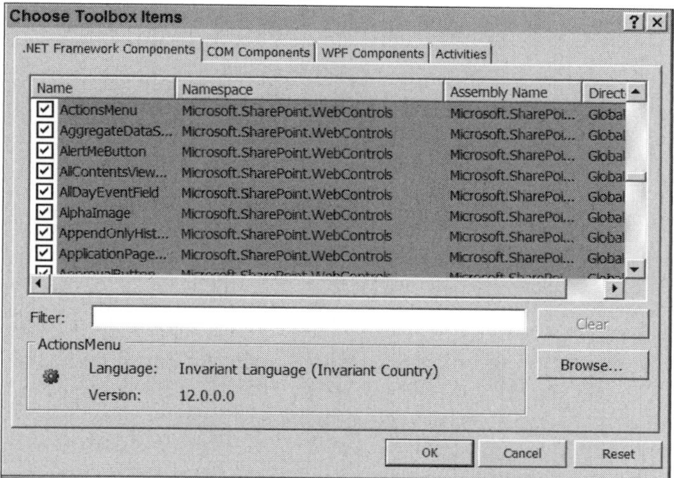

Figure 2-13: The Choose Toolbox Items dialog displaying SharePoint server controls

As Figure 2-14 shows, the SharePoint Controls tab now contains the SharePoint components that you can drag and drop onto the design surface.

Figure 2-14: The Toolbox tab displaying the SharePoint server controls

10. Next, go ahead and add Listing 2-15 to the Default.aspx file.

Listing 2-15: The content of the Default.aspx file

```
<%@ Page Language="C#" MasterPageFile="~/_layouts/application.master"
Inherits="Microsoft.SharePoint.WebControls.LayoutsPageBase" %>
```

Note that the MasterPageFile attribute of the @Page directive is set to the following:

```
~/_layouts/application.master
```

The application.master is the master page that every application page should use. This ensures that your custom application pages have the same look and feel as other SharePoint pages. This also means that every application page is a content page. A content page can contain page directives, server-side and client-side script elements, and Content server controls. Each Content server control must override the content of a specific ContentPlaceHolder server control in the application.master master page.
Your custom application page must set the ContentPlaceHolderId property of each Content server control to the ID property of its associated ContentPlaceHolder. The application.master master page comes with twenty different ContentPlaceHolder server controls whose content you can override to add your own custom contents. Your custom application page can override any or none of these content placeholders.

As Listing 2-15 shows, the Inherits attribute of the @Page directive is set to the following value:

```
Inherits="Microsoft.SharePoint.WebControls.LayoutsPageBase"
```

This means that the application page inherits from a base class named LayoutsPageBase in the Microsoft.SharePoint.WebControls namespace. This seems to be a departure from a normal ASP.NET page, which inherits from a base class named Page in the System.Web.UI namespace. This is really not a departure because LayoutsPageBase inherits from Page and extends its functionality to add support for SharePoint-related properties and methods. For example, LayoutsPageBase exposes a property of type SPSite named Site, which returns an SPSite object that represents the current site collection, and a property of type SPWeb named Web, which returns an SPWeb object that represents the current site. Therefore, as a best practice, your custom application pages should always inherit from LayoutsPageBase rather than Page to take advantage of the SharePoint-related methods and properties of LayoutsPageBase.

In this example you're going to override the content of a ContentPlaceHolder server control named PlaceHolderMain to add your own custom content:

1. Go ahead and add a Content tag to the Default.aspx file as follows:

```
<%@ Page Language="C#" MasterPageFile="~/_layouts/application.master"
Inherits="Microsoft.SharePoint.WebControls.LayoutsPageBase" %>

<asp:Content ID="Main" ContentPlaceHolderID="PlaceHolderMain" runat="server">

</asp:Content>
```

2. Next, drag the ListViewByQuery control from the SharePoint Controls tab and drop it onto the design surface within the opening and closing tags of the Content tag like so. You can optionally directly enter the boldfaced portion of the following code listing instead of dragging and dropping the control from the Toolbox:

```
<%@ Page Language="C#" MasterPageFile="~/_layouts/application.master"
Inherits="Microsoft.SharePoint.WebControls.LayoutsPageBase" %>

<%@ Register Assembly="Microsoft.SharePoint, Version=12.0.0.0, Culture=neutral,
PublicKeyToken=71e9bce111e9429c"Namespace="Microsoft.SharePoint.WebControls"
TagPrefix="cc1" %>
<asp:Content ID="Main" ContentPlaceHolderID="PlaceHolderMain" runat="server">
<cc1:ListViewByQuery ID="ListViewByQuery1" runat="server" />
</asp:Content>
```

If you use the drag-and-drop approach, Visual Studio automatically adds the preceding boldfaced portion. Note that the @Register directive shown in the boldfaced portion registers the associated tag prefix for the Microsoft.SharePoint.WebControl namespace. Now it's time to add some inline custom code to initialize the ListViewByQuery server control.

3. Go ahead and add the <script> block shown in Listing 2-16 to the Default.aspx file.

Listing 2-16: The content of the Default.aspx file

```
<%@ Page Language="C#" MasterPageFile="~/_layouts/application.master"
Inherits="Microsoft.SharePoint.WebControls.LayoutsPageBase" %>

<%@ Register Assembly="Microsoft.SharePoint, Version=12.0.0.0, Culture=neutral,
PublicKeyToken=71e9bce111e9429c"
Namespace="Microsoft.SharePoint.WebControls" TagPrefix="cc1" %>

<%@ Import Namespace="Microsoft.SharePoint" %>

<script runat="server">
  void Page_Load(object sender, EventArgs e)
  {
    SPList list = this.Web.Lists["Clients"];
    SPView view = list.Views["All contacts"];
    SPQuery query = new SPQuery(view);
    query.ViewFields = "<FieldRef Name='LinkTitle'/>" +
                       "<FieldRef Name='FirstName'/>" +
                       "<FieldRef Name='Company'/>" +
                       "<FieldRef Name='WorkCity'/>";
    query.Query = "<Where>" +
                    "<Eq>" +
                      "<FieldRef Name='Company' />" +
                      "<Value Type='Text'>Company1</Value>" +
                    "</Eq>" +
                  "</Where>" +
                  "<OrderBy>" +
                    "<FieldRef Name='LinkTitle' />" +
                  "</OrderBy>";
```

(continued)

Listing 2-16 *(continued)*

```
      ListViewByQuery1.List = list;
      ListViewByQuery1.Query = query;

    }
  </script>

  <asp:Content ID="Main" ContentPlaceHolderID="PlaceHolderMain" runat="server">
    <cc1:ListViewByQuery ID="ListViewByQuery1" runat="server" />
  </asp:Content>
```

The custom application page inherits two properties named Site and Web from its base class, which return an SPSite and an SPWeb object that respectively represent the current site collection and site as discussed earlier.

The Page_Load uses "Clients" as an index into the Lists SPListCollection collection property of the SPWeb object to return a reference to the SPList object that represents the Clients list:

```
      SPList list = this.Web.Lists["Clients"];
```

Next, Page_Load accesses the SPView object that represents the default view of the Clients list:

```
      SPView view = list.Views["All contacts"];
```

Page_Load then instantiates an SPQuery object and initializes its properties:

```
      SPQuery query = new SPQuery(view);
      query.ViewFields = "<FieldRef Name='LinkTitle'/>" +
                         "<FieldRef Name='FirstName'/>" +
                         "<FieldRef Name='Company'/>" +
                         "<FieldRef Name='WorkCity'/>";
      query.Query = "<Where>" +
                      "<Eq>" +
                        "<FieldRef Name='Company' />" +
                        "<Value Type='Text'>Company1</Value>" +
                      "</Eq>" +
                    "</Where>" +
                    "<OrderBy>" +
                      "<FieldRef Name='LinkTitle' />" +
                    "</OrderBy>";
```

Page_Load finally assigns the preceding SPList and SPQuery objects to the List and Query properties of the ListViewByQuery server control:

```
      ListViewByQuery1.List = list;
      ListViewByQuery1.Query = query;
```

The ListViewByQuery server control internally calls the GetItems method on the SPList object, passing in the SPQuery object to return an SPListItemCollection collection that contains the SPListItem objects that represent the query results. The ListViewByQuery server control finally displays these SPListItem objects in a table.

So far you've learned how to implement a simple application page such as Default.aspx that contains inline code. Next, you need to deploy this application page to the LAYOUTS directory in the following location on the file system of the front-end web server:

```
Local_Drive:\Program Files\Common Files\microsoft shared\Web Server Extensions\12\
TEMPLATE
```

Every application page must be deployed into the LAYOUTS directory.

As a best practice, you should create a new directory inside the LAYOUTS directory and then deploy your application page to this directory to avoid filename conflicts with other application pages. Now go ahead and create a directory named WSSMOSSProgCh2_1 inside the LAYOUTS directory and copy the Default.aspx page into this directory.

That's it! You have now a deployed custom application page that can be accessed from any SharePoint site within the farm where you deployed the Default.aspx page. The URL of this application page consists of two parts, where the first part is the URL of the target SharePoint site and the second part is

```
/_layouts/WSSMOSSProg_ch2_1/Default.aspx
```

This is possible because SharePoint creates a virtual directory named _layouts for each IIS web site, which maps into the following physical directory on the file system of the web server, when it is configuring the web site for SharePoint:

```
Local_Drive:\Program Files\Common Files\microsoft shared\Web Server Extensions\12\
TEMPLATE\LAYOUTS
```

Thanks to this mapping, you can simply copy your custom application pages into the LAYOUTS directory on the file system of the web server and rest assured that it will automatically be available to all SharePoint sites running on the web server. You do not have to deploy your custom application pages to each SharePoint site. A single deployment does the trick!

Figure 2-15 shows you what you'll see if you access Default.aspx from your browser. Note that the ListViewByQuery server control displays the content of the Client list in a table as discussed earlier.

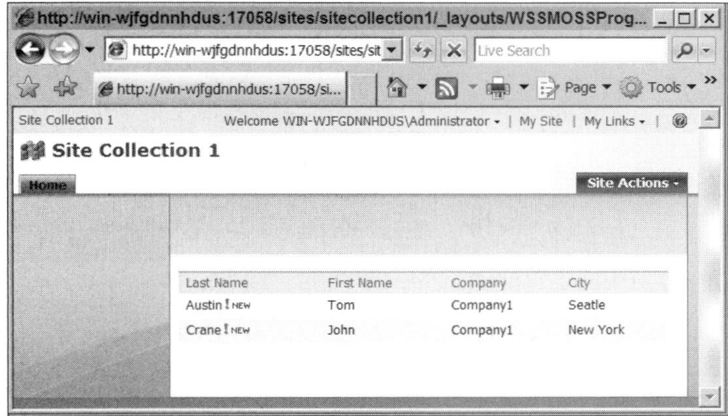

Figure 2-15: The page containing a ListViewByQuery server control

As you saw, you manually deployed the Default.aspx to the WSSMOSSProCh2_1 folder under the LAYOUTS folder in the front-end Web server. Next, you learn how to automate this.

It is a good practice to create the same folder hierarchy as the front-end web server in your Class Library project to ease the deployment process. As such, go ahead and add a new folder named TEMPLATE to the root directory of the Class Library project. Then add a subfolder named LAYOUTS to this TEMPLATE folder. Finally, add a subfolder named WSSMOSSProCh2_1 to this LAYOUTS folder. This basically creates the same folder hierarchy as the front-end web server where you want to deploy the Default.aspx page.

Now, move the Default.aspx file from the root folder of the class library to the WSSMOSSProCh2_1 folder. Next add the following batch file named mybatchfile.bat to the root folder of the Class Library project:

```
@SET TEMPLATE="c:\program files\common files\microsoft shared\web server
extensions\12\Template"

Echo Copying files to TEMPLATES directory
xcopy /e /y TEMPLATE\* %TEMPLATE%

IISRESET
```

Now right-click the Class Library project in the Solution Explorer of Visual Studio and select the Properties option as shown in Figure 2-16.

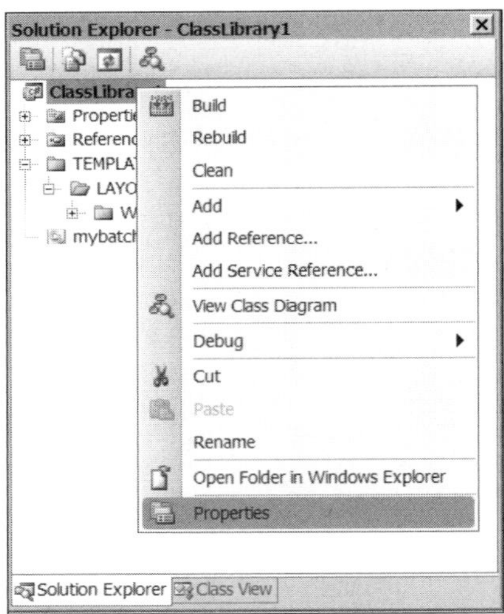

Figure 2-16: The popup menu that contains the Properties menu option

This will launch the Properties pane shown in Figure 2-17.

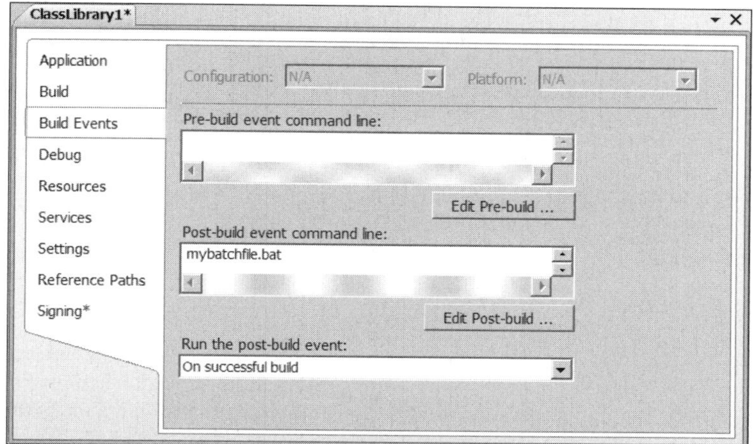

Figure 2-17: The Properties pane

Switch to the Build Events tab as shown in Figure 2-17 and add the following to the "Post-build event command line" text field:

```
cd $(ProjectDir)
mybatchfile.bat
```

Every time you build the Class Library project, it will now automatically run the mybatchfile.bat, which in turn automatically deploys the Default.aspx file to the WSSMOSSProCh2_1 folder in the front-end web server.

Code-Behind Approach

So far you've learned how to implement and deploy custom application pages that include inline code. Next, you learn how to implement and deploy custom application pages that do not directly include inline code. Instead this code is stored in a separate code-behind file.

Now go ahead and add a new text file named Default2.aspx to the WSSMOSSProCh2_1 folder of the previously discussed Class Library project in Visual Studio 2008. Now add Listing 2-17 to the Default2 .aspx file.

Listing 2-17: The content of the Default2.aspx file

```
<%@ Page Language="C#" MasterPageFile="~/_layouts/application.master"
Inherits="Default2, ClassLibrary1, Version=1.0.0.0, Culture=neutral,
PublicKeyToken=" %>

<%@ Register Assembly="Microsoft.SharePoint, Version=12.0.0.0, Culture=neutral,
PublicKeyToken=71e9bce111e9429c"
Namespace="Microsoft.SharePoint.WebControls" TagPrefix="cc1" %>

<asp:Content ID="Main" ContentPlaceHolderID="PlaceHolderMain" runat="server">
  <cc1:ListViewByQuery ID="ListViewByQuery1" runat="server" />
</asp:Content>
```

Note the differences between Listings 2-16 and 2-17:

- The Inherits attributes of the @Page directives in Listings 2-16 and 2-17 are respectively set to Microsoft.SharePoint.WebControls.LayoutsPageBase and Default2. This means that the Default.aspx custom application page inherits from Microsoft.SharePoint.WebControl. LayoutsPageBase, whereas the Default2.aspx custom application page inherits from the Default2 class. The Default2 class is discussed shortly.
- The Inherits attribute in Listing 2-17 contains the information about the assembly that contains the Default2 class. This information consists of four parts: assembly name, version, culture, and public key token. You'll learn shortly how to specify the public key token parameter. These four parameters together define a strong name for an assembly. This is necessary because you have to deploy the assembly that contains the Default2 class, that is, the code behind, to the GAC and only strong-named assemblies can be installed in the GAC.
- Note that the Inherits attribute in Listing 2-16 does not contain the assembly information because Microsoft.SharePoint.WebControls.LayoutsPageBase is in Microsoft.SharePoint.dll assembly, which is a standard SharePoint assembly.
- Listing 2-16 does not contain the script block that contains the inline code because the inline code is moved to the Default2.aspx.cs code-behind file.
- Listing 2-17 does not contain the @Import directive because the Default2.aspx custom application page does not contain inline code. As you'll see shortly, this inline code is moved to the Default2.aspx.cs code-behind file.

Next, go ahead and add a new Class (.cs file) item named Default2.aspx.cs to the Class Library project and add the code shown in Listing 2-18 to this file. Notice that this file contains the same inline code shown in Listing 2-16. Also note that the Default2 class inherits the Microsoft.SharePoint.WebControls. LayoutsPageBase rather than Page.

Listing 2-18: The content of the Default2.aspx.cs file

```
using System;
using Microsoft.SharePoint;
using Microsoft.SharePoint.WebControls;

public partial class Default2 : LayoutsPageBase
{
  protected ListViewByQuery ListViewByQuery1;

  protected void Page_Load(object sender, EventArgs e)
  {
    SPList list = this.Web.Lists["Clients"];
    SPView view = list.Views["All contacts"];
    SPQuery query = new SPQuery(view);
    query.ViewFields = "<FieldRef Name='LinkTitle'/>" +
                       "<FieldRef Name='FirstName'/>" +
                       "<FieldRef Name='Company'/>" +
                       "<FieldRef Name='WorkCity'/>";
    query.Query = "<Where>" +
                    "<Eq>" +
                      "<FieldRef Name='Company' />" +
                      "<Value Type='Text'>Company1</Value>" +
                    "</Eq>" +
                  "</Where>" +
                  "<OrderBy>" +
                    "<FieldRef Name='LinkTitle' />" +
                  "</OrderBy>";
    ListViewByQuery1.List = list;
    ListViewByQuery1.Query = query;
  }
}
```

As discussed earlier, you must deploy the Default2.aspx custom application page to the LAYOUTS directory on the file system of the front-end web server. How about the deployment of the Default2.aspx.cs code-behind file?

In normal ASP.NET development, when you add a new Web Form with the “Place Code in Separate File” checkbox toggled on, Visual Studio automatically sets the value of:

- The CodeFile attribute of the @Page directive to the path to the code-behind file:

```
<%@ Page Language="C#" AutoEventWireup="true" CodeFile="Default.aspx.cs"
Inherits="Default2" %>
```

- The Inherits attribute of the @Page directive to the fully qualified name of the type of the code-behind class including its complete namespace containment hierarchy:

```
<%@ Page Language="C#" AutoEventWireup="true" CodeFile="Default.aspx.cs"
Inherits="Default2" %>
```

At runtime when the .aspx file is accessed for the first time, ASP.NET uses the value of the CodeFile attribute to locate the code-behind file and the value of the Inherits attribute to determine the code-behind class within this file. It then compiles both .aspx and its associated code-behind files into a single class that inherits from the Page base class.

SharePoint does not support dynamic compilation of the code-behind file. Instead it expects you to:

- Compile the code-behind file into a strongly-named assembly
- Install the assembly in the GAC
- Add the assembly information including assembly name, version, culture, and public key token to the Inherits attribute

You can optionally use an @Assembly directive to introduce the assembly information instead of adding this information to the Inherits attribute.

As you can see, the value of the CodeFile attribute, which specifies the path to the code-behind file, is not used. Instead SharePoint expects the Inherits attribute to contain both the type and assembly information about the code-behind class, which is Default2 in this case.

You could manually compile the code-behind file into a strongly-named assembly. However, the better way to go is to configure Visual Studio as follows. First, right-click the Class Library project in the Solution Explorer and select the Properties menu item as shown in Figure 2-17.

This launches the Properties dialog shown in Figure 2-18.

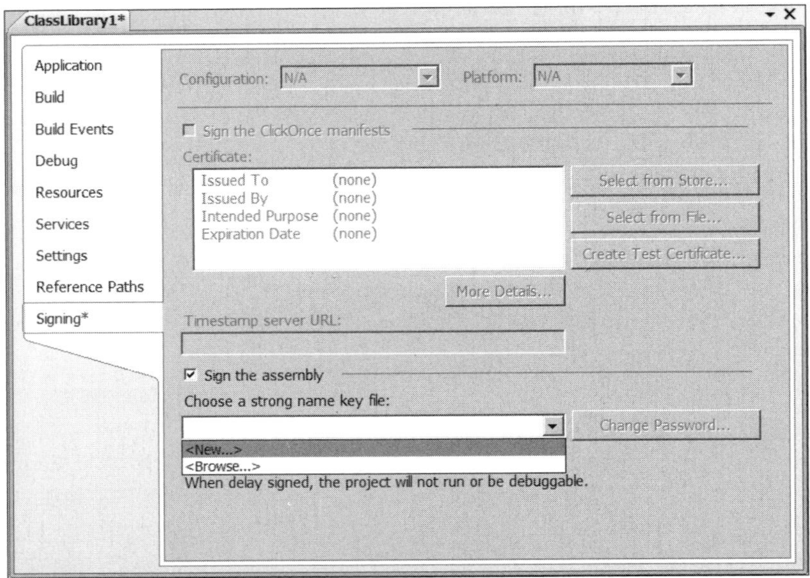

Figure 2-18: The Signing tab in the Properties pane

Switch to the Signing tab. Drop down the "Choose a strong name key file" list and select <NEW> as shown in Figure 2-18 to launch the Create Strong Name Key File dialog box shown in Figure 2-19.

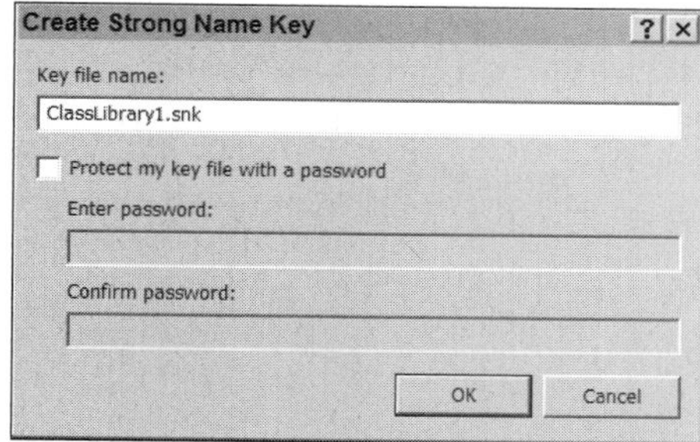

Figure 2-19: The Create Strong Name Key dialog

Enter a name for the key file and click OK. This will generate the key file and add the file to the root directory of the Class Library project. When you attempt to build the project, Visual Studio will automatically use the key to sign the assembly.

Note that the Default2.aspx.cs file contains the following declaration as shown in Listing 2-18:

```
protected ListViewByQuery ListViewByQuery1;
```

This is very different from the normal ASP.NET development in a Visual Studio web site project where you do not need to declare the server controls that you add to the .aspx file because the Visual Studio automatically does this behind the scenes every time you build the project.

Now build the Class Library project to create the strongly-named assembly. Use Windows Explorer to install this assembly in the GAC. Right-click the assembly in the GAC and select the Properties menu item to launch the dialog shown in Figure 2-20. Copy the public key token and paste it back into the Inherits attribute of the @Page directive in the Default2.aspx file like so:

```
<%@ Page Language="C#" MasterPageFile="~/_layouts/application.master"
Inherits="Default2, ClassLibrary1, Version=1.0.0.0, Culture=neutral,
PublicKeyToken=566105b43a7965be" %>
```

From this point on you don't have to worry about the pubic key token anymore, because as long as you're using the same key file every build will generate the assembly with the same public key token.

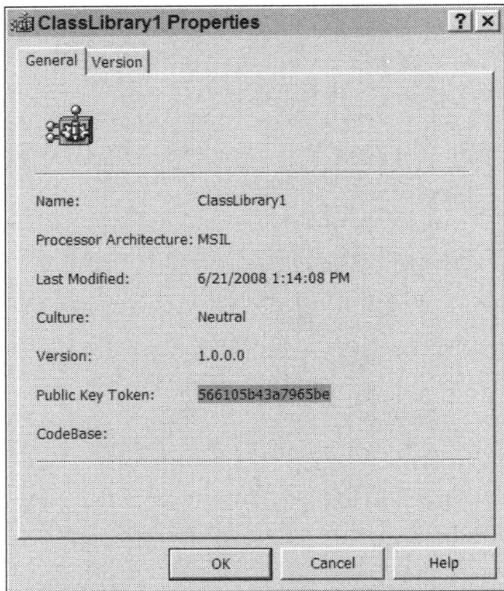

Figure 2-20: The Properties dialog

Next add the boldfaced portions in the following code listing to the mybatchfile.bat file:

```
@SET TEMPLATE="c:\program files\common files\microsoft shared\web server
extensions\12\Template"
@SET GACUTIL="c:\Program Files\Microsoft Visual Studio 8\SDK\v2.0\Bin\gacutil.exe"

Echo Installing ClassLibrary1.dll in GAC
%GACUTIL% -if bin\debug\ClassLibrary1.dll

xcopy bin\debug\ClassLibrary1.pdb
C:\WINDOWS\assembly\GAC_MSIL\ClassLibrary1\1.0.0.0__566105b43a7965be /s /Y

Echo Copying files to TEMPLATES directory
xcopy /e /y TEMPLATE\* %TEMPLATE%

IISRESET
```

As you can see, this batch file uses the gacutil command-line utility to automatically install the assembly to the GAC every time you build the project.

Now if you access the following URL from your browser you should see the same page shown in Figure 2-15:

```
http://SiteURL/WSSMOSSProgCh2_1/default2.aspx
```

In other words, the end result of the inline and code-behind approaches is the same. The biggest advantage of the code-behind approach is the separation of business logic from the user interface.

Accessing the default2.aspx page by its URL is not very user friendly, is it? Next, you learn how to add a menu item to the Site Actions menu to access the default2.aspx page. You need to use CAML to add a new item to a SharePoint menu or toolbar. As discussed earlier, the CAML element that does the trick is an element named <CustomAction>. Listing 2-19 presents the XML document adding a menu item titled Launch Default2 Page to the SharePoint Site Actions menu. Save this document in a file named default2.xml and add this file to the Class Library project.

Listing 2-19: The XML document that adds a menu item to Site Actions menu

```
<?xml version="1.0" encoding="utf-8" ?>
<Elements xmlns="http://schemas.microsoft.com/sharepoint/">
 <CustomAction
  Id="38A70C3D-A0FB-4c0f-B2B8-CC468CF49095"
  GroupId="SiteActions"
  Location="Microsoft.SharePoint.StandardMenu"
  Description="Launches the default2.aspx application page!"
  Sequence="2007"
  ImageUrl="~site/_layouts/images/WSSMOSSProgCh2_1/icon1.gif"
  Title="Launch Default2 Page">
   <UrlAction Url="~site/_layouts/WSSMOSSProgCh2_1/Default2.aspx"/>
  </CustomAction>
</Elements>
```

Keep in mind that the SharePoint Actions menu displays the values of both the Title and Description attributes of the <CustomAction> element to end users. As such you should assign user-friendly values to these two attributes. Also note that the ImageUrl attribute of the <CustomAction> element is set to the virtual path of an icon named icon1.gif. Note that this virtual path begins with the ~site token. SharePoint automatically replaces this token with the actual virtual path of the current site. Also note that SharePoint maps the /_layouts/images virtual path to the following physical path:

```
Local_Drive:\Program Files\Common Files\Microsoft Shared\Web Server
Extensions\12\template\images
```

This means that you must deploy your image files such as icons to the previously discussed physical folder in the file system of the front-end web server. Again, to avoid name conflicts you should create a new directory in this folder and deploy your image files to that folder. For that purpose you should create a subfolder named WSSMOSSProgCh2_1 in the IMAGES folder in the front-end web server.

As discussed earlier, it's a good practice to create the same folder hierarchy in your Class Library project. As such go ahead and add a new subfolder named IMAGES to the TEMPLATE folder in the Class Library project and move the icon1.gif to this subfolder.

Next, you need to implement a feature that references the default2.xml file and to install that feature into the SharePoint farm. Listing 2-20 presents the definition of this feature.

Listing 2-20: The feature.xml file that references the default2.xml file

```
<?xml version="1.0" encoding="utf-8" ?>
<Feature
xmlsn="http://schemas.microsoft.com/sharepoint/"
Id="631BB1D1-DFAD-4f95-A014-1ABB12D73D25"
Description="This feature contains a custom action that launches the Default2
.aspx page!"
Hidden="False"
Title="Default2 Page Launcher"
Scope="Web"
Version="1.0.0.0">
 <ElementManifests>
   <ElementManifest Location="default2.xml"/>
 </ElementManifests>
</Feature>
```

Keep in mind that SharePoint displays the values of the Title and Description attributes to end users on the Site Features page. Also note that you've set the Scope attribute to Web to specify that this feature can only be activated or deactivated at a site level. As you can see, the <ElementManifest> element references the default2.xml file.

You need to deploy your features and the element manifest files that they reference to the FEATURES folder in the file system of the front-end web server.

```
Local_Drive:\Program Files\Common Files\microsoft shared\Web Server
Extensions\12\TEMPLATE\FEATURES
```

As a best practice, you should create a folder inside the FEATURES folder and deploy your feature (feature.xml) and its associated element manifest file (default.xml) to that folder to avoid possible filename conflicts with other files. You'll create a folder named WSSMOSSProgCh2_1.

As discussed, it's a good practice to create the same folder hierarchy in your Class Library project. As such go ahead and add a new subfolder named FEATURES to the root folder of the Class Library project. Then add a subfolder named WSSMOSSProgCh2_1 to this FEATURES folder and add feature.xml (Listing 2-20) and default2.xml (Listing 2-19) to this folder.

After you deploy a feature you need to install it with SharePoint. For that you need to use a command-line tool named stsadm.exe located in the following directory:

```
Local_Drive:\program files\common files\microsoft shared\web server extensions\12\bin\
```

You can automate this process by modifying the mybatchfile.bat file like so:

```
@SET TEMPLATE="c:\program files\common files\microsoft shared\web server
extensions\12\Template"

@SET GACUTIL="c:\Program Files\Microsoft Visual Studio 8\SDK\v2.0\Bin\gacutil.exe"

@SET STSADM="c:\program files\common files\microsoft shared\web server
extensions\12\bin\stsadm"
```

```
Echo Installing ClassLibrary1.dll in GAC
%GACUTIL% -if bin\debug\ClassLibrary1.dll

xcopy bin\debug\ClassLibrary1.pdb
C:\WINDOWS\assembly\GAC_MSIL\ClassLibrary1\1.0.0.0__566105b43a7965be /s /Y

Echo Copying files to TEMPLATES directory
xcopy /e /y TEMPLATE\* %TEMPLATE%

Echo Installing feature
%STSADM% -o installfeature -filename WSSMOSSProgCh2_1\feature.xml -force

IISRESET
```

As a result, every time you build the Class Library project, Visual Studio will automatically run the mybatchfile.bat file, which in turn will automatically install the project assembly in the GAC, copy all the required files to the appropriate folders in the file system of the front-end web server, and install the feature with SharePoint.

After the feature is installed, it can be activated from any site. Recall that you set the Scope attribute of the feature to Web (see Listing 2-20) to specify that the feature can only be activated at site level. Follow these steps to activate the feature at a site level. First, navigate to your site. Next, click the Site Actions menu and select the Site Settings menu item as shown in Figure 2-21.

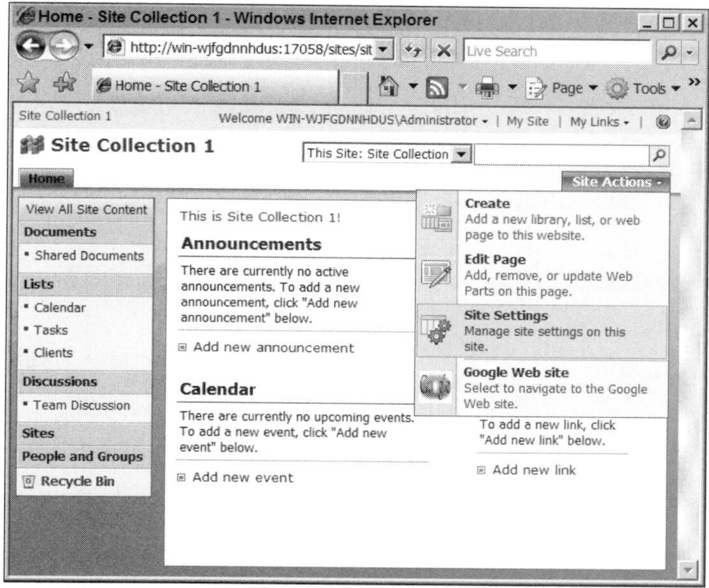

Figure 2-21: The menu that contains the Site Settings menu option

This will take you to the page shown in Figure 2-22. Click the "Site features" link on this page.

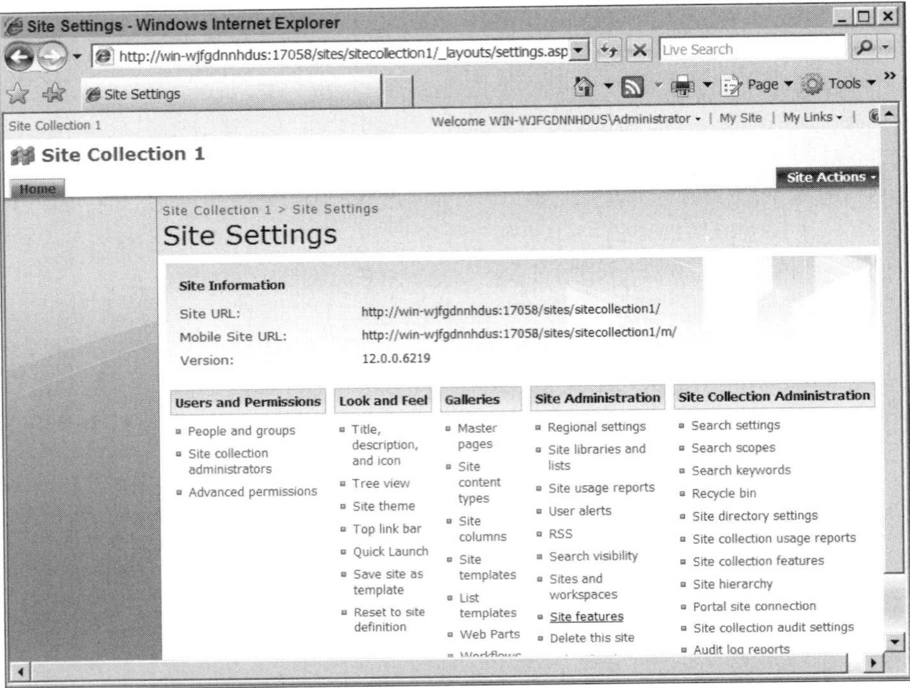

Figure 2-22: The Site Settings page

This will take you to the page shown in Figure 2-23. Locate the feature and click the Activate button to activate it.

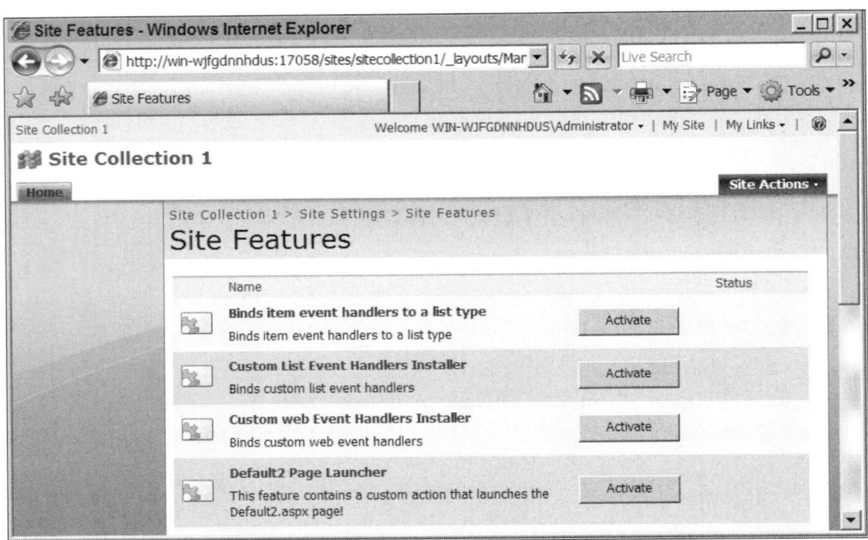

Figure 2-23: The Site Features page

Now click the Site Actions menu and you should see the new menu item listed as shown in Figure 2-24.

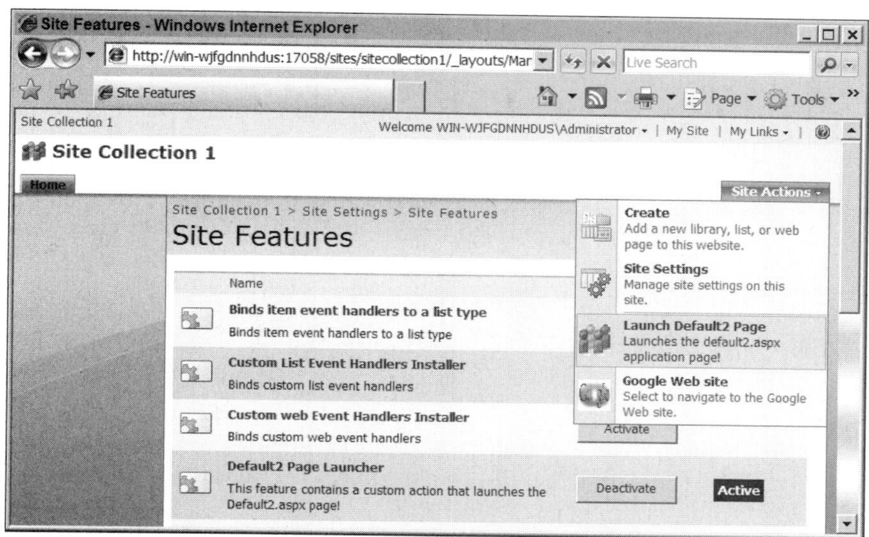

Figure 2-24: The Site Actions menu contains the new menu item

The main problem with the current implementation of the Default2.aspx application page is that it has hard-coded the list whose contents the page displays. Next, you learn how to improve upon the implementation of this page so that it can display the contents of any list. For that you'll use a SharePoint server control named ListView, which is specifically designed to display the items of a given list. Listing 2-21 presents the new implementation of the Default2.aspx application page named Default3.aspx.

Listing 2-21: The new implementation of the Default2.aspx application page

```
<%@ Page Language="C#" MasterPageFile="~/_layouts/application.master"
Inherits="Default3, ClassLibrary1, Version=1.0.0.0, Culture=neutral,
PublicKeyToken=566105b43a7965be" %>

<%@ Register Assembly="Microsoft.SharePoint, Version=12.0.0.0, Culture=neutral,
PublicKeyToken=71e9bce111e9429c"
Namespace="Microsoft.SharePoint.WebControls" TagPrefix="cc1" %>

<asp:Content ID="Main" ContentPlaceHolderID="PlaceHolderMain" runat="server">
  <cc1:ListView ID="ListView1" runat="server" />
</asp:Content>
```

The ListView control exposes a string property named ListId, which must be set to the string representation of the GUID that uniquely identifies the list. What you want to do is to add a new menu item to the Edit Control menu of a list that would allow users to navigate to the Default3.aspx application page where they can view the content of the list. Listing 2-22 presents a new version of the default2.xml named default3.xml, which contains a <CustomAction> element that does just that.

Listing 2-22: The <CustomAction> element that adds a new menu item

```
<?xml version="1.0" encoding="utf-8" ?>
<Elements xmlns="http://schemas.microsoft.com/sharepoint/">
 <CustomAction
  Id="38A70C3D-A0FB-4c0f-B2B8-CC468CF49095"
  GroupId="ActionsMenu"
  Location="Microsoft.SharePoint.StandardMenu"
  Description="Launches the Default3.aspx application page!"
  Sequence="2007"
  ImageUrl="~site/_layouts/images/WSSMOSSProgCh2_1/icon1.gif"
  Title="Launch Default3 Page">
   <UrlAction Url="~site/_layouts/WSSMOSSProgCh2_1/Default3.aspx?ListId={ListId}"/>
  </CustomAction>
</Elements>
```

Notice that you have set the GroupId and Location attributes to ActionsMenu and Microsoft.SharePoint.StandardMenu values to instruct SharePoint to add the new menu item to the ActionsMenu of the SharePoint lists. Also note that the URL value assigned to the URL attribute now contains the querystring ListId={ListId}. SharePoint automatically replaces the {ListId} token with the string representation of the GUID that uniquely identifies the current list.

Next, you need to add a reference to the default3.xml file to the feature.xml file as shown in the boldfaced portion of the following code listing:

```
<?xml version="1.0" encoding="utf-8" ?>
<Feature
xmlsn="http://schemas.microsoft.com/sharepoint/"
Id="631BB1D1-DFAD-4f95-A014-1ABB12D73D25"
Description="This feature contains a custom action that launches the Default2.aspx
page!"
Hidden="False"
Title="Default2 Page Launcher"
Scope="Web"
Version="1.0.0.0">
  <ElementManifests>
    <ElementManifest Location="default2.xml"/>
 <ElementManifest Location="default3.xml"/>
</ElementManifests>
</Feature>
```

Listing 2-23 presents the implementation of the Default3.aspx.cs where you extract the value of the ListId querystring parameter and assign it to the ListId property of the ListView control. This ensures that the ListView control always displays the content of the current list whatever the current list happens to be.

Listing 2-23: The implementation of the Default3.aspx.cs file

```
using System;
using Microsoft.SharePoint;
using Microsoft.SharePoint.WebControls;

public partial class Default3 : LayoutsPageBase
{
  protected ListView ListView1;

  protected void Page_Load(object sender, EventArgs e)
  {
    ListView1.ListId = Request.QueryString["ListId"];
  }
}
```

Next, build the Class Library project and then activate the feature as discussed earlier. Then, navigate to a list and drop down the Edit Control menu of the list as shown in Figure 2-25. You should see a new menu item titled Launch Default3 Page. If you select this item, it will take you to the Default3.aspx page where you can view the content of the list.

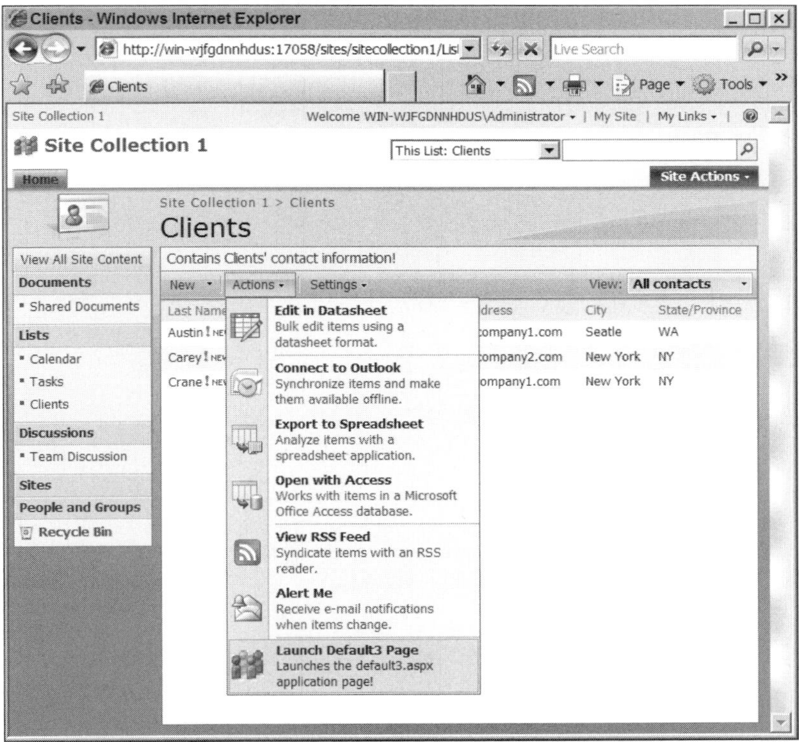

Figure 2-25: The menu that contains the Launch Default3 Page menu option

Summary

This chapter began by presenting the SharePoint Collaboration Application Markup Language (CAML). It then showed you how to use CAML to implement a SharePoint feature. Finally, it dove into SharePoint custom actions and application pages. You learned two different approaches to developing custom application pages. Chapter 3 moves on to the SharePoint list types, where you learn how to implement your own custom list types.

3

List Types

SharePoint virtualizes the underlying IIS and ASP.NET infrastructures enabling you to manage and to organize your collaborative content in terms of abstractions such as site collections, sites, lists, list items, content types, site columns, field types, and so on. Users work with these SharePoint abstractions through the SharePoint forms infrastructure. This and the next few chapters provide an in-depth coverage of these SharePoint abstractions and SharePoint forms infrastructure. The main focus of this chapter is list types and the skills you need to learn to implement custom list types.

What Is SharePoint Forms Infrastructure, Anyway?

SharePoint data are stored in SharePoint lists and document libraries, which are actually special types of lists. To help you understand the role of SharePoint forms infrastructure, let's walk through a typical scenario, which consists of the following steps:

1. Creating a new list from a list type.
2. Adding a new list item to this list.
3. Updating a list item in this list.
4. Viewing a list item in this list.

As you're walking through these steps, it will raise questions that are answered in this and the next chapters as you learn more about the SharePoint forms infrastructure. These questions are raised so you know up front some of the issues that this infrastructure addresses.

Creating a New List

In this section you create a new list and raise some of the related questions that the SharePoint forms infrastructure addresses. Now navigate to the create.aspx page shown in Figure 3-1.

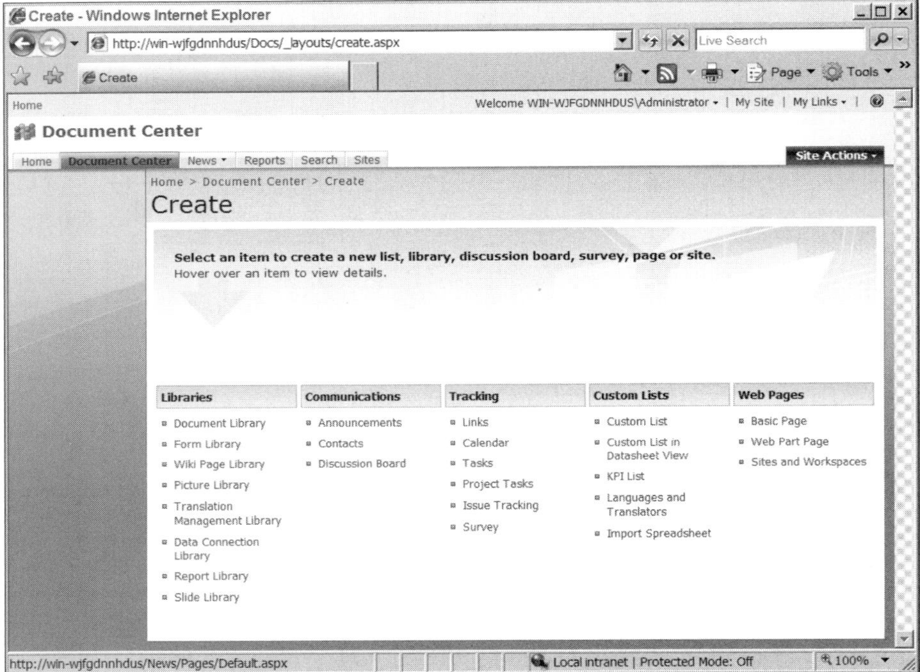

Figure 3-1: The create.aspx page

As you can see, the create.aspx page displays the list of available list types from which you can create new lists. You may be wondering how SharePoint knows the list types that are available and which categories to display each list type. The answer to this question is covered next.

Start by selecting the Survey list type. This will take you to the new.aspx page shown in Figure 3-2.

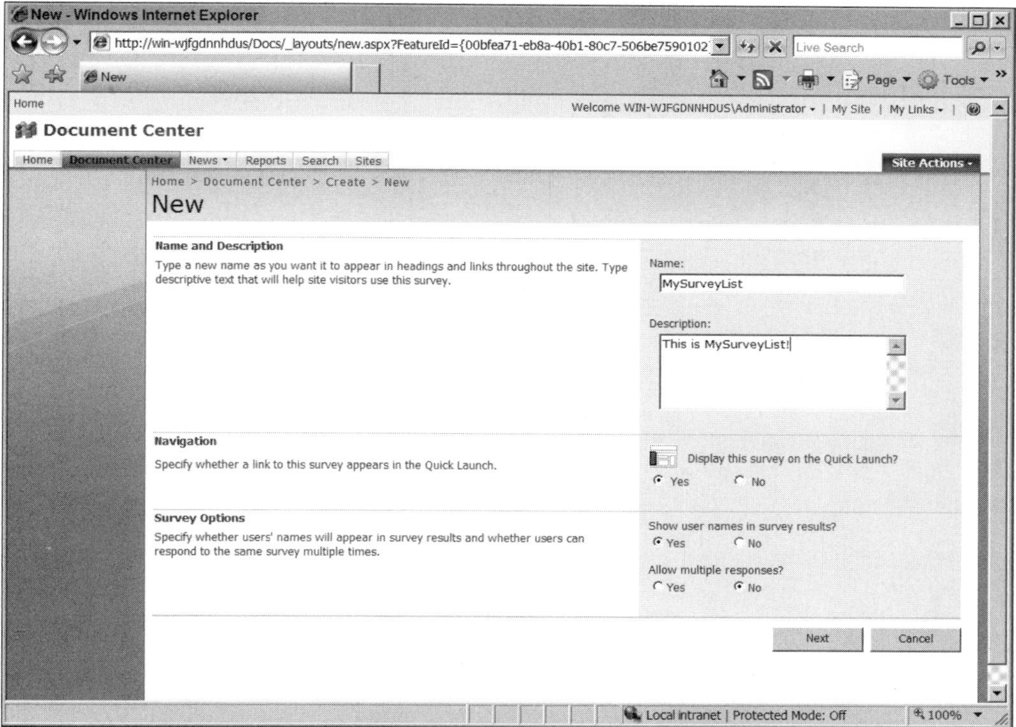

Figure 3-2: The new.aspx page

Enter a name and a description for the new list and click Next to navigate to the page shown in Figure 3-3. Enter a question with possible answers.

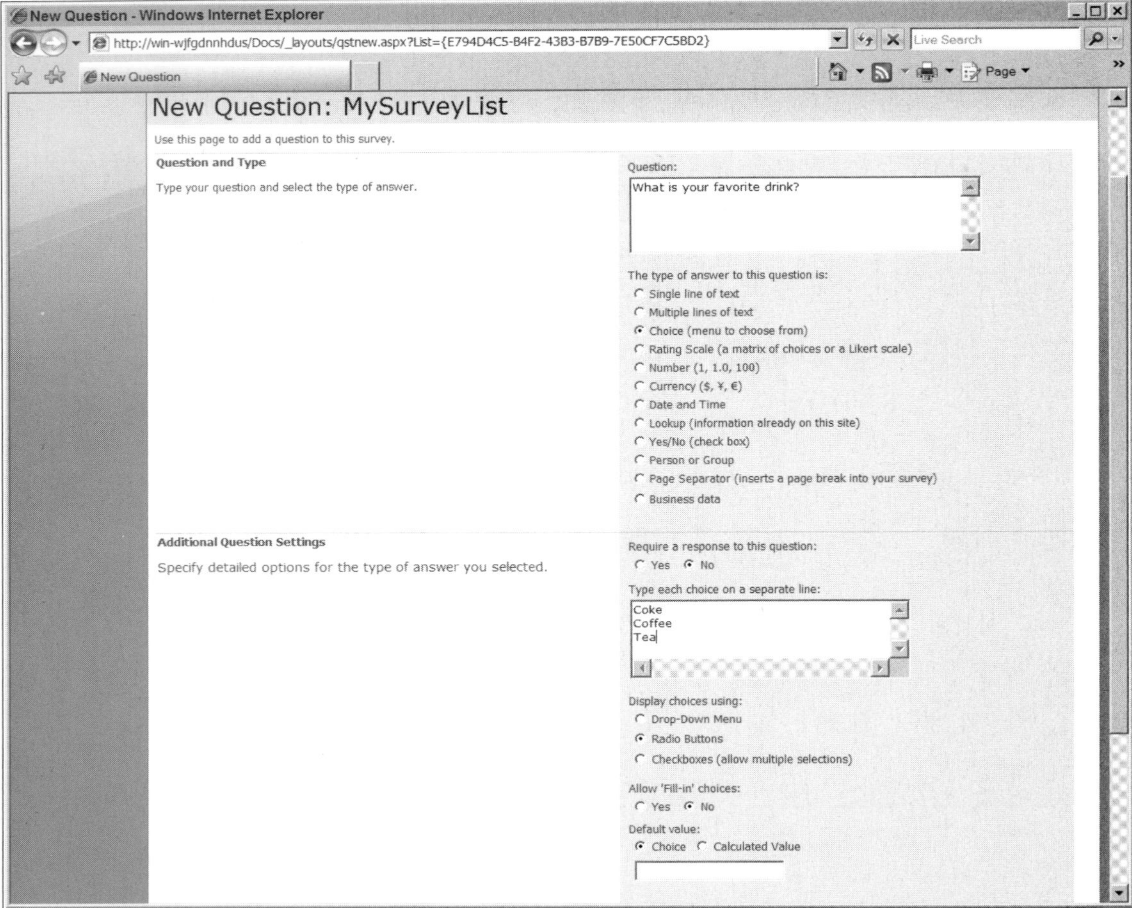

Figure 3-3: Adding a question to a survey list

Note that this page consists of a textbox where you can enter the survey question, a bunch of radio buttons specifying the possible types of answer to this question, a section labeled "Requires a response to this question" with two radio buttons, Yes and No, and many other possible choices for format.

As you can see, this page is tailored toward the type of list you're provisioning. If you're provisioning a list from a different list type, you'd be shown a page with different GUI elements.

Click the Finish button to create the list. Then navigate to the overview.aspx page that displays the list, as shown in Figure 3-4.

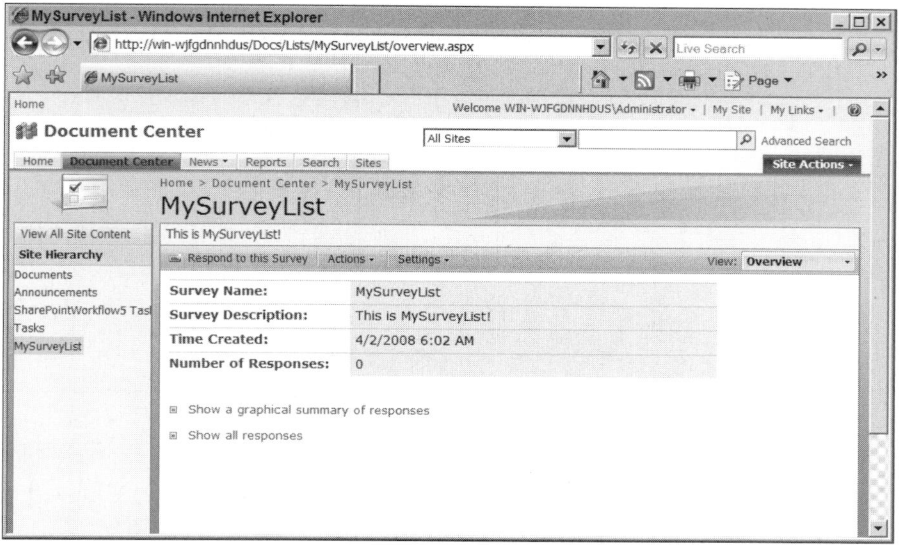

Figure 3-4: The MySurveyList SharePoint list

Adding a New List Item

Click the Respond to this Survey menu bar button shown in Figure 3-4. This will take you to the NewForm.aspx page shown in Figure 3-5.

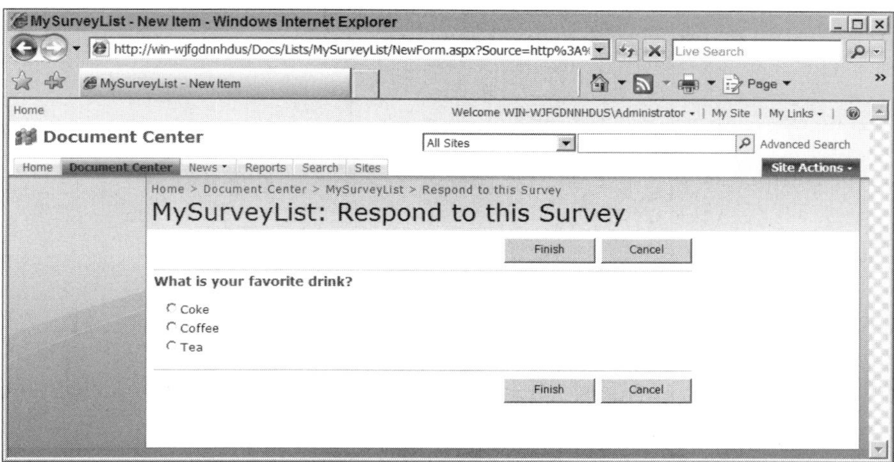

Figure 3-5: The NewForm.aspx page

The NewForm.aspx page is an example of a new list item form because it allows you to add a new list item to a list. As you can see, this new list item form contains the following GUI elements: two Finish and Cancel buttons, a label that displays the survey question, and a set of radio buttons that display the possible answers. The GUI elements that the new list item form displays varies from one list type to another.

Next, go ahead and click one of the Finish buttons to add the new list item to your list. Then, navigate to the AllItems.aspx page by clicking the "Show all responses" link to view all list items as shown in Figure 3-6. This page is an example of a list view.

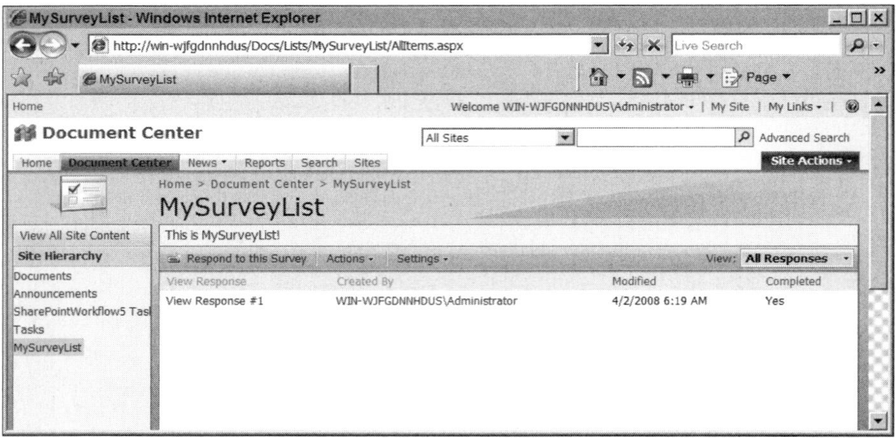

Figure 3-6: The AllItems.aspx page

Note that the list view form consists of a table containing a header row where the list field names are rendered as hyperlinks. You can click a header hyperlink to sort the table data based on the specified list field. The table also contains one data row for each list item added to the list where the list field values are rendered.

Viewing a List Item

Note that the Edit Control Block (ECB) menu of the Title field of each row contains a menu option named View Response as shown in Figure 3-7.

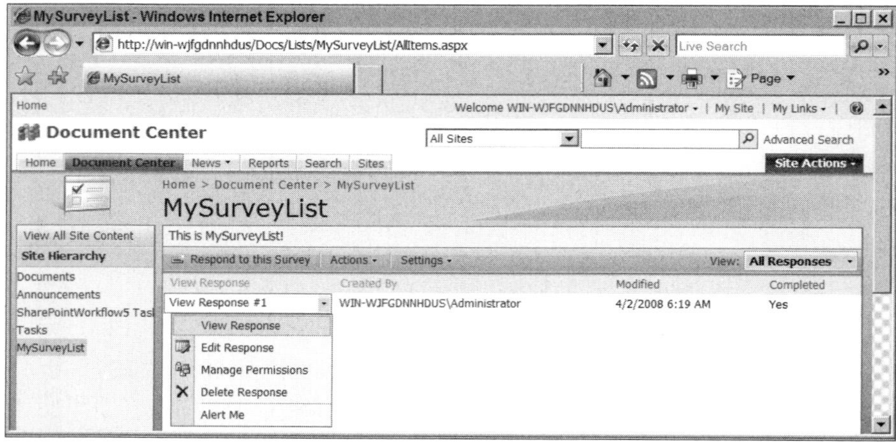

Figure 3-7: The View Response menu option

Select the View Response menu option. This will take you to the DispForm.aspx page shown in Figure 3-8. This page displays a list item.

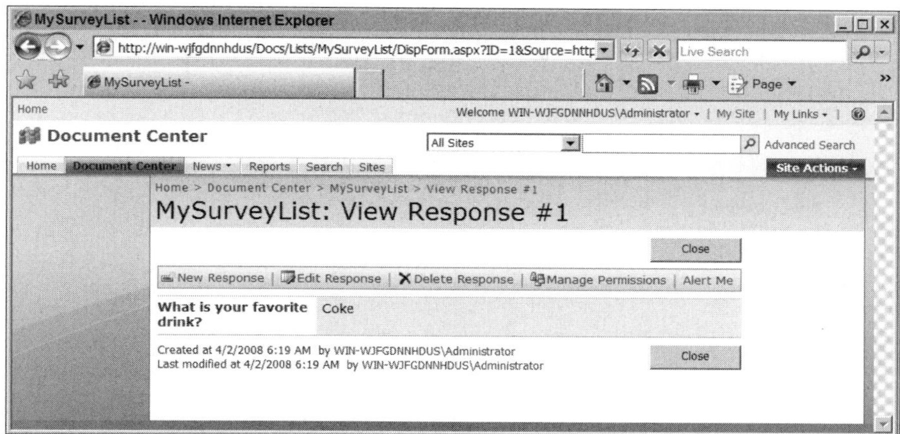

Figure 3-8: The DispForm.aspx page

As you can see, this display list item form consists of the following GUI elements: a header that displays the list name and list item title, two Close buttons, a menu bar of actions such as New Response, Edit Response, Delete Response, and so on, and a row of two columns that displays the question and the respective answer. The GUI elements that the display list item form displays vary from one list type to another.

Editing a List Item

As you can see from Figure 3-7, the ECB menu on the Title field of each list item in the list view page (AllItems.aspx) contains a menu option named Edit Response. Select this option. This will take you to the EditForm.aspx page shown in Figure 3-9. This page is an example of an edit list item form.

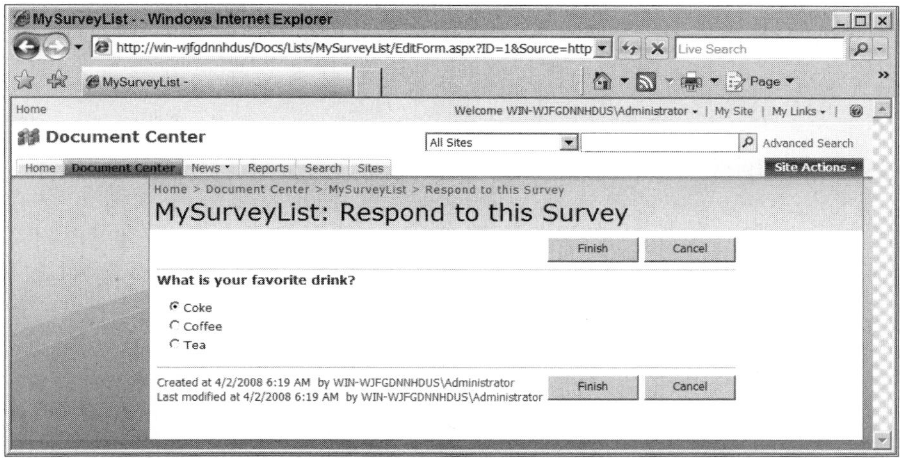

Figure 3-9: The EditForm.aspx page

As you can see, the edit list item form consists of these GUI elements: a header that displays the list name and list item title, two Finish and two Cancel buttons, the survey question, and three radio buttons displaying the possible answers. Also note that one of the radio buttons is selected. This radio button displays the current field value. Again, as you can see, the edit list item form contains GUI elements that are specific to the type of list to which the current list item belongs.

Display, New, and Edit List Item Forms

The answers to any questions regarding list view forms (AllItems.aspx), display list item forms (DispForm.aspx), new list item forms (NewForm.aspx), and edit list item forms (EditForm.aspx), as well as many other similar questions lie in the SharePoint forms infrastructure, as you'll see throughout the remaining chapters in the book (as well as some of the sections found in this chapter).

As an example, consider the display, new, and edit list item forms. As you'll see later in this chapter, a list type is defined in an XML file named schema.xml. This XML file is deployed through a SharePoint feature to a subfolder under a feature-specific folder on the file system of the front-end web server. As the name suggests, the schema.xml file defines the schema for the list type. This schema supports an element named <Forms>, which can contain one or more child elements named <Form>. Each <Form> element specifies a particular type of form. For example, Listing 3-1 shows an excerpt from the schema.xml file, which defines the schema for the survey list type.

Listing 3-1: An excerpt from the schema.xml file that defines the schema from the survey list type

```
<List Title="Vote/Survey" Url="Lists/voting" BaseType="4">
  <MetaData>
    <Forms>
      <Form Type="DisplayForm" Url="DispForm.aspx" Template="ListForm"
      SetupPath="pages\form.aspx" WebPartZoneID="Main" />
      <Form Type="EditForm" Url="EditForm.aspx" Template="SurveyForm"
      SetupPath="pages\form.aspx" WebPartZoneID="Main" />
      <Form Type="NewForm" Url="NewForm.aspx" Template="SurveyForm"
      SetupPath="pages\form.aspx" WebPartZoneID="Main" />
    </Forms>
  </MetaData>
</List>
```

This schema.xml file is located in a subfolder named Survey, under a feature-specific folder named SurveyList, on the file system of the front-end web server:

```
Local_Drive:\Program Files\Common Files\Microsoft Shared\web server
extensions\12\TEMPLATE\FEATURES\SurveysList\Survey
```

The <Form> element supports the following attributes:

- **Type.** This required attribute specifies the type of form that the <Form> element describes. The possible values are DisplayForm, EditForm, or NewForm. The <Form> elements with Type attribute values of DisplayForm, EditForm, and NewForm describe a display list item form, an edit list item form, and a new list item form, respectively:

```
<Form Type="DisplayForm" ... />
<Form Type="EditForm" ... />
<Form Type="NewForm" ... />
```

- **SetupPath.** This optional attribute specifies the relative path to the folder in the setup directory that contains the page template from which the form that this <Form> element describes is provisioned. This setup directory is normally the following directory on the file system of the front-end web server:

```
Local_Drive:\Program Files\Common Files\microsoft shared\Web Server Extensions\12\
TEMPLATE
```

  The SetupPath attributes for all <Form> elements in Listing 3-1 are set to pages\form.aspx. The standard SharePoint TEMPLATE folder (which is the setup directory) contains a subfolder named Pages, which contains the form.aspx page template from which display the list item form, edit list item form, and new list item form site pages are provisioned.

  As you can see, the display, edit, and new list item form site pages are all provisioned from the same pages\form.aspx page template:

```
<Form SetupPath="pages\form.aspx" ... />
<Form SetupPath="pages\form.aspx" ... />
<Form SetupPath="pages\form.aspx" ... />
```

- **URL.** This required attribute specifies the relative URL to the form site page that is provisioned from the page template specified in the SetupPath attribute. In the case of a document library, all three types of form site pages (that is, display, edit, and new list item form site pages) are provisioned into a subfolder named Forms under the root folder of the document library. This means that the URL specified in the URL attribute is relative to the forms folder. In the case of a standard SharePoint list, all three types of form site pages are provisioned into a subfolder under the root folder of the list. This means that the URL specified in the URL attribute is relative to this folder.

  As you can see from Listing 3-1, the display, edit, and new list item form site pages of the survey list type are provisioned into form site pages named DispForm.aspx, EditForm.aspx, and NewForm.aspx:

```
<Form Url="DispForm.aspx" ... />
<Form Url="EditForm.aspx" ... />
<Form Url="NewForm.aspx" ... />
```

In this case, the URL of the survey list in this excerpt is Lists/Voting. This means that the absolute URL to the list is:

```
http://ServerName/Site1/Lists/Voting
```

- Therefore, the absolute URLs to the display, edit, and new list item form site pages are:

```
http://ServerName/Site1/Lists/Voting/DispForm.aspx
http://ServerName/Site1/Lists/Voting/EditForm.aspx
http://ServerName/Site1/Lists/Voting/NewForm.aspx
```

- **WebPartZoneID.** The form that the <Form> element describes contains an instance of the Microsoft.SharePoint.WebPartPages.WebPartZone server control. This optional attribute specifies the ID attribute value of this control. SharePoint uses this ID attribute value to locate this control within the form. Once located, it adds an instance of the Microsoft.SharePoint.WebPartPages.ListFormWebPart Web part to this WebPartZone server control:

```
<Form WebPartZoneID="Main" ... />
<Form WebPartZoneID="Main" ... />
<Form WebPartZoneID="Main" ... />
```

- **Template.** The ListFormWebPart server control (the one added to the form that the <Form> element describes) loads the form-rendering template that has its ID attribute value specified in the Template optional attribute. This form-rendering template is located in an .ascx file, in the following folder on the file system of the front-end web server:

```
Local_Drive:\Program Files\Common Files\microsoft shared\Web Server
Extensions\12\TEMPLATE\CONTROLTEMPLATES
```

This form-rendering template specifies what gets rendered in the form that the <Form> element describes. In other words, the form-rendering templates determine the GUI elements that are rendered in these forms. If you're wondering, a form-rendering template is an instance of a server control named RenderingTemplate, which is declared in an .ascx file. RenderingTemplate and form-rendering templates are discussed in more depth later on in the chapter.

As you can see from Listing 3-1, a form-rendering template with the ID attribute value of ListForm is used to render the display list item form for a survey list, and a form-rendering template with the ID attribute value of SurveyForm is used to render the edit and new list item forms for a survey list:

```
<Form Type="DisplayForm" Url="DispForm.aspx" Template="ListForm"
SetupPath="pages\form.aspx" WebPartZoneID="Main" />
<Form Type="EditForm" Url="EditForm.aspx" Template="SurveyForm"
SetupPath="pages\form.aspx" WebPartZoneID="Main" />
<Form Type="NewForm" Url="NewForm.aspx" Template="SurveyForm"
SetupPath="pages\form.aspx" WebPartZoneID="Main" />
```

Note that these two form-rendering templates are defined in an .ascx file named DefaultTemplates.ascx in the following folder on the file system of the front-end web server:

```
Local_Drive:\Program Files\Common Files\microsoft shared\Web Server
Extensions\12\TEMPLATE\CONTROLTEMPLATES
```

You'll get a closer look at these two form-rendering templates shortly.

- **UseLegacyForm.** Set this optional attribute to True to use CAML rendering instructions within the opening and closing tags of the <Form> element. These instructions are used to show SharePoint how to render the form that the <Form> element represents. As its name suggests, this attribute exists for backward compatibility. You're strongly discouraged from specifying the rendering logic of a form within the opening and closing tags of the <Form> element. Instead, you should use a form-rendering template to render the form and to assign the ID attribute value of this form-rendering template to the Template attribute as discussed earlier.

As I mentioned previously, all three display, edit, and new list item forms for a survey list are provisioned from the same form.aspx page. This means that the form.aspx page is a page template and that the display, edit, and new list item forms are site pages that are provisioned from this page template. Because the display, edit, and new list item forms are site pages, they follow the same rules as other site pages. For example, they cannot contain inline code and they are processed in no-compile mode. They are also stored in the content database when they're customized, just like other site pages. The display, edit, and new list item forms are content pages and thus use the default.aspx master page, which is the master page for all site pages.

Page Template for Display, Edit, and New List Item Forms

Listing 3-2 presents the form.aspx page template from which the display, edit, and new list item form site pages are provisioned. As discussed earlier, this page template is located in the Pages subfolder of the TEMPLATE folder in the file system of the front-end web server.

Listing 3-2: The form.aspx page

```
<%@ Page Language="C#" MasterPageFile="~masterurl/default.master"
Inherits="Microsoft.SharePoint.WebPartPages.WebPartPage,Microsoft.SharePoint,
Version=12.0.0.0,Culture=neutral,PublicKeyToken=71e9bce111e9429c" %>

<%@ Register TagPrefix="SharePoint" Namespace="Microsoft.SharePoint.WebControls"
Assembly="Microsoft.SharePoint, Version=12.0.0.0, Culture=neutral,
PublicKeyToken=71e9bce111e9429c" %>

<%@ Register TagPrefix="Utilities" Namespace="Microsoft.SharePoint.Utilities"
Assembly="Microsoft.SharePoint, Version=12.0.0.0, Culture=neutral,
PublicKeyToken=71e9bce111e9429c" %>

<%@ Import Namespace="Microsoft.SharePoint" %>

<%@ Register TagPrefix="WebPartPages" Namespace="Microsoft.SharePoint.WebPartPages"
Assembly="Microsoft.SharePoint, Version=12.0.0.0, Culture=neutral,
PublicKeyToken=71e9bce111e9429c" %>

<asp:Content ContentPlaceHolderID="PlaceHolderPageTitle" runat="server">
  <SharePoint:ListFormPageTitle runat="server" />
</asp:Content>

<asp:Content ContentPlaceHolderID="PlaceHolderPageTitleInTitleArea" runat="server">
  <SharePoint:ListProperty Property="LinkTitle" runat="server" ID="ID_LinkTitle" />
  :
  <SharePoint:ListItemProperty ID="ID_ItemProperty" MaxLength="40"
```

(continued)

Listing 3-2 *(continued)*

```
  runat="server" />
</asp:Content>

<asp:Content ContentPlaceHolderID="PlaceHolderPageImage" runat="server">
  <img src="/_layouts/images/blank.gif" width="1" height="1" alt="">
</asp:Content>

<asp:Content ContentPlaceHolderID="PlaceHolderLeftNavBar" runat="server" />

<asp:Content ContentPlaceHolderID="PlaceHolderMain" runat="server">
  <table cellpadding="0" cellspacing="0" id="onetIDListForm">
    <tr>
      <td>
        <WebPartPages:WebPartZone runat="server" FrameType="None" ID="Main"
        Title="loc:Main" />
        <img src="/_layouts/images/blank.gif" width="590" height="1" alt="">
      </td>
    </tr>
  </table>
</asp:Content>

<asp:Content ContentPlaceHolderID="PlaceHolderTitleLeftBorder" runat="server">
  <table cellpadding="0" height="100%" width="100%" cellspacing="0">
    <tr>
      <td class="ms-areaseparatorleft">
        <img src="/_layouts/images/blank.gif" width="1" height="1" alt="">
      </td>
    </tr>
  </table>
</asp:Content>

<asp:Content ContentPlaceHolderID="PlaceHolderTitleAreaClass" runat="server">
  <script id="onetidPageTitleAreaFrameScript">
    document.getElementById("onetidPageTitleAreaFrame").className=
"ms-areaseparator";
  </script>
</asp:Content>

<asp:Content ContentPlaceHolderID="PlaceHolderBodyAreaClass" runat="server">
  <style type="text/css">
    .ms-bodyareaframe
    {
      padding: 8px;
      border: none;
    }
  </style>
</asp:Content>

<asp:Content ContentPlaceHolderID="PlaceHolderBodyLeftBorder" runat="server">
  <div class='ms-areaseparatorleft'>
```

```
      <img src="/_layouts/images/blank.gif" width="8" height="100%" alt="">
    </div>
  </asp:Content>

  <asp:Content ContentPlaceHolderID="PlaceHolderTitleRightMargin" runat="server">
    <div class='ms-areaseparatorright'>
      <img src="/_layouts/images/blank.gif" width="8" height="100%" alt="">
    </div>
  </asp:Content>

  <asp:Content ContentPlaceHolderID="PlaceHolderBodyRightMargin" runat="server">
    <div class='ms-areaseparatorright'>
      <img src="/_layouts/images/blank.gif" width="8" height="100%" alt="">
    </div>
  </asp:Content>

  <asp:Content ContentPlaceHolderID="PlaceHolderTitleAreaSeparator" runat="server" />
```

As you can see, form.aspx, like any other content page, consists of a bunch of <asp:Content> tags where each tag provides content for a specific content placeholder within the default.master master page. At runtime, ASP.NET merges the form site page provisioned from the form.aspx page template and the default.master pages into a single page, which is then served to the end user.

Note that most <asp:Content> tags in the form.aspx page contain one or more SharePoint server controls from the Microsoft.SharePoint.WebControls namespace. These server controls together render the associated form; that is, a display, edit, or new list item form. As you can see, the display, edit, and new list item forms consist of a bunch of server controls where each server control renders a portion of the form as follows.

The following <asp:Content> tag contains a ListFormPageTitle server control that provides the content for the PlaceHolderPageTitle content placeholder declared within the default.master page:

```
<asp:Content ContentPlaceHolderID="PlaceHolderPageTitle" runat="server">
  <SharePoint:ListFormPageTitle runat="server" />
</asp:Content>
```

As the following excerpt from the default.master page shows, the PlaceHolderPageTitle content placeholder is located within the <Title> element:

```
<Title ID=onetidTitle>
  <asp:ContentPlaceHolder id=PlaceHolderPageTitle runat="server"/>
</Title>
```

As such, the ListFormPageTitle server control renders the page title, which is the string that goes within the opening and closing tags of the <Title> element. This string is what is shown to end users when they try to bookmark the form. As you'll see later, the ListFormPageTitle server control (like many other SharePoint server controls) is well aware of the SharePoint contextual information, such as the current list and its title. The rendering logic within the Render method of the ListFormPageTitle server control renders the title of the list as the page title.

As Listing 3-2 shows, form.aspx then uses the following <asp:Content> tag to provide content for a content placeholder named PlaceHolderPageTitleInTitleArea:

```
<asp:Content ContentPlaceHolderID="PlaceHolderPageTitleInTitleArea" runat="server">
  <SharePoint:ListProperty Property="LinkTitle" runat="server" ID="ID_LinkTitle" />
  :
  <SharePoint:ListItemProperty ID="ID_ItemProperty" MaxLength="40"
  runat="server" />
</asp:Content>
```

This <asp:Content> tag renders the text that goes into the title area of form.aspx. As you can see, this Content server control contains a ListProperty and a ListItemProperty server control. As you'll see in Chapter 4, the ListProperty and ListItemProperty server controls are well aware of the SharePoint contextual information, such as current list and current list item. The rendering logic in their Render methods render the list name and list item title, respectively.

As Listing 3-2 shows, form.aspx then uses the following <asp:Content> tag to provide content for a content placeholder named PlaceHolderMain:

```
<asp:Content ContentPlaceHolderID="PlaceHolderMain" runat="server">
  <table cellpadding="0" cellspacing="0" id="onetIDListForm">
    <tr>
      <td>
        <WebPartPages:WebPartZone runat="server" FrameType="None" ID="Main"
        Title="loc:Main" />
        <img src="/_layouts/images/blank.gif" width="590" height="1" alt="">
      </td>
    </tr>
  </table>
</asp:Content>
```

This <asp:Content> renders the content that goes into the body of the form.aspx page. As you can see, this Content server control contains a Microsoft.SharePoint.WebPartPages.WebPartZone Web part zone. As mentioned earlier, SharePoint adds a Microsoft.SharePoint.WebPartPages.ListFormWebPart Web part to this Web part zone. As such, the ListFormWebPart Web part is the one that renders the body of a display, edit, or new list item form.

ListFormWebPart

Listing 3-3 presents the portion of the internal implementation of the ListFormWebPart Web part.

Listing 3-3: The ListFormWebPart Web part

```
public sealed class ListFormWebPart : WebPart
{
  private bool renderListFormWebPart;
  public bool HideIfNoPermissions { get; set; }

  protected override void OnInit(EventArgs e)
  {
```

```
    // ...
    if (this.HideIfNoPermissions)
    {
      // ...
      if (this.list != null)
      {
        if (this.ControlMode != SPControlMode.New)
        {
          if (this.ControlMode != SPControlMode.Edit)
          {
            if (this.ControlMode == SPControlMode.Display)
              this.renderListFormWebPart =
                !this.list.DoesUserHavePermissions(
                    SPBasePermissions.EmptyMask | SPBasePermissions.ViewListItems);
          }
          else
            this.renderListFormWebPart =
              !this.list.DoesUserHavePermissions(SPBasePermissions.EditListItems);
        }
        else
          this.renderListFormWebPart =
            !this.list.DoesUserHavePermissions(
                    SPBasePermissions.EmptyMask | SPBasePermissions.AddListItems);
      }
      if (this.renderListFormWebPart)
      {
        this.ChromeType = PartChromeType.None;
        this.Hidden = true;
      }
    }
    // ...
  }

  [TemplateContainer(typeof(TemplateContainer)),
  Browsable(false), DefaultValue((string)null)]
  public ITemplate Template
  {
    get
    {
      if (this.template == null && this.TemplateName != null)
        this.template =
                SPControlTemplateManager.GetTemplateByName(this.TemplateName);

      return this.template;
    }
    set { this.template = value; }
  }

  public string TemplateName
  {
    get
```

(continued)

Listing 3-3 *(continued)*

```
    {
      if (this.templateName == null)
      {
        // ...
        if (this.ItemContext != null)
        {
          SPContentType contentType = this.ItemContext.ContentType;
          if (contentType != null)
          {
            switch (this.ControlMode)
            {
              case SPControlMode.Display:
                this.templateName = contentType.DisplayFormTemplateName;
                break;

              case SPControlMode.Edit:
                this.templateName = contentType.EditFormTemplateName;
                break;

              case SPControlMode.New:
                this.templateName = contentType.NewFormTemplateName;
                break;
            }
            if (!string.IsNullOrEmpty(this.templateName))
              return this.templateName;
          }
        }
        this.templateName = this.form.TemplateName;
      }
      return this.templateName;
    }
    set { this.templateName = value; }
  }

  protected override void CreateChildControls()
  {
    if (!this.renderListFormWebPart && this.Template != null)
    {
      this.Controls.Clear();
      TemplateContainer templateContainer = new TemplateContainer();
      templateContainer.ControlMode = this.ControlMode;
      templateContainer.ItemContext = this.ItemContext;
      this.Template.InstantiateIn(templateContainer);
      this.Controls.Add(templateContainer);
    }
  }
}
```

As Listing 3-3 shows, the ListFormWebPart Web part supports a template property named Template. This template property, just like any other template property, uses a private field as its backing store, which is a template in this case. This template property, like any other template property, is a read-write property. This means that an ITemplate object can be explicitly assigned to this property. As you can see from

Listing 3-3, the getter of the Template property first checks whether the template field has been set (that is, whether the value of the property has been explicitly specified). If so, it simply returns a reference to the ITemplate object that the template private field references. If not, it invokes a static method named GetTemplateByName on a class named SPControlTemplateManager, passing in the value of the TemplateName property:

```
this.template = SPControlTemplateManager.GetTemplateByName(this.TemplateName);
```

The TemplateName property contains the ID property value of a RenderingTemplate server control in an .ascx file in the ControlTemplates folder on the file system of the front-end web server.

When a web application starts, SharePoint automatically loads all .ascx files in the ControlTemplates folder. The GetTemplateByName static method simply returns a reference to the ITemplate object that the Template property of the RenderingTemplate server control with the specified ID property value references. As you can see, the Template property of ListFormWebPart returns a reference to one of two objects: either an ITemplate object that is explicitly assigned to the property through its setter or an ITemplate object that the Template property of the RenderingTemplate server control (whose ID property value is specified in the TemplateName property of ListFormWebPart) references.

Next, let's take a look at the internal implementation of the TemplateName property shown in Listing 3-3. TemplateName is a read-write property that uses a private field named templateName as its backing store. This means that the value of this property can be explicitly set. In other words, you can add a new .ascx file that contains a RenderingTemplate server control to the ControlTemplates folder and assign the ID attribute value of this server control to the TemplateName property.

As Listing 3-3 shows, the getter of TemplateName first checks whether the templateName field has been explicitly set, that is, whether the *value* of this property has been explicitly set. If so, it simply returns the value of this field. If not, it takes these steps to determine the value of this field. First, it accesses a reference to the SPContentType object that represents the current content type:

```
SPContentType contentType = this.ItemContext.ContentType;
```

You can talk about current content type here because a display, edit, or new list item form displays, edits, or creates a new list item, which is of a specific content type. A content type is defined in a CAML-based XML file and deployed to SharePoint through a feature. This CAML-based XML field supports an element named <XmlDocuments>, which can contain one or more <XmlDocument> child elements. An <XmlDocument> child element can contain any valid XML document. One of these XML documents is a document with the document element named <FormTemplates>, which is used to specify the display, edit, and new list item forms:

```
<XmlDocuments>
  <XmlDocument
  NamespaceURL="http://schemas.microsoft.com/sharepoint/v3/contenttype/forms">
    <FormTemplates
    xmlns="http://schemas.microsoft.com/sharepoint/v3/contenttype/forms">
      <Display>ListForm</Display>
      <Edit>ListForm</Edit>
      <New>ListForm</New>
    </FormTemplates>
  </XmlDocument>
</XmlDocuments>
```

Note that the <FormTemplates> document element supports three child elements named <Display>, <Edit>, and <New>, whose contents specify the ID property values of form-rendering templates declared in an .ascx file in the ControlTemplates folder. As you'll see later, a form-rendering template is declared as a <SharePoint:RenderingTemplate> tag in an .ascx file. As such, the contents of the <Display>, <Edit>, and <New> elements are the ID attribute values of <SharePoint:RenderingTemplate> tags in an .ascx file in the ControlTemplates folder.

The getter of TemplateName next determines the control mode of the ListFormWebPart Web part. If it is in the Display mode, it assigns the value of the DisplayFormTemplateName property of the SPContentType object to the templateName. The DisplayFormTemplateName property returns the value specified within the opening and closing tags of the <Display> element, which is the ID attribute value of a <SharePoint:RenderingTemplate> tag in an .ascx file:

```
case SPControlMode.Display:
  this.templateName = contentType.DisplayFormTemplateName;
  break;
```

If it is in Edit mode, it assigns the value of the EditFormTemplateName property of the SPContentType object to templateName. The EditFormTemplateName property returns the value specified within the opening and closing tags of the <Edit> element:

```
case SPControlMode.Edit:
  this.templateName = contentType.EditFormTemplateName;
  break;
```

If it is in New mode, it assigns the value of the NewFormTemplateName property of the SPContentType object to templateName. This property returns the value specified within the opening and closing tags of the <New> element:

```
case SPControlMode.New:
  this.templateName = contentType.NewFormTemplateName;
  break;
```

If templateName is still null or empty string, the getter of TemplateName assigns the value of the TemplateName property of the SPForm object that represents the current form (which could be a display, edit, or new list item form) to templateName:

```
this.templateName = this.form.TemplateName;
```

Recall that a list type is defined in a schema.xml file, which can contain one <Form> element to describe each type of list item form. This <Form> element features an attribute named Template that specifies the ID property value of the form-rendering template that renders the form that the <Form> element describes. Keep in mind that a form-rendering template is represented by a <SharePoint:RenderingTemplate> tag in an .ascx file in the ControlTemplates folder. As such, the Template attribute on a <Form> element specifies the ID attribute value of a <SharePoint:RenderingTemplate> tag.

Listing 3-4 presents the internal implementation of the TemplateName property of the SPForm class.

Listing 3-4: The SPForm class

```
public class SPForm
{
  public string TemplateName
  {
    get
    {
      string namedStringItem = SPGlobal.GetNamedStringItem(this.node,
                                                          "Template");
      if (!string.IsNullOrEmpty(namedStringItem))
        return namedStringItem;
      if (this.Forms.List.BaseType != SPBaseType.DocumentLibrary)
      {
        if (this.Forms.List.BaseType == SPBaseType.Survey)
        {
          if (this.Type != PAGETYPE.PAGE_DISPLAYFORM)
            return "SurveyForm";
          return "ListForm";
        }
        return "ListForm";
      }
      return "DocumentLibraryForm";
    }
  }
}
```

As you can see, this property first accesses the value of the Template attribute on the <Form> element that describes the form that the SPForm object represents. Keep in mind that this form could be a display, edit, or new list item form:

```
string namedStringItem = SPGlobal.GetNamedStringItem(this.node, "Template");
```

If the <Form> element does not specify a value for the Template attribute, it then takes these steps to determine a default template name. If the current list is not a document library but its base type is survey, it returns SurveyForm as the template name if the form that the SPForm object represents is an edit or new list item form, and ListForm as the template name if the form that the SPForm object represents is a display list item form. If the current list is not a document library and its base type is not survey either, it returns ListForm as the template name for all three types of forms. If the current list is a document library, it returns DocumentLibraryForm as the template name.

The DefaultTemplates.ascx file in the ContentTemplates folder contains RenderingTemplate server controls with ID property values of ListForm, SurveyForm, and DocumentLibraryForm. Listing 3-5 presents an excerpt from DefaultTemplates.ascx that contains the RenderingTemplate server control with the ID property value of ListForm. As just discussed, all standard list types (non-document library lists) use the ListItem template form for all three types of forms. The only exception to this rule is the edit and new list item forms of the survey-based list types, which use the SurveyForm form template.

Listing 3-5: The RenderingTemplate server control with ID property value of "ListForm"

```
<SharePoint:RenderingTemplate ID="ListForm" runat="server">
  <Template>
    <SPAN id='part1'>
      <SharePoint:InformationBar runat="server"/>
      <wssuc:ToolBar CssClass="ms-formtoolbar" id="toolBarTbltop"
      RightButtonSeparator=" " runat="server">
        <Template_RightButtons>
          <SharePoint:NextPageButton runat="server"/>
          <SharePoint:SaveButton runat="server"/>
          <SharePoint:GoBackButton runat="server"/>
        </Template_RightButtons>
      </wssuc:ToolBar>
      <SharePoint:FormToolBar runat="server"/>
      <TABLE class="ms-formtable" style="margin-top: 8px;" border="0"
      cellpadding="0" cellspacing="0" width="100"%>
        <SharePoint:ChangeContentType runat="server"/>
        <SharePoint:FolderFormFields runat="server"/>
        <SharePoint:ListFieldIterator runat="server"/>
        <SharePoint:ApprovalStatus runat="server"/>
        <SharePoint:FormComponent TemplateName="AttachmentRows" runat="server"/>
      </TABLE>
      <table cellpadding="0" cellspacing="0" width="100"%>
        <tr>
          <td class="ms-formline">
            <IMG SRC="/_layouts/images/blank.gif" width="1" height="1" alt="">
          </td>
        </tr>
      </table>
      <TABLE cellpadding="0" cellspacing="0" width="100"% style="padding-top: 7px">
        <tr>
          <td width="100"%>
            <SharePoint:ItemHiddenVersion runat="server"/>
            <SharePoint:ParentInformationField runat="server"/>
            <SharePoint:InitContentType runat="server"/>
            <wssuc:ToolBar CssClass="ms-formtoolbar" id="toolBarTbl"
            RightButtonSeparator=" " runat="server">
              <Template_Buttons>
                <SharePoint:CreatedModifiedInfo runat="server"/>
              </Template_Buttons>
              <Template_RightButtons>
                <SharePoint:SaveButton runat="server"/>
                <SharePoint:GoBackButton runat="server"/>
              </Template_RightButtons>
            </wssuc:ToolBar>
          </td>
        </tr>
      </TABLE>
    </SPAN>
    <SharePoint:AttachmentUpload runat="server"/>
  </Template>
</SharePoint:RenderingTemplate>
```

The ASP.NET page parser first parses the markup enclosed within the opening and closing tags of the <Template> child element of the <SharePoint:RenderingTemplate> element shown in Listing 3-5 into a dynamically generated class that implements the ITemplate interface. It then dynamically compiles this class into an assembly and loads the assembly into the current application domain. Finally it dynamically instantiates an instance of this class and assigns this instance to the Template property of the RenderingTemplate server control.

As discussed earlier, the getter of the Template property of the ListFormWebPart Web part invokes the GetTemplateByName static method to return a reference to the ITemplate object that the ASP.NET page parser has assigned to the Template property of the RenderingTemplate server control and assigns this reference to the template private field.

As you can see from Listing 3-5, the <Template> child element of the <SharePoint:RenderingTemplate> element contains the markup that the ListFormWebPart Web part renders in a display, edit, or new list item form for all SharePoint standard lists (non-document library lists) with the exception of the edit and new list item forms of the survey-based lists. Keep in mind that the ListFormWebPart Web part provides the content for the PlaceHolderMain content placeholder, which is the body of the display, edit, or new list item form.

Next, you take a look at a couple of main server controls declared within the opening and closing tags of the <Template> child element of the <RenderingTemplate> tag in Listing 3-5. The first one is the FormToolBar server control that renders the form toolbar, which includes the action buttons such as New Response and Edit Response as shown in Figure 3-8.

```
<SharePoint:FormToolBar runat="server"/>
```

The second one is the ListFieldIterator server control that iterates through the list item fields and renders their names and values into the form:

```
<SharePoint:ListFieldIterator runat="server"/>
```

So far, you've learned that the ListFormWebPart Web part defines a template property named Template that references the ITemplate object that the ASP.NET page parser creates and assigns to the Template property of the RenderingTemplate server control with the ID property value of ListItem declared in the DefaultTemplates.ascx file in the ControlTemplates folder. Next, let's take a look at the implementation of the CreateChildControls method of the ListFormWebPart Web part shown in Listing 3-3 to see how this method manages to use this ITemplate object.

CreateChildControls first clears the Controls collection as usual:

```
this.Controls.Clear();
```

Then, it instantiates an instance of a class named TemplateContainer. As the name suggests, a TemplateContainer server control acts as a container into which the ITemplate object is rendered:

```
TemplateContainer templateContainer = new TemplateContainer();
```

Next, CreateChildControls assigns the values of the ControlMode and ItemContext properties of ListFormWebPart to the ControlMode and ItemContext properties of the TemplateContainer server control. The ItemContext property of a SharePoint server control references the SPContext object that represents the SharePoint context within which the server control is rendered, and the ControlMode enumeration property represents the control mode of the server control with the possible values of DisplayMode, EditMode, and NewMode. Many SharePoint server controls expose the ItemContext property. This means that many SharePoint server controls are rendered within a specific SharePoint context:

```
templateContainer.ControlMode = this.ControlMode;
templateContainer.ItemContext = this.ItemContext;
```

Next, CreateChildControls invokes the InstantiateIn method on the ITemplate object that the Template property of the ListFormWebPart Web part references to render this object into the TemplateContainer server control:

```
this.Template.InstantiateIn(templateContainer);
```

Finally, it adds the TemplateContainer server control and its content to the Controls collection of the ListFormWebPart Web part:

```
this.Controls.Add(templateContainer);
```

This means that the ListFormWebPart Web part by default ends up rendering the markup specified within the opening and closing tags of the <Template> child element of the <SharePoint:RenderingTemplate> element with the ID property value of one of the following:

- **ListForm.** This value is used if the Web part is in the Display, Edit, or New mode and the current list is a non-survey-based non-document library list. It is also used if the Web part is in Display mode and the current list is a survey-based list.
- **SurveyList.** This value is used if the Web part is in the Edit or New mode and the current list is a survey-based list.
- **DocumentLibrary.** This value is used if the Web part is in the Display, Edit, or New mode and the current list is a document library.

You have several different options for customizing what the ListFormWebPart Web part renders. One option is to implement an .ascx file that contains a <SharePoint:RenderingTemplate> element with the same ID property value of ListForm, SurveyForm, or DocumentLibrary and then add this file to the ControlTemplates folder on the file system of the front-end web server. Remember that the getter of the Template property of the ListFormWebPart Web part invokes the GetTemplateByName static method to return a reference to the ITemplate object that the ASP.NET page parser creates. It is then assigned to the Template property of the RenderingTemplate server control with the ID property value of ListItem, SurveyForm, or DocumentLibrary.

As you'll see later, when the GetTemplateByName static method is called for the first time, it stores the references to the ITemplate objects assigned to the Template properties of all RenderingTemplate server controls declared in the DefaultTemplates.ascx file in an internal table. If the ControlTemplates folder contains an .ascx file that declares a RenderingTemplate server control with the same ID property value as one of the standard RenderingTemplate server controls declared in the DefaultTemplates.ascx file, the GetTemplateByName static method replaces the reference to the ITemplate object assigned to the

Template property of the standard RenderingTemplate server control with the reference to the ITemplate object assigned to the Template property of the non-standard RenderingTemplate server control.

You should not introduce duplicate custom form-rendering templates, that is, form-rendering templates with the same ID attribute values. In other words, each standard form-rendering template declared in the DefaultTemplates.ascx file should be overridden once per SharePoint web application.

As you might imagine, overriding the ListForm, SurveyForm, or DocumentLibrary form templates with one of your own is not such a good idea because it will affect all SharePoint lists. Keep in mind that all non-survey-based, non-document library SharePoint lists use the ListForm form-rendering template in Display, Edit, and New modes, all survey-based SharePoint lists use the ListForm form-rendering template in Display mode and the SurveyForm form template in Edit and New modes, and all document libraries use the DocumentLibrary form-rendering template in Display, Edit, and New modes.

As a result, you shouldn't override the ListForm, SurveyForm, or DocumentLibrary form templates. Instead you should implement a custom list type that uses custom form-rendering templates. The next section shows you how to implement a custom list type.

For the same reasons, you should not override the form-rendering templates for a standard SharePoint content type either. Instead you should implement a custom content type that uses custom form-rendering templates.

As you may have noticed, I intentionally did not discuss list view forms such as AllItems.aspx. As the name suggests, a list view form displays a particular view of a SharePoint list, whereas different views of a list are rendered differently. The next question you may be wondering about is how a list view form knows to render a given list view. The very next section answers your questions.

List Types

Every SharePoint list is provisioned from a list type. Because Visual Studio (among many other benefits) provides IntelliSense support for XML manipulation, you'll use it in the following exercise as you learn how to use CAML to define a list type.

In this section you implement a custom list type named Tasks1, which duplicates the standard SharePoint Tasks list type. Follow these steps to implement a custom list type (note that each step also specifies what you need to do in that step to implement your custom list type Tasks1):

1. If you haven't done so already, copy the CAML schema files into the following Visual Studio folder on your machine to enable IntelliSense support for CAML:

```
Local_Drive:\Program Files\Microsoft Visual Studio 9.0\Xml\Schemas
```

The CAML schema files are made up of four files named CoreDefinitions.xsd, camlView.xsd, camlQuery.xsd, and wss.xsd, which are located in the following folder on your machine:

```
Local_Drive:\Program Files\Common Files\microsoft shared\Web Server
Extensions\12\TEMPLATE\XML
```

2. Launch Visual Studio.
3. Create a Class Library project. Name this Class Library project ClassLibrary1. This is the class library that will contain your Tasks1 custom list type.
4. Delete the Class1.cs file.
5. Add a new folder named TEMPLATE to the Class Library project.
6. Add a subfolder named FEATURES to the TEMPLATE folder from Step 5.
7. Add a feature-specific subfolder to the FEATURES folder from Step 6. Create a feature-specific folder named Tasks1List for your Tasks1 custom type example. This means that you'll be deploying your sample list type to SharePoint via a SharePoint feature named Tasks1List.
8. Add an XML file named feature.xml to the feature-specific subfolder from Step 7. As you'll see later, you'll use this feature to deploy your Tasks1 list type to SharePoint.
9. Add a subfolder named ListTemplates to the feature-specific folder from Step 6. This step is not mandatory, but will help you to organize things.
10. Add an XML file to the ListTemplates subfolder. This XML file by convention has the same name as your custom list type. As you'll see later in this chapter, this XML file is the element manifest file that defines your list template. Name this XML file Tasks1.xml for your sample list type because your sample list type is a list type named Tasks1.
11. Add a subfolder to the feature-specific folder from Step 7. This subfolder by convention has the same name as your custom list type. Name this subfolder Tasks1 for your sample list type because your sample list type is a list type named Tasks1.
12. Add an XML file named schema.xml to the subfolder from Step 11. You must name this XML file schema.xml.
13. Implement the feature.xml from Step 8, the element manifest XML file from Step 10, and the schema.xml file from Step 12. You'll implement these files for your custom Tasks1 list type shortly.
14. Add a text file named mybatchfile.bat to the Class Library project. You'll implement this file for your custom Tasks1 list type shortly.
15. Add a post-build event to Visual Studio (as discussed in Chapter 2) to have it execute the mybatchfile.bat file every time the project is built:

```
cd $(ProjectDir)
mybatchfile.bat
```

Figure 3-10 presents the folder structure for the Class Library project that contains your Tasks1 custom list type.

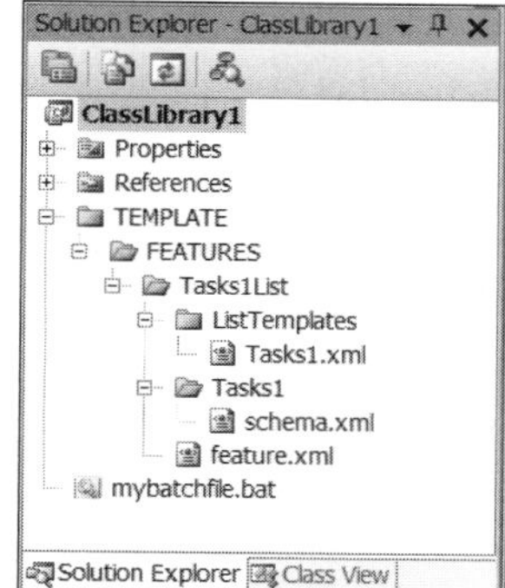

Figure 3-10: The folder hierarchy of the project

Next, you'll implement the mybatchfile.bat file as shown in Listing 3-6.

Listing 3-6: The content of mybatchfile.bat file

```
@SET TEMPLATE="c:\program files\common files\microsoft shared\web server
extensions\12\Template"
@SET STSADM="c:\program files\common files\microsoft shared\web server
extensions\12\bin\stsadm"

Echo Copying the files from the project to the TEMPLATE folder
xcopy /e /y TEMPLATE\* %TEMPLATE%

Echo Installing the Tasks1List feature with SharePoint
%STSADM% -o InstallFeature -filename Tasks1List\feature.xml -force

Echo Restarting IIS for changes to take effect
IISRESET
```

Next, you'll implement the feature that deploys the Tasks1 list type. Listing 3-7 presents the content of the feature.xml file.

Listing 3-7: The content of the feature.xml file

```
<?xml version="1.0" encoding="utf-8" ?>
<Feature xmlns="http://schemas.microsoft.com/sharepoint/"
 Id="{8D6E4CFC-A0A2-4769-BC3D-8B63DD030A24}"
 Description="This feature contains Tasks1 list type."
 Hidden="False"
 Scope="Web"
 Title="Tasks1 list type Feature"
 Version="1.0.0.0">
  <ElementManifests>
    <ElementManifest Location="ListTemplates\Tasks1.xml"/>
  </ElementManifests>
</Feature>
```

As discussed in the previous chapter, you can use the GuidGen.exe command-line utility to generate the GUID that you need to assign to the Id attribute on this <Feature> element. Note that this feature references the Tasks1.xml element manifest file, which is located in the ListTemplates folder. Listing 3-8 presents the content of this file.

Listing 3-8: The Tasks1.xml file

```
<?xml version="1.0" encoding="utf-8"?>
<Elements xmlns="http://schemas.microsoft.com/sharepoint/">
  <ListTemplate
  Name="Tasks1"
  Type="10010"
  BaseType="0"
  OnQuickLaunch="TRUE"
  SecurityBits="11"
  Sequence="600"
  DisplayName="Tasks1"
  Description="This is Tasks1 list type."
  Image="/_layouts/images/ittask.gif"/>
</Elements>
```

Note that you have set the xmlns attribute on the <Elements> document element to the following value so that you can take advantage of the Visual Studio IntelliSense support:

```
xmlsn="http://schemas.microsoft.com/sharepoint/"
```

As this listing shows, the <Elements> document element contains a child element named <ListTemplate>, which is used to define your Tasks1 list template. Note that the Name attribute on this child element is set to "Tasks1," which is the name of the folder that contains the schema.xml file. The Type attribute is set to 10010, which is an integer that uniquely identifies your Tasks1 list template. Here are the descriptions of the attributes of the <ListTemplate> element:

- **AllowDeletion.** Set this optional Boolean attribute to specify whether list instances provisioned from this list template can be deleted.
- **BaseType.** Set this required attribute to one of the possible values of 0, 1, 2, 3, or 4 to specify the base type for this list template.
- **Description.** Set this optional attribute to specify a short description for the list template.
- **DisplayName.** Set this required attribute to specify a display name for the list template.
- **FeatureId.** Set this optional attribute to the GUID of the feature that references the element manifest file that contains the definition of this list template.
- **Hidden.** Set this optional Boolean attribute to specify whether this list template should be available on the create.aspx page for provisioning lists.
- **HiddenList.** Set this optional Boolean attribute to specify whether lists provisioned from this list are hidden.
- **Image.** Set this optional attribute to specify the URL to an icon that represents a list.

- **Name.** Set this required attribute to specify an internal name for this list template. SharePoint uses this internal name to locate the folder that contains the schema.xml file that defines this list type.
- **OnQuickLaunch.** Set this optional Boolean attribute to specify whether lists provisioned from this list type should be displayed on the Quick Launch bar.
- **SecurityBits.** Set this optional string attribute to specify the security bits for this list type. The string that you assign to this attribute must contain two digits. The possible values for the first digit are 1 and 2, where 1 means users can read all list items on the lists provisioned from this list type and 2 means users can read only their own list items. The possible values for the second digit are 1, 2, and 3, where 1 means users can edit all list items on the lists provisioned from this list, 2 means user can edit only their own list items, and 3 means users cannot edit list items. As you can see, the first digit specifies the read-access permission on the list items and the second digit specifies the write-access permission on the list items. Keep in mind this attribute is only applicable to non-document library lists.
- **Sequence.** Set this optional integer attribute to specify the order in which this list template appears on the create.aspx page. If you don't specify a value for this attribute, SharePoint will display this list template at the bottom of the create.aspx page together with other list templates whose Sequence attributes are not set.
- **Type.** Set this optional integer value to specify a unique identifier for the list template. This identifier must be unique within the feature. It doesn't have to be unique across feature definitions or site definitions. This attribute must have the same value as the Type attribute on the <List> element that defines the schema of the list type. The <List> element is discussed shortly.
- **Unique.** Set this optional Boolean attribute to true to specify that this list type can be provisioned from only when a site is being created from a site template and cannot be provisioned from through SharePoint object mode or after the site has been provisioned. This basically makes the list type hidden. As such this list type will not appear on the create.aspx page.

The following table displays the value of the Type attribute for the standard SharePoint list types.

Value	Description
100	Generic list
101	Document library
102	Survey
103	Links list
104	Announcements list
105	Contacts list
106	Events list
107	Tasks list
108	Discussion board

(Continued)

Value	Description
109	Picture library
110	Data sources
111	Site template gallery
112	User Information list
113	Web Part gallery
114	List template gallery
115	XML Form library
116	Master pages gallery
117	No-Code Workflows
118	Custom Workflow Process
119	Wiki Page library
120	Custom grid for a list
130	Data Connection library
140	Workflow History
150	Gantt Tasks list
200	Meeting Series list
201	Meeting Agenda list
202	Meeting Attendees list
204	Meeting Decisions list
207	Meeting Objectives list
210	Meeting text box
211	Meeting Things To Bring list
212	Meeting Workspace Pages list
300	Portal Sites list
301	Blog Posts list
302	Blog Comments list
303	Blog Categories list
1100	Issue tracking
1200	Administrator tasks list
2002	Personal document library
2003	Private document library

The schema.xml file is where the schema of the list type is defined. Because your Tasks1 custom list type duplicates the standard SharePoint Tasks list type, copy the content of the schema.xml file that defines the schema of the standard SharePoint Tasks list type and paste it into the schema.xml file in your Class Library project. You can access the schema.xml file that defines the schema of the standard SharePoint Tasks list type from the following folder on the file system of the front-end web server:

```
Local_Drive:\Program Files\Common Files\microsoft shared\Web Server
Extensions\12\TEMPLATE\FEATURES\TasksList\Tasks
```

Listing 3-9 presents the portion of the schema.xml file that defines the Tasks1 list type.

Listing 3-9: The portion of the schema.xml file

```
<?xml version="1.0" encoding="utf-8"?>
<List
xmlsn:ows="Microsoft SharePoint"
Title="Tasks1"
FolderCreation="FALSE"
Direction="RTL"
Url="Lists/Tasks1"
BaseType="0">
  <MetaData>
    <ContentTypes>
      ...
    </ContentTypes>
    <Fields>
      ...
    </Fields>
    <Views>
      ...
    </Views>
    <Forms>
      ...
    </Forms>
  </MetaData>
</List>
```

As you can see, the document element of the schema.xml file is an element named <List>. This element features the following attributes:

- **BaseType.** Use this optional attribute to specify the base type for this list type.
- **Default.** Use this optional attribute to specify whether the list referenced in the Onet.xml file be created whenever a site is provisioned from the site definition. If this attribute is set to false, the list instance will not be provisioned from this list type but will be available for later provisioning.
- **Description.** Use this optional attribute to specify a description for the list type. Note that this attribute is mandatory in an Onet.xml file when adding a list type to a site definition. Also note that the value of this attribute overrides the value contained within the <DefaultDescription> child element of the <List> document element.
- **Direction.** Use this required attribute to specify the direction of reading order for this list type. The possible values are RTL (**R**ight **T**o **L**eft), LTR (**L**eft **T**o **R**ight), and none.

- **DisableAttachments.** Use this attribute to disable attachments in the list.
- **EnableContentTypes.** Use this attribute to enable content type management for lists provisioned from this list type.
- **Id.** Use this optional attribute to specify a GUID that uniquely identifies the list type.
- **Name.** Use this required attribute to specify an internal name for the list type.
- **RootWebOnly.** Use this optional Boolean attribute to specify whether list instances can only be provisioned from this list type in the top-level site of a site collection.
- **Title.** Use this required attribute to specify a title for the list type.
- **Type.** Use this optional integer attribute to specify the type of the list type. Note that this attribute and the Type attribute on the <ListTemplate> element have the same values.
- **URL.** Use this optional attribute to specify the site relative virtual path for the list type. As Listing 3-9 shows, this attribute is set to Lists/Tasks1 in your case. This means that the absolute URL to this list is:

```
http://EnterDomainNameHere/EnterSitePathHere/Lists/Tasks1
```

As Listing 3-9 shows, the <List> element supports a child element named <MetaData>, which supports the following child elements:

- **ContentTypes.** Use this child element to specify the content types that this list type supports.
- **Fields.** Use this child element to specify the columns for this list type.
- **Views.** Use this child element to specify views for this list type.
- **Forms.** Use this child element to specify the display, edit, and new list item forms for this list type.

As you can see from the following excerpt, the Tasks1 list type supports two content types:

```
<ContentTypes>
  <ContentTypeRef ID="0x0108">
    <Folder TargetName="Task2" />
  </ContentTypeRef>
  <ContentTypeRef ID="0x0120" />
</ContentTypes>
```

Note that each <ContentTypeRef> child element of the <ContentTypes> element references a content type with a specific content type ID. You can access the content type ID of standard content types from the ctypeswss.xml element manifest file in the following folder on the file system of the front-end web server:

```
Local_Drive:\Program Files\Common Files\microsoft shared\Web Server
Extensions\12\TEMPLATE\FEATURES\ctypes
```

The Tasks1 list type references two content types with the content type ID of 0x0108 (Task content type) and 0x0120 (Folder content type) as defined in the following excerpts from the ctypeswss.xml element manifest file:

```
<ContentType ID="0x0108"
Name="$Resources:Task"
Group="$Resources:List_Content_Types"
Description="$Resources:TaskCTDesc"
Version="0"
V2ListTemplateName="tasks">
  <FieldRefs>
    <FieldRef ID="{a8eb573e-9e11-481a-a8c9-1104a54b2fbd}" Name="Priority" />
    <FieldRef ID="{c15b34c3-ce7d-490a-b133-3f4de8801b76}" Name="Status" />
    <FieldRef ID="{d2311440-1ed6-46ea-b46d-daa643dc3886}" Name="PercentComplete" />
    <FieldRef ID="{53101f38-dd2e-458c-b245-0c236cc13d1a}" Name="AssignedTo" />
    <FieldRef ID="{7662cd2c-f069-4dba-9e35-082cf976e170}" Name="Body" />
    <FieldRef ID="{64cd368d-2f95-4bfc-a1f9-8d4324ecb007}" Name="StartDate" />
    <FieldRef ID="{cd21b4c2-6841-4f9e-a23a-738a65f99889}" Name="DueDate" />
  </FieldRefs>
</ContentType>

<ContentType ID="0x0120"
Name="$Resources:Folder"
Group="$Resources:Folder_Content_Types"
Description="$Resources:FolderCTDesc"
Sealed="TRUE"
Version="0">
  <FieldRefs>
    <FieldRef ID="{fa564e0f-0c70-4ab9-b863-0177e6ddd247}" Name="Title"
    Required="FALSE" Hidden="TRUE"/> <!-- Title -->
    <FieldRef ID="{8553196d-ec8d-4564-9861-3dbe931050c8}" Name="FileLeafRef"
    Hidden="FALSE" Required="TRUE"/> <!-- FileLeafRef -->
  </FieldRefs>
</ContentType>
```

This means that the Tasks1 list type inherits the Priority, Status, PercentComplete, AssignedTo, Body, StartDate, and DueDate columns from the first content type and the Title and FileLeafRef columns from the second content type.

As Listing 3-9 shows, the <MetaData> element supports a child element named <Fields> where you must specify the field or column definitions that the Tasks1 list type supports. You must use a separate <Field> child element inside the <Fields> element to specify each field or column definition:

```
<Fields>
  <Field ID="{a8eb573e-9e11-481a-a8c9-1104a54b2fbd}" Type="Choice" Name="Priority"
  DisplayName="$Resources:core,Priority;"
  SourceID="http://schemas.microsoft.com/sharepoint/v3" StaticName="Priority">
    <CHOICES>
      <CHOICE>$Resources:core,Priority_High;</CHOICE>
      <CHOICE>$Resources:core,Priority_Normal;</CHOICE>
      <CHOICE>$Resources:core,Priority_Low;</CHOICE>
    </CHOICES>
    <MAPPINGS>
```

(continued)

(continued)

```
      <MAPPING Value="1">$Resources:core,Priority_High;</MAPPING>
      <MAPPING Value="2">$Resources:core,Priority_Normal;</MAPPING>
      <MAPPING Value="3">$Resources:core,Priority_Low;</MAPPING>
    </MAPPINGS>
    <Default>$Resources:core,Priority_Normal;</Default>
  </Field>

  <Field Type="Choice" ID="{c15b34c3-ce7d-490a-b133-3f4de8801b76}" Name="Status"
  DisplayName="$Resources:core,Tasks_Status;"
  SourceID="http://schemas.microsoft.com/sharepoint/v3" StaticName="Status">
    <CHOICES>
      <CHOICE>$Resources:core,Tasks_NotStarted;</CHOICE>
      <CHOICE>$Resources:core,Tasks_InProgress</CHOICE>
      <CHOICE>$Resources:core,Tasks_Completed</CHOICE>
      <CHOICE>$Resources:core,Tasks_Deferred</CHOICE>
      <CHOICE>$Resources:core,Tasks_Waiting</CHOICE>
    </CHOICES>
    <MAPPINGS>
      <MAPPING Value="1">$Resources:core,Tasks_NotStarted;</MAPPING>
      <MAPPING Value="2">$Resources:core,Tasks_InProgress</MAPPING>
      <MAPPING Value="3">$Resources:core,Tasks_Completed</MAPPING>
      <MAPPING Value="4">$Resources:core,Tasks_Deferred</MAPPING>
      <MAPPING Value="5">$Resources:core,Tasks_Waiting</MAPPING>
    </MAPPINGS>
    <Default>$Resources:core,Tasks_NotStarted;</Default>
  </Field>

  <Field ID="{d2311440-1ed6-46ea-b46d-daa643dc3886}" Type="Number"
  Name="PercentComplete" Percentage="TRUE" Min="0" Max="1"
  DisplayName="$Resources:core,Percent_Complete;"
  SourceID="http://schemas.microsoft.com/sharepoint/v3"
  StaticName="PercentComplete" />

  <Field ID="{53101f38-dd2e-458c-b245-0c236cc13d1a}" Type="User" List="UserInfo"
  Name="AssignedTo" DisplayName="$Resources:core,Assigned_To;"
  SourceID="http://schemas.microsoft.com/sharepoint/v3" StaticName="AssignedTo" />

  <Field ID="{50d8f08c-8e99-4948-97bf-2be41fa34a0d}" Type="User" List="UserInfo"
  Name="TaskGroup" DisplaceOnUpgrade="TRUE"
  DisplayName="$Resources:core,Task_Group;" ReadOnlyEnforced="TRUE"
  SourceID="http://schemas.microsoft.com/sharepoint/v3" StaticName="TaskGroup" />

  <Field ID="{7662cd2c-f069-4dba-9e35-082cf976e170}" Type="Note" RichText="TRUE"
  Name="Body" DisplayName="$Resources:core,Description;" Sortable="FALSE"
  SourceID="http://schemas.microsoft.com/sharepoint/v3" StaticName="Body" />

  <Field ID="{64cd368d-2f95-4bfc-a1f9-8d4324ecb007}" Type="DateTime"
  Name="StartDate" DisplayName="$Resources:core,Start_Date;" Format="DateOnly"
  SourceID="http://schemas.microsoft.com/sharepoint/v3" StaticName="StartDate">
    <Default>[today]</Default>
  </Field>
```

```
    <Field Type="DateTime" ID="{cd21b4c2-6841-4f9e-a23a-738a65f99889}" Name="DueDate"
    DisplayName="$Resources:core,Due_Date;" Format="DateOnly"
    SourceID="http://schemas.microsoft.com/sharepoint/v3" StaticName="DueDate" />

  </Fields>
```

Each content type contains references to the field or column definitions that it supports. Even though the <ContentTypes> section of the schema.xml file references the content types that contain references to these field or column definitions, you still have to explicitly include the field definitions in the <Fields> section of the file. This is because SharePoint does not automatically copy the field definitions that these content types reference to the list type when you're adding content types declaratively through the <ContentTypes> section. If you add a content type to a list type through the SharePoint object model, SharePoint automatically copies the field definitions that the content type references to the Fields collection of the list.

Note that each <Field> element inside the <Fields> element contains the same information that the associated <Field> element in the fieldswss.xml element manifest file in the following folder presents:

```
C:\Program Files\Common Files\microsoft shared\Web Server
Extensions\12\TEMPLATE\FEATURES\fields
```

In other words, the <Fields> element of the schema.xml file contains the actual definition of the fields as opposed to references to these fields. That is, you must duplicate the same field definition inside the <Fields> element of the schema.xml file. As just mentioned, this is because SharePoint does not copy these field definitions into the list type definition when you add a content type declaratively.

As Listing 3-9 shows, the <MetaData> element supports a child element named <Views> where you must define the views that the list type supports. The <Views> element contains one <View> element for each view, which contains CAML rendering instructions for rendering the view. As an example, take a look at one of these views named All Tasks. As you'll see later in this chapter, after you deploy the Tasks1 list type to SharePoint, you can provision a list from this list type. Figure 3-11 shows a list named Tasks1 provisioned from this list type.

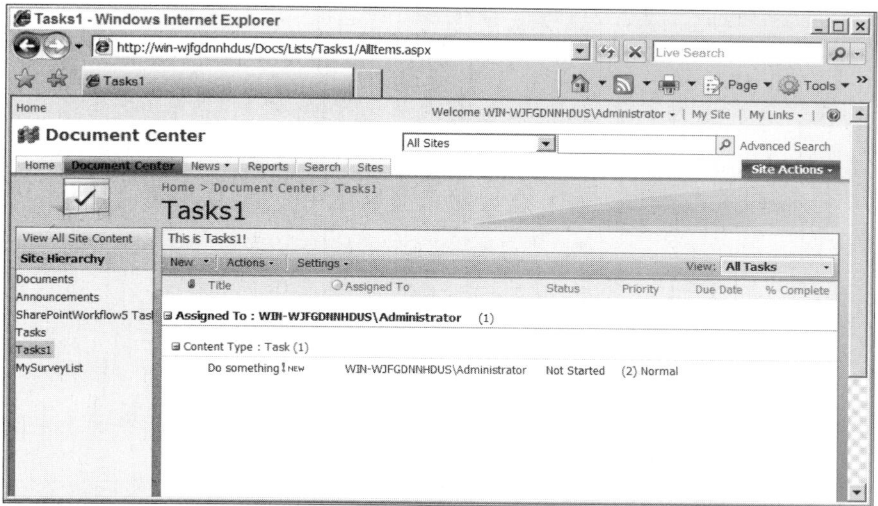

Figure 3-11: A Tasks1 list instance

Note that this figure contains a drop-down list box named View, which allows you to select a view from the list of views defined in the <Views> section of the Tasks1 list type (see Figure 3-12).

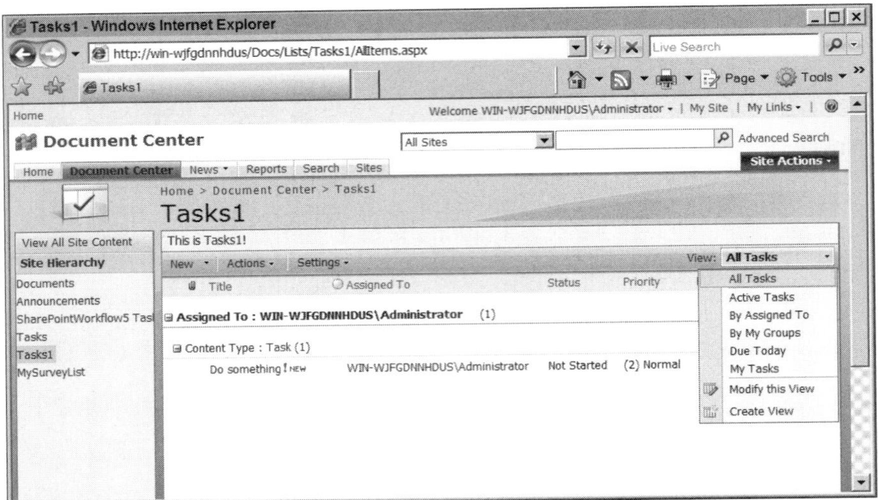

Figure 3-12: The menu displaying the list of views

Listing 3-10 presents a portion of the schema.xml file.

Listing 3-10: A portion of the schema.xml file

```
<List Title="MyTasks">
  <MetaData>
    <Views>
      <View BaseViewID="1" Type="HTML" WebPartZoneID="Main" Url="AllItems.aspx"
      DisplayName="$Resources:core,All_Tasks;" DefaultView="TRUE"
      SetupPath="pages\viewpage.aspx" ImageUrl="/_layouts/images/issues.png">
        ...
      </View>

      <View BaseViewID="2" Type="HTML" WebPartZoneID="Main"
      DisplayName="$Resources:core,My_Tasks;" SetupPath="pages\viewpage.aspx"
      ImageUrl="/_layouts/images/issues.png" Url="MyItems.aspx" ReqAuth="TRUE">
        ...
      </View>

      <View BaseViewID="3" Type="HTML" WebPartZoneID="Main"
      DisplayName="$Resources:core,Due_Today;" SetupPath="pages\viewpage.aspx"
      ImageUrl="/_layouts/images/issues.png" Url="duetoday.aspx">
        ...
      </View>
```

```
        <View BaseViewID="4" Type="HTML" WebPartZoneID="Main"
        DisplayName="$Resources:core,Active_Tasks;" SetupPath="pages\viewpage.aspx"
        ImageUrl="/_layouts/images/issues.png" Url="active.aspx">
          ...
        </View>

        <View BaseViewID="5" Type="HTML" WebPartZoneID="Main"
        DisplayName="$Resources:core,By_Assigned_To;" SetupPath="pages\viewpage.aspx"
        ImageUrl="/_layouts/images/issues.png" Url="byowner.aspx">
          ...
        </View>

        <View BaseViewID="8" Type="HTML" WebPartZoneID="Main"
        DisplayName="$Resources:core,By_My_Groups;" SetupPath="pages\viewpage.aspx"
        ImageUrl="/_layouts/images/issues.png" Url="MyGrTsks.aspx" ReqAuth="TRUE">
          ...
        </View>
      </Views>
    </MetaData>
  </List>
```

As you can see, the schema.xml file contains one <View> element for each view listed in the View drop-down list shown in Figure 3-12. Note that the DisplayName attribute on each <View> element pulls the locale-specific text from the core.resx file, which is located in the following folder on the file system of the front-end web server:

```
Local_Drive:\Program Files\Common Files\microsoft shared\Web Server
Extensions\12\Resources
```

The View drop-down list shown in Figure 3-12 displays the values of the DisplayName properties of the views specified in the schema.xml file. When you select a view from this drop-down list box, SharePoint navigates to the page whose URL is given by the Url attribute on the <View> element that represents the selected view. For example, if you select the All Tasks view from this drop-down list box, SharePoint navigates to the AllItems.aspx page, which is the value of the URL attribute on the <View> element in the schema.xml file that represents the All Tasks view, as shown in the boldfaced portion of the following excerpt from the schema.xml file:

```
        <View BaseViewID="1" Type="HTML" WebPartZoneID="Main" Url="AllItems.aspx"
        DisplayName="$Resources:core,All_Tasks;" DefaultView="TRUE"
        SetupPath="pages\viewpage.aspx" ImageUrl="/_layouts/images/issues.png"
          . . .
        </View>
```

As the preceding excerpt shows, the DefaultView attribute on the <View> element that represents the All Tasks view is set to True to specify that this view is the default view of the Tasks1 list type.

The pages whose URLs are specified in the URL attributes of the <View> elements in the schema.xml file (see Listing 3-10) contain a Web part zone whose ID is given by the WebPartZoneID attribute on the associated <View> element. For example, the AllItems.aspx page whose URL is specified in the Url attribute of the <View> element that represents the All Tasks view contains a Web part zone with an ID value of Main, which is the value of the WebPartZoneID attribute on this <View> element, as you can see from the boldfaced portions of the following excerpt:

```
<View BaseViewID="1" Type="HTML" WebPartZoneID="Main" Url="AllItems.aspx"
DisplayName="$Resources:core,All_Tasks;" DefaultView="TRUE"
SetupPath="pages\viewpage.aspx" ImageUrl="/_layouts/images/issues.png">
  ...
</View>
```

SharePoint uses the value of this attribute to locate this Web part zone and to add a ListViewWebPart Web part into this Web part zone. This ListViewWebPart Web part uses the CAML rendering instructions specified within the <View> element to render the view.

A <View> element supports an attribute named Type, which specifies the rendering type. The possible values are HTML, Chart, and Pivot. A <View> element also supports an attribute named BaseViewID, which you must set to an integer that uniquely identifies the view among other views of the list type.

The main responsibility of a <View> element is to provide the ListViewWebPart Web part with CAML rendering instructions for rendering the associated view. As an example, take a look at the <View> element that represents the All Tasks view as shown in Listing 3-11.

Listing 3-11: The <View> element that represents the All Tasks view

```
<View BaseViewID="1" Type="HTML" WebPartZoneID="Main"
DisplayName="$Resources:core,All_Tasks;" DefaultView="TRUE" MobileView="True"
MobileDefaultView="False" SetupPath="pages\viewpage.aspx"
ImageUrl="/_layouts/images/issues.png" Url="AllItems.aspx">
  <GroupByHeader>
    ...
  </GroupByHeader>
  <GroupByFooter>
    ...
  </GroupByFooter>
  <ViewHeader>
    ...
  </ViewHeader>
  <ViewBody>
    ...
  </ViewBody>
  <ViewFooter>
    ...
  </ViewFooter>
  <Toolbar Type="Standard" />
  <ViewFields>
    <FieldRef Name="Attachments" />
    <FieldRef Name="LinkTitle" />
    <FieldRef Name="AssignedTo" />
    <FieldRef Name="Status" />
    <FieldRef Name="Priority" />
    <FieldRef Name="DueDate" />
    <FieldRef Name="PercentComplete" />
  </ViewFields>
  <Query>
```

```
      <OrderBy>
        <FieldRef Name="ID" />
      </OrderBy>
    </Query>
  </View>
```

As this code listing shows, the <View> element contains the following child elements:

- **<GroupByHeader>.** This child element contains the CAML rendering instructions that render the HTML for the Group By header.
- **<GroupByFooter>.** This child element contains the CAML rendering instructions that render the HTML for the Group By footer.
- **<ViewHeader>.** This child element contains the CAML rendering instruction that renders the HTML for the header of the view.
- **<ViewBody>.** This child element contains the CAML rendering instruction that renders the HTML for the body of the view.
- **<ViewFooter>.** This child element contains the CAML rendering instruction that renders the HTML for the footer of the view.
- **<RowLimit>.** This child element specifies the maximum number of rows to display on a page. When this maximum is reached, the Next and Previous buttons are rendered to allow users to see the rest of the rows.
- **<ViewFields>.** This child element specifies the fields that the view contains. When a view is selected from the View drop-down list box, only the fields specified in this child element are rendered.
- **<Query>.** This child element specifies the CAML query that returns the data rows for this view.

The following sections discuss some of the child elements contained in the <View> element representing the All Tasks view.

GroupByHeader

The <GroupByHeader> child element of the <View> element that represents the All Tasks view contains the CAML rendering instructions that render the HTML that displays the UI portion of Figure 3-11 shown in Figure 3-13.

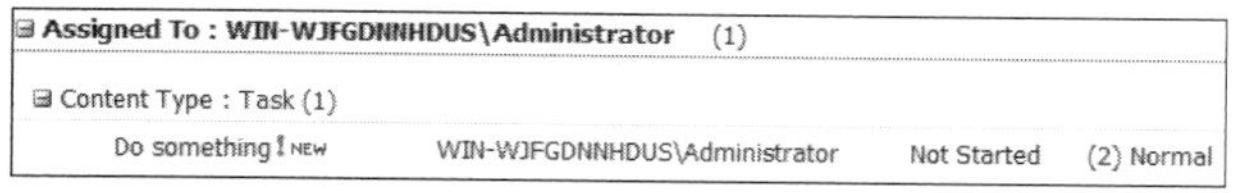

Figure 3-13: The group by header UI for the All Tasks view

Listing 3-12 presents the content of the <GroupByHeader> child element.

Listing 3-12: The <GroupByHeader> child element of the <View> element

```
<GroupByHeader>
  <HTML><![CDATA[<TBODY id="titl]]></HTML>
  <GetVar Name="GroupByLevelString" />
  <HTML><![CDATA[" groupString="]]></HTML>
  <GetVar Name="GroupByValueString" />
  <HTML><![CDATA["><TR><TD colspan="100"]]></HTML>
  <Switch>
    <Expr>
      <GetVar Name="GroupByIndent" />
    </Expr>
    <Case Value="0">
      <HTML><![CDATA[ class="ms-gb" ]]></HTML>
    </Case>
    <Default>
      <HTML><![CDATA[ class="ms-gb2" ]]></HTML>
    </Default>
  </Switch>
  <HTML>
    <![CDATA[
      nowrap><img src="/_layouts/images/blank.gif" alt="" height=1 width=
    ]]>
  </HTML>
  <GetVar Name="GroupByIndent" />
  <HTML>
    <![CDATA[
      ><a href="javascript:" onclick="javascript:ExpCollGroup('
    ]]>
  </HTML>
  <GetVar Name="GroupByLevelString" />
  <HTML><![CDATA[','img_]]></HTML>
  <GetVar Name="GroupByLevelString" />
  <HTML><![CDATA[');return false;"><img id="img_]]></HTML>
  <GetVar Name="GroupByLevelString" />
  <HTML><![CDATA[" src="/_layouts/images/minus.gif" alt="]]></HTML>
  <HTML>$Resources:groupExpColl;</HTML>
  <HTML><![CDATA[" border="0"></a> ]]></HTML>
  <HTML><![CDATA[<a href="javascript:" onclick="javascript:ExpCollGroup(']]></HTML>
  <GetVar Name="GroupByLevelString" />
  <HTML><![CDATA[','img_]]></HTML>
  <GetVar Name="GroupByLevelString" />
  <HTML><![CDATA[');return false;">]]></HTML>
  <GetVar Name="GroupByField" HTMLEncode="TRUE" />
  <HTML><![CDATA[</a> : ]]></HTML>
  <GetVar Name="GroupByValue" />
  <HTML><![CDATA[</TD></TR></TBODY>]]></HTML>
</GroupByHeader>
```

Listing 3-13 presents the HTML that the <GroupByHeader> element generates.

Listing 3-13: The HTML that the <GroupByHeader> element generates

```
<TBODY id="titl1-1_" groupString="">
  <TR>
    <TD colspan="100" class="ms-gb" nowrap>
      <img src="/_layouts/images/blank.gif" alt="" height=1 width=0>
      <a href="javascript:"
      onclick="javascript:ExpCollGroup('1-1_','img_1-1_');return false;">
        <img id="img_1-1_" src="/_layouts/images/minus.gif"
        alt="$Resources:groupExpColl" border="0">
      </a> 
      <a href="javascript:"
      onclick="javascript:ExpCollGroup('1-1_','img_1-1_');return false;">
        Assigned To
      </a> : 
      <nobr>
        <span>
          <A ONCLICK="GoToLink(this);return false;"
          HREF="/Docs/_layouts/userdisp.aspx?ID=1">
            WIN-WJFGDNNHDUS\Administrator
          </A>
          <img border="0" height="1" width="3"
          src="/_layouts/images/blank.gif" alt="" />
          <img border="0" height="12" width="12"
          src="/_layouts/images/blank.gif" alt=""/>
        </span>
      </nobr>
      <span style="font-weight: lighter">
        &#8206;(1)
      </span>
    </TD>
  </TR>
</TBODY>
<TBODY id="titl1-1_1_" groupString="">
  <TR>
    <TD colspan="100" class="ms-gb2" nowrap>
      <img src="/_layouts/images/blank.gif" alt="" height=1 width=10>
      <a href="javascript:"
      onclick="javascript:ExpCollGroup('1-1_1_','img_1-1_1_');return false;">
        <img id="img_1-1_1_" src="/_layouts/images/minus.gif"
        alt="$Resources:groupExpColl" border="0">
      </a> 
      <a href="javascript:"
      onclick="javascript:ExpCollGroup('1-1_1_','img_1-1_1_');return false;">
        Content Type
      </a>
      : Task
      <span style="font-weight: lighter">
        &#8206;(1)
      </span>
    </TD>
  </TR>
</TBODY>
```

Next, you'll walk you through the CAML-rendering instructions specified in the <GroupByHeader> element to see how this element generates the HTML shown in Listing 3-13.

As you can see, the <GroupByHeader> element performs these tasks to generate this HTML. First, it uses an <HTML> CAML rendering element to render the opening tag of the first <TBody> element shown in Listing 3-13:

```
<HTML><![CDATA[<TBODY id="titl]]></HTML>
```

Because the schema.xml as an XML file must be a valid XML, the content of the preceding <HTML> CAML rendering element is placed within <![CDATA[and]]> to escape the < character. This <HTML> CAML rendering element renders the following HTML into the output stream:

```
<TBODY id="titl
```

Next, the <GroupByHeader> element uses a <GetVar> element to get and to render the value of the GroupByLevelString global variable right after the preceding HTML:

```
<GetVar Name="GroupByLevelString" />
```

This <GetVar> element returns and renders the *string 1-1_* into the output stream, which is the value of the GroupByLevelString variable. This value makes sense because you're rendering the first Group By level shown in Figure 3-13.

So far, the output HTML is as follows:

```
<TBODY id="titl1-1_
```

Next, the <GroupByHeader> element uses the following <HTML> CAML rendering element to render the string *" groupString="* into the output stream:

```
<HTML><![CDATA[" groupString="]]></HTML>
```

So far, the output HTML is as follows:

```
<TBODY id="titl1-1_" groupString="
```

Next, the <GroupByHeader> uses another <GetVar> element to render the value of the GroupByValueString variable as the value of the groupString attribute shown in the preceding line:

```
<GetVar Name="GroupByValueString" />
```

The value of this variable happens to be an empty string. Next, <GroupByHeader> uses the following <HTML> CAML rendering element to render the string *"><TR><TD colspan="100"* into the output stream:

```
<HTML><![CDATA["><TR><TD colspan="100"]]></HTML>
```

So far, the output HTML looks like the following:

```
<TBODY id="titl1-1_" groupString="">
  <TR>
    <TD colspan="100"
```

I've added indentations and placed different pieces of HTML on different lines to make the HTML more readable. The actual HTML does not contain these indentations and everything is rendered on the same line.

Next, <GroupByHeader> uses a <Switch> CAML element to determine what to render next. This element operates in a way that is similar to the C# switch construct. Recall that the C# switch construct uses an expression to determine which case statement to execute next. The <Switch> element contains a sub-element named <Expr>, which is used to specify the switching expression. In this case, the <Expr> element contains a <GetVar> sub-element that returns the value of the GroupByIndent variable. The <Switch> element uses the value of this variable to determine which <Case> sub-element to execute next. In this case, this value is zero. This means that the <Case> sub-element with the Value attribute of zero is executed. This <Case> sub-element renders the string *class="ms-gb"* into the output stream:

```
<Switch>
  <Expr>
    <GetVar Name="GroupByIndent" />
  </Expr>
  <Case Value="0">
    <HTML><![CDATA[ class="ms-gb" ]]></HTML>
  </Case>
  <Default>
    <HTML><![CDATA[ class="ms-gb2" ]]></HTML>
  </Default>
</Switch>
```

Note that the <Switch> element (just like its C# switch counterpart) contains a <Default> element, which is executed when none of the <Case> sub-elements have the same value as the switching expression.

So far, the output HTML looks like the following:

```
<TBODY id="titl1-1_" groupString="">
  <TR>
    <TD colspan="100" class="ms-gb"
```

Next, <GroupByHeader> uses the following <HTML> CAML element:

```
<HTML>
  <![CDATA[
    nowrap><img src="/_layouts/images/blank.gif" alt="" height=1 width=
  ]]>
</HTML>
```

to render the following string:

```
nowrap><img src="/_layouts/images/blank.gif" alt="" height=1 width=
```

So far, the output HTML looks like this:

```
<TBODY id="titl1-1_" groupString="">
  <TR>
    <TD colspan="100" class="ms-gb" nowrap>
      <img src="/_layouts/images/blank.gif" alt="" height=1 width=
```

Next, <GroupByHeader> uses a <GetVar> element to render the value of the GroupByIndent variable, which is zero in this case. As the name implies, the GroupByIndent variable specifies the amount of indentation:

```
<GetVar Name="GroupByIndent" />
```

So far, the output HTML looks like this:

```
<TBODY id="titl1-1_" groupString="">
  <TR>
    <TD colspan="100" class="ms-gb" nowrap>
      <img src="/_layouts/images/blank.gif" alt="" height=1 width=0
```

Next, <GroupByHeader> uses the following <HTML> CAML element:

```
<HTML>
  <![CDATA[
    ><a href="javascript:" onclick="javascript:ExpCollGroup('
  ]]>
</HTML>
```

to render the following string

```
><a href="javascript:" onclick="javascript:ExpCollGroup('
```

So far, the output HTML looks like the following:

```
<TBODY id="titl1-1_" groupString="">
  <TR>
    <TD colspan="100" class="ms-gb" nowrap>
      <img src="/_layouts/images/blank.gif" alt="" height=1 width=0>
      <a href="javascript:"
      onclick="javascript:ExpCollGroup('
```

Next, <GroupByHeader> uses another <GetVar> element to render the value of the GroupByLevelString variable. Recall that the value of this variable is *1-1_*:

```
<GetVar Name="GroupByLevelString" />
```

Therefore, the output HTML is as follows:

```
<TBODY id="titl1-1_" groupString="">
  <TR>
    <TD colspan="100" class="ms-gb" nowrap>
```

```
<img src="/_layouts/images/blank.gif" alt="" height=1 width=0>
<a href="javascript:"
onclick="javascript:ExpCollGroup('1-1_
```

Then, <GroupByHeader> uses the following <HTML> CAML element:

```
<HTML><![CDATA[',''img_]]></HTML>
```

to render the following string

```
','img_
```

So far, the output HTML is as follows:

```
<TBODY id="titl1-1_" groupString="">
  <TR>
    <TD colspan="100" class="ms-gb" nowrap>
      <img src="/_layouts/images/blank.gif" alt="" height=1 width=0>
      <a href="javascript:"
      onclick="javascript:ExpCollGroup('1-1_','img_
```

Then, <GroupByHeader> uses a <GetVar> element to render the value of the GroupByLevelString variable, which is *1_1_*:

```
  <GetVar Name="GroupByLevelString" />
<TBODY id="titl1-1_" groupString="">
  <TR>
    <TD colspan="100" class="ms-gb" nowrap>
      <img src="/_layouts/images/blank.gif" alt="" height=1 width=0>
      <a href="javascript:"
      onclick="javascript:ExpCollGroup('1-1_','img_1-1_
```

Next, <GroupByHeader> uses the following <HTML> CAML element:

```
<HTML><![CDATA[');return false;"><img id="img_]]></HTML>
```

to render the following string:

```
');return false;"><img id="img_
```

So far, the output HTML is as follows:

```
<TBODY id="titl1-1_" groupString="">
  <TR>
    <TD colspan="100" class="ms-gb" nowrap>
      <img src="/_layouts/images/blank.gif" alt="" height=1 width=0>
      <a href="javascript:"
      onclick="javascript:ExpCollGroup('1-1_','img_1-1_');return false;">
        <img id="img_
```

As you can see, <GroupByHeader> keeps using the CAML rendering elements such as <HTML> and <GetVar> to render the output HTML piece by piece:

```
<GetVar Name="GroupByLevelString" />
<HTML><![CDATA[" src="/_layouts/images/minus.gif" alt="]]></HTML>
<HTML>$Resources:groupExpColl;</HTML>
<HTML><![CDATA[" border="0"></a> ]]></HTML>
<HTML><![CDATA[<a href="javascript:" onclick="javascript:ExpCollGroup(']]></HTML>
<GetVar Name="GroupByLevelString" />
<HTML><![CDATA[','img_]]></HTML>
<GetVar Name="GroupByLevelString" />
<HTML><![CDATA[');return false;">]]></HTML>
<GetVar Name="GroupByField" HTMLEncode="TRUE" />
<HTML><![CDATA[</a> : ]]></HTML>
<GetVar Name="GroupByValue" />
<HTML><![CDATA[</TD></TR></TBODY>]]></HTML>
```

Note that the CAML rendering instructions used within the <GroupByHeader> element only render a single <TBODY> element and its constituent child elements and attributes. However, as you can see from Listing 3-13, the output HTML contains two <TBODY> elements. This means that the <GroupByHeader> element is executed twice, once for each group. This is because the All Tasks view contains two groups, one contained in the other, as shown in Figure 3-12. As you can see, the CAML-rendering instructions contained within the <GroupByHeader> sub-element of a <View> element is executed once for each group within the view.

<GroupByFooter>

Listing 3-14 presents the content of the <GroupByFooter> sub-element of the <View> element that represents the All Tasks view.

Listing 3-14: The <GroupByFooter> element

```
<GroupByFooter>
  <Switch>
    <Expr>
      <GetVar Name="GroupByIndent" />
    </Expr>
    <Case Value="0">
      <HTML><![CDATA[<TBODY id="foot]]></HTML>
      <GetVar Name="GroupByLevelString" />
      <HTML><![CDATA[_"></TBODY>]]></HTML>
    </Case>
    <Default />
  </Switch>
  <Switch>
    <Expr>
      <GetVar Name="GroupByCollapse" />
    </Expr>
    <Case Value="TRUE">
      <HTML><![CDATA[<SCRIPT>ExpCollGroup(']]></HTML>
```

```
        <GetVar Name="GroupByLevelString" />
        <HTML><![CDATA[','img_]]></HTML>
        <GetVar Name="GroupByLevelString" />
        <HTML><![CDATA[');</SCRIPT>]]></HTML>
      </Case>
      <Default />
    </Switch>
  </GroupByFooter>
```

As the name suggests, <GroupByFooter> renders the HTML that displays the footer of a group. As you can see from Listing 3-14, <GroupByFooter> uses a <Switch> element to determine what to render next. The <Expr> sub-element of this <Switch> element uses a <GetVar> element that returns the value of the GroupByIndent variable and uses this value as the switching expression:

```
      <Expr>
        <GetVar Name="GroupByIndent" />
      </Expr>
```

In this case, this value is zero. This means that the <Case> element with the Value attribute value of zero is executed:

```
      <Case Value="0">
        <HTML><![CDATA[<TBODY id="foot]]></HTML>
        <GetVar Name="GroupByLevelString" />
        <HTML><![CDATA[_"></TBODY>]]></HTML>
      </Case>
```

This <Case> element first uses an <HTML> CAML element to render the following string:

```
  <TBODY id="foot
```

Next, it uses a <GetVar> element to render the value of the GroupByLevelString variable, which is *1-1_* in this case. Finally, it uses another <HTML> element to render the string *"></TBODY>*. Therefore, this <Case> element renders the following HTML into the output stream:

```
  <TBODY id="foot1-1_"></TBODY>
```

Next, <GroupByFooter> uses another <Switch> element to determine what to render next.
The <Expr> sub-element of this <Switch> element uses a <GetVar> element to return the value of the GroupByCollapse variable and uses this value as the switching expression:

```
      <Expr>
        <GetVar Name="GroupByCollapse" />
      </Expr>
```

The value of this variable in this case is FALSE. This means that the <Case> element with the Value attribute value of TRUE will not be executed. Instead the <Default> element is executed. Because this element does not render anything, the footer for this group is simply:

```
  <TBODY id="foot1-1_"></TBODY>
```

Just like <GroupByHeader>, <GroupByFooter> is executed once for each group in the view. Recall that the switching expression in the case of the first <Switch> sub-element of <GroupByFooter> is the value of the GroupByIndent variable. This variable in the case of the second group shown in Figure 3-12 is no longer zero because this group is indeed indented. This means that the <Default> sub-element of the first <Switch> element gets executed. Because this sub-element does not render anything, there is no rendering contribution from the first <Switch> sub-element of <GroupByFooter> element for the second group.

Recall that the switching expression in the case of the second <Switch> sub-element of <GroupByFooter> is the value of the GroupByCollapse variable, which is FALSE in the case of the second group because the second group, just like the first group, is not collapsed (see Figure 3-12). As such, the rendering contribution of the second <Switch> element is also nothing in the case of the second group. Therefore, <GroupByFooter> provides no rendering contribution in the case of the second group.

<ViewFields>

Listing 3-15 presents the content of the <ViewFields> child element of the <View> element that represents the All Tasks view.

Listing 3-15: The <ViewFields> element

```
<ViewFields>
  <FieldRef Name="Attachments" />
  <FieldRef Name="LinkTitle" />
  <FieldRef Name="AssignedTo" />
  <FieldRef Name="Status" />
  <FieldRef Name="Priority" />
  <FieldRef Name="DueDate" />
  <FieldRef Name="PercentComplete" />
</ViewFields>
```

As you can see, <ViewFields> specifies the fields or columns that the All Tasks view supports. In other words, if you select this view from the View drop-down list box shown in Figure 3-12, you'll only see the fields or columns specified within the <ViewFields> element.

<Query>

Listing 3-16 presents the content of the <Query> child element of the <View> element that represents the All Tasks view.

Listing 3-16: The <Query> element

```
<Query>
  <OrderBy>
    <FieldRef Name="ID" />
  </OrderBy>
</Query>
```

The <Query> element specifies the CAML query that returns the data rows for this view. As you can see, the All Tasks view returns all data rows and sorts them by the ID field.

<ViewBody>

Listing 3-17 presents the content of the <ViewBody> child element of the <View> element that represents the All Tasks view.

Listing 3-17: The <ViewBody> element

```
<ViewBody>
  <HTML><![CDATA[<TR class="]]></HTML>
  <GetVar Name="AlternateStyle" />
  <HTML><![CDATA[">]]></HTML>
  <IfEqual>
    <Expr1>
      <GetVar Name="AlternateStyle" />
    </Expr1>
    <Expr2>ms-alternating</Expr2>
    <Then>
      <SetVar Scope="Request" Name="AlternateStyle">
      </SetVar>
    </Then>
    <Else>
      <SetVar Scope="Request" Name="AlternateStyle">ms-alternating</SetVar>
    </Else>
  </IfEqual>
  <Fields>
    <HTML><![CDATA[<TD Class="]]></HTML>
    <FieldSwitch>
      <Expr>
        <Property Select="ClassInfo" />
      </Expr>
      <Case Value="Menu">
        <HTML><![CDATA[ms-vb-title" height="100%]]></HTML>
      </Case>
      <Case Value="Icon">ms-vb-icon</Case>
      <Default>
        <FieldSwitch>
          <Expr>
            <Property Select="Type" />
            <PresenceEnabled />
          </Expr>
          <Case Value="UserTRUE">ms-vb-user</Case>
          <Case Value="UserMultiTRUE">ms-vb-user</Case>
          <Default>ms-vb2</Default>
        </FieldSwitch>
      </Default>
    </FieldSwitch>
    <HTML><![CDATA[">]]></HTML>
    <Field />
    <HTML><![CDATA[</TD>]]></HTML>
  </Fields>
  <HTML><![CDATA[</TR>]]></HTML>
</ViewBody>
```

Listing 3-18 shows the output HTML that the CAML rendering instructions within the <ViewBody> element generate. These CAML rendering instructions are executed once for each data row that the CAML query specified in the <Query> element returns. Each execution of these CAML rendering instructions renders a data row returned from this CAML query.

Because the *MyTasks List Instance 1* list instance contains only a single item (because the CAML query in this case returns only a single data row), this output HTML contains a single <TR> element to render this data row. If your list instance contained more than one item and the CAML query returned more than one data row, this output HTML would contain one <TR> element for each data row. Note that the <TR> element that renders this single data row contains one <TD> element to render the value of each field of the data row.

Listing 3-18: The output HTML that the <ViewBody> element generates

```
<TR class="">
  <td class="ms-vh-group" width=20px>
    <img height=1px width=20px src='/_layouts/images/blank.gif' alt=''>
  </td>
  <TD Class="ms-vb2"></TD>

  <TD Class="ms-vb-title" height="100%">
    <table height="100%" cellspacing=0 class="ms-unselectedtitle"
    onmouseover="OnItem(this)" CTXName="ctx1" Id="1"
    Url="/Docs/Lists/Tasks1/1_.000"
    DRef="Docs/Lists/Tasks1"
    Perm="0x7fffffffffffffff" Type="" Ext=""
    Icon="icgen.gif||" OType="0" COUId="" HCD="" CSrc="" MS="0" CType="Task"
    CId="0x010800A484B5FA8C591C4484B0561226210922" UIS="512" SUrl="">
      <tr>
        <td width="100%" Class="ms-vb">
          <a onfocus="OnLink(this)"
          href="/Docs/Lists/Tasks1/DispForm.aspx?ID=1"
          ONCLICK="GoToLink(this);return false;" target="_self">
            Do something
            <img src="/_layouts/images/blank.gif" class="ms-hidden" border=0
            width=1 height=1 alt="Use SHIFT+ENTER to open the menu (new window).">
          </a>
          <IMG SRC="/_layouts/1033/images/new.gif" alt="New">
        </td>
        <td>
          <img src="/_layouts/images/blank.gif" width=13
          style="visibility:hidden" alt="">
        </td>
      </tr>
    </table>
  </TD>
  <TD Class="ms-vb-user">
    <table cellpadding=0 cellspacing=0 dir="">
      <tr>
        <td style="padding-right: 3px;">
          <img title="" alt="No presence information" name="imnmark" border="0"
```

```
            valign="middle" height="12" width="12"
            src="/_layouts/images/blank.gif" >
          </td>
          <td style="padding: 1px 0px 0px 0px;" class="ms-vb">
            <A ONCLICK="GoToLink(this);return false;"
            HREF="/Docs/_layouts/userdisp.aspx?ID=1">
              WIN-WJFGDNNHDUS\Administrator
            </A>
          </td>
        </tr>
      </table>
    </TD>
    <TD Class="ms-vb2">Not Started</TD>
    <TD Class="ms-vb2">(2) Normal</TD>
    <TD Class="ms-vb2"><NOBR></NOBR></TD>
    <TD Class="ms-vb2"><DIV ALIGN=RIGHT></DIV></TD>
  </TR>
```

Next, you'll walk through the CAML rendering instructions contained within the <ViewBody> element as shown in Listing 3-17.

<ViewBody> first uses an <HTML> CAML element to render *<TR class="*:

```
    <HTML><![CDATA[<TR class="]]></HTML>
```

Next, it uses a <GetVar> element to render the value of the AlternateStyle variable, which is an empty string:

```
    <GetVar Name="AlternateStyle" />
```

Then, it uses an <HTML> CAML element to render ">:

```
    <HTML><![CDATA[">]]></HTML>
```

So far, the output HTML looks like this:

```
  <TR class="">
```

Next, <ViewBody> uses the <IfEqual>, <Then>, and <Else> elements to determine what to render next. These elements operate very similarly to the C# if, if else, and else constructs. Recall that these C# constructs use a branching condition. A branching condition in C# consists of two operands. The <Expr1> and <Expr2> sub-elements of the <IfEqual> element specify the left and right operands of the equality that the <IfEqual> element represents. The <Expr1> element uses a <GetVar> element to return the value of the AlternateStyle, which is an empty string, and uses this value as the left operand:

```
      <Expr1>
        <GetVar Name="AlternateStyle" />
      </Expr1>
```

The <Expr2> element uses ms-alternating as the right operand:

```
      <Expr2>ms-alternating</Expr2>
```

Because in this case the value of AlternateSyle, which is an empty string, is not equal to ms-alternating, <ViewBody> skips the execution of the <Then> element and executes the <Else> element. The <Else> element contains a <SetVar> element that sets the value of the AlternateStyle variable to ms-alternating value. Note that the Scope attribute on the <SetVar> element is set to Request to specify that the AlternateStyle variable is a global variable:

```
<Then>
  <SetVar Scope="Request" Name="AlternateStyle">
  </SetVar>
</Then>
<Else>
  <SetVar Scope="Request" Name="AlternateStyle">ms-alternating</SetVar>
</Else>
```

Next, <ViewBody> then uses the <Fields> element to iterate through the view fields. Note that the <Fields> element is equivalent to <ForEach Select="Fields/Field">. Recall that the view fields are specified within the <Fields> sub-element of the <View> element that represents the view (see Listing 3-15).

<ViewBody> takes these steps for each enumerated field. First, it uses an <HTML> CAML element to render *<TD Class="*:

```
<HTML><![CDATA[<TD Class="]]></HTML>
```

<ViewBody> then uses a <FieldSwitch> element to determine what to render next. The <FieldSwitch> element also operates very similarly to a C# switch. The <Expr> child element of the <FieldSwitch> element specifies the switching expression. In this case, this child element uses a <Property> element to return the value of the ClassInfo property of the enumerated field and uses this value as the switching expression.

As Listing 3-15 shows, the All Tasks view contains seven fields named Attachments, LinkTitle, AssignedTo, Status, Priority, DueDate, and PercentComplete. The value of the ClassInfo property of the LinkTitle field is Menu. The value of the ClassInfo property of other fields is neither Menu nor Icon. This means that the <Case Value="Menu"> element is executed in the case of the LinkTitle field and the <Default> is executed in the case of other fields. Next, you'll enumerate through these fields one by one to see what gets rendered into the output stream starting with the first field, Attachments.

Because the ClassInfo property of the Attachments field is neither Menu nor Icon, the <Default> sub-element of the <FieldSwitch> element gets executed:

```
<Default>
  <FieldSwitch>
    <Expr>
      <Property Select="Type" />
      <PresenceEnabled />
    </Expr>
    <Case Value="UserTRUE">ms-vb-user</Case>
    <Case Value="UserMultiTRUE">ms-vb-user</Case>
    <Default>ms-vb2</Default>
  </FieldSwitch>
</Default>
```

The <Default> element contains a <FieldSwitch> element. The <Expr> sub-element of this <FieldSwitch> element uses a concatenation of the value of the Type property of the Attachments field and the Boolean value that specifies whether the presence is enabled to determine which <Case> element to execute. In this case, this concatenation is neither UserTRUE nor UserMultiTRUE. This means that the <Default> element gets executed. This <Default> element simply returns ms-vb2. Therefore, the output HTML looks like this:

```
<TD Class="ms-vb2
```

As you can see from Listing 3-17, at this point the <FieldSwitch> element returns and the next CAML element, which is the following <HTML> element, is executed:

```
<HTML><![CDATA[">]]></HTML>
```

Therefore, the output HTML now looks like this:

```
<TD Class="ms-vb2">
```

Next, the following CAML element is executed:

```
    <Field />
```

This element returns the formatted value of the Attachments field. This formatted value in this case is an empty string. Next, the following CAML element is executed:

```
    <HTML><![CDATA[</TD>]]></HTML>
```

Therefore, the output HTML now looks like this:

```
<TD Class="ms-vb2"></TD>
```

So far, you've seen how the CAML-rendering instructions render the Attachments field. Next, you see how it renders the LinkTitle field. This means that the next iteration of the <Fields> element is now executed. Recall that the <Fields> element is equivalent to the <ForEach Select="Fields/Field"> element.

```
  <Fields>
    <HTML><![CDATA[<TD Class="]]></HTML>
    <FieldSwitch>
      <Expr>
        <Property Select="ClassInfo" />
      </Expr>
      <Case Value="Menu">
        <HTML><![CDATA[ms-vb-title" height="100%]]></HTML>
      </Case>
      <Case Value="Icon">ms-vb-icon</Case>
      <Default>
        <FieldSwitch>
          <Expr>
            <Property Select="Type" />
            <PresenceEnabled />
          </Expr>
          <Case Value="UserTRUE">ms-vb-user</Case>
```

(continued)

(continued)

```
            <Case Value="UserMultiTRUE">ms-vb-user</Case>
            <Default>ms-vb2</Default>
          </FieldSwitch>
        </Default>
      </FieldSwitch>
      <HTML><![CDATA[">]]></HTML>
      <Field />
      <HTML><![CDATA[</TD>]]></HTML>
    </Fields>
```

The next iteration starts all over again by executing the following <HTML> CAML element:

```
<HTML><![CDATA[<TD Class="]]></HTML>
```

Therefore, the output HTML now looks like this:

```
<TD Class="ms-vb2"></TD>
<TD Class="
```

Next, the <FieldSwitch> element is executed. Because the ClassInfo property of the LinkTitle field is Menu, the following <Case> element is executed:

```
      <Case Value="Menu">
        <HTML><![CDATA[ms-vb-title" height="100%]]></HTML>
      </Case>
```

As a result, the output HTML is now:

```
<TD Class="ms-vb2"></TD>
<TD Class="ms-vb-title" height="100%
```

At this point, the <FieldSwitch> element returns and the following <HTML> element is executed:

```
<HTML><![CDATA[">]]></HTML>
```

As a result, the output HTML becomes:

```
<TD Class="ms-vb2"></TD>
<TD Class="ms-vb-title" height="100%">
```

Next, the <Field> element executes:

```
    <Field />
```

This element simply returns the formatted value of the LinkTitle field, which is:

```
  <table height="100%" cellspacing=0 class="ms-unselectedtitle"
    onmouseover="OnItem(this)" CTXName="ctx1" Id="1"
    Url="/Docs/Lists/Tasks1/1_.000"
    DRef="Docs/Lists/Tasks1"
    Perm="0x7fffffffffffff" Type="" Ext=""
```

```
      Icon="icgen.gif||" OType="0" COUId="" HCD="" CSrc="" MS="0" CType="Task"
      CId="0x010800A484B5FA8C591C4484B0561226210922" UIS="512" SUrl="">
        <tr>
          <td width="100%" Class="ms-vb">
            <a onfocus="OnLink(this)"
            href="/Docs/Lists/Tasks1/DispForm.aspx?ID=1"
            ONCLICK="GoToLink(this);return false;" target="_self">
              Do something
              <img src="/_layouts/images/blank.gif" class="ms-hidden" border=0
              width=1 height=1 alt="Use SHIFT+ENTER to open the menu (new window).">
            </a>
            <IMG SRC="/_layouts/1033/images/new.gif" alt="New">
          </td>
          <td>
            <img src="/_layouts/images/blank.gif" width=13
            style="visibility:hidden" alt="">
          </td>
        </tr>
      </table>
```

Therefore, the output HTML now becomes:

```
    <TD Class="ms-vb2"></TD>
    <TD Class="ms-vb-title" height="100%">
      <table height="100%" cellspacing=0 class="ms-unselectedtitle"
      onmouseover="OnItem(this)" CTXName="ctx1" Id="1"
      Url="/Docs/Lists/Tasks1/1_.000"
      DRef="Docs/Lists/Tasks1"
      Perm="0x7fffffffffffffff" Type="" Ext=""
      Icon="icgen.gif||" OType="0" COUId="" HCD="" CSrc="" MS="0" CType="Task"
      CId="0x010800A484B5FA8C591C4484B0561226210922" UIS="512" SUrl="">
        <tr>
          <td width="100%" Class="ms-vb">
            <a onfocus="OnLink(this)"
            href="/Docs/Lists/Tasks1/DispForm.aspx?ID=1"
            ONCLICK="GoToLink(this);return false;" target="_self">
              Do something
              <img src="/_layouts/images/blank.gif" class="ms-hidden" border=0
              width=1 height=1 alt="Use SHIFT+ENTER to open the menu (new window).">
            </a>
            <IMG SRC="/_layouts/1033/images/new.gif" alt="New">
          </td>
          <td>
            <img src="/_layouts/images/blank.gif" width=13
            style="visibility:hidden" alt="">
          </td>
        </tr>
      </table>
```

Next, the following <HTML> element is executed, which simply adds the </TD> to the end of the previous listing:

```
      <HTML><![CDATA[</TD>]]></HTML>
```

This wraps up the second iteration of the <Fields> element. If you follow the same arguments for the other iterations of this element, you'll arrive at the output HTML shown in Listing 3-18.

List Provisioning

The previous section showed you how to implement and add a list type to SharePoint. Recall that you created a class library in Visual Studio that contains everything needed to implement and to deploy your Tasks1 custom list type. Go ahead and build this Class Library project. Thanks to the postbuild event that you added earlier on, this will automatically execute the mybatchfile.bat batch file, which in turn will deploy your Tasks1 custom list type to SharePoint.

This section shows you how to provision a list instance from a list type such as your Tasks1 custom list type. In general, there are three ways to provision a list instance from a list type:

1. Graphical via SharePoint user interface
2. Declarative via SharePoint feature
3. Imperative via SharePoint object model

Graphical List Provisioning

To use the SharePoint user interface to provision a list instance from a list type, navigate to the /_layouts/create.aspx application page and select the desired list type. Figure 3-14 uses your Tasks1 list type under the Custom Lists group to provision a list instance.

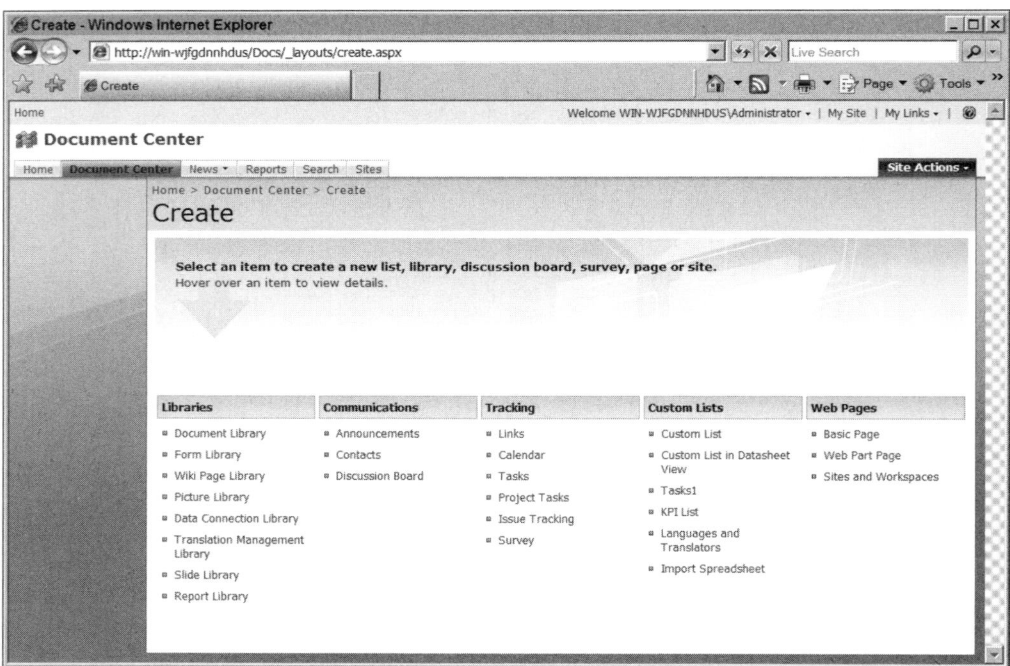

Figure 3-14: The create.aspx page

Click the Tasks1 list type to navigate to the /_layouts/new.aspx application page shown in Figure 3-15. Enter a name and a description for the list instance and use the Yes and No toggles to specify whether a link to this list instance appears in the Quick Launch bar.

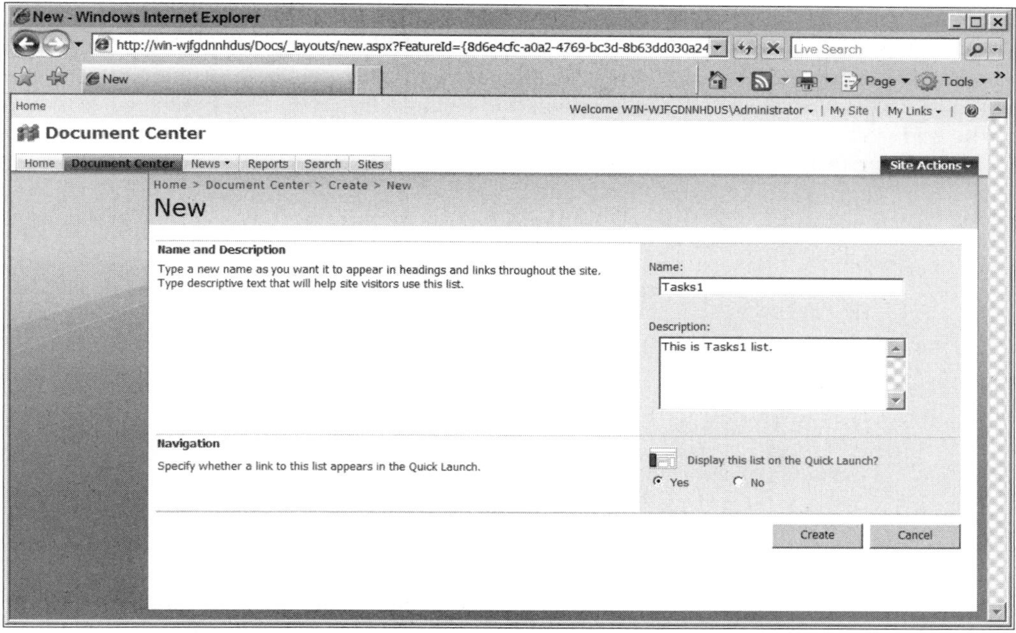

Figure 3-15: The new.aspx page

Next, click the Create button. This will take you the /Lists/Tasks1/AllItems.aspx page shown in Figure 3-16.

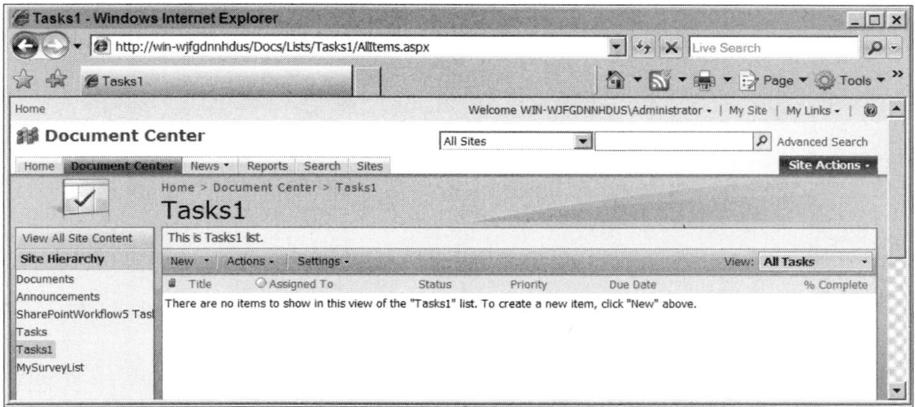

Figure 3-16: The AllItems.aspx page

Declarative List Provisioning

The previous section showed you how to use the SharePoint user interface to provision a list from a list type. This section shows you how to use CAML to provision a list from a list type. You must then use a SharePoint feature to deploy your CAML-based list to SharePoint.

Listing 3-19 presents a CAML-based element manifest file named Tasks1ListInstance.xml that contains the CAML instructions for provisioning a list instance from Tasks1 list type.

Listing 3-19: The Tasks1ListInstance.xml file

```
<?xml version="1.0" encoding="utf-8" ?>
<Elements
xmlsn="http://schemas.microsoft.com/sharepoint/">
  <ListInstance
  Description="This is an instance of Tasks1 list type!"
  FeatureId="{8D6E4CFC-A0A2-4769-BC3D-8B63DD030A24}"
  Id="1"
  OnQuickLaunch="True"
  RootWebOnly="False"
  TemplateType="10010"
  Title="Tasks1"
  Url="Lists/Tasks1">
    <Data>
      <Rows>
        <Row>
          <Field Name="Title">Do something else!</Field>
          <Field Name="Status">Not Started</Field>
          <Field Name="Priority">Normal</Field>
        </Row>
      </Rows>
    </Data>
  </ListInstance>
</Elements>
```

You must use the <ListInstance> CAML element to provision a list from a list type. This element supports the following attributes:

- **Description.** Use this optional attribute to provide a short description for the list instance.
- **FeatureId.** Use this attribute to specify the Id attribute value of the SharePoint feature that references the element manifest file that defines the list template from which this list instance is being provisioned. If you don't specify a value for this attribute, SharePoint assumes that the feature that contains this list instance also contains the list type.
- **Id.** Use this required attribute to specify an integer identifier to uniquely identify this list instance from others in the same the feature.
- **OnQuickLaunch.** Use this optional Boolean attribute to specify whether to add a link to the Quick Launch bar.
- **RootWebOnly.** Use this optional Boolean attribute to specify whether the list instance can be provisioned within the top-level site of a site collection.

- **TemplateType.** Use this required integer attribute to specify the Type attribute value of the <ListTemplate> element that defines the list template from which this list instance is being provisioned.
- **Title**. Use this required attribute to specify the title of the list instance.
- **URL**. Use this required attribute to specify a site-relative URL for this list instance. This is normally a forward slash — separated list of two substrings where the first substring is Lists and the second substring is the value of the Title attribute.

The <ListInstance> element supports a single element named <Data> where you can specify default rows for the list instance. The <Data> element supports a single element named <Rows>. You must use a separate <Row> element within the <Rows> element to specify each default data row. You must also use a separate <Field> element within the <Row> element for each required field to specify the value of each field. The <Field> element supports an attribute named Name that you must set to the name of the field whose value is being set.

```
<Row>
  <Field Name="Title">Do something else!</Field>
  <Field Name="Status">Not Started</Field>
  <Field Name="Priority">Normal</Field>
</Row>
```

Listing 3-20 presents the feature that references the Tasks1ListInstance.xml element manifest file.

Listing 3-20: The feature that references the MyTasksListInstance.xml element manifest

```
<?xml version="1.0" encoding="utf-8" ?>
<Feature xmlns="http://schemas.microsoft.com/sharepoint/"
 Id="{706DC585-A073-494f-A842-67CD174AA759}"
 Description="This feature contains Tasks1 list type!"
 Hidden="False"
 Scope="Web"
 Title="Tasks1 list type feature"
 Version="1.0.0.0">
  <ElementManifests>
    <ElementManifest Location="ListTemplates\Tasks1.xml"/>
    <ElementManifest Location="Tasks1ListInstance.xml"/>
  </ElementManifests>
</Feature>
```

Note that in this case both the Tasks1.xml element manifest, which contains that definition of the Tasks list template, and Tasks1ListInstance.xml element manifest, which contains the list provisioning CAML instructions, are deployed through the same feature. As such, you don't have to specify the value of the FeatureId attribute on the <ListInstance> element.

If you deploy this feature and activate it in a site, the feature will automatically provision a list instance from the list type, add the specified data row to the list instance, and add a link to the Quick Launch bar.

Imperative List Provisioning

The previous two sections showed you how to use the SharePoint user interface to provision a list from a list type and how to add rows to the list in graphical fashion, and how to use CAML to provision a list from a list type and how to add rows to the list in declarative fashion. This section shows you how to use the SharePoint object model to provision a list from a list type and how to add rows to the list in imperative fashion.

In general, there are three main ways to use SharePoint object model:

- Implement a SharePoint component such as a WebPart control, application page, site page, or similar that runs within SharePoint. Such components can directly access the SharePoint object model.
- Implement a web, Windows, or console application that runs locally on the server where SharePoint is running. Such applications can also directly access the SharePoint object model.
- Implement a client web service such as a web, Windows, or console application that runs on a remote machine where SharePoint is not installed and uses SharePoint web services to indirectly use the SharePoint object model.

You have seen examples of the first two approaches in Chapters 1 and 2. In this section, you use the third approach to access the SharePoint object model indirectly to provision a list instance from the Tasks list type and to add a row to this list instance.

Launch Visual Studio and create a new ASP.NET web site named WebSite. Right-click the WebSite project in the Solution Explorer and select Add Web Reference from the pop-up menu as shown in Figure 3-17.

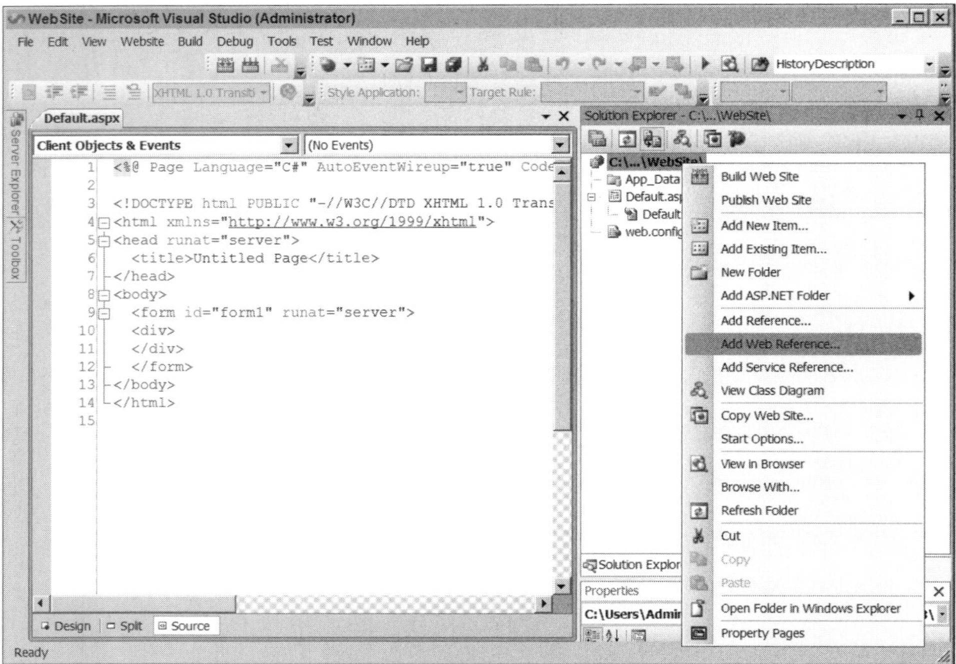

Figure 3-17: Adding a Web Reference

This will pop up the Add Web Reference dialog shown in Figure 3-18.

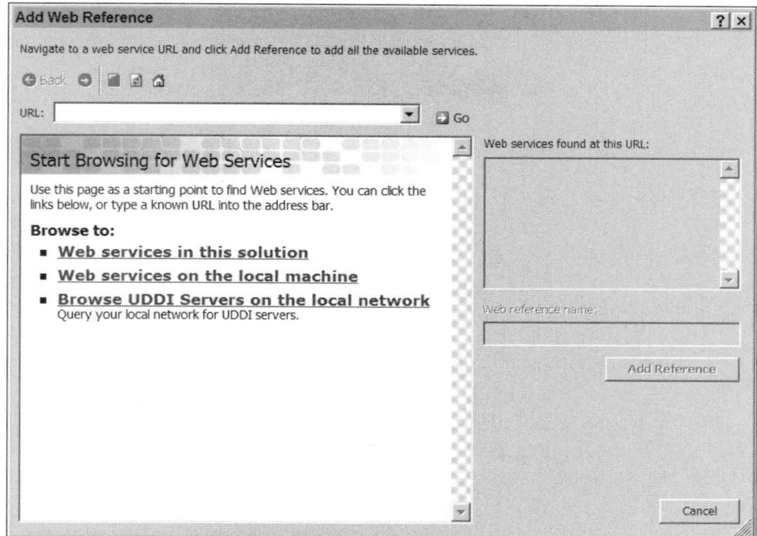

Figure 3-18: The Add Web Reference dialog box

All SharePoint services are located in the _vti_bin virtual directory. When SharePoint is taking an IIS web site through a one-time transformation process to transform it into a SharePoint web application, it adds the _vti_bin virtual directory to the IIS web site as shown in the highlighted portion of Figure 3-19. This figure is a snapshot of the IIS Manager.

If you're running SharePoint on a Windows 2003 server, you have access to a version of the IIS Manager that is different from the one shown in Figure 3-19.

Figure 3-19: The IIS Manager displaying the _vti_bin virtual directory

Click the Basic Settings link on the Actions pane in Figure 3-19 to launch the Edit Virtual Directory dialog shown in Figure 3-20.

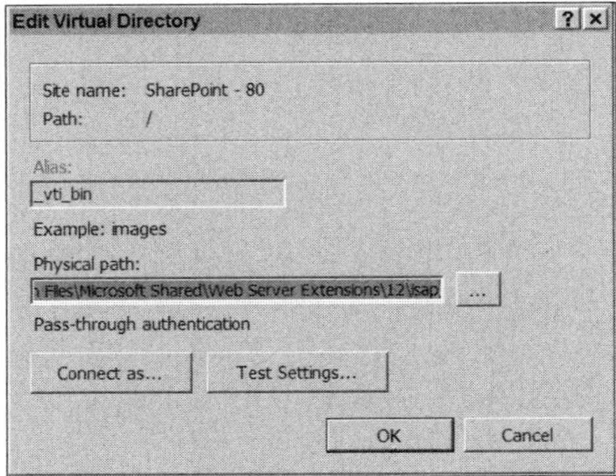

Figure 3-20: The Edit Virtual Directory dialog

As you can see from this figure, SharePoint has mapped the following physical path on the file system of the front-end web server to the _vti_bin virtual directory:

```
Local_Drive:\Program Files\Common Files\Microsoft Shared\Web Server Extensions\12\
isapi
```

In other words, SharePoint web services are placed in the preceding physical folder, which is mapped to the _vti_bin virtual directory. This enables you to use the following virtual path to access any SharePoint web service:

```
http://DomainOrServer/SitePath/_vti_bin/WebServiceName.asmx
```

The DomainOrServer is the name of the server where SharePoint is running. SitePath is the virtual path of the SharePoint site. The WebServiceName is the name of the SharePoint Web service. In your case, you need to use a SharePoint web service named Lists.asmx.

Next, you need to enter the virtual path of the WSDL document that describes the SharePoint web service in the URL textbox in Figure 3-18. This virtual path is normally as follows:

```
http://DomainOrServer/SitePath/_vti_bin/WebServiceName.asmx?wsdl
```

In your case, you're interested in the Lists.asmx web service. Enter the following virtual path in the URL textbox in Figure 3-17:

```
http://DomainOrServer/SitePath/_vti_bin/Lists.asmx?wsdl
```

Don't forget to replace DomainOrServer and SitePath with the appropriate values. This should activate the Add Reference button as shown in Figure 3-21.

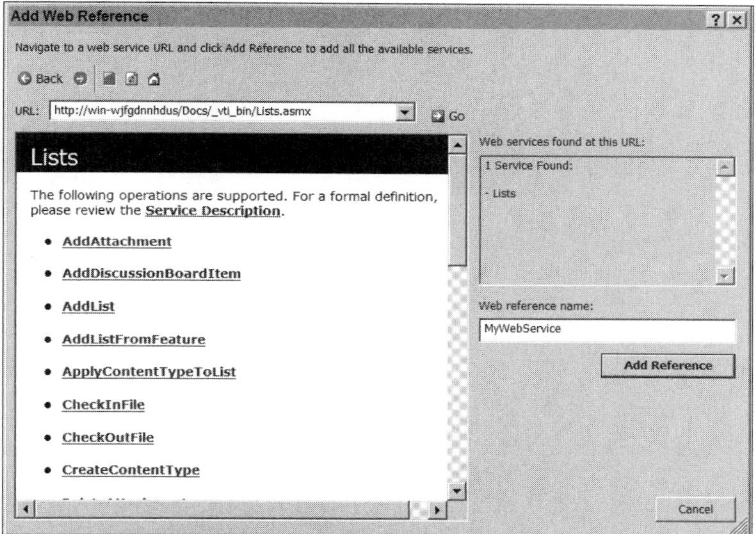

Figure 3-21: The Add Web Reference dialog displaying the web service

Enter MyWebService as the web reference name and click Add Reference. This will automatically:

1. Download the WSDL document that describes the Lists.asmx web service.
2. Parse the WSDL document and generate the code for a proxy class named Lists. The value that you entered into the web reference name, that is, MyWebService, is automatically used as the namespace of this proxy class.
3. Compile this code into an assembly.
4. Add the assembly to the web site project.

To use this SharePoint web service, first you need to instantiate an instance of the MyWebService.Lists proxy class. Next, you need to invoke the appropriate method of this instance. That's all!

Listing 3-21 presents the content of the web page that uses the Lists.asmx SharePoint web service to provision a list instance from the Tasks1 list type.

Listing 3-21: A web page that uses the Lists.asmx web service to provision a list from the Tasks1 list type

```
<%@ Page Language="C#" %>

<!DOCTYPE html PUBLIC "-//W3C//DTD XHTML 1.0 Transitional//EN"
"http://www.w3.org/TR/xhtml1/DTD/xhtml1-transitional.dtd">
<script runat="server">
  void Page_Load(object sender, EventArgs e)
  {
    MyWebService.Lists lists = new MyWebService.Lists();
    lists.Credentials = System.Net.CredentialCache.DefaultCredentials;
    Guid featureGuid = new Guid("{706DC585-A073-494f-A842-67CD174AA759}");
    lists.AddListFromFeature("Tasks2",
                         "This is Tasks2 list instance!", featureGuid, 10010);
  }
</script>

<html xmlns="http://www.w3.org/1999/xhtml">
<head runat="server">
  <title>Untitled Page</title>
</head>
<body>
  <form id="form1" runat="server">
  <div>
  </div>
  </form>
</body>
</html>
```

Follow these steps to use the Lists.asmx web service to provision a list from a list type:

1. Instantiate an instance of the proxy class:

```
MyWebService.Lists lists = new MyWebService.Lists();
```

Set the Credentials property on the proxy instance:

```
lists.Credentials = System.Net.CredentialCache.DefaultCredentials;
```

You must set the Credentials property to the ICredential object that contains the credentials of the user making the call to the web service. The CredentialCache class exposes a static property named DefaultCredentials that references an ICredential object that contains the system credentials for the security context in which the application is running. Because an ASP.NET web application such as the one you're using uses Windows credentials by default, this ICredential object contains the Windows credentials of the user running this application. Keep in mind that the DefaultCredentials is only applicable to NTLM, negotiate, and Kerberos-based authentication.

3. Create a GUID that represents the GUID of the feature that contains your Tasks1 list type. You can copy and paste this GUID from Listing 3-21:

```
Guid featureGuid = new Guid("{706DC585-A073-494f-A842-67CD174AA759}");
```

4. Invoke the AddListFromFeature method on the proxy instance:

```
lists.AddListFromFeature("Tasks2",
                         "This is Tasks2 list instance!", featureGuid, 10010);
```

Here is the declaration of this method:

```
public XmlNode AddListFromFeature ( string listName, string description,
                                    Guid featureID, int templateID)
```

As you can see, this method takes four parameters as follows:

- **listName.** Use this parameter to specify a name for the list instance being provisioned.
- **description.** Use this parameter to specify a short description for the list instance you're provisioning.
- **featureID.** Use this parameter to pass the GUID that uniquely identifies the SharePoint feature that contains the list type from which the list instance is being provisioned.
- **templateID.** Use this parameter to specify the integer ID that uniquely identifies the list type from which the list instance is being provisioned.

Custom List Item Forms

As discussed earlier, the <List> element that defines the schema of a list type supports a child element named <MetaData>, which in turn supports a child element named <Forms>, which in turn supports one or more child elements named <Form>. Each <Form> child element represents a specific type of form. There are in general three types of forms known as display list item form, edit list item form, and new list item form. As discussed earlier, the Type attribute on a <Form> element specifies the type of form the element represents.

A <Form> element tells SharePoint to provision a form of the type specified in the Type attribute with the URL specified in the Url attribute from the page template specified in the SetupPath attribute and to provision a ListFormWebPart Web part into the WebPartZone Web part zone specified in the WebPartZoneID attribute located inside the provisioned form. As discussed earlier, this ListFormWebPart Web part uses a form template to render the body of the provisioned form.

For example, the standard SharePoint Tasks list type definition contains three <Form> elements as follows:

```
<List Title="Tasks1" Url="Lists/Tasks1" ...>
  <MetaData>
    <Forms>
      <Form Type="DisplayForm" Url="DispForm.aspx" SetupPath="pages\form.aspx"
      WebPartZoneID="Main" />
      <Form Type="EditForm" Url="EditForm.aspx" SetupPath="pages\form.aspx"
      WebPartZoneID="Main" />
      <Form Type="NewForm" Url="NewForm.aspx" SetupPath="pages\form.aspx"
      WebPartZoneID="Main" />
    </Forms>
  </MetaData>
</List>
```

The first <Form> element instructs SharePoint to provision a form of the DisplayForm type with the DispForm.aspx URL from the form.aspx page template located in the pages subfolder of the TEMPLATE folder and to provision a ListFormWebPart Web part into the WebPartZone Web part with the ID attribute value of Main inside this provisioned DispForm.aspx site page.

Follow these steps to add support for a custom display list item form, edit list item form, or new list item form for a custom list type:

1. Implement a custom page template.
2. Create a subfolder under the TEMPLATE folder in the file system of the front-end web server.
3. Copy the custom page template from Step 1 into the subfolder from Step 2.
4. Add a <Form> child element to the <Forms> child element of the <MetaData> element of the <List> element that defines the schema of the custom list type.
5. Set the Type attribute on the <Form> element from Step 4 to DisplayForm to provision a display list item form, to EditForm to provision an edit list item form, or to NewForm to provision a new list item form.
6. Set the SetupPath attribute to the name of the subfolder from Step 2 followed by a backward slash (\) followed by the name of the custom page template file.
7. Set the Url attribute to the name of the form being provisioned.
8. Set the WebPartZoneID attribute to the ID attribute of the WebPartZone Web part zone in the provisioned form where you want SharePoint to provision a ListViewWebPart Web part.

The previous sections implemented a list type named Tasks1, which duplicates the standard SharePoint Tasks list type. As an example, go ahead and create a new folder named pages1 under the TEMPLATE folder and copy the forms.aspx page template from the pages folder to the pages1 folder. Then rename this page template to forms1.aspx. Next, go ahead and modify the <Form> elements in the Tasks1 list type definition as follows:

```
<List Title="Tasks1" Url="Lists/Tasks1" ...>
  <MetaData>
    <Forms>
      <Form Type="DisplayForm" Url="DispForm1.aspx" SetupPath="pages1\form1.aspx"
      WebPartZoneID="Main" />
      <Form Type="EditForm" Url="EditForm1.aspx" SetupPath="pages1\form1.aspx"
      WebPartZoneID="Main" />
      <Form Type="NewForm" Url="NewForm1.aspx" SetupPath="pages1\form1.aspx"
      WebPartZoneID="Main" />
    </Forms>
  </MetaData>
</List>
```

Now, if you select the View Item or Edit Item from the ECB menu of a list item in a list provisioned from the Tasks1 list type or New Item from the menu bar of a list view page such as AllItems.aspx that displays a list provisioned from this list type, SharePoint will take you to the DispForm1.aspx, EditForm1.aspx, or NewForm1.aspx page instead of the standard DispForm.aspx, EditForm.aspx, or NewForm.aspx pages.

Summary

Collaborative content management in SharePoint is achieved through an extensible flexible data model based on abstractions such as site collections, sites, lists, list items, content types, and so on. Users work with these abstractions through SharePoint forms infrastructure. This chapter began by presenting an introduction to SharePoint collaborative content management and forms infrastructure. It then dove into list types, views, and list instances, which are some of the most important data model abstractions in SharePoint. You learned how each view of a list type contains the CAML rendering instructions that are used in list view pages such as AllItems.aspx to render the view.

Chapter 4 covers more of these data model abstractions and you'll also learn how the SharePoint forms infrastructure manages to render these abstractions in the SharePoint user interface.

Form-Rendering Controls

As discussed in the previous chapter, SharePoint virtualizes the underlying IIS and ASP.NET infrastructures, enabling you to manage and organize your collaborative content in terms of abstractions such as site collections, sites, lists, list items, content types, site columns, field types, and so on. Users work with these SharePoint abstractions through SharePoint forms infrastructure. Form-rendering server controls form a major portion of the SharePoint forms infrastructure. This chapter provides an in-depth coverage of these server controls.

SharePoint Rendering Server Controls

Figure 4-1 presents the class hierarchy of the SharePoint forms infrastructure. The following sections discuss some of the main classes of this diagram.

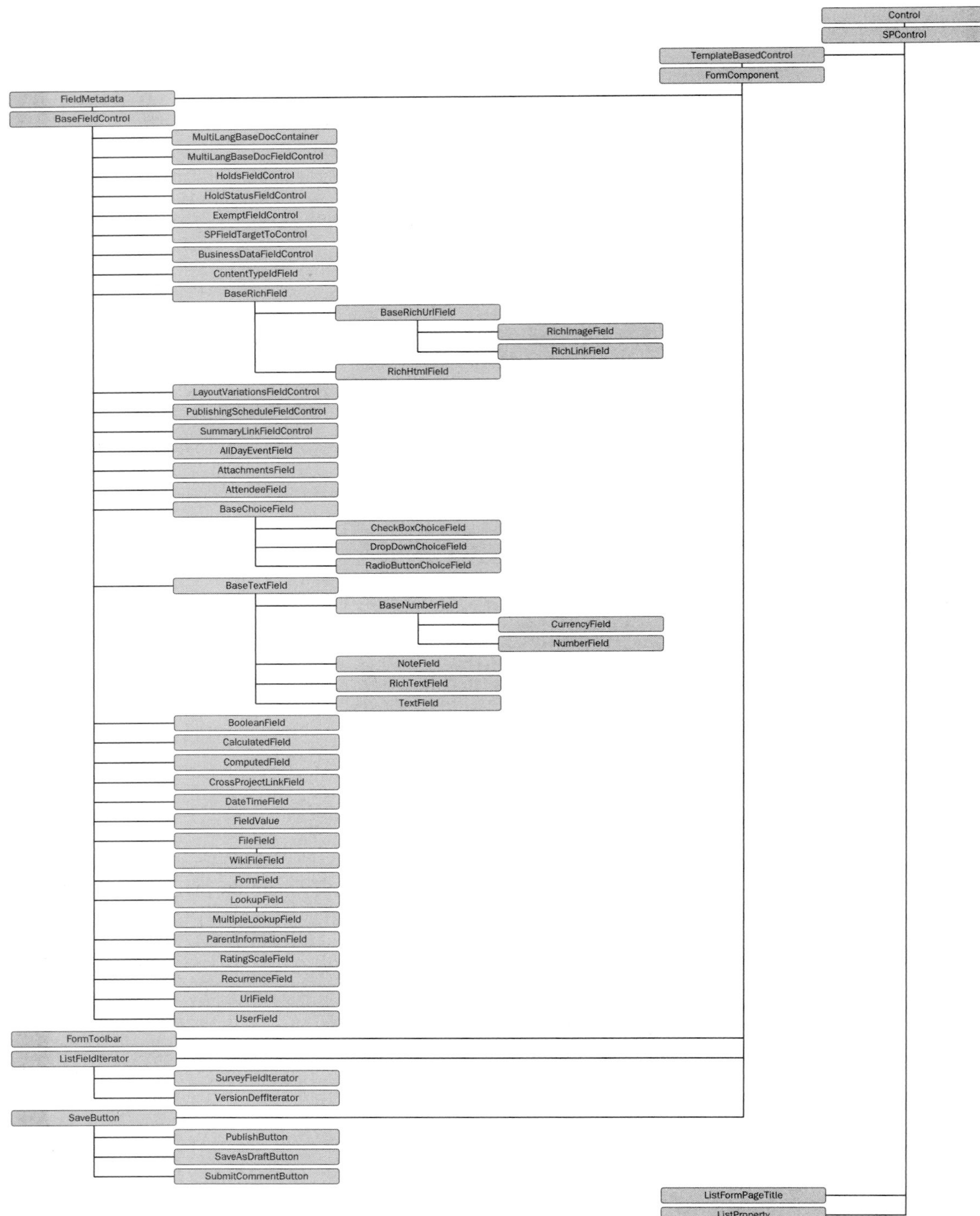

Figure 4-1: The class hierarchy of the SharePoint forms infrastructure

SPControl

As you can see from Figure 4-1, SPControl inherits from the ASP.NET Control base class and extends its functionality to provide methods for getting and setting the SharePoint context in which the server control is rendered. This SharePoint context includes the site collection, site, and web application wherein an HTTP request is processed.

Listing 4-1 presents some of the main members of SPControl class.

Listing 4-1: Some of the main members of SPControl

```
public class SPControl : Control, IDesignTimeHtmlProvider, IDesignerEventAccessor
{
  public static SPSite GetContextSite(HttpContext context);
  public static SPWeb GetContextWeb(HttpContext context);
  public static SPWebApplication GetContextWebApplication(HttpContext context);

  public Uri PageUri { get; set; }
}
```

Here is the description of some of the members of SPControl:

- **GetContextSite.** This static method takes an HttpContext object representing an HTTP request and returns an SPSite object that represents the site collection where the request is being processed.
- **GetContextWeb.** This static method takes an HttpContext object that represents an HTTP request and returns an SPWeb object that represents the site where the request is being processed.
- **GetContextWebApplication.** This static method takes an HttpContext object that represents an HTTP request and returns an SPWebApplication that represents the web application where the request is being processed.
- **PageUri.** This gets or sets the Uri object that represents the URI of the page that contains the SPControl server control where the request is being processed.

Because the GetContextSite, GetContextWeb, and GetContextWebApplication methods take an HttpContext object as their arguments, these methods can only be used within the managed code running within a MOSS or WSS context. For example, you can use these methods in a WebPart server control and an application page. The following code snippet shows how to use these methods:

```
SPSite siteCollection = SPControl.GetContextSite(HttpContext.Current);
SPWeb site = SPControl.GetContextWeb(HttpContext.Current);
SPWebApplication webApplication =
                              SPControl.GetContextWebApplication(HttpContext.Current);
```

ListFormPageTitle

Recall from the previous chapter that the form.aspx page template, from which the standard SharePoint display list item site page (DispForm.aspx), edit list item site page (EditForm.aspx), and new list item site page (NewForm.aspx) are provisioned includes the following <asp:Content> tag. This tag contains a ListFormPageTitle server control that provides the content for the PlaceHolderPageTitle content placeholder declared within the default.master page:

```
<asp:Content ContentPlaceHolderID="PlaceHolderPageTitle" runat="server">
  <SharePoint:ListFormPageTitle runat="server" />
</asp:Content>
```

As the following excerpt from the default.master page shows, the PlaceHolderPageTitle content placeholder is located within the <Title> element:

```
<Title ID=onetidTitle>
  <asp:ContentPlaceHolder id=PlaceHolderPageTitle runat="server"/>
</Title>
```

As such, the ListFormPageTitle server control renders the page title, which is the string that goes within the opening and closing tags of the <Title> element. This string is what is shown to end users when they try to bookmark the display, edit, or new list item forms. As Listing 4-2 shows, the ListFormPageTitle server control, like many other SharePoint server controls, is aware of the SharePoint contextual information such as the current list and its title. The rendering logic within the Render method of the ListFormPageTitle server control renders the title of the list as the page title.

Listing 4-2: The internal implementation of the ListFormPageTitle server control

```
public sealed class ListFormPageTitle : SPControl
{
  [SharePointPermission(SecurityAction.Demand, ObjectModel = true)]
  protected override void Render(HtmlTextWriter output)
  {
    SPFormContext formContext = SPContext.Current.FormContext;
    SPList list = SPContext.Current.List;

    if ((formContext == null) || (list == null))
      return;

    output.Write(SPHttpUtility.HtmlEncode(list.Title));
    if (formContext.FormMode == SPControlMode.New)
    {
      output.Write(" - ");
      output.Write(SPHttpUtility.HtmlEncode(
                    SPResource.GetString("NewFormTitleNewItem", new object[0])));
      return;
    }

    SPListItem listItem = SPContext.Current.ListItem;
    if (listItem == null)
      return;

    if (list.AllowContentTypes &&
```

```
          listItem.ContentTypeId.IsChildOf(SPBuiltInContentTypeId.Link))
        {
          string url = (string)listItem.GetValue("URL", false);
          string str = string.Empty;
          if (!string.IsNullOrEmpty(url))
          {
            int i = url.IndexOf(',');
            if (i > -1)
            {
              if (i < (url.Length - 1))
                str = url.Substring(i + 1);
            }
          }
          if (!string.IsNullOrEmpty(str))
          {
            output.Write(" - ");
            output.Write(SPHttpUtility.HtmlEncode(
                                        SPUtility.SummarizeText(str, 40)));
          }
        }
        else if (list.BaseType != SPBaseType.DocumentLibrary)
        {
          output.Write(" - ");
          output.Write(SPHttpUtility.HtmlEncode(
                                        SPUtility.SummarizeText(listItem.Title, 40)));
        }
        else if ((list.BaseTemplate != SPListTemplateType.WebPageLibrary) &&
                 (list.BaseTemplate != SPListTemplateType.PictureLibrary))
        {
          output.Write(" - ");
          output.Write(SPHttpUtility.HtmlEncode(
                                        SPUtility.SummarizeText(listItem.Name, 40)));
        }
      }
    }
```

Next, you'll walk through the implementation of the Render method to see how ListFormPageTitle renders the page title. The implementation of this method reveals one of the main differences between SharePoint server controls and regular ASP.NET server controls, which is that SharePoint server controls are rendered within a specific SharePoint context. This enables a SharePoint server control to access SharePoint contextual information such as current web application, site collection, site, list, list item, and so on. This type of contextual information is not available to regular ASP.NET server controls. As the internal implementation of ListFormPageTitle shows, a SharePoint server control can use this SharePoint contextual information in its rendering logic.

The Render method first accesses the SPFormContext object representing the form context that ListFormPageTitle server control is rendered in:

```
SPFormContext formContext = SPContext.Current.FormContext;
```

At this point it accesses the SPList object that represents the current SharePoint list. Keep in mind that ListFormPageTitle is normally used within a display, edit, or new list item form, which then displays, edits, or creates a new list item in a SharePoint list. The SPList object represents this SharePoint list:

```
SPList list = SPContext.Current.List;
```

Next, the Render method renders the title of the current list:

```
output.Write(SPHttpUtility.HtmlEncode(list.Title));
```

At this point, the Render method determines whether the current form is a new list item form (New mode). It does this by using the value of the FormMode enumeration property of the SPFormContext object representing the form context within which the ListFormPageTitle server control is rendered. If so, it first renders the " - " string and then pulls the localized value for the "NewFormTitleNewItem" resource key for the current culture from the resource file and renders this value:

```
output.Write(" - ");
        output.Write(SPHttpUtility.HtmlEncode(
                      SPResource.GetString("NewFormTitleNewItem", new object[0])));
```

If the current form is in the Display mode, meaning if the current form is a display list item form, the Render method takes these steps to retrieve and to render the list item title. First it accesses the SPListItem object that represents the current list item. The display list item then displays:

```
SPListItem listItem = SPContext.Current.ListItem;
```

Next, the Render method uses the AllowContentTypes property of the SPList object representing the current list to determine whether the user has enabled content types on the current list. As you can see, a SharePoint server control has access to detailed information, such as whether the user has enabled content types on the current list. Access to such SharePoint contextual information enables you to develop pretty powerful server controls in SharePoint, which cannot be developed in ASP.NET.

The SPListItem object that represents the current list item exposes a property of the ContentTypeId type named ContentTypeId, which returns a reference to a ContentTypeId object representing the content type ID of the current list item. The Render method invokes the IsChildOf method on this ContentTypeId object to determine whether the content type of the current list item inherits from the Link content type.

If the content types are enabled on the current list and if the content type of the current list item inherits from the Link content type, the Render method performs these tasks:

- Accesses the value of the URL field, which is a comma-separated list of strings:

```
string url = (string)listItem.GetValue("URL", false);
```

- Extracts these strings and concatenates them into a single string:

```
string str = null;
if (!string.IsNullOrEmpty(url))
{
  int i = url.IndexOf(',');
  if (i > -1)
```

```
            {
              if (i < (url.Length - 1))
                str = url.Substring(i + 1);
            }
          }
```

- Renders the string " - " followed by this single string:

```
output.Write(" - ");
output.Write(SPHttpUtility.HtmlEncode(SPUtility.SummarizeText(str, 40)));
```

If the content types are not enabled or if the current list item is not of the Link content type, the Render method determines whether the current list is a document library. If not, that is, if the current list is a standard SharePoint list, it first renders the string " - " and then renders the title of the current list item:

```
output.Write(" - ");
output.Write(SPHttpUtility.HtmlEncode(
                                 SPUtility.SummarizeText(listItem.Title, 40)));
```

If the current list is indeed a document library, the Render method checks whether it is a web page library or a picture library. If so, it first renders the string " - " and then pulls the localized value of the name of the current list item from the resources file and renders it:

```
output.Write(" - ");
output.Write(SPHttpUtility.HtmlEncode(
                                      SPUtility.SummarizeText(listItem.Name, 40)));
```

ListProperty

Recall from Chapter 3 that form.aspx uses the following <asp:Content> tag to provide content for a content placeholder named PlaceHolderPageTitleInTitleArea:

```
<asp:Content ContentPlaceHolderID="PlaceHolderPageTitleInTitleArea" runat="server">
  <SharePoint:ListProperty Property="LinkTitle" runat="server" ID="ID_LinkTitle" />
  :
  <SharePoint:ListItemProperty ID="ID_ItemProperty" MaxLength="40"
  runat="server" />
</asp:Content>
```

This <asp:Content> tag renders the text that goes into the title area of form.aspx. As you can see, this Content server control contains a ListProperty and a ListItemProperty server control, which render the name of the current list and the title of the current list item, respectively.

The following code listing presents the internal implementation of the ListProperty server control, which inherits from the SPControl base class:

```
public class ListProperty : SPControl
{
  private string cssClass;
  private string list;
  private string property;

  protected override void Render(HtmlTextWriter writer)
  {
    if (this.Context == null)
      return;

    SPWeb site = SPControl.GetContextWeb(this.Context);
    SPRequest request = site.Request;
    SPList list = SPContext.Current.List;
    string listProperty;

    if (((this.List == null) && (list != null)) &&
         (( listProperty = this.Property) != null))
    {
      if (listProperty == "Title")
      {
        if (!string.IsNullOrEmpty(list.Title))
          this.RenderValue(writer, SPHttpUtility.HtmlEncode(list.Title));
        return;
      }

      if (listProperty == "Description")
      {
        if (!string.IsNullOrEmpty(list.Description))
          this.RenderValue(writer, SPHttpUtility.NoEncode(
                      SPUtility.AutoHyperLinking(site, list.Description)));
        return;
      }
    }

    if (this.Property == "RelativeFolderPath")
    {
      string rootFolder = this.Context.Request.QueryString["RootFolder"];
      rootFolder = site.MeetingInformation.GetListViewRootFolder(this.List,
                                                           rootFolder, null);
      if (string.IsNullOrEmpty(rootFolder))
        this.Property = null;

      else if (rootFolder != "*")
        request.SetVar(site.Url, "RootFolder", rootFolder);
    }

    if (string.IsNullOrEmpty(this.List) || string.IsNullOrEmpty(this.Property))
      return;

    SPStringCallback callback = new SPStringCallback();
```

```
    request.RenderListProperty(base.PageUri.ToString(), this.List,
                               this.Property, callback);
    if (!string.IsNullOrEmpty(callback.StringResult))
      this.RenderValue(writer, callback.StringResult);
  }

  private void RenderValue(HtmlTextWriter writer, string s)
  {
    if (this.CssClass == null)
    {
      writer.Write(s);
      return;
    }

    writer.Write("<div class='");
    SPHttpUtility.HtmlEncode(this.CssClass, writer);
    writer.Write("'>");
    writer.Write(SPHttpUtility.NoEncode(s));
    writer.Write("</div>");
  }

  public string CssClass
  {
    get { return this.cssClass; }
    set { this.cssClass = value; }
  }

  public string Property
  {
    get { return this.property; }
    set { this.property = value; }
  }

  public string List
  {
    get
    {
      if (this.list == null)
      {
        if (SPContext.Current.ListId != Guid.Empty)
          this.list = SPContext.Current.ListId.ToString("B");
      }
      return this.list;
    }
    set { this.list = value; }
  }
}
```

Now we'll walk you through the implementation of the Render method of the ListProperty server control, where you can see for yourself how this server control takes full advantage of the SharePoint contextual information available to it through its base class (SPControl) in its rendering logic.

The Render method first checks whether the Context property is null. ListProperty, like any other server control, inherits this property from the ASP.NET Control base class. This property is of the HttpContext type. The Render method does not render anything if the Context property is null because there can't be a current list if there is no HttpContext object.

If the Context property is not null, the Render method takes these steps. First, it invokes the GetContextWeb static method of the SPControl class, passing in the HttpContext object representing the current HTTP request, which returns a reference to the SPWeb object representing the current site:

```
SPWeb site = SPControl.GetContextWeb(this.Context);
```

Next it accesses the SPRequest object that represents the current request:

```
request = site.Request;
```

The Render method then accesses the SPList object that represents the current SharePoint list. Keep in mind that the ListProperty server control is used in a display, edit, or new list item form, which displays, edits, or creates a new list item in a SharePoint list. The SPList object represents this SharePoint list:

```
SPList list = SPContext.Current.List;
```

Next, Render accesses the value assigned to the Property property of the ListProperty server control. Recall from Listing 3-2 that the display, edit, or new list item form where the ListProperty server control is declared sets the value of the Property property as shown in the following excerpt from Listing 3-2:

```
<asp:Content ContentPlaceHolderID="PlaceHolderPageTitleInTitleArea" runat="server">
  <SharePoint:ListProperty Property="LinkTitle" runat="server" ID="ID_LinkTitle" />
  :
  <SharePoint:ListItemProperty ID="ID_ItemProperty" MaxLength="40"
  runat="server" />
</asp:Content>
```

If the value of the Property property is set to Title, the Render method uses the RenderValue method to render the title of the current list and then returns:

```
this.RenderValue(writer, SPHttpUtility.HtmlEncode(list.Title));
return;
```

If the value of the Property property is set to Description, the Render method uses the RenderValue method to render the description of the current list and then returns:

```
this.RenderValue(writer, SPHttpUtility.NoEncode(
                  SPUtility.AutoHyperLinking(site, list.Description)));
return;
```

TemplateBasedControl

As you can see from Figure 4-1, TemplateBasedControl inherits from SPControl and extends its functionality to add support for templates. Listing 4-3 presents the internal implementation of TemplateBasedControl.

Listing 4-3: The internal implemenation of TemplateBasedControl

```
[PersistChildren(false),
ParseChildren(true)]
public class TemplateBasedControl : SPControl, INamingContainer
{
  private ITemplate template;
  private TemplateContainer templateContainer;
  private string templateName;
  private TemplateOverride templateOverride;
  private SPWeb web;
  private ITemplate alternateTemplate;
  private string alternateTemplateName;
  private ITemplate customAlternateTemplate;
  private ITemplate customTemplate;
  private SPContext renderContext;

  public static TemplateBasedControl GetParentTemplateBasedControl(Control control)
  {
    for (Control control1 = control.Parent; (control1 != null) &&
                             !(control1 is HtmlForm); control1 = control1.Parent)
    {
      if (control1 is TemplateBasedControl)
        return (TemplateBasedControl)control1;
    }

    return null;
  }

  protected override void OnLoad(EventArgs e)
  {
    base.OnLoad(e);
    this.EnsureChildControls();
  }

  protected override void CreateChildControls()
  {
    ITemplate template = null;
    if ((this.TemplateOverride != TemplateOverride.None) ||
                                                  (this.ControlTemplate == null))
    {
      if ((this.TemplateOverride != TemplateOverride.Template) &&
          ((this.TemplateOverride != TemplateOverride.Both) ||
                                                        (this.Template == null)))
      {
        if ((this.TemplateOverride == TemplateOverride.AlternateTemplate) ||
            ((this.TemplateOverride == TemplateOverride.Both) &&
              (this.AlternateTemplate != null)))
          template = this.AlternateTemplate;
      }

      else
```

(continued)

Listing 4-3 *(continued)*

```
        template = this.Template;
      }

      else
        template = this.ControlTemplate;

      if (template == null)
      {
        base.CreateChildControls();
        return;
      }

      this.Controls.Clear();
      template.InstantiateIn(this.TemplateContainer);
      this.Controls.Add(this.TemplateContainer);
    }

    protected override void Render(HtmlTextWriter output)
    {
      this.EnsureChildControls();
      base.Render(output);
    }

    public override ControlCollection Controls
    {
      get
      {
        this.EnsureChildControls();
        return base.Controls;
      }
    }

    protected virtual ITemplate ControlTemplate
    {
      get { return this.Template; }
    }

    [TemplateContainer(typeof(TemplateContainer))]
    public ITemplate AlternateTemplate
    {
      get
      {
        if (this.alternateTemplate == null && this.AlternateTemplateName != null)
          this.alternateTemplate =
              SPControlTemplateManager.GetTemplateByName(this.AlternateTemplateName);

        return this.alternateTemplate;
      }
      set { this.alternateTemplate = value; }
    }

    public string AlternateTemplateName
```

```
{
  get
  {
    if (this.alternateTemplateName == null)
      this.alternateTemplateName = this.DefaultAlternateTemplateName;

    return this.alternateTemplateName;
  }
  set { this.alternateTemplateName = value; }
}

[PersistenceMode(PersistenceMode.InnerProperty),
TemplateContainer(typeof(TemplateContainer))]
public ITemplate CustomAlternateTemplate
{
  get { return this.customAlternateTemplate; }
  set
  {
    this.customAlternateTemplate = value;
    this.alternateTemplate = value;
  }
}

protected virtual string DefaultAlternateTemplateName
{
  get { return null; }
}

protected virtual string DefaultTemplateName
{
  get { return null; }
}

[PersistenceMode(PersistenceMode.InnerProperty),
TemplateContainer(typeof(TemplateBasedControl))]
public ITemplate CustomTemplate
{
  get { return this.customTemplate; }
  set
  {
    this.customTemplate = value;
    this.template = value;
  }
}

public SPContext RenderContext
{
  get
  {
    if (this.renderContext == null)
```

(continued)

Listing 4-3 *(continued)*

```
      {
        TemplateBasedControl parent = GetParentTemplateBasedControl(this);
        if (parent == null)
          this.renderContext = SPContext.Current;
        else
          this.renderContext = parent.RenderContext;
      }
      return this.renderContext;
    }
    set { this.renderContext = value; }
  }

  public virtual TemplateContainer TemplateContainer
  {
    get
    {
      if (this.templateContainer == null)
        this.templateContainer = new TemplateContainer();

      return this.templateContainer;
    }
  }

  [TemplateContainer(typeof(TemplateBasedControl))]
  public ITemplate Template
  {
    get
    {
      if (this.template == null && this.TemplateName != null)
        this.template =
                    SPControlTemplateManager.GetTemplateByName(this.TemplateName);

      return this.template;
    }
    set { this.template = value; }
  }

  public virtual SPWeb Web
  {
    get
    {
      if (this.web == null)
      {
        if (this.renderContext == null)
          this.web = SPControl.GetContextWeb(this.Context);

        else
          this.web = this.renderContext.Web;
      }
```

```
        return this.web;
      }
    }

    public string TemplateName
    {
      get
      {
        if (this.templateName == null)
          this.templateName = this.DefaultTemplateName;

        return this.templateName;
      }
      set { this.templateName = value; }
    }

    protected TemplateOverride TemplateOverride
    {
      get { return this.templateOverride; }
      set { this.templateOverride = value; }
    }
  }
```

As you can see from Listing 4-3, TemplateBasedControl exposes the templates discussed in the following sections.

Template Property

TemplateBasedControl renders this template unless otherwise instructed. As such this is the main template. As Listing 4-3 shows, this template is a read-write property. Explicitly assign your own ITemplate object to this property to have TemplateBasedControl render your own ITemplate object. As you can see from Listing 4-3, the getter of the Template property checks whether an ITemplate object has been explicitly assigned to it. If so, it simply returns this ITemplate object. If not, it calls a static method named GetTemplateByName on a class named SPControlTemplateManager to return the ITemplate object assigned to the Template property of the RenderingTemplate server control whose ID property value is specified in the TemplateName property of TemplateBasedControl.

As you can see, you have two options to have TemplateBasedControl render your own ITemplate object. One option is to assign your ITemplate object directly to the Template property of TemplateBasedControl as discussed earlier. Another option is to assign the ID property value of a RenderingTemplate server control to the TemplateName property of TemplateBasedControl to have TemplateBasedControl automatically pick up the ITemplate object assigned to the Template property of the RenderingTemplate server control. The first approach is discussed later in this chapter. But first, this section covers the second approach.

As you can see from Listing 4-4, RenderingTemplate is a server control that inherits from the ASP.NET Control base class and extends its functionality to add support for a single property of the ITemplate type named Template.

Listing 4-4: The RenderingTemplate server control

```
[ParseChildren(true),
PersistChildren(false)]
public sealed class RenderingTemplate : Control
{
  private ITemplate renderTemplate;

  [PersistenceMode(PersistenceMode.InnerProperty),
  TemplateContainer(typeof(RenderingTemplateContainer))]
  public ITemplate Template
  {
    get { return this.renderTemplate; }
    set { this.renderTemplate = value; }
  }
}
```

As Listing 4-4 illustrates, RenderingTemplate is annotated with the ParseChildren(true) metadata attribute to instruct the ASP.NET page parser to parse the content enclosed within the opening and closing tags of the <Template> child element of the <RenderingTemplate> element (which represents the RenderingTemplate server control on an .ascx file) as the value of the Template property of the RenderingTemplate server control as opposed to its child control. In other words, it tells the ASP.NET page parser that the <Template> tag represents the Template property of the RenderingTemplate server control as opposed to the child control of this server control. Without the ParseChildren(true) metadata, the ASP.NET page parser would treat the <Template> tag as the child control of the RenderingTemplate server control.

This enables you to use a <Template> element within the opening and closing tags of the <RenderingTemplate> and specify whatever HTML and server controls are deemed appropriate within the opening and closing tags of the <Template> element. The page parser will automatically parse the content enclosed within the opening and closing tags of the <Template> element into a class that implements the ITemplate interface. The page parser then dynamically compiles this class into an assembly, loads the assembly into the application domain, dynamically instantiates an instance of this class, and assigns this instance to the Template property of the RenderingTemplate server control.

RenderingTemplate server controls are declared in .ascx files deployed to the following folder on the file system of the front-end web server:

```
Local_Drive:\Program Files\Common Files\Microsoft Shared\Web Server
Extensions\12\Template\ControlTemplates
```

SharePoint ships with standard .ascx file named DefaultTemplates.ascx that contains several RenderingTemplate server controls. This means that you can simply assign the ID attribute value of one of the <SharePoint:RenderingTemplate> tags in these .ascx files to the TemplateName property of a TemplateBasedControl-derived server control to have this server control pick up and render the ITemplate object that the ASP.NET page parser dynamically instantiates and assigns to the Template property of the RenderingTemplate server control as just discussed. This basically enables the TemplateBasedControl-derived server control to delegate the responsibility of rendering the appropriate HTML markup text to the <Template> child element of the <SharePoint:RenderingTemplate> element in an .ascx file in the ControlTemplates folder on the file system of the front-end web server. The great thing about this delegation is that you can have the same TemplateBasedControl-derived server control render completely different HTML markup text by simply assigning the ID attribute value of a different <SharePoint:RenderingTemplate> tag to its TemplateName property.

You're not limited to using the standard <SharePoint:RenderingTemplate> tags declared in the DefaultTemplates.ascx file in the ControlTemplates folder. You can also implement your own .ascx files that contain <SharePoint:RenderingTemplate> tags and deploy them to the ControlTemplates folder. The following code listing shows an example:

```
<% @Control Language="C#" %>
<% @Register TagPrefix="SharePoint" Namespace="Microsoft.SharePoint.WebControls"
Assembly="Microsoft.SharePoint, Version=12.0.0.0, Culture=neutral, PublicKeyToken=
71e9bce111e9429c" %>

<SharePoint:RenderingTemplate ID="MyRenderingTemplate" runat="server">
  <Template>
    Use HTML, ASP.NET server control, and/or SharePoint server control tags here
  </Template>
</SharePoint:RenderingTemplate>
```

There are two ways to have a TemplateBasedControl-derived server control use the ITemplate object that the ASP.NET page parser dynamically creates and assigns to the Template property of the RenderingTemplate server control. One way is to directly assign the ID attribute value of the <SharePoint:RenderingTemplate> tag, which is MyRenderingTemplate in this case, to the TemplateName property of the TemplateBasedControl-derived server control. This can be done because the TemplateName property is a writable property as shown in the boldfaced portion of the following excerpt from Listing 4-3:

```
public string TemplateName
{
  get
  {
    if (this.templateName == null)
      this.templateName = this.DefaultTemplateName;

    return this.templateName;
  }
  set { this.templateName = value; }
}
```

Another approach is to implement a server control that directly or indirectly inherits from TemplateBasedControl. This server control can then override the DefaultTemplateName property of TemplateBasedControl to return the ID attribute value of the desired <SharePoint:RenderingTemplate> tag:

```
protected override string DefaultTemplateName
{
  get { return "MyRenderingTemplate"; }
}
```

This is possible because of two factors. First, the DefaultTemplateName property is overridable because it's marked as virtual. Second, the getter of the TemplateName property returns the value of the DefaultTemplateName property if its value has not been directly set, as you can see from the boldfaced portion of the following excerpt from Listing 4-3:

```
public string TemplateName
  {
    get
    {
      if (this.templateName == null)
        this.templateName = this.DefaultTemplateName;

      return this.templateName;
    }
    set { this.templateName = value; }
  }
```

Note that the TemplateName property of TemplateBasedControl is not overridable. The only way to indirectly override this property is to override the DefaultTemplateName property.

As you can see, you'll need to write code to assign the ID attribute value of the desired <SharePoint:RenderingTemplate> tag to the TemplateName property. Where should this code go? It all depends on the specific requirements of your application. You have numerous places to stick this code: a feature event handler, WebPart server control, application page, page template, and so on.

If you really need to implement a TemplateBasedControl-derived control that can dynamically pick up the ID attribute value of a desired <SharePoint:RenderingTemplate> tag, your override of the DefaultTemplateName property can pick up its value from the web.config of the SharePoint Web application.

As you can see from the following excerpt from Listing 4-3, the getter of the Template property of TemplateBasedControl invokes the GetTemplateByName static method on the SPControlTemplateManager class, passing in the value of the TemplateName property of TemplateBasedControl if the value of the Template property has not been explicitly set:

```
[TemplateContainer(typeof(TemplateBasedControl))]
public ITemplate Template
{
  get
  {
    if (this.template == null && this.TemplateName != null)
      this.template =
            SPControlTemplateManager.GetTemplateByName(this.TemplateName);

    return this.template;
  }
  set { this.template = value; }
}
```

Listing 4-5 presents the internal implementation of the SPControlTemplateManager class.

Listing 4-5: The internal implementation of SPControlTemplateManager

```
public sealed class SPControlTemplateManager : Control, INamingContainer
{
  private static object syncObject = new object();
  private static Hashtable templateCollection;

  private static void PopulateTemplateCollection()
  {
    if ((templateCollection == null) && (HttpContext.Current != null))
    {
      lock (syncObject)
      {
        if (templateCollection == null)
        {
          templateCollection = new Hashtable();
          DirectoryInfo controlTemplatesDir =
             new DirectoryInfo(
                     HttpContext.Current.Server.MapPath("/_controltemplates/"));
          FileInfo[] files = controlTemplatesDir.GetFiles("*.ascx");

          foreach (FileInfo info in files)
          {
            Page page = new Page();
            page.AppRelativeTemplateSourceDirectory = "~";
            Control control = page.LoadControl(
                                    "/_controltemplates/" + info.FileName);

            IEnumerator enumerator = control.Controls.GetEnumerator();
            Control control2;
            while (enumerator.MoveNext())
            {
              control2 = (Control)enumerator.Current;
              if (control2 is RenderingTemplate)
                templateCollection[control2.ID] =
                                 ((RenderingTemplate)control2).Template;
            }
          }
        }
      }
    }
  }

  public static ITemplate GetTemplateByName(string templateName)
  {
    if (HttpContext.Current != null && !string.IsNullOrEmpty(templateName))
    {
      PopulateTemplateCollection();
      ITemplate template = (ITemplate)templateCollection[templateName];
      return template;
    }
    return null;
  }
}
```

we'll walk you through the implementation of the GetTemplateByName method next. As you can see, this method takes a single string parameter that contains the ID attribute value of a <SharePoint:RenderingTemplate> tag in an .ascx file in the ControlTemplates folder. The method first invokes another method named PopulateTemplateCollection to populate a local Hashtable named templateCollection with the ITemplate objects that the Template properties of all RenderingTemplate server controls in all .ascx files in the ControlTemplates folder reference:

```
PopulateTemplateCollection();
```

Next, the method uses the ID attribute value of the specified <SharePoint:RenderingTemplate> tag as an index into the templateCollection Hashtable to return a reference to the ITemplate object assigned to the Template property of this RenderingTemplate server control:

```
ITemplate template = (ITemplate)templateCollection[templateName];
```

As you can see, the GetTemplateByName method takes the ID property value of a RenderingTemplate server control declared in one of the .ascx files in the ControlTemplates folder and returns a reference to the ITemplate object assigned to the Template property of this RenderingTemplate server control.

Next, we'll walk you through the internal implementation of the PopulateTemplateCollection method. This method first checks whether the templateCollection Hashtable has already been populated. If so, it simply returns. If not, it performs these tasks to populate this Hashtable. First, it instantiates the templateCollection Hashtable:

```
templateCollection = new Hashtable();
```

It now instantiates a DirectoryInfo object that represents the ControlTemplates folder on the file system of the front-end web server. Recall that this folder contains all the .ascx files deployed to SharePoint, including both the standard .ascx files that ship with SharePoint and your own custom .ascx files:

```
DirectoryInfo controlTemplatesDir =
      new DirectoryInfo(HttpContext.Current.Server.MapPath("/_controltemplates/"));
```

Then, it invokes the GetFiles method on this DirectoryInfo object, passing in *.ascx to return an array of FileInfo objects. Each FileInfo object in this array represents an .ascx file in the ControlTemplates folder:

```
FileInfo[] files = controlTemplatesDir.GetFiles("*.ascx");
```

Next, it iterates through these FileInfo objects and performs these tasks for each enumerated FileInfo object. First, it creates a Page object and specifies "~" as the relative template source directory:

```
Page page = new Page();
page.AppRelativeTemplateSourceDirectory = "~";
```

Next, it invokes the LoadControl method on this Page object, passing in the relative path of the enumerated .ascx file. The LoadControl method under the hood uses the ASP.NET page parser to parse the enumerated .ascx file into a dynamically generated class, compiles this class into an assembly, loads the assembly into the current application domain, instantiates an instance of this class, and returns this instance. Note that LoadControl returns the instance as a generic Control type:

```
Control control = page.LoadControl("/_controltemplates/" + info.FileName);
```

Next, it accesses the IEnumerator object that knows how to enumerate the child controls of the server control returned from the LoadControl method:

```
IEnumerator enumerator = control.Controls.GetEnumerator();
```

Then, it uses this IEnumerator object to iterate through these child controls and takes these steps for each enumerated child control. It checks whether the child control is of the RenderingTemplate type. If so, it uses the ID property value of the child control as an index into the templateCollection Hashtable to store a reference to the Template property of the child control. Keep in mind that this Template property references an ITemplate object that the ASP.NET page parser dynamically generates and assigns to this property:

```
if (control2 is RenderingTemplate)
  templateCollection[control2.ID] = ((RenderingTemplate)control2).Template;
```

As you can see, thanks to the PopulateTemplateCollection static method of the SPControlTemplateManager, you can implement a custom .ascx file that contains a <SharePoint:RenderingTemplate> tag and deploy this file to the ControlTemplates folder, and rest assured that it will be automatically loaded when the web application starts or restarts. Because the getter of the Template property of TemplateBasedControl invokes the GetTemplateByName static method on the SPControlTemplateManager class (see Listing 4-3), passing in the value of the TemplateName property, this getter will automatically pick up the ITemplate object that the ASP.NET page parser assigns to the Template property of your custom RenderingTemplate server control when it parses the <SharePoint:RenderingTemplate> tag that represents your server control in the respective .ascx file.

Just in case you're wondering which .ascx file in the ControlTemplates folder contains the standard SharePoint RenderingTemplate server controls, the answer is DefaultTemplates.ascx. You can configure a TemplateBasedControl to use any of these RenderingTemplate server controls as discussed earlier.

Before wrapping up this section, I'd like to make one last comment about the Template property. This property is not annotated with the PersistenceMode(PersistenceMode.InnerProperty) metadata attribute, contrary to what you would expect from a template property of a templated control. This metadata attribute instructs a visual designer such as Visual Studio to persist the value of the template property as an inner property, that is, as a child element (<Template>) of the element that represents the templated control in an .aspx or .ascx file. This means that the Template property of TemplateBasedControl is not intended to be set through the standard ASP.NET templating procedure where you specify this value by adding HTML and server controls to the tag that represents this property in the .aspx or .ascx file (<Template>).

AlternateTemplate Property

The preceding section discussed the Template property of TemplateBasedControl, which is the main template. TemplateBasedControl renders this main template unless otherwise instructed. There could be circumstances where the main template may not be appropriate. TemplateBasedControl supports another template named AlternateTemplate for these circumstances. As the name suggests, this template acts as an alternate to the main template. The following excerpt from Listing 4-3 presents the implementation of the AlternateTemplate property of TemplateBasedControl:

```
[TemplateContainer(typeof(TemplateContainer))]
public ITemplate AlternateTemplate
{
  get
  {
    if (this.alternateTemplate == null && this.AlternateTemplateName != null)
      this.alternateTemplate =
          SPControlTemplateManager.GetTemplateByName(this.AlternateTemplateName);

    return this.alternateTemplate;
  }
  set { this.alternateTemplate = value; }
}
```

As you can see, the AlternateTemplate property is writable. This means that you can assign your own custom ITemplate object directly to this property to have TemplateBasedControl render your template. The getter of the AlternateTemplate property first checks whether an ITemplate object has been explicitly assigned to it. If so, it returns this ITemplate object. If not, it invokes the GetTemplateByName static method on the SPControlTemplateManager class, passing in the value of a property named AlternateTemplateName. This static method returns a reference to the ITemplate object that the ASP.NET page parser creates and assigns to the Template property of the RenderingTemplate server control whose ID property value is specified in the AlternateTemplateName property.

As the following excerpt from Listing 4-3 shows, the AlternateTemplateName property of TemplateBasedControl is a read-write property:

```
public string AlternateTemplateName
{
  get
  {
    if (this.alternateTemplateName == null)
      this.alternateTemplateName = this.DefaultAlternateTemplateName;

    return this.alternateTemplateName;
  }
  set { this.alternateTemplateName = value; }
}
```

Because the AlternateTemplateName property is writable, you can directly assign a value to it. This value must be the ID attribute value of a <SharePoint:RenderingTemplate> tag in an .ascx file in the ControlTemplates folder. This <SharePoint:RenderingTemplate> tag basically contains the HTML and server controls that make up the alternate template. The getter of the AlternateTemplateName property first checks whether a value has been directly assigned to it. If so, it simply returns this value. If not, it returns the value of the DefaultAlternateTemplateName property.

Note that the AlternateTemplateName property of TemplateBasedControl is not overridable. There are only two ways to set the value of this property. You can either directly assign a value to the property or use a different value for the DefaultAlternateTemplateName property. The following excerpt from Listing 4-3 presents the implementation of the DefaultAlternateTemplateName property:

```
protected virtual string DefaultAlternateTemplateName
{
  get { return null; }
}
```

Note that this property is not writable. The only way to have this property return a different value is to override it. Here is an example:

```
protected override string DefaultAlternateTemplateName
{
  get { return "MyAlternateTemplate"; }
}
```

When you override this property, you must return a string that contains the ID attribute value of a <SharePoint:RenderingTemplate> tag in an .ascx file in the ControlTemplates folder.

If you need to dynamically specify the value that the DefaultAlternateTemplateName property returns, you can override this property to include the logic that retrieves this value from the web.config file of the current web application.

TemplateOverride

As you can see from Listing 4-3, TemplateBasedControl exposes a property of the TemplateOverride enumeration type named TemplateOverride:

```
protected TemplateOverride TemplateOverride
{
  get { return this.templateOverride; }
  set { this.templateOverride = value; }
}
```

Listing 4-6 presents the definition of the TemplateOverride enumeration type.

Listing 4-6: The TemplateOverride enumeration type

```
public enum TemplateOverride
{
  None,
  Template,
  AlternateTemplate,
  Both
}
```

Here is the description of these enumeration values:

- **Template.** Assign this value to the TemplateOverride property of a TemplateBasedControl server control to instruct this server control to use the ITemplate object that the Template property of the server control references. In other words, this enumeration value instructs the TemplateBasedControl server control to use the main template.
- **AlternateTemplate.** Assign this value to the TemplateOverride property of a TemplateBasedControl server control to instruct this server control to use the ITemplate object that the AlternateTemplate property of the server control references. In other words, this enumeration value instructs the TemplateBasedControl server control to use the alternate template.
- **Both.** Assign this value to the TemplateOverride property of a TemplateBasedControl server control to instruct this server control to use the ITemplate object that the Template property of the server control references unless this property returns null, in which case use the ITemplate object that the AlternateTemplate property of the server control references. In other words, this enumeration value instructs the TemplateBasedControl server control to use the main template unless the main template is null, in which case use the alternate template.
- **None.** Assign this value to the TemplateOverride property of a TemplateBasedControl server control to instruct this server control to use the ITemplate object that the ControlTemplate property of the server control references. The next section discusses the ControlTemplate property.

ControlTemplate

The following excerpt from Listing 4-3 presents the implementation of the ControlTemplate property of TemplateBasedControl:

```
protected virtual ITemplate ControlTemplate
{
  get { return this.Template; }
}
```

As you can see, the ControlTemplate property is a read-only property that returns the ITemplate object that the Template property references, which is the main template. In other words, if you set the TemplateOverride property of a TemplateBasedControl to the enumeration value of None to let the ControlTemplate property decide what template to use, TemplateBasedControl will use the main template by default.

Because the ControlTemplate property is not writable, the only way you can have this property to return a different ITemplate object is to override the property.

CreateChildControls

The following excerpt from Listing 4-3 presents the implementation of the CreateChildControls method of TemplateBasedControl:

```
protected override void CreateChildControls()
{
  ITemplate template = null;
  if ((this.TemplateOverride != TemplateOverride.None) ||
                                                   (this.ControlTemplate == null))
  {
    if ((this.TemplateOverride != TemplateOverride.Template) &&
        ((this.TemplateOverride != TemplateOverride.Both) ||
                                                         (this.Template == null)))
    {
      if ((this.TemplateOverride == TemplateOverride.AlternateTemplate) ||
          ((this.TemplateOverride == TemplateOverride.Both) &&
             (this.AlternateTemplate != null)))
        template = this.AlternateTemplate;
    }

    else
      template = this.Template;
  }

  else
    template = this.ControlTemplate;

  if (template == null)
  {
    base.CreateChildControls();
    return;
  }

  this.Controls.Clear();
  template.InstantiateIn(this.TemplateContainer);
  this.Controls.Add(this.TemplateContainer);
}
```

As you can see, this method checks the value of the TemplateOverride property. If this value is set to None and if the ControlTemplate property is not null, it uses the ITemplate object that the ControlTemplate property returns:

```
else
  template = this.ControlTemplate;
```

If this value is set to Template or Both and if the Template property is not null, it uses the ITemplate object that the Template property returns:

```
else
  template = this.Template;
```

If this value is set to Both but the Template property is null or if this value is set to AlternateTemplate and AlternateTemplate is not null, it uses the ITemplate object that the AlternateTemplate property returns:

```
template = this.AlternateTemplate;
```

If none of the preceding conditions are met, that is, if no template is available, the CreateChildControls method simply invokes the CreateChildControls method of its base class and returns. If any of the preceding conditions are met, that is, if a template is available (whether it is the main template, alternate template, or a template returned from the ControlTemplate property), it performs these tasks. First, it clears the Controls collection:

```
this.Controls.Clear();
```

Then, it invokes the InstantiateIn method on the template, passing in the value of the TemplateContainer property of TemplateBasedControl. The InstantiateIn method internally adds the child controls specified within the ITemplate object that the Template property of the respective RenderingTemplate server control references to the server control that the TemplateContainer property references. (Keep in mind that these child controls basically represent the markup specified within the opening and closing tags of the <Template> child element of the respective <SharePoint:RenderingTemplate> element.)

```
template.InstantiateIn(this.TemplateContainer);
```

Finally, it adds the server control that the TemplateContainer property references to the Controls collection:

```
this.Controls.Add(this.TemplateContainer);
```

The following excerpt from Listing 4-3 shows the implementation of the TemplateContainer property:

```
public virtual TemplateContainer TemplateContainer
{
  get
  {
    if (this.templateContainer == null)
      this.templateContainer = new TemplateContainer();

    return this.templateContainer;
  }
}
```

As you can see, this property simply instantiates and returns an instance of a server control named TemplateContainer. Note that TemplateContainer inherits from TemplateBasedControl. That is why the Template and AlternateTemplate properties are both annotated with the TemplateContainer (typeof(TemplateBasedControl)) metadata attribute, as you can see from the boldfaced portions of the following code listing:

```
[TemplateContainer(typeof(TemplateBasedControl))]
public ITemplate Template
{
  get { ... }
  set { ... }
}

[TemplateContainer(typeof(TemplateContainer))]
public ITemplate AlternateTemplate
{
  get { ... }
  set { ... }
}
```

As the name implies, the TemplateContainerAttribute metadata attribute specifies the type of template containers that the specified template uses. A template container is a server control that contains the child controls specified in the ITemplate object that the Template property of the respective RenderingTemplate server control references. When the ASP.NET page parser is parsing the HTML and server controls specified within the opening and closing tags of the respective <Template> child element on the .ascx file, it adds the respective child server controls to an instance of the template container whose type is specified by the TemplateContainerAttribute metadata attribute, which is the TemplateContainer server control in this case.

CustomTemplate and CustomAlternateTemplate

The previous sections discussed three important templates of a TemplateBasedControl server control: ControlTemplate, Template, and AlternateTemplate. As Listing 4-3 shows, a TemplateBasedControl server control also exposes two more template properties named CustomTemplate and CustomAlternateTemplate. As you saw previously, the CreateChildControls method of a TemplateBasedControl server control does not use CustomTemplate or CustomAlternateTemplate. Because CreateChildControls is the only place in a server control where the child controls are created, you maybe wondering what CustomTemplate and CustomAlternateTemplate are for.

The following excerpt from Listing 4-3 presents the implementation of the CustomTemplate and CustomAlternateTemplate properties:

```
[PersistenceMode(PersistenceMode.InnerProperty),
TemplateContainer(typeof(TemplateBasedControl))]
public ITemplate CustomTemplate
{
  get { return this.customTemplate; }
  set
  {
    this.customTemplate = value;
    this.template = value;
  }
}

[PersistenceMode(PersistenceMode.InnerProperty),
TemplateContainer(typeof(TemplateContainer))]
```

(continued)

(continued)

```
public ITemplate CustomAlternateTemplate
{
  get { return this.customAlternateTemplate; }
  set
  {
    this.customAlternateTemplate = value;
    this.alternateTemplate = value;
  }
}
```

As you can see, when you assign ITemplate objects to the CustomTemplate and CustomAlternateTemplate properties, the setters of these properties assign these ITemplate objects to the template and alternateTemplate fields, respectively. As you can see from the boldfaced portions of the following excerpts, the Template and AlternateTemplate properties respectively use the template and alternateTemplate fields as their backing stores:

```
public ITemplate AlternateTemplate
{
  get
  {
    if (this.alternateTemplate == null && this.AlternateTemplateName != null)
      this.alternateTemplate =
          SPControlTemplateManager.GetTemplateByName(this.AlternateTemplateName);

    return this.alternateTemplate;
  }
  set { this.alternateTemplate = value; }
}

public ITemplate Template
{
  get
  {
    if (this.template == null && this.TemplateName != null)
      this.template =
                  SPControlTemplateManager.GetTemplateByName(this.TemplateName);

    return this.template;
  }
  set { this.template = value; }
}
```

Note that the getters of the Template and AlternateTemplate properties bypass the logic that invokes the GetTemplateByName method of the SPControlTemplateManager class if the template and alternateTemplate fields are not null.

As you can see, by setting the CustomTemplate and CustomAlternateTemplate properties you're basically providing a custom main template and custom alternate templates for a TemplateBasedControl server control.

RenderContext

As the following excerpt from Listing 4-3 shows, a TemplateBasedControl server control exposes a property named RenderContext, which returns an SPContext object that represents the SharePoint context within which the server control is rendered:

```
public SPContext RenderContext
{
  get
  {
    if (this.renderContext == null)
    {
      TemplateBasedControl parent = GetParentTemplateBasedControl(this);
      if (parent == null)
        this.renderContext = SPContext.Current;
      else
        this.renderContext = parent.RenderContext;
    }
    return this.renderContext;
  }
  set { this.renderContext = value; }
}
```

Note that the RenderContext property is writable. For example, a WebPart server control can set this property to the current SPContext. The getter of this property returns the RenderContext of its first ancestor TemplateBasedControl if this property has not been explicitly set. Note that the GetParentTemplateBasedControl method returns the first ancestor TemplateBasedControl of the current TemplateBasedControl server control:

```
public static TemplateBasedControl GetParentTemplateBasedControl(Control control)
{
  for (Control control1 = control.Parent; (control1 != null) &&
                              !(control1 is HtmlForm); control1 = control1.Parent)
  {
    if (control1 is TemplateBasedControl)
      return (TemplateBasedControl)control1;
  }
  return null;
}
```

You can use the SPContext object that the RenderContext property of a TemplateBasedControl server control references to access the SharePoint context. This is the context within which the server control is rendered. This SharePoint context includes the following contextual information:

- RenderContext.Site for the current SharePoint site collection
- RenderContext.Web for the current SharePoint site
- RenderContext.Site.WebApplication for the current SharePoint web application
- RenderContext.List for the current SharePoint list
- RenderContext.ListItem for the current SharePoint list item

A TemplateBasedControl server control also exposes a property named Web, which returns the SPWeb object that represents the current site, as you can see from the following excerpt from Listing 4-3:

```
public virtual SPWeb Web
{
  get
  {
    if (this.web == null)
    {
      if (this.renderContext == null)
        this.web = SPControl.GetContextWeb(this.Context);

      else
        this.web = this.renderContext.Web;
    }
    return this.web;
  }
}
```

FormComponent

As you can see from Figure 4-1, FormComponent inherits from TemplateBasedControl. As the name implies, FormComponent is the base class from which all form-rendering controls inherit directly or indirectly. In addition, FormComponent is also the base class from which all field-rending controls inherit directly or indirectly. A form-rendering control renders a SharePoint item, whereas a field-rendering control renders a SharePoint item field. The SharePoint object model ships with two base classes named SPItem and SPField whose instances represent SharePoint items and fields, respectively.

Listing 4-7 presents the internal implementation of the SPItem abstract base class.

Listing 4-7: The SPItem abstract class

```
[SharePointPermission(SecurityAction.LinkDemand, ObjectModel = true),
SharePointPermission(SecurityAction.InheritanceDemand, ObjectModel = true)]
public abstract class SPItem
{
  public const int InvalidItemId = 0;
  protected SPFieldCollection Fields;
  internal const int NewItemId = -1;

  public abstract void Delete();
  public abstract void Update();

  public virtual SPFieldCollection Fields
  {
    get { return this.Fields; }
    set { this.Fields = value; }
  }

  public virtual int ID
```

```
    {
      get { return 0; }
      set { }
    }

    public abstract object this[string fieldName] { get; set; }
    public abstract object this[int index] { get; set; }
  }
```

Note that SPItem exposes methods and properties that enable form- and field-rendering controls to deal with SharePoint items in an abstract fashion. For example, a call to the Delete and Update abstract methods of SPItem deletes or updates the current SharePoint item in the underlying data store. SPItem exposes a property of the SPFieldCollection type named Fields, which contains references to the SPField objects that represent the current item's fields.

You may be wondering why SPItem has its own Fields collection. This is because different items in a list can be of different content types, where each content type may have its own set of fields.

The ID property of SPItem gets or sets the integer that uniquely identifies the current SharePoint item among other items in the same SharePoint list. SPItem comes with two indexer properties that take a field name or an integer and respectively return the field value of the item field with the specified name or the field value of the item field with the specified index. Also note that SPItem is annotated with two code access security metadata attributes to demand its subclasses and callers to have permission to use the SharePoint object model.

Listing 4-8 presents the internal implementation of FormComponent.

Listing 4-8: The internal implementation of FormComponent

```
[PersistChildren(false),
ParseChildren(true)]
public class FormComponent : TemplateBasedControl
{
  private Guid listId = Guid.Empty;
  private SPControlMode renderMode;
  private string instanceItemId;
  private SPContext itemContext;
  private int itemId;

  protected override void OnPreRender(EventArgs e)
  {
    base.OnPreRender(e);
    if (this.ControlMode != SPControlMode.Display)
      ScriptLink.Register(this.Page, "form.js", true);
  }

  internal static Control GetParentFormComponentControl(Control control)
  {
    Control parent = control.Parent;
    while ((parent != null) && !(parent is HtmlForm))
```

(continued)

Listing 4-8 *(continued)*

```
    {
      if (parent is FormComponent || parent is TemplateContainer)
        return parent;

      parent = parent.Parent;
    }
    return null;
  }

  public SPControlMode ControlMode
  {
    get
    {
      if (this.renderMode == SPControlMode.Invalid)
      {
        Control parent = GetParentFormComponentControl(this);
        if (parent != null)
        {
          if (!(parent is FormComponent))
            this.renderMode =
                       ((TemplateContainer)parent).ControlMode;
          else
            this.renderMode =
                            ((FormComponent)parent).ControlMode;
        }

        if (this.renderMode == SPControlMode.Invalid)
        {
          SPContext context = SPContext.GetContext(this.Context);
          this.renderMode = context.FormContext.FormMode;
        }

        if (this.renderMode == SPControlMode.Invalid)
        {
          string strControlMode = this.Context.Request.QueryString["ControlMode"];
          if (!string.IsNullOrEmpty(strControlMode))
          {
            try
            {
              this.renderMode =
                (SPControlMode)Enum.Parse(typeof(SPControlMode),
                                          strControlMode, true);
            }
            catch (ArgumentException)
            {
              this.renderMode = SPControlMode.Invalid;
            }
          }
        }
```

```
        if (((this.renderMode == SPControlMode.Invalid) &&
             (SPContext.Current != null)) && SPContext.Current.IsDesignTime)
          this.renderMode = SPControlMode.Display;

        if (this.renderMode == SPControlMode.Invalid)
          throw new SPException("Control mode is not set!");
      }
      return this.renderMode;
    }
    set
    {
      if (value == SPControlMode.Invalid)
        throw new ArgumentException();
      this.renderMode = value;
    }
  }

  public SPFieldCollection Fields
  {
    get { return this.ItemContext.Fields; }
  }

  public SPItem Item
  {
    get { return this.ItemContext.Item; }
  }

  public SPContext ItemContext
  {
    get
    {
      if (this.itemContext == null)
      {
        SPContext itemContext = null;
        Control parent = GetParentFormComponentControl(this);
        if (parent != null)
        {
          if (!(parent is FormComponent))
            itemContext =
                     ((TemplateContainer)parent).ItemContext;
          else
            itemContext = ((FormComponent)parent).ItemContext;
        }

        ...

        if (itemContext == null)
          this.itemContext = SPContext.GetContext(this.Context);

        else
        {
          this.itemContext = itemContext;
          if ((this.renderMode == SPControlMode.Invalid) &&
              !this.itemContext.FormContext.IsMixedModeForm)
```

(continued)

Listing 4-8 *(continued)*

```
              this.renderMode = this.itemContext.FormContext.FormMode;
          }
          this.itemContext.FormContext.FormMode = this.ControlMode;
        }
        return this.itemContext;
      }
      set { this.itemContext = value; }
    }

    public int ItemId
    {
      get
      {
        if ((this.ControlMode != SPControlMode.New) && (this.itemId == 0))
          this.itemId = this.ItemContext.ItemId;
        return this.itemId;
      }
      set { this.itemId = value; }
    }

    public SPList List
    {
      get { return this.ItemContext.List; }
    }

    public Guid ListId
    {
      get
      {
        if (this.listId == Guid.Empty)
          this.listId = this.ItemContext.ListId;

        return this.listId;
      }
      set { this.listId = value; }
    }

    public SPListItem ListItem
    {
      get { return this.ItemContext.ListItem; }
    }
  }
```

ControlMode

This read-write property gets or sets an SPControlMode enumeration value that specifies the rendering mode for a form component server control (display, edit, or new). Keep in mind that a form component server control could be a form-rendering or a field-rendering control. Listing 4-9 presents the definition of the SPControlMode enumeration type.

Listing 4-9: The SPControlMode enumeration

```
public enum SPControlMode
{
  Invalid,
  Display,
  Edit,
  New
}
```

Because the ControlMode property of a form component server control is a read-write property, the rendering mode of the control can be explicitly set. As Listing 4-8 shows, the ControlMode property uses a private field named renderMode as its backing store. When the ControlMode property of a form component server control is being explicitly set, the setter of this property simply sets the value of this field as expected.

The getter of this property first checks whether the renderMode field has been explicitly set, that is, whether the rendering mode for this form component has been explicitly specified. If so, it simply returns the SPControlMode enumeration value assigned to the renderMode field.

If not, it takes these steps to determine the rendering mode for the form component. First, it invokes the GetParentFormComponentControl method to return a reference to the first ancestor form component or first ancestor template container of the current form component:

```
        Control parent = GetParentFormComponentControl(this);
```

If the current form component does indeed have a form component or template container ancestor, it simply assigns the value of the ControlMode property of this ancestor to the renderMode field. That means that the current form component inherits the rendering mode of its first ancestor form component or first ancestor template container:

```
        if (parent != null)
        {
          if (!(parent is FormComponent))
            this.renderMode =
                     ((TemplateContainer)parent).ControlMode;
          else
            this.renderMode =
                         ((FormComponent)parent).ControlMode;
        }
```

You may be wondering under what circumstances a form component server control could have a template container as an ancestor. This happens, for example, when you declare a form component within the opening and closing tags of the <Template> element of a <SharePoint:RenderingTemplate> element in an .ascx file in the ControlTemplates folder and then assign the ID attribute value of this <SharePoint:RenderingTemplate> element to the TemplateName property of another form component. As discussed earlier, the form component renders the ITemplate object that the Template property of this RenderingTemplate server control references into a template container server control, which is then added to the Controls collection of the form component. This means that the form component declared within the opening and closing tags of the <Template> element now becomes the child server control of this form component.

If the current form component does not have a form component or template container ancestor, it uses the rendering mode of the current list item form. The current SPContext exposes a property named FormContext, which references an SPFormContext object that provides information about the context that is specific to the list item form. This SPFormContext object features a property of the SPControlMode type named FormMode, which gets the rendering mode of the current list item form:

```
if (this.renderMode == SPControlMode.Invalid)
{
  SPContext context = SPContext.GetContext(this.Context);
  this.renderMode = context.FormContext.FormMode;
}
```

If the rendering mode of the current list item form has not been set, it accesses and uses the value of a query string parameter named ControlMode, which specifies the rendering mode of the current page. In other words, the current form component inherits the rendering mode of the current page:

```
string str = this.Context.Request.QueryString["ControlMode"];
if (!string.IsNullOrEmpty(str))
{
  try
  {
    this.renderMode =
      (SPControlMode)Enum.Parse(typeof(SPControlMode),
            this.Context.Request.QueryString["ControlMode"], true);
  }
  catch (ArgumentException)
  {
    this.renderMode = SPControlMode.Invalid;
  }
}
```

ItemContext

As you can see from Listing 4-8, FormComponent features a read-write property named ItemContext, which gets or sets the SPContext object that represents the SharePoint context for the current SharePoint item. Because ItemContext is a writable property, its value can be explicitly set.

Note that this property uses a private field named itemContext as its backing store. The getter of this property first checks whether this private field has been explicitly set. If so, it returns the value of this field.

If the item context for the form component has not been explicitly set, the getter uses the GetParentFormComponentControl method to determine whether the current form component has an ancestor form component or template container. If so, the current form component inherits the item context of this ancestor form component or template container:

```
bool flag;
SPContext itemContext = null;
Control parent = GetParentFormComponentControl(this);
if (parent != null)
```

```
      {
        if (!(parent is FormComponent))
          itemContext =
                  ((TemplateContainer)parent).ItemContext;
        else
          itemContext = ((FormComponent)parent).ItemContext;
      }
```

If not, it uses the current SPContext as its item context:

```
        this.itemContext = SPContext.GetContext(this.Context);
```

Fields

As Listing 4-8 shows, FormComponent exposes a read-only collection property of the SPFieldCollection type named Fields, which returns a reference to the SPFieldCollection object referenced by the Fields property of the item context. The Fields collection property of FormComponent contains references to all SPField objects that represent the fields of the current SharePoint item:

```
public SPFieldCollection Fields
{
  get { return this.ItemContext.Fields; }
}
```

Item

As you can see from Listing 4-8, FormComponent exposes a read-only property of the SPItem type named Item, which returns a reference to the SPItem object that the Item property of the item context references. The Item property of FormComponent basically returns a reference to the SPItem object that represents the current SharePoint item:

```
public SPItem Item
{
  get { return this.ItemContext.Item; }
}
```

ItemId

As Listing 4-8 illustrates, FormComponent exposes a read-write property of the integer type named ItemId, which returns the ID of the current SharePoint item. Note that this integer ID uniquely identifies the SharePoint item among other items in the SharePoint list:

```
public int ItemId
{
  get
  {
    if ((this.ControlMode != SPControlMode.New) && (this.itemId == 0))
      this.itemId = this.ItemContext.ItemId;
    return this.itemId;
  }
  set { this.itemId = value; }
}
```

List

As Listing 4-8 shows, FormComponent features a read-only property named List, which returns a reference to the SPList object that represents the current SharePoint list. This property returns the value of the List property of the item context:

```
public SPList List
{
  get { return this.ItemContext.List; }
}
```

ListId

As you can see from Listing 4-8, FormComponent contains a read-write property named ListId, which gets or sets the GUID that uniquely identifies the current SharePoint list. If the value of this property is not set explicitly, it simply returns the value of the ListId property of the item context:

```
public Guid ListId
{
  get
  {
    if (this.listId == Guid.Empty)
      this.listId = this.ItemContext.ListId;

    return this.listId;
  }
  set { this.listId = value; }
}
```

ListItem

As Listing 4-8 demonstrates, FormComponent has a read-only property named ListItem, which returns a reference to the SPListItem object that represents the current list item:

```
public SPListItem ListItem
{
  get { return this.ItemContext.ListItem; }
}
```

Note that this property returns the value of the ListItem property of the item context. The following code listing shows the internal implementation of the ListItem property of the item context:

```
public SPListItem ListItem
{
  get
  {
    if (this.Item is SPListItem)
      return (SPListItem) this.Item;
    return null;
  }
}
```

As you can see, this property determines whether the current list item is of the SPListItem type. If so, it casts the SPItem object referenced by the Item property to the SPListItem type and returns it. Therefore, both the ListItem and Item properties of FormComponent return the same object if the current list item is of the SPListItem type. If you use the Item property, you have to do the type casting yourself.

FormToolBar

Recall that Listing 3-5 presents the <SharePoint:RenderingTemplate> tag with the ID attribute value of ListForm. As a reminder, the ListFormWebPart Web part contained within every list item page (such as the display list item, edit list item, and new list item forms) renders markup content specified within the opening and closing tags of the <Template> child element of this <SharePoint:RenderingTemplate> element. As the following excerpt from Listing 3-5 shows, this markup contains a FormToolBar server control that renders the form toolbar, which includes the action buttons such as New Response and Edit Response as shown in Figure 3-8:

```
<SharePoint:RenderingTemplate ID="ListForm" runat="server">
  <Template>
    <SPAN id='part1`prime;>
      <SharePoint:InformationBar runat="server"/>
      ...
  <SharePoint:FormToolBar runat="server"/>
      ...
  </Template>
</SharePoint>
```

As you can see from Figure 4-1, FormToolbar inherits from FormComponent. Listing 4-10 presents a portion of the internal implementation of FormToolbar.

Listing 4-10: The FormToolbar form-rendering control

```
public class FormToolBar : FormComponent
{
  protected override void CreateChildControls()
  {
    base.CreateChildControls();
    ToolBar toolbarControl =
                  (ToolBar)this.TemplateContainer.FindControl("toolBarTbl");
    ...
    if (base.ControlMode != SPControlMode.Display)
    {
      RequiredFieldMessage child = new RequiredFieldMessage();
      toolbarControl.RightButtons.Controls.Add(child);
    }
    ...
  }

  protected override string DefaultTemplateName
  {
    get
```

(continued)

Listing 4-10 *(continued)*

```
      {
        string templateName = string.Empty;
        if (base.ItemContext.FormContext.Form != null)
          templateName = base.ItemContext.FormContext.Form.ToolbarTemplateName;

        if (string.IsNullOrEmpty(templateName))
        {
          if (base.List != null)
          {
            if (base.List.BaseType != SPBaseType.DocumentLibrary)
            {
              switch (base.ControlMode)
              {
                case SPControlMode.Display:
                  if (base.ItemContext.IsCurrentItemVersion)
                    return "DisplayFormToolBar";
                  return "DisplayFormVersionToolBar";

                case SPControlMode.New:
                  return "NewFormToolBar";

                case SPControlMode.Edit:
                  return "EditFormToolBar";
              }
            }

            else
            {
              switch (base.ControlMode)
              {
                case SPControlMode.Display:
                  if (base.ItemContext.IsCurrentItemVersion)
                    return "DocLibDisplayFormToolBar";
                  return "DocLibDisplayFormVersionToolBar";

                case SPControlMode.New:
                  return "UploadFormToolBar";

                case SPControlMode.Edit:
                  return "DocLibEditFormToolBar";
              }
            }
          }
        }
        return templateName;
      }
    }
  }
```

As you can see, FormToolBar overrides the DefaultTemplateName property. Recall that by default the Template property references the ITemplate object that the Template property of a RenderingTemplate server control whose ID property value is specified in the DefaultTemplateName property references. As discussed earlier, this RenderingTemplate server control is declared in an .ascx file located in the ControlTemplates folder. By default, this .ascx file is the standard DefaultTemplates.ascx file.

Next, we'll walk you through the implementation of the DefaultTemplateName property. This property first accesses the SPForm object that represents the current form, which could be a display list item form, edit list item form, or new list item form. It then accesses the value of the ToolbarTemplateName property of this SPForm object:

```
string templateName = null;
if (base.ItemContext.FormContext.Form != null)
  templateName = base.ItemContext.FormContext.Form.ToolbarTemplateName;
```

The ToolbarTemplateName property returns the ID property value of a predefined RenderingTemplate server control, that is, "ToolbarTemplate". If there is no predefined RenderingTemplate server control with this ID property value, the DefaultTemplateName property takes these steps to determine the default control template name. First, it checks whether the current list is a document library. If not, it checks the control mode of the FormToolBar server control. If it is in Display mode, that is, if it is used in a display list item form (DispForm.aspx), it checks whether this display list item form is displaying the current version of the current list item. If so, it returns the string "DisplayFormToolBar". That is, the FormToolBar server control will render the ITemplate object that the Template property of the RenderingTemplate server control with the ID property value of "DisplayFormToolBar" references.

If you examine the DefaultTemplate.ascx file located in the ControlTemplates folder, you'll see that it does indeed contain a <SharePoint:RenderingTemplate> tag with the ID attribute value of "DisplayFormToolBar":

```
<SharePoint:RenderingTemplate ID="DisplayFormToolBar" runat="server">
 <Template>
    <script>
    recycleBinEnabled =
         <SharePoint:ProjectProperty Property="RecycleBinEnabled" runat="server"/>;
    </script>
    <wssuc:ToolBar CssClass="ms-toolbar" id="toolBarTbl" runat="server"
    FocusOnToolbar=true>
      <Template_Buttons>
        <SharePoint:EnterFolderButton runat="server"/>
        <SharePoint:NewItemButton runat="server"/>
        <SharePoint:EditItemButton runat="server"/>
        <SharePoint:EditSeriesButton runat="server"/>
        <SharePoint:DeleteItemButton runat="server"/>
        <SharePoint:ClaimReleaseTaskButton runat="server"/>
        <SharePoint:ManagePermissionsButton runat="server"/>
        <SharePoint:ManageCopiesButton runat="server"/>
        <SharePoint:ApprovalButton runat="server"/>
        <SharePoint:WorkflowsButton runat="server"/>
        <SharePoint:AlertMeButton runat="server"/>
        <SharePoint:VersionHistoryButton runat="server"/>
      </Template_Buttons>
    </wssuc:ToolBar>
 </Template>
</SharePoint:RenderingTemplate>
```

Note that this RenderingTemplate server control uses standard SharePoint controls such as NewItemButton, EditItemButton, and so on to render the standard toolbar action buttons that appear on a display list item form. One way to customize what the FormToolBar server control renders is to implement an .ascx file that contains a <SharePoint:RenderingTemplate> tag with the same ID attribute value of "DisplayFormToolBar" and deploy this file to the ControlTemplates folder. You can then use standard SharePoint controls such as NewItemButton, EditItemButton, and so on or your own custom server control inside the <Template> child element of this <SharePoint:RenderingTemplate> element to instruct the FormToolBar server control what to render in the toolbar of a display list item form. However, this approach has a downside, that is, it will affect all SharePoint forms where the FormToolBar server control is used.

Now back to the implementation of the DefaultTemplateName property. If the display list item form is not displaying the current version of the current list item, this property returns "DisplayFormVersionToolBar". If you examine the DefaultTemplates.ascx file, you'll notice that it does include a <SharePoint:RenderingTemplate> tag with the ID attribute value of "DisplayFormVersionToolBar" as follows:

```
<SharePoint:RenderingTemplate ID="DisplayFormVersionToolBar" runat="server">
  <Template>
    <wssuc:ToolBar id="toolBarTbl" runat="server" FocusOnToolbar=true>
      <Template_Buttons>
        <SharePoint:DeleteItemVersionButton runat="server"/>
       <SharePoint:RestoreItemVersionButton runat="server"/>
       <SharePoint:VersionHistoryButton runat="server"/>
     </Template_Buttons>
   </wssuc:ToolBar>
</Template>
</SharePoint:RenderingTemplate>
```

Note that this RenderingTemplate server control uses standard SharePoint server controls such as DeleteItemVersionButton and RestoreItemVersionButton to render the standard version-dependent action buttons in the toolbar that appears in a display list item form. Again, one way to customize what the FormToolBar server control renders when the form is not displaying the current version of the current list item is to implement an .ascx file that contains a <SharePoint:RenderingTemplate> tag with the same ID attribute value of "DisplayFormVersionToolBar" and deploy this file to the ControlTemplates folder. You can then use whatever standard or custom server controls are deemed appropriate within this <SharePoint:RenderingTemplate> tag.

Now back to the implementation of the DefaultTemplateName property. If the FormToolBar server control is in Edit mode, that is, if the list item form in which the FormToolBar server control is used is an edit list item form (EditForm.aspx), the property returns "EditFormToolBar", which is the ID property value of the RenderingTemplate server control that determines what the FormToolBar server control will render in the toolbar of the edit list item form.

Here is an excerpt from the DefaultTemplates.ascx file that declares this RenderingTemplate server control:

```
<SharePoint:RenderingTemplate ID="EditFormToolBar" runat="server">
  <Template>
    <script>
      recycleBinEnabled =
        <SharePoint:ProjectProperty Property="RecycleBinEnabled" runat="server"/>;
    </script>
    <wssuc:ToolBar CssClass="ms-toolbar" id="toolBarTbl"
    RightButtonSeparator=" " runat="server">
      <Template_Buttons>
        <SharePoint:AttachmentButton runat="server"/>
        <SharePoint:EditSeriesButton runat="server"/>
        <SharePoint:DeleteItemButton runat="server"/>
        <SharePoint:ClaimReleaseTaskButton runat="server"/>
      </Template_Buttons>
    </wssuc:ToolBar>
  </Template>
</SharePoint:RenderingTemplate>
```

As you can see, this template control uses the standard SharePoint server controls such as AttachmentButton and DeleteItemButton to render the standard action buttons such as Attach File and Delete Item in the toolbar of an edit list item form (EditForm.aspx). Recall that users select the Edit Item menu option from the ECB menu to navigate to this form.

Now back to the implementation of the DefaultTemplateName property. If the FormToolBar server control is in New mode, that is, if it is used in a new list item form (NewForm.aspx), this property returns "NewFormToolBar", which is the ID property value of the RenderingTemplate control template that determines what the FormToolBar server control renders in the toolbar of a new list item form.

The following excerpt from DefaultTemplates.ascx presents the declaration of this control template:

```
<SharePoint:RenderingTemplate ID="NewFormToolBar" runat="server">
  <Template>
    <wssuc:ToolBar CssClass="ms-toolbar" id="toolBarTbl"
    RightButtonSeparator=" " runat="server">
      <Template_Buttons>
        <SharePoint:AttachmentButton runat="server"/>
      </Template_Buttons>
    </wssuc:ToolBar>
  </Template>
</SharePoint:RenderingTemplate>
```

As you can see, this control template uses the SharePoint AttachmentButton server control to render the Attach File action button in the toolbar of a new list item form.

So far, you've looked at what the DefaultTemplateName property returns if the current list is not a document library. Next, you see what this property returns if the current list is a document library. If the FormToolBar server control resides in a display list item form and if the form is not displaying the current version of the current list item, the property returns "DocLibDisplayFormToolBar", which is the ID property value of the following RenderingTemplate control template from the DefaultTemplates.ascx file:

```
<SharePoint:RenderingTemplate ID="DocLibDisplayFormToolBar" runat="server">
  <Template>
    <script>
      recycleBinEnabled = <SharePoint:ProjectProperty Property="RecycleBinEnabled"
                          runat="server"/>;
    </script>
    <wssuc:ToolBar CssClass="ms-toolbar" id="toolBarTbl" runat="server"
    FocusOnToolbar="true">
      <Template_Buttons>
        <SharePoint:EnterFolderButton runat="server"/>
        <SharePoint:EditItemButton runat="server"/>
        <SharePoint:DeleteItemButton runat="server"/>
        <SharePoint:ManagePermissionsButton runat="server"/>
        <SharePoint:ManageCopiesButton runat="server"/>
        <SharePoint:CheckInCheckOutButton runat="server"/>
        <SharePoint:VersionHistoryButton runat="server"/>
        <SharePoint:WorkflowsButton runat="server"/>
        <SharePoint:AlertMeButton runat="server"/>
        <SharePoint:ApprovalButton runat="server"/>
      </Template_Buttons>
    </wssuc:ToolBar>
  </Template>
</SharePoint:RenderingTemplate>
```

As you can see, this control template uses the SharePoint EditItemButton, DeleteItemButton, ManagePermissionsButton, ManageCopiesButton, CheckInCheckOutButton, WorkflowsButton, and AlertButton to render typical Edit Item, Delete Item, Manage Permissions, Manage Copies, Check Out, Workflows, and Alert Me action buttons in the toolbar of a display list item form as shown in Figure 4-2.

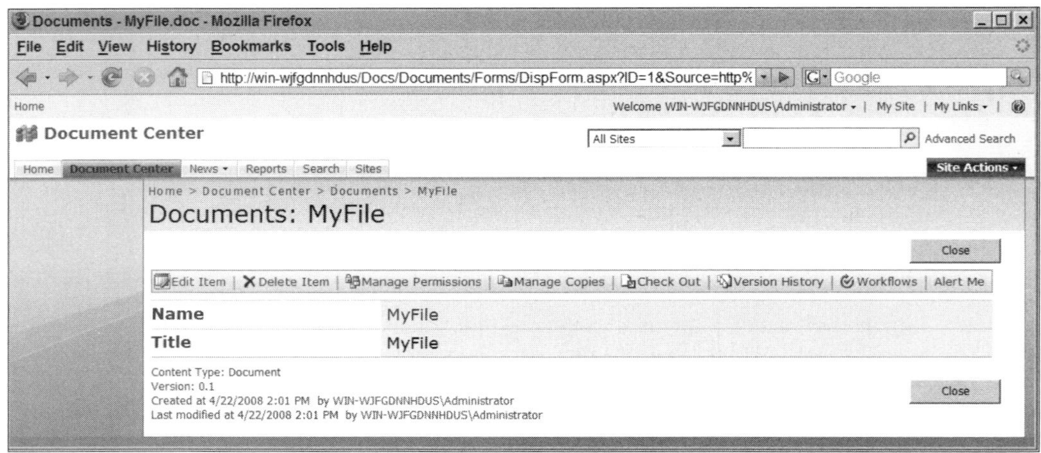

Figure 4-2: The toolbar of a document library's display list item

If the FormToolBar server control resides in an edit list item form, the property returns "DocLibEditFormToolBar", which is the ID property value of the following RenderingTemplate control template in the DefaultTemplates.ascx file:

```
<SharePoint:RenderingTemplate ID="DocLibEditFormToolBar" runat="server">
  <Template>
    <script>
      recycleBinEnabled = <SharePoint:ProjectProperty Property="RecycleBinEnabled"
                          runat="server"/>;
    </script>
    <wssuc:ToolBar CssClass="ms-toolbar" id="toolBarTbl"
    RightButtonSeparator=" " runat="server">
      <Template_Buttons>
        <SharePoint:DeleteItemButton runat="server"/>
      </Template_Buttons>
    </wssuc:ToolBar>
  </Template>
</SharePoint:RenderingTemplate>
```

As you can see, this control template uses a DeleteItemButton server control to render the Delete Item action button in the toolbar of an edit list item form.

Next, you'll take a look at the internal implementation of the CreateChildControls method of FormToolBar. As Listing 4-10 shows, this method first invokes the CreateChildControls method of its base class. Recall that the base class implementation of this method first accesses the ITemplate object that the Template property of the RenderingTemplate control template references. This is the same RenderingTemplate control template whose ID property value is specified in the DefaultTemplateName property. The base class implementation of the CreateChildControls method then instantiates a TemplateContainer server control and loads the child controls within this ITemplate object into this server control and finally adds this TemplateContainer server control to the Controls collection.

The CreateChildControls method of FormToolBar then invokes the FindControl method on this TemplateContainer server control to return a reference to the ToolBar server control with the ID property value of "toolBarTbl". If you look at the excerpts from DefaultTemplates.ascx that you've seen in this section, you'll notice that all RenderingTemplate control templates in these excerpts contain a ToolBar server control with an ID property value of toolBarTbl. This is the server control that contains the standard SharePoint server controls that render the action buttons that go into the toolbar of a form:

```
base.CreateChildControls();
    ToolBar toolbarControl =
                      (ToolBar)this.TemplateContainer.FindControl("toolBarTbl");
```

If the FormToolBar resides in an edit or new list item form, the CreateChildControls method of FormToolBar instantiates a RequiredFieldMessage server control and adds it to the toolbar:

```
    if (base.ControlMode != SPControlMode.Display)
    {
      RequiredFieldMessage child = new RequiredFieldMessage();
      toolbarControl.RightButtons.Controls.Add(child);
    }
```

It is this RequiredFieldMessage server control that renders the asterisk next to a required field. This server control contains the logic that determines which field is required.

RequiredFieldMessage

Listing 4-11 presents the internal implementation of the RequiredFieldMessage server control.

Listing 4-11: The RequiredFieldMessage server control

```
public sealed class RequiredFieldMessage : FormComponent
{
  protected override void OnPreRender(EventArgs e)
  {
    this.EnsureChildControls();
    Control current;
    IEnumerator enumerator = base.FieldControlCollection.GetEnumerator();
    this.Visible = false;
    while (enumerator.MoveNext())
    {
      current = (Control)enumerator.Current;

      if (current.Visible && current is BaseFieldControl &&
          ((BaseFieldControl)current).Field != null &&
          ((BaseFieldControl)current).Field.Required)
      {
        this.Visible = true;
        break;
      }
    }
  }

  protected override string DefaultTemplateName
  {
    get { return "RequiredFieldMessage"; }
  }

  public override bool Visible
  {
    get { return ((base.ControlMode != SPControlMode.Display) && base.Visible); }
    set { base.Visible = value; }
  }
}
```

RequiredFieldMessage, just like many other SharePoint server controls that inherit from TemplateBasedControl, does not directly render its markup. Instead it relies on the RenderingTemplate server control whose ID property value is specified in the DefaultTemplateName property to provide the markup.

As Listing 4-11 shows, the RequiredFieldMessage server control overrides the DefaultTemplateName property to return "RequiredFieldMessage", which is the ID property value of the following RenderingTemplate control template in the DefaultTemplates.ascx file:

```
<SharePoint:RenderingTemplate ID="RequiredFieldMessage" runat="server">
 <Template>
    <span ID="reqdFldTxt" style="white-space: nowrap;padding-right: 3px;"
    class="ms-descriptiontext">
      <asp:literal runat="server" text="<%$Resources:wss,form_required_field%>" />
    </span>
 </Template>
</SharePoint:RenderingTemplate>
```

As you can see, this control template simply pulls the localized value of the form_required_field resource key from the wss.resx file and uses an ASP.NET Literal server control to render this value. If you examine this file, you'll notice that it has the following entry:

```
<data name="form_required_field">
  <value>
    &lt;span class="ms-formvalidation"&gt;*&lt;/span&gt; indicates a required field
  </value>
</data>
```

This means that the RenderingTemplate server control and consequently RequiredFieldMessage render the following markup:

```
<span class="ms-formvalidation">*</span> indicates a required field
```

Note that RequiredFieldMessage overrides the Visible property. The setter of this property simply delegates to the Visible property of the base class. This means that you can still explicitly set the visibility of RequiredFieldMessage:

```
set { base.Visible = value; }
```

The getter of this property returns true only if this property is explicitly set to true and RequiredFieldMessage resides in an edit list item or new list item form:

```
get { return ((base.ControlMode != SPControlMode.Display) && base.Visible); }
```

As Listing 4-11 shows, RequiredFieldMessage overrides the OnPreRender method to include the logic that determines the value of the Visible property. So far you've learned about two out of three factors that affect the visibility of RequiredFieldMessage. The first one is explicitly setting the Visible property. The second one is whether RequiredFieldMessage resides in a new or edit list item form. The OnPreRender method takes care of the third factor, that is, whether the current list item contains any required field. The OnPreRender method takes these steps to make this determination.

First, it invokes the EnsureChildControls method. This method internally invokes the CreateChildControls method if it hasn't already been invoked for the current request. The CreateChildControls method first accesses the ITemplate object that the Template property of the RenderingTemplate control template references. This RenderingTemplate control template is the one whose ID property value is specified in the DefaultTemplateName property, that is, "RequiredFieldMessage". The CreateChildControls method then loads the child controls within this ITemplate object into a TemplateContainer server control and adds this control to the Controls collection:

```
this.EnsureChildControls();
```

The OnPreRender method then accesses the IEnumerator object that knows how to iterate through the field-rendering controls in the FieldControlCollection ArrayList:

```
    IEnumerator enumerator = base.FieldControlCollection.GetEnumerator();
```

The method then sets the Visible property to false:

```
    this.Visible = false;
```

Next, the method iterates through the field-rendering controls in the FieldControlCollection ArrayList searching for a control that meets all these criteria: it's visible, it's a BaseFieldControl, its Field property is not null, and its associated field is required. If it finds a control that meets all these criteria, it sets the Visible property to true:

```
    while (enumerator.MoveNext())
    {
      current = (Control)enumerator.Current;

      if (current.Visible && current is BaseFieldControl &&
         ((BaseFieldControl)current).Field != null &&
         ((BaseFieldControl)current).Field.Required)
      {
        this.Visible = true;
        break;
      }
    }
```

ListFieldIterator

Listing 4-12 presents the internal implementation of the ListFieldIterator server control.

Listing 4-12: The ListFieldIterator server control

```
public class ListFieldIterator : FormComponent
{
  protected override void CreateChildControls()
  {
    this.Controls.Clear();
    for (int i = 0; i < this.Fields.Count; i++)
    {
      if (!this.IsFieldExcluded(this.Fields[i]))
      {
        TemplateContainer container = new TemplateContainer();
        container.FieldName = this.Fields[i].InternalName;
        container.ControlMode = this.ControlMode;
        this.ControlTemplate.InstantiateIn(container);
```

```
          this.Controls.Add(container);
        }
      }
    }

    protected virtual bool IsFieldExcluded(SPField field) { ... }

    protected override string DefaultTemplateName
    {
      get { return "ListFieldIterator"; }
    }

    public string ExcludeFields { get; set; }
  }
```

Recall that Listing 3-5 presents the content of the RenderingTemplate control template with the ID property value of ListForm. This is the control template that the ListFormWebPart Web part uses to render the markup that goes into the body of a display, edit, or new list item form. As the following excerpt from Listing 3-5 shows, this control template uses a ListFieldIterator server control to render the names and values of the list item fields:

```
<SharePoint:RenderingTemplate ID="ListForm" runat="server">
  <Template>
    <SPAN id='part1`prime;>
      ...
      <SharePoint:FormToolBar runat="server"/>
      <TABLE class="ms-formtable" style="margin-top: 8px;" border="0"
      cellpadding="0" cellspacing="0" width="100"%>
        ...
        <SharePoint:ListFieldIterator runat="server"/>
        ...
      </TABLE>
```

As you can see from Listing 4-12, ListFieldIterator exposes a property named ExcludeFields. As the name suggests, this property specifies those fields that ListFieldIterator should not render. The value of this property must be set to a ";#"-separated list of InternalName or Title property values of the fields to exclude. As the previous listing illustrates, the default control template does not exclude any fields from rendering. However, you can override this behavior.

As Listing 4-12 demonstrates, ListFieldIterator also exposes a method named IsFieldExcluded that takes an SPField object that represents a field and returns a Boolean that determines whether the field should be excluded from rendering. The internal logic of this method first checks whether the value of the InternalName or Title property of the field is included in the ExcludeFields property value. If so, it returns true. If not, it uses the following criteria to determine whether the field should be excluded from rendering: the value of the ControlMode property of the ListFieldIterator, the values of the ShowInDisplayForm, Hidden, Type, ShowInNewForm, and ShowInEditForm properties of the field, and the base type of the containing list.

As you can see from Listing 4-12, ListFieldIterator overrides the CreateChildControls method where it performs these tasks. First, it clears the Controls collection as usual:

```
this.Controls.Clear();
```

Then it iterates through the SPField objects in the Fields collection property. These SPField objects represent the list item fields. Keep in mind that the ListFieldIterator server control is used in a display, edit, or new list item form, which displays, edits, or creates a list item. CreateChildControls takes these steps for each enumerated SPField object if the field is not excluded. First it instantiates a TemplateContainer server control:

```
        TemplateContainer container = new TemplateContainer();
```

Then, it sets the ControlMode and FieldName properties of this server control:

```
        container.ControlMode = base.ControlMode;
        container.FieldName = field.InternalName;
```

Next, it invokes the InstantiateIn method on the ITemplate object that the ControlTemplate property of ListFieldIterator references to add the child controls within this object to the TemplateContainer server control:

```
        this.ControlTemplate.InstantiateIn(container);
```

Finally, it adds this server control to the Controls collection of the ListFieldIterator server control:

```
        this.Controls.Add(container);
```

ListFieldIterator inherits the ControlTemplate property from TemplateBasedControl, which provides the following implementation for this property:

```
protected virtual ITemplate ControlTemplate
{
  get { return this.Template; }
}
```

As you can see, the ControlTemplate property simply references the ITemplate object assigned to the Template property, which has the following implementation:

```
[TemplateContainer(typeof(TemplateBasedControl))]
public ITemplate Template
{
  get
  {
    if (this.template == null)
    {
      if (this.TemplateName != null)
        this.template =
                   SPControlTemplateManager.GetTemplateByName(this.TemplateName);
    }
    return this.template;
  }
  set { this.template = value; }
}
```

The Template property invokes the GetTemplateByName method to access a reference to the ITemplate object assigned to the Template property of the control template whose ID property value is specified in the TemplateName property, which in turn has the following implementation:

```
public string TemplateName
{
  get
  {
    if (this.templateName == null)
      this.templateName = this.DefaultTemplateName;

    return this.templateName;
  }

  Set { this.templateName = value; }
}
```

As you can see, the TemplateName property simply returns the value of the DefaultTemplateName property, which has the following implementation:

```
protected override string DefaultTemplateName
{
  get { return "ListFieldIterator"; }
}
```

Therefore, the ControlTemplate property returns a reference to the ITemplate object assigned to the Template property of the RenderingTemplate control template with the ID property value of ListFieldIterator.

You can follow the same pattern in your own custom SharePoint form-rendering controls:

1. Implement an .ascx file that contains a RenderingTemplate control template with a specified ID property value.
2. Deploy this .ascx file to the ControlTemplates folder.
3. Inherit your form-rendering control from FormComponent.
4. Override the DefaultTemplateName property to return a string that contains the ID property value of the RenderingTemplate control template from Step 1.
5. Override the CreateChildControls method only if you need to custom render your form-rendering control. For example, ListFieldIterator overrides this method to filter out excluded fields.

Summary

This chapter provided an in-depth coverage of form-rendering server controls and their internal workings. Through exposure to the internal implementation of these server controls, you also learn the skills that you need to implement your custom form-rendering server controls or to customize SharePoint standard form-rendering server controls. Chapter 5 moves on to the field-rendering server controls.

5

Field Types

As I've discussed in the previous chapters, SharePoint virtualizes the underlying IIS and ASP.NET infrastructures, enabling you to manage and to organize your collaborative content in terms of abstractions such as site collections, sites, lists, list items, content types, field types, site columns, and so on. Field type is one of these abstractions. There are times when your collaborative content cannot be organized through standard field types, but SharePoint enables you to implement your own custom field types and deploy them to SharePoint. This section helps you gain the skills and knowledge you need to implement custom field types.

The discussion starts with the simplest possible scenario and progressively presents more complex situations as the chapter progresses. Developing a custom field type, at a minimum, requires you to implement a field type class and a field type definition. A *field type class* is a .NET class that inherits directly or indirectly from the SPField class. A *field type definition* is an XML document that contains the information that SharePoint uses to render the field type.

SPField

The concept of field or column in SharePoint has rather different meanings in different contexts. First, there is what is known as a site column. A *site column* encapsulates a column definition independent of any list that may use that site column. This means that you can define a site column once, deploy it to a SharePoint site, and use it in any list in that site or its descendant sites. As the name suggests, a site column is scoped to a site and its descendant sites. The SPWeb object that represents a SharePoint site features a collection property named Fields, which is of the SPFieldCollection type. This collection contains SPField objects that represent the site columns of that site. Site columns are discussed in depth in the next chapter.

Secondly, there is what is known as a *list column*. When a site column is added to a list, SharePoint provisions a local copy of the site column definition and adds it to the list. This local copy is known as a list column. As you can see, the relationship between a site column and the list columns provisioned from it is one to many. The SPList object that represents a SharePoint list features a collection property named Fields, which is of the SPFieldCollection type. This collection contains SPField objects that represent the list columns of that list.

Thirdly, there is what I like to call the *list item column*. Because list items of the same list can be of different content types, as discussed thoroughly in next chapter, not every list item has all the list columns that its containing list has. Different types of list items in a list may support different columns. The SPListItem object that represents a list item features a collection property named Fields, which is of the SPFieldCollection type. This collection contains SPField objects that represent the columns of that list item.

So far I've discussed column as a column definition or schema. There is also the concept of field or column as a container of data. This is also represented by SPField or one of its subclasses. As you can see, SPField represents different things in different contexts. Keep this in mind as you're reading through this chapter.

Listing 5-1 presents some of the main methods and properties of the SPField class.

Listing 5-1: The SPField class

```
SharePointPermission(SecurityAction.LinkDemand, ObjectModel = true)]
public class SPField
{
  public SPField(SPFieldCollection fields, string fieldName);
  public SPField(SPFieldCollection fields, string typeName, string displayName);
  public void Delete();
  public virtual object GetFieldValue(string value);
  public virtual string GetFieldValueAsHtml(object value);
  public virtual string GetFieldValueAsText(object value);
  public virtual string GetFieldValueForEdit(object value);
  public virtual string GetValidatedString(object value);
  public virtual void OnAdded(SPAddFieldOptions op);
  public virtual void OnDeleting();
  public virtual void OnUpdated();
  public override string ToString();
  public virtual void Update();
  public void Update(bool pushChangesToLists);

  // Properties
  public virtual string DefaultValue { get; set; }
  public virtual object DefaultValueTyped { get; }
  public string Description { get; set; }
  public string Direction { get; set; }
  public string DisplaySize { get; set; }
  public virtual BaseFieldControl FieldRenderingControl
  {
    get { return null; }
  }
  public SPFieldTypeDefinition FieldTypeDefinition { get; }
  public virtual Type FieldValueType { get; }
  public virtual bool Filterable { get; }
```

```
    public virtual bool FilterableNoRecurrence { get; }
    public string InternalName { get; }
    public SPList ParentList { get; }
    public bool PushChangesToLists { get; set; }
    public bool ReadOnlyField { get; set; }
    public string RelatedField { get; set; }
    public bool Required { get; set; }
    public bool ShowInDisplayForm { get; set; }
    public bool ShowInEditForm { get; set; }
    public bool ShowInListSettings { get; set; }
    public bool ShowInNewForm { get; set; }
    public bool ShowInVersionHistory { get; set; }
    public bool ShowInViewForms { get; set; }
    public virtual bool Sortable { get; }
    public string Title { get; set; }
    public SPFieldType Type { get; set; }
}
```

Here are the descriptions of some of the main methods of SPField, against which you can program from managed code:

- **Delete.** You can use this method to delete the current column
- **GetFieldValue.** As you'll see later, a field type can have a value of a complex .NET type such as a class or struct. The GetFieldValue method takes the string representation of the field value and converts it into an instance of this complex .NET type.
- **GetFieldValueAsHtml.** This method takes the field value object and returns a string that contains the field value in HTML format. SharePoint uses this string to render the field value directly on a page. This string is not used to render the field value on list views (such as AllItems.aspx) or in Display mode (DispForm.aspx). As you'll see later in this chapter, SharePoint uses the rendering logic specified in the RenderPatterns section of the field type definition to render the field value on list views or Display mode. Use GetFieldValueAsHtml if you need to render the field value from managed code.
- **GetFieldValueAsText.** This method takes the field value object and returns a string that contains the field value as plain text.
- **GetFieldValueForEdit.** This method takes the field value object and returns its string representation suitable for rendering the field value in Edit mode in Edit list item form.
- **GetValidatedString.** This method takes the field value object as its argument, validates it, serializes it into its string representation, and returns this serialized string representation.
- **OnAdded.** This method is automatically invoked after the field is added. Override this method in an SPField-derived class if you need to run custom code after a field is added. The SPField class's implementation of this method doesn't do anything.
- **OnDeleting.** This method is automatically invoked before the field is deleted. Override this method in an SPField-derived class if you need to run custom code before a field is deleted. The SPField class's implementation of this method doesn't do anything.
- **OnUpdated.** This method is automatically invoked after the field is updated. Override this method in an SPField-derived class if you need to run custom code after the field schema changes. The SPField class's implementation of this method doesn't do anything.

- **ToString.** This method returns the title of the field.
- **Update.** Invoke this method to commit the changes made to the field. Note that this method has two overloads. The second overload takes a Boolean value as its argument. Invoke this overload and pass true as its argument if you want to push the changes made to the field to all lists where columns based on this field type are used. The first overload calls the second overload under the hood, passing false as its argument.

Here are the descriptions of some of the main properties of the SPField class:

- **CanBeDeleted.** This read-only property returns a Boolean value that specifies whether the field can be deleted.
- **CanToggleHidden.** This read-only property returns a Boolean value that specifies whether the column can be hidden through the user interface.
- **DefaultValue.** This gets or sets the string that contains the default value for the field.
- **DefaultValueTyped.** This gets the default field value object. As you'll see later in this chapter, the field types whose data types are complex .NET data types use a field value class or structure. The DefaultValueTyped property returns an instance of this field value class or structure.
- **Description.** You can use this property to get or set the description for this field.
- **Direction.** You can use this property to get or set the string that specifies the reading order for this field. The possible values are RTL (right-to-left), LTL (left-to-right), and none.
- **DisplaySize.** You can use this property to get or set the string that contains the display size for this field.
- **FieldRenderingControl.** This read-only property returns a BaseFieldControl server control that renders the field in Display, Edit, and New forms, as well as in data form Web parts or pages that use field controls. The SPField class's implementation of this property returns null. That is, by default the RenderingPattern section of the field type definition is used to render the field.
- **FieldTypeDefinition.** You can use this read-only property to access the SPFieldTypeDefinition object that represents the field type definition for this field. A field type definition is an XML document that provides SharePoint with required information to render the field and its value and optionally its variable field type properties. Field type definitions are covered in depth later in this chapter.
- **FieldValueType.** You can use this read-only property to access the Type object that represents the field value class for this field type. A field type with a complex data type normally uses a .NET class or structure known as field value class or type for its data. Field value types are covered in depth later in this chapter.
- **Group.** You can use this property to get or set the group to which the field belongs. SharePoint displays these column groups in the Site Column Gallery shown in Figure 5-1. The default column groups are Base Columns, Core Contact and Calendar Columns, Core Document Columns, Core Task and Issue Columns, Custom Columns, Extended Columns, _Hidden, and Picture Columns. If you set this property to a value that is not included in the preceding list, SharePoint will add a new column group with the name specified in this value and display the field under this column group.

- **Hidden.** You can use this property to get or set a Boolean value that specifies whether the field is hidden. SharePoint does not display hidden fields of a list in the SharePoint user interface.
- **Id.** You can use this read-only property to get the GUID of the field.
- **InternalName.** You can use this read-only string property to access the internal name of the field. As you'll see later, when you implement a custom field type that uses a field-rendering control you need to set the FieldName property of the field-rendering control to the internal name of the field. Note that the internal name of a field is different from its display name. The internal name is the actual name of the field in the underlying data store.
- **ParentList.** You can use this read-only property to access the SPList object that represents the SharePoint list that contains this field.
- **PushChangesToLists.** You can use this property to get or set a Boolean value that specifies whether to push changes that are made to the field template down to the lists where columns based on this field type are used.
- **ReadOnlyField.** You can use this property to get or set a Boolean value that indicates whether the field values can be modified:

```
SPSite siteCollection = SPContext.Current.Site;
SPWeb site = siteCollection.OpenWeb();
SPList someList = site.Lists["SomeList"];
SPListItem item = someList.Items[0];
item.Fields["SomeField"].ReadOnlyField = true;
item.Fields["SomeField"].Update();
```

- **Required.** You can use this property to get or set a Boolean value that specifies whether the field value must be specified.
- **ShowInDisplayForm.** You can use this property to get or set a Boolean value that specifies whether to display this field in the Display list item form (DispForm.aspx).
- **ShowInEditForm.** You can use this property to get or set a Boolean value that specifies whether to display this field in the Edit list item form.
- **ShowInNewForm.** You can use this property to get or set a Boolean value that specifies whether to display this field in the New list item form.
- **ShowInVersionHistory.** You can use this property to get or set a Boolean value that specifies whether to display this field in the version history form. Keep in mind that the version history form renders the string returned from the GetFieldValueAsHtml method.
- **Sortable.** You can use this property to get a Boolean value that specifies whether the field is sortable.

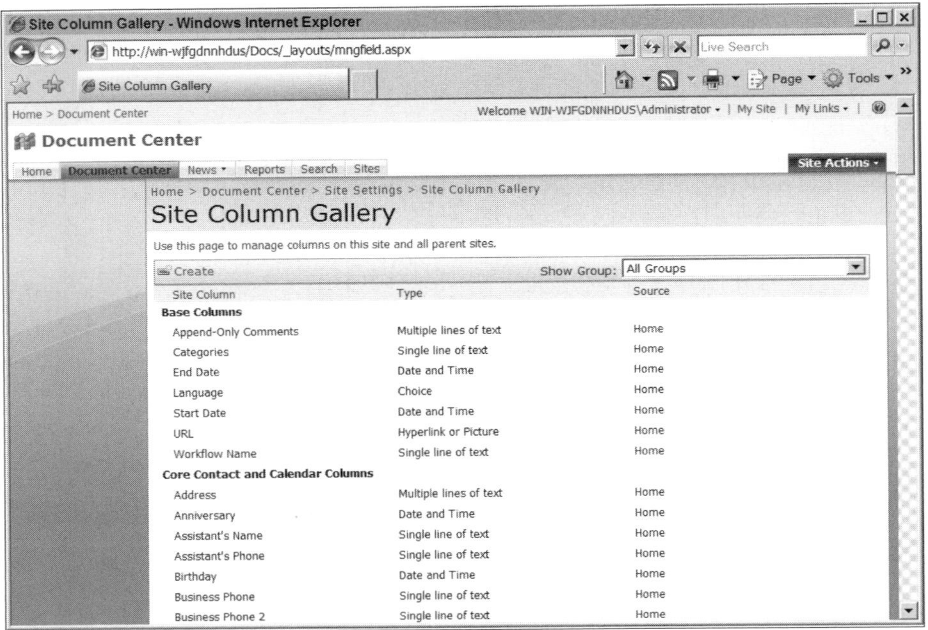

Figure 5-1: Site Column Gallery

As mentioned earlier, you must derive from SPField or one of its subclasses to implement a custom field type. Next, you'll take a look at some of the subclasses of the SPField class from which you can inherit to implement your own custom field types. The internal implementation of these subclasses is discussed to help you gain the skills you need to implement one of your own.

As a best practice, you should use the following naming convention to name your custom field type: *FieldTypeName*Field, where FieldTypeName is the placeholder for the name of your custom field type. This naming convention came about after the SharePoint standard field types were implemented. As such, SharePoint standard field types follow this naming convention: SPField*FieldNameType*, such as SPFieldBoolean, SPFieldText, and so on.

SPFieldBoolean

As the name implies, SPFieldBoolean represents a Boolean field type. Listing 5-2 presents the internal implementation of SPFieldBoolean.

Listing 5-2: The internal implementation of SPFieldBoolean

```
[SharePointPermission(SecurityAction.InheritanceDemand, ObjectModel = true),
SharePointPermission(SecurityAction.LinkDemand, ObjectModel = true)]
public class SPFieldBoolean : SPField
{
  public SPFieldBoolean(SPFieldCollection fields, string fieldName)
    : base(fields, fieldName) { }

  public SPFieldBoolean(SPFieldCollection fields, string typeName,
                        string displayName)
    : base(fields, typeName, displayName) { }

  public override object GetFieldValue(string value)
  {
    if (!string.IsNullOrEmpty(value))
    {
      if (string.Compare(value, "TRUE",
                         StringComparison.InvariantCultureIgnoreCase) != 0 &&
           value != "1" && value != "-1")
        return false;
    }

    else
      return value;

    return true;
  }

  public override string GetFieldValueAsText(object value)
  {
    string rtn;
    if (value == null)
      rtn = string.Empty;
    else if ((bool)value)
      rtn = "Yes";
    else
      rtn = "No";
    return rtn;
  }

  public override object DefaultValueTyped
  {
    get
    {
      if (((string)base.DefaultValueTyped) != "1")
        return false;

      return true;
    }
  }

  public override BaseFieldControl FieldRenderingControl
  {
```

(continued)

Listing 5-2 *(continued)*

```
        get
        {
          BaseFieldControl fieldControl = new BooleanField();
          fieldControl.FieldName = base.InternalName;
          return fieldControl;
        }
      }

      public override Type FieldValueType
      {
        get { return typeof(bool); }
      }
    }
```

First, note that SPFieldBoolean is annotated with the following code access security metadata attribute:

```
[SharePointPermission(SecurityAction.InheritanceDemand, ObjectModel = true),
SharePointPermission(SecurityAction.LinkDemand, ObjectModel = true)]
```

These two metadata attributes respectively demand that the subclasses and callers of SPFieldBoolean have permission to use the SharePoint object model.

Second, note that SPFieldBoolean features two public constructors that delegate to the respective constructors of the SPField class:

```
public SPFieldBoolean(SPFieldCollection fields, string fieldName)
  : base(fields, fieldName) { }

public SPFieldBoolean(SPFieldCollection fields, string typeName,
                      string displayName)
  : base(fields, typeName, displayName) { }
```

You must follow the same pattern in your own custom field types. That is, your field types must expose the same two constructors.

Third, SPFieldBoolean overrides the GetFieldValue method that inherits from SPField. This method takes the string representation of the field value and generates a Boolean value from it. SharePoint returns the return value of GetFieldValue when SPListItem.this["fieldname"] is invoked. Your custom field type override of GetFieldValue should do the same. That is, it should contain the logic that parses the string value passed into GetFieldValue and instantiates and returns an instance of the respective field value type. The field value type in the case of SPFieldBoolean is a Boolean type.

Fourth, SPFieldBoolean overrides the GetFieldValueAsText method that inherits from SPField. This method takes a field value object as its argument and serializes this object into its plain text representation. Your custom field type override of the GetFieldValueAsText method should do the same, That is, it should contain the logic that knows how to serialize the specified field value object into its plain text representation.

Fifth, SPFieldBoolean overrides the DefaultValueTyped read-only property that it inherits from SPField to return the appropriate Boolean value. Your custom field type should also override this property to return an instance of the respective field value type. SharePoint uses this instance when the value of a field based on your field type hasn't been set.

Sixth, SPFieldBoolean overrides the FieldValueType read-only property that it inherits from SPField to return the Type object that represents System.Boolean type. Your custom field type should also override this property to return a Type object that represents the respective field value type.

Lastly, SPFieldBoolean overrides the FieldRenderControl read-only property that it inherits from SPField to instantiate and to return an instance of a field-rendering control named BooleanField. Note that this override assigns the internal name of the field type to the FieldName property of this field-rendering control. Field-rendering controls are discussed later in this chapter. For now, it suffices to say that the field-rendering control that the FieldRenderControl property returns is normally used to render the field in Edit and New list item forms.

SPFieldMultiChoice

As the name suggests, SPFieldMultiChoice represents a fieldchoice field type, that is, a field type that contains multiple values. Listing 5-3 presents a portion of the internal implementation of this field type.

Listing 5-3: The SPMultiChoiceField class

```
[SharePointPermission(SecurityAction.LinkDemand, ObjectModel = true),
SharePointPermission(SecurityAction.InheritanceDemand, ObjectModel = true)]
public class SPFieldMultiChoice : SPField
{
  private StringCollection choices;

  public SPFieldMultiChoice(SPFieldCollection fields, string fieldName):
                                                     base(fields, fieldName)
  {
    this.choices = new StringCollection();
  }

  public SPFieldMultiChoice(SPFieldCollection fields, string typeName,
                            string displayName)
    : base(fields, typeName, displayName)
  {
    this.choices = new StringCollection();
  }

  public override object GetFieldValue(string value)
  {
    if (!string.IsNullOrEmpty(value))
      return new SPFieldMultiChoiceValue(value);

    return null;
  }

  public override string GetFieldValueAsText(object value)
  {
    if (value != null)
```

(continued)

Listing 5-3 *(continued)*

```
    {
      SPFieldMultiChoiceValue value2;
      if (value is SPFieldMultiChoiceValue)
        value2 = (SPFieldMultiChoiceValue)value;

      else
        value2 = new SPFieldMultiChoiceValue((string)value);

      return value2.ToString();
    }
    return string.Empty;
  }

  public StringCollection Choices
  {
    get
    {
      this.InitChoiceCollection();
      return this.choices;
    }
  }

  public override BaseFieldControl FieldRenderingControl
  {
    get
    {
      BaseFieldControl fieldControl = new CheckBoxChoiceField();
      fieldControl.FieldName = base.InternalName;
      return fieldControl;
    }
  }

  public override Type FieldValueType
  {
    get { return typeof(SPFieldMultiChoiceValue); }
  }

  public override bool Sortable
  {
    get { return false; }
  }
}
```

Note that both constructors of SPFieldMultiChoice instantiate a StringCollection where the field values are stored:

```
this.choices = new StringCollection();
```

As you can see from Listing 5-3, SPFieldMultiChoice features a public property that returns a reference to this StringCollection. Therefore, you can iterate through the strings in this StringCollection to access the field values.

As Listing 5-3 shows, SPFieldMultiChoice's override of GetFieldValue instantiates an SPFieldMultiChoiceValue instance, passing in the string representation of the specified field value:

```
public override object GetFieldValue(string value)
{
  if (!string.IsNullOrEmpty(value))
    return new SPFieldMultiChoiceValue(value);

  return null;
}
```

Because SPFieldMultiChoice contains a complex data type, which consists of multiple values, it makes use of what is known as field value type or class. The SPFieldMultiChoiceValue class is the field value type or class in this case. A field value type is a .NET class or struct whose instances contain the field values for a specified field type. If your custom field type supports a complex data type, you should consider implementing a custom field value type. There is no requirement as to from which base class you should inherit your custom field value type. As a matter of fact, a field value type does not have to inherit from any type.

As Listing 5-3 illustrates, SPFieldMultiChoice's override of GetFieldValueAsText follows the typical implementation pattern that you should also follow in your own override of this method. First, it checks whether the field value passed into the method is null. If so, it simply returns an empty string. Your custom field type override of GetFieldValueAsText should also return an empty string if the field value is null.

If the field value passed into the method is not null, it performs these tasks. First, it checks whether the field value is of the SPFieldMultiChoiceValue type. If so, it simply casts the value to the SPFieldMultiChoiceValue type:

```
if (value is SPFieldMultiChoiceValue)
   value2 = (SPFieldMultiChoiceValue)value;
```

If not, it assumes that the field value passed into the method is the string representation of the field value object. Therefore, it instantiates an SPFieldMultiChoiceValue object, passing in this string representation:

```
else
  value2 = new SPFieldMultiChoiceValue((string)value);
```

Your custom field type override of GetFieldValueAsText should follow the same implementation pattern. That is, it should check whether the field value passed in the method is of the field value type associated with your custom field type. If so, it should cast the value to the respective field value type. If not, it should assume that the field value passed into the method is the string representation of the actual field value object and instantiate an instance of the respective field value type, passing in this string representation.

As Listing 5-3 demonstrates, SPFieldMultiChoice's override of GetFieldValueAsText finally returns the return value of the ToString method of the field value object:

```
return value2.ToString();
```

This is possible because the ToString method of the SPFieldMultiChoiceValue field value type returns the string representation of the field value object. As you can see, SPFieldMultiChoice's override of GetFieldValueAsText simply delegates the responsibility of serializing the field value object into its string representation to the ToString method of the field value object.

Your custom field type override of GetFieldValueAsText should do the same thing. That is, it should delegate to the ToString method of the respective field value object. This also means that your custom field value type should override the ToString method that it inherits from System.Object to serialize the field value object into its string representation.

As you can see from Listing 5-3, SPFieldMultiChoice overrides the FieldValueType read-only property to return a Type object that represents the type of its associated field value type, that is, SPFieldMultiChoiceValue:

```
public override Type FieldValueType
{
  get { return typeof(SPFieldMultiChoiceValue); }
}
```

Also note that SPFieldMultiChoice overrides FieldRenderingControl to instantiate and return an instance of its respective field-rendering control, that is, CheckBoxChoiceField. SharePoint uses this control to render fields of the SPFieldMultiChoice field type in the New and Edit list item forms:

```
public override BaseFieldControl FieldRenderingControl
{
  get
  {
    BaseFieldControl fieldControl = new CheckBoxChoiceField();
    fieldControl.FieldName = base.InternalName;
    return fieldControl;
  }
}
```

Next, take a look at the SPFieldMultiChoiceValue field value type as shown in Listing 5-4.

Listing 5-4: The SPFieldMultiChoiceValue field value type

```
[Serializable,
SharePointPermission(SecurityAction.InheritanceDemand, ObjectModel = true),
SharePointPermission(SecurityAction.LinkDemand, ObjectModel = true)]
public class SPFieldMultiChoiceValue
{
  private const string delimiter = ";#";
  private ArrayList choiceValues;

  public SPFieldMultiChoiceValue()
  {
    this.choiceValues = new ArrayList();
  }

  [SharePointPermission(SecurityAction.Demand, ObjectModel = true)]
  public override string ToString()
  {
    StringBuilder stringBuilder = new StringBuilder(0xff);
    int num = 0;
    while (num < this.choiceValues.Count)
    {
      if (!string.IsNullOrEmpty((string)this.choiceValues[num]))
      {
        stringBuilder.Append(";#");
        stringBuilder.Append(this.choiceValues[num]);
      }
      num++;
    }

    if (stringBuilder.Length <= 0)
      return string.Empty;

    stringBuilder.Append(";#");
    return stringBuilder.ToString();
  }

  public SPFieldMultiChoiceValue(string fieldValue)
  {
    this.choiceValues = new ArrayList();
    if (!string.IsNullOrEmpty(fieldValue))
    {
      if (!fieldValue.StartsWith(Delimiter))
        fieldValue = ";#" + fieldValue + ";#";

      int fieldIndex;
      for (int i = 2; i < fieldValue.Length; i = fieldIndex + 2)
      {
        fieldIndex = fieldValue.IndexOf(";#", i);
        if (fieldIndex < 0)
          return;

        if (fieldIndex > i)
        {
```

(continued)

Listing 5-4 *(continued)*

```
            string str = fieldValue.Substring(i, fieldIndex - i);
            this.choiceValues.Add(str);
          }
        }
      }
    }

    public string this[int index]
    {
      get
      {
        if (this.choiceValues.Count != 0)
          return (string)this.choiceValues[index];

        return string.Empty;
      }
    }

    public bool FillInChoice { get; set; }

    public void Add(string choiceValue)
    {
      this.choiceValues.Add(choiceValue);
    }

    public int Count
    {
      get { return this.choiceValues.Count; }
    }

    public static string Delimiter
    {
      get { return ";#"; }
    }
  }
```

SPFieldMultiChoiceValue follows the typical implementation pattern of a field value type as follows. First, it is annotated with the SerializableAttribute metadata attribute so its instances can be serialized and stored. You should always annotate your custom field value types with the SerializableAttribute metadata attribute. The only exception to this rule is those field value types whose instances cannot be serialized due to the fact that they're context-dependent. You'll see an example of this later in this chapter.

Second, SPFieldMultiChoiceValue is annotated with the following two code access security metadata attributes to demand that its subclasses and callers must have permission to use the SharePoint object model:

```
SharePointPermission(SecurityAction.InheritanceDemand, ObjectModel = true),
SharePointPermission(SecurityAction.LinkDemand, ObjectModel = true)
```

Third, it exposes two constructors where the first constructor takes no arguments and the second constructor takes a single string argument. Your custom field value types should also expose the same two constructors. Your custom field values can optionally expose other constructors as needed.

The string argument that the second constructor takes is nothing but the string representation of the respective field value object. As Listing 5-4 shows, this constructor simply parses this string representation and loads its content into an internal ArrayList. Note that this constructor expects this string representation to have a specific format. That is, this string must contain a ";#"-separated list of substrings that may or may not start with ";#".

The constructor of your custom field value type should follow a similar implementation pattern. That is, it should parse the string passed into it as its argument and load the content of this string in some internal storage. This constructor must expect a string with a specific format. You as the field value type developer decide what this format should be. Keep in mind that this string is the string representation of the field value object.

Fourth, SPFieldMultiChoiceValue overrides the ToString method that inherits from System.Object where it simply loads the content of the internal ArrayList discussed earlier into a string of ";#"-separated substrings that starts and ends with ";#". As such, the ToString method returns the string representation of the field value object. As you saw earlier in Listing 5-3, the GetFieldValueAsText method of SPFieldMultiChoice simply delegates to the ToString method of SPFieldMultiChoiceValue.

Your custom field value type should also override the ToString method to return the string representation of the field value object. Your custom field class's implementation of GetFieldValueAsText should then simply delegate to the ToString method of your custom field value type.

SPFieldChoice

As the name implies, SPFieldChoice represents a choice field type. Listing 5-5 contains the portion of the internal implementation of SPFieldChoice.

Listing 5-5: The SPFieldChoice class

```
[SharePointPermission(SecurityAction.InheritanceDemand, ObjectModel = true),
SharePointPermission(SecurityAction.LinkDemand, ObjectModel = true)]
public class SPFieldChoice : SPFieldMultiChoice
{
  public SPFieldChoice(SPFieldCollection fields, string fieldName)
    : base(fields, fieldName) { }

  public SPFieldChoice(SPFieldCollection fields, string typeName,
                       string displayName)
    : base(fields, typeName, displayName) { }

  public override object GetFieldValue(string value)
  {
    return value;
  }

  public SPChoiceFormatType EditFormat
  {
    get
    {
      string fieldAttributeValue = base.GetFieldAttributeValue("Format", 0x10);
      if (fieldAttributeValue != null)
```

(continued)

Listing 5-5 *(continued)*

```
        {
          while (fieldAttributeValue != string.Empty)
          {
            return (SPChoiceFormatType)Enum.Parse(
                              SPChoiceFormatType.Dropdown.GetType(), fieldAttributeValue);
          }
        }
        return SPChoiceFormatType.Dropdown;
      }
      set
      {
        base.SetFieldAttributeValue("Format", Convert.ToString(value));
      }
    }

    public override BaseFieldControl FieldRenderingControl
    {
      get
      {
        BaseFieldControl fieldControl;
        switch (this.EditFormat)
        {
          case SPChoiceFormatType.Dropdown:
            fieldControl = new DropDownChoiceField();
            break;

          case SPChoiceFormatType.RadioButtons:
            fieldControl = new RadioButtonChoiceField();
            break;

          default:
            return null;
        }
        fieldControl.FieldName = base.InternalName;
        return fieldControl;
      }
    }

    public override Type FieldValueType
    {
      get { return typeof(string); }
    }
  }
```

Because SPFieldMultiChoice provides most of the functionality that SPFieldChoice must support, SPFieldChoice inherits from SPFieldMultiChoice. The main functionality that SPFieldChoice adds to SPFieldMultiChoice is the ability to use a DropDownChoiceField or RadioButtonChoiceField to render the SPFieldChoice field type in the New and Edit list item forms. Also note that the SPFieldChoice field type does not use SPFieldMultiChoiceValue as its field value type because the SPFieldChoice field type only supports the string data type. As such, the SPFieldChoice field type overrides FieldValueType to return a Type object that represents the type of System.String.

As you can see, just because you inherit your custom field type from another field type does not mean that your custom field type must use its base class's field value type or inherit from it. Your custom field type can use an entirely different field value type.

Field Type Definition

As mentioned earlier, at a minimum you must implement a custom field class and define a field type definition in order to implement a custom field type. The previous section discussed field classes. This section covers field type definitions.

A field type definition is an XML document that provides SharePoint with the necessary information to render the respective field type in the Display, Edit, and New control modes and on list view pages such as AllItem.aspx.

The previous section discussed three field classes named SPFieldBoolean, SPFieldMultiChoice, and SPFieldChoice. As an example, this section discusses the field type definition for the SPFieldChoice field type. The field type definitions for all standard SharePoint field types are in an XML file named FLDTYPES.xml, which is located in the following folder on the file system of the front-end web server:

```
Local_Drive:\Program Files\Common Files\microsoft shared\Web Server
Extensions\12\TEMPLATE\XML
```

Listing 5-6 presents the field type definition for the SPFieldChoice field type.

Listing 5-6: The field type definition for the SPFieldChoice field type

```
<FieldType>
  <Field Name="TypeName">Choice</Field>
  <Field Name="TypeDisplayName">$Resources:core,fldtype_choice;</Field>
  <Field Name="TypeShortDescription">$Resources:core,fldtype_choice_desc;</Field>
  <Field Name="InternalType">Choice</Field>
  <Field Name="SQLType">nvarchar</Field>
  <Field Name="FieldTypeClass">Microsoft.SharePoint.SPFieldChoice</Field>
  <Field Name="ParentType"></Field>
  <Field Name="Sortable">TRUE</Field>
  <Field Name="Filterable">TRUE</Field>
  <RenderPattern Name="HeaderPattern">
    <Switch>
      <Expr>
        <Property Select='Filterable'/>
      </Expr>
      <Case Value="FALSE"> </Case>
      <Default>
        <Switch>
          <Expr>
            <GetVar Name='Filter'/>
          </Expr>
          <Case Value='1'>
```

(continued)

Listing 5-6 *(continued)*

```
        <HTML><![CDATA[<SELECT ID="diidFilter]]></HTML>
        <Property Select='Name'/>
        <HTML>                  <![CDATA[" TITLE=]]></HTML>
        <HTML>"$Resources:core,501;</HTML>
        <Property Select='DisplayName' HTMLEncode='TRUE'/>
        <HTML><![CDATA[" OnChange='FilterField("]]></HTML>
        <GetVar Name="View"/>
        <HTML><![CDATA[",]]></HTML>
        <ScriptQuote>
          <Property Select='Name' URLEncode="TRUE"/>
        </ScriptQuote>
        <HTML>
          <![CDATA[
            ,this.options[this.selectedIndex].value,
             this.selectedIndex);' dir="
          ]]></HTML>
        <Property Select="Direction" HTMLEncode="TRUE"/>
        <HTML><![CDATA[">]]></HTML>
        <FieldFilterOptions BooleanTrue="$Resources:core,fld_yes;"
        BooleanFalse="$Resources:core,fld_no;"
        NullString="$Resources:core,fld_empty;"
        AllItems="$Resources:core,fld_all;" />
        <HTML><![CDATA[</SELECT><BR>]]></HTML>
      </Case>
    </Switch>
  </Default>
</Switch>
<Switch>
  <Expr>
    <Property Select='Sortable'/>
  </Expr>
  <Case Value="FALSE">
    <Property Select='DisplayName' HTMLEncode="TRUE"/>
  </Case>
  <Default>
    <Switch>
      <Expr>
        <GetVar Name='SortDisable'/>
      </Expr>
      <Case Value='TRUE'>
        <Property Select='DisplayName' HTMLEncode="TRUE"/>
      </Case>
      <Default>
        <HTML><![CDATA[<A ID="diidSort]]></HTML>
        <Property Select='Name'/>
        <HTML>         <![CDATA[" onfocus="OnFocusFilter(this)" TITLE=]]></HTML>
        <HTML>"$Resources:core,500;</HTML>
        <Property Select='DisplayName' HTMLEncode='TRUE'/>
        <HTML>
```

```
                <![CDATA[
                  " HREF="javascript:" OnClick="javascript:return
                  OnClickFilter(this,event);"
                ]]></HTML>
              <HTML><![CDATA[ SORTINGFIELDS="]]></HTML>
              <FieldSortParams HTMLEncode="TRUE"/>
              <HTML><![CDATA[">]]></HTML>
              <Property Select='DisplayName' HTMLEncode="TRUE"/>
              <HTML>
                <![CDATA[
                  <img src="/_layouts/images/blank.gif" class="ms-hidden" border=0
                  width=1 height=1 alt="
                ]]></HTML>
              <HTML>$Resources:OpenMenuKeyAccessible;</HTML>
              <HTML><![CDATA[">]]></HTML>
              <HTML><![CDATA[</A><IMG SRC="]]></HTML>
              <FieldSortImageURL/>
              <HTML><![CDATA[" ALT="]]></HTML>
              <Switch>
                <Expr>
                  <GetVar Name='SortDir'/>
                </Expr>
                <Case Value='Asc'>
                  <HTML>$Resources:core,150;</HTML>
                </Case>
                <Case Value='Desc'>
                  <HTML>$Resources:core,151;</HTML>
                </Case>
                <Default>
                  <HTML></HTML>
                </Default>
              </Switch>
              <HTML><![CDATA[" BORDER=0>]]></HTML>
            </Default>
          </Switch>
        </Default>
      </Switch>
      <HTML><![CDATA[<IMG SRC="]]></HTML>
      <FieldFilterImageURL/>
      <HTML><![CDATA[" BORDER=0 ALT="">]]></HTML>
    </RenderPattern>
    <RenderPattern Name="DisplayPattern">
      <Column HTMLEncode="TRUE"/>
    </RenderPattern>
    <RenderPattern Name="EditPattern">
      <HTML><![CDATA[<SCRIPT>fld = new ChoiceField(frm,]]></HTML>
      <ScriptQuote>
        <Property Select="Name"/>
      </ScriptQuote>
      <HTML>,</HTML>
```

(continued)

Listing 5-6 *(continued)*

```
<ScriptQuote>
  <Property Select="DisplayName"/>
</ScriptQuote>
<HTML>,</HTML>
<ScriptQuote>
  <Column/>
</ScriptQuote>
<HTML>); fld.format = "</HTML>
<Property Select="Format"/>
<HTML>"; </HTML>
<Switch>
  <Expr>
    <Property Select="FillInChoice"/>
  </Expr>
  <Case Value="TRUE">fld.fFillInChoice = true;</Case>
</Switch>
<ForEach Select="CHOICES/CHOICE">
  <HTML>fld.AddChoice(</HTML>
  <ScriptQuote>
    <Property Select="."/>
  </ScriptQuote>
  <HTML>, </HTML>
  <ScriptQuote>
    <Property Select="Value"/>
  </ScriptQuote>
  <HTML>);</HTML>
</ForEach>
<Switch>
  <Expr>
    <Property Select="Required"/>
  </Expr>
  <Case Value="TRUE">fld.fRequired = true;</Case>
</Switch>
<HTML><![CDATA[fld.IMEMode="]]></HTML>
<Switch>
  <Expr>
    <Property Select="Type"/>
  </Expr>
  <Case Value="Lookup">
    <HTML><![CDATA[inactive]]></HTML>
  </Case>
  <Case Value="DateTime">
    <HTML><![CDATA[inactive]]></HTML>
  </Case>
  <Case Value="GridChoice">
    <HTML><![CDATA[inactive]]></HTML>
  </Case>
  <Case Value="Calculated">
    <HTML><![CDATA[inactive]]></HTML>
  </Case>
```

```
        <Case Value="Currency">
          <HTML><![CDATA[inactive]]></HTML>
        </Case>
        <Case Value="Number">
          <HTML><![CDATA[inactive]]></HTML>
        </Case>
        <Case Value="User">
          <HTML><![CDATA[inactive]]></HTML>
        </Case>
        <Case Value="Boolean">
          <HTML><![CDATA[inactive]]></HTML>
        </Case>
        <Default>
          <Property Select="IMEMode" HTMLEncode="TRUE"/>
        </Default>
      </Switch>
      <HTML><![CDATA[";]]></HTML>
      <HTML><![CDATA[fld.BuildUI();</SCRIPT>]]></HTML>
    </RenderPattern>
    <RenderPattern Name="NewPattern" DisplayName="NewPattern">
      <HTML><![CDATA[<SCRIPT>fld = new ChoiceField(frm,]]></HTML>
      <ScriptQuote>
        <Property Select="Name"/>
      </ScriptQuote>
      <HTML>,</HTML>
      <ScriptQuote>
        <Property Select="DisplayName"/>
      </ScriptQuote>
      <HTML>,</HTML>
      <ScriptQuote>
        <Column/>
      </ScriptQuote>
      <HTML>); fld.format = "</HTML>
      <Property Select="Format"/>
      <HTML>"; </HTML>
      <Switch>
        <Expr>
          <Property Select="FillInChoice"/>
        </Expr>
        <Case Value="TRUE">fld.fFillInChoice = true;</Case>
      </Switch>
      <ForEach Select="CHOICES/CHOICE">
        <HTML>fld.AddChoice(</HTML>
        <ScriptQuote>
          <Property Select="."/>
        </ScriptQuote>
        <HTML>, </HTML>
        <ScriptQuote>
          <Property Select="Value"/>
        </ScriptQuote>
        <HTML>);</HTML>
      </ForEach>
```

(continued)

Listing 5-6 *(continued)*

```
    <Switch>
      <Expr>
        <Property Select="Required"/>
      </Expr>
      <Case Value="TRUE">fld.fRequired = true;</Case>
    </Switch>
    <HTML><![CDATA[fld.IMEMode="]]></HTML>
    <Switch>
      <Expr>
        <Property Select="Type"/>
      </Expr>
      <Case Value="Lookup">
        <HTML><![CDATA[inactive]]></HTML>
      </Case>
      <Case Value="DateTime">
        <HTML><![CDATA[inactive]]></HTML>
      </Case>
      <Case Value="GridChoice">
        <HTML><![CDATA[inactive]]></HTML>
      </Case>
      <Case Value="Calculated">
        <HTML><![CDATA[inactive]]></HTML>
      </Case>
      <Case Value="Currency">
        <HTML><![CDATA[inactive]]></HTML>
      </Case>
      <Case Value="Number">
        <HTML><![CDATA[inactive]]></HTML>
      </Case>
      <Case Value="User">
        <HTML><![CDATA[inactive]]></HTML>
      </Case>
      <Case Value="Boolean">
        <HTML><![CDATA[inactive]]></HTML>
      </Case>
      <Default>
        <Property Select="IMEMode" HTMLEncode="TRUE"/>
      </Default>
    </Switch>
    <HTML><![CDATA[";]]></HTML>
    <HTML><![CDATA[fld.BuildUI();</SCRIPT>]]></HTML>
  </RenderPattern>
</FieldType>
```

As Listing 5-6 illustrates, every field type definition has a root element named <FieldType>, which contains the rest of the field type definition. As you can see from the following excerpt, this <FieldType> element contains several <Field> and <RenderPattern> elements:

```
<FieldType>
  <Field Name="TypeName">Choice</Field>
  <Field Name="TypeDisplayName">$Resources:core,fldtype_choice;</Field>
  <Field Name="TypeShortDescription">$Resources:core,fldtype_choice_desc;</Field>
```

```
    <Field Name="InternalType">Choice</Field>
    <Field Name="SQLType">nvarchar</Field>
    <Field Name="FieldTypeClass">Microsoft.SharePoint.SPFieldChoice</Field>
    <Field Name="ParentType"></Field>
    <Field Name="Sortable">TRUE</Field>
    <Field Name="Filterable">TRUE</Field>

    <RenderPattern Name="HeaderPattern">
    </RenderPattern>
    <RenderPattern Name="DisplayPattern">
    </RenderPattern>
    <RenderPattern Name="EditPattern">
    </RenderPattern>
    <RenderPattern Name="NewPattern" DisplayName="NewPattern">
    </RenderPattern>
  </FieldType>
```

Each <Field> element specifies a specific characteristic of the SPFieldChoice field type as named in the Name attribute of the element:

- The <Field> element whose name attribute is set to TypeName specifies the name of the field type, which is Choice in this case.
- The <Field> element whose name attribute is set to TypeDisplayName specifies a display name for the field type. Because display name is locale-specific, this <Field> pulls the localized display name from the core.resx resource file.
- The <Field> element whose name attribute is set to TypeShortDescription specifies a short description for the field type. Once again because this short description is locale-specific, this <Field> pulls the localized short description from the core.resx resource file.
- The <Field> element whose name attribute is set to FieldTypeClass specifies the fully qualified name of the field class. The fully qualified name of your custom field class must contain a comma-separated list of five items: namespace-qualified name of your custom field class, name of the strong-named assembly that contains your custom field class, the version of this assembly, the culture of this assembly, and the public key token of this assembly. As you can see, you must compile your custom field class into a strong-named assembly and deploy this assembly to the Global Assembly Cache. You'll see an example of this later in this chapter.

Next, you learn about the <RenderPattern> child elements of the <FieldType> element. A <RenderPattern> element supports an attribute named Name with values of HeaderPattern, DisplayPattern, EditPattern, and NewPattern:

- A HeaderPattern type of RenderPattern contains the CAML rendering instructions for rendering the header of the field type.
- A DisplayPattern type of RenderPattern contains the CAML rendering instructions for rendering the field type in Display mode (DispForm.aspx) and in list view forms such as AllItems.aspx.
- An EditPattern type of RenderPattern contains the CAML rendering instructions for rendering the field type in Edit mode.
- A NewPattern type of RenderPattern contains the CAML rendering instructions for rendering the field type in New mode.

Some of these RenderPatterns are discussed in the following sections. To help you understand the implementation of these RenderPatterns, add a column of the SPFieldChoice type to a SharePoint list. To do so, you need to select the Create Column option from the Settings menu to navigate to the Create Column page shown in Figure 5-2.

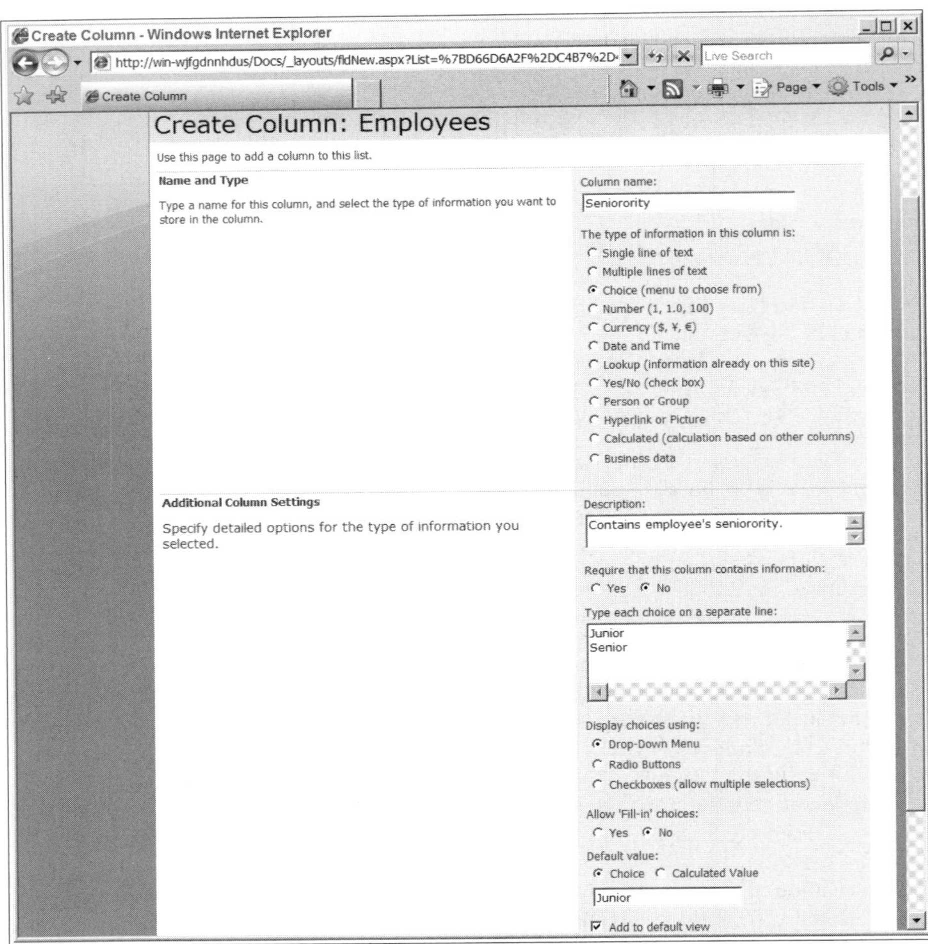

Figure 5-2: The Create Column page Add caption

As you can see, the Create Column page renders two types of field type properties. One type includes those properties that all field types have in common, such as column name, data type, description, and whether the column is required, that is, whether a value must be specified for this column. The second type includes properties that are specific to each field type. Because these properties vary from one field type to another, they're known as variable field type properties. The Create Column page renders the variable field type properties inside the Additional Column Settings section.

Now go ahead and enter Seniority as the column name and then check the Choice (menu to choose from) toggle as the data type. Note that as soon as you check the Choice toggle, the UI shown in Figure 5-3 is added to the Additional Column Settings section.

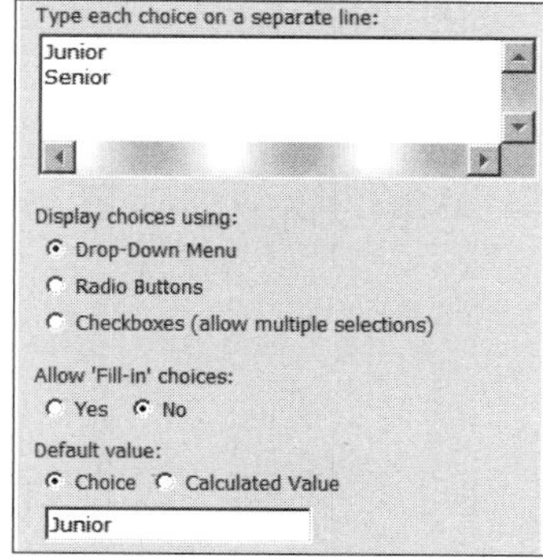

Figure 5-3: The Additional Column Settings section

This UI renders the variable field type properties of the Choice field type. As you'll see later, the CAML rendering instructions specified in the PropertySchema of the field type definition of a field type are used to render the UI that enables users to set the variable field type properties in the Create Column (fldNew.aspx), Edit Column (FldEdit.aspx), New Site Column (fldnew.aspx), and Change Site Column (fldedit.aspx) pages. Unfortunately, none of the standard field types that ship with SharePoint follow this rule. In other words, these pages hard-code the rendering logic.

Enter Junior and Senior in the top text box shown in Figure 5-3.

Figure 5-4 shows the list with the Seniority column of the Choice type added.

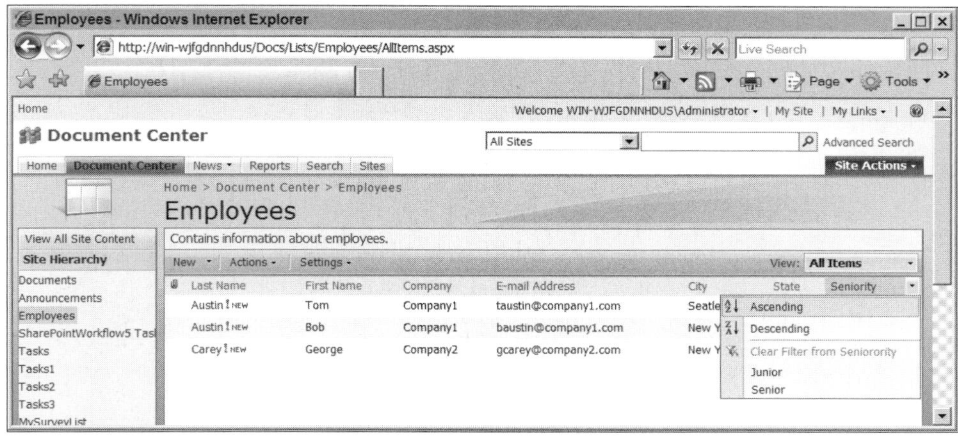

Figure 5-4: The AllItems.aspx page

As you can see, the AllItems.aspx page renders a header for the Seniority column, which contains Ascending, Descending, Clear Filter from Seniority, Junior, and Senior menu options. As you'll see later, the CAML rendering instructions specified in the HeaderPattern type of RenderPattern in the field type definition of the SPFieldChoice field type are used to render this header.

Now go ahead and select the Edit Item option from the ECB of a list item in Figure 5-4 to navigate to the EditForm.aspx page shown in Figure 5-5.

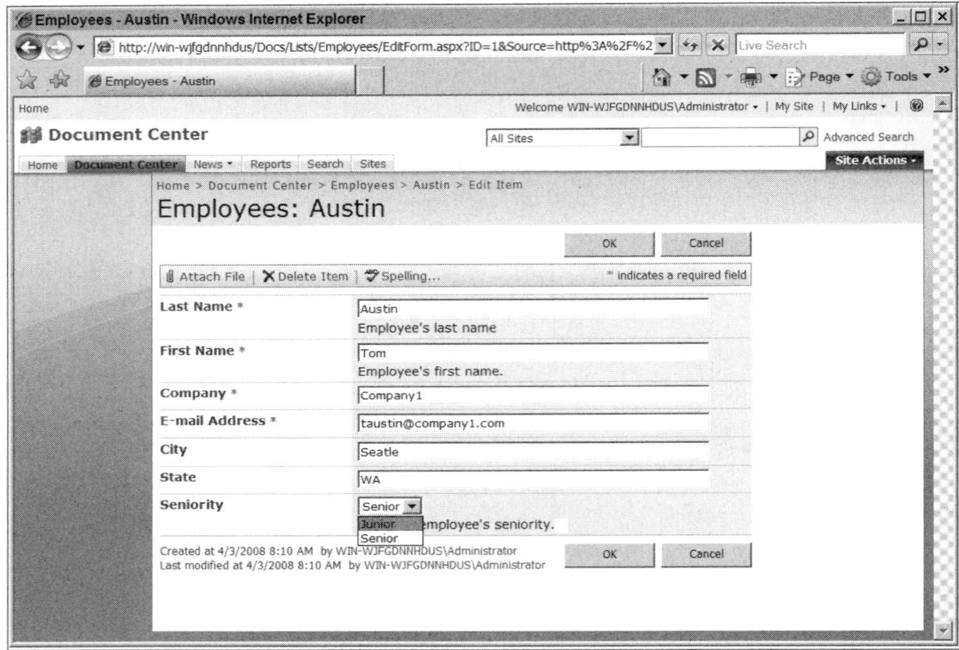

Figure 5-5: The edit list item page

Note that the EditForm.aspx renders a UI that consists of a label titled Seniority and a drop-down list box with two values of Junior and Senior. As you'll see later, the CAML rendering instructions specified in the EditPattern type of RenderPattern in the field type definition of the SPFieldChoice field type are used to render this UI.

Now go ahead and select Senior from this drop-down list field and click the OK button in Figure 5-5. This should take you back to the AllItems.aspx page shown in Figure 5-6.

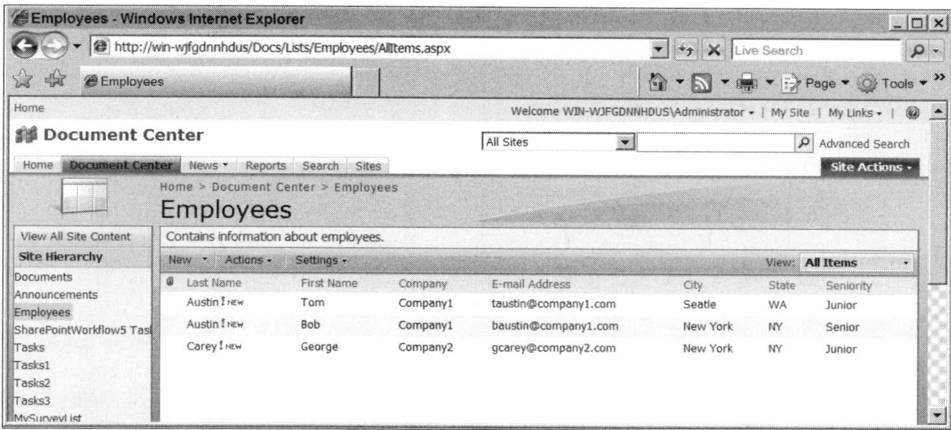

Figure 5-6: The AllItems.aspx page

As you can see from Figure 5-6, the AllItems.aspx page renders each value in the Seniority column, which is of the Choice type, as a simple text. As you'll see later, the CAML rendering instructions specified in the DisplayPattern type of RenderPattern in the field type definition of the SPFieldChoice field type are used to render the values in the Seniority column.

Next, click the New button shown in Figure 5-6 to navigate to the NewForm.aspx page shown in Figure 5-7.

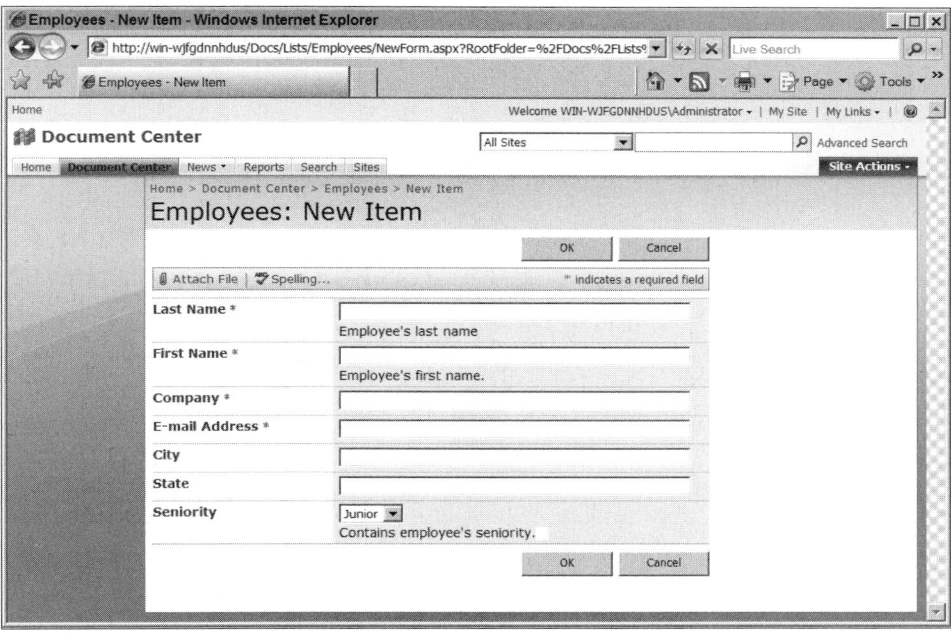

Figure 5-7: The NewForm.aspx page

Note that the NewForm.aspx page renders a UI that consists of a label titled Seniority and a drop-down list box with the values of Junior and Senior. As you'll see later, the CAML rendering instructions specified in the NewPattern type of RenderPattern in the field type definition of the SPFieldChoice field type are used to render this UI.

In summary:

- CAML rendering instructions specified in the PropertySchema of the field type definition of a field type are used to render the UI that enables users to set the variable field type properties in the Create Column (fldNew.aspx), Edit Column (FldEdit.aspx), New Site Column (fldnew.aspx), and Change Site Column (fldedit.aspx) pages.
- Unfortunately none of the standard SharePoint field types follow this rule. In other words, the renderings of these field types are hard-coded in these pages. The only exception is the User and Lookup field types. These two field types use field-rendering controls, which are discussed later in this chapter.
- Even though none of the standard SharePoint field types make use of the PropertySchema element, you should use this element to specify the CAML rendering instructions for rendering the UI that enables users to set the variable field type properties of your custom field types.
- CAML rendering instructions specified in the DisplayPattern type of RenderPattern in the field type definition are used to render the field type in pages such as DispForm.aspx and AllItems.aspx that display the value of a field type.
- CAML rendering instructions specified in the HeaderPattern type of RenderPattern in the field type definition of a field type are used to render the header of the field type in pages such as DispForm.aspx and AllItems.aspx that display the value of a field type.
- CAML rendering instructions specified in the EditPattern type of RenderPattern in the field type definition of a field type are used to render the field type in an edit list item page such as EditForm.aspx.
- CAML rendering instructions specified in the NewPattern type of RenderPattern in the field type definition of a field type are used to render the field type in a new list item page such as NewForm.aspx.

HeaderPattern

This section examines the CAML rendering instructions in the HeaderPattern type of RenderPattern. As mentioned earlier, these CAML rendering instructions are used to render the header of the SPFieldChoice field type in pages such as DispForm.aspx and AllItems.aspx.

However, first take a look at the output HTML that these CAML rendering instructions generate. For that, you need to navigate to one of the previously mentioned pages in your browser and use the View Source menu option of your browser to view this output HTML. The boldfaced portion of the following excerpt presents the output HTML that the CAML rendering instructions in the HeaderPattern type of RenderPattern generate inside the AllItems.aspx page:

```
<th nowrap scope="col" class="ms-vh2">
  <div style="width: 100%; position: relative; left: 0; top: 0;">
    <table style="width: 100%;" sortable="" sortdisable="" filterdisable=""
    filterable="" name="Seniority" ctxnum="1" displayname="Seniority"
fieldtype="Choice"
    resulttype=""
    sortfields="FilterField1=Seniority&amp;FilterValue1=Junior&amp;
                SortField=Seniority&amp;SortDir=Asc&amp;
                View=%7b1C4DFCD2%2d20BB%2d465B%2dAB88%2d349F780F8D83%7d"
    height="100%" cellspacing="1" cellpadding="0" class="ms-unselectedtitle"
    onmouseover="OnMouseOverFilter(this)">
      <tr>
        <td width="100%" class="ms-vb" nowrap>
          <a id="diidSortSeniority" onfocus="OnFocusFilter(this)"
          title="Sort by Seniority" href="javascript:"
          onclick="javascript:return OnClickFilter(this,event);"
          sortingfields="FilterField1=Seniority&amp;FilterValue1=Junior&amp;
                         SortField=Seniority&amp;SortDir=Asc&amp;
                         View=%7b1C4DFCD2%2d20BB%2d465B%2dAB88%2d349F780F8D83%7d">
            Seniority
            <img src="/_layouts/images/blank.gif" class="ms-hidden" border="0"
            width="1" height="1"
            alt="Use SHIFT+ENTER to open the menu (new window)."/>
          </a>
          <img src="/_layouts/images/rsort.gif" alt="Sort Descending" border="0"/>
          <img src="/_layouts/images/filter.gif" border="0" alt=""/>
        </td>
        <td style="position: absolute;">
          <img src="/_layouts/images/blank.gif" width="13px"
          style="visibility: hidden" alt="">
        </td>
      </tr>
    </table>
  </div>
</th>
```

Now that you have seen the final output HTML in its entirety, walk through the CAML rendering instructions in the HeaderPattern to see how these instructions manage to render this HTML. As Listing 5-6 shows, the HeaderPattern starts with a <Switch> element to determine what to render first. The <Expr> child element of this <Switch> element uses the value of the Filterable property of the field type as the switching expression:

```
<Expr>
  <Property Select='Filterable'/>
</Expr>
```

Recall from Listing 5-6 that the following <Field> element specifies the value of TRUE for the Filterable property of the field type:

```
<Field Name="Filterable">TRUE</Field>
```

Therefore, the <Switch> element renders the <Default> element, which in turn uses another <Switch> element to determine what to render next. The <Expr> child element of this <Switch> element uses the value of the Filter variable as the switching expression:

```
<Expr>
  <GetVar Name='Filter'/>
</Expr>
```

Because the Filter variable is not set to one nothing gets rendered. Next, <RenderPattern> executes another <Switch> element. The <Expr> child element of this <Switch> element uses the value of the Sortable property as the switching expression:

```
<Expr>
  <Property Select='Sortable'/>
</Expr>
```

Recall from Listing 5-6 that the following <Field> element specifies the value of TRUE for the Sortable property of the field type:

```
<Field Name="Sortable">TRUE</Field>
```

Therefore, the <Switch> element renders its <Default> element. The <Default> element uses another <Switch> element to determine what to render next. The <Expr> child element of this <Switch> element uses the value of the SortDisable variable as the switching expression:

```
<Expr>
  <GetVar Name='SortDisable'/>
</Expr>
```

Because this variable is set to FALSE in this case, the <Default> child element of this <Switch> element executes. This <Default> element first uses the following <HTML> CAML element to render *<A ID="diidsort*:

```
<HTML><![CDATA[<A ID="diidSort]]></HTML>
```

Therefore, the output HTML of the HeaderPattern type of RenderPattern is:

```
<A ID="diidSort
```

Next, the <Default> element renders the value of the Name property of the field type, which is "Seniority":

```
<Property Select='Name'/>
```

Therefore, the output HTML of the HeaderPattern type of RenderPattern now becomes:

```
<A ID="diidSortSeniority
```

Next, the <Default> element uses the following <HTML> CAML element

```
<HTML><![CDATA[" onfocus="OnFocusFilter(this)" TITLE=]]></HTML>
```

to render the following text:

```
" onfocus="OnFocusFilter(this)" TITLE=
```

As a result, the output HTML of the HeaderPattern now becomes:

```
<A ID="diidSortSeniority" onfocus="OnFocusFilter(this)" TITLE=
```

Next, the <Default> element uses the following <HTML> CAML element, which in turn uses a resource reference to pull the value of the TITLE attribute on the <A> element, which is *"Sort by"*, from the core.resx resource file:

```
                <HTML>"$Resources:core,500;</HTML>
```

The output HTML of the HeaderPattern now becomes:

```
<A ID="diidSortSeniority" onfocus="OnFocusFilter(this)" TITLE="Sort by
```

Then, the <Default> element renders the value of the DisplayName property of the field type in HTML-encoded format, which is "Seniority":

```
                <Property Select='DisplayName' HTMLEncode='TRUE'/>
```

The output HTML of the HeaderPattern is now:

```
<A ID="diidSortSeniority" onfocus="OnFocusFilter(this)" TITLE="Sort by Seniority"
```

Next, <Default> uses the following <HTML> CAML element

```
                <HTML>
                  <![CDATA[
                    " HREF="javascript:" OnClick="javascript:return
                    OnClickFilter(this,event);"
                  ]]></HTML>
```

to render the following into the output stream:

```
" HREF="javascript:" OnClick="javascript:return OnClickFilter(this,event);"
```

The output HTML is now:

```
<A ID="diidSortSeniority" onfocus="OnFocusFilter(this)" TITLE="Sort by Seniority"
HREF="javascript:" OnClick="javascript:return OnClickFilter(this,event);"
```

Then, <Default> uses the <HTML> element

```
                <HTML><![CDATA[ SORTINGFIELDS="]]></HTML>
```

to render

```
 SORTINGFIELDS="
```

Next, <Default> renders the field sort parameters in HTML-encoded format:

```
<FieldSortParams HTMLEncode="TRUE"/>
```

The output HTML then becomes:

```
<A ID="diidSortSeniority" onfocus="OnFocusFilter(this)"
title="Sort by Seniority" href="javascript:"
onclick="javascript:return OnClickFilter(this,event);"
sortingfields="FilterField1=Seniority&amp;FilterValue1=Junior&amp;SortField=Seniority
&amp;SortDir=Asc&amp;View=%7b1C4DFCD2%2d20BB%2d465B%2dAB88%2d349F780F8D83%7d
```

<Default> then uses another <HTML> CAML element to render the closing tag of the <a> element:

```
<HTML><![CDATA[">]]></HTML>
```

Next, <Default> renders the value of the DisplayName property of the field type in HTML-encoded format, which is "Seniority":

```
<Property Select='DisplayName' HTMLEncode="TRUE"/>
```

So far, the output HTML is:

```
<A ID="diidSortSeniority" onfocus="OnFocusFilter(this)"
title="Sort by Seniority" href="javascript:"
onclick="javascript:return OnClickFilter(this,event);"
sortingfields="FilterField1=Seniority&amp;FilterValue1=Junior&amp;SortField=Seniority
&amp;SortDir=Asc&amp;View=%7b1C4DFCD2%2d20BB%2d465B%2dAB88%2d349F780F8D83%7d">
  Seniority
```

Next, <Default> uses the following <HTML> element

```
<HTML>
  <![CDATA[
    <img src="/_layouts/images/blank.gif" class="ms-hidden" border=0
    width=1 height=1 alt="
  ]]>
</HTML>
```

to render the following into the output stream:

```
<img src="/_layouts/images/blank.gif" class="ms-hidden" border=0 width=1
height=1 alt="
```

Then, <Default> uses the following <HTML> element, which in turn uses a resource reference to pull the localized value of the alt attribute on the preceding <img> element from the resource file:

```
<HTML>$Resources:OpenMenuKeyAccessible;</HTML>
```

Next, <Default> uses another <HTML> element to render the closing tag of the <img> element:

```
<HTML><![CDATA[">]]></HTML>
```

Here is what the output HTML looks like so far:

```
<a id="diidSortSeniority" onfocus="OnFocusFilter(this)"
title="Sort by Seniority" href="javascript:"
onclick="javascript:return OnClickFilter(this,event);"
sortingfields="FilterField1=Seniority&amp;FilterValue1=Junior&amp;
               SortField=Seniority&amp;SortDir=Asc&amp;
               View=%7b1C4DFCD2%2d20BB%2d465B%2dAB88%2d349F780F8D83%7d">
  Seniority
  <img src="/_layouts/images/blank.gif" class="ms-hidden" border="0"
  width="1" height="1"
  alt="Use SHIFT+ENTER to open the menu (new window)."/>
```

Keep in mind that I'm reformatting the output HTML to make it more readable. In reality the entire content of the output HTML is rendered on the same line.

Next, <Default> uses this <HTML>

```
<HTML><![CDATA[</A><IMG SRC="]]></HTML>
```

to render this:

```
</A><IMG SRC="
```

Then, <Default> retrieves the field sort image URL and renders it as the value of the SRC attribute on the preceding <IMG> element:

```
<FieldSortImageURL/>
```

Next, <Default> uses this <HTML>

```
<HTML><![CDATA[" ALT="]]></HTML>
```

to render this:

```
" ALT="
```

Then, <Default> uses a <Switch> element to determine what to render next. The <Expr> child element of this <Switch> element uses the value of the SortDir variable as the switching expression:

```
<Expr>
  <GetVar Name='SortDir'/>
</Expr>
```

Depending on whether the value of the SortDir variable is "Asc" or "Desc", the <Switch> element renders the appropriate <Case> child element. Note that each <Case> element simply uses an <HTML> element, which in turn uses a resource reference to pull the appropriate localized text from the resource file:

```
<Case Value='Asc'>
  <HTML>$Resources:core,150;</HTML>
</Case>
<Case Value='Desc'>
  <HTML>$Resources:core,151;</HTML>
</Case>
```

Also note that if the value of the SortDir variable is neither "Asc" nor "Des", the <Switch> element renders nothing:

```
<Default>
  <HTML></HTML>
</Default>
```

Next, the <Default> child element of the original <Switch> element uses an <HTML> element to render the closing tag of the <IMG> element:

```
<HTML><![CDATA[" BORDER=0>]]></HTML>
```

Here is what the output HTML looks like so far:

```
<a id="diidSortSeniority" onfocus="OnFocusFilter(this)"
  title="Sort by Seniority" href="javascript:"
  onclick="javascript:return OnClickFilter(this,event);"
  sortingfields="FilterField1=Seniority&amp;FilterValue1=Junior&amp;
                SortField=Seniority&amp;SortDir=Asc&amp;
                View=%7b1C4DFCD2%2d20BB%2d465B%2dAB88%2d349F780F8D83%7d">
    Seniority
    <img src="/_layouts/images/blank.gif" class="ms-hidden" border="0"
    width="1" height="1"
    alt="Use SHIFT+ENTER to open the menu (new window)."/>
  </a>
  <img src="/_layouts/images/rsort.gif" alt="Sort Descending" border="0"/>
```

Next, <Default> uses this

```
<HTML><![CDATA[<IMG SRC="]]></HTML>
```

to render this:

```
<IMG SRC="
```

Then, <Default> retrieves the field filter image URL and renders it as the value of the SRC attribute on the preceding <IMG> element:

```
<FieldFilterImageURL/>
```

Finally, <Default> uses this

```
<HTML><![CDATA[" BORDER=0 ALT="">]]></HTML>
```

to render this:

```
" BORDER=0 ALT=""
```

Here is what the final output HTML that the HeaderPattern type of RenderPattern looks like:

```
<a id="diidSortSeniority" onfocus="OnFocusFilter(this)"
title="Sort by Seniority" href="javascript:"
onclick="javascript:return OnClickFilter(this,event);"
sortingfields="FilterField1=Seniority&amp;FilterValue1=Junior&amp;
               SortField=Seniority&amp;SortDir=Asc&amp;
               View=%7b1C4DFCD2%2d20BB%2d465B%2dAB88%2d349F780F8D83%7d">
  Seniority
  <img src="/_layouts/images/blank.gif" class="ms-hidden" border="0"
  width="1" height="1"
  alt="Use SHIFT+ENTER to open the menu (new window)."/>
</a>
<img src="/_layouts/images/rsort.gif" alt="Sort Descending" border="0"/>
<img src="/_layouts/images/filter.gif" border="0" alt=""/>
```

DisplayPattern

This section examines the CAML rendering instructions in the <RenderPattern> element whose Name attribute is set to DisplayPattern. Recall that these CAML rendering instructions are used in pages such as DispForm.aspx and AllItems.aspx to render the SPFieldChoice field type.

As the following excerpt from Listing 5-6 shows, this <RenderPattern> simply renders the HTML-encoded value of the SPFieldChoice field type:

```
<RenderPattern Name="DisplayPattern">
  <Column HTMLEncode="TRUE"/>
</RenderPattern>
```

For example, in the case of Figure 5-6 this renders one of the values in the Seniority column, that is, Junior, Senior, or Junior.

EditPattern

This section examines the CAML rendering instructions in the <RenderPattern> element whose Name attribute is set to EditPattern. Recall that these CAML rendering instructions are used in an edit list item page such as EditForm.aspx to render the SPFieldChoice field type in Edit mode. As Figure 5-5 shows, these CAML rendering instructions render a UI that consists of a label title Seniority and a drop-down list box with two values of Junior and Senior.

Take a look at the output HTML that the CAML rendering instructions in the <RenderPattern> element with the Name attribute value of EditPattern generate. For that, you need to navigate to an edit list item page such as EditForm.aspx shown in Figure 5-5 in your browser and use the View Source menu option of your browser to view this output HTML. The following excerpt presents this output HTML:

```
<TD nowrap="true" valign="top" width="190px" class="ms-formlabel">
  <H3 class="ms-standardheader">
    <nobr>Seniority</nobr>
  </H3>
</TD>
<TD valign="top" class="ms-formbody" width="400px">
  <!-- FieldName="Seniority" FieldInternalName="Seniority"
FieldType="SPFieldChoice" -->
  <span dir="none">
    <select name="ctl00$m$g_a4c758d4_9bae_4f98_9a5a_38feff95bba7$ctl00$ctl04$ctl17$
                  ctl00$ctl00$ctl04$ctl00$DropDownChoice"
    id="ctl00_m_g_a4c758d4_9bae_4f98_9a5a_38feff95bba7_ctl00_ctl04_ctl17
        _ctl00_ctl00_ctl04_ctl00_DropDownChoice" title="Seniority"
    class="ms-RadioText">
      <option selected="selected" value="Junior">Junior</option>
      <option value="Senior">Senior</option>
    </select>
    <br>
  </span>
</TD>
```

Next, walk through the CAML rendering instructions in the <RenderPattern> element with the Name attribute value of EditPattern to see how these instructions render the preceding HTML.

As you can see from Listing 5-6, this <RenderPattern> element begins by rendering the first portion of a <script> block:

```
    <HTML><![CDATA[<SCRIPT>fld = new ChoiceField(frm,]]></HTML>
```

Therefore, the output HTML is now:

```
<SCRIPT>
  fld = new ChoiceField(frm,
```

As you can see, this script block instantiates a JavaScript class named ChoiceField. This JavaScript class is defined in a JavaScript file named BFORM.js, which is located in the following folder on the file system of the front-end web server:

```
Local_Drive:\Program Files\Common Files\microsoft shared\Web Server
Extensions\12\TEMPLATE\LAYOUTS\1033
```

The ChoiceField JavaScript is responsible for rendering the choice field. As you can see, the <RenderPattern> of your custom field type definition does not have to directly render the output HTML. Instead it can render the JavaScript code that knows how to render the output HTML.

Next, <RenderPattern> renders the value of the Name property of the field, which is Seniority, in script-quoted format:

```
<ScriptQuote>
  <Property Select="Name"/>
</ScriptQuote>
```

As a result, the output HTML now becomes:

```
<SCRIPT>
  fld = new ChoiceField(frm, "Seniority"
```

Next, <RenderPattern> renders the comma that separates the next parameter of the ChoiceField function from the "Seniority" parameter:

```
<HTML>,</HTML>
```

Then, <RenderPattern> renders the value of the DisplayName property of the SPFieldChoice field type, which is "Seniority", as the third parameter of the ChoiceField constructor:

```
<ScriptQuote>
  <Property Select="DisplayName"/>
</ScriptQuote>
```

Next, <RenderPattern> renders the comma that separates the next parameter of the ChoiceField function from the "Seniority" parameter:

```
<HTML>,</HTML>
```

Then, <RenderPattern> renders the value of the current value of the field in script-quoted format as the fourth parameter of the ChoiceField function:

```
<ScriptQuote>
  <Column/>
</ScriptQuote>
```

The current value of the field depends on which list item you're editing. For example, if you're editing the first list item shown in Figure 5-6, the current field value is Junior. In this case, the output HTML is:

```
<SCRIPT>
  fld = new ChoiceField(frm, "Seniority", "Seniority", "Junior"
```

Next, <RenderPattern> renders the closing brace of the ChoiceField constructor and the fld.format=" expression:

```
<HTML>); fld.format = "</HTML>
```

The output HTML then becomes:

```
<SCRIPT>
  fld = new ChoiceField(frm, "Seniority", "Seniority", "Junior");
  fld.format = "
```

Then, <RenderPattern> renders the value of the Format property of the SPFieldChoice field type followed by a semicolon:

```
        <Property Select="Format"/>
        <HTML>"; </HTML>
```

The Format property is one of those properties that are known as variable field type properties. The variable field type property of a field type such as SPFieldChoice is a property whose value varies from one column to another column based on the field type. As such, the column creator must specify the value of the variable field properties on the Create Column (fldNew.aspx), Edit Column (FldEdit.aspx), New Site Column (fldnew.aspx), or Change Site Column (fldedit.aspx) page. For example, as Figures 5-2 and 5-3 show, the New Site Column page renders the UI shown in Figure 5-3 that contains a section titled Display Choices Using:, which presents column creators with three options of Drop-Down Menu, Radio Buttons, and Checkboxes (Allow Multiple Selections). Column creators choose one of these options to set the value of the Format property of the SPFieldChoice field type. Assuming the column creator has selected the Drop-Down Menu option, the output HTML is:

```
    <SCRIPT>
      fld = new ChoiceField(frm, "Seniority", "Seniority", "Junior");
      fld.format = "Dropdown";
```

Next, <RenderPattern> uses a <Switch> element to determine what to render next. The <Expr> child element of this <Switch> element uses the value of the FillInChoice property of the SPFieldChoice field type as the switching expression:

```
          <Expr>
            <Property Select="FillInChoice"/>
          </Expr>
```

The FillInChoice property is also a variable field type property. Column creators must specify the value of this property through the Create Column (fldNew.aspx), Edit Column (FldEdit.aspx), New Site Column (fldnew.aspx), or Change Site Column (fldedit.aspx) page. For example, as you can see from Figures 5-2 and 5-3 the New Site Column page renders the UI shown in Figure 5-3 that contains a section titled Allow 'Fill-in' Choices, which presents column creators with two options of Yes and No to specify the value of the FillInChoice property of the SPFieldChoice field type. Column selectors select the Yes option to set the value of the FillInChoice property to TRUE and No option to set it to FALSE.

If the column creator has selected the Yes option, the <Case> elements with the Value attribute value of TRUE get executed:

```
          <Case Value="TRUE">fld.fFillInChoice = true;</Case>
```

As a result, the output HTML becomes:

```
    <SCRIPT>
      fld = new ChoiceField(frm, "Seniority", "Seniority", "Junior");
      fld.format = "Dropdown";
      fld.fFillInChoice = true;
```

Next, <RenderPattern> executes a <ForEach> element whose Select attribute is set to "CHOICES/CHOICE":

```
<ForEach Select="CHOICES/CHOICE">
```

The <ForEach> element operates very similarly to the C# for each statement. The content of this element is rendered once for each choice. Recall that the SPFieldChoice field type offers users a list of options to choose from. This <ForEach> element iterates through these options. In this case, the Seniority field offers two options of Junior and Senior. This means that the content of the <ForEach> element is executed twice: once for the Junior option and the other time for the Senior option.

First, consider the Junior option. The <ForEach> first renders fld.AddChoice(:

```
<HTML>fld.AddChoice(</HTML>
```

Then, it renders the name of the Junior option, that is, the string "Junior", in script-quoted format:

```
<ScriptQuote>
  <Property Select="."/>
</ScriptQuote>
```

Next, it renders the comma that separates the previous parameter from the next:

```
<HTML>, </HTML>
```

Then, it renders the value of the Junior option, which is "Junior" again, in script-quoted format followed by a semicolon:

```
<ScriptQuote>
  <Property Select="Value"/>
</ScriptQuote>
<HTML>);</HTML>
```

<ForEach> repeats the same steps for the Senior option. As a result, the output HTML becomes:

```
<SCRIPT>
  fld = new ChoiceField(frm, "Seniority", "Seniority", "Junior");
  fld.format = "Dropdown";
  fld.fFillInChoice = true;
  fld.AddChoice("Junior", "Junior");
  fld.AddChoice("Senior", "Senior");
```

Next, <RenderPattern> uses a <Switch> element to determine what to render next. The <Expr> child element of this <Switch> element uses the value of the Required property of the Seniority SPFieldChoice field type as the switching expression:

```
<Expr>
  <Property Select="Required"/>
</Expr>
```

Column creators specify the value of the Required property in the Create Column (fldNew.aspx), Edit Column (FldEdit.aspx), New Site Column (fldnew.aspx), or Change Site Column (fldedit.aspx) page. For example, as Figure 5-2 shows, the Create Column page contains a section titled Require That This Column Contains Information, with two options of Yes and No. Column creators select the Yes option to set the value of the Required property to TRUE and the No option to set it to FALSE.

If the Required property is set to TRUE, the <Case> element with the Value attribute value of TRUE is executed:

```
<Case Value="TRUE">fld.fRequired = true;</Case>
```

As you can see, this <Case> element simply renders a *fld.fRequired=true;* statement. As a result, the output HTML of the <RenderPattern> element with the Name value of EditPattern becomes this so far:

```
<SCRIPT>
  fld = new ChoiceField(frm, "Seniority", "Seniority", "Junior");
  fld.format = "Dropdown";
  fld.fFillInChoice = true;
  fld.AddChoice("Junior", "Junior");
  fld.AddChoice("Senior", "Senior");
  fld.fRequired = true;
```

Next, the <RenderPattern> element uses this <HTML> CAML element to render *fld.IMEMode="*:

```
<HTML><![CDATA[fld.IMEMode="]]></HTML>
```

As such, the output HTML becomes:

```
<SCRIPT>
  fld = new ChoiceField(frm, "Seniority", "Seniority", "Junior");
  fld.format = "Dropdown";
  fld.fFillInChoice = true;
  fld.AddChoice("Junior", "Junior");
  fld.AddChoice("Senior", "Senior");
  fld.fRequired = true;
  fld.IMEMode = "
```

Next, the <RenderPattern> element uses a <Switch> element to determine what to render next. The <Expr> child element of this <Switch> element uses the value of the Type property of the Seniority SPFieldChoice field type as the switching expression:

```
<Expr>
  <Property Select="Type"/>
</Expr>
```

This <Switch> statement basically uses the value of the Type property to determine the IME mode, which is assigned as the value of the IMEMode property on the fld ChoiceField object:

```
        <Case Value="Lookup">
          <HTML><![CDATA[inactive]]></HTML>
        </Case>
        <Case Value="DateTime">
          <HTML><![CDATA[inactive]]></HTML>
        </Case>
        <Case Value="GridChoice">
          <HTML><![CDATA[inactive]]></HTML>
        </Case>
        <Case Value="Calculated">
          <HTML><![CDATA[inactive]]></HTML>
        </Case>
        <Case Value="Currency">
          <HTML><![CDATA[inactive]]></HTML>
        </Case>
        <Case Value="Number">
          <HTML><![CDATA[inactive]]></HTML>
        </Case>
        <Case Value="User">
          <HTML><![CDATA[inactive]]></HTML>
        </Case>
        <Case Value="Boolean">
          <HTML><![CDATA[inactive]]></HTML>
        </Case>
        <Default>
          <Property Select="IMEMode" HTMLEncode="TRUE"/>
        </Default>
```

Next, the <RenderPattern> element renders ";

```
      <HTML><![CDATA[";]]></HTML>
```

Finally, the <RenderPattern> element renders fld.BuildUI();</SCRIPT>, which builds the UI that render the Seniority SPFieldChoice field type in Edit mode:

```
      <HTML><![CDATA[fld.BuildUI();</SCRIPT>]]></HTML>
```

Here is the final output HTML that the <RenderPattern> element with the Name attribute value of EditPattern generates:

```
  <SCRIPT>
    fld = new ChoiceField(frm, "Seniority", "Seniority", "Junior");
    fld.format = "Dropdown";
    fld.fFillInChoice = true;
    fld.AddChoice("Junior", "Junior");
    fld.AddChoice("Senior", "Senior");
    fld.fRequired = true;
    fld.IMEMode = "inactive";
    fld.BuildUI();
  </SCRIPT>
```

NewPattern

As you can see from Listing 5-6, in this case the <RenderPattern> element with the Name attribute value of NewPattern contains the same CAML rendering instructions as the <RenderPattern> element with the Name attribute value of EditPattern. However, this may not be true in general. In other words, you don't have to use the same CAML rendering instructions in both cases.

Field-Rendering Controls

As discussed in the previous sections, to implement a custom field type, you must at a minimum implement a custom field type class and a custom field type definition. As you saw, the field type definition can contain <RenderPattern> elements with Name attribute values of DisplayPattern, EditPattern, and NewPattern to specify the CAML rendering instructions for rending the field type in Display, New, and Edit modes and in list view pages such as AllItems.aspx.

This rendering approach limits the rendering capabilities of your custom field type to what you can achieve with CAML rendering instructions. Another downside of this approach is that you cannot perform UI-level data validation through CAML.

For most common scenarios CAML rendering instructions are sufficient for rending a field type in the Display mode (DispForm.aspx) and in list view pages such as AllItems.aspx because such rendering normally does not require complex UI and because data validation is not an issue in Display mode. As such, you should render your custom field types in Display mode through the CAML rendering instructions that you specify in a <RenderPattern> element of your field type definition.

If you cannot render the type of UI that you want for your field type in Edit and New modes through CAML rendering instructions and/or if you want to perform complex data validation, you should use a field-rendering control to render your field type in Edit and New modes instead of the <RenderPattern> element.

Every field-rendering server control directly or indirectly inherits from the FieldMetadata server control discussed in the next section.

FieldMetadata

FieldMetadata is the base class from which all field-rendering controls directly or indirectly inherit. As such, it provides the base functionality for field-rendering controls. Listing 5-7 presents the internal implementation of FieldMetadata.

Listing 5-7: The internal implementation of FieldMetadata

```
[SharePointPermission(SecurityAction.LinkDemand, ObjectModel = true),
AspNetHostingPermission(SecurityAction.LinkDemand,
                        Level = AspNetHostingPermissionLevel.Minimal),
SharePointPermission(SecurityAction.InheritanceDemand, ObjectModel = true),
AspNetHostingPermission(SecurityAction.InheritanceDemand,
                        Level = AspNetHostingPermissionLevel.Minimal)]
public class FieldMetadata : FormComponent
{
  private int displaySize;
  private string fieldName;
  private SPField field;

  public virtual int DisplaySize
  {
    get
    {
      if (this.displaySize == 0 && this.Parent != null)
      {
        if (this.Parent is FieldMetadata)
          this.displaySize = ((FieldMetadata)this.Parent).DisplaySize;
        else if (this.Parent.Parent is FieldMetadata)
          this.displaySize = ((FieldMetadata)this.Parent.Parent).DisplaySize;
        if (((this.displaySize != 0) || (this.Field == null)) ||
              string.IsNullOrEmpty(this.Field.DisplaySize))
          return this.displaySize;

        this.displaySize = Convert.ToInt32(this.Field.DisplaySize,
                                      CultureInfo.InvariantCulture);
      }
      return this.displaySize;
    }
    set { this.displaySize = value; }
  }

  public SPField Field
  {
    get
    {
      if (this.field != null)
        return this.field;

      if (base.Fields == null)
        return null;

      this.field = base.Fields.GetFieldByInternalName(this.FieldName, false);
      if ((this.field == null) && (base.Item != null))
        this.field = base.Item.Fields.GetFieldByInternalName(this.FieldName,
                                                                    false);
      if (this.field == null)
        this.field = base.Fields.GetFieldByDisplayName(this.FieldName, false);
```

(continued)

Listing 5-7 *(continued)*

```
        if ((this.field == null) && (base.Item != null))
          this.field = base.Item.Fields.GetFieldByDisplayName(this.FieldName, false);
        return this.field;
      }
    }

    public string FieldName
    {
      get
      {
        if (string.IsNullOrEmpty(this.fieldName))
        {
          Control parentTemplateBasedControl =
            TemplateBasedControl.GetParentTemplateBasedControl(this);
          while (true)
          {
            if (((parentTemplateBasedControl == null) ||
                    (parentTemplateBasedControl is FieldMetadata)) ||
                    (parentTemplateBasedControl is TemplateContainer))
            {
              if (parentTemplateBasedControl is FieldMetadata)
                this.fieldName =
                          ((FieldMetadata)parentTemplateBasedControl).FieldName;
              else if (parentTemplateBasedControl is TemplateContainer)
                this.fieldName =
                        ((TemplateContainer)parentTemplateBasedControl).FieldName;
              break;
            }
            parentTemplateBasedControl =
              TemplateBasedControl.GetParentTemplateBasedControl(
                                               parentTemplateBasedControl);
          }
        }
        return this.fieldName;
      }
      set { this.fieldName = value; }
    }

    public override bool Visible
    {
      [SharePointPermission(SecurityAction.Demand, ObjectModel = true)]
      get
      {
        if (this.Field == null)
          return false;
        return base.Visible;
      }
      [SharePointPermission(SecurityAction.Demand, ObjectModel = true)]
      set { base.Visible = value; }
    }
  }
```

FieldName

As you can see from Listing 5-7, FieldMetadata exposes a string read-write property named FieldName, which gets or sets the name of the current item field. If the value of this property is not explicitly set, the getter of this property takes these steps to set the value. First, it invokes the GetParentTemplateBasedControl static method on the TemplateBasedControl class to return a reference to the first TemplateBasedControl ancestor of the current FieldMetadata:

```
Control parentTemplateBasedControl =
                                    TemplateBasedControl.GetParentTemplateBasedControl(this);
```

If this first TemplateBasedControl ancestor is a FieldMetadata, the current FieldMetadata simply inherits the field name of this ancestor:

```
this.fieldName = ((FieldMetadata)parentTemplateBasedControl).FieldName;
```

If the first TemplateBasedControl ancestor is a TemplateContainer, the current FieldMetadata simply inherits the field name from this ancestor:

```
this.fieldName = ((TemplateContainer)parentTemplateBasedControl).FieldName;
```

Field

As you can see from Listing 5-7, FieldMetadata exposes a read-only property of the SPField type named Field, which returns a reference to the SPField object that represents the current SharePoint field. This property performs these tasks to access this reference. First, it invokes the GetFieldByInternalName method on the SPFieldCollection object that the Fields collection property of the base class references, passing in the field name. This method returns a reference to the SPField object in the Fields collection with the specified *internal* field name:

```
this.field = base.Fields.GetFieldByInternalName(this.FieldName, false);
```

If the Fields collection does not contain an SPField object with the specified internal field name, the Field property invokes the GetFieldByInternalName method on the Fields collection property of the SPItem object that represents the current SharePoint item. This method returns a reference to the SPField object in the Fields collection with the specified *internal* field name:

```
this.field = base.Item.Fields.GetFieldByInternalName(this.FieldName, false);
```

If the Fields collection of the SPItem object that represents the current SharePoint item does not contain an SPField object with the specified internal field name either, the Field property assumes that the FieldName property does not contain the internal field name and instead contains the display name. As such, it invokes the GetFieldByDisplayName method on the SPFieldCollection object that the Fields collection property of the base class references, passing in the field name. This method returns a reference to the SPField object in the Fields collection with the specified display name:

```
this.field = base.Fields.GetFieldByDisplayName(this.FieldName, false);
```

If the Fields collection of the base class does not contain a reference to an SPField object with the specified display name, the Field property invokes the GetFieldByDisplayName method on the SPFieldCollection object that the SPItem object that represents the current SharePoint item references.

This method returns a reference to the SPField object in this Fields collection with the specified display name:

```
this.field = base.Item.Fields.GetFieldByDisplayName(this.FieldName, false);
```

DisplaySize

The DisplaySize property of FieldMetadata gets or sets an integer that specifies the maximum number of characters of the value of the field that the field-rendering control should display. Because this property is writable, its value can be specified explicitly. If the value of this property is not set, the getter of the property performs these tasks to specify the value. If the parent server control of the field-rendering control is a FieldMetadata, it uses the value of the DisplaySize property of the parent. In other words, the current FieldMetadata inherits the display size of its parent FieldMetadata:

```
            if (this.Parent is FieldMetadata)
              this.displaySize = ((FieldMetadata)this.Parent).DisplaySize;
```

If the parent of the current FieldMetadata is not a FieldMetadata itself, the getter checks whether its grandparent is a FieldMetadata. If so, the current FieldMetadata inherits the display size of its grandparent FieldMetadata:

```
            else if (this.Parent.Parent is FieldMetadata)
              this.displaySize = ((FieldMetadata)this.Parent.Parent).DisplaySize;
```

If neither the parent nor the grandparent of the current FieldMetadata is a FieldMetadata, the current FieldMetadata inherits the display size of the SPField object that represents the current item field:

```
              this.displaySize = Convert.ToInt32(this.Field.DisplaySize,
                                                 CultureInfo.InvariantCulture);
```

Visible

As you can see from Listing 5-7, FieldMetadata features a read-write Boolean property named Visible, which gets or sets the visibility of the current FieldMetadata. As you can see, FieldMetadata overrides the Visible property of its base class to add two new features. First, it annotates both the getter and setter methods with the following code access security metadata attribute to demand that the callers must have permission to use the SharePoint object model:

```
    [SharePointPermission(SecurityAction.Demand, ObjectModel = true)]
```

Second, the getter returns false if the SPField object that represents the current item field is null, that is, if there is no current item field:

```
        if (this.Field == null)
          return false;
```

CompositeField

Listing 5-8 presents the internal implementation of CompositeField. As you can see, CompositeField inherits from FieldMetadata.

Listing 5-8: The CompositeField field-rendering server control

```
[ParseChildren(true),
PersistChildren(false),
SharePointPermission(SecurityAction.LinkDemand, ObjectModel = true),
AspNetHostingPermission(SecurityAction.LinkDemand,
                        Level = AspNetHostingPermissionLevel.Minimal),
SharePointPermission(SecurityAction.InheritanceDemand, ObjectModel = true),
AspNetHostingPermission(SecurityAction.InheritanceDemand,
                        Level = AspNetHostingPermissionLevel.Minimal)]
public class CompositeField : FieldMetadata
{
  protected override string DefaultTemplateName
  {
    get
    {
      if (base.ControlMode != SPControlMode.Display)
        return "CompositeField";
      return "DisplayCompositeField";
    }
  }

  public override bool Visible
  {
    [SharePointPermission(SecurityAction.Demand, ObjectModel = true)]
    get { return (!base.Field.Hidden && base.Visible); }

    [SharePointPermission(SecurityAction.Demand, ObjectModel = true)]
    set { base.Visible = value; }
  }
}
```

CompositeField follows the typical implementation pattern discussed earlier. It overrides the DefaultTemplateName property where it returns "DisplayCompositeField" if it is in Display mode, that is, if it resides in a display list item form and it returns "CompositeField" if it is in an edit or new list item form. These two strings, as you may have already guessed, are the ID property values of two RenderingTemplate control templates declared in the DefaultTemplates.ascx file as shown in the following excerpts from this file:

```
<SharePoint:RenderingTemplate ID="DisplayCompositeField" runat="server">
  <Template>
    <TD nowrap="true" valign="top" width="165px" class="ms-formlabel">
      <H3 class="ms-standardheader">
        <SharePoint:FieldLabel runat="server"/>
      </H3>
    </TD>
    <TD valign="top" class="ms-formbody" width="450px" ID="SPField"
      <SharePoint:FieldProperty PropertyName='Type' runat='server'/>">
      <SharePoint:FormField runat="server"/>
      <SharePoint:AppendOnlyHistory runat="server"/>
    </TD>
  </Template>
```

(continued)

(continued)

```
</SharePoint:RenderingTemplate>

<SharePoint:RenderingTemplate ID="CompositeField" runat="server">
  <Template>
    <TD nowrap="true" valign="top" width="190px" class="ms-formlabel">
      <H3 class="ms-standardheader">
        <SharePoint:FieldLabel runat="server"/>
      </H3>
    </TD>
    <TD valign="top" class="ms-formbody" width="400px">
      <SharePoint:FormField runat="server"/>
      <SharePoint:FieldDescription runat="server"/>
      <SharePoint:AppendOnlyHistory runat="server"/>
    </TD>
  </Template>
</SharePoint:RenderingTemplate>
```

Note that the only difference between these two control templates is that the DisplayCompositeField control template uses a FieldProperty server control, whereas the CompositeField control template uses a FieldDescription server control. Note that both control templates use a FieldLabel server control to render the field name, a FormField server control to render the field value, and an AppendOnlyHistory server control to render the history version. As you can see, these two control templates render the complete information about a given field including its name, value, version history, and description, hence the name composite field. In a way, a CompositeField field-rendering control composes a FieldLabel, a FieldProperty/FieldDescription, a FormField, and an AppendOnlyHistory field-rendering control through its associated RenderingTemplate server control to provide complete information about a specified field.

FieldDescription

Listing 5-9 presents the implementation of FieldDescription, which inherits from FieldMetadata. Recall that the RenderingTemplate server control associated with the CompositeField field-rendering control uses a FieldDescription field-rendering server control.

Listing 5-9: The FieldDescription field-rendering server control

```
[PersistChildren(false),
ParseChildren(true),
SharePointPermission(SecurityAction.LinkDemand, ObjectModel = true),
AspNetHostingPermission(SecurityAction.LinkDemand,
                        Level = AspNetHostingPermissionLevel.Minimal),
SharePointPermission(SecurityAction.InheritanceDemand, ObjectModel = true),
AspNetHostingPermission(SecurityAction.InheritanceDemand,
                        Level = AspNetHostingPermissionLevel.Minimal)]
public class FieldDescription : FieldMetadata
{
  [SharePointPermission(SecurityAction.Demand, ObjectModel = true)]
  protected override void Render(HtmlTextWriter writer)
  {
    if (!string.IsNullOrEmpty(base.Field.Description))
      writer.Write(SPHttpUtility.NoEncode(
                  SPUtility.AutoHyperLinking(this.Web, base.Field.Description)));
```

```
    }

    public override bool Visible
    {
      [SharePointPermission(SecurityAction.Demand, ObjectModel = true)]
      get
      {
        return ((((base.ControlMode != SPControlMode.Display) &&
                 !string.IsNullOrEmpty(base.Field.Description)) &&
                 (base.Field.Type != SPFieldType.User)) && base.Visible);
      }

      [SharePointPermission(SecurityAction.Demand, ObjectModel = true)]
      set { base.Visible = value; }
    }
  }
```

As the name suggests, FieldDescription renders the description of a field. As you can see, FieldDescription overrides the Render method where it simply writes out the value of the Description property of the SPField object that represents the field.

FieldProperty

Listing 5-10 contains the code for the FieldProperty field-rendering server control, which inherits from FieldMetadata. Recall that the RenderingTemplate server control associated with the CompositeField field-rendering server control uses a FieldProperty field-rendering control.

Listing 5-10: The FieldProperty field-rendering server control

```
[SharePointPermission(SecurityAction.LinkDemand, ObjectModel = true),
AspNetHostingPermission(SecurityAction.LinkDemand,
                        Level = AspNetHostingPermissionLevel.Minimal),
SharePointPermission(SecurityAction.InheritanceDemand, ObjectModel = true),
AspNetHostingPermission(SecurityAction.InheritanceDemand,
                        Level = AspNetHostingPermissionLevel.Minimal)]
public class FieldProperty : FieldMetadata
{
  [SharePointPermission(SecurityAction.Demand, ObjectModel = true)]
  protected override void Render(HtmlTextWriter writer)
  {
    if (this.Encode == "HtmlEncodeAllowSimpleTextFormatting")
      SPHttpUtility.HtmlEncodeAllowSimpleTextFormatting(
                         base.Field.GetProperty(this.PropertyName), writer);
    else
      SPHttpUtility.HtmlEncode(base.Field.GetProperty(this.PropertyName), writer);
  }

  public string Encode {get; set; }
  public string PropertyName { get; set; }
}
```

As the name suggests, FieldProperty renders the value of the specified field property in HTML-encoded format. As you can see, FieldProperty extends FieldMetadata to add support for two new properties named Encode and PropertyName. The PropertyName property specifies the name of the field property whose value FieldProperty renders. The Encode property specifies the type of formatting.

As Listing 5-10 shows, FieldProperty overrides the Render method. This override checks whether the Encode property is set to "HtmlEncodeAllowSimpleTextFormatting". If so, it uses the HtmlEncodeAllowSimpleTextFormatting static method of the SPHttpUtility class to render the value of the specified property in HTML-encoded format while preserving spaces and allowing simple text formatting:

```
if (this.Encode == "HtmlEncodeAllowSimpleTextFormatting")
  SPHttpUtility.HtmlEncodeAllowSimpleTextFormatting(
                              base.Field.GetProperty(this.PropertyName), output);
```

If not, it uses the HtmlEncode static method of the SPHttpUtility class to render the value of the specified property in HTML-encoded format:

```
else
  SPHttpUtility.HtmlEncode(base.Field.GetProperty(this.PropertyName), output);
```

As you can see, if you assign any value other than "HtmlEncodeAllowSimpleTextFormatting", FieldProperty renders the value of the field property in an HTML-encoded format.

FieldLabel

Listing 5-11 presents the internal implementation of FieldLabel field-rendering server control. Recall that the RenderingTemplate server control associated with the CompositeField field-rendering control uses a FieldLabel field-rendering control.

Listing 5-11: The FieldLabel field-rendering server control

```
[PersistChildren(false),
ParseChildren(true),
SharePointPermission(SecurityAction.LinkDemand, ObjectModel = true),
AspNetHostingPermission(SecurityAction.LinkDemand,
                        Level = AspNetHostingPermissionLevel.Minimal),
SharePointPermission(SecurityAction.InheritanceDemand, ObjectModel = true),
AspNetHostingPermission(SecurityAction.InheritanceDemand,
                        Level = AspNetHostingPermissionLevel.Minimal)]
public class FieldLabel : FieldMetadata
{
  private ITemplate displayTemplate;
  private string displayTemplateName;

  protected override ITemplate ControlTemplate
  {
    get
    {
      if (base.Field != null)
      {
        if (base.ControlMode != SPControlMode.Display)
```

```
        {
          if (!base.Field.Required)
            return base.Template;
          return base.AlternateTemplate;
        }
        return this.DisplayTemplate;
      }
      return null;
    }
  }

  protected override string DefaultAlternateTemplateName
  {
    get { return "FieldLabelRequired"; }
  }

  protected virtual string DefaultDisplayTemplateName
  {
    get { return "FieldLabelForDisplay"; }
  }

  protected override string DefaultTemplateName
  {
    get { return "FieldLabelDefault"; }
  }

  [TemplateContainer(typeof(FormComponent))]
  public ITemplate DisplayTemplate
  {
    get
    {
        if (this.displayTemplate == null && this.DisplayTemplateName != null)
        this.displayTemplate =
              SPControlTemplateManager.GetTemplateByName(this.DisplayTemplateName);
      return this.displayTemplate;
    }
    set { this.displayTemplate = value; }
  }

  public string DisplayTemplateName
  {
    get
    {
      if (this.displayTemplateName == null)
        this.displayTemplateName = this.DefaultDisplayTemplateName;
      return this.displayTemplateName;
    }
    set { this.displayTemplateName = value; }
  }
}
```

FieldLabel overrides the DefaultTemplateName and DefaultAlternateTemplateName properties to respectively return "FieldLabelDefault" and "FieldLabelRequired", which are the ID property values of two RenderingTemplate server controls in the DefaultTemplates.ascx file as shown in the following excerpt from this file:

```
<SharePoint:RenderingTemplate ID="FieldLabelDefault" runat="server">
  <Template>
    <nobr>
      <SharePoint:FieldProperty PropertyName="Title" runat="server"/>
    </nobr>
  </Template>
</SharePoint:RenderingTemplate>

<SharePoint:RenderingTemplate ID="FieldLabelRequired" runat="server">
  <Template>
    <nobr>
      <SharePoint:FieldProperty PropertyName="Title" runat="server"/>
      <span class="ms-formvalidation"> *</span>
    </nobr>
  </Template>
</SharePoint:RenderingTemplate>
```

As you can see, both of these server controls use a FieldProperty field-rendering server control to render the value of the Title property of the field in HTML-encoded format. The FieldLabelRequired RenderingTemplate server control also renders an asterisk to specify that the field is required.

FieldLabel adds support for a new template property named DisplayTemplate. FieldLabel follows the typical template implementation pattern to add support for this template property:

- It defines a read-only default template name property, which returns a string that contains the ID property value of a RenderingTemplate server control in an .ascx file in the ControlTemplates folder.

```
protected virtual string DefaultDisplayTemplateName
{
  get { return "FieldLabelForDisplay"; }
}
```

- The DefaultTemplates.ascx file contains the following RenderingTemplate server control with the ID property value of "FieldLabelForDisplay":

```
<SharePoint:RenderingTemplate ID="FieldLabelForDisplay" runat="server">
  <Template>
    <a name="SPBookmark_<SharePoint:FieldProperty PropertyName='InternalName'
runat='server'/>" />
    <SharePoint:FieldProperty PropertyName="Title" runat="server"/>
  </Template>
</SharePoint:RenderingTemplate>
```

- As you can see, this RenderingTemplate server control uses a FieldProperty field-rendering server control to render the value of the Title property of the field in HTML-encoded format. The control also adds a bookmark whose name contains the value of the InternalName field property in HTML-encoded format.
- It defines a read-write template name property that uses a private field as a backing store. The getter of this property assigns the value of the property defined in the previous step to this private field if the value of the private field hasn't been explicitly set:

```
public string DisplayTemplateName
{
  get
  {
    if (this.displayTemplateName == null)
      this.displayTemplateName = this.DefaultDisplayTemplateName;
    return this.displayTemplateName;
  }
  set { this.displayTemplateName = value; }
}
```

- It defines a new read-write template property that uses a private field as a backing store. The getter of this property first checks whether an ITemplate object has been explicitly assigned to its backing storage private field. If so, it returns a reference to this object. If not, it invokes the GetTemplateByName static method on the SPControlTemplateManager class, passing in the value of the property defined in the previous step. The getter assigns the ITemplate object that the GetTemplateByName static method returns to the backing storage private field:

```
[TemplateContainer(typeof(FormComponent))]
  public ITemplate DisplayTemplate
  {
    get
    {
      if (this.displayTemplate == null)
      {
        while (this.DisplayTemplateName != null)
        {
          this.displayTemplate =
              SPControlTemplateManager.GetTemplateByName(this.DisplayTemplateName);
          break;
        }
      }
      return this.displayTemplate;
    }
    set { this.displayTemplate = value; }
  }
```

- It overrides the ControlTemplate property to include the logic that determines when to return the ITemplate object assigned to the template property defined in the previous step:

```
protected override ITemplate ControlTemplate
{
  get
  {
    if (base.Field != null)
    {
      if (base.ControlMode != SPControlMode.Display)
      {
        if (!base.Field.Required)
          return base.Template;
        return base.AlternateTemplate;
      }
      return this.DisplayTemplate;
    }
    return null;
  }
}
```

- In this case, the ControlTemplate property returns the ITemplate object assigned to the Template property if the FieldLabel field-rendering server control is not in Display mode (that is, this server control does not reside on a display list item form) and the field is not required, returns the ITemplate object assigned to the AlternateTemplate property if the FieldLabel field-rendering server control is not in Display mode but the field is required, and returns the ITemplate object assigned to the DisplayTemplate property if the FieldLabel field-rendering control is on a display list item form.

BaseFieldControl

SharePoint does not make use of the ASP.NET validator server controls. Instead BaseFieldControl, which is the base class for all field-rendering controls, directly implements the ASP.NET IValidator interface. Listing 5-12 presents the definition of this interface.

Listing 5-12: The IValidator interface

```
[AspNetHostingPermission(SecurityAction.InheritanceDemand,
                         Level=AspNetHostingPermissionLevel.Minimal), AspNetHosting
Permission(SecurityAction.LinkDemand,
                        Level=AspNetHostingPermissionLevel.Minimal)]
public interface IValidator
{
  void Validate();
  string ErrorMessage { get; set; }
  bool IsValid { get; set; }
}
```

As you can see, IValidator exposes a method named Validate. The IValidator implementor must implement this method to incorporate the appropriate data validation logic. This logic must set the IsValid property to true if the validation succeeds and to false otherwise. This logic must also set the ErrorMessage property if the validation fails. Note that IValidator is annotated with the appropriate code access security metadata attributes to demand its implementors and callers have at least the ASP.NET Minimal trust level (<trust level="Minimal"/>).

Listing 5-13 presents the BaseFieldControl class's implementation of the members of the IValidator interface.

Listing 5-13: The BaseFieldControl class's implmentation of IValidator

```
public abstract class BaseFieldControl: FieldMetadata, IValidator
{
  private string errorMessage;
  private bool isValid;

  [SharePointPermission(SecurityAction.Demand, ObjectModel=true)]
  public virtual void Validate() { }

  public string ErrorMessage
  {
    [SharePointPermission(SecurityAction.Demand, ObjectModel=true)]
    get { return this.errorMessage; }

    [SharePointPermission(SecurityAction.Demand, ObjectModel=true)]
    set { this.errorMessage = value; }
  }

  public bool IsValid
  {
    [SharePointPermission(SecurityAction.Demand, ObjectModel=true)]
    get { return this.isValid; }

    [SharePointPermission(SecurityAction.Demand, ObjectModel=true)]
    set { this.isValid = value; }
  }

  ...
}
```

As you can see from Listing 5-13, the BaseFieldControl class's implementation of the Validate method doesn't contain any validation logic. It is the responsibility of the subclasses of BaseFieldControl to override this method to include the appropriate data validation logic. Note that the Validate method validates the value of the Value property of BaseFieldControl. The Value property is the UI value, that is, the value that BaseFieldControl displays in its UI, not the value of the SPField object whose FieldRenderingControl property returns a reference to the BaseFieldControl server control. The ItemFieldValue property of BaseFieldControl returns the value of this SPField object. The Validate method does not validate the value of the ItemFieldValue property. It is the responsibility of the GetValidatedString method of the SPField object to validate the field value. The BaseFieldControl subclasses' implementation of Validate must set the IsValid property to false if the data validation fails and to true otherwise. The BaseFieldControl subclasses' implementation of Validate must also set the ErrorMessage property to the appropriate error message if the validation fails.

Besides implementing the IValidator interface, BaseFieldControl also exposes new methods and properties as discussed in the following sections. These methods and properties are common among all field-rendering controls.

CssClass

BaseFieldControl exposes a read-write string property named CssClass, which gets or sets the CSS class name that the subclasses of BaseFieldControl can assign to the server control or HTML they use to render the current field. It is important to realize that BaseFieldControl does not make any use of the CssClass property. It simply defines it as shown in Listing 5-14.

Listing 5-14: The CssClass property

```
public abstract class BaseFieldControl: FieldMetadata, IValidator
{
  protected BaseFieldControl()
  {
    this.cssClass = "ms-input";
    ...
  }

  public virtual string CssClass
  {
    get { return this.cssClass; }
    set { this.cssClass = value; }
  }
}
```

Note that BaseFieldControl specifies a CSS class named "ms-input" as the value of the CssClass property. The "ms-input" CSS class is defined in the core.css file in the following folder on the file system of the front-end web server:

```
Local_Drive:\Program Files\Common Files\microsoft shared\Web Server
Extensions\12\TEMPLATE\LAYOUTS\1033
```

The core.css file defines the "ms-input" CSS class as follows:

```
.ms-input
{
  font-size:8pt;
  font-family:Verdana,sans-serif;
}
```

As mentioned, it is the responsibility of the subclasses of BaseFieldControl to assign the value of the CssClass property to the server control or HTML element that renders the field. For example, there is a subclass named BaseTextField whose CreateChildControls method assigns the value of the CssClass property to the TextBox server control that renders the field as shown in the following code listing:

```
public abstract class BaseTextField: BaseFieldControl
{
  protected override void CreateChildControls()
  {
    base.CreateChildControls();
    if ((base.ControlMode != SPControlMode.Display) && (base.Field != null))
    {
      this.textBox = (TextBox) this.TemplateContainer.FindControl("TextField");
      this.textBox.TabIndex = this.TabIndex;
      this.textBox.CssClass = this.CssClass;
      ...
    }
  }
}
```

Note that the CssClass property is marked as virtual. This means that the subclasses of BaseFieldControl can override this property to return a value other than "ms-input". As a matter of fact, BaseTextField overrides this property as follows:

```
public override string CssClass
{
  get
  {
    if (this.cssClass == null)
    {
      if (this.DisplaySize <= 0)
        this.cssClass = "ms-long";
      else
        this.cssClass = "ms-input";
    }
    return this.cssClass;
  }

  set { this.cssClass = value; }
}
```

DisableInputFieldLabel

This property gets or sets a Boolean value that specifies whether the default input field label should be used on the New and Edit forms. Set this value to true if you don't want the default input field label to be used on the New and Edit forms. As you can see from the following code listing, this property cannot be overridden. It can only be set.

```
private bool disableInputFieldLabel = false;
public bool DisableInputFieldLabel
{
  get { return this.disableInputFieldLabel; }
  set { this.disableInputFieldLabel = value; }
}
```

DisplayTemplate and DisplayTemplateName

BaseFieldControl follows the typical implementation pattern for adding a new template to add a new template, which is used to render the field in Display mode, that is, when the field is not in Edit or New mode:

- Defines a new read-write virtual string property named DisplayTemplateName, which specifies the ID attribute value of a <RenderingTemplate> element in an .ascx file in the ControlTemplates folder on the file system of the front-end web server:

```
private string displayTemplateName;

public virtual string DisplayTemplateName
{
  get { return this.displayTemplateName; }
  set { this.displayTemplateName = value; }
}
```

- Defines a new read-write virtual property of the ITemplate type named DisplayTemplate:

```
private ITemplate displayTemplate;

[TemplateContainer(typeof(FormComponent))]
public ITemplate DisplayTemplate
{
  get
  {
    if (this.displayTemplate == null && this.DisplayTemplateName != null)
      this.displayTemplate =
             SPControlTemplateManager.GetTemplateByName(this.DisplayTemplateName);

    return this.displayTemplate;
  }
  set { this.displayTemplate = value; }
}
```

- The getter of this template property, like the getter of any other template property, checks whether the value of the property has been explicitly specified. Because this property is writable, you can directly assign an ITemplate object to the property to set its value. If the value of the property has not been explicitly set, the getter invokes the GetTemplateByName static method on the SPControlTemplateManager class, passing in the value of the DisplayTemplateName property. Recall that the DisplayTemplateName property specifies the ID attribute value of a <SharePoint:RenderingTemplate> element in an .ascx file in the ControlTemplates folder. As discussed earlier, the GetTemplateByName property returns a reference to the ITemplate object that the ASP.NET page parser dynamically creates and assigns to the Template property of the RenderingTemplate server control. As you can see, the getter simply assigns this ITemplate object to the displayTemplate field that it uses as its backing store.
- Overrides the CreateChildControls method as follows:

```
[SharePointPermission(SecurityAction.Demand, ObjectModel=true)]
protected override void CreateChildControls()
{
  if ((base.ControlMode == SPControlMode.Display) &&
```

```
        (this.DisplayTemplate != null))
      base.Template = this.DisplayTemplate;

    if ((base.ControlMode != SPControlMode.Display) ||
        (this.DisplayTemplate != null))
      base.CreateChildControls();
  }
```

- Note that BaseFieldControl's override of CreateChildControl first sets the Template property to reference the ITemplate object that the DisplayTemplate property references and then invokes the CreateChildControls method of its base class. As discussed earlier, the CreateChildControls method of the base class renders the ITemplate object referenced by the Template property.

ItemFieldValue

BaseFieldControl exposes a read-write property of the System.Object type named ItemFieldValue, which gets or sets the value of the SPField object whose FieldRenderingControl property references the BaseFieldControl server control. Listing 5-15 presents the simplified version of the internal implementation of this property.

Listing 5-15: The simplified version of the internal implementation of ItemFieldValue

```
public virtual object ItemFieldValue
{
  get
  {
    if (base.Field == null)
      return null;

    if (base.ControlMode == SPControlMode.New)
      return base.Field.DefaultValueTyped;

    else if (base.ItemContext.ListItemVersion == null && base.Item != null)
    {
      object obj = base.Item[base.Field.InternalName];
      if (obj != null)
        return obj;

      else
      {
        if (((base.ItemContext != null) &&
            (base.ItemContext.FormContext != null)) &&
            base.ItemContext.FormContext.UploadMode)
          return base.Field.DefaultValueTyped;
        return null;
      }
    }

    return base.ItemContext.ListItemVersion[base.Field.InternalName];
  }
  set { base.Item[base.Field.InternalName] = value; }
}
```

As you can see, ItemFieldValue returns null if there is no SPField object associated with BaseFieldControl:

```
if (base.Field == null)
    return null;
```

If BaseFieldControl is in New mode, ItemFieldValue returns the value of the DefaultValueTyped property of the SPField object whose FieldRenderingControl property references the BaseFieldControl server control. The DefaultValueTyped property returns an instance of the field value type associated with the SPField object.

```
if (base.ControlMode == SPControlMode.New)
    return base.Field.DefaultValueTyped;
```

If the ListItemVersion property of the item context is not null, ItemFieldValue uses the internal name of the SPField object whose FieldRenderingControl property references the BaseFieldControl server control as an index into the SPListItemVersion object that the ListItemVersion property references to return the value of the field:

```
return base.ItemContext.ListItemVersion[base.Field.InternalName];
```

The ListItemVersion property of the item context references the SPListItemVersion object that represents the current version of the current SharePoint list item.

If the ListItemVersion property of the item context is null, ItemFieldValue uses the internal name of the SPField object whose FieldRenderingControl property references the current BaseFieldControl server control as an index into the SPItem object that the Item property references to return the value of the field:

```
        object obj = base.Item[base.Field.InternalName];
        if (obj != null)
          return obj;
```

If this value is null as well, ItemFieldValue returns the value of the DefaultValueTyped property of the SPField object:

```
        if (((base.ItemContext != null) &&
              (base.ItemContext.FormContext != null)) &&
              base.ItemContext.FormContext.UploadMode)
            return base.Field.DefaultValueTyped;
          return null;
```

ListItemFieldValue

BaseFieldControl exposes another read-write property of the System.Object type named ListItemFieldValue that simply delegates to the ItemFieldValue property:

```
public virtual object ListItemFieldValue
{
  get { return this.ItemFieldValue; }
  set { this.ItemFieldValue = value; }
}
```

TabIndex

BaseFieldControl contains a property of the short type named TabIndex, which gets or sets the tab order of the control on the page. The TabIndex is zero by default. This means that by default the control has no tab order. However, the subclasses of BaseFieldControl can override this property to return a different value.

```
private short tabIndex = 0;

public virtual short TabIndex
{
  get { return this.tabIndex; }
  set { this.tabIndex = value; }
}
```

Note that BaseFieldControl makes no use of the TabIndex property. It simply defines it. It is up to the subclasses of BaseFieldControl to use this property. For example, the BaseTextField server control's override of the CreateChildControls method assigns the value of this property to the TabIndex property of the TextBox server control that renders the field:

```
public abstract class BaseTextField: BaseFieldControl
{
  protected override void CreateChildControls()
  {
    base.CreateChildControls();
    if ((base.ControlMode != SPControlMode.Display) && (base.Field != null))
    {
      this.textBox = (TextBox) this.TemplateContainer.FindControl("TextField");
      this.textBox.TabIndex = this.TabIndex;
      this.textBox.CssClass = this.CssClass;
      ...
    }
  }
}
```

Value

BaseFieldControl has a virtual property of the System.Object type named Value, which gets or sets the value in the UI. This is different from the ItemFieldValue property, which gets or sets the value of the SPField object that represents the SharePoint field. As you can see from the following code listing, BaseFieldControl's implementation of the getter of the Value property returns null. Note that BaseFieldControl does not provide implementation for the setter of this property:

```
public virtual object Value
{
  get { return null; }
  set { }
}
```

If you inherit directly from BaseFieldControl to implement a field-rendering control, you must override the Value property. For example, BaseTextField directly inherits from BaseFieldControl. As such, it overrides the Value property as follows:

```
public abstract class BaseTextField: BaseFieldControl
{
  public override object Value
  {
    get { return this.Text; }
    set
    {
      if (base.Field != null)
        this.Text = base.Field.GetFieldValueForEdit(value);
    }
  }

  public virtual string Text
  {
    get
    {
      this.EnsureChildControls();
      if (this.textBox == null)
        return null;

      return this.textBox.Text;
    }
    set
    {
      this.EnsureChildControls();
      if (this.textBox != null)
        this.textBox.Text = value;
    }
  }

  protected override void CreateChildControls()
  {
    base.CreateChildControls();
```

```
        if ((base.ControlMode != SPControlMode.Display) && (base.Field != null))
        {
          this.textBox = (TextBox) this.TemplateContainer.FindControl("TextField");
          ...
        }
      }
      ...
    }
```

As you can see from the BaseTextField's override of the CreateChildControls method, BaseTextField uses a TextBox server control to render its associated field. BaseTextField exposes a string property named Text whose getter and setter delegate to the Text property of this TextBox server control. The getter of the Value property simply returns the value of the Text property, which is nothing but the value entered into the TextBox server control. The setter of the Value property invokes the GetFieldValueForEdit method on the associated SPField object and assigns the return value of this method to the Text property, which is then automatically assigned to the Text property of the TextBox server control.

AllowFirstFocus

BaseFieldControl exposes a virtual read-only Boolean property named AllowFirstFocus, which returns a Boolean value that specifies whether the page is allowed to set the initial focus to the BaseFieldControl on loading. As you can see from the following code listing, BaseFieldControl's implementation of this property always returns true. However, the subclasses of BaseFieldControl can override this property to include the logic that determines which value to return.

```
protected virtual bool AllowFirstFocus
{
  get { return true; }
}
```

CanCacheRenderedFieldValue

BaseFieldControl has a read-write Boolean property named CanCacheRenderedFieldValue, which gets or sets a Boolean value that specifies whether the rendered field value (the value of the Value property) can be locally cached. As you can see from the following, BaseFieldControl's implementation of this property returns true:

```
private bool canCacheRenderedFieldValue = true;
protected bool CanCacheRenderedFieldValue
{
  get { return this.canCacheRenderedFieldValue; }
  set { this.canCacheRenderedFieldValue = value; }
}
```

Note that this property is not overridable. The only way to change the value of the property is to set its value.

HasPostBackEditData

BaseFieldControl has a read-only Boolean property named HasPostBackEditData, which gets a Boolean value that specifies whether the BaseFieldControl server control's data might have changed due to a postback. As you can see from the following code, BaseFieldControl's implementation of this property returns true if the previous control mode of BaseFieldControl was New or Edit:

```
protected virtual bool HasPostBackEditData
{
  get
  {
    return ((SPControlMode.New == this.PreviousControlMode) ||
            (SPControlMode.Edit == this.PreviousControlMode));
  }
}
```

Note that this property is overridable.

IsFieldValueCached

BaseFieldControl exposes a Boolean read-only property named IsFieldValueCached, which returns a Boolean value that specifies whether the value of the BaseFieldControl server control has been cached. Note that this property is not overridable. The subclasses of BaseFieldControl must check the value of this property before they attempt to access the database.

```
private bool isFieldValueCached;
protected bool IsFieldValueCached
{
  get { return this.isFieldValueCached; }
}
```

PreviousControlMode

The PreviousControlMode property returns an SPControlMode enumeration value that specifies the control mode of the BaseFieldControl before the last postback:

```
protected virtual SPControlMode PreviousControlMode
{
  get
  {
    if (this.ViewState["PreviousControlMode"] != null)
      return (SPControlMode) this.ViewState["PreviousControlMode"];

    return SPControlMode.Invalid;
  }
}
```

Focus

As the name suggests, the Focus method sets the focus to the BaseFieldControl field-rendering control. Note that the BaseFieldControl base class's implementation of Focus doesn't do anything. It is the responsibility of its subclasses to override Focus to include that logic that actually sets the focus to the field-rendering control:

```
[SharePointPermission(SecurityAction.Demand, ObjectModel=true)]
public override void Focus() { }
```

UpdateFieldValueInItem

The BaseFieldControl base class's implementation of this method assigns the value of the Value property to the ItemFieldValue property. In other words, it sets the value of the underlying field to the value that the user has entered into the UI of the field-rendering control. Note that if any exception occurs, this field sets the IsValid property to false and assigns the error message to the ErrorMessage property:

```
public virtual void UpdateFieldValueInItem()
{
  if (this.Visible)
  {
    try
    {
      if (this.Parent is FormField &&
          !string.Equals(this.ItemFieldValue.ToString(), this.Value.ToString()))
        ((FormField)this.Parent).OnValueChanged(EventArgs.Empty);

      this.ItemFieldValue = this.Value;
    }
    catch (SPFieldValidationException exception)
    {
      this.IsValid = false;
      this.ErrorMessage = exception.Message;
    }
  }
}
```

Validate

The Validate method validates the value of the Value property, that is, the value that the user has entered into the UI of the BaseFieldControl field-rendering control. It does not validate the value of the underlying field. Note that the BaseFieldControl base class's implementation of Validate doesn't do anything. It is the responsibility of the subclasses of this base class to override the Validate method to incorporate the logic that validates the value of the Value property. The subclass must set the value of the IsValid property to false and assign an error message to the ErrorMessage property if the validation fails. Otherwise it must set the IsValid property to true.

```
[SharePointPermission(SecurityAction.Demand, ObjectModel=true)]
public virtual void Validate() { }
```

RegisterFieldControl

As you can see from the following code fragment, RegisterFieldControl adds the BaseFieldControl control to the FieldControlCollection collection and the Validators collection of the containing page:

```
protected virtual void RegisterFieldControl()
{
  base.FieldControlCollection.Add(this);
  this.Page.Validators.Add(this);
}
```

RenderFieldForDisplay

As the name suggests, this method renders the BaseFieldControl field-rendering control in Display mode, that is, when it resides on a list view page such as AllItem.aspx or a display list item page such as DispForm.aspx. The BaseFieldControl base class's implementation of this method renders the field on a display list item page as it does on a list view page. Override this method if you want to provide a different rendering on a display list item page versus a list view page.

```
protected virtual void RenderFieldForDisplay(HtmlTextWriter output)
{
  ...
}
```

RenderFieldForInput

As the name implies, this method renders the BaseFieldControl field-rendering control in Edit or New mode, that is, when it resides on an edit list item page such as EditForm.aspx or a new list item page such as NewForm.aspx page. The BaseFieldControl field-rendering control's implementation of this method first invokes the Render method to render the control and then invokes the RenderValidationMessage method to render the error message (if any):

```
protected virtual void RenderFieldForInput(HtmlTextWriter output)
{
  base.Render(output);
  this.RenderValidationMessage(output);
}
```

RenderValidationMessage

This method doesn't render anything if the IsValid property is set to true. If the IsValid property is set to true, that is, if the data validation has failed, this method checks whether the ErrorMessage property has been set. If not, it sets the value of this property to a generic error message. The method then HTML-encodes the value of the ErrorMessage property and renders this HTML-encoded value within a <span> element:

```
protected virtual void RenderValidationMessage(HtmlTextWriter output)
{
  if (!this.IsValid)
  {
    if (string.IsNullOrEmpty(this.ErrorMessage))
      this.ErrorMessage = "InvalidFieldValue";

    output.Write("<span class=\"ms-formvalidation\">");
    SPHttpUtility.HtmlEncode(this.ErrorMessage, output);
    output.Write("</span><br>");
  }
}
```

FormField

FormField is a generic field-rendering control that inherits from BaseFieldControl. FormField instantiates basic field control of a specified type. Listing 5-16 presents the internal implementation of the FormField field-rendering server control.

Listing 5-16: The FormField field-rendering server control

```
[SharePointPermission(SecurityAction.LinkDemand, ObjectModel = true),
AspNetHostingPermission(SecurityAction.LinkDemand,
                        Level = AspNetHostingPermissionLevel.Minimal),
SharePointPermission(SecurityAction.InheritanceDemand, ObjectModel = true),
AspNetHostingPermission(SecurityAction.InheritanceDemand,
                        Level = AspNetHostingPermissionLevel.Minimal)]
public class FormField : BaseFieldControl
{
  private static readonly object ValueChangedEventKey = new object();
  private BaseFieldControl childControl;

  public event EventHandler ValueChanged
  {
    add { base.Events.AddHandler(ValueChangedEventKey, value); }
    remove { base.Events.RemoveHandler(ValueChangedEventKey, value); }
  }

  [SharePointPermission(SecurityAction.Demand, ObjectModel = true)]
  protected override void CreateChildControls()
  {
    this.Controls.Clear();
    if (!base.IsFieldValueCached && (base.Field != null))
    {
      Control parent = this.Parent;
      while ((parent != null) && !(parent is HtmlForm))
      {
        if (!(parent is ListFormWebPart))
          parent = parent.Parent;

        if (((ListFormWebPart)parent).Hidden)
        {
          this.Visible = false;
          return;
        }
      }

      if (this.childControl == null)
      {
        this.childControl = base.Field.FieldRenderingControl;
        if (this.childControl == null)
          return;
        this.Controls.Add(this.childControl);
      }

      this.childControl.ControlMode = base.ControlMode;
      if (base.TemplateName != null)
        this.childControl.TemplateName = base.TemplateName;
      if (base.Template != null)
        this.childControl.Template = base.Template;
      if (base.AlternateTemplateName != null)
        this.childControl.AlternateTemplateName = base.AlternateTemplateName;
```

(continued)

Listing 5-16 *(continued)*

```
      if (base.AlternateTemplate != null)
        this.childControl.AlternateTemplate = base.AlternateTemplate;
      if (this.DisplayTemplateName != null)
        this.childControl.DisplayTemplateName = this.DisplayTemplateName;
      if (base.DisplayTemplate != null)
        this.childControl.DisplayTemplate = base.DisplayTemplate;
      if (!string.IsNullOrEmpty(base.InputFieldLabel))
        this.childControl.InputFieldLabel = base.InputFieldLabel;
      if (this.DisplaySize > 0)
        this.childControl.DisplaySize = this.DisplaySize;
    }
  }

  [SharePointPermission(SecurityAction.Demand, ObjectModel = true)]
  public override void Focus()
  {
    this.EnsureChildControls();
    if (this.childControl != null)
      this.childControl.Focus();
  }

  protected internal void OnValueChanged(EventArgs e)
  {
    EventHandler handler = (EventHandler)base.Events[ValueChangedEventKey];
    if (handler != null)
      handler(this, e);
  }

  protected override void RegisterFieldControl() { }

  public override void UpdateFieldValueInItem() { }

  public override object Value
  {
    get
    {
      this.EnsureChildControls();
      if (this.childControl != null)
        return this.childControl.Value;
      return null;
    }
    set
    {
      this.EnsureChildControls();
      if (this.childControl != null)
        this.childControl.Value = value;
    }
  }
}
```

A FormField field-rendering server control wraps another field-rendering server control enabling you to use the same field-rendering server control on a list form to render different types of field-rendering server controls. Take a look at an example of a list form that uses a FormField field-rendering server control. The DefaultTemplates.ascx file in the ControlTemplates folder on the file system of the front-end web server contains a RenderingTemplate server control with the ID property value of CompositeField as shown in Listing 5-17.

Listing 5-17: The RenderingTemplate server control with the ID property value of CompositeField

```
<SharePoint:RenderingTemplate ID="CompositeField" runat="server">
  <Template>
    <TD nowrap="true" valign="top" width="190px" class="ms-formlabel">
      <H3 class="ms-standardheader">
        <SharePoint:FieldLabel runat="server"/>
      </H3>
    </TD>
    <TD valign="top" class="ms-formbody" width="400px">
      <SharePoint:FormField runat="server"/>
      <SharePoint:FieldDescription runat="server"/>
      <SharePoint:AppendOnlyHistory runat="server"/>
    </TD>
  </Template>
</SharePoint:RenderingTemplate>
```

As you can see, this rendering template renders two columns. The first column contains a FieldLabel field-rendering server control. The second column contains three field-rendering server controls, that is, a FormField, a FieldDescription, and an AppendOnlyHistory field-rendering server control.

ValueChanged and OnValueChanged

FormField has only two new members. FormField inherits the rest of its members from its base class. The two new members are ValueChanged and OnValueChanged. The ValueChanged member is an event and the OnValueChanged member is a method that raises this event. As you can see, FormField follows the typical .NET event implementation pattern to implement the ValueChanged event:

- Defines and instantiates a static read-only field that will be used as the event key:

```
private static readonly object ValueChangedEventKey = new object();
```

- Defines an event property whose add and remove methods delegate to the AddHandler and RemoveHandler methods of the Events collection, respectively. Note that the event key is used as an index into the Events collection to add or to remove an event handler from the collection:

```
public event EventHandler ValueChanged
{
  add { base.Events.AddHandler(ValueChangedEventKey, value); }
  remove { base.Events.RemoveHandler(ValueChangedEventKey, value); }
}
```

- Implements a protected virtual method that raises the event:

```
protected internal void OnValueChanged(EventArgs e)
{
  EventHandler handler = (EventHandler)base.Events[ValueChangedEventKey];
  if (handler != null)
    handler(this, e);
}
```

Recall that the UpdateFieldValueInItem method of BaseFieldControl invokes the OnValueChanged method on the FormField.

If you're wondering who calls the OnValueChanged method to raise the ValueChanged event, the answer is the UpdateFieldValueInItem method of the base class, that is, BaseFieldControl, as shown in the following code fragment:

```
public virtual void UpdateFieldValueInItem()
{
  if (this.Visible)
  {
    try
    {
      if (this.Parent is FormField &&
          !string.Equals(this.ItemFieldValue.ToString(), this.Value.ToString()))
        ((FormField)this.Parent).OnValueChanged(EventArgs.Empty);

      this.ItemFieldValue = this.Value;
    }
    catch (SPFieldValidationException exception)
    {
      this.IsValid = false;
      this.ErrorMessage = exception.Message;
    }
  }
}
```

Recall that UpdateFieldValueInItem updates the value of the underlying field with the value that the user has entered into the UI of the field-rendering control. As the preceding code fragment shows, UpdateFieldValueInItem invokes the OnValueChanged method if the value that the user has entered into the UI is different from the value of the field.

CreateChildControls

As Listing 5-16 shows, FormField overrides CreateChildControls where it takes these steps. First, it walks up the containment control hierarchy of the FormField control until it locates the ListFormWebPart server control. Recall that SharePoint automatically adds a ListFormWebPart server control to every list form. If this server control is hidden, CreateChildControls sets the Visible property to false and returns because there is no point in creating child controls when the containing ListFormWebPart server control is hidden:

```
Control parent = this.Parent;
while ((parent != null) && !(parent is HtmlForm))
{
  if (!(parent is ListFormWebPart))
    parent = parent.Parent;

  else (((ListFormWebPart)parent).Hidden)
  {
    this.Visible = false;
    return;
  }
}
```

Next, CreateChildControls accesses the field-rendering control that the FieldRenderingControl property of the respective field references and adds it to the Controls collection. In other words, FormField renders this field-rendering control:

```
this.childControl = base.Field.FieldRenderingControl;
if (this.childControl == null)
  return;
this.Controls.Add(this.childControl);
```

Next, CreateChildControls assigns the ControlMode, TemplateName, Template, AlternateTemplateName, AlternateTemplate, DisplayTemplateName, DisplayTemplate, InputFieldLabel, and DisplaySize properties of FormField to the field-rendering control that this control encapsulates. As such, you can use these properties of the FormField control to set the respective properties of the encapsulated field-rendering control:

```
this.childControl.ControlMode = base.ControlMode;
if (base.TemplateName != null)
  this.childControl.TemplateName = base.TemplateName;
if (base.Template != null)
  this.childControl.Template = base.Template;
if (base.AlternateTemplateName != null)
  this.childControl.AlternateTemplateName = base.AlternateTemplateName;
if (base.AlternateTemplate != null)
  this.childControl.AlternateTemplate = base.AlternateTemplate;
if (this.DisplayTemplateName != null)
  this.childControl.DisplayTemplateName = this.DisplayTemplateName;
if (base.DisplayTemplate != null)
  this.childControl.DisplayTemplate = base.DisplayTemplate;
if (!string.IsNullOrEmpty(base.InputFieldLabel))
  this.childControl.InputFieldLabel = base.InputFieldLabel;
if (this.DisplaySize > 0)
  this.childControl.DisplaySize = this.DisplaySize;
```

Focus

FormField overrides Focus to invoke the Focus method on the encapsulated field-rendering control to set the mouse focus to this control:

```
[SharePointPermission(SecurityAction.Demand, ObjectModel = true)]
public override void Focus()
{
  this.EnsureChildControls();
  if (this.childControl != null)
    this.childControl.Focus();
}
```

Value

FormField overrides Value to delegate to the Value property of the encapsulated field-rendering control:

```
public override object Value
{
  get
  {
    this.EnsureChildControls();
    if (this.childControl != null)
      return this.childControl.Value;
    return null;
  }
  set
  {
    this.EnsureChildControls();
    if (this.childControl != null)
      this.childControl.Value = value;
  }
}
```

Variable Field Type Property Rendering

The New Site Column, Change Site Column, Create Column, and Change Column pages render two types of field type properties. One type includes those properties that all field types have in common such as column name, data type, description, and whether the column is required, that is, whether a value must be specified for the column. The second type includes properties that are specific to each field type.

How would you tell the New Site Column, Change Site Column, Create Column, and Change Column pages how to render the variable field type properties of a field type? In general, you have two ways to instruct these pages to render these properties. One approach is to define a property schema for the field type. This property schema instructs these pages how to render the variable field type properties of the field type. Another approach is to implement a user control known as a variable field type property editor and have these pages host this user control. The following sections discuss both approaches.

Property Schema

A property schema for a field type is defined in the field type definition. The <FieldType> element that represents a field type definition supports a child element named <PropertySchema>. This child element has no attributes and supports a single child element named <Fields>. The <Fields> element has no attributes and supports one or more child elements named <Field>. Each <Field> child element represents a variable field type property of the field type. The <Field> element supports the following required attributes:

- **Name.** You can set this attribute to the name of the variable field type property that the <Field> element represents.
- **DisplayName.** You can set this attribute to the display name of the variable field type property that the <Field> element represents. SharePoint displays the value of this attribute in the Additional Column Settings section on the New Site Column and Create Column pages.
- **Type.** You can use this attribute to specify the data type of the variable field type property that the <Field> element represents. SharePoint uses the value of this attribute to determine what type of control to render to hold the value of the variable field type property in the UI.
- **MaxLength.** You can use this attribute to specify the maximum length, in characters, of the value of the variable field type property that the <Field> element represents can contain.
- **DisplaySize.** You can use this attribute to specify the length, in characters, of the control that holds the value of the variable field type in the UI.

This approach to rendering variable field type properties has the following downsides:

- It limits the rendering of a variable field type property to what can be achieved through the attributes on the <Field> element that represents the property. This approach allows you to specify the display name of the property and to specify the length of the control that holds the property value in the UI. However, it doesn't allow you to specify the type of this control other than setting the Type attribute. It is SharePoint that decides what type of control to render based on the value of the Type attribute.
- It won't allow you to validate the value that the column creator or editor enters in the UI as the value of the property.

Variable Field Type Property Editor

This approach to rendering variable field type properties of a field type gives you complete control over the UI and data validation. You decide what control to present to the column creator or editor and how to validate the data that the column creator or editor enters into the control.

Take these steps to implement and to deploy a variable field type property editor:

1. Implement a user control (.ascx).
2. Implement a code-behind class for the user control from Step 1. This code-behind class must meet the following two requirements:
    - It must derive directly from the UserControl base class or a class that derives directly or indirectly from the UserControl base class
    - It must implement the IFieldEditor interface

3. Compile the code-behind class from Step 2 into the same strong-named assembly as the field type class and install this assembly in the Global Assembly Cache.
4. Set the Inherits attribute on the @Control directive in the .ascx file from Step 1 to the fully assembly-namespace-qualified name of the code-behind class from Step 2. The fully assembly-namespace-qualified name of a type consists of five parts: fully namespace-qualified name of the type including its complete namespace containment hierarchy plus the type name, the name of the assembly that contains the type, the version, culture, and public key token for this assembly.
5. Create a subfolder in the following folder on the file system of the front-end web server:

```
Local_Drive:\Program Files\Common Files\microsoft shared\Web Server
Extensions\12\TEMPLATE\CONTROLTEMPLATES
```

6. Deploy the user control .ascx file from Step 1 to the subfolder from Step 5.
7. Add a <Field> child element to the <FieldType> element that defines the field type definition.
8. Set the Name attribute on the <Field> child element from Step 5 to FieldEditorUserControl.
9. Specify the relative URL of the .ascx file from Step 1 within the opening and closing tags of the <Field> child element from Step 7. This URL consists of two parts separated by the \ character. The first part is the relative URL of the following folder on the file system of the front-end web server:

```
Local_Drive:\Program Files\Common Files\microsoft shared\Web Server
Extensions\12\TEMPLATE\CONTROLTEMPLATES
```

When SharePoint is transforming an IIS web site into a SharePoint web application, it adds a virtual directory named _controltemplates to this web site and maps it to the ControlTemplates folder. As such, the web application-relative URL of this folder is

```
/_controltemplates
```

The second part is the name of the subfolder from Step 5 plus the name of the .ascx file from Step 1.

The <Field> element from Step 7 instructs SharePoint to host the .ascx file from Step 1 in the New Site Column, Change Site Column, Create Column, or Change Column pages. SharePoint uses the relative URL specified within the opening and closing tags of this <Field> element to locate this .ascx file. Keep in mind that this .ascx file contains the variable field type property editor, which provides the column creator or editor with the appropriate UI to specify or to edit the values of the variable field type properties of the field type. The code-behind class of this variable field type property editor contains custom data processing and validation logic.

Implementing a Custom Field Type

Follow these steps to implement a custom field type:

1. Implement a custom field value type if your custom field type class requires one.
2. Implement a custom field-rendering server control to render your custom field type in Edit and New modes, that is, when it resides in an edit list item page such as EditForm.aspx or a new list item page such as NewForm.aspx. This step is not mandatory. It becomes mandatory when one or both of the following conditions are met:
    - The rendering that you have in mind for your custom field type cannot be achieved through CAML rendering instructions in an EditPattern or NewPattern type of RenderPattern in the field type definition.
    - You need to validate the data that the user enters into the UI of your custom field type. Keep in mind that we're talking about the validation of the value of the Value property of the field-rendering control, not the value of the ItemFieldValue property.
3. Implement a custom validation rule. Do this step if you need to validate the field value.
4. Implement a custom field type class.
5. Implement a custom variable field type property editor user control. This step is not mandatory. It becomes mandatory when one or both of the following conditions are met:
    - The rendering that you have in mind for your custom variable field type properties cannot be achieved through CAML rendering instructions in a PropertySchema in the field type definition.
    - You need to validate the data that the user enters into the UI of your custom variable field type properties. Keep in mind that we're talking about the validation of the values that the column creator or editor enters into the variable field type property UI on the New Site Column, Change Site Column, Create Column, and Change Column pages for the variable field type properties, not the values that a user enters into the field UI on the edit list item page or new list item page.
6. Compile your custom field value type (if any), custom field-rendering control (if any), custom field type class, and code-behind class for your custom variable field type property editor user control (if any) into a strong-named assembly and install this assembly in the Global Assembly Cache.
7. Implement a custom field type definition and save it as an XML file that follows this naming convention:

```
fldtypes_YourOrganizationName_YourFieldTypeName.xml
```

    It is very important that this XML file follows the fldtype*.xml naming format, otherwise your custom type will not show up on the SharePoint user interface.

8. Deploy your custom field type definition to the following folder on the file system of the front-end web server:

```
Local_Drive:\Program Files\Common Files\Microsoft Shared\web server
extensions\12\TEMPLATE\XML
```

Because all field types are deployed to the same folder you should include the name of your organization in the name of the XML file that contains your field type definition as discussed in Step 7 to avoid possible name conflicts with third-party field types.

Next, you'll use this eight-step recipe to implement and to deploy a custom field type. Go ahead and launch Visual Studio 2008. Create a Class Library project. Delete the Class1.cs file. Follow the steps discussed in the previous chapters to configure Visual Studio to compile the project into a strong-named assembly. Copy the CAML schema files discussed in the previous chapters to the following folder if you haven't done so yet so you can take advantage of the IntelliSense support when you're implementing the field type definition:

```
C:\Program Files\Microsoft Visual Studio 9.0\Xml\Schemas
```

If you have installed Visual Studio 2008 in a folder other than Program Files, you need to copy these schema files to the Schemas folder under that folder.

You also need to add a reference to Microsoft.SharePoint.dll and System.Web to this Class Library project. The Microsoft.SharePoint DLL is located in the following folder on your machine:

```
Local_Drive:\Program Files\Common Files\microsoft shared\Web Server
Extensions\12\ISAPI
```

Implementing a Custom Field Type Class

Follow these steps to implement a custom field type class:

1. Choose a base field type class to inherit from. To do so, list the features that your custom field type must support. Then search through the following standard field type classes or your own custom field type classes for a field type class that supports more of these features: SPFieldBoolean, SPFieldChoice, SPFieldCurrency, SPFieldDateTime, SPFieldLookup, SPFieldMultiChoice, SPFieldMultiColumn, SPFieldMultiLineText, SPFieldNumber, SPFieldRatingScale, SPFieldText, SPFieldUrl, and SPFieldUser. In this case, use the SPFieldText as the base field type class.
2. Determine which methods and/or properties of the base field type class from Step 1 you need to override to add support for the features that this base field type class does not support out-of-the-box. In this case, override the FieldRenderingControl property and GetValidatedString method.
3. Implement a custom field type class that inherits from the base field type class from Step 1 and overrides the methods and/or properties from Step 2. In this case, implement a custom field type named MyFieldTypeField, which inherits from SPFieldText and overrides its FieldRenderingControl and GetValidatedString members.

4. Implement custom variable field type properties for your field type class if necessary. In this case, implement the following two custom variable field type properties for your MyFieldTypeField custom field type class:

    - **UseListBox.** This Boolean custom variable field type property specifies whether the respective custom field-rendering control will use a ListBox server control or the default RadioButtonList server control.
    - **AvailableItems.** This string property contains the item names and values that the ListBox or RadioButtonList server control will display to users.

5. Your custom field type class must support these two constructors:

```
public MyFieldTypeField(SPFieldCollection fields, string fieldName)
  : base(fields, fieldName) { }

public MyFieldTypeField(SPFieldCollection fields, string typeName,
                        string displayName)
  : base(fields, typeName, displayName) { }
```

Listing 5-18 presents the implementation of the MyFieldTypeField custom field type class.

Listing 5-18: The MyFieldTypeField custom field type class

```
using System;
using System.IO;
using System.Security.Permissions;
using System.Text;
using System.Xml;
using System.Web;
using System.Web.UI;
using System.Web.UI.WebControls;
using System.Web.UI.HtmlControls;
using Microsoft.SharePoint;
using Microsoft.SharePoint.WebControls;
using System.ComponentModel;
using System.Configuration;
using System.Diagnostics;

namespace ClassLibrary1
{


  public class MyFieldTypeField : SPFieldText
  {

    public MyFieldTypeField(SPFieldCollection fields, string fieldName)
      : base(fields, fieldName) { }

    public MyFieldTypeField(SPFieldCollection fields, string typeName,
                            string displayName)
      : base(fields, typeName, displayName) { }

    public override BaseFieldControl FieldRenderingControl
```

(continued)

Listing 5-18 *(continued)*

```
        {
          get
          {
            BaseFieldControl control = new MyFieldTypeFieldControl();
            control.FieldName = this.InternalName;
            return control;
          }
        }

        public bool UseListBox
        {
          get
          {
            return (bool)this.GetCustomProperty("UseListBox");
          }
          set
          {
            this.SetCustomProperty("UseListBox", value);
          }
        }

        public string AvailableItems
        {
          get
          {
            return (string)this.GetCustomProperty("AvailableItems");
          }
          set
          {
            this.SetCustomProperty("AvailableItems", value);
          }
        }
      }
    }
```

Note that MyFieldTypeField overrides FieldRenderingControl where it instantiates a MyFieldTypeFieldControl field-rendering control, sets its FieldName property, and finally returns the control. This field-rendering control is discussed in the next section.

Also note that MyFieldTypeField exposes two variable field type properties named UseListIndex and AvailableItems. As you can see, the getters and setters of these two properties delegate to the GetCustomProperty and SetCustomProperty methods, respectively. MyFieldTypeField inherits these two methods from the SPField base class. The GetCustomProperty method takes the name of a custom variable field type property and returns the value of the property as an object. The SetCustomProperty method takes the name and value of a custom variable field type property and assigns the value to the property. Note that these two methods work in conjunction with the <PropertySchema> element in the respective field type definition.

Implementing a Custom Field-Rendering Control

Listing 5-19 presents the implementation of the MyFieldTypeFieldControl field-rendering control.

Listing 5-19: The MyFieldTypeFieldControl field-rendering control

```
using System;
using System.IO;
using System.Security.Permissions;
using System.Text;
using System.Xml;
using System.Web;
using System.Web.UI;
using System.Web.UI.WebControls;
using System.Web.UI.HtmlControls;
using Microsoft.SharePoint;
using Microsoft.SharePoint.WebControls;
using System.ComponentModel;
using System.Configuration;
using System.Diagnostics;

namespace ClassLibrary1
{
  public class MyFieldTypeFieldControl : BaseFieldControl
  {
    protected ListControl myFieldTypeListControl;
    protected override string DefaultTemplateName
    {
      get
      {

        string defaultTemplateName = "MyFieldTypeRadioButtonListRenderingTemplate";
        MyFieldTypeField tfield = this.Field as MyFieldTypeField;
        if (tfield.UseListBox)
          defaultTemplateName = "MyFieldTypeListBoxRenderingTemplate";

        return defaultTemplateName;
      }
    }

    public override object Value
    {
      get
      {
        this.EnsureChildControls();
        return this.myFieldTypeListControl.SelectedValue;
      }
      set
      {
        EnsureChildControls();
```

(continued)

Listing 5-19 *(continued)*

```
          this.myFieldTypeListControl.SelectedValue = (string)this.ItemFieldValue;
        }
      }

      protected override void CreateChildControls()
      {
        if (this.Field == null || this.ControlMode == SPControlMode.Display)
          return;
        base.CreateChildControls();

        this.myFieldTypeListControl =
              (ListControl)TemplateContainer.FindControl("MyFieldTypeListControl");

        if (this.myFieldTypeListControl == null)
          throw new Exception("The user control does not contain the ListControl!");

        if (!this.Page.IsPostBack)
        {
          MyFieldTypeField tfield = this.Field as MyFieldTypeField;
          string str = tfield.AvailableItems;
          string[] items = str.Split(';');
          string[] texts = new string[items.Length];
          string[] values = new string[items.Length];

          for (int i = 0; i < items.Length; i++)
          {
            string[] str2 = items[i].Split(',');
            texts[i] = str2[0];
            values[i] = str2[1];
          }

          for (int j = 0; j < texts.Length; j++)
          {
            this.myFieldTypeListControl.Items.Add(new ListItem(texts[j], values[j]));
          }
        }
      }
    }
  }
```

As Listing 5-19 shows, the MyFieldTypeFieldControl field-rendering control overrides the DefaultTemplateName property to specify the ID property value of the default RenderingTemplate server control. This override returns "MyFieldTypeRadioButtonListRenderingTemplate" if the UseListBox variable field type property is not set. Otherwise it returns "MyFieldTypeListBoxRenderingTemplate".

As you can see from Listing 5-19, the MyFieldTypeFieldControl field-rendering control also overrides the CreateChildControls method as follows. First, it checks whether the respective field is null or the field-rendering control is in Display mode. If so, it returns. As you can see, the MyFieldTypeFieldControl field-rendering control is not used in the display method. Instead the CAML rendering instructions specified in the DisplayPattern type of RenderPattern in the field type definition are used to render the field in Display mode. In other words, the field-rendering control is used only to render the field type in Edit or New mode:

```
if (this.Field == null || this.ControlMode == SPControlMode.Display)
  return;
```

Next, it invokes the CreateChildControls method of the base class. This is important because it is this method that adds the child controls in the ITemplate object referenced by the Template property of the RenderingTemplate server control specified in the DefaultTemplateName property to the Controls collection of the MyFieldTypeFieldControl field-rendering control:

```
base.CreateChildControls();
```

Next, it invokes the FindControl method on the template container server control referenced by the TemplateContainer property to return a reference to the ListControl server control with the ID property value of "MyFieldTypeListControl". This will be clear when you take a look at the RenderingTemplate server control specified in the DefaultTemplateName property:

```
this.myFieldTypeListControl =
       (ListControl)TemplateContainer.FindControl("MyFieldTypeListControl");
```

Next, it takes these steps if the page is being accessed for the first time. First, it accesses the respective MyFieldTypeField field:

```
MyFieldTypeField tfield = this.Field as MyFieldTypeField;
```

Then, it accesses the value of the AvailableItems variable field type property:

```
string str = tfield.AvailableItems;
```

This property contains the item names and values that you would like the MyFieldTypeListControl ListControl server control to display to users:

```
string[] items = str.Split(';');
string[] texts = new string[items.Length];
string[] values = new string[items.Length];

for (int i = 0; i < items.Length; i++)
{
  string[] str2 = items[i].Split(',');
  texts[i] = str2[0];
  values[i] = str2[1];
}
```

Finally, it adds items with the preceding names and values to the ListControl server control:

```
for (int j = 0; j < texts.Length; j++)
{
  this.myFieldTypeListControl.Items.Add(new ListItem(texts[j], values[j]));
}
```

As Listing 5-19 shows, the MyFieldTypeFieldControl field-rendering control overrides the Value property where both the getter and setter of this property first invoke the EnsureChildControl method. This method internally invokes the CreateChildControls method if necessary. This ensures that the ListControl server control has already been created and added to the Controls collection before the getter and setter access this server control.

Note that the getter simply returns the value of the SelectedValue property of the ListControl server control, which is the value that the user has selected for this field when the user is editing the field value or adding a new field value. The getter assigns the value of the ItemFieldValue property to the SelectedValue property of the ListControl server control. The ItemFieldValue property contains the value of the field in the underlying data content.

As you saw, the DefaultTemplateName property of the MyFieldTypeFieldControl field-rendering control returns "MyFieldTypeListBoxRenderingTemplate" or "MyFieldTypeRadioButtonListRenderingTemplate", which are the ID property values of the RenderingTemplate server controls declared in Listing 5-20.

Listing 5-20: The RenderingTemplate server controls that the MyFieldTypeFieldControl field-rendering control uses

```
<%@ Control Language="C#" Debug="true" %>
<%@ Assembly Name="Microsoft.SharePoint, Version=12.0.0.0, Culture=neutral,
PublicKeyToken=71e9bce111e9429c" %>
<%@ Register TagPrefix="SharePoint" Assembly="Microsoft.SharePoint,
Version=12.0.0.0, Culture=neutral, PublicKeyToken=71e9bce111e9429c"
             Namespace="Microsoft.SharePoint.WebControls" %>

<SharePoint:RenderingTemplate ID="MyFieldTypeListBoxRenderingTemplate"
runat="server">
  <Template>
    <asp:ListBox ID="MyFieldTypeListControl" runat="server" />
  </Template>
</SharePoint:RenderingTemplate>

<SharePoint:RenderingTemplate ID="MyFieldTypeRadioButtonListRenderingTemplate"
runat="server">
  <Template>
    <asp:RadioButtonList ID="MyFieldTypeListControl" runat="server" />
  </Template>
</SharePoint:RenderingTemplate>
```

As you can see, both RenderingTemplate server controls contain a ListControl server control with the ID property value of MyFieldTypeListControl. Note that the first RenderingTemplate server control uses a ListBox server control, whereas the second RenderingTemplate server control uses a RadioButtonList server control. You need to deploy the .ascx file shown in Listing 5-20 to the following folder in your machine:

```
CC:\Program Files\Common Files\microsoft shared\Web Server
Extensions\12\TEMPLATE\CONTROLTEMPLATES
```

Implementing a Field Type Definition

Listing 5-21 presents the field type definition for your custom field type.

Listing 5-21: The field type definition for your custom field type

```
<?xml version="1.0" encoding="utf-8" ?>
<FieldTypes>
  <FieldType>
    <Field Name="TypeName">MyFieldType</Field>
    <Field Name="ParentType">Text</Field>
    <Field Name="TypeDisplayName">My Field Type</Field>
    <Field Name="TypeShortDescription">My Field Type</Field>
    <Field Name="UserCreatable">TRUE</Field>
    <Field Name="ShowInListCreate">TRUE</Field>
    <Field Name="ShowInSurveyCreate">TRUE</Field>
    <Field Name="ShowInDocumentLibraryCreate">TRUE</Field>
    <Field Name="ShowInColumnTemplateCreate">TRUE</Field>
    <Field Name="FieldTypeClass">ClassLibrary1.MyFieldTypeField, ClassLibrary1,
Version=1.0.0.0, Culture=neutral, PublicKeyToken=4597a8072c121508</Field>
    <RenderPattern Name="DisplayPattern">
      <Switch>
        <Expr>
          <Column/>
        </Expr>
        <Case Value="">
        </Case>
        <Default>
          <HTML>
            <![CDATA[
              <span style="background-color:blue;color:yellow;font-bold:true">
            ]]>
          </HTML>
          <Column HTMLEncode="TRUE"/>
          <HTML><![CDATA[</span>]]></HTML>
        </Default>
      </Switch>
    </RenderPattern>
    <PropertySchema>
      <Fields>
        <Field Name="AvailableItems"
               DisplayName="Available Items"
               MaxLength="200"
               DisplaySize="100"
               Type="Text"/>
        <Field Name="UseListBox"
               DisplayName="Use ListBox"
               MaxLength="200"
               DisplaySize="100"
               Type="Boolean"/>
      </Fields>
    </PropertySchema>
  </FieldType>
</FieldTypes>
```

As you can see from Listing 5-21, this field type definition contains a property schema that describes the AvailableItems and UseListBox variable field type properties. Also note that this field type definition contains a DisplayPattern type of RenderPattern that specifies the CAML rendering instructions for rendering your custom field type in Display mode, that is, when it is used on a display list item or list view page. As Listing 5-21 illustrates, this RenderPattern uses a <Switch> element to determine what to render. Note that the <Expr> child element of this <Switch> element specifies the value of the field as the switching expression:

```
<Expr>
  <Column/>
</Expr>
```

If this value is an empty string, the <Switch> element executes the <Case> child element, which does nothing:

```
<Case Value="">
</Case>
```

If this value is not an empty string, the <Switch> element executes the <Default> child element. This child element first uses an <HTML> CAML rendering instruction element to render the opening tag of a <span> element with a style attribute value of " background-color:blue;color:yellow;font-bold:true":

```
<HTML>
  <![CDATA[<span style="background-color:blue;color:yellow;font-bold:true">]]>
</HTML>
```

Next, it renders the value of the field:

```
<Column HTMLEncode="TRUE"/>
```

Finally, it uses another <HTML> CAML rendering instruction element to render the closing tag of the <span> element:

```
<HTML><![CDATA[</span>]]></HTML>
```

Using the Custom Field Type

Following the recipe discussed earlier, you need to compile your custom field type class and custom field-rendering control into a strong-named assembly and install the assembly in the Global Assembly Cache. Next, you need to deploy your field type definition file to the following folder:

```
Local_Drive:\Program Files\Common Files\microsoft shared\Web Server
Extensions\12\TEMPLATE\XML
```

Finally, you need to deploy the .ascx file that contains your RenderingTemplate server controls to the following folder:

```
Local_Drive:\Program Files\Common Files\microsoft shared\Web Server
Extensions\12\TEMPLATE\CONTROLTEMPLATES
```

Next, navigate to your favorite SharePoint list. Select the Create Column menu option from the Settings menu bar button to navigate to the FldNewEx.aspx page shown in Figure 5-8. As you can see this page shows the custom field type (My Field Type) among the list of available field types.

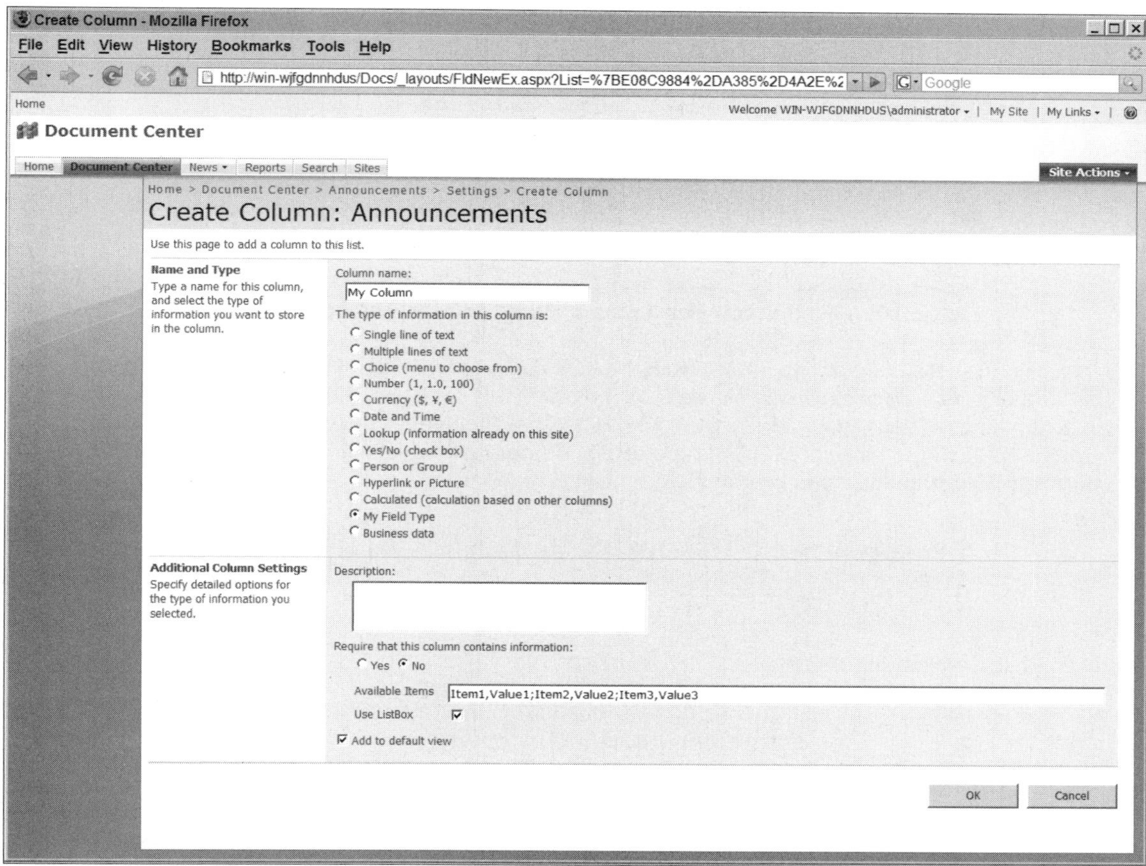

Figure 5-8: The Create Column page

Toggle on My Field Type to select your custom field type, enter a name for the column, enter a value in the Available Items text field, and toggle on the Use ListBox checkbox. Make sure the value that you enter into the Available Items text field follows the format discussed earlier. Next, click OK to go back to the list as shown in Figure 5-9. Note that a new column is added to the list. Nothing is rendered in this new column. This is because the <Switch> element specified in the <RenderPattern> element in the field type definition executes the following <Case> element, which does nothing:

```
<Case Value="">
</Case>
```

Figure 5-9: A list that contains a column based on your custom field type

Next, select the Edit Item menu option from the ECB menu of a list item in this list to navigate to the EditForm.aspx page shown in Figure 5-10. Note that this page uses a ListBox control to render the possible values of your custom field type. This is because the RenderingTemplate server control with the ID attribute value of MyFieldTypeListBoxRenderingTemplate, which contains a ListBox server control, is used to render your custom field type in Edit mode.

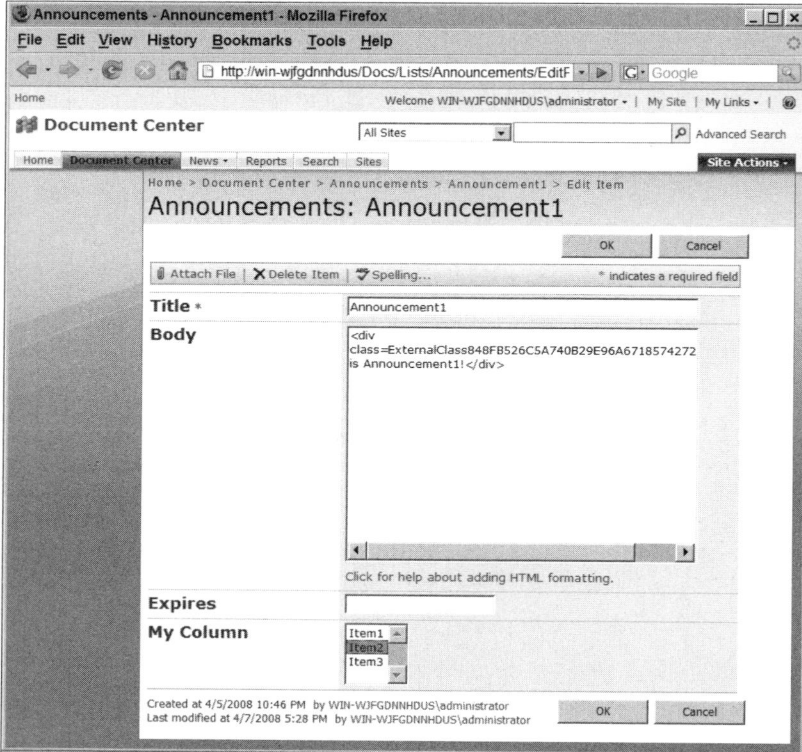

Figure 5-10: The edit list item form

Next, click the OK button in Figure 5-10 to navigate back to the list as shown in Figure 5-11. Note that the column now contains the value of the of the field type. This is because the <Switch> element specified in the <RenderPattern> element executes the <Default> element:

```
<Default>
  <HTML>
    <![CDATA[
      <span style="background-color:blue;color:yellow;font-bold:true">
    ]]>
  </HTML>
  <Column HTMLEncode="TRUE"/>
  <HTML><![CDATA[</span>]]></HTML>
</Default>
```

The <Default> element renders the value of the field within the opening and closing tags of a <span> element with the style attribute value of "background-color:blue;color:yellow;font-bold:true", which explains why the text is rendered in yellow, bold, and with a blue background.

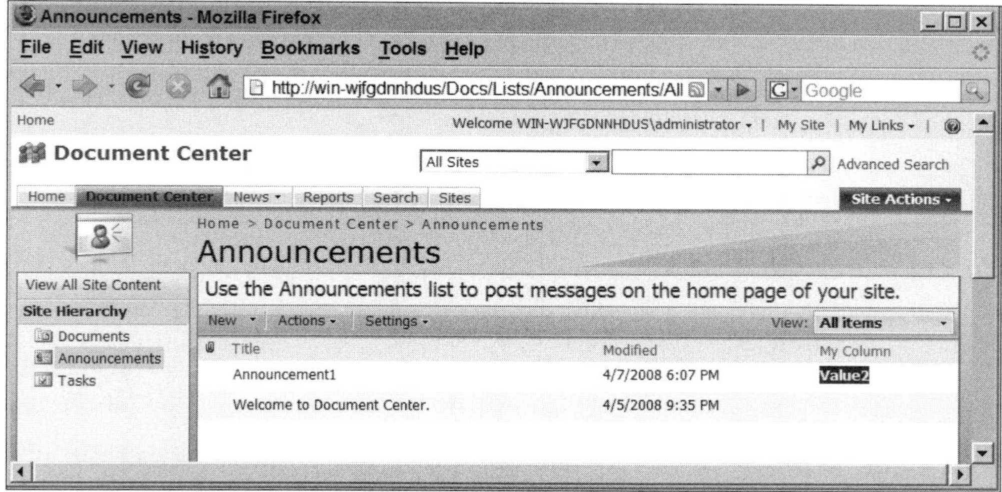

Figure 5-11: The AllItems.aspx page

Summary

This chapter discussed field types in detail and showed you how to implement your own custom field types. The chapter provided you with an in-depth coverage of the internal implementation of the standard SharePoint field types where you saw the techniques used to implement these field types and how to use these techniques in your own field types. The chapter then presented recipes for implementing field types and used them to implement a custom field type.

The next chapter moves on to the next SharePoint abstraction known as site columns, which are based on field types. The next chapter also covers site content types, which reference site columns.

6

Site Columns and Site Content Types

As discussed in previous chapters, SharePoint virtualizes the underlying IIS and ASP.NET infrastructures, enabling you to manage and to organize your collaborative content in terms of abstractions such as site collections, sites, lists, list items, content types, field types, site columns, and so on. Site columns, site content types, and site definitions are three of these abstractions. This chapter helps you gain the skills that you need to implement your own custom site columns and site content types.

Site Columns

Chapter 5 showed one way to create a new column based on a field type such as the custom field type. The column that you created via this approach is not reusable across lists and is created as part of the list on which it is created. As such, it is an integral part of the list itself because it can't be detached from the list to be added to another list.

SharePoint allows you to encapsulate a SharePoint column or field schema in a component known as a site column so it can be reused across lists. As the name implies, a site column is defined at the site level. A site column is available to all descendant sites of the site in which it is defined. This means that it can be added to any list in any descendant site. If you want to implement a site column that can be added to any list in any site in a given site collection, you need to make the site column available at the top-level site of the site collection.

When a site column is added to a list, SharePoint adds a local copy of the site column definition to the list. This local copy is known as a list column. When you modify a list column definition, your updates have no impact on the site column definition from which the list column definition was copied. When you modify a site column definition, you can optionally push the changes down to all list column definitions that were copied from it.

You'll first use the SharePoint user interface to create a site column in the next section. Then you'll dive into developing a site column using CAML.

Graphical Approach

Start by navigating to the Site Column Gallery as shown in Figure 6-1.

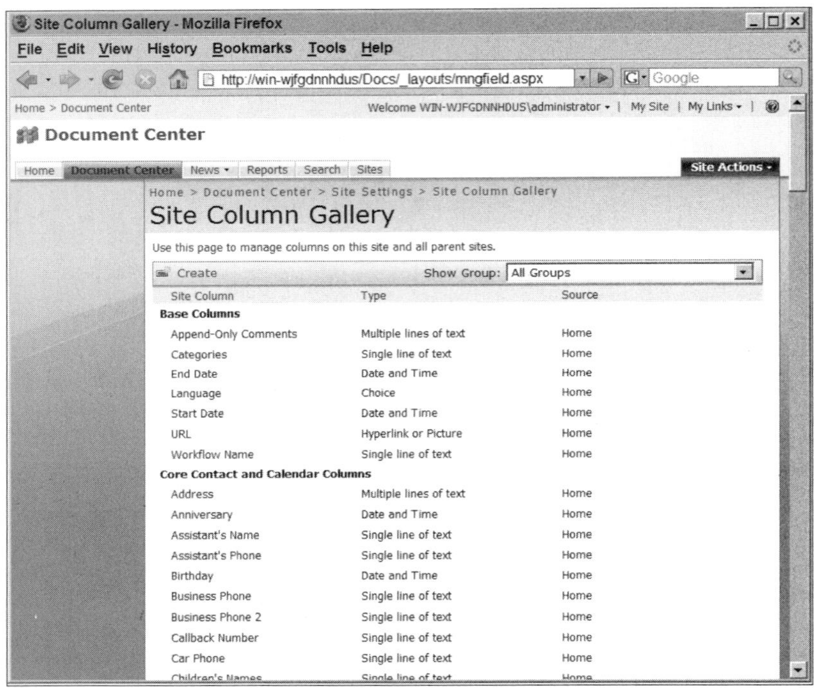

Figure 6-1: Site Column Gallery

Click the Create button to navigate to the New Site Column page shown in Figure 6-2. This page allows you to specify the properties of the new site column such as column name, field type (recall from the previous chapter that you can implement and add your own field type to this list), column group, and so on.

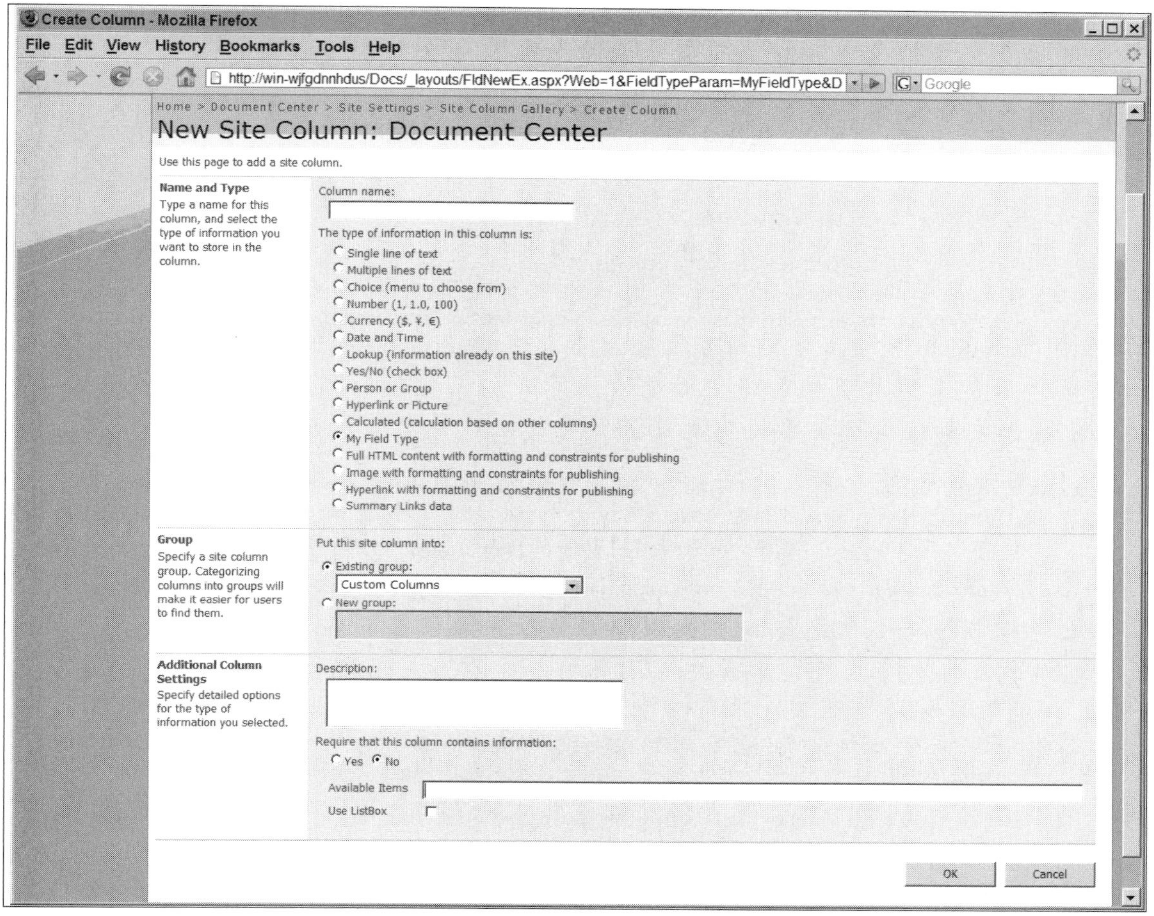

Figure 6-2: The New Site Column page

The site column that you create through the SharePoint user interface is considered a user customization and is stored in the content database. As such, it is not a deployable component and cannot be used across site collections, web applications, and so on.

Declarative Approach

You can use CAML to implement your custom site column declaratively in an XML file, which is then referenced by a SharePoint feature. This XML file can contain one or more site column definitions. The document element of this XML file is an element named <Elements>:

```
<Elements xmlns="http://schemas.microsoft.com/sharepoint"/>
  ...
</Elements>
```

This document element supports a child element named <Fields>, where you must define your site columns. You must use a separate <Field> element inside the <Fields> element to define each site column:

```
<Elements xmlns=http://schemas.microsoft.com/sharepoint>
  <Field ... />
  <Field ... />
  ...
</Elements>
```

The Field element supports the following attributes:

- **ID.** You can use this attribute to specify a GUID that uniquely identifies your site column. You can use the guidgen.exe utility discussed in the previous chapters to generate and to copy and paste the GUID:

```
<Field ID="{a8eb573e-9e11-481a-a8c9-1104a54b2fbd}" ... />
```

- **Group.** You can use this attribute to specify the name of the group to which you want your site column to belong. The Site Column Gallery page, shown in Figure 6-1, lists each site column under its group. Grouping enables end users to easily locate your site column in this gallery.
- **Name.** You can use this attribute to specify an internal name for your site column.
- **DisplayName.** You can use this attribute to specify a display name for your site column.
- **Type.** You can use this attribute to specify the field type on which your site column is based. This field type must be one of the standard or custom field types discussed earlier.
- **Sealed.** You can use this attribute to specify whether your site column can be modified. Set this attribute to true to prevent others from modifying your site column.
- **ReadOnly.** You can use this attribute to specify whether the data stored in this site column can be edited through the SharePoint user interface.
- **Hidden.** You can use this attribute to specify whether your site column should be displayed in the SharePoint user interface.
- **RowOrdinal.** You can use this attribute to specify the index of a cell in a row where you want your site column to be placed.
- **Description**. You can use this attribute to specify a short description for the site column.
- **AllowDeletion.** You can use this Boolean attribute to specify whether the site column can be deleted.
- **CanToggleHidden.** You can use this Boolean attribute to specify whether the site column can be hidden through the user interface.
- **DisplaySize.** You can use this string attribute to specify a display size for the site column.
- **Filterable.** You can use this attribute to specify whether the site column can be filtered.
- **ShowInDisplayForm.** You can use this attribute to specify whether this site column is displayed in a display list item form.
- **ShowInEditForm.** You can use this attribute to specify whether this site column is displayed in an edit list item form.

- **ShowInNewForm.** You can use this attribute to specify whether this site column is displayed in a new list item form.
- **ShowInViewForm.** You can use this attribute to specify whether this site column is displayed in a list view form.
- **Required.** You can use this attribute to specify whether this site column requires a value.
- **Sortable.** You can use this attribute to specify whether this site column can be sorted.
- **SourceId.** You can use this attribute to specify the namespace (such as http://schemas.microsoft.com/sharepoint/v3 or http://schemas.microsoft.com/sharepoint/v3/fields) that defines the site column or to specify the GUID of a list in which the field is created through the user interface.
- **StaticName.** You can use this attribute to specify the internal name of the site column.

The <Field> element supports a child element named <Choices>, which is applicable only when you set the Type attribute to Choice. As the name suggests, the <Choices> element is where you specify the possible values of your site column. Use a separate <Choice> element inside the <Choices> element to specify each possible value.

Follow these steps to implement and to deploy a custom site column:

1. Copy the CAML schema files to the following folder if you haven't done it already so you can take full advantage of the Visual Studio IntelliSense support when you're writing the CAML that defines your custom site column:

```
Local_Drive:\Program Files\Microsoft Visual Studio 9.0\Xml\Schemas
```

   These CAML schema files define the schema types that belong to the http://schemas.microsoft.com/sharepoint/ namespace.

2. Create a feature-specific folder under the following folder on the file system of the front-end web server:

```
Local_Drive:\Program Files\Common Files\microsoft shared\Web Server
Extensions\12\TEMPLATE\FEATURES
```

   In this case you'll create a folder named MyCustomColumn for a custom site column named MyCustomColumn that you'll implement in this section.

3. Add an XML file named feature.xml to the folder from Step 2. This file will define the feature that references the custom site column definition.
4. Add another XML file to the folder from Step 2. Name this XML file MyCustomColumn.xml in this case. This file will define the MyCustomColumn site column.
5. Open the XML files from Steps 3 and 4 in Visual Studio and implement them.
6. Use the STSADM command-line utility to install the feature. Here is the command you'll use in this case:

```
stsadm -o installfeature -name MyCustomColumn
```

7. Activate the feature in a SharePoint site to add your custom site column to the site's site columns.

Listing 6-1 presents the implementation of the MyCustomColumn.xml file, which defines the MyCustomColumn site column.

Listing 6-1: A site column definition based on the custom field type

```
<?xml version="1.0" encoding="utf-8" ?>
<Elements xmlns="http://schemas.microsoft.com/sharepoint/">
  <Field
    AllowDeletion="TRUE"
    Description="This is MyCustomColumn"
    DisplayName="My Custom Column"
    DisplaySize="100"
    Group="My Custom Group"
    Hidden="FALSE"
    ID="{19FB9422-D586-4c8c-A6B6-BD1B9CD12FD9}"
    ReadOnly="FALSE"
    Required="FALSE"
    SourceID="http://schemas.microsoft.com/sharepoint/v3"
    ShowInDisplayForm="TRUE"
    ShowInEditForm="TRUE"
    ShowInNewForm="TRUE"
    ShowInViewForms="TRUE"
    Type="Choice"
    Name="MyCustomColumn"
    Filterable="TRUE"
    HeaderImage="/_layouts/images/actionlhd.gif"
    DisplayImage="/_layouts/images/actionlhd.gif"
    Height="200"
    Sealed="FALSE"
    RowOrdinal="3"
    Sortable="TRUE"
    StaticName="MyCustomColumn"
    Width="100">
    <CHOICES>
      <CHOICE>Item1</CHOICE>
      <CHOICE>Item2</CHOICE>
      <CHOICE>Item3</CHOICE>
      <CHOICE>Item4</CHOICE>
    </CHOICES>
    <Default>Item2</Default>
  </Field>
</Elements>
```

Notice that you've set the xmlns attribute on the <Elements> document element to http://schemas.microsoft.com/sharepoint/ so you can take advantage of the Visual Studio IntelliSense support. Note that the <Field> element supports a child element named <Choices>, which you can use to specify enumeration values if your site column is based on the Choice field type. You must use a separate <Choice> child element within the <Choices> element to define each enumeration value. In this case you've defined four enumeration values of Item1, Item2, Item3, and Item4.

Listing 6-2 presents the implementation of the feature.xml file, which references the MyCustomColumn .xml file.

Listing 6-2: The feature.xml file

```
<?xml version="1.0" encoding="utf-8" ?>
<Feature
xmlsn="http://schemas.microsoft.com/sharepoint/"
Description="This is MyCustomColumn feature!"
Hidden="FALSE"
Id="{7CAD78D5-5418-4355-B834-4B15FDADC8DA}"
Scope="Site"
Title="MyCustomColumn Feature"
Version="1.0.0.0">
  <ElementManifests>
    <ElementManifest Location="MyCustomColumn.xml" />
  </ElementManifests>
</Feature>
```

If you install and activate this feature and navigate to the Site Column Gallery, you should see a new group named My Custom Group that contains the custom site column as shown in Figure 6-3.

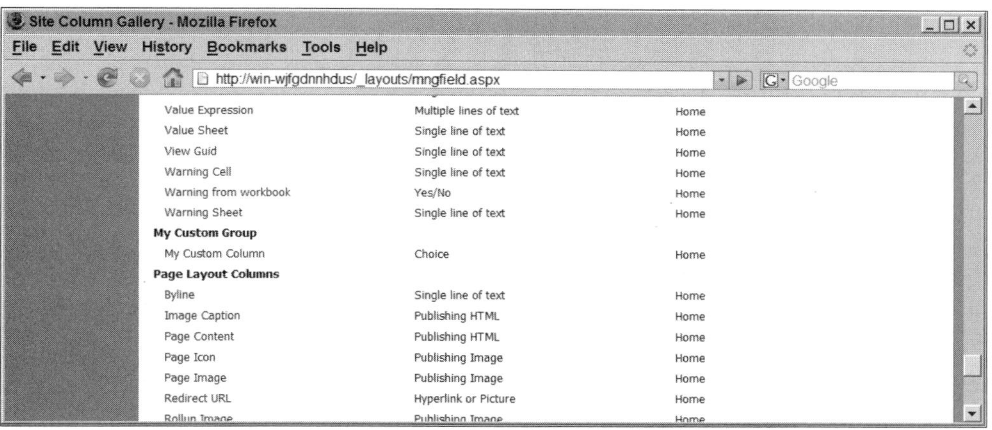

Figure 6-3: Groups in the Site Column Gallery

Next, click the My Custom Column link shown in Figure 6-3 to navigate to the Change Column page shown in Figure 6-4.

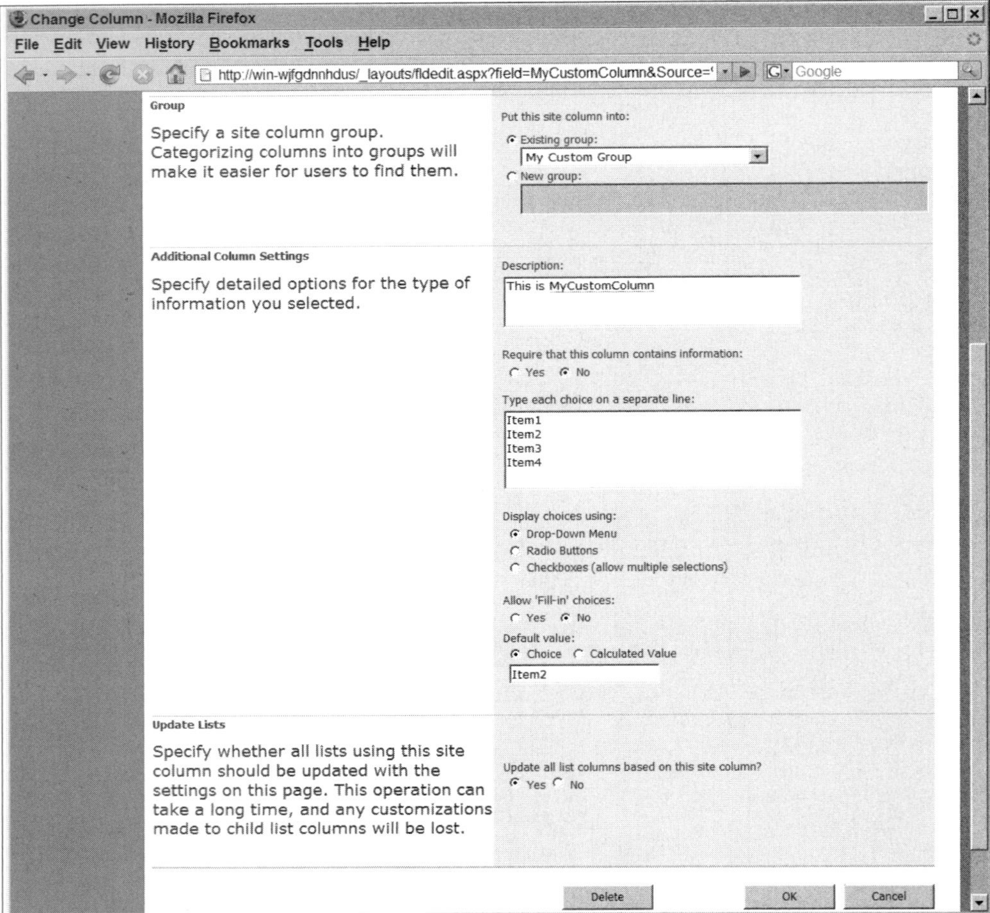

Figure 6-4: The Change Column page

Note that:

- The text area labeled Type Each Choice on a Separate Line contains all the choices that you've defined within the <Choices> element in the site column definition.
- The Allow 'Fill-in' Choices option is set to No because you did not set the FillInChoice attribute on the <Field> element that defines the site column. The default is false.
- The default value is set to Item2, which is the value that the <Default> child element of the <Field> element specifies.
- The Update All List Columns Based on This Site Column? option is set to Yes. This means that updates made to this site column will be automatically propagated to all list columns copied from this site column.

When a site column is added to a list, SharePoint makes a local copy of the site column definition and adds that local copy to the list. This local copy is known as a list column. Because changes made to a list column definition are made to a local copy, these changes will have no effect on the site column definition from which the list column definition was copied. This also means that changes made to a site column definition will have no effect on the list column copied from it unless you explicitly instruct SharePoint to propagate the changes. This is exactly what the Update All List Columns Based on This Site Column radio button list on the Change Site Column page is for.

Next, you'll use the site column in a list. Navigate to the AllItems.aspx page that displays your favorite list. Select the List Settings menu option from the Settings menu on this page to navigate to the listedit .aspx page where you can edit the list. In the Columns section of this page click the "Add from existing site columns" link to navigate to the AddFieldFromTemplate.aspx page as shown in Figure 6-5.

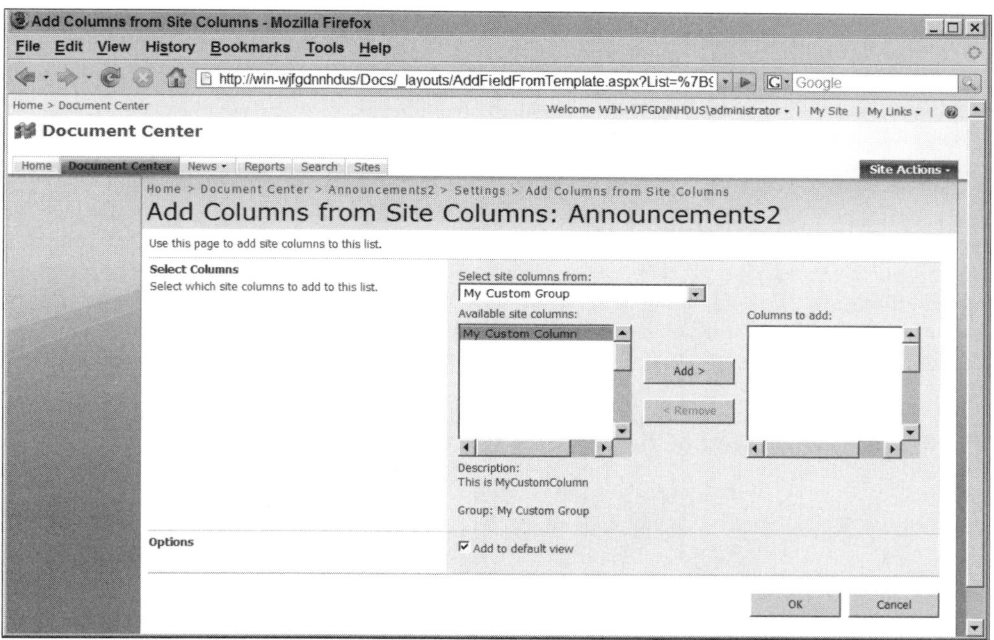

Figure 6-5: The AddFieldFromTemplate.aspx page

Note that this page contains a drop-down list box titled Select Site Columns From, which displays the My Custom Column among many other groups. Go ahead and add the My Custom Column to the list. SharePoint automatically makes a local copy of the My Custom Column site column definition and adds this local copy to the list.

As you can see from Figure 6-6, the My Custom Column displays whatever text is specified within the opening and closing tags of the respective <Choice> child element of the <Choices> element in the list column definition.

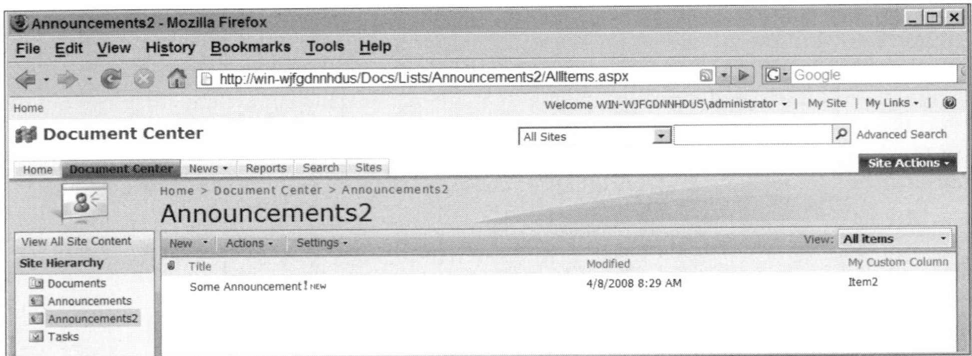

Figure 6-6: A list that uses the custom site column

However, you may want to map the text specified within the opening and closing tags of a <Choice> element to a value that makes more sense to your application. The <Field> element that defines a site column supports a child element named <Mappings>, which enables you to define mappings from the text specified in the <Choice> elements to values that make more sense to your application. You have to use a separate <Mapping> child element within the <Mappings> element to define each mapping. Listing 6-3 presents a new version of the My Site Column site column definition that makes use of mappings.

Listing 6-3: A new version of the My Site Column site column

```
<?xml version="1.0" encoding="utf-8" ?>
<Elements xmlns="http://schemas.microsoft.com/sharepoint/">
  <Field
    AllowDeletion="TRUE"
    Description="This is MyCustomColumn"
    DisplayName="My Custom Column"
    DisplaySize="100"
    Group="My Custom Group"
    Hidden="FALSE"
    ID="{19FB9422-D586-4c8c-A6B6-BD1B9CD12FD9}"
    ReadOnly="FALSE"
    Required="FALSE"
    SourceID="http://schemas.microsoft.com/sharepoint/v3"
    ShowInDisplayForm="TRUE"
    ShowInEditForm="TRUE"
    ShowInNewForm="TRUE"
    ShowInViewForms="TRUE"
    Type="Choice"
    Name="MyCustomColumn"
```

```
      Filterable="TRUE"
      HeaderImage="/_layouts/images/actionlhd.gif"
      DisplayImage="/_layouts/images/actionlhd.gif"
      Height="200"
      Sealed="FALSE"
      RowOrdinal="3"
      Sortable="TRUE"
      StaticName="MyCustomColumn"
      Width="100">
      <CHOICES>
        <CHOICE>Item1</CHOICE>
        <CHOICE>Item2</CHOICE>
        <CHOICE>Item3</CHOICE>
        <CHOICE>Item4</CHOICE>
      </CHOICES>
      <Default>Item2</Default>
      <MAPPINGS>
        <MAPPING Value="Value1">Item1</MAPPING>
        <MAPPING Value="Value2">Item2</MAPPING>
        <MAPPING Value="Value3">Item3</MAPPING>
        <MAPPING Value="Value4">Item4</MAPPING>
      </MAPPINGS>
    </Field>
  </Elements>
```

SPListItem["My Custom Column"] will then return the value of the Value attribute of the respective <Mapping> element as opposed to the text specified within the opening and closing tags of the respective <Choice> elements.

Site Content Types

It's all about content management! One very useful approach to managing your collaborative content is to categorize or group it in different types or categories. You can then implement a separate site content type to represent each category or type of collaborative content. You define a site content type regardless of which SharePoint list will store the collaborative content type that this site content type represents. In other words, site content types are location-agnostic. This means that all the same settings that you specify for a site content type will be used in all SharePoint lists where this site content type is used. These settings include:

- **Columns.** As mentioned, a site content type represents a category or type of collaborative content. A site content type represents the attributes of this collaborative content as columns. This means that you can define all columns of your site content type in one location and rest assured that the same columns will show up on all lists where your site content type is used.
- **Workflows.** A site content type is more than just a set of columns. It also has behaviors. You can associate one or more workflow templates with your site content type and rest assured that the same workflow association will be available on all list items that are of your site content type.
- **Forms.** You can optionally associate custom forms with your site content types. These forms enable users to edit, create, and view list items of your site content types.

Site content types are extensible in that you can store XML data in them and access them from your application.

This enables you to manage the settings for your site content type in a centralized location. This way you can ensure lists that use your site content type all use the same columns, workflows, and forms.

As the name suggests, a site content type is created at the site level and is available to all lists in that site and all descendant sites of that site. If you want to make your site content type available to all sites in a site collection, you need to add your site content type to the top-level site of the site collection.

When you add a site content type to a list, SharePoint creates a local copy of the site content type definition and adds this local copy to the list. This local copy is known as a list content type definition. Because all changes made to a list content type are made to this local copy of the original site content type definition, these changes do not affect the original site content type definition. This also means that changes made to the original site content type definition will have no effect on the list content types copied from that site content type unless you specifically ask SharePoint to propagate the changes from the site content type to all list content types copied from it.

When you add a site content type to a list, SharePoint creates local copies of all columns that the site content type references and adds these local copies to the list if the list already does not contain the same columns. These local copies appear as columns on the list.

One of the great advantages of site content types is that you can add multiple site content types to the same SharePoint list. This enables you to maintain heterogeneous collaborative content in the same list.

You must inherit your site content type from another site content type. This enables you to create a hierarchy of site content types much like a hierarchy of .NET classes. You can start with implementing a base site content type that specifies settings common to all other site content types in your application such as columns and forms (edit, view, and new list item forms). You can then implement one or more site content types that inherit from this base content type. These site content types in turn can act as base content types from which you can inherit other content types.

A derived site content type, just like a derived class, inherits some of its base content type's aspects while overriding some selected ones such as altering, removing, or adding columns and specifying different edit, view, or new list item forms. A site content type can inherit from a single site content type. As a matter of fact class inheritance in .NET has the same limitation.

There are times when you want to prevent others from making changes to a site content type definition. There are two ways to achieve this goal. One approach is to set the ReadOnly property of the site content type to true to mark your site content type as read-only. Those who want to change your site content type must explicitly set the ReadOnly property to false before they can make changes. Another approach is to set the Sealed property of your site content type to true to mark your site content type as sealed. Those who want to change your site content type must explicitly set the Sealed property to false before they can make changes. Only those with site collection administration privileges are allowed to change the value of this property. Also note that changes cannot be pushed down from the parent site content type to the site content type because the site content type is sealed. Keep in mind that no matter which approach you take you can never prevent others from inheriting from your site content type.

Let's use the SharePoint user interface to create a site content type. Navigate to the Site Content Type Gallery page shown in Figure 6-7.

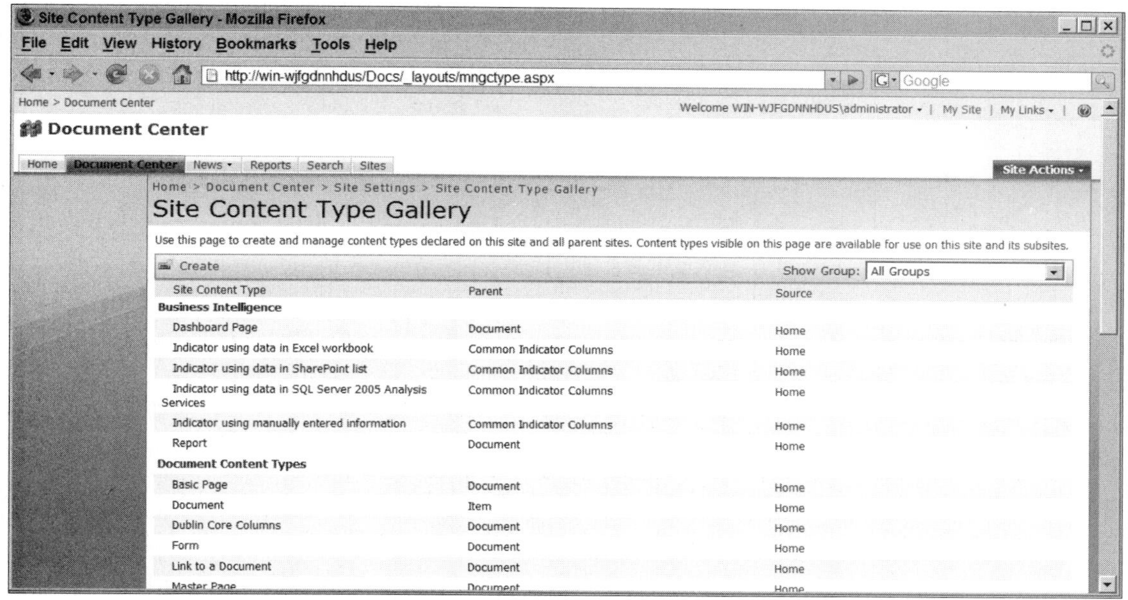

Figure 6-7: Site Content Type Gallery

This page contains all site content types available in the current site. Note that site content types are placed in different groups. Now click the Create button to navigate to the New Site Content Type page shown in Figure 6-8.

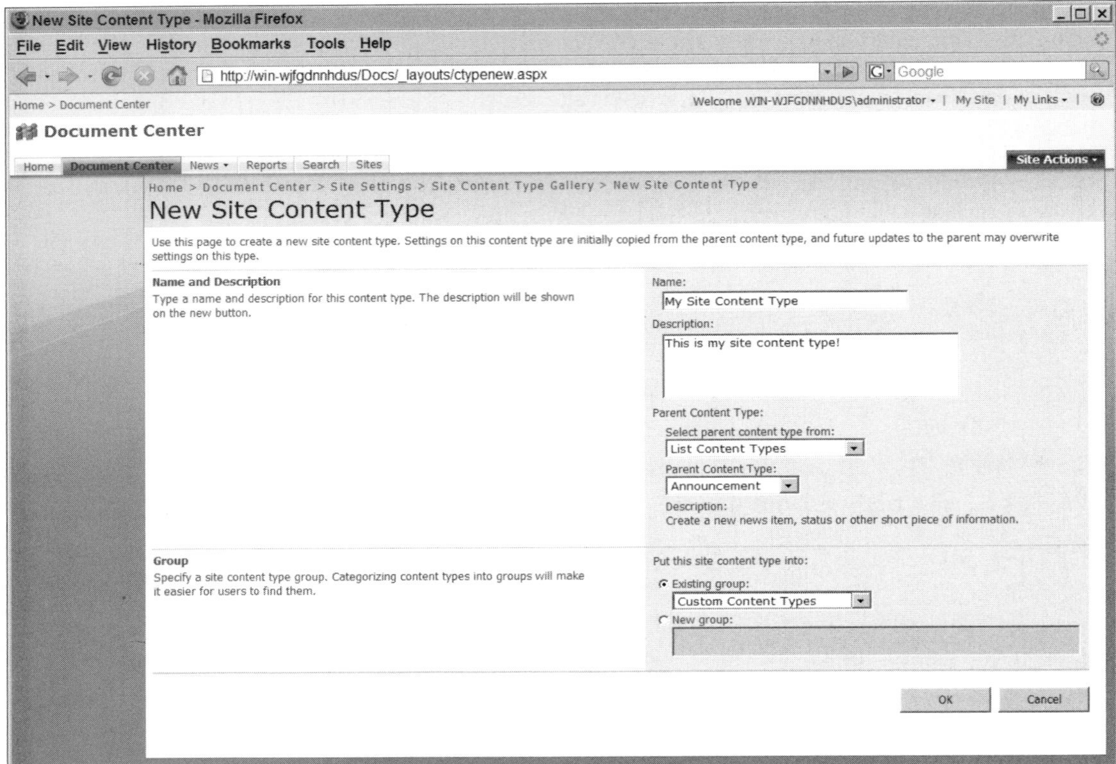

Figure 6-8: The New Site Content Type page

As you can see, a site content type has a name, a description, a parent content type, and a group. Every site content type inherits from another site content type known as the parent content type. Enter a name and description for the new site content type and select a parent content type from which to inherit the new site content type. Finally, click OK to navigate to the ManageContentType.aspx page shown in Figure 6-9.

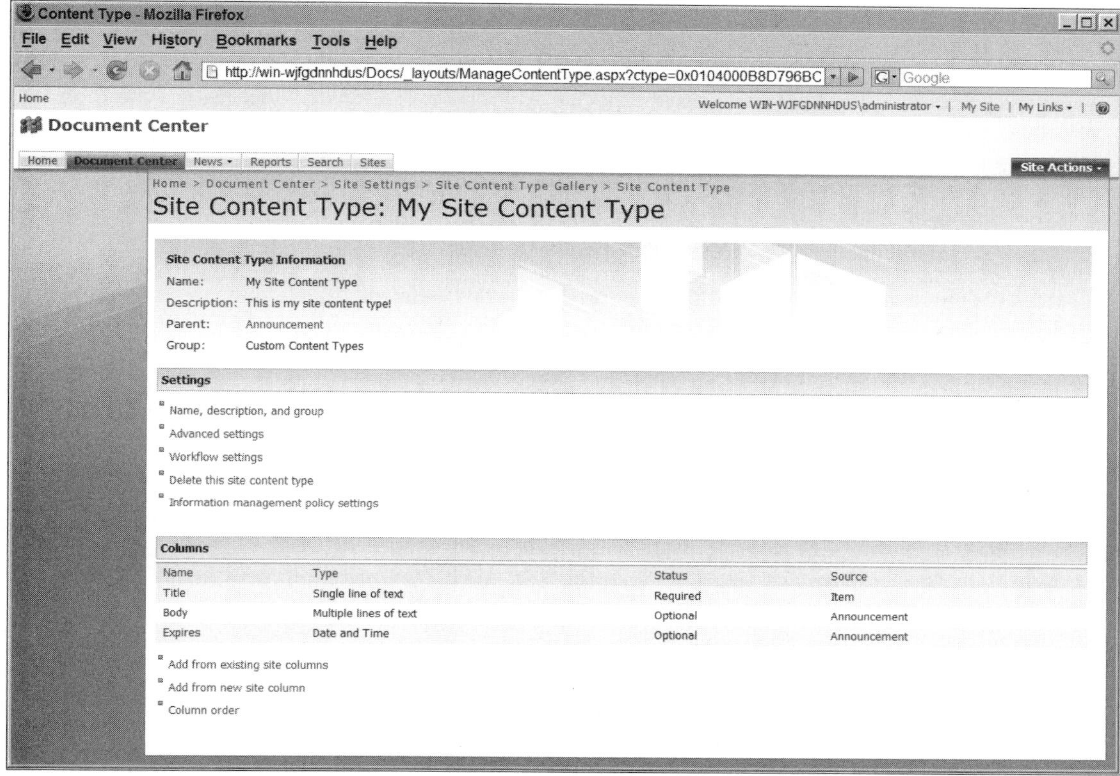

Figure 6-9: The manage content type page

As you can see from the Columns section of this page, the new site content type has inherited the Body and Expires columns from the Announcements content type, which you picked as the parent content type. Also note that the new site content type inherits the Title column from the Item content type. This is because the Announcements content type inherits from the Item content type.

Creating a site content type through the SharePoint user interface has its own pluses and minuses. Among the pluses is the ease of development as you've just seen. Among the minuses is the fact that a site content type created through the SharePoint user interface is considered site customization. As such, it is not an independent, deployable component that could be deployed to other sites.

Another approach to site content type development is through CAML. This enables you to implement your site content type in CAML and deploy it to any site that supports the base content type from which your site content type inherits.

Next, take a look at the implementation of three site content types to help you gain the skills you need to implement your own site content types. Here is the idea behind these three site content types. There is a SharePoint list known as a Tasks list. As the name suggests, the list items in this SharePoint list are tasks assigned to specific people. A SharePoint workflow is normally associated with a SharePoint task, which maintains the SharePoint tasks that the workflow creates as part of its execution logic. For example, an approval workflow may create a task and assign it to an approver. An approver is then responsible for updating and marking the task as complete to enable the workflow to resume its execution.

There is a standard SharePoint site content type named WorkflowTask, which defines the common columns that a typical task needs. However, these columns are generic columns that apply to all tasks. If the type of task that your workflow needs to create requires additional columns, you'll need to implement custom site content types for that purpose. As an example, consider a large organization that is organizing a conference for a selected group of employees. Interested employees are required to send a request to their respective managers and get their manager's approval before they can participate in this conference. Because the conference lasts for days, employees must also get their manager's approval for the days they wish to participate. To keep the discussions focused you'll assume every request is made for consecutive days. Now, imagine that you want to create a workflow to automate the process through which an employee makes a request to participate in the conference and the manager and the personnel approve or deny the request. Such a workflow will then need to create tasks that will contain custom columns such as employee first and last names and requested number of days in addition to the typical columns that the WorkflowTask site content type provides. As such, you'll implement three site content types and store them in an XML file named ConferenceRequestSiteContentTypes.xml. This XML file is an example of what is known as an element manifest file. Listing 6-4 presents the content of this XML file.

Listing 6-4: The content of the ConferenceRequestSiteContentTypes.xml file

```
<?xml version="1.0" encoding="utf-8" ?>
<Elements xmlns="http://schemas.microsoft.com/sharepoint/">
  <ContentType
    ID="0x01080100A3440F3CB4E74e5e8B4CF07BAEBAB9B1"
    Name="ConferenceRequestContentType"
    Description="Provision a new ConferenceRequestContentType"
    Version="0"
    Group="Conference Request Content Types" >
    <FieldRefs>
      <FieldRef ID="{C936B73E-5607-462f-9623-5AACD5765CBF}"
      Name="EmployeeFirstName" DisplayName="Employee First Name" />
      <FieldRef ID="{481FD88F-4964-4924-A25B-FF1C3882CD0F}" Name="EmployeeLastName"
      DisplayName="Employee Last Name" />
      <FieldRef ID="{7FF39930-F6CD-4728-8000-9AA39B50995F}"
      Name="ConferenceStartDate" DisplayName="Conference Start Date" />
      <FieldRef ID="{D5601EC5-FCE3-4ea8-ABA6-8A1503DB8D22}" Name="ConferenceEndDate"
      DisplayName="Conference End Date" />
      <FieldRef ID="{7E26EA7A-A5A6-4dc3-B257-442FB62E84EB}" Name="EntitledDays"
      DisplayName="Entitled Days" />
    </FieldRefs>
  </ContentType>

  <ContentType
    ID="0x01080100A3440F3CB4E74e5e8B4CF07BAEBAB9B101"
    Name="ManagerContentType"
    Description="Provision a new ManagerContentType"
    Version="0"
```

```
    Group="Conference Request Content Types" >
    <FieldRefs>
      <FieldRef ID="{D90A2BE9-0230-4d0e-8C33-192CF9F54A27}" Name="ManagerComment"
      DisplayName="Manager Comment" />
      <FieldRef ID="{29BBEEC4-BE8E-4efb-9646-F4A132222B45}" Name="ManagerApproval"
      DisplayName="Manager Approval" />
    </FieldRefs>
  </ContentType>

  <ContentType
    ID="0x01080100A3440F3CB4E74e5e8B4CF07BAEBAB9B10101"
    Name="PersonnelContentType"
    Description="Provision a new PersonnelContentType"
    Version="0"
    Group="Conference Request Content Types" >
    <FieldRefs>
      <FieldRef ID="{4296281E-3EC8-42d6-AD17-7CCB52483E66}" Name="PersonnelComment"
      DisplayName="Personnel Comment" />
      <FieldRef ID="{D382F1DA-5FA5-4478-A2F8-C96FCE95293C}"
      Name="PersonnelApproval" DisplayName="Personnel Approval" />
    </FieldRefs>
  </ContentType>
</Elements>
```

As you can see, this element manifest file, like any other element manifest file, has a document element named <Elements>. This document element contains three <ContentType> child elements that define the ConferenceRequestContentType, ManagerContentType, and PersonnelContentType site content types, respectively. The value of the ID attribute of a <ContentType> element is known as the content type ID of the site content type that the element defines. As a matter of fact, the SharePoint object model comes with a class named SPContentTypeId whose instances represent the content type IDs of SharePoint content types.

Note that the value of the ID attribute on the <ContentType> element that defines the ConferenceRequest ContentType site content type, that is, the content type ID of the ConferenceRequestContentType site content type, consists of the following parts:

- **0x010801.** This hexadecimal number is the content type ID of a standard SharePoint site content type named WorkflowTask. The WorkflowTask site content type, like any other standard SharePoint site content type, is defined in an element manifest file named ctypeswss.xml, which is located in the following folder on the file system of the front-end web server:

```
Local_Drive:\Program Files\Common Files\microsoft shared\Web Server
Extensions\12\TEMPLATE\FEATURES\ctypes
```

The following excerpt from ctypes.xml presents the definition of the WorkflowTask site content type:

```
<ContentType
ID="0x010801"
Name="$Resources:WorkflowTask"
Group="_Hidden"
Hidden="TRUE"
Description="$Resources:WorkflowTaskCTDesc"
Version="0">
  <FieldRefs>
    <FieldRef ID="{58ddda52-c2a3-4650-9178-3bbc1f6e36da}" Name="Link" />
    <FieldRef ID="{16b6952f-3ce6-45e0-8f4e-42dac6e12441}"
    Name="OffsiteParticipant" />
    <FieldRef ID="{4a799ba5-f449-4796-b43e-aa5186c3c414}"
    Name="OffsiteParticipantReason" />
    <FieldRef ID="{18e1c6fa-ae37-4102-890a-cfb0974ef494}" Name="WorkflowOutcome" />
    <FieldRef ID="{e506d6ca-c2da-4164-b858-306f1c41c9ec}" Name="WorkflowName" />
    <FieldRef ID="{ae069f25-3ac2-4256-b9c3-15dbc15da0e0}" Name="GUID" />
    <FieldRef ID="{8d96aa48-9dff-46cf-8538-84c747ffa877}" Name="TaskType" />
    <FieldRef ID="{17ca3a22-fdfe-46eb-99b5-9646baed3f16}" Name="FormURN" />
    <FieldRef ID="{78eae64a-f5f2-49af-b416-3247b76f46a1}" Name="FormData" />
    <FieldRef ID="{8cbb9252-1035-4156-9c35-f54e9056c65a}" Name="EmailBody" />
    <FieldRef ID="{47f68c3b-8930-406f-bde2-4a8c669ee87c}"
    Name="HasCustomEmailBody" />
    <FieldRef ID="{cb2413f2-7de9-4afc-8587-1ca3f563f624}"
    Name="SendEmailNotification" />
    <FieldRef ID="{4d2444c2-0e97-476c-a2a3-e9e4a9c73009}" Name="PendingModTime" />
    <FieldRef ID="{35363960-d998-4aad-b7e8-058dfe2c669e}" Name="Completed" />
    <FieldRef ID="{1bfee788-69b7-4765-b109-d4d9c31d1ac1}" Name="WorkflowListId" />
    <FieldRef ID="{8e234c69-02b0-42d9-8046-d5f49bf0174f}" Name="WorkflowItemId" />
    <FieldRef ID="{1c5518e2-1e99-49fe-bfc6-1a8de3ba16e2}"
    Name="ExtendedProperties" />
  </FieldRefs>
</ContentType>
```

The WorkflowTask site content type defines the columns that appear in all workflow task lists. As you can see from this excerpt, the ID attribute of the WorkflowTask site content type is set to 0x010801, which is the same value with which the content type ID of the ConferenceRequestContentType begins. This tells SharePoint that the ConferenceRequestContentType site content type inherits from the WorkflowTask site content type. This means that the ConferenceRequestContentType site content type inherits all the columns that the WorkflowTask site content type references.

- **00.** This hexadecimal number is used to separate the content type ID of the base site content type, which is 0x010801 in this case, from the rest of the content type ID of the derived content type, which is discussed in the next bulleted item.
- **A3440F3CB4E74e5e8B4CF07BAEBAB9B1.** This is a GUID that uniquely identifies the ConferenceRequestContentType site content type from all other content types that inherit from the same base site content type, which is the WorkflowTask site content type in this case.

As you can see from Listing 6-4, the ConferenceRequestContentType site content type references five site columns named EmployeeFirstName, EmployeeLastName, and ConferenceStartDate, ConferenceEndDate, and EntitledDays (specifies the number of days the employee is entitled to):

```
<FieldRefs>
  <FieldRef ID="{C936B73E-5607-462f-9623-5AACD5765CBF}"
  Name="EmployeeFirstName" DisplayName="Employee First Name" />
  <FieldRef ID="{481FD88F-4964-4924-A25B-FF1C3882CD0F}" Name="EmployeeLastName"
  DisplayName="Employee Last Name" />
  <FieldRef ID="{7FF39930-F6CD-4728-8000-9AA39B50995F}"
  Name="ConferenceStartDate" DisplayName="Conference Start Date" />
  <FieldRef ID="{D5601EC5-FCE3-4ea8-ABA6-8A1503DB8D22}" Name="ConferenceEndDate"
  DisplayName="Conference End Date" />
  <FieldRef ID="{7E26EA7A-A5A6-4dc3-B257-442FB62E84EB}" Name="EntitledDays"
  DisplayName="Entitled Days" />
</FieldRefs>
```

In other words, the ConferenceRequestContentType site content type extends the columns that it inherits from the WorkflowTask site content type to add support for these five site columns. This means that when you add the ConferenceRequestContentType site content type to a SharePoint list, it will add the columns that it inherits from the WorkflowTask site content type plus the preceding five columns. The definitions of these five site columns are presented later in this section.

As you can see from Listing 6-4, the ConferenceRequestContentTypes.xml element manifest file also defines a site content type named ManagerContentType. The ID attribute of the <ContentType> element that defines this site content type, like the ID attribute of any other <ContentType> element, specifies the content type ID of the site content type that the <ContentType> element defines. As Listing 6-4 illustrates, this content type ID consists of the following sections:

- **0x01080100A3440F3CB4E74e5e8B4CF07BAEBAB9B1.** This is nothing but the content type ID of the ConferenceRequestContentType site content type. This means that the ManagerContentType site content type inherits from the ConferenceRequestContentType site content type. As such it inherits all the site column references that the ConferenceRequestContentType site content type contains. This includes those site column references that the ConferenceRequestContentType site content type inherits from the WorkflowTask site content type plus the five site column references that the ConferenceRequestContentType site content type contains, that is, EmployeeFirstName, EmployeeLastName, ConferenceStartDate, ConferenceEndDate, and EntitledDays.
- **01.** This hexadecimal number uniquely identifies the ManagerContentType site content type from all other site content types that inherit from the ConferenceRequestContentType site content type.

As you can see from Listing 6-4, the ManagerContentType site content type references two new site columns named ManagerComment and ManagerApproval:

```
<FieldRefs>
  <FieldRef ID="{D90A2BE9-0230-4d0e-8C33-192CF9F54A27}" Name="ManagerComment"
  DisplayName="Manager Comment" />
  <FieldRef ID="{29BBEEC4-BE8E-4efb-9646-F4A132222B45}" Name="ManagerApproval"
  DisplayName="Manager Approval" />
</FieldRefs>
```

As Listing 6-4 illustrates, the ConferenceRequestContentTypes.xml element manifest file also defines a site content type named PersonnelContentType. As you can see, the content type ID of this site content type consists of the following sections:

- **0x01080100A3440F3CB4E74e5e8B4CF07BAEBAB9B101.** This is nothing but the content type ID of the ManagerContentType site content type. This means that the PersonnelContentType site content type inherits from the ManagerContentType site content type. As such it inherits all the site column references that the ManagerContentType site content type contains. This includes those site column references that the ManagerContentType site content type inherits from the ConferenceRequestContentType site content type plus the two site column references that the ManagerContentType site content type contains, that is, ManagerApproval and ManagerComment.
- **01.** This hexadecimal number uniquely identifies the PersonnelContentType site content type from all other site content types that inherit from the ManagerContentType site content type.

As you can see from Listing 6-4, the PersonnelContentType site content type references two new site columns named PersonnelComment and PersonnelApproval:

```
<FieldRefs>
  <FieldRef ID="{D90A2BE9-0230-4d0e-8C33-192CF9F54A27}" Name="PersonnelComment"
  DisplayName="Personnel Comment" />
  <FieldRef ID="{29BBEEC4-BE8E-4efb-9646-F4A132222B45}"
  Name="PersonnelApproval" DisplayName="Personnel Approval" />
</FieldRefs>
```

Listing 6-5 presents the content of another element manifest file named ConferenceRequestSiteColumns .xml that defines the site columns that the ConferenceRequestContentType, ManagerContentType, and PersonnelContentType site content types reference.

Listing 6-5: The content of the ConferenceRequestSiteColumns.xml file

```
<?xml version="1.0" encoding="utf-8" ?>
<Elements xmlns="http://schemas.microsoft.com/sharepoint/">
  <Field
    ID="{C936B73E-5607-462f-9623-5AACD5765CBF}"
    Name="EmployeeFirstName"
    SourceID="http://schemas.microsoft.com/sharepoint/v3"
    StaticName="EmployeeFirstName"
    Group="Conference Request Site Columns"
    DisplayName="Employee First Name"
    Type="Text" />

  <Field
    ID="{481FD88F-4964-4924-A25B-FF1C3882CD0F}"
    Name="EmployeeLastName"
    SourceID="http://schemas.microsoft.com/sharepoint/v3"
    StaticName="EmployeeLastName"
    Group="Conference Request Site Columns"
    DisplayName="Employee Last Name"
    Type="Text" />

  <Field
    ID="{7FF39930-F6CD-4728-8000-9AA39B50995F}"
```

```
    Name="ConferenceStartDate"
    SourceID="http://schemas.microsoft.com/sharepoint/v3"
    StaticName="ConferenceStartDate"
    Group="Conference Request Site Columns"
    DisplayName="Conference Start Date"
    Type="DateTime" />

  <Field
    ID="{D5601EC5-FCE3-4ea8-ABA6-8A1503DB8D22}"
    Name="ConferenceEndDate"
    SourceID="http://schemas.microsoft.com/sharepoint/v3"
    StaticName="ConferenceEndDate"
    Group="Conference Request Site Columns"
    DisplayName="Conference End Date"
    Type="DateTime" />

  <Field
    ID="{7E26EA7A-A5A6-4dc3-B257-442FB62E84EB}"
    Name="EntitledDays"
    SourceID="http://schemas.microsoft.com/sharepoint/v3"
    StaticName="EntitledDays"
    Group="Conference Request Site Columns"
    DisplayName="EntitledDays"
    Type="Number" />

  <Field
    ID="{D90A2BE9-0230-4d0e-8C33-192CF9F54A27}"
    Name="ManagerComment"
    SourceID="http://schemas.microsoft.com/sharepoint/v3"
    StaticName="ManagerComment"
    Group="Conference Request Site Columns"
    DisplayName="Manager Comment"
    Type="Note" />

  <Field
    ID="{29BBEEC4-BE8E-4efb-9646-F4A132222B45}"
    Name="ManagerApproval"
    SourceID="http://schemas.microsoft.com/sharepoint/v3"
    StaticName="ManagerApproval"
    Group="Conference Request Site Columns"
    DisplayName="Manager Approval"
    Type="Boolean" />

  <Field
    ID="{4296281E-3EC8-42d6-AD17-7CCB52483E66}"
    Name="PersonnelComment"
    SourceID="http://schemas.microsoft.com/sharepoint/v3"
    StaticName="PersonnelComment"
    Group="Conference Request Site Columns"
    DisplayName="Personnel Comment"
    Type="Note" />

  <Field
    ID="{D382F1DA-5FA5-4478-A2F8-C96FCE95293C}"
```

(continued)

Listing 6-5 *(continued)*

```
      Name="PersonnelApproval"
      SourceID="http://schemas.microsoft.com/sharepoint/v3"
      StaticName="PersonnelApproval"
      Group="Conference Request Site Columns"
      DisplayName="Personnel Approval"
      Type="Boolean" />
</Elements>
```

As you can see, this element manifest file contains a bunch of <Field> elements each defining a site column. The ID attribute of each <Field> element must be set to a GUID that uniquely identifies the site column. Use the guidgen.exe utility to generate and to copy and paste the required GUIDs. The Type attribute of each <Field> element specifies the data type of the site column that the element defines. As you can see, a site column does not define its own data type. Instead it uses an existing data type. Also note that the ID attribute of a <Field> element that defines a site column does not follow the same pattern as the ID attribute of a <ContentType> element that defines a site content type. In other words, the ID attribute of a <Field> element that defines a site column does not contain the ID attribute value of another site column. This means that you cannot inherit from a site column to define a new site column. This is very different from content types where you must inherit your site content type from another site content type.

Listings 6-4 and 6-5, respectively, present the contents of the ConferenceRequestContentTypes.xml and ConferenceRequestSiteColumns.xml element manifest files that define the ConferenceRequestContentType, ManagerContentType, and PersonnelContentType site content types and the site columns that these site content types reference. Next, you need to implement a feature that references these element manifest files as shown in Listing 6-6.

Listing 6-6: The feature that references the element manifest files that define the site columns and site content types

```
<?xml version="1.0" encoding="utf-8" ?>
<Feature
Id="AC1C2E35-20BE-4418-917F-34AB8689F711"
Title="Conference Request Feature"
Description="This is Conference Request Feature!"
Version="1.0.0.0"
Scope="Site"
ReceiverAssembly="Microsoft.Office.Workflow.Feature, Version=12.0.0.0,
                  Culture=neutral, PublicKeyToken=71e9bce111e9429c"
ReceiverClass="Microsoft.Office.Workflow.Feature.WorkflowFeatureReceiver"
xmlsn="http://schemas.microsoft.com/sharepoint/">
  <ElementManifests>
    <ElementManifest Location="ConferenceRequestSiteColumns.xml"/>
    <ElementManifest Location="ConferenceRequestSiteContentTypes.xml"/>
  </ElementManifests>
  <Properties>
    <Property Key="GloballyAvailable" Value="true" />
    <!-- Value for RegisterForms key indicates the path to the forms relative to
feature file location -->
    <!-- if you don't have forms, use *.xsn -->
    <Property Key="RegisterForms" Value="*.xsn" />
  </Properties>
</Feature>
```

Next you need to take these steps:

1. Create a feature-specific folder named ConferenceRequest under the FEATURES folder in the following folder on the file system of the front-end web server:

```
Local_Drive:\Program Files\Common Files\microsoft shared\Web Server
Extensions\12\TEMPLATE
```

2. Copy the feature.xml feature file whose content is shown in Listing 6-6 into the ConferenceRequest folder.
3. Copy the ConferenceRequestContentTypes.xml and ConferenceRequestSiteColumns.xml element manifest files whose contents are shown in Listings 6-4 and 6-5 into the ConferenceRequest folder.
4. Run the STSADM.exe command-line utility to install the feature:

```
stsadm.exe -o installfeature -name ConferenceRequest
```

   Note that the -name switch expects the name of the feature-specific folder under which the feature.xml file is stored, which is the ConferenceRequest folder in the case.
5. Run the STSADM.exe command-line utility or use the SharePoint user interface to activate the feature in your favorite site.

Activating the feature on a site makes the ConferenceRequestContentType, ManagerContentType, and PersonnelContentType site content types and the site columns that they reference available to all SharePoint lists in that site and its descendant sites. In other words, you can add these site content types to any SharePoint list in that site and its descendant sites. In this case, you would like to add these content types to the Tasks list.

Next, go ahead and use the SharePoint user interface to add the ManagerContentType site content type to the Tasks list. Because the ManagerContentType site content type inherits from the ConferenceRequestContentType site content type, you do not need to add the ConferenceRequestContentType site content type to the task list.

Now go ahead and add a new task of the ManagerContentType type to the task list. Next, select Edit Item from the ECB menu to navigate to the EditForm.aspx page shown in Figure 6-10.

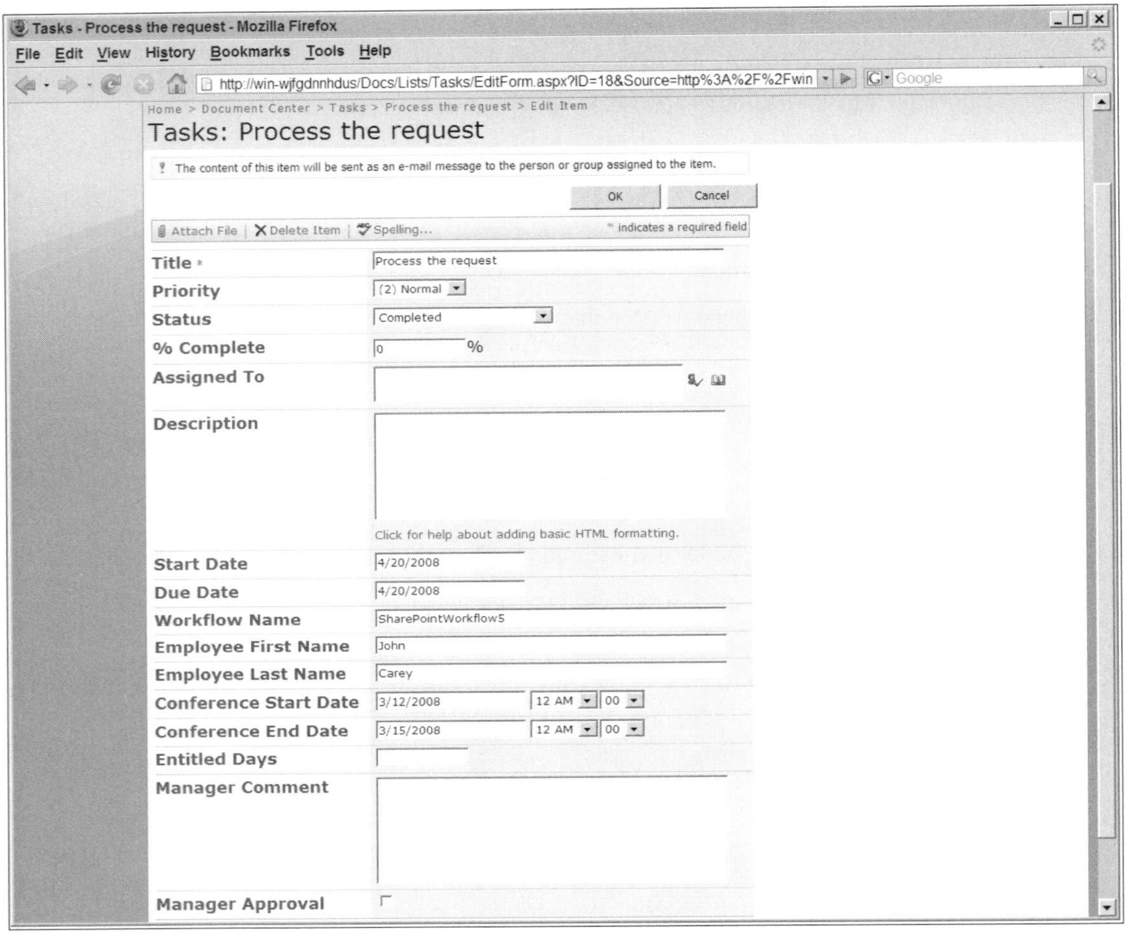

Figure 6-10: The edit form

Note that SharePoint automatically renders the custom columns that the ManagerContentType and ConferenceRequestContentType content types reference. You may be wondering how SharePoint knows how to render these columns. The answer lies in the field types on which these custom columns are based. As discussed in the previous chapter, each field type specifies how it should be rendered in a page such as DispForm.asxp, NewForm.aspx, and EditForm.aspx.

Next, you'll learn how to develop a custom edit task form to replace the SharePoint standard edit task form (EditForm.aspx). You'll develop an application page named ManagerContentTypeEditTaskForm .aspx that does just that.

Listing 6-7 presents the implementation of this page. Create a Class Library project named ClassLibrary1 in Visual Studio. Add a new text file named ManagerContentTypeEditTaskForm.aspx to this class library and add the content of Listing 6-7 to this file. Next, configure Visual Studio to compile the project into a strong-named assembly.

Listing 6-7: The ManagerContentTypeEditTaskForm.aspx page

```
<%@ Page Language="C#" MasterPageFile="~/_layouts/application.master"
EnableSessionState="true"
ValidateRequest="False" Inherits="ClassLibrary1.ManagerContentTypeEditTaskForm" %>

<%@ Assembly Name="ClassLibrary1, Version=1.0.0.0, Culture=neutral,
PublicKeyToken=dc3f8dd98d3e6a2d" %>

<%@ Register TagPrefix="SharePoint" Namespace="Microsoft.SharePoint.WebControls"
Assembly="Microsoft.SharePoint, Version=12.0.0.0, Culture=neutral,
PublicKeyToken=71e9bce111e9429c" %>

<%@ Register TagPrefix="Utilities" Namespace="Microsoft.SharePoint.Utilities"
Assembly="Microsoft.SharePoint, Version=12.0.0.0, Culture=neutral,
PublicKeyToken=71e9bce111e9429c" %>

<%@ Register TagPrefix="wssuc" TagName="InputFormSection"
Src="/_controltemplates/InputFormSection.ascx" %>

<%@ Register TagPrefix="wssuc" TagName="InputFormControl"
Src="/_controltemplates/InputFormControl.ascx" %>

<%@ Register TagPrefix="wssuc" TagName="ButtonSection"
Src="/_controltemplates/ButtonSection.ascx" %>

<asp:Content ID="Main" ContentPlaceHolderID="PlaceHolderMain" runat="server">
  <SharePoint:FormDigest ID="FormDigest1" runat="server" />
  <asp:Table CellSpacing="0" CellPadding="0" BorderWidth="0">
    <wssuc:InputFormSection Title="First name"
    Description="Employee first name"
    runat="server">
      <template_inputformcontrols>
        <wssuc:InputFormControl runat="server">
          <Template_Control>
            <asp:Label ID="FirstNameLbl" font-bold="true" width="300"
            runat="server"/>
          </Template_Control>
        </wssuc:InputFormControl>
      </template_inputformcontrols>
    </wssuc:InputFormSection>

    <wssuc:InputFormSection Title="Last name"
    Description="Employee last name"
    runat="server">
      <template_inputformcontrols>
```

(continued)

Listing 6-7 *(continued)*

```
        <wssuc:InputFormControl runat="server">
          <Template_Control>
            <asp:Label ID="LastNameLbl" font-bold="true" width="300"
            runat="server"/>
          </Template_Control>
        </wssuc:InputFormControl>
      </template_inputformcontrols>
    </wssuc:InputFormSection>

    <wssuc:InputFormSection Title="Starting date"
    Description="Starting date"
    runat="server">
      <template_inputformcontrols>
        <wssuc:InputFormControl runat="server">
          <Template_Control>
            <asp:Label ID="StartingDateLbl" font-bold="true" width="300"
            runat="server"/>
          </Template_Control>
        </wssuc:InputFormControl>
      </template_inputformcontrols>
    </wssuc:InputFormSection>

    <wssuc:InputFormSection Title="Ending date"
    Description="Ending date."
    runat="server">
      <template_inputformcontrols>
        <wssuc:InputFormControl runat="server">
          <Template_Control>
            <asp:Label ID="EndingDateLbl" font-bold="true" width="300"
            runat="server"/>
          </Template_Control>
        </wssuc:InputFormControl>
      </template_inputformcontrols>
    </wssuc:InputFormSection>

    <wssuc:InputFormSection Title="Days"
    Description="Days the employee is entitled to."
    runat="server">
      <template_inputformcontrols>
        <wssuc:InputFormControl runat="server">
          <Template_Control>
            <asp:Label ID="DaysLbl" font-bold="true" width="300"
            runat="server"/>
          </Template_Control>
        </wssuc:InputFormControl>
      </template_inputformcontrols>
    </wssuc:InputFormSection>

    <wssuc:InputFormSection Title="Manager Comment"
    Description="Enter an optional comment" runat="server">
```

```
        <template_inputformcontrols>
          <wssuc:InputFormControl runat="server">
            <Template_Control>
              <SharePoint:InputFormTextBox Title="Manager Comment"
              ID="ManagerCommentTbx" runat="server" TextMode="MultiLine"
              Columns="50" Rows="6"/>
            </Template_Control>
          </wssuc:InputFormControl>
        </template_inputformcontrols>
      </wssuc:InputFormSection>

      <wssuc:ButtonSection runat="server" ShowStandardCancelButton="false">
        <template_buttons>
          <asp:PlaceHolder runat="server">
            <asp:Button runat="server" OnClick="ApproveCallback"
            Text="Approve Request" />
            <asp:Button runat="server" OnClick="DenyCallback"
            Text="Deny Request" />
            <asp:Button runat="server" OnClick="CancelCallback" Text="Cancel" />
          </asp:PlaceHolder>
        </template_buttons>
      </wssuc:ButtonSection>
    </asp:Table>
  </asp:Content>

  <asp:Content ID="Content1" ContentPlaceHolderID="PlaceHolderPageTitle" runat="server">
    <%= PlaceHolderPageTitleContent %>
  </asp:Content>

  <asp:Content ID="Content2" ContentPlaceHolderID="PlaceHolderPageTitleInTitleArea"
  runat="server">
    <%= PlaceHolderPageTitleInTitleAreaContent %>
  </asp:Content>
```

Because you're taking over the rendering of the entire edit task form, you have to take the required steps to render the form chrome to ensure that the custom form has the same look and feel as the rest of the pages in the site. This is an easy task to accomplish considering the fact that the custom edit task form is an application page and just like any other application page uses the application.master master page. This master page renders the chrome for you. As such the @Page directive in Listing 6-7 contains the following attribute:

```
MasterPageFile="~/_layouts/application.master"
```

The edit task form, like any other content page, consists of bunch of <asp:Content> tags, each providing content for a specific content placeholder in the application.master page. More specifically, the custom edit task form provides contents for the PlaceHolderMain, PlaceHolderPageTitle, and PlaceHolderPageTitleInTitleArea content placeholders.

As Listing 6-7 shows, the content that the edit task form provides for the PlaceHolderMain content placeholder consists of five labels that display the employee's first and last names, starting and ending dates, and the number of days to which the employee is entitled, a textbox where the manager can enter a comment, and three buttons that allow the manager to approve or deny the request or cancel the form for now.

You must deploy the ManagerContentTypeEditTaskForm.aspx page to the LAYOUTS subfolder of the following folder on the file system of the front-end web server:

```
Local_Drive:\Program Files\Common Files\microsoft shared\Web Server
Extensions\12\TEMPLATE\LAYOUTS
```

As a best practice, you should create a folder under the LAYOUTS folder and deploy your page there as opposed to deploying your page directly to the LAYOUTS folder itself to avoid possible name-conflicts with other pages deployed to the same folder. In this case, create a folder named ConferenceRequest under the LAYOUTS folder and deploy the ManagerContentTypeEditTaskForm.aspx page to that folder.

Note that the @Page directive in Listing 6-8 contains an Inherits attribute that specifies a code-behind class named ManagerContentTypeEditTaskForm:

```
Inherits="ClassLibrary1.ManagerContentTypeEditTaskForm"
```

This code-behind class is where the behavior of the edit task form is implemented. Also note that this code-behind class is compiled into a strong-named assembly and deployed to the Global Assembly Cache.

```
<%@ Assembly Name="ClassLibrary1, Version=1.0.0.0, Culture=neutral,
PublicKeyToken=dc3f8dd98d3e6a2d" %>
```

Listing 6-8 presents the implementation of the ManagerContentTypeEditTaskForm code-behind class. Add a new Class file named ManagerContentTypeEditTaskForm.cs to the project and add the contents of Listing 6-8 to this file. Also add a reference to the Microsoft.SharePoint.dll assembly, which is located in the following folder on your machine:

```
Local_Drive:\Program Files\Common Files\Microsoft Shared\Web Server
Extensions\12\ISAPI
```

You also need to add a reference to the System.Web.dll assembly.

Listing 6-8: The ManagerContentTypeEditTaskForm code-behind class

```
using System;
using System.IO;
using System.Text;
using System.Web;
using System.Web.UI;
using System.Web.UI.WebControls;
using System.Web.UI.HtmlControls;
using System.Xml;
using System.Xml.Serialization;
using Microsoft.SharePoint;
using Microsoft.SharePoint.Utilities;
using Microsoft.SharePoint.WebControls;
using Microsoft.SharePoint.Workflow;
using System.Collections;

namespace ClassLibrary1
{
  public class ManagerContentTypeEditTaskForm : LayoutsPageBase
  {
    protected string PlaceHolderPageTitleContent;
    protected string PlaceHolderPageTitleInTitleAreaContent;

    protected SPList targetTasksList;
    SPListItem targetTask;


    protected Label FirstNameLbl;
    protected Label LastNameLbl;
    protected Label StartingDateLbl;
    protected Label EndingDateLbl;
    protected Label DaysLbl;
    protected InputFormTextBox ManagerCommentTbx;

    protected override void OnLoad(EventArgs e)
    {
      targetTasksList = Web.Lists[new Guid(Request.Params["List"])];
      targetTask =
               targetTasksList.GetItemById(int.Parse(Request.Params["ID"]));

      PlaceHolderPageTitleContent = "Process Request";
      PlaceHolderPageTitleInTitleAreaContent = "Process Request";

      if (!this.Page.IsPostBack)
      {
        this.FirstNameLbl.Text = (string)targetTask["EmployeeFirstName"];
        this.LastNameLbl.Text = (string)targetTask["EmployeeLastName"];
        this.StartingDateLbl.Text = targetTask["StartDate"].ToString();
        this.EndingDateLbl.Text = targetTask["EndDate"].ToString();
        this.DaysLbl.Text = targetTask["Days"].ToString();
      }
```

(continued)

Listing 6-8 *(continued)*

```
    }

    public void CancelCallback(object sender, EventArgs e)
    {
      SPUtility.Redirect(targetTasksList.DefaultViewUrl, SPRedirectFlags.Default,
                         HttpContext.Current);
    }

    public void ApproveCallback(object sender, EventArgs e)
    {
      try
      {
        Hashtable taskProperties = new Hashtable();
        taskProperties["TaskStatus"] = "Completed";
        taskProperties["ManagerApproval"] = true;
        taskProperties["ManagerComment"] = this.ManagerCommentTbx.Text;
        SPWorkflowTask.AlterTask(targetTask, taskProperties, true);
      }

      catch (Exception exception)
      {
        SPUtility.Redirect("Error.aspx", SPRedirectFlags.RelativeToLayoutsPage,
                           HttpContext.Current,
            "ErrorText=" + SPHttpUtility.UrlKeyValueEncode(exception.Message));
      }

      SPUtility.Redirect(targetTasksList.DefaultViewUrl, SPRedirectFlags.Default,
                         HttpContext.Current);
    }

    public void DenyCallback(object sender, EventArgs e)
    {
      try
      {
        Hashtable taskProperties = new Hashtable();
        taskProperties["TaskStatus"] = "Completed";
        taskProperties["ManagerApproval"] = false;
        taskProperties["ManagerComment"] = this.ManagerCommentTbx.Text;
        SPWorkflowTask.AlterTask(targetTask, taskProperties, true);
      }

      catch (Exception exception)
      {
        SPUtility.Redirect("Error.aspx", SPRedirectFlags.RelativeToLayoutsPage,
                           HttpContext.Current,
            "ErrorText=" + SPHttpUtility.UrlKeyValueEncode(exception.Message));
      }

      SPUtility.Redirect(targetTasksList.DefaultViewUrl, SPRedirectFlags.Default,
                         HttpContext.Current);
    }
  }
}
```

ManagerContentTypeEditTaskForm, like any other application page code-behind class, inherits from the LayoutsPageBase base class. This base class is fully aware of the SharePoint context within which the form is executing such as what the current site or site collection is and contains public properties such Web and Site that expose the current SharePoint context. An application page code-behind class inherits these properties and can use them to access the current SharePoint context.

As you can see from Listing 6-8, ManagerContentTypeEditTaskForm overrides the OnLoad method where it performs these tasks. First, it retrieves the value of a query string parameter named List. This value is the string representation of the GUID of the SharePoint tasks list. Next, it creates the actual GUID and uses it as an index into the Lists collection property of the SPWeb object that represents the current site to return a reference to an SPList object that represents the tasks list:

```
targetTasksList = Web.Lists[new Guid(Request.Params["List"])];
```

ManagerContentTypeEditTaskForm inherits the Web property from LayoutsPageBase. This property references the SPWeb object that represents the current site. This is an example of the SharePoint contextual information to which I referred earlier.

Next, OnLoad accesses the value of a query string parameter named ID, which is the string representation of the ID of the current task. OnLoad then converts this string into an integer and passes it into the GetItemById method of the SPList object that represents the current task list to return a reference to the SPListItem object that represents the current task:

```
targetTask = targetTasksList.GetItemById(Convert.ToInt32(Request.Params["ID"]));
```

If the page is being loaded for the first time, OnLoad accesses the values of the EmployeeFirstName, EmployeeLastName, StartDate, EndDate, and Days fields of the current task and renders them in their respective labels:

```
        this.FirstNameLbl.Text = (string)targetTask["EmployeeFirstName"];
        this.LastNameLbl.Text = (string)targetTask["EmployeeLastName"];
        this.StartingDateLbl.Text = targetTask["StartDate"].ToString();
        this.EndingDateLbl.Text = targetTask["EndDate"].ToString();
        this.DaysLbl.Text = targetTask["Days"].ToString();
```

As Listing 6-8 shows, the custom edit task form registers methods named ApproveCallback and DenyCallback as event handlers for the Click events of the Approve Request and Deny Request buttons, respectively. As you can see from Listing 6-8, both event handlers use a similar logic. This logic begins with instantiating a Hashtable:

```
Hashtable taskProperties = new Hashtable();
```

Then it sets the TaskStatus field of the current task to "Completed" to mark the task as completed:

```
        taskProperties["TaskStatus"] = "Completed";
```

Next, it sets the ManagerApproval field of the current task to true if the Approve Request button is clicked. Otherwise its sets it to false:

```
        taskProperties["ManagerApproval"] = true;
```

Next, it sets the ManagerComment field to the comment that the manager has entered the comment textbox:

```
        taskProperties["ManagerComment"] = this.ManagerCommentTbx.Text;
```

Finally, it invokes a static method named AlterTask to a class named SPWorkflowTask, passing in the SPListItem object that represents the current task and the Hashtable that contains the field values:

```
        SPWorkflowTask.AlterTask(targetTask, taskProperties, true);
```

This method updates the current task in the content database.

So far you've implemented the ManagerContentTypeEditTaskForm.aspx page and its code-behind class. Next, you need to update the element manifest file that defines the ManagerContentType site content type to add a reference to the ManagerContentTypeEditTaskForm.aspx page. Recall that you've defined this site content type in an element manifest file named ConferenceRequestContentTypes.xml, which you deployed to the following feature-specific folder on the file system of the front-end web server:

```
Local_Drive:\Program Files\Common Files\microsoft shared\Web Server Extensions\12\
TEMPLATE\FEATURES\ConferenceRequest
```

Listing 6-9 presents an excerpt from this element manifest file.

Listing 6-9: The ManagerContentType site content type

```
<?xml version="1.0" encoding="utf-8" ?>
<Elements xmlns="http://schemas.microsoft.com/sharepoint/">
  ...
  <ContentType
    ID="0x01080100A3440F3CB4E74e5e8B4CF07BAEBAB9B101"
    Name="ManagerContentType"
    Description="Provision a new ManagerContentType"
    Version="0"
    Group="Conference Request Content Types" >
    <FieldRefs>
      <FieldRef ID="{D90A2BE9-0230-4d0e-8C33-192CF9F54A27}" Name="ManagerComment"
      DisplayName="Manager Comment" />
      <FieldRef ID="{29BBEEC4-BE8E-4efb-9646-F4A132222B45}" Name="ManagerApproval"
      DisplayName="Manager Approval" />
    </FieldRefs>

    <XmlDocuments>
      <XmlDocument
   NamespaceURI="http://schemas.microsoft.com/sharepoint/v3/contenttype/forms/url">
        <FormUrls
        xmlns="http://schemas.microsoft.com/sharepoint/v3/contenttype/forms/url">
          <Edit>_layouts/ConferenceRequest/ManagerContentTypeEditTaskForm.aspx</Edit>
        </FormUrls>
      </XmlDocument>
    </XmlDocuments>

  </ContentType>
  . . .
</Elements>
```

As you can see from the boldfaced portion of this XML fragment, you've added an element named <XmlDocuments> as the child element of the <ContentType> element that defines the ManagerContentType site content type. This child element is the main extensibility point of a site content type. To extend a site content type, you simply add one or more <XmlDocument> child elements to the <XmlDocuments> element. You can include any valid XML document between the opening and closing tags of each <XmlDocument> child element. You can then access these XML documents through the SharePoint object model to do whatever is deemed necessary.

SharePoint uses the same extensibility point of a site content type to enable you to add support for custom list item forms including display list item forms, edit list item forms, and new list item forms for a site content type. All you need to do is to:

1. Add an <XmlDocument> child element to the <XmlDocuments> element.
2. Add a <FormUrls> child element to the <XmlDocument> element from Step 1.
3. Add one or more of the following child elements to the <FormUrls> element from Step 2:
    - **An <Edit> child element.** You must specify the URL to your custom edit list item form within the opening and closing tags of this child element.
    - **A <Display> child element.** You must specify the URL to your custom view list item form within the opening and closing tags of this child element.
    - **A <New> child element.** You must specify the URL to your custom new list item form within the opening and closing tags of this child element.

In this case, you're only interested in adding support for a custom edit list item or task form. As such, the <FormUrls> element only contains the <Edit> child element to provide a reference to the ManagerContentTypeEditTaskForm.aspx application page.

Note that when you update a site content type, the update does not affect the list content types that were provisioned from the site content type. You have to either explicitly push the changes down to these list content types or remove these list content types from their lists and add the site content type back in these lists. This is because when you add a site content type to a list, SharePoint adds a local copy of the site content type definition to the list. This local copy is known as a list content type. As such changes made to a site content type do not affect the list content types provisioned from it.

After propagating the changes made to the ManagerContentType site content type to the list content type provisioned from it, go ahead and create a task with the ManagerContentType type. Select Edit Item. SharePoint should direct you to the ManagerContentTypeEditTaskForm.aspx application page as shown in Figure 6-11.

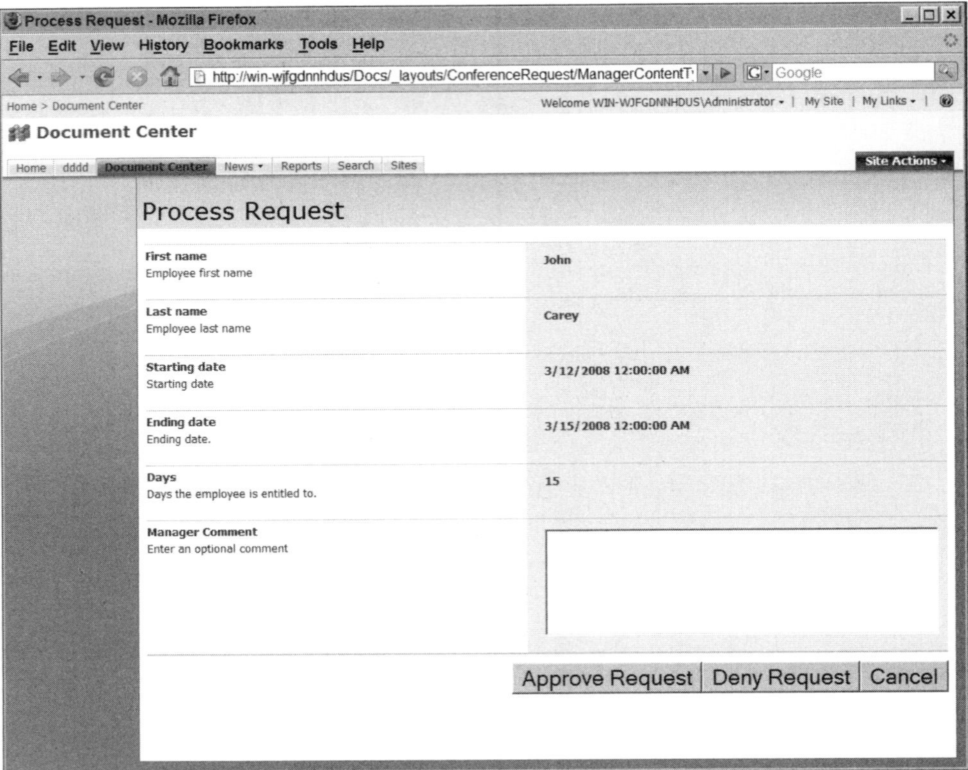

Figure 6-11: Your custom task edit form

Summary

This chapter provided an in-depth coverage of site columns and site content types and showed you how to implement your own custom site columns and site content types and deploy them to SharePoint. The next chapter moves on to the next SharePoint abstraction known as site definitions.

7

Site Definitions and Site Provisioning Providers

This chapter dives into site definitions and site provisioning providers and uses examples to show you how to implement your own custom site definitions and site provisioning providers.

Site Definitions

A site definition contains zero or more site definition configurations from which SharePoint sites are provisioned. In other words, a site definition configuration acts as a template from which sites are provisioned.

Take these steps to implement and to deploy a site definition:

1. Copy the CAML schema files to the following folder if you haven't already done it so you can take full advantage of the Visual Studio IntelliSense support when you're writing the CAML that defines your custom site definition:

```
Local_Drive:\Program Files\Microsoft Visual Studio 9.0\Xml\Schemas
```

   These CAML schema files define the schema types that belong to the http://schemas.microsoft.com/sharepoint/ namespace.

2. Launch Visual Studio 2008 and create a Class Library project.
3. Add an XML file named onet.xml to the Class Library project from Step 2.
4. Add an XML file named WebTemp*UniqueString*.xml to the Class Library project from Step 2 where UniqueString must be a unique string. In this case, name this file WebTempMyWebTemp.xml.
5. Add a text file named mybatchfile.bat to the Class Library project from Step 2.

6. Add a post-build event to Visual Studio as discussed in the previous chapter to have it execute the mybatchfile.bat file every time the project is built:

```
cd $(ProjectDir)
mybatchfile.bat
```

Next, implement the mybatchfile.bat file as shown in the following listing:

```
xcopy /e /y onet.xml "c:\program files\common files\microsoft shared\web server
extensions\12\Template\SiteTemplates\MySiteDefinition\XML\onet.xml"

xcopy /e /y WebTempMyWebTemp.xml "c:\program files\common files\microsoft shared\
web server extensions\12\Template\1033\XML\WebTempMyWebTemp.xml"

xcopy /e /y default.aspx "c:\program files\common files\microsoft shared\web server
extensions\12\Template\SiteTemplates\MySiteDefinition\default.aspx"

xcopy /e /y defaultdws.aspx "c:\program files\common files\microsoft shared\web
server extensions\12\Template\SiteTemplates\MySiteDefinition\defaultdws.aspx"

IISRESET
```

As you can see, this batch file takes these steps:

1. Creates a folder in the SiteTemplates folder on the file system of the front-end web server. This folder must have the same name as your custom site template. In this case, you'll implement a custom site template named MySiteDefinition.
2. Creates a folder named XML in the folder from Step 1. This folder must be named XML.
3. Copies the onet.xml file from this Class Library project to the XML folder from Step 2.
4. Copies the WebTemp*UniqueString*.xml file to the XML subfolder of the 1033 subfolder of the Template folder on the files system of the front-end web server. In this case, this will copy the WebTempMyWebTemp.xml file.
5. Copies an .aspx page named default.aspx to the folder from Step1.The default.aspx page is discussed later in this chapter.
6. Copies an .aspx page named defaultdws.aspx to the folder from Step1. The default.aspx page is discussed later in this chapter.
7. Runs IISRESET to reset IIS. This is necessary because IIS caches site definitions.

As you can see, every site definition consists of two XML files named onet.xml and WebTempUniqueString.xml. The following sections take a look at the implementation of these two files. As a best practice, you should copy the onet.xml and WebTemp*.xml files of a standard SharePoint site definition and modify these copies to meet your specific requirements. In this case you'll use the standard STS SharePoint site definition.

onet.xml

The onet.xml files of all standard SharePoint site definitions and custom site definitions are located in a folder named XML under a folder named after the site definition under the SiteTemplates folder on the file system of each front-end web server. Listing 7-1 presents the content of the onet.xml file of the standard STS SharePoint site definition. This file is located in the following folder on your machine:

```
Local_Drive:\Program Files\Common Files\microsoft shared\Web Server
Extensions\12\TEMPLATE\SiteTemplates\sts\xml
```

Now go ahead and copy the content of this file into the onet.xml file in this Class Library project.

Listing 7-1: The onet.xml file of the STS site definition

```
<?xml version="1.0" encoding="utf-8"?>
<Project
Title="$Resources:onet_TeamWebSite;"
Revision="2"
ListDir="$Resources:core,lists_Folder;"
xmlns:ows="Microsoft SharePoint">
  <NavBars>
    <NavBar Name="$Resources:core,category_Top;"
    Separator="&amp;nbsp;&amp;nbsp;&amp;nbsp;"
    Body="&lt;a ID='onettopnavbar#LABEL_ID#' href='#URL#'
          accesskey='J'&gt;#LABEL#&lt;/a&gt;" ID="1002" />
    <NavBar Name="$Resources:core,category_Documents;"
    Prefix="&lt;table border=0 cellpadding=4 cellspacing=0&gt;"
    Body="&lt;tr&gt;&lt;td&gt;&lt;table border=0 cellpadding=0
          cellspacing=0&gt;&lt;tr&gt;&lt;td&gt;&lt;img
          src='/_layouts/images/blank.gif' ID='100' alt=''
          border=0&gt;&amp;nbsp;&lt;/td&gt;&lt;td valign=top&gt;&lt;a
          ID=onetleftnavbar#LABEL_ID#
          href='#URL#'&gt;#LABEL#&lt;/td&gt;&lt;/tr&gt;&lt;/table&gt;&lt;
                /td&gt;&lt;/tr&gt;"
    Suffix="&lt;/table&gt;" ID="1004" />
    <NavBar Name="$Resources:core,category_Lists;"
    Prefix="&lt;table border=0 cellpadding=4 cellspacing=0&gt;"
    Body="&lt;tr&gt;&lt;td&gt;&lt;table border=0 cellpadding=0
          cellspacing=0&gt;&lt;tr&gt;&lt;td&gt;&lt;img
          src='/_layouts/images/blank.gif' ID='100' alt=''
          border=0&gt;&amp;nbsp;&lt;/td&gt;&lt;td valign=top&gt;&lt;a
          ID=onetleftnavbar#LABEL_ID#
          href='#URL#'&gt;#LABEL#&lt;/td&gt;&lt;/tr&gt;&lt;
          /table&gt;&lt;/td&gt;&lt;/tr&gt;"
    Suffix="&lt;/table&gt;" ID="1003" />
    <NavBar Name="$Resources:core,category_Discussions;"
    Prefix="&lt;table border=0 cellpadding=4 cellspacing=0&gt;"
    Body="&lt;tr&gt;&lt;td&gt;&lt;table border=0 cellpadding=0
          cellspacing=0&gt;&lt;tr&gt;&lt;td&gt;&lt;img
          src='/_layouts/images/blank.gif' ID='100' alt=''
          border=0&gt;&amp;nbsp;&lt;/td&gt;&lt;td valign=top&gt;&lt;a
```

(continued)

Listing 7-2 *(continued)*

```
            ID=onetleftnavbar#LABEL_ID#
            href='#URL#'&gt;#LABEL#&lt;/td&gt;&lt;/tr&gt;&lt;
            /table&gt;&lt;/td&gt;&lt;/tr&gt;"
      Suffix="&lt;/table&gt;" ID="1006" />
      <NavBar Name="$Resources:core,category_Sites;"
      Prefix="&lt;table border=0 cellpadding=4 cellspacing=0&gt;"
      Body="&lt;tr&gt;&lt;td&gt;&lt;table border=0 cellpadding=0
            cellspacing=0&gt;&lt;tr&gt;&lt;td&gt;&lt;img
            src='/_layouts/images/blank.gif' ID='100' alt=''
            border=0&gt;&amp;nbsp;&lt;/td&gt;&lt;td valign=top&gt;&lt;a
            ID=onetleftnavbar#LABEL_ID#
             href='#URL#'&gt;#LABEL#&lt;/td&gt;&lt;/tr&gt;&lt;
            /table&gt;&lt;/td&gt;&lt;/tr&gt;"
      Suffix="&lt;/table&gt;" ID="1026" />
      <NavBar Name="$Resources:core,category_People;"
      Prefix="&lt;table border=0 cellpadding=4 cellspacing=0&gt;"
      Body="&lt;tr&gt;&lt;td&gt;&lt;table border=0 cellpadding=0
            cellspacing=0&gt;&lt;tr&gt;&lt;td&gt;&lt;img
            src='/_layouts/images/blank.gif' ID='100' alt=''
            border=0&gt;&amp;nbsp;&lt;/td&gt;&lt;td valign=top&gt;&lt;a
            ID=onetleftnavbar#LABEL_ID#
            href='#URL#'&gt;#LABEL#&lt;/td&gt;&lt;/tr&gt;&lt;
            /table&gt;&lt;/td&gt;&lt;/tr&gt;"
      Suffix="&lt;/table&gt;" ID="1027" />
    </NavBars>
    <ListTemplates>
    </ListTemplates>
    <DocumentTemplates>
    </DocumentTemplates>
    <Configurations>
      <Configuration ID="-1" Name="NewWeb" />
      <Configuration ID="0" Name="Default">
        <Lists>
          <List FeatureId="00BFEA71-E717-4E80-AA17-D0C71B360101" Type="101"
          Title="$Resources:core,shareddocuments_Title;"
          Url="$Resources:core,shareddocuments_Folder;"
          QuickLaunchUrl="$Resources:core,shareddocuments_Folder;
                          /Forms/AllItems.aspx" />
          <List FeatureId="00BFEA71-6A49-43FA-B535-D15C05500108" Type="108"
          Title="$Resources:core,discussions_Title;"
          Url="$Resources:core,lists_Folder;/$Resources:core,discussions_Folder;"
          QuickLaunchUrl="$Resources:core,lists_Folder;/
                          $Resources:core,discussions_Folder;/AllItems.aspx"
          EmailAlias="$Resources:core,discussions_EmailAlias;" />
          <List FeatureId="00BFEA71-D1CE-42de-9C63-A44004CE0104" Type="104"
          Title="$Resources:core,announceList;"
          Url="$Resources:core,lists_Folder;/$Resources:core,announce_Folder;">
            <Data>
              <Rows>
                <Row>
                  <Field Name="Title">$Resources:onetid11;</Field>
                  <Field Name="Body">$Resources:onetid12;</Field>
                  <Field Name="Expires">&lt;ows:TodayISO/&gt;</Field>
```

```
          </Row>
        </Rows>
      </Data>
    </List>
    <List FeatureId="00BFEA71-2062-426C-90BF-714C59600103" Type="103"
    Title="$Resources:core,linksList;"
    Url="$Resources:core,lists_Folder;/$Resources:core,links_Folder;" />
    <List FeatureId="00BFEA71-EC85-4903-972D-EBE475780106" Type="106"
    Title="$Resources:core,calendarList;"
    Url="$Resources:core,lists_Folder;/$Resources:core,calendar_Folder;"
    QuickLaunchUrl="$Resources:core,lists_Folder;/
                    $Resources:core,calendar_Folder;/Calendar.aspx"
    EmailAlias="$Resources:core,calendar_EmailAlias;" />
    <List FeatureId="00BFEA71-A83E-497E-9BA0-7A5C597D0107" Type="107"
    Title="$Resources:core,taskList;"
    Url="$Resources:core,lists_Folder;/$Resources:core,tasks_Folder;"
    QuickLaunchUrl="$Resources:core,lists_Folder;/
                    $Resources:core,tasks_Folder;/AllItems.aspx" />
  </Lists>
  <Modules>
    <Module Name="Default" />
  </Modules>
  <SiteFeatures>
    <!-- BasicWebParts Feature -->
    <Feature ID="00BFEA71-1C5E-4A24-B310-BA51C3EB7A57" />
    <!-- Three-state Workflow Feature -->
    <Feature ID="FDE5D850-671E-4143-950A-87B473922DC7" />
  </SiteFeatures>
  <WebFeatures>
    <Feature ID="00BFEA71-4EA5-48D4-A4AD-7EA5C011ABE5" />
    <!-- TeamCollab Feature -->
    <Feature ID="F41CC668-37E5-4743-B4A8-74D1DB3FD8A4" />
    <!-- MobilityRedirect -->
  </WebFeatures>
</Configuration>
<Configuration ID="1" Name="Blank">
  <Lists />
  <Modules>
    <Module Name="DefaultBlank" />
  </Modules>
  <SiteFeatures>
    <!-- BasicWebParts Feature -->
    <Feature ID="00BFEA71-1C5E-4A24-B310-BA51C3EB7A57" />
    <!-- Three-state Workflow Feature -->
    <Feature ID="FDE5D850-671E-4143-950A-87B473922DC7" />
  </SiteFeatures>
  <WebFeatures>
    <Feature ID="00BFEA71-4EA5-48D4-A4AD-7EA5C011ABE5" />
    <!-- TeamCollab Feature -->
    <Feature ID="F41CC668-37E5-4743-B4A8-74D1DB3FD8A4" />
    <!-- MobilityRedirect -->
  </WebFeatures>
</Configuration>
```

(continued)

Listing 5-2 *(continued)*

```
    <Configuration ID="2" Name="DWS">
      <Lists>
        <List FeatureId="00BFEA71-E717-4E80-AA17-D0C71B360101" Type="101"
        Title="$Resources:core,shareddocuments_Title;"
        Url="$Resources:core,shareddocuments_Folder;" />
        <List FeatureId="00BFEA71-6A49-43FA-B535-D15C05500108" Type="108"
        Title="$Resources:core,discussions_Title;"
        Url="$Resources:core,lists_Folder;/$Resources:core,discussions_Folder;"
        QuickLaunchUrl="$Resources:core,lists_Folder;/
                        $Resources:core,discussions_Folder;" />
        <List FeatureId="00BFEA71-D1CE-42de-9C63-A44004CE0104" Type="104"
        Title="$Resources:core,announceList;"
        Url="$Resources:core,lists_Folder;/$Resources:core,announce_Folder;">
          <Data>
            <Rows>
              <Row>
                <Field Name="Title">$Resources:onetid11;</Field>
                <Field Name="Body">$Resources:onetid12;</Field>
                <Field Name="Expires">&lt;ows:TodayISO/&gt;</Field>
              </Row>
            </Rows>
          </Data>
        </List>
        <List FeatureId="00BFEA71-2062-426C-90BF-714C59600103" Type="103"
        Title="$Resources:core,linksList;"
        Url="$Resources:core,lists_Folder;/$Resources:core,links_Folder;" />
        <List FeatureId="00BFEA71-EC85-4903-972D-EBE475780106" Type="106"
        Title="$Resources:core,calendarList;"
        Url="$Resources:core,lists_Folder;/$Resources:core,calendar_Folder;"
        QuickLaunchUrl="$Resources:core,lists_Folder;/
                        $Resources:core,calendar_Folder;/Calendar.aspx" />
        <List FeatureId="00BFEA71-A83E-497E-9BA0-7A5C597D0107" Type="107"
        Title="$Resources:core,taskList;"
        Url="$Resources:core,lists_Folder;/$Resources:core,tasks_Folder;" />
      </Lists>
      <Modules>
        <Module Name="DWS" />
      </Modules>
      <SiteFeatures>
        <!-- BasicWebParts Feature -->
        <Feature ID="00BFEA71-1C5E-4A24-B310-BA51C3EB7A57" />
        <!-- Three-state Workflow Feature -->
        <Feature ID="FDE5D850-671E-4143-950A-87B473922DC7" />
      </SiteFeatures>
      <WebFeatures>
        <Feature ID="00BFEA71-4EA5-48D4-A4AD-7EA5C011ABE5" />
        <!-- TeamCollab Feature -->
        <Feature ID="F41CC668-37E5-4743-B4A8-74D1DB3FD8A4" />
        <!-- MobilityRedirect -->
      </WebFeatures>
    </Configuration>
```

```
    </Configurations>
    <Modules>
      <Module Name="Default" Url="" Path="">
        <File Url="default.aspx" NavBarHome="True">
          <View
          List="$Resources:core,lists_Folder;/$Resources:core,announce_Folder;"
          BaseViewID="0" WebPartZoneID="Left" />
          <View
          List="$Resources:core,lists_Folder;/$Resources:core,calendar_Folder;"
          BaseViewID="0" RecurrenceRowset="TRUE" WebPartZoneID="Left"
          WebPartOrder="2" />
          <AllUsersWebPart WebPartZoneID="Right" WebPartOrder="1">
            <![CDATA[
              <WebPart xmlns="http://schemas.microsoft.com/WebPart/v2"
              xmlns:iwp="http://schemas.microsoft.com/WebPart/v2/Image">
                <Assembly>
                  Microsoft.SharePoint, Version=12.0.0.0, Culture=neutral,
                  PublicKeyToken=71e9bce111e9429c
                </Assembly>
                <TypeName>Microsoft.SharePoint.WebPartPages.ImageWebPart</TypeName>
                <FrameType>None</FrameType>
                <Title>$Resources:wp_SiteImage;</Title>
                <iwp:ImageLink>/_layouts/images/homepage.gif</iwp:ImageLink>
                <iwp:AlternativeText>
                  $Resources:core,sitelogo_wss;
                </iwp:AlternativeText>
              </WebPart>
            ]]>
          </AllUsersWebPart>
          <View
          List="$Resources:core,lists_Folder;/$Resources:core,links_Folder;"
          BaseViewID="0" WebPartZoneID="Right" WebPartOrder="2" />
          <NavBarPage Name="$Resources:core,nav_Home;" ID="1002" Position="Start" />
          <NavBarPage Name="$Resources:core,nav_Home;" ID="0" Position="Start" />
        </File>
      </Module>
      <Module Name="DefaultBlank" Url="" Path="">
        <File Url="default.aspx" NavBarHome="True" Type="Ghostable">
          <AllUsersWebPart WebPartZoneID="Right" WebPartOrder="1">
            <![CDATA[
              <WebPart xmlns="http://schemas.microsoft.com/WebPart/v2"
              xmlns:iwp="http://schemas.microsoft.com/WebPart/v2/Image">
                <Assembly>
                  Microsoft.SharePoint, Version=12.0.0.0, Culture=neutral,
                  PublicKeyToken=71e9bce111e9429c
                </Assembly>
                <TypeName>Microsoft.SharePoint.WebPartPages.ImageWebPart</TypeName>
                <FrameType>None</FrameType>
                <Title>$Resources:wp_SiteImage;</Title>
                <iwp:ImageLink>/_layouts/images/homepage.gif</iwp:ImageLink>
                <iwp:AlternativeText>
                  $Resources:core,sitelogo_wss;
                </iwp:AlternativeText>
              </WebPart>
```

(continued)

Listing 5-2 *(continued)*

```
        ]]>
      </AllUsersWebPart>
      <NavBarPage Name="$Resources:core,nav_Home;" ID="1002" Position="Start" />
      <NavBarPage Name="$Resources:core,nav_Home;" ID="0" Position="Start" />
    </File>
  </Module>
  <Module Name="DWS" Url="">
    <File Url="defaultdws.aspx" Name="default.aspx">
      <View
      List="$Resources:core,lists_Folder;/$Resources:core,announce_Folder;"
      BaseViewID="3" WebPartZoneID="Top" />
      <View
      List="$Resources:core,lists_Folder;/$Resources:core,links_Folder;"
      BaseViewID="3" WebPartZoneID="Right" WebPartOrder="2" />
      <View
      List="$Resources:core,shareddocuments_Folder;" BaseViewID="6"
      WebPartZoneID="Left" />
      <View
      List="$Resources:core,lists_Folder;/$Resources:core,tasks_Folder;"
      BaseViewID="7" WebPartZoneID="Left" WebPartOrder="2" />
      <AllUsersWebPart WebPartZoneID="Right" WebPartOrder="1">
        <![CDATA[
          <WebPart xmlns="http://schemas.microsoft.com/WebPart/v2">
            <Assembly>
              Microsoft.SharePoint, Version=12.0.0.0, Culture=neutral,
              PublicKeyToken=71e9bce111e9429c
            </Assembly>
            <TypeName>Microsoft.SharePoint.WebPartPages.MembersWebPart</TypeName>
            <Title>$Resources:wp_Members;</Title>
            <Description>$Resources:wp_Members_Desc;</Description>
            <FrameType>Standard</FrameType>
            <IsVisible>true</IsVisible>
          </WebPart>
        ]]>
      </AllUsersWebPart>
      <NavBarPage Name="$Resources:core,nav_Home;" ID="1002" Position="Start" />
      <NavBarPage Name="$Resources:core,nav_Home;" ID="0" Position="Start" />
    </File>
  </Module>
</Modules>
<ServerEmailFooter>$Resources:ServerEmailFooter;</ServerEmailFooter>
</Project>
```

As Listing 7-1 shows, the document element of a onet.xml file is an element named <Project>, which features the following important attributes:

- **Title.** You can use this attribute to specify a title for your site definition. SharePoint displays this title in the Template Selection section of the New SharePoint Site web page as shown in Figure 7-1. Note that Listing 7-1 uses a resource reference to pull the localized title from the localized resource file as opposed to hard-coding this title:

```
Title="$Resources:onet_TeamWebSite;"
```

When SharePoint parses a onet.xml file, it replaces resource references with the actual resource values, which is the string "Team Site" in this case.

If you provision a site from a site definition and visit the following URL, you should see the localized site definition:

```
http://SiteURL/_vti_bin/owssvr.dll?Cmd=GetProjSchema
```

The SiteURL is the URL of the site that was provisioned from the site definition. IIS caches the localized site definition of each site definition for the lifetime of the web application. The preceding URL basically accesses this cached localized site definition.

- ❑ **ListDir.** You can use this attribute to specify the folder for the lists in the sites provisioned from this site definition. Again, note that Listing 7-1 uses a resource reference to pull the folder name from the resource file as opposed to hard-coding it:

```
ListDir="$Resources:core,lists_Folder;"
xmlsn:ows="Microsoft SharePoint"
```

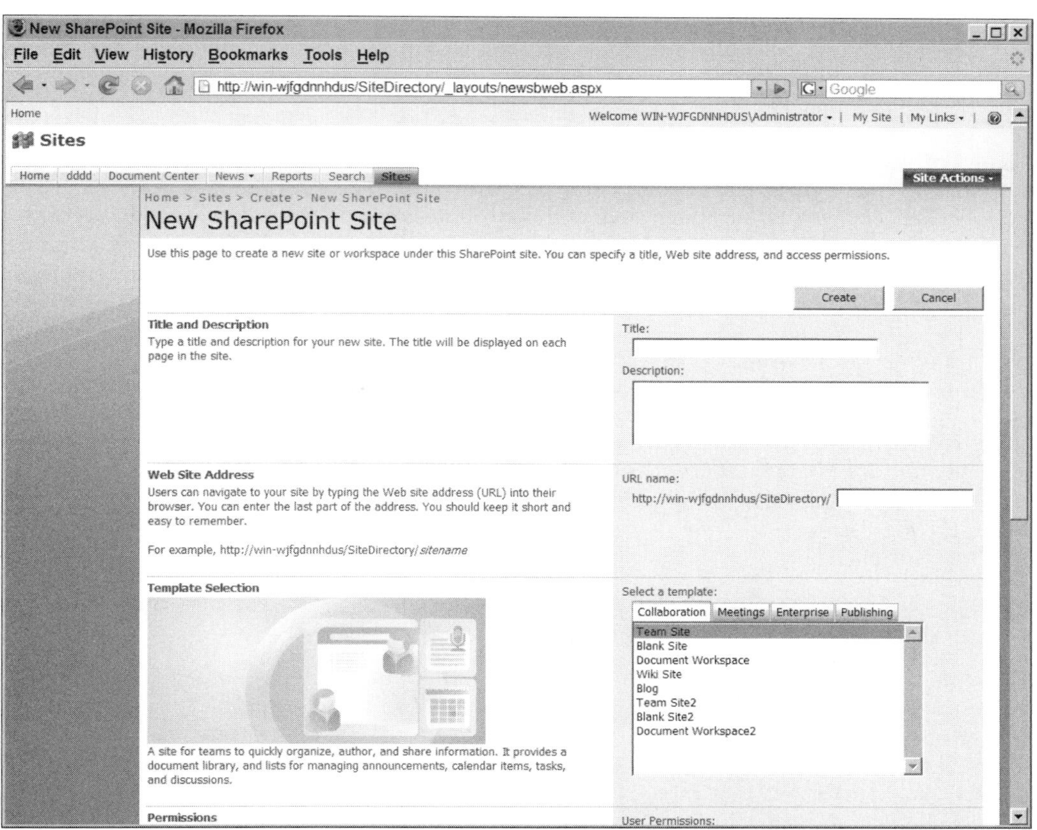

Figure 7-1: The New SharePoint Site page

As Listing 7-1 shows, the <Project> document element supports the following main child elements:

- **<NavBars>.** This child element defines the navigation bars for the site definition.
- **<Configurations>.** This child element defines different configurations of the site definition. It is these configurations that act as templates from which sites are provisioned. That is, the Template Selection section of the New SharePoint Site web page shown in Figure 7-1 displays these configurations.
- **<Modules>.** This child element defines the modules of the site definition. A module is used to provision one or more files into a site upon site creation.

These child elements are discussed in the following sections.

<NavBars>

As Listing 7-1 shows, <NavBars> contains child elements named <NavBar>. As the name suggests, a <NavBar> element defines a navigation bar in a site provisioned from the site definition. The <NavBar> element supports the following attributes:

- **Name.** Use this attribute to specify the text that appears in the heading of the navigation bar. Note that Listing 7-1 uses a resource reference to pull this text from a localized resource file:

```
Name="$Resources:core,category_Documents;"
```

- **Prefix.** Use this attribute to specify the opening tag(s) of the containing HTML element(s) of the HTML that renders the navigation bar. The containing HTML element is normally a <table> HTML element. As such, the value of this attribute is normally the XML-encoded version of the string "<table . . . >". You must XML-encode this HTML because the value of this attribute, like the value of any other XML attribute, must a be valid XML attribute value. More specifically, you must replace the "<" and ">" characters with "<" and ">" strings:

```
Prefix="&lt;table border=0 cellpadding=4 cellspacing=0&gt;"
```

- **Body.** Use this attribute to specify the HTML that goes within the containing HTML element(s) of the HTML that renders the navigation bar. Every navigation bar consists of zero or more hyperlinks. SharePoint uses the value of this attribute to render each hyperlink. In the case of Listing 7-1, the value of the Body attribute is set to the XML-encoded version of the following HTML:

```
<tr>
  <td>
    <table border="0" cellpadding="0" cellspacing="0">
      <tr>
        <td>
          <img src="/_layouts/images/blank.gif" id="100" alt="" border="0" /> 
        </td>
        <td valign="top">
          <a href="#URL">#LABEL#</a>
```

```
          </td>
        </tr>
      </table>
    </td>
  </tr>
```

When SharePoint parses the value of the Body attribute, it replaces the #URL# and #LABEL# with the target URL and label of the respective hyperlink. Every hyperlink in a navigation bar is represented by a <NavBarLink> element, which is added as the child element of the <NavBar> element that represents the navigation bar. As you can see, none of the navigation bars defined in Listing 7-1 contain <NavBarLink> child elements. However, you can add <NavBarLink> elements in your own custom site definitions. Here is an example:

```
<NavBar Name="$Resources:core,category_Documents;"
Prefix="&lt;table border='0' cellpadding='4' cellspacing=0&gt;"
Body="&lt;tr&gt;&lt;td&gt;&lt;table border='0' cellpadding='0'
      cellspacing='0'&gt;&lt;tr&gt;&lt;td&gt;&lt;img
      src='/_layouts/images/blank.gif' ID='100' alt=''
      border='0'&gt;&amp;nbsp;&lt;/td&gt;&lt;td valign=top&gt;&lt;a
      ID=onetleftnavbar#LABEL_ID#
      href='#URL#'&gt;#LABEL#&lt;/td&gt;&lt;/tr&gt;&lt;/table&gt;&lt;
            /td&gt;&lt;/tr&gt;"
Suffix="&lt;/table&gt;" ID="1004">
  <NavBarLink Name="MyHyperLink1" Url="SiteRelativeURL1" />
  <NavBarLink Name="MyHyperLink2" Url="SiteRelativeURL2" />
  <NavBarLink Name="MyHyperLink3" Url="SiteRelativeURL3" />
</NavBar>
```

As you can see, the <NavBarLink> element supports the following two attributes:

- ❑ **Name.** Use this attribute to specify the label of the hyperlink. SharePoint replaces the #LABEL# in the Body attribute with this value when it is using the HTML specified in the Body attribute to render this hyperlink.
- ❑ **Url.** Use this attribute to specify the site-relative target URL of the hyperlink. SharePoint replaces the #URL# in the Body attribute with this value when it is using the HTML specified in the Body attribute to render this hyperlink. Two examples of a site-relative URL are _layouts/MyApplicationPage.aspx and Lists/MyList/AllItems.aspx.

❑ **Suffix.** Use this attribute to specify the XML-encoded version of the closing tag(s) of the containing HTML element(s), which is normally the XML-encoded version of "</table>":

```
Suffix="&lt;/table&gt;"
```

In summary, add a <NavBar> child element to the <NavBars> element of the onet.xml file of a site definition to add a new navigation bar to sites provisioned from the site definition. The Prefix, Body, and Suffix attributes of this <NavBar> child element must tell SharePoint how to render the navigation bar and its containing hyperlinks, as discussed earlier.

<Configurations>

Sites are not provisioned from the site definition itself. Instead they're provisioned from a site definition configuration specified in the site definition. A site definition can contain zero or more site definition configurations. A site definition that does not contain a site definition configuration is an abstract site definition from which no site can be provisioned.

SharePoint comes with a site definition named Global. The onet.xml file of every site definition is located in a folder named XML in a subfolder with the same name as the site definition in the following folder on the file system of each front-end web server:

```
Local_Drive:\Program Files\Common Files\microsoft shared\Web Server
Extensions\12\TEMPLATE\SiteTemplates
```

The only exception to this rule is the Global site definition whose onet.xml file is located in a folder named XML in a subfolder with the same name as the site definition (Global) in the following folder on the file system of each front-end web server:

```
Local_Drive:\Program Files\Common Files\microsoft shared\Web Server
Extensions\12\TEMPLATE\Global
```

Listing 7-2 presents the portion of the onet.xml file of the Global site definition.

Listing 7-2: The portion of the onet.xml file of the Global site definition

```
<?xml version="1.0" encoding="utf-8"?>
<Project Title="$Resources:onet_TeamWebSite;" ListDir="$Resources:core,lists_
Folder;"
xmlns:ows="Microsoft SharePoint">
  <NavBars>
  </NavBars>
  <ListTemplates>
    <ListTemplate Name="mplib" DisplayName="$Resources:MasterPageGallery;"
    Description="$Resources:global_onet_mplib_desc;" SetupPath="global\lists\mplib"
    Type="116" BaseType="1" Path="GLOBAL" Hidden="TRUE" HiddenList="TRUE"
    NoCrawl="TRUE" Unique="TRUE" Catalog="TRUE" OnQuickLaunch="FALSE"
    SecurityBits="11" AllowDeletion="FALSE" AllowEveryoneViewItems="TRUE"
    Image="/_layouts/images/itdl.gif" AlwaysIncludeContent="TRUE"
    DocumentTemplate="100" />

    <ListTemplate Name="users" DisplayName="$Resources:userinfo_schema_listtitle;"
    Description="$Resources:global_onet_userinfo_desc;"
    SetupPath="global\lists\users" Type="112" BaseType="0" Hidden="TRUE"
    Unique="TRUE" RootWebOnly="TRUE" Catalog="TRUE" DontSaveInTemplate="TRUE"
    HiddenList="TRUE" OnQuickLaunch="FALSE" SecurityBits="11" AllowDeletion="FALSE"
    AllowEveryoneViewItems="TRUE" CacheSchema="TRUE"
    Image="/_layouts/images/users.gif" />

    <ListTemplate Name="webtemp"
    DisplayName="$Resources:core,sitetemplategalleryList;"
    Description="$Resources:core,sitetemplategalleryList_Desc;"
    SetupPath="global\lists\webtemp" Type="111" BaseType="1" Hidden="TRUE"
```

```
    FolderCreation="FALSE" DontSaveInTemplate="TRUE" HiddenList="TRUE"
    NoCrawl="TRUE" Unique="TRUE" RootWebOnly="TRUE" Catalog="TRUE"
    OnQuickLaunch="FALSE" SecurityBits="11" AllowDeletion="FALSE"
    Image="/_layouts/images/itdl.gif" DocumentTemplate="100" />

    <ListTemplate Name="wplib" DisplayName="$Resources:core,webpartgalleryList;"
    Description="$Resources:core,webpartgalleryList_Desc;"
    SetupPath="global\lists\wplib" Type="113" BaseType="1" Hidden="TRUE"
    HiddenList="TRUE" NoCrawl="TRUE" FolderCreation="FALSE" Unique="TRUE"
    RootWebOnly="TRUE" Catalog="TRUE" OnQuickLaunch="FALSE" SecurityBits="11"
    AllowDeletion="FALSE" Image="/_layouts/images/itdl.gif"
    DontSaveInTemplate="TRUE" DocumentTemplate="100" />

    <ListTemplate Name="listtemp"
    DisplayName="$Resources:core,listtemplategalleryList;"
    Description="$Resources:core,listtemplategalleryList_Desc;"
    SetupPath="global\lists\listtemp" Type="114" BaseType="1" Hidden="TRUE"
    HiddenList="TRUE" NoCrawl="TRUE" FolderCreation="FALSE" Unique="TRUE"
    RootWebOnly="TRUE" Catalog="TRUE" OnQuickLaunch="FALSE" SecurityBits="11"
    AllowDeletion="FALSE" Image="/_layouts/images/itdl.gif"
    DontSaveInTemplate="TRUE" DocumentTemplate="100" />
  </ListTemplates>

  <BaseTypes>
    <BaseType Title="Generic List" Image="/_layouts/images/itgen.gif" Type="0">
      <MetaData>
        <Fields>
          ...
        </Fields>
      </MetaData>
    </BaseType>

    <BaseType Title="Document Library" Image="/_layouts/images/itdl.gif" Type="1">
      <MetaData>
        <Fields>
          ...
        </Fields>
      </MetaData>
    </BaseType>

    <BaseType Title="Discussion Forum" Image="/_layouts/images/itdisc.gif"
    Type="3">
      <MetaData>
        <Fields>
          ...
        </Fields>
      </MetaData>
    </BaseType>

    <BaseType Title="Vote or Survey" Image="/_layouts/images/itsurvey.gif"
    Type="4">
      <MetaData>
```

(continued)

Listing 7-2 *(continued)*

```
          <Fields>
            ...
          </Fields>
        </MetaData>
      </BaseType>

      <BaseType Title="Issues List" Image="/_layouts/images/itgen.gif" Type="5">
        <MetaData>
          <Fields>
            ...
          </Fields>
        </MetaData>
      </BaseType>

    </BaseTypes>

    <Configurations>
      <Configuration ID="0" Name="Default"
      MasterUrl="_catalogs/masterpage/default.master">
        <SiteFeatures>
          <Feature ID="CA7BD552-10B1-4563-85B9-5ED1D39C962A" />
          <!--Fields-->
          <Feature ID="695B6570-A48B-4A8E-8EA5-26EA7FC1D162" />
          <!--Ctypes-->
        </SiteFeatures>
        <WebFeatures>
        </WebFeatures>
        <Lists>
          <List Title="$Resources:core,MasterPageGallery;" Type="116"
          Url="_catalogs/masterpage" />
          <List Title="$Resources:core,userinfo_schema_listtitle;" Type="112"
          Url="_catalogs/users" RootWebOnly="TRUE" />
          <List Title="$Resources:core,sitetemplategalleryList;" Type="111"
          Url="_catalogs/wt" RootWebOnly="TRUE" />
          <List Type="113" Title="$Resources:core,webpartgalleryList;"
          Url="_catalogs/wp" RootWebOnly="TRUE" />
          <List Type="114" Title="$Resources:core,listtemplategalleryList;"
          Url="_catalogs/lt" RootWebOnly="TRUE" />
        </Lists>
        <Modules>
          <Module Name="DefaultMasterPage" />
        </Modules>
      </Configuration>
    </Configurations>
    <Modules>
      <Module Name="DefaultMasterPage" List="116" Url="_catalogs/masterpage"
      RootWebOnly="FALSE">
        <File Url="default.master" Type="GhostableInLibrary"
        IgnoreIfAlreadyExists="TRUE" />
      </Module>
    </Modules>
  </Project>
```

As you can see from Listing 7-2, the Global site definition takes these steps:

- It defines the following five base list types from which all other list types in SharePoint inherit:
  - Generic List (Type=0)
  - Document Library (Type=1)
  - Discussion Forum (Type=2)
  - Vote or Survey (Type=3)
  - Issues List (Type=4)

  When you provision a site from any standard SharePoint or custom site definition, SharePoint automatically adds these base list types to the site. Thanks to the Global site definition, the onet .xml file of your custom site definition does not have to (in fact, it mustn't) define these five base types.
- It defines a site definition configuration named Default. When you provision a site from any standard SharePoint or custom site definition, SharePoint automatically provisions the site from this configuration as well as the configuration of the site definition from which the site is being provisioned. As Listing 7-2 shows, the Default site definition configuration performs these tasks:
  - It activates the feature that defines standard SharePoint site columns:

```
<SiteFeatures>
  <Feature ID="CA7BD552-10B1-4563-85B9-5ED1D39C962A" />
  <!--Fields-->
  <Feature ID="695B6570-A48B-4A8E-8EA5-26EA7FC1D162" />
  <!--Ctypes-->
</SiteFeatures>
```

  This feature is named fields, and like any other feature, it is located in a folder with the same name as the feature (fields in this case) in the following folder:

```
C:\Program Files\Common Files\microsoft shared\Web Server Extensions\12\TEMPLATE\
FEATURES
```

  These site columns are defined in an element manifest file named fieldswss.xml, which is referenced from this feature.

  - It activates the feature that defines standard SharePoint site content types:

```
<SiteFeatures>
  <Feature ID="CA7BD552-10B1-4563-85B9-5ED1D39C962A" />
  <!--Fields-->
  <Feature ID="695B6570-A48B-4A8E-8EA5-26EA7FC1D162" />
  <!--Ctypes-->
</SiteFeatures>
```

- It provisions instances of the Master Page Gallery, User Information List, Site Template Gallery, Web Part Gallery, and List Template Gallery list types. Note that the RootWebOnly attributes on the <List> elements that provision the latter four list types are set to TRUE. This means that the instances of the latter four list types are provisioned only if the site being provisioned is a top-level site of the current site collection. In other words, every site collection can have single instances of the User Information List, Site Template Gallery, Web Part Gallery, and List Template Gallery list types.

```
<Lists>
  <List Title="$Resources:core,MasterPageGallery;" Type="116"
  Url="_catalogs/masterpage" />
  <List Title="$Resources:core,userinfo_schema_listtitle;" Type="112"
  Url="_catalogs/users" RootWebOnly="TRUE" />
  <List Title="$Resources:core,sitetemplategalleryList;" Type="111"
  Url="_catalogs/wt" RootWebOnly="TRUE" />
  <List Type="113" Title="$Resources:core,webpartgalleryList;"
  Url="_catalogs/wp" RootWebOnly="TRUE" />
  <List Type="114" Title="$Resources:core,listtemplategalleryList;"
  Url="_catalogs/lt" RootWebOnly="TRUE" />
</Lists>
```

- It provisions the file that the module named DefaultMasterPage represents:

```
<Modules>
  <Module Name="DefaultMasterPage" />
</Modules>
```

This module is defined outside of this site definition configuration as shown in the following excerpt from Listing 7-2:

```
<Modules>
  <Module Name="DefaultMasterPage" List="116" Url="_catalogs/masterpage"
  RootWebOnly="FALSE">
    <File Url="default.master" Type="GhostableInLibrary"
    IgnoreIfAlreadyExists="TRUE" />
  </Module>
</Modules>
```

You must define the modules of your site definition outside of your site definition's configurations in an element named <Modules> and reference them from these configurations. This enables you to define a module once and reference it from different configurations.

Each module is defined by a <Module> child element inside the <Modules> element. In general, a <Module> is used to provision one or more files where each file is represented by a <File> child element inside the <Module> element.

The <Module> element supports an attribute named Name, which must be set to a value that uniquely identifies the module from other modules defined within the site definition. Site definition configurations use the value of this attribute to reference the module.

The <Module> element also supports an attribute named List. Set this attribute to the integer identifier of a list type. This attribute is applicable in cases such as Listing 7-2 where the <Module> element is used to provision a file into a list. The List attribute basically specifies the list type of the list. In the case of Listing 7-2, the List attribute is set to 116 because this <Module> element is used to provision an instance of the default.master file into the Master Page Gallery of the site being provisioned. The integer identifier of the master page gallery list type is 116.

The <Module> element also features an attribute named Url, which is used to specify the site-relative URL for the file being provisioned. In the case of Listing 7-2, the file being provisioned is an instance of the default.master master page, which is being provisioned into the Master Page Gallery list and the site-relative URL of the Master Page Gallery list is _catalogs/masterpage.

The <Module> element supports a Boolean attribute named RootWebOnly, which specifies whether the file should be provisioned only when the site being provisioned is a top-level site in the current site collection. In the case of Listing 7-2, this attribute is set to *false* because each site has its own Master Page Gallery and therefore an instance of the default.master master page must be provisioned into the site's Master Page Gallery regardless of whether the site being provisioned is a top-level site.

The <Module> element supports one or more <File> child elements where each <File> element provisions a specific file. As such, a <Module> element represents provisioning of one or more files. In the case of Listing 7-2, the <Module> element contains a single <File> element. Therefore, this <Module> element provisions a single file.

The <File> element supports an attribute named Url, which determines the URL of the provisioned file with respect to the URL specified in the Url attribute on the <Module> element. Recall that the URL specified in the Url attribute on the <Module> element is site-relative and is set to _catalogs/masterpage, which is the site-relative URL of the Master Page Gallery. As such, the Url attribute on the <File> element specifies the URL of the provisioned file relative to the Master Page Gallery. Therefore the site-relative URL of the provisioned default.master master page becomes:

```
_catalogs/masterpage/default.master
```

The <File> element also features an attribute named Type, which is set to GhostableInLibrary in the case of Listing 7-2 because the default.master file is being provisioned into the Master Page Gallery, which is a document library.

As you can see, the Global site definition saves you from implementing the SharePoint components just discussed in your site definition. Now that you have a good understanding of the Global site definition and its role in site provisioning, let's get back to the discussion of the <Configurations> element of the onet.xml file of a site definition.

The <Configurations> element is where you define the configurations from which sites are provisioned. Each configuration is defined by a <Configuration> child element of this <Configurations> element. As Listing 7-1 shows, the <Configurations> element contains three main <Configuration> elements that define three site definition configurations from which sites can be provisioned.

The <Configuration> element features two important attributes named ID and Name, which must be set to an integer identifier and the name of the configuration. As Listing 7-1 shows, the STS site definition contains three configurations with the ID values of 0, 1, and 2, respectively, and with the Name attribute values of Default, Blank, and DWS.

The <Configuration> element supports the following child elements:

- **<Lists>.** This child element provisions instances of the specified list types upon site creation.
- **<Modules>.** This child element provisions instances of the specified files upon site creation. You saw an example of this in the discussion of the Global site definition.
- **<SiteFeatures>.** This element activates the specified site collection–level features upon site creation if the site being provisioned is a top-level site in the current site collection.
- **<WebFeatures>.** This element activates the specified site-level features upon site creation regardless of whether the site being provisioned is a top-level site.

Note that referencing a feature (site or web feature) from a site definition automatically activates the feature upon site creation. This is equivalent to performing the activatefeature operation on the stsadm .exe command-line utility.

Next, you walk through the implementation of the Default, Blank, and DWS configurations of the STS site definition to help you gain the skills you need to implement your own configurations.

Default Configuration

The <Lists> child element of the <Configuration> element that defines the default configuration provisions the instances of the specified list types upon site creation. The <Lists> element contains a <List> child element, which provisions a specific list.

The <List> element supports an attribute named FeatureId, which must be set to the value of the Id attribute of the <Feature> element that defines the feature that references the element manifest file that defines the list type from which the <List> element provisions the list. For example, consider the first <List> element of the <Lists> child element of the default configuration:

```
<Configuration ID="0" Name="Default">
  <Lists>
    <List FeatureId="00BFEA71-E717-4E80-AA17-D0C71B360101" Type="101"
    Title="$Resources:core,shareddocuments_Title;"
    Url="$Resources:core,shareddocuments_Folder;"
    QuickLaunchUrl="$Resources:core,shareddocuments_Folder;
                    /Forms/AllItems.aspx" />
  ...
</Configuration>
```

The FeatureId attribute on this <List> element is set to the value of the Id attribute of the following <Feature> element, which is located in the feature.xml file in the following folder:

```
Local_Drive:\Program Files\Common Files\microsoft shared\Web Server Extensions\12\
TEMPLATE\FEATURES\DocumentLibrary
```

Here is the content of this feature.xml file:

```
<?xml version="1.0" encoding="utf-8"?>
<Feature Id="00BFEA71-E717-4E80-AA17-D0C71B360101"
Title="$Resources:core,documentlibraryFeatureTitle;"
Description="$Resources:core,documentlibraryFeatureDesc;"
Version="1.0.0.0"
Scope="Web"
Hidden="TRUE"
DefaultResourceFile="core"
xmlsn="http://schemas.microsoft.com/sharepoint/">
  <ElementManifests>
    <ElementManifest Location="ListTemplates\DocumentLibrary.xml" />
  </ElementManifests>
</Feature>
```

The <List> element also supports an attribute named Type, which must be set to the value of the Type attribute of the <ListTemplate> element that defines the list type from which the <List> element provisions the list. This <ListTemplate> element is located in an element manifest file that the previously mentioned feature references. For example, the previous feature references an element manifest file named DocumentLibrary.xml, which contains the <ListTemplate> element as shown in the following:

```
<?xml version="1.0" encoding="utf-8"?>
<Elements xmlns="http://schemas.microsoft.com/sharepoint/">
  <ListTemplate Name="doclib" Type="101" BaseType="1" OnQuickLaunch="TRUE"
  SecurityBits="11" Sequence="110" DisplayName="$Resources:core,doclibList;"
  Description="$Resources:core,doclibList_Desc;" Image="/_layouts/images/itdl.gif"
  DocumentTemplate="101"/>
</Elements>
```

The Type attribute on the <List> element is set to the value of the Type attribute on this <ListTemplate> element.

The <List> element supports an attribute named Title, which specifies the title of the list being provisioned. SharePoint displays this title to users. Note that Listing 7-1 uses a resource reference to pull the value of this title from a resource file as opposed to hard-coding it. Here is an example:

```
Title="$Resources:core,discussions_Title;"
```

The <List> element supports an attribute named Url, which specifies the site-relative URL of the list being provisioned. This is the URL that users use to access the list. Again, note that Listing 7-1 uses a resource reference to pull this URL from a resource file. Here is an example:

```
        Url="$Resources:core,lists_Folder;/$Resources:core,discussions_Folder;"
```

The <List> element supports a Boolean attribute named QuickLaunchUrl, which specifies the URL of the hyperlink that represents this list on the Quick Launch bar. Listing 7-1 uses a resource reference to pull this URL from a resource file. Here is an example:

```
        QuickLaunchUrl="$Resources:core,lists_Folder;/
                        $Resources:core,discussions_Folder;/AllItems.aspx"
```

Note that SharePoint uses the CAML rendering instructions specified in the Body attribute of the <NavBar> elements that represent the Quick Launch bar to render the hyperlink that represents this list. The CAML rendering instructions were discussed in the previous section.

In summary, the default configuration of the STS site definition shown in Listing 7-1 provisions six lists from list templates of type 101 (Document Library), 103 (Links list), 104 (Announcements list), 106 (Events list), 107 (Tasks list), and 108 (Discussion board). As you can see, the default configuration basically provisions instances of all collaborative lists that a team site needs.

As Listing 7-1 shows, the <List> element that provisions an instance of the Announcements list type (104) also provisions a row in this list upon site creation:

```
<List FeatureId="00BFEA71-D1CE-42de-9C63-A44004CE0104" Type="104"
Title="$Resources:core,announceList;"
Url="$Resources:core,lists_Folder;/$Resources:core,announce_Folder;">
  <Data>
    <Rows>
      <Row>
        <Field Name="Title">$Resources:onetid11;</Field>
        <Field Name="Body">$Resources:onetid12;</Field>
        <Field Name="Expires">&lt;ows:TodayISO/&gt;</Field>
      </Row>
    </Rows>
  </Data>
</List>
```

This means that when a site is provisioned from the default configuration, this row is automatically added to this list. Note that the STS site definition (see Listing 7-1) uses resource references to pull the default values of the Title and Body fields from a localized resource as opposed to hard-coding these values.

As Listing 7-1 illustrates, the default configuration also provisions the files that a module named Default contains:

```
<Modules>
  <Module Name="Default" />
</Modules>
```

As discussed earlier, all modules are defined outside of site definition configurations so several configurations can reference and share the same modules. Modules are discussed later in this chapter.

As Listing 7-1 shows, the default configuration activates the BasicWebParts and Three-state Workflow features if the site being provisioned is a top-level site:

```
<SiteFeatures>
  <!-- BasicWebParts Feature -->
  <Feature ID="00BFEA71-1C5E-4A24-B310-BA51C3EB7A57" />
  <!-- Three-state Workflow Feature -->
  <Feature ID="FDE5D850-671E-4143-950A-87B473922DC7" />
</SiteFeatures>
```

Next, take a look at these two features starting with the BasicWebParts feature. The feature.xml file of the BasicWebParts feature is located in the following folder:

```
Local_Drive:\Program Files\Common Files\microsoft shared\Web Server
Extensions\12\TEMPLATE\FEATURES\BasicWebParts
```

Here is the content of this file:

```
<?xml version="1.0" encoding="utf-8"?>
<Feature Id="00BFEA71-1C5E-4A24-B310-BA51C3EB7A57"
Title="$Resources:core,basicwebpartsFeatureTitle;"
Description="$Resources:core,basicwebpartsFeatureDesc;"
ImageUrl="WssBasicWebPartsFeature.gif"
Scope="Site"
Hidden="TRUE"
DefaultResourceFile="core"
xmlsn="http://schemas.microsoft.com/sharepoint/">
  <ElementManifests>
    <ElementManifest Location="elements.xml" />
  </ElementManifests>
</Feature>
```

You can learn a lot from examining how things are done in standard SharePoint features and components. For example, note that the Title and Description attributes on this <Feature> element use resource references to pull the localized values from the localized resource as opposed to hard-coding them. This is important because SharePoint displays these two values to users. In general, you should use a resource reference anywhere you're using text that will be displayed to users.

This feature references an element manifest file named elements.xml as follows:

```
<?xml version="1.0" encoding="utf-8"?>
<Elements xmlns="http://schemas.microsoft.com/sharepoint/">
  <Module Name="WebPartPopulation" List="113" Url="_catalogs/wp"
  RootWebOnly="TRUE">
    <File Url="MSContentEditor.dwp" Type="GhostableInLibrary" />
    <File Url="MSPageViewer.dwp" Type="GhostableInLibrary" />
    <File Url="MSImage.dwp" Type="GhostableInLibrary" />
    <File Url="MSMembers.dwp" Type="GhostableInLibrary" />
    <File Url="MSSimpleForm.dwp" Type="GhostableInLibrary" />
    <File Url="MSUserDocs.dwp" Type="GhostableInLibrary" />
    <File Url="MSUserTasks.dwp" Type="GhostableInLibrary" />
    <File Url="MSXml.dwp" Type="GhostableInLibrary" />
  </Module>
</Elements>
```

As you can see, this feature contains a module that provisions eight Web part description files into the Web Part Gallery. Note that the RootWebOnly attribute is set to TRUE because such provisioning can only be done if the current site is a top-level site. Keep in mind that every site collection can contain a single Web Part Gallery, which is available to all its descendant sites. These eight Web parts are basic Web parts that every team site needs.

So far, I've covered one of the two site collection-scoped features that the default configuration activates, that is, the BasicWebPart feature. The second site collection–scoped feature is the Three-state Workflow feature:

```
      <SiteFeatures>
        <!-- BasicWebParts Feature -->
        <Feature ID="00BFEA71-1C5E-4A24-B310-BA51C3EB7A57" />
        <!-- Three-state Workflow Feature -->
        <Feature ID="FDE5D850-671E-4143-950A-87B473922DC7" />
      </SiteFeatures>
```

As this example shows, your site definition activates this feature upon site creation.

As Listing 7-1 shows, the default configuration also activates two site-scoped features named TeamCollab and MobilityRedirect:

```
    <WebFeatures>
      <Feature ID="00BFEA71-4EA5-48D4-A4AD-7EA5C011ABE5" />
      <!-- TeamCollab Feature -->
      <Feature ID="F41CC668-37E5-4743-B4A8-74D1DB3FD8A4" />
      <!-- MobilityRedirect -->
    </WebFeatures>
  </Configuration>
```

The TeamCollab feature is an interesting feature because it uses a technique known as feature dependency. Feature dependency enables you to package several features in one feature and activate them all by activating the containing feature. The following listing presents the feature.xml file of the TeamCollab feature:

```
<?xml version="1.0" encoding="utf-8"?>
<Feature Id="00BFEA71-4EA5-48D4-A4AD-7EA5C011ABE5"
Title="$Resources:core,teamcollabFeatureTitle;"
Description="$Resources:core,teamcollabFeatureDesc;"
ImageUrl="WssTeamCollaborationFeature.gif"
ImageUrlAltText=""
Scope="Web"
DefaultResourceFile="core"
xmlsn="http://schemas.microsoft.com/sharepoint/">
  <ActivationDependencies>

    <!-- AnnouncementsList Feature -->
    <ActivationDependency FeatureId="00BFEA71-D1CE-42de-9C63-A44004CE0104" />

    <!-- ContactsList Feature -->
    <ActivationDependency FeatureId="00BFEA71-7E6D-4186-9BA8-C047AC750105" />

    <!-- CustomList Feature -->
    <ActivationDependency FeatureId="00BFEA71-DE22-43B2-A848-C05709900100" />

    <!-- DataSourceLibrary Feature -->
    <ActivationDependency FeatureId="00BFEA71-F381-423D-B9D1-DA7A54C50110"/>

    <!-- DiscussionsList Feature -->
    <ActivationDependency FeatureId="00BFEA71-6A49-43FA-B535-D15C05500108" />

    <!-- DocumentLibrary Feature -->
    <ActivationDependency FeatureId="00BFEA71-E717-4E80-AA17-D0C71B360101" />

    <!-- EventsList Feature -->
    <ActivationDependency FeatureId="00BFEA71-EC85-4903-972D-EBE475780106" />

    <!-- GanttTasksList Feature -->
```

```
      <ActivationDependency FeatureId="00BFEA71-513D-4CA0-96C2-6A47775C0119" />

      <!-- GridList Feature -->
      <ActivationDependency FeatureId="00BFEA71-3A1D-41D3-A0EE-651D11570120" />

      <!-- IssuesList Feature -->
      <ActivationDependency FeatureId="00BFEA71-5932-4F9C-AD71-1557E5751100" />

      <!-- LinksList Feature -->
      <ActivationDependency FeatureId="00BFEA71-2062-426C-90BF-714C59600103" />

      <!-- NoCodeWorkflowLibrary Feature -->
      <ActivationDependency FeatureId="00BFEA71-F600-43F6-A895-40C0DE7B0117" />

      <!-- PictureLibrary Feature -->
      <ActivationDependency FeatureId="00BFEA71-52D4-45B3-B544-B1C71B620109" />

      <!-- SurveysList Feature -->
      <ActivationDependency FeatureId="00BFEA71-EB8A-40B1-80C7-506BE7590102" />

      <!-- TasksList Feature -->
      <ActivationDependency FeatureId="00BFEA71-A83E-497E-9BA0-7A5C597D0107" />

      <!-- WebPageLibrary Feature -->
      <ActivationDependency FeatureId="00BFEA71-C796-4402-9F2F-0EB9A6E71B18" />

      <!-- WorkflowProcessLibrary Feature -->
      <ActivationDependency FeatureId="00BFEA71-2D77-4A75-9FCA-76516689E21A" />

      <!-- WorkflowHistoryList Feature -->
      <ActivationDependency FeatureId="00BFEA71-4EA5-48D4-A4AD-305CF7030140" />

      <!-- XmlFormLibrary Feature -->
      <ActivationDependency FeatureId="00BFEA71-1E1D-4562-B56A-F05371BB0115" />

    </ActivationDependencies>
  </Feature>
```

As you can see, the TeamCollab feature uses an <ActivationDependency> element to define an activation dependency on the feature whose GUID is specified in the FeatureId attribute of the element. When a feature such as the TeamCollab feature, which defines activation dependencies, is activated it automatically forces the activation of the features that these activation dependencies reference. Feature activation dependency allows you to activate or deactivate a bunch of features in one shot through another feature (TeamCollab in this case).

The features that the TeamCollab feature activates basically contain the collaborative list types such as TasksList, XmlFormLibrary, and so on. This means that the default configuration of the STS site definition automatically makes these list types available to the sites provisioned from this configuration. In other words, these provisioned sites can provision instances of these list types if needed. Note that activating these features does not provision instances of these list types; it simply makes them available for provisioning if needed.

Blank Configuration

As Listing 7-1 shows, the blank configuration of the STS site configuration does not provision any lists:

```
<Lists />
```

However, it provisions the files that a module named DefaultBlank represent. Modules are discussed later in this chapter.

As Listing 7-1 illustrates, the blank configuration also activates the same site collection– and site-scoped features as the default configuration:

```
<Configuration ID="1" Name="Blank">
  <Lists />
  <Modules>
    <Module Name="DefaultBlank" />
  </Modules>
  <SiteFeatures>
    <!-- BasicWebParts Feature -->
    <Feature ID="00BFEA71-1C5E-4A24-B310-BA51C3EB7A57" />
    <!-- Three-state Workflow Feature -->
    <Feature ID="FDE5D850-671E-4143-950A-87B473922DC7" />
  </SiteFeatures>
  <WebFeatures>
    <Feature ID="00BFEA71-4EA5-48D4-A4AD-7EA5C011ABE5" />
    <!-- TeamCollab Feature -->
    <Feature ID="F41CC668-37E5-4743-B4A8-74D1DB3FD8A4" />
    <!-- MobilityRedirect -->
  </WebFeatures>
</Configuration>
```

DWS Configuration

As you can see from Listing 7-1, the DWS configuration of the STS site definition provisions instances of the same list types that the default configuration provisions, that is, list templates of type 101 (Document Library), 103 (Links list), 104 (Announcements list), 106 (Events list), 107 (Tasks list), and 108 (Discussion board). As such, the DWS configuration, just like the default configuration, provisions instances of all collaborative lists that a team site needs:

```
<Lists>
  <List FeatureId="00BFEA71-E717-4E80-AA17-D0C71B360101" Type="101"
  Title="$Resources:core,shareddocuments_Title;"
  Url="$Resources:core,shareddocuments_Folder;" />
  <List FeatureId="00BFEA71-6A49-43FA-B535-D15C05500108" Type="108"
  Title="$Resources:core,discussions_Title;"
  Url="$Resources:core,lists_Folder;/$Resources:core,discussions_Folder;"
  QuickLaunchUrl="$Resources:core,lists_Folder;/
                  $Resources:core,discussions_Folder;" />
  <List FeatureId="00BFEA71-D1CE-42de-9C63-A44004CE0104" Type="104"
  Title="$Resources:core,announceList;"
  Url="$Resources:core,lists_Folder;/$Resources:core,announce_Folder;">
    <Data>
```

```
          <Rows>
            <Row>
              <Field Name="Title">$Resources:onetid11;</Field>
              <Field Name="Body">$Resources:onetid12;</Field>
              <Field Name="Expires"><ows:TodayISO/></Field>
            </Row>
          </Rows>
        </Data>
      </List>
      <List FeatureId="00BFEA71-2062-426C-90BF-714C59600103" Type="103"
      Title="$Resources:core,linksList;"
      Url="$Resources:core,lists_Folder;/$Resources:core,links_Folder;" />
      <List FeatureId="00BFEA71-EC85-4903-972D-EBE475780106" Type="106"
      Title="$Resources:core,calendarList;"
      Url="$Resources:core,lists_Folder;/$Resources:core,calendar_Folder;"
      QuickLaunchUrl="$Resources:core,lists_Folder;/
                      $Resources:core,calendar_Folder;/Calendar.aspx" />
      <List FeatureId="00BFEA71-A83E-497E-9BA0-7A5C597D0107" Type="107"
      Title="$Resources:core,taskList;"
      Url="$Resources:core,lists_Folder;/$Resources:core,tasks_Folder;" />
    </Lists>
```

Note that the <List> element that provisions an instance of the Announcements list type (104) also provisions a row in this list upon site creation:

```
      <List FeatureId="00BFEA71-D1CE-42de-9C63-A44004CE0104" Type="104"
      Title="$Resources:core,announceList;"
      Url="$Resources:core,lists_Folder;/$Resources:core,announce_Folder;">
        <Data>
          <Rows>
            <Row>
              <Field Name="Title">$Resources:onetid11;</Field>
              <Field Name="Body">$Resources:onetid12;</Field>
              <Field Name="Expires"><ows:TodayISO/></Field>
            </Row>
          </Rows>
        </Data>
      </List>
```

This means that when a site is provisioned from the DWS configuration, this row is automatically added to this list. Note that the STS site definition uses resource references to pull the default values of the Title, Body, and Expires fields from a localized resource as opposed to hard-coding these values.

As Listing 7-1 shows, the DWS configuration provisions the files that a module named DWS represents. These files are discussed later in this chapter.

```
    <Modules>
      <Module Name="DWS" />
    </Modules>
```

Finally, as Listing 7-1 illustrates, the DWS configuration activates the same site collection–scoped and site-scoped features as the default configuration:

```
    <SiteFeatures>
      <!-- BasicWebParts Feature -->
      <Feature ID="00BFEA71-1C5E-4A24-B310-BA51C3EB7A57" />
      <!-- Three-state Workflow Feature -->
      <Feature ID="FDE5D850-671E-4143-950A-87B473922DC7" />
    </SiteFeatures>
    <WebFeatures>
      <Feature ID="00BFEA71-4EA5-48D4-A4AD-7EA5C011ABE5" />
      <!-- TeamCollab Feature -->
      <Feature ID="F41CC668-37E5-4743-B4A8-74D1DB3FD8A4" />
      <!-- MobilityRedirect -->
    </WebFeatures>
  </Configuration>
```

<Modules>

As discussed earlier, the default, blank, and DWS configurations of the STS site definition respectively provision the files that the modules named Default, Blank, and DWS represent. These modules are discussed in this section.

Default Module

Listing 7-3 presents the Default module.

Listing 7-3: The Default module

```
<Module Name="Default" Url="" Path="">
  <File Url="default.aspx" NavBarHome="True">
    <View
    List="$Resources:core,lists_Folder;/$Resources:core,announce_Folder;"
    BaseViewID="0" WebPartZoneID="Left" />

    <View
    List="$Resources:core,lists_Folder;/$Resources:core,calendar_Folder;"
    BaseViewID="0" RecurrenceRowset="TRUE" WebPartZoneID="Left"
    WebPartOrder="2" />

    <AllUsersWebPart WebPartZoneID="Right" WebPartOrder="1">
      <![CDATA[
        <WebPart xmlns="http://schemas.microsoft.com/WebPart/v2"
        xmlns:iwp="http://schemas.microsoft.com/WebPart/v2/Image">
          <Assembly>
            Microsoft.SharePoint, Version=12.0.0.0, Culture=neutral,
            PublicKeyToken=71e9bce111e9429c
          </Assembly>
          <TypeName>Microsoft.SharePoint.WebPartPages.ImageWebPart</TypeName>
          <FrameType>None</FrameType>
          <Title>$Resources:wp_SiteImage;</Title>
          <iwp:ImageLink>/_layouts/images/homepage.gif</iwp:ImageLink>
          <iwp:AlternativeText>
```

```
              $Resources:core,sitelogo_wss;
            </iwp:AlternativeText>
          </WebPart>
        ]]>
      </AllUsersWebPart>

      <View
      List="$Resources:core,lists_Folder;/$Resources:core,links_Folder;"
      BaseViewID="0" WebPartZoneID="Right" WebPartOrder="2" />

      <NavBarPage Name="$Resources:core,nav_Home;" ID="1002" Position="Start" />

      <NavBarPage Name="$Resources:core,nav_Home;" ID="0" Position="Start" />

    </File>
  </Module>
```

This module provisions a site page from a page template named default.aspx. This site page will be the homepage for the site being provisioned. Because the Url attribute on the <Module> element is set to an empty string, the site-relative URL of this provisioned site page will be default.aspx. The Path attribute on the <Module> element is set to an empty string because the default.aspx page template itself is located at the root folder of the STS site definition as shown in Figure 7-2.

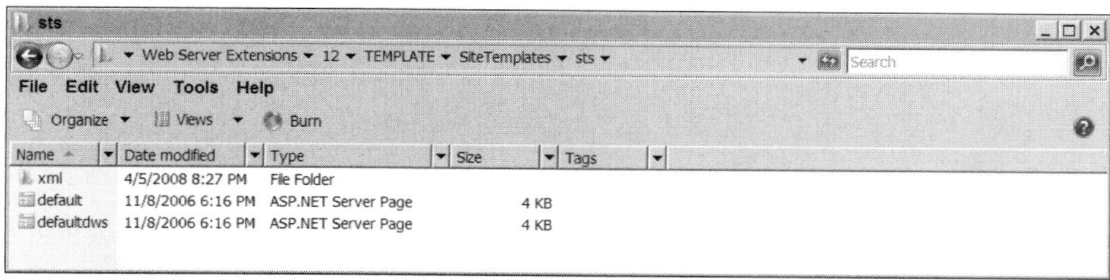

Figure 7-2: The root folder of sts site definition

As Listing 7-3 shows, the <Module> element contains a single <File> element because this module provisions a single file. This <File> element contains the following <View> element:

```
      <View
      List="$Resources:core,lists_Folder;/$Resources:core,announce_Folder;"
      BaseViewID="0" WebPartZoneID="Left" />
```

This <View> element provisions a ListViewWebPart Web part into the WebPartZone zone with the ID attribute value of Left to display the view of the Lists/Announcements list with the base view ID of zero. Recall from the discussions in the previous sections that the default configuration has already provisioned this Lists/Announcements list.

Listing 7-4 presents a portion of the default.aspx page shown in Figure 7-2. As you can see from the boldfaced portion of this listing, this page contains two WebPartZone zones with the ID attribute values of Left and Right.

Listing 7-4: The default.aspx page

```
<%@ Page language="C#" MasterPageFile="~masterurl/default.master"
Inherits="Microsoft.SharePoint.WebPartPages.WebPartPage,Microsoft.SharePoint,
Version=12.0.0.0,Culture=neutral,PublicKeyToken=71e9bce111e9429c" %>
...
<asp:Content ContentPlaceHolderId="PlaceHolderMain" runat="server">
<table cellspacing="0" border="0" width="100%">
  ...
  <tr>
     <td>
       <table width="100%" cellpadding=0 cellspacing=0
       style="padding: 5px 10px 10px 10px;">
         <tr>
  <td valign="top" width="70%">
           <WebPartPages:WebPartZone runat="server" FrameType="TitleBarOnly"
            ID="Left" Title="loc:Left" /> 
  </td>
  <td> </td>
  <td valign="top" width="30%">
           <WebPartPages:WebPartZone runat="server" FrameType="TitleBarOnly"
            ID="Right" Title="loc:Right" /> 
  </td>
  <td> </td>
</tr>
      </table>
    </td>
  </tr>
</table>
</asp:Content>
```

Listing 7-5 presents a portion of the view of the Announcements list with the base view ID value of zero. This listing is an excerpt from the following file:

```
Local_Drive:\Program Files\Common Files\microsoft shared\Web Server Extensions\12\
TEMPLATE\FEATURES\AnnouncementsList\Announce\schema.xml
```

Listing 7-5: The view with the base view ID value of zero

```
<?xml version="1.0" encoding="utf-8"?>
<List xmlns:ows="Microsoft SharePoint" Title="$Resources:100;" FolderCreation="FALSE"
Direction="$Resources:Direction;" Url="Lists/Announcements"
BaseType="0">
  <MetaData>
    ...
    <Views>
      <View BaseViewID="0" FreeForm="TRUE" Type="HTML">
        <ViewHeader>
          ...
        </ViewHeader>
        <ViewBody>
```

```
      ...
    </ViewBody>
    <ViewFooter>
      ...
    </ViewFooter>
    ...
    <Query>
      <Where>
        <Or>
          <IsNull>
            <FieldRef Name="Expires" />
          </IsNull>
          <Geq>
            <FieldRef Name="Expires">
            </FieldRef>
            <Value Type="DateTime">
              <Today>
              </Today>
            </Value>
          </Geq>
        </Or>
      </Where>
      <OrderBy>
        <FieldRef Name="Modified" Ascending="FALSE">
        </FieldRef>
      </OrderBy>
    </Query>
    <ViewFields>
      <FieldRef Name="LinkTitleNoMenu" Explicit="TRUE">
      </FieldRef>
      <FieldRef Name="Body" Explicit="TRUE">
      </FieldRef>
      <FieldRef Name="Author" Explicit="TRUE">
      </FieldRef>
      <FieldRef Name="Modified" Explicit="TRUE">
      </FieldRef>
      <FieldRef Name="Attachments" Explicit="TRUE">
      </FieldRef>
    </ViewFields>
    <RowLimit>5</RowLimit>
  </View>
```

As discussed earlier in this book, a view provides a ListViewWebPart Web part with the CAML rendering instructions to render the view. As the <Query> element of this view shows, this view basically renders those announcement records whose expiration date is greater than or equal to today's date and sorts these records in descending order based on the value of the Modified field. As the <ViewFields> element shows, this view renders the LinkTitleNoMenu, Body, Author, Modified, and Attachments fields.

As Listing 7-3 illustrates, the <File> element also contains an <AllUsersWebPart> element that provisions the specified Web part into the WebPartZone zone with the ID attribute value of Right on the provisioned default.aspx site page:

```
<AllUsersWebPart WebPartZoneID="Right" WebPartOrder="1">
  <![CDATA[
    <WebPart xmlns="http://schemas.microsoft.com/WebPart/v2"
    xmlns:iwp="http://schemas.microsoft.com/WebPart/v2/Image">
      <Assembly>
        Microsoft.SharePoint, Version=12.0.0.0, Culture=neutral,
        PublicKeyToken=71e9bce111e9429c
      </Assembly>
      <TypeName>Microsoft.SharePoint.WebPartPages.ImageWebPart</TypeName>
      <FrameType>None</FrameType>
      <Title>$Resources:wp_SiteImage;</Title>
      <iwp:ImageLink>/_layouts/images/homepage.gif</iwp:ImageLink>
      <iwp:AlternativeText>
        $Resources:core,sitelogo_wss;
      </iwp:AlternativeText>
    </WebPart>
  ]]>
</AllUsersWebPart>
```

This Web part is provisioned upon site creation. The content of the <AllUsersWebPart> element is nothing but the Web part definition document that describes the Web part. Every Web part description contains a document element named <WebPart>, which supports the following child elements:

- **<Assembly>.** Specifies the fully qualified name of the assembly that contains the Web part. If the assembly is strong-named, this fully qualified name is the strong name of the assembly, which contains the assembly name, version, culture, and public key token. If the assembly is not strong-named and is deployed to the bin directory of the current web application, this fully qualified name is the name of the assembly.
- **<TypeName>.** This specifies the namespace-qualified name of the type of the Web part.
- **<FrameType>.** This specifies the type of Web part chrome.
- **<Title>.** This specifies the title of the Web part description. Note that Listing 7-3 uses a resource reference to pull the localized title from the localized resource. This is because the title is shown to users in the SharePoint user interface.

As Listing 7-3 shows, the <File> element of the default module also contains the following <View> element:

```
<View
List="$Resources:core,lists_Folder;/$Resources:core,links_Folder;"
BaseViewID="0" WebPartZoneID="Right" WebPartOrder="2" />
```

This <View> element provisions a ListViewWebPart into the WebPartZone zone with the ID attribute value of Right to display the view of the Lists/Links list with the base view ID of zero. Recall from the previous sections that the default configuration has already provisioned the Lists/Links list.

Listing 7-6 presents the portion of the definition of this view.

Listing 7-6: A portion of the view

```
<?xml version="1.0" encoding="utf-8"?>
<List xmlns:ows="Microsoft SharePoint" Title="$Resources:core,linksList;"
Direction="$Resources:core,Direction;" OrderedList="TRUE"
Url="$Resources:core,lists_Folder;/$Resources:core,links_Folder;" BaseType="0"
DisableAttachments="
TRUE">
  <MetaData>
    <Views>
      <View BaseViewID="0" Type="HTML" OrderedView="TRUE">
        <ViewHeader>
          ...
        </ViewHeader>
        <ViewBody>
          ...
        </ViewBody>
        <ViewFooter>
          ...
        </ViewFooter>
        ...
        <Query>
          <OrderBy>
            <FieldRef Name="Order" Ascending="TRUE">
            </FieldRef>
          </OrderBy>
        </Query>
        <ViewFields>
          <FieldRef Name="URL" Explicit="TRUE">
          </FieldRef>
          <FieldRef Name="URLNoMenu">
          </FieldRef>
        </ViewFields>
        <RowLimit>20</RowLimit>
      </View>
```

This view, like any other view, presents the ListViewWebPart Web part with the CAML rendering instructions to render the view. As you can see from the <Query> element, this view renders all links in ascending order based on the value of the Order field. As <ViewFields> illustrates, this view renders the URL and URLNoMenu fields.

Default Blank Module

Listing 7-7 presents the default blank module.

Listing 7-7: The default blank module

```
<Module Name="DefaultBlank" Url="" Path="">
  <File Url="default.aspx" NavBarHome="True" Type="Ghostable">
    <AllUsersWebPart WebPartZoneID="Right" WebPartOrder="1">
      <![CDATA[
        <WebPart xmlns="http://schemas.microsoft.com/WebPart/v2"
        xmlns:iwp="http://schemas.microsoft.com/WebPart/v2/Image">
          <Assembly>
            Microsoft.SharePoint, Version=12.0.0.0, Culture=neutral,
            PublicKeyToken=71e9bce111e9429c
          </Assembly>
          <TypeName>Microsoft.SharePoint.WebPartPages.ImageWebPart</TypeName>
          <FrameType>None</FrameType>
          <Title>$Resources:wp_SiteImage;</Title>
          <iwp:ImageLink>/_layouts/images/homepage.gif</iwp:ImageLink>
          <iwp:AlternativeText>
            $Resources:core,sitelogo_wss;
          </iwp:AlternativeText>
        </WebPart>
      ]]>
    </AllUsersWebPart>
    <NavBarPage Name="$Resources:core,nav_Home;" ID="1002" Position="Start" />
    <NavBarPage Name="$Resources:core,nav_Home;" ID="0" Position="Start" />
  </File>
</Module>
```

The default blank module contains a single <File> element because it provisions a single site page from a page template named default.aspx. This site page will be the homepage for the site provisioned from the blank configuration. Note that the homepages of the sites provisioned from the default and blank configurations are provisioned from the same page template. This page template is the default.aspx page shown in Figure 7-2. Even though these two homepages are provisioned from the same page template, they will be very different from one another because the default blank and default modules use different provisioning instructions. The previous section discussed the provisioning instructions that the default module uses. This section discusses the provisioning instructions that the default blank module uses.

As Listing 7-7 shows, the <File> element uses an <AllUsersWebPart> element to provision a Web part with the specified characteristics into the WebPartZone zone with the ID attribute value of Right. In other words, the default blank module does not provision the ListViewWebPart Web parts that the default module did. Hence the name blank.

DWS Module

Listing 7-8 presents the DWS module.

Listing 7-8: The DWS module

```
    <Module Name="DWS" Url="">
      <File Url="defaultdws.aspx" Name="default.aspx">
        <View
        List="$Resources:core,lists_Folder;/$Resources:core,announce_Folder;"
        BaseViewID="3" WebPartZoneID="Top" />

        <View
        List="$Resources:core,lists_Folder;/$Resources:core,links_Folder;"
        BaseViewID="3" WebPartZoneID="Right" WebPartOrder="2" />

        <View
        List="$Resources:core,shareddocuments_Folder;" BaseViewID="6"
        WebPartZoneID="Left" />

        <View
        List="$Resources:core,lists_Folder;/$Resources:core,tasks_Folder;"
        BaseViewID="7" WebPartZoneID="Left" WebPartOrder="2" />

        <AllUsersWebPart WebPartZoneID="Right" WebPartOrder="1">
          <![CDATA[
            <WebPart xmlns="http://schemas.microsoft.com/WebPart/v2">
              <Assembly>
                Microsoft.SharePoint, Version=12.0.0.0, Culture=neutral,
                PublicKeyToken=71e9bce111e9429c
              </Assembly>
              <TypeName>Microsoft.SharePoint.WebPartPages.MembersWebPart</TypeName>
              <Title>$Resources:wp_Members;</Title>
              <Description>$Resources:wp_Members_Desc;</Description>
              <FrameType>Standard</FrameType>
              <IsVisible>true</IsVisible>
            </WebPart>
          ]]>
        </AllUsersWebPart>

        <NavBarPage Name="$Resources:core,nav_Home;" ID="1002" Position="Start" />
        <NavBarPage Name="$Resources:core,nav_Home;" ID="0" Position="Start" />
      </File>
    </Module>
  </Modules>
```

Contrary to the default and default blank modules, the DWS module provisions the homepage of the site provisioned from the DWS configuration from a page template named defaultdws.aspx as opposed to default.aspx. The defaultdws.aspx page template is in the same folder as the default.aspx page as shown in Figure 7-2. Note that the Name attribute on the <File> element in Listing 7-8 is set to default.aspx. This means that the homepage of the site provisioned from the DWS configuration has the same name as the homepages of the sites provisioned from the default and blank configurations.

Listing 7-9 presents the portion of the defaultdws.aspx page template.

Listing 7-9: The portion of the defaultdws.aspx page template

```
<%@ Page Language="C#" MasterPageFile="~masterurl/default.master"
Inherits="Microsoft.SharePoint.WebPartPages.WebPartPage,Microsoft.SharePoint,
Version=12.0.0.0,Culture=neutral,PublicKeyToken=71e9bce111e9429c" %>
...
<asp:Content ContentPlaceHolderID="PlaceHolderMain" runat="server">
  <table cellspacing="0" border="0" width="100%">
    ...
    <tr>
      <td>
        <table width="100%" cellpadding="0" cellspacing="0"
        style="padding: 5px 10px 10px 10px;">
          <tr>
            <td valign="top" width="100%">
              <WebPartPages:WebPartZone runat="server" FrameType="TitleBarOnly"
              ID="Top" Title="loc:Top" />
               
            </td>
            <td>
               
            </td>
          </tr>
        </table>
      </td>
    </tr>
    <tr>
      <td>
        <table width="100%" cellpadding="0" cellspacing="0"
        style="padding: 5px 10px 10px 10px;">
          <tr>
            <td valign="top" width="70%">
              <WebPartPages:WebPartZone runat="server" FrameType="TitleBarOnly"
              ID="Left" Title="loc:Left" />
               
            </td>
            <td>
               
            </td>
            <td valign="top" width="30%">
              <WebPartPages:WebPartZone runat="server" FrameType="TitleBarOnly"
              ID="Right" Title="loc:Right" />
               
            </td>
            <td>
               
            </td>
          </tr>
        </table>
      </td>
    </tr>
  </table>
</asp:Content>
```

As you can see, the defaultdws.aspx page template contains three WebPartZone zones with the ID attribute values of Top, Left, and Right.

As Listing 7-8 shows, the DWS module performs these provisioning tasks:

- Provisions a ListViewWebPart Web part into the WebPartZone zone with the ID attribute value of Top to display the Announcements list view with the base view of 3:

```
<View
List="$Resources:core,lists_Folder;/$Resources:core,announce_Folder;"
BaseViewID="3" WebPartZoneID="Top" />
```

- Provisions a ListViewWebPart Web part into the WebPartZone zone with the ID attribute value of Right to display the Links list view with the base view of 3:

```
<View
List="$Resources:core,lists_Folder;/$Resources:core,links_Folder;"
BaseViewID="3" WebPartZoneID="Right" WebPartOrder="2" />
```

- Provisions a ListViewWebPart Web part into the WebPartZone zone with the ID attribute value of Left to display the shared documents list view with the base view of 6:

```
<View
List="$Resources:core,shareddocuments_Folder;" BaseViewID="6"
WebPartZoneID="Left" />
```

- Provisions a ListViewWebPart Web part into the WebPartZone zone with the ID attribute value of Left to display the Tasks list view with the base view of 7:

```
<View
List="$Resources:core,lists_Folder;/$Resources:core,tasks_Folder;"
BaseViewID="7" WebPartZoneID="Left" WebPartOrder="2" />
```

- Provisions a Web part with the specified characteristics into the WebPartZone zone with the ID attribute value of Right:

```
<AllUsersWebPart WebPartZoneID="Right" WebPartOrder="1">
  <![CDATA[
    <WebPart xmlns="http://schemas.microsoft.com/WebPart/v2">
      <Assembly>
        Microsoft.SharePoint, Version=12.0.0.0, Culture=neutral,
        PublicKeyToken=71e9bce111e9429c
      </Assembly>
      <TypeName>Microsoft.SharePoint.WebPartPages.MembersWebPart</TypeName>
      <Title>$Resources:wp_Members;</Title>
      <Description>$Resources:wp_Members_Desc;</Description>
      <FrameType>Standard</FrameType>
      <IsVisible>true</IsVisible>
    </WebPart>
  ]]>
</AllUsersWebPart>
```

WebTemp*.xml

All standard WSS 3.0 site definitions share the same WebTemp.xml file, which is located in the following folder on the file system of the front-end web server:

```
Local_Drive:\program files\common files\microsoft shared\web server extensions\12\
Template\1033\XML\
```

Listing 7-10 presents the content of the WebTemp.xml file.

Listing 7-10: The WebTemp.xml file

```
<?xml version="1.0" encoding="utf-8"?>
<Templates xmlns:ows="Microsoft SharePoint">

  <Template Name="GLOBAL" SetupPath="global" ID="0">
    <Configuration ID="0" Title="Global template" Hidden="TRUE" ImageUrl=""
    Description="This template is used for initializing a new site." />
  </Template>

  <Template Name="STS" ID="1">
    <Configuration ID="0" Title="Team Site" Hidden="FALSE"
    ImageUrl="/_layouts/images/stsprev.png"
    Description="A site for teams to quickly organize, author, and share
                 information. It provides a document library, and lists for
                 managing announcements, calendar items, tasks, and discussions."
    DisplayCategory="Collaboration" />

    <Configuration ID="1" Title="Blank Site" Hidden="FALSE"
    ImageUrl="/_layouts/images/blankprev.png"
    Description="A blank site for you to customize based on your requirements."
    DisplayCategory="Collaboration" AllowGlobalFeatureAssociations="False" />

    <Configuration ID="2" Title="Document Workspace" Hidden="FALSE"
    ImageUrl="/_layouts/images/dwsprev.png"
    Description="A site for colleagues to work together on a document. It provides
                 a document library for storing the primary document and supporting
                 files, a tasks list for assigning to-do items, and a links list
                 for resources related to the document."
    DisplayCategory="Collaboration" />
  </Template>

  <Template Name="MPS" ID="2">
    <Configuration ID="0" Title="Basic Meeting Workspace" Hidden="FALSE"
    ImageUrl="/_layouts/images/mwsprev.png"
    Description="A site to plan, organize, and capture the results of a meeting. It
                 provides lists for managing the agenda, meeting attendees, and
                 documents." DisplayCategory="Meetings" />
    <Configuration ID="1" Title="Blank Meeting Workspace" Hidden="FALSE"
    ImageUrl="/_layouts/images/blankmwsprev.png"
    Description="A blank meeting site for you to customize based on your
                 requirements." DisplayCategory="Meetings" />
    <Configuration ID="2" Title="Decision Meeting Workspace" Hidden="FALSE"
```

```
    ImageUrl="/_layouts/images/decisionmwsprev.png"
    Description="A site for meetings that track status or make decisions. It
                provides lists for creating tasks, storing documents, and
                recording decisions." DisplayCategory="Meetings" />
    <Configuration ID="3" Title="Social Meeting Workspace" Hidden="FALSE"
    ImageUrl="/_layouts/images/socialmwsprev.png"
    Description="A site to plan social occasions. It provides lists for tracking
                attendees, providing directions, and storing pictures of the
                event."
    DisplayCategory="Meetings" />
    <Configuration ID="4" Title="Multipage Meeting Workspace" Hidden="FALSE"
    ImageUrl="/_layouts/images/multipagemwsprev.png"
    Description="A site to plan, organize, and capture the results of a meeting. It
                provides lists for managing the agenda and meeting attendees in
                addition to two blank pages for you to customize based on your
                requirements."
    DisplayCategory="Meetings" />
  </Template>

  <Template Name="CENTRALADMIN" ID="3">
    <Configuration ID="0" Title="Central Admin Site" Hidden="TRUE" ImageUrl=""
    Description="A site for central administration. It provides Web pages and links
                for application and operations management." />
  </Template>

  <Template Name="WIKI" ID="4">
    <Configuration ID="0" Title="Wiki Site" Hidden="FALSE"
    ImageUrl="/_layouts/images/wikiprev.png"
    Description="A site for a community to brainstorm and share ideas. It provides
                Web pages that can be quickly edited to record information and
                then linked together through keywords"
    DisplayCategory="Collaboration" />
  </Template>

  <Template Name="BLOG" ID="9">
    <Configuration ID="0" Title="Blog" Hidden="FALSE"
    ImageUrl="/_layouts/images/blogprev.png"
    Description="A site for a person or team to post ideas, observations, and
                expertise that site visitors can comment on."
    DisplayCategory="Collaboration" />
  </Template>

</Templates>
```

As you can see, a WebTemp*.xml file has a document element named <Templates>, which contains one or more <Template> elements where each <Template> element represents a site definition. The <Template> element features an attribute called Name, which specifies the name of the site definition that the element represents. This name must be the name of the site definition folder under the SiteTemplates folder. The <Template> element also features an attribute named ID, which uniquely identifies the template among other templates in the farm. You must set the ID attribute value of your own custom templates to a number greater than 10000 to avoid possible conflicts with the current and future SharePoint standard site templates.

Note that Listing 7-10 contains a <Template> element that represents the Global site definition:

```
<Template Name="GLOBAL" SetupPath="global" ID="0">
  <Configuration ID="0" Title="Global template" Hidden="TRUE" ImageUrl=""
  Description="This template is used for initializing a new site." />
</Template>
```

The SetupPath attribute is set to global, which is the name of the folder under the Template folder where the Global site definition resides. Keep in mind that the folder path specified in the SetupPath attribute is always with respect to the Template folder. Also keep in mind that the path specified in the SetupPath is a folder path, not a site-relative path.

A <Template> element contains one or more <Configuration> elements that map to the <Configuration> elements specified in the <Configurations> section of the respective onet.xml. As a matter of fact, the ID attribute value of a <Configuration> element in a <Template> element is the same as the ID attribute value of its corresponding <Configuration> element in the <Configurations> element.

The <Configuration> element in the <Configurations> section of the onet.xml file provides the actual implementation and definition of the configuration, whereas the corresponding <Configuration> element in the respective <Template> element provides the information that is displayed to users in the Template Selection section of the New SharePoint Site web page shown in Figure 7-1 as follows:

- The value of the Title attribute on this <Configuration> element is rendered as the name of the configuration in the list of the configurations shown in the Template Selection section (see Figure 7-1).
- The value of the Hidden Boolean attribute specifies whether SharePoint should display this configuration in the list of available configurations in the Template Selection section.
- The value of the ImageUrl attribute specifies the icon that SharePoint displays when the user selects the configuration in the Template Selection section.
- The value of the Description attribute is rendered as the description of the configuration in the Template Selection section.
- The value of the DisplayCategory attribute tells SharePoint in which tab in the Template Selection section to render the name of the configuration. If this attribute is set to a category that does not have an associated tab, SharePoint automatically creates a tab for that category.

A site definition configuration is identified by a pound sign-separated list of two substrings where the second substring contains the value of the ID attribute of the <Configuration> element that defines the configuration, and the first substring contains the value of the Name attribute of the <Template> element that represents the site definition that contains the configuration. For example, sts#0 identifies the first configuration of the STS site definition.

When you're using the SharePoint object model or STSADM command-line utility to provision a site from a site definition configuration, you must use this identification to identify the configuration to SharePoint:

```
stsadm -o createsite -url http://localhost/mysite1 -ownerlogin ServerName\
Username -owneremail someone@somewhere.com -siteTemplate sts#0
```

Site Definition Best Practices

The following sections discuss a few best practices that you should follow when you're implementing a site definition.

List Provisioning

As you saw from Listing 7-1, the configuration of the STS site definition, like the configuration of many other SharePoint standard site definitions, uses the <Lists> element, which contains the instructions for provisioning lists from specified list types. As a best practice, you should *not* follow this pattern in your own site definition. Instead you should encapsulate these list provisioning instructions in features and reference these features from your site definition.

As an example, you'll implement a version of the STS site definition that follows this best practice. As discussed earlier, every site definition consists of two XML files named onet.xml and WebTemp*.xml. Listing 7-11 presents the content of the WebTempMyWebTemp.xml file for this version of the STS site definition. Add this file to the root of the Class Library project that you created earlier in this chapter.

Listing 7-11: The WebTempMyWebTemp.xml file

```
<?xml version="1.0" encoding="utf-8"?>
<Templates xmlns:ows="Microsoft SharePoint">
  <Template Name="STS2" ID="10020">
    <Configuration
    ID="0"
    Title="Team Site 2"
    Hidden="FALSE"
    ImageUrl="/_layouts/images/stsprev.png"
    Description="This is Team Site 2."
    DisplayCategory="My Site Templates" />

    <Configuration
    ID="1"
    Title="Blank Site 2"
    Hidden="FALSE"
    ImageUrl="/_layouts/images/blankprev.png"
    Description="This is Blank Site 2."
    DisplayCategory="My Site Templates" />

    <Configuration
    ID="2"
    Title="Document Workspace 2"
    Hidden="FALSE"
    ImageUrl="/_layouts/images/dwsprev.png"
    Description="This is Document Workspace 2."
    DisplayCategory="My Site Templates" />
  </Template>
</Templates>
```

The WebTempMyWebTemp.xml file, like any other WebTemp*.xml file, contains a document element named <Templates>. This document element contains a <Template> child element that references the site definition configurations of this custom STS site definition. Note that the Name attribute on this <Template> element is set to STS2, which is the name of this custom site definition. This means that the folder that contains this site definition must be named STS2. Also note that the ID attribute on the <Template> element is set to a number larger than 10000. The value of this attribute must be unique within the farm. As you can see from Listing 7-11, the <Template> element contains three <Configuration> child elements that reference the site definition configuration of this STS2 site definition. As Listing 7-11 shows, the DisplayCategory attributes on these three <Configuration> child elements are set to "My Site Templates" to instruct SharePoint to create a new tab with the My Site Templates heading for this site definition configuration if this tab has not already been created.

Go ahead and copy the WebTempMyWebTemp.xml file into the following folder on the file system of the front-end web server:

```
Local_Drive:\Program Files\Common Files\microsoft shared\Web Server
Extensions\12\TEMPLATE\1033\XML
```

Next, navigate to the following folder on the file system of the front-end web server:

```
Local_Drive:\Program Files\Common Files\microsoft shared\Web Server
Extensions\12\TEMPLATE\SiteTemplates
```

Then, copy and paste the sts folder and rename the new folder sts2. The new folder should contain the XML folder and the default.aspx and defaultdws.aspx files shown in Figure 7-2. The XML folder should contain the onet.xml file shown in Listing 7-1. The default.aspx and defaultdws.aspx files were covered in Listings 7-4 and 7-9.

The goal is to remove the <List> child elements of the <Lists> element from the onet.xml file because you want to remove these list provisioning instructions from the onet.xml and encapsulate them in an element manifest file, which is referenced from a feature. You'll then add a reference to this feature in this configuration.

Listing 7-12 presents the content of the element manifest file named MyListInstances.xml, which contains the instructions for provisioning list instances of the Document Library, Discussion Board, Announcements, Links, Events, and Tasks list types.

Listing 7-12: The MyListInstances.xml file

```
<?xml version="1.0" encoding="utf-8" ?>
<Elements
xmlsn="http://schemas.microsoft.com/sharepoint/">
  <ListInstance
  Description="Provisions a Document Library list."
  FeatureId="00BFEA71-E717-4E80-AA17-D0C71B360101"
  Id="1"
  OnQuickLaunch="True"
  RootWebOnly="False"
  TemplateType="101"
  Title="$Resources:core,shareddocuments_Title;"
  Url="$Resources:core,shareddocuments_Folder;" />

  <ListInstance
  Description="Provisions a Discussion board list."
  FeatureId="00BFEA71-6A49-43FA-B535-D15C05500108"
  Id="2"
  OnQuickLaunch="True"
```

```
    RootWebOnly="False"
    TemplateType="108"
    Title="$Resources:core,discussions_Title;"
    Url="$Resources:core,lists_Folder;/$Resources:core,discussions_Folder;" />

    <ListInstance
    Description="Provisions a Announcements list."
    FeatureId="00BFEA71-D1CE-42de-9C63-A44004CE0104"
    Id="3"
    OnQuickLaunch="True"
    RootWebOnly="False"
    TemplateType="104"
    Title="$Resources:core,announceList;"
    Url="$Resources:core,lists_Folder;/$Resources:core,announce_Folder;">
      <Data>
        <Rows>
          <Row>
            <Field Name="Title">$Resources:core,onetid11;</Field>
            <Field Name="Body">$Resources:core,onetid12;</Field>
            <Field Name="Expires"><ows:TodayISO/></Field>
          </Row>
        </Rows>
      </Data>
    </ListInstance>

    <ListInstance
    Description="Provisions a Links list."
    FeatureId="00BFEA71-2062-426C-90BF-714C59600103"
    Id="4"
    OnQuickLaunch="True"
    RootWebOnly="False"
    TemplateType="103"
    Title="$Resources:core,linksList;"
    Url="$Resources:core,lists_Folder;/$Resources:core,links_Folder;" />

    <ListInstance
    Description="Provisions an Events  list."
    FeatureId="00BFEA71-EC85-4903-972D-EBE475780106"
    Id="5"
    OnQuickLaunch="True"
    RootWebOnly="False"
    TemplateType="106"
    Title="$Resources:core,calendarList;"
    Url="$Resources:core,lists_Folder;/$Resources:core,calendar_Folder;" />

    <ListInstance
    Description="Provisions a Tasks list."
    FeatureId="00BFEA71-A83E-497E-9BA0-7A5C597D0107}"
    Id="6"
    OnQuickLaunch="True"
    RootWebOnly="False"
    TemplateType="107"
    Title="$Resources:core,taskList;"
    Url="$Resources:core,lists_Folder;/$Resources:core,tasks_Folder;" />

</Elements>
```

As you can see, MyListInstances.xml, like any other element manifest file, has a document element named <Elements>. This document element contains six <ListInstance> elements, each provisioning one of six list instances. Note that the Title and Url attributes on each <ListInstance> use resource references to pull the localized title and URL from the localized resource. I've hard-coded the values of the Description attributes on purpose so you know what type of list each <ListInstance> element provisions. You should use localized values for the Description attributes as well in your own applications.

Listing 7-13 presents the feature.xml file that references the MyListInstances.xml element manifest file.

Listing 7-13: The feature.xml file

```
<?xml version="1.0" encoding="utf-8" ?>
<Feature xmlns="http://schemas.microsoft.com/sharepoint/"
Id="{1E0CFC51-DD21-4321-9D6B-81FC4B6AEE1A}"
Description="This feature provisions list instances upon activation."
Hidden="False"
Scope="Web"
Title="My List Instances Feature"
Version="1.0.0.0">
  <ElementManifests>
    <ElementManifest Location="MyListInstances.xml"/>
  </ElementManifests>
</Feature>
```

Now go ahead and create a feature-specific folder named MyListInstances in the following folder on the file system of the front-end web server:

```
Local_Drive:\Program Files\Common Files\microsoft shared\Web Server
Extensions\12\TEMPLATE\FEATURES
```

Next, copy the feature.xml file shown in Listing 7-13 and the MyListInstances.xml file shown in Listing 7-12 into this MyListInstances folder. Then use the following stsadm command line to install the feature:

```
"C:\Program Files\Common Files\microsoft shared\Web Server Extensions\12\bin\
stsadm.exe" -o installfeature -name MyListInstances
```

This step is important. You must install the feature that provisions the list instances before you attempt to provision a site from a site definition configuration that references this feature. Otherwise you would get the error shown in Figure 7-3 when you try to provision the site.

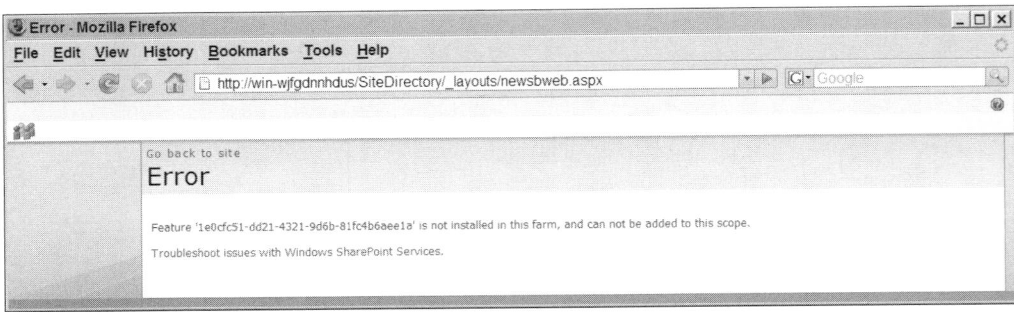

Figure 7-3: Error received if you fail to install the feature that provisions list instances

Next, you need to remove the <List> elements that provision these lists from the onet.xml file and add a reference to the feature that provisions these lists. Listing 7-14 presents the new version of the onet.xml with these changes.

Listing 7-14: The onet.xml file

```
<?xml version="1.0" encoding="utf-8"?>
<Project Title="$Resources:onet_TeamWebSite;" Revision="2"
ListDir="$Resources:core,lists_Folder;" xmlns:ows="Microsoft SharePoint">
  <NavBars>
    ...
  </NavBars>
  <ListTemplates>
  </ListTemplates>
  <DocumentTemplates>
    ...
  </DocumentTemplates>
  <Configurations>
    <Configuration ID="-1" Name="NewWeb" />
    <Configuration ID="0" Name="Default">
      <Modules>
        <Module Name="Default" />
      </Modules>
      <SiteFeatures>
        <!-- BasicWebParts Feature -->
        <Feature ID="00BFEA71-1C5E-4A24-B310-BA51C3EB7A57" />
        <!-- Three-state Workflow Feature -->
        <Feature ID="FDE5D850-671E-4143-950A-87B473922DC7" />
      </SiteFeatures>
      <WebFeatures>
        <Feature ID="00BFEA71-4EA5-48D4-A4AD-7EA5C011ABE5" />
        <!-- TeamCollab Feature -->
        <Feature ID="F41CC668-37E5-4743-B4A8-74D1DB3FD8A4" />
        <!-- MobilityRedirect -->
        <Feature ID="{1E0CFC51-DD21-4321-9D6B-81FC4B6AEE1A}" />
      </WebFeatures>
    </Configuration>
    <Configuration ID="1" Name="Blank">
      <Lists />
      <Modules>
        <Module Name="DefaultBlank" />
      </Modules>
      <SiteFeatures>
        <!-- BasicWebParts Feature -->
        <Feature ID="00BFEA71-1C5E-4A24-B310-BA51C3EB7A57" />
        <!-- Three-state Workflow Feature -->
        <Feature ID="FDE5D850-671E-4143-950A-87B473922DC7" />
      </SiteFeatures>
      <WebFeatures>
        <Feature ID="00BFEA71-4EA5-48D4-A4AD-7EA5C011ABE5" />
        <!-- TeamCollab Feature -->
        <Feature ID="F41CC668-37E5-4743-B4A8-74D1DB3FD8A4" />
```

(continued)

Listing 7-2 *(continued)*

```
        <!-- MobilityRedirect -->
      </WebFeatures>
    </Configuration>
    <Configuration ID="2" Name="DWS">
      <Modules>
        <Module Name="DWS" />
      </Modules>
      <SiteFeatures>
        <!-- BasicWebParts Feature -->
        <Feature ID="00BFEA71-1C5E-4A24-B310-BA51C3EB7A57" />
        <!-- Three-state Workflow Feature -->
        <Feature ID="FDE5D850-671E-4143-950A-87B473922DC7" />
      </SiteFeatures>
      <WebFeatures>
        <Feature ID="00BFEA71-4EA5-48D4-A4AD-7EA5C011ABE5" />
        <!-- TeamCollab Feature -->
        <Feature ID="F41CC668-37E5-4743-B4A8-74D1DB3FD8A4" />
        <!-- MobilityRedirect -->
        <Feature ID="{1E0CFC51-DD21-4321-9D6B-81FC4B6AEE1A}" />
      </WebFeatures>
    </Configuration>
  </Configurations>
  <Modules>
    . . .
  </Modules>
  <ServerEmailFooter>$Resources:ServerEmailFooter;</ServerEmailFooter>
</Project>
```

As the boldfaced portions of Listing 7-14 show, the <WebFeatures> elements of the default and DWS site definition configurations contain a <Feature> child element that references the feature whose activation provisions the team collaboration lists discussed earlier. Note that the <WebFeatures> element of a site definition configuration does not install the referenced features. It only activates them. That is why you must install every feature that a site definition configuration references.

Next, test this custom site definition by provisioning a site from the Team Site 2 site definition configuration of this site definition. Navigate to the newsbweb.aspx page shown in Figure 7-4. This page allows you to provision a site from a desired site definition configuration.

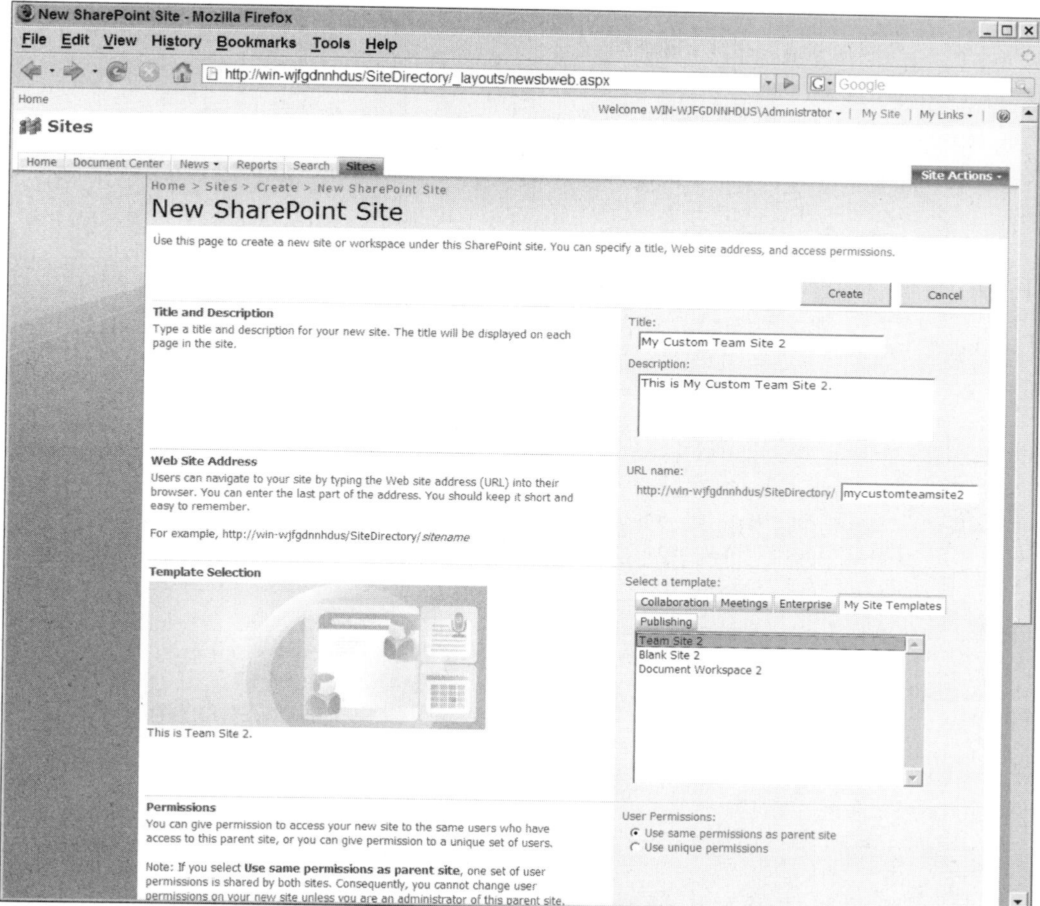

Figure 7-4: Page allowing you to provision a site from a desired site definition configuration

Note that setting the DisplayCategory attributes on the <Configuration> elements in WebTempMyWebTemp.xml file shown in Listing 7-11 has caused SharePoint to create a new tab titled My Site Templates, which contains all three of the site definition configurations (see Figure 7-4). Enter a title, description, and URL for the new site. Switch to the My Site Templates tab, select Team Site 2, and click the Create button. This will create the site shown in Figure 7-5.

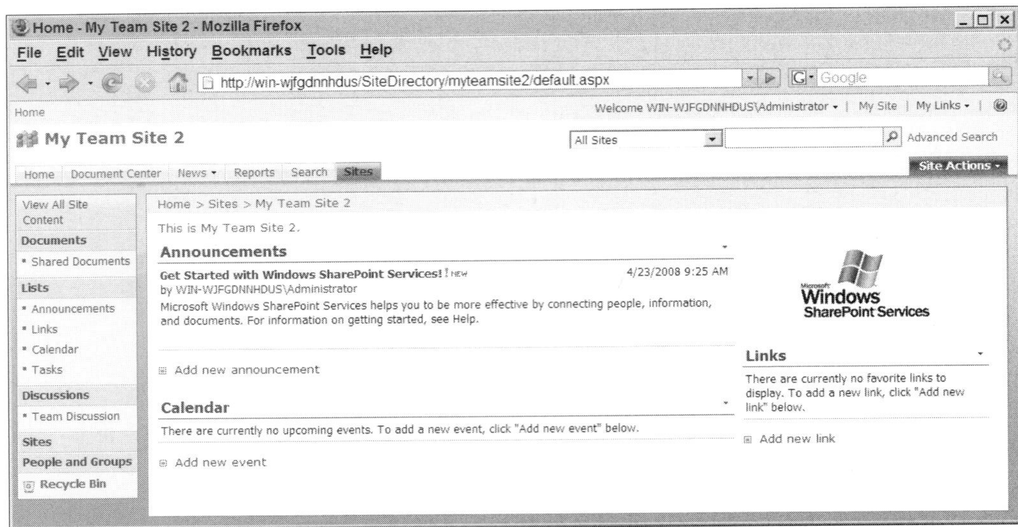

Figure 7-5: The My Team Site 2 site

Note that the Quick Launch bar contains links to the lists that this feature provisions. This is because Listing 7-12 sets the OnQuickLaunch attributes on <ListInstance> elements that provision these lists to true. Next, go ahead and click the Announcements link in the Quick Launch bar to navigate to the AllItems.aspx page that displays the Announcement lists that this feature has provisioned as shown in Figure 7-6. Note that this list contains a list item because the <ListInstance> element that provisions the Announcements list also adds this list item to this list as shown in Listing 7-12.

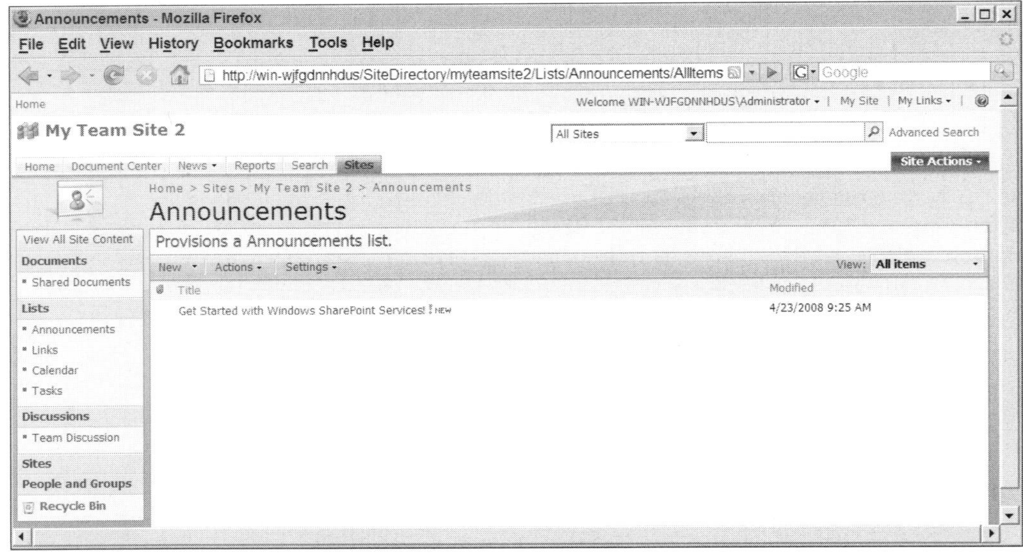

Figure 7-6: The AllItems.aspx page displaying the Announcements list

Modules

As you saw from Listing 7-1, the <Project> element in an onet.xml file supports an element named <Modules> where you can define the modules for your site definition. As a best practice, you should *not* define your modules inside your site definition. Instead you should define your modules in features and reference those features from your site definition. The only exception to this rule is cases such as the homepage for your site definition. You should contain the module that provisions the homepage of your site definition in the site definition itself. You saw a few examples of this earlier in this chapter.

Site Provisioning Provider

A site definition provides a complete business solution package that users can use out-of-the-box by simply provisioning a site from one of the site definition's configurations through the SharePoint user interface. Most of the functionalities of such a complete business solution package can be implemented through CAML. However, there could be functionalities whose implementation may require managed code. For such functionalities you can implement a component known as a site provisioning provider.

A site provisioning provider is a .NET class that inherits from an abstract base class named SPWebProvisioningProvider. This abstract base class is in the Microsoft.SharePoint namespace in the Microsoft.SharePoint.dll assembly. As Listing 7-15 shows, this base class exposes an abstract method named Provision. Your custom site provisioning provider must implement this method.

Listing 7-15: The SPWebProvisioningProvider base class

```
[SharePointPermission(SecurityAction.InheritanceDemand, ObjectModel=true),
SharePointPermission(SecurityAction.LinkDemand, ObjectModel=true)]
public abstract class SPWebProvisioningProvider
{
  public abstract void Provision(SPWebProvisioningProperties props);
}
```

Note that the SPWebProvisioningProvider abstract base class is annotated by the following code access security metadata attributes:

```
[SharePointPermission(SecurityAction.InheritanceDemand, ObjectModel=true),
SharePointPermission(SecurityAction.LinkDemand, ObjectModel=true)]
```

These metadata attributes demand the callers and inheritors of the SPWebProvisioningProvider base class to have permission to use the SharePoint object model.

When a user provisions a site from one of your custom site definitions' configuration, SharePoint takes the following steps right after the site is provisioned:

1. Instantiates an instance of a class named SPWebProvisioningProperties. As Listing 7-16 shows, this class exposes the following two properties:
   - **Data.** Returns a string that contains the value of the ProvisionData attribute on the <Configuration> element in the WebTemp*.xml file from which the site was provisioned.
   - **Web.** Returns a reference to an SPWeb object that represents the provisioned site.

Note that the setters of both Data and Web properties are marked as internal. Therefore, you cannot set these two properties. You can only read them. Also note that SPWebProvisioningProperties is marked with the following metadata attribute to demand its callers to have permission to use the SharePoint object model because the Web property references an SPWeb object, which is part of the SharePoint object model:

```
SharePointPermission(SecurityAction.LinkDemand, ObjectModel = true)
```

2. Sets the Web property of the SPWebProvisioningProperties object from Step 1 to reference an SPWeb object that represents the provisioned site.
3. Assigns the value of the ProvisionData attribute on the <Configuration> element in the WebTemp*.xml file from which the site was provisioned. You can use this attribute to pass data from the WebTemp*.xml file to your custom site provisioning provider.
4. Reads the value of the ProvisionClass attribute on the <Configuration> element in the WebTemp*.xml file from which the site was provisioned. You must set this attribute to the fully namespace-qualified name of your custom site provisioning provider.
5. Reads the value of the ProvisionAssembly attribute on the <Configuration> element in the WebTemp*.xml file from which the site was provisioned. You must set this attribute to the strong name of the assembly that contains your custom site provisioning provider. The strong name of an assembly consists of four parts: assembly name, version, culture, and public key token.
6. Loads the assembly from Step 5 into the application domain if it hasn't already been loaded.
7. Uses .NET reflection to instantiate an instance of your custom site provisioning provider.
8. Invokes the Provision method of the site provisioning provider instance from Step 7 and passes the SPWebProvisioningProvider object into this method as its argument.

Your custom site provisioning provider's implementation of the Provision method can then use the Web and Data properties of this SPWebProvisioningProvider object to access the SPWeb object that represents the provisioned site and the value of the ProvisionData attribute. Listing 7-17 presents a simple example of a site provisioning provider whose Provision method simply assigns the value of the ProvisionData attribute to the Title property of the provisioned site.

Listing 7-16: The SPWebProvisioningProperties type

```
[SharePointPermission(SecurityAction.LinkDemand, ObjectModel = true),
SharePointPermission(SecurityAction.InheritanceDemand, ObjectModel = true)]
public sealed class SPWebProvisioningProperties
{
  private string data;
  private SPWeb web;

  public string Data
  {
    get { return this.data; }
    internal set { this.data = value; }
  }

  public SPWeb Web
  {
    get { return this.web; }
    internal set { this.web = value; }
  }
}
```

Listing 7-17: The CustomProvisioningProvider.cs

```
using Microsoft.SharePoint;

namespace ClassLibrary2
{
  public class CustomProvisioningProvider: SPWebProvisioningProvider
  {
    public override void Provision(SPWebProvisioningProperties props)
    {
      props.Web.ApplyWebTemplate("STS2#0");
      props.Web.Title = props.Data;
      props.Web.Update();
    }
  }
}
```

Now go ahead and launch Visual Studio. Choose File ⇨ New Project to create a new Class Library project. Add a reference to the Microsoft.SharePoint.dll assembly, which is located in the following folder:

```
Local_Drive:\Program Files\Common Files\microsoft shared\Web Server Extensions\12\
ISAPI
```

Rename the Class1.cs file to CustomProvisioningProvider.cs and add the code shown in Listing 7-17 to this file.

A custom provisioning provider must be compiled into a strong-named assembly and deployed to the Global Assembly Cache (GAC) before it can be used. Follow these steps to configure Visual Studio to compile this custom provisioning provider into a strong-named assembly. Right-click the project in the Solution Explorer and select Properties as shown in Figure 7-7.

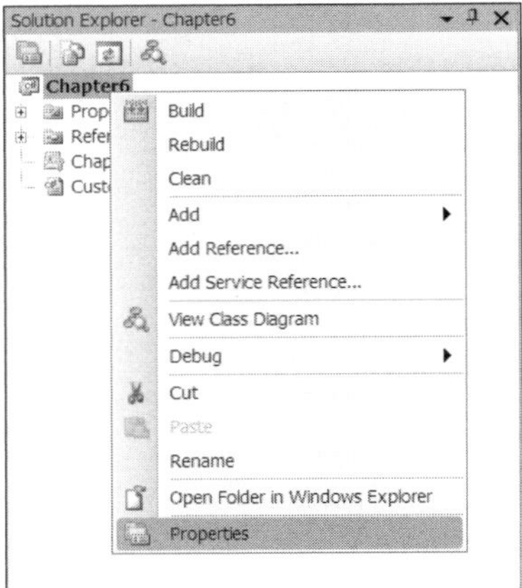

Figure 7-7: The popup menu displaying the Properties option

Switch to the Signing tab and check the Sign the Assembly box as illustrated in Figure 7-8.

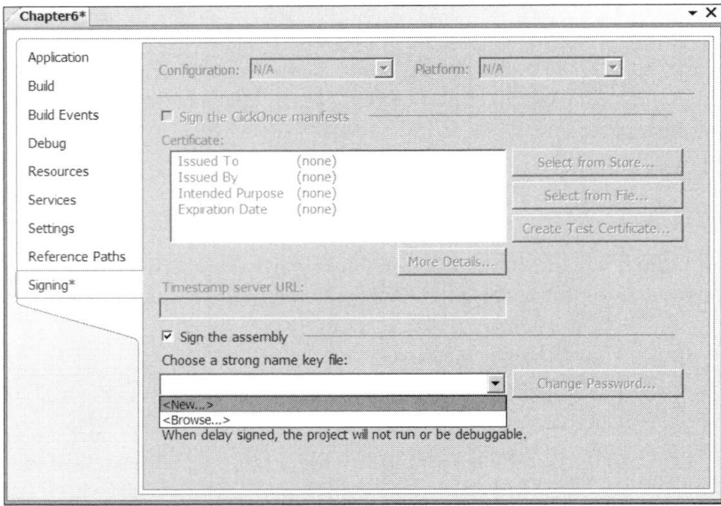

Figure 7-8: The Properties window

Next, select the New menu option from the drop-down list box shown in Figure 7-8 to launch the Create Strong Name Key dialog shown in Figure 7-9. Enter a name for the key file, uncheck the Protect My Key File with a Password toggle, and click OK. This will create a key file and add it to the root directory of this project. Visual Studio will use this key file to sign the assembly.

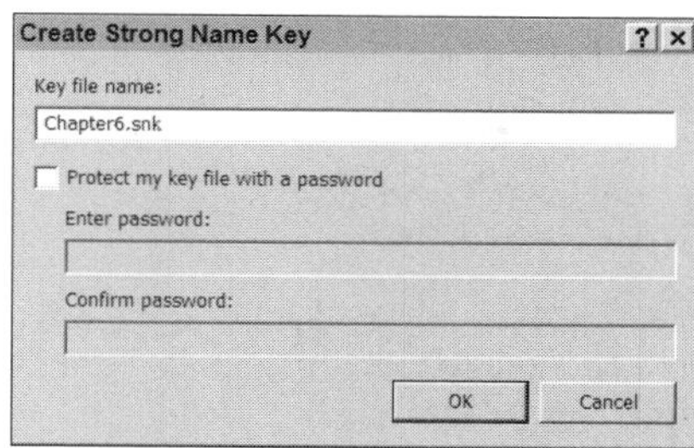

Figure 7-9: The Create Strong Name Key dialog

Next, you see how to configure Visual Studio to install the assembly in the GAC automatically every time the project is built. Switch to the Build Events tab in the Properties window as illustrated in Figure 7-10. Enter the following in the Post-Build Event Command Line textbox:

```
"c:\Program Files\Microsoft Visual Studio 8\SDK\v2.0\Bin\gacutil.exe" -if
"$(TargetPath)"
```

Visual Studio will automatically run this gacutil command-line utility to install the assembly in the GAC every time the project is built successfully.

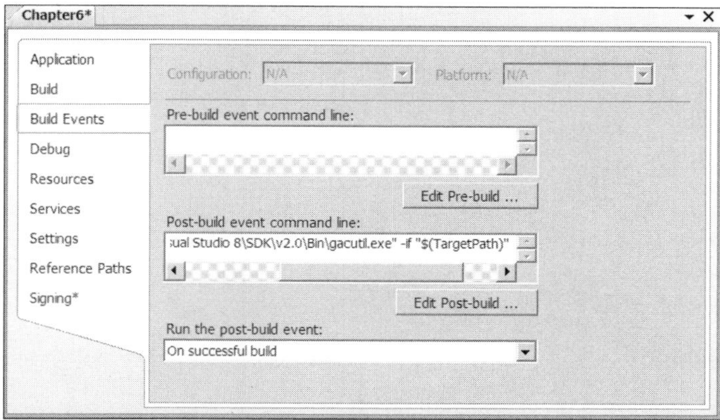

Figure 7-10: Adding the post-build event command line

Next, you need to make the required changes to the WebTempMyWebTemp.xml file as shown in Listing 7-18.

Listing 7-18: The new version of WebTempMyWebTemp.xml file

```
<?xml version="1.0" encoding="utf-8"?>
<Templates xmlns:ows="Microsoft SharePoint">
  <Template Name="STS2" ID="10020">
    <Configuration ID="3" Title="Team Site 2"
    Hidden="FALSE"
    ImageUrl="/_layouts/images/stsprev.png"
    Description="This is Team Site 2."
    DisplayCategory="My Site Templates"
    ProvisionClass="ClassLibrary.CustomProvisioningProvider"
    ProvisionAssembly="ClassLibrary, Version=1.0.0.0, Culture=neutral,
PublicKeyToken=2b56bd310cddb0e3"
    ProvisionData="My Team Site 2" />

    <Configuration
    ID="0"
    Title="Team Site 2"
    Hidden="TRUE"
    ImageUrl="/_layouts/images/stsprev.png"
    Description="This is Team Site 2."
    DisplayCategory="My Site Templates" />

    <Configuration
    ID="1"
    Title="Blank Site 2"
    Hidden="FALSE"
    ImageUrl="/_layouts/images/blankprev.png"
    Description="This is Blank Site 2."
    DisplayCategory="My Site Templates" />

    <Configuration
    ID="2"
    Title="Document Workspace 2"
    Hidden="FALSE"
    ImageUrl="/_layouts/images/dwsprev.png"
    Description="This is Document Workspace 2."
    DisplayCategory="My Site Templates" />
  </Template>
</Templates>
```

Recall that this custom STS2 site definition supports the following three configurations:

- Team Site 2 (STS2#0)
- Blank Site 2 (STS2#1)
- Document Space 2 (STS2#2)

Also recall that a site provisioning provider provides a way to customize site provisioning from a configuration. The first order of business is to choose the site provisioning that you want to customize. In this case, you would like to customize site provisioning from the Team Site 2 (STS2#0). Next, you need to define a new configuration with the same attributes as the configuration whose site provisioning is being customized, that is, the Team Site 2 in this case. You'll then configure this new configuration with this site provisioning provider. This new configuration is shown in boldface in Listing 7-18. Note that the old Team Site 2 (STS2#2) whose site provisioning is being customized is still there. However, you've set its Hidden attribute to TRUE so SharePoint does not display the old Team Site 2 to users. Because the new configuration has the same attributes as the old one, the new configuration appears to users to be the old one. Note that the ID attribute of the new configuration (3) is different from the old one (2).

Because every configuration in the WebTemp*.xml file must reference a configuration with the same ID value in the respective onet.xml file, you also need to add this configuration to the onet.xml file as shown in Listing 7-19. Note that the new configuration does not contain references to any modules, site features, or web features. The new configuration acts like a proxy for the old configuration.

Listing 7-19: The new version of the onet.xml file

```
<?xml version="1.0" encoding="utf-8"?>
<Project Title="$Resources:onet_TeamWebSite;" Revision="2"
ListDir="$Resources:core,lists_Folder;" xmlns:ows="Microsoft SharePoint">
  <NavBars>
    . . .
  </NavBars>
  <DocumentTemplates>
    . . .
  </DocumentTemplates>
  <Configurations>
    <Configuration ID="-1" Name="NewWeb" />
    <Configuration ID="3" Name="Default2" />
    <Configuration ID="0" Name="Default">
      <Modules>
        <Module Name="Default" />
      </Modules>
      <SiteFeatures>
        <!-- BasicWebParts Feature -->
        <Feature ID="00BFEA71-1C5E-4A24-B310-BA51C3EB7A57" />
        <!-- Three-state Workflow Feature -->
        <Feature ID="FDE5D850-671E-4143-950A-87B473922DC7" />
      </SiteFeatures>
      <WebFeatures>
        <Feature ID="00BFEA71-4EA5-48D4-A4AD-7EA5C011ABE5" />
        <!-- TeamCollab Feature -->
        <Feature ID="F41CC668-37E5-4743-B4A8-74D1DB3FD8A4" />
        <!-- MobilityRedirect -->
        <Feature ID="{1E0CFC51-DD21-4321-9D6B-81FC4B6AEE1A}" />
      </WebFeatures>
    </Configuration>
    . . .
  </Configurations>
  <Modules>
    . . .
  </Modules>
  <ServerEmailFooter>$Resources:ServerEmailFooter;</ServerEmailFooter>
</Project>
```

When a user provisions a site from this new configuration, SharePoint automatically invokes the Provision method shown in Listing 7-17. As you can see, this method first accesses the SPWeb object that represents the site provisioned from this new configuration and then invokes the ApplyWebTemplate method on this SPWeb object:

```
props.Web.ApplyWebTemplate("STS2#0");
```

Note that the Provision method passes the string that identifies the old Team Site 2 (STS2#0) into the ApplyWebTemplate method. This method applies the old Team Site 2 configuration to the site provisioned from the new configuration. This basically simulates what would be the case if the user had provisioned the site from the old Team Site 2 configuration.

The Provision method then assigns the value of the ProvisionData attribute to the Title property of the provisioned site:

```
        props.Web.Title = props.Data;
```

The Provision method finally invokes the Update method to commit the changes:

```
        props.Web.Update();
```

The important point to take away from these discussions is that the configuration identifier that you pass into the ApplyWebTemplate method mustn't be the identifier of the configuration from which the user has provisioned the site on which this method is invoked.

This is because the ApplyWebTemplate method triggers a site provisioning from the configuration with the identifier specified in its argument, which in turn triggers the reinvocation of the Provision method, which in turn triggers the reinvocation of the ApplyWebTemplate method, and so on. In other words, you'll get stuck in an infinite loop! If you were to configure the old configuration (STS2#0) with this site provisioning provider and if you were to pass the same configuration identifier (STS2#0) into the ApplyWebTemplate method, the following sequence would take place. The user would provision a site from the old configuration (STS2#2) through the SharePoint user interface. This would trigger the invocation of the Provision method, which would invoke the ApplyWebTemplate method, passing in the old configuration identifier (STS2#2). The ApplyWebTemplate method would trigger another site provisioning from the old configuration, which would trigger the reinvocation of the Provision method, which would reinvoke the ApplyWebTemplate method, and so on. That is why you introduced a new configuration with a different identifier (STS2#3), configured this new configuration with this site provisioning provider, and passed the identifier of the old configuration (STS2#0) as an argument into the ApplyWebTemplate method to avoid an infinite loop.

As you can see from the boldfaced portion of Listing 7-18, you need to access the public key token of theassembly to use it in the value of the ProvisionAssembly attribute. There are different ways to access the public key token of the assembly. Earlier in this book I showed you one way to do this. That approach requires you to navigate to the assembly folder in the Windows Explorer, right-click the assembly, and select the Properties option from the popup menu to launch the Properties dialog. You can then copy and paste the public key token from this dialog. Here is another approach: Select the Tools ⇨ External Tools menu option from the Tools menu of Visual Studio to launch the External Tools dialog shown in Figure 7-11.

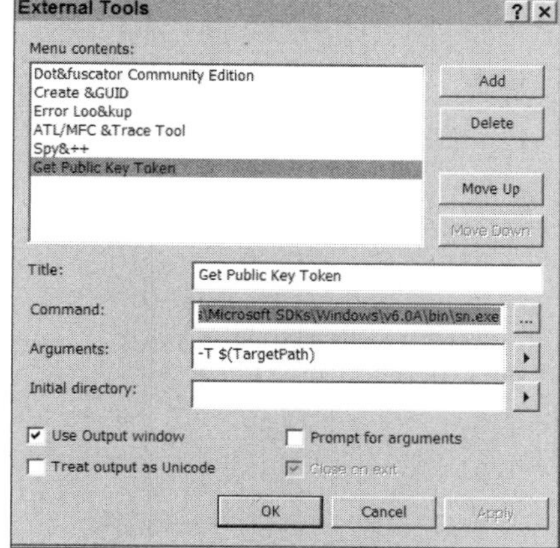

Figure 7-11: The External Tools dialog

Click the Add button. Enter "Get Public Key Token" as the title for the tool. Enter the following command line in the Command textbox:

```
C:\Program Files\Microsoft SDKs\Windows\v6.0A\bin\sn.exe
```

The path to the sn.exe command-line utility could be different on your machine.

Enter the following into the Arguments textbox:

```
-T $(TargetPath)
```

Check the Use Output Window toggle.

These settings will add a menu option named Get Public Key Token in the Tools menu of Visual Studio as shown in Figure 7-12.

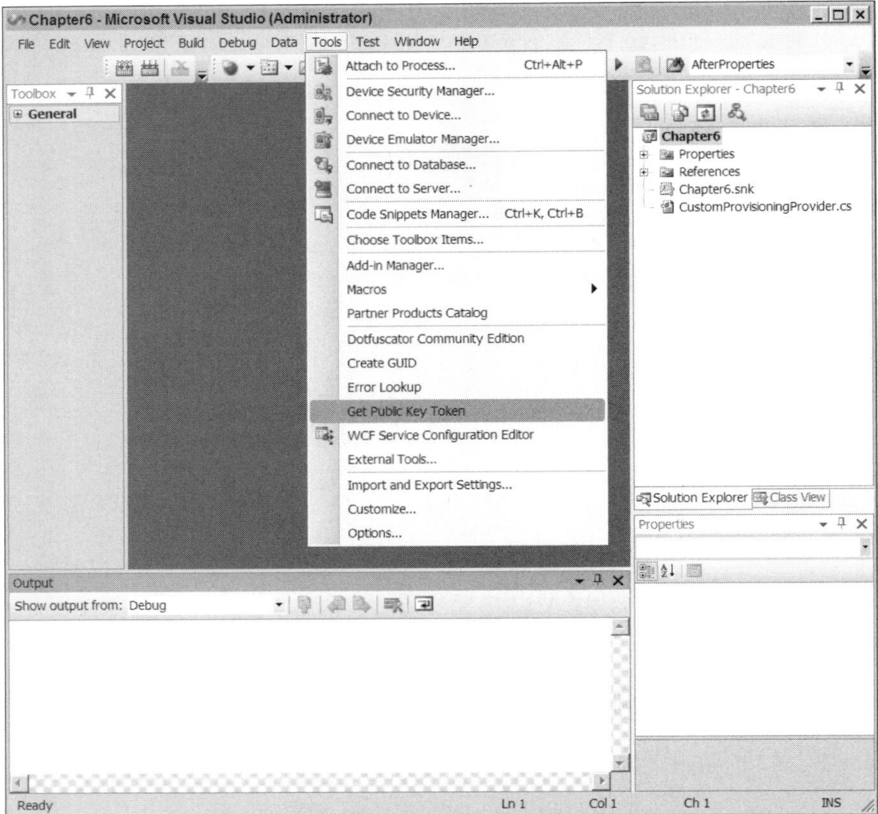

Figure 7-12: The Tools menu display the Get Public Key Token menu option

Next build the project. Then select the Get Public Key Token menu option. Visual Studio will automatically run the sn.exe tool with the -T $(TargetPath) switch to extract the public key token and print it into the output window as shown in Figure 7-13.

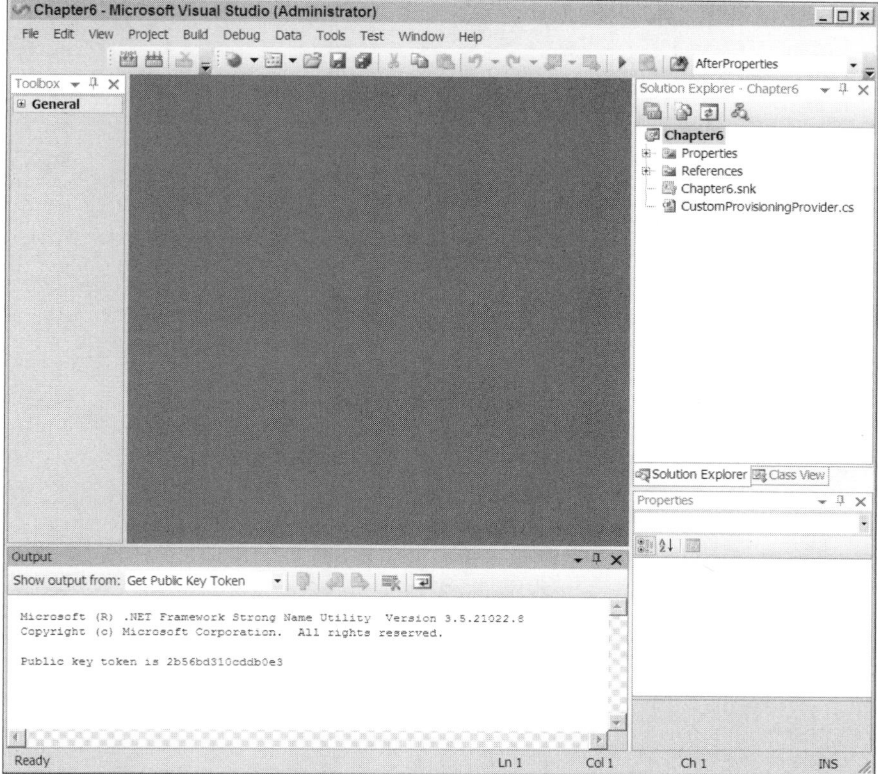

Figure 7-13: The output window displaying the public key token

Don't forget to run the iisreset command line. Next, navigate to the newsbweb.aspx page shown in Figure 7-14 to create a new site from the new Team Site 2 site definition configuration (STS2#3) of this custom sts2 site definition.

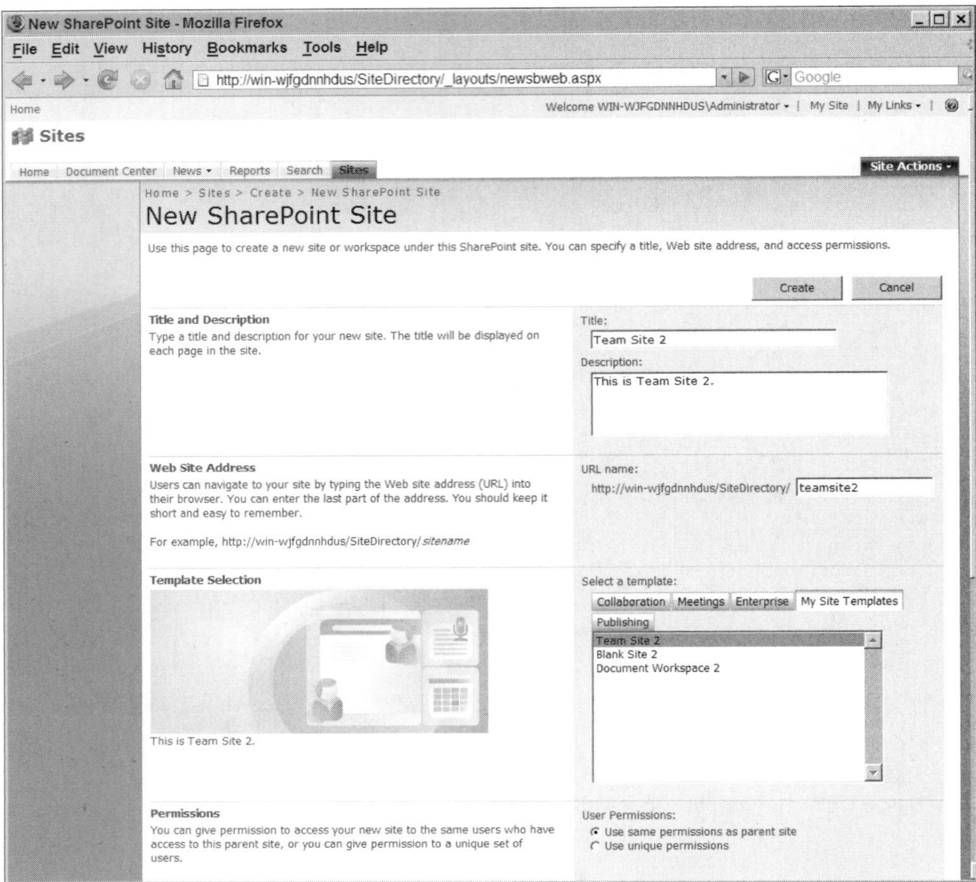

Figure 7-14: The newsbweb.aspx page

As Figure 7-15 shows, this site provisioning provider has changed the title of the provisioned site from Team Site 2 to My Team Site 2. This was a simple example but it shows you everything you need to know to implement complex site provisioning providers.

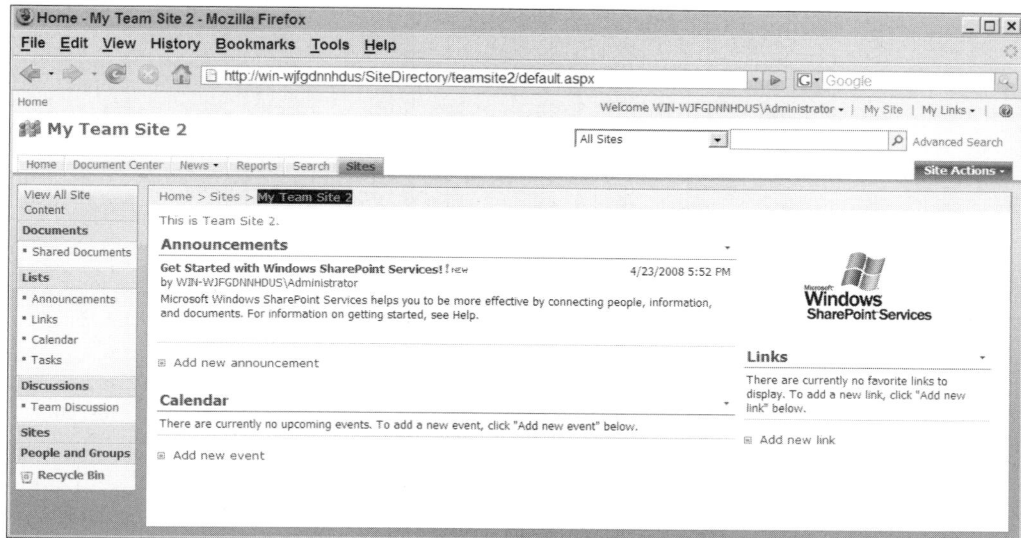

Figure 7-15: The title change caused by the site provisioning provider

Summary

This chapter covered site definitions and site provisioning providers in detail and used examples to show you how to implement your own custom site definitions and site provisioning providers.

8

Advanced SharePoint Programming

The next two chapters dive into advanced SharePoint programming topics. This chapter covers the following:

- ❑ Web configuration modification via the SharePoint object model
- ❑ Extending the STSADM command-line utility to add support for custom operations
- ❑ Feature receivers
- ❑ Developing custom timer jobs
- ❑ Feature dependency
- ❑ Feature stapling

Web Configuration Modification

As discussed earlier, you can think of a site definition as a complete SharePoint solution, which is mostly implemented in CAML but partly implemented in managed code through a site provisioning provider. As a complete SharePoint solution, your site definition should encapsulate and support anything that the clients need to use the site provisioned from the site definition. Some of the functionality that you include in a site definition may require adding one or more entries to the web.config file of the web application when clients provision a site from the site definition.

You may be thinking, "What is so difficult about adding a few entries into a web.config file of a web application?" This may not be an issue in a stand-alone web server. However, this may lead to problems in a server farm. As discussed, SharePoint virtualizes IIS web sites into web applications. The same web application is mapped into numerous IIS web sites in the server farm. These IIS web sites may or may not be on the same web server. Manually adding configuration entries into the web.config of a web application leads to the following problems:

- Manually adding the same configuration entries to the web.config file for every single IIS web site associated with the web application on every single web server in the server farm is an error-prone operation and could easily lead into a mess.
- Even after manually adding the same configuration entries to the web.config files of all the IIS web sites, your job is still not done because:
    - New IIS web sites on the existing web servers in the server farm may be transformed to the same web application.
    - New web servers could be added to the server farm. The IIS web sites of these web servers may be transformed to the same web application.
- You have to constantly remember to add the same configuration entries for the lifetime of the web application. Again, this is a very error-prone and unmanageable process.

SharePoint comes with a class named SPWebApplication, whose instances represent SharePoint web applications. This class exposes a collection property named WebConfigModifications, which contains objects of type SPWebConfigModification. Each SPWebConfigModification object in this collection represents a specific configuration modification, meaning the addition or removal of a configuration entry from the respective web.config file.

Listing 8-1 presents the internal implementation of the SPWebConfigModification class.

Listing 8-1: The internal implementation of the SPWebConfigModification class

```
[SharePointPermission(SecurityAction.LinkDemand, ObjectModel = true)]
public sealed class SPWebConfigModification : SPAutoSerializingObject
{
  [Persisted]
  private string name;
  [Persisted]
  private string owner;
  [Persisted]
  private uint sequence;
  [Persisted]
  private SPWebConfigModificationType type;
  [Persisted]
  private string value;
  [Persisted]
  private string xPath;

  public SPWebConfigModification()
  {
    this.sequence = 0x10000;
    this.owner = string.Empty;
    this.value = string.Empty;
  }

  public SPWebConfigModification(string name, string xpath)
  {
```

```
    this.sequence = 0x10000;
    this.owner = string.Empty;
    this.value = string.Empty;
    this.Name = name;
    this.Path = xpath;
  }

  [SharePointPermission(SecurityAction.Demand, ObjectModel = true)]
  public override bool Equals(object obj)
  {
    SPWebConfigModification modification = obj as SPWebConfigModification;
    return ((((modification != null) &&
            (this.Name.Equals(modification.Name) &&
            this.Path.Equals(modification.Path))) &&
            (this.Value.Equals(modification.Value) &&
            this.Type.Equals(modification.Type))) &&
            this.Owner.Equals(modification.Owner));
  }

  [SharePointPermission(SecurityAction.Demand, ObjectModel = true)]
  public override int GetHashCode()
  {
    return (this.Name + this.Path).GetHashCode();
  }

  public string Name
  {
    get { return this.name; }
    set { this.name = value; }
  }

  public string Owner
  {
    get { return this.owner; }
    set { this.owner = value; }
  }

  public string Path
  {
    get { return this.xPath; }
    set { this.xPath = value; }
  }

  public uint Sequence
  {
    get { return this.sequence; }
    set { this.sequence = value; }
  }

  public SPWebConfigModificationType Type
```

(continued)

Listing 8-1 *(continued)*

```
    {
      get { return this.type; }
      set { this.type = value; }
    }

    public string Value
    {
      get { return this.value; }
      set { this.value = value; }
    }

    // Nested Types
    public enum SPWebConfigModificationType
    {
      EnsureChildNode,
      EnsureAttribute,
      EnsureSection
    }
  }
```

Listing 8-1 demonstrates a number of things:

- SPWebConfigModification inherits from SPAutoSerializingObject. This means that SPWebConfigModification objects in the WebConfigModifications collection of a web application are serialized into the configuration database.
- All fields of SPWebConfigModification are marked with the Persisted metadata attribute, indicating that these fields are serialized into the configuration database. Note that these fields are used as the backing stores for the public properties of SPWebConfigModification. As such, the values assigned to the properties of an SPWebConfigModification are serialized into the configuration database.
- SPWebConfigModification presents the following properties:
    - **Value.** You can set this property to a string containing the entry you want to add to or remove from the web.config file. For example, the following value for the Value property adds an <add> element with the specified attributes to or removes an <add> element with the specified attributes from the web.config file:

```
SPWebConfigModification modification = new SPWebConfigModification();
modification.Value = "<add verb='*' path='MyFile.myextension' " +
 "type='MyNamespace.MyHandler, MyAssembly, Version=1.0.0.0, " +
 "Culture=neutral, PublicKeyToken=b03f5f7f11d50a3a' />";
```

- **Name.** You can set this property to an XPath expression that selects the node specified in the Value property. For example, the following XPath expression selects the <add> element in the previous example:

```
modification.Name = "add[@path='MyFile.myextension']";
```

- **Path.** You can set this property to an XPath expression that selects the parent node of the node specified in the Value property. For example, the following XPath expression selects the <httpHandlers> node where the previous <add> is to be added:

```
Modification.Path = "configuration/system.web/httpHandlers";
```

- **Owner.** You can set this property to a string that will act as the owner of this modification. The owner is normally the full name of the executing assembly. You can use Assembly.GetExecutingAssembly( ).FullName to access the full name of the executing assembly:

```
Modification.Owner = Assembly.GetExecutingAssembly().FullName;
```

- **Sequence.** You can set this property to a number to specify the position of the node being added in the parent node. In some scenarios the position of a child node matters. For example, if you are adding an <add> element to <httpModules> to add a new HTTP module, the position does matter because the modules are processed in the order in which they're added. Therefore, if your module needs to run before another module, you have to make sure that it is added on top of that module.

```
Modification.Sequence = 10;
```

- **Type.** You can set this property to an SPWebConfigModificationType enumeration value to have SharePoint ensure a section, child node, or attribute as described next.

SPWebConfigModification contains a nested enumeration type named SPWebConfigModificationType with the following possible values:

- **EnsureSection.** You can use this enumeration value to instruct SharePoint to ensure that only a single instance of the node specified in the Value property is ever added to the configuration file, regardless of how many attempts are made to add the node. You can also use this value to ensure the uniqueness of a node in a web.config file. This comes in very handy in cases where the web.config may or may not contain a node that you're adding and you want to make sure that if the web.config file contains the node it is not added for the second time.
- **EnsureChildNode.** You can use this enumeration value to instruct SharePoint to ensure that the node specified in the Value property of the SPWebConfigModification object is the child node of the parent node specified in the Path property of the object.
- **EnsureAttribute.** You can use this enumeration value to instruct SharePoint to ensure the attribute.

When you need to add an entry to or remove an entry from the web.config file of a web application, you should write managed code where you should instantiate an SPWebConfigModification object, populate its properties with the appropriate values, and add this object to the WebConfigModifications collection property of the SPWebApplication object that represents the web application. When the changes are finally committed to the WebConfigModifications, SharePoint does the following:

- Automatically adds the specified entries to or removes the specified entries from the web.config files of all existing IIS web sites that map into the web application. These IIS web sites could be on different web servers in the server farm.
- Automatically adds the specified entries to or removes the specified entries from the web.config files of all IIS web sites that are transformed into the same web application in the future. Again, these IIS web sites could be on new web servers that are added to the server farm after you've committed the changes.

Next, you'll implement an HTTP handler named RssHandler. My goal is twofold. First, I'll use this example to show you how to use SPWebConfigModification to add entries to the web.config file of a web application. Second, I'll use this example to show you how to implement your own custom HTTP handlers and deploy them to SharePoint.

Follow these steps to implement and to deploy a custom HTTP handler to SharePoint:

1. Launch Visual Studio and create a Class Library project. Go ahead and create a Class Library project for your RSS handler.
2. Use the steps discussed earlier to configure Visual Studio to compile this project into a strong-named assembly. Go ahead and do this configuration for your class library.
3. Use the steps discussed in the previous chapter to configure Visual Studio to install this assembly into the Global Assembly Cache. Recall that this requires you to add a post event, which executes the following command every time the project is compiled:

```
"Local_Drive:\Program Files\Microsoft Visual Studio 8\SDK\v2.0\Bin\gacutil.exe" -if
"$(TargetPath)"
```

   You could also install the assembly into the local bin directory of the web application. If you decide to use this option, you must grant your assembly the required permissions. For example, as you'll see later in this section, your RSS handler needs to use the SQL client to connect to the database. Code access security is discussed later in this book.

4. Write a class that implements the IHttpHandler interface.
5. Add the required entries to the web.config file of the web application. These entries are discussed shortly.

RSS

Really Simple Syndication (RSS) is a format for syndicating news. This section briefly describes RSS 2.0 in preparation for the next section, where you learn how to develop an HTTP handler named RssHandler to dynamically generate RSS for your web site. Listing 8-2 shows an example of an RSS document.

Listing 8-2: An example of RSS

```
<?xml version="1.0" encoding="utf-8"?>
<rss version="2.0">
  <channel>
    <title>New Articles On greatarticles.com</title>
    <link>http://www.articles.com</link>
    <description>List of newly published articles on articles.com</description>
    <item>
      <title>ASP.NET 2.0</title>
      <description>Discusses new ASP.NET 2.0 features</description>
      <link>http://localhost:1507/CreditCardForm/Smith.aspx</link>
    </item>
    <item>
      <title>View State Management</title>
      <description>In-depth coverage of view state management</description>
```

```
      <link>http://localhost:1507/CreditCardForm/Murray.aspx</link>
    </item>
    <item>
      <title>XSLT</title>
      <description>Discusses common applications of XSLT</description>
      <link>http://localhost:1507/CreditCardForm/Brown.aspx</link>
    </item>
    <item>
      <title>Introduction to XML</title>
      <description>Provides an introduction to XML</description>
      <link>http://localhost:1507/CreditCardForm/Smith.aspx</link>
    </item>
    <item>
      <title>XML Web Services</title>
      <description>In-depth coverage of XML Web services</description>
      <link>http://localhost:1507/CreditCardForm/Murray.aspx</link>
    </item>
  </channel>
</rss>
```

As Listing 8-2 shows, RSS is an XML document with a document element named <rss>. The document element has a mandatory attribute named version. This section covers version 2.0. The <rss> element has a single child element named <channel>. The <channel> element has three required elements named <title>, <link>, and <description>. The <channel> element may also contain zero or more <item> elements. Listing 8-2 shows three child elements of the <item> element: <title>, <description>, and <link>.

RssHandler

You could use a data-bound control such as Repeater to generate an RSS document. The problem with this approach is that every time the user accesses the document, the request goes through the typical page life cycle even though the RSS document doesn't contain any HTML markup text. To avoid the overhead of normal ASP.NET request processing, this section implements a custom HTTP handler named RssHandler to replace the normal page handler.

RssHandler implements the IHttpHandler interface. This interface exposes a method named ProcessRequest and a property named IsReusable. ProcessRequest does just what its name says it does — it processes the client request. The IsReusable Boolean property specifies whether the same instance of the HTTP handler should be used to process different requests. Your custom HTTP handler's implementation of IsReusable should return false:

```
bool IHttpHandler.IsReusable
{
  get { return false; }
}
```

Listing 8-3 shows the implementation of the RssHandler HTTP handler. You need to add references to the System.Web.dll and System.Configuration.dll assemblies because these assemblies contain the IHttpHandler interface and ConnectionStringSettings class, respectively.

Listing 8-3: The RssHandler HTTP handler

```
using System;
using System.Data;
using System.Configuration;
using System.Web;
using System.Web.Security;
using System.Web.UI;
using System.Web.UI.WebControls;
using System.Web.UI.WebControls.WebParts;
using System.Web.UI.HtmlControls;
using System.Data.Common;
using System.Xml;

namespace ClassLibrary1
{
  /// <summary>
  /// Summary description for RssHandler
  /// </summary>
  public class RssHandler : IHttpHandler
  {

    #region IHttpHandler Members

    bool IHttpHandler.IsReusable
    {
      get { return false; }
    }
    DbDataReader GetDataReader()
    {
      ConnectionStringSettings cssettings =
ConfigurationManager.ConnectionStrings["MyConnectionString"];

      DbProviderFactory provider =
DbProviderFactories.GetFactory(cssettings.ProviderName);
      DbConnection con = provider.CreateConnection();
      con.ConnectionString = cssettings.ConnectionString;
      DbCommand com = provider.CreateCommand();
      com.Connection = con;
      com.CommandText = "Select * From Articles";
      con.Open();
      return com.ExecuteReader(CommandBehavior.CloseConnection);
    }

    void IHttpHandler.ProcessRequest(HttpContext context)
    {
      DbDataReader reader = GetDataReader();
      XmlWriterSettings settings = new XmlWriterSettings();
      settings.Indent = true;
      context.Response.ContentType = "text/xml";
      using (XmlWriter writer = XmlWriter.Create(context.Response.OutputStream,
settings))
      {
        writer.WriteStartDocument();
```

```
        writer.WriteStartElement("rss");
        writer.WriteAttributeString("version", "2.0");
        writer.WriteStartElement("channel");
        writer.WriteElementString("title", "New Articles On greatarticles.com");
        writer.WriteElementString("link", "http://www.greatarticles.com");
        writer.WriteElementString("description", "The list of newly published
articles ongreatarticles.com");
        while (reader.Read())
        {
          writer.WriteStartElement("item");
          writer.WriteElementString("title", (string)reader["Title"]);
          writer.WriteElementString("description", (string)reader["Abstract"]);
          writer.WriteElementString("link", "http://localhost/articles?author=" +
(string)reader["AuthorName"] + ".aspx");
          writer.WriteEndElement();
        }
        writer.WriteEndElement();
        writer.WriteEndElement();
        writer.WriteEndDocument();
      }
    }

    #endregion
  }
}
```

As Listing 8-3 shows, the ProcessRequest method first sets the content type to text/xml to inform the clients of the application that the RSS document contains XML data:

```
context.Response.ContentType = "text/xml";
```

Then it retrieves all the article data rows from the Articles database table. Each data row contains three columns (Title, Abstract, and AuthorName):

```
DbDataReader reader = GetDataReader();
```

Then it creates an instance of the XmlWriter class. This instance will be used to dynamically generate the RSS document from the retrieved article data rows:

```
XmlWriterSettings settings = new XmlWriterSettings();
settings.Indent = true;
using (XmlWriter writer = XmlWriter.Create(context.Response.OutputStream,settings))
```

Because the Create method takes the output stream as its argument, the XML writer will directly write into the response's output stream.

Keep in mind that you're trying to dynamically generate an RSS document similar to the one shown in Listing 8-1. As Listing 8-3 shows, the ProcessRequest generates the RSS document line by line. In Listing 8-1, the first line of the RSS document is the XML declaration:

```
<?xml version="1.0" encoding="utf-8"?>
```

ProcessRequest calls the WriteStartDocument method of the XML writer to start the document and add the XML declaration on the top of the RSS document.

The second line of the RSS document is the opening tag of the rss element and its version attribute:

```
<rss version="2.0">
```

ProcessRequest calls the WriteStartElement and WriteAttributeString methods of the XML writer to render the opening tag of the rss element and its version attribute, respectively:

```
writer.WriteStartElement("rss");
writer.WriteAttributeString("version", "2.0");
```

The third line of the RSS document is the opening tag of the channel element:

```
<channel>
```

ProcessRequest calls the WriteStartElement method to render the opening tag of the channel element.

The fourth, fifth, and sixth lines of the RSS document are the title, link, and description sub-elements of the channel element:

```
<title>New Articles On greatarticles.com</title>
<link>http://www.greatarticles.com</link>
<description>List of newly published articles on articles.com</description>
```

ProcessRequest calls the WriteElementString method three times to generate the title, link, and description child elements of the channel element:

```
writer.WriteElementString("title", "New Articles On articles.com");
writer.WriteElementString("link", "http://www.greatarticles.com");
writer.WriteElementString("description",
"List of newly published articles on articles.com");
```

The RSS document may have zero or more item elements, where each item element contains three elements named title, description, and link:

```
<item>
  <title>ASP.NET 2.0</title>
  <description>Discusses new ASP.NET 2.0 features</description>
  <link>http://localhost/authors.aspx?author=Smith.aspx</link>
</item>
```

ProcessRequest enumerates the retrieved article data rows and renders an item element for each enumerated data row. The first line of each item element is the opening tag of the item element:

```
<item>
```

ProcessRequest calls the WriteStartElement method to render the opening tag of the item element:

```
writer.WriteStartElement("item");
```

ProcessRequest accesses the Title and Abstract columns of the enumerated data row and passes the value of each column into the WriteAttributeString method to generate the title and description elements and their contents:

```
writer.WriteElementString("title",(string)reader["Title"]);
writer.WriteElementString("description",(string)reader["Abstract"]);
```

ProcessRequest accesses the AuthorName column of the enumerated data row, which is then used to generate the URL of the document that contains the articles of the specified author:

```
writer.WriteElementString("link", "http://localhost:1507/CreditCardForm/" +
(string)reader["AuthorName"] + ".aspx");
```

The last line of each item element is the closing tag of the item element:

```
</item>
```

ProcessRequest calls the WriteEndElement method to render the closing tag of the item element:

```
writer.WriteEndElement();
```

ProcessRequest then calls the WriteEndElement method to render the closing tag of the channel element. Finally, ProcessRequest calls the WriteEndElement method to render the closing tag of the rss element.

Next, you'll walk through the implementation of the GetDataReader method. As Listing 8-3 illustrates, this method uses the string "MyConnectionString" as an index into the ConnectionStrings static collection property of the ConfigurationManager static class to return a reference to the ConnectionStringSettings object that represents the respective connection string in the web.config file of the current web application:

```
ConnectionStringSettings cssettings =
                        ConfigurationManager.ConnectionStrings["MyConnectionString"];
```

The RssHandler HTTP handler expects the <connectionStrings> section of the web.config file to contain an entry for the respective connection string as follows:

```
<connectionStrings>
  <add name="MyConnectionString"
  connectionString="Data Source=ServerName;Initial Catalog=DataBaseName;
                    Integrated Security=SSPI"
  providerName="System.Data.SqlClient" />
</connectionStrings>
```

Next, GetDataReader invokes the GetFactory static method on the DbProviderFactories static class, passing in the name of the provider that was retrieved from the web.config file (which is System.Data .SqlClient in the previous configuration entry) to instantiate and to return a reference to the DbProviderFactory object that represents the respective provider factory (in the case of configuration entry, this provider factory represents the SQL client):

```
DbProviderFactory provider =
                          DbProviderFactories.GetFactory(cssettings.ProviderName);
```

Next, GetDataReader invokes the CreateConnection method on this provider factory to instantiate a DbConnection object that represents a connection to the database:

```
DbConnection con = provider.CreateConnection();
```

Then, it configures this DbConnection object with the connection string that was retrieved from the web.config file:

```
con.ConnectionString = cssettings.ConnectionString;
```

Next, it creates a DbCommand object to represent a database command and configures it with the newly created connection and this SQL Select command.

You'll need to add the following two entries to the web.config file of the current web application for this RssHandler HTTP handler to work:

```
<configuration>
  <connectionStrings>
    <add name="MyConnectionString"
    connectionString="Data Source=ServerName;Initial Catalog=DataBaseName;
                      Integrated Security=SSPI"
    providerName="System.Data.SqlClient" />
  </connectionStrings>

  <system.web>
    <httpHandlers>
      <add verb="*" path="MyFile.myextension"
      type="ClassLibrary1.RssHandler, ClassLibrary1, Version=1.0.0.0,
Culture=neutral,
            PublicKeyToken=2b56bd310cddb0e3" />
    </httpHandlers>
  </system.web>
</configuration>
```

The first entry adds the connection string. The second registers the RssHandler as an HTTP handler for a web resource named MyFile.myextension. Every HTTP handler entry is to handle requests for web resources with a specific file extension. You can choose any file extension that you want as long as it is unique. At runtime, the ASP.NET HTTP Runtime Pipeline automatically reads this entry from the web.config file and uses the type information specified in the type attribute of the <add> element registered by your HTTP handler to instantiate your HTTP handler. You must set the type attribute to the fully assembly-namespace-qualified name of your HTTP handler, which includes the fully namespace-qualified name of your HTTP handler and the strong name of the assembly that contains your HTTP handler. Keep in mind that the strong name of the assembly consists of the assembly name, version, culture, and public key token.

In a normal ASP.NET environment, there is also a third requirement in addition to adding the previous two entries to the web.config file. You must also add an entry to the IIS metabase to instruct IIS to pass the requests for the file extensions that your handler handles to the aspnet_isapi.dll ISAPI extension module. This ISAPI extension module in turn passes the requests to ASP.NET. This is not needed in SharePoint because SharePoint has already added an entry to the IIS metabase to have IIS pass all requests for all file extensions to the aspnet_isapi.dll ISAPI extension module.

For the reasons discussed earlier, you shouldn't add the previous two entries to the web.config file of the current web application manually. Instead you should use an SPWebConfigModification object to have SharePoint add these entries on your behalf. This requires you to write managed code. Where should this managed code go? There are several options, such as:

- A site provisioning provider associated with a site definition configuration
- A feature receiver
- A console application that runs locally on a web server in the server farm

Listing 8-4 modifies the site provisioning provider developed earlier to use three SPWebConfigModification objects to add the required entries to the web.config files of all the existing and future IIS web sites that map into the current web application. You'll need to add a reference to the Microsoft.SharePoint.dll assembly as discussed earlier in this chapter. Don't forget to replace EnterServerName and EnterDataBase with your server and database names. Also don't forget to replace the PublicKeyToken attribute with the actual public key token of your assembly.

Listing 8-4: The site provisioning provider that adds entries to web.config

```
using Microsoft.SharePoint;
using Microsoft.SharePoint.Administration;
using System.Reflection;

namespace ClassLibrary1
{
  public class CustomProvisioningProvider : SPWebProvisioningProvider
  {
    public override void Provision(SPWebProvisioningProperties props)
    {
      props.Web.ApplyWebTemplate("STS10#0");
      props.Web.Title = props.Data;
      props.Web.Update();

      using (SPSite siteCollection = new SPSite(props.Web.Site.ID))
      {
        using (SPWeb site = siteCollection.OpenWeb(props.Web.ID))
        {
          site.AllowUnsafeUpdates = true;
          SPWebApplication app = siteCollection.WebApplication;

          SPWebConfigModification modification1 = new SPWebConfigModification();
          modification1.Path = "configuration";
          modification1.Name = "connectionStrings";
          modification1.Value = "<connectionStrings></connectionStrings>";
          modification1.Owner = Assembly.GetExecutingAssembly().FullName;
          modification1.Sequence = 100;
          modification1.Type =
                 SPWebConfigModification.SPWebConfigModificationType.EnsureSection;
          app.WebConfigModifications.Add(modification1);

          SPWebConfigModification modification2 = new SPWebConfigModification();
          modification2.Path = "configuration/connectionStrings";
```

(continued)

Listing 8-4 *(continued)*

```
                modification2.Name = "add[@name='MyConnectionString']";
                modification2.Value = "<add name='MyConnectionString' " +
                                      "connectionString='Data Source=EnterServerName;" +
                                      "Initial Catalog=EnterDatabaseName;" +
                                      "Integrated Security=SSPI' " +
                                      "providerName='System.Data.SqlClient' />";
                modification2.Owner = Assembly.GetExecutingAssembly().FullName;
                modification2.Sequence = 100;
                modification2.Type =
                      SPWebConfigModification.SPWebConfigModificationType.EnsureSection;
                app.WebConfigModifications.Add(modification2);

                SPWebConfigModification modification3 = new SPWebConfigModification();
                modification3.Path = "configuration/system.web/httpHandlers";
                modification3.Name = "add[@path='MyFile.myextension']";
                modification3.Value = "<add verb='*' " +
                                      "path='MyFile.myextension' " +
                                      "type='ClassLibrary1.RssHandler, ClassLibrary1, " +
                                      "Version=1.0.0.0, Culture=neutral, " +
                                      "PublicKeyToken=0b0dae5bc88b512c' />";
                modification3.Owner = Assembly.GetExecutingAssembly().FullName;
                modification3.Sequence = 100;
                modification3.Type =
                      SPWebConfigModification.SPWebConfigModificationType.EnsureSection;
                app.WebConfigModifications.Add(modification3);

                SPWebService service = SPFarm.Local.Services.GetValue<SPWebService>();
                service.ApplyWebConfigModifications();
            }
        }
      }
    }
  }
```

Your site provisioning provider first uses the WebApplication property of the SPSite object that represents the current site collection to access a reference to the SPWebApplication object representing the current SharePoint web application:

```
SPWebApplication app = siteCollection.WebApplication;
```

Note that your site provisioning provider creates three SPWebConfigModification objects. The first object adds the <connectionStrings> element to the web.config file. This is to ensure that the web.config file already contains this element before you attempt to add an entry for your own connection string. Keep in mind that your entry goes within the opening and closing tags of the <connectionStrings> element. As Listing 8-4 shows, your site provisioning provider sets the Path property on the first SPWebConfigModification object to the "configuration" XPath expression. This XPath expression selects the parent of the <connectionString> element, which is the <configuration> document element:

```
            modification1.Path = "configuration";
```

Then, it sets the Name property on this SPWebConfigModification object to the "connectionStrings" XPath expression. This XPath expression selects the <connectionString> element, which is the element being added:

```
modification1.Name = "connectionStrings";
```

SharePoint uses the values of the Path and Name properties to track this modification throughout the lifetime of the current web application. For example, every time a new web server is added to the current server farm and an IIS web site on this web server is mapped into this web application, SharePoint evaluates the XPath expression specified in the Path property to locate the parent node, which is the <connectionStrings> node in this case, and then evaluates the XPath expression specified in the Name property to determine where to stick the child node, which is the <add> node in this case.

As Listing 8-4 shows, this site provisioning provider then sets the Value property on this SPWebConfigModification object to the actual node being added:

```
modification1.Value = "<connectionStrings></connectionStrings>";
```

Next, it sets the Owner property to the full name of the current assembly. SharePoint uses the value of this property for tracking the modification:

```
modification1.Owner = Assembly.GetExecutingAssembly().FullName;
```

Next, it sets the Sequence property to specify where in the parent node the new child node should be inserted:

```
modification1.Sequence = 100;
```

Then, it sets the Type property to EnsureSection enumeration value:

```
modification1.Type =
        SPWebConfigModification.SPWebConfigModificationType.EnsureSection;
```

Finally, it adds this SPWebConfigModification object to the WebConfigModifications collection property of the SPWebApplication object that represents the current web application:

```
app.WebConfigModifications.Add(modification1);
```

Note that you set the Type property to EnsureSection, ensuring the <connectionStrings> element is added once to the web.config file. This is important because users may provision multiple sites from this site definition configuration in the same web application. Your site provisioning provider is bound to be called each time a new site is provisioned from this configuration. As such, if you're adding an entry to the web.config file through a site provisioning provider, you must use the EnsureSection enumeration value to avoid duplicate entries in the web.config file of the same web application.

Note that if you attempt to add an entry to a parent node such as <connectionString> and the node does not exist in the web.config file, users will get the error shown in Figure 8-1 when they try to provision a site from this configuration.

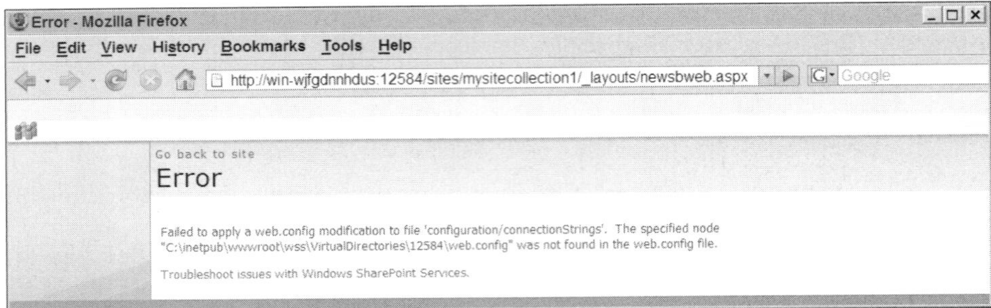

Figure 8-1: The error message shown when an attempt is made to add an entry to a non-existent connectionStrings parent node

As Listing 8-4 shows, after adding the first modification, this site provisioning provider proceeds with the addition of the second modification, which is responsible for adding an entry for this connection string to the <connnectionStrings> element that you just added.

Listing 8-4 first instantiates an SPWebConfigModification object:

```
SPWebConfigModification modification2 = new SPWebConfigModification();
```

Then, it sets its Path property to the "configuration/connectionStrings" XPath expression. This XPath expression selects the <connectionStrings> element, which is the parent node of the node that you want to add:

```
modification2.Path = "configuration/connectionStrings";
```

Next, it sets its Name property to the "add[@name='MyConnectionString']" XPath expression. This XPath expression selects the <add> element that you want to add:

```
modification2.Name = "add[@name='MyConnectionString']";
```

Then, it sets its Value property to the actual node that you want to add:

```
modification2.Value = "<add name='MyConnectionString' " +
                      "connectionString='Data Source=ServerName;" +
                      "Initial Catalog=DatabaseName" +
                      "Integrated Security=SSPI' " +
                      "providerName='System.Data.SqlClient' />";
```

Finally, it sets the Owner, Sequence, and Type properties and then adds the object to the WebConfigModifications collection as usual:

```
            modification2.Owner = Assembly.GetExecutingAssembly().FullName;
            modification2.Sequence = 100;
            modification2.Type =
                SPWebConfigModification.SPWebConfigModificationType.EnsureSection;
            app.WebConfigModifications.Add(modification2);
```

As Listing 8-4 shows, this site provisioning provider then adds the third modification, which adds the entry that registers this RssReader HTTP handler with the current web application:

```
            SPWebConfigModification modification3 = new SPWebConfigModification();
            modification3.Path = "configuration/system.web/httpHandlers";
            modification3.Name = "add[@path='MyFile.myextension']";
            modification3.Value = "<add verb='*' " +
                                  "path='MyFile.myextension' " +
                                  "type='ClassLibrary1.RssHandler, ClassLibrary1, " +
                                  "Version=1.0.0.0, Culture=neutral, " +
                                  "PublicKeyToken=2b56bd310cddb0e3' />";
            modification3.Owner = Assembly.GetExecutingAssembly().FullName;
            modification3.Sequence = 100;
            modification3.Type =
                SPWebConfigModification.SPWebConfigModificationType.EnsureSection;
            app.WebConfigModifications.Add(modification3);
```

Listing 8-4 finally takes these two steps to commit the modifications. First, it accesses a reference to the SPWebService object that represents the current web service:

```
            SPWebService service = SPFarm.Local.Services.GetValue<SPWebService>();
```

Then it invokes the ApplyWebConfigModifications method on this SPWebService object to apply these modifications to the web.config files of all IIS web sites in all web servers in the server farm, which map to the current web application:

```
            service.ApplyWebConfigModifications();
```

Next, add a new XML file named WebTempMyWebTemp2.xml to the following folder on your machine:

```
Local_Drive:\Program Files\Common Files\microsoft shared\Web Server
Extensions\12\TEMPLATE\1033\XML
```

Then, add the content of the following listing to the WebTempMyWebTemp2.xml file:

```
<?xml version="1.0" encoding="utf-8"?>
<Templates xmlns:ows="Microsoft SharePoint">
  <Template Name="STS2" ID="10050">
    <Configuration ID="3" Title="Team Site 2"
    Hidden="FALSE"
    ImageUrl="/_layouts/images/stsprev.png"
    Description="This is Team Site 2."
    DisplayCategory="My Site Templates2"
```

(continued)

(continued)

```
    ProvisionClass="ClassLibrary1.CustomProvisioningProvider"
    ProvisionAssembly="ClassLibrary1, Version=1.0.0.0, Culture=neutral,
PublicKeyToken=ed4f2e3fc6b1b0e0"
    ProvisionData="My Team Site 2" />

    <Configuration
    ID="0"
    Title="Team Site 2"
    Hidden="TRUE"
    ImageUrl="/_layouts/images/stsprev.png"
    Description="This is Team Site 2."
    DisplayCategory="My Site Templates2" />

    <Configuration
    ID="1"
    Title="Blank Site 2"
    Hidden="FALSE"
    ImageUrl="/_layouts/images/blankprev.png"
    Description="This is Blank Site 2."
    DisplayCategory="My Site Templates2" />

    <Configuration
    ID="2"
    Title="Document Workspace 2"
    Hidden="FALSE"
    ImageUrl="/_layouts/images/dwsprev.png"
    Description="This is Document Workspace 2."
    DisplayCategory="My Site Templates2" />
  </Template>
</Templates>
```

Note that the values of the ProvisionClass and ProvisionAssembly attributes are set to the fully namespace-qualified name of your custom provisioning provider and its containing assembly, respectively:

```
ProvisionClass="ClassLibrary1.CustomProvisioningProvider"
ProvisionAssembly="ClassLibrary1, Version=1.0.0.0, Culture=neutral,
PublicKeyToken=ed4f2e3fc6b1b0e0"
```

Note that both the WebTempMyWebTemp.xml file (discussed in the previous chapter) and the WebTempMyWebTemp2.xml file use the same STS2 site definition. As this example clearly shows, you can have two templates using the same site definition. Each template can then be configured to use a different custom provisioning provider to run different custom code.

Now go ahead and build the project. This should automatically build the strong-named assembly that contains your RSS handler and custom site provisioning provider and install it in the GAC. Next, reset IIS to have IIS pick up the new template. Then follow the steps discussed in the previous chapter to create a new site from your site template. Note that the DisplayCategory attribute in the WebTempMyWebTemp.xml file is set to My Site Templates2 to instruct SharePoint to place your template in a separate tab titled My Site Templates2 in the page that enables users to provision a site from your site template.

If you access the MyFile.myextension file, you should get the result shown in Figure 8-2.

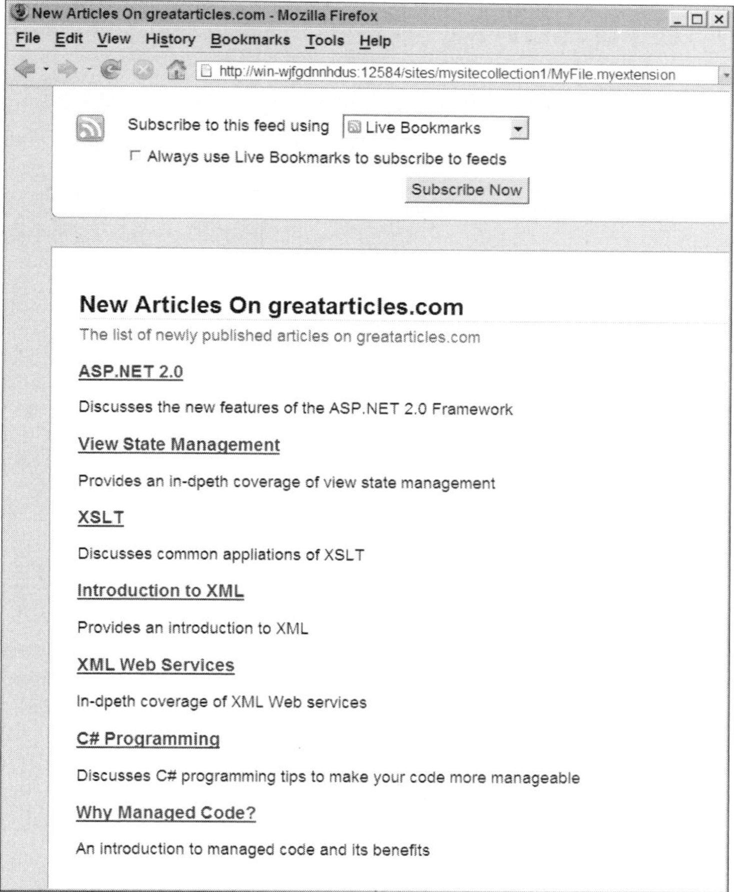

Figure 8-2: The page showing the RSS feed

Figure 8-3 presents the schema of the table that Figure 8-2 uses.

Table - dbo.Articles

ArticleId	Title	AuthorName	Abstract
1	ASP.NET 2.0	Smith	Discusses the new features of the ASP.NET 2.0 Framework
2	View State Management	Murray	Provides an in-dpeth coverage of view state management
3	XSLT	Brown	Discusses common applations of XSLT
4	Introduction to XML	Smith	Provides an introduction to XML
5	XML Web Services	Murray	In-dpeth coverage of XML Web services
6	C# Programming	Brown	Discusses C# programming tips to make your code more manageable
7	Why Managed Code?	Brown	An introduction to managed code and its benefits

Figure 8-3: The database table used to generate the RSS document

Extending STSADM

This section shows you how to extend the STSADM command-line utility to add support for new operations. Follow these steps to extend STSADM:

1. Launch Visual Studio, create a Class Library project, and add a reference to the Microsoft.SharePoint.dll assembly.
2. Use the steps discussed earlier to configure Visual Studio to compile this project into a strong-named assembly.
3. Use the steps discussed earlier to configure Visual Studio to install this assembly into the Global Assembly Cache.
4. Choose an appropriate name for your custom operation.
5. Write a class that implements the ISPStsadmCommand interface.
6. Write an XML file to describe your new operation to the STSADM command-line utility.
7. Deploy this XML file to the following folder on your machine:

```
Local_Drive:\Program Files\Common Files\Microsoft Shared\web server extensions\12\
CONFIG
```

Next, you'll use these steps to add support for a new operation named modifywebconfig. As the name suggests, this operation will allow users to add a specified modification to or remove a specified modification from the web.config files of all IIS web sites mapped into the specified web application.

As mentioned, you need to write a class that implements the ISPStsadmCommand interface. Listing 8-5 presents the definition of this interface.

Listing 8-5: The ISPStsadmCommand interface

```
[SharePointPermission(SecurityAction.InheritanceDemand, ObjectModel=true),
SharePointPermission(SecurityAction.LinkDemand, ObjectModel=true)]
public interface ISPStsadmCommand
{
  string GetHelpMessage(string command);
  int Run(string command, StringDictionary keyValues, out string output);
}
```

As you can see, this interface features the following two methods that every command class must implement:

- **GetHelpMessage.** The STSADM command-line utility calls this method and passes the command or operation name into this method. Your custom command class's implementation of this method must return a string that specifies to users which parameters are supported by your custom operation.
- **Run.** The STSADM command-line utility calls this method and passes the operation name, a StringDictionary that contains the parameter names and values, and an out string. Your custom command class's implementation of this method must use these parameter values, execute the necessary code, and populate the output string with the appropriate message. The STSADM command-line utility displays this message to users when the operation completes.

Because the STSADM command-line utility passes the operation name into the GetHelpMessage and Run methods, you can use the same command class to handle more than one operation. Your command class's implementation of these methods should then use the operation name to determine what code it needs to execute to process the operation.

Listing 8-6 presents the implementation of a custom command class named ModifyWebConfig.

Listing 8-6: The ModifyWebConfig custom command class

```
using System;
using Microsoft.SharePoint;
using Microsoft.SharePoint.StsAdmin;
using System.Collections.Specialized;
using Microsoft.SharePoint.Administration;
using System.Text;

namespace ClassLibrary2
{
  public class ModifyWebConfig : ISPStsadmCommand
  {
    protected string GetHelpMessage(string command)
    {
      return "-url <full url to a site collection in SharePoint> " +
             "-path <XPath expression that selects the parent node> " +
             "-name <XPath expression that selects the node being added> " +
             "-value <node being added> " +
             "-owner <owner> " +
             "-sequence <order of the node among other nodes> " +
             "-type <type of modification (EnsureAttribute, EnsureChildNode, and
EnsureSection> " +
             "-action <add or remove>";
    }

    protected int Run(string command, StringDictionary keyValues, out string
output)
    {
      if (!keyValues.ContainsKey("url"))
        throw new InvalidOperationException("The url parameter was not specified.");
```

(continued)

Listing 8-6 *(continued)*

```
      if (!keyValues.ContainsKey("path"))
        throw new InvalidOperationException("The path parameter was not specified.");

      if (!keyValues.ContainsKey("name"))
        throw new InvalidOperationException("The name parameter was not specified.");

      if (!keyValues.ContainsKey("value"))
        throw new InvalidOperationException("The value parameter was not specified.");

      if (!keyValues.ContainsKey("owner"))
        throw new InvalidOperationException("The owner parameter was not specified.");

      if (!keyValues.ContainsKey("sequence"))
        throw new InvalidOperationException("The sequence parameter was
not specified.");

      if (!keyValues.ContainsKey("type"))
        throw new InvalidOperationException("The type parameter was not specified.");

      if (!keyValues.ContainsKey("action"))
        throw new InvalidOperationException("The action parameter was not specified.");

      String url = keyValues["url"];
      String path = keyValues["path"];
      String name = keyValues["name"];
      String value = keyValues["value"];
      String owner = keyValues["owner"];
      String sequence = keyValues["sequence"];
      String type = keyValues["type"];
      String action = keyValues["action"];

      try
      {
        using (SPSite site = new SPSite(url))
        {
          SPWebApplication app = site.WebApplication;
          SPWebConfigModification modification = new SPWebConfigModification();
          modification.Path = path;
          modification.Name = name;
          modification.Value = value;
          modification.Owner = owner;
          modification.Sequence = uint.Parse(sequence);
          type = type.ToLower();
          action = action.ToLower();
```

```
          switch (type)
          {
            case "ensureattribute":
              modification.Type =
SPWebConfigModification.SPWebConfigModificationType.EnsureAttribute;
              break;
            case "ensurechildnode":
              modification.Type =
SPWebConfigModification.SPWebConfigModificationType.EnsureChildNode;
              break;
            case "ensuresection":
              modification.Type =
SPWebConfigModification.SPWebConfigModificationType.EnsureSection;
              break;
          }

          if (action == "add")
            app.WebConfigModifications.Add(modification);
          else
            app.WebConfigModifications.Remove(modification);

          SPWebService service = SPFarm.Local.Services.GetValue<SPWebService>();
          service.ApplyWebConfigModifications();
        }
      }

      catch (Exception e)
      {
        throw new InvalidOperationException(e.Message);
      }

      output = "The specified modification was applied";

      return 0;
    }

    #region ISPStsadmCommand Members

    string ISPStsadmCommand.GetHelpMessage(string command)
    {
      return this.GetHelpMessage(command);
    }

    int ISPStsadmCommand.Run(string command, StringDictionary keyValues, out string
output)
    {
      return this.Run(command, keyValues, out output);
    }

    #endregion
  }
}
```

Note that ModifyWebConfig uses the C# interface implementation pattern to implement the GetHelpMessage and Run methods of the ISPStsadmCommand interface. Follow these steps to use this pattern to implement the methods of an interface:

1. For each method of the interface, implement a protected virtual method with the same signature as the interface method. Keep in mind that the signature of a method includes the method name, parameter types, and return type.
2. Implicitly implement each method of the interface. Make sure that the implicit implementation of an interface method meets the following two important requirements:
    - Qualifies the name of the method with the name of the interface
    - Does not use an access modifier such as public, protected, and so on
3. The method that implicitly implements an interface method delegates to the respective method from Step 1; the method from Step 1 has the same signature as the method that implicitly implements the interface method.

The C# interface implementation pattern enables the subclasses of your class to override your class's implementation of the interface by overriding the respective protected methods without having to directly implement the interface.

Following the C# interface implementation pattern, Listing 8-6 contains two methods named ISPStsadmCommand.GetHelpMessage and ISPStsadmCommand.Run, which implicitly implement the GetHelpMessage and Run methods of the ISPStsadmCommand interface. Note that these methods delegate to the GetHelpMessage and Run protected virtual methods.

Next, you'll walk through the implementation of the GetHelpMessage and Run protected virtual methods. As Listing 8-6 shows, the GetHelpMessage method returns a string that contains the help message:

```
return "-url <full url to a site collection in SharePoint> " +
       "-path <XPath expression that selects the parent node> " +
       "-name <XPath expression that selects the node being added> " +
       "-value <node being added> " +
       "-owner <owner> " +
       "-sequence <order of the node among other nodes> " +
       "-type <type of modification (EnsureAttribute, EnsureChild, and
EnsureSection> " +
       "-action <add or remove>";
```

Your command operation, like any other STSADM command operation, supports command-line switches. Users use these command-line switches to provide the Run method of the respective command class with the complete information that it needs to execute the code that handles the operation. Your custom STSADM operation supports the following command-line switches:

- **-url.** The user uses this switch to specify the URL of a site collection in the desired web application.
- **-path.** The user uses this switch to specify the XPath expression that selects the parent node of the node being added or removed.

- **-name.** The user uses this switch to specify the XPath expression that selects the node being added or removed.
- **-value.** The user uses this switch to specify the actual node being added or removed.
- **-owner.** The user uses this switch to specify an owner for the modification.
- **-sequence.** The user uses this switch to specify the position of the node being added or removed with respect to other nodes in the same parent node.
- **-type.** The user uses this switch to specify the type of the modification. The possible values are ensureattribute, ensurechildnode, and ensuresection.
- **-action.** The user uses this switch to specify whether to add or to remove the node. The possible values are add and remove.

As Listing 8-6 demonstrates, the Run method first examines the StringDictionary argument to ensure that the user has indeed entered values for all switches. If a switch is missing, Run raises an InvalidOperationException:

```
if (!keyValues.ContainsKey("url"))
  throw new InvalidOperationException("The url parameter was not specified.");

if (!keyValues.ContainsKey("path"))
  throw new InvalidOperationException("The path parameter was not specified.");

if (!keyValues.ContainsKey("name"))
  throw new InvalidOperationException("The name parameter was not specified.");

if (!keyValues.ContainsKey("value"))
  throw new InvalidOperationException("The value parameter was not specified.");

if (!keyValues.ContainsKey("owner"))
  throw new InvalidOperationException("The owner parameter was not specified.");

if (!keyValues.ContainsKey("sequence"))
  throw new InvalidOperationException("The sequence parameter was not specified.");

if (!keyValues.ContainsKey("type"))
  throw new InvalidOperationException("The type parameter was not specified.");

if (!keyValues.ContainsKey("action"))
  throw new InvalidOperationException("The action parameter was not specified.");
```

It then uses each switch name as an index into the StringDictionary to return the value of the switch:

```
String url = keyValues["url"];
String path = keyValues["path"];
String name = keyValues["name"];
String value = keyValues["value"];
String owner = keyValues["owner"];
String sequence = keyValues["sequence"];
String type = keyValues["type"];
String action = keyValues["action"];
```

The Run method then instantiates an SPSite object to represent the site collection whose URL is specified as the value of the url switch. As a best practice, you should always instantiate an SPSite object within a using statement to ensure that the Dispose method of the object is automatically invoked when the object goes out of scope:

```
SPSite site = new SPSite(url);
```

The Run method then uses the WebApplication property of this SPSite object to access a reference to the SPWebApplication object that represents the web application that contains the site collection:

```
SPWebApplication app = site.WebApplication;
```

Next, the Run method instantiates an SPWebConfigModification object and assigns the values of the path, name, value, owner, sequence, and type command-line switches to the respective properties of this object. Note that Run invokes the Add method on the WebConfigModifications collection if the user has set the value of the action switch to add. Otherwise, it invokes the Remove method:

```
if (action == "add")
  app.WebConfigModifications.Add(modification);
else
  app.WebConfigModifications.Remove(modification);
```

Run then applies the modification:

```
SPWebService service = SPFarm.Local.Services.GetValue<SPWebService>();
service.ApplyWebConfigModifications();
```

Finally, Run returns a message indicating that everything went fine and the specified modification was applied:

```
output = "The specified modification was applied";
```

Listing 8-7 presents the XML file that describes this custom STSADM operation to the STSADM command-line utility.

Listing 8-7: The XML file that describes this custom STSADM operation

```
<?xml version="1.0" encoding="utf-8" ?>
<commands>
  <command
  name="modifywebconfig"
  class="ClassLibrary2.ModifyWebConfig, ClassLibrary2, Version=1.0.0.0,
Culture=neutral, PublicKeyToken=693829e6dcd41d14"/>
</commands>
```

This XML file has a document element named <commands>, which contains one <command> element that describes each custom STSADM operation or command. Because you've only defined one command, the <commands> document element contains a single <command> element. The <command> element exposes the following two attributes:

- **name.** You must assign the name of your operation to this attribute. This is the name that the user will use as the value of the -o switch when it executes the STSADM command-line utility.
- **class.** You must assign the fully namespace assembly–qualified name of your custom command class to this attribute.

Figure 8-4 shows this custom operation in action.

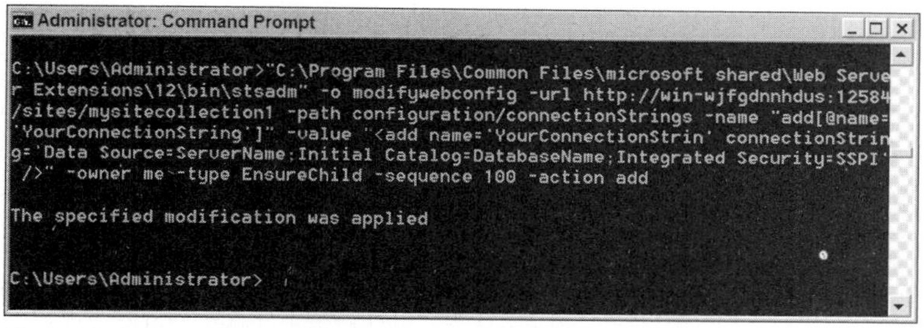

```
Administrator: Command Prompt

C:\Users\Administrator>"C:\Program Files\Common Files\microsoft shared\Web Serve
r Extensions\12\bin\stsadm" -o modifywebconfig -url http://win-wjfgdnnhdus:12584
/sites/mysitecollection1 -path configuration/connectionStrings -name "add[@name=
'YourConnectionString']" -value '<add name='YourConnectionStrin' connectionStrin
g='Data Source=ServerName;Initial Catalog=DatabaseName;Integrated Security=SSPI'
 />" -owner me -type EnsureChild -sequence 100 -action add

The specified modification was applied

C:\Users\Administrator>
```

Figure 8-4: The modifywebconfig operation in action

Feature Receiver

As you've seen throughout this book, you can use features to deploy a variety of SharePoint components such as site columns and site content types, just to name a few. Features also support a very powerful event model that you can use to execute custom code when a feature is activated or installed. To do so, you need to implement a class known as a feature receiver. Follow these steps to implement and to deploy a feature receiver:

1. Launch Visual Studio 2008 and create a Class Library project.
2. Follow the steps discussed earlier to configure Visual Studio to compile this project into a strong-named assembly and to install the assembly in the GAC every time the project is built.
3. Follow the steps discussed earlier to add the Get Public Key Token tool to the Tools menu of Visual Studio if you haven't done it already so you can easily retrieve the public key token of the assembly. You're going to need this public key token later.
4. Add a class to this Class Library project.
5. Derive this class from the SPFeatureReceiver abstract base class. Add a reference to the Microsoft.SharePoint.dll assembly.

6. Implement all four methods of the abstract base class. You must implement all four methods because all four methods are abstract methods.

7. Add the CAML schema files to the Schema directory of your Visual Studio installation if you haven't done so already; it provides Visual Studio IntelliSense support.

8. Add a feature.xml file to this Class Library project and implement a feature as usual. For example, this feature could be used to deploy site columns or site content types. Don't forget to set the xmlns attribute on the <Feature> element to http://schemas.microsoft.com/sharepoint/ so you can take advantage of Visual Studio IntelliSense support as you're writing the CAML that implements the feature.

9. Set the ReceiverClass attribute on the <Feature> element to the fully namespace-qualified name of your feature receiver class from Step 4.

10. Set the ReceiverAssembly attribute on the <Feature> element to the strong name of the assembly that contains your feature receiver class.

Listing 8-8 presents the definition of the SPFeatureReceiver abstract base class from which every feature receiver class must inherit.

Listing 8-8: The SPFeatureReceiver abstract base class

```
[SharePointPermission(SecurityAction.LinkDemand, ObjectModel=true),
SharePointPermission(SecurityAction.InheritanceDemand, ObjectModel=true)]
public abstract class SPFeatureReceiver
{
  public abstract void FeatureActivated(SPFeatureReceiverProperties properties);
  public abstract void FeatureDeactivating(SPFeatureReceiverProperties properties);
  public abstract void FeatureInstalled(SPFeatureReceiverProperties properties);
  public abstract void FeatureUninstalling(SPFeatureReceiverProperties properties);
}
```

The SPFeatureReceiver abstract base class exposes the following four abstract methods that every feature receiver must implement:

- **FeatureActivated.** SharePoint automatically invokes this method and passes an SPFeatureReceiverProperties object into it when the feature is activated. A feature can be activated through the SharePoint user interface, SharePoint object model, or SharePoint web services. Implement this method to include the custom code to be executed when the feature is activated.

- **FeatureDeactivating.** SharePoint automatically invokes this method and passes an SPFeatureReceiverProperties object into it when the feature is about to be deactivated. A feature can be deactivated through the SharePoint user interface, SharePoint object model, or SharePoint web services. Implement this method to include the custom code that to be executed when the feature is about to be deactivated.

- **FeatureInstalled.** SharePoint automatically invokes this method and passes an SPFeatureReceiverProperties object into it when the feature is installed. Implement this method to include the custom code to be executed when the feature is installed.

- **FeatureUninstalling.** SharePoint automatically invokes this method and passes an SPFeatureReceiverProperties object when the feature is about to be uninstalled. Implement this method to include the custom code to be executed when the feature is about to be uninstalled.

Listing 8-9 presents the implementation of a feature receiver named MyFeatureReceiver.

Listing 8-9: The MyFeatureReceiver class

```
using System;
using Microsoft.SharePoint;
using Microsoft.SharePoint.Administration;
using System.Reflection;

namespace ClassLibrary3
{
  public class MyFeatureReceiver: SPFeatureReceiver
  {
    public override void FeatureActivated(SPFeatureReceiverProperties properties)
    {
    }

    public override void FeatureDeactivating(SPFeatureReceiverProperties
properties)
    {
    }

    public override void FeatureInstalled(SPFeatureReceiverProperties properties)
    {
      SPWebApplication app;
      SPSite siteCollection = properties.Feature.Parent as SPSite;
      if (siteCollection != null)
        app = siteCollection.WebApplication;
      else
      {
        SPWeb site = properties.Feature.Parent as SPWeb;
        app = site.Site.WebApplication;
      }

      SPWebConfigModification modification1 = new SPWebConfigModification();
      modification1.Path = "configuration";
      modification1.Name = "connectionStrings";
      modification1.Value = "<connectionStrings></connectionStrings>";
      modification1.Owner = Assembly.GetExecutingAssembly().FullName;
      modification1.Sequence = 100;
      modification1.Type =
SPWebConfigModification.SPWebConfigModificationType.EnsureSection;
      app.WebConfigModifications.Add(modification1);

      SPWebConfigModification modification2 = new SPWebConfigModification();
      modification2.Path = "configuration/connectionStrings";
      modification2.Name = "add[@name='MyConnectionString']";
      modification2.Value = "<add name='MyConnectionString' " +
                            "connectionString='Data Source=WIN-
WJFGDNNHDUS\\OFFICESERVERS;Initial Catalog=D:\\MINE2\\AUTHORREVIEW\\793507
CH08\\CODE\\CUSTOMHTTPHANDLER\\APP_DATA\\CHAPTER8DB4.MDF;" +
 "Integrated Security=SSPI' " +
 "providerName='System.Data.SqlClient' />";
```

(continued)

Listing 8-9 *(continued)*

```
        modification2.Owner = Assembly.GetExecutingAssembly().FullName;
        modification2.Sequence = 100;
        modification2.Type =
                SPWebConfigModification.SPWebConfigModificationType.EnsureChildNode;
        app.WebConfigModifications.Add(modification2);

        SPWebConfigModification modification3 = new SPWebConfigModification();
        modification3.Path = "configuration/system.web/httpHandlers";
        modification3.Name = "add[@path='MyFile.myextension']";
        modification3.Value = "<add verb='*' " +
   "path='MyFile.myextension' " +
   "type='Chapter6.RssHandler, Chapter6, Version=1.0.0.0, " +
   "Culture=neutral, PublicKeyToken=2b56bd310cddb0e3' />";
        modification3.Owner = Assembly.GetExecutingAssembly().FullName;
        modification3.Sequence = 100;
        modification3.Type =
                SPWebConfigModification.SPWebConfigModificationType.EnsureChildNode;
        app.WebConfigModifications.Add(modification3);

        SPWebService service = SPFarm.Local.Services.GetValue<SPWebService>();
        service.ApplyWebConfigModifications();
      }

      public override void FeatureUninstalling(SPFeatureReceiverProperties
   properties)
      {
        SPWebApplication app;
        SPSite siteCollection = properties.Feature.Parent as SPSite;
        if (siteCollection != null)
          app = siteCollection.WebApplication;
        else
        {
          SPWeb site = properties.Feature.Parent as SPWeb;
          app = site.Site.WebApplication;
        }

        SPWebConfigModification modification1 = new SPWebConfigModification();
        modification1.Path = "configuration";
        modification1.Name = "connectionStrings";
        modification1.Value = "<connectionStrings></connectionStrings>";
        modification1.Owner = Assembly.GetExecutingAssembly().FullName;
        modification1.Sequence = 100;
        modification1.Type =
  SPWebConfigModification.SPWebConfigModificationType.EnsureSection;
        app.WebConfigModifications.Remove(modification1);

        SPWebConfigModification modification2 = new SPWebConfigModification();
        modification2.Path = "configuration/connectionStrings";
        modification2.Name = "add[@name='MyConnectionString']";
        modification2.Value = "<add name='MyConnectionString' " +
                              "connectionString='Data Source=WIN-
```

```
WJFGDNNHDUS\\OFFICESERVERS;Initial Catalog=D:\\MINE2\\AUTHORREVIEW\\793507
CH08\\CODE\\CUSTOMHTTPHANDLER\\APP_DATA\\CHAPTER8DB4.MDF;" +
                                                "Integrated Security=SSPI' " +
                                "providerName='System.Data.SqlClient' />";
        modification2.Owner = Assembly.GetExecutingAssembly().FullName;
        modification2.Sequence = 100;
        modification2.Type =
SPWebConfigModification.SPWebConfigModificationType.EnsureChildNode;
        app.WebConfigModifications.Remove(modification2);

        SPWebConfigModification modification3 = new SPWebConfigModification();
        modification3.Path = "configuration/system.web/httpHandlers";
        modification3.Name = "add[@path='MyFile.myextension']";
        modification3.Value = "<add verb='*' " +
                             "path='MyFile.myextension' " +
                            "type='Chapter6.RssHandler, Chapter6, Version=1.0.0.0, " +
                                 "Culture=neutral, PublicKeyToken=2b56bd310cddb0e3'
/>";
        modification3.Owner = Assembly.GetExecutingAssembly().FullName;
        modification3.Sequence = 100;
        modification3.Type =
SPWebConfigModification.SPWebConfigModificationType.EnsureChildNode;
        app.WebConfigModifications.Remove(modification3);

        SPWebService service = SPFarm.Local.Services.GetValue<SPWebService>();
        service.ApplyWebConfigModifications();
      }
    }
  }
```

Because the feature receiver does not need to execute custom code when the feature is activated or being deactivated, its implementation of the FeatureActivated and FeatureDeactivating methods does not do anything. Your feature receiver's implementation of the FeatureInstalled method adds the necessary entries for this RssHandler to the web.config files of all IIS web sites mapped to the current web application. Your feature receiver's implementation of the FeatureUninstalling method does the opposite; it removes the entries from these web.config files.

Note that the only difference between adding a modification and removing it is in the method that is invoked on the WebConfigModifications collection property of the SPWebApplication object. Otherwise, everything else remains the same. You must invoke the Remove method to remove a modification and the Add method to add the modification. Removing a modification still requires you to instantiate an SPWebConfigModification object and set its properties.

As Listing 8-9 shows, the Type properties of the SPWebConfigModification object that adds an entry for this connection string and an entry that registers your RssHandler are both set to EnsureChildNode as opposed to EnsureSection; the same feature cannot be installed twice in the same web application. These two entries are bound to be added only once to the web.config files. This is true especially considering the fact that this custom feature receiver's implementation of the FeatureUninstalling method removes these entries from these configuration files.

Listing 8-10 presents the feature.xml file for this feature.

Listing 8-10: The feature.xml file

```
<?xml version="1.0" encoding="utf-8" ?>
<Feature xmlns="http://schemas.microsoft.com/sharepoint/"
 Id="{43595619-7883-410d-8725-242B4E6E1AB0}"
 Title="MyFeature"
 Description="This feature executes MyFeatureReceiver."
 Hidden="FALSE"
 Scope="Site"
 ReceiverClass="ClassLibrary3.MyFeatureReceiver"
 ReceiverAssembly="ClassLibrary3, Version=1.0.0.0, Culture=neutral, PublicKeyToken=
7a55bf94d561a051" />
```

The boldfaced portions of Listing 8-10 set the ReceiverClass and ReceiverAssembly attributes in the <Feature> element to the fully namespace-qualified name of this feature receiver class and the strong name of the assembly that contains your feature receiver class.

Developing Custom Timer Jobs

There are times when you need to perform a given task on a scheduled basis. This is where SharePoint timer jobs come into play. The SharePoint Timer Service (owstimer.exe) is the SharePoint component that runs the scheduled jobs.

This section shows you how to implement your own custom timer job, associate it with a service or web application, and specify a schedule for when it should run.

Follow these steps to implement a custom timer job:

1. Launch Visual Studio and create a Class Library project and add a reference to the Microsoft.SharePoint.dll assembly.
2. Use the steps discussed earlier to configure Visual Studio to compile this project into a strong-named assembly.
3. Use the steps discussed earlier to configure Visual Studio to install this assembly into the Global Assembly Cache every time the project is compiled.
4. Write a class that inherits from the SPJobDefinition base class.
5. Associate your custom timer job with a service, web application, or a specific server.
6. Specify a schedule for when your custom timer job should run.

Listing 8-11 presents the definition of the SPJobDefinition base class.

Listing 8-11: The SPJobDefinition base class

```
public class SPJobDefinition : SPPersistedObject
{
  public SPJobDefinition();

  public SPJobDefinition(string name, SPService service,
                         SPServer server, SPJobLockType lockType);

  public SPJobDefinition(string name, SPWebApplication webApplication,
                         SPServer server, SPJobLockType lockType);

  public override void Delete();
  public virtual void Execute(Guid targetInstanceId);
  public override void Update();

  public bool IsDisabled { get; set; }
  public DateTime LastRunTime { get; }
  public SPJobLockType LockType { get; }
  public bool Retry { get; set; }
  public SPSchedule Schedule { get; set; }
  public SPServer Server { get; }
  public SPService Service { get; }
  public string Title { get; set; }
  public SPWebApplication WebApplication { get; }
}
```

As Listing 8-11 shows, SPJobDefinition supports three public constructors. The first one is the default constructor. The second one takes the following parameters:

- **name.** This is the name of the timer job. The name uniquely identifies a timer job, differentiating it from other timer jobs in the same SharePoint service or web application. As you'll see later, the SPService object that represents the service that a timer job is associated with and the SPWebApplication object that represents the web application that a timer job is associated with both expose a collection property named JobDefinitions; it contains references to the SPJobDefinition objects that represent the timer jobs associated with the service or web application. The name of the timer job uniquely identifies the timer job among other timer jobs in this JobDefinitions collection.
- **service.** This references the SPService object that represents the specific SharePoint service with which you would like to associate the timer job being created.
- **server.** This references the SPServer object that represents the specific server with which you would like to associate the timer job being created.
- **lockType.** You can use this parameter to specify the type of lock for the timer job being created. This property is of the SPJobLockType enumeration type defined as follows:

```
public enum SPJobLockType
{
  None,
  ContentDatabase,
  Job
}
```

Here is the description of each enumeration value:

- **None.** No locks
- **ContentDatabase.** The content database is locked before the timer job starts running.
- **Job.** The timer job itself is locked before the timer job starts running. This ensures that the same timer job is not run on more than one machine at a time.

The third constructor of SPJobDefinition takes the same parameters as the second constructor except for the second parameter. The second parameter in the second constructor references the SPService object that represents the specific SharePoint service with which you would like to associate the timer job being created, whereas the second parameter in the third constructor references the SPWebApplication object that represents the specific SharePoint web application with which you would like to associate the timer job being created. Therefore, use the second constructor if you want to associate your timer job with a specific SharePoint service and use the third constructor if you want to associate your timer job with a specific SharePoint web application. Both constructors allow you to optionally specify a specific server.

SPJobDefinition exposes the following public properties:

- **IsDisabled.** This gets or sets a Boolean value that specifies whether the timer job is disabled. You can disable a timer job from within your managed code in addition to the SharePoint Central Administration web application. This means that you can install a timer job in SharePoint and enable/disable it when you need to.
- **LastRunTime.** This gets a DateTime object that specifies the time when the timer job was last executed. A timer job is a scheduled job that is executed on a regular basis.
- **LockType.** This gets the lock type for the timer job.
- **Retry.** This gets or sets a Boolean value that specifies whether the timer job should be retried if it ends abnormally.
- **Schedule.** This gets or sets the SPSchedule object that represents the schedule for when the timer job should run.
- **Server.** This gets a reference to the SPServer object that represents the specific server with which the timer job is associated.
- **Service.** This gets a reference to the SPService object that represents the specific SharePoint service with which the timer job is associated. SPService is the base class for SharePoint services. For example, SPWebService inherits from SPService. SPService exposes the following property:

```
public SPJobDefinitionCollection JobDefinitions { get; }
```

The JobDefinitions collection contains references to all SPJobDefinition objects that represent timer jobs associated with the service.

- **Title.** This gets or sets the title of the timer job. The SharePoint Central Administration displays this title to users.
- **WebApplication.** This gets a reference to the SPWebApplication object that represents the specific SharePoint web application with which the timer job is associated. SPWebApplication exposes the following property:

```
public SPJobDefinitionCollection JobDefinitions { get; }
```

The JobDefinitions collection contains references to all SPJobDefinition objects that represent timer jobs associated with the web application.

Here are descriptions of the methods of the SPJobDefinition class:

- **Delete.** This method deletes the timer job represented by the SPJobDefinition object on which this method is invoked.
- **Execute.** This method executes the timer job represented by the SPJobDefinition object on which this method is invoked. Note that this method takes the GUID as its only argument. This parameter contains the GUID of the target content database if the timer job is processing a content database. Otherwise it contains GUID.Empty. Your timer job's implementation of this method can use this GUID to access a reference to the SPContentDatabase object that represents the content database that your timer job is processing. The SPContentDatabase object exposes a collection property named Sites, which contains references to the SPSite objects that represent the site collections that use the content database that the SPContentDatabase object represents. As such, your timer job's implementation of the Execute method can access the SPSite object that it needs from this Sites collection. You'll see an example of this later in this section.
- **Update.** This method causes the timer job to save its state and to propagate changes to all servers in the server farm.

The SPSchedule class is the base class for all schedule classes. SharePoint comes with the schedule classes discussed in the following sections.

SPOneTimeSchedule

Instantiate an instance of SPOneTimeSchedule and assign it to the Schedule property of your timer job to have SharePoint execute your timer job at a random time during the specified time range. SPOneTimeSchedule exposes a constructor that takes a DateTime object as its argument. You can use this argument to specify this time range.

SPMinuteSchedule

SPMinuteSchedule inherits from SPSchedule and extends its functionality to add support for three properties:

```
public sealed class SPMinuteSchedule : SPSchedule
{
  public int BeginSecond { get; set; }
  public int EndSecond { get; set; }
  public int Interval { get; set; }
}
```

Instantiate an instance of SPMinuteSchedule and assign it to the Schedule property of your timer job to have SharePoint execute your timer job at a random time during the specified time range at a specified frequency. Use the BeginSecond and EndSecond properties to specify the time range and the Interval property to specify the frequency at which your timer job is run. This frequency must be in minutes. The default value for the Interval property is 5. This means that by default SharePoint runs your timer job every 5 minutes. For example, if you set the BeginSecond to 10 and the EndSecond to 30, by default SharePoint will run your timer job every 5 minutes at a random time within the 10th and 30th seconds of each minute.

SPHourlySchedule

SPHourlySchedule extends SPSchedule and adds support for two more properties:

```
public sealed class SPHourlySchedule : SPSchedule
{
  public int BeginMinute { get; set; }
  public int EndMinute { get; set; }
}
```

If you need to run your timer object on an hourly basis, instantiate an SPHourlySchedule object and assign it to the Schedule property of your timer object. SharePoint runs your timer job at a random time during the time range specified by the BeginMinute and EndMinute properties. For example, if you set the BeginMinute to 0 and EndMinute to 30, SharePoint will run your timer job at a random time during the first half of each hour.

SPDailySchedule

SPDailySchedule extends SPSchedule to add support for six new properties:

```
public class SPDailySchedule : SPSchedule
{
  public int BeginHour { get; set; }
  public int BeginMinute { get; set; }
  public int BeginSecond { get; set; }
  public int EndHour { get; set; }
  public int EndMinute { get; set; }
  public int EndSecond { get; set; }
}
```

Use SPDailySchedule to run your timer job on daily basis. SharePoint runs your timer job at a random time during the time range specified by the BeginHour, BeginMinute, BeginSecond, EndHour, EndMinute, and EndSecond properties. For example, if you set the BeginHour to 8, BeginMinute to 2, BeginSecond to 5, EndHour to 10, EndMinute to 20, and EndSecond to 30, SharePoint will run your timer job at a random time between 08:02:05 o'clock and 10:20:30 o'clock of each day.

SPMonthlySchedule

SPMonthlySchedule inherits from SPDailySchedule and defines two new properties:

```
public class SPMonthlySchedule : SPDailySchedule
{
  public int BeginDay { get; set; }
  public int EndDay { get; set; }
}
```

Because SPMonthlySchedule derives from SPDailySchedule, it inherits the same BeginHour, BeginMinute, BeginSecond, EndHour, EndMinute, and EndSecond properties from SPDailySchedule. Use SPMonthlySchedule to run your timer job on monthly basis. SharePoint runs your timer job at a random time during the time range specified by the BeginDay, BeginHour, BeginMinute, BeginSecond, EndDay, EndHour, EndMinute, and EndSecond properties. For example, if you set BeginDay to 3, BeginHour to 8, BeginMinute to 2, BeginSecond to 5, EndDay to 20, EndHour to 10, EndMinute to 20, and EndSecond to 30, SharePoint will run your timer job at a random time between 08:02:05 AM on the 3rd of each month and 10:20:30 AM on the 20th of each month.

SPWeeklySchedule

SPWeeklySchedule inherits SPDailySchedule and adds support for two new properties:

```
public sealed class SPWeeklySchedule : SPDailySchedule
{
  public DayOfWeek BeginDayOfWeek { get; set; }
  public DayOfWeek EndDayOfWeek { get; set; }
}
```

Because SPWeeklySchedule derives from SPDailySchedule, it inherits the same BeginHour, BeginMinute, BeginSecond, EndHour, EndMinute, and EndSecond properties from SPDailySchedule. Note that SPWeeklySchedule features two new properties of the DayOfWeek enumeration type defined as follows:

```
public enum DayOfWeek
{
  Sunday,
  Monday,
  Tuesday,
  Wednesday,
  Thursday,
  Friday,
  Saturday
}
```

Use SPWeeklySchedule to run your timer job on weekly basis. SharePoint runs your timer job at a random time during the time range specified by the BeginDayOfWeek, BeginHour, BeginMinute, BeginSecond, EndDayOfWeek, EndHour, EndMinute, and EndSecond properties. For example, if you set the BeginDayOfWeek to Tuesday, BeginHour to 8, BeginMinute to 2, BeginSecond to 5, EndDayOfWeek to Thursday, EndHour to 10, EndMinute to 20, and EndSecond to 30, SharePoint will run your timer job at a random time between 08:02:05 AM on Tuesdays and 10:20:30 AM on Thursdays of each week.

SPYearlySchedule

SPYearlySchedule derives from SPMonthlySchedule and defines two new properties:

```
public sealed class SPYearlySchedule : SPMonthlySchedule
{
  public int BeginMonth { get; set; }
  public int EndMonth { get; set; }
}
```

Because SPYearlySchedule derives from SPMonthlySchedule, it inherits the same BeginDay, BeginHour, BeginMinute, BeginSecond, EndDay, EndHour, EndMinute, and EndSecond properties from SPMonthlySchedule.

Use SPYearlySchedule to run your timer job on yearly basis. SharePoint runs your timer job at a random time during the time range specified by the BeginMonth, BeginDay, BeginHour, BeginMinute, BeginSecond, EndMonth, EndDay, EndHour, EndMinute, and EndSecond properties. For example, if you set the BeginMonth to 2, BeginDay to 3, BeginHour to 8, BeginMinute to 2, BeginSecond to 5, EndMonth to 5, EndDay to 20, EndHour to 10, EndMinute to 20, and EndSecond to 30, SharePoint will run your timer job at a random time between 08:02:05 AM on February 3 and 10:20:30 AM on May 20 of each year.

Next, you'll use the recipe discussed earlier to implement a custom timer job named HighPriorityBugAlert. Here is the idea behind this timer job. You have a custom list named Bugs where information about new bugs found in a software product is stored. This list has a column named Priority with possible values of Low, Medium, and High. The HighPriorityBugAlert timer job monitors the Bugs list on regular basis and adds an item to the Announcements list if it finds a High priority bug.

Listing 8-12 presents the implementation of this custom timer job.

Listing 8-12: The HighPriorityBugAlert timer job

```
using System;
using Microsoft.SharePoint;
using Microsoft.SharePoint.Administration;
using Microsoft.SharePoint.Utilities;

namespace ClassLibrary4
{
  public class HighPriorityBugAlert: SPJobDefinition
  {
    public HighPriorityBugAlert() : base() { }

    public HighPriorityBugAlert(string name, SPWebApplication webApplication,
                                SPServer server, SPJobLockType lockType)
      : base(name, webApplication, server, lockType) { }

    public HighPriorityBugAlert(string name, SPService service,
                                SPServer server, SPJobLockType lockType)
      : base(name, service, server, lockType) { }

    public override void Execute(Guid targetInstanceId)
    {
      SPWebApplication webApplication = this.Parent as SPWebApplication;
      SPContentDatabase contentDb = webApplication.ContentDatabases[targetInstanceId];

      SPQuery query = new SPQuery();
      query.ViewFields = @"<FieldRef Name='Title'/><FieldRef Name='BugPriority'/>";
      query.Query = @"<Where>" +
                    "<Eq>" +
                      "<FieldRef Name='BugPriority' />" +
                      "<Value Type='Text'>High</Value>" +
```

```
                    "</Eq>" +
                  "</Where>";
      SPList bugs = contentDb.Sites[0].AllWebs["Docs"].Lists["Bugs"];
      SPListItemCollection items = bugs.GetItems(query);
      string body = "<b>New high priority bugs:</b><br/>";
      foreach (SPListItem item in items)
      {
        body += item.Title + "<br/>";
      }

      SPList announcements = contentDb.Sites[0].AllWebs["Docs"].
Lists["Announcements"];
      SPListItem announcement = announcements.Items.Add();
      announcement["Title"] = "High Priority Bugs";
      announcement["Body"] = body;
      announcement.Update();
    }
  }
}
```

As Listing 8-12 illustrates, your custom timer job, like any other timer job, exposes a few constructors that delegate to the constructors of its base class. Your custom timer job, like any other timer job, overrides the Execute method. Next, you'll walk through the implementation of this method. This method first accesses a reference to the SPWebApplication object that represents the web application with which your timer job is associated:

```
SPWebApplication webApplication = this.Parent as SPWebApplication;
```

You'll see later in this section how to associate your timer job with a web application. Next, the method uses the GUID passed into it as its argument as an index into the ContentDatabases collection property of the SPWebApplication object to return a reference to the SPContentDatabase object that represents the content database that the timer job is processing. The ContentDatabases collection contains references to the SPContentDatabase objects that represent the content databases associated with the web application that the SPWebApplication represents.

```
SPContentDatabase contentDb = webApplication.ContentDatabases[targetInstanceId];
```

Next, the Execute method instantiates an SPQuery object to represent a CAML query that you're about to define:

```
      SPQuery query = new SPQuery();
```

Then, it sets the ViewFields property of this SPQuery object to a string that specifies the fields that this CAML query returns:

```
      query.ViewFields = @"<FieldRef Name='Title'/><FieldRef Name='BugPriority'/>";
```

Next, it sets the Query property of this SPQuery object to a string that contains the actual CAML query. This CAML query returns bug records with a BugPriority field value of High:

```
query.Query = @"<Where>" +
                  "<Eq>" +
                    "<FieldRef Name='BugPriority' />" +
                    "<Value Type='Text'>High</Value>" +
                  "</Eq>" +
                "</Where>";
```

Then, it accesses a reference to the SPList object that represents the Bugs list, where the bug records are kept:

```
SPList bugs = contentDb.Sites[0].AllWebs["Docs"].Lists["Bugs"];
```

As you can see, this custom timer job assumes that the bug records are kept in a SharePoint list named Bugs in a site named Docs in the first site collection in the Sites collection of the content database.

Next, the Execute method invokes the GetItems method on the SPList object that represents the Bugs SharePoint list, passing in the SPQuery object that represents your CAML query to return an SPListItemCollection object that contains references to the SPListItem objects that represent high priority bug records:

```
SPListItemCollection items = bugs.GetItems(query);
```

The Execute method then iterates through these SPListItem objects and accesses the value of the Title field:

```
string body = "<b>New high priority bugs:</b><br/>";
foreach (SPListItem item in items)
{
  body += item.Title + "<br/>";
}
```

Finally, the Execute method accesses the SPList object that represents the Announcements list and adds a new announcement:

```
SPList announcements =
                  contentDb.Sites[0].AllWebs["Docs"].Lists["Announcements"];
SPListItem announcement = announcements.Items.Add();
announcement["Title"] = "High Priority Bugs";
announcement["Body"] = body;
announcement.Update();
```

Next, you need to install your custom timer job with SharePoint. Listing 8-13 presents a feature that does this for you. Don't forget to assign the public key token of your assembly to the PublicKeyToken parameter. Deploy the feature to the front-end web server and activate it as discussed earlier.

Listing 8-13: A feature that installs your custom timer job

```
<?xml version="1.0" encoding="utf-8" ?>
<Feature xmlns="http://schemas.microsoft.com/sharepoint/"
 Id="{E71BCB01-5C10-42f7-B531-0F9B355AFB7A}"
 Title="HighPriorityBugAlert Feature"
 Description="This feature contains HighPriorityBugAlert timer job."
 Hidden="FALSE"
 Scope="Site"
 ReceiverClass="ClassLibrary4.HighPriorityBugAlertFeatureReceiver"
 ReceiverAssembly="ClassLibrary4, Version=1.0.0.0, Culture=neutral,
PublicKeyToken=2b56bd310cddb0e3"
  AlwaysForceInstall="true" ActivateOnDefault="false">
</Feature>
```

Note that this feature references a feature receiver named HighPriorityBugAlertFeatureReceiver. Listing 8-14 presents the implementation of this feature receiver.

Listing 8-14: Your custom feature receiver

```
using System;
using Microsoft.SharePoint;
using Microsoft.SharePoint.Administration;
using System.Reflection;

namespace ClassLibrary4
{
  class MyFeatureReceiver : SPFeatureReceiver
  {
    public override void FeatureActivated(SPFeatureReceiverProperties properties)
    {
      SPWebApplication app;
      SPSite siteCollection = properties.Feature.Parent as SPSite;
      if (siteCollection != null)
        app = siteCollection.WebApplication;
      else
      {
        SPWeb site = properties.Feature.Parent as SPWeb;
        app = site.Site.WebApplication;
      }

      foreach (SPJobDefinition job in app.JobDefinitions)
      {
        if (job.Name == "HighPriorityBugAlert")
          job.Delete();
      }

      HighPriorityBugAlert timerJob =
           new HighPriorityBugAlert("HighPriorityBugAlert", app, null,
SPJobLockType.ContentDatabase);

      SPMinuteSchedule schedule = new SPMinuteSchedule();
```

(continued)

Listing 8-14 *(continued)*

```
        schedule.BeginSecond = 0;
        schedule.EndSecond = 59;
        schedule.Interval = 5;
        timerJob.Schedule = schedule;
        timerJob.Update();
      }

      public override void FeatureDeactivating(SPFeatureReceiverProperties
properties)
      {
        SPWebApplication app;
        SPSite siteCollection = properties.Feature.Parent as SPSite;
        if (siteCollection != null)
          app = siteCollection.WebApplication;
        else
        {
          SPWeb site = properties.Feature.Parent as SPWeb;
          app = site.Site.WebApplication;
        }

        foreach (SPJobDefinition job in app.JobDefinitions)
        {
          if (job.Name == "HighPriorityBugAlert")
            job.Delete();
        }
      }

      public override void FeatureInstalled(SPFeatureReceiverProperties properties)
      {
      }

      public override void FeatureUninstalling(
                                          SPFeatureReceiverProperties properties)
      {
      }
    }
  }
```

Next, you'll walk through the implementation of the FeatureActivated method shown in Listing 8-14. This method first accesses a reference to the SPWebApplication object that represents the current web application:

```
        SPWebApplication app;
        SPSite siteCollection = properties.Feature.Parent as SPSite;
        if (siteCollection != null)
          app = siteCollection.WebApplication;
        else
        {
          SPWeb site = properties.Feature.Parent as SPWeb;
          app = site.Site.WebApplication;
        }
```

Then, it iterates through the SPJobDefinition objects in the JobDefinitions collection of this web application and deletes this timer job because you're about to create a new instance of your timer job:

```
foreach (SPJobDefinition job in app.JobDefinitions)
{
  if (job.Name == "HighPriorityBugAlert")
    job.Delete();
}
```

Next, it instantiates your timer job. Note that this method passes the reference to the SPWebApplication object into the constructor that instantiates your timer job. This basically associates your timer job with the current web application:

```
HighPriorityBugAlert timerJob =
     new HighPriorityBugAlert("HighPriorityBugAlert", app, null,
SPJobLockType.ContentDatabase);
```

Next, the FeatureActivated method instantiates an SPMinuteSchedule schedule:

```
SPMinuteSchedule schedule = new SPMinuteSchedule();
```

It then sets the properties of this schedule object, assigns the object to the Schedule property of your timer job, and invokes the Update method on your timer job so that it saves its state and propagates the changes to all servers in the server farm:

```
schedule.BeginSecond = 0;
schedule.EndSecond = 59;
schedule.Interval = 5;
timerJob.Schedule = schedule;
timerJob.Update();
```

This schedule object instructs SharePoint to run this timer job at a random time every five minutes.

Next, you'll walk through the implementation of the FeatureDeactivated method. As Listing 8-14 shows, this method first accesses the SPWebApplication object that represents the current web application as usual. Then it searches the JobDefinitions collection of the current web application for the SPJobDefinition object that represents this timer job. Finally, it deletes the timer job:

```
foreach (SPJobDefinition job in app.JobDefinitions)
{
  if (job.Name == "HighPriorityBugAlert")
    job.Delete();
}
```

Feature Activation

SharePoint provides you with five different approaches to activate a feature:

1. The ManageFeatures.aspx application page displays the list of installed features and enables you to activate or deactivate them:

```
http://SiteURL/_layouts/ManageFeatures.aspx?Scope=...
```

2. Any feature that is referenced from a configuration in a site definition is automatically activated when a site is provisioned from the configuration.
3. The activatefeature operation of the STSADM command-line utility can be used to activate features from the command line.
4. Any feature that is referenced from an <ActivationDependency> element of another feature is automatically activated when the other feature is activated.
5. Any feature that is stapled to a configuration in a site definition is automatically activated when a site is provisioned from the configuration.

You have seen numerous examples of the first three feature activation approaches throughout this book. The last two approaches are discussed in the following two sections.

Feature Dependency

You saw an example of feature dependency in the previous chapter. Recall that the TeamCollab feature defines activation dependencies on features that contain collaborative list types such as TasksList, XmlFormLibrary, and so on. When a feature such as TeamCollab is activated, SharePoint automatically activates all features that the activation dependencies defined within the feature reference. For example, the activation of the TeamCollab feature automatically activates features that contain collaborative list types.

Activation dependency is used in the following two scenarios:

- It enables you to bundle a bunch of features in a single feature so they can be activated or deactivated in one shot. The TeamCollab feature is an example of this scenario.
- If a feature depends on one or more other features, you should define activation dependencies inside the feature that references these features to force their activation every time the feature is activated. This ensures that all the features on which a feature depends are activated before the feature itself is activated.

Because you've seen an example of the first scenario, this section only covers an example of the second scenario. As you may recall, the ConferenceRequestSiteContentType, ManagerSiteContentType, and PersonnelSiteContentType site content types developed in the previous chapters reference the EmployeeFirstName, EmployeeLastName, ConferenceStartDate, ConferenceEndDate, EntitledDays, ManagerComment, ManagerApproval, PersonnelComment, and PersonnelApproval site columns. Next, you'll develop two features. The first feature references the ConferenceRequestSiteColumns.xml element manifest file that defines these site columns. Listing 6-5 presents the content of this element manifest file.

The second feature references the ConferenceRequestSiteContentTypes.xml element file that defines these site content types. Listing 6-4 presents the content of this element manifest file.

Listing 8-15 presents the feature.xml file for the first feature. As you can see, the <Feature> element that defines this feature contains an <ElementsManifests> child element, which contains an <ElementManifest> child element that references the ConferenceRequestSiteColumns.xml element manifest file.

Listing 8-15: The feature that references the ConferenceRequestSiteColumns.xml file

```
<?xml version="1.0" encoding="utf-8" ?>
<Feature
Id="{41E52AFB-01FA-4134-8A42-82BD2133CE10}"
Title="Conference Request Site Columns Feature"
Description="This is Conference Request Feature!"
Version="1.0.0.0"
Scope="Site"
xmlsn="http://schemas.microsoft.com/sharepoint/">
  <ElementManifests>
    <ElementManifest Location="ConferenceRequestSiteColumns.xml"/>
  </ElementManifests>
</Feature>
```

Listing 8-16 presents the feature.xml file for the second feature. The <Feature> element that defines this feature contains the following child elements:

- **<ActivationDependencies>.** This contains an <ActivationDependency> child element that references the first feature.
- **<ElementManifests>.** This contains an <ElementManifest> child element that references the ConferenceRequestSiteContentTypes.xml element manifest file.

Listing 8-16: A feature with activation dependencies

```
<?xml version="1.0" encoding="utf-8" ?>
<Feature
Id="{08930DAF-E95D-49fb-A771-419598E5F13E}"
Title="Conference Request Site Content Types Feature"
Description="This is Conference Request Feature!"
Version="1.0.0.0"
Scope="Site"
xmlsn="http://schemas.microsoft.com/sharepoint/">
  <ActivationDependencies>
    <ActivationDependency FeatureId="{41E52AFB-01FA-4134-8A42-82BD2133CE10}"/>
  </ActivationDependencies>

  <ElementManifests>
    <ElementManifest Location="ConferenceRequestSiteContentTypes.xml"/>
  </ElementManifests>
</Feature>
```

The preceding setup means that the activation of the second feature will automatically force the activation of the first feature.

Feature Stapling

This section discusses feature stapling. Recall from Chapter 7 that any feature referenced from a site definition configuration is automatically activated when a user provisions a site from the site definition configuration. This is great for those features that are directly referenced from the <SiteFeatures> or <WebFeatures> child element of the <Configuration> element that represents the site definition configuration. What if you have one or more features that are not directly referenced from the <SiteFeatures> or <WebFeatures> child element of this <Configuration> element but you still want these features to be activated when a user provisions a site from the site definition configuration that this <Configuration> element represents?

For example, you may have one or more features that you want automatically activated every time a user provisions a site from the Team Site (STS#0) site definition configuration even though these features are not directly referenced from the <SiteFeatures> or <WebFeatures> child elements of the <Configuration> element that represents the Team Site site definition configuration. This is where feature stapling comes into play. Here is how it works:

1. Identify the desired site definition configurations.
2. Identify those features that you want to be automatically activated every time users provision sites from the site definition configurations identified in Step 1.
3. Implement a feature. The <Feature> element that defines this feature must contain one <FeatureSiteTemplateAssociation> element for each feature/site definition configuration pair. Each <FeatureSiteTemplateAssociation> associates a feature with a specific site definition configuration. You must respectively set the Id and TemplateName attributes on each <FeatureSiteTemplateAssociation> element to the GUID of the feature and to the site definition configuration identifier.

The same feature (from Step 3) can staple several features to several site definition configurations. As an example, you'll staple the feature that defines the ConferenceRequestContentType, ManagerContentType, and PersonnelContentType site content types (see Listing 8-16) to the Team Site (STS#0) site definition configuration. Listing 8-17 presents the feature.xml file that does the stapling.

Listing 8-17: A stapling feature

```
<?xml version="1.0" encoding="utf-8" ?>
<Feature
Id="{3E7C4914-372E-4221-BF0F-93D9358BA5CC}"
Title="Conference Site Content Types Stapling Feature"
Description="This feature staples conference site content types feature to Team
sites"
Version="1.0.0.0"
Scope="Site"
xmlsn="http://schemas.microsoft.com/sharepoint/">
  <ElementManifests>
    <ElementManifest Location="FeatureSiteTemplateAssociations.xml"/>
  </ElementManifests>
</Feature>
```

The <Feature> element that defines the stapling feature contains an <ElementManifests> element, which contains an <ElementManifest> element that references the element manifest file that defines the associations between the features and site definition configurations.

Listing 8-18 presents the FeatureSiteTemplateAssociations.xml element manifest file that defines the association between the conference request content types feature (shown back in Listing 8-16) and the Team Site (STS#0) site definition configuration.

Listing 8-18: The FeatureSiteTemplateAssociations.xml file

```
<?xml version="1.0" encoding="utf-8" ?>
<Elements xmlns="http://schemas.microsoft.com/sharepoint/">
  <FeatureSiteTemplateAssociation
  Id="{08930DAF-E95D-49fb-A771-419598E5F13E}"
  TemplateName="STS#0" />
</Elements>
```

This element manifest file contains a <FeatureSiteTemplateAssociation> whose Id attribute is set to the GUID of the feature that contains the conference request content types and whose TemplateName attribute is set to STS#0, which is the identifier for the Team Site site definition configuration.

Note that the value of the Scope attribute on the <Feature> element defining the stapling feature plays a significant role. As an example, consider the stapling feature defined in Listing 8-17:

- If you set the Scope attribute to Web, the activation of the stapling feature will staple the conference request site content types feature to the Team Site site definition configuration at the current site and any of its child sites. This means that provisioning a new site at the current site or any of its child sites from the Team Site site definition configuration will automatically activate the conference request site content types feature for the new site.
- If you set the Scope attribute to Site, the activation of the stapling feature will staple the conference request site content types feature to the Team Site site definition configuration at any of the child sites of the current site collection. This means that provisioning a new site at any of the child sites of the current site collection from the Team Site site definition configuration will automatically activate the conference request site content types feature for the new site.
- If you set the Scope attribute to WebApplication, the activation of the stapling feature will staple the conference request site content types feature to the Team Site site definition configuration at any of the child sites of any of the child site collections of the current web application. This means that provisioning a new site at any of the child sites of any of the child site collections of the current Web application from the Team Site site definition configuration will automatically activate the conference request site content types feature for the new site.
- If you set the Scope attribute to Farm, the activation of the stapling feature will staple the conference request site content types feature to the Team Site site definition configuration at any of the child sites of any of the child site collections of any of the web applications of the current farm. This means that provisioning a new site at any of the child sites of any of the child site collections of any of the web applications of the current farm from the Team Site site definition configuration will automatically activate the conference request site content types feature for the new site.

Another important factor is the site definition configuration to which the stapling feature staples one or more feature. For example, the stapling feature defined in Listing 8-17 staples the conference request site content types feature to the Team Site (STS#0) site definition configuration. Listing 8-19 presents a new version of the FeatureSiteTemplateAssociations.xml element manifest file that associates the conference request site content types feature with the Global site definition configuration (Global#0).

Regardless of from which specific site definition configuration a site is provisioned, it is also provisioned from the Global site definition configuration. Here is the effect of the Scope attribute value when a feature is stapled to the Global site definition configuration (Global#0):

- If you set the Scope attribute to Web, the activation of the stapling feature will staple the conference request site content types feature to any site definition configuration at the current site and any of its child sites. This means that provisioning a new site at the current site or any of its child sites from any site definition configuration will automatically activate the conference request site content types feature for the new site.
- If you set the Scope attribute to Site, the activation of the stapling feature will staple the conference request site content types feature to any site definition configuration at any of the child sites of the current site collection. This means that provisioning a new site at any of the child sites of the current site collection from any site definition configuration will automatically activate the conference request site content types feature for the new site.
- If you set the Scope attribute to WebApplication, the activation of the stapling feature will staple the conference request site content types feature to any site definition configuration at any of the child sites of any of the child site collections of the current web application. This means that provisioning a new site at any of the child sites of any of the child site collections of the current Web application from any site definition configuration will automatically activate the conference request site content types feature for the new site.
- If you set the Scope attribute to Farm, the activation of the stapling feature will staple the conference request site content types feature to any site definition configuration at any of the child sites of any of the child site collections of any of the web applications of the current farm. This means that provisioning a new site at any of the child sites of any of the child site collections of any of the web applications of the current farm from any site definition configuration will automatically activate the conference request site content types feature for the new site.

Listing 8-19: The FeatureSiteTemplateAssociations.xml file

```
<?xml version="1.0" encoding="utf-8" ?>
<Elements xmlns="http://schemas.microsoft.com/sharepoint/">
  <FeatureSiteTemplateAssociation
  Id="{08930DAF-E95D-49fb-A771-419598E5F13E}"
  TemplateName="GLOBAL#0" />
</Elements>
```

Summary

This chapter covered web configuration modification via SharePoint object model, extending the STSADM command line utility, feature receivers, custom timer jobs, feature dependencies, and feature stapling in detail.The next chapter moves on to event receivers, where you'll learn how to respond to events raised by SharePoint lists, list items, and sites.

9

Event Receivers

This chapter provides in-depth coverage of the three main types of event receivers and uses numerous examples to help you gain the skills you need to implement your own event receivers. The chapter starts with list event receivers, which enable you to respond to events that SharePoint lists fire. Next, item event receivers are discussed. You can use these event receivers to execute custom code in response to events that a list item raises. Finally, the chapter looks at web event receivers, which enable you to run custom code when a site fires a specified event.

Overview

SharePoint lists, list items, and sites fire events before and after certain actions take place. You can register event handlers for these events so that they run custom code before and after the respective actions take place. There are two types of events for this purpose:

- **Before events.** These are the events that SharePoint lists, list items, and sites fire before certain actions take place, which is the reason for its name. You can register event handlers for Before events that run application-specific logic to determine whether the respective actions should be allowed to take place. If not, your event handlers can cancel these actions.
- **After events.** These are the events that SharePoint lists, list items, and sites fire after certain actions take place, hence the name After events. You can register event handlers for After events to run application-specific logic. Your event handlers cannot cancel the respective actions because they've already taken place.

Implementing event handlers for the Before and After events that SharePoint lists, list items, and sites fire is very different from implementing event handlers for events raised in a typical .NET class. SharePoint comes with three base classes named SPListEventReceiver, SPItemEventReceiver, and SPWebEventReceiver. Each base class contains one public virtual method for each Before or After event. If you want to respond to a Before or After event, you must implement a class that inherits from one of these event receiver base classes and override the respective public virtual method. As such, these public virtual methods are known as event handlers and your class is known as an event receiver.

The SPListEventReceiver, SPItemEventReceiver, and SPWebEventReceiver classes inherit from a base class named SPEventReceiverBase, shown in Listing 9-1.

Listing 9-1: The SPEventReceiver class

```
[SharePointPermission(SecurityAction.InheritanceDemand, ObjectModel=true),
SharePointPermission(SecurityAction.LinkDemand, ObjectModel=true)]
public class SPEventReceiverBase
{
  protected void DisableEventFiring();
  protected void EnableEventFiring();
}
```

Note that this class is annotated with two code access security metadata attributes that demand its callers and inheritors to have permission to access the SharePoint object model. This class exposes two methods as follows:

- **DisableEventFiring.** Invoke this method as the first statement in the body of your event handler, if your event handler needs to take an action that triggers an event. This avoids repetitive calls into your event handler.
- **EnableEventFiring.** Invoke this method as the last statement in the body of your event handler if you've invoked the DisableEventFiring method. Your event handler must call this method if it calls the DisableEventFiring method.

List Event Receiver

Listing 9-2 presents the definition of the SPListEventReceiver base class.

Listing 9-2: The SPListEventReceiver base class

```
[SharePointPermission(SecurityAction.LinkDemand, ObjectModel=true),
SharePointPermission(SecurityAction.InheritanceDemand, ObjectModel=true)]
public class SPListEventReceiver : SPEventReceiverBase
{
  public virtual void FieldAdded(SPListEventProperties properties);
  public virtual void FieldAdding(SPListEventProperties properties);
  public virtual void FieldDeleted(SPListEventProperties properties);
  public virtual void FieldDeleting(SPListEventProperties properties);
  public virtual void FieldUpdated(SPListEventProperties properties);
  public virtual void FieldUpdating(SPListEventProperties properties);
}
```

As you can see, the SPListEventReceiver event receiver base class contains the following six event handlers:

- **FieldAdded.** Your custom event receiver must override this event handler to handle the FieldAdded event. Note that this event is an After event, meaning that the respective SharePoint list fires this event after a column definition is added to the list.
- **FieldAdding.** Your custom event receiver must override this event handler to handle the FieldAdding event. Note that this event is a Before event, so the respective SharePoint list fires this event before a column definition is added to the list. Your custom event handler can contain an application-specific logic that determines whether to allow the column definition to be added to the list.
- **FieldDeleted.** Your custom event receiver must override this event handler to handle the FieldDeleted event. Note that this event is an After event, that is, the respective SharePoint list fires this event after a column definition is deleted from the list.
- **FieldDeleting.** Your custom event receiver must override this event handler to handle the FieldDeleting event. Note that this event is a Before event, that is, the respective SharePoint list fires this event before a column definition is deleted from the list. Your custom event handler can contain an application-specific logic that determines whether to allow the column definition to be deleted from the list.
- **FieldUpdated.** Your custom event receiver must override this event handler to handle the FieldUpdated event. Note that this event is an After event, with the respective SharePoint list firing this event after a column definition is updated.
- **FieldUpdating.** Your custom event receiver must override this event handler to handle the FieldUpdating event. Note that this event is a Before event, meaning that the respective SharePoint list fires this event before a column definition is updated. Your custom event handler can contain an application-specific logic that determines whether to allow the column definition to be updated.

As Listing 9-2 shows, all event handlers of the SPListEventReceiver list event receiver base class take an argument of type SPListEventProperties. When the respective SharePoint list raises the FieldAdding, FieldAdded, FieldDeleting, FieldDeleted, FieldUpdating, or FieldUpdated event, it creates an SPListEventProperties object and passes it into the respective event handler.

Listing 9-3 presents the public properties of this type.

Listing 9-3: The SPListEventProperties type

```
[SharePointPermission(SecurityAction.LinkDemand, ObjectModel=true),
SharePointPermission(SecurityAction.InheritanceDemand, ObjectModel=true)]
public sealed class SPListEventProperties : SPEventPropertiesBase
{
  public SPEventReceiverType EventType { get; }
  public SPField Field { get; }
  public string FieldName { get; }
  public string FieldXml { get; }
  public SPList List { get; }
```

(continued)

Listing 9-3 *(continued)*

```
    public Guid ListId { get; }
    public string ListTitle { get; }
    public Guid SiteId { get; }
    public string UserDisplayName { get; }
    public string UserLoginName { get; }
    public SPWeb Web { get; }
    public Guid WebId { get; }
    public string WebUrl { get; }
}
```

Here are the descriptions of these properties:

- **Field.** This gets a reference to the SPField object that represents the column definition that the event affects. Keep in mind that the event is one of the following events: FieldAdding, FieldAdded, FieldDeleting, FieldDeleted, FieldUpdating, or FieldUpdated.
- **FieldName.** This gets the name of the column definition that the event affects.
- **FieldXml.** This gets the actual column definition XML document that the event affects.
- **List.** This gets a reference to the SPList object that represents the SharePoint list that raised the event.
- **ListId.** This gets the GUID that uniquely identifies the SharePoint list that raised the event.
- **ListTitle.** This gets the title of the SharePoint list that raised the event.
- **SiteId.** This gets the GUID that uniquely identifies the site collection that contains the SharePoint list that raised the event.
- **UserDisplayName.** This gets the display name of the user that caused the event to fire.
- **UserLoginName.** This gets the login name of the user that caused the event to fire.
- **Web.** This gets a reference to the SPWeb object that represents the SharePoint site that contains the SharePoint list that fired the event.
- **WebId.** This gets the GUID that uniquely identifies the SharePoint site that contains the SharePoint list that fires the event.
- **WebUrl.** This gets the URL of the SharePoint site that contains the SharePoint list that fires the event.
- **EventType.** This gets an SPEventReceiverType enumeration value that specifies the type of the event. The following code listing presents the definition of this enumeration type:

```
public enum SPEventReceiverType
{
  ContextEvent = 0x7ffe,
  EmailReceived = 0x4e20,
  FieldAdded = 0x2775,
  FieldAdding = 0x65,
  FieldDeleted = 0x2777,
  FieldDeleting = 0x67,
  FieldUpdated = 0x2776,
```

```
    FieldUpdating = 0x66,
    InvalidReceiver = -1,
    ItemAdded = 0x2711,
    ItemAdding = 1,
    ItemAttachmentAdded = 0x2717,
    ItemAttachmentAdding = 7,
    ItemAttachmentDeleted = 0x2718,
    ItemAttachmentDeleting = 8,
    ItemCheckedIn = 0x2714,
    ItemCheckedOut = 0x2715,
    ItemCheckingIn = 4,
    ItemCheckingOut = 5,
    ItemDeleted = 0x2713,
    ItemDeleting = 3,
    ItemFileConverted = 0x271a,
    ItemFileMoved = 0x2719,
    ItemFileMoving = 9,
    ItemUncheckedOut = 0x2716,
    ItemUncheckingOut = 6,
    ItemUpdated = 0x2712,
    ItemUpdating = 2,
    SiteDeleted = 0x27d9,
    SiteDeleting = 0xc9,
    WebDeleted = 0x27da,
    WebDeleting = 0xca,
    WebMoved = 0x27db,
    WebMoving = 0xcb
}
```

SPEventPropertiesBase

As Listing 9-3 shows, SPListEventProperties inherits from SPEventPropertiesBase, which is defined in Listing 9-4. This means that SPListEventProperties inherits the properties of SPEventPropertiesBase. As you'll see later, SPItemEventProperties and SPWebEventProperties also inherit from SPEventPropertiesBase.

Listing 9-4: The SPEventPropertiesBase class

```
[SharePointPermission(SecurityAction.InheritanceDemand, ObjectModel=true),
SharePointPermission(SecurityAction.LinkDemand, ObjectModel=true)]
public class SPEventPropertiesBase
{
  public bool Cancel { get; set; }
  public string ErrorMessage { get; set; }
  public string ReceiverData { get; }
  public SPEventReceiverStatus Status { get; set; }
}
```

Here are the descriptions of the properties of SPEventPropertiesBase:

- **Cancel.** This gets or sets a Boolean value that determines whether the action that caused the Before event to fire should be canceled. Obviously, this property is only applicable to event handlers for Before events such as FieldAdding, FieldDeleting, and FieldUpdating. Your event handler can set this property to True to have the action canceled.
- **ErrorMessage.** This gets or sets a string that contains an error message. Your event handler can set this property to an appropriate error message. SharePoint displays this message to users. For example, an event handler for a Before event, which needs to cancel the action that caused the event to fire, should assign an appropriate error message to this property in addition to setting the Cancel property to True.
- **ReceiverData.** This gets a string that contains data about the event.
- **Status.** This gets or sets an SPEventReceiverStatus enumeration value, which specifies the status of the event. Here is the definition of this enumeration:

```
public enum SPEventReceiverStatus
{
  Continue,
  CancelNoError,
  CancelWithError
}
```

Here are the descriptions of these enumeration values:

- **CancelNoError.** This enumeration value specifies that the event is canceled, but no error message is displayed.
- **CancelWithError.** This enumeration value specifies that the event is canceled and an error message is displayed.
- **Continue.** This enumeration value specifies that the event continues, that is, it is not canceled.

As shown in Listing 9-4, the SPEventPropertiesBase class is annotated with two instances of the SharePointPermissionAttribute code access security metadata attributes for demanding the callers and inheritors of this class to have the permission to access the SharePoint object model. This means that if you implement a Web part that uses SPEventPropertiesBase and if you deploy your Web part assembly to the local bin directory of a web application, you must grant this assembly the permission to access the SharePoint object model. Otherwise the .NET security system will fire a SecurityException exception when your Web part attempts to access SPEventPropertiesBase.

Implementing a Custom List Event Receiver

Next, you'll take a look at an example of the scenario where you may want to implement a custom list event receiver. If you have a specific SharePoint list and you want to prevent users from adding a new column definition to the list and from updating and deleting the existing column definitions of the list, you can implement an event receiver that overrides the FieldAdding, FieldUpdating, and FieldDeleting event handlers to cancel the column addition, update, or deletion action as shown in the following code listing:

```
using System;
using Microsoft.SharePoint;

namespace ClassLibrary1
{
  public class MyListEventReceiver1 : SPListEventReceiver
  {
    public override void FieldAdding(SPListEventProperties properties)
    {
      properties.ErrorMessage = "New column definitions cannot be added to the " +
                                properties.ListTitle + " list.";
      properties.Cancel = true;
    }

    public override void FieldDeleting(SPListEventProperties properties)
    {
      properties.ErrorMessage = "The column definitions of the list " +
                                properties.ListTitle + " cannot be deleted.";
      properties.Cancel = true;
    }

    public override void FieldUpdating(SPListEventProperties properties)
    {
      properties.ErrorMessage = "The column definitions of the list " +
                                properties.ListTitle + " cannot be updated.";
      properties.Cancel = true;
    }
  }
}
```

Note that all three of these event handlers first set the ErrorMessage to an appropriate error message and then set the Cancel property to true to cancel the addition, deletion, or update operation.

After you implement your custom list event receiver, you must compile it into a strong-named assembly and install this assembly in the Global Assembly Cache to make your custom list event receiver available to SharePoint. The easiest way to go about this is to:

1. Create a Class Library project.
2. Add a C# source file containing your custom list event receiver to this project.
3. Configure Visual Studio to compile the project into a strong-named assembly.
4. Add a post event to have Visual Studio execute the following command every time the project is built:

```
"Local_Drive:\Program Files\Microsoft Visual Studio 8\SDK\v2.0\Bin\gacutil.exe" -if
"$(TargetPath)"
```

Next, you need to bind the event handlers of your custom list event receiver to a SharePoint list. You have three options, which are discussed in more detail in the following sections:

- Bind the event handlers of your list event receiver to a list type.
- Bind your event handlers to a specific list.
- Bind your list event handlers to a site content type.

Binding List Event Handlers to a List Type

Binding your event handlers to a list type provides you with the following two benefits:

- Because you bind your event handlers to a list type as opposed to a specific list, your event handlers are automatically bound to all list instances of that list type, which are instantiated after your event handlers are bound to the list type. This enables you to bind your event handlers to all these list instances and unbind your event handlers from all these list instances in one shot.
- Binding event handlers to a list type does not require writing custom code because it is all done declaratively in CAML.

Binding your event handlers to a list type has the following two downsides:

- It does not allow you to bind your event handlers to a specific list instance.
- It requires you to use a feature scoped at site level to bind your event handlers. This means that you cannot use it in a feature scoped at other levels such as site collection.

Here is what you need to do to bind your event handlers to a list type. First you need to implement a feature that references an element manifest file as shown in Listing 9-5.

Listing 9-5: Your feature

```
<?xml version="1.0" encoding="utf-8" ?>
<Feature xmlns="http://schemas.microsoft.com/sharepoint/"
Id="{6070B044-8F01-4557-A837-86DB7B2E7E5D}"
Hidden="False"
Description="Binds custom list event handlers"
Title="Custom List Event Handlers Installer"
Scope="Web">
  <ElementManifests>
    <ElementManifest Location="elements.xml" />
  </ElementManifests>
</Feature>
```

Second, this element manifest file must use a Receivers element to bind your event handlers as shown in Listing 9-6. Don't forget to replace the value of the PublicKeyToken attribute with the actual public key token of the assembly that contains your custom list event receiver.

Listing 9-6: Your element manifest file

```
<?xml version="1.0" encoding="utf-8" ?>
<Elements xmlns="http://schemas.microsoft.com/sharepoint/">
  <Receivers ListTemplateId="100">
    <Receiver>
      <Name>Field Adding</Name>
      <Type>FieldAdding</Type>
      <Class>ClassLibrary1.MyListEventReceiver1</Class>
      <Assembly>ClassLibrary1, Version=1.0.0.0, Culture=neutral,
PublicKeyToken=6c5894e55cb0f391</Assembly>
      <Data>Adding a Column Definition</Data>
      <SequenceNumber>100</SequenceNumber>
    </Receiver>
    <Receiver>
      <Name>Field Updating</Name>
      <Type>FieldUpdating</Type>
      <Class>ClassLibrary1.EventReceivers.MyListEventReceiver1</Class>
      <Assembly>ClassLibrary1, Version=1.0.0.0, Culture=neutral,
PublicKeyToken=6c5894e55cb0f391</Assembly>
      <Data>Updating a Column Definition</Data>
      <SequenceNumber>101</SequenceNumber>
    </Receiver>
    <Receiver>
      <Name>Field Deleting</Name>
      <Type>FieldDeleting</Type>
      <Class>ClassLibrary1.EventReceivers.MyListEventReceiver1</Class>
      <Assembly>ClassLibrary1, Version=1.0.0.0, Culture=neutral,
PublicKeyToken=6c5894e55cb0f391</Assembly>
      <Data>Deleting a Column Definition</Data>
      <SequenceNumber>102</SequenceNumber>
    </Receiver>
  </Receivers>
</Elements>
```

Note that the ListTemplateId attribute on the <Receivers> element is set to 100, which is the integer identifier of the SharePoint generic or custom list type. This means that this <Receivers> element binds your event handlers to the custom list type instances. As Listing 9-6 shows, the Receivers element contains three Receiver elements. Each receiver element binds a specific event handler. The <Receiver> element supports the following child elements:

- **<Name>.** This specifies a friendly name for this binding.
- **<Type>.** This specifies the name of the event handler being bound.
- **<Class>.** This specifies the fully namespace-qualified name of the type of the event receiver that contains the event handler being bound.
- **<Assembly>.** This specifies the strong name of the assembly that contains the event receiver.
- **<Data>**. This specifies extra data.
- **<SequenceNumber>.** This specifies a sequence number.

Next, you'll need to deploy the feature file shown in Listing 9-5 and the element manifest file shown in Listing 9-6 to a feature-specific folder in the Features system folder in the file system of each front-end web server in the server farm. In this case, go ahead and create a folder named BindingToAListType in the FEATURES folder and copy the feature.xml (Listing 9-5) and elements.xml (Listing 9-6) files to this folder.

Next, you need to use the Installfeature operation of the STSADM command-line utility to install this feature:

```
"Local_Drive:\program files\common files\microsoft shared\web server extensions\12\
bin\stsadm" -o installfeature -name BindingToAListType
```

Then you need to activate the feature:

```
"Local_Drive:\program files\common files\microsoft shared\web server extensions\12\
bin\stsadm" -o activatefeature -name BindingToAListType -url EnterSiteURLHere
```

After installing and activating the feature in your favorite site, go ahead and create a custom list in that site. Then try to add a new column to the list, or delete an existing column from the list, or update an existing column in the list. You should be directed to a page that displays the error message that the respective event handler assigned to the ErrorMessage property of the SPListEventProperties object.

Binding List Event Handlers to a List Instance

So far, I've discussed the first approach to binding your list event handlers by binding them to a list type. Another approach is to bind your list event handlers to a specific list. This requires writing custom code and using the SharePoint object model. First, you need to implement a feature that uses a feature receiver. You'll add custom code to this feature receiver where you'll use the SharePoint object model to bind your event handlers to a specific list instance. Listing 9-7 presents this feature.

Listing 9-7: Your feature

```
<?xml version="1.0" encoding="utf-8" ?>
<Feature xmlns="http://schemas.microsoft.com/sharepoint/"
Id="{20FF80BB-83D9-41bc-8FFA-E589067AF783}"
Title="Installs MyFeatureReceiver"
Description="Installs MyFeatureReceiver" Hidden="False" Version="1.0.0.0" Scope="Site"
ReceiverClass="ClassLibrary1.MyFeatureReceiver"
ReceiverAssembly="ClassLibrary1, Version=1.0.0.0, Culture=neutral,
PublicKeyToken=6c5894e55cb0f391">
</Feature>
```

Note that the Scope attribute on the <Feature> element that defines this feature is set to Site, which means that the feature is scoped at the site collection level. As you can see, you don't have to use a feature scoped at site level. As the ReceiverClass attribute shows, you're using a feature receiver named MyFeatureReceiver to bind your event handlers. Listing 9-8 presents the implementation of this feature receiver.

Listing 9-8: The MyFeatureReceiver feature receiver

```
using System;
using Microsoft.SharePoint;

namespace ClassLibrary1
{
  public class MyFeatureReceiver: SPFeatureReceiver
  {
    public override void FeatureActivated(SPFeatureReceiverProperties properties)
    {
      SPSite siteCollection = properties.Feature.Parent as SPSite;
      SPWeb site = siteCollection.AllWebs["Docs"];
      SPList list = site.Lists["MyList"];
      SPEventReceiverDefinition rd = list.EventReceivers.Add();
      rd.Name = "My Event Receiver";
      rd.Class = "ClassLibrary1.MyListEventReceiver1";
      rd.Assembly = "ClassLibrary1, Version=1.0.0.0, Culture=neutral,
PublicKeyToken=6c5894e55cb0f391";
      rd.Data = "My Event Receiver data";
      rd.Type = SPEventReceiverType.FieldAdding;
      rd.Update();
    }

    public override void FeatureDeactivating(SPFeatureReceiverProperties properties)
    {
      SPSite sitecollection = properties.Feature.Parent as SPSite;
      SPWeb site = sitecollection.AllWebs["Docs"];
      SPList list = site.Lists["MyList"];
      foreach (SPEventReceiverDefinition rd in list.EventReceivers)
      {
        if (rd.Name == "My Event Receiver")
          rd.Delete();
      }
    }

    public override void FeatureInstalled(SPFeatureReceiverProperties properties)
    {
    }

    public override void FeatureUninstalling(SPFeatureReceiverProperties properties)
    {
    }
  }
}
```

Next, you'll walk through the implementation of the FeatureActivated method. This method first accesses a reference to the SPSite object that represents the current site collection:

```
SPSite siteCollection = properties.Feature.Parent as SPSite;
```

Next, it accesses a reference to the SPWeb object that represents the Docs site:

```
      SPWeb site = siteCollection.AllWebs["Docs"];
```

Then, it accesses a reference to the SPList object that represents the MyList list instance. The MyList instance is an instance of the generic or custom list type:

```
SPList list = site.Lists["MyList"];
```

Next, it invokes the Add method on the EventReceivers collection property of this SPList object to create and to return a reference to an SPEventReceiverDefinition object that you will use to bind your event handler to the list:

```
SPEventReceiverDefinition rd = list.EventReceivers.Add();
```

As you can see, every list maintains its event receiver definitions in its EventReceivers collection.

FeatureActivated then specifies a name for this event receiver definition. This name uniquely identifies this event receiver definition among other event receiver definitions of the list. Event receiver definitions are named entities:

```
rd.Name = "My Event Receiver";
```

Next, it provides the event receiver definition with the fully namespace-qualified name of the event receiver that contains the event handler that the event receiver definition will bind to the list:

```
rd.Class = "Chapter6.EventReceivers.MyListEventReceiver1";
```

Then, it provides the event receiver definition with the strong name of the assembly that contains this event receiver:

```
rd.Assembly = "Chapter6, Version=1.0.0.0, Culture=neutral,
PublicKeyToken=2b56bd310cddb0e3";
```

Next, it specifies the context data that you would like to associate with the event receiver definition:

```
rd.Data = "My Event Receiver data";
```

Then, it specifies the event handler that you want the event receiver definition to bind to the list:

```
rd.Type = SPEventReceiverType.FieldAdding;
```

Finally, it invokes the Update method on the event receiver definition to commit the changes:

```
rd.Update();
```

Next, you'll walk through the implementation of the FeatureDeactivated method shown in Listing 9-8. This method first accesses a reference to the SPSite object that represents the current site collection:

```
SPSite sitecollection = properties.Feature.Parent as SPSite;
```

Then, it accesses a reference to the SPWeb object that represents the Docs site:

```
SPWeb site = sitecollection.AllWebs["Docs"];
```

Next, it accesses a reference to the SPList object that represents the MyList list:

```
SPList list = site.Lists["MyList"];
```

Then, it searches through the EventReceivers collection of the MyList list for the "My Event Receiver" event receiver definition and deletes it. As you can see, the name of an event receiver definition is used to access it in this collection:

```
foreach (SPEventReceiverDefinition rd in list.EventReceivers)
{
  if (rd.Name == "My Event Receiver")
    rd.Delete();
}
```

Listing 9-9 presents the definition of the SPEventReceiverDefinition class.

Listing 9-9: The SPEventReceiverDefinition class

```
[SharePointPermission(SecurityAction.InheritanceDemand, ObjectModel=true),
SharePointPermission(SecurityAction.LinkDemand, ObjectModel=true)]
public sealed class SPEventReceiverDefinition
{
  public void Delete();
  public void Update();

  public string Assembly { get; set; }
  public string Class { get; set; }
  public string Data { get; set; }
  public string Name { get; set; }
  public Guid SiteId { get; }
  public SPEventReceiverType Type { get; set; }
  public Guid WebId { get; }
}
```

Here are the descriptions of the properties of SPEventReceiverDefinition:

- **Assembly.** This gets or sets the strong name of the assembly that contains the event receiver, which contains the event handler that the event receiver definition binds.
- **Class.** This gets or sets the fully namespace-qualified name of the event receiver class.
- **Data.** This gets or sets the context data that you want to associate with the event receiver definition.
- **Name.** This gets or sets the name of the event receiver definition. Event receiver definitions are named entities. This name is used to locate the event receiver definition.
- **SiteId.** This gets the GUID identifier of the site collection in which the event receiver definition binds the respective event handler.
- **Type.** This gets or sets the SPEventReceiverType enumeration value that represents the event handler that event receiver definition binds.
- **WebId.** This gets the GUID identifier of the site in which the event receiver definition binds the respective event handler.

Here are the descriptions of the methods of SPEventReceiverDefinition:

- **Delete.** This deletes the event receiver definition.
- **Update.** This updates the event receiver definition.

Next, you need to build the event receiver class shown in Listing 9-8 into a strong-named assembly and deploy this assembly to the Global Assembly Cache.

Then, you need to deploy the feature file shown in Listing 9-7 to a feature-specific folder in the Features system folder in the file system of each front-end web server in the server farm. In this case, go ahead and create a folder named BindingToAListInstance in the FEATURES folder and copy the feature.xml (Listing 9-7) file to this folder.

Next, you need to use the Installfeature operation of the STSADM command-line utility to install this feature:

```
"Local_Drive:\program files\common files\microsoft shared\web server extensions\12\
bin\stsadm" -o installfeature -name BindingToAListInstance
```

Then you need to activate the feature:

```
"Local_Drive:\program files\common files\microsoft shared\web server extensions\12\
bin\stsadm" -o activatefeature -name BindingToAListInstance -url
EnterSiteCollectionURLHere
```

After installing and activating the feature in your favorite site, create a custom list there. Then try to add a new column to the list. You should be directed to a page that displays the error message that the respective event handler assigned to the ErrorMessage property of the SPListEventProperties object.

Binding List Event Handlers to a Site Content Type

The previous two sections showed you how to bind your list event handlers to a list type and a list instance. This section shows you how to bind your list event handlers to a site content type. This approach provides you with the following benefits:

- Your event handlers are automatically bound to all list content types provisioned from that site content type. This enables you to bind your list event handlers to all these list content types and unbind your event handlers from all these list content types in one shot.
- Binding list event handlers to a site content type does not require writing custom code because it is all done declaratively in CAML.

But binding your list event handlers to a site content type has a down side. It does not allow you to bind your list event handlers to a specific list content type.

Here is what you need to do to bind your list event handlers to a site content type. First, you need to implement a feature that references an element manifest file as shown in Listing 9-10.

Listing 9-10: The feature.xml file

```
<?xml version="1.0" encoding="utf-8" ?>
<Feature xmlns="http://schemas.microsoft.com/sharepoint/"
Id="{C89612C7-0F72-4bd3-AE64-3B3B1B98C656}"
Hidden="False"
Description="Binds event handlers to your site content type"
Title="Custom List Event Handlers Installer"
Scope="Site">
  <ElementManifests>
    <ElementManifest Location="elements.xml" />
  </ElementManifests>
</Feature>
```

Listing 9-11 presents the content of the elements.xml element manifest file.

Listing 9-11: The elements.xml file

```
<?xml version="1.0" encoding="utf-8" ?>
<Elements xmlns="http://schemas.microsoft.com/sharepoint/">
  <ContentType ID="0x010402"
  Name="MyAnnouncement"
  Group="My Custom Content Types"
  Description="Provisions a MyAnnouncement content type."
  Version="0">
    <FieldRefs>
      <FieldRef ID="{a8eb573e-9e11-481a-a8c9-1104a54b2fbd}" Name="Priority" />
      <FieldRef ID="{6df9bd52-550e-4a30-bc31-a4366832a87f}" Name="Comment" />
    </FieldRefs>
    <XmlDocuments>
      <XmlDocument NamespaceURI="http://schemas.microsoft.com/sharepoint/events">
        <events:Receivers xmlns:events="http://schemas.microsoft.com/sharepoint/
events">
          <events:Receiver>
            <events:Name>Field Adding</events:Name>
            <events:Type>FieldAdding</events:Type>
            <events:Class>ClassLibrary1.MyListEventReceiver1</events:Class>
            <events:Assembly>ClassLibrary1, Version=1.0.0.0, Culture=neutral,
PublicKeyToken=6c5894e55cb0f391</events:Assembly>
          </events:Receiver>
          <events:Receiver>
            <events:Name>Field Deleting</events:Name>
            <events:Type>FieldDeleting</events:Type>
            <events:Class>ClassLibrary1.MyListEventReceiver1</events:Class>
            <events:Assembly>ClassLibrary1, Version=1.0.0.0, Culture=neutral,
PublicKeyToken=6c5894e55cb0f391</events:Assembly>
          </events:Receiver>
          <events:Receiver>
            <events:Name>Field Updating</events:Name>
            <events:Type>FieldUpdating</events:Type>
```

(continued)

Listing 9-3 *(continued)*

```
              <events:Class>ClassLibrary1.MyListEventReceiver1</events:Class>
              <events:Assembly>ClassLibrary1, Version=1.0.0.0, Culture=neutral,
PublicKeyToken=6c5894e55cb0f391</events:Assembly>
            </events:Receiver>
          </events:Receivers>
        </XmlDocument>
      </XmlDocuments>
    </ContentType>
</Elements>
```

As you can see, this element manifest file defines a site content type named MyAnnouncement, with the content type ID of 0x010402. This site content type inherits from the Announcement site content type (0x0104) to add two new site column references:

```
      <FieldRef ID="{a8eb573e-9e11-481a-a8c9-1104a54b2fbd}" Name="Priority" />
      <FieldRef ID="{6df9bd52-550e-4a30-bc31-a4366832a87f}" Name="Comment" />
```

The <ContentType> element that defines a site content type supports a child element named <XmlDocuments>. This child element supports zero or more <XmlDocument> child elements. As the name suggests, you can stick any valid XML document within the opening and closing tags of an <XmlDocument>. SharePoint supports an XML document with elements and attributes that belong to the following XML namespace:

```
http://schemas.microsoft.com/sharepoint/events
```

The document element of this XML document is an element named <Receivers>, which supports one or more instances of an element named <Receiver>. Each <Receiver> element is used to bind a specific list or item event handler to the site content type. Listing 9-11 binds the FieldAdding, FieldDeleting, and FieldUpdating event handlers of your list event receiver to the MyAnnouncement site content type.

Next, you'll need to deploy the feature file shown in Listing 9-10 and the element manifest file shown in Listing 9-11 to a feature-specific folder in the Features system folder in the file system of each front-end web server in the server farm. In this case, go ahead and create a folder named BindingToASiteContentType in the FEATURES folder and copy the feature.xml (Listing 9-10) and elements.xml (Listing 9-11) files to this folder.

Next, you need to use the Installfeature operation of the STSADM command-line utility to install this feature:

```
"Local_Drive:\program files\common files\microsoft shared\web server
extensions\12\bin\stsadm" -o installfeature -name BindingToASiteContentType
```

Then you need to activate the feature:

```
"Local_Drive:\program files\common files\microsoft shared\web server
extensions\12\bin\stsadm" -o activatefeature -name BindingToASiteContentType -url
EnterSiteCollectionURLHere
```

After installing and activating the feature in your favorite site, add the MyAnnouncement site content type to your favorite list. This will automatically create a local copy of this site content type known as a list content type and add this local copy to your list. Then try to delete one of the columns of this list content type. You should be directed to a page that displays the error message that the respective event handler assigned to the ErrorMessage property of the SPListEventProperties object.

Binding List Event Handlers to a List Content Type

The preceding section showed you how to bind your list event handlers to a site content type. The downside of this approach is that your list event handlers are bound to all list content types provisioned from that site content type. There are times when you want to bind your list event handlers to a specific list content type. This section shows you how to do this. First, you need to implement a feature that is configured with a feature receiver as shown in Listing 9-12.

Listing 9-12: The feature.xml file

```
<?xml version="1.0" encoding="utf-8" ?>
<Feature xmlns="http://schemas.microsoft.com/sharepoint/"
Id="{E667C78E-3AB8-4846-913F-F42E7FAAC69F}"
Title="Installs MyFeatureReceiver2"
Description="Installs MyFeatureReceiver2" Hidden="False" Version="1.0.0.0" Scope="Site"
ReceiverClass="ClassLibrary1.MyNewFeatureReceiver"
ReceiverAssembly="ClassLibrary1, Version=1.0.0.0, Culture=neutral,
PublicKeyToken=6c5894e55cb0f391">
</Feature>
```

Listing 9-13 presents the implementation of the MyNewFeatureReceiver feature receiver.

Listing 9-13: The MyNewFeatureReceiver feature receiver

```
using System;
using Microsoft.SharePoint;
  .
namespace ClassLibrary1
{
  public class MyNewFeatureReceiver: SPFeatureReceiver
  {
    public override void FeatureActivated(SPFeatureReceiverProperties properties)
    {
      SPSite siteCollection = properties.Feature.Parent as SPSite;
      SPWeb site = siteCollection.AllWebs["Docs"];
      SPList list = site.Lists["MyList50"];
      SPContentTypeId listContentTypeId = new SPContentTypeId("0x010403");
      SPContentType listContentType = list.ContentTypes[listContentTypeId];

      SPEventReceiverDefinition rd = listContentType.EventReceivers.Add();
      rd.Name = "My Event Receiver";
      rd.Class = "ClassLibrary1.MyListEventReceiver1";
      rd.Assembly = "ClassLibrary1, Version=1.0.0.0, Culture=neutral,
PublicKeyToken=6c5894e55cb0f391";
      rd.Data = "My Event Receiver data";
```

(continued)

Listing 9-3 *(continued)*

```
      rd.Type = SPEventReceiverType.FieldDeleting;
      rd.Update();
    }

    public override void FeatureDeactivating(SPFeatureReceiverProperties properties)
    {
      SPSite sitecollection = properties.Feature.Parent as SPSite;
      SPWeb site = sitecollection.AllWebs["Docs"];
      SPList list = site.Lists["MyList50"];
      SPContentTypeId listContentTypeId = new SPContentTypeId("0x010403");
      SPContentType listContentType = list.ContentTypes[listContentTypeId];
      foreach (SPEventReceiverDefinition rd in listContentType.EventReceivers)
      {
        if (rd.Name == "My Event Receiver")
          rd.Delete();
      }
    }

    public override void FeatureInstalled(SPFeatureReceiverProperties properties)
    {
    }

    public override void FeatureUninstalling(SPFeatureReceiverProperties properties)
    {
    }
  }
}
```

Next, you'll walk through the implementation of the FeatureActivated method. This method first accesses the SPList object that represents the desired list as discussed earlier:

```
      SPSite siteCollection = properties.Feature.Parent as SPSite;
      SPWeb site = siteCollection.AllWebs["Docs"];
      SPList list = site.Lists["MyList50"];
```

Then, it instantiates an SPContentTypeId object to represent the ID of the desired list content type:

```
      SPContentTypeId listContentTypeId = new SPContentTypeId("0x010403");
```

Next, it uses this SPContentTypeId object as an index into the ContentTypes collection property of the SPList object to return a reference to the SPContentType object that represents the desired list content type. The ContentTypes collection property of an SPList object contains references to the SPContentType objects that represent the list content types on the list that the SPList object represents:

```
      SPContentType listContentType = list.ContentTypes[listContentTypeId];
```

Next, it invokes the Add method on the EventReceivers collection property of the SPContentType object to create and to return a reference to an SPEventReceiverDefinition object that you will use to bind your list event handler to the list content type that the SPContentType object represents. The ContentTypes collection property of an SPList object contains references to the SPContentType objects that represent the list content types of the SharePoint list that the SPList object represents.

```
        SPEventReceiverDefinition rd = listContentType.EventReceivers.Add();
```

Next, it sets the properties of this SPEventReceiverDefinition object as discussed earlier:

```
        rd.Name = "My Event Receiver";
        rd.Class = "ClassLibrary1.MyListEventReceiver1";
        rd.Assembly = "ClassLibrary1, Version=1.0.0.0, Culture=neutral,
  PublicKeyToken=6c5894e55cb0f391";
        rd.Data = "My Event Receiver data";
        rd.Type = SPEventReceiverType.FieldDeleting;
        rd.Update();
```

Listing 9-13 assumes that the MyList50 SharePoint list contains a list content type with the content type ID of 0x010403. The following listing presents the definition of the site content type associated with this list content type:

```
<?xml version="1.0" encoding="utf-8" ?>
<Elements xmlns="http://schemas.microsoft.com/sharepoint/">
  <ContentType ID="0x010403"
  Name="NewAnnouncements"
  Group="My Custom Content Types"
  Description="Provisions a NewAnnouncement content type."
  Version="0">
    <FieldRefs>
      <FieldRef ID="{a8eb573e-9e11-481a-a8c9-1104a54b2fbd}" Name="Priority" />
      <FieldRef ID="{6df9bd52-550e-4a30-bc31-a4366832a87f}" Name="Comment" />
    </FieldRefs>
  </ContentType>
</Elements>
```

Here is the feature that installs this site content type:

```
<?xml version="1.0" encoding="utf-8" ?>
<Feature xmlns="http://schemas.microsoft.com/sharepoint/"
Id="{F199675B-7A5A-49ad-944F-3F89F9D677E1}"
Title="Installs NewAnnouncements"
Description="Installs NewAnnouncements" Hidden="False" Version="1.0.0.0" Scope="Site">
  <ElementManifests>
    <ElementManifest Location="elements.xml"/>
  </ElementManifests>
</Feature>
```

You'll need to install and to activate this feature before you attempt to install the feature shown in Listing 9-12. You also need to create a list named MyList50 and add the previous site content type to this list before you attempt to activate the feature shown in Listing 9-12.

Now you'll need to build the feature receiver class shown in Listing 9-13 into a strong-named assembly and deploy this assembly to the Global Assembly Cache. Then you need to deploy the feature file shown in Listing 9-12 to a feature-specific folder in the Features system folder in the file system of each front-end web server in the server farm. In this case, go ahead and create a folder named BindingToAListContentType in the FEATURES folder and copy the feature.xml (Listing 9-12) file to this folder.

Next, you need to use the Installfeature operation of the STSADM command-line utility to install this feature:

```
"Local_Drive:\program files\common files\microsoft shared\web server extensions\12\
bin\stsadm" -o installfeature -name BindingToAListContentType
```

Then you need to activate the feature:

```
"Local_Drive:\program files\common files\microsoft shared\web server extensions\12\
bin\stsadm" -o activatefeature -name BindingToAListContentType -url
EnterSiteCollectionURLHere
```

After installing and activating the feature in your favorite site, go ahead and try to delete one of the columns of the list content type with the content type ID of 0x010403 from the MyList50 list. You should be directed to a page that displays the error message that the respective event handler assigned to the ErrorMessage property of the SPListEventProperties object.

Item Event Receiver

The previous section showed you how to implement your own custom list event handlers and bind them to a list type, list instance, site content type, or list content type. This section shows you how to implement your own custom item event handlers and bind them to a site content type or a list.

The first order of business is to implement an item event receiver, which is a class that inherits directly or indirectly from a base class named SPItemEventReceiver as defined in Listing 9-14.

Listing 9-14: The SPItemEventReceiver class

```
[SharePointPermission(SecurityAction.InheritanceDemand, ObjectModel=true),
SharePointPermission(SecurityAction.LinkDemand, ObjectModel=true)]
public class SPItemEventReceiver : SPEventReceiverBase
{
  public virtual void ItemAdded(SPItemEventProperties properties);
  public virtual void ItemAdding(SPItemEventProperties properties);
  public virtual void ItemAttachmentAdded(SPItemEventProperties properties);
  public virtual void ItemAttachmentAdding(SPItemEventProperties properties);
  public virtual void ItemAttachmentDeleted(SPItemEventProperties properties);
  public virtual void ItemAttachmentDeleting(SPItemEventProperties properties);
  public virtual void ItemCheckedIn(SPItemEventProperties properties);
  public virtual void ItemCheckedOut(SPItemEventProperties properties);
  public virtual void ItemCheckingIn(SPItemEventProperties properties);
  public virtual void ItemCheckingOut(SPItemEventProperties properties);
  public virtual void ItemDeleted(SPItemEventProperties properties);
  public virtual void ItemDeleting(SPItemEventProperties properties);
  public virtual void ItemFileConverted(SPItemEventProperties properties);
  public virtual void ItemFileMoved(SPItemEventProperties properties);
  public virtual void ItemFileMoving(SPItemEventProperties properties);
  public virtual void ItemUncheckedOut(SPItemEventProperties properties);
  public virtual void ItemUncheckingOut(SPItemEventProperties properties);
  public virtual void ItemUpdated(SPItemEventProperties properties);
  public virtual void ItemUpdating(SPItemEventProperties properties);
}
```

The methods of SPItemEventReceiver are known as item event handlers because each method is automatically invoked when its respective event is fired. For example, the ItemAdded event handler is invoked after an item is added to the SharePoint list. Because none of the methods of this base class are marked as abstract, your custom item event receiver can override the desired item event handlers without having to provide implementation for all these event handlers. This is very different from a feature receiver where your custom feature receiver must implement all four methods of the SPFeatureReceiver base class.

Here are the descriptions of some of the event handlers that SPItemEventReceiver contains:

- **ItemAdding.** This is invoked before an item is added to the respective list. Your event receiver's implementation of this event handler can run application-specific code to determine whether to allow the item to be added.
- **ItemAdded.** This is invoked after an item is added to the respective list.
- **ItemDeleting.** This is invoked before an item is deleted from the list. Your event receiver's implementation of this event handler can execute application-specific validation logic and cancel the item deletion operation if it fails to validate.
- **ItemDeleted.** This is invoked after an item is deleted from the list.
- **ItemUpdating.** This is invoked before an item in the list is updated. Your event receiver's implementation of this event handler can execute application-specific validation logic and cancel the item update operation if it fails to validate.
- **ItemUpdated.** This is invoked after an item in the list is updated.
- **ItemCheckingIn.** This is invoked before an item is checked in. Your event receiver's implementation of this event handler can execute application-specific validation logic and cancel the item check-in operation if it fails to validate.
- **ItemCheckedIn.** This handler is invoked after an item is checked in.
- **ItemCheckingOut.** This is invoked before an item is checked out. Your event receiver's implementation of this event handler can execute application-specific validation logic and cancel the item check-out operation if it fails to validate.
- **ItemCheckedOut.** This event handler is invoked after an item is checked out.

Note that all the event handlers of SPItemEventReceiver take a single argument of type SPItemEventProperties as defined in Listing 9-15.

Listing 9-15: The SPItemEventProperties type

```
[SharePointPermission(SecurityAction.LinkDemand, ObjectModel=true),
SharePointPermission(SecurityAction.InheritanceDemand, ObjectModel=true)]
public sealed class SPItemEventProperties : SPEventPropertiesBase, IDisposable
{
  [SharePointPermission(SecurityAction.Demand, ObjectModel=true)]
  public void Dispose();
  public SPWeb OpenWeb();
```

(continued)

Listing 9-3 *(continued)*

```
    public SPItemEventDataCollection AfterProperties { get; }
    public string AfterUrl { get; }
    public SPItemEventDataCollection BeforeProperties { get; }
    public string BeforeUrl { get; }
    public int CurrentUserId { get; }
    public SPEventReceiverType EventType { get; }
    public Guid ListId { get; }
    public SPListItem ListItem { get; }
    public int ListItemId { get; }
    public string ListTitle { get; }
    public string RelativeWebUrl { get; }
    public Guid SiteId { get; }
    public string UserDisplayName { get; }
    public string UserLoginName { get; }
    public bool Versionless { get; }
    public string WebUrl { get; }
}
```

Here are the descriptions of the properties of SPItemEventProperties:

- **AfterUrl.** This gets the URL of the item after the event is fired.
- **BeforeUrl.** This gets the URL of the item before the event is fired.
- **CurrentUserId.** This gets the current user ID, which is the user ID of the user who caused the event to fire.
- **EventType.** This gets the type of the event.
- **ListId.** This gets the GUID identifier of the SharePoint list to which the item belongs.
- **ListItem.** This gets a reference to the SPListItem object that represents the item.
- **ListItemId.** This gets the integer identifier of the item.
- **ListTitle.** This gets the title of the SharePoint list to which the item belongs.
- **RelativeWebUrl.** This gets the server-relative URL of the site in which the event occurs.
- **SiteId.** This gets the GUID identifier of the site collection in which the event is fired.
- **UserDisplayName.** This gets the display name of the user that caused the event to fire.
- **UserLoginName.** This gets the login name of the user that caused the event to fire.
- **WebUrl.** This gets the absolute URL of the site where the event is fired.
- **AfterProperties.** This gets a reference to the SPItemEventDataCollection object that contains the field names and values of the item after the event is fired.
- **BeforeProperties.** This gets a reference to the SPItemEventDataCollection object that contains the field names and values of the item before the event is fired.

The SPItemEventDataCollection class internally stores field names and values in a hashtable. This class exposes an indexer property that takes the name of a field and returns its value.

Next, you'll implement a custom item event receiver named MyItemEventReceiver and deploy it to SharePoint. Listing 9-16 presents the implementation of your custom item event receiver. Go ahead and launch Visual Studio 2008 and add a new Class Library project named ClassLibrary2. Add a reference to Microsoft.SharePoint.dll assembly. Then configure Visual Studio to compile the project into a strong-named assembly and add a post event to have Visual Studio automatically install the assembly in the GAC every time the project is built. Next change the name of the Class1.cs file to MyItemEventReceiver.cs and add the content of Listing 9-16 to this file.

Listing 9-16: The MyItemEventReceiver item event receiver

```
using System;
using Microsoft.SharePoint;
using Microsoft.SharePoint.Utilities;
using System.Net.Mail;

namespace ClassLibrary2.ItemEventReceiver
{
  public class MyItemEventReceiver : SPItemEventReceiver
  {
    private bool ValidateFieldValues(SPItemEventDataCollection fields,
                                     out string errorMessage)
    {
      // Use application-specific validation logic to validate field values and to
      // set the error message if any
      errorMessage = "";
      double myColumnValue = double.Parse(fields["MyColumn1"].ToString());
      if (myColumnValue > 100)
      {
        errorMessage =
                  "The value of the MyColumn1 column cannot be greater than 100!";
        return false;
      }
      return true;
    }

    public override void ItemAdding(SPItemEventProperties properties)
    {
      string errorMessage;
      if (!ValidateFieldValues(properties.AfterProperties, out errorMessage))
      {
        properties.ErrorMessage = errorMessage;
        properties.Status = SPEventReceiverStatus.CancelWithError;
        properties.Cancel = true;
      }
    }

    public override void ItemAdded(SPItemEventProperties properties)
    {
      string body = "The new item " + properties.ListItem.Title +
                    " was added to the list " +
                    properties.ListTitle;
```

(continued)

Listing 9-16 *(continued)*

```
        MailMessage message = new MailMessage("admin@somewhere.com",
                                "EnterToEmailAddress", "New Item Added", body);

        SmtpClient client = new SmtpClient();
        client.Send(message);
      }

      public override void ItemUpdating(SPItemEventProperties properties)
      {
        string errorMessage;
        if (!ValidateFieldValues(properties.AfterProperties, out errorMessage))
        {
          properties.ErrorMessage = errorMessage;
          properties.Status = SPEventReceiverStatus.CancelWithError;
          properties.Cancel = true;
        }
      }

      public override void ItemUpdated(SPItemEventProperties properties)
      {
        string body = "The item " + properties.ListItem.Title + " in list " +
                      properties.ListTitle + " was updated";
        MailMessage message = new MailMessage("admin@somewhere.com",
                                "EnterToEmailAddress", "Item Updated", body);

        SmtpClient client = new SmtpClient();
        client.Send(message);
      }
    }
  }
```

MyItemEventReceiver, like any other item event receiver, inherits from SPItemEventReceiver. MyItemEventReceiver contains four event handlers: ItemAdding, ItemAdded, ItemUpdating, and ItemUpdated. Note that both the ItemAdding and ItemUpdating event handlers use a private method named ValidateFieldValues, which contains application-specific validation logic to validate the field values of the item being added. The field values are contained in the AfterProperties property of the SPItemEventProperties object that SharePoint passes into the ItemAdding and ItemUpdating event handlers.

As Listing 9-16 shows, ItemAdding and ItemUpdating first validate the field values. If this validation fails, they set the ErrorMessage and Status properties of the SPItemEventProperties object and cancel the add or update operation:

```
properties.ErrorMessage = errorMessage;
properties.Status = SPEventReceiverStatus.CancelWithError;
properties.Cancel = true;
```

ItemAdded and ItemUpdated use the ASP.NET MailMessage and SmtpClient classes to send an email to a specified email address stating that a new item is added or updated. The constructor of the MailMessage takes the following four parameters:

- From email address
- To email address
- Email subject
- Email body

Note that ItemAdded and ItemUpdated use the Title property of the ListItem property of the SPItemEventReceiver object and the ListTitle property of this object to access the titles of the item and the list that contains the item. They then include these two titles in the email body:

```
string body = "The item " + properties.ListItem.Title + " in list " +
                    properties.ListTitle + " was updated";
```

SmtpClient uses the configuration settings specified in the web.config file of the web application to determine the SMTP outgoing server and the credentials (if necessary). Listing 9-17 presents the section of the web.config file that contains these settings.

Listing 9-17: A portion of web.config

```
<configuration>
  <system.net>
    <mailSettings>
      <smtp>
        <network host="HostGoesHere" port="25" />
      </smtp>
    </mailSettings>
  </system.net>
</configuration>
```

As you can see, <system.net> contains a child element named <mailSettings>, which contains a child element named <smtp>, which in turn contains a child element named <network>, which is used to specify the SMTP outgoing mail server. <network> supports the following two attributes:

- **host.** You'll want to assign the address of the SMTP outgoing mail server to this attribute.
- **port.** The port number 25 is normally used.

You can use the STSADM command-line utility that you developed earlier to add the <mailSettings> entry to the web.config file of the web application.

Next, you'll need to compile MyItemEventReceiver shown in Listing 9-16 to a strong-named assembly and install this assembly in the Global Assembly Cache. Next, you'll see how to bind the item event handlers of your item event receiver. You have several options that are discussed in the following sections.

Binding Item Event Handlers to a Site Content Type

The first option is to bind these item event handlers to a site content type. Here is what you need to do to bind your item event handlers to a site content type. First, you need to implement a feature that references an element manifest file as shown in Listing 9-18.

Listing 9-18: The feature.xml file

```
<?xml version="1.0" encoding="utf-8" ?>
<Feature xmlns="http://schemas.microsoft.com/sharepoint/"
Id="{324ED9EA-7B95-4c79-AB4F-0BB8E648096D}"
Hidden="False"
Description="Binds item event handlers to your site content type"
Title="Binds item event handlers to your site content type"
Scope="Site">
  <ElementManifests>
    <ElementManifest Location="elements.xml" />
  </ElementManifests>
</Feature>
```

Next, you need to implement this element manifest file as shown in Listing 9-19.

Listing 9-19: The element manifest file

```
<?xml version="1.0" encoding="utf-8" ?>
<Elements xmlns="http://schemas.microsoft.com/sharepoint/">
  <ContentType ID="0x010409"
  Name="NewAnnouncementsType"
  Group="My Custom Content Types"
  Description="Provisions a NewAnnouncementsType content type."
  Version="0">
    <FieldRefs>
      <FieldRef ID="{A3C0A7D7-5D3B-4966-AB64-FEF29ECEBDBC}" Name="MyColumn1" />
    </FieldRefs>
    <XmlDocuments>
      <XmlDocument NamespaceURI="http://schemas.microsoft.com/sharepoint/events">
        <Receivers xmlns="http://schemas.microsoft.com/sharepoint/events">
          <Receiver>
            <Name>Item Adding</Name>
            <Type>ItemAdding</Type>
            <Class>ClassLibrary2.ItemEventReceiver.MyItemEventReceiver</Class>
            <Assembly>ClassLibrary2, Version=1.0.0.0, Culture=neutral,
PublicKeyToken=fa0f9b97611d4862</Assembly>
          </Receiver>
          <Receiver>
            <Name>Item Added</Name>
            <Type>ItemAdded</Type>
            <Class>ClassLibrary2.ItemEventReceiver.MyItemEventReceiver</Class>
            <Assembly>ClassLibrary2, Version=1.0.0.0, Culture=neutral,
PublicKeyToken=fa0f9b97611d4862</Assembly>
          </Receiver>
          <Receiver>
            <Name>Item Updating</Name>
```

```
                <Type>ItemUpdating</Type>
                <Class>ClassLibrary2.ItemEventReceiver.MyItemEventReceiver</Class>
                <Assembly>ClassLibrary2, Version=1.0.0.0, Culture=neutral,
PublicKeyToken=fa0f9b97611d4862</Assembly>
              </Receiver>
              <Receiver>
                <Name>Item Updated</Name>
                <Type>ItemUpdated</Type>
                <Class>ClassLibrary2.ItemEventReceiver.MyItemEventReceiver</Class>
                <Assembly>ClassLibrary2, Version=1.0.0.0, Culture=neutral,
PublicKeyToken=fa0f9b97611d4862</Assembly>
              </Receiver>
            </Receivers>
          </XmlDocument>
        </XmlDocuments>
  </ContentType>
  <Field ID="{A3C0A7D7-5D3B-4966-AB64-FEF29ECEBDBC}"
  Name="MyColumn1"
  SourceID="http://schemas.microsoft.com/sharepoint/v3"
  StaticName="MyColumn1"
  Group="My Site Columns"
  RowOrdinal="0"
  DisplayName="My Column1"
  Type="Number"
  Hidden="False">
  </Field>
</Elements>
```

As Listing 9-19 shows, this element manifest file defines a custom site content type named NewAnnouncementsType with the content type ID of 0x010405, which inherits from the Announcements site content type (0x0104) and adds a reference to a custom site column named MyColumn1. Note that this element manifest file also contains the definition of the MyColumn1 custom site column.

As discussed earlier, the <ContentType> element that defines a site content type supports a child element named <XmlDocuments>, which in turn supports one or more instances of a child element named <XmlDocument>. As thoroughly discussed earlier, you can use an XML document with the document element named <Receivers> within the opening and closing tags of an <XmlDocument> to bind your event handlers to the site content type.

Next, you need to deploy the feature file shown in Listing 9-18 and the element manifest file shown in Listing 9-19 to a feature-specific folder in the Features system folder in the file system of each front-end web server in the server farm. Next, you need to use the installfeature and activatefeature operations of the STSADM command-line utility to install and to activate this feature. After installing and activating the feature in your favorite site, add the NewAnnouncementsType site content type to your favorite list. This will automatically create a local copy of this site content type known as a list content type and add this local copy to your list. Then try to add an item with the NewAnnouncementsType content type with the MyColumn1 field value greater than 100. You should be directed to a page that displays the error message that the respective event handler assigned to the ErrorMessage property of the SPListEventProperties object. Next, add an item with the NewAnnouncementsType content type with the MyColumn1 field value less than 100. You should get an email from SharePoint stating that the item has been added to the list.

Binding Item Event Handlers to a List Instance

Another option is to bind your item event handlers to a specific list in your site. First, you'll need to implement a feature that uses a feature receiver as shown in Listing 9-20.

Listing 9-20: The feature.xml file

```
<?xml version="1.0" encoding="utf-8" ?>
<Feature xmlns="http://schemas.microsoft.com/sharepoint/"
Id="{71376DA3-C6D7-4ab1-88D2-1645BFD32C64}"
Title="Installs MyNewFeatureReceiver2"
Description="Installs MyNewFeatureReceiver2" Hidden="False" Version="1.0.0.0"
Scope="Site"
ReceiverClass="ClassLibrary2.MyNewFeatureReceiver2"
ReceiverAssembly=" ClassLibrary2, Version=1.0.0.0, Culture=neutral,
PublicKeyToken=fa0f9b97611d4862">
</Feature>
```

Listing 9-21 contains the code for the feature receiver that this feature uses.

Listing 9-21: The feature receiver

```
using System;
using Microsoft.SharePoint;

namespace ClassLibrary2
{
  public class MyNewFeatureReceiver2: SPFeatureReceiver
  {
    public override void FeatureActivated(SPFeatureReceiverProperties properties)
    {
      SPSite siteCollection = properties.Feature.Parent as SPSite;
      SPWeb site = siteCollection.OpenWeb();
      SPList list = site.Lists["MyList100"];

      SPEventReceiverDefinition rd = list.EventReceivers.Add();
      rd.Name = "My Item Event Receiver";
      rd.Class = " ClassLibrary2.ItemEventReceiver.MyItemEventReceiver";
      rd.Assembly = " ClassLibrary2, Version=1.0.0.0, Culture=neutral,
PublicKeyToken=fa0f9b97611d4862";
      rd.Data = "My Event Receiver data";
      rd.Type = SPEventReceiverType.ItemAdded;
      rd.Update();
    }

    public override void FeatureDeactivating(
                                   SPFeatureReceiverProperties properties)
    {
      SPSite sitecollection = properties.Feature.Parent as SPSite;
      SPWeb site = sitecollection.OpenWeb();
      SPList list = site.Lists["MyList100"];

      foreach (SPEventReceiverDefinition rd in list.EventReceivers)
```

```
            {
              if (rd.Name == "My Item Event Receiver")
                rd.Delete();
            }
        }

        public override void FeatureInstalled(SPFeatureReceiverProperties properties)
        {
        }

        public override void FeatureUninstalling(
                                          SPFeatureReceiverProperties properties)
        {
        }
    }
}
```

Next, you'll walk through the implementation of the FeatureActivated method. This method first accesses the SPList object that represents the SharePoint list as usual:

```
        SPSite siteCollection = properties.Feature.Parent as SPSite;
        SPWeb site = siteCollection.OpenWeb();
        SPList list = site.Lists["MyList100"];
```

Then, it invokes the Add method on the EventReceivers collection property of this SPList object to instantiate and to return a reference to an SPEventReceiverDefinition object, which will be used to bind the ItemAdded event handler to the list:

```
        SPEventReceiverDefinition rd = list.EventReceivers.Add();
```

Finally, it sets the properties of this SPEventReceiverDefinition object and invokes the Update method on the object as usual:

```
        rd.Name = "My Item Event Receiver";
        rd.Class = "ClassLibrary2.ItemEventReceiver.MyItemEventReceiver";
        rd.Assembly = "ClassLibrary2, Version=1.0.0.0, Culture=neutral,
  PublicKeyToken=fa0f9b97611d4862";
        rd.Data = "My Event Receiver data";
        rd.Type = SPEventReceiverType.ItemAdded;
        rd.Update();
```

Next, you need to build the project. Then, you need to deploy the feature file shown in Listing 9-20 to a feature-specific folder in the Features system folder in the file system of each front-end web server in the server farm. Next, you need to use the installfeature operation of the STSADM command-line utility to install this feature. Then add a new list named MyList100 to your favorite site. Next add a new column named MyColumn1 to this list. Keep in mind that this column must be a Number column. Finally, activate the feature in this site. Now if you add an item to the list, you should get an email stating that the specified item has been added to the list.

Web Event Receiver

This section shows you how to implement web event handlers and bind them to a site. The first order of business is to implement a class known as a web event receiver, which inherits from a base class named SPWebEventReceiver as defined in Listing 9-22.

Listing 9-22: The SPWebEventReceiver class

```
[SharePointPermission(SecurityAction.InheritanceDemand, ObjectModel=true),
SharePointPermission(SecurityAction.LinkDemand, ObjectModel=true)]
public class SPWebEventReceiver : SPEventReceiverBase
{
  public virtual void SiteDeleted(SPWebEventProperties properties);
  public virtual void SiteDeleting(SPWebEventProperties properties);
  public virtual void WebDeleted(SPWebEventProperties properties);
  public virtual void WebDeleting(SPWebEventProperties properties);
  public virtual void WebMoved(SPWebEventProperties properties);
  public virtual void WebMoving(SPWebEventProperties properties);
}
```

The methods of SPWebEventReceiver are known as web event handlers because they're automatically invoked when their respective events are fired. Here are the descriptions of these web event handlers:

- **SiteDeleting.** This web event handler is invoked before a site collection is deleted. Because this event handler handles the SiteDeleting Before event, your web event receiver's override of this event handler can cancel the site collection deletion if it violates application-specific validation logic.
- **SiteDeleted.** This web event handler is invoked after a site collection is deleted.
- **WebDeleting.** This web event handler is invoked before a site is deleted. Because this event handler handles the WebDeleting Before event, your web event receiver's override of this event handler can cancel the site deletion if it violates application-specific validation logic.
- **WebDeleted.** This web event handler is invoked after a site is deleted.
- **WebMoving.** This web event handler is invoked before a site is moved. Because this event handler handles the WebMoving Before event, your web event receiver's override of this event handler can cancel the site move if it violates application-specific validation logic.
- **WebMoved.** This web event handler is invoked after a site is moved.

As Listing 9-22 shows, all web event handlers take a single argument of type SPWebEventProperties, which is defined as shown in Listing 9-23.

Listing 9-23: The SPWebEventProperties type

```
[SharePointPermission(SecurityAction.InheritanceDemand, ObjectModel=true),
SharePointPermission(SecurityAction.LinkDemand, ObjectModel=true)]
public sealed class SPWebEventProperties : SPEventPropertiesBase
{
  public SPEventReceiverType EventType { get; }
  public string FullUrl { get; }
  public string NewServerRelativeUrl { get; }
  public string ServerRelativeUrl { get; }
```

```
    public Guid SiteId { get; }
    public string UserDisplayName { get; }
    public string UserLoginName { get; }
    public SPWeb Web { get; }
    public Guid WebId { get; }
  }
```

Here are the descriptions of the properties of SPWebEventProperties type:

- **EventType.** This gets an SPEventReceiverType enumeration value that specifies the type of the event.
- **FullUrl.** This gets the absolute URL of the site that fired the event.
- **NewServerRelativeUrl.** This gets the server-relative URL of the site after it has moved.
- **ServerRelativeUrl.** This gets the server-relative URL of the site that fired the event.
- **SiteId.** This gets the GUID identifier of the site collection in which the event was fired.
- **UserDisplayName.** This gets the display name of the user that caused the event to fire.
- **UserLoginName.** This gets the login name of the user that caused the event to fire.
- **Web.** This gets a reference to the SPWeb object that represents the site that fired the event.
- **WebId.** This gets the GUID identifier of the site that fired the event.

Next, you'll implement a custom web event receiver named MyWebEventReceiver. Listing 9-24 presents the implementation of this web event receiver. Go ahead and create a new Class Library project named ClassLibrary3. Rename the Class1.cs file to MyWebWebEventReceiver.cs and copy the content of Listing 9-24 into this file. Next, configure Visual Studio to compile the project into strong-named assembly and add a post event to have Visual Studio install the assembly in the GAC every time the project is built. Don't forget to add a reference to the Microsoft.SharePoint.dll assembly.

Listing 9-24: The MyWebEventReceiver web event receiver

```
using System;
using Microsoft.SharePoint;
using System.Net.Mail;

namespace ClassLibrary3
{
  public class MyWebEventReceiver : SPWebEventReceiver
  {
    public override void WebDeleted(SPWebEventProperties properties)
    {
      string body = "The site " + properties.FullUrl + " was deleted.";
      MailMessage message = new MailMessage("admin@somewhere.com",
                                "ToEmailAddress", "Site Deleted", body);

      SmtpClient client = new SmtpClient();
      client.Send(message);
    }
  }
}
```

This web event receiver contains a single web event handler called WebDeleted. As you can see, this web event handler sends an email to a specified email address when a site is deleted. Note that this web event handler contains the value of the FullUrl property of the SPWebEventProperties object in the email body.

Next, you'll see how to bind this web event handler to a site. You have several options, as discussed in the following sections.

Binding a Web Event Handler to an Existing Site

You have several options for binding a web event handler to an existing site. One option is to use a feature receiver. Another option is to implement a console application. The latter option requires console access to the web server, but many system administrators do not like to give console access to developers. In this section, you'll use the former option. Here is how it works.

First, implement a feature that uses a feature receiver as shown in Listing 9-25.

Listing 9-25: The feature.xml file

```
<?xml version="1.0" encoding="utf-8" ?>
<Feature xmlns="http://schemas.microsoft.com/sharepoint/"
Id="{F398089B-CDB7-43f2-9E16-1651990EB887}"
Hidden="False"
Description="Binds custom web event handlers"
Title="Custom web Event Handlers Installer"
Scope="Web"
ReceiverClass="ClassLibrary3.MyNewFeatureReceiver3"
ReceiverAssembly="ClassLibrary3, Version=1.0.0.0, Culture=neutral,
PublicKeyToken=df663a77cbaeeca1">
</Feature>
```

Listing 9-26 presents the implementation of this feature receiver. Go ahead and add a new source file named MyNewFeatureReceiver3.cs to the project and add the content of Listing 9-26 to this file.

Listing 9-26: The feature receiver

```
using System;
using Microsoft.SharePoint;

namespace ClassLibrary3
{
  public class MyNewFeatureReceiver3: SPFeatureReceiver
  {
    public override void FeatureActivated(SPFeatureReceiverProperties properties)
    {
      SPWeb site = properties.Feature.Parent as SPWeb;

      SPEventReceiverDefinition rd = site.EventReceivers.Add();
      rd.Name = "My Event Receiver";
      rd.Class = "ClassLibrary3.MyWebEventReceiver";
      rd.Assembly = "ClassLibrary3, Version=1.0.0.0, Culture=neutral,
PublicKeyToken=df663a77cbaeeca1";
      rd.Data = "My Event Receiver data";
```

```
            rd.Type = SPEventReceiverType.WebDeleted;
            rd.Update();
        }

        public override void FeatureDeactivating(
                                        SPFeatureReceiverProperties properties)
        {
            SPWeb site = properties.Feature.Parent as SPWeb;

            foreach (SPEventReceiverDefinition rd in site.EventReceivers)
            {
                if (rd.Name == "My Event Receiver")
                    rd.Delete();
            }
        }

        public override void FeatureInstalled(SPFeatureReceiverProperties properties)
        {
        }

        public override void FeatureUninstalling(
                                        SPFeatureReceiverProperties properties)
        {
        }
    }
}
```

As you can see, the FeatureActivated method first accesses a reference to the SPWeb object that represents the current web site:

```
            SPWeb site = properties.Feature.Parent as SPWeb;
```

Then, it invokes the Add method on the EventReceivers collection property of this SPWeb object to instantiate and to return a reference to the SPEventReceiverDefinition object that you will use to bind your web event handler to the current site. As you can see, the EventReceivers collection property of an SPWeb object contains references to the SPEventReceiverDefinition objects that bind web event handlers to the site that the SPWeb object represents:

```
            SPEventReceiverDefinition rd = site.EventReceivers.Add();
```

Next, FeatureActivated specifies a unique name for this SPEventReceiverDefinition:

```
            rd.Name = "My Event Receiver";
```

Then, it specifies the MyWebEventReceiver class as the web event receiver:

```
            rd.Class = "ClassLibrary3.MyWebEventReceiver";
            rd.Assembly = "ClassLibrary3, Version=1.0.0.0, Culture=neutral,
    PublicKeyToken=df663a77cbaeeca1";
```

Next, it specifies the WebDeleted web event handler as the web event handler that you want to bind to the current site:

```
rd.Type = SPEventReceiverType.WebDeleted;
```

Next, you need to build the project. Then, you need to deploy the feature file shown in Listing 9-25 to a feature-specific folder in the Features system folder in the file system of each front-end web server in the server farm. Next, you need to use the installfeature and activatefeature operations of the STSADM command-line utility to install and to activate this feature. After installing and activating the feature in your favorite site, go ahead and delete the site. You should get an email stating that the specified site has been deleted.

Binding a Web Event Handler to an Existing Site Definition Configuration

The previous section implemented a feature that uses a feature receiver to bind a web event handler to a specific site. This section shows you how to use the same feature to bind the web event handler to an existing site definition configuration as opposed to a specific site. When you bind a web event handler to a site definition configuration it gets bound to all sites provisioned from that site definition configuration.

Listing 9-27 presents a stapling feature that staples your web event handler to the STS#0 site definition configuration. Introduced in Chapter 8, feature stapling allows you to attach a feature to a site definition configuration without modifying it so that you can add this feature to all new instances of sites created using that site definition. Sites already created will not have the feature activated.

Listing 9-27: The stapling feature

```
<?xml version="1.0" encoding="utf-8" ?>
<Feature
Id="{D245F7A1-C95A-4b25-9378-FB171C03E5C9}"
Title="Stapling Feature"
Description="This feature staples your feature to Team sites"
Version="1.0.0.0"
Scope="Site"
xmlsn="http://schemas.microsoft.com/sharepoint/">
  <ElementManifests>
    <ElementManifest Location="elements.xml"/>
  </ElementManifests>
</Feature>
```

Listing 9-28 presents the content of the element manifest file that your stapling feature references.

Listing 9-28: The element manifest file

```
<?xml version="1.0" encoding="utf-8" ?>
<Elements xmlns="http://schemas.microsoft.com/sharepoint/">
  <FeatureSiteTemplateAssociation
  Id="{F398089B-CDB7-43f2-9E16-1651990EB887}"
  TemplateName="STS#0" />
</Elements>
```

Note that the Id attribute on the <FeatureSiteTemplateAssociation> element is set to the GUID identifier of the feature shown in Listing 9-25 and TemplateName attribute is set to the identifier of the Team Site site definition configuration.

Note that the value of the Scope attribute on the <Feature> element that defines the stapling feature (see Listing 9-27) plays a significant role:

- If you set the Scope attribute to web, the web event handler will be bound to any Team child site in the site where the stapling feature is activated provided that the Team child site is provisioned after the feature is activated.
- If you set the Scope attribute to Site, the web event handler will be bound to any Team site in the site collection where the stapling feature is activated provided that the Team child site is provisioned after the feature is activated.
- If you set the Scope attribute to WebApplication, the web event handler will be bound to any Team site in any site collection in the web application where the stapling feature is activated provided that the Team child site is provisioned after the feature is activated.
- If you set the Scope attribute to Farm, the web event handler will be bound to any Team site in any site collection in any web application in the farm where the stapling feature is activated provided that the Team child site is provisioned after the feature is activated.

Another important factor is the site definition configuration to which the stapling feature staples your feature. For example, the stapling feature defined in Listing 9-27 staples your feature to the Team Site (STS#0) site definition configuration. Listing 9-29 presents a new version of the element manifest file that associates your feature with the Global site definition configuration (Global#0).

Because regardless of from which specific site definition configuration a site is provisioned, it is also provisioned from the Global site definition configuration:

- If you set the Scope attribute to web, the web event handler will be bound to any child site in the site where the stapling feature is activated provided that the child site is provisioned after the feature is activated.
- If you set the Scope attribute to Site, the web event handler will be bound to any site in the site collection where the stapling feature is activated provided that the site is provisioned after the feature is activated.
- If you set the Scope attribute to WebApplication, the web event handler will be bound to any site in any site collection in the web application where the stapling feature is activated provided that the site is provisioned after the feature is activated.
- If you set the Scope attribute to Farm, the web event handler will be bound any site in any site collection in any web application in the farm where the stapling feature is activated provided that the site is provisioned after the feature is activated.

As you can see, you can bind the web event handler to any site in any site collection in any web application in a farm by simply setting the Scope attribute to Farm and associating your feature with the Global site definition configuration (GLOBAL#0).

Listing 9-29: The elements.xml file

```
<?xml version="1.0" encoding="utf-8" ?>
<Elements xmlns="http://schemas.microsoft.com/sharepoint/">
  <FeatureSiteTemplateAssociation
  Id="{F398089B-CDB7-43f2-9E16-1651990EB887}"
  TemplateName="GLOBAL#0" />
</Elements>
```

Binding a Web Event Handler to a New Site Definition Configuration (First Approach)

The preceding section showed you how to use feature stapling to bind your web event handlers to an existing site definition configuration. This section shows you how to bind your web event handlers to a new site definition configuration. There are two ways to do this. The first approach is discussed in this section and the second approach is discussed in the next section.

As discussed earlier, any feature that is referenced from the <SiteFeatures> or <WebFeatures> element of a site definition configuration is automatically activated upon site creation. This is equivalent to running the activatefeature operation of the STSADM command-line utility on the feature. Recall that you implemented a custom site definition configuration named STS2#3. This site definition configuration under the hood uses the STS2#0 site definition configuration (see Listing 7-14). Listing 9-30 presents a new version of the portion of the onet.xml file for the STS2 site definition.

Listing 9-30: The onet.xml file for STS2 site definition

```
<?xml version="1.0" encoding="utf-8"?>
<Project Title="$Resources:onet_TeamWebSite;" Revision="2" ListDir="$Resources:
core,lists_Folder;" xmlns:ows="Microsoft SharePoint">
  <NavBars>
    ...
  </NavBars>
  <ListTemplates>
  </ListTemplates>
  <DocumentTemplates>
    ...
  </DocumentTemplates>
  <Configurations>
    <Configuration ID="-1" Name="NewWeb" />
    <Configuration ID="0" Name="Default">
      <Modules>
        <Module Name="Default" />
      </Modules>
      <SiteFeatures>
        <!-- BasicWebParts Feature -->
        <Feature ID="00BFEA71-1C5E-4A24-B310-BA51C3EB7A57" />
        <!-- Three-state Workflow Feature -->
        <Feature ID="FDE5D850-671E-4143-950A-87B473922DC7" />
```

```
        </SiteFeatures>
        <WebFeatures>
          <Feature ID="00BFEA71-4EA5-48D4-A4AD-7EA5C011ABE5" />
          <!-- TeamCollab Feature -->
          <Feature ID="F41CC668-37E5-4743-B4A8-74D1DB3FD8A4" />
          <!-- MobilityRedirect -->
          <Feature ID="{1E0CFC51-DD21-4321-9D6B-81FC4B6AEE1A}" />
          <Feature ID="{F398089B-CDB7-43f2-9E16-1651990EB887}" />
        </WebFeatures>
    </Configuration>
      <Configuration ID="1" Name="Blank">
  <Lists />
        <Modules>
          <Module Name="DefaultBlank" />
        </Modules>
        <SiteFeatures>
          <!-- BasicWebParts Feature -->
          <Feature ID="00BFEA71-1C5E-4A24-B310-BA51C3EB7A57" />
          <!-- Three-state Workflow Feature -->
          <Feature ID="FDE5D850-671E-4143-950A-87B473922DC7" />
        </SiteFeatures>
         <WebFeatures>
          <Feature ID="00BFEA71-4EA5-48D4-A4AD-7EA5C011ABE5" />
          <!-- TeamCollab Feature -->
          <Feature ID="F41CC668-37E5-4743-B4A8-74D1DB3FD8A4" />
          <!-- MobilityRedirect -->
          <Feature ID="{F398089B-CDB7-43f2-9E16-1651990EB887}" />
         </WebFeatures>
    </Configuration>
      <Configuration ID="2" Name="DWS">
        <Modules>
          <Module Name="DWS" />
        </Modules>
        <SiteFeatures>
          <!-- BasicWebParts Feature -->
          <Feature ID="00BFEA71-1C5E-4A24-B310-BA51C3EB7A57" />
          <!-- Three-state Workflow Feature -->
          <Feature ID="FDE5D850-671E-4143-950A-87B473922DC7" />
          </SiteFeatures>
  <WebFeatures>
          <Feature ID="00BFEA71-4EA5-48D4-A4AD-7EA5C011ABE5" />
          <!-- TeamCollab Feature -->
          <Feature ID="F41CC668-37E5-4743-B4A8-74D1DB3FD8A4" />
          <!-- MobilityRedirect -->
          <Feature ID="{1E0CFC51-DD21-4321-9D6B-81FC4B6AEE1A}" />
          <Feature ID="{F398089B-CDB7-43f2-9E16-1651990EB887}" />
        </WebFeatures>
      </Configuration>
    </Configurations>
    <Modules>
      ...
    </Modules>
    <ServerEmailFooter>$Resources:ServerEmailFooter;</ServerEmailFooter>
  </Project>
```

As you can see, the boldfaced portions of Listing 9-30 reference the feature shown in Listing 9-25. Recall that this feature binds a web event handler to a site. Because these boldfaced portions, that is, these references to this feature, are included in the <WebFeatures> elements of the Team Site, Blank Site, and Document Spaces site definition configurations, this feature is automatically activated every time a new site is provisioned from one of these site definition configurations. This means that your web event handler will be automatically bound to any site provisioned from one of these site definition configurations.

Binding a Web Event Handler to a New Site Definition Configuration (Second Approach)

If you're implementing a custom site definition, you can use a site provisioning provider to bind your web event handlers to your site definition configurations. This means that your web event handlers will automatically be bound to all sites provisioned form these site definition configurations. Recall that you implemented a custom site definition configuration named STS2#3 and configured it with a site provisioning provider. In this section, you'll add code to this site provisioning provider to bind your web event handler to this site definition configuration.

Listing 9-31 presents the implementation of this custom site provisioning provider.

Listing 9-31: The site provisioning provider

```
using Microsoft.SharePoint;
using Microsoft.SharePoint.Administration;
using System.Reflection;

namespace ClassLibrary3
{
  public class MySiteProvisioningProvider : SPWebProvisioningProvider
  {
    public override void Provision(SPWebProvisioningProperties props)
    {
      props.Web.ApplyWebTemplate("STS2#0");
      props.Web.Title = props.Data;
      props.Web.Update();

      using (SPSite siteCollection = new SPSite(props.Web.Site.ID))
      {
        using (SPWeb site = siteCollection.OpenWeb(props.Web.ID))
        {
          site.AllowUnsafeUpdates = true;
          SPWebApplication app = siteCollection.WebApplication;

          SPWebConfigModification modification1 = new SPWebConfigModification();
          modification1.Path = "configuration/appSettings";
          modification1.Name = "add[@key='MyKey']";
          modification1.Value = "<add key='MyKey' value='" + props.Web.ID.ToString()
+ "' />";
          modification1.Owner = Assembly.GetExecutingAssembly().FullName;
          modification1.Sequence = 100;
```

```
            modification1.Type =
                SPWebConfigModification.SPWebConfigModificationType.EnsureChildNode;
            app.WebConfigModifications.Add(modification1);

            SPWebService service = SPFarm.Local.Services.GetValue<SPWebService>();
            service.ApplyWebConfigModifications();

            SPEventReceiverDefinition rd = site.EventReceivers.Add();
            rd.Name = "My Event Receiver";
            rd.Class = "ClassLibrary3.MyWebEventReceiver2";
            rd.Assembly = "ClassLibrary3, Version=1.0.0.0, Culture=neutral,
PublicKeyToken=df663a77cbaeeca1";
            rd.Data = "My Event Receiver data";
            rd.Type = SPEventReceiverType.WebDeleted;
            rd.Update();
          }
        }
      }
    }
  }
```

As you can see, the Provision method performs these tasks. First, it applies the STS2#0 site definition configuration. Recall that this configuration duplicates the standard STS configuration:

```
        props.Web.ApplyWebTemplate("STS2#0");
```

Next, it uses the provisioning data specified in the WebTemp*.xml file as the title of the site being provisioned:

```
        props.Web.Title = props.Data;
```

Then, it commits this change:

```
        props.Web.Update();
```

Next, it accesses a reference to the SPWeb object that represents the site being provisioned:

```
        using (SPSite siteCollection = new SPSite(props.Web.Site.ID))
        {
          using (SPWeb site = siteCollection.OpenWeb(props.Web.ID))
          {
```

Next, it accesses a reference to the SPWebApplication object that represents the web application in which the site is being provisioned:

```
            SPWebApplication app = siteCollection.WebApplication;
```

Next, it creates an SPWebConfigModification object to represent the configuration modification that you're about to make. This modification adds an entry to the <appSettings> section of the web.config files of all IIS web sites that map into the web application:

```
            SPWebConfigModification modification1 = new SPWebConfigModification();
```

Then, it sets the Path property on the SPWebConfigModification object to the XPath expression that selects the parent node, which is <appSettings> in this case:

```
            modification1.Path = "configuration/appSettings";
```

Next, it sets the Name property on the SPWebConfigModification object to the XPath expression that selects the node you want to add to the <appSettings> parent node:

```
            modification1.Name = "add[@key='MyKey']";
```

Then, it assigns the actual node being added to the Value property of the SPWebConfigModification object. As you can see, this node is an <add> element that supports two attributes named key and value where the value attribute is set to the GUID identifier of the site being provisioned:

```
    modification1.Value = "<add key='MyKey' value='" + props.Web.ID.ToString() + "'
  />";
```

Next, it specifies EnsureChildNode as the modification type:

```
            modification1.Type =
                SPWebConfigModification.SPWebConfigModificationType.EnsureChildNode;
```

Then, it invokes the Add method on the WebConfigModifications collection property of the SPWebApplication object to add the new SPWebConfigModification object to this collection:

```
            app.WebConfigModifications.Add(modification1);
```

Next, it accesses a reference to the SPWebService object that represents the current web service and invokes the ApplyWebConfigModifications method on this object to add the specified <add> entry to the <appSettings> section of the web.config files of all IIS web sites that map into the web application:

```
            SPWebService service = SPFarm.Local.Services.GetValue<SPWebService>();
            service.ApplyWebConfigModifications();
```

Then, Provision invokes the Add method on the EventReceivers collection property of the SPWeb object that represents the site being provisioned to instantiate and to return a reference to an SPEventReceiverDefinition object, which will be used to bind your WebDeleted web event handler to the site being provisioned:

```
            SPEventReceiverDefinition rd = site.EventReceivers.Add();
```

Next, it specifies a unique name for this event receiver definition:

```
            rd.Name = "My Event Receiver";
```

Then, it specifies the fully namespace-qualified name of the web event receiver that contains your WebDeleted web event handler:

```
            rd.Class = "ClassLibrary3.MyWebEventReceiver2";
```

Next, it specifies the strong name of the assembly that contains this web event receiver:

```
            rd.Assembly = "ClassLibrary3, Version=1.0.0.0, Culture=neutral,
PublicKeyToken=df663a77cbaeeca1";
```

Then, it specifies WebDeleted as the web event handler that you want to bind to the site being provisioned:

```
            rd.Type = SPEventReceiverType.WebDeleted;
```

As you can see, you've moved the code that binds your WebDeleted web event handler inside the Provision method of your site provisioning provider to ensure that this event handler is bound to every site provisioned from your site configuration.

Listing 9-32 presents the implementation of your web event receiver.

Listing 9-32: Your web event receiver

```
using System;
using Microsoft.SharePoint;
using System.Net.Mail;
using Microsoft.SharePoint.Administration;
using System.Reflection;

namespace ClassLibrary3
{
  public class MyWebEventReceiver2 : SPWebEventReceiver
  {
    public override void WebDeleted(SPWebEventProperties properties)
    {
      properties.Web.AllowUnsafeUpdates = true;
      SPWebApplication app = properties.Web.Site.WebApplication;

      SPWebConfigModification modification1 = new SPWebConfigModification();
      modification1.Path = "configuration/appSettings";
      modification1.Name = "add[@key='MyKey']";
      modification1.Value = "<add key='MyKey' value='" + properties.WebId
.ToString() + "' />";
      modification1.Owner = Assembly.GetExecutingAssembly().FullName;
      modification1.Sequence = 100;
      modification1.Type =
            SPWebConfigModification.SPWebConfigModificationType.EnsureChildNode;
      app.WebConfigModifications.Remove(modification1);

      SPWebService service = SPFarm.Local.Services.GetValue<SPWebService>();
      service.ApplyWebConfigModifications();
    }
  }
}
```

As you can see, your WebDeleted web event handler first creates an SPWebConfigModification object and sets its properties to the same exact values as your site provisioning provider. The only difference is that your WebDeleted web event handler invokes the Remove method instead to the Add method to remove the SPWebConfigModification object from the WebConfigModifications collection property of the SPWebApplication object that represents the web application:

```
app.WebConfigModifications.Remove(modification1);
```

When your WebDeleted web event handler finally invokes the ApplyWebConfigModifications method on the SPWebService object, the <add> entry that your site provisioning provider added to the <appSettings> configuration section is automatically removed.

In general, you should perform runtime site-specific operations such as adding site-specific entries to the web.config file (recall that the value attribute of the <add> entry is set to the GUID identifier of the site, which is a site-specific value, which you can access only at runtime) inside the Provision method of your site provisioning provider. You should also bind your web event handlers from within the Provision method as well. Your WebDeleted web event handler must clean up resources such as web.config when the site is deleted. For example, the site-specific <add> entry should be removed when the respective site is deleted.

Summary

This chapter covered the three types of event receivers, including list, item, and web event receivers. You saw examples of these three event receiver types and learned how to bind them to the appropriate SharePoint entities.

Chapter 10 moves on to SharePoint Web parts, where you learn how to implement your own custom Web parts and deploy them to SharePoint.

10

SharePoint Web Parts

SharePoint Web parts work on top of the ASP.NET Web Parts Framework. As such, this chapter begins with an overview of the ASP.NET Web Parts Framework and its components. The main goal of this overview is three-fold. First, the ASP.NET Web Parts Framework is the foundation upon which the SharePoint Web parts are built. Second, SharePoint extends and replaces some of the extensible components of the ASP.NET Web Parts Framework. These extensibility points and replacements are pointed out during the overview. Third, some aspects of the ASP.NET Web Parts Framework are not applicable in SharePoint. These differences are pointed out during the overview as well.

What Is the ASP.NET Web Parts Framework?

A complex framework such as the ASP.NET Web Parts Framework can easily overwhelm you if you're new to it. When you're learning a complex framework, it normally helps if you first get an overview of the main components before diving into their details. This is exactly what this section does.

The ASP.NET Web Parts Framework enables you to componentize an ASP.NET page into a set of server controls, where each control occupies a particular region or zone on the page. These server controls are known as WebZone controls because they all directly or indirectly derive from the WebZone base class. A WebZone server control is a composite control that contains one or more child server controls. These child controls are known as Part controls because they all directly or indirectly derive from the Part base class.

The ASP.NET Web Parts Framework comes with three descendants of the Part base class, which means that there are three types of Part server controls:

- **WebPart.** WebPart server controls make up the User Interface (UI) of an ASP.NET web page. You can think of WebPart controls as the building blocks of the UI of a web page.

- **EditorPart.** EditorPart server controls provide end users with the appropriate UIs to personalize the properties of the WebPart controls that make up the UI of a page.
- **CatalogPart.** CatalogPart server controls provide end users with a catalog or list of WebPart controls to choose from.

The ASP.NET Web Parts Framework comes with four descendants of the WebZone base class, which means that there are four types of WebZone server controls:

- **WebPartZone.** WebPartZone server controls are composite controls that contain the WebPart controls that make up the UI of a web page.
- **EditorZone.** EditorZone server controls are composite controls that contain the EditorPart controls that provide users with the appropriate UI to personalize the properties of the WebPart controls that make up the UI of a web page.
- **CatalogZone.** CatalogZone server controls are composite controls that contain the CatalogPart controls that provide users with the catalog or list of WebPart controls to choose from.
- **ConnectionsZone.** A ConnectionsZone server control provides users with the appropriate UI to perform the following tasks:
    - Establish connections between WebPart controls that make up the UI of a page so they can share data
    - Remove existing connections between WebPart controls to stop them from sharing data
    - Personalize the connections between WebPart controls

The ASP.NET Web Parts Framework comes with four descendants of the EditorPart base class, which means that there are four types of EditorPart server controls: AppearanceEditorPart, LayoutEditorPart, BehaviorEditorPart, and PropertyGridEditorPart. These four EditorPart controls provide end users with the appropriate UIs to respectively personalize the appearance, layout, behavior, and custom properties of the WebPart controls that make up the UI of an ASP.NET web page.

The ASP.NET Web Parts Framework comes with three subclasses of the CatalogPart base class, which means that there are three types of CatalogPart controls:

- **DeclarativeCatalogPart.** A DeclarativeCatalogPart control provides end users with the catalog or list of all available WebPart controls that users can add to the WebPartZone controls on the page. Figure 10-1 shows how SharePoint renders its declarative catalog part. The users are presented with links such as Home Gallery and Server Gallery, which present them with the list of available WebPart controls to choose from.
- **PageCatalogPart.** Users have the option of closing existing WebPart controls. The ASP.NET Web Parts Framework automatically adds these WebPart controls to the PageCatalogPart composite control. In other words, the PageCatalogPart control provides the end users with the catalog or list of closed WebPart controls that users can add back to the page. Figure 10-2 shows how SharePoint renders its page catalog part. The users are presented with a link named Closed Web Parts, which presents them with the list of closed Web part controls to choose from.

- **ImportCatalogPart.** An ImportCatalogPart control provides users with the appropriate UI to import WebPart controls as XML files. Figure 10-3 shows how SharePoint renders its import catalog part control. The users use the Browse button to navigate to the folder that contains the Web part description file that describes the WebPart control that they want to import into SharePoint.

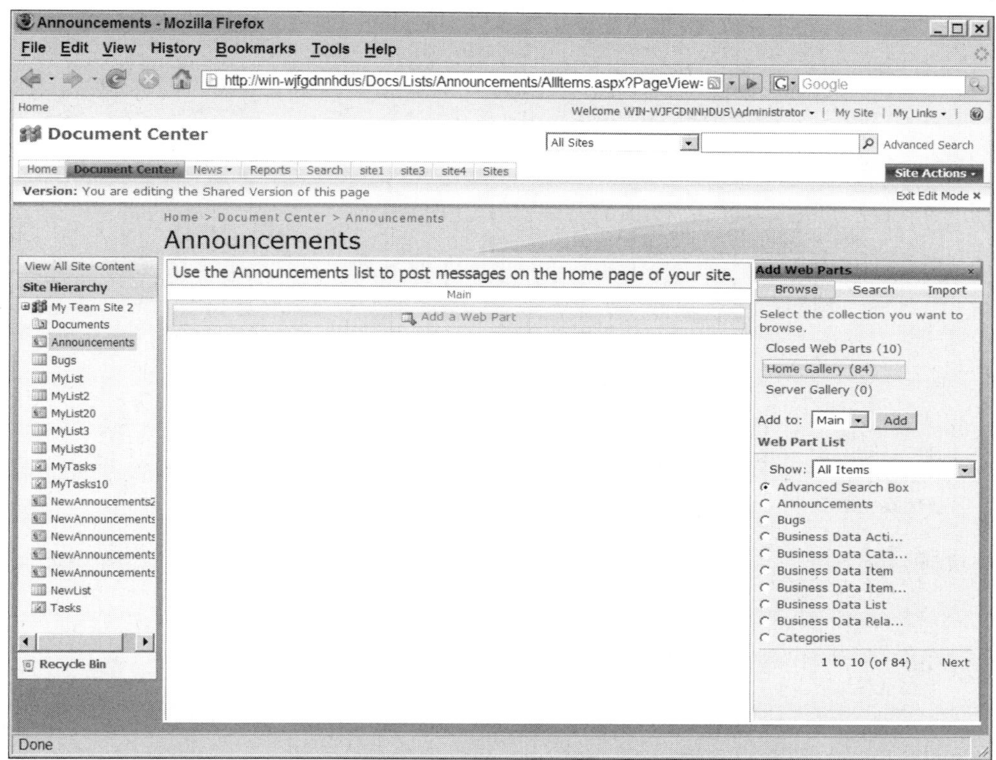

Figure 10-1: SharePoint page displaying declarative catalog part

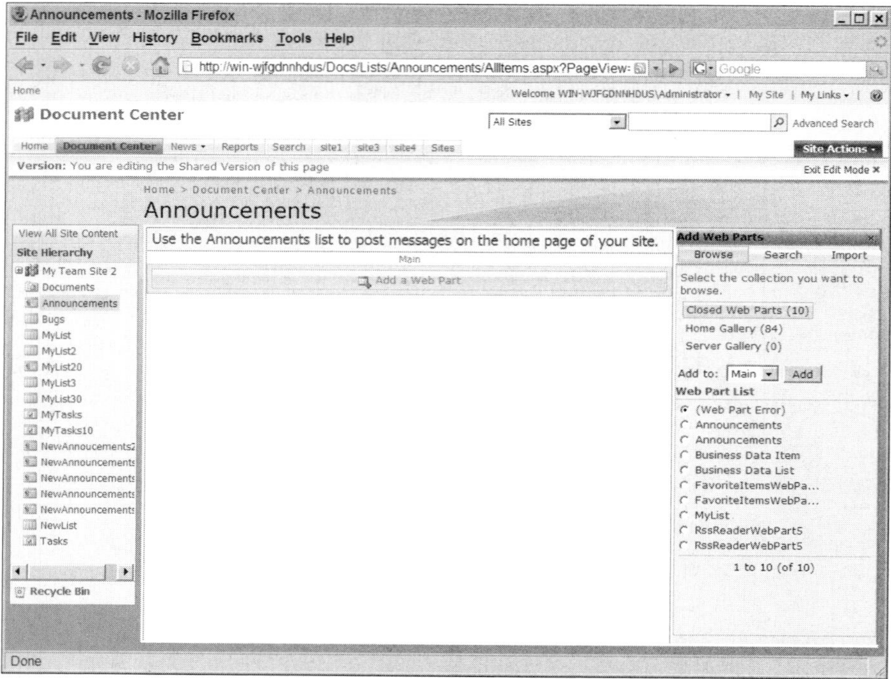

Figure 10-2: SharePoint page displaying page catalog part

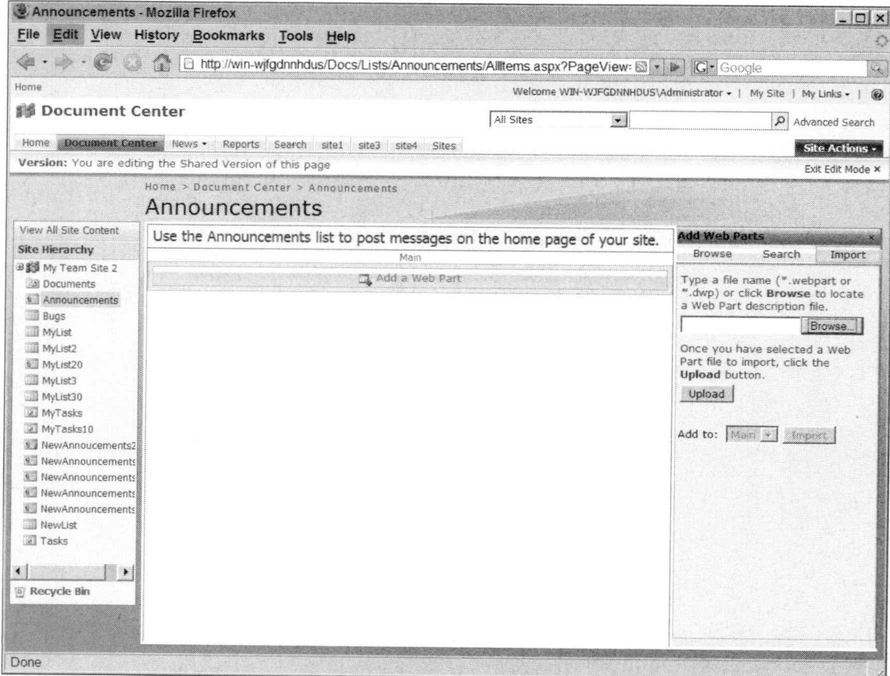

Figure 10-3: SharePoint page displaying import catalog part

The ASP.NET Web Parts Framework comes with a server control named WebPartManager whose main responsibility is to manage all the zones and parts declared on an ASP.NET page. Every Web parts page can have one and only one WebPartManager control. WebPartManager also switches a Web parts page from one display mode to another.

So, what is a Web part? A Web part is a server control that allows users to personalize its following aspects right from their browsers:

- Users can dynamically access the WebPart control from the catalog or list of available WebPart controls and add the control to a given WebPartZone composite control.
- Users can use the WebPartZone control's UI to dynamically remove, minimize, and restore the WebPart control.
- Users can close the WebPart control and access it again from the catalog or list of closed WebPart controls.
- Users can dynamically import the WebPart control.
- Users can dynamically personalize the appearance, layout, behavior, and custom properties of the WebPart control.
- Users can dynamically move the WebPart control from one WebPartZone composite control to another.
- Users can connect the WebPart control to another WebPart control so they can share data.

SharePoint Extensions to ASP.NET Web Parts Framework

This section presents the SharePoint extensions to the ASP.NET Web Parts Framework.

SPWebPartManager

As mentioned earlier, every Web parts page must contain an instance of a server control named WebPartManager. As its name suggests, this server control manages parts and zones, Web parts connections, and so on. SharePoint ships with a server control named SPWebPartManager that inherits from the ASP.NET WebPartManager. The SPWebPartManager server control contains the logic that stores Web parts-related data in the content database.

Every SharePoint Web parts page must contain a single instance of SPWebPartManager. As the following excerpt shows, the default.master file, which is the master page for SharePoint site pages, contains a single declaration of the SPWebPartManager server control:

```
...
<%@ Register Tagprefix="WebPartPages" Namespace="Microsoft.SharePoint.WebPartPages"
Assembly="Microsoft.SharePoint, Version=12.0.0.0, Culture=neutral,
PublicKeyToken=71e9bce111e9429c" %>
...
<html>
  ...
  <body ...>
    <form runat="server" ...>
    <WebPartPages:SPWebPartManager id="m" runat="Server" />
    ...
</form>
  </body>
</html>
```

If your page templates use this master page, they automatically inherit this server control. As such, your page templates must not add another instance of this server control. For the most part, you normally don't interact directly with this server control.

WebPartZone

As discussed earlier, every Web parts page must contain one or more instances of the ASP.NET WebPartZone server controls. These server controls host the WebPart server controls that make up the UI of the page. One of the responsibilities of a WebPartZone server control is to render the chrome that surrounds a WebPart server control. The ASP.NET WebPartZone server control does not hard-code the logic that renders the chrome. Instead it delegates the responsibility of rendering the chrome to an instance of a class named WebPartChrome. The ASP.NET WebPartZone exposes a protected virtual method named CreateWebPartChrome whose sole function is to instantiate and to return an instance of the appropriate subclass of the WebPartChrome class:

```
protected virtual WebPartChrome CreateWebPartChrome();
```

SharePoint ships with a server control named WebPartZone that inherits from the ASP.NET WebPartZone server control.

```
public sealed class WebPartZone : WebPartZone, INamingContainer { ... }
```

Note that the SharePoint WebPartZone is a sealed class. This means you cannot develop a custom WebPartZone class in SharePoint because a sealed class prevents derivation.

The SharePoint WebPartZone server control overrides the CreateWebPartChrome method that it inherits from the ASP.NET WebPartZone server control to instantiate and to return an instance of a subclass of the WebPartChrome class named SPChrome:

```
public sealed class SPChrome : WebPartChrome { ... }
```

This SPChrome instance is responsible for rendering the SharePoint-specific chrome around WebPart server controls on a SharePoint Web parts page. Because the SharePoint WebPartZone is a sealed class and because the only way to have the framework use a different type of chrome class to render the chrome is by inheriting from the WebPartZone class and overriding its CreateWebPartChrome, you cannot use a different type of chrome class to change the chrome rendering.

The following listing shows an excerpt from the default.aspx page template from which SharePoint Team Site and Blank Site homepages are provisioned:

```
<%@ Page language="C#" MasterPageFile="~masterurl/default.master"
Inherits="Microsoft.SharePoint.WebPartPages.WebPartPage,Microsoft.SharePoint,
Version=12.0.0.0,Culture=neutral,PublicKeyToken=71e9bce111e9429c" %>

<%@ Register Tagprefix="WebPartPages" Namespace="Microsoft.SharePoint.WebPartPages"
Assembly="Microsoft.SharePoint, Version=12.0.0.0, Culture=neutral,
PublicKeyToken=71e9bce111e9429c" %>

...

<asp:Content ID="Content11" ContentPlaceHolderID="PlaceHolderMain" runat="server">
  <table cellspacing="0" border="0" width="100%">
    <tr>
      <td class="ms-pagebreadcrumb">
        <asp:SiteMapPath SiteMapProvider="SPContentMapProvider" ID="ContentMap"
       SkipLinkText="" NodeStyle-CssClass="ms-sitemapdirectional" runat="server" />
      </td>
    </tr>
    <tr>
      <td class="ms-webpartpagedescription">
        <SharePoint:ProjectProperty ID="ProjectProperty3" Property="Description"
        runat="server" />
      </td>
    </tr>
    <tr>
      <td>
        <table width="100%" cellpadding="0" cellspacing="0"
        style="padding: 5px 10px 10px 10px;">
          <tr>
            <td valign="top" width="70%">
              <WebPartPages:WebPartZone runat="server" FrameType="TitleBarOnly"
              ID="Left" Title="loc:Left" />
            </td>
            <td valign="top" width="30%">
              <WebPartPages:WebPartZone runat="server" FrameType="TitleBarOnly"
              ID="Right" Title="loc:Right" />
            </td>
          </tr>
        </table>
      </td>
    </tr>
  </table>
</asp:Content>
```

As you can see from the boldfaced portions of this listing, the default.aspx page template follows these steps:

1. Sets the MasterPageFile attribute on the @Page directive to reference the default.master file, which is the master page for every SharePoint site page:

```
<%@ Page language="C#" MasterPageFile="~masterurl/default.master" ... %>
```

   Note that the default.aspx page template does not directly contain an instance of the SPWebPartManager server control because it inherits the SPWebPartManager server control declared within the default.master page. Keep in mind that when a content page such as default .aspx is requested, it is merged with its associated master page to form a single page. As discussed earlier, a single page cannot contain more than one instance of the SPWebPartManager server control.

   If you're writing your own custom site definition where you're implementing a custom page template for the site homepage, you should follow the same implementation pattern. That is, you should implement this custom page template as a content page that uses the default.master master page as its master page.

2. Declares an @Register directive to register a tag prefix named WebPartPages, which references the Microsoft.SharePoint.WebPartPages namespace in the Microsoft.SharePoint.dll assembly:

```
<%@ Register Tagprefix="WebPartPages" Namespace="Microsoft.SharePoint.WebPartPages"
Assembly="Microsoft.SharePoint, Version=12.0.0.0, Culture=neutral,
PublicKeyToken=71e9bce111e9429c" %>
```

   You should do the same in your custom page template for your custom site homepage.

3. Declares two instances of the <WebPartPages:WebPartZone> server controls:

```
<td valign="top" width="70%">
  <WebPartPages:WebPartZone runat="server" FrameType="TitleBarOnly"
  ID="Left"
  Title="loc:Left" />
</td>
<td valign="top" width="30%">
  <WebPartPages:WebPartZone runat="server" FrameType="TitleBarOnly"
  ID="Right" Title="loc:Right" />
</td>
```

   Note that your custom page templates must use <WebPartPages:WebPartZone> where the WebPartPages prefix references the Microsoft.SharePoint.WebPartPages namespace as opposed to <asp:WebPartZone> because your page templates must use the SharePoint WebPartZone as opposed to the ASP.NET WebPartZone.

Editor and Catalog Zones

Editor and catalog zones host editor and catalog parts. As discussed earlier, an editor part is a server control that provides end users with the appropriate UI to edit a WebPart server control on a Web parts page. A catalog part is a server control that provides end users with the catalog of WebPart server controls to choose from.

SharePoint ships with a base class named WebPartPage in the Microsoft.SharePoint.WebPartPages namespace in the Microsoft.SharePoint.dll assembly, which contains the logic that automatically adds the required editor and catalog zones to a Web parts page. All you have to do is to inherit your Web parts page from this base class.

The following listing shows the @Page directive of the default.aspx page, which is the page template from which SharePoint Team Site and Blank Site homepages are provisioned:

```
<%@ Page language="C#" MasterPageFile="~masterurl/default.master"
Inherits="Microsoft.SharePoint.WebPartPages.WebPartPage,Microsoft.SharePoint,
Version=12.0.0.0,Culture=neutral,PublicKeyToken=71e9bce111e9429c" %>
```

As you can see, the Inherits attribute on the @Page directive references the WebPartPage base class. If you're implementing a custom page template, you should set the Inherits attribute on the @Page directive of your custom page template to the same value or a code-behind class that inherits from WebPartPage.

Switching Display Modes

A Web parts page can be in different display modes. When you implement a Web parts page in ASP.NET, your page must contain the logic that allows end users to switch the page from one display mode to another. For example, end users switch from the default browse display mode to edit display mode so they can personalize the properties of the WebPart server controls on the page. The WebPartPage base class in the Microsoft.SharePoint.WebPartPages namespace in the Microsoft.SharePoint.dll assembly contains the logic that enables users to switch display modes. As such, if you set the Inherits attribute on the @Page directive of your custom page template to the value discussed in the previous section, your Web parts page will automatically inherit from the WebPartPage base class and consequently you don't have to worry about the display mode-switching logic.

Developing WebPart Server Controls

There are two different approaches to developing a WebPart server control in ASP.NET. The first approach allows you to turn any of the following server controls into a WebPart control without writing a single line of code:

- ASP.NET standard server controls, such as Calendar
- Custom server controls
- User controls

All you need to do is place any of these server controls within the opening and closing tags of the <ZoneTemplate> child element of an <asp:WebPartZone> element on your ASP.NET Web parts page. At runtime, the ASP.NET Web Parts Framework automatically wraps your server control in an instance of a control named GenericWebPart that derives from the WebPart base class. This wrapper allows your server control to act like a normal WebPart control at runtime.

The SharePoint Web Parts Framework does not support this approach. Both SharePoint and ASP.NET support a second approach to Web part development, which requires you to implement a server control that directly or indirectly inherits from the WebPart base class. You'll use this approach later in this chapter to develop Web parts.

Main Components of the Web Parts Framework

Figure 10-4 shows the class or control diagram for the main Web parts controls. The ASP.NET Web Parts Framework is a component-based architecture that consists of pluggable and replaceable components. In other words, it supports what is known as plug-and-play, where you can plug your own custom components into the framework.

This is all possible because the components of the framework talk to one another through well-defined APIs. In other words, the only dependency between these components is the APIs through which they communicate. These APIs shield these components from the specific types of components they are communicating with. As such, the components of the framework have no knowledge of the actual types of components they are talking to. This means that it doesn't matter what type of component is being used as long as the component complies with the specified API.

The ASP.NET Web Parts Framework uses base classes such as WebPart, EditorPart, CatalogPart, WebPartZoneBase, EditorZoneBase, and CatalogZoneBase to define the APIs that all components must implement. In other words, the methods and properties of each base class define an API as follows:

- **WebPart.** This defines the API for the Web parts controls that make up the UI of a Web parts page. You can plug your own custom WebPart control into the framework if your custom control implements the WebPart API.
- **EditorPart.** This defines the API that are used to edit the WebPart controls. You can plug your own custom EditorPart control into the framework if your custom control implements the EditorPart API.
- **CatalogPart.** This defines the API for the Web parts controls that provide users with a catalog of WebPart controls to choose from.
- **WebPartZoneBase.** This defines the API for the Web parts controls that act as containers for the WebPart controls.
- **EditorZoneBase.** This defines the API for the Web parts controls that act as containers for the EditorPart controls.
- **CatalogZoneBase.** This defines the API for the Web parts controls that act as containers for the CatalogPart controls.

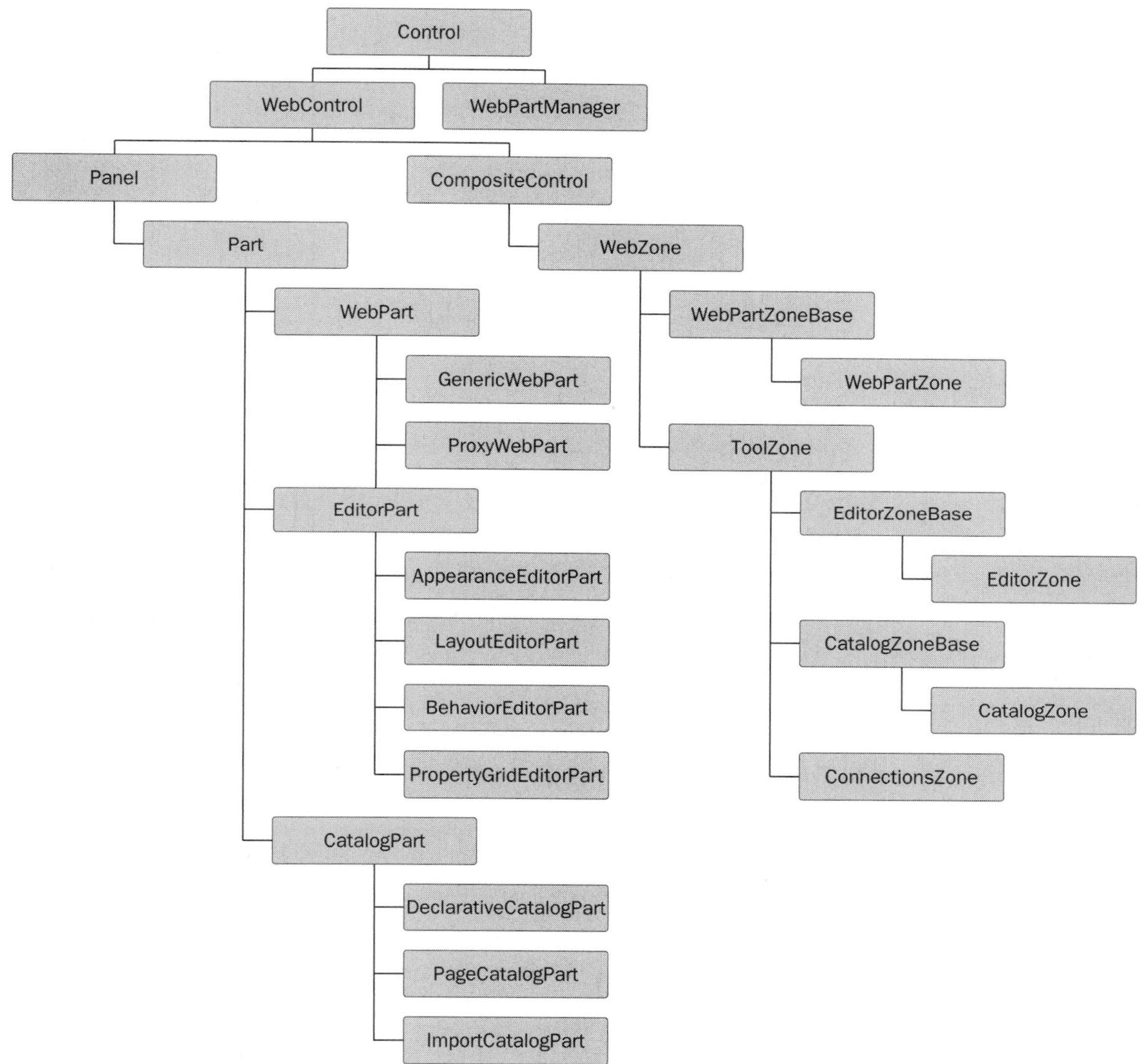

Figure 10-4: The class diagram for the main Web parts controls

Part

As Figure 10-4 shows, the Part base class derives from the Panel class. Part has three subclasses: WebPart, EditorPart, and CatalogPart. The Part base class encapsulates those properties that all these subclasses have in common:

```
public virtual PartChromeState ChromeState {get; set;}
public virtual PartChromeType ChromeType {get; set;}
public virtual string Description {get; set;}
public virtual string Title {get; set;}
```

- **ChromeState.** This is a property of type PartChromeState enumeration that specifies whether a part control is in minimized or normal state. The possible values are PartChromeState. Minimized and PartChromeState.Normal.
- **ChromeType.** This is a property of type PartChromeType enumeration that specifies the type of chrome that frames a part control. The possible values are:
    - **PartChromeType.BorderOnly.** This is a border without a title bar.
    - **PartChromeType.TitleOnly.** This is a title bar without a border.
    - **PartChromeType.TitleAndBorder.** This is both a title bar and a border.
    - **PartChromeType.Default.** This inherits the containing zone's PartChromeType setting.
    - **PartChromeType.None.** This has neither title bar nor border.
- **Description.** This is a short description of what the part control does. ToolTips and CatalogZone controls display this description to end users.
- **Title.** This gets or sets the text that appears in the title bar of a part control.

As you'll see later, another thing that these three subclasses have in common is that all of them are composite controls; that is, they're all composed of other server controls, which means that these subclasses, like all composite controls, should derive from the CompositeControl base class.

Therefore, these subclasses must derive from two base classes: Part, which contains all their common properties, and CompositeControl. This isn't possible because C# and VB.NET don't support class multiple inheritance. That's why the Part base class literally implements all the functionality that the CompositeControl supports:

- Overriding the Controls collection to call the EnsureChildControls:

```
public override ControlCollection Controls
{
  get
  {
    EnsureChildControls();
    return base.Controls;
  }
}
```

Becasue part controls such as your own custom WebPart controls directly or indirectly inherits from Part, they do not need to override the Controls collection to invoke the EnsureChildControls.

- Implementing INamingContainer interface:

```
public abstract class Part : Panel, INamingContainer,
                             ICompositeControlDesignerAccessor
```

Becasue part controls such as your own custom WebPart controls directly or indirectly inherits from Part, they do not need to implement the INamingContainer interface.

- Overriding the DataBind method:

```
public override void DataBind()
{
  OnDataBinding(EventArgs.Empty);
  EnsureChildControls();
  DataBindChildren();
}
```

- Implementing the ICompositeControlDesignerAccessor interface. This interface exposes a single method named ReCreateChildControls that allows designer developers to re-create the child controls of a composite control on the design surface. This is useful if you want to develop a custom designer for your composite control. A designer is a component that allows page developers to work with your custom composite control in a designer such as Visual Studio:

```
public abstract class Part : Panel, INamingContainer,
                             ICompositeControlDesignerAccessor
```

In summary, the Part base class is a simple composite control that exposes four simple properties named ChromeState, ChromeType, Description, and Title.

Web Part

As you saw in Figure 10-4, the WebPart control derives from the Part control and implements the IWebPart, IWebActionable, and IWebEditable interfaces, as discussed in the following sections. Listing 10-1 contains the definition of the IWebPart interface. As this code listing shows, this interface exposes six properties that every WebPart control must support to enhance the user experience.

Listing 10-1: The IWebPart interface

```
public interface IWebPart
{
  string CatalogIconImageUrl { get; set; }
  string Description { get; set; }
  string Subtitle { get; }
  string Title { get; set; }
  string TitleIconImageUrl { get; set; }
  string TitleUrl { get; set; }
}
```

The following list describes these properties:

- **CatalogIconImageUrl.** This specifies the URL to an image that the CatalogZone control uses to represent the WebPart control.
- **Description.** This is a short description of what the WebPart control does. ToolTips and CatalogZone controls display this description to end users.
- **Title.** This is the text that appears in the title bar of a WebPart control.
- **Subtitle.** This is the text that appears in the title bar of a WebPart control as a subtitle.
- **TitleIconImageUrl.** This specifies the URL to an image that the title bar of a WebPart control uses to represent the control.
- **TitleUrl.** This specifies the URL to a page that contains more information about the WebPart control.

The Web part control implements these properties of the IWebPart interface. If you implement a custom control that derives from the WebPart base class, your control doesn't have to implement the properties of the IWebPart interface because the base class has already implemented all these properties.

This section implements a custom WebPart control named RssReaderWebPart that derives from the WebPart base class to show you how to develop your own custom WebPart controls. Listing 10-2 contains the code for RssReaderWebPart custom WebPart control. The following sections discuss the implementation of the members of this control.

Listing 10-2: The RssReaderWebPart Web part

```
using System.Web.UI.WebControls.WebParts;
using System.Web.UI.WebControls;
using System.Web.UI;
using System;
using System.Collections;
using System.Web.Profile;
using System.Data.SqlClient;
using System.Configuration;
using System.Web;
using System.Collections.Generic;
using System.Xml;
using System.IO;
using System.ComponentModel;
using System.Collections.Specialized;

namespace WebPartsChapter
{
  public class RssReaderWebPart : WebPart
  {
    Table table;
    private string rssUrl;
    [Personalizable(true)]
    [WebBrowsable()]
```

```
public virtual string RssUrl
{
  get { return rssUrl; }
  set { rssUrl = value; }
}

protected virtual void AddContainer()
{
  table = new Table();
  table.CellSpacing = 5;
  Controls.Add(table);
}
protected virtual void AddItemToContainer(XmlReader reader)
{
  string link = string.Empty; ;
  string title = string.Empty;
  string description = string.Empty;

  while (reader.Read())
  {
    if (reader.NodeType == XmlNodeType.Element)
    {
      if (reader.Name == "link")
        link = reader.ReadElementContentAsString();

      else if (reader.Name == "title")
        title = reader.ReadElementContentAsString();

      else if (reader.Name == "description")
        description = reader.ReadElementContentAsString();
    }
  }

  TableRow row = new TableRow();
  table.Rows.Add(row);
  TableCell cell = new TableCell();
  row.Cells.Add(cell);

  HyperLink hyperLink = new HyperLink();
  hyperLink.NavigateUrl = link;
  hyperLink.Text = title;
  hyperLink.Font.Bold = true;
  cell.Controls.Add(hyperLink);
  LiteralControl lc = new LiteralControl("<br/>");
  cell.Controls.Add(lc);
  Label label = new Label();
  label.Text = description;
  cell.Controls.Add(label);
}
protected override void CreateChildControls()
{
  Controls.Clear();
```

(continued)

Listing 10-2 *(continued)*

```
        if (string.IsNullOrEmpty(rssUrl))
        {
          ChildControlsCreated = true;
          return;
        }

        using (XmlReader reader = XmlReader.Create(rssUrl))
        {
          AddContainer();
          reader.MoveToContent();
          reader.ReadToDescendant("channel");
          reader.ReadToDescendant("item");
          do
          {
            using (XmlReader itemReader = reader.ReadSubtree())
            {
              AddItemToContainer(itemReader);
            }
          } while (reader.ReadToNextSibling("item"));
        }
        ChildControlsCreated = true;
      }
    }
  }
```

RssUrl

The RssReaderWebPart control exposes a property named RssUrl that must be set to the URL of the RSS feed, as shown in Listing 10-2. RssUrl is marked with the [Personalizable(true)] metadata attribute to store the value in the personalization data store. Note that the RssUrl property uses a private field as its backing store. You cannot use the ViewState collection of the RssReaderWebPart control as the backing store of the property that you want the Web Parts Framework to store in the personalization data store because the value of this property is stored in and retrieved from the personalization data store as opposed to the page's view state. The page's view state is the suitable data store across page postbacks.

CreateChildControls

As Listing 10-2 illustrates, CreateChildControls uses an XmlReader to stream in the RSS document. When reading XML data such as RSS documents, you have three options as follows:

- You can use the XmlReader streaming XML API to read in the XML document in streaming fashion.
- You can use the XPathNavigator random-access XML API to read in the XML document in cursor-style fashion.
- You can use the XmlDocument random-access DOM XML API to load the XML document into an XmlDocument.

Here is a handy rule of thumb: Stream your XML unless you have a good reason not to do so. When you think about it, you don't really need to access the data in the RSS document in a random fashion.

The CreateChildControls method then calls the AddContainer method to create the container control that will contain the entire contents of the RssReaderWebPart control. This method is discussed shortly. Notice that this method is marked as protected virtual to allow subclasses of the RssReaderWebPart control to use a different type of container control. This is an example of how you can make your custom WebPart controls more extensible:

```
AddContainer();
```

The method then calls the MoveToContent method of the XmlReader to position the reader on the document element, the <rss> element:

```
reader.MoveToContent();
```

It then calls the ReadToDescendant method of the XmlReader to move the reader from the <rss> element to the <channel> element. You have to constantly be aware of the node on which the XmlReader is currently positioned because the outcome of the XmlReader's methods, such as ReadToDescendant, depends on where the reader is currently positioned:

```
reader.ReadToDescendant("channel");
```

Next, the method calls the ReadToDescendant method of the XmlReader to move the reader from the <channel> element to the first <item> element:

```
reader.ReadToDescendant("item");
```

The CreateChildControls method then enters a do-while loop. In each iteration of the loop, the method calls the ReadSubtree method of the XmlReader. The ReadSubtree method returns a new XmlReader positioned on the same node as the original XmlReader. You can reposition this XmlReader independently of its parent XmlReader. In other words, when you exit an iteration and are about to invoke the ReadToNextSibling method on the parent XmlReader, the parent XmlReader is still positioned at the same node at which it was positioned when you entered the iteration:

```
using (XmlReader itemReader = reader.ReadSubtree())
```

The CreateChildControls method then calls the AddItemToContainer method and passes the new XmlReader into it. This method is discussed shortly.

```
AddItemToContainer(itemReader);
```

Then it calls the ReadToNextSibling method of the original XmlReader to move the reader from the current <item> node to the next <item> node:

```
reader.ReadToNextSibling("item")
```

AddContainer

As Listing 10-2 shows, the AddContainer method uses a Table control as the container that contains the entire contents of the RssReaderWebPart control. Because this method is marked as protected virtual, you can override it to use a different container.

AddItemToContainer

Listing 10-2 illustrates the implementation of the AddItemToContainer method. The AddItemToContainer method uses the Name property of the XmlReader to locate the <link>, <title>, and <description> sub-elements of the current <item> element. It then calls the ReadElementContentAsString method of the XmlReader to read the content within the opening and closing tags of the <link>, <title>, and <description> sub-elements.

Deploying a Custom WebPart Server Control

Follow these steps to implement and to deploy a custom Web part server control to SharePoint:

1. Launch Visual Studio and create a Class Library project. Go ahead and create a Class Library project named WebPartsChapter.
2. Configure Visual Studio to compile your custom Web parts into a strong-named assembly. Go ahead and do this configuration for the WebPartsChapter.
3. Implement a class that inherits from the WebPart base class directly or indirectly. You did this step in the previous section where you developed a Web part named RssReaderWebPart, which inherits from the WebPart base class. Go ahead and add a source file named RssReaderWebPart .cs to the project and add the content of Listing 10-2 to this source file.
4. Add the following assembly-level metadata attribute to the AssemblyInfo.cs file:

```
[assembly: System.Security.AllowPartiallyTrustedCallers]
```

   The role of this assembly-level metadata attribute is discussed in the next chapter. For now it suffices to say that this metadata attribute is only applicable to strong-named assemblies.

5. Install the assembly that contains your custom WebPart server control in GAC or the bin directory of the target SharePoint web application. You can add a post-build event to Visual Studio as discussed in the previous chapters to automate this installation.
6. Open the web.config file of the SharePoint web application where you want to use your custom WebPart server control and add a <SafeControl> entry to the <SafeControls> section of this configuration file to register your custom WebPart server control as a safe control:

```
<SafeControl
Assembly="WebPartsChapter, Version=1.0.0.0, Culture=neutral,
          PublicKeyToken=9db0c35d16bdcc98"
Namespace="WebPartsChapter"
TypeName="*"
Safe="True" />
```

As discussed earlier in this book, it is not a good idea to manually edit the web.config file because of the following two important factors:

- You have to manually make the same edits to all web.config files of all IIS web sites that map into the target SharePoint web application. Keep in mind that the SharePoint web application is a SharePoint abstraction that may map to numerous IIS web sites on different web servers in the server farm.
- You have to manually make the same edits to the web.config files of the IIS web sites that will be mapped to the same web application in the future. New web servers may be added to the server farm that may contain IIS web sites that map to the same SharePoint web application.

Clearly manual edits to web.config are not scalable and are error-prone. Chapter 12 shows you how to add these safe control entries to a SharePoint solution package to have SharePoint take control of adding these entries to the web.config files of the current or future IIS web sites that map to the same SharePoint web application.

7. Create a .webpart XML file that describes your custom WebPart server control. This XML file is discussed shortly.
8. Add this .webpart XML file to the Web Part Gallery of the target site collection. Keep in mind that every site collection has a single Web Part Gallery whose contents are available to all sites in that site collection. The Web Part Gallery is basically a document library that maintains the .webpart XML files that describe the available WebPart server controls. After adding this .webpart XML file to the Web Part Gallery you can navigate to any site page in the site collection and use the SharePoint user interface to access and to add your custom WebPart server control to a web part zone on the site page.

Bin versus GAC

As mentioned, you can deploy the assembly that contains your custom WebPart server control to the GAC or the local bin directory of a SharePoint web application. If you plan on deploying the assembly to the GAC, you must strong-name the assembly because only strong-named assemblies can be installed in the GAC. The GAC is where shared assemblies reside. These are the assemblies that all SharePoint web applications on the server computer can access and use. Because every assembly in the GAC is electronically signed, when a web application attempts to load an assembly the CLR loads the assembly only if the assembly is coming from where it claims it's coming from and has not been tampered with. That is why only strong-named assemblies can be installed in the GAC.

Here is an important question: Should you install the assembly that contains your custom WebPart server control in the GAC or the local bin directory of a web application? To find the answer to this question, take a look at the pros and cons of each installation approach. Installing an assembly in the GAC makes the assembly available to every SharePoint web application running on the server machine. This is both good and bad. It's good because a single deployment makes your custom WebPart server control available to all web applications. If you install your assembly in the local bin directory of a web application, your custom WebPart server control is only available to the pages in that web application.

The con is that all assemblies in the GAC are executed in full trust code access security mode. That is, the CLR fully trusts the code in these assemblies. Assemblies in the local bin directory of a SharePoint web application, on the other hand, are partially trusted. This means that the CLR applies the configured code access security policies to ensure that the code in the assembly has the proper permissions.

The CLR would not allow the code to perform an operation for which it does not have the proper permissions. As a best practice, you should always install the assembly that contains your custom WebPart server control in the local bin directory of a SharePoint web application to take full advantage of the CLR code access security enforcement.

To help you gain a better understanding of trust level and its role, take a look at the trust levels in a WSS web application. If you open the web.config file of a WSS web application you should see the following XML fragment:

```
<system.web>
  <securityPolicy>

    <trustLevel
    name="WSS_Medium"
    policyFile="C:\Program Files\Common Files\Microsoft Shared\Web Server
                Extensions\12\config\wss_mediumtrust.config" />

    <trustLevel
    name="WSS_Minimal"
    policyFile="C:\Program Files\Common Files\Microsoft Shared\Web Server
                Extensions\12\config\wss_minimaltrust.config" />

  </securityPolicy>

  <trust level="WSS_Minimal" originUrl="" />
</system.web>
```

As you can see, <system.web> contains a child element named <securityPolicy>, which contains two instances of a child element named <trustLevel>. As the name suggests, a <trustLevel> element is used to define a trust level. This element features an attribute named name, which specifies the name of the trust level. As you can see, trust levels are named entities. The <trustLevel> element also features an attribute named policyFile that specifies the physical path to the policy file that contains the set of permissions associated with the trust level. In a way, you can think of a trust level as a canned set of permissions. As the preceding XML fragment shows, WSS defines two trust levels named WSS_Minimal and WSS_Medium whose associated set of permissions are specified in the wss_minimaltrust.config and wss_mediumtrust.config files in the following folder on the file system of the front-end web server:

```
Local_Drive:\Program Files\Common Files\Microsoft Shared\Web Server Extensions\12\
config\
```

As the preceding XML fragment shows, the web.config file of a WSS web application contains a <trust> element whose level attribute is set to WSS_Minimal. This means that by default every WSS web application runs in WSS_Minimal trust level, which basically gives the assembly the permission to execute and nothing more. If your custom WebPart server control needs more permission, you can take one of these two approaches to raise the trust level:

1. Raise the trust level of the entire SharePoint web application. For example, you can change the trust level of a WSS 3.0 web application from WSS_Minimal to WSS_Medium. To do so, open the web.config file of the SharePoint web application and search for the <trust> element and change the value of the level attribute on this element to WSS_Medium. This approach is highly discouraged because:

- Raising the trust level of the entire SharePoint web application unnecessarily raises the trust level for all assemblies residing in the bin directory of the application.
- Raising the trust level gives your assemblies the permissions that it does not need.
- There is no guarantee that the web application on the production server will have the required trust level.

2. Create a new policy file and define a new trust level that gives your assembly the exact permissions that it needs and set the level attribute on the <trust> element to the name of this new trust level. Because the new policy file is deployed to the production server, you can rest assured that the production server will also support the new trust level. It is highly recommended that you use this approach to raise the trust level for your custom WebPart server control. The next chapter dives into code access security where you'll learn a great deal about this very important security topic. Chapter 12 shows you how to include your code access security settings in the solution package to have SharePoint automatically create a new policy file with the required permission sets for you.

Web Part Description File

As mentioned earlier, you must create a .webpart XML file that describes your custom WebPart server control and add this file to the Web Part Gallery of the target site collection. Keep in mind that the Web Part Gallery is a document library that maintains the .webpart XML files that describe the available WebPart server controls.

The .webpart description file of a WebPart control contains all the information about the control, including the fully qualified name of the type of the control, the complete information about the assembly that contains the type, and the values of properties of the control. You can think of the Web part description file as a recipe that SharePoint uses to generate a WebPart control of a specific type with specific settings.

Listing 10-3 shows a description file that describes an ASP.NET Calendar control with the specified settings. As you can see, this description file has a document element named <webParts> that contains a <webPart> child element, which represents an ASP.NET Calendar WebPart control.

As Listing 10-3 illustrates, the <webPart> element has two child elements, <metaData> and <data>. The <metaData> element itself contains two child elements, <type> and <importErrorMessage>. The <type> child element exposes an attribute named name that contains the following information:

- The fully qualified name of the type of the WebPart control, including its complete namespace containment hierarchy, such as System.Web.UI.WebControls.Calendar.
- The complete information about the assembly that contains the type. This information contains the assembly name, version, culture, and public key token, such as System.Web, Version=2.0.0.0, Culture=neutral, PublicKeyToken=b03f5f7f11d50a3a if the assembly is strong-named.

The <importErrorMessage> child element, on the other hand, contains the error message that will be shown to the user if the import operation fails.

The <data> element contains two child elements, <properties> and <genericWebPartProperties>. The description file only populates one of these two properties. If the control doesn't derive from the WebPart control such as an ASP.NET control, custom control, or user control, only the

<genericWebPartProperties> element is populated and the <properties> element is left empty. Listing 10-3 presents an example of this case where the description file describes an ASP.NET Calendar control. As discussed earlier SharePoint does not support runtime WebPart server controls. In other words, SharePoint expects every WebPart server control to inherit from the WebPart base class directly or indirectly.

If the control derives from the WebPart control, such as the RssReaderWebPart control, only the <properties> element is populated and the <genericWebPartProperties> element is left empty.

Both the <properties> and <genericWebPartProperties> elements contain the same type of child element, <property>. Each <property> element represents a property of the WebPart control. The name and type attributes of a <property> element are set to the name and data type of the property that the element represents. The value of the property that the element represents is placed within the opening and closing tags of the <property> element.

Listing 10-3: An example of a description file

```
<?xml version="1.0" encoding="utf-8"?>
<webParts>
  <webPart xmlns="http://schemas.microsoft.com/WebPart/v3">
    <metaData>
      <type
      name="System.Web.UI.WebControls.Calendar, System.Web, Version=2.0.0.0,
            Culture=neutral, PublicKeyToken=b03f5f7f11d50a3a" />
      <importErrorMessage>Cannot import this Web Part.</importErrorMessage>
    </metaData>
    <data>
      <properties />
      <genericWebPartProperties>
        <property name="AllowClose" type="bool">True</property>
        <property name="Width" type="unit" />
        <property name="AllowMinimize" type="bool">True</property>
        <property name="AllowConnect" type="bool">True</property>
        <property name="ChromeType" type="chrometype">Default</property>
        <property name="TitleIconImageUrl" type="string" />
        <property name="Description" type="string" />
        <property name="Hidden" type="bool">False</property>
        <property name="TitleUrl" type="string" />
        <property name="AllowEdit" type="bool">True</property>
        <property name="Height" type="unit" />
        <property name="HelpUrl" type="string" />
        <property name="Title" type="string">Calendar</property>
        <property name="CatalogIconImageUrl" type="string" />
        <property name="Direction" type="direction">NotSet</property>
        <property name="ChromeState" type="chromestate">Normal</property>
        <property name="AllowZoneChange" type="bool">True</property>
        <property name="AllowHide" type="bool">True</property>
        <property name="HelpMode" type="helpmode">Navigate</property>
        <property name="ExportMode" type="exportmode">All</property>
      </genericWebPartProperties>
    </data>
  </webPart>
</webParts>
```

As part of deployment of your custom WebPart server control, you must create a .webpart XML file that describes your custom WebPart server control and add this description file to the Web Parts Gallery of the target site collection. You have several different options when it comes to creating a .webpart XML file, as discussed in the following sections.

Graphical Approach

One approach is to navigate to the Web Parts Gallery of the target site collection as shown in Figure 10-5. Here is the top-level site relative URL to this page:

```
/_catalogs/wp/Forms/AllItems.aspx
```

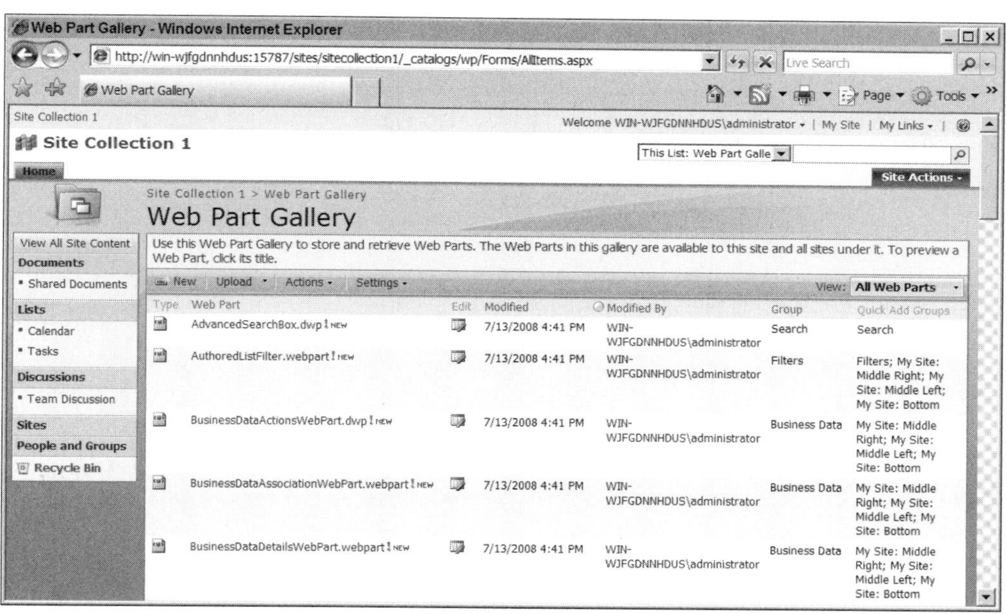

Figure 10-5: The Web Part Gallery

Next, click the New button to navigate to the page shown in Figure 10-6.

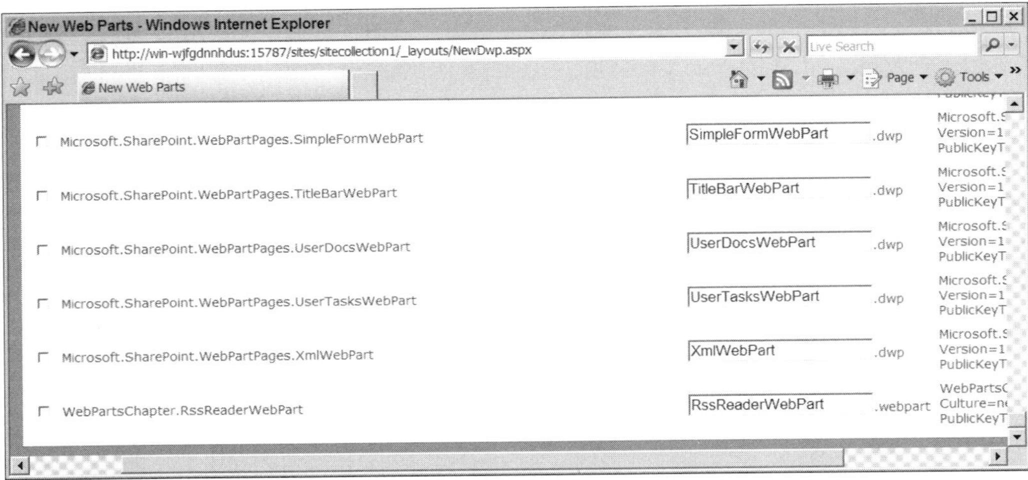

Figure 10-6: The New Web Parts page

This page displays the list of all safe WebPart server controls in the assemblies residing in the bin directory of the current SharePoint web application and the assemblies residing in the Global Assembly Cache. Recall that a safe WebPart server control is a control with a <SafeControl> entry in the <SafeControls> section of the web.config file of the current SharePoint web application. As you can see, this page only displays safe WebPart server controls.

Search for your WebPart server control in this page, which is the RssReaderWebPart control in this case. Select the checkbox for this control and enter a name for the .webpart XML file. Next, click the Populate Gallery button. This will automatically create a .webpart description file for your custom WebPart server control and add this description file to the Web Part Gallery as shown in the highlighted portion of Figure 10-7.

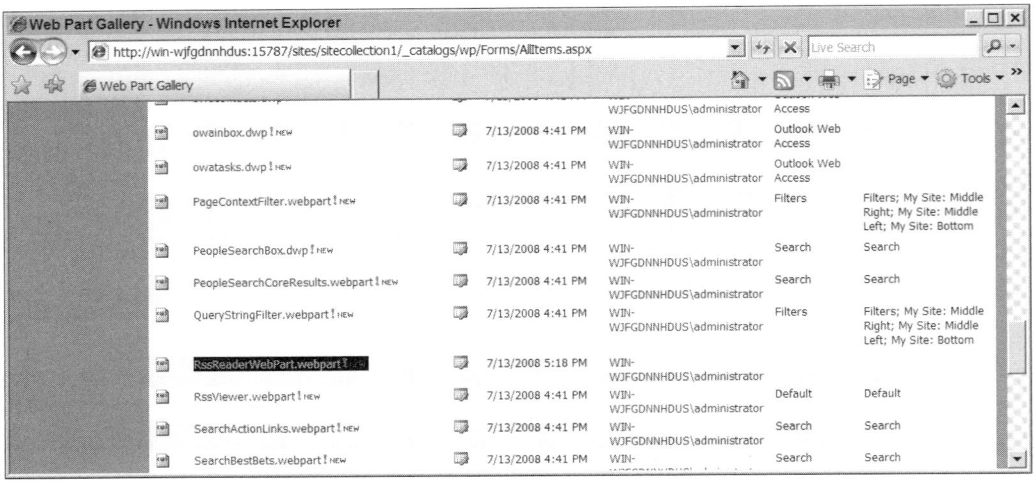

Figure 10-7: The Web Part Gallery

Declarative Approach

Because the .webpart description file is an XML file with a well-defined schema, you can implement this file yourself as shown in Listing 10-4.

Listing 10-4: The Web part description file for the RssReaderWebPart control

```
<?xml version="1.0" encoding="utf-8"?>
<webParts>
  <webPart xmlns="http://schemas.microsoft.com/WebPart/v3">
    <metaData>
      <type
      name="WebPartsChapter.RssReaderWebPart, WebPartsChapter, Version=1.0.0.0,
            Culture=neutral, PublicKeyToken=9db0c35d16bdcc98" />
      <importErrorMessage>Cannot import this Web Part.</importErrorMessage>
    </metaData>
    <data>
    <properties>
      <property name="Title" type="string">RssReaderWebPart</property>
   </properties>
    </data>
</webPart>
</webParts>
```

Next, you need to upload this file to the Web Part Gallery of the target site collection. You have two options. You can do this graphically through the SharePoint user interface, or you can do this through a SharePoint feature. The graphical approach is covered first.

Navigate to the same page shown in Figure 10-5. However, this time around click the Upload button instead of the New button to upload this .webpart description file to the Web Part Gallery of the site collection. Clicking the Upload button takes you to the page shown in Figure 10-8.

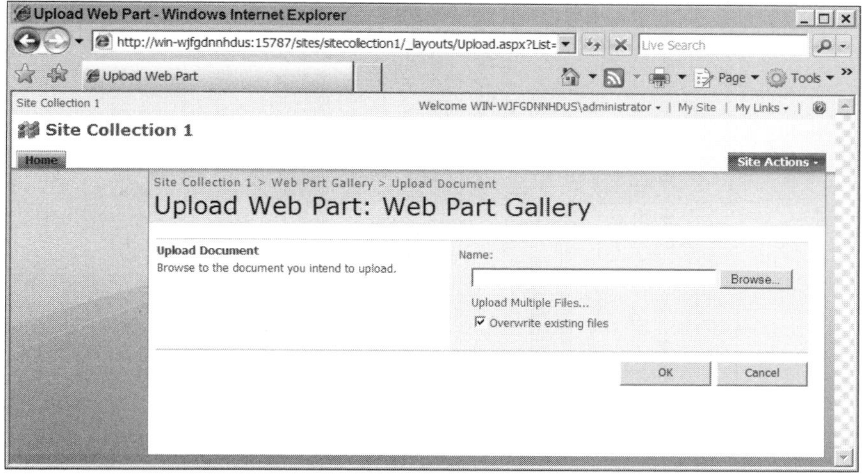

Figure 10-8: The Upload Web Part page

Click the Browse button, navigate to the folder where the .webpart description file for your custom WebPart server control resides, and select this file. Then click the OK button as shown in Figure 10-8 to upload the file to the Web Part Gallery of the site collection.

Even though this graphical approach is quite simple, it is not a recommended practice. As a best practice, you should take these steps to add your .webpart description file to the Web Part Gallery:

1. Create a feature as shown in Listing 10-5. Note that this feature is scoped at site collection level because you want to add this .webpart description file to the Web Part Gallery, which is a site collection-level gallery. Recall that each site collection has a single instance of the Web Part Gallery. As you can see, this feature references another file named elements.xml, which is shown in Listing 10-6.
2. Create an application-specific folder under the FEATURES folder on file system of the front-end web server and copy the feature.xml and the elements.xml files into this directory. In this case, create a directory named CustomServerControls and copy the files shown in Listings 10-5 and 10-6 to this folder.
3. Create a subfolder named dwp under this application-specific folder and copy the .webpart description file into this folder. In this case, create the dwp subfolder under the CustomServerControls folder and copy the RssReaderWebPart.webpart file shown in Listing 10-4 into this subfolder.
4. Use the STSADM command-line utility to install the feature.
5. Activate the feature at the site collection level. This will automatically provision this RssReaderWebPart.webpart file into the Web Part Gallery of the site collection. In other words, it will add a copy of this RssReaderWebPart.webpart file to the content database.

Listing 10-5: The feature that is used to upload the Web part description file

```
<?xml version="1.0" encoding="utf-8" ?>
<Feature
  Id="{8BF2AD8E-7547-47f4-84D8-8067CF9211CC}"
  Title="RSS Reader WebPart Server Control Feature"
  Description="Contains the RSS Reader WebPart Server Control"
  Hidden="FALSE"
  Scope="Site"
  xmlns="http://schemas.microsoft.com/sharepoint/">
  <ElementManifests>
    <ElementManifest Location="elements.xml"/>
  </ElementManifests>
</Feature>
```

Listing 10-6: The elements.xml file

```
<?xml version="1.0" encoding="utf-8" ?>
<Elements xmlns="http://schemas.microsoft.com/sharepoint/">
  <Module
  Name="RssReaderWebPart"
  Path="dwp"
  List="113"
  Url="_catalogs/wp"
  RootWebOnly="true">
    <File Url="RssReaderWebPart.webpart" Type="GhostableInLibrary" >
      <Property Name="Group" Value="My Custom WebPart Server Controls" />
    </File>
  </Module>
</Elements>
```

Next, you'll walk through the implementation of the elements.xml file shown in Listing 10-6. As you can see, this file contains a single <Module> element named RssReaderWebPart. Note that the Path attribute on this <Module> element is set to "dwp," which is the name of the subfolder that you created under the CustomServerControls folder where you deployed the feature. Keep in mind that the value of the Path attribute represents the full folder path to the subfolder from the folder within which the elements.xml file resides. In this case the elements.xml file resides in the CustomServerControls folder.

Note that the List attribute on the <Module> element is set to "113," which identifies the Web Part Gallery, which is the SharePoint list into which you want to provision the RssReaderWebPart.webpart file. The Url attribute on the <Module> element is set to "_catalogs/wp," which is the top-level site relative URL of the Web Part Gallery where the RssReaderWebPart.webpart file is provisioned.

The RootWebOnly attribute on the <Module> element is set to "true" to specify that this module provisions the RssReaderWebPart.webpart file only into a site collection level list. This makes sense because the Web Part Gallery is a top site level gallery.

Note that the <Module> element contains a single <File> element that specifies the file to provision. The Url attribute on this <File> element is set to the name of this .webpart description file. Recall that the Url attribute specifies the relative URL of the provisioned file.

The <File> element contains a single <Property> child element that defines a new group for this .webpart description file. The value of this property appears in the Group column of the page that displays the content of the Web Part Gallery. As you saw, you have two options when it comes to provisioning your .webpart description file into a Web Part Gallery. The first option uses the SharePoint user interface. This provisions your .webpart description file into the Web Part Gallery of the current site collection. The second option uses a feature that can be activated in any site collection and consequently your .webpart description file can be provisioned into the Web Part Gallery of any site collection. Keep in mind that activating the feature in a site collection automatically provisions your .webpart description file into the Web Part Gallery of the site collection.

Next, take these steps to see the RssReaderWebPart in action. Navigate to your favorite site page. Select the Edit Page option from the Site Actions menu to enter the Edit Page mode and add the RssReaderWebPart to this page as shown in Figure 10-9. You should see the RssUrl textfield under Miscellaneous.

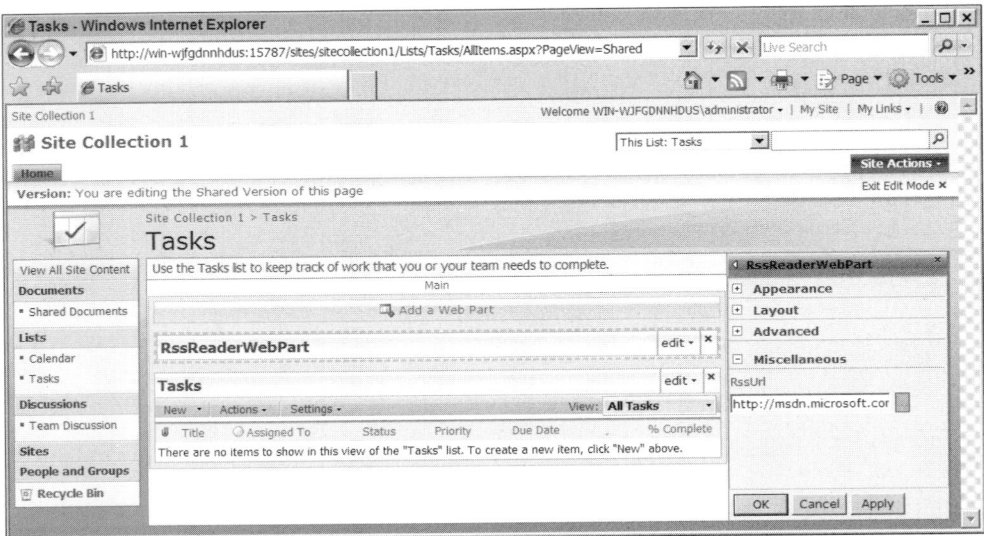

Figure 10-9: A page in Edit mode that contains the RssReaderWebPart

Enter the URL to your favorite RSS feed and click the OK button. Next, exit the Edit mode. You should see the result shown in Figure 10-10.

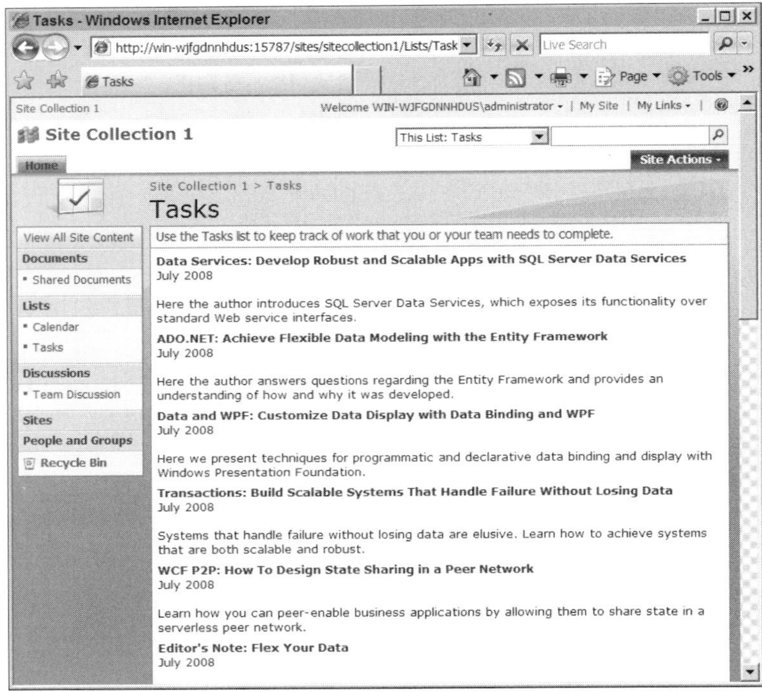

Figure 10-10: The RssReaderWebPart in action

Implementing IWebPart

As discussed, if you implement a custom control that derives from the WebPart control, you don't have to implement the IWebPart interface because the WebPart base class has already implemented the properties of this interface. However, there are times when a custom control that derives from the WebPart control may still need to implement some of the properties of this interface to provide its own custom implementation.

For example, this section implements a new version of the RssReaderWebPart control named RssReaderWebPart2 that overrides the TitleIconImageUrl properties to provide a default icon if the page developer hasn't specified an icon, as shown in Listing 10-7.

Listing 10-7: The CatalogIconImageUrl and TitleIconImageUrl properties

```
using System.Web.UI.WebControls.WebParts;

namespace WebPartsChapter
{

  public class RssReaderWebPart2 : RssReaderWebPart
  {
    public override string TitleIconImageUrl
    {
      get
      {
        return ViewState["TitleIconImageUrl"] != null ?
               (string)ViewState["TitleIconImageUrl"] :
                                                   "_layouts/images/contact.gif";
      }
      set { ViewState["TitleIconImageUrl"] = value; }
    }
  }
}
```

IWebActionable

Web parts support what are known as verbs. A verb is an action UI element such as a button and link that the user can click to perform an action on the Web part. Figure 10-11 shows the standard Web part verbs, which enable users to minimize, close, and delete a WebPart server control.

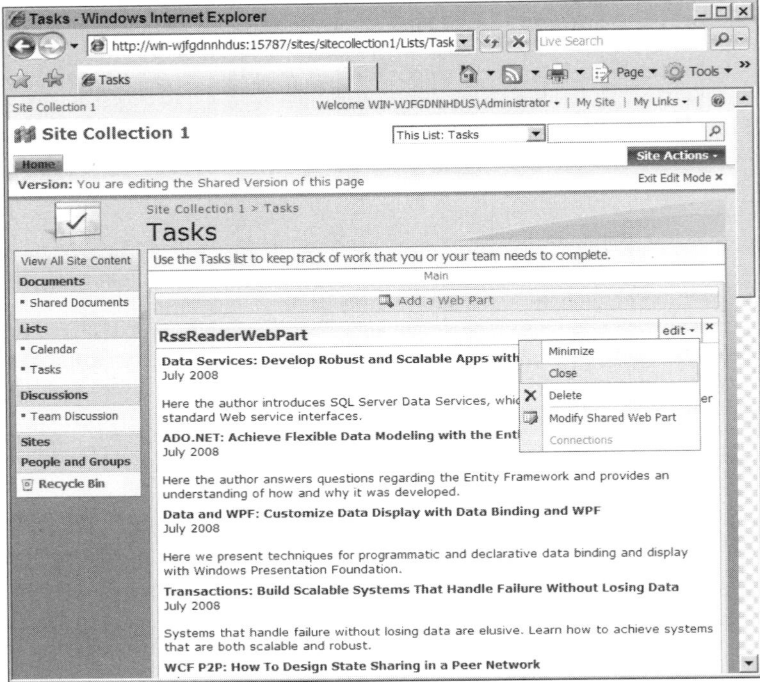

Figure 10-11: Standard Web part verbs

The ASP.NET Web Parts Framework represents each verb with an instance of a class named WebPartVerb. Listing 10-8 contains the declaration of the members of the WebPartVerb class.

Listing 10-8: The WebPartVerb class

```
public class WebPartVerb : IStateManager
{
  public WebPartVerb(string id, string clientClickHandler);
  public WebPartVerb(string id, WebPartEventHandler serverClickHandler);
  public WebPartVerb(string id, WebPartEventHandler serverClickHandler,
                     string clientClickHandler);
  public virtual bool Checked { get; set; }
  public string ClientClickHandler { get; }
  public virtual string Description { get; set; }
  public virtual bool Enabled { get; set; }
  public string ID { get; }
  public virtual string ImageUrl { get; set; }
  public WebPartEventHandler ServerClickHandler { get; }
  public virtual string Text { get; set; }
  protected StateBag ViewState { get; }
  public virtual bool Visible { get; set; }
  protected virtual void LoadViewState(object savedState);
  protected virtual object SaveViewState();
```

```
    void IStateManager.LoadViewState(object savedState);
    object IStateManager.SaveViewState();
    void IStateManager.TrackViewState();
    protected virtual void TrackViewState();
    protected virtual bool IsTrackingViewState { get; }
    bool IStateManager.IsTrackingViewState { get; }
  }
```

As this code listing shows, the WebPartVerb class is nothing but a bag of properties that manages its property values across page postbacks. These properties contain information about the verb that the class represents:

- **Checked.** This specifies whether the user has already selected the verb.
- **ClientClickHandler.** This contains the name of the client-side handler (such as a JavaScript function) for the client-side event that the verb raises when the user selects it.
- **Description.** This is a short description of what the verb does. When the user moves the mouse pointer over the verb, the tooltip displays this description.
- **Enabled.** This specifies whether the verb is enabled. When an application is in a state where certain actions aren't allowed, you can disable the associated verbs to prevent users from selecting them.
- **ID.** This contains a string that uniquely identifies the verb among other verbs.
- **ImageUrl.** This specifies the URL to the image that represents the verb.
- **ServerClickHandler.** The server-side handler that's called when the user selects the verb.
- **Text.** This specifies the text for the verb.
- **Visible.** This specifies whether the verb is visible.

In general there are two types of verbs: standard and custom. Standard verbs such as Close and Remove are automatically added without any coding effort on your part. The Web Parts Framework also allows you to add your own custom verbs to a WebPart control.

To accomplish this task, you must implement the IWebActionable interface to add your custom verb to a WebPart control. Listing 10-9 contains the definition of this interface, which exposes a single collection property of type WebPartVerbCollection named Verbs.

Listing 10-9: The IWebActionable interface

```
public interface IWebActionable
{
  WebPartVerbCollection Verbs { get; }
}
```

WebPartVerbCollection is a collection of WebPartVerb objects where each object represents a verb on the WebPart control.

EditorPart

The EditorPart control defines the API for Web parts controls that are used to edit WebPart controls. You can plug your own custom EditorPart control into the Web Parts Framework, provided that your custom control implements the EditorPart API. This section helps you understand this API and shows you how to develop custom EditorPart controls that implement the API.

As shown in Figure 10-4, the EditorPart control derives from the Part class and is the base class for all EditorPart controls such as AppearanceEditorPart, LayoutEditorPart, BehaviorEditorPart, and PropertyGridEditorPart. As discussed, EditorPart controls are used to edit the properties of the WebPart controls that make up the UI of a Web parts page.

Listing 10-10 illustrates the main properties and methods of the EditorPart base class.

Listing 10-10: The EditorPart base class

```
public abstract class EditorPart : Part
{
  public abstract bool ApplyChanges();
  public abstract void SyncChanges();
  protected WebPartManager WebPartManager { get; }
  protected WebPart WebPartToEdit { get; }
  protected EditorZoneBase Zone { get; }
}
```

The following list describes the main methods and properties of the EditorPart base class:

- **ApplyChanges().** This applies the changes the user has made in the EditorPart control's UI to the WebPart being edited.
- **SyncChanges().** This gets the current values of the WebPart being edited and applies them to the EditorPart control to allow the user edit them.
- **WebPartManager.** This references the WebPartManager.
- **WebPartToEdit.** This references the WebPart control being edited.
- **Zone.** This references the EditorZone control that contains the EditorPart control.

Listing 10-10 shows that the EditorPart API consists of two important abstract methods named ApplyChanges and SyncChanges. Your custom EditorPart control must implement these two methods as discussed in the following section.

Developing Custom EditorPart Controls

This section develops a custom EditorPart control named RssReaderEditorPart to show you how to implement the EditorPart API to override the ApplyChanges and SyncChanges methods to write your own custom EditorPart controls.

The RssReaderEditorPart custom EditorPart control will be used to edit the RssUrl property of a new version of the RSS reader WebPart control named RssReaderWebPart3, which is discussed later in this chapter.

Listing 10-11 presents the implementation of the RssReaderEditorPart custom EditorPart control.

Listing 10-11: The RssReaderEditorPart custom EditorPart control

```
using System;
using System.Web.UI;
using System.Web.UI.WebControls;
using System.Web.UI.WebControls.WebParts;

namespace WebPartsChapter
{
  /// <summary>
  /// Summary description for RssReaderEditorPart
  /// </summary>
  public class RssReaderEditorPart : EditorPart
  {
    public RssReaderEditorPart()
    {
      Title = "RSS Feeds";
    }

    public override ControlCollection Controls
    {
      get
      {
        EnsureChildControls();
        return base.Controls;
      }
    }

    DropDownList ddl;
    protected override void CreateChildControls()
    {
      Controls.Clear();

      ddl = new DropDownList();
      ddl.Items.Add(
         new ListItem("MSDN: Just Publised", "http://msdn.microsoft.com/rss.xml"));
      ddl.Items.Add(
        new ListItem("MSDN ASP.NET", "http://msdn.microsoft.com/asp.net/rss.xml"));
      Controls.Add(ddl);
    }

    public override bool ApplyChanges()
```

(continued)

Listing 10-11 *(continued)*

```
      {
        RssReaderWebPart3 rssReader = WebPartToEdit as RssReaderWebPart3;
        EnsureChildControls();
        rssReader.RssUrl = ddl.SelectedValue;
        return true;
      }

      public override void SyncChanges()
      {
        RssReaderWebPart3 rssReader = WebPartToEdit as RssReaderWebPart3;
        EnsureChildControls();
        ddl.SelectedIndex =
                         ddl.Items.IndexOf(ddl.Items.FindByValue(rssReader.RssUrl));
      }
    }
  }
```

The members of this control are discussed in the following sections.

CreateChildControls

The main responsibility of this method is to create the drop-down list box that enables users to select an RSS feed and populate it with the list of available RSS feeds. The method first clears the Controls collection:

```
Controls.Clear();
```

Next, it instantiates a DropDownList:

```
ddl = new DropDownList();
```

Then, it populates this DropDownList with two RSS feeds:

```
        ddl.Items.Add(
           new ListItem("MSDN: Just Publised", "http://msdn.microsoft.com/rss.xml"));
        ddl.Items.Add(
          new ListItem("MSDN ASP.NET", "http://msdn.microsoft.com/asp.net/rss.xml"));
```

Finally, it adds this DropDownList to the Controls collection:

```
        Controls.Add(ddl);
```

SyncChanges

The RssReaderEditorPart control, like all EditorPart controls, implements the SyncChanges method as shown in Listing 10-11. The main responsibility of the SyncChanges method is to set the selected value of the drop-down list box to the current user's favorite RSS feed. SyncChanges first accesses the RssReaderWebPart3 being edited:

```
RssReaderWebPart3 rssReader = WebPartToEdit as RssReaderWebPart3;
```

Next, it invokes the EnsureChildControls method to ensure that the drop-down list box has been created. This method internally calls the CreateChildControls method if it hasn't already been called:

```
EnsureChildControls();
```

Finally, it sets the selected index of the drop-down list box to the index of the item that represents the current user's favorite RSS feed:

```
ddl.SelectedIndex = ddl.Items.IndexOf(ddl.Items.FindByValue(rssReader.RssUrl));
```

ApplyChanges

RssReaderEditorPart also implements the ApplyChanges method, as all EditorPart controls must, as illustrated in Listing 10-11. The main responsibility of ApplyChanges is to apply the changes the user has made in the RssReaderEditorPart control to the RssReaderWebPart3 control. ApplyChanges first accesses the RssReaderWebPart3 control being edited:

```
RssReaderWebPart3 rssReader = WebPartToEdit as RssReaderWebPart3;
```

Next, it invokes the EnsureChildControls method to ensure that the drop-down list box has been created:

```
EnsureChildControls();
```

Finally, it assigns the selected value of the drop-down list box to the RssUrl property of the RssReaderWebPart3 control:

```
        rssReader.RssUrl = ddl.SelectedValue;
```

RssReaderWebPart3 Control

This section implements the RssReaderWebPart3 control that the RssReaderEditorPart edits. This control, like all other Web part controls, derives from the WebPart base class. Listing 10-12 contains the implementation of the RssReaderWebPart3 control.

Listing 10-12: The RssReaderWebPart3 control

```
using System.Web.UI.WebControls.WebParts;
using System;
using System.Collections;

namespace WebPartsChapter
{
  public class RssReaderWebPart3 : RssReaderWebPart
  {
    [Personalizable(true)]
    [WebBrowsable(false)]
    public override string RssUrl
    {
      get { return base.RssUrl; }
      set { base.RssUrl = value; }
    }

    private EditorPartCollection editorParts;
    public override EditorPartCollection CreateEditorParts()
    {
      if (editorParts == null)
      {
        ArrayList editors = new ArrayList();
        RssReaderEditorPart editorPart = new RssReaderEditorPart();
        editorPart.ID = ID + "RssReaderEditorPart";
        editors.Add(editorPart);
        editorParts = new EditorPartCollection(editors);
      }
      return editorParts;
    }
  }
}
```

The IWebEditable interface allows you to associate your custom EditorPart control with the WebPart control that your custom EditorPart control is designed to edit. Listing 10-13 contains the definition of this interface. Every Web part control must implement this interface. When you derive from the WebPart base class to implement a custom Web part control, you shouldn't explicitly implement this interface because the base class has implemented the interface.

Listing 10-13: The IWebEditable interface

```
public interface IWebEditable
{
  EditorPartCollection CreateEditorParts();
  object WebBrowsableObject { get; }
}
```

As Listing 10-13 shows, the interface exposes a property named WebBrowsableObject, which references the Web part control being edited. The WebPart base class provides the following implementation for this property:

```
public virtual object WebBrowsableObject
{
  get {return this;}
}
```

The IWebEditable interface also exposes a method named CreateEditorParts whose main responsibility is to instantiate custom EditorPart controls associated with the Web part control and populate an EditorPartCollection with the instantiated custom EditorPart controls and return the collection.

The following fragment presents the WebPart base class's implementation of the CreateEditorParts method:

```
public virtual EditorPartCollection CreateEditorParts()
{
  return EditorPartCollection.Empty;
}
```

As this fragment shows, Web part controls by default aren't associated with any custom EditorPart controls. If you want users to use your own custom EditorPart controls to edit a WebPart control, your WebPart control must override the CreateEditorParts method to instantiate and return the specified custom EditorPart controls. The RssReaderWebPart3 custom WebPart control overrides this method to instantiate and return an RssReaderEditorPart custom EditorPart control as shown in Listing 10-12.

You may be wondering how custom EditorPart controls such as RssReaderEditorPart are added to the EditorZone zone and how the CreateEditorParts method fits in all this.

The methods and properties of the EditorZoneBase base class define the API that all editor zones such as EditorZone must honor. This API includes a collection property of type EditorPartCollection named EditorParts as shown in Listing 10-14.

Listing 10-14: The EditorParts property of the EditorZoneBase base class

```
private EditorPartCollection editorParts;
public EditorPartCollection EditorParts
{
  get
  {
    if (editorParts == null)
    {
      EditorPartCollection myEditorParts = WebPartToEdit.CreateEditorParts();
      editorParts = new EditorPartCollection(myEditorParts, CreateEditorParts());
    }
    return editorParts;
  }
}
```

The EditorZoneBase base class exposes a property of type Web part named WebPartToEdit that references the WebPart control being edited. As Listing 10-14 shows, the EditorParts property calls the

CreateEditorParts method of the WebPart control being edited, such as the CreateEditorParts method of the RssReaderWebPart3 control, to access the custom EditorPart controls associated with the WebPart control:

```
EditorPartCollection myEditorParts = WebPartToEdit.CreateEditorParts();
```

It then calls the CreateEditorParts method of the EditorZoneBase class to access the standard EditorPart controls that are already added to the EditorZone control. Keep in mind that SharePoint adds its own standard editor part control.

Finally, it combines the custom and standard EditorPart controls in a single EditorPartCollection and returns the collection:

```
editorParts = new EditorPartCollection(myEditorParts, CreateEditorParts());
```

As you can see, your custom editor part control does not replace the standard SharePoint editor part control. It complements it. As such, you need to instruct the SharePoint editor part control not to display the same property whose value is set through your custom editor part control. To do so, you need to annotate your property with the WebBrowsable(false) metadata attribute.

```
[Personalizable(true)]
[WebBrowsable(false)]
public override string RssUrl
{
  get { return base.RssUrl; }
  set { base.RssUrl = value; }
}
```

Figure 10-12 presents the custom editor part in action.

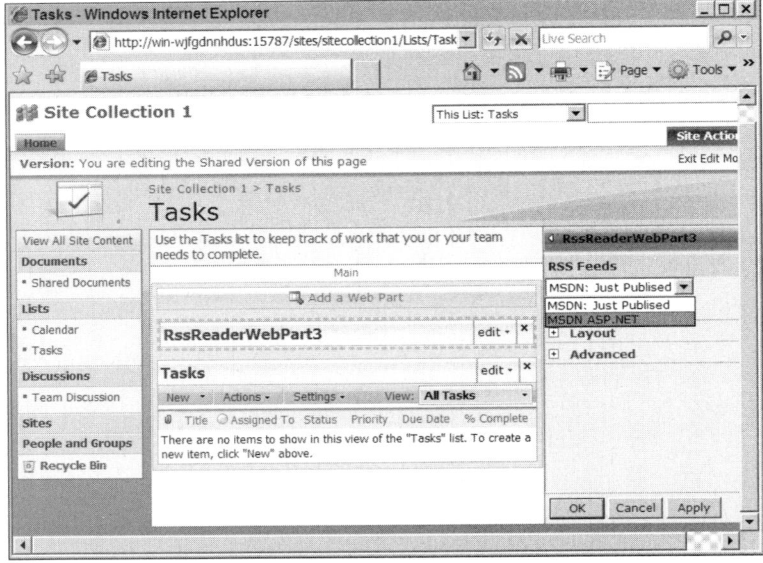

Figure 10-12: The RssReaderEditorPart editor part in action

Templated Web Parts

In general, there are two approaches to server control development. The first approach, which is known as custom control development, is done entirely in code where you have to implement a class that inherits directly or indirectly from the Control base class. The second approach, which is known as user control development, is more like developing an ASP.NET page. The second approach provides you with the following important benefits:

- You can use a drag-and-drop WYSIWYG approach to develop your user control in the Visual Studio environment with minimal efforts. You can't do the same with custom controls.
- Programmers who feel more comfortable with declarative programming languages such as XHTML and XML should feel at home with user controls where they can use XHTML-like tags to declaratively develop the control without writing a lot of code in a procedural language such as C# or VB.NET. The page framework parses this declarative code into .NET managed code. In other words, user controls make life easy on declarative programmers by putting the burden of generating the code on the page framework. Custom controls, on the other hand, put the burden of writing the code entirely on the programmer. Custom controls are on the other extreme of the programming spectrum where nothing can be implemented in an XHTML-like language.

This section shows a development approach that enables you to take advantage of both user control and custom control development approaches in your own custom Web parts. Who says you can't have your cake and eat it too!

TemplateBasedWebPart

You'll implement a base class named TemplateBasedWebPart from which you can inherit to implement your own custom Web parts. This base class implements the infrastructure that delegates the responsibility of rendering your Web part's markup text to a RenderingTemplate server control declared in an .ascx file deployed to the following folder on the file system of each front-end web server:

```
Local_Drive:\Program Files\Common Files\microsoft shared\Web Server
Extensions\12\TEMPLATE\CONTROLTEMPLATES
```

Listing 10-15 presents the implementation of the TemplateBasedWebPart base class. Add a source file named TemplateBasedWebPart.cs to your Class Library project and add the content of this code listing to this source file. You'll also need to add references to the Microsoft.SharePoint.dll and Microsoft .SharePoint.Security.dll assemblies.

Listing 10-15: The TemplateBasedWebPart base class

```
using System;
using System.Web.UI;
using System.Web.UI.WebControls.WebParts;
using Microsoft.SharePoint.WebControls;
using Microsoft.SharePoint;
using Microsoft.SharePoint.Security;
using System.Security.Permissions;
using System.Web;
```

(continued)

Listing 10-15 *(continued)*

```
using System.Web.UI.HtmlControls;

namespace WebPartsChapter
{
  [PersistChildren(false),
   ParseChildren(true),
   SharePointPermission(SecurityAction.LinkDemand, ObjectModel = true),
   SharePointPermission(SecurityAction.InheritanceDemand, ObjectModel = true)]
  public class TemplateBasedWebPart : WebPart
  {
    protected virtual string DefaultTemplateName
    {
      get { return null; }
    }

    private string templateName;
    public string TemplateName
    {
      get
      {
        if (string.IsNullOrEmpty(this.templateName))
          this.templateName = this.DefaultTemplateName;
        return this.templateName;
      }

      set { this.templateName = value; }
    }

    private ITemplate template;

    [TemplateContainer(typeof(TemplateContainer))]
    public ITemplate Template
    {
      get
      {
        if (this.template == null && !string.IsNullOrEmpty(this.TemplateName))
          this.template =
                   SPControlTemplateManager.GetTemplateByName(this.TemplateName);
        return this.template;
      }
      set { this.template = value; }
    }

    protected virtual string DefaultAlternateTemplateName
    {
      get { return null; }
    }

    private string alternateTemplateName;
    public string AlternateTemplateName
    {
      get
      {
```

```
    if (string.IsNullOrEmpty(this.alternateTemplateName))
      this.alternateTemplateName = this.DefaultAlternateTemplateName;
    return this.alternateTemplateName;
  }

  set { this.alternateTemplateName = value; }
}

private ITemplate alternateTemplate;

[TemplateContainer(typeof(TemplateContainer))]
public ITemplate AlternateTemplate
{
  get
  {
    if (this.alternateTemplate == null &&
                       !string.IsNullOrEmpty(this.AlternateTemplateName))
      this.alternateTemplate =
        SPControlTemplateManager.GetTemplateByName(this.AlternateTemplateName);
    return this.alternateTemplate;
  }
  set { this.alternateTemplate = value; }
}

protected virtual ITemplate ControlTemplate
{
  get { return this.Template; }
}

private TemplateOverride templateOverride;
protected TemplateOverride TemplateOverride
{
  get { return this.templateOverride; }
  set { this.templateOverride = value; }
}

private TemplateContainer templateContainer;
public virtual TemplateContainer TemplateContainer
{
  get
  {
    if (this.templateContainer == null)
      this.templateContainer = new TemplateContainer();
    return this.templateContainer;
  }
}

[SharePointPermission(SecurityAction.Demand, ObjectModel = true)]
protected override void CreateChildControls()
{
  ITemplate template = null;
  if (this.TemplateOverride == TemplateOverride.None)
    template = this.ControlTemplate;

  else if (this.TemplateOverride == TemplateOverride.Template)
```

(continued)

Listing 10-15 *(continued)*

```
        template = this.Template;

      else if (this.TemplateOverride == TemplateOverride.AlternateTemplate)
        template = this.AlternateTemplate;

      else if (this.TemplateOverride == TemplateOverride.Both)
      {
        template = this.Template;
        if (template == null)
          template = this.AlternateTemplate;
      }

      if (template == null)
      {
        base.CreateChildControls();
        return;
      }

      this.Controls.Clear();
      template.InstantiateIn(this.TemplateContainer);
      this.Controls.Add(this.TemplateContainer);
      this.ChildControlsCreated = true;
    }

    public virtual SPWeb Web
    {
      get { return SPControl.GetContextWeb(this.Context); }
    }

    public override ControlCollection Controls
    {
      [SharePointPermission(SecurityAction.Demand, ObjectModel = true)]
      get
      {
        this.EnsureChildControls();
        return base.Controls;
      }
    }

    [SharePointPermission(SecurityAction.Demand, ObjectModel = true)]
    protected override void OnLoad(EventArgs e)
    {
      base.OnLoad(e);
      this.EnsureChildControls();
    }

    [SharePointPermission(SecurityAction.Demand, ObjectModel = true)]
    protected override void Render(HtmlTextWriter output)
    {
      this.EnsureChildControls();
      base.Render(output);
    }
  }
}
```

The implementation of the members of this class is discussed in the following sections.

Templates

As Listing 10-15 shows, TemplateBasedWebPart exposes three templates:

- Main Template
- Alternate Template
- Control Template

TemplateBasedWebPart exposes a protected property named TemplateOverride, which is of the TemplateOverride enumeration type defined as follows:

```
public enum TemplateOverride
{
  None,
  Template,
  AlternateTemplate,
  Both
}
```

Note that the TemplateOverride property is marked as protected to ensure that only subclasses of TemplateBaseWebPart could get and set the value of this property. Here is the description of these enumeration values:

- **Template.** A subclass sets the value of the TemplateOverride property to Template to instruct the CreateChildControls method to use the main template.
- **AlternateTemplate.** A subclass sets the value of the TemplateOverride property to AlternateTemplate to instruct the CreateChildControls method to use the alternate template.
- **Both.** A subclass sets the value of the TemplateOverride property to Both to instruct the CreateChildControls method to use the main template if the main template is not null and to use the alternate template otherwise.
- **None.** A subclass sets the value of the TemplateOverride property to None to instruct the CreateChildControls method to use the control template.

The main, alternate, and control templates are discussed in the following sections.

Main Template

As Listing 10-15 shows, TemplateBasedWebPart exposes three members that together provide support for the main template:

- **DefaultTemplateName.** This read-only property is marked as protected virtual to enable the subclasses of TemplateBasedWebPart to override it to return the ID property value of the RenderingTemplate server control that provides the default rendering for the main template of the Web part. Every subclass must come with an .ascx file deployed to the ControlTemplates folder, which contains the RenderingTemplate server control whose ID property value the DefaultTemplateName returns.

- **TemplateName.** This read-write property gets or sets the ID property value of the RenderingTemplate server control that provides the rendering for the main template of the Web part. Note that this property is *not* marked as virtual. However, the getter of this property returns the value of the DefaultTemplateName property if the TemplateName property has not been explicitly set. As such, a subclass can effectively override the value of the TemplateName property through overriding the DefaultTemplateName property. Because TemplateName is a public property, its value can be directly set. Note that TemplateName does not use the value of the DefatulTemplateName property if its value has been directly set.
- **Template.** This read-write property gets or sets the ITemplate object that contains the child controls of the Web part. As Listing 10-30 shows, the getter of this property first checks whether its value has been explicitly set. If not, it invokes the GetTemplateByName static method on the SPControlTemplateManager class, passing in the value of the TemplateName property:

```
this.template = SPControlTemplateManager.GetTemplateByName(this.TemplateName);
```

When the GetTemplateByName method is invoked for the first time (that is, for the first request to the web application that triggers the invocation of this method), the method takes these steps:

- Loads all .ascx files in the ControlTemplates folder. The loading process uses the ASP.NET parser to parse the content of these .ascx files into their respective server controls. For example, the <SharePoint:RenderingTemplate> tags, which are used in some of these .ascx files, are parsed into RenderingTemplate server controls. Note that the ASP.NET parser parses the content of the <Template> subelement of each <SharePoint:RenderingTemplate> element into a class that implements the ITemplate interface, instantiates an instance of this class, and assigns this instance to the Template property of the respective RenderingTemplate server control.
- Stores references to the ITemplate objects that the ASP.NET parser has assigned to the Template properties of respective RenderingTemplate server controls in an internal collection. Note that each reference is stored under the ID property value of the respective RenderingTemplate server control

The GetTemplateByName method uses the value passed into it as its argument, which is the value of the TemplateName property in this case, as an index into the internal collection where the references to the ITemplate objects are maintained to return a reference to the ITemplate object assigned to the Template property of the RenderingTemplate server control whose ID property value is specified in the TemplateName property. The Template property of TemplateBasedWebPart returns the ITemplate object assigned to the Template property of the RenderingTemplate server control whose ID property value is specified in the TemplateName property.

Alternate Template

As Listing 10-15 shows, TemplateBasedWebPart exposes the following three properties that work together to provide support for the alternate template:

- **DefaultAlternateTemplateName.** This read-only protected property plays a similar role as the DefaultTemplateName property. A subclass of TemplateBasedWebPart overrides this property to return the ID property value of the RenderingTemplate server control that provides default rendering for the alternate template.

- **AlternateTemplateName.** This read-write public property plays a similar role as TemplateName property. The getter of this property returns the value of the DefaultAlternateTemplateName property if the value of the property has not been explicitly set. This property basically returns the ID property value of the RenderingTemplate server control that provides rendering for the alternate template, which may or may not be the default rendering.

- **AlternateTemplate.** This read-write property returns a reference to the ITemplate object assigned to the Template property of the RenderingTemplate server control whose ID property value is given by the AlternateTemplateName property. As Listing 10-15 shows, the getter of this property uses the GetTemplateByName static method to access the reference to this ITemplate object.

Control Template

As Listing 10-15 shows, the TemplateBasedWebPart class' implementation of the ControlTemplate property simply returns the value of the Template property. However, a subclass of TemplateBasedWebPart can override this property to include the logic that returns a different value.

CreateChildControls

As Listing 10-15 shows, CreateChildControls uses the control template if the TemplateOverride property is set to None, the main template if this property is set to Template, and alternate template if this property is set to AlternateTemplate. Note that if the TemplateOverride property is set to Both, CreateChildControls uses the main template if the main template is not null and uses the alternate template otherwise:

```
ITemplate template = null;
if (this.TemplateOverride == TemplateOverride.None)
  template = this.ControlTemplate;

else if (this.TemplateOverride == TemplateOverride.Template)
  template = this.Template;

else if (this.TemplateOverride == TemplateOverride.AlternateTemplate)
  template = this.AlternateTemplate;

else if (this.TemplateOverride == TemplateOverride.Both)
{
  template = this.Template;
  if (template == null)
    template = this.AlternateTemplate;
}
```

After determining which template to use, CreateChildControls first clears the Controls collection:

```
this.Controls.Clear();
```

Then, it loads the child controls contained within the template into the template container:

```
template.InstantiateIn(this.TemplateContainer);
```

Next, it adds the template container to the Controls collection of the Web part:

```
this.Controls.Add(this.TemplateContainer);
```

Finally, it sets the ChildControlsCreated method to true:

```
this.ChildControlsCreated = true;
```

Because the EnsureChildControls method could be invoked multiple times and because the EnsureChildControls method does not invoke the CreateChildControls method if the ChildControlsCreated property is set to true, you must set this property to true to signal the EnsureChildControls method not to invoke the CreateChildControls method anymore. Otherwise the CreateChildControls method could be invoked multiple times.

Web

As the following excerpt from Listing 10-15 shows, TemplateBasedWebPart exposes a public property named Web, which is of the SPWeb type. This read-only property returns a reference to the SPWeb object that represents the current SharePoint site:

```
public virtual SPWeb Web
{
  get { return SPControl.GetContextWeb(this.Context); }
}
```

TemplateBasedWebPart1

This section implements a Web part named TemplateBasedWebPart1, which inherits from TemplateBasedWebPart1 developed in the previous section. Listing 10-16 presents the implementation of this Web part. Add a source file named TemplateBasedWebPart1.cs to your project and add the content of Listing 10-16 to this source file.

Listing 10-16: The TemplateBasedWebPart1 Web part

```
using System;
using Microsoft.SharePoint.WebControls;
using Microsoft.SharePoint.Security;
using System.Security.Permissions;
using System.Web.UI.WebControls;
using System.Web.UI.WebControls.WebParts;
using System.Web.UI;

namespace WebPartsChapter
{
  public class TemplateBasedWebPart1 : TemplateBasedWebPart
  {
    [SharePointPermission(SecurityAction.Demand, ObjectModel = true)]
    protected override void OnInit(EventArgs e)
```

```
    {
      base.OnInit(e);
      this.TemplateOverride = TemplateOverride.None;
    }

    protected override string DefaultTemplateName
    {
      get { return "TemplateBasedWebPart1RenderingTemplate"; }
    }

    protected override void CreateChildControls()
    {
      base.CreateChildControls();
      if (this.Web == null)
        return;

      ListBox listBox = (ListBox)this.TemplateContainer.FindControl("ListBox1");

      listBox.Items.Add(
          new ListItem("Current User ID: " +
                       this.Web.CurrentUser.ID.ToString(),
                       "This is current user ID."));
      listBox.Items.Add(
          new ListItem("Site Description: " + this.Web.Description,
                       "This is Site Description."));
      listBox.Items.Add(
          new ListItem("Site ID: " + this.Web.ID.ToString(), "This is Site ID."));
    }
  }
}
```

As you can see, TemplateBasedWebPart1 overrides the OnInit method to set the value of the TemplateOverride property to None to instruct CreateChildControls to use the control template:

```
this.TemplateOverride = TemplateOverride.None;
```

As Listing 10-16 shows, TemplateBasedWebPart1 also overrides the DefaultTemplateName property to return "TemplateBasedWebPart1RenderingTemplate," which is the ID property value of the RenderingTemplate server control that provides the default rendering for the main template. Listing 10-17 presents the .ascx file where this RenderingTemplate server control is declared. Save the content of this listing into a file named TemplateBasedWebPart1.ascx and deploy this file to the following folder on your machine:

```
Local_Drive:\Program Files\Common Files\microsoft shared\Web Server Extensions\12\
TEMPLATE\CONTROLTEMPLATES
```

Listing 10-17: The .ascx file that contains the "TemplateBasedWebPart1RenderingTemplate" RenderingTemplate server control

```
<%@ Control Language="C#" %>
<%@ Register TagPrefix="SharePoint" Namespace="Microsoft.SharePoint.WebControls"
Assembly="Microsoft.SharePoint, Version=12.0.0.0, Culture=neutral,
PublicKeyToken=71e9bce111e9429c" %>

<SharePoint:RenderingTemplate ID="TemplateBasedWebPart1RenderingTemplate"
runat="server">
 <Template>
    <asp:ListBox ID="ListBox1" runat="server" />
 </Template>
</SharePoint:RenderingTemplate>
```

As you can see, this RenderingTemplate server control contains a ListBox server control.

As Listing 10-15 shows, TemplateBasedWebPart1 overrides the CreateChildControls method as follows. First, it invokes the CreateChildControls method of the TemplateBasedWebPart base class. Recall that this base class loads the template container with the child controls contained within the ITemplate object that the Template property of the RenderingTemplate server control references:

```
base.CreateChildControls();
```

Next, the CreateChildControls method of TemplateBasedWebPart1 invokes the FindControl method on the template container to return a reference to the ListBox server control:

```
      ListBox listBox = (ListBox)this.TemplateContainer.FindControl("ListBox1");
```

It then adds three pieces of information about the current SharePoint site to this ListBox server control:

```
      listBox.Items.Add(
          new ListItem("Current User ID: " +
                       this.Web.CurrentUser.ID.ToString(),
                       "This is current user ID."));
      listBox.Items.Add(
          new ListItem("Site Description: " + this.Web.Description,
                       "This is Site Description."));
      listBox.Items.Add(
          new ListItem("Site ID: " + this.Web.ID.ToString(), "This is Site ID."));
```

Deploying Web Parts

Follow the same steps discussed earlier in this chapter to deploy TemplateBasedWebPart and TemplateBasedWebPart1 to SharePoint. The only additional step in this case is that you have to also deploy the .ascx file that contains the RenderingTemplate server control to the ControlTemplates folder of each front-end web server.

Connecting WebPart Controls

To make the discussions more concrete, this section develops two WebPart controls named RssReaderWebPart4 and FavoriteItemWebPart, both of which are shown in Figure 10-13.

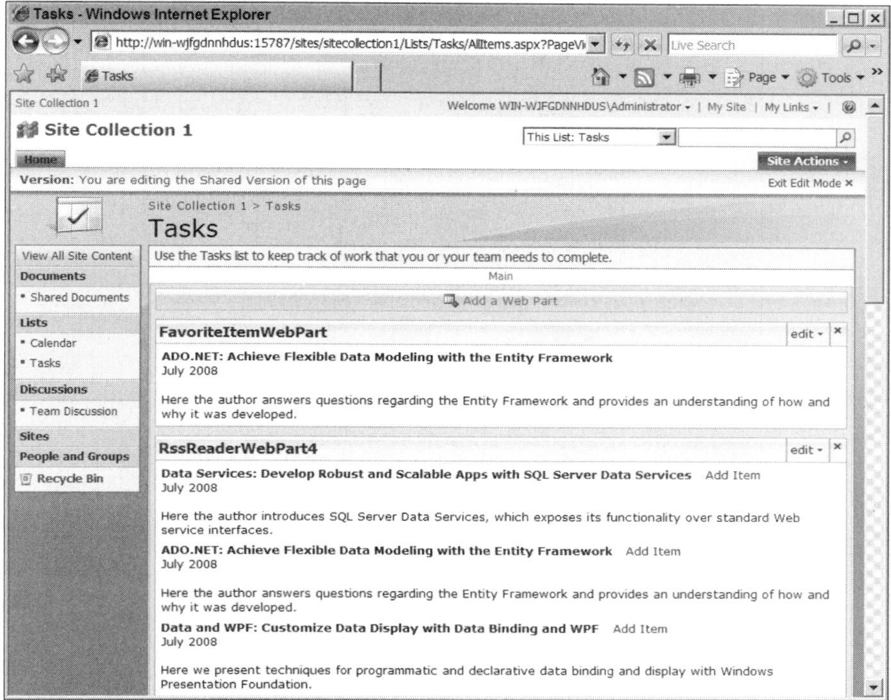

Figure 10-13: A page displaying two connected Web parts

The RssReaderWebPart4 control, like its predecessor RssReaderWebPart3, downloads and displays the current user's favorite RSS feed. As discussed, each RSS feed consists of one or more items where each item contains the following information:

- Title
- Link
- Description

Like its predecessor, RssReaderWebPart4 uses a hyperlink to display the title of each item and a label to display its description. As Figure 10-13 shows, RssReaderWebPart4 does one more thing that its predecessor doesn't do — each displayed item in RssReaderWebPart4 includes a LinkButton named "Add Item." When the user clicks a LinkButton associated with an item, RssReaderWebPart4 sends the complete information about the selected item (its title, link, and description) to the FavoriteItemWebPart control.

This raises the following question: How does RssReaderWebPart4 send the selected item's title, link, and description to the FavoriteItemWebPart control? If you're familiar with the ASP.NET Web Parts Framework, you know the answer to this question. RssReaderWebPart4 uses the ASP.NET Web parts connection feature to send the data to FavoriteItemWebPart control.

However, because the purpose of this section is to help you understand the ASP.NET Web parts connection feature from the inside out, step back and consider the following question: If you didn't have access to the ASP.NET Web parts connection feature, how would you implement the feature that allows RssReaderWebPart4 to send an item's title, link, and description to the FavoriteItemWebPart control when the user clicks the "Add Item" LinkButton associated with the item?

One way to do this is to define a new interface named IItem that exposes three properties named Title, Link, and Description as shown in Listing 10-18.

Listing 10-18: The Item class

```
public interface IItem
{
  string ItemTitle { get;}
  string ItemDescription  { get;}
  string ItemLink  { get;}
}
```

You could then write a new class named Item that implements the IItem interface:

```
public class Item : IItem
{
  private string title;
  public string ItemTitle
  {
    get {return title;}
    set {title = value;}
  }

  private string link;
  public string ItemLink
  {
    get {return link;}
    set { link = value;}
  }

  private string description;
  public string ItemDescription
  {
    get {return description;}
    set { description = value;}
  }
}
```

You would then implement and add a new method named AddItem to the FavoriteItemWebPart control. This method takes an instance of the IItem interface and stores it in a local field, as shown in Listing 10-19.

Listing 10-19: The FavoriteItemWebPart control

```
public class FavoriteItemWebPart : WebPart
{
  ...
  IItem item;
  public void AddItem(IItem item)
  {
    this.item = item;
  }
  ...
}
```

Next, you would implement and add a new method named GetSelectedItem to the RssReaderWebPart4 control. This method takes no argument and returns an instance of the IItem interface that contains the information about the selected item.

Then, in the callback method for the Click event of the Add Item button (shown in Listing 10-20), you would call the GetSelectedItem of the RssReaderWebPart4 control to return the IItem instance that contains the title, link, and description of the selected item:

```
IItem item = GetSelectedItem();
```

Then you'd call the AddItem method of the FavoriteItemWebPart control and pass the IItem instance into it:

```
part.AddItem(item);
```

Listing 10-20: The RssReaderWebPart4 control

```
public class RssReaderWebPart4 : WebPart
{
  ...
  private void CallbackMethodForClickEvent(object sender, EventArgs e)
  {
    IItem item = GetSelectedItem();
    FavoriteItemWebPart part = GetReferenceToFavoriteItemWebPart();
    part.AddItem(item);
  }
}
```

This solution seems to address the question that was raised previously: How does RssReaderWebPart4 send the selected item's title, link, and description to FavoriteItemWebPart control? If that's the case, why do you need the ASP.NET Web parts connection feature when you already have a simple solution?

If you examine Listing 10-20 more closely, you'll notice the CallbackMethodForClickEvent method of RssReaderWebPart4 directly uses the FavoriteItemWebPart control, which means that RssReaderWebPart4 is tied to the FavoriteItemWebPart control. In other words, RssReaderWebPart4 can service one and only one type of control, FavoriteItemWebPart, and can't service any other types of controls.

Therefore, RssReaderWebPart4 shouldn't send data directly to the FavoriteItemWebPart control. What you need is a third component that retrieves the data from RssReaderWebPart4 and passes it along to FavoriteItemWebPart. The ASP.NET Web Parts Framework comes with a class named WebPartConnection that acts as this third component. This class includes a method (call it ExchangeData) that retrieves the data from RssReaderWebPart4 and passes it to the FavoriteItemWebPart control.

How would you implement the ExchangeData method of the WebPartConnection class? Listing 10-21 shows one possible implementation for this method. This implementation calls the GetSelectedItem method of the RssReaderWebPart4 control to return the IItem instance that contains the title, link, and description of the selected item:

```
IItem item = provider.GetSelectedItem();
```

Then it calls the AddItem method of the FavoriteItemWebPart control and passes the IItem instance into it:

```
consumer.AddItem(item);
```

Listing 10-21: The first version of the WebPartConnection class

```
public class WebPartConnection
{
  RssReaderWebPart4 provider;
  FavoriteItemWebPart consumer;
  public void ExchangeData()
  {
    IItem item = provider.GetSelectedItem();
    consumer.AddItem (item);
  }
}
```

Obviously the implementation that Listing 10-21 presents for WebPartConnection class suffers from the same problem as Listing 10-20 — this implementation ties the WebPartConnection class to the RssReaderWebPart4 and FavoriteItemWebPart controls and doesn't allow it to work with other types of controls.

Later in this section, you'll see an implementation of the WebPartConnection class that resolves this problem. Before diving into that implementation, you need to examine a very important concept that the ExchangeData method shown in Listing 10-21 promotes. The ExchangeData method first calls the GetSelectedItem method to get the data from RssReaderWebPart4 and then calls the AddItem method to pass the data to FavoriteItemWebPart control. In other words, you can think of the WebPartConnection as a connection channel between the GetSelectedItem and AddItem methods, which means that you can think of the methods themselves as connection points where one connection point (the GetSelectedItem method) acts as a data provider and the other connection point (the AddItem method) acts as a data consumer, as shown in Figure 10-14.

Provider Connection Point ⟶ Consumer Connection Point

Figure 10-14: A Web part connection

The provider connection point is characterized by the following characteristics:

- The type of data provider control, in this case, RssReaderWebPart4
- The method of the data provider control that is called when the connection is established, in this case, GetSelectedItem
- The type of object that the data provider control provides, in this case, IItem

The consumer connection point, on the other hand, is characterized by the following characteristics:

- The type of data consumer control, in this case, FavoriteItemWebPart
- The method of the data consumer control that is called when the connection is established, in this case, AddItem
- The type of object that the data consumer control consumes, in this case, IItem

The ASP.NET Web Parts Framework comes with two classes named ProviderConnectionPoint and ConsumerConnectionPoint that represent the provider and consumer connection points shown in Figure 10-14. Listing 10-22 contains the code for the ProviderConnectionPoint class. This class allows you to represent the provider connection point in a generic fashion as follows:

1. The constructor of this class takes a System.Type object as its third argument. This object is the generic representation of the data provider control.
2. The constructor takes a MethodInfo object as its first argument. This object is the generic representation of the method of the data provider control that is called when the connection is established.
3. The constructor takes a System.Type object as its second argument. This object is the generic representation of the type of object that the data provider control provides.
4. The class exposes a method named GetObject that allows you to call the data provider method (the method that provides the data) in generic fashion.

Listing 10-22: The ProviderConnectionPoint class

```
public class ProviderConnectionPoint : ConnectionPoint
{
  public ProviderConnectionPoint(MethodInfo callbackMethod,Type interfaceType,
                                 Type controlType, string displayName, string id,
                                 bool allowsMultipleConnections);
   public virtual object GetObject(Control control)
   {
     return base.CallbackMethod.Invoke(control, null);
   }
}
```

Listing 10-23 contains the code for the ConsumerConnectionPoint class. This class allows you to represent the consumer connection point shown in Figure 10-10 in a generic fashion as follows:

1. The constructor of this class takes a System.Type object as its third argument. This object is the generic representation of the data consumer control.
2. The constructor takes a MethodInfo object as its first argument. This object is the generic representation of the method of the data consumer control that is called when the connection is established.
3. The constructor takes a System.Type object as its second argument. This object is the generic representation of the type of object that the data consumer control consumes.
4. The class exposes a method named SetObject that allows you to call the data consumer method (the method that consumes the data) in generic fashion.

Listing 10-23: The ConsumerConnectionPoint class

```
public class ConsumerConnectionPoint : ConnectionPoint
{
  public ConsumerConnectionPoint(MethodInfo callbackMethod,
                                 Type interfaceType,
                                 Type controlType, string displayName, string id,
                                 bool allowsMultipleConnections);
  public virtual void SetObject(Control control, object data)
  {
    CallbackMethod.Invoke(control, new object[] { data });
  }
}
```

Listing 10-24 shows the version of WebPartConnection that uses the ProviderConnectionPoint and ConsumerConnectionPoint classes. As this code listing shows, the new version of ExchangeData calls the GetObject method of the ProviderConnectionPoint to invoke the data provider control's method (the method that provides data) in generic fashion and return the object that contains the data:

```
object obj = this.ProviderConnectionPoint.GetObject(this.Provider.ToControl());
```

It then calls the SetObject method of the ConsumerConnectionPoint and passes the data object into it to invoke the data consumer control's method (the method that consumer data) in generic fashion.

Listing 10-24: The final version of the WebPartConnection class

```
public sealed class WebPartConnection
{
  internal void ExchangeData()
  {
    object obj = this.ProviderConnectionPoint.GetObject(this.Provider.ToControl());
    this.ConsumerConnectionPoint.SetObject(this.Consumer.ToControl(),obj);
  }
  public WebPart Consumer {get;}
  public WebPart Provider {get;}
  public ConsumerConnectionPoint ConsumerConnectionPoint {get;}
  public ProviderConnectionPoint ProviderConnectionPoint {get;}
}
```

As these discussions show, every connection between two WebPart controls is represented by an instance of the WebPartConnection class. Connecting two WebPart controls means creating an instance of the WebPartConnection class. As a matter of fact, WebPartManager exposes a method named ConnectWebParts that simply creates and returns an instance of the WebPartConnection class. In Web parts jargon, though, there is a difference between connecting two WebParts and activating the connection. Two WebParts are connected when the appropriate WebPartConnection object has been created and added to the WebPartManager control's list of connections. A connection is activated when the ExchangeData (the name of the method is immaterial) method of the WebPartConnection object associated with the connection is called, that is, when the data is exchanged.

Implementing Web Parts that Support Connections

Now that you have learned how Web part connections work from inside out, let's get down to the implementation of the RssReaderWebPart4 and FavoriteItemWebPart Web parts. First, review what these two controls do. RssReaderWebPart4 downloads and displays the user's favorite RSS feed. This RSS feed consists of one or more items, where each item contains the following information: title, link, and description.

As Figure 10-13 shows, each displayed item in RssReaderWebPart4 includes a LinkButton named AddItem. When the user clicks a LinkButton associated with an item, the RssReaderWebPart4 control provides FavoriteItemWebPart with an object of type IItem that contains the title, link, and description of the selected item. FavoriteItemWebPart, on its part, displays the selected item.

Listing 10-25 presents the implementation of RssReaderWebPart4. Add a source file named RssReaderWebPart4.cs to your project and add the content of this code listing to this file.

Listing 10-25: The RssReaderWebPart4 Web part

```
using System.Web.UI.WebControls.WebParts;
using System.Web.UI.WebControls;
using System.Web.UI;
using System;
using System.Collections;
using System.Xml;

namespace WebPartsChapter
{
  public class RssReaderWebPart4 : WebPart, IItem
  {
    Table table;
    private string rssUrl;

    [Personalizable(true)]
    [WebBrowsable(false)]
    public virtual string RssUrl
    {
      get { return rssUrl; }
      set { rssUrl = value; }
    }

    public RssReaderWebPart4()
```

(continued)

Listing 10-25 *(continued)*

```
{
  this.AllowConnect = true;
}

private EditorPartCollection editorParts;
public override EditorPartCollection CreateEditorParts()
{
  if (editorParts == null)
  {
    ArrayList editors = new ArrayList();
    RssReaderEditorPart2 editorPart = new RssReaderEditorPart2();
    editorPart.ID = ID + "RssReaderEditorPart2";
    editors.Add(editorPart);
    editorParts = new EditorPartCollection(editors);
  }
  return editorParts;
}

protected virtual void AddContainer()
{
  table = new Table();
  table.CellSpacing = 5;
  Controls.Add(table);
}

protected virtual void AddItemToContainer(XmlReader reader)
{
  string link = string.Empty; ;
  string title = string.Empty;
  string description = string.Empty;

  while (reader.Read())
  {
    if (reader.NodeType == XmlNodeType.Element)
    {
      if (reader.Name == "link")
        link = reader.ReadElementContentAsString();

      else if (reader.Name == "title")
        title = reader.ReadElementContentAsString();

      else if (reader.Name == "description")
        description = reader.ReadElementContentAsString();
    }
  }

  TableRow row = new TableRow();
  table.Rows.Add(row);
  TableCell cell = new TableCell();
  row.Cells.Add(cell);

  HyperLink hyperLink = new HyperLink();
```

```
      hyperLink.NavigateUrl = link;
      hyperLink.Text = title;
      hyperLink.Font.Bold = true;
      cell.Controls.Add(hyperLink);
      LiteralControl lc;

      lc = new LiteralControl("   ");
      cell.Controls.Add(lc);
      LinkButton btn = new LinkButton();
      btn.Text = "Add Item";
      btn.CommandArgument = table.Rows.GetRowIndex(row).ToString();
      btn.Command += new CommandEventHandler(SelectCommandCallback);
      cell.Controls.Add(btn);

      lc = new LiteralControl("<br/>");
      cell.Controls.Add(lc);
      Label label = new Label();
      label.Text = description;
      cell.Controls.Add(label);
    }

    protected override void CreateChildControls()
    {
      Controls.Clear();
      if (string.IsNullOrEmpty(rssUrl))
      {
        ChildControlsCreated = true;
        return;
      }

      using (XmlReader reader = XmlReader.Create(rssUrl))
      {
        AddContainer();
        reader.MoveToContent();
        reader.ReadToDescendant("channel");
        reader.ReadToDescendant("item");
        do
        {
          using (XmlReader itemReader = reader.ReadSubtree())
          {
            AddItemToContainer(itemReader);
          }
        } while (reader.ReadToNextSibling("item"));
      }
      ChildControlsCreated = true;
    }

    private string title;
    public virtual string ItemTitle
    {
      get { return title; }
    }

    private string description;
```

(continued)

Listing 10-25 *(continued)*

```
    public virtual string ItemDescription
    {
      get { return description; }
    }

    private string link;
    public virtual string ItemLink
    {
      get { return link; }
    }

    [ConnectionProvider("Send item to")]
    public IItem ProvideSelectedItem()
    {
      return this;
    }

    void SelectCommandCallback(object sender, CommandEventArgs e)
    {
      int rowIndex = int.Parse(e.CommandArgument.ToString());
      TableRow row = table.Rows[rowIndex];
      TableCell cell = row.Cells[0];
      HyperLink hyperLink = cell.Controls[0] as HyperLink;
      title = hyperLink.Text;
      link = hyperLink.NavigateUrl;
      Label label = cell.Controls[4] as Label;
      description = label.Text;
    }

    string IItem.ItemTitle
    {
      get { return this.ItemTitle; }
    }

    string IItem.ItemDescription
    {
      get { return this.ItemDescription; }
    }

    string IItem.ItemLink
    {
      get { return this.ItemLink; }
    }
  }
}
```

As Listing 10-25 shows, RssReaderWebPart4 implements the IItem interface. Strictly speaking this is not a requirement. Your data provider WebPart control does not have to implement the interface even though in most cases it does. Instead you could write a separate class that implements this interface and have your data provider WebPart control return an instance of this class.

Note that Listing 10-25 marks the provider method, ProvideSelectedItem, with the ConnectionProviderAttribute metadata attribute. This metadata attribute takes a string argument, which SharePoint displays in the Connections menu.

This ConnectionProviderAttribute metadata attribute serves the following purposes:

- Your data provider control, like all controls or classes, may expose numerous methods, which makes it impossible for the WebPartManager control to know which method provides the data. The ConnectionProviderAttribute metadata attribute tells the WebPartManager that the method marked with this attribute is the method that provides the data.
- The ConnectionProviderAttribute metadata attribute takes two important arguments that the WebPartManager must pass to the constructor of the ProviderConnectionPoint class when it's creating an instance of the class. These arguments are displayName and id. The displayName argument provides a friendly name for the connection point. SharePoint displays this friendly name in the Connections menu. The id argument is used to identify the connection point when the data provider supports more than one connection point.

Note from Listing 10-25 that RssReaderWebPart4 makes use of a new version of your RSS reader editor part as follows:

```
using System;
using System.Web.UI;
using System.Web.UI.WebControls;
using System.Web.UI.WebControls.WebParts;

namespace WebPartsChapter
{
  /// <summary>
  /// Summary description for RssReaderEditorPart
  /// </summary>
  public class RssReaderEditorPart2 : EditorPart
  {
    public RssReaderEditorPart2()
    {
      Title = "RSS Feeds";
    }

    public override ControlCollection Controls
    {
      get
      {
        EnsureChildControls();
        return base.Controls;
      }
    }

    DropDownList ddl;
    protected override void CreateChildControls()
    {
      Controls.Clear();

      ddl = new DropDownList();
```

(continued)

(continued)

```
      ddl.Items.Add(
         new ListItem("Wrox",
                        "http://www.wrox.com/WileyCDA/feed/RSS_WROX_ALLNEW.xml"));
      ddl.Items.Add(
        new ListItem("MSDN Magazine",
          "http://msdn.microsoft.com/en-us/magazine/rss/default.aspx?issue=tue"));
      Controls.Add(ddl);
    }

    public override bool ApplyChanges()
    {
      RssReaderWebPart4 rssReader = WebPartToEdit as RssReaderWebPart4;
      EnsureChildControls();
      rssReader.RssUrl = ddl.SelectedValue;
      return true;
    }

    public override void SyncChanges()
    {
      RssReaderWebPart4 rssReader = WebPartToEdit as RssReaderWebPart4;
      EnsureChildControls();
      ddl.SelectedIndex =
                        ddl.Items.IndexOf(ddl.Items.FindByValue(rssReader.RssUrl));
    }
  }
}
```

Listing 10-26 presents the implementation of FavoriteItemWebPart. Add a source file named FavoriteItemWebPart.cs to your project and add the content of this code listing to this source file.

Listing 10-26: The FavoriteItemWebPart Web part

```
using System;
using System.Data;
using System.Configuration;
using System.Web;
using System.Web.Security;
using System.Web.UI;
using System.Web.UI.WebControls;
using System.Web.UI.WebControls.WebParts;
using System.Web.UI.HtmlControls;

namespace WebPartsChapter
{
  public class FavoriteItemWebPart : WebPart
  {
    public FavoriteItemWebPart()
    {
      Title = "My Favorite Item";
      this.ScrollBars = ScrollBars.Auto;
```

```
      this.AllowConnect = true;
    }

    private IItem item;

    [ConnectionConsumer("Get item from")]
    public void ConsumeSelectedItem(IItem item)
    {
      this.item = item;
    }

    Table table;

    protected override void CreateChildControls()
    {
      Controls.Clear();

      if (item == null)
      {
        ChildControlsCreated = true;
        return;
      }

      table = new Table();
      table.CellSpacing = 5;
      Controls.Add(table);

      string title = item.ItemTitle;
      string link = item.ItemLink;
      string description = item.ItemDescription;

      TableRow row = new TableRow();
      table.Rows.Add(row);
      TableCell cell = new TableCell();
      row.Cells.Add(cell);

      HyperLink hyperLink = new HyperLink();
      hyperLink.NavigateUrl = link;
      hyperLink.Text = title;
      hyperLink.Font.Bold = true;
      cell.Controls.Add(hyperLink);
      LiteralControl lc = new LiteralControl("<br/>");
      cell.Controls.Add(lc);
      Label label = new Label();
      label.Text = description;
      cell.Controls.Add(label);

      ChildControlsCreated = true;
    }
  }
}
```

As Listing 10-26 shows, FavoriteItemWebPart marks its consumer method, which is the ConsumeSelectedItem method, with the ConnectionConsumerAttribute metadata attribute. Note that the implementation of a data consumer method normally consists of one line of code, where the method assigns the data object to a private field of the same type.

The ConnectionConsumerAttribute metadata attribute serves the same two purposes discussed before, specifically, it tells the WebPartManager that the method marked with the attribute is the method that consumes the data, and it provides the WebPartManager control with the values of the displayName and id parameters that the control must pass to the constructor of the ConsumerConnectionPoint class when it's creating an instance of the class.

As Listing 10-25 shows, the RssReaderWebPart4 control implements a method named AddItemToContainer that adds an item to the control. The implementation of this method is the same as RssReaderWebPart3 with one main difference. This method also renders the "Add Item" LinkButton and registers a method named SelectCommandCallback as the callback for the Click event of the LinkButton.

Note that the SelectCommandCallback method extracts the title, link, and description values associated with the selected item and assigns them to the title, link, and description private fields of the RssReaderWebPart4 control. Recall that the RssReaderWebPart4 control implements the IItem interface where its implementation of the ItemTitle, ItemLink, and ItemDescription properties of this interface return the values of the title, link, and description private fields (see Listing 10-25).

The SelectCommandCallback method doesn't directly send the data to FavoriteItemWebPart control as Listing 10-21 did. The method leaves the responsibility of sending the values of its ItemTitle, ItemLink, and ItemDescription properties to the Web Parts Framework.

Also notice that the FavoriteItemsWebPart control marks its ConsumeSelectedItem method with the [ConnectionConsumerAttribute("Get the item")] attribute to specify this method as the method that consumes the data that the RssReaderWebPart4 control provides. Notice that this method simply assigns the item that the provider provides to a private field of type IItem named item. The Web Parts Framework automatically calls the ConsumeSelectedItem method, which means that the value of the item private field is automatically set to the IItem object that the provider provides:

```
private IItem item;
[ConnectionConsumer("Item")]
public void ConsumeSelectedItem(IItem item)
{
  this.item = item;
}
```

As Listing 10-26 shows, the FavoriteItemWebPart control overrides the CreateChildControls method where it checks whether the item private field has been set. If it has, it's an indication that the RssReaderWebPart4 provider has provided a new item. The control then uses a hyperlink and a label to respectively display the title and description of the item (see Listing 10-26).

The current implementation of the RssReaderWebPart4 control renders the "Add Item" LinkButton even when RssReaderWebPart4 is no longer connected. This causes usability problems because end users may still try to click these LinkButtons not realizing they're no longer active. Next, you'll implement a new version of the control named RssReaderWebPart5 that fixes this problem. Listing 10-27 presents the implementation of RssReaderWebPart5.

Listing 10-27: The RssReaderWebPart5 Web part

```
using System.Web.UI.WebControls.WebParts;
using System.Web.UI.WebControls;
using System.Web.UI;
using System;
using System.Collections;
using System.Xml;

namespace WebPartsChapter
{
  public class RssReaderWebPart5 : WebPart, IItem
  {
    Table table;
    private string rssUrl;
    [Personalizable(true)]
    [WebBrowsable(false)]
    public virtual string RssUrl
    {
      get { return rssUrl; }
      set { rssUrl = value; }
    }

    bool renderAddItemLink;
    [Personalizable(true)]
    public bool RenderAddItemLink
    {
      get { return this.renderAddItemLink; }
      set { renderAddItemLink = value; }
    }

    protected override void OnInit(EventArgs e)
    {
      base.OnInit(e);
      this.WebPartManager.WebPartsDisconnected +=
                 new WebPartConnectionsEventHandler(WebPartsDisconnectedCallback);
      this.WebPartManager.WebPartsConnected +=
                  new WebPartConnectionsEventHandler(WebPartsConnectedCallback);
    }

    void WebPartsConnectedCallback(object sender, WebPartConnectionsEventArgs e)
    {
      if (e.Provider.Equals(this))
        renderAddItemLink = true;
    }

    void WebPartsDisconnectedCallback(object sender, WebPartConnectionsEventArgs e)
    {
      if (e.Provider.Equals(this))
        renderAddItemLink = false;
    }

    private EditorPartCollection editorParts;
```

(continued)

Listing 10-27 *(continued)*

```
public override EditorPartCollection CreateEditorParts()
{
  if (editorParts == null)
  {
    ArrayList editors = new ArrayList();
    RssReaderEditorPart3 editorPart = new RssReaderEditorPart3();
    editorPart.ID = ID + "RssReaderEditorPart3";
    editors.Add(editorPart);
    editorParts = new EditorPartCollection(editors);
  }
  return editorParts;
}

protected virtual void AddContainer()
{
  table = new Table();
  table.CellSpacing = 5;
  Controls.Add(table);
}

protected virtual void AddItemToContainer(XmlReader reader)
{
  string link = string.Empty; ;
  string title = string.Empty;
  string description = string.Empty;

  while (reader.Read())
  {
    if (reader.NodeType == XmlNodeType.Element)
    {
      if (reader.Name == "link")
        link = reader.ReadElementContentAsString();

      else if (reader.Name == "title")
        title = reader.ReadElementContentAsString();

      else if (reader.Name == "description")
        description = reader.ReadElementContentAsString();
    }
  }

  TableRow row = new TableRow();
  table.Rows.Add(row);
  TableCell cell = new TableCell();
  row.Cells.Add(cell);

  HyperLink hyperLink = new HyperLink();
  hyperLink.NavigateUrl = link;
  hyperLink.Text = title;
  hyperLink.Font.Bold = true;
  cell.Controls.Add(hyperLink);
```

```
    LiteralControl lc;

    if (RenderAddItemLink)
    {

      lc = new LiteralControl("   ");
      cell.Controls.Add(lc);
      LinkButton btn = new LinkButton();
      btn.Text = "Add Item";
      btn.CommandArgument = table.Rows.GetRowIndex(row).ToString();
      btn.Command += new CommandEventHandler(SelectCommandCallback);
      cell.Controls.Add(btn);
    }

    lc = new LiteralControl("<br/>");
    cell.Controls.Add(lc);
    Label label = new Label();
    label.Text = description;
    cell.Controls.Add(label);
  }

  protected override void CreateChildControls()
  {
    Controls.Clear();
    if (string.IsNullOrEmpty(rssUrl))
    {
      ChildControlsCreated = true;
      return;
    }

    using (XmlReader reader = XmlReader.Create(rssUrl))
    {
      AddContainer();
      reader.MoveToContent();
      reader.ReadToDescendant("channel");
      reader.ReadToDescendant("item");
      do
      {
        using (XmlReader itemReader = reader.ReadSubtree())
        {
          AddItemToContainer(itemReader);
        }
      } while (reader.ReadToNextSibling("item"));
    }
    ChildControlsCreated = true;
  }

  private string title;
  public string ItemTitle
  {
    get { return title; }
  }

  private string description;
```

(continued)

Listing 10-27 *(continued)*

```
    public string ItemDescription
    {
      get { return description; }
    }

    private string link;
    public string ItemLink
    {
      get { return link; }
    }

    [ConnectionProvider("Send item to")]
    public IItem ProvideSelectedItem()
    {
      return this;
    }

    void SelectCommandCallback(object sender, CommandEventArgs e)
    {
      int rowIndex = int.Parse(e.CommandArgument.ToString());
      TableRow row = table.Rows[rowIndex];
      TableCell cell = row.Cells[0];
      HyperLink hyperLink = cell.Controls[0] as HyperLink;
      title = hyperLink.Text;
      link = hyperLink.NavigateUrl;
      Label label = cell.Controls[4] as Label;
      description = label.Text;
    }

    string IItem.ItemTitle
    {
      get { return this.ItemTitle; }
    }

    string IItem.ItemDescription
    {
      get { return this.ItemDescription; }
    }

    string IItem.ItemLink
    {
      get { return this.ItemLink; }
    }
  }
}
```

RssReaderWebPart5 exposes a new Boolean property named RenderAddItemLink as shown in the following code fragment:

```
bool renderAddItemLink;
[Personalizable(true)]
public bool RenderAddItemLink
{
  get { return this.renderAddItemLink; }
  set { renderAddItemLink = value; }
}
```

Notice that the code fragment marks the RenderAddItemLink property with the [Personalizable(true)] attribute to instruct the personalization infrastructure to store the value of this property in the underlying personalization data store.

RssReaderWebPart5 then modifies the implementation of the AddItemToContainer method of RssReaderWebPart4 as shown in Listing 10-27. This implementation is the same as the one shown in Listing 10-25 with one difference — the addition of the if statement that checks the value of RenderAddItemLink property to determine whether the "Add Item" LinkButton should be rendered.

When the end user connects and disconnects a WebPart control, WebPartManager raises the WebPartsConnected and WebPartsDisconnected events. RssReaderWebPart5 overrides the OnInit method to respectively register the WebPartsConnectedCallback and WebPartsDisconnectedCallback methods as callbacks for the WebPartsConnected and WebPartsDisconnected events, as shown in Listing 10-27.

As the following code fragment illustrates, the WebPartsConnectedCallback and WebPartsDisconnectedCallback methods set the value of the RenderAddItemLink property to true and false, respectively:

```
void WebPartsConnectedCallback(object sender, WebPartConnectionsEventArgs e)
{
  if (e.Provider.Equals(this))
    renderAddItemLink = true;
}

void WebPartsDisconnectedCallback(object sender, WebPartConnectionsEventArgs e)
{
  if (e.Provider.Equals(this))
    renderAddItemLink = false;
}
```

Because you've replaced RssReaderWebPart4 with a new Web part called RssReaderWebPart5 you also need to implement a new editor part named RssReaderEditorPart3 as shown in Listing 10-28.

Listing 10-28: The RssReaderEditorPart3 editor part

```
using System;
using System.Web.UI;
using System.Web.UI.WebControls;
using System.Web.UI.WebControls.WebParts;
using Microsoft.SharePoint;
using Microsoft.SharePoint.WebControls;

namespace WebPartsChapter
{
  /// <summary>
  /// Summary description for RssReaderEditorPart
  /// </summary>
  public class RssReaderEditorPart3 : EditorPart
  {
    public RssReaderEditorPart3()
    {
      Title = "RSS Feeds";
    }

    public override ControlCollection Controls
    {
      get
      {
        EnsureChildControls();
        return base.Controls;
      }
    }

    DropDownList ddl;
    protected override void CreateChildControls()
    {
      Controls.Clear();

      ddl = new DropDownList();
      ddl.Items.Add(
         new ListItem("Wrox",
                      "http://www.wrox.com/WileyCDA/feed/RSS_WROX_ALLNEW.xml"));
      ddl.Items.Add(
        new ListItem("MSDN Magazine",
           "http://msdn.microsoft.com/en-us/magazine/rss/default.aspx?issue=tue"));

      Controls.Add(ddl);
    }

    public override bool ApplyChanges()
    {
      RssReaderWebPart5 rssReader = WebPartToEdit as RssReaderWebPart5;
      if (rssReader != null)
      {
        EnsureChildControls();
        rssReader.RssUrl = ddl.SelectedValue;
```

```
            }
            return true;
        }

        public override void SyncChanges()
        {
            RssReaderWebPart5 rssReader = WebPartToEdit as RssReaderWebPart5;
            if (rssReader != null)
            {
                EnsureChildControls();
                ddl.SelectedIndex =
                          ddl.Items.IndexOf(ddl.Items.FindByValue(rssReader.RssUrl));
            }
        }
    }
}
```

Note that the ApplyChanges and SyncChanges methods of RssReaderEditorPart3 editor part use RssReaderWebPart5 as the Web part to edit. Also note that RssReaderWebPart5's implementation of CreateEditorParts instantiates an instance of RssReaderEditorPart3 as shown in Listing 10-27.

Figure 10-15 presents the situation where the RssReaderWebPart5 and FavoriteItemWebPart Web parts are not connected. As you can see, RssReaderWebPart5 does not display the Add Item link.

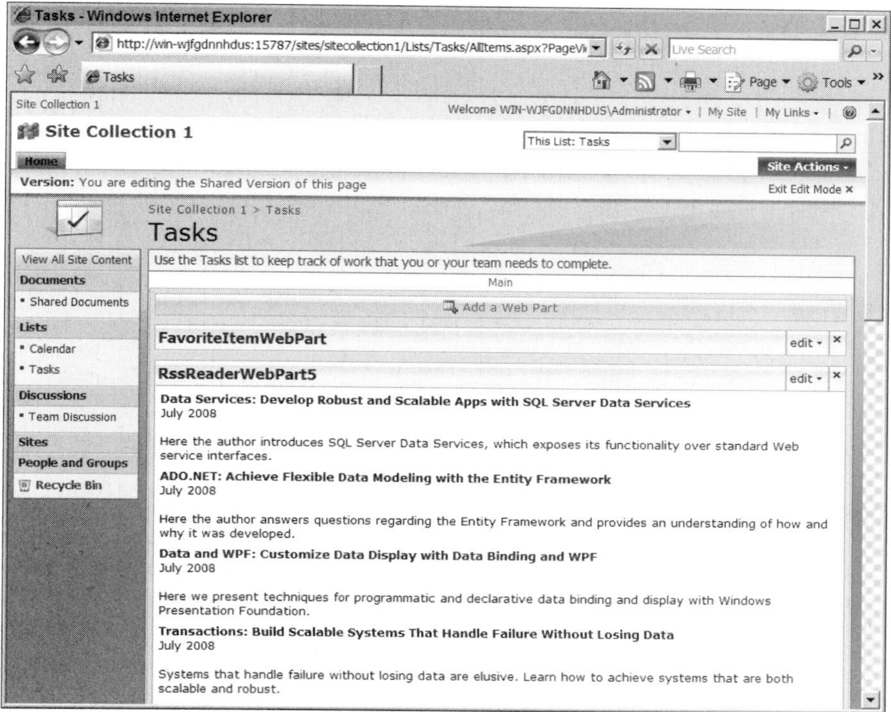

Figure 10-15: The Web parts in disconnected mode

Now if you go ahead and connect the Web parts, the Add Item link will show up as usual.

Next, implement a new Web part named RssReaderWebPart6 and a new editor part named RssReaderEditorPart4, which respectively extend the functionality of RssReaderWebPart5 and RssReaderEditorPart3. The main goal is to teach you the techniques that you need to implement more complex Web part and editor part server controls. Even though these server control development techniques are used to implement RssReaderEditorPart4, they are equally applicable to Web parts.

Before diving into the implementation of this Web part and its associated editor part, let's see what they look like in action as shown in Figure 10-16.

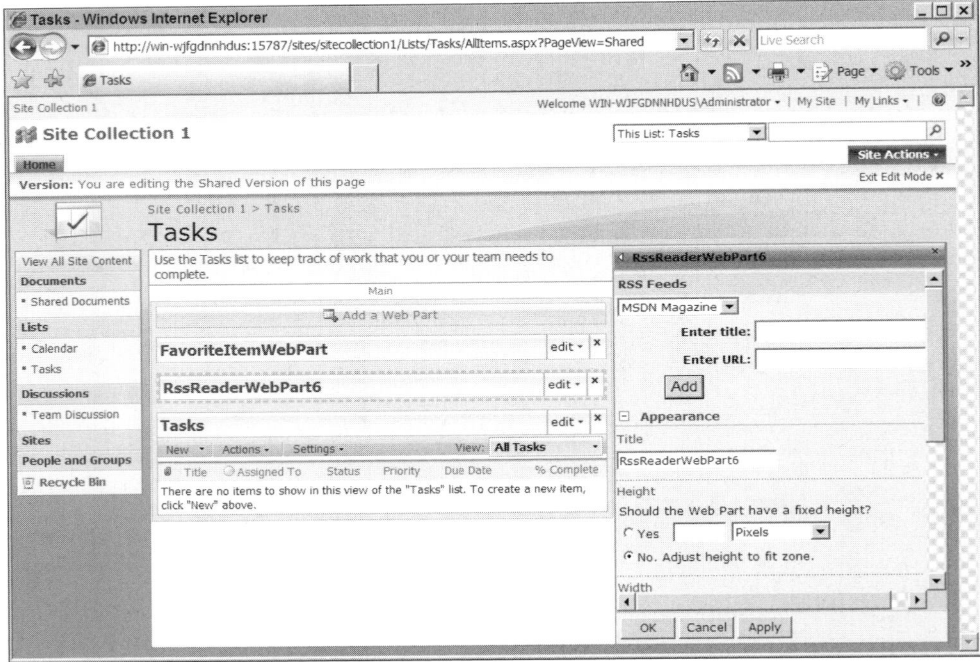

Figure 10-16: The new RSS reader editor part in action

As this figure illustrates, RssReaderEditorPart4 contains the following elements:

- A drop-down list box to display the list of available feeds.
- Two textboxes and an Add button for adding new feeds to the drop-down list box. The user enters the new feed title and URL in these textboxes and hits the Add button to add the new feed to the drop-down list box.

Listing 10-29 presents the implementation of RssReaderWebPart6 Web part.

Listing 10-29: The RssReaderWebPart6 Web part

```
using System.Web.UI.WebControls.WebParts;
using System.Web.UI.WebControls;
using System.Web.UI;
using System;
using System.Collections;
using System.Xml;

namespace WebPartsChapter
{
  public class RssReaderWebPart6 : WebPart, IItem, IPersonalizable
  {
    Table table;
    private string rssUrl;
    [Personalizable(true)]
    [WebBrowsable(false)]
    public virtual string RssUrl
    {
      get { return rssUrl; }
      set { rssUrl = value; }
    }

    bool renderAddItemLink;
    [Personalizable(true)]
    public bool RenderAddItemLink
    {
      get { return this.renderAddItemLink; }
      set { renderAddItemLink= value; }
    }

    protected override void OnInit(EventArgs e)
    {
      base.OnInit(e);
      this.WebPartManager.WebPartsDisconnected +=
                  new WebPartConnectionsEventHandler(WebPartsDisconnectedCallback);
      this.WebPartManager.WebPartsConnected +=
                   new WebPartConnectionsEventHandler(WebPartsConnectedCallback);
    }

    void WebPartsConnectedCallback(object sender, WebPartConnectionsEventArgs e)
    {
      if (e.Provider.Equals(this))
        renderAddItemLink = true;
    }

    void WebPartsDisconnectedCallback(object sender, WebPartConnectionsEventArgs e)
    {
      if (e.Provider.Equals(this))
        renderAddItemLink = false;
```

(continued)

Listing 10-29 *(continued)*

```
    }

    private EditorPartCollection editorParts;
    public override EditorPartCollection CreateEditorParts()
    {
      if (editorParts == null)
      {
        ArrayList editors = new ArrayList();
        RssReaderEditorPart4 editorPart = new RssReaderEditorPart4();
        editorPart.ID = ID + "RssReaderEditorPart4";
        editors.Add(editorPart);
        editorParts = new EditorPartCollection(editors);
      }
      return editorParts;
    }

    protected virtual void AddContainer()
    {
      table = new Table();
      table.CellSpacing = 5;
      Controls.Add(table);
    }

    protected virtual void AddItemToContainer(XmlReader reader)
    {
      string link = string.Empty; ;
      string title = string.Empty;
      string description = string.Empty;

      while (reader.Read())
      {
        if (reader.NodeType == XmlNodeType.Element)
        {
          if (reader.Name == "link")
            link = reader.ReadElementContentAsString();

          else if (reader.Name == "title")
            title = reader.ReadElementContentAsString();

          else if (reader.Name == "description")
            description = reader.ReadElementContentAsString();
        }
      }

      TableRow row = new TableRow();
      table.Rows.Add(row);
      TableCell cell = new TableCell();
      row.Cells.Add(cell);

      HyperLink hyperLink = new HyperLink();
      hyperLink.NavigateUrl = link;
      hyperLink.Text = title;
```

```
        hyperLink.Font.Bold = true;
        cell.Controls.Add(hyperLink);
        LiteralControl lc;

        if (RenderAddItemLink)
        {

          lc = new LiteralControl("   ");
          cell.Controls.Add(lc);
          LinkButton btn = new LinkButton();
          btn.Text = "Add Item";
          btn.CommandArgument = table.Rows.GetRowIndex(row).ToString();
          btn.Command += new CommandEventHandler(SelectCommandCallback);
          cell.Controls.Add(btn);
        }

        lc = new LiteralControl("<br/>");
        cell.Controls.Add(lc);
        Label label = new Label();
        label.Text = description;
        cell.Controls.Add(label);
      }
      protected override void CreateChildControls()
      {
        Controls.Clear();
        if (string.IsNullOrEmpty(rssUrl))
        {
          ChildControlsCreated = true;
          return;
        }

        using (XmlReader reader = XmlReader.Create(rssUrl))
        {
          AddContainer();
          reader.MoveToContent();
          reader.ReadToDescendant("channel");
          reader.ReadToDescendant("item");
          do
          {
            using (XmlReader itemReader = reader.ReadSubtree())
            {
              AddItemToContainer(itemReader);
            }
          } while (reader.ReadToNextSibling("item"));
        }
        ChildControlsCreated = true;
      }

      #region IItem Members

      private string title;
      public string ItemTitle
      {
        get { return title; }
```

(continued)

Listing 10-29 *(continued)*

```
    }

    private string description;
    public string ItemDescription
    {
      get { return description; }
    }

    private string link;
    public string ItemLink
    {
      get { return link; }
    }

    #endregion

    [ConnectionProvider("Send item to")]
    public IItem ProvideSelectedItem()
    {
      return this;
    }

    void SelectCommandCallback(object sender, CommandEventArgs e)
    {
      int rowIndex = int.Parse(e.CommandArgument.ToString());
      TableRow row = table.Rows[rowIndex];
      TableCell cell = row.Cells[0];
      HyperLink hyperLink = cell.Controls[0] as HyperLink;
      title = hyperLink.Text;
      link = hyperLink.NavigateUrl;
      Label label = cell.Controls[4] as Label;
      description = label.Text;
    }

    #region IItem Members

    string IItem.ItemTitle
    {
      get { return this.ItemTitle; }
    }

    string IItem.ItemDescription
    {
      get { return this.ItemDescription; }
    }

    string IItem.ItemLink
    {
      get { return this.ItemLink; }
    }

    #endregion
```

```
    private ArrayList titles;
    public ArrayList Titles
    {
      get { return titles; }
      set { titles = value; }
    }

    private ArrayList urls;
    public ArrayList Urls
    {
      get { return urls; }
      set { urls = value; }
    }

    #region IPersonalizable Members

    private bool isDirty;
    protected internal bool IsDirty
    {
      get { return isDirty; }
      set { isDirty = value; }
    }

    bool IPersonalizable.IsDirty
    {
      get { return IsDirty; }
    }

    void IPersonalizable.Load(PersonalizationDictionary state)
    {
      if (state == null)
        return;

      if (state["Titles"] != null)
        titles = state["Titles"].Value as ArrayList;

      if (state["Urls"] != null)
        urls = state["Urls"].Value as ArrayList;
    }

    void IPersonalizable.Save(PersonalizationDictionary state)
    {
      if ((titles != null) && (titles.Count != 0))
        state["Titles"] =
                    new PersonalizationEntry(titles, PersonalizationScope.User);

      if ((urls != null) && (urls.Count != 0))
        state["Urls"] = new PersonalizationEntry(urls, PersonalizationScope.User);
    }

    #endregion
  }
}
```

The main focus in this code listing is on the boldfaced portions. Note that RssReaderWebPart6 exposes two ArrayList properties, named Titles and Urls, which contain the user's favorite feed titles and URLs. As you'll see later, the DropDownList server control in the RssReaderEditorPart4 editor part displays these feeds. RssReaderWebPart6 implements an interface named IPersonalizable to store the Titles and Urls properties in and to retrieve the Titles and Urls properties from the personalization store.

The Web parts personalization infrastructure provides Web parts controls with two different mechanisms to store their personalization data or state in and restore their personalization data or state from the underlying personalization data store.

Web parts controls can mark their properties with the [Personalizable(true)] metadata attribute to instruct the Web parts personalization infrastructure to store their values in and to restore their values from the personalization data store. The RssReaderWebPart6 control uses this approach to store the value of its RssUrl property in the personalization data store as shown in the following code fragment:

```
private string rssUrl;
[Personalizable(true)]
[WebBrowsable()]
public string RssUrl
{
get { return rssUrl; }
set { rssUrl = value; }
}
```

Web parts controls can directly implement the IPersonalizable interface to store their property values in and to restore their property values from the personalization data store. As you'll see in this section, RssReaderWebPart6 uses this approach to store the contents of its Titles and Urls collections in the personalization data store.

Listing 10-30 contains the definition of the IPersonalizable interface.

Listing 10-30: The IPersonalizable interface

```
public interface IPersonalizable
{
  void Load(PersonalizationDictionary state);
  void Save(PersonalizationDictionary state);
  bool IsDirty { get; }
}
```

The members of this interface are as follows:

- **Load.** The Web parts personalization infrastructure calls the Load method of a Web parts control and passes a PersonalizationDictionary collection into it. This collection contains the control's saved personalization data. It's the responsibility of the Load method to restore the state of the Web Part control from this collection.

- **Save.** The Web parts personalization infrastructure calls the Save method of a Web parts control and passes a PersonalizationDictionary collection into it. It's the responsibility of the Save method to store the control's personalization data into this collection.
- **IsDirty.** This specifies whether the personalization data of the Web parts control has changed ("dirty").

The Web parts personalization infrastructure calls the Save method of the control to allow the control to save its personalization data if the control has been marked as dirty.

PersonalizationDictionary is a collection of PersonalizationEntry objects where each object contains a piece of personalization data, such as the value of a property. The following code contains the definition of the PersonalizationEntry class:

```
public sealed class PersonalizationEntry
{
  public PersonalizationEntry(object value, PersonalizationScope scope);
  public PersonalizationEntry(object value, PersonalizationScope scope,
  bool isSensitive);
  public bool IsSensitive { get; set; }
  public PersonalizationScope Scope { get; set; }
  public object Value { get; set; }
}
```

The following are the properties of the PersonalizationEntry class:

- **Value.** This is the personalization data that the PersonalizationEntry entry contains.
- **Scope.** This is the personalization scope of the personalization data that the PersonalizationEntry entry contains. The possible values are PersonalizationScope.Shared and PersonalizationScope.User, where the former specifies that the personalization data is shared among all users and the latter specifies that the personalization data only applies to the current user.
- **IsSensitive.** This specifies whether the personalization data that the PersonalizationEntry entry contains includes sensitive information.

As the boldfaced portions of Listing 10-29 illustrate, the RssReaderWebPart6 control implements the Save method to store the contents of the Titles and Urls collections to the underlying personalization data store. The Save method stores the content of each collection in a PersonalizationEntry entry and adds the entry to the PersonalizationDictionary that the Web parts personalization infrastructure passes into it.

```
void IPersonalizable.Save(PersonalizationDictionary state)
{
  if ((titles != null) && (titles.Count != 0))
    state["Titles"] =
                 new PersonalizationEntry(titles, PersonalizationScope.User);

  if ((urls != null) && (urls.Count != 0))
    state["Urls"] = new PersonalizationEntry(urls, PersonalizationScope.User);
}
```

The boldfaced portion of Listing 10-29 also presents the RssReaderWebPart6 control's implementation of the Load method where the method retrieves the PersonalizationEntry entries that contain the title texts and URLs of the current user's favorite RSS feeds and respectively adds the contents of these entries to the Titles and Urls collections of the RssReaderWebPart6 control:

```
void IPersonalizable.Load(PersonalizationDictionary state)
{
  if (state == null)
    return;

  if (state["Titles"] != null)
    titles = state["Titles"].Value as ArrayList;

  if (state["Urls"] != null)
    urls = state["Urls"].Value as ArrayList;
}
```

The RssReaderWebPart6 control exposes an internal read-write property named IsDirty. As you'll see later, the ApplyChanges method of the RssReaderEditorPart4 control sets the value of the IsDirty property of the RssReaderWebPart6 control to true to mark the control as dirty. As mentioned, the Web parts personalization infrastructure calls the Save method of a control to allow the control to save its personalization data if the control is marked dirty:

```
private bool isDirty;
protected internal bool IsDirty
{
  get { return isDirty; }
  set { isDirty = value; }
}
```

The RssReaderWebPart6 control's implementation of the IsDirty property of the IPersonalization interface calls the preceding IsDirty property as follows:

```
bool IPersonalizable.IsDirty
{
  get { return IsDirty; }
}
```

Listing 10-31 presents the implementation of the RssReaderEditorPart4 editor part.

Listing 10-31: The RssReaderEditorPart4 editor part

```
using System;
using System.Web.UI;
using System.Web.UI.WebControls;
using System.Web.UI.WebControls.WebParts;
using Microsoft.SharePoint;
using Microsoft.SharePoint.WebControls;
using System.Collections;

namespace WebPartsChapter
{
  /// <summary>
  /// Summary description for RssReaderEditorPart
  /// </summary>
  public class RssReaderEditorPart4 : EditorPart
  {
    public RssReaderEditorPart4()
    {
      Title = "RSS Feeds";
    }

    public override ControlCollection Controls
    {
      get
      {
        EnsureChildControls();
        return base.Controls;
      }
    }

    DropDownList ddl;
    TextBox titletbx;
    TextBox urltbx;
    Label titlelbl;
    Label urllbl;
    Button btn;

    protected override void CreateChildControls()
    {
      Controls.Clear();

      ddl = new DropDownList();
      titletbx = new TextBox();
      urltbx = new TextBox();
      titlelbl = new Label();
      titlelbl.Text = "Enter title: ";
      urllbl = new Label();
      urllbl.Text = "Enter URL: ";
      btn = new Button();
      btn.Text = "Add";
      btn.Click += new EventHandler(Btn_Click);
      Controls.Add(ddl);
```

(continued)

Listing 10-31 *(continued)*

```
    Controls.Add(titletbx);
    Controls.Add(urltbx);
    Controls.Add(titlelbl);
    Controls.Add(urllbl);
    Controls.Add(btn);

    ChildControlsCreated = true;
  }

  void Btn_Click(object sender, EventArgs e)
  {
    string title = titletbx.Text;
    string url = urltbx.Text;
    ddl.Items.Add(new ListItem(title, url));
  }

  protected override void RenderContents(HtmlTextWriter writer)
  {
    writer.RenderBeginTag(HtmlTextWriterTag.Tr);
    writer.AddStyleAttribute(HtmlTextWriterStyle.Width, "100%");
    writer.RenderBeginTag(HtmlTextWriterTag.Td);
    ddl.RenderControl(writer);
    writer.RenderEndTag();
    writer.RenderEndTag();

    writer.RenderBeginTag(HtmlTextWriterTag.Tr);
    writer.AddAttribute(HtmlTextWriterAttribute.Align, "right");
    writer.AddStyleAttribute(HtmlTextWriterStyle.FontWeight, "bold");
    writer.RenderBeginTag(HtmlTextWriterTag.Td);
    titlelbl.RenderControl(writer);
    writer.RenderEndTag();
    writer.AddAttribute(HtmlTextWriterAttribute.Align, "left");
    writer.RenderBeginTag(HtmlTextWriterTag.Td);
    titletbx.RenderControl(writer);
    writer.RenderEndTag();
    writer.RenderEndTag();

    writer.RenderBeginTag(HtmlTextWriterTag.Tr);
    writer.AddAttribute(HtmlTextWriterAttribute.Align, "right");
    writer.AddStyleAttribute(HtmlTextWriterStyle.FontWeight, "bold");
    writer.RenderBeginTag(HtmlTextWriterTag.Td);
    urllbl.RenderControl(writer);
    writer.RenderEndTag();
    writer.AddAttribute(HtmlTextWriterAttribute.Align, "left");
    writer.RenderBeginTag(HtmlTextWriterTag.Td);
    urltbx.RenderControl(writer);
    writer.RenderEndTag();
    writer.RenderEndTag();

    writer.RenderBeginTag(HtmlTextWriterTag.Tr);
    writer.AddAttribute(HtmlTextWriterAttribute.Align, "center");
    writer.RenderBeginTag(HtmlTextWriterTag.Td);
```

```
      btn.RenderControl(writer);
      writer.RenderEndTag();
      writer.RenderEndTag();
    }

    protected override HtmlTextWriterTag TagKey
    {
      get { return HtmlTextWriterTag.Table; }
    }

    public override bool ApplyChanges()
    {
      RssReaderWebPart6 rssReader = WebPartToEdit as RssReaderWebPart6;

      if (rssReader.Titles == null)
        rssReader.Titles = new ArrayList();
      if (rssReader.Urls == null)
        rssReader.Urls = new ArrayList();

      rssReader.Titles.Clear();
      rssReader.Urls.Clear();

      foreach (ListItem item in ddl.Items)
      {
        rssReader.Titles.Add(item.Text);
        rssReader.Urls.Add(item.Value);
      }

      rssReader.RssUrl = ddl.SelectedValue;

      rssReader.IsDirty = true;
      return true;
    }

    public override void SyncChanges()
    {
      RssReaderWebPart6 rssReader = WebPartToEdit as RssReaderWebPart6;
      if (rssReader.Titles == null || rssReader.Urls == null)
        return;

      EnsureChildControls();
      for (int i = 0; i < rssReader.Titles.Count; i++)
        ddl.Items.Add(new ListItem(rssReader.Titles[i].ToString(),
                      rssReader.Urls[i].ToString()));

      ddl.SelectedIndex =
                ddl.Items.IndexOf(ddl.Items.FindByValue(rssReader.RssUrl));
    }
  }
}
```

As Listing 10-31 shows, RssReaderEditorPart4 exposes the following seven members:

- ApplyChanges
- SyncChanges
- CreateChildControls
- RenderContents
- TagKey
- Btn_Click
- Controls

Next, the discussion moves to the implementation of these members starting with Controls. RssReaderEditorPart4, like any other composite server control, overrides the Controls property to invoke the EnsureChildControls method. This method internally invokes the CreateChildControls method if it hasn't already been invoked to create the child controls. Next, you'll walk through the implementation of ApplyChanges. Recall that the Web Parts Framework invokes this method when the user clicks the OK button to commit the changes. This method basically applies the changes to the Web part that the editor part edits. As Listing 10-31 shows, ApplyChanges first accesses the Web part:

```
RssReaderWebPart6 rssReader = WebPartToEdit as RssReaderWebPart6;
```

Then, it instantiates the Titles and Urls properties of the Web part if they haven't already been instantiated:

```
if (rssReader.Titles == null)
  rssReader.Titles = new ArrayList();
if (rssReader.Urls == null)
  rssReader.Urls = new ArrayList();
```

Next, it clears them:

```
rssReader.Titles.Clear();
rssReader.Urls.Clear();
```

Then, it iterates through the feeds displayed in the drop-down list box and adds their titles to the Titles collection and their URLs to the Urls collection of the Web part:

```
foreach (ListItem item in ddl.Items)
{
  rssReader.Titles.Add(item.Text);
  rssReader.Urls.Add(item.Value);
}
```

Next, it assigns the URL of the selected feed to the RssUrl property of the Web part:

```
rssReader.RssUrl = ddl.SelectedValue;
```

Finally, it marks the Web part as dirty so the Web parts personalization infrastructure calls the Save method on the Web part to have the Web part save the contents of the Titles and Urls collections into the personalization data store:

```
rssReader.IsDirty = true;
```

Next, you'll walk through the implementation of the SyncChanges method. Recall that Web Parts Framework invokes this method to allow the editor part to populate itself with the current values of the appropriate properties of the Web part. As Listing 10-31 shows, this method first accesses the Web part:

```
RssReaderWebPart6 rssReader = WebPartToEdit as RssReaderWebPart6;
```

Then, it populates the drop-down list box with the titles and URLs of the current user's favorite feeds:

```
for (int i = 0; i < rssReader.Titles.Count; i++)
  ddl.Items.Add(new ListItem(rssReader.Titles[i].ToString(),
                rssReader.Urls[i].ToString()));
```

Finally, its sets the SelectedIndex property of the drop-down list box so it displays the current user's selected favorite feed:

```
ddl.SelectedIndex =
              ddl.Items.IndexOf(ddl.Items.FindByValue(rssReader.RssUrl));
```

RssReaderEditorPart4, like any other composite server control, follows the typical implementation pattern of a composite server control. First, it overrides the TagKey property to specify the containing HTML element of the server control as a whole. RssReaderEditorPart4's implementation of this property specifies the <table> HTML element as the containing HTML element for the markup text that RssReaderEditorPart4 generates. Keep in mind that the containing HTML element is the outermost HTML element that contains the rest of the HTML element that the control generates:

```
protected override HtmlTextWriterTag TagKey
{
  get { return HtmlTextWriterTag.Table; }
}
```

RssReaderEditorPart4, like any other composite server control, overrides the CreateChildControls method to create its child controls. You cannot create the child controls of your composite control in the constructor of the control. You must create all your composite control's child controls inside the CreateChildControls method. As Listing 10-31 shows, the RssReaderEditorPart4's implementation of CreateChildControls first clears the Controls collection because you're about to re-create the child controls:

```
Controls.Clear();
```

Then, it instantiates and initializes the child controls one by one:

```
ddl = new DropDownList();
titletbx = new TextBox();
urltbx = new TextBox();
titlelbl = new Label();
titlelbl.Text = "Enter title: ";
urllbl = new Label();
urllbl.Text = "Enter URL: ";
btn = new Button();
btn.Text = "Add";
```

Next, it registers the Btn_Click method as an event handler for the Click event of the Add button:

```
btn.Click += new EventHandler(Btn_Click);
```

Then, it adds all child controls to the Controls collection. You must add the child controls to the Controls collection after you initialize them. Any changes you make in the child controls after they're added to the Controls collection will be stored in the page's view state. Because the page's view state is stored in the page itself, this unnecessarily increases the page size and degrades the performance.

```
Controls.Add(ddl);
Controls.Add(titletbx);
Controls.Add(urltbx);
Controls.Add(titlelbl);
Controls.Add(urllbl);
Controls.Add(btn);
```

Finally, CreateChildControls sets the ChildControlsCreated property to true. This step is important because the EnsureChildControls method internally checks the value of this property and invokes the CreateChildControls method if this property is false. Keep in mind that the EnsureChildControls method could be invoked multiple times during the same request. Setting this property to true ensures that the child controls are instantiated only once:

```
ChildControlsCreated = true;
```

As just mentioned, CreateChildControls method registers the Btn_Click method as an event handler for the Click event of the Add button. As Listing 10-31 shows, this method simply retrieves the feed title and URL from the respective textfields and adds them to the drop-down list box:

```
string title = titletbx.Text;
string url = urltbx.Text;
ddl.Items.Add(new ListItem(title, url));
```

Next, you'll walk through the RssReaderEditorPart4's implementation of the RenderContents method. As just discussed, the CreateChildControls method is where a control creates and initializes its child controls and adds them to the Controls collection. The RenderContents method is where the control actually renders its child controls. This is where a control uses HTML formatting to lay out its child controls on the containing page. As the RssReaderEditorPart4's implementation of the RenderControls method shows, this control lays out its child controls in a tabular manner where the drop-down list box is in the first row, the feed title label and textfield are in the second row, the feed URL label and textbox are in the third row, and the Add button is in the fourth row.

Note that the CreateChildControls method does not instantiate the formatting controls such as table, table rows, and table cells. You shouldn't treat these formatting controls as child controls of your composite controls. As the name implies, the formatting controls are there to format and lay out the child controls. They themselves are not child controls. If you treat them as child controls and instantiate and add them to the Controls collection of your composite control, their states will be stored in the page's view state and consequently it will unnecessarily increase the size of the page.

As Listing 10-31 shows, RenderContents takes these steps to render the first row. First, it renders the opening tag of the <tr> HTML element:

```
writer.RenderBeginTag(HtmlTextWriterTag.Tr);
```

Then, it renders the opening tag of the <td> HTML element and its width attribute:

```
writer.AddStyleAttribute(HtmlTextWriterStyle.Width, "100%");
writer.RenderBeginTag(HtmlTextWriterTag.Td);
```

Next, it renders the drop-down list box within the opening and closing tags of this <td> HTML element:

```
ddl.RenderControl(writer);
```

Then, it renders the closing tag of the <td> HTML element:

```
writer.RenderEndTag();
```

Finally, it renders the closing tag of the <tr> HTML element:

```
writer.RenderEndTag();
```

RenderContents repeats the same process to render the other rows.

Summary

This chapter used several examples to show you how to implement custom Web parts and deploy them to SharePoint. As discussed, you should deploy your Web part assemblies to the local bin directory of your web applications so you can take advantage of code access security. The next chapter provides in-depth coverage of .NET code access security.

11

Code Access Security (CAS)

Role-based security works by using the roles in which an authenticated user is to authorize what the user can and cannot access. Such a user-centric authorization mechanism assumes that as long as the user is authorized everything should be working as it was configured. This overlooks the fact that a trustworthy user normally executes pieces of code coming from different sources. These pieces of code execute under the trustworthy user's security context. Some of these pieces of code could be malicious, and others might have bugs that could be used by malicious code to mount an attack. Still others may have bugs that could cause the code to do things that it is not authorized to do. The security problems in these situations do not stem from the fact that the user is untrustworthy or malicious. The security problems arise from the code itself. Code Access Security (CAS) authorizes code, not users, and determines whether a piece of code has the permission to access a protected resource or perform a protected operation. If the code does not have the required permission, the runtime's security system will not allow the code to access the protected resource or perform the protected operation. Another related issue is the fact that users do need to run code that originates from untrustworthy sources. Code Access Security enables administrators to establish a security context or sandbox where code that originates from variety of sources can execute without compromising the security of the system. In other words, CAS is a solution that prevents untrustworthy code from performing privileged actions.

Code Access Security provides the following important benefits among many others:

- Prevents malicious code from accessing protected resources and performing protected operations
- Prevents malicious code from using trustworthy code to access protected resources and operations
- Prevents a bug in trustworthy code from getting unauthorized access to protected resources and operations
- Enables users to execute code originating from a variety of untrustworthy sources within a security sandbox established by the local security policy

- Allows you to trust code to varying degrees based on the identity of the code, which also includes the location where the code originated. In other words, the trust is not all or nothing. There are degrees of trust based on the identity of the code. This minimizes the amount of code that you have to fully trust.
- Minimizes the likelihood that malicious code can take advantage of the vulnerabilities of your trustworthy code because you can explicitly specify not only what permissions your code must be granted to operate properly but also what permission your code should never be granted. This reduces your liability.

As you'll see in this chapter, CAS plays a fundamental role in SharePoint Web part solutions. This chapter provides in-depth coverage of CAS and shows how to take advantage of it in your own code.

What CAS Provides

Code Access Security (CAS) enables you to do the following:

- Define individual permissions or permission sets for accessing various protected resources and operations.
- Define code groups where each code group is assigned a specific permission set. Each code group explicitly specifies a code membership condition that the given code must meet in order to be a member of the group. All code members of a code group have the permissions specified in the permission set assigned to the code group.
- Request the runtime security system to grant your assembly specified permissions or permission sets. Keep in mind that an assembly is the unit of security in the .NET Framework. The runtime grants permission to assemblies, not individual classes, methods, events, or properties in the assembly. As such, security requests are always made at the assembly level. Keep in mind that just because an assembly makes a security request does not mean that the runtime security system will grant the assembly the requested permissions. The runtime security system uses the local security policy to determine whether to grant the assembly the requested permissions.
- As you'll see later in this chapter, an assembly can make the following three types of security requests:
    - **Minimal.** An assembly makes a minimal security request to let the runtime know that the assembly cannot operate properly without requested permissions. This enables the runtime to determine whether to load the assembly into memory. The runtime will not load the assembly if the local security policy does not allow the assembly to have the requested permissions. This is a great way to catch problems at load time as opposed to runtime. As such, your Web part assembly should explicitly make minimal security requests for permissions that they have to have to operate properly. This will enable you to catch the security problems at load time.
    - **Optional.** An assembly makes an optional security request to let the runtime know that the assembly can still operate properly without the requested permissions. The runtime will still load the assembly even if the local security policy does not allow the assembly to have the requested optional permissions. When the assembly finally attempts to access the protected resource or operation for which it does not have the permission, the runtime will throw a security exception. As a best practice, your code must catch these security exceptions and handle them accordingly.

- **Refuse.** An assembly makes a refuse security request to let the runtime know that the assembly must never be granted the specified permissions. This enables you to prevent malicious code from taking advantage of the vulnerabilities of your code to access protected resources or operations. It also prevents bugs in your code to cause it to access these resources or operations to do things that it should not do. The runtime will not grant your code the permissions even if the local security policy allows your code to have these permissions.

- Grant your assemblies the minimum permissions they need to operate properly. As mentioned earlier, an assembly can request the runtime to be granted specified permissions or permission sets. The runtime uses the local security policy to determine whether to grant the assembly the requested permissions. Therefore, if you know that your assembly cannot operate properly without the specified permissions, you can use Code Access Security to add entries for your assembly to the local security policy so your assembly is granted the minimum permissions it needs to operate properly. As you'll see later, the local security policy grants permissions to code groups. In other words, the unit of security at the local security policy level is a code group, not an assembly. That said, you could set the code membership condition of a code group so that the code group only contains a single assembly. As a matter of fact, this is how SharePoint creates the code groups that it needs to add to the local security policy from the solution package. This is discussed further later in this book.
- Demand the callers of your classes and class members to have specific permissions or permission sets before they can call into your classes and their members. This reduces your liability by preventing less trusted code to use your code to access protected resources or operations for which they are not granted the required permissions. At runtime, when a piece of code attempts to access your code, the runtime security system walks the call stack and compares the granted permissions of each caller in the stack to the demanded permissions. If even one caller in the call stack does not have the demanded permissions, the runtime security system throws a security exception and prevents the caller from accessing your code.

It is very important to realize that every piece of managed code goes through the runtime security system's security checks. It is ultimately the local security policy on the local machine that determines which permissions an assembly is granted. Because different machines are bound to have different local security policies you can never know whether your assembly will be granted the permissions that it needs to operate properly. The same assembly that runs perfect on the development box may fail measurably on the deployment box because these two computers have two different local security policies.

You should not assume that the local security policy will grant the permissions that your assembly needs. As a best practice, you should always target for the minimum trust level. The minimum trust level in WSS is known as WSS_Minimal. You should never assume that the deployment box will have the WSS_Medium trust level, which is the next trust level after the WSS_Minimal trust level. If your assembly must have certain permissions, you should explicitly add entries for your assembly to the local security policy when deploying your assembly.

Security Syntax

As discussed earlier, your code needs to make security requests to be granted specific permissions and to make security demands to its caller to have or *not* have specific permissions. This means that your code needs to interact with the runtime security system. The .NET Framework provides two types of security syntax that your code can use to interact with the runtime security system, as discussed in the following sections.

Declarative Security Syntax

Every permission or permission set is represented by a security metadata attribute with which you can annotate your assemblies, classes, and class members to make a security request or demand. For example, the following permissions are represented by the SharePointPermissionAttribute metadata attribute:

- Permission to access the SharePoint object model
- Permission to impersonate
- Permission to save to database on Get requests

As you can see, a security metadata attribute could represent more than one permission. A security metadata attribute normally exposes properties. You must set these properties to specify which of the permissions that the security metadata attribute represents you're interested in. For example, the SharePointPermission metadata attribute exposes the following Boolean properties:

- **ObjectModel.** Set this property to true to make a security request or demand for accessing the SharePoint object model.
- **Impersonate.** Set this property to true to make a security request or demand for impersonation.
- **UnSafeSaveOnGet.** Set this property to true to make a security request or demand for saving to database on Get requests.

Every security metadata attribute also takes a SecurityAction enumeration value as its argument. Pass the appropriate SecurityAction enumeration value into a security metadata attribute to specify the type of security call. Listing 11-1 presents the definition of the SecurityAction enumeration type.

Listing 11-1: The SecurityAction enumeration type

```
[Serializable, ComVisible(true)]
public enum SecurityAction
{
  Assert = 3,
  Demand = 2,
  Deny = 4,
  InheritanceDemand = 7,
  LinkDemand = 6,
  PermitOnly = 5,
  RequestMinimum = 8,
  RequestOptional = 9,
  RequestRefuse = 10
}
```

Here are the descriptions of these enumeration values:

- **Assert.** Use this SecurityAction enumeration value to tell the runtime that if the callers of your code have the permissions represented by the security metadata attribute they should be allowed to access your code regardless of whether callers higher in the call stack have these permissions. This is used in what is known as security overrides, which are rarely used and are not covered in this book.

- **Demand.** Use this SecurityAction enumeration value to tell the runtime to walk the call stack to ensure that all callers in the stack have the permissions represented by the security metadata attribute. The runtime will throw an exception and deny access to your code if even one caller in the call stack does not have these permissions.
- **Deny.** Use this SecurityAction enumeration value to tell the runtime to deny access to the resources or operations (specified by the security metadata attribute) to the caller even if the caller has been granted the permissions represented by the security metadata attribute.
- **InheritanceDemand.** Annotate your class with a security metadata attribute and pass this SecurityAction enumeration value into the attribute to tell the runtime that a class must have the permissions represented by the security metadata attribute to inherit from your class. Or annotate a virtual member of your class with a security metadata attribute and pass this SecurityAction enumeration value into the attribute to tell the runtime that a subclass must have the permissions represented by the security metadata attribute to override this method.
- **LinkDemand.** Use this SecurityAction enumeration value to tell the runtime that the immediate caller must have the permissions represented by the security metadata attribute. The main difference between Demand and LinkDemand is that contrary to Demand, LinkDemand does not cause the runtime to walk the call stack.
- **PermitOnly.** Use this SecurityAction enumeration value to tell the runtime that only resources and operations specified by this security metadata attribute can be accessed. The runtime will not allow access to any other resources and operations even if the code is granted the permissions to do so.
- **RequestMinimum.** Use this SecurityAction enumeration value to tell the runtime that your assembly must be granted the permissions represented by this security metadata attribute to operate properly. The runtime will not load your assembly if the local security policy does not grant your assembly the requested permissions.
- **RequestOptional.** Use this SecurityAction enumeration value to tell the runtime that your assembly can still operate properly even if the permissions represented by this security metadata attribute are not granted. The runtime grants your assembly these optional permissions if the local security policy allows it. However, if the local security policy does not allow your assembly to have these optional permissions, the runtime will still load your assembly but it will throw a security exception if your assembly attempts to access the protected resources or operations for which it is not granted the required permissions. As a best practice, your code should catch these security exceptions and handle them accordingly.

  This SecurityAction enumeration value has a side effect. Because you use this SecurityAction enumeration value to specify optional permissions, the runtime assumes that your assembly does not need other permissions. By using this SecurityAction enumeration value, you're indirectly telling the runtime that your assembly must not be granted permissions that are not specified in this security metadata attribute.
- **RequestRefuse.** Use this SecurityAction enumeration value to tell the runtime that your assembly must never be granted the permissions represented by this security metadata attribute even if the local security policy allows your assembly to have these permissions.

You can use the declarative security syntax to make both security requests and security demands.

You can also use this syntax to make security overrides. Security overrides are rarely used and are beyond the scope of this book.

Security requests are always made at the assembly level. Here is an example:

```
[assembly : SharePointPermission(SecurityAction.RequestMinimum, ObjectModel=true,
Impersonate=true, UnSafeSaveOnGet=true)]
```

This assembly-level security metadata attribute requests the runtime to grant the assembly the permission to access the SharePoint object model, the permission to impersonate, and the permission to save to the database on the Get requests. Note that the SecurityAction.RequestMinimum enumeration value has been passed into this attribute to tell the runtime that this assembly will not operate properly without these three permissions. This means that the runtime will not load this assembly into memory if the local security policy does not allow the assembly to be granted these three permissions.

Where should assembly-level security metadata attributes go? You have two options. You can add this on top of any source code file in your project. Or you can add it to the AssemblyInfo.cs file of your project. The AssemblyInfo.cs file is the recommended place for assembly-level attributes.

Imperative Security Syntax

Every permission or permission set is represented by a permission class. The imperative security syntax can be used to make security demands and overrides but not requests. Security requests can only be made at the assembly level using assembly-level security metadata attributes.

Because imperative security demands are made within your managed code, the first order of business is to determine where to place this security demand in your code. The runtime will not allow the code following a security demand to execute if the code does not have the permissions that the permission object represents. Therefore, you should insert the security demand right before the code that you want to protect. Here is an example:

```
public void MyMethod()
{
  ...
  SharePointPermission perm =
                       new SharePointPermission(PermissionState.Unrestricted);
  perm.ObjectModel = true;
  perm.Demand();
  SPWeb site = SPContext.Current.Web;
  ...
}
```

The code that follows the call into the Demand method will be executed only if all the callers in the call stack are granted the permission to access the SharePoint object model. Note that this security demand has no impact on the code that comes before the call into the Demand method. The situation would be different if you were to use the declarative security syntax to annotate MyMethod with the SharePointPermissionAttribute metadata attribute:

```
 [SharePointPermission(SecurityAction.Demand, ObjectModel=true, Unrestricted=true)]
public void MyMethod()
{
  ...
  SPWeb site = SPContext.Current.Web;
  ...
}
```

In this case, the whole MyMethod method including the code that comes before the call into the SPContext.Current.Web and the code that comes after it is protected. In other words, only if all the callers in the call stack are granted the permission to access the SharePoint object model would the runtime allow the access to this method. The imperative security syntax allows more granular control over what gets protected. For example, in this case you may not need to protect the code that comes before the SPContext.Current.Web.

These steps need to be taken in order to use the imperative security syntax:

- Identify the code that you need to protect.
- Identify the permission class that represents the permissions that you want to demand the callers to have.
- Instantiate an instance of the permission class right before the code that you want to protect.
- Set the appropriate properties of this permission object. Recall that a permission object may represent more than one permission. You need to set the appropriate properties of the permission object to specify which permissions your callers must have to access the code.
- Invoke the Demand method on the permission object. The call into the Demand method causes the runtime security check to occur where the runtime walks the call stack. What happens to the code that follows the call into the Demand method depends on two factors. One factor is whether or not the runtime security check fails. If it does, the runtime will throw an exception. Another factor is whether you have encapsulated the call into the Demand method in a try block and whether you're catching the security exception that the runtime raises. If you do indeed catch the exception and handle it accordingly, the code following the call into the Demand method could run as is.

GAC versus Bin

Any assembly deployed to the Global Assembly Cache (GAC) executes with full trust. Any assembly deployed to the local bin directory of a SharePoint web application executes within the security context (also known as sandbox) established by the local code access security policy. As such, the code that runs from the local bin directory of a web application is only allowed to access resources and perform operations for which it has been granted the required permissions. Follow these best code access security practices in your own applications:

- Deploy your Web part assemblies to the local bin directory of your web application as opposed to the GAC to ensure that your Web parts only access protected resources and perform protected operations for which they have been granted permissions.
- If you have one or more Web parts that require more permissions than others, compile these Web parts in their own assembly and grant this assembly higher permissions as opposed to putting all your Web parts in one assembly and granting this big assembly higher permissions. Keep in mind that assembly is the unit of security.

- If you have an assembly that requires a higher level of trust, you should grant that assembly the permission it needs as opposed to raising the local trust level because raising the local trust level raises the trust level for all assemblies in the bin directory. This will all be clear by the end of this chapter.
- As you have seen throughout this book, certain SharePoint components such as feature receivers and event receivers must be deployed to the GAC. If your SharePoint solution contains these components plus Web parts, you should compile your Web parts in a separate assembly so you can deploy them to the local bin directory of your web application where you can benefit from the local code access security policy.
- Your clients should be able to deploy your Web part assemblies to the bin directory of their web applications where the WSS_Minimal trust level is used. If you have a Web part assembly that requires more permissions, you must explicitly grant these permissions through custom code access security settings. This will enable your assembly to run under the WSS_Minimal trust level. Your assembly should not expect the trust level to be higher than WSS_Minimal.

Security Demands

If your code accesses a protected resource or operation and if you're concerned that unauthorized code may use your code to access this protected resource or operation, your code should demand its callers to have or not have a specific permission or permission set to call your code. Note that you could make a security demand for callers *not* to have a specific permission or set of permissions. For example, if your code reads a file but does not update it and if you're concerned that a caller may use your code to update the file, you can demand the caller not to have the write access to the file to reduce your liability.

A security demand can be applied to:

- A class to demand that the callers have the specified permissions to perform the following tasks:
    - Instantiate the class.
    - Access the members of the class. You can apply a security demand to a class to protect all members of the class.
    - Inherit from the class.
- A method in a class to demand the callers to have the specified permissions to perform the following tasks:
    - Call the method (Demand or LinkDemand)
    - Override the method (InheritanceDemand)
- A property in a class to demand the callers to have the specified permissions to perform the following tasks:
    - Call the getter of the property
    - Call the setter of the property
    - Override the property
    - An event in a class.

Note that you cannot use security demands to protect assemblies or fields in a class. As you can see, if you have a field in a class that you need to protect, you should turn it into a property. If you apply a security demand to a class, it applies to all members of the class. If you apply a security demand to a member of a class, it only applies to that member and will override the security demands applied to the class. Here is an example:

```
[SharePointPermission(SecurityAction.Demand, ObjectModel=true)]
public class MyClass
{
  [SharePointPermission(SecurityAction.LinkDemand, Impersonate=true)]
  public void MyMethod()
  {
    ...
  }

  public void MyOtherMethod()
  {
    ...
  }

  public string MyProperty
  {
    get { ... }
    set { ... }
  }
}
```

In this example, all callers of the MyOtherMethod and MyProperty members in the call stack are demanded to have permission to access the SharePoint object model. This does not apply to the callers of the MyMethod method because this method specifies its own security requirements, which overrides the security requirements specified at the class level. MyMethod demands its immediate callers to have the permission to impersonate. It does not demand them to have the permission to access the SharePoint object model.

In general there are three types of security demands that are discussed in the following sections: Demand, LinkDemand, and InheritanceDemand. All security demands cause the runtime to walk the call stack to perform security checks on all callers in the stack. The only exception to this rule is LinkDemand, which causes the runtime to perform a security check only on the immediate caller.

Demand

This type of security demand causes the runtime security system to walk the call stack and check the granted permissions of all callers to ensure that every single caller in the call stack has the demanded permission. This helps prevent luring attacks, which happen when a less-trusted code calls highly trusted code to access a protected resource or operation for which the less-trusted code does not have the demanded permission. Here is an example. Method A calls Method B, which demands its caller to have permission Perm 1. Because Method A has been granted the Perm 1 permission it can access Method B. Now imagine a Method C, which has not been granted the Perm 1 permission, calls Method A, which in turn calls Method B. Because the runtime security system walks the call stack, it finds out that Method C has not been granted the permission. As such, the runtime security system does not allow Method A to call into Method B and raises the SecurityException exception.

There are two ways to make a security demand: declarative and imperative. The declarative approach requires you to take these steps to secure a class, a method in a class, an event in a class, or a property in a class:

1. Annotate the class, method, event, or property with the permission metadata attribute that represents the permission that you want to demand the callers to have or not to have.
2. Pass the enumeration value of SecurityAction. Demand as an argument into this permission metadata attribute.
3. Set the appropriate properties of the permission metadata attribute. A permission metadata attribute may represent a bunch of permissions where each permission is associated with a property. You need to set these properties to specify which permissions you want to demand.

The imperative approach can only be used inside a method or property. It cannot be used on a class or a member as a whole.

Most .NET classes make the appropriate security demands. As such, you should not make the same security demands to protect access to these .NET classes. Doing so would trigger redundant call stack walks. You should make security demands to protect custom resources and operations. For example, the SPWebApplication class is annotated with two instances of the SharePointPermission metadata attribute:

```
[SharePointPermission(SecurityAction.InheritanceDemand, ObjectModel=true),
SharePointPermission(SecurityAction.LinkDemand, ObjectModel=true)]
public class SPWebApplication : SPPersistedUpgradableObject,
                                IBackupRestore, IMigratable
{
   ...
}
```

The first permission metadata attribute demands the subclasses of the SPWebApplication class to have the permission to access the SharePoint object model. The second permission metadata attribute demands the immediate callers of this class to have the permission to access the SharePoint object model. If your code accesses the SPWebApplication class, you do not need to make the same security demands. Note that the SPWebApplication class only demands its immediate callers to have the permission to access the SharePoint object model. It does not demand other callers higher in the call stack to have the same permission. If your code is running in the environment where you're concerned about luring attacks where less trusted code may use your code to access the SPWebApplication class, you can make a security demand for all callers in the stack using the SecurityAction.Demand option.

Link Demand

Making a link demand does not cause a call stack walk. The actual security check is performed at the just-in-time compilation phase where the direct links to your code such as method calls are examined to determine whether the direct caller has the specified permissions. If not, a security exception is raised at load time.

Inheritance Demand

An inheritance demand can only be specified declaratively and only applies to classes and nonstatic class members. When an attempt is made to execute a class that inherits from a class protected by an inheritance demand, the runtime performs a security check to determine whether the derived class has been granted the demanded permissions. If not, the runtime will not allow the derived class to run.

Security Requests

As a best practice, your assembly should make security requests for the permissions that it needs. Security requests must be made at the assembly level using the declarative syntax. They cannot be made at the class or class member level. They cannot be made using the imperative approach either. The compiler stores the security requests made through these assembly-level permission metadata attributes into the assembly manifest. At load time, the runtime accesses this metadata and uses the local security policy to determine whether to grant your assembly the requested permissions.

Technically speaking your assembly does not have to make security requests. However, doing so provides the following important benefits among many others:

- The assembly that makes security requests for the minimum permissions that it needs to operate properly will not run unless it is granted these minimum permissions. If the assembly is running, it has been granted these permissions. This means that you don't have to litter your code with unnecessary security checks to determine whether your code has been granted these permissions. This also means that you don't have to litter your code with unnecessary catch blocks that handle security exceptions because the runtime allows your code to execute only after it is granted these minimum permissions.
- If the assembly that explicitly requests the permissions that it needs and the permissions that it must not be granted is misused by malicious code or misbehaves due to a bug, it cannot perform unauthorized access to the protected resources and operations because it simply does not have the permissions to do so.
- The assembly that explicitly requests the permissions that it needs makes it possible for the administrators to add the required entries to the local security policy to grant the assembly these minimum permissions if they choose to do so. Otherwise, there would be no way for administrators to know what permissions the assembly needs to operate properly.

Keep in mind that making a security request has absolutely no effect on whether the runtime will grant the specified permissions to the assembly. It can only make the runtime not to grant permissions. It is only the local security policy that determines whether an assembly should be granted the requested permissions.

In general there are three types of security requests: minimum, optional, and refuse. These security request types are discussed in the following sections.

Minimum

Pass the SecurityAction.RequestMinimum enumeration value into an assembly-level permission metadata attribute to tell the runtime that the assembly needs the permissions that the permission metadata attribute represents to run. The runtime will not run the assembly if the assembly cannot be granted these minimum permissions.

One of the great things about the SecurityAction.RequestMinimum option is that your assembly will still be granted all the permissions that the local security policy allows your assembly to have even though your assembly did not specifically request all of these permissions. In other words, this option does not deprive your assembly from getting all the permissions that the local security policy allows your assembly to have. It can only specify which permissions are required at the minimum.

Here is an example:

```
[assembly : SharePointPermission(SecurityAction.RequestMinimum, ObjectModel=true)]
```

Optional

Pass the SecurityAction.RequestOptional enumeration value into an assembly-level permission metadata attribute to tell the runtime that your assembly needs the permissions that the permission metadata attribute represents but it can run without them. At load time, the runtime grants these permissions to your assembly if the local security policy allows your assembly to have these permissions. However, the runtime will allow your assembly to run even if your assembly is not granted these optional permissions. When your assembly finally attempts to access the protected resources or operations for which it was not granted the optional permissions, the runtime will throw a security exception. Because your assembly specifies these permissions as optional and consequently tells the runtime to allow your assembly to run even when it is not granted these permissions, you have to use catch blocks in your code to catch the security exceptions that the runtime throws. This is very different from the SecurityAction.RequestMinimum option where you don't need to litter your code with such catch blocks because the runtime will not allow your code to run if it is not granted the requested permissions.

One downside of the SecurityAction.RequestOptional option is that it implicitly tells the runtime not to grant your assembly those permissions that are not explicitly requested even though the local security policy allows your assembly to have those permissions. When you use the SecurityAction .RequestOptional option to specify the optional permissions, you should also use the Security Action.RequestMinimum option to specify the required permissions. Otherwise, your assembly will only be granted the requested optional permissions if the local security policy allows your assembly to have these permissions.

Here is an example of the optional security request:

```
[assembly : SharePointPermission(SecurityAction.RequestOptional, ObjectModel=true)]
```

Refuse

Pass the SecurityAction.RequestRefuse enumeration value into an assembly-level permission metadata attribute to tell the runtime that your assembly must not be granted the permissions that the permission metadata attribute represents. The runtime will not grant your assembly these permissions even if the local security policy allows your assembly to have these permissions.

Here is the idea behind the SecurityAction.RequestRefuse option. As discussed earlier, it is the local security policy that determines what permissions an assembly can be granted. As such, your assembly may be granted permissions that it does not need. Malicious code can easily exploit these unnecessary permissions to do damage through your code. As a best practice, you should identify the permissions that your assembly does not need and that malicious code could exploit and use the SecurityAction .RequestRefuse option to tell the runtime that your assembly mustn't be granted these permissions.

Here is an example of the SecurityAction.RequestRefuse option:

```
[assembly : SharePointPermission(SecurityAction.RequestRefuse, ObjectModel=true)]
```

So far we've discussed how to use the three types of security requests, that is, minimum, optional, and refuse, to make security requests for individual permissions. Another option is to make these three types of security requests for what is known as named permission sets. As the name suggests, a named permission set is a named set of permissions. The .NET Framework comes with these standard named permission sets: Nothing, Execution, FullTrust, Internet, LocalIntranet, and SkipVerification. You must use the PermissionSetAttribute assembly-level permission metadata attribute to make a security request for a named permission set. Here is an example:

```
[assembly : PermissionSetAttribute(SecurityAction.RequestMinimum,Name="Execution")]
```

As you can see, the PermissionSetAttribute permission metadata attribute supports a property named Name that must be set to the name of the named permission set. This property can only be assigned the name of a standard named permission set.

Granting Permissions

The previous two sections discussed security demands and requests. As you saw, an assembly should make security requests for minimum permissions that it needs to run, optional permissions, and permissions that it must never be granted. Security requests for minimum and optional permissions do not influence the runtime in any way to give the assembly the requested permissions. It is the local security policy that determines what permissions can be granted to an assembly. The local security policy is implemented in configuration files known as policy files, which are located in the following folder in the file system of each front-end web server:

```
Local_Drive:\Program Files\Common Files\microsoft shared\Web Server Extensions\12\
CONFIG
```

Each policy file specifies a set of permissions that each code group can be granted. As the name suggests, a code group specifies a group of code. This enables system administrators to group code based on some grouping criteria and grant each group a specific set of permissions. To help you understand the structure of a policy file, examine wss_minimaltrust.config, which is one of the policy files that comes with a typical WSS installation. This policy file, like any other policy file, is located in the 12\CONFIG folder. Listing 11-2 presents this policy file.

Listing 11-2: The wss_minimaltrust.config policy file

```
<configuration>
  <mscorlib>
    <security>
      <policy>
        <PolicyLevel version="1">
          <SecurityClasses>
            <SecurityClass
            Name="AllMembershipCondition"
            Description="System.Security.Policy.AllMembershipCondition, mscorlib,
Version=2.0.0.0, Culture=neutral, PublicKeyToken=b77a5c561934e089"/>
            <SecurityClass
            Name="AspNetHostingPermission"
            Description="System.Web.AspNetHostingPermission, System,
Version=2.0.0.0, Culture=neutral, PublicKeyToken=b77a5c561934e089"/>
            <SecurityClass
            Name="FirstMatchCodeGroup"
            Description="System.Security.Policy.FirstMatchCodeGroup, mscorlib,
Version=2.0.0.0, Culture=neutral, PublicKeyToken=b77a5c561934e089"/>
            <SecurityClass
            Name="NamedPermissionSet"
            Description="System.Security.NamedPermissionSet"/>
            <SecurityClass
            Name="SecurityPermission"
            Description="System.Security.Permissions.SecurityPermission, mscorlib,
Version=2.0.0.0, Culture=neutral, PublicKeyToken=b77a5c561934e089"/>
            <SecurityClass
            Name="StrongNameMembershipCondition"
            Description="System.Security.Policy.StrongNameMembershipCondition,
mscorlib, Version=2.0.0.0, Culture=neutral, PublicKeyToken=b77a5c561934e089"/>
            <SecurityClass
            Name="UnionCodeGroup"
            Description="System.Security.Policy.UnionCodeGroup, mscorlib,
Version=2.0.0.0, Culture=neutral, PublicKeyToken=b77a5c561934e089"/>
            <SecurityClass
            Name="UrlMembershipCondition"
            Description="System.Security.Policy.UrlMembershipCondition, mscorlib,
Version=2.0.0.0, Culture=neutral, PublicKeyToken=b77a5c561934e089"/>
            <SecurityClass
            Name="WebPartPermission"
            Description="Microsoft.SharePoint.Security.WebPartPermission,
Microsoft.SharePoint.Security, Version=12.0.0.0, Culture=neutral,
PublicKeyToken=71e9bce111e9429c"/>
            <SecurityClass
            Name="ZoneMembershipCondition"
            Description="System.Security.Policy.ZoneMembershipCondition, mscorlib,
 Version=2.0.0.0, Culture=neutral, PublicKeyToken=b77a5c561934e089"/>
          </SecurityClasses>
```

```
<NamedPermissionSets>
  <PermissionSet
  class="NamedPermissionSet"
  version="1"
  Unrestricted="true"
  Name="FullTrust"
  Description="Allows full access to all resources" />
  <PermissionSet
  class="NamedPermissionSet"
  version="1"
  Name="Nothing"
  Description="Denies all resources, including the right to execute" />
  <PermissionSet
  class="NamedPermissionSet"
  version="1"
  Name="SPRestricted">
    <IPermission
    class="AspNetHostingPermission"
    version="1"
    Level="Minimal" />
    <IPermission
    class="SecurityPermission"
    version="1"
    Flags="Execution" />
    <IPermission class="WebPartPermission"
    version="1"
    Connections="True" />
  </PermissionSet>
</NamedPermissionSets>
<CodeGroup
class="FirstMatchCodeGroup"
version="1"
PermissionSetName="Nothing">
  <IMembershipCondition
  class="AllMembershipCondition"
  version="1" />
  <CodeGroup
  class="UnionCodeGroup"
  version="1"
  PermissionSetName="FullTrust">
    <IMembershipCondition
    class="UrlMembershipCondition"
    version="1"
    Url="$AppDirUrl$/_app_bin/*" />
  </CodeGroup>
  <CodeGroup
  class="UnionCodeGroup"
  version="1"
  PermissionSetName="SPRestricted">
    <IMembershipCondition
    class="UrlMembershipCondition"
    version="1"
    Url="$AppDirUrl$/*" />
  </CodeGroup>
```

(continued)

Listing 11-2 *(continued)*

```
            <CodeGroup
            class="UnionCodeGroup"
            version="1"
            PermissionSetName="FullTrust">
              <IMembershipCondition
              class="UrlMembershipCondition"
              version="1"
              Url="$CodeGen$/*" />
            </CodeGroup>
            <CodeGroup class="UnionCodeGroup" version="1" PermissionSetName="Nothing">
              <IMembershipCondition
              class="ZoneMembershipCondition"
              version="1"
              Zone="MyComputer" />
              <CodeGroup
              class="UnionCodeGroup"
              version="1"
              PermissionSetName="FullTrust"
              Name="Microsoft_Strong_Name"
              Description="This code group grants code signed with the Microsoft
strong name full trust. ">
                <IMembershipCondition
                class="StrongNameMembershipCondition"
                version="1"
PublicKeyBlob="002400000480000094000000060200000024000052534131000400000100010007D1FA5
7C4AED9F0A32E84AA0FAEFD0DE9E8FD6AEC8F87FB03766C834C99921EB23BE79AD9D5DCC1DD9AD23613
2102900B723CF980957FC4E177108FC607774F29E8320E92EA05ECE4E821C0A5EFE8F1645C4C0C93C1A
B99285D622CAA652C1DFAD63D745D6F2DE5F17E5EAF0FC4963D261C8A12436518206DC093344D5AD293"/>
              </CodeGroup>
              <CodeGroup
              class="UnionCodeGroup"
              version="1"
              PermissionSetName="FullTrust"
              Name="Ecma_Strong_Name"
              Description="This code group grants code signed with the ECMA strong
name full trust. ">
                <IMembershipCondition
                class="StrongNameMembershipCondition"
                version="1"
                PublicKeyBlob="00000000000000000400000000000000" />
              </CodeGroup>
            </CodeGroup>
          </CodeGroup>
        </PolicyLevel>
      </policy>
    </security>
  </mscorlib>
</configuration>
```

As you can see from Listing 11-2, the code access security policy is specified in an element named <PolicyLevel>, which contains three child elements named <SecurityClasses>, <NamedPermissionSets>, and <CodeGroup>:

```
<PolicyLevel version="1">
  <SecurityClasses>
    ...
  </SecurityClasses>
  <NamedPermissionSets>
    ...  </NamedPermissionSets>
  <CodeGroup>
    ...
  </CodeGroup>
</PolicyLevel>
```

The <SecurityClasses> element is where the security classes are declared. Each security class is declared in a separate <SecurityClass> child element of the <SecurityClasses> element. The <SecurityClass> supports two attributes named Name and Description. The Name attribute provides a friendly name for the security class and the Description attribute contains the fully assembly namespace–qualified name of the security class. The rest of the policy file uses this friendly name to refer to the security class. For example, the following <SecurityClass> declares the AllMembershipCondition security class:

```
<SecurityClasses>
  <SecurityClass
  Name="AllMembershipCondition"
  Description="System.Security.Policy.AllMembershipCondition, mscorlib,
Version=2.0.0.0, Culture=neutral, PublicKeyToken=b77a5c561934e089"/>
  ...
</SecurityClasses>
```

The <NamedPermissionSets> element is where the permission sets for code groups are defined. Each named permission set is defined in a separate <PermissionSet> element. This element supports the following important attributes:

- **class.** This specifies a security class for the permission set. This is basically the friendly name of a security class declared in the <SecurityClasses> element. Set this to NamedPermissionSet because we're defining a named permission set.
- **version.** This specifies a version for the named permission set.
- **Name.** This specifies a name for the permission set. As you'll see later, the web.config file of a SharePoint web application uses this name to reference the permission set.
- **Description.** This specifies a short description for the permission set.

The <PermissionSet> element supports zero or more <IPermission> child elements. Each <IPermission> child element defines a permission. The <IPermission> child element supports the following attributes:

- **class.** This specifies the security class that represents the permission. This is the friendly name of a security class declared in the <SecurityClasses> element.
- **version.** This specifies a version for the permission.

As Listing 11-2 shows, the wss_minimaltrust.config file defines a permission set named SPRestricted as follows:

```
<PermissionSet
class="NamedPermissionSet"
version="1"
Name="SPRestricted">

  <IPermission
  class="AspNetHostingPermission"
  version="1"
  Level="Minimal" />

  <IPermission
  class="SecurityPermission"
  version="1"
  Flags="Execution" />

  <IPermission class="WebPartPermission"
  version="1"
  Connections="True" />

</PermissionSet>
```

As you can see, the SPRestricted permission set contains three permissions, which are represented by the AspNetHostingPermission, SecurityPermission, and WebPartPermission security classes. The Level property on the AspNetHostingPermission security class is set to Minimal to grant the respective code groups the minimal level of ASP.NET hosting permission. The Flags property on the SecurityPermission security class is set to Execution to grant the respective code groups the permission to execute. The Connections property on the WebPartPermission security class is set to True to grant the respective code group the permission for Web part to Web part connections.

As Listing 11-2 shows, the <CodeGroup> element is the root of a hierarchy of code groups. Each code group in this hierarchy is represented by a separate <CodeGroup> element. The <CodeGroup> element supports the following attributes:

- **class.** This specifies the security class that determines the type of code group. This is the friendly name of a security class declared in the <SecurityClasses> element.
- **version.** This specifies a version for the code group.
- **PermissionSetName.** This specifies a permission set for the code group. This is the value of the Name attribute of a <PermissionSet> child element in the <PermissionSets> element. This means that the code group is granted the permissions specified in the permission set.

The <CodeGroup> element supports a single <IMembershipCondition> child element and one or more <CodeGroup> child elements. The <IMembershipCondition> element specifies the condition that given code must meet to be a member of the code group. The permission set whose name is specified in the PermissionSetName attribute is granted to all members of the code group.

As mentioned, code groups form a hierarchy of code groups with a single root code group. The CLR begins with the top of the code group hierarchy. The root code group hierarchy in Listing 11-2 is the FirstMatchCodeGroup code group. Note that this code group uses the AllMembershipCondition membership condition. This condition matches every code group, hence the name FirstMatchCodeGroup. The PermissionSetName attribute on the root code group is set to Nothing, which is the name of the permission set that grants no permissions to the code group, not even the permission to execute. This means that every code group originally has no permissions.

```
<CodeGroup
class="FirstMatchCodeGroup"
version="1"
PermissionSetName="Nothing">
  <IMembershipCondition
  class="AllMembershipCondition"
  version="1" />
```

The root code group contains four UnionCodeGroup code groups. The first UnionCodeGroup code group uses the UrlMembershipCondition membership condition with the Url property value of $AppDirUrl$/_app_bin/*. This basically specifies that any code that originates from the _app_bin folder of the web application is a member of this code group. This folder is located in the root directory of each web application, which is normally the following folder in the file system of each front-end web server in the server farm:

```
Local_Drive:\inetpub\wwwroot\wss\VirtualDirectories\WebApplicationName
```

The $AppDirUrl$ maps to this root folder. If you check out the _app_bin folder, you'll see that it contains the following assemblies:

- Microsoft.Office.DocumentManagement.Pages.dll
- Microsoft.Office.officialfileSoap.dll
- Microsoft.Office.Policy.Pages.dll
- Microsoft.Office.SlideLibrarySoap.dll
- Microsoft.Office.Workflow.Pages.dll
- Microsoft.Office.WorkflowSoap.dll
- Microsoft.SharePoint.ApplicationPages.dll

The code that these assemblies contain is a member of this UnionCodeGroup code group. As Listing 11-2 shows, the PermissionSetName attribute on this code group is set to FullTrust. This means that the members of this code group, that is, the preceding assemblies, are fully trusted. The _app_bin folder is for SharePoint infrastructural assemblies. You should not add custom assemblies to this folder.

```
<CodeGroup
class="UnionCodeGroup"
version="1"
PermissionSetName="FullTrust">
  <IMembershipCondition
  class="UrlMembershipCondition"
  version="1"
  Url="$AppDirUrl$/_app_bin/*" />
</CodeGroup>
```

The second UnionCodeGroup code group that the root code group contains uses the UrlMembershipCondition membership condition with the URL property value of $AppDirUrl$/*. This basically specifies that any code that originates from the root folder of the web application is a member of this code group. As Listing 11-2 shows, the PermissionSetName attribute on this code group is set to SPRestricted. This means that the members of this code group have the permissions specified in the SPRestricted permission set discussed earlier.

```
<CodeGroup
class="UnionCodeGroup"
version="1"
PermissionSetName="SPRestricted">
  <IMembershipCondition
  class="UrlMembershipCondition"
  version="1"
  Url="$AppDirUrl$/*" />
</CodeGroup>
```

Note that the members of the first UnionCodeGroup code group are also the members of the second UnionCodeGroup code group. This means that the members of the first UnionCodeGroup code group have the permissions that the members of the second code group have plus the permissions that their own code group grants them.

The third UnionCodeGroup code group that the root code group contains uses the UrlMembershipCondition membership condition with the URL attribute value of $CodeGen$/*. This basically specifies that any code that originates from this folder is a member of this group. As Listing 11-2 shows, the PermissionSetName attribute on this code group is set to FullTrust. This means that the members of this code group are fully trusted.

```
<CodeGroup
class="UnionCodeGroup"
version="1"
PermissionSetName="FullTrust">
  <IMembershipCondition
  class="UrlMembershipCondition"
  version="1"
  Url="$CodeGen$/*" />
</CodeGroup>
```

The fourth UnionCodeGroup code group that the root code group contains uses the ZoneMembershipCondition membership condition with the Zone attribute value of MyComputer. This basically specifies that any code that originates from this zone is a member of this group. As Listing 11-2 shows, the PermissionSetName attribute on this code group is set to Nothing. This means that the members of this code group have no permissions, not even the permission to execute.

```
<CodeGroup class="UnionCodeGroup" version="1" PermissionSetName="Nothing">
  <IMembershipCondition
  class="ZoneMembershipCondition"
  version="1"
  Zone="MyComputer" />
```

This code group contains two child code groups. The first child code group is UnionCodeGroup that uses the StrongNameMembershipCondition membership condition with the specified PublicKeyBlob property. This public key blob is basically the public key blob of assemblies signed with the Microsoft strong name.

This basically specifies that any code in any assembly signed with this strong name is a member of this code group. As Listing 11-2 shows, the PermissionSetName attribute on this code group is set to FullTrust. This means that the members of this code group are fully trusted. Keep in mind that the runtime traverses the code group hierarchy from top to bottom. This means that the code that belongs to this code group first passes the membership condition of the parent code group where the code gets no permissions at all (recall that the PermissionSetName attribute on the parent code group is set to Nothing). The code then passes the membership condition of this code group where it is granted full trust:

```
    <CodeGroup
    class="UnionCodeGroup"
    version="1"
    PermissionSetName="FullTrust"
    Name="Microsoft_Strong_Name"
    Description="This code group grants code signed with the Microsoft strong name
full trust. ">
      <IMembershipCondition
      class="StrongNameMembershipCondition"
      version="1"
PublicKeyBlob="002400000480000094000000060200000024000052534131000400000100010007D1FA
57C4AED9F0A32E84AA0FAEFD0DE9E8FD6AEC8F87FB03766C834C99921EB23BE79AD9D5DCC1DD9AD23613
2102900B723CF980957FC4E177108FC607774F29E8320E92EA05ECE4E821C0A5EFE8F1645C4C0C93C1AB
99285D622CAA652C1DFAD63D745D6F2DE5F17E5EAF0FC4963D261C8A12436518206DC09334D5AD293"/>
    </CodeGroup>
```

The second child code group is a UnionCodeGroup code group that uses the StrongNameMembershipCondition membership condition with the specified PublicKeyBlob property. This public key blob is basically the public key blob of assemblies signed with the ECMA strong name. This basically specifies that any code in any assembly signed with this strong name is a member of this code group. As Listing 11-2 shows, the PermissionSetName attribute on this code group is set to FullTrust. This means that the members of this code group are fully trusted:

```
    <CodeGroup
    class="UnionCodeGroup"
    version="1"
    PermissionSetName="FullTrust"
    Name="Ecma_Strong_Name"
    Description="This code group grants code signed with the ECMA strong name full
trust. ">
      <IMembershipCondition
      class="StrongNameMembershipCondition"
      version="1"
      PublicKeyBlob="00000000000000000400000000000000" />
    </CodeGroup>
```

As you can see, the CLR walks the code group hierarchy specified in the policy file from top to bottom to determine the code groups to which a given code belongs. Because each code group is granted a specified permission set, the CLR easily figures out the permission set granted to the code. The code can only have the permissions specified in the local policy file. The CLR will not grant the code any more permissions than specified in this file even if the code has requested these extra permissions.

The security policy file is only half the story. The second half is in the web.config file of the web application. As Listing 11-3 shows, this web.config file contains a configuration section named <securityPolicy>, which contains one or more <trustLevel> child elements.

Listing 11-3: The portion of the web.config file

```
<?xml version="1.0" encoding="UTF-8" standalone="yes"?>
<configuration>
  <system.web>
    <securityPolicy>
      <trustLevel name="WSS_Medium" policyFile="C:\Program Files\Common Files\
Microsoft Shared\Web Server Extensions\12\config\wss_mediumtrust.config" />
      <trustLevel name="WSS_Minimal" policyFile="C:\Program Files\Common Files\
Microsoft Shared\Web Server Extensions\12\config\wss_minimaltrust.config" />
      <trustLevel name="WSS_Custom" policyFile="C:\Program Files\Common Files\
Microsoft Shared\Web Server Extensions\12\config\wss_custom_wss_mediumtrust
.config" />
    </securityPolicy>
  </system.web>
  <trust level="WSS_Minimal" originUrl="" />
</configuration>
```

As the name suggests, each <trustLevel> element defines a trust level. The <trustLevel> element supports the following two attributes:

- **name.** This specifies a unique name for the trust level.
- **policyFile.** This specifies the full folder path to the policy file for the trust level.

As Listing 11-3 shows, the web.config file defines several trust levels. The question is which trust level is used. The answer lies in the <trust> element of the web.config file:

```
<trust level="WSS_Minimal" originUrl="" />
```

The <trust> element specifies the trust level that is used. This element supports an attribute named level, which is set to the name of the trust level. By default, this is set to the WSS_Minimal trust level for WSS installations. As Listing 11-3 shows, the wss_minimaltrust.config policy file discussed earlier in this section is the policy file for this trust level.

Following the discussions of this section, you should be able to implement your own custom security policy file to grant the assemblies that contain your custom Web parts the permissions that the custom Web parts need to operate properly. For example, if your custom Web parts need to access the SharePoint object model, the default WSS_Minimal trust level will not permit it. Therefore, you need to take these steps to grant your custom Web parts the required permission:

- Follow the discussions of this section to implement a policy file that grants your custom Web parts the permission to access the SharePoint object model.
- Add a new <trustLevel> element to the web.config file of the web application.
- Pick a unique name for your custom trust level and assign it to the name attribute on this <trustLevel> element.
- Set the policyFile attribute on this <trustLevel> element to the full folder path to your custom policy file.
- Assign the name of your custom trust level to the level attribute on the <trust> element.

Because this approach requires you to modify the web.config file, you should use the SPWebConfigModification class in managed code to modify this file as discussed earlier in this book. This ensures that these changes are propagated to:

- The web.config files of all IIS web sites, which map to the web application, in all existing front-end web servers in the server farm.
- The web.config files of all IIS web sites, which map to the web application, in all front-end web servers that will be added in the future.

The next chapter discusses the SharePoint deployment, where you learn how to add code access security entries to a solution manifest to have SharePoint automatically create the appropriate policy file for you. This saves you from having to modify the web.config file and create the policy file yourself. As such, you should always add your code access security settings to the solution manifest as opposed to creating the policy file yourself. The discussions of this section should put you in a much better position to understand the structure of the code access security entries that you need to add to a solution manifest.

AllowPartiallyTrustedCallersAttribute

When you strong-name an assembly, .NET automatically places a LinkDemand for FullTrust on every public or protected method on every publicly accessible class in the assembly. This means that the CLR will only allow fully trusted callers to call into the public or protected methods of the publicly accessible classes in the assembly. As discussed earlier, all assemblies in the bin directory of a SharePoint web application execute in partially trusted mode. If any of these assemblies attempts to call into a strong-named assembly, the CLR will raise an exception. Because strong-named assemblies are normally installed in the GAC, this protects these shared assemblies from malicious code.

If you want to enable partially trusted code to access your Web part and if you're strong-naming the assembly that contains your Web part, you'll need to add the AllowPartiallyTrustedCallersAttribute assembly-level attribute:

```
[assembly: System.Security.AllowPartiallyTrustedCallers()]
```

This instructs the compiler *not* to place the LinkDemand for FullTrust on the public or protected methods of the publicly accessible classes in the assembly. Keep in mind that this introduces a security hole in your application because you're allowing partially trusted callers to call into your assembly. If you choose to do so, you must take extra precaution to ensure that your assembly does not contain a code that introduces security risks. Also keep in mind that the AllowPartiallyTrusedCallersAttribute is only applicable when you're strong-naming the assembly. This attribute will have no effect if you're not strong-naming your assembly.

Summary

This chapter provided in-depth coverage of Code Access Security to set the stage for the next chapter, where you learn how to add code access security entries to your solution manifest to grant your Web part assemblies the permissions they need to function properly.

12

Deployment

This chapter provides in-depth coverage of the SharePoint deployment, allowing you to learn how to package your SharePoint solution in a single deployment package and deploy it as a single unit.

Why Use a SharePoint Solution Package?

Deploying a SharePoint solution involves one or more of these main tasks:

- Copying template files in the appropriate folders in the TEMPLATE folder on the file system of each front-end web server. These template files include:
  - Feature files and element manifest files referenced by these feature files. These files are copied into feature-specific subfolders of the FEATURES folder of the TEMPLATE folder.
  - Field type definition files, which are copied into the XML subfolder of the TEMPLATE folder.
  - Page template files that onet.xml files use to provision homepage site pages. These page template files are copied into the site template–specific subfolders of the SITETEMPLATES folder of the TEMPLATE folder.
  - Application pages, which are copied into the application-specific subfolders of the LAYOUTS subfolder of the TEMPLATE folder.
  - Image files, which are copied into the application-specific subfolders of the IMAGES subfolder of the TEMPLATE folder.
  - schema.xml files, which define the schemas of list types. These files are copied into the list-specific subfolders of the feature-specific subfolders of the FEATURES subfolder of the TEMPLATE folder. Keep in mind that the feature that contains a list

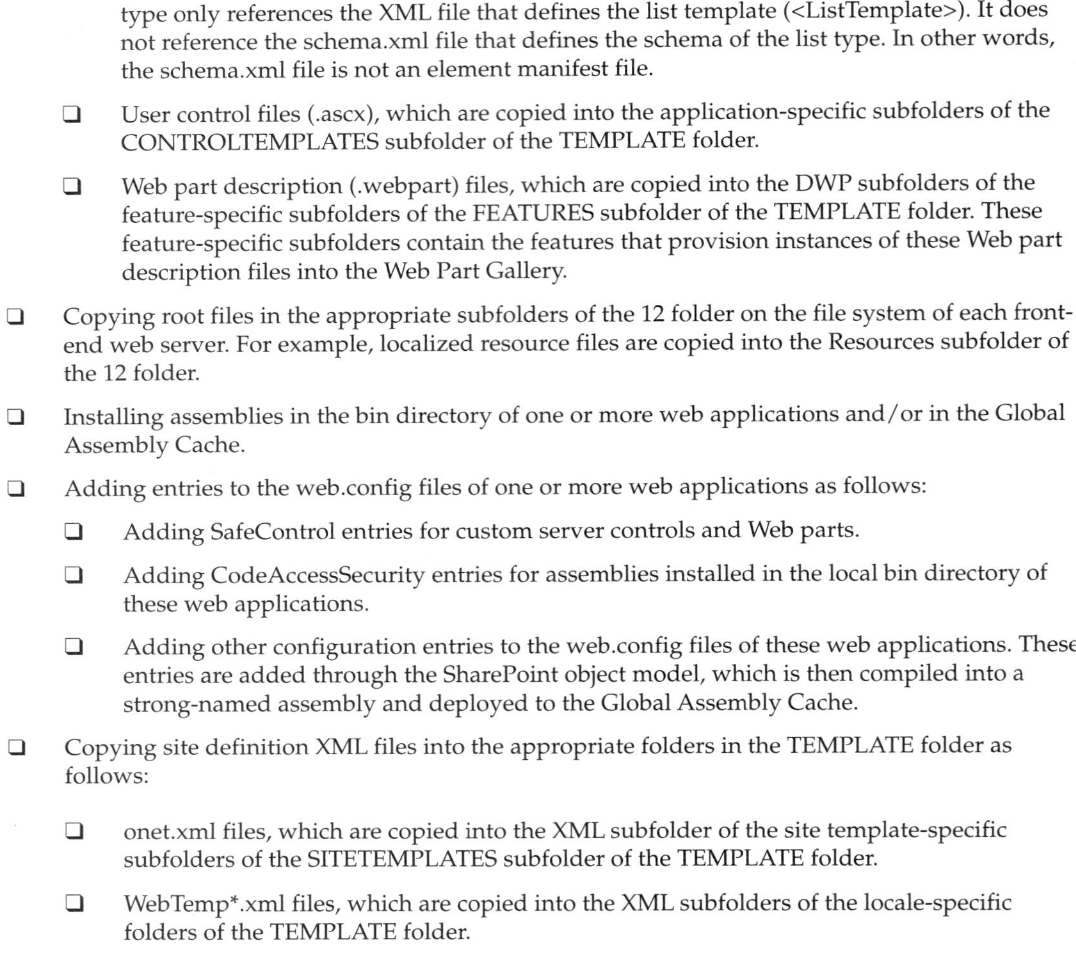

type only references the XML file that defines the list template (<ListTemplate>). It does not reference the schema.xml file that defines the schema of the list type. In other words, the schema.xml file is not an element manifest file.

- User control files (.ascx), which are copied into the application-specific subfolders of the CONTROLTEMPLATES subfolder of the TEMPLATE folder.
- Web part description (.webpart) files, which are copied into the DWP subfolders of the feature-specific subfolders of the FEATURES subfolder of the TEMPLATE folder. These feature-specific subfolders contain the features that provision instances of these Web part description files into the Web Part Gallery.

- Copying root files in the appropriate subfolders of the 12 folder on the file system of each front-end web server. For example, localized resource files are copied into the Resources subfolder of the 12 folder.
- Installing assemblies in the bin directory of one or more web applications and/or in the Global Assembly Cache.
- Adding entries to the web.config files of one or more web applications as follows:
    - Adding SafeControl entries for custom server controls and Web parts.
    - Adding CodeAccessSecurity entries for assemblies installed in the local bin directory of these web applications.
    - Adding other configuration entries to the web.config files of these web applications. These entries are added through the SharePoint object model, which is then compiled into a strong-named assembly and deployed to the Global Assembly Cache.
- Copying site definition XML files into the appropriate folders in the TEMPLATE folder as follows:
    - onet.xml files, which are copied into the XML subfolder of the site template-specific subfolders of the SITETEMPLATES subfolder of the TEMPLATE folder.
    - WebTemp*.xml files, which are copied into the XML subfolders of the locale-specific folders of the TEMPLATE folder.

The examples and recipes presented in the previous chapters of this book used a manual approach to perform these main deployment tasks in order to make the steps involved in the deployment of SharePoint solutions explicit so you can gain better understanding of these steps. For example, as you saw, this manual approach required you to directly create the required folders in the file system of each front-end web server and copy the required files into these folders.

This manual approach was taken for educational purposes. You should not use this manual approach to deploy your SharePoint solutions to a production machine. Instead you should use SharePoint solution packages as discussed in this chapter. A SharePoint solution package automatically creates the specified folders and copies the specified files to these folders.

Implementing a SharePoint solution package requires you to know what files you need to deploy and to which folders on the file system of each front-end web server in the server farm to deploy these files. The manual approach used in the previous chapters explicitly specified what these files are and where they should be deployed. With that knowledge in mind, this chapter shows you how to use SharePoint solution packages to avoid the pitfalls with the manual approach. SharePoint solution packages enable you to compress all your deployment files into a single compressed file, which is then deployed as a single unit.

Cabinet and DDF Files

Because the compressed file into which you add all your SharePoint deployment files is a cabinet file with the .wsp extension, first you need to gain a solid understanding of how to compress a library of files into a cabinet file and how to specify the layout of these files inside the cabinet file. As you'll see later, the layout of these files inside of a cabinet file comes into play when SharePoint deploys the cabinet file to the front end web servers in a server farm.

You must use the MAKECAB operating system command-line utility to create a cabinet file. You must feed this command-line utility a file known as a Data Description File (.ddf), which instructs this command-line utility which files to add into the cabinet file, how to lay out these files inside the cabinet file, what name and extension to use for the cabinet file, and in which directory to place the cabinet file. Because a SharePoint solution package is a cabinet file with the .wsp extension, the data description file that you feed the MAKECAB command-line utility should instruct this utility to create a cabinet file with the .wsp extension.

The following MAKECAB command-line utility compresses the files specified in the cab.ddf into a cabinet file based on the structure or layout specified in the cab.ddf. In other words, the specified files are laid out inside the.wsp file as instructed in the cab.ddf file.

```
makecab /f cab.ddf
```

A Data Description File (.ddf) consists of two parts: header and body. The header tells the MAKECAB utility what name and extension to use for the cabinet file and in which directory to create the cabinet file. The body tells the MAKECAB utility what files to compress into the cabinet file and how to lay out these files in the cabinet file.

Listing 12-1 presents an example of a simple data description file named cab.ddf.

Listing 12-1: A simple data description file

```
;** Header **
.Option Explicit
.Set CabinetNameTemplate=cab.wsp
.set DiskDirectoryTemplate=CDROM
.Set CompressionType=MSZIP
.Set UniqueFiles="ON"
.Set Cabinet=on
.Set DiskDirectory1=cab

;** Body **
MyDir1\MyFile1.txt MyCabDir1\MyTextFiles\MyFile1.txt
MyDir2\MyImage1.jpg MyCabDir1\MyImageFiles\MyImage1.jpg
```

Use the CabinetNameTemplate header to tell MAKECAB what name and extension to use for the cabinet file. SharePoint solution packages should always use the extension .wsp. Use the DiskDirectory1 header to tell MAKECAB in which folder (from the folder in which the MAKECAB utility runs) to create the cabinet file or the SharePoint solution package. If the folder does not already exist, MAKECAB automatically creates this folder.

As Listing 12-1 shows, the body of a data description file contains a bunch of lines where each line consists of two parts. The first part provides the full folder path (from the folder in which the MAKECAB utility runs) of the file to add to the cabinet file. For example, the first part of the first line of the body of the ddf file shown in Listing 12-1 is as follows:

```
MyDir1\MyFile1.txt
```

This tells the MAKECAB command-line utility to add the MyFile1.txt, which is in the MyDir1 subfolder of the folder where the utility is running, into the cabinet file.

The second part of a line in the body of a ddf file provides the full folder path of the location in the cabinet file where to add the file specified in the first part. For example, the second part of the first line of the body of the ddf file shown in Listing 12-1 is as follows:

```
MyCabDir1\MyTextFiles\MyFile1.txt
```

This tells the MAKECAB utility to add the MyDir1\MyFile1.txt file as MyFile1.txt to a folder named MyTextFiles in a folder named MyCabDir1 in the cabinet file. If the cabinet file does not already contain the MyCabDir1 folder, the MAKECAB utility creates this folder. If the MyCabDir1 folder does not already contain the MyTextFiles folder, the MAKECAB utility creates this folder as well.

As Listing 12-1 shows, you can add any type of file such as text and image files into a cabinet file. Note that when the second line of the body of the ddf file shown in Listing 12-1 runs, MAKECAB retrieves the MyImage1.jpg image file from the MyDir2 subfolder of the folder in which the MAKECAB utility is running and adds it as MyImage1.jpg to a folder named MyImageFiles in the MyCabDir1 folder. As you can see, in this case, the cabinet file will contain a single folder named MyCabDir1, which contains two subfolders named MyTextFiles and MyImageFiles, which in turn contains the MyFile1.txt and MyImage1.jpg files, respectively. To see this in action, go ahead and create a folder named Testing on your local drive. Then create two subfolders named MyDir1 and MyDir2 in the Testing folder. Next, create a text file named MyFile1.txt and add it to the MyDir1 folder. Then, download a jpg file from your favorite site, name the file MyImage1.jpg, and add it to the MyDir2 folder. Next, create another text file inside the Testing directory, name this text file cab.ddf, and add the content of Listing 12-1 to this text file. Finally, run the MAKECAB utility from the Testing folder as follows:

```
MAKECAB /f cab.ddf
```

This should create a subfolder named cab in the folder from which you ran the MAKECAB utility. If you change directory to this subfolder, you should see a file named cab.wsp in this subfolder. This is the cabinet file. Next, download and install your favorite cabinet file viewer and open this cab.wsp file in the viewer. The viewer should show you the content of this cabinet file, which consists of a single folder named MyCabDir1, which contains two subfolders named MyTextFiles and MyImageFiles. If you change folders in the viewer to the MyTextFiles and MyImageFiles folders you should see the MyImage1.txt and MyFile1.jpg in these two folders.

As this example clearly shows, the .ddf file tells the MAKECAB utility not only to add the MyFile1.txt and MyImage1.jpg to the cabinet file, but also to create a specified hierarchy of folders in the cabinet file and to place these files in specific folders in this hierarchy.

Solution Manifest

So far you've learned a great deal about the ddf file and its role in creating a cabinet file. Creating a cabinet file is only half the story. When a solution package (the cabinet file with .wsp extension) is deployed to SharePoint, SharePoint needs to decompress the files in the solution package and deploy them. This raises the following questions:

- How does SharePoint know what types of files the solution package contains?
- How does SharePoint know in which folders in the folder hierarchy in the cabinet file each file type is located?
- How does SharePoint know where to deploy these files in the file system of each front-end web server in the server farm? As you've seen throughout this book, different types of files are deployed into different folders in the file system of each front-end web server. For example, feature files are deployed into feature-specific folders in the Features folder, whereas the field type definition files are deployed into the XML subfolder of the Template folder.
- Deployment of some types of files requires creation of new folders. For example, deployment of a new feature requires creation of a feature-specific subfolder in the Features folder. How does SharePoint know what folders to create and where in the file system of each front-end web server to create them?

As you can see, SharePoint needs to know in which folder in the solution package each deployment file is located, to which folder in the file system of each front-end web server to deploy each deployment file, whether to create a new folder for a deployment file, and what to name the new folder (if any) and in which folder in the file system of each front-end web server to create the new folder (if any).

To address these SharePoint needs, every solution package also contains a special file named solution manifest (manifest.xml). This file, in conjunction with the cabinet folder hierarchy in which each deployment file resides, provides SharePoint with the complete information to decompress and to deploy the deployment files into the right folders in the file system of each front-end web server in the server farm.

Listing 12-2 presents the complete structure of the manifest.xml file. Note that not every manifest.xml file uses all these elements and attributes.

Listing 12-2: The complete structure of the manifest.xml file

```
<?xml version="1.0" encoding="utf-8" ?>
<Solution xmlns="http://schemas.microsoft.com/sharepoint/" SolutionId="">
  <Assemblies>
    <Assembly DeploymentTarget="GlobalAssemblyCache | WebApplication" Location="">
      <SafeControls>
        <SafeControl Assembly="" Namespace="" TypeName="" Safe="True | False"/>
        <SafeControl Assembly="" Namespace="" TypeName="" Safe="True | False"/>
      </SafeControls>
      <ClassResources>
        <ClassResource FileName="" Location="" />
        <ClassResource FileName="" Location="" />
      </ClassResources>
    </Assembly>
  </Assemblies>

  <ApplicationResourceFiles>
    <ApplicationResourceFile Location=""/>
    <ApplicationResourceFile Location=""/>
  </ApplicationResourceFiles>

  <CodeAccessSecurity>
    <PolicyItem>
      <PermissionSet class="NamedPermissionSet" Description="" Name="" version="">
        <IPermission class="Fully-assembly-namespace-qualified Name of the
permission class" .../>
        <IPermission class="Fully-assembly-namespace-qualified Name of the
permission class" .../>
      </PermissionSet>
      <Assemblies>
        <Assembly Name="" PublicKeyBlob="" Version=""/>
        <Assembly Name="" PublicKeyBlob="" Version=""/>
      </Assemblies>
    </PolicyItem>
    <PolicyItem>
      <PermissionSet class="NamedPermissionSet" Description="" Name="" version="">
        <IPermission class="Fully-assembly-namespace-qualified Name of the
permission class" .../>
        <IPermission class="Fully-assembly-namespace-qualified Name of the
permission class" .../>
      </PermissionSet>
      <Assemblies>
        <Assembly Name="" PublicKeyBlob="" Version=""/>
        <Assembly Name="" PublicKeyBlob="" Version=""/>
      </Assemblies>
    </PolicyItem>
```

```
    </CodeAccessSecurity>

    <DwpFiles>
      <DwpFile FileName="" Location="" />
      <DwpFile FileName="" Location="" />
    </DwpFiles>

    <FeatureManifests>
      <FeatureManifest Location=""/>
      <FeatureManifest Location=""/>
    </FeatureManifests>

    <Resources>
      <Resource Location=""/>
      <Resource Location=""/>
    </Resources>

    <RootFiles>
      <RootFile Location=""/>
      <RootFile Location=""/>
    </RootFiles>

    <SiteDefinitionManifests>
      <SiteDefinitionManifest Location="">
        <WebTempFile Location=""/>
      </SiteDefinitionManifest>
      <SiteDefinitionManifest Location="">
        <WebTempFile Location=""/>
      </SiteDefinitionManifest>
    </SiteDefinitionManifests>

    <TemplateFiles>
      <TemplateFile Location=""/>
      <TemplateFile Location=""/>
    </TemplateFiles>
  </Solution>
```

As you can see, a solution manifest is an XML file with a document element named <Solution>, which supports an attribute named SolutionId. You must set this attribute to a GUID that uniquely identifies the solution package. Use the guidgen.exe utility discussed earlier to generate and copy and paste a GUID as the value of this attribute. As you can see, a solution package just like a feature is identified by a GUID.

The elements and attributes that you need to use to implement your solution manifest XML file belong to the following namespace:

```
http://microsoft.schemas.com/sharepoint/
```

This namespace is defined in the CAML schema files. Copy these files into the Schema directory in the installation directory of Visual Studio on your machine if you haven't done it already and assign this namespace to the xmlns attribute on the <Solution> element to take advantage of the Visual Studio IntelliSense support when you're implementing your solution manifest.

The <Solution> document element supports the following important child elements:

- **<FeatureManifests>.** This child element instructs SharePoint which features to copy to which folders in the FEATURES system folder of each front-end web server in the server farm and to install these features. Note that this child element does not instruct SharePoint to activate these features. You still have to activate them.
- **<TemplateFiles>.** This child element instructs SharePoint which template files to copy to which folders in the TEMPLATE system folder of each front-end web server in the server farm.
- **<SiteDefinitionManifests>.** This child element instructs SharePoint which site definition files to copy to which folders in the system directory of each front-end web server in the server farm. Recall that site definition files are the onet.xml and webtemp*.xml files.
- **<Assemblies>.** This child element instructs SharePoint which assemblies to install in the Global Assembly Cache and which assemblies to install in the local bin directory of the web application in each front-end web server in the server farm.
- **<RootFiles>.** This child element instructs SharePoint which files to install in which folders in the 12 system folder of each front-end web server in the server farm.
- **<CodeAccessSecurity>.** This child element instructs SharePoint which code access security settings to use for which assemblies.
- **<DwpFiles>.** This child element instructs SharePoint which Web part description files to copy to the Web Part Gallery of each site collection in the web application.
- **<Resources>.** This child element instructs SharePoint which resources to install.
- **<ApplicationResourceFiles>.** This child element instructs SharePoint which application resource files to install. These resource files are used in application pages.

Deployment Scenarios

As you saw in the previous section, you can deploy all kinds of deployment files through a SharePoint solution package including feature and element manifest files, template files, site definition files, assemblies, root files, Web part description files, resource files, and even add safe control entries to the web.config file and code access security settings for specified assemblies. This does not mean that every SharePoint solution package must deploy all these files. Different deployment scenarios require deployment of different types of files. A couple of these deployment scenarios are discussed in the following sections.

Deploying a SharePoint Web Part Solution

This section shows you how to implement a solution package for a SharePoint Web part solution. A SharePoint Web part solution consists of one or more of the following components that are deployed to the appropriate folders in the file system of each front-end web server in the server farm:

- **Assemblies containing the compiled code for custom Web parts.** These assemblies are installed in the local bin directory of the web application or the Global Assembly Cache. As a best practice, you should always install your Web part assemblies to the local bin directory of the web application where your code runs in the security context established by the local security policy.

- **.ascx files used in custom Web parts.** These .ascx files are deployed into the ControlTemplates folder in the file system of each front-end web server in the server farm.
- **Other files such as image files used in custom Web parts.** These image files are deployed into the Images folder in the file system of each front-end web server in the server farm.
- **Web part description files for custom Web parts.** These files are normally deployed into a folder named DWP in the feature-specific folders that contain the features that reference the element manifest files that provision these files into the Web Part Gallery.
- **Element manifest files that provision Web part description files into the Web Part Gallery.** These files are deployed into the feature-specific folders that contain the features that reference these files.
- **Feature files that reference the element manifest files that provision Web part description files into the Web Part Gallery.** These files are deployed into the feature-specific folders in the Features folder in the file system of each front-end web server in the server farm.
- **Safe control entries that register custom Web parts as safe controls.** These safe control entries are maintained in the web application as custom web.config files.
- **Code access security settings for custom Web parts.** These code access security settings are maintained in the 12\config folder as custom policy files.

SharePoint enables you to encapsulate all the previous components of your Web part solution in a single solution package, which can then be deployed as a single unit to the server farm, which in turn pushes this single unit of deployment out to all front-end web servers in the server farm.

Next, you'll walk through an example to help you understand this deployment scenario. Launch Visual Studio 2008 and create a new Class Library project. Right-click the project in the Solution Explorer and select the Properties menu option to launch the Properties window. Switch to the Application tab in the Properties window. Enter "WebPartsChapter" into both the Assembly Name and Default Namespace textbox fields. Then switch to the Signing tab and follow the steps discussed earlier to create a key file for the project. Next, switch to the Build Events tab and enter the following into the Post-Build Event Command Line textbox:

```
cd $(ProjectDir)
mybatchfile.bat
```

Then, go back to the Solution Explorer and add references to the System.Web.dll, Microsoft.SharePoint.dll, and Microsoft.SharePoint.Security.dll assemblies, which are located in the following folder in the file system of the front-end web server where you're running Visual Studio 2008:

```
Local_Drive:\Program Files\Common Files\Microsoft Shared\Web Server Extensions\12\ISAPI
```

Next, add the following code access security assembly-level metadata attribute to the AssemblyInfo.cs file under the Properties folder in the Solution Explorer:

```
[assembly: System.Security.AllowPartiallyTrustedCallers()]
```

As discussed in the previous chapter, this assembly-level metadata attribute instructs the compiler *not* to place the LinkDemand for FullTrust on the public or protected methods of the publicly accessible classes in the assembly so partially trusted code could call into these publicly accessible classes. Next, right-click the project in the Solution Explorer and use the Add ⇨ New Item option to add the following files to the root directory of the project:

- A text file named cab.ddf
- An XML file named manifest.xml
- An XML file named feature.xml
- An XML file named elements.xml
- A text file named mybatchfile.bat
- **A class file named TemplateBasedWebPart.cs.** Go ahead and copy Listing 10-15 into this file. Recall that this code listing contains the implementation of the TemplateBasedWebPart custom Web part.
- **A class file named TemplateBasedWebPart1.cs.** Go ahead and copy Listing 10-16 into this file. Recall that this code listing contains the implementation of the TemplateBasedWebPart1 custom Web part.
- **An XML file named TemplateBasedWebPart1.webpart**. This file is discussed shortly.
- **A user control (.ascx) file named TemplateBasedWebPart1.ascx.** Go ahead and copy Listing 10-17 into this file. Recall that this code listing contains the RenderingTemplate server control whose ID property value is given by the DefaultTemplateName property of the TemplateBasedWebPart1 custom Web part. As you may recall, this custom Web part renders the markup content specified within the opening and closing tags of the <Template> element that represents the Template property of this RenderingTemplate server control.

Next, go ahead and copy Listing 12-3 into the TemplateBasedWebPart1.webpart file. This listing contains the Web part description file for the TemplateBasedWebPart1 custom Web part. After you build the project, use the Get Public Key Token external tool that you added to the Tools menu of Visual Studio to access the public key token of the assembly and use this public key token in the value of the name attribute on the <type> element in the Web part description file shown in Listing 12-3.

Listing 12-3: The Web part description file for TemplateBasedWebPart1

```
<?xml version="1.0" encoding="utf-8"?>
<webParts>
  <webPart xmlns="http://schemas.microsoft.com/WebPart/v3">
    <metaData>
      <type
      name="WebPartsChapter.TemplateBasedWebPart1,WebPartsChapter, Version=1.0.0.0,
Culture=neutral, PublicKeyToken=7a0b3ae00d1d1f55" />
      <importErrorMessage>Cannot import this Web Part.</importErrorMessage>
    </metaData>
    <data>
      <properties>
        <property name="Title" type="string">Template Based Web Part 1</property>
      </properties>
    </data>
  </webPart>
</webParts>
```

Next, copy Listing 12-4 into the elements.xml file. This listing contains the element manifest that provisions the TemplateBasedWebPart1.webpart Web part description file into the Web Part Gallery.

Listing 12-4: The elements.xml file

```
<?xml version="1.0" encoding="utf-8" ?>
<Elements xmlns="http://schemas.microsoft.com/sharepoint/">
  <Module
  Name="MyCustomWebParts"
  Path="dwp"
  List="113"
  Url="_catalogs/wp"
  RootWebOnly="true">
    <File Url="TemplateBasedWebPart1.webpart" Type="GhostableInLibrary" >
      <Property Name="Group" Value="My Custom Web Parts" />
    </File>
  </Module>
</Elements>
```

Then, copy Listing 12-5 into the feature.xml file. This listing contains the feature that references the element manifest file that provisions the TemplateBasedWebPart1.webpart Web part description file.

Listing 12-5: The feature.xml file

```
<?xml version="1.0" encoding="utf-8" ?>
<Feature
xmlsn="http://schemas.microsoft.com/sharepoint/"
 Id="{8FD05FB7-DA2D-45c5-8A3C-4704CE4D85B9}"
 Description="This feature deploys our Web part description files"
 Hidden="FALSE"
 Scope="Site"
 Title="Our Web Part description file feature">
  <ElementManifests>
    <ElementManifest Location="elements.xml"/>
  </ElementManifests>
 </Feature>
```

Next, copy Listing 12-6 into the cab.ddf file. This listing contains the Data Description File that instructs the MAKECAB operating system command-line utility which files and in which layout to compress into the solution package file.

Listing 12-6: The data description file

```
; * Data description file for deploying our SharePoint Web part solution *
.Option Explicit
.Set CabinetNameTemplate=cab.wsp
.set DiskDirectoryTemplate=CDROM
.Set CompressionType=MSZIP
.Set UniqueFiles="ON"
.Set Cabinet=on
.Set DiskDirectory1=cab

manifest.xml manifest.xml
```

(continued)

Listing 12-6 *(continued)*

```
feature.xml MyCustomWebParts\feature.xml
elements.xml MyCustomWebParts\elements.xml
TemplateBasedWebPart1.webpart Features\MyCustomWebParts\DWP\TemplateBasedWebPart1
.webpart
TemplateBasedWebPart1.ascx CONTROLTEMPLATES\TemplateBasedWebPart1.ascx
bin\Debug\WebPartsChapter.dll WebPartsChapter.dll
```

As Listing 12-6 shows, the CabinetNameTemplate header of the cab.ddf file tells the MAKECAB utility to name the cabinet file cab.wsp and use the .wsp as the file extension, which is the file extension that SharePoint expects. The DiskDirectory1 header tells the MAKECAB utility to create a subfolder named cab in the folder from which the utility is running and place this cab.wsp file in this subfolder. Because you'll run the MAKECAB utility from the root folder of the Class Library project, the MAKECAB utility will create the cab folder in the root folder of the project.

Next, you'll walk through the body of the data description file shown in Listing 12-6. Note that each line in the body consists of two parts separated by space. The first part of each line is the full folder path of a file from the folder in which MAKECAB runs. Because you'll run MAKECAB from the root folder of the Class Library project, this full folder path is from the root folder of the project. The second part of each line is the full folder path of a file from the root of the cab.wsp cabinet file. Each line in the body of the data description file instructs MAKECAB to copy the file whose full folder path is specified in the first part from the Class Library project into the file whose full folder path is specified in the second part in the cab.wsp cabinet file.

The first line in the body of the data description file shown in Listing 12-6 instructs MAKECAB to copy the manifest.xml file from the root folder of the project into the root of the cab.wsp cabinet file:

```
manifest.xml manifest.xml
```

Note that if you had stored the manifest.xml file into a folder named cab in the root folder of the project, the first line would be:

```
cab\manifest.xml manifest.xml
```

This is because the first part of the line specifies the full folder path from the folder in which MAKECAB runs, which is the root folder the project in this case. Keep in mind that you must always copy the manifest.xml file into the root of the cab.wsp cabinet file. You mustn't copy it into a subfolder in the root of this cabinet file.

The second line tells MAKECAB to copy the feature.xml file from the root folder of the project into the MyCustomWebParts folder in the cab.wsp cabinet file. MAKECAB automatically creates the MyCustomWebParts folder in the root of the cab.wsp cabinet file:

```
feature.xml MyCustomWebParts\feature.xml
```

Again, note that if you had stored the feature.xml file into a folder named MyCustomWebParts in the root folder of the project, the second line would be:

```
MyCustomWebParts\feature.xml MyCustomWebParts\feature.xml
```

This would tell MAKECAB to copy the feature.xml file from the MyCustomWebParts folder in the root folder of the project into the MyCustomWebParts folder in the root of the cab.wsp cabinet file.

The third line tells MAKECAB to copy the elements.xml file from the root folder of the project into the MyCustomWebParts folder in the cab.wsp cabinet file:

```
elements.xml MyCustomWebParts\elements.xml
```

Your data description file must always instruct MAKECAB to copy the element manifest files into the same folder in the cabinet file where the feature that references these element manifest files resides.

The fourth line tells MAKECAB to copy the TemplateBasedWebPart1.webpart file from the root folder of the project into the DWP subfolder of the MyCustomWebParts subfolder of the Features folder in the root of the cab.wsp cabinet file:

```
TemplateBasedWebPart1.webpart Features\MyCustomWebParts\DWP\TemplateBasedWebPart1
.webpart
```

Note that MAKECAB automatically creates the Features folder in the root of the cab.wsp cabinet file, the MyCustomWebParts subfolder in the Features folder, and the DWP subfolder in the MyCustomWebParts folder.

Note that if you had stored the TemplateBasedWebPart1.webpart file into a subfolder named DWP under a subfolder named MyCustomWebParts under a subfolder named Features under a folder named Template in the root folder of the project, the fourth line would be:

```
Template\Features\MyCustomWebParts\DWP\TemplateBasedWebPart1.webpart Features\
MyCustomWebParts\DWP\TemplateBasedWebPart1.webpart
```

This would tell MAKECAB to copy the TemplateBasedWebPart1.webpart file from the DWP subfolder of the MyCustomWebParts subfolder of the Features subfolder of the Template subfolder in the root folder of the project into the DWP subfolder of the MyCustomWebParts subfolder of the Features subfolder in the root of the cab.wsp cabinet file. As you can see, the file being copied can be in an arbitrary folder structure in the project as long as the full folder path of the file from the folder from which MAKECAB runs is specified. This full folder path in this case is from the root folder of the project because you'll run MAKECAB from the root folder of the project.

The fifth line in the body of the data description file shown in Listing 12-6 tells MAKECAB to copy the TemplateBasedWebPart1.ascx file from the root folder of the project into the ControlTemplates folder in the root of the cab.wsp cabinet file. MAKECAB automatically creates the ControlTemplates folder in the root of the cab.wsp cabinet file:

```
TemplateBasedWebPart1.ascx CONTROLTEMPLATES\TemplateBasedWebPart1.ascx
```

The sixth line tells MAKECAB to copy the WebPartsChapter.dll assembly from the Release folder in the bin directory of the project into the root of the cab.wsp cabinet file:

```
bin\Debug\WebPartsChapter.dll WebPartsChapter.dll
```

As discussed earlier, the file being copied can be in an arbitrary folder structure in the project as long as the first part of the line that copies the file specifies the full folder path from the folder in which you run MAKECAB. How about the folder structure in the cab.wsp cabinet file? Can you copy the file into an arbitrary folder structure in the cab.wsp cabinet file? What is the significance of the folder structure in the cab.wsp cabinet file into which the file is copied?

The folder structure in the cab.wsp cabinet file into which the file is copied must mimic the folder structure into which SharePoint must deploy the file in the file system of each front-end web server in the server farm. In other words, the folder structure in the cab.wsp cabinet file into which a file is copied tells the SharePoint runtime into which folder structure in the file system of each front-end web server in the server farm to deploy the file. SharePoint automatically creates the required folder structure if the file system does not already contain the structure.

This raises the following questions. Which folder structure in the file system of each front-end web server in the server farm do the second parts (shown in boldfaced in the following excerpt from Listing 12-6) of the lines in the body of the data description file shown in Listing 12-6 represent?

```
manifest.xml manifest.xml

feature.xml MyCustomWebParts\feature.xml

elements.xml MyCustomWebParts\elements.xml

TemplateBasedWebPart1.webpart Features\MyCustomWebParts\DWP\TemplateBasedWebPart1
.webpart

TemplateBasedWebPart1.ascx CONTROLTEMPLATES\TemplateBasedWebPart1.ascx

bin\Debug\WebPartsChapter.dll WebPartsChapter.dll
```

The answer to these questions is in the manifest.xml file shown in Listing 12-7.

Listing 12-7: The manifest.xml file

```
<?xml version="1.0" encoding="utf-8" ?>
<Solution
xmlsn="http://schemas.microsoft.com/sharepoint/"
SolutionId="{4D99C209-7842-4d78-871D-80C6EDC813C7}">
  <FeatureManifests>
    <FeatureManifest Location="MyCustomWebParts\feature.xml"/>
  </FeatureManifests>

  <TemplateFiles>
    <TemplateFile Location="ControlTemplates\TemplateBasedWebPart1.ascx"/>
    <TemplateFile Location="Features\MyCustomWebParts\DWP\TemplateBasedWebPart1
.webpart"/>
  </TemplateFiles>

  <Assemblies>
    <Assembly DeploymentTarget="WebApplication" Location="WebPartsChapter.dll">
      <SafeControls>
        <SafeControl
        Assembly="WebPartsChapter, Version=1.0.0.0, Culture=neutral,
PublicKeyToken=7a0b3ae00d1d1f55"
        Namespace="WebPartsChapter"
        TypeName="*"
        Safe="True"/>
      </SafeControls>
    </Assembly>
```

```
  </Assemblies>

  <CodeAccessSecurity>
    <PolicyItem>
      <PermissionSet
      class="NamedPermissionSet"
      Description="Specifies permission set for my custom Web parts"
version="2">
        <IPermission class="Microsoft.SharePoint.Security.SharePointPermission,
Microsoft.SharePoint.Security, Version=12.0.0.0, Culture=neutral,
PublicKeyToken=71e9bce111e9429c"
        version="2" ObjectModel="True" />
      </PermissionSet>
      <Assemblies>
      <Assembly Name="WebPartsChapter, Version=1.0.0.0, Culture=neutral,
PublicKeyToken=7a0b3ae00d1d1f55"/>
      </Assemblies>
    </PolicyItem>
  </CodeAccessSecurity>
</Solution>
```

As you can see, this manifest file like any other manifest file contains a document element named <Solution>, which features an attribute named SolutionId, which is set to a GUID that uniquely identifies the solution package in the server farm. Use the GUIDGEN utility to generate the GUID. Don't forget to copy the CAML XML schema file into the Schema directory of your Visual Studio installation and set the xmlns attribute on the <Solution> element to http://schemas.microsoft.com/sharepoint/ so you can take advantage of the Visual Studio IntelliSense support as you're writing the manifest file.

Next, you'll walk through the implementation of this manifest file. As Listing 12-7 shows, a manifest file contains elements such as <FeatureManifest>, <TemplateFile>, and <Assembly> that expose an attribute named Location. The Location attribute on each of these elements specifies a full folder path in the cab.wsp cabinet file.

As you can see from Listing 12-7, the <FeatureManifests> element contains a <FeatureManifest> element whose Location attribute is set to MyCustomWebParts\feature.xml, which is the full folder path to the feature.xml file in the cab.wsp cabinet file:

```
<FeatureManifests>
  <FeatureManifest Location="MyCustomWebParts\feature.xml"/>
</FeatureManifests>
```

Here is how SharePoint deduces the system folder structure into which it needs to deploy this feature.xml file:

- The <FeatureManifest> element itself is a signal to SharePoint that the file that the Location attribute references is a feature file that must be deployed into a feature-specific folder (if any) in the Features folder in the file system of each front-end web server in the server farm.
- SharePoint then treats the MyCustomWebParts folder specified in the Location attribute as the name of this feature-specific folder. SharePoint automatically creates this folder in the Features folder in the file system of each front-end web server in the server farm if it hasn't already been created.

SharePoint not only copies the feature file, but also copies all the element manifest files that the feature file references into the feature-specific folder. In this case, SharePoint automatically copies the elements.xml manifest file into the MyCustomWebParts folder in the file system of each front-end web server in the server farm. As you can see, you do not need to and mustn't specify the element manifest files in the manifest.xml file.

After copying the feature files and the element manifest files that these feature files reference, SharePoint installs these features. This is equivalent to performing the installfeature operation on the STSADM command-line utility for each feature. Note that SharePoint does not activate these features. It only installs them. You still need to activate them.

As you can see from Listing 12-7, the <TemplateFiles> element contains a <TemplateFile> element whose Location attribute is set to ControlTemplates\TemplateBasedWebPart1.ascx, which is the full folder path to the TemplateBasedWebPart1.ascx file in the cab.wsp cabinet file and a <TemplateFile> element whose Location attribute is set to Features\MyCustomWebParts\DWP\TemplateBasedWebPart1.webpart, which is the full folder path to the TemplateBasedWebPart1.webpart file in the cab.wsp cabinet file:

```
  <TemplateFiles>
    <TemplateFile Location="ControlTemplates\TemplateBasedWebPart1.ascx"/>
    <TemplateFile
Location="Features\MyCustomWebParts\DWP\TemplateBasedWebPart1.webpart"/>
</TemplateFiles>
```

Here is how SharePoint deduces the system folder structure into which it needs to deploy files such as the TemplateBasedWebPart1.ascx and TemplateBasedWebPart1.webpart files specified in the <TemplateFile> elements:

- The <TemplateFile> element itself is a signal to SharePoint that the file that the Location attribute of the element references is a template file that must be deployed into a folder structure in the Template folder in the file system of each front-end web server in the server farm.
- SharePoint then treats the folder path specified in the Location attribute as a folder path from the Template folder. SharePoint automatically creates this folder structure in the Template folder in the file system of each front-end web server in the server farm if it hasn't already been created. Because the file system already contains the ControlTemplates folder, SharePoint simply copies the TemplateBasedWebPart1.ascx file into this folder in the file system of each front-end web server in the server farm. Things are different with the TemplateBasedWebPart1.webpart file. In this case, SharePoint creates a DWP subfolder in the MyCustomWebParts folder and deploys the TemplateBasedWebPart1.webpart file into this subfolder. Because the <FeatureManifest> element instructed SharePoint to create the MyCustomWebParts feature-specific folder, SharePoint does not attempt to re-create this folder.

As Listing 12-7 shows, the manifest element contains an <Assembly> element whose Location attribute is set to WebPartsChapter.dll, which is the full folder path to the WebPartsChapter.dll assembly in the cab.wsp cabinet file. In this case, this assembly is located in the root of this cabinet file:

```
  <Assemblies>
    <Assembly DeploymentTarget="WebApplication" Location="WebPartsChapter.dll">
      <SafeControls>
        <SafeControl
        Assembly="WebPartsChapter, Version=1.0.0.0, Culture=neutral,
PublicKeyToken=7a0b3ae00d1d1f55"
```

```
        Namespace="WebPartsChapter"
        TypeName="*"
        Safe="True"/>
      </SafeControls>
    </Assembly>
  </Assemblies>
```

Note that the <Assembly> element features an attribute named DeploymentTarget with the following possible values:

- **WebApplication.** Set this attribute to this value to instruct SharePoint to deploy the assembly to the local bin directory of the web application.
- **GlobalAssemblyCache.** Set this attribute to this value to instruct SharePoint to install the assembly in the Global Assembly Cache. Keep in mind that only strong-named assemblies can be installed in the GAC.

Note that the <Assembly> element contains a child element named <SafeControls> where you can specify safe control entries for your custom Web parts. Each <SafeControl> element follows the same exact schema as the <SafeControl> element of the web.config file. SharePoint creates a new web.config file in the root directory of the web application. This new web.config file contains the safe control entries that you specify in your manifest.xml file. As you can see, SharePoint does not update the main web.config file. Each time you deploy a Web part solution package, SharePoint creates a new web.config file whose name contains the date and time of the deployment. This enables SharePoint to keep track of deployed solution packages. Thanks to this tracking mechanism, you can retract a deployed SharePoint solution and rest assured that when a deployed SharePoint solution package is retracted and deleted all safe control entries associated with the solution package are deleted as well.

As Listing 12-7 shows, the manifest file contains an element named <CodeAccessSecurity>. Use this element to specify code access security settings for the assemblies that you deploy to the local bin directory of your web application. Keep in mind that these code access security settings do not apply to assemblies that you deploy to the Global Assembly Cache because all assemblies in the Global Assembly Cache run in full trust mode.

The <CodeAccessSecurity> element can contain one or more <PolicyItem> elements. Each <PolicyItem> element defines a specific code access security policy, which applies to specific assemblies:

```
  <CodeAccessSecurity>
    <PolicyItem>
      <PermissionSet
      class="NamedPermissionSet"
      Description="Specifies permission set for my custom Web parts"
      version="2">
        <IPermission class="Microsoft.SharePoint.Security.SharePointPermission,
Microsoft.SharePoint.Security, Version=12.0.0.0, Culture=neutral,
PublicKeyToken=710e9bce111e9429c"
        version="2" ObjectModel="True" />
      </PermissionSet>
      <Assemblies>
        <Assembly Name="WebPartsChapter, Version=1.0.0.0, Culture=neutral,
PublicKeyToken=7a0b3ae00d1d1f55"/>
      </Assemblies>
    </PolicyItem>
  </CodeAccessSecurity>
```

Note that the <PolicyItem> supports a child element named <PermissionSet>. Does this child element sound familiar? You got it! This is the same <PermissionSet> element discussed in the previous chapter. Recall that this element is used in a policy file to specify a set of permissions where each permission is specified by an <IPermission> child element of the <PermissionSet> element. Also recall that the policy file defines a bunch of code groups where each code group is assigned a permission set. In other words, all code members of the same code group share the same permissions specified in the permission set.

When a solution package is deployed, the <PermissionSet> elements specified in the solution manifest are added to the <NamedPermissionSets> element of a custom policy file maintained by SharePoint. This custom policy file, like any other policy file, is located in the following system folder in the file system of each front-end web server in the server farm:

```
Local_Drive:\Program Files\Common Files\microsoft shared\Web Server Extensions\12\CONFIG
```

Note that the <PolicyItem> element (see Listing 12-7) contains a child element named <Assemblies>, which specifies the assemblies to which the new custom policy applies. Note that each assembly is specified in an <Assembly> element whose name attribute is set to the strong name of the assembly. When a solution package is deployed, SharePoint creates a new code group for each assembly specified in the <Assemblies> element and adds this code group to the <CodeGroup> element of the custom policy file. For example, in the case of Listing 12-7, SharePoint adds the <CodeGroup> element shown in boldface to the main <CodeGroup> element:

```
<CodeGroup class="FirstMatchCodeGroup" version="1" PermissionSetName="Nothing">
  <IMembershipCondition class="AllMembershipCondition" version="1" />
  <CodeGroup class="UnionCodeGroup" version="1"
  PermissionSetName="cab.wsp-4D99C209-7842-4d78-871D-80C6EDC813C7">
    <IMembershipCondition version="1"
    Name="WebPartsChapter, Version=1.0.0.0, Culture=neutral,
PublicKeyToken=7a0b3ae00d1d1f55"
    class="UrlMembershipCondition"
    Url="$AppDirUrl$/bin/WebPartsChapter, Version=1.0.0.0, Culture=neutral,
PublicKeyToken=7a0b3ae00d1d1f55.dll" />
  </CodeGroup>
</CodeGroup>
```

Note that the PermissionSetName attribute on this <CodeGroup> is set to a value that consists of two parts separated by a hyphen (-). The first part is the name of the solution package file including its .wsp file extension. The second part is the GUID identifier of the solution, that is, the value of the SolutionId attribute of the <Solution> document element of the solution manifest file. As discussed in the previous chapter, each <CodeGroup> element must contain an <IMembershipCondition> child element whose function is to specify the code group membership. As the boldfaced portion of the preceding listing shows, the class attribute on this <IMembershipCondition> element is set to UrlMembershipCondition. This means that any code that originates from the URL specified in the Url attribute is a member of this code group. The Url attribute in this case is set to the following value:

```
Url="$AppDirUrl$/bin/WebPartsChapter, Version=1.0.0.0, Culture=neutral,
PublicKeyToken=7a0b3ae00d1d1f55.dll"
```

This basically says that the WebPartsChapter assembly in the local bin directory of the web application is the member of this code group. In other words, this code group has only one member.

As you see, if you specify your code access security settings in the solution package, you save yourself from having to:

- Create a new policy file because SharePoint creates a custom policy file for you
- Create a new <CodeGroup> because SharePoint creates it for you
- Add the <PermissionSet> to the new policy file because SharePoint does it for you

Another very important benefit of including your code access security settings in the solution package is as follows. If you were to create the new policy file, you would have to then edit the web.config file of the web application to reference the new policy file and to specify the new policy file as the current policy file for your application. As discussed thoroughly in this book, it is not a good idea to directly edit the web.config file. It is simply not scalable and is error-prone in server farms that consist of numerous web servers where you have to make the same changes in all web.config files of the same application in all these web servers. In addition, you have to also make the same changes when new web servers, which include IIS web sites mapped to the same web application, are added to the farm. Besides, you would have to roll back all changes when a solution package is rolled back.

Adding your code access security settings to the solution package delegates all these responsibilities to SharePoint.

Note that the <Assembly> child element of the <Assemblies> element of the <PolicyItem> element in a solution package (see Listing 12-7) also supports an attribute named PublicKeyBlob. You can use this attribute instead of the Name attribute. As the name suggests, the PublicKeyBlob attribute must be set to a public key BLOB. A BLOB is used to store the public key portion of a public/private key pair. The private key is used to sign the assembly. The CLR uses the public key to determine whether the assembly is indeed signed by the associated private key. Public key BLOBs are not encrypted because the public keys within are not secret.

You can assign the public key BLOB of the assembly to the PublicKeyBlob attribute of the <Assembly> element to apply the respective code access security policy to all assemblies signed with the same private key. As you can see, the Name attribute provides more granularity than the PublicKeyBlob because it enables you to apply the respective code access security policy to a specific assembly as opposed to all assemblies signed with the same private key.

Follow these steps to access the public key BLOB of an assembly. Launch a Visual Studio Command Prompt. Enter ildasm to launch the IL DASM tool shown in Figure 12-1.

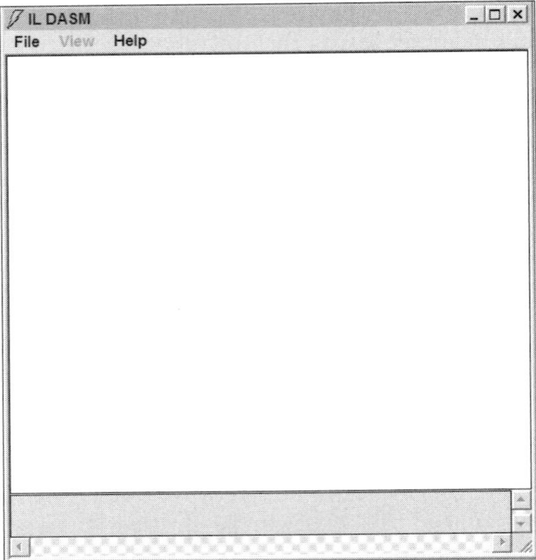

Figure 12-1: IL DASM

Use the File ⇨ Open menu and navigate to the folder that contains the assembly and select the assembly to load the assembly as shown in Figure 12-2.

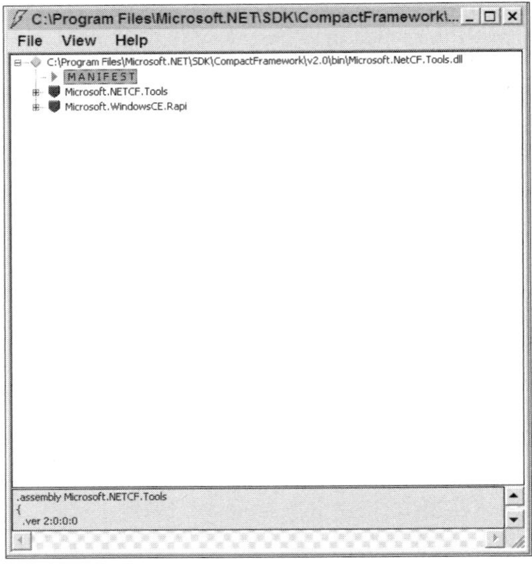

Figure 12-2: Displaying assembly info in IL DASM

Double-click the MANIFEST node to launch the window shown in Figure 12-3. This window displays the assembly manifest. Scroll down this window to locate the public key BLOB of the assembly as highlighted in Figure 12-3.

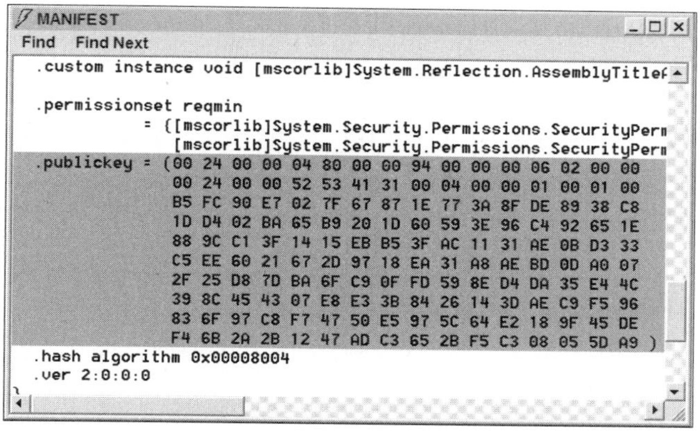

Figure 12-3: Assembly Manifest

So far, you've learned how to create a SharePoint solution package (.wsp) file. The next order of business is to use the STSADM command-line utility to copy the solution package file into the solution store of the configuration database to make it available to the server farm. STSADM comes with an operation named addsolution, which installs the solution package into the solution store. This operation supports a switch named -filename. You must use this switch to specify the full folder path to your solution package file from the folder where you run STSADM:

```
stsadm -o addsolution -filename cab\cab.wsp
```

After adding your solution package file to the solution store of the configuration database, you need to deploy this file to the front-end web servers in the server farm. The STSADM command-line utility comes with an operation named deploysolution, which does that for you. This operation supports a switch named -name, which you must use to specify the name of the solution package including its .wsp file extension:

```
stsadm -o deploysolution -name cab.wsp -immediate -allowCasPolicies -url
http://localhost
```

Note that the deploysolution operation supports the -allowCasPolicies switch, which you must use if your solution package contains code access security settings. You need to use this switch because the Web part solution package specifies code access security settings for the Web part assembly. Also note that the deploysolution operation supports a switch named -url. You must use this switch to specify the URL of a SharePoint Web application if your solution package adds entries to the Web.config file. Our solution package adds a safe control entry to the Web.config file to register our Web part as a safe control. As such, we must specify the URL of our Web application.

As discussed earlier, the solution manifest contains a reference to the SharePoint feature that provisions the Web part definition file into the Web Part Gallery. Because deploying a solution package only installs the referenced features without actually activating them, next you need to activate this feature:

```
stsadm -o activatefeature -name MyCustomWebParts -url http://localhost
```

You can automate the entire process of creating, installing, and deploying a solution package by writing a batch file as shown in Listing 12-8.

Listing 12-8: The mybatchfile.bat file

```
if Exist cab\cab.wsp Del cab\cab.wsp
makecab /f cab.ddf

@SET STSADM="c:\program files\common files\microsoft shared\web server
extensions\12\bin\stsadm"

%STSADM% -o deactivatefeature -name MyCustomWebParts -url http://localhost

%STSADM% -o retractsolution -name cab.wsp -immediate -url http://localhost
%STSADM% -o execadmsvcjobs
%STSADM% -o deletesolution -name cab.wsp -override
%STSADM% -o execadmsvcjobs

%STSADM% -o addsolution -filename cab\cab.wsp
%STSADM% -o execadmsvcjobs
%STSADM% -o deploysolution -name cab.wsp -immediate -allowGacDeployment -
allowCasPolicies -url http://localhost
%STSADM% -o execadmsvcjobs

%STSADM% -o activatefeature -name MyCustomWebParts -url http://localhost
```

This batch file takes these steps. First, it checks whether the cab folder contains the solution package file. If so, it deletes the file because you're about to re-create this solution package file:

```
if Exist cab\cab.wsp Del cab\cab.wsp
```

Next, it runs the MAKECAB operating system command-line utility to create the solution package file:

```
makecab /f cab.ddf
```

Then it defines an alias for the full folder path to the STSADM command-line utility. Your batch file should not make the assumption that the path to this utility has been set in the client's environment:

```
@SET STSADM="c:\program files\common files\microsoft shared\web server
extensions\12\bin\stsadm"
```

Next, it performs the deactivatefeature operation of STSADM to deactivate the feature that provisions the Web part description file into the Web Part Gallery:

```
%STSADM% -o deactivatefeature -name MyCustomWebParts -url http://localhost
```

Then, it performs the retractsolution operation of STSADM to retract the solution package if it has already been deployed to SharePoint because you're about to redeploy this solution package:

```
%STSADM% -o retractsolution -name cab.wsp -immediate -url http://localhost
```

The retractsolution operation internally creates a timer job to do the actual retraction. As discussed earlier in this book, timer jobs are inherently asynchronous. This is a problem in a script that contains a bunch of commands because each command must be executed after the previous command has completed its execution. To solve this problem, STSADM comes with an operation named execadmsvcjobs, which executes all scheduled timer jobs synchronously and waits for these timer jobs to complete their executions. As you can see from Listing 12-8, the batch file performs the execadmsvcjobs operation on STSADM right after performing the retractsolution operation to force the timer job that the retractsolution operation created to run synchronously:

```
%STSADM% -o execadmsvcjobs
```

The batch file then performs the deletesolution operation of STSADM to remove the solution package file from the solution store of the configuration database because you're about to copy a new solution package to the solution store:

```
%STSADM% -o deletesolution -name cab.wsp -override
```

The deletesolution operation just like the retractsolution operation creates a timer job to do the actual deletion. For the same reasons just discussed, the batch file performs the execadmsvcjobs operation on STSADM to run this timer job immediately. As mentioned the execadmsvcjobs operation waits for the timer job to complete before it returns:

```
%STSADM% -o execadmsvcjobs
```

The batch file then performs the addsolution operation on STSADM to add the solution package file to the solution store of the configuration database:

```
%STSADM% -o addsolution -filename cab\cab.wsp
```

The batch file once again performs the execadmsvcjobs operation to run this timer job synchronously:

```
%STSADM% -o execadmsvcjobs
```

Next, the batch file uses the deploysolution operation to deploy the solution package:

```
%STSADM% -o deploysolution -name cab.wsp -immediate -allowCasPolicies -url
http://localhost
```

The deploysolution operation internally creates a timer job, which is handled by the front-end web servers in the server farm. Thanks to this timer job the solution package is deployed to all front-end web servers in the server farm. The batch file performs the execadmsvcjobs operation to run this timer job and wait for it to complete. This means that the STSADM returns only when the solution package has been deployed to all front-end web servers in the server farm:

```
%STSADM% -o execadmsvcjobs
```

Finally, the batch file activates the feature that provisions the Web part definition file into the Web Part Gallery:

```
%STSADM% -o activatefeature -name MyCustomWebParts -url http://localhost
```

Deploying a SharePoint Site Definition Solution

This section implements a solution package that deploys a SharePoint site definition solution. A SharePoint site definition solution is a SharePoint solution that contains one or more site definitions. Recall that every site definition consists of the following deployment files:

- **onet.xml.** This file contains the actual definition of the site definition and its configurations. This file must be deployed to a folder named XML under a site definition-specific folder under the SiteTemplates system folder in the file system of each front-end web server in the server farm.
- **WebTemp*.xml.** This file references the site definition configurations defined in the onet.xml file and specifies attributes such as title and description that are displayed in the Template Selection section of the New SharePoint Site page (newsbweb.aspx).
- **Home page templates.** These are the page templates from which the respective modules in the onet.xml provision the home pages for the sites provisioned from the site definition configurations defined in the onet.xml file. These page template files are normally deployed to the root folder of the site definition-specific folder under the SiteTemplates system folder in the file system of each front-end web server in the server farm.
- **Assemblies.** These are the assemblies that contain the site provisioning providers of the respective site definition configurations defined in the onet.xml and referenced in the WebTemp*.xml file. These assemblies must be installed into the Global Assembly Cache.

Next is an example to show you to how to implement a solution package to deploy a SharePoint site definition solution. Follow these steps for this example:

1. Launch Visual Studio 2008 and create a Class Library project. Add a reference to the Microsoft.SharePoint.dll assembly.
2. Follow the steps discussed earlier to configure Visual Studio to compile this project into a strong-named assembly. Follow the steps discussed earlier to set the Assembly Name and Default Namespace to STS2.
3. Follow the steps discussed earlier to add the following post-build event:

```
cd $(ProjectDir)
mybatchfile.bat
```

4. Add a C# source file named CustomProvisioningProvider.cs to this project and add the code shown in Listing 7-17 (shown in Chapter 7) to this file. Recall that this code listing contains the implementation of the custom site provisioning provider.
5. Add an XML file named WebTempMyWebTemp.xml to this project and add the XML document shown in Listing 12-9 to this file.

6. Add an XML file named onet.xml to this project and add the XML document shown in Listing 7-19 to this file. Recall that Listing 7-19 is a modified version of the onet.xml file of the SharePoint standard STS site definition, which is located in the following system folder in the file system of each web server in the server farm:

```
Local_Drive:\Program Files\Common Files\microsoft shared\Web Server Extensions\12\
TEMPLATE\SiteTemplates\sts\xml
```

   Note that Listing 7-19 does not contain the entire content of the onet.xml file. As such you need to get the rest of this file from the onet.xml file of the standard STS site definition.

7. Add an .aspx file named default.aspx to this project and add the content of the default.aspx file of the SharePoint standard STS site definition, which is located in the following system folder, to this file:

```
Local_Drive:\Program Files\Common Files\microsoft shared\Web Server Extensions\12\
TEMPLATE\SiteTemplates\sts
```

8. Add an .aspx file named defaultdws.aspx to this project and add the content of the defaultdws.aspx file of the SharePoint standard STS site definition, which is located in the following system folder, to this file:

```
Local_Drive:\Program Files\Common Files\microsoft shared\Web Server Extensions\12\
TEMPLATE\SiteTemplates\sts
```

9. Add an XML file named cab.ddf to this project.
10. Add a text file named mybatchfile.bat to this project.
11. Add an XML file named manifest.xml to this project.

Listing 12-9 presents the content of the WebTempMyWebTemp.xml file.

Listing 12-9: The WebTempMyWebTemp.xml file

```
<?xml version="1.0" encoding="utf-8"?>
<Templates xmlns:ows="Microsoft SharePoint">
  <Template Name="STS2" ID="10020">
    <Configuration ID="3" Title="Team Site 2"
    Hidden="FALSE"
    ImageUrl="/_layouts/images/stsprev.png"
    Description="This is Team Site 2."
    DisplayCategory="My Site Templates"
    ProvisionClass="ClassLibrary2.CustomProvisioningProvider"
    ProvisionAssembly="STS2, Version=1.0.0.0, Culture=neutral,
PublicKeyToken=2aa68f1f0dc981dd"
    ProvisionData="My Team Site 2" />

    <Configuration
    ID="0"
    Title="Team Site 2"
    Hidden="TRUE"
    ImageUrl="/_layouts/images/stsprev.png"
```

(continued)

Listing 12-9 *(continued)*

```
    Description="This is Team Site 2."
    DisplayCategory="My Site Templates" />

    <Configuration
    ID="1"
    Title="Blank Site 2"
    Hidden="FALSE"
    ImageUrl="/_layouts/images/blankprev.png"
    Description="This is Blank Site 2."
    DisplayCategory="My Site Templates" />

    <Configuration
    ID="2"
    Title="Document Workspace 2"
    Hidden="FALSE"
    ImageUrl="/_layouts/images/dwsprev.png"
    Description="This is Document Workspace 2."
    DisplayCategory="My Site Templates" />
  </Template>
</Templates>
```

Next, you need to implement the cab.ddf, manifest.xml, and mybatchfile.bat files. Listing 12-10 presents the implementation of the mybatchfile.bat file.

Listing 12-10: The mybatchfile.bat file

```
if Exist cab\cab.wsp Del cab\cab.wsp
makecab /f cab.ddf

@SET STSADM="c:\program files\common files\microsoft shared\web server extensions\
12\bin\stsadm"

%STSADM% -o retractsolution -name cab.wsp -immediate
%STSADM% -o execadmsvcjobs
%STSADM% -o deletesolution -name cab.wsp -override
%STSADM% -o execadmsvcjobs

%STSADM% -o addsolution -filename cab\cab.wsp
%STSADM% -o execadmsvcjobs
%STSADM% -o deploysolution -name cab.wsp -immediate -allowGacDeployment
%STSADM% -o execadmsvcjobs
```

As you can see, this batch file is very similar to the batch file discussed in the previous section. The main difference is that this batch file performs the deploysolution operation with the -allowGacDeployment switch. This is because contrary to the previous section you're now deploying the assembly, which contains the site provisioning provider, to the Global Assembly Cache.

Listing 12-11 presents the implementation of the cab.ddf file.

Listing 12-11: The cab.ddf file

```
 ; * STS2 Solution *
 .Option Explicit
 .Set CabinetNameTemplate=cab.wsp
 .set DiskDirectoryTemplate=CDROM
 .Set CompressionType=MSZIP
 .Set UniqueFiles="ON"
 .Set Cabinet=on
 .Set DiskDirectory1=cab

manifest.xml manifest.xml
default.aspx SiteTemplates\sts2\default.aspx
defaultdws.aspx SiteTemplates\sts2\defaultdws.aspx
onet.xml sts2\XML\onet.xml
WebTempMyWebTemp.xml 1033\XML\WebTempMyWebTemp.xml
bin\Debug\STS2.dll STS2.dll
```

As you can see, this data description file performs these tasks:

1. Copies the manifest.xml file from the project to the root of the cab.wsp file.
2. Copies the default.aspx file from the project to the sts2 subfolder of the SiteTemplates folder in the root of the cab.wsp file.
3. Copies the defaultdws.aspx file from the project to the sts2 subfolder of the SiteTemplates folder in the root of the cab.wsp file.
4. Copies the onet.xml file from the project to the XML subfolder of the sts2 folder in the root of the cab.wsp file.
5. Copies the WebTempMyWebTemp.xml file from the project to the XML subfolder of the 1033 folder in the root of the cab.wsp file.
6. Copies the STS2.dll assembly from the Debug subfolder of the bin folder of the project to the root of the cab.wsp file.

Listing 12-12 presents the implementation of the solution manifest file.

Listing 12-12: The manifest.xml file

```
<?xml version="1.0" encoding="utf-8" ?>
<Solution
xmlsn="http://schemas.microsoft.com/sharepoint/"
SolutionId="{AC39CF01-68BA-422f-A589-8BDF963836C3}">

  <TemplateFiles>
    <TemplateFile Location="SiteTemplates\sts2\default.aspx"/>
    <TemplateFile Location="SiteTemplates\sts2\defaultdws.aspx"/>
  </TemplateFiles>

  <SiteDefinitionManifests>
    <SiteDefinitionManifest Location="STS2">
      <WebTempFile Location="1033\XML\WebTempMyWebTemp.XML"/>
    </SiteDefinitionManifest>
  </SiteDefinitionManifests>

  <Assemblies>
    <Assembly DeploymentTarget="GlobalAssemblyCache"
    Location="STS2.dll" />
  </Assemblies>
</Solution>
```

The following <TemplateFile> element in this solution manifest

```
<TemplateFile Location="SiteTemplates\sts2\default.aspx"/>
```

instructs SharePoint to copy the default.aspx file from the sts2 subfolder of the SiteTemplates folder in the root of the cab.wsp file to the sts2 subfolder of the SiteTemplates folder in the Template system folder.

The following <TemplateFile> element in this solution manifest

```
<TemplateFile Location="SiteTemplates\sts2\defaultdws.aspx"/>
```

instructs SharePoint to copy the defaultdws.aspx file from the sts2 subfolder of the SiteTemplates folder in the root of the cab.wsp file to the sts2 subfolder of the SiteTemplates folder in the Template system folder.

The following <SiteDefinitionManifest> element in this solution manifest

```
<SiteDefinitionManifest Location="STS2">
```

instructs SharePoint to copy the onet.xml file from the sts2 subfolder of the SiteTemplates folder in the root of the cab.wsp file to the sts2 subfolder of the SiteTemplates folder in the Template system folder.

The following <WebTempFile> element in this solution manifest

```
<WebTempFile Location="1033\XML\WebTempMyWebTemp.XML"/>
```

instructs SharePoint to copy the WebTempMyWebTemp.xml file from the XML subfolder of the 1033 folder in the root of the cab.wsp file to the XML subfolder of the 1033 folder in the Template system folder.

The following <Assembly> element in this solution manifest

```
<Assembly DeploymentTarget="GlobalAssemblyCache" Location="STS2.dll" />
```

instructs SharePoint to install the STS2.dll from the root of the cab.wsp file into the Global Assembly Cache.

Summary

This chapter showed you how to implement a SharePoint solution package to deploy your SharePoint solution and provided you with examples where you learned how to implement solution packages for your SharePoint Web part and site definition solutions.

The next chapter moves on to the SharePoint topic of Business Data Catalog (BDC), where you learn how to use the BDC markup language to implement your own BDC application definition files.

13

Business Data Catalog

Enterprise Application Integration (EAI) is a major challenge facing any corporation that needs to integrate data from a disparate array of Line of Business (LOB) applications into a unified presentation layer. This presentation layer in this case is a SharePoint portal site. The Business Data Catalog (BDC) enables a SharePoint portal site to bring in business data from various database and web service LOB applications and expose them as if they were SharePoint data. This enables the users of the SharePoint portal site to view data from these back-end database and web service LOB applications as if they were viewing SharePoint data.

All you need to do is add metadata for your database or web service LOB application to the BDC metadata repository. This metadata must describe everything that the BDC needs to know to fetch the business data from the LOB application including how to connect to the application, which methods to call on the application to fetch the business data, and which parameters to pass into these methods. Because the BDC is implemented as a Microsoft Office SharePoint Server 2007 (MOSS) shared service, metadata is stored in the Share Services database, which is a standard SQL Server database. This database contains tables where metadata is stored. As you can see, the metadata for a LOB application is stored as relational data.

The BDC introduces a special XML markup language that you can use to describe a database or web service LOB application in XML format. The XML file that contains this XML document is known as a BDC application definition file because it defines or describes the LOB application to the BDC. This chapter provides in-depth coverage of this XML markup language and its associated schema.

Once the metadata for a LOB application is added to the metadata repository, the BDC automatically takes care of establishing a connection to the back-end LOB application and fetching the business data without a single line of code on your part. The BDC automatically takes care of everything for you.

BDC Metadata XML Schema

The BDC comes with a special XML markup language that you can use to define the metadata for your database and web service LOB applications declaratively without writing a single line of code. This metadata is an XML document, which must comply with the BDC metadata XML schema. This XML schema is defined in a file named BdcMetadata.xsd, which is located in the bin folder of your MOSS 2007 installation folder. This chapter provides in-depth coverage of the BDC metadata XML schema to help you gain the skills you need to create metadata for your own database and web service LOB applications.

As the excerpt from BdcMetadata.xsd shown in Listing 13-1 illustrates, BdcMetadata.xsd defines the XML namespace shown in boldface, which is the namespace that contains all the BDC XML schema types, elements, and attributes that you need to use to create metadata for your LOB applications.

Listing 13-1: The portion of BdcMetadata.xsd that specifies the target namespace

```
<xs:schema
xmlsn:xs="http://www.w3.org/2001/XMLSchema"
xmlsn:bdc="http://schemas.microsoft.com/office/2006/03/BusinessDataCatalog"
targetNamespace="http://schemas.microsoft.com/office/2006/03/BusinessDataCatalog"
elementFormDefault="qualified">
</xs:schema>
```

Note that the elementFormDefault attribute on the <xs:schema> document element is set to "qualified" to specify that all XML elements defined within the BdcMetadata.xsd file belong to this namespace.

If you're using Visual Studio to write the application definition XML file, take one of these approaches to take advantage of the IntelliSense support. The first approach requires you to take these steps:

- Use the schemaLocation attribute on the <LobSystem> document element to reference the http://schemas.microsoft.com/office/2006/03/BusinessDataCatalog namespace and the BdcMetadata.xsd file that defines the namespace as shown in Listing 13-2.
- Add a copy of the BdcMetadata.xsd file to your working folder.

Listing 13-2: The <LobSystem> document element

```
<LobSystem
xmlsn="http://schemas.microsoft.com/office/2006/03/BusinessDataCatalog"
xmlsn:xsi="http://www.w3.org/2001/XMLSchema-instance"
xsi:schemaLocation="http://schemas.microsoft.com/office/2006/03/BusinessDataCatalog
BDCMetadata.xsd">
  . . .
</LobSystem>
```

The second approach requires you to add a copy of the BdcMetadata.xsd file to the Schemas subfolder of the Xml folder under your Visual Studio installation folder, which is normally:

```
Local_Drive:\Program Files\Microsoft Visual Studio 9.0\Xml\Schemas
```

The schema types and elements that BdcMetadata.xsd defines are discussed in the following sections.

MetadataObject

Listing 13-3 shows an excerpt from BdcMetadata.xsd that defines the MetadataObject schema type.

Listing 13-3: The MetadataObject schema type

```
<xs:complexType name="MetadataObject" abstract="true">
  <xs:sequence>
    <xs:element name="LocalizedDisplayNames" type="bdc:LocalizedDisplayNames"
    minOccurs="0" maxOccurs="1"/>
    <xs:element name="Properties" type="bdc:Properties" minOccurs="0"
    maxOccurs="1"/>
  </xs:sequence>
  <xs:attribute name="Name" type="xs:string" use="required"/>
  <xs:attribute name="DefaultDisplayName" type="xs:string"/>
  <xs:attribute name="IsCached" type="xs:boolean"/>
</xs:complexType>
```

Notice that the MetadataObject schema type is an abstract schema type. As you'll see throughout this chapter, this schema type is the base schema type from which many other BDC schema types inherit. According to this schema type, any XML element such as <LobSystem> whose schema type inherits from the MetadataObject schema type can contain:

- A sequence of two optional (minOccurs=0) elements as follows:
  - <LocalizedDisplayNames>, which is of the LocalizedDisplayNames schema type
  - <Properties>, which is of the Properties schema type
- Note that any XML element of the MetadataObject schema type such as <LobSystem> can only contain single instances of the <LocalizedDisplayNames> and <Properties> elements (maxOccurs=1).
- Three attributes as follows:
  - Name, which is of the string schema type. Use the Name attribute to name the metadata object. Every metadata object in the BDC is named.
  - DefaultDisplayName, which is of the string schema type.
  - IsCached, which is of the Boolean schema type.
- Notice that only the Name attribute is required (use="required").

As the name implies, the <LocalizedDisplayNames> child element of an XML element of the MetadataObject schema type specifies localized display names for the metadata object. As you'll see later in this chapter, the <LocalizedDisplayNames> child element specifies one localized display name for each desired locale.

The Name attribute is used to identify and name a metadata object in the metadata repository. The DefaultDisplayName attribute contains the default display name that is displayed to users if a localized display name has not been specified for the current locale. If the <LocalizedDisplayNames> child element has specified a localized display name for the current locale, the SharePoint user interface displays this localized display name instead of the default display name specified in the

DefaultDisplayName attribute. If a localized display name has not been specified for the current locale and a default display name has not been specified either, the SharePoint user interface displays the value of the Name attribute, which is the name of the metadata object.

The <Properties> child element of an XML element of the MetadataObject schema type specifies its properties. Different types of metadata objects expose different properties. You can think of the <Properties> child element as a generic collection where you can specify the names, .NET types, and values of the properties of a metadata object.

As mentioned earlier, the metadata for a business application is stored as relational data in the metadata repository, which is the standard Shared Services SQL Server database. This means that the BDC must connect to this database to fetch the metadata. Set the IsCached attribute on an XML element of the MetadataObject schema type to true to instruct the BDC to cache this metadata object after it is fetched from the Shared Services database to improve performance. If you set the value of the IsCached attribute to "false," the BDC will not cache the metadata object. This enables you to cache only frequently used metadata objects.

IndividuallySecurableMetadataObject

Listing 13-4, which is an excerpt from BdcMetadata.xsd, presents the definition of the IndividuallySecurableMetadataObject schema type.

Listing 13-4: The IndividuallySecurableMetadataObject schema type

```
<xs:complexType name="IndividuallySecurableMetadataObject" abstract="true">
  <xs:complexContent>
    <xs:extension base="bdc:MetadataObject">
      <xs:sequence>
        <xs:element name="AccessControlList" type="bdc:AccessControlList"
        minOccurs="0" maxOccurs="1"/>
      </xs:sequence>
    </xs:extension>
  </xs:complexContent>
</xs:complexType>
```

As you can see, the IndividuallySecurableMetadataObject schema type extends the MetadataObject schema type to add support for an optional (minOccurs=0) element named <AccessControlList>, which is of the AccessControlList schema type. As the name implies, the <AccessControlList> element is used to specify the access control list (ACL) for the metadata object. As you'll see later, the ACL specifies which principals have which rights on the metadata object. In other words, you can secure access to the IndividuallySecurableMetadataObject metadata objects individually by setting their ACLs. The ACLs of the metadata objects whose schema type do not inherit from the IndividuallySecurableMetadataObject schema type cannot be directly specified because these metadata objects inherit the ACLs of their first individually securable metadata object ancestors. As such you cannot secure access to these metadata objects individually, that is, you cannot set their ACLs. Their security is determined by their first individually securable metadata object ancestors.

Note that an XML element of the IndividuallySecurableMetadataObject schema type can contain only a single instance of the <AccessControlList> child element (maxOccurs=1).

Because the IndividuallySecurableMetadataObject schema type inherits from the MetadataObject schema type, an XML element of the IndividuallySecurableMetadataObject schema type can contain the same Name, DefaultDisplayName, and IsCached attributes and the same optional <LocalizedDisplayNames> and <Properties> child elements that the MetadataObject schema type defines, in addition to the optional <AccessControlList> child element, which the IndividuallySecurableMetadataObject schema type defines.

LocalizedDisplayNames

Recall from Listing 13-3 that the MetadataObject schema type defines an optional child element named <LocalizedDisplayNames>, which is of the LocalizedDisplayNames schema type. Listing 13-5 presents an excerpt from BdcMetadata.xsd that defines the LocalizedDisplayNames schema type.

Listing 13-5: The LocalizedDisplayNames schema type

```
<xs:complexType name="LocalizedDisplayNames">
  <xs:sequence>
    <xs:element name="LocalizedDisplayName" type="bdc:LocalizedDisplayName"
    minOccurs="1" maxOccurs="unbounded"/>
  </xs:sequence>
</xs:complexType>
```

According to this schema type, the <LocalizedDisplayNames> element must contain at least one instance of a child element named <LocalizedDisplayName>, which is of the LocalizedDisplayName schema type as defined in Listing 13-6.

Listing 13-6: The LocalizedDisplayName schema type

```
<xs:complexType name="LocalizedDisplayName" mixed="true">
  <xs:attribute name="LCID" type="xs:integer" use="required"/>
</xs:complexType>
```

Notice that:

- The mixed attribute of the <xs:complexType> schema element that defines the LocalizedDisplayName schema type is set to true to allow you to specify the localized display name within the opening and closing tags of a <LocalizedDisplayName> element.
- The LocalizedDisplayName schema type defines a required attribute of the integer schema type named LCID. You must set this attribute to the integer value that uniquely identifies the locale for the localized display name specified within the opening and closing tags of the <LocalizedDisplayName> element. For example, set this attribute to 1033 to specify US English as the locale for the specified localized display name. This means that the SharePoint user interface will display this localized display name only to users whose locale is US English.

The <LocalizedDisplayNames> element contains one <LocalizedDisplayName> child element for each desired locale. Each <LocalizedDisplayName> child element specifies the localized display name of the metadata object for the locale with the specified LCID. At runtime, SharePoint automatically determines the LCID of the current locale of the user, locates the LocalizedDisplayName metadata object with the same LCID attribute value, retrieves the associated localized display name from this LocalizedDisplayName metadata object, and displays the localized display name to the user.

For example, the following XML fragment adds the "Customer" localized display name for a locale with LCID of 1033 and the "Cliente" localized display name for a locale with LCID of 1034 for a metadata object:

```
<LocalizedDisplayNames>
  <LocalizedDisplayName LCID="1033">Customer</LocalizedDisplayName>
  <LocalizedDisplayName LCID="1034">Cliente</LocalizedDisplayName>
</LocalizedDisplayNames>
```

Properties

Recall from Listing 13-3 that the MetadataObject schema type defines an optional child element named <Properties>, which is of the Properties schema type. Listing 13-7 presents the definition of the Properties schema type.

Listing 13-7: The Properties schema type

```
<xs:complexType name="Properties">
  <xs:sequence>
    <xs:element name="Property" type="bdc:Property" minOccurs="1"
    maxOccurs="unbounded"/>
  </xs:sequence>
</xs:complexType>
```

According to this schema type, a <Properties> element must contain at least one instance of an element named <Property>, which is of the Property schema type as defined in Listing 13-8.

Listing 13-8: The Property schema type

```
<xs:complexType name="Property" mixed="true">
  <xs:attribute name="Name" type="xs:string" use="required"/>
  <xs:attribute name="Type" type="xs:string" use="required"/>
</xs:complexType>
```

Note that:

- The mixed attribute is set to true to allow you to specify the value of the respective property of the metadata object within the opening and closing tags of the <Property> element.
- The Property schema type defines a required attribute named Name on the <Property> element, which must be set to the name of the metadata object property whose value is being set.
- The Property schema type defines a required attribute named Type on the <Property> element, which must be set to the fully qualified name of the .NET type of the metadata object property whose value is being set. The fully qualified name of a .NET type must include its complete namespace containment hierarchy in addition to its name.

For example, consider the following XML fragment:

```
<Properties>
  <Property Name="RdbCommandText" Type="System.String">
    SELECT * FROM Product
  </Property>
  <Property Name="RdbCommandType" Type="System.Data.CommandType">
    Text
  </Property>
</Properties>
```

This XML fragment specifies the values of two properties named RdbCommandText and RdbCommandType respectively of the System.String and System.Data.CommandType .NET types.

As mentioned, you must specify the string representation of the value of a metadata object property within the opening and closing tags of the <Property> element that represents the metadata object property. This string representation depends on the .NET type of the metadata object property:

- If the metadata object property is a primitive type such as Int16, Int32, Int64, Single, Double, Decimal, Boolean, String, or Byte, simply insert the value of the property within the opening and closing tags of the <Property> element.
- If the metadata object property is of the System.DateTime type, insert the value of the property in the following format within the opening and closing tags of the <Property> element:

```
"yyyy'-'MM'-'dd HH':'mm':'ss'Z'"
```

- This format is known as universal sortable date and time pattern. Note that your specified value must end with the universal time designator 'Z.'
- If the metadata object property is of the System.Guide type, insert the value of the property in the following format:

```
"XXXXXXXX-XXXX-XXXX-XXXX-XXXXXXXXXXXX"
```

- If the metadata object property is an enumeration type, insert the string representation of the enumeration value.
- If the metadata object property is a serializable type, insert the value of the property in the binary-formatted, base64-encoded string format. A serializable type is a type that is marked with the SerializableAttribute metadata attribute and/or implements the ISerializable interface. You can use one of the .NET binary formatters to serialize a value of a serializable type.

The value of the Type attribute on a <Property> element must be one of the following: System.Int16, System.Int32, System.Int64, System.Single, System.Double, System.Decimal, System.Boolean, System .String, System.Byte, System.UInt16, System.UInt32, System.UInt64, System.Guid, System.String, System.DateTime, or the fully namespace-qualified name of any serializable type.

AccessControlList

Recall from Listing 13-4 that the IndividuallySecurableMetadataObject schema type defines an optional child element named <AccessControlList>, which is of the AccessControlList schema type as defined in Listing 13-9.

Listing 13-9: The AccessControlList schema type

```
<xs:complexType name="AccessControlList">
  <xs:sequence>
    <xs:element name="AccessControlEntry" type="bdc:AccessControlEntry"
    minOccurs="1" maxOccurs="unbounded"/>
  </xs:sequence>
</xs:complexType>
```

According to this schema type, an <AccessControlList> element must contain at least one instance of a child element named <AccessControlEntry>, which is of the AccessControlEntry schema type. Listing 13-10 contains the definition of the AccessControlEntry schema type.

Listing 13-10: The AccessControlEntry schema type

```
<xs:complexType name="AccessControlEntry">
  <xs:sequence>
    <xs:element name="Right" type="bdc:Right" minOccurs="1"
    maxOccurs="unbounded"/>
  </xs:sequence>
  <xs:attribute name="Principal" type="xs:string" use="required"/>
</xs:complexType>
```

As Listing 13-10 shows:

- An <AccessControlEntry> element exposes an attribute named Principal, which must be set to a string that contains the identity name of a principal.
- An <AccessControlEntry> element must contain at least one instance of an element named <Right>, which is of the Right schema type defined in Listing 13-11.

Listing 13-11: The Right schema type

```
<xs:complexType name="Right">
  <xs:attribute name="BdcRight" type="bdc:BdcRightName" use="required"/>
</xs:complexType>
```

As you can see from Listing 13-11, a <Right> element supports a required attribute named BdcRight, which is of the BdcRightName schema type as defined in Listing 13-12.

Listing 13-12: The BdcRightName schema type

```
<xs:simpleType name="BdcRightName">
  <xs:restriction base="xs:string">
    <xs:enumeration value="None"/>
    <xs:enumeration value="Execute"/>
    <xs:enumeration value="Edit"/>
    <xs:enumeration value="SetPermissions"/>
    <xs:enumeration value="SelectableInClients"/>
  </xs:restriction>
</xs:simpleType>
```

As Listing 13-12 illustrates, the BdcRightName schema type is an enumeration with these possible values:

- **None.** Sets the BdcRight attribute on a <Right> element to None so that the principal with the specified identity name has no rights on the metadata object.
- **Execute.** Sets the BdcRight attribute on a <Right> element to Execute so that the specified principal has the right to execute the metadata object. Obviously, this right is only applicable to metadata objects that can be executed. As you'll see later, the only executable metadata objects in the BDC are MethodInstance metadata objects.
- **Edit.** Sets the BdcRight attribute on a <Right> element to Edit so that the specified principal has the right to update, to delete, and to create the metadata object.
- **SetPermissions.** Sets the BdcRight attribute on a <Right> element to SetPermissions so that the specified principal has the right to set permissions on the metadata object. Setting permissions means specifying the ACL for the metadata object. Obviously, this right is only applicable to individually securable metadata objects because only the ACLs of these objects can be specified. Other types of objects inherit the ACLs of their first individually securable metadata object ancestors.
- **SelectableInClients.** Sets the BdcRight attribute on a <Right> element to SelectableInClients so that the specified principal has the right to select and to view the metadata object in clients such as Business Data Web Parts and Business Data Columns. This only applies to two types of metadata objects. ApplicationRegistry and Entity. These two types of metadata objects are discussed later.

Here is an example:

```
<AccessControlList>
  <AccessControlEntry Principal="domainname\username1">
    <Right BdcRight="Edit" />
    <Right BdcRight="SetPermissions" />
  </AccessControlEntry>
  <AccessControlEntry Principal="domainname\username2">
    <Right BdcRight="SelectableInClients" />
  </AccessControlEntry>
</AccessControlList>
```

This example sets two Access Control Entries (ACEs), one for the principal with the identity name "domainname\username1" and one for the principal with the identity name "domainname\username2". The former principal is given the edit and set permissions rights on the metadata object, and the latter is only given the selectable-in-clients right. As such, the first principal can update, delete, and create the metadata object and set its permissions, whereas the second principal can only select and view the metadata object in clients such as Business Data Web Parts and Business Data Columns.

LobSystem Document Element

As the following excerpt from BdcMetadata.xsd shows, BdcMetadata.xsd defines an XML element named <LobSystem>, which is the document element of every BDC application definition file:

```
<xs:element name="LobSystem" type="bdc:LobSystem" />
```

Every XML document has an element known as document element that encapsulates other elements of the document. The document element is different from the root node, which contains the document element and other portions of an XML document such as the XML declaration.

The <LobSystem> document element represents the database or web service LOB application or system that the BDC application definition file describes. As you can see, the <LobSystem> document element is of the LobSystem schema type, which is defined in Listing 13-13.

Listing 13-13: The LobSystem schema type

```
<xs:complexType name="LobSystem">
  <xs:complexContent>
    <xs:extension base="bdc:IndividuallySecurableMetadataObject">
      <xs:sequence>
        <xs:element name="LobSystemInstances" type="bdc:LobSystemInstances"
        minOccurs="0" maxOccurs="1"/>
        <xs:element name="Entities" type="bdc:Entities" minOccurs="0"
        maxOccurs="1"/>
        <xs:element name="Associations" type="bdc:Associations" minOccurs="0"
        maxOccurs="1"/>
      </xs:sequence>
      <xs:attribute name="Type" type="bdc:LobSystemType"/>
      <xs:attribute name="SystemUtility" type="xs:string" use="optional"/>
      <xs:attribute name="ConnectionManager" type="xs:string" use="optional"/>
      <xs:attribute name="EntityInstance" type="xs:string" use="optional"/>
      <xs:attribute name="Version" type="xs:string" use="required"/>
    </xs:extension>
  </xs:complexContent>
</xs:complexType>
```

As Listing 13-13 shows, the LobSystem schema type extends the IndividuallySecurableMetadataObject schema type. According to the LobSystem schema type, a <LobSystem> element can contain:

- A sequence of following optional (minOccurs=0) elements
    - <LobSystemInstances> of the LobSystemInstances schema type
    - <Entities> of the Entities schema type
    - <Associations> of the Associations schema type

- Five attributes:
    - Type, which is of the LobSystemType schema type
    - SystemUtility, which is of the string schema type
    - ConnectionManager, which is of the string schema type
    - EntityInstance, which is of the string schema type
    - Version, which is of the string schema type

Of these five attributes only the Version attribute is required (use="required"). Note that a <LobSystem> element can contain only single instances of the three optional <LobSystemInstances>, <Entities>, and <Associations> elements (maxOccurs=1).

As mentioned, the <LobSystem> document element represents the database or web service LOB application that the application definition file describes. The attributes and child elements of the <LobSystem> document element provide the BDC with all the information it needs to fetch the business data from the LOB application. These attributes and child elements are discussed in more detail in the following sections.

Type Attribute

Use the Type attribute on the <LobSystem> document element to specify the type of the LOB application that the application definition file describes. Note that the Type attribute is of the LobSystemType schema type. As the excerpt from BdcMetadata.xsd shown in Listing 13-14 illustrates, the LobSystemType schema type is an enumeration type with two possible values of Database and WebService.

Listing 13-14: The LobSystemType schema type

```
<xs:simpleType name="LobSystemType">
  <xs:restriction base="xs:string">
    <xs:enumeration value="Database"/>
    <xs:enumeration value="WebService"/>
  </xs:restriction>
</xs:simpleType>
```

Because the BDC supports two types of LOB applications, you can integrate business data from either a database or a web service LOB application into SharePoint.

Version Attribute

Use the Version attribute on the <LobSystem> document element to specify the version of the BDC application definition. Use the major.minor.[build.[revision]] format to specify the value of this attribute. An example of such value is 1.0.0.0. The BDC prevents you from overwriting an existing BDC application definition with another application definition with the same name but a lower version.

SystemUtility

Use the SystemUtility attribute on the <LobSystem> document element to specify the fully qualified name of the type of the system utility including its complete namespace containment hierarchy. A system utility is a class that inherits the AbstractSystemUtility abstract base class shown in Listing 13-15.

Listing 13-15: The AbstractSystemUtility base class

```
internal abstract class AbstractSystemUtility : IDataSystemUtility
{
  public virtual IEntityInstanceEnumerator CreateEntityInstanceDataReader(
       object rawAdapterEntityInstanceStream, SharedEntityState sharedEntityState);
  public abstract void ExecuteStatic(MethodInstance mi, LobSystemInstance si,
                                    ref object[] args);
}
```

Here is the reason why the Business Data Catalog contains this abstract base class. As mentioned, the main goal of the BDC is to integrate data from disparate business data sources into SharePoint. Obviously, different data sources have different data access APIs. There are two challenges involved when it comes to fetching data from various business data sources.

First, the process through which queries are performed on various business data sources varies from one business data source to another. For example, you need to use ADO.NET objects to execute a SQL query on a database, whereas you have to use a web services proxy to invoke a web service method. As Listing 13-15 shows, the AbstractSystemUtility base class exposes a method named ExecuteStatic that allows the BDC to perform a query in generic fashion.

Second, the format of the fetched data varies from one business data source to another. For example, when you use ADO.NET to do a query on a relational database you get back an IDataReader object that contains the data. When you use a web services proxy to do a query on a web service you get back a .NET collection object that contains the data. The BDC comes with an interface named IEntityInstanceEnumerator that wraps this IDataReader or .NET collection allowing the BDC to use the same API to interact with both relational databases and web services. As Listing 13-15 shows, the AbstractSystemUtility abstract base class exposes a method named CreateEntityInstanceDataReader whose main responsibility is to wrap the underlying IDataReader or .NET collection in the appropriate IEntityInstanceEnumerator object.

MOSS comes with two implementations of the AbstractSystemUtility API named DbSystemUtility and WebServiceSystemUtility as shown in Listing 13-16.

Listing 13-16: The DbSystemUtility and WebServiceSystemUtility classes

```
internal class DbSystemUtility : AbstractSystemUtility { . . . }

internal class WebServiceSystemUtility : AbstractSystemUtility, IAuthenticatedWork
{
  . . .
}
```

Assign the fully qualified name of the DbSystemUtility class including its complete namespace containment hierarchy as the value of the SystemUtility attribute on the <LobSystem> document element if the LOB application being described is a database LOB application:

```
Microsoft.Office.Server.ApplicationRegistry.SystemSpecific.Db.DbSystemUtility
```

Assign the fully qualified name of the WebServiceSystemUtility class including its complete namespace containment hierarchy as the value of the SystemUtility attribute if the LOB application is a web service LOB application:

```
Microsoft.Office.Server.ApplicationRegistry.SystemSpecific.WebService
.WebServiceSystemUtility
```

The BDC internally uses the value of the SystemUtility attribute and the .NET reflection to dynamically instantiate an instance of the appropriate system utility object in generic fashion.

ConnectionManager

Use the ConnectionManager attribute on the <LobSystem> document element to specify the fully qualified name of the type of the connection manager including its complete namespace containment hierarchy. The BDC comes with an abstract base class named AbstractConnectionManager that defines the API for connection managers as shown in Listing 13-17.

Listing 13-17: The AbstractConnectionManager base class

```
internal abstract class AbstractConnectionManager : IConnectionManager
{
  public static int ConnectionPoolTimeout;
  protected bool IsThrottled;
  protected Semaphore Pool;
  protected int PoolSize;

  public abstract void CloseConnection(object connection);
  protected void DecrementPool();
  public virtual void FlushConnections();
  public abstract object GetConnection();
  protected void IncrementPool();
  public virtual void Initialize(NamedPropertyDictionary properties);
}
```

This API allows the BDC to manage connections to the underlying LOB system in generic fashion without knowing whether the system is a database or web service LOB system. The Administration object model comes with two implementations of this API named DbConnectionManager and WebServiceConnectionManager as shown in Listing 13-18.

Listing 13-18: The DbConnectionManager and WebServiceConnectionManager classes

```
internal class DbConnectionManager : AbstractConnectionManager, IAuthenticatedWork
{
}

internal class WebServiceConnectionManager : AbstractConnectionManager
{
}
```

Assign the fully qualified name of the DbConnectionManager type including its complete namespace hierarchy as the value of the ConnectionManager attribute on the <LobSystem> document element that represents a LOB application if the LOB application is a database LOB application:

```
Microsoft.Office.Server.ApplicationRegistry.SystemSpecific.Db.DbConnectionManager
```

Assign the fully qualified name of the WebServiceConnectionManager type including its complete namespace containment hierarchy as the value of the ConnectionManager attribute on the <LobSystem> document element that represents a LOB application if the LOB application is a web service LOB application:

```
Microsoft.Office.Server.ApplicationRegistry.SystemSpecific.WebService
.WebServiceConnectionManager
```

The BDC internally uses the value of the ConnectionManager attribute and the .NET reflection to dynamically instantiate the appropriate connection manager object in generic fashion.

EntityInstance

Use the EntityInstance attribute on the <LobSystem> document element that represents a business application to specify the fully qualified name of the type of the entity instance including its complete namespace containment hierarchy. The BDC comes with an abstract base class named AbstractEntityInstance that defines the API for all entity instance types as shown in Listing 13-19.

Listing 13-19: The AbstractEntityInstance abstract base class

```
public abstract class AbstractEntityInstance : AbstractInstance, IEntityInstance
{
  public AbstractEntityInstance(MethodInstance methodInstance,
                 object[] identifierValues, LobSystemInstance lobSystemInstance);
  public AbstractEntityInstance(Entity entity, TypeDescriptor rootTypeDescriptor,
                       object adapterObject, LobSystemInstance lobSystemInstance);
  public virtual DataRow EntityAsDataRow(DataTable tableToAddRowTo);
  protected virtual DataRow EntityAsDataRow(DataTable tableToAddRowTo,
                                        bool formattedFields);
  public virtual DataRow EntityAsFormattedDataRow(DataTable tableToAddRowTo);
  public override object Execute(MethodInstance methodInstanceToExecute,
                              LobSystemInstance lobSystemInstance);
  public override object Execute(MethodInstance methodInstanceToExecute,
                  LobSystemInstance lobSystemInstance, ref object[] overrideArgs);
```

```
    internal virtual object ExecuteInternal(LobSystemInstance lobSystemInstance,
                         LobSystem lobSystem, MethodInstance methodInstanceToExecute,
                         Method methodToExecute, ParameterCollection parameters,
                         ref object[] overrideArgs);
    public string GetActionUrl(Action action);
    public virtual IEntityInstanceEnumerator GetAssociatedInstances(
                                                      Association association);
    public virtual IEntityInstanceEnumerator GetAssociatedInstances(
                                                       string associationName);
    public virtual IEntityInstanceEnumerator GetAssociatedInstances(
                              Association association, FilterCollection filters);
    private DataTable GetEntityAsDataTable(bool format);
    public object GetFormatted(Field field);
    public object GetFormatted(string fieldName);
    public virtual IList<object> GetIdentifierValues();
    public virtual IEntityInstance GetView(string viewName);

    public Entity Entity { get; }
    public virtual DataTable EntityAsDataTable { get; }
    public virtual DataTable EntityAsFormattedDataTable { get; }
}
```

This abstract class defines the API that allows the BDC to interact with both database and web service LOB systems in generic fashion when it needs to execute a method on an entity, get a named view, get identifier values, and so on. The BDC comes with two implementations of this API named DbEntityInstance and WebServiceEntityInstance as shown in Listing 13-20.

Listing 13-20: The DbEntityInstance and WebServiceEntityInstance classes

```
public class DbEntityInstance : AbstractEntityInstance
{
}

public class WebServiceEntityInstance : AbstractEntityInstance
{
}
```

Assign the fully qualified name of the DbEntityInstance type including its complete namespace containment hierarchy as the value of the EntityInstance attribute on the <LobSystem> document element that represents a business application if the business application is a database application:

```
Microsoft.Office.Server.ApplicationRegistry.SystemSpecific.Db.DbEntityInstance
```

Assign the fully qualified name of the WebServiceEntityInstance including its complete namespace containment hierarchy as the value of the EntityInstance attribute on the <LobSystem> document element that represents a business application if the business application is a web service application:

```
Microsoft.Office.Server.ApplicationRegistry.SystemSpecific.WebService
.WebServiceEntityInstance
```

So far you've seen the attributes of the <LobSystem> document element. Next, you should list the child elements that the <LobSystem> document element can contain as follows:

- Because the <LobSystem> document element is of the LobSystem schema type, it can contain a sequence of optional <LobSystemInstances>, <Entities>, and <Associations> child elements (see Listing 13-13):

```
<LobSystem Name="AdventureWorksDW">
  <LobSystemInstances></LobSystemInstances>
  <Entities></Entities>
  <Associations></Associations>
</LobSystem>
```

- Because the LobSystem schema type inherits from the IndividuallySecurableMetadataObject schema type (see Listing 13-13), the <LobSystem> document element can also contain a single instance of the <AccessControlList> child element (see Listing 13-4). This means that you can specify an ACL for the LobSystem metadata object that specifies which principals have which rights on the LobSystem metadata object. For example, the following XML fragment specifies that a principal with the identity name "domainname\username1" has both edit and set permissions rights on the LobSystem metadata object, whereas the principal with the identity name "domainname\username2" only has the selectable-in-clients right on the LobSystem metadata object:

```
<LobSystem Name="AdventureWorksDW">
  <AccessControlList>
    <AccessControlEntry Principal="domainname\username1">
      <Right BdcRight="Edit" />
      <Right BdcRight="SetPermissions" />
    </AccessControlEntry>
    <AccessControlEntry Principal="domainname\username2">
      <Right BdcRight="SelectableInClients" />
    </AccessControlEntry>
  </AccessControlList>
</LobSystem>
```

- Because the IndividuallySecurableMetadataObject schema type inherits from the MetadataObject schema type (see Listing 13-4), the <LobSystem> document element can also contain:
  - A sequence of the <LocalizedDisplayNames> and <Properties> optional child elements
  - Three attributes: Name, DefaultDisplayName, and IsCached, where only the Name attribute is required:

```
<LobSystem Name="AdventureWorksDW" DefaultDisplayName="Adventure Works Data Ware"
IsCached="true">
  <LocalizedDisplayNames>
    <LocalizedDisplayName LCID="1033">Adventure Works DW</LocalizedDisplayName>
  </LocalizedDisplayNames>
  <Properties>
    <Property Name="" Type=""></Property>
  </Properties>
</LobSystem>
```

The <Properties> child element of the <LobSystem> document element is used to specify the properties of the LOB system metadata object. This metadata object supports the following properties for both database and web service LOB applications:

- An optional property named WildcardCharacter, which is of the System.String .NET type with the default value of * (asterisk). As the name suggests, this property is used to specify the wildcard character. Use this property to specify a different wildcard character than the default (*) if the LOB application uses a different wildcard character. For example, a SQL Server database LOB application uses the % character as the wildcard character:

```
<LobSystem Name="AdventureDW">
  <Properties>
    <Property Name="WildcardCharacter" Type="System.String">%</Property>
  </Properties>
</LobSystem>
```

- An optional property named WildcardCharacterEscapeFormat, which is of the System.String .NET type with the default value of \{0}. As the name suggests, this property is used to specify a wildcard character escape format. A wildcard filter uses the wildcard character escape format to escape LOB application-specific wildcard characters in the filter value:

```
<LobSystem Name="AdventureDW">
  <Properties>
    <Property Name="WildcardCharacterEscapeFormat" Type="System.String">
      \{0}
    </Property>
  </Properties>
</LobSystem>
```

A LOB system metadata object supports the following properties only when it represents a web service LOB application:

- **WsdlFetchUrl,** which is of the System.String .NET type. Use this property to specify the URL from which the BDC can fetch the WSDL document for the web service LOB application.
- **WsdlFetchAuthenticationMode,** which is of the Microsoft.Office.Server.ApplicationRegistry .SystemSpecific.WebService.HttpAuthenticationMode .NET type. As Listing 13-21 shows, this type is an enumeration with the following possible values:
  - **RevertToSelf.** Use this value to have the IIS worker process revert to self and to use the identity of the application pool to authenticate to the back-end web service LOB application instead of impersonating and using the user identity to authenticate to the back-end web service LOB application.

    The reason this authentication mode is named RevertToSelf is that the actual identity of the IIS worker process is the identity of its associated application pool. This is an example of what is known as a trusted system authentication model where the middle tier (normally the web server) authenticates to the back-end business database or web service application as a fixed identity.

- **PassThrough.** Use this value to have the operating system pass user credentials through to the back-end web service LOB application. This normally applies in two important scenarios. The first scenario is when both the web server and the back-end web service are running on the same machine. The second scenario is when Kerberos delegation is enabled on your domain. The Kerberos delegation handles the pass through of client credentials from the server running the BDC and the server running the business web service. Both are typical scenarios in most test environments.

  The PassThrough authentication mode is an example of what is known as an impersonation/delegation authentication model where the middle tier (normally the web server) authenticates to the back-end business database or web service application as the identity of the client.

- **WindowsCredentials.** The BDC uses the user's Windows credentials from its single sign-on service to authenticate to the web service LOB application.
- **Credentials.** Use this option if the web service LOB application does not support Windows authentication. The BDC uses the user's credentials from its single sign-on service to authenticate to the web service LOB application through basic or digest authentication. Because basic or digest authentication passes user credentials in clear text you should use SSL to secure the communication channels.

- **WsdlFetchSsoProviderImplementation** is of the System.String .NET type. As just mentioned, both the WindowsCredentials and Credentials authentication modes require the BDC to use the user credentials from its single sign-on (SSO) service to authenticate to the web service LOB application. Use the WsdlFetchSsoProviderImplementation property to specify the fully qualified name of the type of the class that implements the ISsoProvider interface. This tells the BDC to use the specified implementation of this interface to retrieve the user credentials from its single sign-on service.
- **WsdlFetchSsoApplicationId** is of the System.String .NET type. Use this property to specify the ID of the SSO application definition that maintains user credentials. The BDC uses the SSO provider implementation to retrieve user credentials from the LOB application that this SSO application definition describes.
- **WebServiceProxyNamespace** is of the System.String .NET type. Use this property to specify the namespace in which the BDC should generate the web service proxy class.
- **WebServiceProxyProtocol** is of the System.String .NET type. Use this property to specify the protocol through which the BDC should communicate with the web service LOB application. The possible values are Soap (that is, SOAP 1.1), Soap12 (that is, SOAP 1.2), HttpPost, HttpGet, and HttpSoap. The default is Soap.
- **WebServiceProxyType** is of the System.String .NET type. If you do not specify this property, the BDC automatically generates the web service proxy class for you. However, you could generate the web service proxy manually, compile it into a strong-named assembly, install the assembly in the Global Assembly Cache, and reference the web service proxy type from this property.
- **WebProxyServerConfiguration**, which is of the System.String .NET type. Use this property to specify the URL to a web proxy server through which the BDC must route the request for the WSDL document.

Listing 13-21: The HttpAuthenticationMode enumeration type

```
public enum HttpAuthenticationMode
{
  Credentials = 3,
  PassThrough = 0,
  RevertToSelf = 2,
  WindowsCredentials = 4
}
```

Therefore, so far, the <LobSystem> element looks like this:

```
<LobSystem
xmlsn="http://schemas.microsoft.com/office/2006/03/BusinessDataCatalog"
xmlsn:xsi="http://www.w3.org/2001/XMLSchema-instance"
xsi:schemaLocation="http://schemas.microsoft.com/office/2006/03/BusinessDataCatalog
BDCMetadata.xsd"
Type=""
SystemUtility=""
ConnectionManager=""
EntityInstance=""
Version=""
Name=""
DefaultDisplayName=""
IsCached="">
  <LobSystemInstances></LobSystemInstances>
  <Entities></Entities>
  <Associations></Associations>
  <AccessControlList></AccessControlList>
  <LocalizedDisplayNames>
    <LocalizedDisplayName LCID=""></LocalizedDisplayName>
    <LocalizedDisplayName LCID=""></LocalizedDisplayName>
  </LocalizedDisplayNames>
  <Properties>
    <Property Name="" Type=""></Property>
    <Property Name="" Type=""></Property>
  </Properties>
</LobSystem>
```

Use the required Name attribute of the <LobSystem> document element to specify a unique name for the database or web service LOB application that this element represents. Use the DefaultDisplayName attribute to specify a default display name for the LobSystem metadata object. The SharePoint UI displays the value of this attribute as the name of the database or web service LOB application to users if no localized display name is defined for the current culture. Use the <LocalizeDisplayNames> child element to localize the display name of the LobSystem metadata object to the current culture of the user. Use the IsCached attribute of the <LobSystem> document element to specify whether the BDC should cache the LobSystem metadata object to improve performance.

The following table shows the names and schema types of all the attributes of the <LobSystem> document element:

Attribute Name	Schema Type
Type	LobSystemType
SystemUtility	string
ConnectionManager	string
EntityInstance	string
Version	string
Name	string
DefaultDisplayName	string
IsCached	Boolean

The following table shows the names and schema types of all the child elements of the <LobSystem> document element:

Child Element Name	Schema Type
LobSystemInstances	LobSystemInstances
Entities	Entities
Associations	Associations
AccessControlList	AccessControlList
LocalizedDisplayNames	LocalizedDisplayNames
Properties	Properties

So far you've seen all the schema types of all the attributes and child elements of a <LobSystem> element except for the LobSystemInstances, Entities, and Associations schema types, which are discussed in the following sections. For now, you should take a look at a couple of examples.

The first sample BDC application definition file shown in Listing 13-22 describes a database LOB application.

Listing 13-22: The BDC application definition file for a database LOB application

```
<?xml version="1.0" encoding="utf-8" standalone="yes"?>
<LobSystem
xmlsn="http://schemas.microsoft.com/office/2006/03/BusinessDataCatalog"
xmlsn:xsi="http://www.w3.org/2001/XMLSchema-instance"
xsi:schemaLocation="http://schemas.microsoft.com/office/2006/03/BusinessDataCatalog
BDCMetadata.xsd"
Type="Database"
Version="1.0.0.0"
Name="AdventureWorksDW"
SystemUtility="Microsoft.Office.Server.ApplicationRegistry.SystemSpecific.Db
.DbSystemUtility"
ConnectionManager="Microsoft.Office.Server.ApplicationRegistry.SystemSpecific.Db
.DbConnectionManager"
EntityInstance="Microsoft.Office.Server.ApplicationRegistry.SystemSpecific.Db
.DbEntityInstance"
DefaultDisplayName="Adventure Works"
IsCached="true">
  <Properties>
    <Property Name="WildcardCharacter" Type="System.String">%</Property>
  </Properties>
  <LocalizedDisplayNames>
    <LocalizedDisplayName LCID="1033">Adventure Works</LocalizedDisplayName>
  </LocalizedDisplayNames>
  <AccessControlList>
    <AccessControlList Principal="domainname\username1">
      <Right BdcRights="Edit" />
      <Right BdcRights="SetPermissions" />
    </AccessControlList>
  </AccessControlList>
</LobSystem>
```

This LOB application uses the AdventureWorksDW Microsoft SQL Server 2005 sample database. Note that the default installation of SQL Server 2005 does not install this database. However, this database is available as a free download from the Microsoft web site. The BDC application definition file shown in Listing 13-22 performs these tasks:

- Specifies the following XML namespace as the default XML namespace:

```
http://schemas.microsoft.com/office/2006/03/BusinessDataCatalog
```

  Recall that this XML namespace contains the BDC schema types, elements, and attributes.

- Uses the schemaLocation attribute to specify the location of the BdcMetadata.xsd file that defines the preceding namespace. This assumes that you've copied the BdcMetadata.xsd file to your working directory. Another option is to copy this file to the Schemas folder under the Xml folder of your installation of the Visual Studio as discussed earlier. Note that this step is only necessary if you want to take advantage of the Visual Studio IntelliSense support.

- Names the database LOB application "AdventureWorksDW":

```
Name="AdventureWorksDW"
```

- Specifies a version for the BDC application definition. This ensures that no one can override this BDC application definition with another one with a lower version:

```
Version="1.0.0.0"
```

- Specifies a default display name for the database LOB application:

```
DefaultDisplayName="Adventure Works"
```

- Sets the IsCached attribute to true to instruct the BDC to cache the LOB system metadata object to improve performance.
- Specifies the values of the SystemUtility, ConnectionManager, and EntityInstance attributes as discussed earlier. Note that specifying these attributes is optional.
- Sets the Type attribute to "Database" to specify that the LOB application being described is a database:

```
Type="Database"
```

- Sets the value of the WildcardCharacter property to specify the % character as the wildcard character:

```
<Properties>
  <Property Name="WildcardCharacter" Type="System.String">%</Property>
</Properties>
```

  As you'll see later, the value of this property is used by wildcard filters.

- Specifies "Adventure Works" as the localized display name of the LOB system metadata object for the culture with the locale identifier value of 1033:

```
<LocalizedDisplayNames>
  <LocalizedDisplayName LCID="1033">Adventure Works</LocalizedDisplayName>
</LocalizedDisplayNames>
```

- Specifies an ACL for the LOB system metadata object to secure access to this object:

```
<AccessControlList>
  <AccessControlEntry Principal="domainname\username1">
    <Right BdcRights="Edit" />
    <Right BdcRights="SetPermissions" />
  </AccessControlEntry>
</AccessControlList>
```

The second sample BDC application definition file describes a web service LOB application as shown in Listing 13-23.

Listing 13-23: A BDC application definition file that describes a web service LOB application

```
<LobSystem
xmlsn="http://schemas.microsoft.com/office/2006/03/BusinessDataCatalog"
xmlsn:xsi="http://www.w3.org/2001/XMLSchema-instance"
xsi:schemaLocation="http://schemas.microsoft.com/office/2006/03/BusinessDataCatalog
BDCMetadata.xsd"
Type="WebService"
Version="1.0.0.0"
Name="AWSECommerceService"
SystemUtility="Microsoft.Office.Server.ApplicationRegistry.SystemSpecific
.WebService.WebServiceSystemUtility"
ConnectionManager="Microsoft.Office.Server.ApplicationRegistry.SystemSpecific
.WebService.WebServiceConnectionManager"
EntityInstance="Microsoft.Office.Server.ApplicationRegistry.SystemSpecific
.WebService.WebServiceEntityInstance"
DefaultDisplayName="Amazon E-Commerce Web Service"
IsCached="true">
  <Properties>
    <Property Name="WebServiceProxyNamespace" Type="System.String">
      AWSECommerceService
    </Property>
    <Property Name="WsdlFetchAuthenticationMode" Type="System.String">
      PassThrough
    </Property>
    <Property Name="WsdlFetchUrl" Type="System.String">
      http://webservices.amazon.com/AWSECommerceService/AWSECommerceService.wsdl
    </Property>
    <Property Name="WildcardCharacter" Type="System.String">%</Property>
  </Properties>
  <LocalizedDisplayNames>
    <LocalizedDisplayName LCID="1033">
      Amazon E-Commerce Web Service
    </LocalizedDisplayName>
  </LocalizedDisplayNames>
  <AccessControlList>
    <AccessControlEntry Principal="domainname\username1">
      <Right BdcRights="Edit" />
      <Right BdcRights="SetPermissions" />
    </AccessControlEntry>
  </AccessControlList>
</LobSystem>
```

The LOB application described in Listing 13-23 uses the Amazon E-Commerce web service. This BDC application definition file performs these tasks:

- Specifies the default XML namespace
- Specifies the location of the BdcMetadata.xsd file
- Names the LOB application "AWSECommerceService":

```
Name="AWSECommerceService"
```

- Specifies a version for the BDC application definition
- Specifies a default display name for the LOB system metadata object
- Instructs the BDC to cache this LOB system metadata object
- Specifies the values of the SystemUtility, ConnectionManager, and EntityInstance optional attributes as discussed earlier
- Sets the Type attribute to WebService to specify that the LOB application is a web service:

```
Type="WebService"
```

- Sets the value of a property named WebServiceProxyNamespace to AWSECommerceService to specify AWSECommerceService as the namespace in which the BDC will generate the web services proxy class:

```
<Property Name="WebServiceProxyNamespace" Type="System.String">
  AWSECommerceService
</Property>
```

- Sets the value of the WsdlFetchAuthenticationMode property to PassThrough to specify that the BDC should use PassThrough authentication mode to fetch the WSDL document from the amazon.com site:

```
<Property Name="WsdlFetchAuthenticationMode" Type="System.String">
  PassThrough
</Property>
```

- Sets the value of the WsdlFetchUrl property to the URL from which the BDC can fetch the WSDL document that describes the Amazon E-Commerce web service:

```
<Property Name="WsdlFetchUrl" Type="System.String">
  http://webservices.amazon.com/AWSECommerceService/AWSECommerceService.wsdl
</Property>
```

- Sets the value of the WildcardCharacter property to %:

```
<Property Name="WildcardCharacter" Type="System.String">%</Property>
```

- Specifies "Amazon E-Commerce web Service" as the localized display name of the LOB system metadata object for the culture with the locale identifier value of 1033
- Specifies an ACL for the LOB system metadata object to secure access to this object

LobSystemInstances

Recall from Listing 13-13 that a <LobSystem> element can contain an optional element named <LobSystemInstances>, which is of the LobSystemInstances schema type. Listing 13-24 shows an excerpt from the BDCMetadata.xsd file that defines this schema type.

Listing 13-24: The LobSystemInstances schema type

```
<xs:complexType name="LobSystemInstances">
  <xs:sequence>
    <xs:element name="LobSystemInstance" type="bdc:LobSystemInstance"
    minOccurs="1" maxOccurs="2"/>
  </xs:sequence>
</xs:complexType>
```

According to this schema type, the <LobSystemInstances> child element of the <LobSystem> document element must contain at least one and at most two instances of a child XML element named <LobSystemInstance>, which is of the LobSystemInstance schema type defined in Listing 13-25.

Listing 13-25: The LobSystemInstance schema type

```
<xs:complexType name="LobSystemInstance">
  <xs:complexContent>
    <xs:extension base="bdc:MetadataObject"/>
  </xs:complexContent>
</xs:complexType>
```

As you can see, the LobSystemInstance schema type inherits from the MetadataObject schema type discussed earlier. According to the MetadataObject schema type shown in Listing 13-3, the <LobSystemInstance> element can contain single instances of two optional elements named <LocalizedDisplayNames> and <Properties> and three attributes named Name, DefaultDisplayName, and IsCached where only the Name attribute is required.

Use the Name attribute to specify a unique name for the LobSystemInstance metadata object. Use the IsCached attribute to specify whether the BDC should cache the LobSystemInstance metadata object to improve performance. Use the <LocalizedDisplayNames> child element to specify localized display names for desired cultures for the LobSystemInstance metadata object. This allows each user to see a localized display name for the LobSystemInstance metadata object. Use the <Properties> child element to specify the names, types, and values of the properties of the LobSystemInstance metadata object.

As mentioned earlier, the <LobSystemInstances> element can contain up to two <LobSystemInstance> child elements. Here is why and when you would need to use two <LobSystemInstance> child elements. The main responsibility of a LOB system instance metadata object is to provide the Infrastructure component of the BDC with the appropriate authentication settings and connection parameters. The Infrastructure component uses this information at runtime to connect to the back-end LOB application.

There are times when you may need to use two different sets of authentication settings and connection parameters, one for web clients and one specifically for search. In these scenarios you should use two <LobSystemInstance> child elements, one for specifying the authentication settings and connection parameters for web clients and one for specifying the authentication settings and connection parameters for search operations.

A LOB system instance metadata object supports the following properties only when it represents a database LOB application instance:

- **AuthenticationMode.** Specifies which authentication mode the BDC must use to authenticate to the back-end database LOB application. The property is of the

```
Microsoft.Office.Server.ApplicationRegistry.SystemSpecific.Db.DbAuthenticationMode
```

  enumeration type with the following possible values (see Listing 13-26):

  - **RevertToSelf.** Use this value to have the IIS worker process revert to self and to use the identity of the application pool to authenticate to the back-end database LOB application instead of impersonating and using the user identity to authenticate to the back-end database LOB application. This is an example of what is known as a trusted system authentication model where the middle tier (normally the web server) authenticates to the back-end business database or web service application as a fixed identity.
  - **PassThrough.** Use this value to have the operating system pass user credentials through to the back-end database LOB application. This normally applies in two important scenarios. The first scenario is when both the web server and the back-end database are running on the same machine. This is normally the case in a test environment. The second scenario is when Kerberos delegation is enabled on your domain. The Kerberos delegation handles the pass through of client credentials from the server running the BDC and the server running the business database. This is also a typical scenario in most test environments. The PassThrough authentication mode is an example of what is known as an impersonation/delegation authentication model where the middle tier (normally the web server) authenticates to the back-end business database or web service application as the identity of the client.
  - **WindowsCredentials.** Use this value to have the BDC use the user's Windows credentials from its SSO service to authenticate against the back-end database LOB system.
  - **Credentials.** Use this value if the back-end database LOB system does not support Windows credentials and uses database credentials. The BDC retrieves the user credentials from its SSO service and passes them as part of the connection string to the back-end database LOB system.

    This property is optional and defaults to RevertToSelf.

- **DatabaseAccessProvider.** Use this property to specify which data access provider the BDC must use to fetch the business data from the back-end database LOB application. This attribute takes a enumeration of type

```
Microsoft.Office.Server.ApplicationRegistry.SystemSpecific.Db.DbAccessProvider
```

  with the possible values of SqlServer, OleDb, Oracle, and Odbc (see Listing 13-27). This property is optional and defaults to SqlServer.

- **SsoProviderImplementation.** Use this property to specify the fully qualified name of the type of the class that implements the ISsoProvider interface and have the BDC use this implementation to fetch the user credentials from its single sign-on service. This property is required only if you set the AuthenticationMode property to Credentials or WindowsCredentials because these two authentication modes require the BDC to use the user credentials from its single sign-on service to authenticate to the back-end database LOB application.
- **SsoApplicationId.** Use this property to specify the ID of the SSO application definition that describes the LOB application where user credentials are stored. The BDC uses the SSO provider implementation specified in the SsoProviderImplementation property to fetch the user credentials from this LOB application. This property is optional.
- **RdbConnection Data Source.** Use this property to specify the name of the database server instance where the database LOB application resides. This property is optional.
- **RdbConnection Initial Catalog.** Use this property to specify the name of the database. This property is optional.
- **RdbConnection Integrated Security.** Use this property to specify whether to use the integrated security. This property is optional.
- **RdbConnection Pooling.** Use this property to specify whether the connection pooling is enabled.
- **NumberOfConnections.** Use this property to specify the maximum number of simultaneous connections to the back-end database LOB system. This property is optional and defaults to –1, which indicates that there is no upper limit on the number of simultaneous connections.
- **SecondarySsoApplicationId.** Use this property to specify the ID of the SSO application definition that describes the LOB application where the credentials used by the Username and Password filters are stored. These two filters are discussed later in this chapter. This property is optional.

Note that the BDC packs the values of the "RdbConnection Data Source," "RdbConnection Initial Catalog," "RdbConnection Integrated Security," and "RdbConnection Pooling" properties inside the connection string that it uses to connect to the back-end database LOB application.

Listing 13-26: The DbAuthenticationMode enumeration type

```
public enum DbAuthenticationMode
{
  PassThrough = 0,
  RdbCredentials = 3,
  RevertToSelf = 2,
  WindowsCredentials = 4
}
```

Listing 13-27: The DbAccessProvider enumeration type

```
public enum DbAccessProvider
{
  SqlServer,
  OleDb,
  Oracle,
  Odbc
}
```

A LOB system instance metadata object supports the following properties only if it represents a web service LOB application instance:

- **WebServiceAuthenticationMode.** Use this property to specify which authentication mode the BCD must use to authenticate to the back-end web service LOB application to fetch the WSDL document or to invoke a web method. The possible values of this property are RevertToSelf, PassThrough, Credentials, and WindowsCredentials with the same meanings discussed earlier. This property is optional.
- **SsoProviderImplementation.** Use this property to specify the fully namespace-qualified name of the class that implements the ISsoProvider interface and to have the BDC use this implementation to fetch user credentials from its single sign-on service. The BDC uses these credentials to authenticate to the back-end web service LOB application when it needs to fetch the WSDL document or to invoke a web method. This property is required if you set the authentication mode to Credentials or WindowsCredentials because both of these authentication modes require the BDC to fetch the user credentials from its SSO service.
- **WebServiceSsoApplicationId.** Use this property to specify the ID of the web service SSO application definition that describes the LOB application where user credentials are stored. The BDC uses the SSO provider implementation specified in the SsoProviderImplementation property to fetch user credentials from this LOB application. This property is required only if you set the authentication mode to Credentials or WindowsCredentials.
- **WebProxyServerConfiguration.** Use this property to specify the URL for the proxy server through which the BDC must fetch the WSDL document or invoke web methods. This property is optional.
- **NumOfConnections.** Use this property to specify the maximum allowable number of simultaneous connections to the back-end web service LOB application. This property is optional and defaults to –1, which indicates that there is no upper limit on the number of allowable simultaneous connections.
- **SecondarySsoApplicationId.** Use this property to specify the ID of the SSO application definition that describes the LOB application where the usernames and passwords for the Username and Password filters and HTTP and SOAP headers are stored. This property is optional.
- **WebServiceUrlOverride.** Use this property to specify a different URL for the web service than the one specified in the WSDL document. This property is optional.

Listing 13-28 shows what you have so far.

Listing 13-28: The BDC application defintion file

```
<LobSystem
xmlsn="http://schemas.microsoft.com/office/2006/03/BusinessDataCatalog"
xmlsn:xsi="http://www.w3.org/2001/XMLSchema-instance"
xsi:schemaLocation="http://schemas.microsoft.com/office/2006/03/BusinessDataCatalog
BDCMetadata.xsd"
Type=""
SystemUtility=""
ConnectionManager=""
EntityInstance=""
Version=""
Name=""
DefaultDisplayName=""
IsCached="">

  <LobSystemInstances>
    <LobSystemInstance Name="" DefaultDisplayName="" IsCached="">
      <LocalizedDisplayNames>
        <LocalizedDisplayName LCID=""></LocalizedDisplayName>
        <LocalizedDisplayName LCID=""></LocalizedDisplayName>
      </LocalizedDisplayNames>
      <Properties>
        <Property Name="" Type=""></Property>
        <Property Name="" Type=""></Property>
      </Properties>
    </LobSystemInstance>
  </LobSystemInstances>

  <Entities></Entities>
  <Associations></Associations>
  <AccessControlList></AccessControlList>
  <LocalizedDisplayNames>
    <LocalizedDisplayName LCID=""></LocalizedDisplayName>
    <LocalizedDisplayName LCID=""></LocalizedDisplayName>
  </LocalizedDisplayNames>
  <Properties>
    <Property Name="" Type=""></Property>
    <Property Name="" Type=""></Property>
  </Properties>
</LobSystem>
```

Next you'll revisit the database and web service LOB applications discussed in the previous section. Recall that the BDC application definition file shown in Listing 13-22 describes a database LOB application that uses the AdventureWorksDW Microsoft SQL Server 2005 sample database. Listing 13-29 extends Listing 13-22 to add the <LobSystemInstances> element.

Listing 13-29: The BDC application definition XML file for a database LOB application

```
<?xml version="1.0" encoding="utf-8" standalone="yes"?>
<LobSystem . . .>
  <Properties>
    <Property Name="WildcardCharacter" Type="System.String">%</Property>
  </Properties>

  <LobSystemInstances>
    <LobSystemInstance Name="AdventureWorksDWInstance"
    DefaultDisplayName="Adventure Works" IsCached="true">
      <Properties>
        <Property Name="AuthenticationMode"
        Type="Microsoft.Office.Server.ApplicationRegistry.SystemSpecific.
              Db.DbAuthenticationMode">
          PassThrough
        </Property>
        <Property Name="DatabaseAccessProvider"
        Type="Microsoft.Office.Server.ApplicationRegistry.SystemSpecific.
              Db.DbAccessProvider">
          SqlServer
        </Property>
        <Property Name="RdbConnection Data Source" Type="System.String">
          EnterYourAdventureWorksDW2005ServerNameHere
        </Property>
        <Property Name="RdbConnection Initial Catalog" Type="System.String">
          AdventureWorksDW
        </Property>
        <Property Name="RdbConnection Integrated Security" Type="System.String">
          SSPI
        </Property>
      </Properties>

      <LocalizedDisplayNames>
        <LocalizedDisplayName LCID="1033">
          Adventure Works
        </LocalizedDisplayName>
      </LocalizedDisplayNames>

    </LobSystemInstance>
  </LobSystemInstances>

</LobSystem>
```

Listing 13-29 provides an example of a LobSystemInstance metadata object that represents an instance of a database LOB application. Listing 13-30 presents a BDC application definition file that describes a web service LOB application. This listing extends Listing 13-23 to add support for a LobSystemInstance metadata object.

Listing 13-30: A BDC application definition file for a web service LOB application

```
<LobSystem . . .>
  <Properties>
    . . .
  </Properties>

  <LobSystemInstances>
    <LobSystemInstance Name="AWSECommerceService"
    DefaultDisplayName="Amazon E-Commerce Web Service" IsCached="true">
      <Properties>
        <Property Name="WebServiceAuthenticationMode" Type="System.String">
          PassThrough
        </Property>
        <!--
          <Property Name="WebProxyServerConfiguration" Type="System.String">
            EnterYourProxyServerURL
          </Property>
        -->
      </Properties>

      <LocalizedDisplayNames>
        <LocalizedDisplayName LCID="1033">
          Amazon E-Commerce Web Service
        </LocalizedDisplayName>
      </LocalizedDisplayNames>

    </LobSystemInstance>
  </LobSystemInstances>
</LobSystem>
```

Entities

Recall from Listing 13-13 that a <LobSystem> element can contain an optional element named <Entities>, which is of the Entities schema type. Listing 13-31 presents an excerpt from BdcMetadata.xsd that defines the Entities schema type.

Listing 13-31: The Entities schema type

```
<xs:complexType name="Entities">
  <xs:sequence>
    <xs:element name="Entity" type="bdc:Entity" minOccurs="1"
    maxOccurs="unbounded"/>
  </xs:sequence>
</xs:complexType>
```

According to this schema type, the <Entities> child element of the <LobSystem> document element must contain at least one instance of an XML element named <Entity>, which is of the Entity schema type defined in Listing 13-32.

Listing 13-32: The Entity schema type

```
<xs:complexType name="Entity">
  <xs:complexContent>
    <xs:extension base="bdc:IndividuallySecurableMetadataObject">
      <xs:sequence>
        <xs:element name="Identifiers" type="bdc:Identifiers" minOccurs="0"/>
        <xs:element name="Methods" type="bdc:Methods" minOccurs="0"/>
        <xs:element name="Actions" type="bdc:Actions" minOccurs="0"/>
      </xs:sequence>
      <xs:attribute name="EstimatedInstanceCount" type="bdc:InstanceCount"
      default="10000"/>
    </xs:extension>
  </xs:complexContent>
</xs:complexType>
```

As you can see, the Entity schema type extends the IndividuallySecurableMetadataObject schema type. According to the Entity schema type, an <Entity> element can contain:

- A sequence of three optional XML elements as follows:
  - <Identifiers>, which is of the Identifiers schema type
  - <Methods>, which is of the Methods schema type
  - <Actions>, which is of the Actions schema type
- An optional attribute named EstimatedInstanceCount, which is of the InstanceCount schema type with the default value of 10000.

Recall that IndividuallySecurableMetadataObject itself supports three optional child elements named <AccessControlList>, <LocalizedDisplayNames>, and <Properties> and three attributes named Name, DefaultDisplayName, and IsCached where only the Name attribute is required.

Therefore, an <Entity> element altogether can contain six optional child elements named <Identifiers>, <Methods>, <Actions>, <AccessControlList>, <LocalizedDisplayNames>, and <Properties> and four attributes named Name, DefaultDisplayName, IsCached, and EstimatedInstanceCount.

So far you've learned that a LobSystem metadata object represents a database or web service LOB application. A LobSystemInstance metadata object represents an instance of this database or web service LOB application. What does an Entity metadata object represent?

An Entity metadata object represents a business entity in a database or web service LOB application. A business entity in a database or web service LOB application represents a category or type of data. To help you understand what a business entity is in a database and web service LOB application, take a look at examples of these two types of LOB applications.

The first example is the web service LOB application that Listing 13-30 partly defines. Recall that this web service LOB application uses the Amazon E-Commerce web service. This web service exposes an important web method named ItemSearch, which returns a list of items that meet specified search criteria. Therefore, Item is a business entity in this web service LOB application. The equivalent of Item in a database LOB application would be a database table named Items, which contains item instances. There is a difference between an entity and an entity instance. An entity defines a category or type of data, whereas an entity instance is an instance of an entity. For example, the entity instances in the case of a call into the ItemSearch web method are the item instances that the method returns. Or the entity instances in the case of the database LOB application are the item instances, which are stored in table rows.

Listing 13-33 shows what you have so far.

Listing 13-33: The BDC application definition file

```
<LobSystem
xmlsn="http://schemas.microsoft.com/office/2006/03/BusinessDataCatalog"
xmlsn:xsi="http://www.w3.org/2001/XMLSchema-instance"
xsi:schemaLocation ="http://schemas.microsoft.com/office/2006/03/
BusinessDataCatalog BDCMetadata.xsd"
Type=""
SystemUtility=""
ConnectionManager=""
EntityInstance=""
Version=""
Name=""
DefaultDisplayName=""
IsCached="">

  <LobSystemInstances>
    <LobSystemInstance Name="" DefaultDisplayName="" IsCached="">
      <LocalizedDisplayNames>
        <LocalizedDisplayName LCID=""></LocalizedDisplayName>
        <LocalizedDisplayName LCID=""></LocalizedDisplayName>
      </LocalizedDisplayNames>
      <Properties>
        <Property Name="" Type=""></Property>
        <Property Name="" Type=""></Property>
      </Properties>
    </LobSystemInstance>
  </LobSystemInstances>

  <Entities>
    <Entity Name="" DefaultDisplayName="" IsCached="" EstimatedInstanceCount="">
      <AccessControlList>
        <AccessControlList Principal="">
          <Right BdcRights="" />
          <Right BdcRights="" />
        </AccessControlList>
      </AccessControlList>
      <LocalizedDisplayNames>
        <LocalizedDisplayName LCID=""></LocalizedDisplayName>
```

(continued)

Listing 13-33 *(continued)*

```
        </LocalizedDisplayNames>
        <Properties>
          <Property Name="" Type=""></Property>
        </Properties>
        <Identifiers></Identifiers>
        <Methods></Methods>
        <Actions></Actions>
      </Entity>
    </Entities>

    <Associations></Associations>
    <AccessControlList></AccessControlList>
    <LocalizedDisplayNames>
      <LocalizedDisplayName LCID=""></LocalizedDisplayName>
      <LocalizedDisplayName LCID=""></LocalizedDisplayName>
    </LocalizedDisplayNames>
    <Properties>
      <Property Name="" Type=""></Property>
      <Property Name="" Type=""></Property>
    </Properties>
  </LobSystem>
```

An entity metadata object of a LOB system metadata object that represents a database or web service LOB application supports the following properties:

- **Title.** Use this property to specify the name of the TypeDescriptor metadata object that describes the parameter metadata object that represents the title of the entity metadata object. The Business Data features such as Business Data Search and Business Data Columns displays this title to users. In other words, this title is the default title of the entity metadata object in a Business Data feature. This property is optional.
- **__BdcLastModifiedTimestamp.** Use this property to specify the name of the type descriptor metadata object that describes a parameter metadata object that represents the parameter that specifies the last modified date of an entity instance. Use this property to enable incremental search crawls. This property is optional.
- **Audit.** Use this property to specify whether an entry should be written to the Shared Resource Provider's audit log each time one of the method instance metadata objects of the entity metadata object is executed. This property is optional and defaults to true. The possible values of this property are true and false.
- **DefaultAction.** Use this property to specify the text for the hyperlink that displays the default action of the entity metadata object in a Business Data feature. The BDC automatically defines a default action for each entity metadata object. This default action appears as a hyperlink wherever the entity metadata object goes. Users click this hyperlink to view the profile of the entity metadata object.

Next, you'll take a look at a couple of examples. Listing 13-34 presents the first example, which extends Listing 13-29 to define entity metadata objects for the LOB system metadata object that represents the AdventureWorksDW Microsoft SQL Server 2005 sample database.

Listing 13-34: The BDC application definition file that describes the database LOB system

```
<?xml version="1.0" encoding="utf-8" standalone="yes"?>
<LobSystem . . .>
  <Properties>
    <Property Name="WildcardCharacter" Type="System.String">%</Property>
  </Properties>

  <LobSystemInstances>
    <LobSystemInstance Name="AdventureWorksDWInstance"
    DefaultDisplayName="Adventure Works" IsCached="true">
      . . .
    </LobSystemInstance>
  </LobSystemInstances>

  <Entities>
    <Entity EstimatedInstanceCount="10000" Name="Product" IsCached="true"
    DefaultDisplayName="Product">
      <Properties>
        <Property Name="Title" Type="System.String">EnglishProductName</Property>
        <Property Name="DefaultAction" Type="System.String">View Profile</Property>
      </Properties>
      <AccessControlList>
        <AccessControlEntry Principal="domainname1\username1">
          <Right BdcRights="Edit" />
          <Right BdcRights="SetPermissions" />
        </AccessControlEntry>
      </AccessControlList>
      <LocalizedDisplayNames>
        <LocalizedDisplayName LCID="1033">Product</LocalizedDisplayName>
      </LocalizedDisplayNames>
    </Entity>
    <Entity EstimatedInstanceCount="1000" Name="Reseller" IsCached="true"
    DefaultDisplayName="Reseller">
      <Properties>
        <Property Name="__BdcTitle" Type="System.String">ResellerName</Property>
        <Property Name="Title" Type="System.String">ResellerName</Property>
        <Property Name="DefaultAction" Type="System.String">View Profile</Property>
      </Properties>
      <AccessControlList>
        <AccessControlEntry Principal="domainname1\username1">
          <Right BdcRights="Edit" />
          <Right BdcRights="SetPermissions" />
        </AccessControlEntry>
      </AccessControlList>
```

(continued)

Listing 13-34 *(continued)*

```
        <LocalizedDisplayNames>
          <LocalizedDisplayName LCID="1033">Reseller</LocalizedDisplayName>
        </LocalizedDisplayNames>
      </Entity>
      <Entity EstimatedInstanceCount="10000" Name="ProductSubcategory"
      IsCached="true" DefaultDisplayName="Product Subcategory">
        <Properties>
          <Property Name="Title" Type="System.String">
            EnglishProductSubcategoryName
          </Property>
          <Property Name="DefaultAction" Type="System.String">View Profile</Property>
        </Properties>
        <AccessControlList>
          <AccessControlEntry Principal="domainname1\username1">
            <Right BdcRights="Edit" />
            <Right BdcRights="SetPermissions" />
          </AccessControlEntry>
        </AccessControlList>
        <LocalizedDisplayNames>
          <LocalizedDisplayName LCID="1033">
            Product Subcategory
          </LocalizedDisplayName>
        </LocalizedDisplayNames>
      </Entity>
      <Entity EstimatedInstanceCount="10000" Name="ProductCategory"
      IsCached="true" DefaultDisplayName="Product Category">
        <Properties>
          <Property Name="Title" Type="System.String">
            EnglishProductCategoryName
          </Property>
          <Property Name="DefaultAction" Type="System.String">View Profile</Property>
        </Properties>
        <AccessControlList>
          <AccessControlEntry Principal="domainname1\username1">
            <Right BdcRights="Edit" />
            <Right BdcRights="SetPermissions" />
          </AccessControlEntry>
        </AccessControlList>
        <LocalizedDisplayNames>
          <LocalizedDisplayName LCID="1033">Product Category</LocalizedDisplayName>
        </LocalizedDisplayNames>
      </Entity>
    </Entities>

  </LobSystem>
```

The AdventureWorksDW database contains four tables named DimProduct, DimReseller, DimProductSubcategory, and DimProductCategory among many other tables. Listing 13-34 defines four cachable (IsCached=true) entity metadata objects named Product, Reseller, ProductSubcategory, and ProductCategory to represent these four tables and sets the values of the EstimatedInstanceCount and DefaultDisplayName attributes of these entity metadata objects. As the name suggests, the EstimatedInstanceCount attribute specifies the estimated count of the entity instances for the entity metadata object. Business Data features such as Business Data List Web Part use the value of this property when they are rendering these entity instances. For instance, those Business Data features that support paging can use this value to determine how many link buttons they need to render in their paging interface.

Note that this BDC application definition file also defines an ACL for these four entity metadata objects that gives a principal with identity name of domainname1\username1 both the Edit and SetPermissions rights on these entity metadata objects. This means that this principal is allowed to update, delete, and create these entity metadata objects and to set permissions on them. The right to set permissions means that this principal can update, delete, and add access control entries to these four entity metadata objects to specify which principals have which rights to these metadata objects.

Also note that this file specifies localized display names for these four entity metadata objects for the culture with the LCID of 1033. This means that users with this culture will see these localized display names.

This BDC application definition file also sets the values of the Title and DefaultAction properties of these four entity metadata objects:

```
        <Property Name="DefaultAction" Type="System.String">View Profile</Property>
```

Next, you'll take a look at an example of a web service LOB system that defines entity metadata objects. Listing 13-35 extends Listing 13-30 to define entity metadata objects for the LOB system metadata object that represents the Amazon E-Commerce web service LOB application.

Listing 13-35: The BDC application definition file that describes a web service LOB application

```
<LobSystem . . .>
  <Properties>
    . . .
  </Properties>

  <LobSystemInstances>
    <LobSystemInstance Name="AWSECommerceService"
    DefaultDisplayName="Amazon E-Commerce Web Service" IsCached="true">
      . . .
  </LobSystemInstances>

  <Entities>
    <Entity Name="Item" EstimatedInstanceCount="10000"
    DefaultDisplayName="Item" IsCached="true">
      <AccessControlList>
        <AccessControlEntry Principal="domainname1\username1">
          <Right BdcRights="Edit" />
          <Right BdcRights="SetPermissions" />
        </AccessControlEntry>
      </AccessControlList>
      <LocalizedDisplayNames>
        <LocalizedDisplayName LCID="1033">Item</LocalizedDisplayName>
```

(continued)

Listing 13-35 *(continued)*

```
        </LocalizedDisplayNames>
      </Entity>
      <Entity Name="EditorialReview" EstimatedInstanceCount="10000"
      DefaultDisplayName="Editorial Review" IsCached="true">
        <AccessControlList>
          <AccessControlEntry Principal="domainname1\username1">
            <Right BdcRights="Edit" />
            <Right BdcRights="SetPermissions" />
          </AccessControlEntry>
        </AccessControlList>
        <LocalizedDisplayNames>
          <LocalizedDisplayName LCID="1033">Editorial Review</LocalizedDisplayName>
        </LocalizedDisplayNames>
      </Entity>
    </Entities>
  </LobSystem>
```

Listing 13-35 defines an entity metadata object named Item whose instances represent searchable items such as the ones returned from the ItemSearch web method of the Amazon E-Commerce web service. As such, these instances are known as entity instances. Listing 13-35 also defines an entity metadata object named EditorialReview whose instances represent editorial reviews for searchable items. As such, these editorial reviews are also entity instances. Note that Listing 13-35 defines default display names for both Item and EditorialReview metadata objects and sets their IsCached attributes to true to request the BDC to cache these metadata objects to improve performance. Listing 13-35 also sets the ACLs for both Item and EditorialReview metadata objects where it gives both Edit and SetPermissions rights on both metadata objects to a principal with the identity name of domainname1\username1. Finally, Listing 13-35 specifies a localized display name for both metadata objects for the culture with an LCID of 1033.

InstanceCount

Recall from Listing 13-32 that the <Entity> element features an attribute named EstimatedInstanceCount, which is of InstanceCount schema type. Listing 13-36 presents the definition of this schema type.

Listing 13-36: The InstanceCount schema type

```
<xs:simpleType name="InstanceCount">
  <xs:restriction base="xs:integer">
    <xs:minInclusive value="0"/>
  </xs:restriction>
</xs:simpleType>
```

As you can see, the InstanceCount schema type is a restriction of the integer schema type where the minimum allowable value is set to zero. Obviously a negative instance count value does not make sense! Use the EstimatedInstanceCount attribute to specify the estimated count of the entity instances of the entity metadata object. Business Data features use this count when they're displaying the entity instances of the entity metadata object. For example, a Business Data feature may use this count to determine how many link buttons it needs to render in its paging interface.

Identifiers

Recall from Listing 13-32 that the <Entity> element features an optional child element named <Identifiers>, which is of the Identifiers schema type shown in Listing 13-37.

Listing 13-37: The Identifiers schema type

```
<xs:complexType name="Identifiers">
  <xs:sequence>
    <xs:element name="Identifier" type="bdc:Identifier" minOccurs="1"
    maxOccurs="unbounded"/>
  </xs:sequence>
</xs:complexType>
```

According to Listing 13-37, the <Identifiers> element must contain at least one instance of an element named <Identifier>, which is of the Identifier schema type shown in Listing 13-38.

Listing 13-38: The Identifier schema type

```
<xs:complexType name="Identifier">
  <xs:complexContent>
    <xs:extension base="bdc:MetadataObject">
      <xs:attribute name="TypeName" type="xs:string" use="required"/>
    </xs:extension>
  </xs:complexContent>
</xs:complexType>
```

As Listing 13-38 shows, the Identifier schema type extends the MetadataObject schema type. According to the Identifier schema type, an <Identifier> metadata object contains a required attribute named TypeName, which is of the string schema type. Because the MetadataObject schema type supports the optional <LocalizedDisplayNames> and <Properties> elements and the Name, DefaultDisplayName, and IsCached attributes, the <Identifier> element can contain the optional <LocalizedDisplayNames> and <Properties> elements and the Name, DefaultDisplayName, and IsCached attributes where only the Name attribute is required.

So far you've learned that the <Entity> element represents a business entity in a database or web service LOB application and that the <Entity> element can contain the optional <Identifiers> child element, which in turn contains at least one instance of the <Identifier> child element. What does the <Identifiers> child element of the <Entity> element represent? What does the <Identifier> child elements of the <Identifiers> element represent? First, let's remind ourselves of the difference between two important concepts, that is, entity and entity instance. A business entity defines a category or type of data. Entity instances, on the other hand, represent the data themselves. For example, in the case of the Amazon E-Commerce web service LOB application, the Item entity metadata object represents a category of data, that is, searchable items. The entity instances, on the other hand, represent the searchable items themselves such as the items returned from the ItemSearch web method.

In the case of the AdventureWorksDW database LOB application, the Product, ProductSubcategory, ProductCategory, and Reseller entity metadata objects respectively represent the DimProduct, DimProductSubcategory, DimProductCategory, and DimReseller database tables and entity instances represent the rows in these database tables.

The <Identifiers> child element of the <Entity> element represents a set of identifiers or keys whose values uniquely identify business entity instances. For example, in the case of the Amazon E-Commerce web service LOB application this set consists of a single key, that is, ItemId. In this case, the <Identifiers> element represents the set itself and the <Identifier> child element of the <Identifiers> element represents the ItemId key. In this case, the <Identifiers> element contains a single <Identifier> child element because the set contains a single key. In cases where the set contains more than one key you must add a separate <Identifier> child element for each key in the set.

In the case of a database LOB application such as the AdventureWorksDW database LOB application, the database fields that make up the primary key of a database table are the set of identifiers or keys whose values uniquely identify database rows, which are represented by business entity instances. In this case, the <Identifiers> element represents the primary key, and each <Identifier> child element of the <Identifiers> element represents one of the database fields that makes up the primary key.

You must set the Name attribute of an <Identifier> element to the name of the identifier or key that the element represents. For example, in the case of the Item metadata object, which represents the searchable items category in the Amazon E-Commerce web service LOB application, the <Identifier> element represents the ItemId identifier or key, which uniquely identifies an item. As such, you must assign the string "ItemId" as the value of the Name attribute on this <Identifier> element. In the case of the Product metadata object, which represents the DimProduct database table in the AdventureWorksDW database LOB application, the <Identifier> element represents the ProductKey primary key of this database table so you must assign the string "ProductKey" as the value of the Name attribute on this <Identifier> element.

As mentioned, the <Identifiers> child element of an <Entity> element is optional. This means that you could have an entity metadata object without identifier metadata objects. This does not mean that the business entity that the entity metadata object represents does not have identifiers. For example, you may decide to define an entity metadata object that does not have identifier metadata objects to represent a database table even through the database table itself comes with a primary key.

However, keep in mind that if you do choose to define an entity metadata object that does not have identifier metadata objects you will not be able to:

- Search and index its associated entity instances because you need to know the identifiers of the entity instances. For example, you need to know the primary key of an entity instance to query the back-end database for more detailed information about the entity instance.
- Define actions on the entity metadata object.
- Relate or associate the entity metadata object to other entity metadata objects.
- Use in any Business Data features except the Business Data Related List Web Part because any other Business Data feature such as Business Data Columns needs to know the identities of the business entity instances that it displays to operate properly.

There are times that you may not care about any of the preceding features. You may just want to display a blob of data to users. In these scenarios you may choose not to define identifier metadata objects for your entity metadata object.

As mentioned earlier, an <Identifier> element features a required attribute named TypeName that specifies the .NET type of the business identifier that the identifier metadata object represents. The BDC only supports primitive .NET types, that is, System.Boolean, System.Guid, System.Byte, System.Char, System.DateTime, System.Decimal, System.Double, System.Int32, System.Int64, System.Int16, and System.Single.

Listing 13-39 shows what you have so far.

Listing 13-39: The BDC application definition file

```
<LobSystem
xmlsn="http://schemas.microsoft.com/office/2006/03/BusinessDataCatalog"
xmlsn:xsi="http://www.w3.org/2001/XMLSchema-instance"
xsi:schemaLocation="http://schemas.microsoft.com/office/2006/03/BusinessDataCatalog
BDCMetadata.xsd"
Type=""
SystemUtility=""
ConnectionManager=""
EntityInstance=""
Version=""
Name=""
DefaultDisplayName=""
IsCached="">

  <LobSystemInstances>
    <LobSystemInstance Name="" DefaultDisplayName="" IsCached="">
      <LocalizedDisplayNames>
        <LocalizedDisplayName LCID=""></LocalizedDisplayName>
        <LocalizedDisplayName LCID=""></LocalizedDisplayName>
      </LocalizedDisplayNames>
      <Properties>
        <Property Name="" Type=""></Property>
        <Property Name="" Type=""></Property>
      </Properties>
    </LobSystemInstance>
  </LobSystemInstances>

  <Entities>
    <Entity Name="" DefaultDisplayName="" IsCached="" EstimatedInstanceCount="">
      <AccessControlList>
        <AccessControlList Principal="">
          <Right BdcRights="" />
          <Right BdcRights="" />
        </AccessControlList>
      </AccessControlList>
      <LocalizedDisplayNames>
        <LocalizedDisplayName LCID=""></LocalizedDisplayName>
      </LocalizedDisplayNames>
      <Properties>
        <Property Name="" Type=""></Property>
      </Properties>
```

(continued)

Listing 13-39 *(continued)*

```
          <Identifiers>
        <Identifier Name="" DefaultDisplayName="" IsCached="" TypeName="">
          <Properties>
            <Property Name="" Type=""></Property>
            <Property Name="" Type=""></Property>
          </Properties>
          <LocalizedDisplayNames>
            <LocalizedDisplayName LCID=""></LocalizedDisplayName>
            <LocalizedDisplayName LCID=""></LocalizedDisplayName>
          </LocalizedDisplayNames>
        </Identifier>
      </Identifiers>
      <Methods></Methods>
      <Actions></Actions>
    </Entity>
  </Entities>

  <Associations></Associations>

  <AccessControlList></AccessControlList>
  <LocalizedDisplayNames>
    <LocalizedDisplayName LCID=""></LocalizedDisplayName>
    <LocalizedDisplayName LCID=""></LocalizedDisplayName>
  </LocalizedDisplayNames>
  <Properties>
    <Property Name="" Type=""></Property>
    <Property Name="" Type=""></Property>
  </Properties>
</LobSystem>
```

Next, you'll look at a couple of examples. Listing 13-40 extends Listing 13-34 to define identifier metadata objects for the Product, Reseller, ProductSubcategory, and ProductCategory metadata objects of the AdventureWorksDW database LOB application.

Listing 13-40: The BDC application definition file that describes the database LOB system

```
<?xml version="1.0" encoding="utf-8" standalone="yes"?>
<LobSystem . . .>
  <Properties>
    <Property Name="WildcardCharacter" Type="System.String">%</Property>
  </Properties>

  <LobSystemInstances>
    <LobSystemInstance Name="AdventureWorksDWInstance"
    DefaultDisplayName="Adventure Works" IsCached="true">
      . . .
    </LobSystemInstance>
  </LobSystemInstances>

  <Entities>
    <Entity Name="Product" . . .>
```

```
      <Identifiers>
        <Identifier Name="ProductKey" TypeName="System.Int32"
        DefaultDisplayName="Product Key" IsCached="true">
          <LocalizedDisplayNames>
            <LocalizedDisplayName LCID="1033">Product Key</LocalizedDisplayName>
          </LocalizedDisplayNames>
        </Identifier>
      </Identifiers>
      . . .
    </Entity>

    <Entity Name="Reseller" . . .>
      <Identifiers>
        <Identifier Name="ResellerKey" TypeName="System.Int32"
        DefaultDisplayName="Reseller Key" IsCached="true">
          <LocalizedDisplayNames>
            <LocalizedDisplayName LCID="1033">Reseller Key</LocalizedDisplayName>
          </LocalizedDisplayNames>
        </Identifier>
      </Identifiers>
      . . .
    </Entity>

    <Entity Name="ProductSubcategory" . . .>
      <Identifiers>
        <Identifier Name="ProductSubcategoryKey" TypeName="System.Int32"
        DefaultDisplayName="Product Subcategory Key" IsCached="true">
          <LocalizedDisplayNames>
            <LocalizedDisplayName LCID="1033">
              Product Subcategory Key
            </LocalizedDisplayName>
          </LocalizedDisplayNames>
        </Identifier>
      </Identifiers>
      . . .
    </Entity>

    <Entity Name="ProductCategory" . . .>
      <Identifiers>
        <Identifier Name="ProductCategoryKey" TypeName="System.Int32"
        DefaultDisplayName="Product Category Key" IsCached="true">
          <LocalizedDisplayNames>
            <LocalizedDisplayName LCID="1033">
              Product Category Key
            </LocalizedDisplayName>
          </LocalizedDisplayNames>
        </Identifier>

      </Identifiers>
      . . .
    </Entity>
  </Entities>

</LobSystem>
```

As you can see, this code listing defines:

- A cachable identifier metadata object named ProductKey to represent the ProductKey primary key of the DimProduct database table.
- A cachable identifier metadata object named ProductSubcategoryKey to represent the ProductSubcategoryKey primary key of the DimProductSubcategory database table.
- A cachable identifier metadata object named ProductCategoryKey to represent the ProductCategoryKey primary key of the DimProductCategory database table.
- A cachable identifier metadata object named ResellerKey to represent the ResellerKey primary key of the DimReseller database table.

Note that the values of the Name attributes on these <Identifier> elements are set to the names of the primary keys they represent. Also notice that Listing 13-40 defines localized display names for these identifier metadata objects for the culture with an LCID of 1033. This listing also defines default display names for these identifier metadata objects.

Listing 13-41 extends Listing 13-35 to define identifier metadata objects for the Item entity metadata object of the Amazon E-Commerce web service LOB application.

Listing 13-41: The BDC application definition file that describes a web service LOB application

```
<LobSystem . . .>
  <Properties>
    . . .
  </Properties>

  <LobSystemInstances>
    <LobSystemInstance Name="AWSECommerceService"
    DefaultDisplayName="Amazon E-Commerce Web Service" IsCached="true">
      . . .
  </LobSystemInstances>

  <Entities>
    <Entity Name="Item" . . .>
      <Identifiers>
        <Identifier Name="ItemId" TypeName="System.String"
        DefaultDisplayName="Item ID" IsCached="true">
          <LocalizedDisplayNames>
            <LocalizedDisplayName LCID="1033">Item ID</LocalizedDisplayName>
          </LocalizedDisplayNames>
        </Identifier>
      </Identifiers>
      . . .
    </Entity>

    <Entity Name="EditorialReview" . . .>
      . . .
    </Entity>
  </Entities>
</LobSystem>
```

As you can see, the BDC application definition file shown in Listing 13-41 defines an identifier metadata object named ItemId to represent the ItemId key in the Amazon E-Commerce web service LOB application. Note that the EditorReview entity metadata object has no identifier metadata object associated with it. As you can see, not every entity metadata object must have associated identifier metadata objects.

Methods

As Listing 13-32 shows, an <Entity> element can contain an optional child element named <Methods>, which is of the Methods schema type defined in Listing 13-42.

Listing 13-42: The Methods schema type

```
<xs:complexType name="Methods">
  <xs:sequence>
    <xs:element name="Method" type="bdc:Method" minOccurs="1"
    maxOccurs="unbounded"/>
  </xs:sequence>
</xs:complexType>
```

As you can see, the <Methods> element must contain at least one instance of a child element named <Method>, which is of the Method schema type shown in Listing 13-43.

Listing 13-43: The Method schema type

```
<xs:complexType name="Method">
  <xs:complexContent>
    <xs:extension base="bdc:IndividuallySecurableMetadataObject">
      <xs:sequence>
        <xs:element name="FilterDescriptors" type="bdc:FilterDescriptors"
        minOccurs="0" maxOccurs="1"/>
        <xs:element name="Parameters" type="bdc:Parameters" minOccurs="0"
        maxOccurs="1"/>
        <xs:element name="MethodInstances" type="bdc:MethodInstances"
        minOccurs="0" maxOccurs="1"/>
      </xs:sequence>
      <xs:attribute name="IsStatic" type="xs:boolean" default="true"/>
    </xs:extension>
  </xs:complexContent>
</xs:complexType>
```

As Listing 13-43 illustrates, the Method schema type extends the IndividuallySecurableMetadataObject schema type. According to the Method schema type, a <Method> element can contain:

- A sequence of optional elements as follows:
    - <FilterDescriptors>, which is of the FilterDescriptors schema type
    - <Parameters>, which is of the Parameters schema type
    - <MethodInstances>, which is of the MethodInstances schema type

- An attribute named IsStatic, which is of the boolean schema type with the default value of true. Use the IsStatic attribute to specify whether the method must be executed on the entity metadata object statically using Entity.Execute or it must be executed in the context of an entity instance using IEntityInstance.Execute.

Because the Method schema type inherits from the IndividuallySecurableMetadataObject schema type, a method metadata object is an individually securable metadata object and just like any other individually securable metadata object you can specify its access control list (ACL):

```
<Method . . .>
  <AccessControlList>
    <AccessControlEntry Principal="domainname1\username1">
      <Right BdcRight="Edit" />
      <Right BdcRight="SetPermissions" />
    </AccessControlEntry>
  </AccessControlList>
</Method>
```

This example gives the principal with the identity name of domainname1\username1 the right to update, delete, and create the MyMethod method metadata object and to set permissions on it.

Because the Method schema type inherits from the IndividuallySecurableMetadataObject schema type, which in turn inherits from the MetadataObject schema type, a method is a metadata object and just like any other metadata object in the BDC you can:

- Specify the values of its properties:

```
<Method . . .>
  <Properties>
    <Property Name="" Type=""></Property>
    <Property Name="" Type=""></Property>
  </Properties>
  . . .
</Method>
```

- Specify localized display names for it:

```
<Method . . .>
  <LocalizedDisplayNames>
    <LocalizedDisplayName LCID=""></LocalizedDisplayName>
  </LocalizedDisplayNames>
</Method>
```

- Specify a name for it. Keep in mind that every metadata object must have a name because the MetadataObject schema type defines the Name attribute as a required attribute (see Listing 13-3):

```
<Method Name="MyMethod" . . .>
  . . .
</Method>
```

- Specify a default display name for it:

```
<Method DefaultDisplayName="My Method" . . .>
  . . .
</Method>
```

- Specify whether it should be cached:

```
<Method IsCached="true" . . .>
  . . .
</Method>
```

So far you've learned that an entity metadata object represents a business entity in a database or web service LOB application. An entity instance, on the other hand, represents a business entity instance in a database or web service LOB application. What does a method metadata object represent? What do the properties of a method metadata object represent?

A method metadata object represents a business operation on a business entity in a database or web service LOB application. A business operation in a database LOB application is normally a database query in the form of a SQL SELECT statement or a stored procedure. As such, a method metadata object in a database LOB application normally represents a database query. A business operation in a web service LOB application is normally a web method. As such, a method metadata object in a web service LOB application normally represents a web method.

In the case of a database LOB application, a method metadata object supports two properties that you need to set:

- **RdbCommandText.** This property is of the System.String .NET type and specifies the command text, which is normally a SQL SELECT statement or a stored procedure.
- **RdbCommandType.** This property is of the System.Data.CommandType .NET type and specifies the type of the command specified in the RdbCommandText. As Listing 13-44 shows, the CommandType is an enumeration type with possible values of StoredProcedure, TableDirect, and Text.

Listing 13-44: The CommandType enumeration type

```
public enum CommandType
{
  StoredProcedure = 4,
  TableDirect = 0x200,
  Text = 1
}
```

Next you'll take a look at a couple of examples. Listing 13-45 extends Listing 13-40 to define method metadata objects for the entity metadata objects that represent the business entities in the AdventureWorksDW SQL Server 2005 database LOB system.

Listing 13-45: The BDC application definition file that describes the database LOB system

```
<?xml version="1.0" encoding="utf-8" standalone="yes"?>
<LobSystem . . .>
  <Properties>
    <Property Name="WildcardCharacter" Type="System.String">%</Property>
  </Properties>

  <LobSystemInstances>
    <LobSystemInstance Name="AdventureWorksDWInstance"
    DefaultDisplayName="Adventure Works" IsCached="true">
      . . .
    </LobSystemInstance>
  </LobSystemInstances>

  <Entities>
    <Entity Name="Product" . . .>
      <Identifiers>
        <Identifier Name="ProductKey" TypeName="System.Int32" . . .>
          . . .
        </Identifier>
      </Identifiers>
      <Methods>
        <Method Name="GetProducts" DefaultDisplayName="Get Products"
        IsCached="true" IsStatic="true">
          <Properties>
            <Property Name="RdbCommandText" Type="System.String">
              SELECT * FROM DimProduct WHERE (ProductKey &gt;= @MinProductKey) AND
                                             (ProductKey &lt;= @MaxProductKey) AND
                                 (EnglishProductName LIKE @EnglishProductName) AND
                                 (EnglishDescription LIKE @EnglishDescription) AND
                                 (Status='Current')
            </Property>
            <Property Name="RdbCommandType" Type="System.Data.CommandType">
              Text
            </Property>
          </Properties>
          <LocalizedDisplayNames>
            <LocalizedDisplayName LCID="1033">Get Products</LocalizedDisplayNames>
          </LocalizedDisplayNames>
          <AccessControlList>
            <AccessControlEntry Principal="domainname1\username1">
              <Right BdcRight="Edit" />
              <Right BdcRight="SetPermissions" />
            </AccessControlEntry>
          </AccessControlList>
        </Method>
      </Methods>
      . . .
```

```
</Entity>

<Entity Name="Reseller" . . .>
  <Identifiers>
    <Identifier Name="ResellerKey" TypeName="System.Int32" . . .>
      . . .
    </Identifier>
  </Identifiers>
  <Methods>
    <Method Name="ResellerIDEnumerator" IsStatic="true"
    DefaultDisplayName="Reseller ID Enumerator" IsCached="true">
      <Properties>
        <Property Name="RdbCommandText" Type="System.String">
          SELECT ResellerKey FROM DimReseller
        </Property>
        <Property Name="RdbCommandType" Type="System.Data.CommandType">
          Text
        </Property>
      </Properties>
      <LocalizedDisplayNames>
        <LocalizedDisplayName LCID="1033">
          Reseller ID Enumerator
        </LocalizedDisplayNames>
      </LocalizedDisplayNames>
      <AccessControlList>
        <AccessControlEntry Principal="domainname1\username1">
          <Right BdcRight="Edit" />
          <Right BdcRight="SetPermissions" />
        </AccessControlEntry>
      </AccessControlList>
    </Method>
    <Method Name="ResellerFinder" IsStatic="true"
    DefaultDisplayName="Reseller Finder" IsCached="true">
      <Properties>
        <Property Name="RdbCommandText" Type="System.String">
          <![CDATA[
          SELECT ResellerKey, DimReseller.GeographyKey, ResellerAlternateKey,
                 Phone,BusinessType, ResellerName, NumberEmployees,
                 OrderFrequency, FirstOrderYear, LastOrderYear, ProductLine,
                 AddressLine1, AddressLine2, AnnualSales, BankName,
                 MinPaymentAmount, AnnualRevenue, YearOpened, City,
                 StateProvinceCode, StateProvinceName, CountryRegionCode,
                 EnglishCountryRegionName, PostalCode
          FROM DimReseller INNER JOIN DimGeography
               ON DimReseller.GeographyKey = DimGeography.GeographyKey
          WHERE (ResellerKey >= @MinResellerKey) AND
                (ResellerKey <= @MaxResellerKey) AND
                (ResellerName LIKE @ResellerName)
          ]]>
        </Property>
        <Property Name="RdbCommandType" Type="System.Data.CommandType">
          Text
        </Property>
```

(continued)

Listing 13-45 *(continued)*

```
        </Properties>
        <LocalizedDisplayNames>
          <LocalizedDisplayName LCID="1033">
            Reseller Finder
          </LocalizedDisplayNames>
        </LocalizedDisplayNames>
        <AccessControlList>
          <AccessControlEntry Principal="domainname1\username1">
            <Right BdcRight="Edit" />
            <Right BdcRight="SetPermissions" />
          </AccessControlEntry>
        </AccessControlList>
      </Method>
    </Methods>
    . . .
  </Entity>

  <Entity Name="ProductSubcategory" . . .>
    <Identifiers>
      <Identifier Name="ProductSubcategoryKey" TypeName="System.Int32" . . .>
        . . .
      </Identifier>
    </Identifiers>
    <Methods>
      <Method Name="GetProductSubcategories" IsStatic="true"
      DefaultDisplayName="Get Product Subcategories" IsCached="true">
        <Properties>
          <Property Name="RdbCommandText" Type="System.String">
            SELECT * FROM DimProductSubcategory
            WHERE (ProductSubcategoryKey &gt;= @MinProductSubcategoryKey) AND
                  (ProductSubcategoryKey &lt;= @MaxProductSubcategoryKey) AND
                  (EnglishProductSubcategoryName LIKE
                                                @EnglishProductSubcategoryName)
          </Property>
          <Property Name="RdbCommandType" Type="System.Data.CommandType">
            Text
          </Property>
        </Properties>
        <LocalizedDisplayNames>
          <LocalizedDisplayName LCID="1033">
            Get Product Subcategories
          </LocalizedDisplayNames>
        </LocalizedDisplayNames>
        <AccessControlList>
          <AccessControlEntry Principal="domainname1\username1">
            <Right BdcRight="Edit" />
            <Right BdcRight="SetPermissions" />
          </AccessControlEntry>
        </AccessControlList>
      </Method>
```

```
      <Method Name="GetProducts" IsStatic="true"
      DefaultDisplayName="Get Products" IsCached="true">
        <Properties>
          <Property Name="RdbCommandText" Type="System.String">
            SELECT * FROM DimProduct
            WHERE ProductSubcategoryKey = @ProductSubcategoryKey AND
                  Status = 'Current'
          </Property>
          <Property Name="RdbCommandType" Type="System.Data.CommandType">
            Text
          </Property>
        </Properties>
        <LocalizedDisplayNames>
          <LocalizedDisplayName LCID="1033">
            Get Products
          </LocalizedDisplayNames>
        </LocalizedDisplayNames>
        <AccessControlList>
          <AccessControlEntry Principal="domainname1\username1">
            <Right BdcRight="Edit" />
            <Right BdcRight="SetPermissions" />
          </AccessControlEntry>
        </AccessControlList>
      </Method>
    </Methods>
    . . .
  </Entity>

  <Entity Name="ProductCategory" . . .>
    <Identifiers>
      <Identifier Name="ProductCategoryKey" TypeName="System.Int32" . . .>
        . . .
      </Identifier>
    </Identifiers>
    <Methods>
      <Method Name="GetProductCategories" IsStatic="true"
      DefaultDisplayName="Get Product Categories" IsCached="true">
        <Properties>
          <Property Name="RdbCommandText" Type="System.String">
            SELECT * FROM DimProductCategory
            WHERE (ProductCategoryKey &gt;= @MinProductCategoryKey) AND
                  (ProductCategoryKey &lt;= @MaxProductCategoryKey) AND
                  (EnglishProductCategoryName LIKE @EnglishProductCategoryName)
          </Property>
          <Property Name="RdbCommandType" Type="System.Data.CommandType">
            Text
          </Property>
        </Properties>
        <LocalizedDisplayNames>
          <LocalizedDisplayName LCID="1033">
            Get Product Categories
          </LocalizedDisplayNames>
        </LocalizedDisplayNames>
```

(continued)

Listing 13-45 *(continued)*

```
          <AccessControlList>
            <AccessControlEntry Principal="domainname1\username1">
              <Right BdcRight="Edit" />
              <Right BdcRight="SetPermissions" />
            </AccessControlEntry>
          </AccessControlList>
        </Method>
        <Method Name="GetProductSubcategories" IsStatic="true"
        DefaultDisplayName="Get Product Subcategories" IsCached="true">
          <Properties>
            <Property Name="RdbCommandText" Type="System.String">
              SELECT * FROM DimProductSubcategory
              WHERE ProductCategoryKey = @ProductCategoryKey
            </Property>
            <Property Name="RdbCommandType" Type="System.Data.CommandType">
              Text
            </Property>
          </Properties>
          <LocalizedDisplayNames>
            <LocalizedDisplayName LCID="1033">
              Get Product Subcategories
            </LocalizedDisplayNames>
          </LocalizedDisplayNames>
          <AccessControlList>
            <AccessControlEntry Principal="domainname1\username1">
              <Right BdcRight="Edit" />
              <Right BdcRight="SetPermissions" />
            </AccessControlEntry>
          </AccessControlList>
        </Method>
      </Methods>
      . . .
    </Entity>
  </Entities>
</LobSystem>
```

The BDC application definition file shown in Listing 13-45 defines a method metadata object named GetProducts on the Product entity metadata object. Recall that the Product entity metadata object represents the DimProduct database table in the AdventureWorksDW SQL Server 2005 database LOB system. Listing 13-45 sets the values of the RdbCommandText and RdbCommandType properties of the GetProducts method metadata object. The value of the RdbCommandText property is set to the following SQL SELECT statement:

```
SELECT * FROM DimProduct
WHERE (ProductKey >= @MinProductKey) AND
      (ProductKey <= @MaxProductKey) AND
      (EnglishProductName LIKE @EnglishProductName) AND
      (EnglishDescription LIKE @EnglishDescription) AND
      (Status='Current')
```

The < (less than) and > (greater than) characters are encoded because the BDC application definition XML file, like any other XML file, must be a valid XML document. Note that the value of the RdbCommandType property is set to Text to specify that the RdbCommandText property contains a SQL SELECT statement. The GetProducts method metadata object basically represents the SQL SELECT statement specified in its RdbCommandText property.

Listing 13-45 defines a method metadata object named ResellerIDEnumerator on the Reseller entity metadata object. Recall that the Reseller entity metadata object represents the DimReseller database table in the AdventureWorksDW SQL Server 2005 database LOB application. Listing 13-45 sets the value of the RdbCommandText property of the ResellerIDEnumerator method metadata object to the following SQL SELECT statement:

```
SELECT ResellerKey FROM DimReseller
```

In other words, the ResellerIDEnumerator method metadata object represents this SQL SELECT statement.

Listing 13-45 defines another method metadata object named ResellerFinder on the Reseller entity metadata object and sets its RdbCommandText property to this SQL SELECT statement:

```
<![CDATA[
SELECT ResellerKey, DimReseller.GeographyKey, ResellerAlternateKey,
       Phone, BusinessType, ResellerName, NumberEmployees,
       OrderFrequency, FirstOrderYear, LastOrderYear, ProductLine,
       AddressLine1, AddressLine2, AnnualSales, BankName,
       MinPaymentAmount, AnnualRevenue, YearOpened, City,
       StateProvinceCode, StateProvinceName, CountryRegionCode,
       EnglishCountryRegionName, PostalCode
FROM DimReseller INNER JOIN DimGeography
     ON DimReseller.GeographyKey = DimGeography.GeographyKey
WHERE (ResellerKey >= @MinResellerKey) AND
      (ResellerKey <= @MaxResellerKey) AND
      (ResellerName LIKE @ResellerName)
]]>
```

Note that in this case, the < and > characters are not encoded because the whole SQL SELECT statement is enclosed within <![CDATA[and]]>. So you have two options: encode the XML invalid characters such as < and > or enclose the entire SQL SELECT statement within <![CDATA[and]]>. The ResellerFinder method metadata object basically represents the previous SQL SELECT statement.

Listing 13-45 defines a method metadata object named GetProductSubcategories on the ProductSubcategory entity metadata object. Recall that this entity metadata object represents the DimProductSubcategory database table. The RdbCommandText property of the GetProductSubcategories method metadata object is set to the SQL SELECT statement, which the method metadata object represents:

```
SELECT * FROM DimProductSubcategory
WHERE (ProductSubcategoryKey >= @MinProductSubcategoryKey) AND
      (ProductSubcategoryKey <= @MaxProductSubcategoryKey) AND
      (EnglishProductSubcategoryName LIKE @EnglishProductSubcategoryName)
```

Listing 13-45 defines another method metadata object named GetProducts on the same ProductSubcategory entity metadata object. A BDC application definition file can define multiple method metadata objects on the same entity metadata object. The RdbCommandText property of the GetProducts method metadata object is set to the SQL SELECT statement that the method metadata object represents:

```
SELECT * FROM DimProduct
WHERE ProductSubcategoryKey = @ProductSubcategoryKey AND Status = 'Current'
```

Recall that the Product metadata object also contains a method metadata object named GetProducts. The name of a method metadata object does not have to be unique within the scope of the BDC application definition file. However, it must be unique within the scope of its parent entity metadata object. In other words, you cannot define two method metadata objects with the same name on the same entity metadata object.

Listing 13-45 also defines a method metadata object named GetProductsCategories on the ProductCategory entity metadata object. Recall that this entity metadata object represents the DimProductCategory database table. The RdbCommandText property of the GetProductsCategories method metadata object is set to the SQL SELECT statement that the method metadata object represents:

```
SELECT * FROM DimProductCategory
 WHERE (ProductCategoryKey >= @MinProductCategoryKey) AND
       (ProductCategoryKey <= @MaxProductCategoryKey) AND
       (EnglishProductCategoryName LIKE @EnglishProductCategoryName)
```

The BDC application definition file shown in Listing 13-45 defines another method metadata object named GetProductSubcategories on the same ProductCategory entity metadata object. The RdbCommandText property of this method metadata object is set to the SQL SELECT statement that the method metadata object represents:

```
SELECT * FROM DimProductSubcategory WHERE ProductCategoryKey = @ProductCategoryKey
```

Note that all method metadata objects defined in Listing 13-45 have their:

- IsCached attribute set to true to have the BDC cache these method metadata objects to improve performance. Strictly speaking you don't have to set the IsCached attribute to true because this is the default value.
- DefaultDisplayName attribute set to specify a default display name for these method metadata objects.
- <LocalizedDisplayNames> child element specified to specify localized display names for these method metadata objects.
- <AccessControlList> child element specified to specify the ACLs for these method metadata objects to secure their access.

So far you've seen examples of method metadata objects for the database LOB application. Next, you'll take a look at examples of method metadata objects for the web service LOB application. Listing 13-46 extends Listing 13-41 to define method metadata objects for the entity metadata objects of the Amazon E-Commerce web service LOB system.

Listing 13-46: The BDC application definition file that describes a web service LOB system

```
<LobSystem . . .>
  <Properties>
    . . .
  </Properties>

  <LobSystemInstances>
    <LobSystemInstance Name="AWSECommerceService"
    DefaultDisplayName="Amazon E-Commerce Web Service" IsCached="true">
      . . .
  </LobSystemInstances>

  <Entities>
    <Entity Name="Item" . . .>
      <Identifiers>
        <Identifier Name="ItemId" TypeName="System.String" . . .>
          . . .
        </Identifier>
      </Identifiers>
      <Methods>
        <Method Name="ItemLookup" DefaultDisplayName="Item Lookup"
        IsCached="true" IsStatic="true">
          <LocalizedDisplayNames>
            <LocalizedDisplayName LCID="1033">
              Item Lookup
            </LocalizedDisplayNames>
          </LocalizedDisplayNames>
          <AccessControlList>
            <AccessControlEntry Principal="domainname1\username1">
              <Right BdcRight="Edit" />
              <Right BdcRight="SetPermissions" />
            </AccessControlEntry>
          </AccessControlList>
          . . .
        </Method>
        <Method Name="ItemSearch" DefaultDisplayName="Item Search"
        IsCached="true" IsStatic="true">
          <LocalizedDisplayNames>
            <LocalizedDisplayName LCID="1033">
              Item Search
            </LocalizedDisplayNames>
          </LocalizedDisplayNames>
          <AccessControlList>
            <AccessControlEntry Principal="domainname1\username1">
              <Right BdcRight="Edit" />
              <Right BdcRight="SetPermissions" />
            </AccessControlEntry>
          </AccessControlList>
          . . .
        </Method>
```

(continued)

Listing 13-46 *(continued)*

```
        </Methods>
        . . .
      </Entity>

      <Entity Name="EditorialReview" . . .>
        <Methods>
          <Method Name="ItemLookup" DefaultDisplayName="Item Lookup"
          IsCached="true" IsStatic="true">
            <LocalizedDisplayNames>
              <LocalizedDisplayName LCID="1033">
                Item Lookup
              </LocalizedDisplayNames>
            </LocalizedDisplayNames>
            <AccessControlList>
              <AccessControlEntry Principal="John">
                <Right BdcRight="Edit" />
                <Right BdcRight="SetPermissions" />
              </AccessControlEntry>
            </AccessControlList>
            . . .
          </Method>
          <Method Name="ItemSearch" DefaultDisplayName="Item Search"
          IsCached="true" IsStatic="true">
            <LocalizedDisplayNames>
              <LocalizedDisplayName LCID="1033">
                Item Search
              </LocalizedDisplayNames>
            </LocalizedDisplayNames>
            <AccessControlList>
              <AccessControlEntry Principal="John">
                <Right BdcRight="Edit" />
                <Right BdcRight="SetPermissions" />
              </AccessControlEntry>
            </AccessControlList>
            . . .
          </Method>
        </Methods>
        . . .
      </Entity>
    </Entities>
  </LobSystem>
```

Listing 13-46 defines two method metadata objects with the same names: ItemLookup and ItemSearch, on both Item and EditorialReview entity metadata objects. These two methods have the same names as the web methods that they represent. You must always set the Name attribute of a method metadata object to the name of the web method that the method metadata object represents.

Notice the big difference between the definitions of the method metadata objects that represent web methods (shown in Listing 13-46) and the method metadata objects that represent database queries (shown in Listing 13-45). As Listing 13-45 shows, the method metadata object that represents a database query exposes a property named RdbCommandText that must be set to the database query and a property named RdbCommandType that must be set to specify the type of the database query. As Listing 13-46 shows, the method metadata object that represents a web method does not expose similar properties because the value of the Name attribute of the <Method> element contains the name of the web method that the method metadata object represents and there is no need for similar properties.

The following code listing shows what you have so far.

```
<LobSystem
xmlsn="http://schemas.microsoft.com/office/2006/03/BusinessDataCatalog"
xmlsn:xsi="http://www.w3.org/2001/XMLSchema-instance"
xsi="http://schemas.microsoft.com/office/2006/03/BusinessDataCatalog
BDCMetadata.xsd"
Type=""
SystemUtility=""
ConnectionManager=""
EntityInstance=""
Version=""
Name=""
DefaultDisplayName=""
IsCached="">

  <LobSystemInstances>
    <LobSystemInstance Name="" DefaultDisplayName="" IsCached="">
      <LocalizedDisplayNames>
        <LocalizedDisplayName LCID=""></LocalizedDisplayName>
        <LocalizedDisplayName LCID=""></LocalizedDisplayName>
      </LocalizedDisplayNames>
      <Properties>
        <Property Name="" Type=""></Property>
        <Property Name="" Type=""></Property>
      </Properties>
    </LobSystemInstance>
  </LobSystemInstances>

  <Entities>
    <Entity Name="" DefaultDisplayName="" IsCached="" EstimatedInstanceCount="">
      <AccessControlList>
        <AccessControlList Principal="">
          <Right BdcRights="" />
          <Right BdcRights="" />
        </AccessControlList>
      </AccessControlList>
      <LocalizedDisplayNames>
        <LocalizedDisplayName LCID=""></LocalizedDisplayName>
      </LocalizedDisplayNames>
      <Properties>
        <Property Name="" Type=""></Property>
      </Properties>
      <Identifiers>
        <Identifier Name="" DefaultDisplayName="" IsCached="" TypeName="">
          <Properties>
            <Property Name="" Type=""></Property>
            <Property Name="" Type=""></Property>
```

(continued)

(continued)

```
          </Properties>
          <LocalizedDisplayNames>
            <LocalizedDisplayName LCID=""></LocalizedDisplayName>
            <LocalizedDisplayName LCID=""></LocalizedDisplayName>
          </LocalizedDisplayNames>
        </Identifier>
      </Identifiers>
      <Methods>
        <Method Name="" DefaultDisplayName="" IsCached="" IsStatic="">
          <LocalizedDisplayNames>
            <LocalizedDisplayName LCID=""></LocalizedDisplayName>
            <LocalizedDisplayName LCID=""></LocalizedDisplayName>
          </LocalizedDisplayNames>
          <Properties>
            <Property Name="" Type=""></Property>
            <Property Name="" Type=""></Property>
          </Properties>
          <FilterDescriptors></FilterDescriptors>
          <Parameters></Parameters>
          <MethodInstances></MethodInstances>
        </Method>
      </Methods>
      <Actions></Actions>
    </Entity>
  </Entities>

  <Associations></Associations>
  <AccessControlList></AccessControlList>
  <LocalizedDisplayNames>
    <LocalizedDisplayName LCID=""></LocalizedDisplayName>
    <LocalizedDisplayName LCID=""></LocalizedDisplayName>
  </LocalizedDisplayNames>
  <Properties>
    <Property Name="" Type=""></Property>
    <Property Name="" Type=""></Property>
  </Properties>
</LobSystem>
```

Parameters

As you can see from Listing 13-43, a <Method> element can contain an optional child element named <Parameters>, which is of the Parameters schema type defined in Listing 13-47.

Listing 13-47: The Parameters schema type

```
<xs:complexType name="Parameters">
  <xs:sequence>
    <xs:element name="Parameter" type="bdc:Parameter" minOccurs="1"
    maxOccurs="unbounded"/>
  </xs:sequence>
</xs:complexType>
```

As this code listing shows, a <Parameters> element must contain at least (minOccurs=1) one instance of a child element named <Parameter>, which is of the Parameter schema type defined in Listing 13-48.

Listing 13-48: The Parameter schema type

```
<xs:complexType name="Parameter">
  <xs:complexContent>
    <xs:extension base="bdc:MetadataObject">
      <xs:sequence>
        <xs:element name="TypeDescriptor" type="bdc:TypeDescriptor"/>
      </xs:sequence>
      <xs:attribute name="Direction" type="bdc:ParameterDirection"
      use="required"/>
      <xs:attribute name="TypeReflectorTypeName" type="xs:string"
      use="optional"/>
    </xs:extension>
  </xs:complexContent>
</xs:complexType>
```

As Listing 13-48 illustrates, the Parameter schema type extends the MetadataObject schema type. According to the Parameter schema type, a <Parameter> element:

- Must contain a single required element named <TypeDescriptor>, which is of the TypeDescriptor schema type
- Two attributes as follows:
  - Direction, which is of the ParameterDirection schema type
  - TypeReflectorTypeName, which is of the string schema type
- Note that only the Direction attribute is required. Listing 13-49 presents the definition of the ParameterDirection schema type.

Listing 13-49: The ParameterDirection schema type

```
<xs:simpleType name="ParameterDirection">
  <xs:restriction base="xs:string">
    <xs:enumeration value="In"/>
    <xs:enumeration value="Out"/>
    <xs:enumeration value="InOut"/>
    <xs:enumeration value="Return"/>
  </xs:restriction>
</xs:simpleType>
```

As you can see, the ParameterDirection is an enumeration type with possible values of In, Out, InOut, and Return.

Because the Parameter schema type inherits from the MetadataObject schema type, the <Parameter> element can contain the optional <LocalizedDisplayNames> and <Properties> child elements and the Name, DefaultDisplayName, and IsCached attributes where only the Name attribute is required.

So far you've learned that a method metadata object is defined on an entity metadata object and represents a business operation that can be performed on the business entity that the entity metadata object represents. Such an operation normally takes some business input parameters and returns some business output parameters that normally contain business entity instances. A parameter metadata object represents a business input or output parameter of a business operation that the method metadata object represents.

For example, a method metadata object in a web service LOB application represents a web method, which is a business operation that takes input parameters and returns output parameters that contain the requested information. For instance, the ItemSearch web method of the Amazon E-Commerce web service takes input parameters that specify the search criteria and returns a collection that contains the search results. A method metadata object in a database LOB application represents a database query such as a SQL SELECT statement or a stored procedure. A SQL SELECT statement or stored procedure normally contains parameters that are used in the WHERE clause to specify the search criteria. A database query returns a collection of rows. This collection is the output parameter of the query.

A parameter metadata object represents an input or output parameter of a web method or database query. The direction of the parameter is determined by the value of the Direction attribute on the <Parameter> element. This value must be one of the values defined in Listing 13-49.

Recall from Listing 13-48 that a <Parameter> element must contain a required child element named <TypeDescriptor>, which is of the TypeDescriptor schema type defined in Listing 13-50.

Listing 13-50: The TypeDescriptor schema type

```
<xs:complexType name="TypeDescriptor">
  <xs:complexContent>
    <xs:extension base="bdc:MetadataObject">
      <xs:sequence>
        <xs:element name="DefaultValues" type="bdc:DefaultValues"
        minOccurs="0" />
        <xs:element name="TypeDescriptors" type="bdc:TypeDescriptors"
        minOccurs="0"/>
      </xs:sequence>
      <xs:attribute name="TypeName" type="xs:string" use="required"/>
      <xs:attribute name="IdentifierEntityName" type="xs:string" use="optional"/>
      <xs:attribute name="IdentifierName" type="xs:string" use="optional"/>
      <xs:attribute name="AssociatedFilter" type="xs:string" use="optional"/>
      <xs:attribute name="IsCollection" type="xs:boolean" default="false"/>
    </xs:extension>
  </xs:complexContent>
</xs:complexType>
```

A parameter metadata object represents a parameter of a web method or a database query. A type descriptor metadata object is defined on a parameter metadata object to describe the web method or database query parameter that the parameter metadata object represents.

As you can see from this code listing, the TypeDescriptor schema type extends the MetadataObject schema type. According to the TypeDescriptor schema type, a <TypeDescriptor> element can contain:

- An optional element named <DefaultValues>, which is of the DefaultValues schema type. As the name suggests, this element specifies a set of default values for the parameter that the type descriptor metadata object describes.

- An optional element named <TypeDescriptors>, which is of the TypeDescriptors schema type. In general there are two kinds of .NET types: simple and complex. A simple .NET type is a non-collection type that does not have properties of its own. System.String is an example of a simple type. A complex .NET type is a type that exposes properties of its own or is a collection. A .NET class with properties is an example of a complex type. IDataReader is an example of a complex collection type because its instances act as containers for .NET objects of type IDataRecord. If the parameter that a type descriptor metadata object describes is of a complex type such as IDataReader, the type descriptor metadata object must contain a <TypeDescriptors> child element to describe the properties of this complex type or the type of the .NET objects that the instances of the type can contain if the type is a collection.
- An optional attribute named TypeName, which is of the string schema type. This attribute specifies the fully qualified name of the type of the parameter that the type descriptor describes. This fully qualified name must contain the complete namespace containment hierarchy of the type. It must also contain the complete information about the assembly that contains the parameter type including assembly name, version, culture, and public key token if the assembly is not a referenced assembly.
- An optional attribute named IdentifierName, which is of the string schema type. This attribute specifies the name of the identifier metadata object that represents an identifier or key of the metadata object. You must set this attribute only if the input or output parameter that the type descriptor metadata object describes is an identifier or key:
    - In the case of output parameters, setting this attribute enables the BDC to identify identity or key output parameters among other output parameters in the entity instances that a business operation such as a web method or database query returns.
    - In the case of input parameters, setting this attribute enables the BDC to identify identity or key input parameters among other input parameters that users pass into a business operation (via a method instance) when they're executing the business operation (via executing the respective method instance). This enables the BDC to insert the values of these parameters into the appropriate type descriptor slots.
- An optional attribute named IdentifierEntityName, which is of the string schema type. This attribute specifies the name of the entity metadata object on which the identifier metadata object associated with the parameter is defined. You must set this attribute only if:
    - The parameter that the type descriptor describes is an identifier or key parameter.
    - The identifier metadata object is defined on a different metadata object than the metadata object on which the type descriptor object is defined. This normally happens when the parameter that the type descriptor object describes is a foreign key.
- An optional attribute named AssociatedFilter, which is of the string schema type. You must set the value of this attribute to the name of a filter descriptor metadata object if the parameter that the type descriptor metadata object describes is a filterable parameter. As you'll see later, users use the SharePoint UI to specify a value for the specified filter descriptor metadata object. When the BDC is about to execute the associated method instance metadata object, it automatically assigns the value of the filter descriptor metadata object to the parameter.

    The filter descriptor metadata object and the AssociatedFilter attribute on the type descriptor metadata object that describes a filterable parameter together enable the BDC to assign the user-specified filter value to the parameter before it executes the associated method instance metadata object. Don't worry about it if you find this a bit confusing. This will all be clear by the end of this chapter.

- An optional attribute named IsCollection, which is of the Boolean schema type with the default value of false. This attribute specifies whether the parameter that the type descriptor metadata object describes is a collection. For example, the execution of an instance of a method metadata object that represents a database query normally returns an output parameter of type IDataReader, which is a collection. Or the execution of an instance of a method metadata object that represents a web method may return a .NET collection object that contains the query results.

Because the TypeDescriptor schema type inherits from the MetadataObject schema type, a <TypeDescriptor> element can contain the <LocalizedDisplayNames> and <Properties> optional child elements and the Name, DefaultDisplayName, and IsCached attributes where only the Name attribute is required.

Recall from Listing 13-50 that a <TypeDescriptor> element can contain an optional child element named <DefaultValues>, which is of the DefaultValues schema type defined in Listing 13-51.

Listing 13-51: The DefaultValues schema type

```
<xs:complexType name="DefaultValues">
  <xs:sequence>
    <xs:element name="DefaultValue" type="bdc:DefaultValue" minOccurs="1"
    maxOccurs="unbounded"/>
  </xs:sequence>
</xs:complexType>
```

Based on this schema type, a <DefaultValues> element must contain at least (minOccurs=1) one instance of a child element named <DefaultValue>, which is of the DefaultValue schema type.

Listing 13-52 presents the definition of the DefaultValue schema type.

Listing 13-52: The DefaultValue schema type

```
<xs:complexType name="DefaultValue" mixed="true">
  <xs:attribute name="MethodInstanceName" type="xs:string" use="required"/>
  <xs:attribute name="Type" type="xs:string" use="required"/>
</xs:complexType>
```

Based on this schema type, a <DefaultValue> element must contain the following two required attributes:

- An attribute named MethodInstanceName, which is of the string schema type. You must set the value of this attribute to the name of the method instance metadata object for which the default value is specified. Method instance metadata objects are discussed later in this chapter.
- An attribute named Type, which is of the string schema type. You must set the value of this attribute to the fully qualified name of the type of the parameter whose default value this <DefaultValue> element specifies. This fully qualified name must contain the complete namespace containment hierarchy of the type in addition to the name of the type.

Note that the mixed attribute on the <xs:complexType> element that defines the DefaultValue schema type is set to true (see Listing 13-52) to enable you to specify the default value of the parameter within the opening and closing tags of the <DefaultValue> element.

Here is the main idea behind the introduction of the <DefaultValues> element. A method metadata object may represent a business operation that takes parameters of complex types. This normally happens in web service LOB applications. Such complex types may themselves expose properties of complex types, which in turn may expose sub properties of complex types, which in turn may expose sub sub properties of complex types, and so on. This requires users to specify the values of all these complex properties no matter how deeply they are nested every time they need to execute these business operations.

To make life easier on users, you can use the <DefaultValues> child element of the type descriptor metadata objects that describe these complex properties to specify meaningful default values. Users can then override only the desired default values when they need to execute these business operations. They do not have to specify the values of all these properties, sub properties, sub sub properties, and so on.

Here is the main idea behind the introduction of the <DefaultValue> elements. A method metadata object represents a business operation such as a database query or web method. A method instance metadata object represents a business operation with a specific set of default values for its parameters. You can define multiple method instance metadata objects on the same method metadata object to execute the same business operation using different default values. Use the <DefaultValue> child element to specify a default value for the parameter for a specific method instance metadata object. In other words, each <DefaultValue> child element of the <DefaultValues> child element of a <TypeDescriptor> element specifies a default value for a different method instance metadata object for the same parameter.

As mentioned earlier, you must specify the default value of a parameter within the opening and closing tags of a <DefaultValue> element. The BDC only supports specifying default values for the following types: System.Int16, System.Int32, System.Int64, System.Single, System.Double, System.Decimal, System.Boolean, System.String, System.Byte, System.UInt16, System.UInt32, System.UInt64, System .Guid, System.DateTime, and any other serializable type.

Recall from Listing 13-50 that a <TypeDescriptor> element, which describes the type of a parameter, must contain a child element named <TypeDescriptors>, which is of the TypeDescriptor schema type, if the parameter is of a complex .NET type or if the parameter is a collection. Listing 13-53 defines the TypeDescriptors schema type.

Listing 13-53: The TypeDescriptors schema type

```
<xs:complexType name="TypeDescriptors">
  <xs:sequence>
    <xs:element name="TypeDescriptor" type="bdc:TypeDescriptor" minOccurs="1"
    maxOccurs="unbounded"/>
  </xs:sequence>
</xs:complexType>
```

According to this schema type, a <TypeDescriptors> element must contain at least one instance of a child element named <TypeDescriptor>, which is of the TypeDescriptor schema type discussed earlier.

Next, you'll extend Listing 13-45 to define a few parameters. Recall that this code listing contains the BDC application definition file that describes the AdventureWorksDW SQL Server 2005 database LOB application to the BDC. As you may recall, Listing 13-45 defines:

- A method metadata object named GetProducts on the Product entity metadata object.
- Two method metadata objects named ResellerIDEnumerator and ResellerFinder on the Reseller entity metadata object.
- Two method metadata objects named GetProductSubcategories and GetProducts on the ProductSubcategory entity metadata object.
- Two method metadata objects named GetProductCategories and GetProductSubcategories on the ProductCategory entity metadata object.

As you can see from Listing 13-45, each method metadata object represents the SQL SELECT statement assigned to its RdbCommandText property. Notice that these SQL SELECT statements contain parameters, which need to be set before these SQL SELECT statements can be executed. Next, you'll define a parameter metadata object for each of these parameters. Because each SQL SELECT statement, when executed, returns a collection of rows, you also need to define a parameter metadata object to represent this collection. This collection is the return parameter.

Listing 13-55 defines parameter metadata objects to represent the parameters of the SQL SELECT statement that the GetProducts method metadata object defined on the Product entity metadata object represents. As Listing 13-54 shows, this SQL SELECT statement, when executed, returns those products from the DimProduct database table whose ProductKey datafields have values less than the value specified in the @MaxProductKey parameter and greater than the value specified in the @MinProductKey parameter, whose EnglishProductName datafields have values that match the pattern specified in the @EnglishProductName parameter, whose EnglishDescription datafields have values that match the pattern specified in the @EnglishDescription parameter, and whose Status datafields have value of "Current."

Listing 13-54: The SQL SELECT statement that the GetProducts method metadata object defined on the Product entity metadata object represents

```
SELECT * FROM DimProduct
WHERE (ProductKey >= @MinProductKey) AND
      (ProductKey <= @MaxProductKey) AND
      (EnglishProductName LIKE @EnglishProductName) AND
      (EnglishDescription LIKE @EnglishDescription) AND
      (Status='Current')
```

Therefore, you need to define four parameter metadata objects to represent the @MinProductKey, @MaxProductKey, @EnglishProductName, and @EnglishDescription parameters. You also need to define a parameter metadata object to represent the outcome of the execution of this SQL SELECT statement.

Listing 13-55: The parameter metadata objects that represent the parameters of the GetProducts method metadata object defined on the Product entity metadata object

```
<?xml version="1.0" encoding="utf-8" standalone="yes"?>
<LobSystem Name="AdventureWorksDW" . . .>
  . . .
  <LobSystemInstances>
    <LobSystemInstance Name="AdventureWorksDWInstance" . . .>
      . . .
    </LobSystemInstance>
  </LobSystemInstances>
  <Entities>
    <Entity Name="Product" . . .>
      <Identifiers>
        <Identifier Name="ProductKey" TypeName="System.Int32" />
      </Identifiers>
      <Methods>
        <Method Name="GetProducts">
          <Properties>
            <Property Name="RdbCommandText" Type="System.String">
              SELECT * FROM DimProduct
              WHERE (ProductKey >= @MinProductKey) AND
                    (ProductKey <= @MaxProductKey) AND
                    (EnglishProductName LIKE @EnglishProductName) AND
                    (EnglishDescription LIKE @EnglishDescription) AND
                    (Status='Current')
            </Property>
            <Property Name="RdbCommandType" Type="System.Data.CommandType">Text
            </Property>
          </Properties>

          <Parameters>
            <Parameter Direction="In" Name="@MinProductKey">
              <TypeDescriptor TypeName="System.Int32" IdentifierName="ProductKey"
              AssociatedFilter="Key" Name="MinProductKey">
                <DefaultValues>
                  <DefaultValue MethodInstanceName="ProductFinderInstance"
                  Type="System.Int32">0</DefaultValue>
                </DefaultValues>
              </TypeDescriptor>
            </Parameter>

            <Parameter Direction="In" Name="@MaxProductKey">
              <TypeDescriptor TypeName="System.Int32" IdentifierName="ProductKey"
              AssociatedFilter="Key" Name="MaxProductKey">
                <DefaultValues>
                  <DefaultValue MethodInstanceName="ProductFinderInstance"
                  Type="System.Int32">99999999</DefaultValue>
                </DefaultValues>
              </TypeDescriptor>
            </Parameter>

            <Parameter Direction="In" Name="@EnglishProductName">
```

(continued)

Listing 13-55 *(continued)*

```
          <TypeDescriptor TypeName="System.String" AssociatedFilter="Name"
          Name="EnglishProductName">
            <DefaultValues>
              <DefaultValue MethodInstanceName="ProductFinderInstance"
              Type="System.String">%</DefaultValue>
              <DefaultValue MethodInstanceName="ProductSpecificFinderInstance"
              Type="System.String">%</DefaultValue>
            </DefaultValues>
          </TypeDescriptor>
        </Parameter>

        <Parameter Direction="In" Name="@EnglishDescription">
          <TypeDescriptor TypeName="System.String"
          AssociatedFilter="Description" Name="EnglishDescription">
            <DefaultValues>
              <DefaultValue MethodInstanceName="ProductFinderInstance"
              Type="System.String">%</DefaultValue>
              <DefaultValue MethodInstanceName="ProductSpecificFinderInstance"
              Type="System.String">%</DefaultValue>
            </DefaultValues>
          </TypeDescriptor>
        </Parameter>

        <Parameter Direction="Return" Name="Products">
          <TypeDescriptor IsCollection="true" Name="ProductDataReader"
          TypeName="System.Data.IDataReader, System.Data, Version=2.0.3600.0,
                    Culture=neutral, PublicKeyToken=b77a5c561934e089">
            <TypeDescriptors>
              <TypeDescriptor Name="ProductDataRecord"
              TypeName="System.Data.IDataRecord, System.Data,
                        Version=2.0.3600.0, Culture=neutral,
                        PublicKeyToken=b77a5c561934e089">
                <TypeDescriptors>
                  <TypeDescriptor TypeName="System.Int32"
                  IdentifierName="ProductKey" Name="ProductKey">
                    <LocalizedDisplayNames>
                      <LocalizedDisplayName
                      LCID="1033">Key</LocalizedDisplayName>
                    </LocalizedDisplayNames>
                  </TypeDescriptor>
                  <TypeDescriptor TypeName="System.String"
                  Name="EnglishProductName">
                    <LocalizedDisplayNames>
                      <LocalizedDisplayName
                      LCID="1033">Name</LocalizedDisplayName>
                    </LocalizedDisplayNames>
                    <Properties>
                      <Property Name="DisplayByDefault"
                      Type="System.Boolean">true</Property>
                    </Properties>
                  </TypeDescriptor>
```

```
                    <TypeDescriptor TypeName="System.String"
                    Name="EnglishDescription">
                      <LocalizedDisplayNames>
                        <LocalizedDisplayName
                        LCID="1033">Description</LocalizedDisplayName>
                      </LocalizedDisplayNames>
                      <Properties>
                        <Property Name="DisplayByDefault"
                        Type="System.Boolean">true</Property>
                      </Properties>
                    </TypeDescriptor>
                    <TypeDescriptor TypeName="System.Decimal" Name="ListPrice">
                      <LocalizedDisplayNames>
                        <LocalizedDisplayName LCID="1033">List Price
                        </LocalizedDisplayName>
                      </LocalizedDisplayNames>
                    </TypeDescriptor>
                    <TypeDescriptor TypeName="System.Decimal"
                    Name="StandardCost">
                      <LocalizedDisplayNames>
                        <LocalizedDisplayName LCID="1033">Standard Cost
                        </LocalizedDisplayName>
                      </LocalizedDisplayNames>
                    </TypeDescriptor>
                    <TypeDescriptor TypeName="System.String" Name="Color">
                      <LocalizedDisplayNames>
                        <LocalizedDisplayName LCID="1033">Color
                        </LocalizedDisplayName>
                      </LocalizedDisplayNames>
                    </TypeDescriptor>
                    <TypeDescriptor TypeName="System.String" Name="Size">
                      <LocalizedDisplayNames>
                        <LocalizedDisplayName LCID="1033">Size
                        </LocalizedDisplayName>
                      </LocalizedDisplayNames>
                    </TypeDescriptor>
                    <TypeDescriptor TypeName="System.String" Name="Class">
                      <LocalizedDisplayNames>
                        <LocalizedDisplayName LCID="1033">Class
                        </LocalizedDisplayName>
                      </LocalizedDisplayNames>
                    </TypeDescriptor>
                    <TypeDescriptor TypeName="System.Int32"
                    Name="DaysToManufacture">
                      <LocalizedDisplayNames>
                        <LocalizedDisplayName LCID="1033">Days To Manufacture
                        </LocalizedDisplayName>
                      </LocalizedDisplayNames>
                    </TypeDescriptor>
                  </TypeDescriptors>
                </TypeDescriptor>
              </TypeDescriptors>
            </TypeDescriptor>
```

(continued)

Listing 13-55 *(continued)*

```
            </Parameter>
          </Parameters>
          . . .
        </Method>
      </Methods>
      . . .
    </Entity>

  </Entities>
</LobSystem>
```

Listing 13-55 defines the following parameter metadata object to represent the @MinProductKey parameter of the SQL SELECT statement shown in Listing 13-54:

```
<Parameter Direction="In" Name="@MinProductKey">
  <TypeDescriptor TypeName="System.Int32" IdentifierName="ProductKey"
  AssociatedFilter="Key" Name="MinProductKey">
    <DefaultValues>
      <DefaultValue MethodInstanceName="ProductFinderInstance"
      Type="System.Int32">0</DefaultValue>
    </DefaultValues>
  </TypeDescriptor>
</Parameter>
```

The Direction attribute on this <Parameter> element is set to the value "In" to specify that this parameter metadata object represents an input parameter. You must always set the value of the Name attribute on a <Parameter> element to the name of the parameter that the parameter metadata object represents (the only exception to this rule is a return parameter because such a parameter does not have a name). In this case, the value of the Name attribute is set to the string "@MinProductKey" because this string contains the name of the parameter that this parameter metadata object represents.

Note that this <Parameter> element contains a <TypeDescriptor> child element that describes the parameter that this parameter metadata object represents. Because a type descriptor is a metadata object (see Listing 13-50), it can contain the optional <LocalizedDisplayNames> and <Properties> child elements and the Name, DefaultDisplayName, and IsCached attributes where only the Name attribute is required. You can name a type descriptor metadata object anything you like as long as it does not violate the XML naming rules.

Recall from Listing 13-50 that a <TypeDescriptor> element must contain a required attribute named TypeName and can contain the IdentifierEntityName, IdentifierName, AssociatedFilter, and IsCollection optional attributes.

You must set the value of the required TypeName attribute on the <TypeDescriptor> element to the fully qualified name of the .NET type of the parameter including its complete namespace containment hierarchy and the complete information about the assembly that contains this type if the type is in an unreferenced assembly. In this case, the TypeName attribute is set to System.String because the @MinProductKey parameter is a string parameter.

Set the value of the IdentifierName optional attribute to the name of the identifier metadata object that represents an identifier or key (normally a primary key datafield in the case of a database LOB application) if the parameter is an identifier or key parameter. In this case, the @MinProductKey parameter specifies the minimum allowable value for the ProductKey datafield, which is the identifier or key in the DimProduct database table. As such, the @MinProductKey parameter is indeed an identifier or key parameter. Therefore, in this case, the value of the IdentifierName attribute is set to "ProductKey," which is the name of the following identifier metadata object that represents the ProductKey primary key datafield:

```
<Entity Name="Product" . . .>
  <Identifiers>
    <Identifier Name="ProductKey" TypeName="System.Int32" />
  </Identifiers>
  . . .
</Entity>
```

Set the value of the IdentifierEntityName optional attribute to the name of the entity metadata object on which the preceding identifier metadata object is defined. If the type descriptor object is defined on the same entity metadata object on which the identifier metadata object is defined, which it is in this case, you do not need to specify the value of the IdentifierEntityName attribute. If you were to specify the value of this attribute, you would set it to the string "Product," which is the name of the Product entity metadata object. You may be wondering when you must set the value of the IdentifierEntityName attribute. This happens when the type descriptor metadata object describes a foreign key parameter. In such a case, you must set the value of the IdentifierEntityName attribute to the name of the entity metadata object that contains the primary key associated with this foreign key parameter.

Set the value of the AssociatedFilter optional attribute to the name of the filter descriptor metadata object that represents a business filter. In this case, the value of this attribute is set to "Key," which is the name of the following filter descriptor metadata object:

```
<FilterDescriptor Type="Comparison" Name="Key" >
  <Properties>
    <Property Name="Comparator" Type="System.String">Equals</Property>
  </Properties>
</FilterDescriptor>
```

This filter descriptor metadata object represents an equality filter. This tells the BDC to use the exact input value as the value of the @MinProductKey parameter. As you'll see later, users will use the SharePoint UI to specify a value for this equality filter descriptor metadata object. The BDC then assigns this value *as is* (because the filter is an equality filter) to the @MinProductKey parameter when it is about to execute the associated SQL SELECT statement.

Set the value of the IsCollection optional attribute to true if the parameter that the parameter metadata object represents is a collection. Recall from Listing 13-50 that the value of this attribute is false by default. Therefore, you do not need to specify this attribute if the parameter that the parameter metadata object represents is not a collection, which is the case here.

The SQL SELECT statement that the GetProducts method metadata object, defined on the Product entity metadata object, represents returns a collection of products that meet the criteria discussed earlier. Therefore, Listing 13-55 defines a parameter metadata object to represent this collection:

```
<Parameter Direction="Return" Name="Products">
  . . .
</Parameter>
```

As you can see, the Direction attribute on this <Parameter> element is set to the value "Return" to specify that this parameter metadata object represents a return value. As discussed earlier, you must set the name of a parameter metadata object that represents an input parameter such as @MinProductKey to the name of the input parameter itself to enable the BDC to determine which parameter metadata object represents which input parameter. Because there is no real parameter name associated with a return value, you can use an arbitrary name. In this case, the name of the parameter metadata object is set to "Products."

This <Parameter> element contains a <TypeDescriptor> child element that describes the return parameter:

```
<Parameter Direction="Return" Name="Products">
  <TypeDescriptor IsCollection="true" Name="ProductDataReader"
  TypeName="System.Data.IDataReader, System.Data, Version=2.0.3600.0,
            Culture=neutral, PublicKeyToken=b77a5c561934e089">
  . . .
</Parameter>
```

The IsCollection attribute of this type descriptor metadata object is set to true to specify that the parameter metadata object represents a collection. The TypeName attribute of this type descriptor metadata object is set to

```
System.Data.IDataReader, System.Data, Version=2.0.3600.0, Culture=neutral,
PublicKeyToken=b77a5c561934e089
```

This value specifies that the collection that the parameter metadata object represents is of the System. Data.IDataReader type, which belongs to the System.Data.dll assembly. Note that this <TypeDescriptor> element contains a <TypeDescriptors> child element that describes the type of the data records in the collection. Because all data records in the IDataReader are of the same type, that is, IDataRecord, the <TypeDescriptors> element only contains a single <TypeDescriptor> child element to describe the IDataRecord type:

```
<Parameter Direction="Return" Name="Products">
  <TypeDescriptor IsCollection="true" Name="ProductDataReader"
  TypeName="System.Data.IDataReader, System.Data, Version=2.0.3600.0,
            Culture=neutral, PublicKeyToken=b77a5c561934e089">
    <TypeDescriptors>
      <TypeDescriptor Name="ProductDataRecord"
       TypeName="System.Data.IDataRecord, System.Data,
                 Version=2.0.3600.0, Culture=neutral,
                 PublicKeyToken=b77a5c561934e089">
      . . .
    </TypeDescriptors>
  </TypeDescriptor>
</Parameter>
```

As Listing 13-55 shows, this <TypeDescriptor> element contains a <TypeDescriptors> child element to describe the datafields that make up the IDataRecord:

```
<TypeDescriptor Name="ProductDataRecord"
TypeName="System.Data.IDataRecord, System.Data,
          Version=2.0.3600.0, Culture=neutral,
          PublicKeyToken=b77a5c561934e089">
  <TypeDescriptors>
    . . .
  </TypeDescriptors>
</TypeDescriptor>
```

As you can see from Listing 13-55, this <TypeDescriptors> element contains one <TypeDescriptor> child element to describe each datafield. The first <TypeDescriptor> child element describes the ProductKey database field:

```
<TypeDescriptor TypeName="System.Int32"
IdentifierName="ProductKey" Name="ProductKey">
  <LocalizedDisplayNames>
    <LocalizedDisplayName
    LCID="1033">Key</LocalizedDisplayName>
  </LocalizedDisplayNames>
</TypeDescriptor>
```

The IdentifierName attribute is set to "ProductKey," which is the name of the identifier metadata object that represents the primary key of the DimProduct database table:

```
<Entity Name="Product" . . .>
  <Identifiers>
    <Identifier Name="ProductKey" TypeName="System.Int32" />
  </Identifiers>
</Entity>
```

Setting the IdentifierName attribute tells the BDC that the database field that this type descriptor metadata object represents is a primary key database field.

The second <TypeDescriptor> child element describes the EnglishProductName database field:

```
<TypeDescriptor TypeName="System.String"
Name="EnglishProductName">
  <LocalizedDisplayNames>
    <LocalizedDisplayName
    LCID="1033">Name</LocalizedDisplayName>
  </LocalizedDisplayNames>
  <Properties>
    <Property Name="DisplayByDefault"
    Type="System.Boolean">true</Property>
  </Properties>
</TypeDescriptor>
```

The value of the Name attribute is set to the name of the database field so it is clear which database field this type descriptor metadata object represents. The DisplayByDefault property of this type descriptor metadata object is set to true to specify that the database field that this type descriptor metadata object represents should be displayed by default.

So far, you've seen examples of parameter metadata objects for a database LOB system. Next, you'll take a look at a few examples of parameter metadata objects for a web service LOB system. You'll also extend Listing 13-46 to define few parameter metadata objects. Recall that this code listing contains the BDC application definition file that describes the Amazon E-Commerce web service LOB application. And that Listing 13-46 defines two method metadata objects named ItemLookup and ItemSearch on the Item and EditorialReview entity metadata objects. The ItemLookup and ItemSearch metadata objects on both Item and EditorialReview entity metadata objects respectively represent the ItemLookup and ItemSearch web methods of the Amazon E-Commerce web service.

Listing 13-56 defines the parameter metadata objects to represent the parameters of the ItemSearch web method that the ItemSearch method metadata object, defined on the Item entity metadata object, represents.

Listing 13-56: The parameter metadata objects that represent the parameters of the ItemSearch web method

```
<LobSystem Name="AWSECommerceService" . . .>
  . . .
  <LobSystemInstances>
    <LobSystemInstance Name="AWSECommerceService">
      . . .
    </LobSystemInstance>
  </LobSystemInstances>

  <Entities>
    <Entity Name="Item">
      <Identifiers>
        <Identifier Name="ItemId" TypeName="System.String"/>
      </Identifiers>
      <Methods>
        <Method Name="ItemLookup">
          <Parameters>
            <Parameter Direction="In" Name="itemLookup">
              <TypeDescriptor
              TypeName="AWSECommerceService.ItemLookup, AWSECommerceService"
              Name="itemLookup">
                <TypeDescriptors>
                  <TypeDescriptor
                  TypeName="AWSECommerceService.ItemLookupRequest[],
                            AWSECommerceService"
                  Name="Request">
                    <TypeDescriptors>
                      <TypeDescriptor
                      TypeName="AWSECommerceService.ItemLookupRequest,
                                AWSECommerceService"
                      Name="RequestObject">
```

```
                <TypeDescriptors>
                  <TypeDescriptor TypeName="System.String[]" Name="ItemId">
                    <TypeDescriptors>
                      <TypeDescriptor TypeName="System.String"
                      AssociatedFilter="ID" IdentifierName="ItemId"
                      Name="ID">
                        <DefaultValues>
                          <DefaultValue Type="System.String"
                          MethodInstanceName="ItemSpecificFinderInstance">
                            0521004810
                          </DefaultValue>
                        </DefaultValues>
                      </TypeDescriptor>
                    </TypeDescriptors>
                  </TypeDescriptor>
                  <TypeDescriptor TypeName="System.String[]"
                  Name="ResponseGroup">
                    <TypeDescriptors>
                      <TypeDescriptor TypeName="System.String"
                      Name="ResponseGroupString">
                        <DefaultValues>
                          <DefaultValue Type="System.String"
                          MethodInstanceName="ItemSpecificFinderInstance">
                            Small
                          </DefaultValue>
                        </DefaultValues>
                      </TypeDescriptor>
                    </TypeDescriptors>
                  </TypeDescriptor>
                </TypeDescriptors>
              </TypeDescriptor>
            </TypeDescriptors>
          </TypeDescriptor>
          <TypeDescriptor TypeName="System.String" Name="SubscriptionId">
            <DefaultValues>
              <DefaultValue Type="System.String"
              MethodInstanceName="ItemSpecificFinderInstance">
                EnterYourSubscriptionIdHere
              </DefaultValue>
            </DefaultValues>
          </TypeDescriptor>
        </TypeDescriptors>
      </TypeDescriptor>
    </Parameter>
    <Parameter Direction="Return" Name="Response">
      <TypeDescriptor
      TypeName="AWSECommerceService.ItemLookupResponse,
                AWSECommerceService"
      Name="response">
        <!--
          The TypeName property of TypeDescriptors for .NET Types found in
          Web service proxy assemblies should be in the form
```

(continued)

Listing 13-56 *(continued)*

```
          Fully.Qualified.TypeName, LobSystemName.
        -->
        <TypeDescriptors>
          <TypeDescriptor
          TypeName="AWSECommerceService.Items[], AWSECommerceService"
          IsCollection="true" Name="Items">
            <TypeDescriptors>
              <TypeDescriptor
              TypeName="AWSECommerceService.Items, AWSECommerceService"
              IsCollection="false" Name="ItemsArray">
                <TypeDescriptors>
                  <TypeDescriptor
                  TypeName="AWSECommerceService.Item[],
                            AWSECommerceService"
                  IsCollection="true" Name="Item">
                    <TypeDescriptors>
                      <TypeDescriptor
                      TypeName="AWSECommerceService.Item,
                                AWSECommerceService"
                      IsCollection="false" Name="ItemArray">
                        <TypeDescriptors>
                          <TypeDescriptor
                          TypeName="System.String" IdentifierName="ItemId"
                          AssociatedFilter="ID" Name="ASIN">
                            <LocalizedDisplayNames>
                              <LocalizedDisplayName LCID="1033">
                                ASIN
                              </LocalizedDisplayName>
                            </LocalizedDisplayNames>
                            <Properties>
                              <Property Name="DisplayByDefault"
                              Type="System.Boolean">
                                true
                              </Property>
                            </Properties>
                          </TypeDescriptor>
                          <TypeDescriptor TypeName="System.String"
                          Name="DetailPageURL">
                            <LocalizedDisplayNames>
                              <LocalizedDisplayName LCID="1033">
                                DetailPageURL
                              </LocalizedDisplayName>
                            </LocalizedDisplayNames>
                            <Properties>
                              <Property Name="DisplayByDefault"
                              Type="System.Boolean">
                                true
                              </Property>
```

```
                                    </Properties>
                                  </TypeDescriptor>
                                </TypeDescriptors>
                              </TypeDescriptor>
                            </TypeDescriptors>
                          </TypeDescriptor>
                        </TypeDescriptors>
                      </TypeDescriptor>
                    </TypeDescriptors>
                  </TypeDescriptor>
                </TypeDescriptors>
              </TypeDescriptor>
            </Parameter>
          </Parameters>
        </Method>
      </Methods>
    </Entity></Entities>
</LobSystem>
```

As you can see, the ItemSearch metadata object supports two parameter metadata objects: one to represent the input parameter of the ItemSearch web method and one to represent the return value of this web method.

As Listing 13-56 shows, the Direction attribute on the first <Parameter> element is set to "In" to specify that this parameter metadata object represents the input parameter of the ItemSearch web method. This parameter metadata object uses the same name as the input parameter that it represents ("itemLookup"):

```
<Parameter Direction="In" Name="itemLookup">
  . . .
</Parameter>
```

As Listing 13-56 shows, the first <Parameter> element contains a <TypeDescriptor> child element that describes the input parameter of the ItemSearch web method. The TypeName attribute specifies the data type of this input parameter. The value of this attribute consists of a comma-separated list of two substrings where the first substring specifies the fully qualified name of the type of the input parameter including its complete namespace containment hierarchy (AWSECommerceService.ItemLookup) and the second substring specifies the name of the LOB system metadata object that represents the Amazon E-Commerce web service LOB application:

```
<Parameter Direction="In" Name="itemLookup">
  <TypeDescriptor Name="itemLookup"
  TypeName="AWSECommerceService.ItemLookup, AWSECommerceService">
    . . .
  </TypeDescriptor>
</Parameter>
```

As Listing 13-56 shows, the preceding <TypeDescriptor> element contains a <TypeDescriptors> child element to describe the properties of the AWSECommerceService.ItemLookup .NET type. This .NET type has two properties named Request and SubscriptionId:

```
<Parameters>
  <Parameter Direction="In" Name="itemLookup">
    <TypeDescriptor TypeName="AWSECommerceService.ItemLookup, AWSECommerceService"
    Name="itemLookup">
      <TypeDescriptors>
        <TypeDescriptor Name="Request"
        TypeName="AWSECommerceService.ItemLookupRequest[], AWSECommerceService">
          . . .
        </TypeDescriptor>
        <TypeDescriptor TypeName="System.String" Name="SubscriptionId">
          . . .
        </TypeDescriptor>
      </TypeDescriptors>
    </TypeDescriptor>
  </Parameter>
</Parameters>
```

The first <TypeDescriptor> child element describes the Request property. The Name attribute on this <TypeDescriptor> child element is set to "Request," which is the name of the property it describes. The TypeName attribute on this <TypeDescriptor> child element is set to the fully qualified name of the type of the property including its complete namespace containment hierarchy, that is, AWSECommerceService.ItemLookupRequest[], plus the name of the LOB system metadata object that represents the Amazon E-Commerce web service LOB application.

The second <TypeDescriptor> child element describes the SubscriptionId property, which is a string. You must set up an account with Amazon.com to receive a subscription ID. This subscription ID must be passed into every single call that the BDC makes to the Amazon E-Commerce web service. To make this possible, this <TypeDescriptor> element contains a <DefaultValues> element, which contains a <DefaultValue> element that specifies the Amazon subscription ID as the default value of the SubscriptionId property to have the BDC to use this value every single time that this method is invoked:

```
<TypeDescriptor TypeName="System.String" Name="SubscriptionId">
  <DefaultValues>
    <DefaultValue Type="System.String"
    MethodInstanceName="ItemSpecificFinderInstance">
      EnterYourSubscriptionIdHere
    </DefaultValue>
  </DefaultValues>
</TypeDescriptor>
```

As Listing 13-56 illustrates, the first <TypeDescriptor> child element contains a <TypeDescriptors> element to describe the type of objects that the AWSECommerceService.ItemLookupRequest[]

array contains. Because this array contains only one type of object, AWSECommerceService.ItemLookupRequest, this <TypeDescriptors> element only contains a single <TypeDescriptor> child element:

```
<TypeDescriptor Name="Request"
TypeName="AWSECommerceService.ItemLookupRequest[], AWSECommerceService">
  <TypeDescriptors>
    <TypeDescriptor Name="RequestObject"
    TypeName="AWSECommerceService.ItemLookupRequest, AWSECommerceService">
      . . .
    </TypeDescriptor>
  </TypeDescriptors>
</TypeDescriptor>
```

This single <TypeDescriptor> child element contains a <TypeDescriptors> child element to describe the properties of the AWSECommerceService.ItemLookupRequest .NET type. Because this .NET type exposes two properties named ItemId and ResponseGroup, this <TypeDescriptors> child element contains two <TypeDescriptor> child elements to describe these two properties:

```
<TypeDescriptor Name="Request"
TypeName="AWSECommerceService.ItemLookupRequest[], AWSECommerceService">
  <TypeDescriptors>
    <TypeDescriptor Name="RequestObject"
    TypeName="AWSECommerceService.ItemLookupRequest, AWSECommerceService">
      <TypeDescriptors>
        <TypeDescriptor TypeName="System.String[]" Name="ItemId">
          <TypeDescriptors>
            <TypeDescriptor TypeName="System.String" Name="ID"
            AssociatedFilter="ID" IdentifierName="ItemId">
              . . .
            </TypeDescriptor>
          </TypeDescriptors>
        </TypeDescriptor>
        <TypeDescriptor TypeName="System.String[]" Name="ResponseGroup">
          <TypeDescriptors>
            <TypeDescriptor TypeName="System.String" Name="ResponseGroupString">
              . . .
            </TypeDescriptor>
          </TypeDescriptors>
        </TypeDescriptor>
      </TypeDescriptors>
    </TypeDescriptor>
  </TypeDescriptors>
</TypeDescriptor>
```

The first <TypeDescriptor> child element describes the ItemId property, which is of the System.String[] type. Note that this <TypeDescriptor> contains a <TypeDescriptors> child element to describe the type of objects that the ItemId array property can contain. Because this property is an array, it contains only one type of object. As such, the <TypeDescriptors> child element contains a single <TypeDescriptor> child element to describe this type:

```
<TypeDescriptor TypeName="System.String" Name="ID"
AssociatedFilter="ID" IdentifierName="ItemId">
  . . .
</TypeDescriptor>
```

As you can see, the TypeName attribute of this <TypeDescriptor> element is set to System.String to specify that the object that this type descriptor metadata object describes is of the string data type. The IdentifierName attribute is set to the name of the following identifier metadata object, which represents the ItemId identifier or key of the business entity that the Item entity metadata object represents:

```
<Entity Name="Item">
  <Identifiers>
    <Identifier Name="ItemId" TypeName="System.String"/>
  </Identifiers>
  . . .
</Entity>
```

This tells the BDC that the parameter that the type descriptor object describes is an identifier or key parameter. That is, the ItemId array property contains the identifier or key of the item being looked up. The AssociatedFilter attribute is set to the name of the following filter descriptor metadata object:

```
<FilterDescriptor Type="Comparison" Name="ID">
  <Properties>
    <Property Name="Comparator" Type="System.String">Equals</Property>
  </Properties>
</FilterDescriptor>
```

As you can see, this filter descriptor metadata object describes an equality filter to instruct the BDC to use the value that the user passes into the method metadata object *as is* as the value of the parameter that the type descriptor metadata object represents. The filter descriptor metadata object is discussed in the next section.

Next is the parameter metadata object that represents the return value of the ItemLookup web method. As Listing 13-56 shows, the Direction attribute on this <Parameter> element is set to "Return" to specify that this parameter metadata object represents a return parameter:

```
<Parameter Direction="Return" Name="Response">
  . . .
</Parameter>
```

This <Parameter> element contains a <TypeDescriptor> child element to describe the return parameter. Note that the TypeName attribute on this <TypeDescriptor> child element is set to the fully qualified name of the .NET data type of the return parameter, that is, AWSECommerceService.

ItemLookupResponse, plus the name of the LOB system metadata object that represents the Amazon E-Commerce LOB application:

```
<Parameter Direction="Return" Name="Response">
  <TypeDescriptor Name="response"
  TypeName="AWSECommerceService.ItemLookupResponse, AWSECommerceService">
    . . .
  </TypeDescriptor>
</Parameter>
```

As Listing 13-56 shows, the preceding <TypeDescriptor> element contains a <TypeDescriptors> element to describe the types of the properties of the AWSECommerceService.ItemLookupResponse .NET type. Because this .NET type only exposes one property named Items, the <TypeDescriptors> element contains a single <TypeDescriptor> child element to describe this property:

```
<Parameter Direction="Return" Name="Response">
  <TypeDescriptor Name="response"
  TypeName="AWSECommerceService.ItemLookupResponse, AWSECommerceService">
    <TypeDescriptors>
      <TypeDescriptor TypeName="AWSECommerceService.Items[], AWSECommerceService"
      IsCollection="true" Name="Items">
        . . .
      </TypeDescriptor>
    </TypeDescriptors>
  </TypeDescriptor>
</Parameter>
```

Note that the IsCollection attribute on this <TypeDescriptor> child element is set to true to specify that the property that this type descriptor metadata object describes is a collection. The TypeName attribute is set to the fully qualified name of the type of this collection, that is, AWSECommerceService.Items[], plus the name of the LOB system metadata object that represents the Amazon E-Commerce web service LOB application.

As Listing 13-56 shows, the preceding <TypeDescriptor> element contains a <TypeDescriptors> child element, which in turn contains a <TypeDescriptor> child element to describe the type of object that the AWSECommerceService.Items[] array contains:

```
<Parameter Direction="Return" Name="Response">
  <TypeDescriptor Name="response"
  TypeName="AWSECommerceService.ItemLookupResponse, AWSECommerceService">
    <TypeDescriptors>
      <TypeDescriptor TypeName="AWSECommerceService.Items[], AWSECommerceService"
      IsCollection="true" Name="Items">
        <TypeDescriptors>
          <TypeDescriptor TypeName="AWSECommerceService.Items, AWSECommerceService"
          IsCollection="false" Name="ItemsArray">
            . . .
          </TypeDescriptor>
        </TypeDescriptors>
      </TypeDescriptor>
    </TypeDescriptors>
  </TypeDescriptor>
</Parameter>
```

The TypeName attribute on this <TypeDescriptor> element is set to the fully qualified name of the type of element called AWSECommerceService.Items, plus the name of the LOB system metadata object.

As Listing 13-56 shows, the preceding <TypeDescriptor> element contains a <TypeDescriptors> child element to describe the properties of the AWSECommerceService.Items type. Because this .NET type only exposes one property named Item, this <TypeDescriptors> element contains a single <TypeDescriptor> child element to describe this property:

```
<Parameter Direction="Return" Name="Response">
  <TypeDescriptor Name="response"
  TypeName="AWSECommerceService.ItemLookupResponse, AWSECommerceService">
    <TypeDescriptors>
      <TypeDescriptor TypeName="AWSECommerceService.Items[], AWSECommerceService"
      IsCollection="true" Name="Items">
        <TypeDescriptors>
          <TypeDescriptor TypeName="AWSECommerceService.Items, AWSECommerceService"
          IsCollection="false" Name="ItemsArray">
            <TypeDescriptors>
              <TypeDescriptor IsCollection="true" Name="Item"
              TypeName="AWSECommerceService.Item[], AWSECommerceService">
                . . .
              </TypeDescriptor>
            </TypeDescriptors>
          </TypeDescriptor>
        </TypeDescriptors>
      </TypeDescriptor>
    </TypeDescriptors>
  </TypeDescriptor>
</Parameter>
```

The TypeName attribute on this <TypeDescriptor> element is set to the fully qualified name of the type of the property, that is, AWSECommerceService.Item[], plus the name of the LOB system metadata object. The IsCollection attribute is set to true to specify that this property is a collection.

As Listing 13-56 shows, the preceding <TypeDescriptor> element contains a <TypeDescriptors> child element to describe the properties of the AWSECommerceService.Item type. Because this type exposes two properties named ASIN and DetailPageUrl, this <TypeDescriptors> element contains two <TypeDescriptor> child elements to describe these two properties:

```
<Parameter Direction="Return" Name="Response">
  <TypeDescriptor Name="response"
  TypeName="AWSECommerceService.ItemLookupResponse, AWSECommerceService">
    <TypeDescriptors>
      <TypeDescriptor TypeName="AWSECommerceService.Items[], AWSECommerceService"
      IsCollection="true" Name="Items">
        <TypeDescriptors>
          <TypeDescriptor TypeName="AWSECommerceService.Items, AWSECommerceService"
          IsCollection="false" Name="ItemsArray">
            <TypeDescriptors>
              <TypeDescriptor IsCollection="true" Name="Item"
              TypeName="AWSECommerceService.Item[], AWSECommerceService">
                <TypeDescriptors>
                  <TypeDescriptor IsCollection="false" Name="ItemArray"
                  TypeName="AWSECommerceService.Item, AWSECommerceService">
```

```
                        <TypeDescriptors>
                          <TypeDescriptor AssociatedFilter="ID" Name="ASIN"
                          TypeName="System.String" IdentifierName="ItemId">
                            <LocalizedDisplayNames>
                              <LocalizedDisplayName LCID="1033">ASIN
                              </LocalizedDisplayName>
                            </LocalizedDisplayNames>
                            <Properties>
                              <Property Name="DisplayByDefault" Type="System.Boolean">
                                true
                              </Property>
                            </Properties>
                          </TypeDescriptor>
                          <TypeDescriptor TypeName="System.String"
                          Name="DetailPageURL">
                            <LocalizedDisplayNames>
                              <LocalizedDisplayName LCID="1033">DetailPageURL
                              </LocalizedDisplayName>
                            </LocalizedDisplayNames>
                            <Properties>
                              <Property Name="DisplayByDefault" Type="System.Boolean">
                                true
                              </Property>
                            </Properties>
                          </TypeDescriptor>
                        </TypeDescriptors>
                      </TypeDescriptor>
                    </TypeDescriptors>
                  </TypeDescriptor>
                </TypeDescriptors>
              </TypeDescriptor>
            </TypeDescriptors>
          </TypeDescriptor>
        </TypeDescriptors>
      </TypeDescriptor>
    </Parameter>
```

The Name attributes on these two <TypeDescriptor> elements are set to the names of the properties that these type descriptor metadata objects represent, which are "ASIN" and "DetailPageURL." The TypeName attributes are set to the fully qualified names of the data types of these two properties, which is System.String. The DisplayByDefault properties of these two type descriptor metadata objects are set to true to specify that the values of these two properties are displayed by default.

Notice that the IdentifierName attribute on the <TypeDescriptor> element that represents the ASIN property is set to the name of the identifier metadata object that represents the identifier or key of the Item entity metadata object to specify that the ASIN property contains the identifier or key value. In general, the return value must always contain the identifier or key value. This is true both in database and web service LOB applications and both in SpecificFinder and Finder method instance metadata objects.

```
<Entity Name="Item">
  <Identifiers>
    <Identifier Name="ItemId" TypeName="System.String" />
  </Identifiers>
</Entity>
```

FilterDescriptors

As you can see from Listing 13-43, a <Method> element can contain an optional child element named <FilterDescriptors>, which is of the FilterDescriptors schema type shown in Listing 13-57.

Listing 13-57: The FilterDescriptors schema type

```
<xs:complexType name="FilterDescriptors">
  <xs:sequence>
    <xs:element name="FilterDescriptor" type="bdc:FilterDescriptor" minOccurs="1"
    maxOccurs="unbounded"/>
  </xs:sequence>
</xs:complexType>
```

Based on this schema type, the <FilterDescriptors> element must contain at least one instance of a child element named <FilterDescriptor>, which is of the FilterDescriptor schema type shown in Listing 13-58.

Listing 13-58: The FilterDescriptor schema type

```
<xs:complexType name="FilterDescriptor">
  <xs:complexContent>
    <xs:extension base="bdc:MetadataObject">
      <xs:attribute name="Type" type="bdc:FilterDescriptorType" use="required"/>
    </xs:extension>
  </xs:complexContent>
</xs:complexType>
```

As Listing 13-58 illustrates, the FilterDescriptor schema type extends the MetadataObject schema type. Based on the FilterDescriptor schema type, a <FilterDescriptor> element features an attribute named Type, which is of the FilterDescriptorType schema type defined in Listing 13-59. Note that this attribute is required.

Listing 13-59: The FilterDescriptorType schema type

```
<xs:simpleType name="FilterDescriptorType">
  <xs:restriction base="xs:string">
    <xs:enumeration value="Limit"/>
    <xs:enumeration value="Wildcard"/>
    <xs:enumeration value="UserContext"/>
    <xs:enumeration value="Username"/>
    <xs:enumeration value="Password"/>
    <xs:enumeration value="LastId"/>
    <xs:enumeration value="SsoTicket"/>
    <xs:enumeration value="UserProfile"/>
    <xs:enumeration value="Comparison"/>
  </xs:restriction>
</xs:simpleType>
```

As you can see from Listing 13-59, the FilterDescriptorType is an enumeration type with possible values of Limit, Wildcard, UserContext, Username, Password, LastId, SsoTicket, UserProfile, and Comparison.

Because the FilterDescriptor schema type inherits from the MetadataObject schema type, a FilterDescriptor object is a metadata object and just like any other metadata object in the BDC you can:

- Specify a name for it. Keep in mind that every metadata object in the BDC must have a name:

```
<FilterDescriptors>
  <FilterDescriptor Name="MyFilter" . . .>
    . . .
  </FilterDescriptor>
  . . .
</FilterDescriptors>
```

- Specify a default display name for it:

```
<FilterDescriptors>
  <FilterDescriptor DefaultDisplayName="My Filter" . . .>
    . . .
  </FilterDescriptor>
  . . .
</FilterDescriptors>
```

- Specify whether the BDC should cache it:

```
<FilterDescriptors>
  <FilterDescriptor IsCached="true" . . .>
    . . .
  </FilterDescriptor>
  . . .
</FilterDescriptors>
```

- Specify localized display names for it:

```
<FilterDescriptors>
  <FilterDescriptor . . .>
    <LocalizedDisplayNames>
      <LocalizedDisplayName LCID="1033">My Filter</LocalizedDisplayName>
      . . .
    </LocalizedDisplayNames>
  </FilterDescriptor>
  . . .
</FilterDescriptors>
```

- Specify its properties:

```
<FilterDescriptors>
  <FilterDescriptor . . .>
    <Properties>
      <Property Name="" Type=""></Property>
      . . .
    </Properties>
  </FilterDescriptor>
  . . .
</FilterDescriptors>
```

So far you've learned that a method metadata object represents a business operation on a business entity in a database or web service LOB application. A business operation in a database LOB application is normally a database query, whereas a business operation in a web service LOB application is normally a web method. As such a method metadata object represents a database query in a database LOB application and a web method in a web service LOB application.

What does a filter descriptor metadata object represent? A filter descriptor metadata object represents a business filter in a database or web service LOB application. A business filter in a database or web service LOB application filters the business entity instances returned from a business operation performed on a business entity. A business filter in a database LOB application filters the database rows returned from a database query. A business filter in a web service LOB application filters the objects returned from a web method. As such, a filter descriptor metadata object normally represents a filter that filters the database rows returned from a database query in a database LOB application and a filter that filters the objects returned from a web method in a web service LOB application.

As Listing 13-43 shows, a filter descriptor metadata object is always defined on a method metadata object. This is because a filter descriptor metadata object represents a filtering on the entity instances returned from the execution of a method metadata object on an entity metadata object. That is why the <FilterDescriptors> element is only used as the child elements of a <Method> element, which itself is the grandchild element of an <Entity> element.

A business filter normally filters business entities based on the values of specific business parameters. For instance, consider the AdventureWorksDW SQL Server 2005 database LOB application. Business entity instances in this case are database table rows and business parameters are the parameters used in a database query such as a SQL SELECT statement or stored procedure. Filtering entity instances in this case means selecting table rows based on the values of specific SQL SELECT statement or stored procedure parameters.

For example, consider the following SQL SELECT statement:

```
SELECT * FROM Customers WHERE CustomerName LIKE @CustomerName
```

This SQL SELECT statement returns those database table rows whose CustomerName column values match the pattern specified in the @CustomerName parameter. The metadata author must take the following two steps to enable users to specify the value of the @CustomerName parameter and to have the BDC use this value when it executes the method instance metadata object that represents the preceding SQL SELECT statement:

1. Define a filter descriptor metadata object of the Wildcard type on the method metadata object that represents the preceding SQL SELECT statement:

```
<Method Name="GetCustomers">
  <FilterDescriptors>
    <FilterDescriptor Type="Wildcard" Name="Name" />
  </FilterDescriptors>
</Method>
```

2. Add a reference to the preceding filter descriptor metadata object to the type descriptor metadata object that describes the @CustomerName parameter:

```
<Method Name="GetCustomers">
  <FilterDescriptors>
    <FilterDescriptor Type="Wildcard" Name="Name" />
  </FilterDescriptors>
  <Parameters>
    <Parameter Name="@CustomerName" Direction="In">
      <TypeDescriptor Name="CustomerName" AssociatedFilter="Name"
      TypeName="System.String">
        . . .
      </TypeDescriptor>
    </Parameter>
  </Parameters>
</Method>
```

3. Add default values for the @CustomerName parameter so users do not have to specify the value of this parameter to execute the method instance metadata object:

```
<Method Name="GetCustomers">
  <FilterDescriptors>
    <FilterDescriptor Type="Wildcard" Name="Name" />
  </FilterDescriptors>
  <Parameters>
    <Parameter Name="@CustomerName" Direction="In">
      <TypeDescriptor Name="CustomerName" AssociatedFilter="Name"
      TypeName="System.String">
        <DefaultValues>
          <DefaultValue MethodInstanceName="GetCustomersInstance"
          TypeName="System.String">%</DefaultValue>
        </DefaultValues>
      </TypeDescriptor>
    </Parameter>
  </Parameters>
</Method>
```

Users then must take these steps to use the previous wildcard filter:

1. Query the metadata repository for the previous filter descriptor metadata object. The SharePoint UI automatically does this for the user for pages such as the one shown in Figure 13-1. Such pages contain a drop-down list that lists the names of all the filter descriptor metadata objects defined on the associated method metadata object.

2. Set the value of this filter descriptor metadata object. For example, they can set the value of this filter to "%smi%" to search for those customers whose name contains "smi." Users typically accomplish this via the SharePoint UI such as the one shown in Figure 13-1. The user simply enters the filter value into the text field shown next to the drop-down list.

3. Query the metadata repository for the finder method instance metadata object. The user normally uses the SharePoint user interface such as the one shown in Figure 13-1 to do this. After the user enters the appropriate value into the text field shown in this figure and hits Enter, the business logic uses the Runtime object model to access the finder method instance metadata object defined on the Product entity metadata object.

4. Execute the metadata instance metadata object. Again this is normally done using the SharePoint user interface such as the one shown in Figure 13-1. After the BDC accesses the finder method instance metadata object on behalf of the user, it locates the type descriptor metadata object that references the filter descriptor metadata object that the user selected and assigns the user's value as the value of this filter descriptor metadata object. The BDC finally uses the Runtime object model to execute this method instance metadata object.

The filter descriptor metadata object and type descriptor metadata object work together to enable users to filter the returned entity instances based on the specified value of a parameter. Because a type descriptor metadata object does not directly contain the filter descriptor metadata object, the same filter descriptor metadata object can be referenced from multiple type descriptor metadata objects.

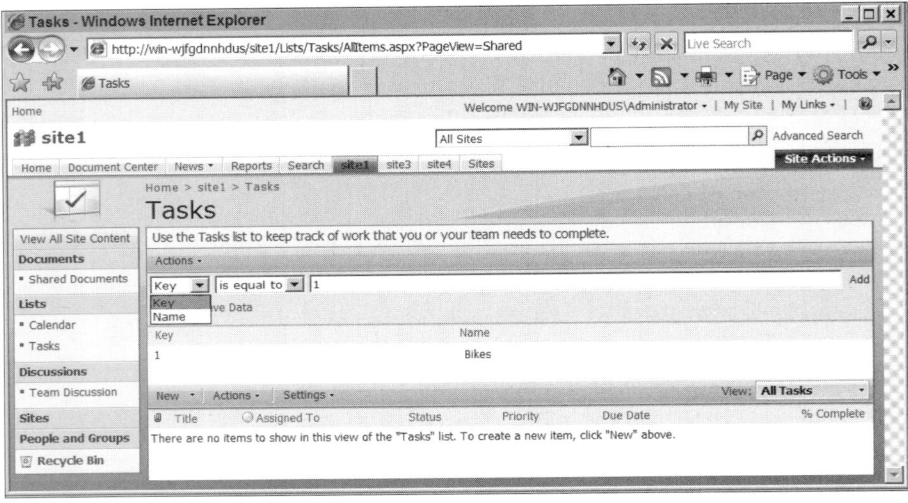

Figure 13-1: A page showing a filter

The BDC supports the following types of filter descriptor metadata objects:

- **Wildcard.** A wildcard filter descriptor metadata object enables a user to filter entity instances based on whether the parameter described by a type descriptor metadata object that references this filter descriptor metadata object matches the pattern that the user specifies as the value.
- **Limit.** A limit filter descriptor metadata object enables a user to filter or limit the number of entity instances to the number that the user specifies as the value of this filter descriptor metadata object. The type descriptor metadata object that references this filter descriptor metadata object describes the parameter, which the underlying business operation uses to limit the number of entity instances. For example, in the case of the following database query, the number n is the parameter:

```
SELECT TOP n From Customers
```

- **UserContext.** A user context filter descriptor metadata object filters entity instances based on the current user's context, in this case, domainname1\username1. The type descriptor metadata object that references this filter descriptor metadata object describes the parameter, which the underlying business operation uses to limit the entity instances to the user context specified in the parameter. For example, in the case of the following database query, @UserContext is the parameter:

```
SELECT From Customers Where UserContext=@UserContext
```

The preceding query enables a user to view only those customer records that the user is authorized to view.

When the BDC encounters a type descriptor metadata object that references the UserContext filter, it automatically sets the value of the parameter that the type descriptor metadata object represents to the current user's context, for example, domainname1\username1. The current user's context is basically the current user's Windows account.

- **UserProfile.** A user profile filter descriptor metadata object filters entity instances based on the value of a specific property of the current user's profile. The type descriptor metadata object that references this filter descriptor metadata object describes the parameter, which the underlying business operation uses to limit the entity instances based on the value of the user profile property specified in the parameter. For example, in the case of the following database query, the @SomeUserProfilePropertyValue datafield is the parameter:

```
SELECT From Customers Where UserProfileProperty=@UserProfileProperty
```

When the BDC encounters a type descriptor metadata object that references the UserProfile filter, it automatically sets the value of the parameter that the type descriptor metadata object represents to the value of the current user's specified user profile property.

A metadata author must define a UserProfile filter as follows:

```
<Method Name="GetCustomers">
  <FilterDescriptors>
    <FilterDescriptor Type="UserProfile" Name="MyFilter">
      <Properties>
        <Property Name="UserProfilePropertyName" Type="System.String">
          SomePropertyName
        </Property>
      </Properties>
    </FilterDescriptor>
  </FilterDescriptors>
</Method>
```

The metadata author needs to set the value of the UserProfilePropertyName property of the UserProfile filter metadata object to the name of the user profile property.

- **Username and Password.** These two filter metadata objects work together to enable the BDC to filter entity instances based on the current user's SSO username and password. The user will be able to view only records that the user is authorized to view. The type descriptor metadata objects that reference these two filter descriptor metadata objects describe the parameters, which the underlying business operation uses to limit the entity instances based on the current user's SSO username and password specified in these two parameters. For example, in the case of the following database query, @SsoUsername and @SsoPassword are the parameters:

```
SELECT From Customers Where SsoUsername=@SsoUsername And SsoPassword=@SsoPassword
```

When the BDC encounters the type descriptor metadata objects that reference the Username and Password filters, it automatically sets the values of these parameters that the type descriptor metadata objects represent to the current user's SSO username and password.

- **SSOTicket.** An SSO ticket filter metadata object enables the BDC to filter entity instances based on the current user's SSO ticket. In other words, the user will be able to view only those records the user is authorized to view. The type descriptor metadata object that references this filter descriptor metadata object describes the parameter, which the underlying business operation uses to limit the entity instances based on the SSO ticket specified in the parameter.

  When the BDC encounters a type descriptor metadata object that references the SSOTicket filter metadata object, it automatically sets the value of the parameter that the type descriptor metadata object represents to the SSO Ticket.

- **LastIdSeen.** This filter metadata object is used in an IdEnumerator method instance to limit the number of returned Ids, which improves performance in the case of non-streaming LOB applications. The type descriptor metadata object that references this filter descriptor metadata object describes the parameter, which the underlying business operation uses to limit the entity instances based on the value specified in the parameter.

  When the BDC encounters a type descriptor metadata object that references the LastIdSeen filter metadata object, it automatically sets the value of the parameter that the type descriptor metadata object represents to the last Id seen. The BDC itself keeps track of the last Id seen.

- **Comparison.** A comparison filter metadata object enables a user to filter entity instances based on a comparison operation. This filter metadata object exposes a property named Comparator that a metadata author must set to specify the type of the comparison operation.

Take a look at an example of a comparison filter metadata object:

```
<Entity Name="Customer">
  <Identifiers>
    <Identifier Name="CustomerId" TypeName="System.String" />
  </Identifiers>
  <Method Name="GetCustomers">
    <Properties>
      <Property Name="RdbCommandText" Type="System.String">
        SELECT * FROM Customers
        WHERE CustomerId <= @MaxCustomerId AND CustomerId >= @MinCustomerId
      </Property>
      <Property Name="RdbCommandType" Type="System.Data.CommandType">
        Text
      </Property>
    </Properties>
    <FilterDescriptors>
      <FilterDescriptor Name="MyFilter" Type="Comparison">
        <Properties>
          <Property Name="Comparator" Type="System.String">Equals</Property>
        </Properties>
      </FilterDescriptor>
    </FilterDescriptors>
    <Parameters>
```

```
        <Parameter Name="@MaxCustomerId" Direction="In">
          <TypeDescriptor Name="MaxCustomerId" AssociatedFilter="MyFilter"
          TypeName="System.Int32" IdentifierName="CustomerId" />
        <Parameter>
        <Parameter Name="@MinCustomerId" Direction="In">
          <TypeDescriptor Name="MinCustomerId" AssociatedFilter="MyFilter"
          TypeName="System.Int32" IdentifierName="CustomerId" />
        <Parameter>
        <Parameter Name="Customers" Direction="In">
          . . .
        </Parameter>
      </Parameters>
      <MethodInstances>
        <MethodInstance Type="Finder" Name="GetCustomersFinder" />
        <MethodInstance Type="SpecificFinder" Name="GetCustomersSpecificFinder" />
      </MethodInstances>
    </Method>
  </Entity>
```

The preceding XML fragment defines an equality comparison filter metadata object named MyFilter. As you can see, this XML fragment defines an entity metadata object named Customer that represents a database table named Customers. This entity metadata object contains an identity metadata object that represents the CustomerId primary key:

```
<Entity Name="Customer">
  <Identifiers>
    <Identifier Name="CustomerId" TypeName="System.String" />
  </Identifiers>
  . . .
</Entity>
```

This XML fragment then defines a method metadata object named GetCustomers on the Customer entity metadata object to represent the following SQL SELECT statement:

```
SELECT * FROM Customers
WHERE CustomerId <= @MaxCustomerId AND CustomerId >= @MinCustomerId
```

This SQL SELECT statement contains two parameters named @MaxCustomerId and @MinCustomerId.

The XML fragment then defines two method instance metadata objects named GetCustomersFinder and GetCustomersSpecificFinder of the Finder and SpecificFinder types, respectively, on the GetCustomers method metadata object:

```
    <MethodInstances>
      <MethodInstance Type="Finder" Name="GetCustomersFinder" />
      <MethodInstance Type="SpecificFinder" Name="GetCustomersSpecificFinder" />
    </MethodInstances>
```

The XML fragment then defines an equality comparison filter metadata object named MyFilter:

```
<FilterDescriptors>
  <FilterDescriptor Name="MyFilter" Type="Comparison">
    <Properties>
      <Property Name="Comparator" Type="System.String">Equals</Property>
    </Properties>
  </FilterDescriptor>
</FilterDescriptors>
```

Note that the type descriptor metadata objects that describe the @MaxCustomerId and @MinCustomerId parameters both reference the same MyFilter equality comparison filter metadata object:

```
<Parameter Name="@MaxCustomerId" Direction="In">
  <TypeDescriptor Name="MaxCustomerId" AssociatedFilter="MyFilter"
  TypeName="System.Int32" IdentifierName="Key" />
<Parameter>
<Parameter Name="@MinCustomerId" Direction="In">
  <TypeDescriptor Name="MinCustomerId" AssociatedFilter="MyFilter"
  TypeName="System.Int32" IdentifierName="Key" />
<Parameter>
```

Also note that these two type descriptor metadata objects reference the same identity metadata object defined on the Customer entity metadata object:

```
<Entity Name="Customer">
  <Identifiers>
    <Identifier Name="CustomerId" TypeName="System.String" />
  </Identifiers>
  . . .
    <Parameters>
      <Parameter Name="@MaxCustomerId" Direction="In">
        <TypeDescriptor Name="MaxCustomerId" AssociatedFilter="MyFilter"
        TypeName="System.Int32" IdentifierName="CustomerId" />
      <Parameter>
      <Parameter Name="@MinCustomerId" Direction="In">
        <TypeDescriptor Name="MinCustomerId" AssociatedFilter="MyFilter"
        TypeName="System.Int32" IdentifierName="CustomerId" />
      <Parameter>
    </Parameters>
  . . .
</Entity>
```

These references to the identity metadata object come into play when the user executes the SpecificFinder method instance metadata object (that is, the method instance metadata object named GetCustomersSpecificFinder), passing in the primary key of the customer about whom detailed information is being queried from the back-end database LOB application. These references to the identity metadata object tell the BDC that the parameters that the associated two type descriptor metadata objects describe (the @MaxCustomerId and @MinCustomerId parameters) are identity or key parameters. As such, the BDC first accesses the value that the user has passed into the SpecificFinder method instance metadata object. Recall that this value is the primary key of the customer record being queried. The BDC then notices that both type descriptor metadata objects also reference the MyFilter equality comparison filter metadata object. This tells the BDC that it must assign this primary key value *as is* to both the @MaxCustomerId and @MinCustomerId parameters. Let's say this primary key value is 100. The end result is that the BDC ends up executing the following SQL SELECT statement on the back-end database:

```
SELECT * FROM Customers
WHERE CustomerId <= 100 AND CustomerId >= 100
```

This SQL SELECT statement in effect returns only the record for the customer with CustomerId value of 100. As you can see, the equality comparison filter metadata object allows you to define and to use two method instance metadata objects of the Finder and SpecificFinder types on the same method metadata object. In effect, you get to run the same SQL SELECT statement to retrieve a set of records (Finder method metadata object) and to retrieve a single record with a specified primary key (SpecificFinder method metadata object).

The filter descriptor metadata object supports the following properties for both database and web service LOB applications:

- **UsedForDisambiguation.** Set this property to *true* to have the Business Data picker to display the list of possible values of the parameter whose type descriptor metadata object references this filter descriptor metadata object for the purpose of not being ambiguous. This property is optional and defaults to false.
- **CaseSensitive.** Set this property to *true* to have the Business Data Web Parts and Business Data Picker tell the user this filter is case sensitive. This property is optional and defaults to false.
- **IsDefault.** Set this property to *true* to have the Business Data Picker to select this filter by default. This property is optional and defaults to false.

Next, you'll look at a couple of examples. Listing 13-60 extends Listing 13-45 to define filter descriptor metadata objects for the method metadata objects that represent business operations in the AdventureWorksDW SQL Server 2005 database LOB system.

Listing 13-60: The BDC application definition file that describes the database LOB system

```
<?xml version="1.0" encoding="utf-8" standalone="yes"?>
<LobSystem . . .>
  . . .
  <Entities>
    <Entity Name="Product" . . .>
      . . .
      <Methods>
        <Method Name="GetProducts" . . .>
          . . .
          <FilterDescriptors>
            <FilterDescriptor Type="Comparison" Name="Key" >
              <Properties>
                <Property Name="Comparator" Type="System.String">Equals</Property>
              </Properties>
            </FilterDescriptor>
            <FilterDescriptor Type="Wildcard" Name="Name">
```

(continued)

Listing 13-60 *(continued)*

```
          <Properties>
            <Property Name="UsedForDisambiguation" Type="System.Boolean">
              true
            </Property>
          </Properties>
        </FilterDescriptor>
        <FilterDescriptor Type="Wildcard" Name="Description" />
      </FilterDescriptors>
      . . .
    </Method>
  </Methods>
  . . .
</Entity>

<Entity Name="Reseller" . . .>
  . . .
  <Methods>
    <Method Name="ResellerIDEnumerator" . . .>
      . . .
    </Method>
    <Method Name="ResellerFinder" . . .>
      . . .
      <FilterDescriptors>
        <FilterDescriptor Type="Wildcard" Name="Name">
          <Properties>
            <Property Name="UsedForDisambiguation" Type="System.Boolean">
              true
            </Property>
          </Properties>
        </FilterDescriptor>
        <FilterDescriptor Type="Comparison" Name="Key" >
          <Properties>
            <Property Name="Comparator" Type="System.String">Equals</Property>
          </Properties>
        </FilterDescriptor>
      </FilterDescriptors>
      . . .
    </Method>
  </Methods>
  . . .
</Entity>

<Entity Name="ProductSubcategory" . . .>
  . . .
  <Methods>
    <Method Name="GetProductSubcategories" . . .>
      . . .
      <FilterDescriptors>
        <FilterDescriptor Type="Comparison" Name="Key" >
          <Properties>
```

```
              <Property Name="Comparator" Type="System.String">Equals</Property>
            </Properties>
          </FilterDescriptor>
          <FilterDescriptor Type="Wildcard" Name="Name">
            <Properties>
              <Property Name="UsedForDisambiguation" Type="System.Boolean">
                true
              </Property>
            </Properties>
          </FilterDescriptor>
        </FilterDescriptors>
        . . .
      </Method>
      <Method Name="GetProducts" . . .>
        . . .
      </Method>
    </Methods>
    . . .
  </Entity>

  <Entity Name="ProductCategory" . . .>
    . . .
    <Methods>
      <Method Name="GetProductCategories" . . .>
        . . .
        <FilterDescriptors>
          <FilterDescriptor Type="Comparison" Name="Key" >
            <Properties>
              <Property Name="Comparator" Type="System.String">Equals</Property>
            </Properties>
          </FilterDescriptor>
          <FilterDescriptor Type="Wildcard" Name="Name">
            <Properties>
              <Property Name="UsedForDisambiguation" Type="System.Boolean">
                true
              </Property>
            </Properties>
          </FilterDescriptor>
        </FilterDescriptors>
        . . .
      </Method>
      <Method Name="GetProductSubcategories" . . .>
        . . .
      </Method>
    </Methods>
    . . .
  </Entity>
</Entities>

</LobSystem>
```

Note that:

- Out of seven methods defined in Listing 13-45, the BDC application definition file shown in Listing 13-60 defines filter metadata objects for only four methods: GetProducts, GetResellerFinder, GetProductSubCategories, and GetProductCategories. Not every method metadata object contains filter metadata objects.
- The filter descriptor metadata objects defined on all these four methods share the same names. This does not introduce name conflicts because filter descriptor metadata objects are defined within the scope of their parent method metadata object. They are never referenced from outside their parent method metadata objects.

Listing 13-61 extends Listing 13-56 to define a few filters. Recall that Listing 13-56 contains the BDC application definition XML file that defines the Amazon E-Commerce web service. As you can see from Listing 13-61, this file defines an equality comparison filter descriptor metadata object named ID on the ItemLookup method metadata object defined on the Item entity metadata object and two equality comparison filter descriptor metadata objects named SearchIndex and Keywords on the ItemSearch method metadata object defined on the Item entity metadata object. This means that the BDC will use the values that the user assigns to these filters as is to the parameters whose type descriptor metadata objects reference these filter descriptor metadata objects.

Listing 13-61: The parameter metadata objects that represent the parameters of the ItemSearch web method

```
<LobSystem Name="AWSECommerceService" . . .>
  . . .
  <Entities>
    <Entity Name="Item">
      <Methods>
        <Method Name="ItemLookup">
          <FilterDescriptors>
            <FilterDescriptor Type="Comparison" Name="ID">
               <Properties>
                 <Property Name="Comparator" Type="System.String">Equals</Property>
               </Properties>
            </FilterDescriptor>
          </FilterDescriptors>
        </Method>

        <Method Name="ItemSearch">
          <FilterDescriptors>
            <FilterDescriptor Type="Comparison" Name="SearchIndex">
              <Properties>
                <Property Name="Comparator" Type="System.String">Equals</Property>
              </Properties>
            </FilterDescriptor>
            <FilterDescriptor Type="Comparison" Name="Keywords">
              <Properties>
                <Property Name="Comparator" Type="System.String">Equals</Property>
              </Properties>
            </FilterDescriptor>
```

```
            </FilterDescriptors>
          </Method>
        </Methods>
      </Entity>
      <Entity Name="EditorialReview">
        <Methods>
          <Method Name="ItemLookup">
            . . .
          </Method>
          <Method Name="ItemSearch">
            . . .
          </Method>
        </Methods>
      </Entity>
    </Entities>
  </LobSystem>
```

Listing 13-62 shows what you have so far.

Listing 13-62: The BDC application definition file

```
<LobSystem
xmlsn="http://schemas.microsoft.com/office/2006/03/BusinessDataCatalog"
xmlsn:xsi="http://www.w3.org/2001/XMLSchema-instance"
xsi="http://schemas.microsoft.com/office/2006/03/BusinessDataCatalog BDCMetadata
.xsd"
Type=""
SystemUtility=""
ConnectionManager=""
EntityInstance=""
Version=""
Name=""
DefaultDisplayName=""
IsCached="">

  <LobSystemInstances>
    <LobSystemInstance Name="" DefaultDisplayName="" IsCached="">
      <LocalizedDisplayNames>
        <LocalizedDisplayName LCID=""></LocalizedDisplayName>
        <LocalizedDisplayName LCID=""></LocalizedDisplayName>
      </LocalizedDisplayNames>
      <Properties>
        <Property Name="" Type=""></Property>
        <Property Name="" Type=""></Property>
      </Properties>
    </LobSystemInstance>
  </LobSystemInstances>

  <Entities>
    <Entity Name="" DefaultDisplayName="" IsCached="" EstimatedInstanceCount="">
      <AccessControlList>
```

(continued)

Listing 13-62 *(continued)*

```
      <AccessControlList Principal="">
        <Right BdcRights="" />
        <Right BdcRights="" />
      </AccessControlList>
    </AccessControlList>
    <LocalizedDisplayNames>
      <LocalizedDisplayName LCID=""></LocalizedDisplayName>
    </LocalizedDisplayNames>
    <Properties>
      <Property Name="" Type=""></Property>
    </Properties>
    <Identifiers>
      <Identifier Name="" DefaultDisplayName="" IsCached="" TypeName="">
        <Properties>
          <Property Name="" Type=""></Property>
          <Property Name="" Type=""></Property>
        </Properties>
        <LocalizedDisplayNames>
          <LocalizedDisplayName LCID=""></LocalizedDisplayName>
          <LocalizedDisplayName LCID=""></LocalizedDisplayName>
        </LocalizedDisplayNames>
      </Identifier>
    </Identifiers>
    <Methods>
      <Method Name="" DefaultDisplayName="" IsCached="" IsStatic="">
        <LocalizedDisplayNames>
          <LocalizedDisplayName LCID=""></LocalizedDisplayName>
          <LocalizedDisplayName LCID=""></LocalizedDisplayName>
        </LocalizedDisplayNames>
        <Properties>
          <Property Name="" Type=""></Property>
          <Property Name="" Type=""></Property>
        </Properties>
        <FilterDescriptors>
          <FilterDescriptor Name="" DefaultDisplayName="" IsCached=""
          IsStatic="" Type="">
            <LocalizedDisplayNames>
              <LocalizedDisplayName LCID=""></LocalizedDisplayName>
              <LocalizedDisplayName LCID=""></LocalizedDisplayName>
            </LocalizedDisplayNames>
            <Properties>
              <Property Name="" Type=""></Property>
              <Property Name="" Type=""></Property>
            </Properties>
          </FilterDescriptor>
        </FilterDescriptors>
        <Parameters></Parameters>
        <MethodInstances></MethodInstances>
      </Method>
    </Methods>
    <Actions></Actions>
  </Entity>
```

```
    </Entities>

    <Associations></Associations>
    <AccessControlList></AccessControlList>
    <LocalizedDisplayNames>
      <LocalizedDisplayName LCID=""></LocalizedDisplayName>
      <LocalizedDisplayName LCID=""></LocalizedDisplayName>
    </LocalizedDisplayNames>
    <Properties>
      <Property Name="" Type=""></Property>
      <Property Name="" Type=""></Property>
    </Properties>
  </LobSystem>
```

MethodInstances

As you can see from Listing 13-43, a <Method> element can contain an optional child element named <MethodInstances>, which is of the MethodInstances schema type defined in Listing 13-63.

Listing 13-63: The MethodInstances schema type

```
<xs:complexType name="MethodInstances">
  <xs:sequence>
    <xs:element name="MethodInstance" type="bdc:MethodInstance" minOccurs="1"
    maxOccurs="unbounded"/>
  </xs:sequence>
</xs:complexType>
```

Based on the MethodInstances schema type, a <MethodInstances> element must contain at least one instance of a child element named <MethodInstance>, which is of the MethodInstance schema type defined in Listing 13-64.

Listing 13-64: The MethodInstance schema type

```
<xs:complexType name="MethodInstance">
  <xs:complexContent>
    <xs:extension base="bdc:IndividuallySecurableMetadataObject">
      <xs:attribute name="Type" type="bdc:MethodInstanceType" use="required"/>
      <xs:attribute name="ReturnParameterName" type="xs:string" use="required"/>
      <xs:attribute name="ReturnTypeDescriptorName" type="xs:string"
      use="optional"/>
      <xs:attribute name="ReturnTypeDescriptorLevel"
      type="bdc:ReturnTypeDescriptorLevel" use="optional"/>
    </xs:extension>
  </xs:complexContent>
</xs:complexType>
```

The MethodInstance schema type extends the IndividuallySecurableMetadataObject schema type. This makes every method instance metadata object an individually securable metadata object. Recall that you can directly specify the ACL on an individually securable metadata object to secure its access. According to the MethodInstance schema type shown in Listing 13-64, a <MethodInstance> element contains:

- A required attribute named Type, which is of the MethodInstanceType schema type
- A required attribute named ReturnParameterName, which is of the string schema type
- An optional attribute named ReturnTypeDescriptorName, which is of the string schema type
- An optional attribute named ReturnTypeDescriptorLevel, which is of the ReturnTypeDescriptorLevel schema type

Listing 13-65 presents the definition of the MethodInstanceType schema type.

Listing 13-65: The MethodInstanceType schema type

```
<xs:simpleType name="MethodInstanceType">
  <xs:restriction base="xs:string">
    <xs:enumeration value="Finder"/>
    <xs:enumeration value="SpecificFinder"/>
    <xs:enumeration value="ViewAccessor"/>
    <xs:enumeration value="GenericInvoker"/>
    <xs:enumeration value="IdEnumerator"/>
    <xs:enumeration value="Scalar"/>
    <xs:enumeration value="AccessChecker"/>
  </xs:restriction>
</xs:simpleType>
```

The MethodInstanceType schema type is a restriction of the string schema type that restricts the value of the MethodInstanceType attribute on a <MethodInstance> element to the following values: Finder, SpecificFinder, IdEnumerator, Scalar, AccessChecker, ViewAccessor, and GenericInvoker.

Listing 13-66 presents the definition of the ReturnTypeDescriptorLevel schema type.

Listing 13-66: The ReturnTypeDescriptorLevel schema type

```
<xs:simpleType name="ReturnTypeDescriptorLevel">
  <xs:restriction base="xs:integer">
    <xs:minInclusive value="0"/>
    <xs:maxInclusive value="9"/>
  </xs:restriction>
</xs:simpleType>
```

The ReturnTypeDescriptorLevel schema type is a restriction of the integer schema type that restricts the value of the ReturnTypeDescriptorLevel attribute on a <MethodInstance> element to an integer value between 0 and 9. As such, the BDC supports only ten type descriptor levels. In other words, it supports complex properties with up to ten sub-property levels.

So far you've learned that a method metadata object represents a business operation in a LOB application. As discussed earlier, a business operation in a database LOB application is normally a database query such as a SQL SELECT statement or stored procedure and in a web service LOB application it is normally a web method. In other words, a method metadata object represents a database query or a web method. What is a method instance metadata object for?

Next, you'll learn the reasons why you need method instance metadata objects and how to use them in your BDC application definition files. Here is the first reason.

As discussed earlier, a business operation (normally a database query or web method) contains parameters that must be specified before the business operation can be executed. Expecting a user to specify all required parameters of a business operation every time the user needs to execute the business operation puts lot of burden on the user if these parameters are of a complex type. For example, consider a web method that takes a complex parameter of a .NET type named A, which exposes two complex properties of .NET types named A1 and A2 where A1 exposes three complex properties of .NET types named A11, A12, and A13 and A2 exposes four complex properties of .NET types named A21, A22, A23, and A24. This could go on and on up to ten levels of hierarchy. Recall that the BDC supports only ten levels of hierarchy.

```
<Method Name="MyWebMethod">
  <Parameters>
    <Parameter Name="MyParameter" Direction="In">
      <TypeDescriptor TypeName="A" Name="MyParameter">
        <TypeDescriptors>
          <TypeDescriptor TypeName="A1" Name="MyParameter1">
            <TypeDescriptors>
              <TypeDescriptor TypeName="A11" Name="MyParameter11">
                . . .
              </TypeDescriptor>
              <TypeDescriptor TypeName="A12" Name="MyParameter12">
                . . .
              </TypeDescriptor>
              <TypeDescriptor TypeName="A13" Name="MyParameter12">
                . . .
              </TypeDescriptor>
            </TypeDescriptors>
          </TypeDescriptor>
          <TypeDescriptor TypeName="A2" Name="MyParameter1">
            <TypeDescriptors>
              <TypeDescriptor TypeName="A21" Name="MyParameter11">
                . . .
              </TypeDescriptor>
              <TypeDescriptor TypeName="A22" Name="MyParameter12">
                . . .
              </TypeDescriptor>
              <TypeDescriptor TypeName="A23" Name="MyParameter11">
                . . .
              </TypeDescriptor>
              <TypeDescriptor TypeName="A24" Name="MyParameter12">
                . . .
              </TypeDescriptor>
            </TypeDescriptors>
          </TypeDescriptor>
        </TypeDescriptors>
      </TypeDescriptor>
    </Parameter>

    <Parameter Name="MyItems" Direction="Return">
    </Parameter>
  </Parameters>
</Method>
```

As you can see, the user must specify several values at each type hierarchy level in order to execute the web method. This is simply too taxing for the user.

In these cases, to make life easier on users, the metadata author should take these three steps:

- Determine several sets of default values for the parameters of the business operation.
- Define a method instance metadata object for each set of default values. For instance, if there are five sets of default values, the metadata author needs to define a separate method instance metadata object for each set.
- Use the <DefaultValues> element inside each leaf <TypeDescriptor> element to define default values. A leaf <TypeDescriptor> element is a <TypeDescriptor> element that does not contain a <TypeDescriptors> element. Each <DefaultValue> element in a given <DefaultValues> element must specify the default value for the associated parameter for a specific method instance metadata object.

Here is an example:

```
<Method Name="MyWebMethod">
  <Parameters>
    <Parameter Name="MyParameter" Direction="In">
      <TypeDescriptor TypeName="A" Name="MyParameter">
        <TypeDescriptors>
          <TypeDescriptor TypeName="A1" Name="MyParameter1">
            <TypeDescriptors>
              <TypeDescriptor TypeName="A11" Name="MyParameter11">
                <DefaultValues>
                  <DefaultValue MethodInstanceName="MethodInstance1"
                  Type="A11">...</DefaultValue>
                  <DefaultValue MethodInstanceName="MethodInstance2"
                  Type="A11">...</DefaultValue>
                </DefaultValues>
              </TypeDescriptor>
              <TypeDescriptor TypeName="A12" Name="MyParameter12">
                <DefaultValue MethodInstanceName="MethodInstance1"
                Type="A12">...</DefaultValue>
                <DefaultValue MethodInstanceName="MethodInstance2"
                Type="A12">...</DefaultValue>
              </TypeDescriptor>
              <TypeDescriptor TypeName="A13" Name="MyParameter12">
                <DefaultValue MethodInstanceName="MethodInstance1"
                Type="A13">...</DefaultValue>
                <DefaultValue MethodInstanceName="MethodInstance2"
                Type="A13">...</DefaultValue>
              </TypeDescriptor>
            </TypeDescriptors>
          </TypeDescriptor>
          <TypeDescriptor TypeName="A2" Name="MyParameter1">
            <TypeDescriptors>
              <TypeDescriptor TypeName="A21" Name="MyParameter11">
                <DefaultValue MethodInstanceName="MethodInstance1"
                Type="A21">...</DefaultValue>
```

```
              <DefaultValue MethodInstanceName="MethodInstance2"
              Type="A21">...</DefaultValue>
            </TypeDescriptor>
            <TypeDescriptor TypeName="A22" Name="MyParameter12">
              <DefaultValue MethodInstanceName="MethodInstance1"
              Type="A22">...</DefaultValue>
              <DefaultValue MethodInstanceName="MethodInstance2"
              Type="A22">...</DefaultValue>
            </TypeDescriptor>
            <TypeDescriptor TypeName="A23" Name="MyParameter11">
              <DefaultValue MethodInstanceName="MethodInstance1"
              Type="A23">...</DefaultValue>
              <DefaultValue MethodInstanceName="MethodInstance2"
              Type="A23">...</DefaultValue>
            </TypeDescriptor>
            <TypeDescriptor TypeName="A24" Name="MyParameter12">
              <DefaultValue MethodInstanceName="MethodInstance1"
              Type="A24">...</DefaultValue>
              <DefaultValue MethodInstanceName="MethodInstance2"
              Type="A24">...</DefaultValue>
            </TypeDescriptor>
          </TypeDescriptors>
        </TypeDescriptor>
      </TypeDescriptors>
    </TypeDescriptor>
  </Parameter>

  <Parameter Name="MyItems" Direction="Return">
    . . .
  </Parameter>
</Parameters>

<MethodInstances>
  <MethodInstance Name="MethodInstance1" Type="Finder"
  ReturnParameterName="MyItems" />
  <MethodInstance Name="MethodInstance2" Type="Finder"
  ReturnParameterName="MyItems" />
</MethodInstances>
</Method>
```

This XML fragment defines two sets of default values and defines a method instance metadata object named MethodInstance1 for the first set of default values and a method instance metadata object named MethodInstance2 for the second set of default values. The users who like to execute the web method that the MyWebMethod method metadata object represents with the first set of default values need to execute the method instance metadata object named MethodInstance1. The users who like to execute the web method that the MyWebMethod method metadata object represents with the second set of default values need to execute the method instance metadata object named MethodInstance2.

In summary, the first reason for the introduction of method instance metadata objects is to enable users to execute the same business operation using different sets of default values. Here is the second reason for the introduction of method instance metadata objects.

As discussed earlier, a <MethodInstance> element features the following attributes:

- **Type.** Use this required attribute to specify the type of the method instance metadata object. This attribute is discussed later in this chapter. The following XML fragment defines two method instance metadata objects of the Finder and SpecificFinder types on the same method metadata object named MyWebMethod:

```
<Method Name="MyWebMethod">
  <Parameters>
    . . .
  </Parameters>

  <MethodInstances>
    <MethodInstance Name="MethodInstance1" Type="Finder"
    ReturnParameterName="MyItems" />
    <MethodInstance Name="MethodInstance2" Type="SpecificFinder"
    ReturnParameterName="MyItems" />
  </MethodInstances>
</Method>
```

- **ReturnParameterName.** Set this required attribute to the name of the parameter metadata object that represents the return parameter of the method metadata object on which the method instance metadata object is defined:

```
<Method Name="MyWebMethod">
  <Parameters>
    . . .
    <Parameter Name="MyItems" Direction="Return">
      . . .
    </Parameter>
  </Parameters>

  <MethodInstances>
    <MethodInstance Name="MethodInstance1" Type="Finder"
    ReturnParameterName="MyItems" />
    <MethodInstance Name="MethodInstance2" Type="SpecificFinder"
    ReturnParameterName="MyItems" />
  </MethodInstances>
</Method>
```

- **ReturnTypeDescriptorName.** Set this optional attribute to the name of the type descriptor metadata object that describes the structure of the return value of the method instance metadata object.

- **ReturnTypeDescriptorLevel.** Set this optional attribute to the integer value that represents the hierarchy level at which the type descriptor object that describes the return value resides.

The second reason for the introduction of method instance metadata objects is to enable users to fetch only the desired information about the returned entity instances. To do this, the metadata author must define method instance metadata objects that use different values for the ReturnTypeDescriptorName to return different portions or sub data structures of the main data structure. Users who are interested in fetching a specific sub data structure can execute the associated method instance metadata object. This allows users to execute the same underlying business operation to retrieve different sub data structures.

Here is the third reason for the introduction of method instance metadata objects. As discussed earlier, a <MethodInstance> element supports an attribute named Type with the possible values of Finder, SpecificFinder, IdEnumerator, Scalar, AccessChecker, ViewAccessor, and GenericInvoker. This allows users to use different types of method instance metadata objects to execute the same underlying business operation to achieve different results, as described in the following sections.

Finder

As the name suggests, a finder method instance metadata object finds and returns entity instances from a back-end database or web service LOB application. This raises the following question: How does a finder method instance metadata object know which entity instances to return? This is where the filterable parameters of the business operation that the finder method instance metadata object represents come into play. Recall that a business operation is a database query in the case of a database LOB application and a web method in the case of a web service LOB application. Users set the values of the desired filter descriptor metadata objects, which are defined on the respective method metadata object, to specify which entity instances a finder method instance metadata object must return. Each entity instance that a finder method instance metadata object returns must contain the identifier or key of the entity instance. This allows the user to invoke a specific finder method instance metadata object, passing in the identifier or key of an entity instance, to retrieve more detailed information about the entity instance. The entity instance that a specific finder method instance metadata object returns must also contain the identifier or key of the entity instance.

A finder method instance metadata object does not take an entity instance identifier or key as a parameter, whereas a specific finder method instance metadata object takes an entity instance identifier or key as a parameter. This is because a finder method instance metadata object returns a collection of entity instances that meet the criteria specified in the filterable parameters, whereas a specific finder method instance metadata object returns a single entity instance whose identifier or key is specified in the parameter passed into the specific finder method instance metadata object.

Both finder and specific finder method instance metadata objects are static. Every entity metadata object should contain a finder and a specific finder method instance metadata object. The only exception to this rule is an entity metadata object that is only reachable through association. Such an entity metadata object must not contain a finder or specific finder method instance metadata object. The EditorialReview entity metadata object in the Amazon E-Commerce web service is an example of such an entity metadata object.

If your entity metadata object does not contain a finder method instance metadata object, it cannot be used in a Business Data List Web Part because this Web part uses the finder method instance metadata object to retrieve the entity instances from the back-end database or web service LOB application. If your entity metadata object does not contain a specific finder method instance metadata object:

- It cannot be used in any Business Data features except the Business Data Related List Web Part. This is because all these Business Data features under the hood use the specific finder method instance metadata object.
- It cannot contain actions because when users select an action the associated URL passes the identifier or key of the entity instance as the value of a query string, which is subsequently used in a specific finder method instance metadata object to retrieve more detailed information about the entity instance.

- It cannot be searched or indexed because searching and indexing involves invoking the specific finder method instance metadata object.

Every entity metadata object can contain only a single instance of a finder method instance metadata object and a single instance of a specific finder method instance metadata object.

Enterprise Search and Indexing

An IdEnumerator method instance metadata object returns entity instance identifiers or keys. The following database query presents an example of a business operation that an IdEnumerator method instance metadata object represents:

```
SELECT CustomerId FROM Customers
```

As you can see this database query simply returns the primary key values of the customer records.

The BDC comes with a filter named LastIdSeen that you can use to improve the performance of non-streaming LOB applications such as web services. For this to work, you need to take two steps. First, you need to define an IdEnumerator method instance metadata object that takes a filterable parameter that filters entity instance identifiers or keys. The following database query presents an example of a business operation that such an IdEnumerator method instance metadata object represents:

```
SELECT CustomerId FROM Customers WHERE CustomerId >= @LastIdSeen ORDER BY CustomerId
```

Second, define a filter descriptor metadata object of the LastIdSeen type and reference this filter descriptor metadata object from the type descriptor metadata object that describes the previous filterable parameter.

You can improve the performance of a non-streaming LOB application even more if you take these extra steps. First, define an IdEnumerator method instance metadata object that limits the number of returned identifiers or keys to a preset number. The following database query presents an example of a business operation that such an IdEnumerator method instance metadata object represents:

```
SELECT TOP n CustomerId FROM Customers WHERE CustomerId >= @LastIdSeen ORDER BY
CustomerId
```

Second, define a filter descriptor metadata object of the Limit type.

A BDC search crawl involves two steps. First, the BDC executes an IdEnumerator method instance metadata object to retrieve the list of entity instance identifiers or keys. Next, the BDC executes a specific finder method instance metadata object, passing in an entity instance identifier or key to retrieve the detailed information about the entity instance.

You can perform what is known as an incremental crawl if you take these steps. First, define an IdEnumerator method instance metadata object that returns not only the identifier or key of each entity instance but also the value that determines when the entity instance was last modified. The following database query presents an example of a business operation that the IdEnumerator method represents:

```
SELECT CustomerId, LastModified FROM Customers
```

Second, assign the name of the type descriptor metadata object that describes the last modified return parameter to the __BdcLastModifiedTimestamp property of the entity metadata object.

Every entity metadata object can contain zero or one IdEnumerator method instance metadata object.

Scalar

A scalar method instance metadata object returns a single value. The following database query is an example of a business operation that a scalar method instance metadata object represents:

```
SELECT COUNT(*) FROM Customers WHERE CustomerName LIKE @CustomerName
```

As you can see, a scalar method instance metadata object can take filterable parameters.

Actions

Recall from Listing 13-32 that an <Entity> element can contain an optional child element named <Actions>, which is of the Actions schema type shown in Listing 13-67.

Listing 13-67: The Actions schema type

```
<xs:complexType name="Actions">
  <xs:sequence>
    <xs:element name="Action" type="bdc:Action" minOccurs="1"
    maxOccurs="unbounded"/>
  </xs:sequence>
</xs:complexType>
```

Based on the Actions schema type, an <Actions> element must contain at least one instance of an element named <Action>, which is of the Action schema type defined in Listing 13-68.

Listing 13-68: The Action schema type

```
<xs:complexType name="Action">
  <xs:complexContent>
    <xs:extension base="bdc:MetadataObject">
      <xs:sequence>
        <xs:element name="ActionParameters" type="bdc:ActionParameters"
        minOccurs="0"/>
      </xs:sequence>
      <xs:attribute name="Position" type="bdc:ActionPosition" use="required"/>
      <xs:attribute name="IsOpenedInNewWindow" type="xs:boolean"
      default="false"/>
      <xs:attribute name="Url" type="xs:string" use="required"/>
      <xs:attribute name="ImageUrl" type="xs:string"/>
    </xs:extension>
  </xs:complexContent>
</xs:complexType>
```

The Action schema type extends the MetadataObject schema type. According to the Action schema type, an <Action> element contains:

- Zero or more instances of a child element named <ActionParameters>, which is of the ActionParameters schema type
- A required attribute named Position, which is of the ActionPosition schema type
- A required attribute named IsOpenedInNewWindow, which is of the Boolean type with the default value of false
- A required attribute named Url, which is of the string type
- An optional attribute named ImageUrl, which is of the string type

Because the Action schema type inherits the MetadataObject schema type, an <Action> element can contain the optional <LocalizedDisplayNames> and <Properties> child elements and the Name, DefaultDisplayName, and IsCached attributes in addition to the <ActionParameters> child element and the Position, IsOpenedInNewWindows, Url, and ImageUrl attributes:

```
<Action Name="" DefaultDisplayName="" IsCached="" Position=""
IsOpenedInNewWindows="" Url="" ImageUrl="">
  <ActionParameters></ActionParameters>
  <LocalizedDisplayNames></LocalizedDisplayNames>
  <Properties></Properties>
</Action>
```

As Listing 13-69 shows, an ActionPosition schema type is a restriction of the integer schema type where the minimum allowable value for the Position attribute is set to one.

Listing 13-69: The ActionPosition schema type

```
<xs:simpleType name="ActionPosition">
  <xs:restriction base="xs:integer">
    <xs:minInclusive value="1"/>
  </xs:restriction>
</xs:simpleType>
```

Listing 13-70 contains the definition of the ActionParameters schema type.

Listing 13-70: The ActionParameters schema type

```
<xs:complexType name="ActionParameters">
  <xs:sequence>
    <xs:element name="ActionParameter" type="bdc:ActionParameter" minOccurs="1"
    maxOccurs="unbounded"/>
  </xs:sequence>
</xs:complexType>
```

Base on this schema type, an <ActionParameters> element must contain at least one instance of a child element named <ActionParameter>, which is of the ActionParameter schema type defined in Listing 13-71.

Listing 13-71: The ActionParameter schema type

```
<xs:complexType name="ActionParameter">
  <xs:complexContent>
    <xs:extension base="bdc:MetadataObject">
      <xs:attribute name="Index" type="bdc:Ordinal" use="required"/>
    </xs:extension>
  </xs:complexContent>
</xs:complexType>
```

The ActionParameter schema type derives from the MetadataObject schema type. Based on the ActionParameter schema type, an <ActionParameter> element must contain a required attribute named Index, which is of the Ordinal schema type shown in Listing 13-72.

Listing 13-72: The Ordinal schema type

```
<xs:simpleType name="Ordinal">
  <xs:restriction base="xs:integer">
    <xs:minInclusive value="0"/>
  </xs:restriction>
</xs:simpleType>
```

The Ordinal schema type is a restriction of the integer schema type that specifies zero as the minimum allowable value for the Index attribute.

Because the ActionParameter schema type inherits the MetadataObject schema type, an <ActionParameter> element can contain the optional <LocalizedDisplayNames> and <Properties> child elements and the Name, DefaultDisplayName, and IsCached attributes in addition to the Index attribute:

```
<Action Name="" DefaultDisplayName="" IsCached="" Position=""
IsOpenedInNewWindows="" Url="" ImageUrl="">
  <ActionParameters>
    <ActionParameter Name="" DefaultDisplayName="" IsCached="" Index="">
      <LocalizedDisplayNames></LocalizedDisplayNames>
      <Properties></Properties>
    </ActionParameter>

    <ActionParameter Name="" DefaultDisplayName="" IsCached="" Index="">
      <LocalizedDisplayNames></LocalizedDisplayNames>
      <Properties></Properties>
    </ActionParameter>
  </ActionParameters>
  <LocalizedDisplayNames></LocalizedDisplayNames>
  <Properties></Properties>
</Action>
```

What does an action metadata object represent in a LOB application? What does an action parameter metadata object represent in a LOB application? What are the roles of the Position, IsOpenedInNewWindows, Url, ImageUrl, and Index attributes? What do they signify in a LOB application?

As the name suggests, an action metadata object represents an action that users can perform on the entity metadata object on which the action metadata object is defined. An action is rendered as a hyperlink and goes in the SharePoint UI wherever the entity metadata object on which the action metadata object is defined goes. An action normally provides users with a link back to the user interface of the LOB application where users can edit data.

Use the ImageUrl attribute to specify the absolute or relative virtual path of the icon that you want SharePoint to display for your action. Use the Url attribute to specify the target URL for the action. This target URL could be the URL to the target page where users will be redirected when they click the action link. Such an URL normally contains query string parameters with the following format:

```
Url="http://MySite/MyPage?P1={0}&P2={1}&P3={2}"
```

Each placeholder in this query string maps to an <ActionParameter> element with the same index. For example, the {0} placeholder maps to the <ActionParameter> element with the index attribute value of 0. Use the IsOpenedInNewWindows attribute to tell SharePoint whether to display the target page in a new window.

You must set the Name attribute on an <ActionParameter> element to the name of a type descriptor metadata object that describes a return parameter of the specific finder method instance metadata object of the entity metadata object on which the action metadata object is defined. Keep in mind that every entity metadata object can have only one specific finder method instance metadata object. Each action parameter metadata object is bound to a specific type descriptor metadata object in the return parameters of the specific finder method instance metadata object of the entity metadata object. This enables the BDC to determine the values of these action parameter metadata objects and stick them into the appropriate placeholders in the Url attribute value of the <Action> element.

Associations

Recall from Listing 13-13 that a <LobSystem> element can contain an optional child element named <Associations>, which is of the Associations schema type defined in Listing 13-73.

Listing 13-73: The Associations schema type

```
<xs:complexType name="Associations">
  <xs:sequence>
    <xs:element name="Association" type="bdc:Association" minOccurs="1"
    maxOccurs="unbounded"/>
  </xs:sequence>
</xs:complexType>
```

According this schema type, an <Associations> element must contain at least one instance of a child element named <Association>, which is of the Association schema type as defined in Listing 13-74.

Listing 13-74: The Association schema type

```
<xs:complexType name="Association">
  <xs:complexContent>
    <xs:extension base="bdc:IndividuallySecurableMetadataObject">
      <xs:sequence>
        <xs:element name="SourceEntity" type="bdc:SourceEntity" minOccurs="1"
        maxOccurs="unbounded"/>
        <xs:element name="DestinationEntity" type="bdc:DestinationEntity"
        minOccurs="1" maxOccurs="1"/>
      </xs:sequence>
      <xs:attribute name="AssociationMethodEntityName" type="xs:string"
      use="required"/>
      <xs:attribute name="AssociationMethodName" type="xs:string"
      use="required"/>
      <xs:attribute name="AssociationMethodReturnParameterName" type="xs:string"
      use="required"/>
      <xs:attribute name="AssociationMethodReturnTypeDescriptorName"
      type="xs:string" use="optional"/>
      <xs:attribute name="AssociationMethodReturnTypeDescriptorLevel"
      type="bdc:ReturnTypeDescriptorLevel" use="optional"/>
    </xs:extension>
  </xs:complexContent>
</xs:complexType>
```

The Association schema type extends the IndividuallySecurableMetadataObject schema type. As such, an association metadata object is an individually securable metadata object whose ACL can be directly specified. Based on the Association schema type defined in Listing 13-74, an <Association> element contains:

- At least one instance of a child element named <SourceEntity>, which is of the SourceEntity schema type
- A single instance of a child element named <DestinationEntity>, which is of the DestinationEntity schema type
- A required attribute named AssociationMethodEntityName, which is of the string schema type
- A required attribute named AssociationMethodName, which is of the string schema type
- A required attribute named AssociationMethodReturnParameterName, which is of the string schema type
- An optional attribute named AssociationMethodReturnTypeDescriptorName, which is of the string schema type
- An optional attribute named AssociationMethodReturnTypeDescriptorLevel, which is of the ReturnTypeDescriptorLevel schema type discussed earlier

Because the Association schema type inherits the IndividuallySecurableMetadataObject schema type, an <Association> element can contain the optional <AccessControlList> child element. Because the IndividuallySecurableMetadataObject schema type inherits the MetadataObject schema type, an

<Association> element can also contain the optional <LocalizedDisplayNames> and <Properties> child elements and the Name, DefaultDisplayName, and IsCached attributes:

```
<Association Name="" DefaultDisplayName="" IsCached=""
AssociationMethodEntityName=""
AssociationMethodName=""
AssociationMethodReturnParameterName=""
AssociationMethodReturnTypeDescriptorName=""
AssociationMethodReturnTypeDescriptorLevel="">
  <LocalizedDisplayNames></LocalizedDisplayNames>
  <Properties></Properties>
  <AccessControlList></AccessControlList>
  <SourceEntity></SourceEntity>
  <DestinationEntity></DestinationEntity>
</Association>
```

Based on the SourceEntity schema type defined in Listing 13-75, a <SourceEntity> element contains a required attribute named Name, which is of the string schema type.

Listing 13-75: The SourceEntity schema type

```
<xs:complexType name="SourceEntity">
  <xs:attribute name="Name" type="xs:string" use="required"/>
</xs:complexType>
```

According to the DestinationEntity schema type shown in Listing 13-76, a <DestinationEntity> element contains a required attribute named Name, which is of the string schema type.

Listing 13-76: The DestinationEntity schema type

```
<xs:complexType name="DestinationEntity">
  <xs:attribute name="Name" type="xs:string" use="required"/>
</xs:complexType>
```

As the name implies, an association metadata object represents an association between two or more business entities where each business entity is represented by an entity metadata object. An association between business entities is normally a SQL SELECT statement or stored procedure in the case of a database LOB application and a web method in the case of a web service LOB application. For example, the following SQL SELECT statement presents an association between the Customers, Orders, and Distributors database tables, which are business entities in a database LOB application:

```
SELECT OrderName, CustomerName, DistributorName FROM
Customers, Orders, Distributors
```

Because every business operation such as the preceding SQL SELECT statement is represented by a method metadata object in the BDC and because every method metadata object in the BDC is defined on an entity metadata object, the method metadata object that represents an association such as the preceding SQL SELECT statement must be defined on the entity metadata object that represents one of the business entities such as Customers, Orders, or Distributors that are involved in the definition of the business operation. As such, the <Association> element contains the following two required attributes:

- **AssociationMethodName.** Set this attribute to the name of the method instance metadata object that represents the association between the business entities. Such a method instance metadata object is known as an association method instance metadata object.
- **AssociationMethodEntityName.** Set this attribute to the name of the entity metadata object that contains the association method instance metadata object.

The <Association> element also supports a third required attribute named AssociationReturnParameterName that you must set to the name of the type descriptor metadata object that describes the return parameter of the association method instance metadata object. The <Association> element also features the following two optional attributes:

- **AssociationMethodReturnTypeDescriptorName.** Set this attribute to the name of the return type descriptor metadata object that describes the desired sub data structure of the return data structure to have the association method instance metadata object return only the desired sub data structure.
- **AssociationMethodReturnTypeDescriptorLevel.** Set this attribute to an integer value between 0 and 9 to specify the return type descriptor level.

As discussed earlier, an association is a business operation which is normally a SQL SELECT statement or stored procedure in a database and a web method in a web service:

```
SELECT OrderName, CustomerName, DistributorName FROM
Customers, Orders, Distributors
```

An association business operation, like any other business operation, returns business entity instances. These business entity instances, like all other business entity instances, are instances of a business entity. The business entity whose instances an association business operation returns is known as a destination entity. For example, in the case of the preceding SQL SELECT statement you can think of the data rows returned from this database query as data rows of a logical table named CustomerOrderDistributor. In this case, this logical table is the destination entity. Other business entities such as the Customers, Orders, and Distributors tables in this example are the source entities. As this example shows, business entities such as the CustomerOrderDistributor can be reached only through an association business operation. Such business entities cannot contain Finder and SpecificFinder method instance metadata objects. The EditorialReview entity metadata object is an example of such an entity metadata object. The destination entity does not have be a logical entity such as CustomerOrderDistributor. You'll see an example of this later in this section.

As you can imagine, every association metadata object can have only a single destination entity, whereas it can have multiple source entities:

```
<Association Name="MyAssociation"
AssociationMethodName="MyAssociationMethod"
AssociationMethodEntityName="Customers"
AssociationMethodReturnParameterName="ReturnParameter"
AssociationMethodReturnTypeDescriptorName="ReturnTypeDescriptor"
AssociationMethodReturnTypeDescriptorLevel="1">
  <SourceEntity Name="Customers" />
  <SourceEntity Name="Orders" />
  <SourceEntity Name="Distributors" />
  <DestinationEntity Name="CustomerOrderDistributor" />
</Association>
```

Figure 13-2 shows an example where an association is used. The top part of the page shown in this figure is a Business Data Catalog List Web Part, which is configured to display the list of records from the DimProductCategory table in the AdventureWorksDW database that match the pattern specified as the value of the selected filter on the top of this Web part. The bottom part of the page is a Business Data Catalog Related List Web Part, which is connected to the previous Business Data Catalog List Web Part to display the list of the records from the DimProductSubcategory table that relate to the record selected in the Business Data Catalog List Web Part.

When the user selects a product category from the list of product categories shown in the Business Data Catalog List Web Part, the following sequence of events takes place:

1. The Runtime object model is used to read the association metadata object that associates the ProductCategory and ProductSubcategory entity metadata objects from the metadata repository. The following excerpt from the BDC application definition file presents the definition of this association metadata object:

```
<Association Name="ProductCategoryToProductSubcategory"
AssociationMethodEntityName="ProductCategory"
AssociationMethodName="GetProductSubcategories"
AssociationMethodReturnParameterName="ProductSubcategories">
  <SourceEntity Name="ProductCategory" />
  <DestinationEntity Name="ProductSubcategory" />
</Association>
```

   The ProductSubcategory entity metadata object is an example of an entity metadata object that represents a real destination business entity, that is, a real table in the underlying database LOB application. The ProductCategorytoProductSubcategory association metadata object is not the only way to reach the ProductSubcategory entity metadata object instances.

2. The Runtime object model is used to read the values of the AssociationMethodName and AssociationMethodEntityName attributes of the association metadata object from the metadata repository to determine the names of the association method metadata object and the entity metadata object that contains the association method metadata object. As the XML fragment from Step 1 shows, the association method metadata object in this case is an association metadata object named GetProductSubcategories that is defined on an entity metadata object named ProductCategory.

3. The Runtime object model is used to read the association method metadata object with the specified name that is defined on the entity metadata object with the specified name from the metadata repository. The following excerpt from the BDC application definition file presents the GetProductSubcategories association method metadata object:

```
<Entity EstimatedInstanceCount="10000" Name="ProductCategory">
  <Methods>
    <Method Name="GetProductSubcategories">
      <Parameters>
        <Parameter Direction="In" Name="@ProductCategoryKey">
          <TypeDescriptor TypeName="System.Int32"
          IdentifierName="ProductCategoryKey" Name="ProductCategoryKey" />
        </Parameter>
        <Parameter Direction="Return" Name="ProductSubcategories">
          <TypeDescriptor
          TypeName="System.Data.IDataReader, System.Data, Version=2.0.3600.0,
                    Culture=neutral, PublicKeyToken=b77a5c561934e089"
          IsCollection="true" Name="ProductSubcategoryDataReader">
            <TypeDescriptors>
              <TypeDescriptor
              TypeName="System.Data.IDataRecord, System.Data, Version=2.0.3600.0,
                        Culture=neutral, PublicKeyToken=b77a5c561934e089"
              Name="ProductSubcategoryDataRecord">
                <TypeDescriptors>
                  <TypeDescriptor TypeName="System.Int32"
                  IdentifierEntityName="ProductSubcategory"
                  IdentifierName="ProductSubcategoryKey"
                  Name="ProductSubcategoryKey" />
                  <TypeDescriptor TypeName="System.String"
                  Name="EnglishProductSubcategoryName" />
                </TypeDescriptors>
              </TypeDescriptor>
            </TypeDescriptors>
          </TypeDescriptor>
        </Parameter>
      </Parameters>
    </Method>
  </Methods>
</Entity>
```

4. The Runtime object model is used to execute the association method metadata object, passing in the product category key of the selected product category in the Business Data Catalog List Web Part. The Business Data Catalog Related List Web Part then displays the entity instances returned from the association method metadata object.

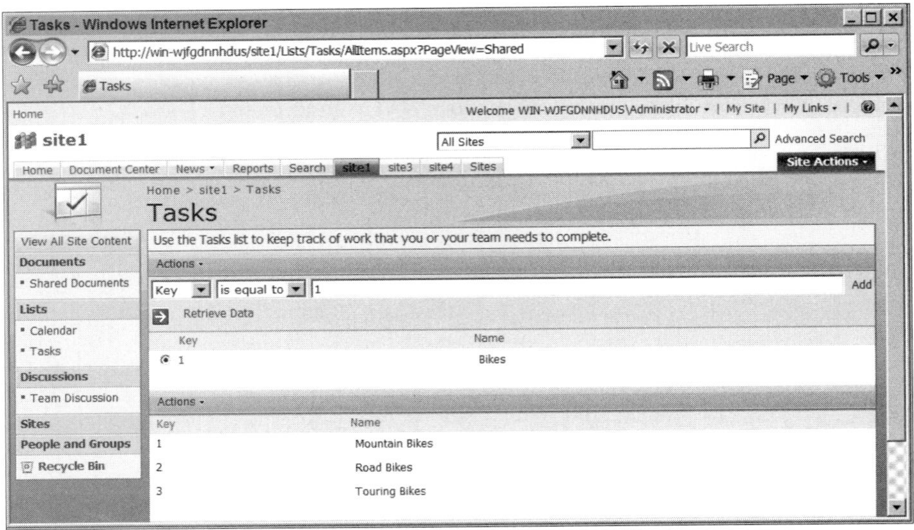

Figure 13-2: A page displaying an association

Example

The previous sections of this chapter showed you how to use the BDC XML markup language to describe a LOB business application to the BDC. This section shows you how to upload your BDC application definition XML file to the BDC. Launch the SharePoint 3.0 Central Administration web application as shown in Figure 13-3.

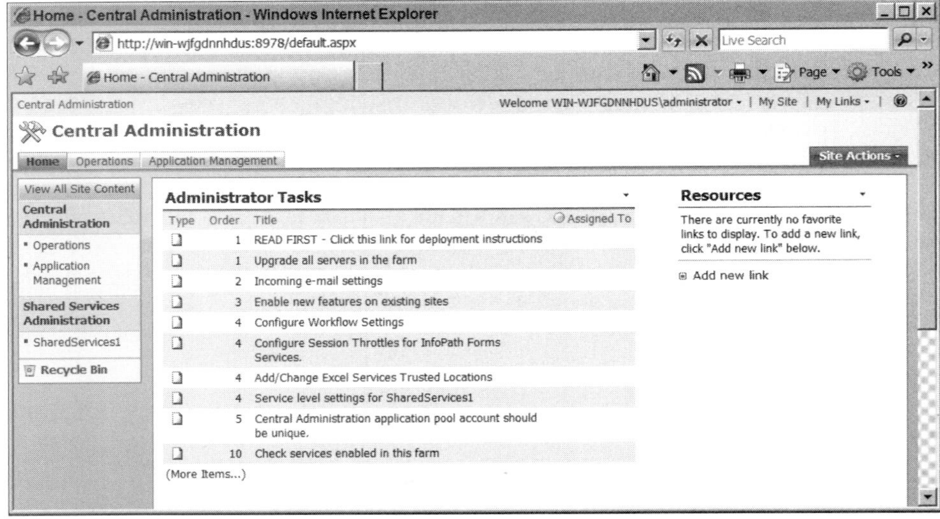

Figure 13-3: The SharePoint 3.0 Central Administration web application

The default installation of the SharePoint 3.0 Central Administration web application normally creates and configures a default shared service provider named SharedServices1 (see Figure 13-3). Clicking this default shared service provider takes you to the page shown in Figure 13-4, where you can manage shared services such as the BDC.

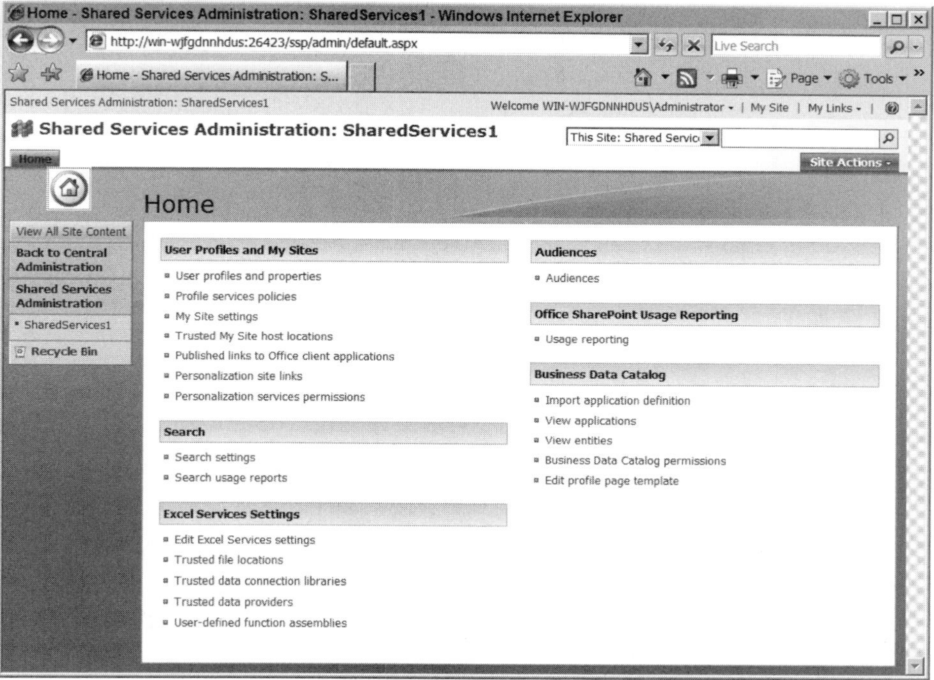

Figure 13-4: Shared Services Administration

Click the "Import application definition" link under the Business Data Catalog section to navigate to the page shown in Figure 13-5, where you can import your BDC application definition file.

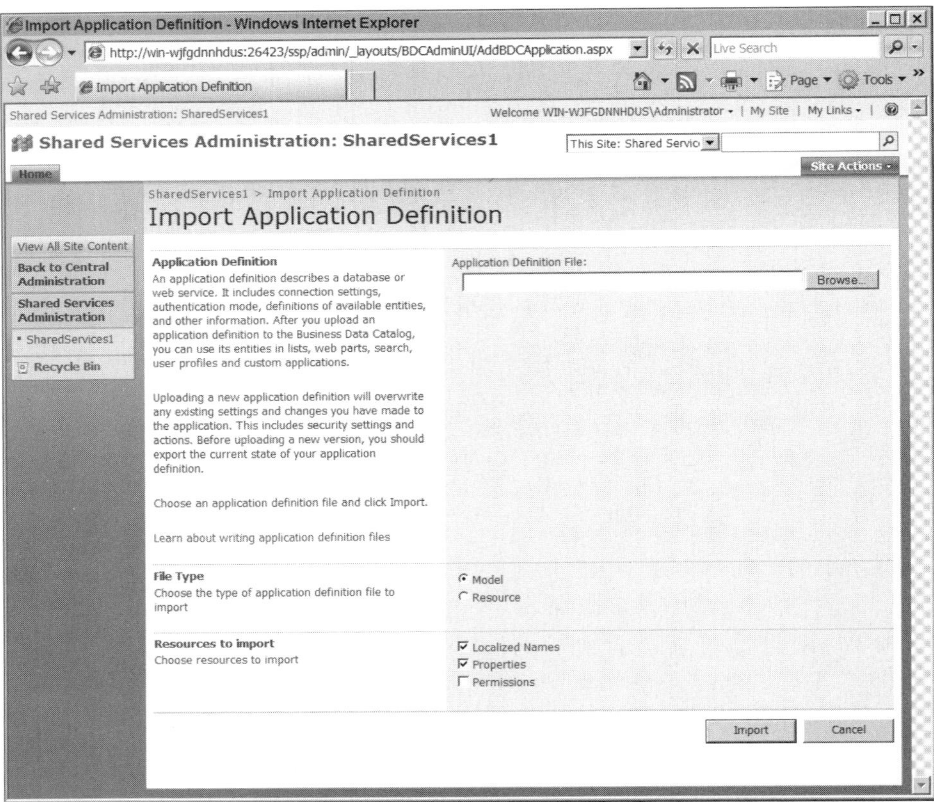

Figure 13-5: The Import Application Definition page

Click the Browse button and browse to the folder that contains the BDC application definition XML file and upload the file. Uploading a file may take a minute or so during which the BDC validates your BDC application definition file and creates profile pages for the entity metadata objects defined in this file. If everything goes fine, the upload process should take you a page that contains a message stating that the application definition was successfully imported.

Click the OK button in this page to go to the page shown in Figure 13-6 if you've uploaded the AdventureWorksDW SQL Server 2005 application definition XML file and the page shown in Figure 13-7 if you've uploaded the Amazon E-Commerce web service application definition XML file. Note that in the case of the Amazon E-Commerce web service application definition XML file, you'll get a warning saying that the BDC could not generate a profile page for the EditorialReview entity metadata object because this entity metadata object does not contain identifier metadata objects. This is an expected behavior. Profile pages can be created only for those entity metadata objects that contain identifier metadata objects. If you check out the EditorialReview entity metadata object defined in the Amazon E-Commerce web service application definition XML file you'll notice that this entity metadata object does not contain any identifier metadata objects. This is because this entity metadata object is an association entity metadata object, that is, it can be reached only through the association method instance metadata object specified in the following XML fragment:

```
<Associations>
  <Association AssociationMethodEntityName="EditorialReview"
  AssociationMethodName="ItemLookup"
  AssociationMethodReturnParameterName="Response"
  AssociationMethodReturnTypeDescriptorName="EditorialReviews"
  Name="EditoralReviewsForItem">
    <SourceEntity Name="Item"/>
    <DestinationEntity Name="EditorialReview"/>
  </Association>
</Associations>
```

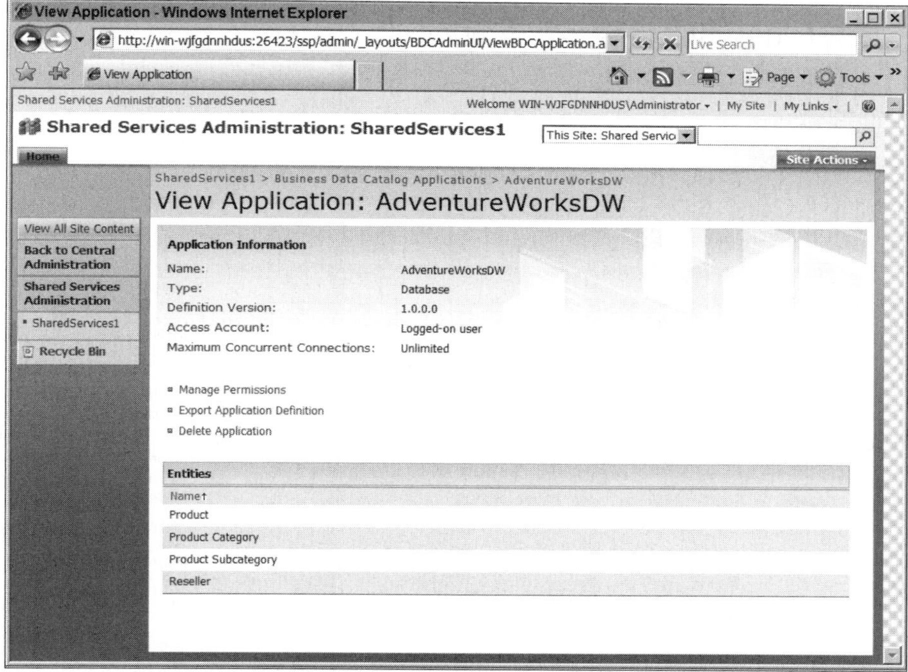

Figure 13-6: The View Application page showing AdventureWorksDW

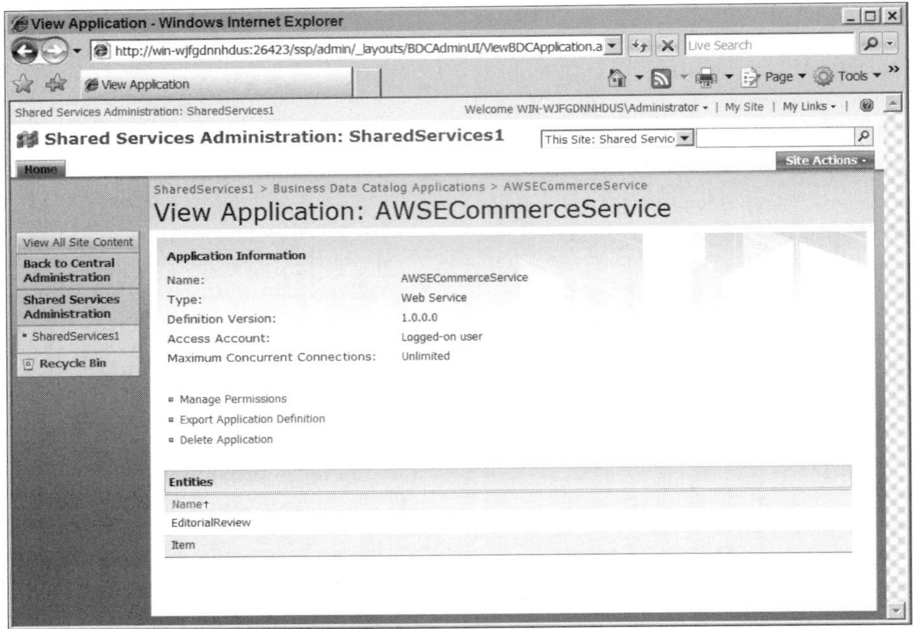

Figure 13-7: The View Application page showing AWSECommerceService

The pages shown in Figures 13-6 and 13-7 consist of two parts. The top part displays information about the LOB application that the BDC application definition file defines including the name of the LOB application (the value of the Name attribute on the <LobSystem> element), its type (the value of the Type attribute on the <LobSystem> element, which shows whether the LOB application is a web service or database), its version (the value of the Version attribute on the <LobSystem> element), and so on. The bottom part displays the names of the entity metadata objects defined in your BDC application definition. The AdventureWorksDW application definition defines four entity metadata objects named Product, ProductCategory, Product SubCategory, and Reseller. The Amazon E-Commerce application definition defines two entity metadata objects named EditorialReview and Item.

Note that if an entity metadata object or the LOB system metadata object contains a localized display name for the current culture, the pages shown in Figures 13-6 and 13-7 display this localized display name. If an entity metadata object or the LOB system metadata object does not contain a localized display name for the current culture, these pages display the default display name if the DefaultDisplayName attribute is set. Otherwise they simply display the name of the metadata object.

Note that the bottom part of the pages shown in Figures 13-6 and 13-7 contains a link titled Manage Permission. This link takes you to the page shown in Figure 13-8 in the case of the AdventureWorksDW SQL Server 2005 LOB application and to the page shown in Figure 13-9 in the case of the Amazon E-Commerce web service LOB application where you can specify which principals have which rights on the LOB system metadata object that represents the current LOB application.

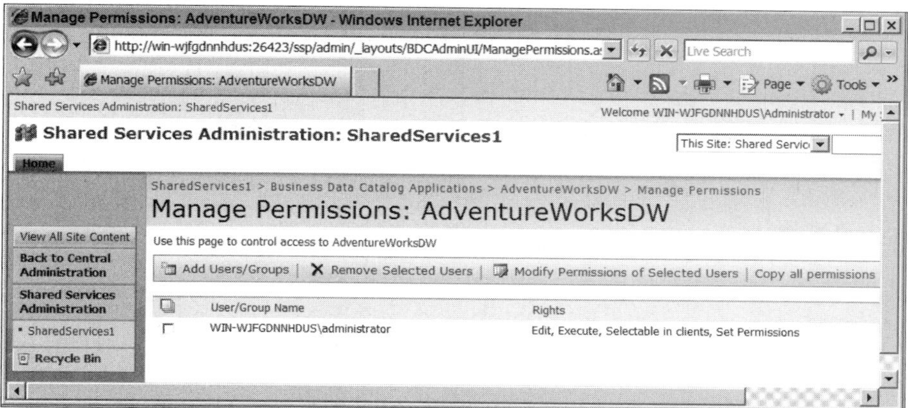

Figure 13-8: The Manage Permissions page showing permissions for AdventureWorksDW

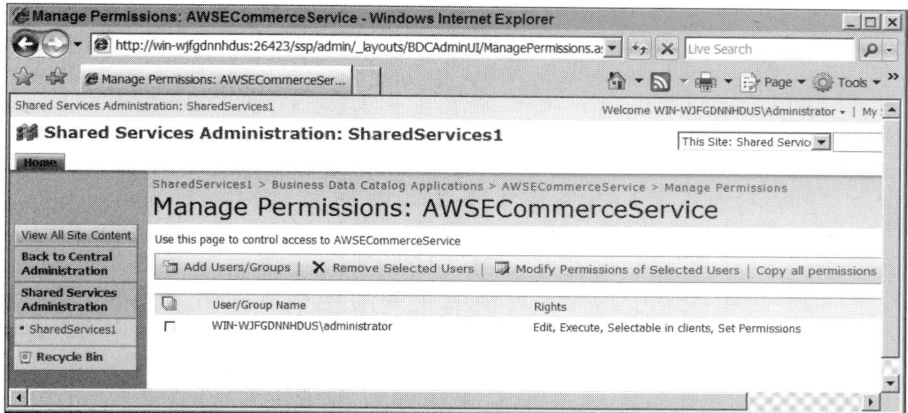

Figure 13-9: The Manage Permissions page showing permissions for AWSECommerceService

The pages shown in Figures 13-8 and 13-9 present you with the list of available principals where each principal is rendered as a link, which respectively takes you the pages shown in Figure 13-10 in the case of the AdventureWorksDW SQL Server 2005 database LOB application and Figure 13-11 in the case of the Amazon E-Commerce web service LOB application, where you can specify which rights this principal has on the LOB system metadata object that represents the current LOB application.

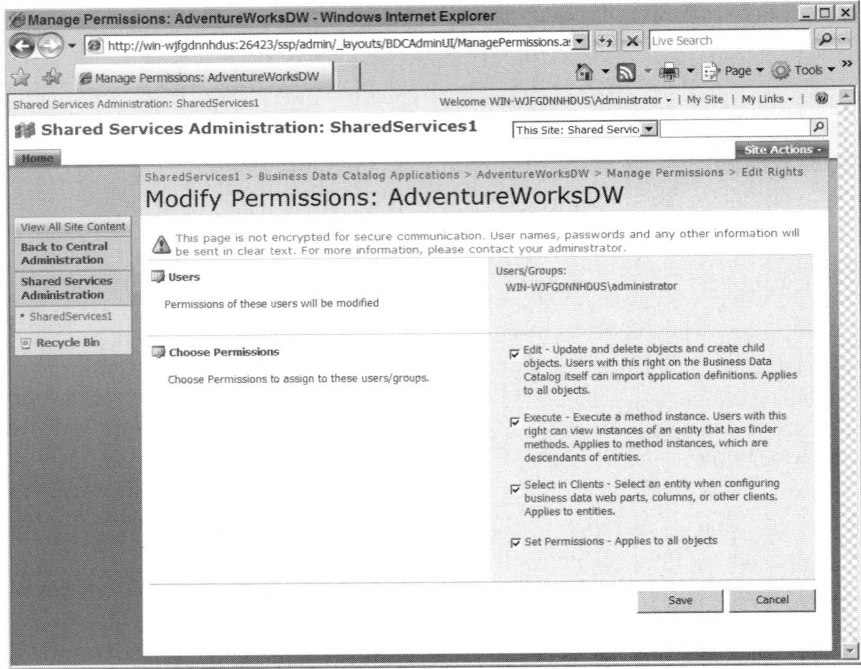

Figure 13-10: The Modify Permissions page for AdventureWorksDW

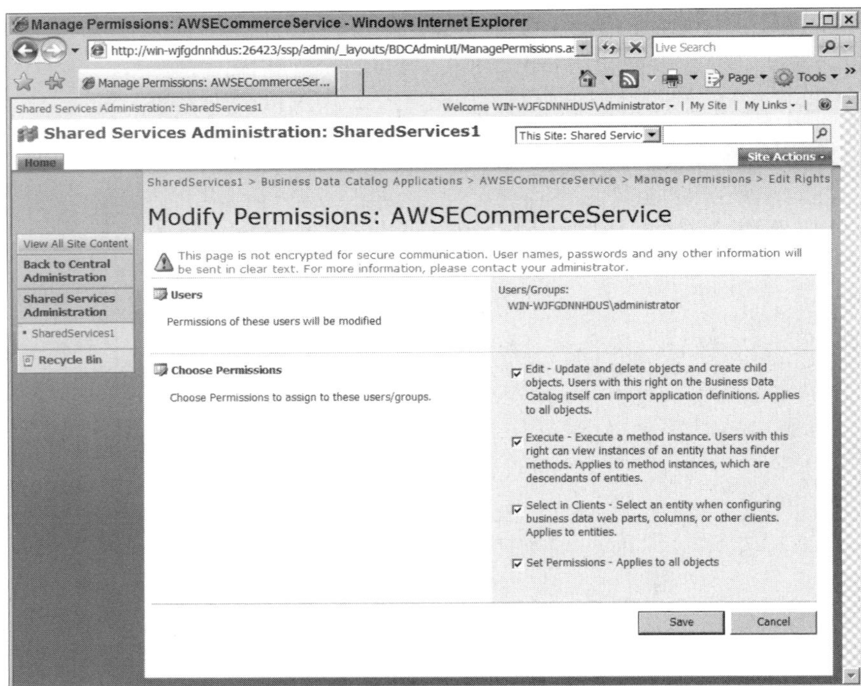

Figure 13-11: The Modify Permissions page for AWSECommerceService

Now back to the pages shown in Figures 13-6 and 13-7. The top part of these pages contains a link titled Export Application Definition, which allows you to export the current BDC application definition as an XML file. This link takes you to the page shown in Figure 13-12 in the case of the AdventureWorksDW SQL Server 2005 database LOB application and Figure 13-13 in the case of the Amazon E-Commerce web service LOB application.

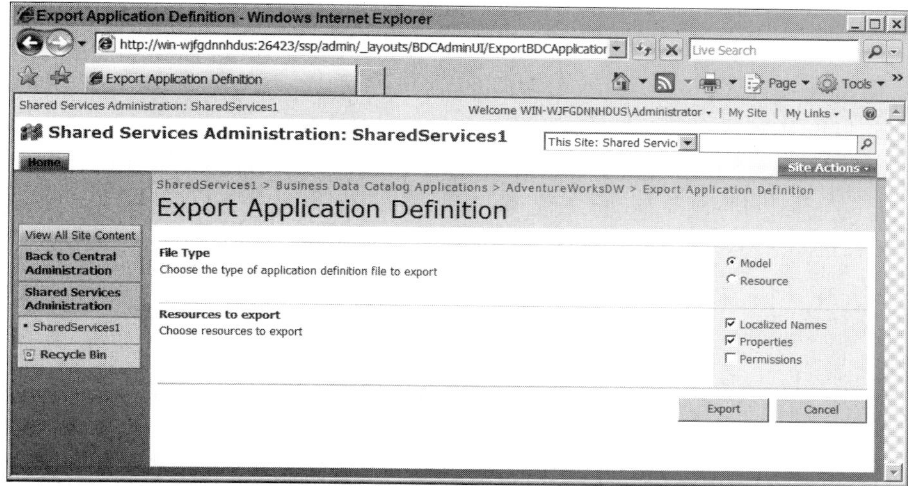

Figure 13-12: The Export Application Definition page for AdventureWorksDW

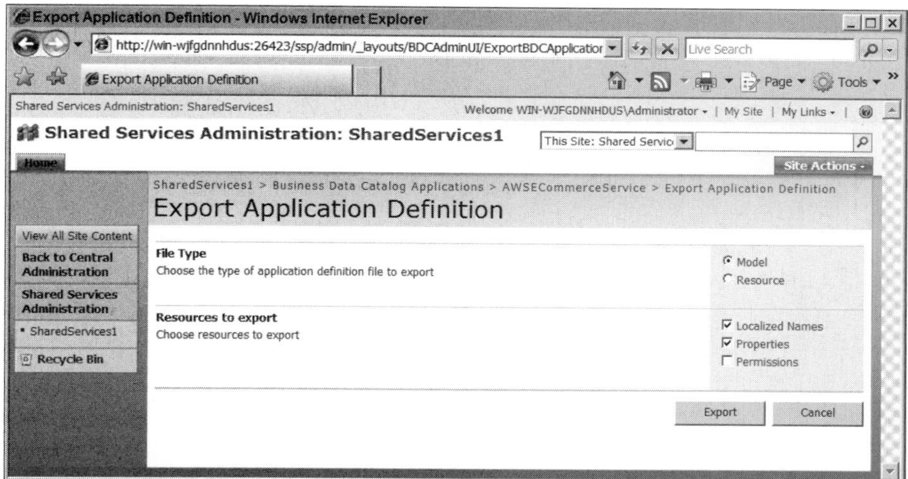

Figure 13-13: The Export Application Definition page for AWSECommerceService

In this page you can choose whether you want to export a Model or Resource application definition file. You can also choose whether you want to export localized names, properties, and/or permissions. You may be wondering why anyone would want to export an application definition XML file that he or she has already uploaded into the BDC. The answer lies in the fact that there are three different ways to add metadata to the metadata repository: declarative via a BDC application definition file, imperative via Administration object model, and graphical via the SharePoint user interface. You have already seen a graphical example where you can use the Manage Permissions link shown in Figure 13-6 or 13-7 to navigate to the page where you can add an access control list metadata object or an access control entry to the LOB system metadata object. The Export Application Definition link allows you to export all the metadata added through these three different means into a BDC application definition XML file. If you click the Export button shown in Figure 13-12 or 13-13, it will pop up a dialog asking you to specify a location and file name for the BDC application definition XML file being exported.

Now refer back to the page shown in Figure 13-6 or 13-7. This page renders each entity metadata object as a link, which takes you the page shown in Figure 13-14 in the case of the Product entity metadata object defined in the AdventureWorksDW SQL Server database LOB application and Figure 13-15 in the case of the EditorialReview entity metadata object defined in the Amazon E-Commerce web service LOB application, where you can view more information about the entity metadata object and manage certain aspects of the object.

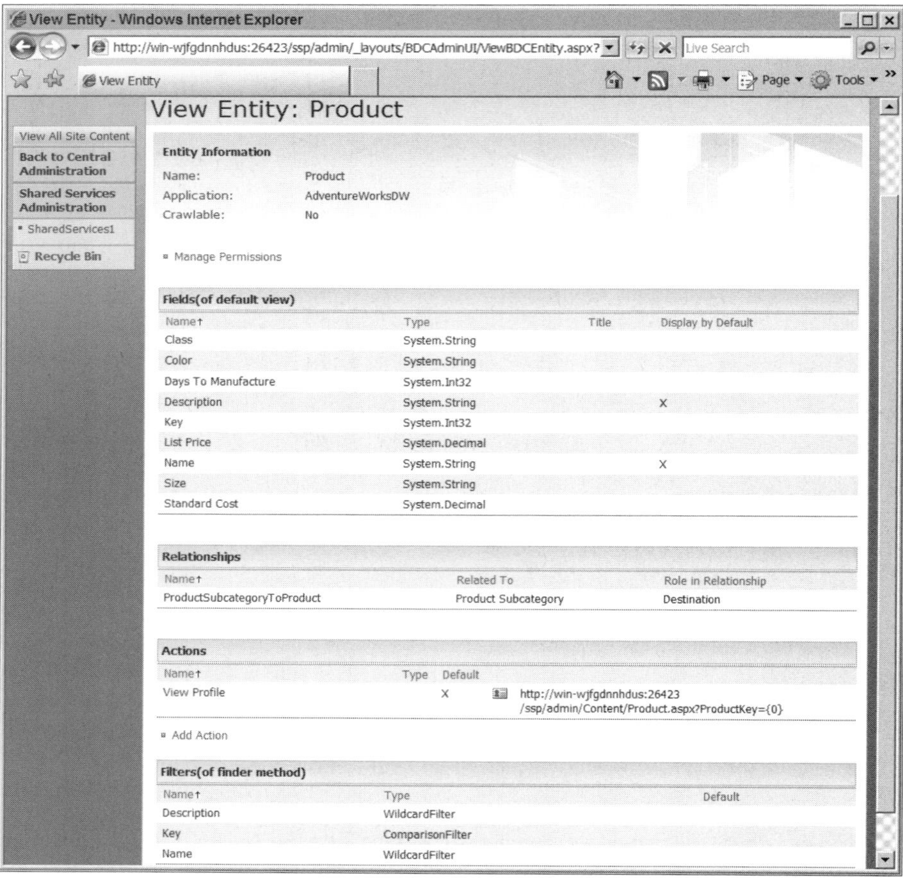

Figure 13-14: The View Entity page showing the Product entity

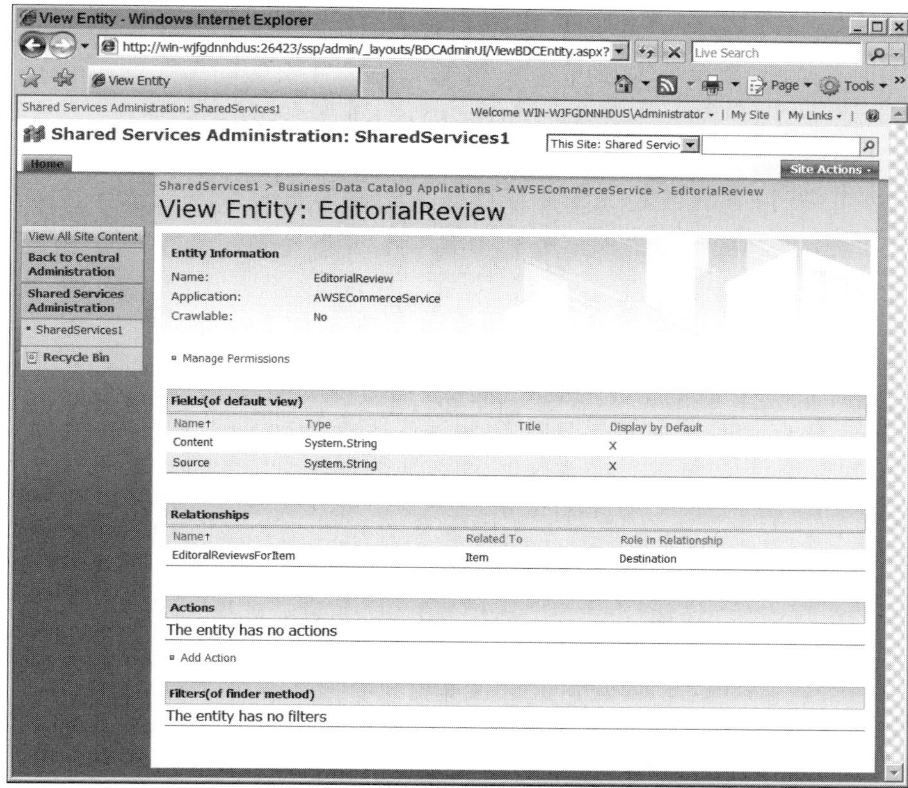

Figure 13-15: The View Entity page showing the EditorialReview page

The page shown in Figure 13-14 or 13-15 contains four tables as follows. The first table displays information about the return parameter of the finder method metadata object defined on the current entity metadata object. Keep in mind that every entity metadata object can have only one finder method metadata object. Recall that the return parameter of a finder method metadata object is a collection of data records. Also recall that the type descriptor metadata object that describes the return parameter contains one type descriptor metadata object to describe each field in the return parameter. Listing 13-77 shows an excerpt from the AdventureWorksDW SQL Server 2005 database application definition, which presents the type descriptor metadata object that describes the return parameter of the GetProducts finder method metadata object defined on the Product entity metadata object.

Listing 13-77: An excerpt from the AdventureWorksDW application definition

```
<LobSystem Name="AdventureWorksDW">
  <Entities>
    <Entity Name="Product">
      <Methods>
        <Method Name="GetProducts">
          <Parameters>
            <Parameter Direction="Return" Name="Products">
              <TypeDescriptor Name="ProductDataReader" IsCollection="true"
              TypeName="System.Data.IDataReader, System.Data, Version=2.0.3600.0,
                        Culture=neutral, PublicKeyToken=b77a5c561934e089" >
                <TypeDescriptors>
                  <TypeDescriptor Name="ProductDataRecord"
                  TypeName="System.Data.IDataRecord, System.Data,
                            Version=2.0.3600.0, Culture=neutral,
                            PublicKeyToken=b77a5c561934e089">
                    <TypeDescriptors>

                      <TypeDescriptor Name="ProductKey" TypeName="System.Int32"
                      IdentifierName="ProductKey">
                        <LocalizedDisplayNames>
                          <LocalizedDisplayName LCID="1033">
                            Key
                          </LocalizedDisplayName>
                        </LocalizedDisplayNames>
                      </TypeDescriptor>

                      <TypeDescriptor Name="EnglishProductName"
                      TypeName="System.String">
                        <LocalizedDisplayNames>
                          <LocalizedDisplayName LCID="1033">
                            Name
                          </LocalizedDisplayName>
                        </LocalizedDisplayNames>
                        <Properties>
                          <Property Name="DisplayByDefault" Type="System.Boolean">
                            true
                          </Property>
                        </Properties>
                      </TypeDescriptor>

                      <TypeDescriptor Name="EnglishDescription"
                      TypeName="System.String">
                        <LocalizedDisplayNames>
                          <LocalizedDisplayName LCID="1033">
                            Description
                          </LocalizedDisplayName>
                        </LocalizedDisplayNames>
                        <Properties>
```

```
            <Property Name="DisplayByDefault" Type="System.Boolean">
              true
            </Property>
          </Properties>
        </TypeDescriptor>

        <TypeDescriptor Name="ListPrice" TypeName="System.Decimal">
          <LocalizedDisplayNames>
            <LocalizedDisplayName LCID="1033">
              List Price
            </LocalizedDisplayName>
          </LocalizedDisplayNames>
        </TypeDescriptor>

        <TypeDescriptor Name="StandardCost"
        TypeName="System.Decimal" >
          <LocalizedDisplayNames>
            <LocalizedDisplayName LCID="1033">
              Standard Cost
            </LocalizedDisplayName>
          </LocalizedDisplayNames>
        </TypeDescriptor>

        <TypeDescriptor TypeName="System.String" Name="Color">
          <LocalizedDisplayNames>
            <LocalizedDisplayName LCID="1033">
              Color
            </LocalizedDisplayName>
          </LocalizedDisplayNames>
        </TypeDescriptor>

        <TypeDescriptor TypeName="System.String" Name="Size">
          <LocalizedDisplayNames>
            <LocalizedDisplayName LCID="1033">
              Size
            </LocalizedDisplayName>
          </LocalizedDisplayNames>
        </TypeDescriptor>

        <TypeDescriptor TypeName="System.String" Name="Class">
          <LocalizedDisplayNames>
            <LocalizedDisplayName LCID="1033">
              Class
            </LocalizedDisplayName>
          </LocalizedDisplayNames>
        </TypeDescriptor>

        <TypeDescriptor Name="DaysToManufacture"
        TypeName="System.Int32">
          <LocalizedDisplayNames>
            <LocalizedDisplayName LCID="1033">
              Days To Manufacture
```

(continued)

Listing 13-77 *(continued)*

```
                        </LocalizedDisplayName>
                      </LocalizedDisplayNames>
                    </TypeDescriptor>
                  </TypeDescriptors>
                </TypeDescriptor>
              </TypeDescriptors>
            </TypeDescriptor>
          </Parameter>
        </Parameters>
      </Method>
    </Methods>
  </Entity>
 </Entities>
</LobSystem>
```

The first table in Figure 13-14 has nine rows where each row maps into one of the type descriptor metadata objects shown in boldface in the preceding code listing. Notice that the Name column of each row displays the localized display name that its associated type descriptor metadata object specifies. The type column of each row displays the value of the TypeName attribute of its associated type descriptor metadata object. The DisplayByDefault column of each row displays the value of the DisplayByDefault property of its associated type descriptor metadata object.

Listing 13-78 shows an excerpt from the Amazon E-Commerce web service application definition, which presents the type descriptor metadata object that describes the return parameter of the ItemSearch finder method metadata object defined on the EditorialReview entity metadata object.

Listing 13-78: An excerpt from the Amazon E-Commerce web service application definition

```
<LobSystem Name="AWSECommerceService">
  <Entities>
    <Entity Name="EditorialReview">
      <Methods>
        <Method Name="ItemSearch">
          <Parameters>
            <Parameter Direction="Return" Name="Response">
              <TypeDescriptor Name="response"
              TypeName="AWSECommerceService.ItemLookupResponse,
                         AWSECommerceService">
                <TypeDescriptors>
                  <TypeDescriptor
                  TypeName="AWSECommerceService.Items[], AWSECommerceService"
                  IsCollection="true" Name="Items">
                    <TypeDescriptors>
                      <TypeDescriptor
                      TypeName="AWSECommerceService.Items, AWSECommerceService"
                      IsCollection="false" Name="ItemsArray">
                        <TypeDescriptors>
                          <TypeDescriptor
```

```
                    TypeName="AWSECommerceService.Item[],
                              AWSECommerceService"
                    IsCollection="true" Name="Item">
                      <TypeDescriptors>
                        <TypeDescriptor
                        TypeName="AWSECommerceService.Item,
                                  AWSECommerceService"
                        IsCollection="false" Name="ItemArray">
                          <TypeDescriptors>
                            <TypeDescriptor
                            TypeName="AWSECommerceService.EditorialReview[],
                                      AWSECommerceService"
                            IsCollection="true" Name="EditorialReviews">
                              <TypeDescriptors>
                                <TypeDescriptor
                               TypeName="AWSECommerceService.EditorialReview,
                                         AWSECommerceService"
                                IsCollection="false" Name="EditorialReview">
                                  <TypeDescriptors>

                                    <TypeDescriptor TypeName="System.String"
                                    IsCollection="false" Name="Content">
                                      <LocalizedDisplayNames>
                                        <LocalizedDisplayName LCID="1033">
                                          Content
                                        </LocalizedDisplayName>
                                      </LocalizedDisplayNames>
                                      <Properties>
                                        <Property Name="DisplayByDefault"
                                        Type="System.Boolean">true</Property>
                                      </Properties>
                                    </TypeDescriptor>

                                    <TypeDescriptor TypeName="System.String"
                                    Name="Source">
                                      <LocalizedDisplayNames>
                                        <LocalizedDisplayName
                                        LCID="1033">
                                          Source
                                        </LocalizedDisplayName>
                                      </LocalizedDisplayNames>
                                      <Properties>
                                        <Property Name="DisplayByDefault"
                                        Type="System.Boolean">true</Property>
                                      </Properties>
                                    </TypeDescriptor>

                                  </TypeDescriptors>
                                </TypeDescriptor>
                              </TypeDescriptors>
                            </TypeDescriptor>
                          </TypeDescriptors>
```

(continued)

Listing 13-78 *(continued)*

```
                                </TypeDescriptor>
                              </TypeDescriptors>
                            </TypeDescriptor>
                          </TypeDescriptors>
                        </TypeDescriptor>
                      </TypeDescriptors>
                    </TypeDescriptor>
                  </TypeDescriptors>
                </TypeDescriptor>
              </Parameter>
            </Parameters>
          </Method>
        </Methods>
      </Entity>
    </Entities>
  </LobSystem>
```

The rows in the first table in Figure 13-15 map into the type descriptor metadata objects shown in boldface in the preceding code listing. Note that the Name column of each row displays the localized display name specified in its associated type descriptor metadata object. The Type column of each row displays the value of the TypeName attribute of its associated type descriptor metadata object. The Display by Default column of each row displays the value of the DisplayByDefault property of its associated type descriptor metadata object. The first table contains two rows because the type descriptor metadata object that describes the return parameter of the finder method metadata object of the EditorialReview entity metadata object contains two type descriptor metadata objects.

So far, you've seen the first table in Figures 13-14 and 13-15. The rows in the second table of these two figures display information about the association metadata objects that associate the current entity metadata object — which is the Product entity metadata object in Figure 13-14 and the EditorialReview entity metadata object in Figure 13-15 — with other entity metadata objects defined in the current BDC application definition.

The second table in Figure 13-14 contains a single row because the BDC application definition defines a single association metadata object that associates the Product entity metadata object to the ProductSubcategory entity metadata object as can be seen from the following excerpt fro the BDC application definition:

```
<Association Name="ProductSubcategoryToProduct"
AssociationMethodEntityName="ProductSubcategory" AssociationMethodName="GetProducts"
AssociationMethodReturnParameterName="Products" IsCached="true">
  <SourceEntity Name="ProductSubcategory" />
  <DestinationEntity Name="Product" />
</Association>
```

The second table has three columns named Name, Related To, and Role in Relationship. The first column displays the name of the association metadata object, that is, the value of the Name attribute in the preceding XML fragment. The second column displays the name of the entity metadata object to which this association metadata object relates the Product entity metadata object. In this case the second column displays the value of the Name attribute on the <SourceEntity> element in the preceding XML fragment. The third column specifies what role the Product entity metadata object plays in the association. According to the preceding XML fragment, the Product entity metadata object plays the role of the destination entity metadata object in this association.

The second table in Figure 13-15 contains a single row because the BDC application definition defines a single association metadata object that associates the EditorialReview entity metadata object to the Item entity metadata object as shown in the following excerpts from the BDC application definition:

```
<Association Name="EditoralReviewsForItem"
AssociationMethodEntityName="EditorialReview"
AssociationMethodName="ItemLookup"
AssociationMethodReturnParameterName="Response"
AssociationMethodReturnTypeDescriptorName="EditorialReviews">
  <SourceEntity Name="Item"/>
  <DestinationEntity Name="EditorialReview"/>
</Association>
```

The third table in Figure 13-14 or 13-15 displays information about the action metadata objects defined on the current entity metadata object. Every entity metadata object in the BDC, which has one or more identifier metadata objects, automatically supports a default action that takes you to the profile page for the entity metadata object. Note that the web service version (Figure 13-15) does not contain any actions for the EditorialReview entity metadata object because this entity metadata object does not contain any identifier metadata object.

As mentioned earlier, the BDC automatically creates the profile pages when you upload the BDC application definition file into the BDC. Note that this page displays the value of the Url attribute on the <Action> element that represents this action:

```
http://win-wjfgdnnhdus:46649/ssp/admin/Content/Product.aspx?ProductKey={0}
```

This URL takes the user to a page named Product.aspx and passes the value of the ProductKey primary key as the value of the query string parameter named ProductKey. The action metadata object that represents the default action supports an action parameter metadata object with the index value of zero whose name is set to the name of the type descriptor metadata object that describes the return parameter of the specific finder metadata object, which in turn contains the primary key value of the entity instance that this specific finder metadata object returns, as shown in the boldfaced portions of the following XML fragment:

```
<Entity EstimatedInstanceCount="10000" Name="Product">
  <Identifiers>
    <Identifier Name="ProductKey" TypeName="System.Int32" />
  </Identifiers>
  <Methods>
    <Method Name="GetProducts">
      <Parameters>
        . . .
        <Parameter Direction="Return" Name="Products">
          <TypeDescriptor Name="ProductDataReader" IsCollection="true"
          TypeName="System.Data.IDataReader, System.Data, Version=2.0.3600.0,
                    Culture=neutral, PublicKeyToken=b77a5c561934e089">
            <TypeDescriptors>
              <TypeDescriptor Name="ProductDataRecord"
              TypeName="System.Data.IDataRecord, System.Data, Version=2.0.3600.0,
                        Culture=neutral, PublicKeyToken=b77a5c561934e089">
                <TypeDescriptors>
                  <TypeDescriptor Name="ProductKey" TypeName="System.Int32"
                  IdentifierName="ProductKey" >
                  . . .
                  </TypeDescriptor>
                </TypeDescriptors>
              </TypeDescriptor>
            </TypeDescriptors>
          </TypeDescriptor>
        </Parameter>
      </Parameters>
      <MethodInstances>
        <MethodInstance Name="ProductSpecificFinderInstance" Type="SpecificFinder"
        ReturnParameterName="Products" />
      </MethodInstances>
    </Method>
  </Methods>
</Entity>
```

Each action in the page shown in Figure 13-14 is rendered as a link that takes you to the page shown in Figure 13-16 where you can edit the action.

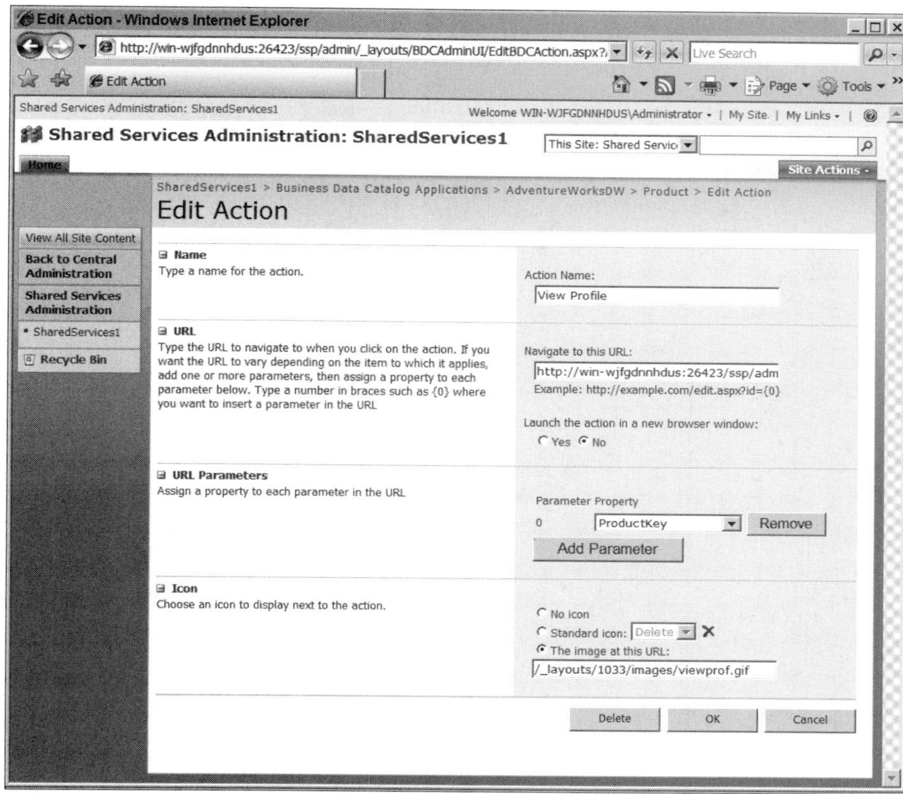

Figure 13-16: The Edit Action page

As you can see, this page allows you to specify the values of the Name, Url, and ImageUrl attributes of the action metadata object and the action parameter metadata objects of the action metadata object in purely graphical fashion. In other words, this page allows you to edit the action metadata object in the underlying metadata repository in graphical fashion. The business logic behind this page under the hood uses the Administration object model to update the action metadata object in the metadata repository.

Note that the page shown in Figure 13-14 also contains a link named Add Action that takes you to the page shown in Figure 13-17, where you can add a new action metadata object to the metadata repository on this entity metadata object. Use the Add Parameter button to add a new action parameter metadata object.

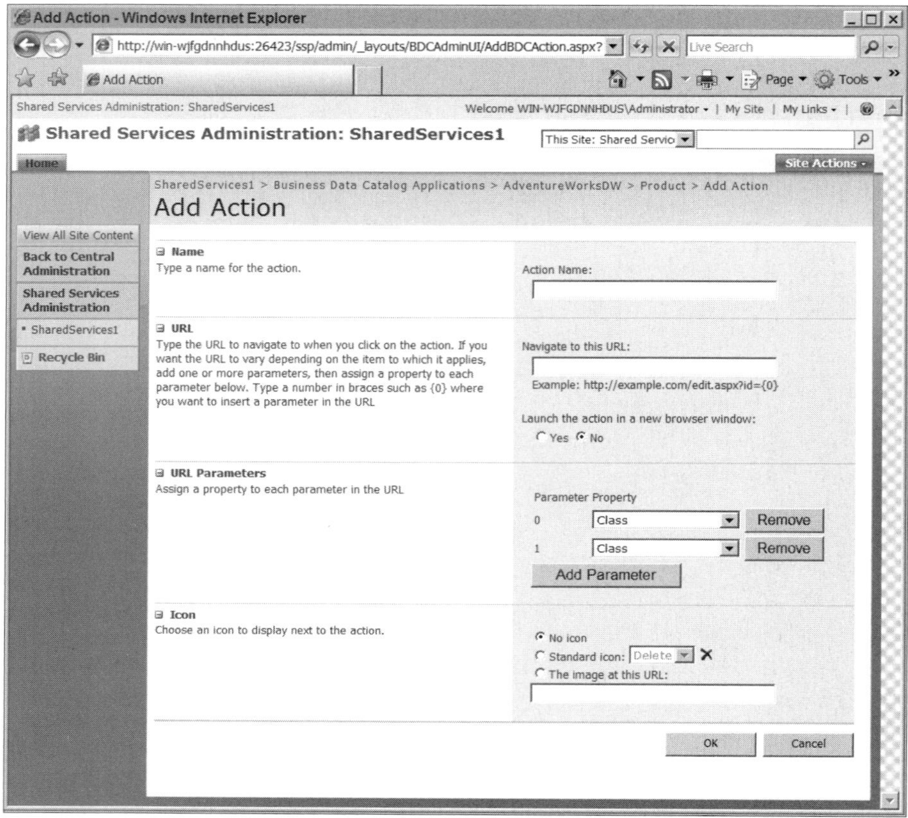

Figure 13-17: The Add Action page

As Figure 13-18 shows, there is a drop-down list that allows you to specify the return parameter whose type descriptor metadata object's name will be bound to the action parameter metadata object being added.

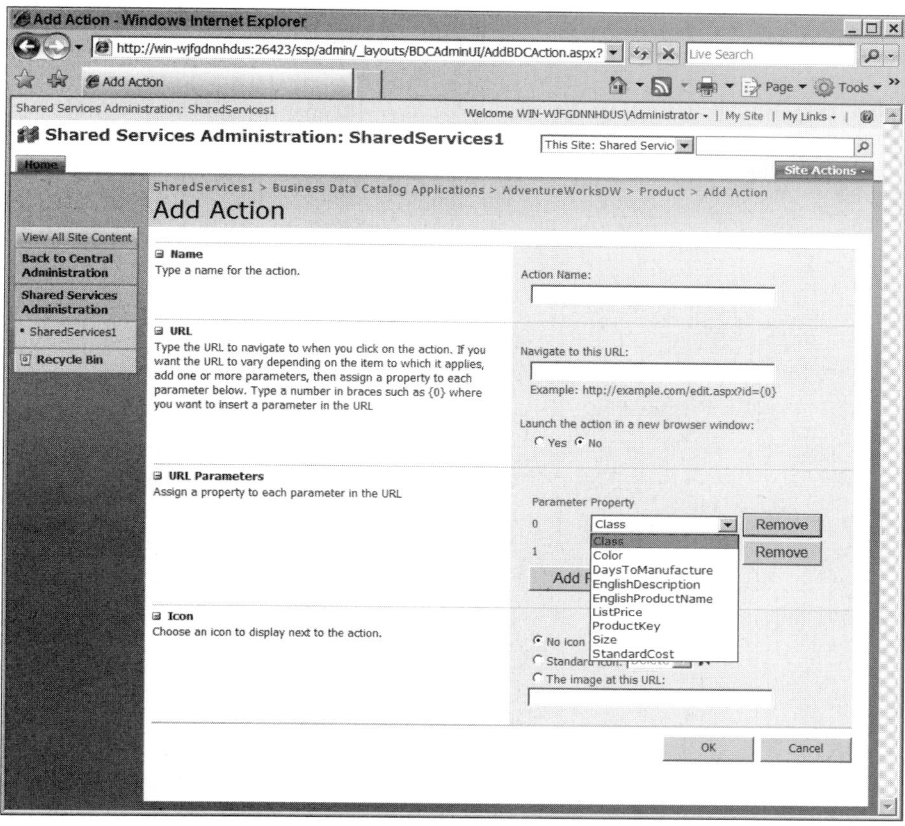

Figure 13-18: The Add Action page displaying the URL parameters

As you can see, this drop-down list displays the list of the names of all return parameters of the specific finder method instance metadata object named ProductSpecificFinderInstance, which is defined on the Product entity metadata object as you can see from Listing 13-79, which shows an excerpt from the BDC application definition.

Listing 13-79: An excerpt from the BDC application definition file

```
<Entity EstimatedInstanceCount="10000" Name="Product">
  <Identifiers>
    <Identifier Name="ProductKey" TypeName="System.Int32" />
  </Identifiers>
  <Methods>
    <Method Name="GetProducts">
      <Parameters>
        . . .
        <Parameter Direction="Return" Name="Products">
          <TypeDescriptor Name="ProductDataReader" IsCollection="true"
          TypeName="System.Data.IDataReader, System.Data, Version=2.0.3600.0,
                    Culture=neutral, PublicKeyToken=b77a5c561934e089">
            <TypeDescriptors>
              <TypeDescriptor Name="ProductDataRecord"
              TypeName="System.Data.IDataRecord, System.Data, Version=2.0.3600.0,
                        Culture=neutral, PublicKeyToken=b77a5c561934e089">
                <TypeDescriptors>
                  <TypeDescriptor Name="ProductKey" TypeName="System.Int32"
                  IdentifierName="ProductKey" />
                  <TypeDescriptor Name="EnglishProductName"
                  TypeName="System.String" />
                  <TypeDescriptor Name="EnglishDescription"
                  TypeName="System.String" />
                  <TypeDescriptor Name="ListPrice" TypeName="System.Decimal" />
                  <TypeDescriptor Name="StandardCost" TypeName="System.Decimal" />
                  <TypeDescriptor Name="Color" TypeName="System.String" />
                  <TypeDescriptor Name="Size" TypeName="System.String" />
                  <TypeDescriptor Name="Class" TypeName="System.String" />
                  <TypeDescriptor Name="DaysToManufacture"
                  TypeName="System.Int32" />
                </TypeDescriptors>
              </TypeDescriptor>
            </TypeDescriptors>
          </TypeDescriptor>
        </Parameter>
      </Parameters>
      <MethodInstances>
        <MethodInstance Name="ProductSpecificFinderInstance" Type="SpecificFinder"
        ReturnParameterName="Products" />
      </MethodInstances>
    </Method>
  </Methods>
</Entity>
```

Also note that the page shown in Figure 13-14 displays the names and types of all filter descriptor metadata objects defined on the GetProducts method instance metadata object as you can see from Listing 13-80, which shows an excerpt from the BDC application definition file.

Listing 13-80: An excerpt from the BDC application definition file

```
<Entity EstimatedInstanceCount="10000" Name="Product">
  <Identifiers>
    <Identifier Name="ProductKey" TypeName="System.Int32" />
  </Identifiers>
  <Methods>
    <Method Name="GetProducts">
      <FilterDescriptors>
        <FilterDescriptor Type="Comparison" Name="Key">
          <Properties>
            <Property Name="Comparator" Type="System.String">Equals</Property>
          </Properties>
        </FilterDescriptor>
        <FilterDescriptor Type="Wildcard" Name="Name">
          <Properties>
            <Property Name="UsedForDisambiguation" Type="System.Boolean">
              true
            </Property>
          </Properties>
        </FilterDescriptor>
        <FilterDescriptor Type="Wildcard" Name="Description" />
      </FilterDescriptors>
      <Parameters>
        . . .
      </Parameters>
      <MethodInstances>
        <MethodInstance Name="ProductFinderInstance" Type="Finder"
        ReturnParameterName="Products" />
      </MethodInstances>
    </Method>
  </Methods>
</Entity>
```

Finally, notice that the page shown in Figure 13-14 or 13-15 contains a link titled Manage Permissions that takes you to the page shown in Figure 13-8 or 13-9 and from there to the page shown in Figure 13-10 or 13-11. These pages allow you to define an ACL on the current entity metadata object.

Index

Symbols

" ;# ", as separator, 229
_vti_bin virtual directory, 155–157
< (less than) and > (greater than) characters (XML), 678, 679

A

AbstractConnectionManager base class (listing), 639
AbstractEntityInstance abstract base class (listing), 640–641
abstractions. *See also* **field types; list types; site columns; site content types; site definitions**
basics of, 97
forms infrastructure and, 163
AbstractSystemUtility base class (listing), 638
AccessControlList schema type, 634–636
Actions schema type, 731–734
activation dependency, 440, 441
Add Action page, BDC and, 757–759
AddContainer method, 504
AddFieldFromTemplate.aspx page, 311
AddItemToContainer method, 504
After events, 445
AllItems.aspx page
adding new list items and, 102
custom field types, using and, 301
field type definition and, 239, 241
list provisioning and, 151, 382
AllowFirstFocus Boolean property, 277
AllowPartiallyTrustedCallersAttribute, 595
<AllUsersWebPart> element, 366
alternate template (TemplateBasedWebPart), 530–531
AlternateTemplate property, 184–185
application pages
basics of, 70–72
code-behind approach. *See* code-behind approach (application pages)
inline approach. *See* inline approach (application pages)
vs. site pages, 70
application pools
basics of, 4–6
defined, 4
iterating through, 17
SPApplicationPool class, 6–8
application.master page, 78
ApplicatonStepManager, InitializeAppInstance method and, 25–26
ApplyChanges method, 521
ApplyWebTemplate method, 390
App_Web_jgyyqxek.0.cs file, 46
architecture (SharePoint), 1–52
ASP.NET hosting environment, 1–3
ASP.NET HTTP runtime pipeline. *See* ASP.NET HTTP runtime pipeline
ASP.NET dynamic compilation. *See* dynamic compilation
form-rendering server controls, 163–164
IIS, 3–6
ISAPIRuntime, 18–19
overview, xxiii
SharePoint Extensions. *See* extensions (SharePoint)
<asp:Content> tags, 109–110
ASP.NET
ASP.NET ISAPI extension module, 4
build environment, 44
dynamic compilation. *See* dynamic compilation
hosting environment, 1–3
ASP.NET HTTP runtime pipeline, 19–52
basics of, 19–23
Http handler factories/handlers/modules, developing custom, 42–52
HttpApplication, 23–26
IHttpHandlerFactory/IHttpHandler. *See* IHttpHandlerFactory/IHttpHandler

ASP.NET HTTP runtime pipeline (continued)
SPHttpApplication, 26–28
SPRequestModule, 28–30
SPVirtualPathProvider, 30–32
ASP.NET Web Parts Framework
AddContainer method, 504
AddItemToContainer method, 504
basics of, 487–491
components, overview of, 496–497
CreateChildControls method, 502–503
deploying custom WebPart server control. *See* WebPart server control, deploying custom
EditorPart controls, 518
IWebActionable interface, 515–517
IWebPart interface, 515
Part base class, 498–499
RssUrl property, 502
SharePoint extensions to, 491–495
templated web parts. *See* templated web parts
WebPart control, 499–502
.aspx page, inline approach and, 73
assemblies
ASP.NET compilation and, 49–50
< Assemblies >, Web part solutions and, 614
defined, 574
<Assembly> child element (<WebPart>), 366
Associations schema type, 734–740
Association schema type (listing), 735
Associations schema type (listing), 734
DestinationEntity schema type (listing), 736
SourceEntity schema type (listing), 736
attributes
of < Association > element, 737
of < DefaultValue > element, 688–689
of < TypeDescriptor > element, 687–688
of <Action> element, 732
of <Form> element, 105–107
of <List> element, 125–126
of <ListTemplate> element, 122–123
of <LobSystem> document element, 642, 646
of <MethodInstance> element, 724, 728
of <Parameter> element, 685
of <SafeControl>, 51
Association schema type, 735
of <CodeGroup> element, 590
of LobSystem schema type, 637. *See also specific* LobSystem schema type attributes
of MetadataObject schema type, 629
of <NamedPermissionSets> element, 589
of <NavBars>, 346
of <PermissionSet> element, 589
supported by <Field> element, 306–307
supported by <ListInstance> CAML element, 152–153
of <trustLevel> element, 594
automating Web part solutions, 618–620

B

BaseFieldControl class, 268–280
AllowFirstFocus Boolean property, 277
BaseFieldControl class' implementation of IValidator (listing), 269
CanCacheRenderedFieldValue Boolean property, 277
CssClass, 270–271
DisableInputFieldLabel, 271
DisplayTemplate/DisplayTemplateName, 272–273
Focus method, 278
HasPostBackEditData Boolean property, 277–278
IsFieldValueCached Boolean property, 278
ItemFieldValue property, 273–274
IValidator interface (listing), 268
ListItemFieldValue property, 275
PreviousControlMode property, 278
RegisterFieldControl, 279
RenderFieldForDisplay method, 280
RenderFieldForInput method, 280
RenderValidationMessage method, 280
TabIndex property, 275
UpdateFieldValueInItem method, 279
Validate method, 279
value virtual property, 276–277
BDC. *See* Business Data Catalog (BDC)
BDC application definition file listings
basic listings, 655, 659–660, 667–668, 721–723
for database LOB application, 647
describing database LOB system, 661–662, 668–669, 674–679, 717–719
describing LOB application, 649, 663–664, 670
describing LOB system, 681–682
for LOB application, 657
XML file for database LOB application, 656
Before events, 445
BeginExecuteUrlForEntireResponse method, 37
bin directory, security of assemblies deployed to, 579–580

Bin, installing web part server controls in, 505–507
binding
item event handlers to list instance, 472–473
item event handlers to site content type, 470–471
list event handlers to list content type, 461–464
list event handlers to list instance, 454–458
list event handlers to list type, 452–454
list event handlers to site content type, 458–461
web event handler to existing site definition configuration, 478–480
web event handler to new site definition configuration, 480–486
web event to existing site, 476–478
blank configuration, 360
Body attribute (<NavBars>), 346
build environment (ASP.NET), 44, 46
BuildSteps method, 26
Business Data Catalog (BDC), 627–761. *See also* BDC application definition file listings
AccessControlList schema type, 634–636
Actions schema type, 731–734
Associations schema type. *See* Associations schema type
BDC metadata XML schema, 628
ConnectionManager attribute, 639–640
Entities schema type. *See* Entities schema type
EntityInstance attribute. *See* EntityInstance attribute on <LobSystem> document element
FilterDescriptors schema type. *See* FilterDescriptors schema type
Identifiers schema type. *See* Identifiers schema type
IndividuallySecurableMetadataObject schema type, 630–631
InstanceCount schema type, 664
LobSystem schema type, 636–637
LobSystemInstances schema type. *See* LobSystemInstances schema type
LobSystemType schema type, 637
LocalizedDisplayName schema type, 631–632
MetadataObject schema type, 629–630
MethodInstances schema type. *See* MethodInstances schema type
Methods schema type. *See* Methods schema type
overview, xxvi
Parameters schema type. *See* Parameters schema type
Properties schema type, 632–633
SystemUtility attribute, 638–639
Type attribute, 637
uploading to BDC. *See* example of uploading to BDC
Version attribute, 637
buttons, used by RenderingTemplate control template, 206

C

C# switch construct, 137
cab.ddf file (listing), 623
cabinet files, 599–601
CAML. *See* Collaborative Application Markup Language (CAML)
CamlQueryRoot type definition (listing), 54
CanCacheRenderedFieldValue Boolean property, 277
CAS. *See* Code Access Security (CAS)
catalog zones, 495
CatalogIconImageUrl/TitleIconImageUrl properties (listing), 515
CatalogPart base class, defined, 496
CatalogPart server controls, defined, 488
CatalogZone server controls, defined, 488
CatalogZoneBase base class, defined, 496
Central Administration web application, launching, 740
Change Column page, 310
child elements
of < Association > element, 735
of < Configuration > element, 353
of < data > element, 507
of < Entity > element, 658
of < Feature > element, 441
of < FormTemplates > document element, 114
< FormUrls > element and, 335
of < metaData > element, 507
of < PolicyLevel > element, 589
of < Project > document element, 346
of < Solution > document element, 604
of < View > element, 133
of < WebPart > document element, 366
of < webPart > element, 507, 508
of <item> element, 402–403
of <LobSystem> document element, 637, 642, 646
of <Metadata> child element, 126, 159
of <Receiver> element, 453
of <Where> element, 55

child elements (continued)
GroupByHeader child element of <View> element, 133–140
of <RenderPattern>, 237–242
ChromeState property, 498
ChromeType property, 498
class hierarchy, SharePoint forms, 163–164
Code Access Security (CAS)
AllowPartiallyTrustedCallersAttribute, 595
benefits of, 573–574
capabilities of, 574–575
declarative security syntax, 576–578
GAC vs. bin, 579–580
imperative security syntax, 578–579
overview, xxvi
permissions, granting. *See* permissions, granting
security demands, 580–583
security requests, 583–585
SecurityAction enumeration type, 576
code access security settings, 615
code-behind approach (application pages), 83–95
<CustomAction> element adding new menu item (listing), 94
Default2.aspx.cs file content (listing), 85
Default3.aspx.cs file implementation (listing), 95
Default.aspx file content (listings), 84
feature.xml file referencing default2.xml file (listing), 90
implementation of Default2.aspx application page (listing), 93
vs. inline approach, 72, 84
XML document adding menu item to Site Actions menu (listing), 89
code listings
AbstractConnectionManager base class, 639
AbstractEntityInstance abstract base class, 640–641
AbstractSystemUtility base class, 638
AccessControlEntry schema type, 634
AccessControlList schema type, 634
Action schema type, 731
ActionParameter schema type, 733
ActionParameters schema type, 732
ActionPosition schema type, 732
Actions schema type, 731
AdventureWorksDW application definition excerpt, 750–752
Amazon E-Commerce web service application definition excerpt, 752–754
application page showing how to access IIS web sites, 9–10
application pools running in local farms, displaying, 7–8
App_Web_jgyyqxek.0.cs file, 46
Association schema type, 735
Associations schema type, 734
BaseFieldControl class' implementation of IValidator, 269
BDC application definition file, 659–660, 667–668, 721–723
BDC application definition file describing database LOB system, 661–662, 668–669, 674–679, 717–719
BDC application definition file describing web service LOB application, 649, 663–664, 670
BDC application definition file describing web service LOB system, 681–682
BDC application definition file excerpt, 760, 761
BDC application definition file for database LOB application, 647
BDC application definition file for web service LOB application, 657
BDC application definition XML file for database LOB application, 656
BDC application definition file, 655
BdcMetadata.xsd portion specifying target namespace, 628
BdcRightName schema type, 635, 636
BeginExecuteUrlForEntireResponse method, 37–38
binding list event handlers to list instance, 454
cab.ddf file, 623
CatalogIconImageUrl/TitleIconImageUrl properties, 515
CommandType enumeration type, 673
Compilation Source, 43
CompositeField field-rendering server control, 261–262
ConferenceRequestSiteColumns.xml file, 322–324
ConferenceRequestSiteColumns.xml file, feature referencing, 441
ConferenceRequestSiteContentTypes.xml file content, 318–319
ConsumerConnectionPoint class, 540
content of feature.xml file, 121
content of mybatchfile.bat file, 121
content of Program.cs file, 59–62
CssClass property, 270
CssClass property, assigning value of, 271

custom feature receiver (timer jobs), 437–439
custom timer jobs, feature to install, 437
<CustomAction> element adding new menu item, 94
CustomProvisioningProvider.cs, 385–388
data description file, 599, 607–608
DbAuthenticationMode enumeration type, 653–654
DbConnectionManager and WebServiceConnectionManager classes, 640
DbEntityInstance and WebServiceEntityInstance classes, 641
DbSystemUtility and WebServiceSystemUtility classes, 638
declarative approach to site columns, 312–313
default blank module, 368
Default Module, 362–364
Default2.aspx.cs file content, 85
Default3.aspx.cs file implementation, 95
Default.aspx file content, 78–81, 84
default.aspx page, 42
default.aspx.cdcab7d2 compiled file, 49
Default.aspx.cs code-behind file, 46
defaultdws.aspx page template, 370–371
DefaultHttpHandler HTTP handler, 35
DefaultValue schema type, 688
DefaultValues schema type, 688
definition of CamlQueryRoot type, 54
definition of ElementManifestReference(s) type, 66
definition of FeatureDefinition type, 64
definition of FieldRefDefinitions type, 57
definition of LogicalJoinDefinition type, 54
definition of LogicalTestDefinition type, 55
definitions of FieldRefDefinition and ValueDefinition types, 56
DestinationEntity schema type, 736
Displaying actual field names, 62–63
DWS module, 369
EditorPart base class, 518
EditorParts property of EditorZoneBase base class, 523–524
element manifest file, 453–454, 470–471, 478–479
elements.xml file, 459–460, 480, 513, 607
Entities schema type, 657
Entity schema type, 658
FavoriteItemWebPart control, 537
feature receiver, 472–473, 476–478
feature referencing element manifest file, 452
feature stapling, 442–443
feature with activation dependencies, 441
FeatureSiteTemplateAssociations.xml file, 443–444
feature.xml file, 309, 378–379, 428, 459, 461, 607
feature.xml file content, 68
feature.xml file referencing default2.xml file, 90
field type definition for custom field types, 297
field type definition for SPFieldChoice field type, 231–236
FieldDescription field-rendering server control, 262–263
FieldLabel field-rendering server control, 264–265
FieldMetadata, internal implementation, 257–258
FieldProperty field-rendering server controls, 263
FilterDescriptor(s) schema type, 708
FilterDescriptorType schema type, 708
form.aspx page, 107–109
FormComponent, internal implementation, 193–196
FormField field-rendering server control, 281–282
FormToolbar form-rendering control, 201–202
GetApplicationInstance method, internal implementation, 21, 22
GoogleMenuItem.xml file content, 68
<GroupByFooter> element, 140–141
<GroupByHeader> child element of <View> element, 134
<GroupByHeader> element generated HTML, 135
HighPriorityBugAlert timer job, 434–436
HTML generated by <GroupByHeader> element, 135
HttpAuthenticationMode enumeration type, 645
<httpModules> section of root web.config file, 23
HttpWorkerRequest API, 2
Identifier(s) schema type, 665
IHttpAsynchronousHandler interface, 36
IHttpHandler interface, 32
IHttpHandlerFactory interface, 33
implementation of Default2.aspx application page, 93
IndividuallySecurableMetadataObject schema type, 630
Init method of SPRequestModule, implementation of, 30
IPersonalizable interface, 562–564
ISPStsadmCommand interface, 416–417
ItemFieldValue simplified version of internal implementation, 273

code listings (continued)
iterating through application pools, 18
IValidator interface, 268
IWebActionable interface, 517
IWebEditable interface, 522–523
IWebPart interface, 499
ListFieldIterator server control, 210–211
ListFormPageTitle server control, internal implementation, 166–167
ListFormWebPart Web part, 110–112
ListItem property, internal implementation, 200
ListProperty, internal implementation, 170–171
<LobSystem> document element, 628, 629
LobSystemInstance schema type, 651
LobSystemInstances schema type, 651
LobSystemType schema type, 637
LocalizedDisplayName(s) schema type, 631
ManagerContentType site content type, 334
ManagerContentTypeEditTaskForm code-behind class, 331–332
ManagerContentTypeEditTaskForm.aspx page, 327–329
manifest.xml file, 610–611, 624
manifest.xml file structure, 602–603
Method schema type, 671
MethodInstance(s) schema type, 723
MethodInstanceType schema type, 724
Methods schema type, 671
ModifyWebConfig custom command class, 417–422
mybatchfile.bat file, 618, 622
MyFeatureReceiver class, 425–427
MyFeatureReceiver feature receiver, 455–457
MyFieldTypeField custom field type class, 291–292
MyFieldTypeFieldControl field-rendering control, 293–294
MyItemEventReceiver item event receiver, 467–469
MyListInstances.xml file, 376–378
MyNewFeatureReceiver feature receiver, 461–464
MyTasksListInstance.xml element manifest, 153
MyWebEventReceiver web event receiver, 475–476
new web application, creating and provisioning, 16
onet.xml file, 379–380, 389–395
onet.xml file for STS2 site definition, 480–482
onet.xml file of STS site definition, 339–344
Ordinal schema type, 733
parameter metadata objects of GetProducts method, 691–694
parameter metadata objects of ItemSearch web method, 698–701, 720–721
Parameter schema type, 685
ParameterDirection schema type, 685
Parameters schema type, 684
portion of onet.xml file of Global site definition, 348–351
ProcessRequest method of HttpRuntime, 19–20
ProcessRequest method of ISAPIRuntime, 19
Properties schema type, 632
Property schema type, 632
ProviderConnectionPoint class, 539–540
<Query> element, 142
RenderingTemplate server control, 178, 296, 534
RenderingTemplate server control with ID property value of CompositeField, 283
RenderingTemplate server control with value of "ListForm", 116
RequiredFieldMessage server control, 208
ReturnTypeDescriptorLevel schema type, 724
Right schema type, 634
RSS example, 402–403
RssHandler HTTP handler, 404–409
RssReaderEditorPart custom EditorPart control, 518–520
RssReaderEditorPart3, implementing, 554–556
RssReaderEditorPart4, 565–571
RssReaderWebPart Web part, 500–502
RssReaderWebPart3 control, 522
RssReaderWebPart4 control, 537–538
RssReaderWebPart4, implementing, 541–546
RssReaderWebPart5, implementing, 548–553
RssReaderWebPart6, implementing, 557–562
schema.xml file excerpt that defines schema from survey list type, 104
schema.xml file (portion of), 125, 130–131
SecurityAction enumeration type, 576–577
SharePoint object model to display web applications in local farm, 14
<SharePoint:RenderingTemplate> tags, deploying, 179
site column definition based on custom field type, 308
site provisioning provider, 482–485
site provisioning provider adding entries to web.config, 409–414
SourceEntity schema type, 736
SPControl main members, 165
SPControlMode enumeration, 197

SPControlTemplateManager, internal implementation, 181
SPEventPropertiesBase class, 449–450
SPEventReceiver class, 446
SPEventReceiverDefinition class, 457–458
SPFeatureReceiver abstract base class, 424
SPField Class, 216–217
SPFieldBoolean, internal implementation, 221–222
SPFieldChoice class, 229–230
SPFieldChoice field type, field type definition for, 231–236
SPFieldMultiChoiceValue field value type, 227–228
SPForm class, 115
SPHttpApplication class, internal implementation, 27–28
SPHttpHandler, internal implementation, 39–41
SPItem abstract class, 192–193
SPItemEventProperties type, 465–466
SPItemEventReceiver class, 464–465
SPJobDefinition base class, 429–431
SPListEventProperties type, 447–449
SPListEventReceiver base class, 446–447
SPMultiChoiceField class, 223–224
SPWebConfigModification class, 398–402
SPWebEventProperties type, 474–475
SPWebEventReceiver class, 474
SPWebProvisioningProperties type, 385
SPWebProvisioningProvider base class, 383–384
SQL SELECT statement and GetProducts method, 690
stapling feature, 478
Tasks1ListInstance.xml file, 152
Tasks1.xml file, 122
TemplateBasedControl, internal implementation, 173–177
TemplateBasedWebPart base class, 525–529
TemplateBasedWebPart1 Web part, 532–533
TemplateOverride enumeration type, 186
type factory, 47–48
TypeDescriptor schema type, 686
TypeDescriptors schema type, 689
view definition portion, 367
<View> element that represents All Tasks view, 132–133
<ViewBody> element, 143
<ViewFields> element, 142
web event receiver, 485–486
web page that uses Lists.asmx web service for provisioning, 158
Web part description file, feature for uploading, 512
Web part description file for RssReaderWebPart control, 511
Web part description for TemplateBasedWebPart1, 606
web.config configuration settings, 469
web.config file, 35, 594
web.config file content, 29
.webpart XML description file example, 508
WebPartConnection class, 538, 540
WebPartVerb class, 516–517
WebServiceEntityInstance classes, 641
WebTempMyWebTemp.xml file, 375–376, 388–389, 621–622
WebTemp.xml file, 372–374
wss_minimaltrust.config policy file, 586–593
XML document adding menu item to Site Actions menu, 89
XML file describing custom STSADM operation, 422–423

<CodeGroup> element, 590

Collaborative Application Markup Language (CAML), 53–69
basics of, 53–57
creating site content type with, 317
to define list types, 119–120
definition of CamlQueryRoot type (listing), 54
definition of FieldRefDefinitions type (listing), 57
definition of LogicalJoinDefinition type (listing), 54
definition of LogicalTestDefinition type (listing), 55
definitions of FieldRefDefinition and ValueDefinition types (listing), 56
feature example, 66–69
features, 63–66
overview, xxiii
queries. *See* queries (CAML)
rendering instructions. *See* rendering instructions (CAML)
schema files, 337
using to declaratively implement site columns. *See* declarative approach to site columns

columns. *See also* field types; site columns
Additional Column Settings section, 239
Change Column page, 310
Create Column page, 299
Create Column page Add caption, 238
creating based on field type, 238–239, 303
list columns, defined, 215–216, 303
list that contains column, 300
various meanings of, 215–216

command-line switches (STSADM), 420–421
command-line utilities
gacutil, 88
MAKECAB operating system, 599–601, 608–609
STSADM, 610–611, 617, 618–619
CommandType enumeration type (listing), 673
Compilation Source, dynamic compilation and, 43
components
of ASP.NET Web Parts Framework, 496–497
of Web part solutions, 604–605
CompositeField server control, 260–262
ConferenceRequestSiteColumns.xml file, feature referencing, 441
ConferenceRequestSiteColumns.xml file (listing), 322–324
ConferenceRequestSiteContentTypes.xml file content (listing), 318–319
configuration database, copying files into, 617
<Configurations> element (site definition), 353
attributes, 353
blank configuration, 360
child elements supported by, 353
Default configuration, 351, 354
default configuration, 354–359
DWS configuration, 360–362
<File> element, 353
Global site definition base list types, 351
Global site definition, onet.xml file of, 348–350
<Modules> element and, 352–353
ConnectionConsumerAttribute, 548
ConnectionManager attribute on <LobSystem>, 639–640
ConnectionProviderAttribute, 545
connections, web parts supporting. *See* web part controls, connecting
ConnectionsZone server controls, defined, 488
consumer connection points, 539
ConsumerConnectionPoint class, 540
<ContentType> element, 471
control template (TemplateBasedWebPart), 531
ControlMode property, 196–198
ControlTemplate property, 186–187
copying files
to deploy SharePoint solutions, 597–598
root files to subfolders, 598
into solution store of configuration database, 617
XML files to TEMPLATE folder, 598
crawls (BDC), 660, 730
create.aspx page, 98, 150
CreateChildControls method
basics of, 187–189, 502–503, 520
of FormToolBar, 207
RssReaderEditorPart4 and, 568–571
templates and, 531–532
CreateChildControls, of FormField, 284–285
creating
columns, 238–239, 303
Create Column page, 299
Create Column page Add caption, 238
new lists, 98–101
new web application, creating and provisioning, 16
new web application (listing), 16
site content types, 315–318
.webpart XML description file, 509–510, 511–514
CssClass property, 270–271
custom control development, 525
custom EditorPart controls, 519, 522–524
custom feature receiver, 437–439
custom field types
custom field-rendering controls, implementing, 293–296
field type definition, implementing, 297–301
implementing, 289–293
site column definition based on (listing), 308
using, 298–301
custom list item forms, 159–161
custom timer jobs. *See* timer jobs, custom
custom verbs, 517
<CustomAction> element adding new menu item (listing), 94
CustomProvisioningProvider.cs, 385–388
CustomTemplate and CustomAlternateTemplate properties, 189–190

D

Data Description File (.ddf), 599–601, 607, 608–609, 623
DbConnectionManager and WebServiceConnectionManager classes (listing), 640
DbEntityInstance and WebServiceEntityInstance classes (listing), 641
DDF files. *See* Data Description File (.ddf)
declarative approach to site columns, 305–313
basics of, 305–308
custom site columns, implementing and deploying, 307
feature.xml file (listing), 309

My Site Column site column, new version (listing), 312–313
site column definition based on custom field type (listing), 308
declarative creation of .webpart Xml file, 511–514
declarative list provisioning, 152–153
declarative security syntax, 576–578
DeclarativeCatalogPart controls, defined, 488
default blank module, 368
default configuration, 351–352, 353–359
Default module, 362–367
Default Web Site (IIS), 8
Default2.aspx application page implementation (listing), 93
Default2.aspx application page, implementing (listing), 93
Default2.aspx.cs file content (listing), 85, 87
default2.xml file, feature xml file referencing (listing), 90
Default3.aspx.cs file implementation (listing), 95
default_aspx class, 4, 5, 45
Default.aspx file content (listings), 78–81, 84
default.aspx page
dynamic compilation and, 42
template, 493–494
default.aspx.cdcab7d2 compiled file (listing), 49
Default.aspx.cs code-behind file, 46
DefaultHttpHandler
basics of, 39
custom handling requests with, 34
internal implementation of, 35
DefaultTemplateName property, 202–203, 204, 205–206
DefaultValue schema type (listing), 688
DefaultValues schema type (listing), 688
demand type (security demands), 581–582
dependency
activation, 440
feature, 440–441
deploying
custom HTTP handler to SharePoint, 402
custom WebPart server controls, 504–505
feature receivers, 423–424
site definitions, 337–338
templated web parts, 534
deployment, 597–625
cabinet and DDF files, 599–601
overview, xxvi
scenarios. *See* site definition solutions; Web part solutions
SharePoint solution packages, 597–599
solution manifest (manifest.xml), 601–604
DeploymentTarget attribute values, 613
derived site content types, 314
Description attribute, 374
DestinationEntity schema type (listing), 736
DisableEventFiring method, 446
DisableInputFieldLabel property, 271
Discussion Forum type, 351
DispForm.aspx page, 103, 104
display modes, switching (Web parts page), 495
display/new/edit list item forms, 104–119
form.aspx page (listing), 107–109
ListFormWebPart. *See* ListFormWebPart
page template for, 107–110
schema.xml file excerpt that defines schema from survey list type (listing), 104
DisplayCategory attribute, 374
DisplayPattern, CAML rendering and, 249
DisplaySize property, 260
DisplayTemplate virtual property, 272–273
DisplayTemplateName virtual string property, 272–273
document element (XML), 636
Document Library type, 351
DocumentLibrary value, ID property value of, 118
DWS
configuration, 360–362
module, 369–371
dynamic compilation, 42–52
App_Web_jgyyqxek.0.cs file, 46
code-behind files and, 86
Compilation Source, 43
default.aspx page (listing), 42
default.aspx.cdcab7d2 compiled file (listing), 49
Default.aspx.cs code-behind file, 46
type factory and, 47–48

E

EditForm.aspx page, 103, 104
editing. *See also* display/new/edit list item forms
list items, 103–104
editor zones, 494–495
EditorialReview page, 749
EditorPart base class, defined, 496
EditorPart controls
ApplyChanges method, 521
basics, 518
CreateChildControls method, 520

EditorPart controls (continued)
custom, 519, 522–524
RssReaderEditorPart control, 518–520
RssReaderWebPart3 control, 521–524
SyncChanges method, 521
EditorPart server controls, defined, 488
EditorZone server controls, defined, 488
EditorZoneBase base class, defined, 496
EditPattern, CAML rendering and, 249–255
element manifest file
item event receiver, 470–471
list event receiver, 453–454
web event receiver, 478–479
ElementManifestReference(s) type definition (listing), 66
<ElementManifests> element, 440
elements.xml file, 459–460, 480, 513, 607
EnableEventFiring method, 446
EnsureChildControls method, 532
enterprise search and indexing, 730–731
Entities schema type, 657–664
BDC application definition file describing database LOB system (listing), 661–662
BDC application definition file describing web service LOB application, 663–664
BDC application definition file (listing), 659–660
Entities schema type (listing), 657
Entity schema type (listing), 658
EntityInstance attribute on <LobSystem> document element, 640–651
AbstractEntityInstance abstract base class (listing), 640–641
attributes of <LobSystem> document element, 646
BDC application definition file describing web service LOB application (listing), 649
BDC application definition file for database LOB application (listing), 647
child elements of <LobSystem> document element, 646
DbEntityInstance and WebServiceEntityInstance classes (listing), 641
HttpAuthenticationMode enumeration type (listing), 645
enumeration
CommandType enumeration type (listing), 673
enumeration values of TemplateOverride enumeration type, 186
HttpAuthenticationMode enumeration type (listing), 645
SecurityAction enumeration type, 576
SecurityAction enumeration values, 576–577
SecurityAction.Request enumeration values, 584–585
SPControlMode enumeration (listing), 197
TemplateOverride enumeration type (listing), 186
EstimatedInstanceCount attribute, 664
event handlers
Init method of HTTP modules and, 24
SPItemEventReceiver, 465
web event handlers, 474
event receivers
item event receiver. *See* item event receiver
list event receiver. *See* list event receiver
overview, xxv, 445–446
SPEventReceiver class, 446
web event receiver. *See* web event receiver
events, of HttpApplication, 24–25
example of uploading to BDC, 740–761
Add Action page, 757–759
excerpt from the AdventureWorksDW application definition (listing), 750–752
excerpt from the Amazon E-Commerce web service application definition (listing), 752–754
excerpt from the BDC application definition file (listing), 760, 761
Export Application Definition page, 747–748
Import Application Definition page, 741–742
launch SharePoint 3.0 Central Administration web application, 740
Manage Permissions page, 744–745
Modify Permissions page, 745–746
Shared Services Administration, 741
View Application page, 742–744
View Entity page, 748–749, 756
ExchangeData method, 538
ExcludeFields property, 211
Execute method, of IExecutionStep object, 34
ExecuteStage method, ApplicationStepManager and, 26
Export Application Definition link, 747, 748
Export Application Definition page, BDC and, 747–748
eXtensible Markup Language (XML)
< (less than) and > (greater than) characters and, 678, 679
BDC and, 627
BDC metadata XML schema, 628
CAML and features, 63
document element, 636

feature.xml, 63
files. *See* XML files
XML element of
IndividuallySecurableMetadataObject, 630–631
XML schema of CAML, 53–57
extensions (SharePoint), 6–18
SPApplicationPool, 6–8
SPIisWebSite, 8–11
SPWebApplication, 11–14
SPWebApplicationBuilder, 14–16
SPWebService, 16–18
External Tools dialog, 391

F

FavoriteItemWebPart control, 537
FavoriteItemWebPart Web part, 546–548
feature activation
approaches for, 440
feature dependency, 440–441
feature referencing
ConferenceRequestSiteColumns.xml file, 441
feature stapling, 442–443
feature with activation dependencies, 441
FeatureSiteTemplateAssociations.xml file,
443–444
feature receivers
binding item event handlers and, 472–473
binding web event handlers and, 476–478
feature.xml file, 428
implementing and deploying, 423–424
MyFeatureReceiver class, 425–427
SPFeatureReceiver abstract base class, 424
FeatureActivated method, 462
FeatureDefinition type definition (listing), 64
features
basics in CAML, 63–66
defined, 63
example of, 66–69
FEATURES folder, 90
Site Actions menu, 91–93
feature.xml file
content, 121
listings, 309, 378, 459, 461, 607
<Field> element
attributes supported by, 306–307
of SPFieldChoice field type, 237
Field event handlers, 447
field names (CAML), displaying (listing), 62–63
Field property, of FieldMetadata, 259–260
field-rendering controls, 256–286
BaseFieldControl. *See* BaseFieldControl class
CompositeField server control, 260–262
FieldDescription, 262–263
FieldLabel, 264–268
FieldMetadata. *See* FieldMetadata
FieldProperty, 263–264
FormField. *See* FormField
field type definition
<RenderPattern>, 237–242
additional columns settings, 239
AllItems.aspx page and, 239, 241
Create Column page Add caption, 238
defined, 215
DisplayPattern, 249
edit list item page, 240
EditPattern, 249–255
HeaderPattern type of RenderPattern, 242–249
implementing, 297–298
NewForm.aspx page, 241
NewPattern, 256
for SPFieldChoice field type (listing), 231–236
field types
creating columns based on, 238–239, 303
custom, 298–301
custom field-rendering control, implementing,
293–296
custom, implementing, 289–293
field-rendering controls. *See* field-rendering controls
field type class, defined, 215
field type definition. *See* field type definition
overview, xxiv
SPField. *See* SPField
variable field type property rendering, 286–289
**FieldDescription field-rendering server control,
262–263**
FieldLabel field-rendering server control, 264–268
FieldMetadata, 256–262
DisplaySize property, 260
Field property, 259–260
FieldMetadata, internal implementation (listing),
257–258
FieldName, 259
Visible property, 260
FieldName string property, 259
**FieldProperty field-rendering server control,
263–264**
**FieldRefDefinition and ValueDefinition types
definitions (listing), 56**
FieldRefDefinitions type definition (listing), 57

<Fields> element, 129
Fields property, 199
<File> child elements, 353
<File> element, 353
files
added to root directory (web part solution), 606
copying into solution store of configuration database, 617
copying to deploy SharePoint solutions, 597–598
copying to subfolders (root files), 598
copying to TEMPLATE folder (XML files), 598
deployment files (site definition solutions), 620
dynamically generated, for ASP.NET applications, 48
image files, deploying to folders, 89
filter descriptors, 712–714
FilterDescriptors schema type
BDC application definition file describing database LOB system (listing), 717–719
BDC application definition file (listing), 721–723
FilterDescriptor schema type (listing), 708
FilterDescriptors schema type (listing), 708
FilterDescriptorType schema type (listing), 708
parameter metadata objects of ItemSearch web method (listing), 720–721
finder method, 729–730
FlushResponse method, 2
Focus method
of BaseFieldControl class, 278
of FormField, 286
<Form> element
attributes of, 105–107
custom list item forms and, 159, 160
SetupPath element of, 105
form-rendering server controls, 163–213
architecture, 163–164
FormComponent class. *See* FormComponent class
FormToolBar, 201–208
ListFieldIterator, 210–213
ListFormPageTitle, 166–169
ListProperty, 169–172
overview, xxiv
RequiredFieldMessage, 208–210
SPControl class, 165
TemplateBasedControl. *See* TemplateBasedControl
FormComponent class, 192–201
ControlMode property, 196–198
Fields property, 199
FormComponent, internal implementation (listing), 193–196
Item property, 199
ItemContext property, 198–199
Itemid property, 199
List property, 200
ListId property, 200
ListItem property, 200–201
SPControlMode enumeration, 197
SPItem abstract class (listing), 192–193
FormField, 280–286
CreateChildControls, 284–285
Focus method, 286
FormField field-rendering server control (listing), 281–282
RenderingTemplate server control with ID property value of CompositeField (listing), 283
Value property, 286
ValueChanged and OnValue Changed members, 283–284
forms
custom list item forms, 159–161
form.aspx page (listing), 107–109
form.aspx page template, 107–110
forms infrastructure. *See also* form-rendering server controls
abstractions and, 163
display/new/edit list item forms. *See* display/new/edit list item forms
list items, editing, 103–104
list items, viewing, 102–103
new list items, adding, 101–102
new lists, creating, 98–101
FormToolBar server control, 201–208
<FrameType> child element (<WebPart>), 366

G

GAC (Global Assembly Cache)
installing web part server controls in, 505–507
security of assemblies deployed to, 579–580
gacutil command-line utility, 88
GenerateAndCompileAppClassIfNecessary method, 21
Generic List type, 351
GetApplicationInstance method, 20–21, 22
GetContextSite method, 165
GetContextWeb method, 165
GetContextWebApplication method, 165
GetExecuteDelegate method, 3
GetFieldValue, override of, 225–226
GetHelpMessage method, 417
GetTemplateByName static method, 118

ghosted site pages, defined, 30–31
Global Assembly Cache (GAC)
installing web part server controls in, 505–507
security of assemblies deployed to, 579–580
Global site definition
base list types, 351
configuration, 479
onet.xml file and, 348–350
global.asax file, 22, 26
Globally Unique IDentifiers (GUIDs)
CAML XML schema and, 64–65
guidgen.exe tool, 64–65
GoogleMenuItem.xml file content (listing), 68
graphics
graphical approach to site columns, 304–305
graphical creation of .webpart Xml file, 509–510
graphical list provisioning, 150–151
GroupByFooter element, of <View> element, 140–142
GroupByHeader child element
of <View> element, 133–140
HTML generated by, 135
GUIDs (Globally Unique IDentifiers)
CAML XML schema and, 64–65
guidgen.exe tool, 64–65
gyyqxek.out file, 48

H

handlers. *See specific* handlers
HasPostBackEditData Boolean property, 277–278
HeaderPattern type of RenderPattern, 242–249
Hidden Boolean attribute, 374
hierarchy
containment hierarchy, 638, 639, 640, 641, 687
levels (BDC), 726
HighPriorityBugAlert timer job, 434–436
hosting ASP.NET, 1–2
HTML (HyperText Markup Language)
generated by <GroupByHeader> element (listing), 135
generated by <ViewBody> element, 144–145
HTTP handler, deploying, 402
Http handlers, developing custom, 42–52
HTTP Protocol Stack (http.sys), 6
HttpApplication, 23–26
HTTPApplicationFactory, HttpRuntime and, 20
HttpAuthenticationMode enumeration type (listing), 645
HttpExtensionProc function, 18
<httpHandler> section of web.config, 33, 34–35
Httpmodules, developing custom, 42–52
<httpModules>, of web.config file, 23
http.sys, 6
HttpWorker Request, 2–3
HyperText Markup Language (HTML)
generated by <GroupByHeader> element (listing), 135
generated by <ViewBody> element, 144–145

I

ID property values, 118
< Identifier > child element, 665, 666
Identifiers schema type, 665–671
BDC application definition file describing database LOB system (listing), 668–669
BDC application definition file describing web service LOB application (listing), 670
BDC application definition file (listing), 667–668
Identifier schema type (listing), 665
Identifiers schema type (listing), 665
IHttpAsyncHandler interface, 36
IHttpHandlerFactory/IHttpHandler, 32–41
basics of, 32–34
IHttpHandlerFactory interface, 33
SPHttpHandler, 34–42
IHttpModule interface, 24
IIS. *See* Internet Information Services (IIS)
IL DASM tool, 615–616
image files, deploying to folders, 89
ImageUrl attribute, 374
imperative list provisioning, 154–159
imperative security syntax, 578–579
Impersonate property, 576
Import Application Definition page, BDC and, 741–742
ImportCatalogPart controls, defined, 489
INamingContainer interface, 499
indexing, enterprise search and, 730–731
IndividuallySecurableMetadataObject schema type, 630–631
inheritance demands, 583
Init method
of HTTP module, 24
of SPRequestModule, 30, 31
InitializeAppInstance method
ApplicatonStepManager and, 25–26
HTTP modules and, 24

inline approach (application pages), 73–83
basics of, 73–77
vs. code-behind approach, 72, 84
Default.aspx file content (listings), 78–81
IntelliSense support for CAML, 66–67
Internet Information Services (IIS)
IIS Manager, _vti_bin virtual directory and, 155–157
IIS web sites, accessing, 9–10
SharePoint architecture and, 3–6
IPersonalizable interface, 562–564
ISAPIRuntime, 3, 18–19
IsFieldValueCached Boolean property, 278
ISPStsadmCommand interface, 416–417
IsStatic attribute, 672
Issues List type, 351
item event receiver
binding item event handlers to list instance, 472–473
binding item event handlers to site content type, 470–471
MyItemEventReceiver item event receiver, 467–469
SPItemEventProperties type, 465–466
SPItemEventReceiver class, 464–465
web.config configuration settings, 469
Item property, 199
ItemContext property, 198–199
ItemFieldValue property, 273–274
Itemid property, 199
IWebActionable interface, 515–517
IWebEditable interface, 522–523
IWebPart interface, 499, 515

J

jgyyqxek.cmdline file, 48
jgyyqxek.err file, 48

L

LAYOUTS folder
deploying application pages and, 71
deploying application pages to, 81, 82–83
Line of Business (LOB), 627. *See also* EntityInstance attribute on <LobSystem> document element; LobSystemInstances schema type
link demands (security demands), 582
<List> child element, 353–356
list columns, defined, 215–216, 303
<List> element, attributes of, 125–126
list event receiver
binding list event handlers to list content type, 461–464
binding list event handlers to list instance, 454–458
binding list event handlers to list type, 452–454
binding list event handlers to site content type, 458–461
element manifest file, 453–454
feature referencing element manifest file, 452
implementing custom, 450–452
SPEventPropertiesBase, 449–450
SPListEventProperties type, 447–449
SPListEventReceiver base class, 446–447
list item columns, defined, 216
list item forms, custom, 159–161
List property, 200
list provisioning
declarative, 152–153
graphical, 150–151
imperative, 154–159
site definition best practices and, 375–383
list types, 119–150
content of feature.xml file (listing), 121
content of mybatchfile.bat file (listing), 121
custom, 119–120, 160–161
<GroupByFooter>, 140–142
GroupByHeader, 133–140
<GroupByHeader> child element of <View> element (listing), 134
<GroupByHeader> element generated HTML (listing), 135
HTML generated by <ViewBody> element, 144–145
<List> element attributes, 125–126
list provisioning from. *See* list provisioning
<ListTemplate> element attributes, 122–123
overview, xxiii–xxiv
<Query> element (listing), 142
schema.xml file (portion of) (listing), 125, 130–131
Tasks1.xml file (listing), 122
Type attribute values, 123–124
<View> element that represents All Tasks view (listing), 132–133
<ViewBody> element (listing), 143
<ViewFields> element (listing), 142
ListDir attribute (site definitions), 345

ListFieldIterator server control, 210–213
ListFormPageTitle server control, 166–169
ListFormWebPart, 110–119
- ID property values, 118
- ListFormWebPart Web part (listing), 110–112
- RenderingTemplate server control with value of "ListForm" (listing), 116
- SPForm class (listing), 115

ListId property, 200
listings, code. *See* code listings
<ListInstance> CAML element, attributes supported by, 152–153
ListItem property, 200–201
ListItemFieldValue property, 275
ListItemVersion property, 274
ListProperty server control, 169–172
lists
- custom list item forms, 159–161
- display/new/edit list item forms. *See* display/new/edit list item forms
- list items, editing, 103–104
- list items, viewing, 102–103
- list provisioning. *See* list provisioning
- list types. *See* list types
- new list items, adding, 101–102
- new lists, creating, 98–101

Lists.asmx web service to provision a list (listing), 158
<ListTemplate> element, attributes of, 122–123
LOB. *See* Line of Line of Business (LOB)
LobSystem schema type, 636–637
< LobSystemInstances > element, 651
LobSystemInstances schema type, 651–657
- BDC application definition file for web service LOB application (listing), 657
- BDC application definition XML file for database LOB application (listing), 656
- BDC application definition file (listing), 655
- DbAuthenticationMode enumeration type (listing), 653–654
- LobSystemInstance schema type (listing), 651
- LobSystemInstances schema type (listing), 651

local farm
- displaying application pools running in, 7–8
- displaying names of web applications in, 14

LocalizedDisplayName schema type, 631–632
< LocalizedDisplayNames > child element, 629, 631–632
LogicalJoinDefinition type definition (listing), 54
LogicalTestDefinition type definition (listing), 55

M

main template (TemplateBasedWebPart), 529–530
MAKECAB operating system command-line utility, 599–601, 608–609
Manage Permission(s) link, 744, 748, 761
Manage Permissions page, BDC and, 744–745
ManagerContentType site content type (listing), 334
ManagerContentTypeEditTaskForm code-behind class (listing), 331–332
ManagerContentTypeEditTaskForm.aspx page (listing), 327–329
manifest.xml file (solution manifest), 601, 610–611, 624
menus
- <CustomAction> element adding new menu item (listing), 94
- custom menu items added to Site Actions menu, 66–67
- GoogleMenuItem.xml file content, 68
- Site Actions menu, 91–93
- Tab menu option, adding, 73–77
- View Response menu option, 102–103, 104
- XML document adding menu item to Site Actions menu (listing), 89

metadata attribute
- ConnectionConsumerAttribute, 548
- ConnectionProviderAttribute, 545

<MetaData> child element, 126, 127, 129
MetadataObject schema type, 629–630
method metadata objects
- < DefaultValue > elements and, 689
- defined, 672–673, 686, 689, 710, 724
- defining, 674, 680, 682, 685–686
- name conflicts and, 720
- properties supported by, 673
- SQL SELECT statements and, 690, 717
- web methods/database queries and, 682–683

MethodInstances schema type, 723–731
- enterprise search and indexing, 730–731
- finder method and, 729–730
- MethodInstance schema type (listing), 723
- MethodInstances schema type (listing), 723
- MethodInstanceType schema type (listing), 724
- ReturnTypeDescriptorLevel schema type (listing), 724
- scalar method and, 731

methods
of EditorPart base class, 518
of IHttpAsyncHandler interface, 36
of IPersonalizable interface, 562–563
public, SPApplicationPool class, 7
public, SPIisWebSite, 8–9
public, SPWebApplication class, 13
public, SPWebApplicationBuilder class, 15
public, SPWebService class, 17
of SPEventReceiverDefinition, 458
of SPFeatureReceiver abstract base class, 424
of SPField class, 216–218
Methods schema type, 671–684
BDC application definition file describing database LOB system (listing), 674–679
BDC application definition file describing web service LOB system (listing), 681–682
CommandType enumeration type (listing), 673
Method schema type (listing), 671
Methods schema type (listing), 671
Microsoft Office SharePoint Server 2007 (MOSS), 627
minimal security requests, 574
minimum security requests, 584
MobilityRedirect site-scoped feature, 358–359
Modify Permissions page, BDC and, 745–746
ModifyWebConfig custom command class, 417–422
modules
ASP.NET ISAPI extension module, 4
Blank module, 368
Default module, 362–367
DWS module, 369–371
Http handler factories/handlers/modules, developing custom, 42–52
Init method of HTTP modules, 24
Init method of SPRequestModule, implementation of, 30
SPRequestModule, 28–30
MOSS (Microsoft Office SharePoint Server) 2007, 627
MoveToContent method (XmlReader), 503
My Site Column site column, new version (listing), 312–313
mybatchfile.bat file
adding to, 88
content of, 121
implementing, 338
listings, 121, 618, 622
MyCustomColumn.xml file implementation, 308
MyFeatureReceiver class, 425–427
MyFeatureReceiver feature receiver, 455–457
MyFieldTypeField custom field type class (listing), 291–292
MyFieldTypeFieldControl field-rendering control (listing), 293–294
MyItemEventReceiver item event receiver, 467–469
MyListInstances.xml file, 376–378
MyNewFeatureReceiver feature receiver, 461–464
MySurveyList SharePoint list, 101
MyTasksListInstance.xml element manifest (listing), 153
MyWebEventReceiver web event receiver, 475–476

N

Name attribute
Identifiers schema type and, 666, 670
of <LobSystem> document element, 645, 651
naming metadata objects and, 629
of <NavBarLink>, 347
of <NavBars>, 346
of < Identifier > element, 666
< Parameter > element and, 694
<NamedPermissionSets> element, 589
names
of <LobSystem> document element attributes, 646
for custom field types, 220
determining underlying field names (CAML), 62–63
displaying names of web applications in local farm, 14
name conflicts and metadata objects, 720
namespace
BDC XML schema and, 628
default XML, 647
<NavBar> element, 346–347
<NavBarLink> element, 347
new list item forms. *See* display/new/edit list item forms
new.aspx page
creating new lists and, 99
list provisioning and, 151
NewForm.aspx page, 101, 104, 241
NewPattern, CAML rendering and, 256

O

object model
  interacting with, 59
  using, 154
ObjectModel property, 576
onet.xml file, 339–346, 379–380, 389–395
onet.xml file for STS2 site definition, 480–482
optional security requests, 574, 584
<OrderBy> element (CAML), 54, 57
Ordinal schema type (listing), 733
OverrideExecuteUrlPath method, 36

P

PageCatalogPart controls, defined, 488
pages, supported by SharePoint, 70
PageUri method, 165
parameter metadata objects of GetProducts method (listing), 691–694
parameter metadata objects of ItemSearch web method (listing), 698–701, 720–721
Parameters schema type, 684–707
  DefaultValue schema type (listing), 688
  DefaultValues schema type (listing), 688
  parameter metadata objects of GetProducts method (listing), 691–694
  parameter metadata objects of ItemSearch web method (listing), 698–701
  Parameter schema type (listing), 685
  ParameterDirection schema type (listing), 685
  Parameters schema type (listing), 684
  SQL SELECT statement and GetProducts method (listing), 690
  TypeDescriptor schema type (listing), 686
  TypeDescriptors schema type (listing), 689
Part base class, 498–499
permissions, and security metadata attributes, 576
permissions, granting
  overview, 585
  web.config file, 594
  wss_minimaltrust.config policy file, 586–593
<PermissionSet> element, 590
Persisted metadata attribute, 400
PersonalizationDictionary, 563
PersonalizationEntry class, 563–564
PipelineRuntime class, 3
PopulateTemplateCollection static method, 183
Prefix attribute (<NavBars>), 346
PreviousControlMode property, 278
process boundaries (application pools), 4
ProcessRequest method
  of HttpRuntime, 19–20
  of ISAPIRuntime, 3, 19
Program.cs file content (listing), 59–62
properties
  of EditorPart base class, 518
  of entity metadata object of LOB system metadata object, 660
  of field types, 238
  of filter descriptor metadata object, 717
  of IWebPart interface, 500
  of LOB system instance metadata object, 652–653, 654
  of LOB system metadata objects, 643–644
  of a method metadata object, 673
  of PersonalizationEntry class, 563
  public, SPApplicationPool class, 6–7
  public, SPIisWebSite, 8–9
  public, SPWebApplication class, 12
  public, SPWebApplicationBuilder class, 14–15
  public, SPWebService class, 16–17
  of SPEventPropertiesBase, 450
  of SPEventReceiverDefinition, 457
  of SPField class, 216, 218–219
  of SPItemEventProperties type, 466
  of SPListEventProperties type, 448
  of SPWebEventProperties type, 475
  of TemplateBasedWebPart, 530–531
  of WebPartVerb class, 517
< Properties > child element, 643, 651, 685, 694, 732
Properties schema type, 632–633
< Property > element, 632
property schema for field types, 287
provider connection points, 539
ProviderConnectionPoint class, 539–540
Provision method, 390
ProvisionAssembly attribute, 384
ProvisionClass attribute, 384
ProvisionData attribute, 384
provisioning, list. *See* list provisioning
public methods
  SPApplicationPool class, 7
  SPIisWebSite, 8–9
  SPWebApplication class, 13
  SPWebApplicationBuilder class, 15
  SPWebService class, 17

public properties
SPApplicationPool class, 6–7
SPIisWebSite class, 8–9
SPWebApplication class, 12
SPWebApplicationBuilder class, 14–15
SPWebService class, 16–17
PublicKeyBlob, 615, 617
PublicKeyBlob property, 593

Q

queries (CAML), 57–63
content of Program.cs file (listing), 59–62
Displaying actual field names (listing), 62–63
examples of, 58
<Query> element (listing), 142

R

ReadToDescendant method (XmlReader), 503
Really Simple Syndication (RSS), 402–403
<Receivers> element, 453
refuse security requests, 575, 584–585
RegisterFieldControl, 279
RegisterGetVaryByCustomStringHandler method, 28
RenderContext property, 191
RenderFieldForDisplay method, 280
RenderFieldForInput method, 280
rendering
BaseFieldControl, and field rendering, 268
CAML instructions. *See* rendering instructions (CAML)
custom field-rendering control, implementing, 293–296
field-rendering controls, 256, 261, 262–263, 264–265
FormField and, 280–283
RenderingTemplate server control with value of "ListForm", 283
variable field type property rendering, 286–289
rendering instructions (CAML)
basics of, 237, 239–242
DisplayPattern, 249
EditPattern, 249–250
HeaderPattern, 242–243
RenderingTemplate server control (listings), 178, 283, 296, 534
<RenderPattern>
child elements, 237–242
child elements of <FieldType> element, 237–238
DisplayPattern and, 249
EditPattern and, 249–250
HeaderPattern and, 242–243
RenderValidationMessage method, 280
RequiredFieldMessage server control, 208–210
ReturnTypeDescriptorLevel schema type (listing), 724
root files, copying to subfolders, 598
RootWebOnly attribute (<Module>), 353
RSS (Really Simple Syndication), 402–403
RSSHandler
basics of, 403
RssHandler HTTP handler, 404–409
RSSReader
RssReaderEditorPart control, 518–520
RssReaderEditorPart3, implementing, 554–556
RssReaderEditorPart4, 565–571
RssReaderWebPart Web part, 500–502
RssReaderWebPart3 control, 521–524
RssReaderWebPart4 control, 535–536
RssReaderWebPart4, implementing, 541–546
RssReaderWebPart5, implementing, 548–553
RssReaderWebPart6, implementing, 557–562
RssUrl property, 502
Run method, 417, 421–422
runtime class (ASP.NET), 2, 3
Runtime object model, 738, 739

S

<SafeControl>, attributes of, 51
scalar method, 731
schemaLocation attribute, 647
schema.xml file
<Fields> element of, 129
defining schema of list types and, 125
excerpt that defines (listing), 104
portions of (listings), 125, 130–131
Scope attribute (<Feature> element), 479
searching, enterprise, 730–731
security. *See also* Code Access Security (CAS); permissions, granting
code access security settings (Web part solutions), 614–616
declarative security syntax, 576–578
demands, 576–578, 580–583
imperative security syntax, 578–579
inheritance demands, 583

link demands, 582
permissions, and security metadata attributes, 576
refuse security requests, 575
requests, 576–578, 583–585
SecurityAction enumeration type, 576
SecurityAction enumeration values, 576–577
SecurityAction.Request enumeration values, 584–585
<SecurityClasses> element, 589
SelectCommandCallback method, 548
server control development, 525
SetupPath element, of <Form> element, 105
Shared Services Administration, BDC and, 741
SharePoint
3.0 Central Administration web application, launching, 740
creating site content type with, 315–317
object model, web configuration modification via. *See* web configuration modification
SharePoint Timer Service (owstimer.exe), 428
SharePoint solution packages. *See also* site definition solutions; Web part solutions
basics of, 70, 597–599
cabinet and DDF files and, 599–601
solution manifest (manifest.xml), 601–604
SharePointPermission metadata attributes, 576–578
SimpleWorkerRequest, 2
Site Actions menu, adding menu item to (listing), 89
site columns, 303–313
basics of, 303–304
declarative approach. *See* declarative approach to site columns
defined, 215, 303
graphical approach, 304–305
site column gallery, 220, 304, 309
site content types
basics of, 313–315
ConferenceRequestSiteColumns.xml file (listing), 322–324
ConferenceRequestSiteContentTypes.xml file content (listing), 318–319
creating, 315–318
edit task forms, 326–334
element manifest files, feature that references (listing), 324
ID, 319–322
manage content type page, 317
ManagerContentType site content type (listing), 334
ManagerContentTypeEditTaskForm code-behind class (listing), 331–332
ManagerContentTypeEditTaskForm.aspx page (listing), 327–329
overview, xxiv
parts of, 319–322
settings, 313
Site Content Type Gallery, 315
site definition solutions, 620–625
defined, 620
deployment files, 620
example of, 620–624
site definitions
<Modules> element, 383
<Configurations> elements. *See* <Configurations> element (site definition)
default blank module, 368
default module, 362–367
DWS module, 369–371
implementing and deploying, 337–338
list provisioning, 375–383
<NavBar> element, 346–347
onet.xml files, 339–346
WebTemp.xml file, 372–373
site pages
vs. application pages, 70
ghosted, 30–31
unghosted, 31, 51
site provisioning providers
adding entries to web.config with, 409–414
basics, 383
CustomProvisioningProvider.cs, 385–388
onet.xml file, 389–395
SPWebProvisioningProperties type, 385
SPWebProvisioningProvider base class, 383–384
WebTempMyWebTemp.xml file, 388–389
<SiteFeatures> child element, 353
SiteURLs, 345
< Solution > document element child elements, 604
solution packages. *See* SharePoint solution packages
SourceEntity schema type (listing), 736
SPApplicationPool, 6–8
SPAutoSerializingObject, 400
SPControl class main members, 165
SPControlMode enumeration (listing), 197
SPControlTemplateManager, internal implementation (listing), 181

SPDailySchedule, 432
SPEventPropertiesBase, 449–450
SPEventReceiver class, 446
SPEventReceiverDefinition class, 457–458
SPFeatureReceiver abstract base class, 424
SPField, 215–231. ***See also*** **columns**
different meanings of, 215–216
methods of, 217–218
properties of, 218–219
site column gallery, 220
SPFieldBoolean, 220–223
SPFieldChoice, 229–231
SPFieldMultiChoice, 223–229
SPFieldChoice field type field type definition for (listing), 231–236
SPForm class (listing), 115
SPHourlySchedule, 432
SPHttpApplication class
basics of, 26–28
SharePoint applications and, 23
SPHttpHandler
basics of, 34–42
internal implementation of, 39–41
SPIisWebSite, 8–11
SPItem abstract class (listing), 192–193
SPItemEventProperties type, 465–466
SPItemEventReceiver class, 464–465
SPJobDefinition base class, 429–431
SPListEventProperties type, 447–449
SPListEventReceiver base class, 446–447
SPMinuteSchedule, 431–432
SPMonthlySchedule, 432–433
SPOneTimeSchedule, 431
SPRequestModule, 28–30
SPVirtualPathProvider
ASP.NET and, 31–32
basics of, 30–32
SPWebApplication, 11–14
SPWebApplicationBuilder, 14–16
SPWebConfigModification class, 398–402, 595
SPWebConfigModification objects, 410–411
SPWebEventProperties type, 474–475
SPWebEventReceiver class, 474
SPWebPartManager, 491–492
SPWebProvisioningProperties type, 385
SPWebProvisioningProvider base class, 383–384
SPWebService, 16–18
SPWeeklySchedule, 433
SPYearlySchedule, 433–434
SQL SELECT statement and GetProducts method (listing), 690
standard verbs, 517
stapling feature, 442–443, 478
StrongNameMembershipCondition membership condition, 593
STS2 site definition, onet.xml file for, 480–482
STSADM command-line utility
custom operation, 422–423
extending, 416
features and, 612
ISPStsadmCommand interface, 416–417
ModifyWebConfig custom command class, 417–422
solution package files and, 617, 618–619
switches, 420–421
stsadm.exe, 90–91
Suffix attribute (<NavBarLink>), 347
SurveyList value, ID property value of, 118
<Switch> CAML element
of <GroupByFooter>, 142
C# switch construct, 137
switches, command-line (STSADM), 420–421
SyncChanges method, 521
SystemUtility attribute, on <LobSystem>, 638–639

T

Tab menu option, adding with inline approach, 73–77
TabIndex property, 275
Tasks1ListInstance.xml file (listing), 152
Tasks1.xml file (listing), 122
TeamCollab site-scoped feature, 358–359
Template attribute, 106
<Template> element, 374
template files/TEMPLATE folder, 597–598
template property, 177–183
basics of, 177
RenderingTemplate server control (listing), 178
SPControlTemplateManager, internal implementation (listing), 181
TemplateBasedControl, 172–192
AlternateTemplate property, 184–185
ControlTemplate property, 186–187
CreateChildControls method, 187–189
CustomTemplate and CustomAlternateTemplate properties, 189–190
internal implementation of, 172–177
RenderContext property, 191

template property. *See* template property
TemplateOverride property, 185–186
TemplateContainer class, 117–118
TemplateContainerAttribute metadata attribute, 189
templated web parts
deploying, 534
server control development, 525
TemplateBasedWebPart base class, 525–532
TemplateBasedWebPart1, 532–534
TemplateName property, 113–115
TemplateOverride property, 185–186, 529
templates
form.aspx page template, 107–110
Web part description for TemplateBasedWebPart1 (listing), 606
timer jobs, custom
custom feature receiver, 437–439
feature to install, 437
HighPriorityBugAlert timer job, 434–436
implementing, 428
SPDailySchedule, 432
SPHourlySchedule, 432
SPJobDefinition base class, 429–431
SPMinuteSchedule, 431–432
SPMonthlySchedule, 432–433
SPOneTimeSchedule, 431
SPWeeklySchedule, 433
SPYearlySchedule, 433–434
Title attribute (site definitions), 344, 374
<Title> child element (<WebPart>), 366
TitleIconImageUrl properties (listing), 515
toolbars
of document library's display list item, 206–207
FormToolbar form-rendering control, 201–202
toolbox, adding server controls to (Visual Studio), 73–77
trust levels, 506–507
<trustLevel> element, 594
Type attribute
of <Form> element, 105
<LobSystem> and, 637
<Property> element and, 633
values of, 123–124
type factory (listing), 47–48
< TypeDescriptor > child element, 696, 697, 701, 702, 703–706
TypeDescriptor schema type (listing), 686
TypeDescriptors schema type (listing), 689
TypeName attribute, 665, 704, 706, 707
<TypeName> child element (<WebPart>), 366

U

unghosted site pages
compilation and, 51
defined, 31
UnionCodeGroup code groups, 591–593
UnSafeSaveOnGet property, 576
UpdateFieldValueInItem method, 279
URL attribute, 105
Url attribute
of <Module>, 352
of <NavBarLink>, 347
UseLegacyForm attribute, 107
user control development, 525
utilities
gacutil command-line utility, 88
MAKECAB operating system command-line utility, 599–601, 608–609
STSADM command-line utility, 610–611, 617, 618–619

V

Validate method, 279
Value property
of BaseFieldControl class, 276–277
of FormField, 286
ValueChanged and OnValue Changed members, 283–284
values
BdcRightName schema type, 635
ID property values, 118
of Name attributes on < Identifier > elements, 670
of Type attribute, 123–124
variable field type properties
CAML rendering and, 242
defined, 238
variable field type property editor, 287–288
verbs
custom, 517
defined, 515
Version attribute on the <LobSystem>, 637
View Application page, BDC and, 742–744
<View> element
<ViewBody> child element of, 143
<ViewFields> child element and, 142

<View> element (continued)
child elements of, 133, 134
Default module and, 363, 366–367
GroupByFooter element of, 140–142
GroupByHeader child element of, 133–140
that represents All Tasks view (listing), 132–133
View Entity page, BDC and, 748–749, 756
View Response menu option, 102–103, 104
<ViewBody> element (listing), 143
<ViewBody> element, output HTML generated by (listing), 144–145
<ViewFields> element (listing), 142
viewing list items, 102–103
VirtualPathProvider, 31
Visible property, 260
Visual Studio Toolbox, adding server controls to, 73–77
Vote (Survey) type, 351
_vti_bin virtual directory, 155–157

W

web applications. *See* SPWebApplication
web configuration modification
adding entries to web.config with site provisioning provider, 409–414
basics, 397–398
deploying custom HTTP handler to SharePoint, 402
RSS, 402–403
RssHandler, 403
RssHandler HTTP handler, 404–409
SPWebConfigModification class, 398–402
web event receiver
binding web event handler to existing site definition configuration, 478–480
binding web event handler to new site definition configuration, 480–486
binding web event to existing site, 476–478
MyWebEventReceiver web event receiver, 475–476
SPWebEventProperties type, 474–475
SPWebEventReceiver class, 474
web part controls, connecting
ConsumerConnectionPoint class, 540
FavoriteItemWebPart control, 537
FavoriteItemWebPart Web part, 546–548
IPersonalizable interface, 562–564
ProviderConnectionPoint class, 539–540
RssReaderEditorPart3, implementing, 554–556
RssReaderEditorPart4, 565–571
RssReaderWebPart4 control, 535–536
RssReaderWebPart4, implementing, 541–546
RssReaderWebPart5, implementing, 548–553
RssReaderWebPart6, implementing, 557–562
WebPartConnection class, 538, 540
Web part description for TemplateBasedWebPart1 (listing), 606
Web Part Gallery
adding .webpart description files to, 512
defined, 505
Web part solutions, 604–620
< Assemblies > and, 614
automating, 618–620
code access security settings and, 614–616
components of, 604–605
copying file into solution store of configuration database, 617
defined, 604
deploying to front-end web servers, 617
example of, 605–613
Web parts, defined, 491
Web Parts Framework, ASP.NET. *See* ASP.NET Web Parts Framework
web parts, templated. *See* templated web parts
Web public property (SPWeb type), 532
web reference, adding, 154–155
web servers, deploying, 617
web sites. *See also* SPIisWebSite
IIS web sites, accessing, 9–10
for information on BDC namespace, 628
web.config file
adding entries to, 398, 409–414, 598
adding <httpHandlers> to, 34–35
configuration settings, 469
<httpHandler> section of, 33
<httpModules> of, 23
permissions and, 594
SPRequestModule and, 28–29
<WebFeatures> child element, 353
<WebPart> document element, 366
WebPart server control, deploying custom
Bin vs. GAC, 505–507
procedure for, 504–505
.webpart XML description file. *See* .webpart XML description file
WebPart server controls
defined, 487
developing, 495

.webpart XML description file
- declarative approach to creating, 511–514
- example, 508
- graphical approach to creating, 509–510
- overview, 507–508

WebPartManager server control, defined, 491
WebPartPage base class, defined, 495–496
WebPartVerb class, 516–517
WebPartZone server controls
- basics of, 492–494
- defined, 488

WebPartZoneBase base class, defined, 496
WebPartZoneId attribute, 106
WebServiceEntityInstance classes (listing), 641
WebTempMyWebTemp.xml file (listings), 375–376, 388–389, 621–622
WebTemp*.xml file, 372–373
WebZone controls, defined, 487
<Where> element (CAML), 54, 57
wildcard filters
- defined, 643
- descriptor metadata objects, 712
- using, 711–712

WildcardCharacter property, 643
WildcardCharacterEscapeFormat property, 643
worker request class (ASP.NET), 1–2. *See also* HttpWorker Request
.wsp extension (cabinet files), 599
WSS web applications, 506
WSS_Minimal trust level, 575, 580
wss_minimaltrust.config policy file, 586–593

X

XML. *See* eXtensible Markup Language (XML)
XML files. *See also* schema.xml file
- copying to TEMPLATE folder, 598
- file describing custom STSADM operation, 422–423

XML Schema markup language, CAML and, 53–57, 63
<XmlDocuments> child element, 471
XmlReader, 503